Business Law
Principles and Cases
Seventh Edition · UCC

Ronald A. Anderson

Professor of Law and Government,
        Drexel University
Member of the Pennsylvania and Philadelphia Bars
Coauthor of **Business Law**
Author of **Anderson on the Uniform Commercial Code**
        Government and Business
        Social Forces and the Law.
        Anderson's Pennsylvania Civil Practice
        Purdon's Pennsylvania Forms
        Couch's Cyclopedia of Insurance Law
        Insurer's Tort Law
        Hotelman's Basic Law
        Running a Professional Corporation
Consulting Editor of the **Pennsylvania Law Encyclopedia**

Contributing Authors:

Ivan Fox
Professor of Law
    and Chairman,
Business Law Department
Pace University

David P. Twomey
Professor of Law
School of Management
Boston College

Published by

L43 **SOUTH-WESTERN PUBLISHING CO.**

CINCINNATI   WEST CHICAGO, ILL.   DALLAS   PELHAM MANOR, N.Y.   PALO ALTO, CALIF.

ISBN: 0-538-12430-x

Library of Congress Catalog Card Number: 78-64977

3 4 5 6 7 8 D 6 5 4 3 2 1 0

Printed in the United States of America

Preface

The twentieth century world continues to change rapidly. New fact situations and shifting values have produced significant changes in business law. These are presented in this Seventh Edition of BUSINESS LAW PRINCIPLES AND CASES in new chapters and in many new and expanded topics within chapters on traditional subjects.

Law and Law Enforcement Agencies

The importance of law and law enforcement agencies is emphasized. Included is a comprehensive discussion of the federal and state court structure and the procedures involved in a lawsuit from commencement to execution of the judgment.

Social Forces

The unique treatment of social forces in the prior editions is continued in this Seventh Edition. In Chapter 2, Law As an Expression of Social Forces, the specific objectives of the law are discussed against the background of the general objective of creating, maintaining, and restoring order, stability, and justice. The student also learns to think of the law as an evolutionary process and as a synthesis of prior law.

Consumer Protection

The interests of the consumer are being increasingly recognized by federal and state legislation and by administrative regulation. The importance of this area of the law is recognized by Chapter 8, Consumer Protection, which embraces important provisions of the Uniform Consumer Credit Code and the federal Consumer Credit Protection Act. Bait advertising, games of chance as promotional devices, seals of approval, home solicitation sales, referral sales, mail order transactions, credit cards, balloon payments, preservation of consumer defenses, collection methods, protection of credit standing, and consumer remedies are some of the topics in this chapter.

The following topics are examples of those pertaining to consumer protection which are incorporated in other chapters: unordered goods, disclosure in a separate statement for an installment loan, fine print in contracts, domination by seller, unequal bargaining power, unconscionable and oppressive contracts, and consumer protection rescission.

Administrative Agencies

The importance of administrative agencies, particularly those at the federal level, continues to grow. The special character of these agencies is recognized in

Chapter 6. Consideration is given to the administrator's power, the pattern of administrative procedure, and the finality of administrative determination.

Environmental Law

Society increasingly recognizes the social importance of the conservation of natural resources and of the protection of our physical environment. The desire to obtain an unpolluted environment is becoming crystallized into a right, as set forth in Chapter 7, Environmental Law and Community Planning.

Malpractice Liability

The growing area of malpractice lawsuits is recognized. The liability of professionals both to their clients and third persons is discussed fully in Chapter 19.

Franchises

Numerous questions raised by the recent tremendous growth of franchising operations necessitate an understanding of the basic principles of the law involved. These are considered in Chapter 47.

Securities Regulation

The growing importance to the business person of a knowledge of the provisions of the Securities Act of 1933 and the Securities Exchange Act of 1934 has been recognized by an expansion of the material on corporations.

Computers and Other New Topics

The impact of electronic data processing, computers, and retrieval systems is recognized in such topics as defamation by computer, computer programs as property, and computers and corporate management.

Antidiscrimination legislation affects several areas of business law, as reflected by topics dealing with businesses serving the public (restaurants, common carriers of passengers, and hotels and motels), employment, deeds, leases, and insurance.

Numerous other topics include: transfer of title in self-service stores, condominiums, and no-fault insurance.

UCC and UCCC

The rapid growth in the number of court decisions under the Uniform Commercial Code since the publication of the Sixth Edition has necessitated an expanded presentation of the law in such areas as sales, commercial paper, and secured transactions. More evident in the opinions too is the influence of the UCC on contracts in general. An appendix includes the complete 1972 Official Text of the Uniform Commercial Code. Where important to the student, differences found in the 1962 Official Text of the Code are stated in the footnotes.

The Uniform Consumer Credit Code has been adopted in several states. Regardless of the number of additional states that adopt the UCCC, this uniform act is having a definite influence on state legislation concerning consumer credit practices.

Chapter 14, Legality and Public Policy, and Chapter 8, Consumer Protection, incorporate provisions of the UCCC.

Authoritative

The material in this edition has been made up-to-date through an examination of professional publications in the field, new federal legislation, administrative agency regulations, and every reported decision of the federal courts, the state supreme courts, and the intermediate state courts.

Reference is made by the footnotes to uniform statutes, model acts, and restatements of the law as well as to recent cases. In addition to the UCC and UCCC, the uniform statutes and model acts cited pertain to arbitration, anatomical gifts, gifts to minors, aeronautics, fraudulent conveyances, vendor and purchaser risks, disposition of unclaimed property, partnerships, limited partnerships, business corporations, probate, and simultaneous deaths.

Student Supplement

An optional Student Supplement includes for each chapter a review of new legal terms, a study guide consisting of objective questions, and several case problems for which students are required to state in their own words the principle or rule of law that applies.

Tests and Supplementary Case Problems

For evaluative purposes, printed objective tests have been prepared to accompany this text. The instructor may also wish to use selected supplementary case problems that are available.

Contributing Authors

This edition has been enhanced by the outstanding participation of two Contributing Authors—Professor Ivan Fox of Pace University and Professor David P. Twomey of Boston College. Each brought to the project a unique blend of knowledge and experience that substantially facilitated the development of the publication.

A Special Tribute

This edition is the first in over twenty-five years that does not carry the name of Walter A. Kumpf as coauthor. The thousands of students and instructors who have used the editions on which he labored are the beneficiaries of his many contributions to the teaching of business law. His efforts as coauthor and editor, and his friendship are gratefully acknowledged.

R. A. A

Contents

vi

Part 12   ESTATES

Part One • Legal Rights and Social Forces

1 Law and Law Enforcement Agencies

Law has developed because people and society have wanted relationships between people, and between people and government, to conform to certain standards. The rules or laws adopted for this purpose have expressed the social, economic, and moral standards and aspirations of society.

A. NATURE OF LEGAL RIGHTS AND THE LAW

Law consists of the entire body of principles that govern conduct and can be enforced in the courts. If there were no society-made law, no doubt many persons would be guided by principles of moral or natural law. Most people would act in accordance with the dictates of conscience, the precepts of right living that are a part of religion, and the ethical concepts that are generally accepted in the community. Those who would choose to act otherwise, however, would constitute a serious problem for society.

§ 1:1. Legal Rights. What are legal rights? And who has them? In answering these questions, we tend to make the mistake of thinking of the present as being characteristic of what was and what will be. But consider the evolution of the concept of the "rights of the human being" and the right of privacy.

(a) The "Rights of the Human Being" Concept. Our belief in the American way of life and in the concepts on which our society or government is based should not obscure the fact that at one time there was no American way of life. While many religious leaders, philosophers, and poets spoke of the rights and dignity of people, rulers laughed at such pretensions and held people tightly in a society based on status. A noble had the rights of a noble. A warrior had the rights of a warrior. A slave had very few rights at all. In each case, the law saw only status; rights attached not to the human being but to the status.

In the course of time, serfdom displaced slavery in much of the Western world. Eventually feudalism disappeared and, with the end of the Thirty Years War, the modern nation-state began to emerge. Surely one might say that, in such a "new order," a human being had legal rights. No, not as a human being, but only as a subject did one have legal rights. Even when the English colonists settled in America, they brought with them not the rights of human beings but the rights of British subjects. Even when the colonies were within one year of war, the Second Continental Congress presented to King George III the Olive Branch Petition which beseeched the king to recognize the colonists' rights as English subjects. For almost a year the destiny of the colonies hung in the balance with the colonists unable to decide between remaining loyal to the Crown, seeking to obtain recognition of their rights as English subjects (a "status" recognition), or doing something else.

Finally, the ill-advised policies of George III and the eloquence of Thomas Paine's Common Sense tipped the scales and the colonies spoke on July 4, 1776, not in terms of the rights of English subjects but in terms of the rights of people existing independently of any government. Had the American Revolution been lost, the Declaration of Independence would have gone rattling down the corridors of time with many other failures. But the American Revolution was won, and the new government that was established was based upon "human beings" as the building blocks rather than upon "subjects." Rights of human beings replaced the concept of rights of subjects. With this transition, the obligations of a monarch to faithful subjects were replaced by the rights of human beings existing without regard to will or authority of any kind. Since then, America has been going through additional stages of determining what is embraced by the concept of "rights of human beings."

(b) The Right of Privacy. Today everyone recognizes that there is a right of privacy. Before 1890, however, this right did not exist in American law. Certainly those who wrote the Declaration of Independence and the Bill of Rights Amendments to the Constitution were conscious of rights. How can we explain that the law did not recognize a right of privacy until a full century later?

The answer is that at a particular time people worry about the problems which face them. Note the extent of the fears and concern of the framers of the Bill of Rights Amendments to the Constitution. The Fourth Amendment states, "The right of the people to be secure in their persons, houses, papers, and effects, against unreasonable searches and seizures, shall not be violated, and no Warrants shall issue, but upon probable cause, supported by Oath or affirmation, and particularly describing the place to be searched and the persons or things to be seized." The people of 1790 were afraid of a recurrence of the days of George III.

The framers of the Fourth Amendment declared what we today would regard as a segment of privacy—protection from police invasion of privacy. The people of 1790 just were not concerned with invasion of privacy by a private person. While a snooping person could be prosecuted to some extent under a Peeping Tom statute, this was a criminal liability. The victim could not sue for damages for the invasion of privacy.

If we are honest with history, all that we can say is that modern people think highly of privacy and want it to be protected. And, knowing that the law is responsive to the wishes of society, we can also say that the right is protected by government. But note that we should go no further than to say that it is a right which society wishes to protect at the present time. If circumstances arise in our national life of such a nature that privacy will hamper or endanger national defense, we can expect that the "right" of privacy will be limited or modified. We should therefore approach problems relating to rights with an open mind, realizing that there are only such legal rights as we the people, through our legal system, choose to recognize.

§ 1:2. What is the Law? The expression, "a law," is ordinarily used in connection with a statute enacted by a state legislature or the Congress of the United States, such as an act of the federal Congress to provide old-age benefits. However, the statutes enacted by legislative bodies are not the only source of law.

Constitutional law includes the constitutions in force in the particular area or territory. In each state, two constitutions are in force, the state constitution and the national constitution.

Statutory law includes statutes adopted by the lawmakers. Each state has its own legislature and the United States has the Congress, both of which enact laws. In addition, every city, county, or other subdivision has some power to adopt ordinances which, within their sphere of operation, have the same binding effect as legislative acts.

Of great importance are the *administrative regulations,* such as rules of the Securities and Exchange Commission and the National Labor Relations Board. The regulations promulgated by national and state administrative agencies generally have the force of statute and are therefore part of "the law."

Law also includes principles that are expressed for the first time in court decisions. This is *case law.* For example, when a court decides a new question or problem, its decision becomes a *precedent* and stands as the law for that particular problem in the future. This rule that a court decision becomes a precedent to be followed in similar cases is the doctrine of *stare decisis.*

Law also includes treaties made by the United States, and proclamations and orders of the President of the United States or of other public officials.

§ 1:3. Uniform State Laws. To secure uniformity as far as possible, the National Conference of Commissioners on Uniform State Laws, composed of representatives from all the states, has drafted statutes on various business subjects for adoption by the states. The best example of such laws is the Uniform Commercial Code (UCC).[1] The Code regulates the fields of sales of goods; commercial paper, such as checks; secured transactions in personal property; and particular aspects of banking, letters of credit, warehouse receipts, bills of lading, and investment securities.

National uniformity has also been brought about in some areas of consumer protection by the adoption of the federal Consumer Credit Protection Act (CCPA), Title I of which is popularly known as the Truth in Lending Act.[2] A Uniform Consumer Credit Code (UCCC) has been proposed and is now before the states for

---

[1] The Code has been adopted in every state except Louisiana. It has also been adopted in the Virgin Islands and for the District of Columbia. Louisiana has adopted Articles 1, 3, 4, and 5 of the Code. In 1972, a group of amendments to the Code was recommended. These have been adopted in Arizona, Arkansas, California, Colorado, Connecticut, Illinois, Iowa, Kansas, Maine, Minnesota, Mississippi, Nebraska, Nevada, New York, North Carolina, North Dakota, Oregon, Texas, Utah, Virginia, West Virginia, and Wisconsin. The changes made by the 1972 amendments to the UCC are confined mainly to Article 9 on secured transactions.

[2] 15 United States Code § 1601 et seq., and 18 USC § 891 et seq.

possible adoption. To the extent that it is adopted, it will complement the Uniform Commercial Code.[3]

§ 1:4. Classifications of Law. Law is classified in many ways. For example, *substantive law,* which defines the substance of legal rights and liabilities, is contrasted with *procedural law,* which specifies the procedure that must be followed in enforcing those rights and liabilities. The following additional classifications are useful:

(a) Law and Equity. Law is frequently classified as being "law" or "equity." During the early centuries following the Norman Conquest, it was common for subjects of the English Crown to present to the King petitions requesting particular favors or relief that could not be obtained in the ordinary courts of law. The extraordinary or special relief granted by the chancellor, to whom the King referred such matters, was of such a nature as was dictated by principles of justice and equity. This body of principles was called *equity.* While originally applied by separate courts, today the same court usually administers both "law" and "equity."

(b) Classification Based Upon Historical Sources. Law is sometimes classified in terms of its source as the *civil law,* which comes from the Roman civil law, and the *common law,* which is based upon the English common law or the common law that has developed in the United States.

The *law merchant,* which was recognized by early English merchants, has been absorbed to a large extent by the common law. During the centuries that the common law was developing in England, merchants of different nations, trading in all parts of the world, developed their own sets of rules to govern their business transactions. Much of our modern business law relating to commercial paper, insurance, credit transactions, and partnerships originally developed in the law merchant.

B. AGENCIES FOR ENFORCEMENT OF LEGAL RIGHTS

Legal rights are meaningless unless they can be enforced. Government, therefore, provides a system by which the rights of the parties under the law can be determined and enforced. Generally the instrumentality of government by which this is accomplished is a court; the process involved is an action or a lawsuit. Administrative agencies have also been created to enforce law and to determine rights within certain areas. At the same time private agencies have developed as an out-of-court method of dispute determination.

§ 1:5 Courts. A *court* is a tribunal established by government to hear and decide matters properly brought before it, to give redress to the injured or enforce punishment against wrongdoers, and to prevent wrongs. A *court of record* is one in which the proceedings are preserved in an official record. A *court not of record* is a court of which the proceedings are not officially recorded.

---

[3] As of January, 1978, the 1968 version of the Uniform Consumer Credit Code has been adopted in: Colorado, Idaho, Indiana, Oklahoma, South Carolina, Utah, Wisconsin, and Wyoming. This earlier version, however, has been replaced by a 1974 version, which has been adopted in Iowa, Kansas, and Maine.

Each court is empowered to decide certain types or classes of cases. This power is called *jurisdiction*. A court may have original or appellate jurisdiction, or both. A court with *original jurisdiction* has the authority to hear a controversy when it is first brought into court. A court having *appellate jurisdiction,* on the other hand, has authority to review the judgment of an inferior court.

The jurisdiction of a court may be general as distinguished from limited or special. A court having *general jurisdiction* has power to hear and decide all controversies involving legal rights and duties. A court of *limited* or *special jurisdiction* has authority to hear and decide only those cases that fall within a particular class, such as cases in which the amounts are below a specified sum.

Courts are frequently classified in terms of the nature of their jurisdiction. A *criminal court* is one that is established for the trial of crimes, which are regarded as offenses against the public. A *civil court,* on the other hand, is authorized to hear and decide issues involving private rights and duties and also noncriminal public matters. In like manner, courts are classified as equity courts, juvenile courts, probate courts, and courts of domestic relations, upon the basis of their limited jurisdiction.

Each court has inherent power to establish rules necessary to preserve order in the court or to transact the business of the court. An infraction of these rules or the disobedience to any other lawful order, as well as a willful act contrary to the dignity of the court or tending to pervert or obstruct justice, may be punished as *contempt of court.*

§ 1:6. Administrative Agencies. The difficulties of courts administering laws regulating business, labor, agriculture, public utilities, and other phases of the economy led Congress and the state legislatures to establish commissions or agencies of experts to make the rules and to pass upon violations of the rules. Thus we find the Interstate Commerce Commission regulating interstate commerce and passing upon whether conduct of a carrier is a violation of its regulations. The Commission is thus a lawmaker, an executive that enforces the law, and a court which interprets and applies the law. This is also true of the Civil Aeronautics Board, the Federal Trade Commission, the Securities and Exchange Commission, the National Labor Relations Board, and many other federal and state administrative agencies.

Generally an appeal may be taken to court from the action of such an administrative body. The action of the board is usually final, however, with respect to questions of fact when there is substantial evidence to support the decision; but such action may be reversed by the court when the latter disagrees with the board on questions of law.

§ 1:7. Private Agencies. Because of the rising costs, delays, and complexities of litigation, business people often seek to resolve disputes out of court.

(a)   Arbitration. By the use of *arbitration* a dispute is brought before one or more arbitrators who make a decision which the parties have agreed to accept as final. This procedure first reached an extensive use in the field of commercial contracts. Parties to a contract which is to be in effect for some time may specify in the contract that any dispute shall be submitted to arbitrators to be selected by the parties. Arbitration today is encouraged as a means of avoiding expensive litigation and easing the workload of courts. Arbitration enables the parties to present the facts before trained experts because the arbitrators are familiar with the practices that form the background of the dispute.

A Uniform Arbitration Act has been adopted in a number of states.[4] Under this Act and similar statutes, the parties to a contract may agree in advance that all disputes arising thereunder will be submitted to arbitration. In some instances the contract will name the arbitrators for the duration of the contract.

The growth of arbitration has been greatly aided by the American Arbitration Association not only in the development of standards, procedures, and forms for arbitration, but also by the creation of panels of qualified arbitrators from which the parties to a contract may select those who will settle their dispute.

(b) Reference to Third Person. An out-of-court determination of disputes under construction contracts is often made under a term of the contract that any dispute shall be referred to the architect in charge of the construction and that the architect's decision shall be final.

Increasingly, other types of transactions provide for a third person or a committee to decide rights of persons. Thus, employees and an employer may have agreed as a term of the employment contract that claims of employees under retirement and pension plans shall be decided by a designated board or committee. The seller and buyer may have selected a third person to determine the price to be paid for goods. Ordinarily the parties agree that the decision of such a third person or board shall be final and that no appeal or review may be had in any court. In most cases, the referral situation involves the determination of a particular fact in contrast to arbitration which seeks to end a dispute.

(c) Association Tribunals. Many disputes never reach the law courts because both parties to the dispute belong to a group or association and the tribunal created by the group or association disposes of the matter. Thus a dispute between members of a labor union, a stockbrokers' exchange, or a church, may be heard by some board or committee within the association or group. Courts will review the action of such tribunals to determine that a fair and proper procedure was followed but generally the courts will not go any further and will not examine the facts of the case to see if the association tribunal reached the same conclusion that the court would have reached.

C. COURT ORGANIZATION

Courts in the United States are organized in two distinct systems: the federal courts and the state courts. Although created under separate governments, the methods of operation and organization of these two systems are similar.

---

[4] The 1955 version of the Uniform Arbitration Act has been adopted in Alaska, Arizona, Arkansas, Colorado, Delaware, Idaho, Illinois, Indiana, Kansas, Maine, Maryland, Massachusetts, Michigan, Minnesota, Nevada, New Mexico, North Carolina, South Dakota, Texas, and Wyoming. The earlier 1925 version of the Act is in force in Pennsylvania, Utah, and Wisconsin.

§ 1:8. Personnel of Courts.

(a) **Officers of the Court.** The *judge* is the primary officer of the court. A judge is either elected or appointed. *Attorneys* or counselors at law are also officers of the court. They are usually selected by the parties to the controversy—but in some cases by the judge—to present the issues of a case to the court.

The *clerk* of the court is appointed in some of the higher courts but is usually elected to office in the lower courts. The principal duties of the clerks are to enter cases upon the court calendar, to keep an accurate record of the proceedings, to attest the same, and, in some instances, to approve bail bonds and to compute the amount of costs involved.

The *sheriff* is the chief executive of a county. In addition to the duty of maintaining peace and order within the territorial limits of a county, the sheriff has many other duties in connection with the administration of justice in county courts of record: summoning witnesses, taking charge of the jury, preserving order in court, serving writs, carrying out judicial sales, and executing judgments. The *marshals* of the United States perform these duties in the federal courts. In county courts not of record, such as the courts of justices of the peace, these duties, when appropriate, are performed by a *constable.* Some of the duties of the sheriff are now performed by persons known as *court criers;* or by deputy sheriffs, known as *bailiffs.*

(b) **The Jury.** The *jury* is a body of citizens sworn by a court to try to determine by verdict the issues of fact submitted to them. A trial jury consists of not more than twelve persons. The first step in forming a jury is to make a *jury list.* This step consists of the preparation by the proper officers or board of a list of qualified persons from which a jury may be drawn.

A certain number of persons drawn from the jury list constitute the *jury panel.* A trial jury is selected from members of the panel.

§ 1:9. Federal Courts. The federal system of courts includes the following:

(a) **Supreme Court of the United States.** The Supreme Court is the only federal court expressly established by the Constitution. Congress is authorized by the Constitution to create other federal courts.

The Supreme Court has original jurisdiction in all cases affecting ambassadors, other public ministers, and consuls, and in those cases in which a state is a party. Except as regulated by Congress, it has appellate jurisdiction in all cases that may be brought into the federal courts in accordance with the terms of the Constitution. The Supreme Court also has appellate jurisdiction of certain cases that have been decided by the supreme courts of the states. Thousands of cases are filed with this court in a year.

(b) **Courts of Appeals.** The United States, including the District of Columbia, is divided into 11 judicial circuits. Each of the circuits has a court of appeals. These courts are courts of record.

A court of appeals has appellate jurisdiction only and is empowered to review the final decisions of the district courts, except in cases that may be taken directly to the Supreme Court. The decisions of the courts of appeal are final in most cases.

An appeal may be taken on certain constitutional questions. Otherwise, review depends on the discretion of the Supreme Court and, in some cases, of the court of appeals.

(c)   District Courts. The United States, including the District of Columbia, is divided into a number of judicial districts. Some states form a single district, whereas others are divided into two or more districts. District courts are also located in the territories.

The district courts have original jurisdiction in practically all cases that may be maintained in the federal courts. They are the trial courts for civil and criminal cases.

Civil cases that may be brought in these district courts are (a) civil suits brought by the United States; (b) actions brought by citizens of different states claiming land under grants by different states; (c) proceedings under the bankruptcy, internal revenue, postal, copyright, and patent laws; (d) civil cases of admiralty and maritime jurisdiction; (e) actions against national banking associations; and (f) cases between citizens of different states or between citizens of one state and of a foreign state involving $10,000 or more that arise under the federal Constitution, or laws and treaties made thereunder.

(d)   Other Federal Courts. In addition to the Supreme Court, the court of appeals, and the district courts, the following tribunals have been created by Congress to determine other matters as indicated by their titles: Customs Court, Court of Customs and Patent Appeals, Court of Claims, Tax Court,[5] Court of Military Appeals, and the territorial courts.

§ 1:10. State Courts. The system of courts in the various states is organized along lines similar to the federal court system, although differing in details, such as the number of courts, their names, and jurisdiction.

(a)   State Supreme Court. The highest court in most states is known as the Supreme Court. In a few states it may have a different name, such as "Court of Appeals" in New York. The jurisdiction of a supreme court is ordinarily appellate, although in a few instances it is original. In some states the supreme court is required to render an opinion on certain questions that may be referred to it by the legislature or by the chief executive of the state. The decision of the state supreme court is final in all cases not involving the federal Constitution, laws, and treaties.

(b)   Intermediate Courts. In some states intermediate courts have original jurisdiction in a few cases but, in the main, they have appellate jurisdiction of cases removed for review from the county or district courts. They are known as superior, circuit, or district appellate courts. As a general rule, their decisions may be reviewed by the highest state court.

(c)   County and District Courts. These courts of record have appellate jurisdiction of cases tried in the justice of the peace and police courts, as well as general original

---

[5] This court was created originally as a Board of Tax Appeals with the status of an independent agency in the executive branch of the federal government. The Tax Reform Act of 1969 established the official name as United States Tax Court with the status of a court of record under Article I of the Constitution of the United States.

jurisdiction of criminal and civil cases. They also have jurisdiction of wills and guardianship matters, except when, as in some states, the jurisdiction of such cases has been given to special orphans', surrogate, or probate courts.

(d)   Other State Courts. In addition to the foregoing, the following, which are ordinarily not courts of record, have jurisdiction as indicated by their titles: city or municipal courts, police courts, traffic courts, small claims courts, and justice of the peace courts.

D. COURT PROCEDURE

Detailed laws specify how, when, and where a legal dispute can be brought to court. These rules of procedure are necessary in order to achieve an orderly, fair determination of litigation and in order to obtain, as far as humanly possible, the same decisions on the same facts. It is important to remember, however, that there is no uniform judicial procedure. While there are definite similarities, the law of each state may differ from the others. For the most part the uniform laws that have been adopted do not regulate matters of procedure.

In a lawsuit, the person suing is the *plaintiff,* and the person sued is the *defendant.* There may be more than one plaintiff and more than one defendant. If *A* and *B* jointly own an automobile which is damaged by *C,* both *A* and *B* must join in an action against *C.* It is improper for *A* or *B* to sue alone since it is "their" car and not the car of either one alone.

In some instances, several persons, such as shareholders or taxpayers, may bring a *class action* on behalf of themselves and all other persons having the same or similar interest. In some instances, a defendant has the right to bring another person into an action on the ground that such person also has a claim. For example, an insurance company, by the procedure of *interpleader,* may require a person claiming to be entitled to the proceeds of a policy to come into an action brought by another person as beneficiary of the same policy.

By another procedure, a seller sued by a customer for product liability may join the manufacturer as an additional defendant.

§ 1:11. Steps in a Lawsuit.

(a)   Commencement of Action. In the common-law courts an action was commenced by filing an order with the keeper of the court records to issue a writ to the sheriff. This writ of summons ordered the sheriff to inform the defendant to appear before the court on a particular date. This method of commencing an action is still followed in many states.

By way of contrast, an action in a court of equity was begun when the plaintiff filed with the court a *complaint.* No writ was issued, but a copy of the complaint was served on the defendant. In many states and in the federal courts, the reforms of recent years have extended this equity practice to all legal actions. Such actions are today commenced by the filing of the plaintiff's complaint. Some states still preserve the former distinction between law and equity, while others give the plaintiff the option of commencing the action by either method.

(b)   Service of Process. The defendant must be served with *process* (a writ, notice, or summons; or the complaint itself) to give notice that the action is pending and to subject the defendant to the power of the court.

(c)   Pleadings. After process has been served on the defendant and the plaintiff has filed a complaint, the defendant must make some reply after receiving the complaint, generally within 15 or 20 days. If the defendant fails to do so, the plaintiff ordinarily wins the case by default.

Before answering the plaintiff's complaint, the defendant may make certain preliminary objections, such as that the action was brought in the wrong court or that service was not properly made. If the objection is sustained, the case may be ended, depending upon the nature of the objection, or the plaintiff may be allowed to correct the mistake if that is possible. The defendant may also raise the objection, sometimes called a *motion to dismiss* or *demurrer,* that even if the plaintiff's complaint is accepted as true, the plaintiff is still not entitled to any relief.

If the defendant makes an objection but the objection is overruled or dismissed, the defendant must file an *answer,* which either admits or denies some or all of the facts averred by the plaintiff. For example, if the plaintiff declared that the defendant made a contract on a certain date, the defendant may either admit making the contract or deny having done so. An admission of having made the contract does not end the case, for the defendant may then be able to plead defenses, for example, that at a later date the plaintiff and defendant had agreed to set the contract aside.

Without regard to whether the defendant pleads such new matter, the defendant may generally assert a *counterclaim* or *cross complaint* against the plaintiff. Thus the defendant may contend that the plaintiff owes money or is liable for damages and that this liability should be offset against any claim which the plaintiff may have.

After the defendant files an answer, the plaintiff may generally file preliminary objections to the answer. Just as the defendant could raise objections, the plaintiff may, in certain instances, argue that a counterclaim raised by the defendant could not be asserted in that action, that the answer is fatally defective in form, or that it is not legally sufficient. Again the court must pass upon the preliminary objections. When these are disposed of, the pleading stage is ordinarily over.

Generally, all of the pleadings in an action may raise only a few or perhaps one question of law, or a question of fact, or both. Thus the whole case may depend on whether a letter admittedly written by the defendant amounted to an acceptance of the plaintiff's offer, thereby constituting a contract. If this question of law is answered in favor of the plaintiff, a judgment will be entered for the plaintiff; otherwise, for the defendant. By way of contrast, it may be that a certain letter would be an acceptance if it had been written; but the defendant may deny having written it. Here the question is one of fact, and the judgment is entered for the plaintiff if it is determined that the facts happened as claimed by the plaintiff. Otherwise the judgment is entered for the defendant.

If the only questions involved are questions of law, the court will decide the case on the pleadings alone since there is no need for a trial to determine the facts. If questions of fact are involved, then there must be a trial to determine what the facts really were.

(d)   Pretrial Procedure. Many states and the federal courts have adopted other procedural steps that may be employed before the trial, with the purpose of eliminating the need for a trial, simplifying the issues to be tried, or giving the parties information needed for preparation for trial.

(1)   Motion for Judgment on the Pleadings. After the pleadings are closed, many courts permit either party to move for a *judgment on the pleadings.* When such a motion is made, the court examines the record and may then enter a judgment according to the merits of the case as shown by the record.

(2)   Motion for Summary Judgment. In most courts a party may shorten a lawsuit by bringing into court sworn statements and affidavits which show that a claim or defense is false or a sham. This procedure cannot be used when there is substantial dispute of fact concerning the matters to be proved by the use of the affidavits.

(3)   Pretrial Conference. In many courts either party may request the court to call a *pretrial conference,* or the court may take the initiative in doing so. This conference is in substance a round-table discussion by a judge of the court and the attorneys in the case. The object of the conference is to eliminate matters that are not in dispute and to determine what issues remain for litigation.

The pretrial conference is not intended as a procedure to compel the parties to settle their case. It not infrequently results, however, that when the attorneys discuss the matter with the court, they recognize that the differences between the conflicting parties are not so great as contemplated or that one side has less merit than was at first believed; in consequence, a settlement of the case is agreed upon.

(4)   Discovery. The Federal Rules of Civil Procedure and similar rules in a large number of states now permit one party to inquire of the adverse party and of all witnesses about anything relating to the action. This includes asking the adverse party the names of witnesses; asking the adverse party and the witnesses what they know about the case; examining, inspecting, and photographing books, records, buildings, and machines; and making an examination of the physical or mental condition of a party when it has a bearing on the action. These procedures are classed as *discovery.*

Under the prior practice, except for the relatively unusual situation in which a party could obtain information before trial by filing a bill for discovery in equity, a party never knew what witnesses would appear in court for the adverse party or what they would say, or what documentary evidence would be produced.

(5)   Depositions. Ordinarily a witness testifies in court at the time of the trial. In some instances it may be necessary or desirable to take such testimony out of court before the time of the trial. It may be that the witness is aged or infirm or is about to leave the state or country and will not be present when the trial of the action is held. In such case the interested party is permitted to have the testimony, called a *deposition,* of the witness taken outside of the court.

(e)   **Determination of Facts.**

(1)   The Trier of Facts. If the legal controversy is one which in the common-law days would have been tried by a jury, either party to the action has the constitutional right today to demand that the action be tried before a jury. If all parties agree, however, the case may be tried by the court or judge alone without a jury, and in some instances may be referred to a master or a referee appointed by the court to hear the matter.

In equity there is no constitutional right to a jury trial but a chancellor or equity judge may submit questions to a jury. There is the basic difference that in such cases the verdict or decision of the jury is only advisory to the chancellor; that is, the chancellor is not bound by the verdict. In contrast, the verdict of a jury in an action at law is binding on the court unless a basic error is present.

When new causes of action are created by statute, such as the right of an employee to obtain workmen's compensation for an injury arising in the course of employment without regard to whether the employer was negligent, there is no constitutional right to a trial by jury. The trier of facts may accordingly be a judge without a jury, or a special administrative board or agency, such as a Workmen's Compensation Board.

(2)   Basis for Decision. The trier of fact, whether a jury, a judge, a referee, or a board, can only decide questions of fact on the basis of evidence presented before it. Each party offers evidence. The evidence usually consists of the answers of persons to questions in court. Their answers are called *testimony.* The evidence may also include *real evidence,* that is, tangible things, such as papers, books, and records. It is immaterial whether the records are kept in ordinary ledger books or stored on computer tapes because a computer printout of data made for trial is admissible as evidence of the information contained in the computer.[6] In some cases, such as a damage action for improper construction of a building, the trier of fact may be taken to view the building so that a better understanding can be obtained.

The witness who testifies in court is usually a person who had some direct contact with the facts in the case, such as a person who saw the events occur or who heard one of the parties say something. In some instances, it is also proper to offer the testimony of persons who have no connection with the case when they have expert knowledge and their opinions as experts are desired.

A witness who refuses to appear in court may be ordered to do so by a *subpoena,* and may also be compelled to bring relevant papers to the court by a *subpoena duces tecum.* If the witness does not obey the subpoena, the witness may be arrested for contempt of court. In some states the names of the order upon the witness and the procedure for contempt have been changed, but the substance remains the same.

(f)   **Conduct of the Trial.** The conduct of a trial will be discussed in terms of a jury trial. Generally a case is one of several assigned for trial on a certain day or

---

[6] *Transport Indemnity Co. v Seib,* 178 Neb 253, 132 NW2d 871.

during a certain trial period. When the turn of the case is called, the opposing counsel seat themselves at tables in front of the judge and the jury is selected. After the jury is sworn, the attorneys usually make *opening addresses* to the jury. Details vary in different jurisdictions, but the general pattern is that each attorney tells the jury what will be proven. When this step has been completed, the presentation of the evidence by both sides begins.

The attorney for the plaintiff starts with the first witness and asks all the questions desired that are proper. This is called the *direct examination of the witness* since it is made by the attorney calling the witness. After the direct examination has been finished, the opposing counsel asks the same witness other questions in an effort to disprove the prior answers. This is called *cross-examination.*

After the cross-examination has been completed, the attorney for the plaintiff may ask the same witness other questions to overcome the effect of the cross-examination. This is called *redirect examination.* This step in turn may be followed by further examination by the defendant's attorney, called *recross-examination.*

After the examination of the plaintiff's witness has been concluded, the plaintiff's second witness takes the witness stand and is subjected to an examination in the same way as the first. This continues until all of the plaintiff's witnesses have been called. Then the plaintiff "rests," and the defendant calls the first defense witness. The pattern of examination of witnesses is repeated except that now the defendant is calling the witnesses, and the defendant's attorney conducts the direct and redirect examination while the questioning by the plaintiff's attorney is cross- or recross-examination.

After the witnesses of both parties have been examined and all the evidence has been presented, each attorney makes another address, a *summation,* to the jury which sums up the case and suggests that a particular verdict be returned by the jury.

(g)   Charge to the Jury and Verdict. The summation by the attorneys is followed by a *charge* of the judge to the jury. This charge is a résumé of what has happened at the trial and an explanation of the law applicable. At its conclusion, the judge instructs the jury to retire and study the case in the light of the charge and then return a *verdict.* By such instructions, the judge leaves to the jury the problem of determining the facts but states the law that they must apply to such facts as they may find. The jury then retires to secret deliberation in the jury room.

(h)   Taking the Case from the Jury and Attacking the Verdict. At several points during the trial or immediately after it, a party may take a step to end the case or to set aside the verdict which the jury has returned.

> *(1)   Voluntary Nonsuit.* A plaintiff who is dissatisfied with the progress of the trial, may wish to stop the trial and begin again at a later date. In most jurisdictions this can be done by taking a *voluntary nonsuit.*

> *(2)   Compulsory Nonsuit.* After the plaintiff has presented the testimony of all witnesses, the defendant may request the court to enter a nonsuit on the ground that the case presented by the plaintiff does not entitle the plaintiff to recover. This is called a *compulsory nonsuit.*

(3) Mistrial. When necessary to avoid great injustice, the trial court may declare that there has been a *mistrial* and thereby terminate the trial and postpone it to a later date. While either party may move the court to enter a mistrial, it is discretionary with the court whether it does so. A mistrial is commonly entered when the evidence has been of a highly prejudicial character and the trial judge does not believe that the jury can ignore it even when instructed to do so, or when a juror has been guilty of misconduct.

(4) Directed Verdict. After the presentation of all the evidence at the trial, either party may request the court to direct the jury to return a verdict in favor of the requesting party. When the plaintiff would not be entitled to recover even though all the testimony in the plaintiff's favor were believed, the defendant is entitled to have the court direct the jury to return a verdict for the defendant. The plaintiff is entitled to a directed verdict when, even if all the evidence on behalf of the defendant were believed, the jury would still be required to find for the plaintiff. In some states, the defendant may make such a motion at the close of the plaintiff's proof.

(5) New Trial. After the verdict has been returned by the jury, a party may move for a new trial if not satisfied with the verdict or with the amount of damages that has been awarded. If it is clear that the jury made a mistake or if material evidence that could not have been discovered sooner is available, the court will award a new trial and the case will be tried again before another jury.

(6) Judgment N.O.V. If the verdict returned by the jury is clearly wrong as a matter of law, the court may set aside the verdict and enter a judgment contrary to the verdict. This in some states is called a *judgment non obstante veredicto* (notwithstanding the verdict), or as it is abbreviated, a judgment n.o.v.

(i) Judgment and Costs. The court enters a judgment conforming to the verdict unless a new trial has been granted, a mistrial declared after the return of the verdict, or a judgment n.o.v. entered. Generally whoever is the winning party will also be awarded costs in the action. In equity actions or those that had their origin in equity, and in certain statutory proceedings, the court has discretion to award costs to the winner or to divide them between the parties.

Costs ordinarily include the costs of filing papers with the court, the cost of having the sheriff or other officers of the court take official action, the statutory fees paid to the witnesses, the cost of a jury fee, if any, and the cost of printing the record when this is required on appeal. They do not include compensation for the time spent by the party in preparing the case or in being present at the trial, the time lost from work because of the case, or the fee paid to an attorney. Sometimes when a special statutory action is brought, the statute authorizes recovery of a small attorney's fee. Thus, a mechanic's lien statute may authorize the recovery of an attorney's fee of 10 percent of the amount recovered, or a "reasonable attorney's fee." As a general rule, the costs that a party recovers represent only a small part of the total expenses actually sustained in the litigation.

(j)   **Appeal.** After a judgment has been entered, the party who is aggrieved thereby may appeal. This means that a party who wins the judgment but is not awarded as much as had been hoped, as well as a party who loses the case, may take an appeal.

The appellate court does not hear witnesses. It examines the record of the proceedings before the lower court, that is, the file of the case containing all the pleadings, the testimony of witnesses, and the judge's charge, to see if there was an error of law. To assist the court, the attorneys for the parties file arguments or briefs and generally make arguments orally before the court.

If the appellate court does not agree with the application of the law made by the lower court, it generally sets aside or modifies the action of the lower court and enters such judgment as it concludes the lower court should have entered. It may set aside the action of the lower court and send the case back to the lower court with directions to hold a new trial or with directions to enter a new judgment in accordance with the opinion that is filed by the appellate court.

(k)   **Execution.** After a judgment has been entered or after an appeal has been decided, the losing party generally will comply with the judgment of the court. If not, the winning party may then take steps to execute or carry out the judgment.

If the judgment is for the payment of a sum of money, the plaintiff may direct the sheriff or other judicial officer to sell as much of the property of the defendant as is necessary to pay the plaintiff's judgment and the costs of the proceedings and of the execution. Acting under this authorization, the sheriff may make a public sale of the defendant's property and apply the proceeds to the payment of the plaintiff's judgment. In most states the defendant is allowed an exemption of several hundred dollars and certain articles, such as personal clothing and tools of trade.

If the judgment is for the recovery of specific property, the judgment will direct the sheriff to deliver the property to the plaintiff.

If the judgment directs the defendant to do or to refrain from doing an act, it is commonly provided that failure to obey the order is a contempt of court punishable by fine or imprisonment.

§ 1:12. Declaratory Judgment. In this century a new court procedure for settling disputes, authorized by statute, has made its appearance. This is the *declaratory judgment* procedure. Under it a person, when confronted with the early prospect of an actual controversy, may petition the court to decide the question before loss is actually sustained. A copy of the petition is served on all parties. They may file answers. After all the pleadings have been filed, the court then decides the questions involved just as though a lawsuit had been brought.

QUESTIONS AND PROBLEMS

1.   Jones tells you that he has a business dispute with his partner Smith. He does not want to sue Smith. Is there any way in which the dispute can be settled without going to court?

2. Brooks sought to recover damages for breach of contract from Canter in a court action. Should such an action be brought in a court of original jurisdiction or in one of appellate jurisdiction? Why?

3. What is the role of each officer of the court?

4. The Missouri River, which forms part of the boundary line between Kansas and Missouri, suddenly changed its course and formed a new channel several miles west of its old bed. The State of Missouri claimed all of the land between the old and new beds of the river. Would the court with original jurisdiction be the Supreme Court of the United States? Why?

5. Hardy, who lives in Indiana, owes $15,000 to Purdy, who lives in Missouri. Is Purdy entitled to bring action for this amount against Hardy in a federal court? Why?

6. The State of Virginia issued certain bonds under a statute which provided that the bonds were receivable for all taxes. A later statute prohibited the receipt of such bonds for taxes. McCullough brought an action against the state, contending that the second statute impaired the obligation of contract and violated a provision of the federal Constitution. The Supreme Court of Virginia upheld the validity of the second statute. Did its decision settle the question conclusively? Reason?

7. Ames brought an action against Jarvis Co. to recover damages resulting from a breach of contract. No process was served on the defendants, but Ames published notice of the action in the newspaper. Ames secured a judgment against the defendants. Later it was contended that the judgment was not valid. Do you agree? Why?

8. How does each of the following pretrial procedures contribute to the determination of legal disputes?
   (a) Motion for judgment on the pleadings
   (b) Motion for summary judgment
   (c) Pretrial conference
   (d) Discovery

9. A witness is willing to testify concerning certain facts in a case, but he lives in another state. How can his testimony be secured for evidence in the trial?

10. Outline briefly the steps in a trial beginning with the opening statements by the attorneys.

11. The right of privacy is a fundamental right which has always been recognized by American law. Appraise this statement.

12. The right to trial by jury is a fundamental procedure which must always be used whenever any issue of fact is to be determined. Appraise this statement.

2 Law As an Expression of Social Forces

The purpose of law is to provide order, stability, and justice. Thus viewed, the law consists of relatively fixed rules which regulate conduct according to the morality of the community. Proper conduct, as determined by the community, should be allowed or required; improper conduct should be prohibited. Law, then, is a social institution. It is not an end unto itself but is an instrumentality for obtaining social justice.

§ 2:1. Law As Social Justice. Many factors and institutions contribute to molding the concepts of justice. Home and school training, religion, enlightened self-interest, social and business groups, and the various media of modern communication and entertainment— all play a part. It would be a mistake, however, to assume that justice is a universal value which means the same thing to all people. Individual concepts of justice vary in terms of personality, training, and social and economic position. Justice has different meanings to the employer and the employee, to the millionaire and the pauper, to the industrial worker and the farmer, to the retired person and the young adult, to the liberal and the conservative, or to the professor and the student. Absolute justice is unattainable by human beings, but that is no reason why society should ever relent in its efforts to attain as high a level of justice as is humanly possible.

§ 2:2. Objectives of the Law. The objectives of the Constitution of the United States are stated in its preamble. Important statutes frequently include a statement of their objectives. In many instances, however, the objective of the law is not stated or it is expressed in very general terms. Whether stated or not, each law has an objective, and it is helpful in understanding law to know the objectives of the law.

In the following enumeration, the more specific objectives of the law are discussed against the background of our understanding of the general objective of creating and providing order, stability, and justice.[1]

(a) Protection of the State. A number of laws are designed to protect the existing governments, both state and national. Laws condemning treason, sedition, and subversive practices are examples of society taking measures to preserve governmental systems. Less dramatic are the laws that impose taxes to provide for the support of those governments.

---

[1] For a fuller treatment of the social forces, see Ronald A. Anderson, *Social Forces and the Law* (Cincinnati: South-Western Publishing Co., 1969) or Robert N. Corley and Robert Black, *Legal Environment of Business* (New York: McGraw-Hill Book Company, 1973).

(b)   Personal Protection. At an early date, laws developed to protect the individual from being injured or killed. The field of criminal law is devoted to a large extent to the protection of the person. In addition, under civil law a suit can be brought to recover damages for the harm done by the criminal acts. For example, a person who steals an automobile is subject to a penalty imposed by the state in the form of imprisonment or a fine, or both. In addition, the thief is liable to the owner for the money value of the automobile. Over a period of time the protection of personal rights has broadened to include the protection of reputation and privacy and to protect contracts and business relations from malicious interference by outsiders. (See p. 26, Korn v Rennison)

It is a federal offense to knowingly injure, intimidate, or interfere with anyone exercising a basic civil right (such as voting), taking part in any federal government program, or receiving federal assistance. Interference with attendance in a public school or college, with participation in any state or local governmental program, with service as a juror in a state court, or with the use of any public facility (common carrier, hotel, or restaurant) is likewise prohibited when based on race, color, religion, or national origin discrimination.[2]

Protection of the person is expanding to protect economic interest. Laws prohibiting discrimination in employment, in furnishing hotel accommodations and transportation, and in commercial transactions in the sale of property represent an extension of the concept of protecting the person. When membership in a professional association, a labor union, or a trade or business group has economic importance to its members, an applicant can no longer be arbitrarily excluded from the membership, nor may a member be expelled without notice of the charges made and an opportunity to be heard.[3]

(c)   Protection of Public Health, Safety, and Morals. The law seeks to protect the public health, safety, and morals in many ways. (See p. 27, Williams v Indiana) Laws relating to quarantine, food inspection, and compulsory vaccination are designed to protect the public health. Laws regulating highway speeds and laws requiring fire escapes or guard devices around moving parts of factory machinery are for the safety of the public. Laws prohibiting the sale of liquor to minors and those prohibiting obscenity protect the morals of the public.

(d)   Property Protection. Just as laws have developed to protect the individual's physical well-being, laws have developed to protect one's property from damage, destruction, and other harmful acts. As already noted, a thief who steals an automobile is liable civilly to the owner of the automobile for its value and is criminally responsible to the state.

(e)   Title Protection. Because of the importance of ownership of property, one of the objectives of the law has been to protect the title of the owner of property. Thus, if property is stolen, the true owner may recover it from the thief, and even from a person who purchased it in good faith from the thief.

---

[2] Civil Obedience Act of 1968, PL 90-284, 18 United States Code § 245.
[3] Silver v New York Stock Exchange, 373 US 341; Cunningham v Burbank Board of Realtors, 262 CalApp2d 211, 68 CalRptr 653.

(f)   Freedom of Personal Action. In the Anglo-American stream of history, the desire for freedom from political domination gave rise to the American Revolution, and the desire for freedom from economic domination gave rise to the free enterprise philosophy. Today we find freedom as the dominant element in the constitutional provisions for the protection of freedom of religion, press, and speech, and also in such laws as those against trusts or business combinations in restraint of trade by others.

This right of freedom of personal action, however, cannot be exercised by one person in such a way that it interferes to an unreasonable extent with the rights of others. Freedom of speech, for example, does not mean freedom to speak or write a malicious, false statement about another person's character. In effect, this means that one person's freedom of speech must be balanced with another person's right to be free from defamation of character or reputation.

(g)   Freedom of Use of Property. Freedom of action is often stated in terms of freedom of use of property. For example, the owner of an automobile is free to drive the car or not, to say who shall ride in it, to sell or give it away, and so on.

It must be remembered, however, that there are often restrictions on the use of property, such as speed laws governing the automobile, zoning laws regulating buildings, and antipollution laws restricting factories.

(h)   Enforcement of Intent. The law usually seeks to enforce the intent of the contracting parties. This objective is closely related to the concept that the law seeks to protect the individual's freedom of action. For example, if a person provides by will for the distribution of property upon death, the law will generally allow the property to pass to the persons intended by the deceased owner. The law will likewise seek to carry out the intention of the parties to a business transaction.

The extent to which the intent of one person or of several persons will be carried out has certain limitations. Sometimes the intent is not effective unless it is manifested by a particular written formality. For example, a deceased person may have intended to leave property to a friend, but in most states that intent must be shown by a written will signed by the deceased owner. Likewise, in some cases the intent of the parties may not be carried out because the law regards the intent as illegal.

(i)   Protection from Exploitation, Fraud, and Oppression. Many rules of law have developed in the courts and many statutes have been enacted to protect certain groups or individuals from exploitation or oppression by others. (See p. 28, Falcone v Middlesex County Medical Society) Thus, the law developed that a minor (a person under legal age) could set aside contracts, subject to certain exceptions, in order to give the minor an opportunity to avoid a bad bargain.

Persons who buy food that is packed in tin cans are given certain rights against the seller and the manufacturer. Since they cannot see the contents, buyers of such products need special protection from unscrupulous canners. The consumer is also protected by laws against adulteration and poisons in foods, drugs, and household products. Laws prohibiting unfair competition and discrimination, both economic and social, are also designed to protect from oppression.

For the purpose of brevity, "oppression" is used here to include not only conscious wrongdoing by another but also cases where the consequences of another's act causes the victim extreme or oppressive hardship.

(j)   Furtherance of Trade. Society seeks to further trade in a variety of ways, as by establishing a currency as a medium of payment; by recognizing and giving legal effect to installment sales; by adopting special rules for checks, notes, and similar instruments so that they can be widely used as credit devices and substitutes for money; and by enacting laws to mitigate the harmful effects of alternating periods of depression and inflation.

Laws that have been considered in connection with other objectives may also serve to further trade. For example, laws protecting against unfair competition have the objective of furtherance of trade, as well as the objective of protecting certain classes from oppression by others.

(k)   Creditor Protection. Society seeks to protect the rights of creditors and to protect them from dishonest or fraudulent acts of debtors. Initially creditors are protected by the law which declares that contracts are binding and which provides the machinery for the enforcement of contracts, and by the provision of the federal Constitution that prohibits states from impairing the obligation of contracts. Further, creditors may compel a debtor to come into bankruptcy. If the debtor has concealed property or transferred it to a friend in order to hide it from creditors, the law permits the creditors to claim the property for the payment of the debts due them.

(l)   Debtor Rehabilitation. Society has come to regard it as unsound that debtors should be ruined forever by the burden of their debts. The passing centuries have seen the debtor's prison abolished. Bankruptcy laws have been adopted to provide the debtor with a means of starting a new economic life. In times of widespread depression the same objective has been served by special laws that prohibit the foreclosure of mortgages and regulate the amount of the judgments that can be entered against mortgage debtors.

(m)   Stability. Stability is particularly important in all business transactions. When you buy a house, for example, you not only want to know the exact meaning of the transaction under today's law but you also hope that the transaction will have the same meaning in the future.

Because of the objective of stability, the courts will ordinarily follow former decisions unless there is some strong reason to depart from them. When no former case directly bears on the point involved, the desire for stability will influence the courts to reach a decision that is a logical extension of some former decision or which follows a former decision by analogy, rather than to strike off on a fresh path and to reach a decision unrelated to the past.

(n)   Flexibility. If stability were an absolute objective of the law, the cause of justice would often be thwarted. The reason that originally gave rise to a rule of law may have ceased to exist.[4] The rule then appears unjust because it reflects a concept of justice that is outmoded or obsolete. For example, capital punishment which one age believed just, has been condemned by another age as unjust. We must not lose sight of the fact that the rule of law under question was created to further the sense of social justice existing at that time; but our concepts of justice change.

Changes by legislative action in federal and state statutes and local ordinances are relatively easy to make. Furthermore, some statutes recognize the impossibility of laying down in advance a hard and fast rule that will do justice in all cases. The typical modern statute, particularly in the field of regulation of business will often contain an "escape clause" by which a person can escape from the operation of the statute under certain circumstances. Thus, a rent control law may impose a rent ceiling—that is, a maximum above which landlords cannot charge; but it may also authorize a greater charge when special circumstances make it just to allow such exception, as when the landlord has made expensive repairs to the property.

The rule of law may be stated in terms of what a reasonable or prudent person would do. Thus, whether you are negligent in driving your automobile is determined in court by whether you exercised the same degree of care that a prudent person would have exercised under the circumstances in question. This is a vague and variable standard as to how you must drive your car, but it is the only standard that is practical. The alternative would be a detailed motor code specifying how you should drive your car under every situation that might arise, a code that obviously could not foresee every possibility and which certainly would be too long for any driver to know in every detail by memory.

Even constitutions are flexible to the extent that they can be changed by amendment or judicial construction. Constitutions state the procedures for their amendment. Making changes in constitutions is purposely made difficult to serve the objective of stability, but change can be made when the need for change is generally recognized by the people of the state or nation.

(o) Practical Expediency. Frequently the law is influenced by what is practical or expedient in the situation. In some of these situations, the law will strive to make its rules fit the business practices of society. For example, a signature is frequently regarded by the law as including a stamping, printing, or typewriting of a name, in recognition of the business practice of "signing" letters and other instruments by mechanical means. A requirement of a handwritten signature would impose a burden on business that would not be practically expedient. (See p. 29, Louisiana v Hodgeson)

§ 2:3. Conflicting Objectives. The specific objectives of the law sometimes conflict with each other. When this is true, the problem is one of social policy, which in turn means

---

[4] "It is revolting to have no better reason for a rule of law than that it was laid down in the time of Henry IV. It is still more revolting if the grounds upon which it was laid down have vanished long since, and the rule simply persists from blind imitation of the past." Holmes, Collected Papers 187 (1920).

"The law must be stable, but it must not stand still." Roscoe Pound, *Introduction to the Philosophy of Law* (Connecticut: Yale University Press, 1922).

a weighing of social, economic, and moral forces to determine which objective should be furthered. Thus, we find a conflict at times between the objective of the state seeking protection from the conduct of individuals or groups and the objective of freedom of action by those individuals and groups.

For example, while protection of the freedom of the individual urges the utmost freedom of religious belief, society will impose limitations on religious freedom where it believes such freedom will cause harm to the public welfare. (See p. 31, United States v Kuch) Hence, state laws requiring vaccination against smallpox were enforced against the contention that this violated religious principles. Similarly, parents failing to provide medical care for a sick child will be held guilty of manslaughter if the child dies, even though the parents sincerely believed as a matter of religious principle that medical care was improper. In contrast, when the harm contemplated is not direct or acute, religious freedom will prevail, so that a compulsory child education law will not be enforced against Amish parents who as a matter of religion are opposed to state education.[5]

As another example, the objective of protecting title may conflict with the objective of furthering trade. Consider again the example of the stolen property that was sold by the thief to one who purchased it for value and in good faith, without reason to know that the goods had been stolen. If we are to further the objective of protecting the title to the property, we will conclude that the owner can recover the property from the innocent purchaser. This rule, however, will discourage trade, for people will be less willing to buy goods if they run the risk that the goods were stolen and may have to be surrendered. If we instead think only of taking steps to encourage buying and selling, we will hold that the buyer takes a good title because the buyer acted in good faith and paid value. If we do this, we then destroy the title of the original owner and obviously abandon our objective of protecting title to property. As a general rule, American society has followed the objective of protecting title. In some instances, however, the objective of furthering trade is adopted by statute and the buyer is given good title, as in certain cases of commercial paper (notes, drafts, and checks) or of the purchaser from a regular dealer in other people's goods.

§ 2:4. Law As an Evolutionary Process. Law changes as society changes. Let us consider an example of this type of change. When the economy was patterned on a local community unit in which everyone knew each other and each other's product, the concept of "let the buyer beware" expressed a proper basis on which to conduct business. Much of the early law of the sale of goods was predicated on this philosophy. In today's economy, however, with its pattern of interstate, national, and even international activities, the buyer has little or no direct contact with the manufacturer or seller, and the packaging of articles makes their presale examination impossible. Under the circumstances, the consumer must rely on the integrity of others to an increasing degree. Gradually practices that were tolerated and even approved in an earlier era have been condemned and the law has changed to protect the buyer.

Moreover, new principles of law are being developed to meet the new situations that have arisen. Every new invention and every new business practice introduces a

---

[5] Wisconsin v Yoder, 406 US 205 (high school student).

number of situations for which there may be no satisfactory rule of law. For example, how could there have been a law governing the liability of a food canner to the consumer before canning was invented? How could there have been a law relating to stocks and bonds before those instruments came into existence? How could there have been a law with respect to the liability of radio and television broadcasters before such methods of communication were developed?

§ 2:5. Law As a Synthesis. Many rules of law do not further one objective alone. Some rules are combinations of two or more objectives with each objective working toward the same result. In other instances, the objectives oppose each other and the rule of law that emerges is a combination or synthesis of the different objectives.

Law as a synthesis may be illustrated by the law as it relates to contracts for the sale of a house. Originally such a contract could be oral; that is, merely spoken words with nothing in writing to prove that there was such a contract. Of course, there was the practical question of proof—that is, whether the jury would believe that there was such a contract—but no rule of law said that the contract must be evidenced by a writing. This situation made it possible for a witness in court to swear falsely that Jones had agreed to sell Jones' house for a specified sum. Then even though Jones had not made such an agreement, the jury might believe the false witness and Jones would be required to give up the house on terms to which Jones had never agreed. To prevent such a miscarriage of justice, a statute was passed in England in 1677 declaring that contracts for the sale of houses had to be evidenced by a writing.

This law ended the evil of persons lying that there was an oral agreement for the sale of a house, but was justice finally achieved? Not always, for cases arose in which Jones did in fact make an oral agreement to sell land to Smith. Smith would take possession of the land and would make valuable improvements at great expense and effort, and then Jones would have Smith thrown off the land. Smith would defend on the ground that Jones had orally agreed to sell the land. Jones would then say, "Where is the writing that the statute requires?" To this, Smith could only reply there was no writing. No writing meant no enforceable legal agreement; and therefore Smith lost the land, leaving Jones with the land and all the improvements that Smith had made. That certainly was not just.

Gradually the law courts developed the rule that even though the statute required a writing, the courts would enforce an oral contract for the sale of land when the buyer had gone into possession and made valuable improvements of such a nature that it would be difficult to determine what amount of money would be required to make up the loss if the buyer were to be put off the land.

Thus, the law passed through three stages: (a) the original concept that all land contracts could be oral and did not require any written evidence. Because the perjury evil arose under the rule the law swung to (b) the opposite rule that no such contract could be oral without any written evidence. This rule gave rise to the hardship case of the honest buyer under an oral contract who made extensive improvements. The law then swung back, not to the original rule, but to (c) a middle position, combining both (a) and (b), that is, combining the element of a writing requirement as to the ordinary transaction, but allowing oral contracts in the special cases to prevent hardship.

This example is also interesting because it shows the way in which the courts "amend" the law by decision. The flat requirement of the statute was "eroded" by decisions and by exceptions created by the courts in the interest of furthering justice.

§ 2:6. Nature and Purpose of Cases. Following the text in each chapter are cases for analysis and study. They illustrate how certain principles of law are applied in lawsuits by our courts. The information for each case is presented in three parts: (a) the heading, (b) the facts of the case, and (c) the opinion. In this explanation the first case, Korn v Rennison, p. 26, will be used as an example.

(a)   Heading. The heading of the case consists of the title and the source.

    (1)   Title. The title of the case usually consists of the names of the parties to the action. In the illustrative case Korn, as plaintiff, sued Rennison (and others) as defendants.

    The title of an appealed case may not reveal who the plaintiff was in the original or lower court or who the defendant was. When the action is started in the lower court, the first party named is the plaintiff and the second is the defendant. When the case is appealed, the name of the party who takes the appeal may appear first on the records of the higher court, so that if the defendant takes the appeal, the original order of the names of the parties is then reversed.

    (2)   Source. The second part of the heading gives the source of the opinion. The opinion is found in "21 Conn Supp 400, 156 A2d 476." This means that the opinion is found in the 21st volume of the Connecticut Supplement (Conn Supp) reporter beginning at page 400, and that it is also found in the Atlantic (A) sectional reporter[6] in volume 156 of the second series beginning at page 476.

(b)   Facts. The paragraph in smaller type following the heading is a summary of the facts of the case, which provides a background for an understanding and analysis of the opinion. Read the statement of facts for Korn v Rennison. Keep in mind the principles of law that you studied in the chapter. Then read the opinion carefully to see how the court made its decision, what it decided, and whether it agrees with what you thought would be decided.

(c)   Opinion. The opinion of the court includes the name of the judge, excerpts from the reasoning of the court, and the judgment.

    (1)   Judge. At the beginning of the opinion is the name of the judge who wrote it. The opinion in the first case was written by Judge Alcorn. If the case has been appealed, the judge who wrote the opinion is speaking for the entire court, unless otherwise indicated. In cases at the trial level, normally one[7] judge is disposing of the case, as in the Korn case.

    The letter or letters following the name of the judge indicate his rank or title. J. stands for Judge or Justice. (JJ is the plural form.) Other abbreviations

---

[6] See Appendix, footnote 1, for sectional reporters.

[7] In some instances a case at the trial stage is disposed of by three judges instead of one.

include C.J. for Chief Justice or Circuit Judge, D.J. for District Judge, P.J. for Presiding Judge or President Judge, and C. for Chancellor or Commissioner.

(2)   Body of the Opinion. The material following the judge's name is quoted from the opinion of the court. Words enclosed in brackets [ ] did not appear in the original opinion but have been added to explain a legal term, to identify a party, or to clarify a statement. Ellipses (three or four periods) are used to indicate that something has been omitted that is not pertinent to the point of law with which we are concerned at this time.

Decisions vary in length from less than a page to more than a hundred pages, and opinions frequently involve several points of law. Each case in this book has been carefully edited so that the excerpts reprinted here will be convenient for student use.

The edited opinion in Korn v Rennison consists of three paragraphs. In the first paragraph the judge indicates that more than a half-century ago the existence of a right of privacy was recognized by some as a matter of common or nonstatutory law. In the second paragraph he brings the subject up to date, pointing out the present state of the law and the social and scientific factors which influenced the growth of the law. The last paragraph points out the conflict of interests that are involved; and a further recognition of the growth of the law is made, the trend being in favor of a right of privacy. The case then ends with the dismissal of the objection to the plaintiff's claim. The theory is that there is a common-law right of privacy, and consequently it is no defense to say there is no such right.

Opinions do not follow a standard pattern of organization; but usually the well-written opinion will carefully examine the arguments presented by all parties and then explain why the court accepts or rejects those arguments in whole or in part. In this process the opinion may discuss the opinion of the lower court, the decisions in similar cases in other courts, and material from other sources.[8]

(3)   Judgment. The case is concluded with a statement of the court's decision. If the case has been appealed and the court agrees with the lower court, the decision may simply be "Judgment affirmed" or a similar expression. If the appellate court disagrees, the decision may be expressed as "Judgment reversed." "Case remanded" means that the case is returned to the lower court to proceed further in harmony with the appellate court's decision. In lower court cases when the judgment is on a narrow issue, the judgment of the court may be limited to "Objection sustained" or "Objection dismissed."

A judge of the court who disagrees with the majority may simply declare as part of the record that he dissents; or he may file a dissenting opinion, as occurred in the case on page 41.

§ 2:7. Checklist for Case Study. The questions in the following checklist will serve as a guide for the analysis of each case. It should be understood, however, that not every case will provide answers to all of these questions.

---

[8] See Appendix, "How to Find the Law."

(a) **Court.** In what court was the action brought originally, and which court filed the opinion being studied?

(b) **Parties.** Who were the parties to the action? Were they the parties to the original transaction, or were they strangers such as creditors?

(c) **Purpose of the Action.** What was the relief or remedy sought in the action?

(d) **Action Appealed from.** What was done in the lower court which the appellant deemed wrong and from which the appeal was taken?

(e) **Arguments of the Parties.** What were the arguments made by the respective parties?

(f) **Decision of the Court.** What did the court decide?

(g) **Basis for Decision.** On what authority or ground did the court base its decision? Was it common law, decision, statute, Restatement of the Law, text, logic, or the personal belief of the court?

(h) **Appraisal of the Decision.** What social objectives are advanced by the decision? What social objectives are hindered or defeated by the decision? Is the decision socially desirable? Is it practical in application? Does it give rise to any dangers?

CASES FOR CHAPTER 2

Korn v Rennison

21 Conn Supp 400, 156 A2d 476 (1959)

The substance of the complaint was that through an arrangement and agreement between Rennison and other defendants, a photograph of Korn, the plaintiff, was published for advertising purposes in the defendant newspaper without the knowledge, consent, or permission of the plaintiff and in violation of her personal liberties and private rights. As a result, the defendants received monetary benefits and advantages while the plaintiff received none and was subjected to ridicule, embarrassment, vexation, and humiliation. The plaintiff, a minor, brought this action by her mother to recover damages.

ALCORN, J. . . . The defendants argue that . . . a right [of privacy] was not recognized at common law and therefore, in the absence of statute, it cannot exist in Connecticut today. When Samuel D. Warren and Louis D. Brandeis first gave form and substance to the right of privacy in 1890, it was one objective of their discussion in 4 Harvard Law Review 193 to demonstrate that the right found support in common-law principles. Underlying their reasoning is the premise that the common law is not static and its protecting arm does not become immobilized from lack of precedent.

In the years intervening since the right was thus defined, a constantly increasing number of jurisdictions have recognized its independent existence. Press, photography, radio, and television represent elements in constantly changing conditions which impinge upon individual privacy. With the environmental changes of modern living has grown the need that man's inner nature and feelings as well as his body and possessions receive the protection of the law. Hence, the right of privacy has become established. . . .

The line to be drawn between reasonable demands of individual privacy and public interest in legitimate news is not always easy to define, but the boundary is more readily perceived in the case of commercial advertising. . . . No case decided within the last fifteen years has been found in which the existence of a right of privacy has been denied. Decisions which originally denied the right have, with apparently a single exception, since been overruled, modified, or altered by statute. Rhode Island appears to stand alone as an unqualified precedent for denying a recovery in damages for an invasion of the right of privacy. . . .

[Objection of defendants dismissed]

Williams v Indiana

261 Ind 547, 307 NE2d 457 (1974)

A police broadcast stated that a named motel had been robbed by two men using a sawed-off shotgun. The men were reported fleeing in an automobile travelling northwestwardly. Police officers hearing this report assumed that the robbers were seeking to escape to Chicago and went to the nearest intersection of the road leading to that city. They saw a car which they thought might contain the suspects. They trailed the car to another intersection where the better lighting gave a better view of the driver. The police then stopped the car. After it was stopped, the police saw a shotgun in the back of the car and a man attempting to hide on the back seat. The men in the car were arrested and prosecuted for robbery of the motel. They claimed that the evidence of what was learned when their car was stopped could not be admitted at the trial because they had been stopped without a search warrant. This contention was rejected by the trial court and the men were convicted. They appealed.

ARTERBURN, C.J. . . . The sole contention is that the initial stopping of the Appellants' car was unlawful and that, therefore, the fruits of this unlawful seizure must be excluded from the trial. . . .

The legal question that confronts us, to be very specific, is: did the police officers have the right to stop the motorist on the basis of the suspicion created by the meager facts received over the radio and the police officers' calculations from those facts? After the stopping of the Appellants' car, it became immediately apparent without a search, but from open observation (the shotgun and the passenger hiding in the car) that probable cause existed for the arrest of the Appellants. If the stopping was legal, then all that followed was legal. . . . The question is "whether the facts known . . . at the time he (a police officer) stopped the car were sufficient to warrant a man of reasonable caution in the belief that an investigation was appropriate.". . .

In fact, this case presents squarely to us the question whether or not under similar circumstances a roadblock could be set up at certain points where it has reasonably been calculated that fleeing robbers might be apprehended. Justice Jackson of the United States Supreme Court, dissenting from the approval of a seizure and search, realized and noted the problem, commenting as follows:

"If we assume, for example, that a child is kidnapped and the officers throw a roadblock about the neighborhood and search every outgoing car, it would be a drastic and undiscriminating use of the search. The officers might be unable to show probable cause for searching any particular car. However, I should candidly strive hard to sustain such an action, executed fairly and in good faith, because it might be reasonable to subject travelers to that indignity if it was the only way to save a threatened life and detect a vicious crime. But I should not strain to sustain such a roadblock and universal search to salvage a few bottles of bourbon and catch a bootlegger." Brinegar v United States (1948), 338 US 160 at 183. . . . However, the suggestion by Justice Jackson that the right to stop depends upon the enormity of the crime creates an uncertain and hazardous standard for police officers to follow.

In Terry v Ohio (1968), 392 US 1, . . . the United States Supreme Court had before it a situation in which a police officer with thirty (30) years experience on a particular beat became suspicious of the actions of two men who repeatedly and alternately made numerous round-trip strolls past a store window. The officer accosted these men when they were conferring with a third man with whom they had previously conferred during their strolls. In a brief "pat down" or "frisk" the officer discovered concealed weapons on two of the men. In upholding this particular "search and seizure" the Supreme Court said that:

". . . in justifying the particular intrusion the police officer must be able to point to specific and articulable facts which, taken together with rational inferences from those facts, reasonably warrant that intrusion. The scheme of the Fourth Amendment becomes meaningful only when it is assured that at some point the conduct of those charged with enforcing the laws can be subjected to the more detached, neutral scrutiny of a judge who must evaluate the reasonableness of a particular search or seizure in light of the particular circumstances. And in making that assessment it is imperative that the facts be judged against an objective standard: would the facts available to the officer at the moment of the seizure . . . warrant a man of reasonable caution in the belief" that the action taken was appropriate? . . .

Our society has a right to protect itself. What is "unreasonable" under the Fourth Amendment is a function of the totality of conditions existing within our society at any moment in history. Social interests under the police power should give law officers the right to stop users of the highways to check, for instance, their right to use the highway or to check the vehicles for safety standards. . . .

Similarly, we have the searches of passengers boarding airplanes. . . . Such procedures have been very effective in deterring "hijacking," and insofar as our limited observation reveals have met with the traveling public's approval.

We offer the following hypothetical: At a party of, say, twenty or so persons a valuable diamond ring is discovered to be missing from the person of one of the guests. Absent any more information, there would not be probable cause to detain one specific individual from among the persons present, but would it be unreasonable to detain *all* the persons present? A distinction may exist between what is a reasonable restraint of an individual and what is a reasonable restraint of an identifiable group. The interference with citizen liberty described in the above situations may be rationalized on the basis that although there is not probable cause for suspicion of one specific person, probable cause does exist as to an identifiable group (e.g.) those persons using the highways at a certain time and certain place in the aftermath of a crime, those persons boarding airplanes, those persons at the party.

It has been said that constitutional interpretation must conform to the changes which progress has wrought in our society since the adoption of the Constitution. The classic formulation is . . . Chief Justice Marshall's: ". . . we must never forget that it is a constitution we are expounding . . . a constitution, intended to endure for ages to come, and, consequently, to be adapted to the various crises of human affairs." . . .

The automobile has made an alteration in our way of life unforeseen and unforeseeable by the Founding Fathers. It is our duty to be rational and sensible in our constitutional interpretation so that modern society is not damaged or injured by an irrational and unrealistic refusal to recognize the necessities brought about by these changes. The primary purpose of government is the protection of society. An instrument should not be so interpreted as to thwart that main objective.

If the police officers under the facts before us had observed the incriminating evidence inside the car while it was parked on the roadside, there would be no question here as to the right of the officers to arrest the driver and the occupant and to make a further search. . . .

As we previously stated, the question before us is whether or not suspicion such as the officers had in this case is a sufficient basis for the stopping, of an automobile upon the public highway. We believe that it is, and that such pronouncement is a reasonable interpretation of constitutional rights which are rights that belong to the public [the State] as well as to a defendant in a criminal case. Courts have to balance out the rights and have done so in the past. . . .

[Judgment affirmed]

Falcone v Middlesex County Medical Society

34 NJ 582, 170 A2d 791 (1961)

Dr. Falcone was admittedly a licensed and qualified physician and surgeon, holding degrees from a Philadelphia school and from the College of Medicine of the University of Milan, who practiced surgery and obstetrics. He met all the requirements of the bylaws of the Middlesex County Medical Society. The Society, however, refused him membership on the ground that it had an unwritten rule requiring that every applicant have four years of study in a medical school recognized by the American Medical Association. Dr. Falcone did not meet this requirement since the Philadelphia school was not AMA-approved and, although the University of Milan was so approved, the course was not four years. Dr. Falcone brought suit against the Society for refusing to admit him to membership.

JACOBS, J. . . . The Society's declaration of his ineligibility and its refusal to admit him to membership have had seriously adverse economic and professional effects on Dr. Falcone. He was a member of the medical staffs of the Middlesex General Hospital and St. Peter's General Hospital in New Brunswick but was dropped because they, like other hospitals in the area, require that their staff physicians be members of the County Medical Society. It seems entirely evident that Dr. Falcone cannot successfully continue his practice of surgery and obstetrics or properly serve his surgical and obstetric patients without the use of local hospital facilities; he testified that in order to earn a livelihood it is necessary "to belong to the local society" for "otherwise, you cannot use the hospitals." The virtual monopoly which the Society possesses in fact over the use of local hospital facilities results from the well-known interrelationship between the County Society, the State Medical Society, the American Medical Association, and the Joint Commission on Accreditation of Hospitals. . . .

Over thirty years ago Professor Chafee, in his discussion of nonprofit associations, pointed to the distinction between the customary social and fraternal organizations on the one hand and trade unions and professional societies on the other hand; he noted that whereas exclusion or expulsion from a social or fraternal organization may result in little more than hurt feelings, exclusion or expulsion from a trade union or a professional society may result, as here, in deprivation of the invaluable opportunity "to earn a livelihood." . . . In a more recent discussion addressed specially to medical societies, the editors of the Yale Law Journal, after pointing out that exclusion or expulsion from a local medical society results, as a practical matter, in the deprivation of hospital facilities, descriptively noted that "nonmembership amounts to a partial revocation of licensure to practice medicine." 63 Yale LJ 953. . . .

We are here concerned with . . . an organization, membership in which may . . . be viewed as "an economic necessity"; in dealing with such an organization, the court must be particularly alert to the need for truly protecting the public welfare and advancing the interests of justice by reasonably safeguarding the individual's opportunity for earning a livelihood while not impairing the proper standards and objectives of the organization. . . .

When courts originally declined to scrutinize admission practices of membership associations, they were dealing with social clubs, religious organizations, and fraternal associations. Here the policies against judicial intervention were strong, and there were no significant countervailing policies. When the courts were later called upon to deal with trade and professional associations exercising virtually monopolistic control, different factors were involved. The intimate personal relationships which pervaded the social, religious, and fraternal organizations were hardly in evidence and the individual's opportunity of earning a livelihood and serving society in his chosen trade or profession appeared as the controlling policy consideration. . . .

It must be borne in mind that the County Medical Society is not a private voluntary membership association with which the public has little or no concern. It is an association with which the public is highly concerned and which engages in activities vitally affecting the health and welfare of the people. . . . Through its interrelationships, the County Medical Society possesses, in fact, a virtual monopoly over the use of local hospital facilities. As a result it has power, by excluding Dr. Falcone from membership, to preclude him from successfully continuing in his practice of obstetrics and surgery and to restrict patients who wish to engage him as an obstetrician or surgeon in their freedom of choice of physicians. Public policy strongly dictates that this power should not be unbridled but should be viewed judicially as a fiduciary power to be exercised in reasonable and lawful manner for the advancement of the interests of the medical profession and the public generally. . . .

In the light of all of the foregoing, the effort of the County Society to apply its unwritten requirement of four years' attendance at an AMA approved medical college so as to exclude Dr. Falcone from membership, must be viewed as patently arbitrary and unreasonable and beyond the pale of the law. When the County Society engages in action which is designed to advance medical science or elevate professional standards, it should and will be sympathetically supported. When, however, as here, its action . . . runs strongly counter to the public policy of our State and the true interests of justice, it should and will be stricken down. . . .

[Admission ordered]

Louisiana v Hodgeson

(La) 305 So2d 421 (1974)

Hodgeson was prosecuted for manslaughter. Part of the evidence against her was evidence of telephone calls which had been made. This evidence was obtained from the computer printouts of the telephone company. Hodgeson objected that this printout was not admissible because there was no proof of the identity of the persons who had supplied the information to the computer. Hodgeson was convicted and appealed.

DIXON, J. . . . [Defendant specifies as error] the State's introduction into evidence of copies of defendant's telephone bills covering the months of January and February, 1972. Mr. John C. Kling, comptroller-office manager of the East Ascension Telephone Company, testified that the basic data for the telephone bills was compiled by people in his office under his supervision, and was then given to a computer service which calculated and prepared the actual bill. The actual bill denoted the customer, address, amount due for toll and long distance calls and the individual long distance calls. These bills listed the calls which had been made on the defendant's telephone to Dr. C. A. Martello in Baton Rouge, and they were introduced for the purpose of proving communications between defendant and Dr. Martello.

Defendant contends that the evidence was inadmissible because it was hearsay . . . . Its admission confronts this court with the issue of the admissibility of computer printout sheets, the telephone statements in this case, under the recognized exception to the hearsay rule for business records prepared in the ordinary course of business. . . .

The issue of introducing computer printouts of information contained and stored in a computer system has confronted other jurisdictions recently. The majority of cases have been decided under various forms of the Uniform Business Records as Evidence Act.* . . . Louisiana has not adopted this act [and] is therefore not constrained by the language of that statute. The question we must answer is whether such records are admissible in this State and, if so, what standards are to be applied in order to insure (1) necessity and (2) reliability, which are the bases for this exception to the hearsay rule.

The Nebraska Supreme Court confronted this issue first in Transport Indemnity Co. v Seib, 178 Neb. 253, 132 N.W.2d 871 (1965), a suit by an insurance company to collect overdue premiums. The insurance company supplied the raw data to its computer which calculated, according to a programmed formula, the proper premium amount due. Through its data storage facilities and ability to retrieve and process this data, the computer was the company's bookkeeper; the information contained in its storage facilities was the company's record and was accessible only by use of printouts of what was contained

within it. The court found that the printout results of the computer's calculations satisfied the requirements of necessity and reliability and were admissible under the business records exception to the hearsay rule.

The Nebraska result was followed in King v State ex rel. Murdock Acceptance Corp., 222 So.2d 393 (Miss., 1969), where the Mississippi Supreme Court adopted the following rules for the admission of computer records and printouts:

". . . we hold that printout sheets of business records stored on electronic computing equipment are admissible in evidence if relevant and material, without the necessity of identifying, locating, and producing as witnesses the individuals who made the entries in the regular course of business if it is shown (1) that the electronic computing equipment is recognized as standard equipment, (2) the entries are made in the regular course of business at or reasonably near the time of the happening of the event recorded, and (3) the foundation testimony satisfies the court that the sources of information, method and time of preparation were such as to indicate its trustworthiness and justify its admission." (222 So.2d 398).

In adopting these rules as our own, we also note with approval Judge Ely's concurrence in United States v De Georgia, 420 F.2d 889 (9th Cir. 1969), in which he stated:

". . . If a machine is to testify against an accused, the courts must, at the very least, be satisfied with all reasonable certainty that both the machine and those who supply its information have performed their functions with utmost accuracy. Therefore, it is essential that the trial court be convinced of the trustworthiness of the particular records before admitting them into evidence. And it should be convinced by proof presented by the party seeking to introduce the evidence rather than receiving the evidence upon the basis of an inadequate foundation and placing the burden upon the objector to demonstrate its weakness." (420 F.2d 895-896).

In affirming the admissibility of computer records and printouts, we are in accord with the jurisdictions which have confronted the problem of adjusting the tested rule of evidence to the realities

---

* "The Uniform Business Records Evidence Act provides: 'A record of an act, condition or event, shall, insofar as relevant, be competent evidence if the custodian or other qualified witness testifies to its identity and the mode of its preparation, and if it was made in the regular course of business, at or near the time of the act, condition or event, and if, in the opinion of the court, the sources of information, method and time of preparation were such as to justify its admission.' " (9 Uniform Laws Acts 387).

of contemporary business life while insuring the reliability of the information offered at trial. . . .

[Specification of error dismissed and conviction affirmed]

United States v Kuch

summarizing facts

(DC Dist Col) 288 F Supp 439 (1968)

Kuch was indicted for violating the federal Marihuana Tax Act which taxed licensed sellers and prohibited the sale or transfer by an unlicensed person of marihuana or LSD. She defended on the ground of religious freedom. She was an ordained minister of the Neo-American Church and claimed that she was providing the drug for use in the religious services.

GESELL, D.J. . . . The Neo-American Church was incorporated in California in 1965 as a nonprofit corporation. It claims a nationwide membership of about 20,000. At its head is a Chief Boo Hoo. Defendant Kuch is the primate of the Potomac, a position analogized to bishop. She supervises the Boo Hoos in her area. There are some 300 Boo Hoos throughout the country. In order to join the church a member must subscribe to the following principles:

(1) Everyone has the right to expand his consciousness and stimulate visionary experience by whatever means he considers desirable and proper without interference from anyone;

(2) The psychedelic substances, such as LSD, are the true Host of the Church, not drugs. They are sacramental foods, manifestations of the Grace of God, of the infinite imagination of the Self, and therefore belong to everyone;

(3) We do not encourage the ingestion of psychedelics by those who are unprepared.

Building on the central thesis of the group that psychedelic substances, particularly marihuana and LSD, are the true Host, the Church specifies that "it is the Religious *duty* of all members to partake of the sacraments on regular occasions." . . .

The dividing line between what is, and what is not, a religion is difficult to draw. . . . Obviously this question is a matter of delicacy and courts must be ever careful not to permit their own moral and ethical standards to determine the religious implications of beliefs and practices of others. Religions now

accepted were persecuted, unpopular and condemned at their inception.

. . . There is need to develop a sharper line of demarcation between religious activities and personal codes of conduct that lack spiritual import. Those who seek the constitutional protections for their participation in an establishment of religion and freedom to practice its beliefs must not be permitted the special freedoms this sanctuary may provide merely by adopting religious nomenclature and cynically using it as a shield to protect them when participating in antisocial conduct that otherwise stands condemned. In a complex society where the requirements of public safety, health and order must be recognized, those who seek immunity from these requirements on religious grounds must at the very least demonstrate adherence to ethical standards and a spiritual discipline.

The defendant has sought to have the Church designated a religion primarily by emphasizing that ingestion of psychedelic drugs brings about a religious awareness and sharpens religious instincts. There was proof offered that the use of psychedelic drugs may, among other things, have religious implications. Various writings on the subject were received in evidence and testimony was taken from two professors, not members of the Church but having theological interest in the subject, who had themselves taken drugs experimentally and had studied religious manifestations of psychedelic drug ingestion. . . .

Assuming . . . that the Neo-American Church is a genuine religion and that Kuch subscribes fully to its doctrines and thus may invoke the full constitutional guarantees for free religious expression, her contentions are still without merit. The Constitution protects the right to have and to express beliefs. It does not blindly afford the same absolute protection to acts done in the name of or under the impetus of religion. . . .

Defendant misconceives the Constitution and the decisions when she claims in effect an unbridled right to practice her beliefs. The public interest is paramount and if properly determined the Congress may inhibit or prevent acts as opposed to beliefs even where those acts are in accord with religious convictions or beliefs. If individual religious conviction permits one to act contrary to civic duty, public health and the criminal laws of the land, then the right to be let alone in one's belief with all the spiritual peace it guarantees would be destroyed in the resulting breakdown of society. There is abroad among some in the land today a view that the individual is free to do anything he wishes. A nihilistic, agnostic and anti-establishment attitude exists. These beliefs may be held. They may be expressed but where they are antithetical to the interests of others who are not of the same persuasion and contravene criminal statutes legitimately designed to protect society as a whole, such conduct should not find any constitutional sanctuary in the name of religion or otherwise. . . .

. . . The Court concludes that under any common sense view of undisputed facts the full enforcement of the statute here involved is necessary in the public interest and the unintended but obvious restrictions on the practices of defendant's church are wholly permissible.

There is substantial evidence that the use of marihuana creates a health hazard, is often the first step toward serious drug addiction in the progression to heroin, and is frequently associated with the commission of non-drug crimes, often crimes of violence. While all its effects are still unknown and the reactions of users differ, depending on emotional, psychological and frequency-of-use factors, the drug marihuana may often predispose to antisocial behavior and precipitate psychotic episodes. Among other reactions, hallucinations and delusions, impairment of judgment and memory, and confusion and delirium are common. Among chronic users, extremely violent aggressive conduct is manifested. Medical experts, narcotic experts, law enforcement officials, psychologists and proponents of freer marihuana use are not in accord but there is a very substantial body of opinion among individuals in each of these categories which supports the implications of marihuana use summarized above.

. . . To except the members of the Neo-American Church from the regulation of this drug, as Kuch requests, would not amount to some slight exception that would in no way interfere with the purposes of the Marihuana Tax Act. On the contrary, it would permit anyone to violate the law by paying the Church membership fee. The number of marihuana cases in this Court suggests that there are many who would quickly take out membership and the Act would soon be a nullity. . . .

As part of her motion to dismiss the indictment on religious grounds, defendant has also made what may be broadly described as the "peyote" argument. The claim is that she is denied equal protection

in the constitutional sense because members of another religion are permitted under the narcotic laws to use peyote, a similar and at least as harmful an hallucinatory drug.

In People v Woody, 61 Cal 2d 716, 40 Cal Rptr 69, 394 P2d 813 (1964), the California Supreme Court broadly applied the tests of Sherbert v Verner, 374 US 398, 83 S Ct 1790, 10 L Ed 2d 965 (1963), and held that a state statute prohibiting the unauthorized use of peyote could not constitutionally be applied to a member of the Native American Church. The Native American Church, made up of from 30,000 to 250,000 American Indians, had a "long history" of the use of peyote. The court found that:

"Although peyote serves as a sacramental symbol similar to bread and wine in certain Christian churches, it is more than a sacrament. Peyote constitutes in itself an object of worship; prayers are directed to it much as prayers are devoted to the Holy Ghost. . . ." 40 Cal Rptr 69 at 73, 394 P2d 813 at 817.

. . .

Defendant asserts that marihuana is less harmful, or no more harmful, than peyote and that under the reasoning in Woody, she is entitled to an exemption from the Marihuana Tax Act. . . .

The Commissioner of Food and Drugs has exempted peyote, when used by the Native American Church, from regulation under the Drug Abuse Control Amendments to the Federal Food, Drug and Cosmetic Act. . . .

The Court must assume that the FDA [Food and Drug Administration] in granting the peyote exemption acted within its delegated authority. . . . As to marihuana, Congress, rather than delegating responsibility to the FDA, itself determined that there was a clear hazard to health in the use of the drug. That this legislative determination still has validity and a wholly rational basis is demonstrated by the materials submitted to the Court at the hearing on the motion of which the Court takes judicial notice. It is not the function of the Court to go any further behind this legislative determination as to marihuana. . . .

. . . These laws, enacted to preserve public safety, health and order, will be enforced. On the proofs before the Court the statutes are unrelated to the suppression of religion or religious beliefs and there is no denial of defendant's rights under the Constitution of the United States.

[Statute sustained]

decision

QUESTIONS AND CASE PROBLEMS

written and read → responsible

1. What is the general purpose of law?

2. Of the specific objectives of the law, which do you consider to be the most important? Why?

3. (a) When specific objectives of the law conflict in a given situation, which objective prevails?

   (b) Are creditor protection and debtor rehabilitation conflicting specific objectives of the law?

4. (a) How can law be dynamic if stability is one of its specific objectives?

   (b) How do some statutes provide for "built-in" flexibility?

5. Sometimes the development of the law seems to follow a zigzag course. What is the explanation?

6. When O'Brien was prosecuted for burning his draft card, he raised the defense that the right of free speech gave him the privilege to express his disapproval of the draft and of the war in this manner. Was he correct? [United States v O'Brien, 391 US 367]

7. The City of Columbia, South Carolina, provided for the fluoridation of the city water supply. Hall claimed that this deprived him of his constitutional right to drink unfluoridated water since there was no other water supply, and further attacked the validity of the plan on the ground that dental cavities are not contagious and therefore a public health problem did not exist. Was he correct? [Hall v Bates, Mayor of Columbia, 247 SC 511, 148 SE2d 345]

8. The New York Social Services Law authorized the Social Services officials to replace necessary furniture and clothing of welfare recipients who lost such items by fire, flood, or other like catastrophe. Howard was on state welfare. Her clothing was stolen from her apartment by a burglar. She claimed that this was a "catastrophe" and that the Social Service official was required to replace the stolen clothing. Was she correct? [In re Howard, 28 NY2d 434, 271 NE2d 528]

9. Davidson was arrested for loitering. This was her first arrest. The Police Department made the standard police record, taking her photograph and fingerprints. She was acquitted and then brought suit against Dill, the chief of police, to remove her case from the police records or to give her the papers. Dill claimed that she was not entitled to any relief. Was he correct? [Davidson v Dill, 180 Colo 123, 503 P2d 157]

10. The Street of Ships, Inc., owned a floating restaurant, The Robert Fulton. This was a seagoing passenger barge and was certified for use as such by the United States Coast Guard. It was moored to a pier in the city of New York and was opened as a restaurant. There was no intention to take it out to sea. O'Hagan, the Fire Commissioner of New York City, took action against The Robert Fulton because it did not comply with the New York Fire Safety Code which was applicable to "buildings and structures." The owner claimed that the Fulton was a seagoing vessel and not a building or structure and therefore could not be controlled by the City Fire Commissioner. Was he correct? [Street of Ships, Inc. v O'Hagan, 392 NYS2d 531]

11. The Reader's Digest Association published an article on truck hijacking in which it stated that John Doe had taken part in a truck hijacking eleven years before and had thereafter reformed. John Doe sued Reader's Digest for damages for invasion of privacy. It raised the defense that it was not liable because the information was true. Was this a valid defense? [John Doe v Reader's Digest Association, 4 Cal3d 529, 93 CalRptr 866, 483 P2d 34]

3 Criminal Law and Business

In order to preserve our freedom and to protect the rights that give meaning to that freedom, society through rules of law and government imposes certain limitations that apply to everyone. Three areas of the law that determine whether conduct is wrongful are contract law, criminal law, and the law of torts.

A claim based upon contract law arises, for example, when a beneficiary brings suit on a life insurance policy. Contract law in general is discussed in Part 3. Special types of contracts, such as those for sales and insurance, constitute the subject matter of several other parts that follow.

Criminal law is the subject of discussion in this chapter, and the law of torts is discussed in Chapter 4.

A. GENERAL PRINCIPLES

A *crime* is a violation of the law that is punished as an offense against the state or government. While traditionally the victim of a crime received no benefit from the criminal prosecution of a defendant, several states now have statutes providing for varying degrees of financial indemnification to persons injured by criminal acts.

§ 3:1. Classification of Crimes.

(a) Source of Criminal Law. Crimes are classified in terms of their origin as common-law and statutory crimes. Some offenses that are defined by statute are merely declaratory of the common law. Each state has its own criminal law, although a common pattern among the states may be observed.

(b) Seriousness of Offense. Crimes are classified in terms of their seriousness as treason, felonies, and misdemeanors. *Treason* is defined by the Constitution of the United States, which states that "Treason against the United States, shall consist only in levying War against them, or in adhering to their Enemies, giving them Aid and Comfort."

Felonies include the other more serious crimes, such as arson, homicide, and robbery, which are punishable by confinement in prison or by death.

Crimes not classified as treason or felonies are *misdemeanors*. Reckless driving, weighing and measuring goods with scales and measuring devices that have not been inspected, and disturbing the peace by illegal picketing are generally classified as misdemeanors. An act may be a felony in one state and a misdemeanor in another.

(c)   **Nature of Crimes.** Crimes are also classified in terms of the nature of the misconduct. *Crimes mala in se* are crimes that are inherently vicious or, in other words, that are naturally evil as measured by the standards of a civilized community. *Crimes mala prohibita* are crimes that are wrong merely because they are declared wrong by some statute. (See p. 40, United States v Jackson)

§ 3:2. Basis of Criminal Liability.

A crime generally consists of two elements: (a) an act or omission, and (b) a mental state. In the case of some crimes, such as the illegal operation of a business without a license, it is immaterial whether the act causes harm to others. In other cases the defendant's act must be the sufficiently direct cause of harm to another in order to impose criminal liability. (See p. 41, Pennsylvania v Root)

Mental state does not require an awareness or knowledge of guilt. In most crimes it is sufficient that the defendant voluntarily did the act that is criminal, regardless of motive or evil intent. In some instances a particular mental state is required, such as the necessity that a homicide be with malice aforethought to constitute murder. In some cases it is the existence of a specific intent that differentiates the crime committed from other offenses, as an assault with intent to kill is distinguished by that intent from an ordinary assault or an assault with intent to rob.

§ 3:3. Parties to a Crime.

Two or more parties may directly or indirectly contribute to the commission of a crime. At common law participants in the commission of a felony are sometimes known as *principals* and *accessories.*

(a)   **Principals.** Principals may be divided into two classes: (1) *principals in the first degree,* who actually engage in the perpetration of the crime, and (2) *principals in the second degree,* who are actually or constructively present and aid and abet in the commission of the act. For example, a person is a principal in the second degree if that person assists by words of encouragement, stands ready to assist or to give information, or keeps watch to prevent surprise or capture.

The distinction as to degree is frequently abolished by statute so that all persons participating in a crime are principals.

(b)   **Accessories.** Accessories to a crime are also divided into two classes, accessories before the fact and accessories after the fact. An *accessory before the fact* differs from a principal in the second degree only by reason of absence from the scene of the crime. An *accessory after the fact* is a person who knowingly assists one who has committed a felony. Thus, a person, who, after the commission of the crime and with intent to assist the felon, gives warning to prevent arrest or shelters or aids in an escape from imprisonment, is an accessory after the fact.

§ 3:4. Responsibility for Criminal Acts.

In some cases, certain classes of persons are not responsible for their criminal acts.

(a)   **Minors.** Some states have legislation fixing the age of criminal responsibility of minors. At common law, a child under the age of seven was presumed incapable of committing a crime; after the age of fourteen, the child was presumed to have capacity as though an adult; and between the ages of seven and fourteen, no presumption of law arose and it had to be shown that the minor had such capacity. The existence of capacity cannot be presumed from the mere commission of the act.

(b)   Insane Persons. An insane person is not criminally responsible. There is a conflict of opinion over what constitutes such insanity as to excuse a person from criminal responsibility. All courts, however, agree that intellectual weakness alone is not such insanity.

A test commonly applied is the *right-and-wrong test.* The responsibility of the defendant is determined in terms of the ability to understand the nature of the act committed and to distinguish right from wrong in relation to it.

Some courts also use the *irresistible impulse test,* the theory of which is that when the defendant acts under an uncontrollable impulse because of an unsound state of mind caused by disease of any nature, such act is not a voluntary act and the defendant is not criminally responsible. If the mental instability is not caused by disease, the irresistible impulse test is not applied.

In many jurisdictions the right-and-wrong test and the irresistible impulse test have been replaced by the rule stated in the Model Penal Code of the American Law Institute that "A person is not responsible for criminal conduct if at the time of such conduct as a result of mental disease or defect he lacks substantial capacity to appreciate the wrongfulness of his conduct or to conform his conduct to the requirements of the law."

When insanity takes the form of delusions or hallucinations, the defendant is not legally responsible when the imagined facts, if they were true, would justify or excuse the act.

(c)   Intoxicated Persons. Involuntary intoxication relieves a person from criminal responsibility; voluntary intoxication generally does not. An exception to this rule is made in the case of a crime requiring specific intent when the accused was so intoxicated as to be incapable of forming such intent.

(d)   Corporations. The modern tendency is to hold corporations criminally responsible for their acts. A corporation may also be held liable for crimes based upon the failure to act. In some instances, the crime may be defined by statute in such a way that it requires or is interpreted as requiring a living "person" to commit the crime, in which case a corporation cannot be held criminally liable.

Certain crimes, such as perjury, cannot be committed by corporations. It is also usually held that crimes punishable only by imprisonment or corporal punishment cannot be committed by corporations. If the statute imposes a fine in addition to or in lieu of imprisonment or corporal punishment, a corporation may be convicted for the crime. Thus a corporation may be fined for violating the federal antitrust law by conspiring or combining to restrain interstate commerce. A corporation may be fined for committing criminal manslaughter when death has been caused by the corporation's failure to install safety equipment required by statute.

B. SECURITY FROM BUSINESS CRIMES

Many crimes affect business. Some of the more common crimes will be discussed.

§ 3:5. Larceny. *Larceny* is the wrongful or fraudulent taking and carrying away by any person of the personal property of another, with a fraudulent intent to deprive the owner of such property. The place from which the property is taken is generally immaterial, although by statute the offense is sometimes subjected to a greater penalty when property is taken from a particular kind of building, such as a warehouse. Shoplifting is a common form of larceny.

Although the term is broadly used in everyday speech, every unlawful taking is not a larceny. (See p. 42, Lund v Virginia) At common law a defendant taking property of another with the intent to return it was not guilty of larceny. This has been changed in some states so that a person who "borrows" a car for a joyride is guilty of larceny, theft, or some other statutory offense. Statutes in many states penalize as *larceny by trick* the use of any device or fraud by which the wrongdoer obtains the possession of, or title to, personal property from the true owner. In some states all forms of larceny and robbery are consolidated in a statutory crime of theft. At common law there was no single offense of theft.

The concept of property which may be the subject of larceny has been expanded. For example, the theft of computer programs constitutes larceny. Many states have statutes punishing the theft of trade secrets as larceny.

The fact that the person from whom the thief has taken the personal property is not the owner does not constitute a defense to the prosecution of the thief for larceny.

§ 3:6 Robbery. At common law *robbery* was the unlawful taking of personal property of any value from the possession or from the presence of another by means of force or by putting the possessor in fear. It differed from larceny primarily in the use of the force or fear; so that a pickpocket whose act of stealing was unknown to the victim committed larceny but not robbery.

In most states there are special penalties for various forms of aggravated robbery, such as robbery by use of a deadly weapon.

§ 3:7. Burglary. At common law *burglary* was the breaking and entering in the nighttime of the dwelling house of another, with the intent to commit a felony. While one often thinks of burglary as stealing property, any felony would satisfy the definition. The offense was aimed primarily at protecting the habitation and thus illustrates the social objective of protection of the person, in this case the persons living or dwelling in the building.

Modern statutes have eliminated many of the requirements of the common-law definition so that it is immaterial when or where there is an entry to commit a felony, and the elements of breaking and entering are frequently omitted. Under some statutes the offense is aggravated and the penalty is increased in terms of the place where the offense is committed, such as a bank building, freight car, or warehouse. Related statutory offenses have also been created, such as the crime of possessing burglar's tools.

§ 3:8. Arson. At common law *arson* was the willful and malicious burning of the dwelling-house of another. As such, it was designed to protect human life, although the defendant was guilty if there was a burning even though no one was actually hurt. In most states, arson is a felony so that if someone is killed in the resulting fire, the offense is murder by application of the felony-murder rule, under which a homicide, however unintended, occurring in the commission of a felony is automatically classified as murder.

In virtually every state a special offense of *burning to defraud insurers* has been created by statute. However, such burning is not arson when the defendant burns his or her own house to collect the insurance, since the definition of arson requires that the dwelling be that of another person. In many states it is now arson to burn any building owned by another, even though it is not a dwelling.

§ 3:9. Receiving Stolen Goods. The crime of *receiving stolen goods* is the receiving of goods which have been stolen, with knowledge of that fact, and with the intent to deprive the owner of them. It is immaterial that the receiver does not know the identity of the owner or the thief.

§ 3:10. Embezzlement. *Embezzlement* is the fraudulent conversion of property or money owned by another by a person to whom it has been entrusted, as in the case of an employee. It is a statutory crime designed to cover the case of unlawful takings that were not larceny because the wrongdoer did not take the property from the possession of another, and which were not robbery because there was neither a taking nor the use of force or fear.

It is immaterial whether the defendant received the money or property from the victim or from a third person. Thus, an agent commits embezzlement when the agent receives and keeps payments from third persons which the agent should have remitted to the principal.

Generally the fact that the defendant intends to return the property or money embezzled, or does in fact do so, is no defense. However, as a practical matter an embezzler returning what was taken will ordinarily not be prosecuted because the owner will not desire to press charges.

Today every jurisdiction has not only a general embezzlement statute but also various statutes applicable to particular situations, such as embezzlement by trustees, employees, and government officials.

§ 3:11. Obtaining Goods by False Pretenses. In almost all of the states, statutes are directed against obtaining money or goods by means of false pretenses. (See p. 43, California v Randono) These statutes vary in detail and scope. Sometimes the statutes are directed against particular forms of deception, such as using bad checks.

§ 3:12. False Weights, Measures, and Labels. Cheating, defrauding, or misleading the public by the use of false, improper, or inadequate weights, measures, and labels is a crime. Numerous federal and state regulations have been adopted on this subject.

§ 3:13. Swindles and Confidence Games. The act of a person who, intending to cheat and defraud, obtains money or property by trick, deception, fraud, or other device, is an offense known as a *swindle* or *confidence game.* False or bogus checks and spurious coins are frequently employed in swindling operations directed toward business people.

§ 3:14. Counterfeit Money. It is a federal crime to make, to possess with intent to pass, or to pass counterfeit coins, bank notes, or obligations or other securities of the United

States. Legislation has also been enacted against the passing of counterfeit foreign securities or notes of foreign banks.

The various states also have statutes prohibiting the making and passing of counterfeit coins and bank notes. These statutes often provide, as does the federal statute, a punishment for the mutilation of bank notes or the lightening or mutilation of coins.

§ 3:15. Use of Mails to Defraud. Congress has made it a crime to use the mails to further any scheme or artifice to defraud. To constitute the offense, there must be (a) a contemplated or organized scheme to defraud or to obtain money or property by false pretenses, and (b) the mailing or the causing of another to mail a letter, writing, or pamphlet for the purpose of executing or attempting to execute such scheme or artifice. Illustrations of schemes that come within the statute are false statements to secure credit, circulars announcing false cures, false statements to sell stock in a corporation, and false statements as to the origin of a fire and the value of the destroyed goods for the purpose of securing indemnity from an insurance company. Federal law also makes it a crime to use a telegram to defraud.

§ 3:16. Lotteries. There are three elements to a lottery: (a) a payment of money or something of value for the opportunity to win (b) a prize (c) by lot or chance. If these elements appear, it is immaterial that the transaction appears to be a legitimate form of business, or advertising, or that the transaction is called by some name other than a lottery, such as a raffle.

The sending of a chain letter through the mail is generally a federal offense, both as a mail fraud and as an illegal lottery, when the letter solicits contributions or payments for a fraudulent purpose.

In many states, government lotteries are legal.

§ 3:17. Forgery. *Forgery* consists of the fraudulent making or material altering of an instrument, such as a check, which apparently creates or changes a legal liability of another. The instrument must have some apparent legal efficacy to constitute forgery.[1]

Ordinarily forgery consists of signing another's name with intent to defraud. It may also consist of making an entire instrument or altering an existing one. It may result from signing a fictitious name or the offender's own name with the intent to defraud.

When the nonowner of a credit card signs the owner's name on a credit card invoice, such an act is a forgery. In most states a special statute makes it a crime to fraudulently use a credit card. In such a case, the prosecuting attorney may choose either to prosecute the defendant for violation of the forgery statute or the special credit card statute.

§ 3:18. Criminal Libel. A person who falsely defames another without legal excuse or justification may be subject to criminal liability as well as civil liability. *Criminal libel* is based

---

[1]Although the Uniform Commercial Code does not contain any provisions relating to crimes, if the defendant is indicted for forgery of a check, which is a form of commercial paper regulated by the Code, reference will be made to the Code to determine whether the writing in question is a check. Faulkner v Alaska (Alaska) 445 P2d 815.

upon its tendency to cause a breach of the peace. Under some statutes, however, the offense appears to be based upon the tendency to injure another.

No publication or communication to third persons is required in the case of criminal libel. The offense is committed when the defendant communicates the libel directly to the person libeled as well as when it is made known to third persons.

The truth of the statement is a defense in civil libel. In order to constitute a defense to criminal libel, the prevailing view requires that a proper motive on the part of the accused be shown as well as proof that the statement was true.

In a number of states, slander generally or particular kinds of slander have been made criminal offenses by statute.

§ 3:19. Riots and Civil Disorders. Damage to property in the course of a riot or civil disorder is ordinarily a crime to the same extent as though only one wrongdoer were involved. That is, there is larceny, or arson, and so on, depending on the nature of the circumstances, without regard to whether one person or many are involved. In addition, the act of assembling as a riotous mob and engaging in civil disorders is generally some form of crime in itself, without regard to the destruction or theft of property, whether under common-law concepts of disturbing the peace or under modern antiriot statutes.

A state may make it a crime to riot or to incite to riot, although a statute relating to inciting must be carefully drawn to avoid infringing constitutionally protected free speech.

§ 3:20. Conspiracy. When the commission of a crime is agreed to in advance, the participants are guilty of *conspiracy*. This is an independent crime for which they may be prosecuted even though the intended crime is never committed. When a conspiracy exists, each conspirator is criminally liable for the criminal acts of the other conspirators as long as they are done in the course of committing or seeking to commit the planned crime. (See p. 44, Missouri v Sneed)

CASES FOR CHAPTER 3

United States v Jackson

(CA5 Tex) 451 F2d 281 (1971)

The Mercantile Bank of Dallas was holding municipal bonds which had been paid and were to be destroyed. Before this was done, the bonds were apparently stolen. Sixty-five thousand dollars of these bonds were later deposited by Jackson in the Texas Bank and Trust Company with the instructions to collect the amount due and then put the money into a new account which Jackson had just opened under the name of Ed Lee Robbins. Thereafter, Jackson telephoned from Oklahoma to the bank in Dallas to inquire if his account had been

opened. Jackson was told that it would be necessary to sign some additional forms. Jackson then left Oklahoma to go to Texas. On his arrival he was arrested by FBI agents. He was prosecuted for violating the Federal Wire Fraud Act by making the telephone call from Oklahoma to Texas.

RONEY, C.J. . . . The single legal point of defendant's argument . . . is that the telephone call from Tulsa, Oklahoma, to Dallas, Texas, was not an act prohibited by [the federal statute]. He argues that the call was merely made for the purpose of inquiring about the opening of defendant's bank account. He says that this was a legitimate call between client and his bank and had nothing to do with an alleged fraudulent scheme, if one existed.

Defendant's conviction stands or falls on the determination of whether or not the telephone call was made for the purpose of "executing such scheme or artifice."

The Wire Fraud Statute does not require that the scheme be successful, or even that the victim be deceived. It need only be shown that there was a scheme and that interstate wires were "used as a step in the execution of the scheme." . . .

The evidence shows that Jackson's telephone call was a part of the scheme from its inception. Before he left the Texas Bank and Trust Company on May 23rd, Jackson told Mr. Robert Houston that he traveled and that he would be calling. Since Jackson would be unable to withdraw any of the proceeds of the stolen municipal bonds until they had been cashed and his account had been opened, it was impossible for him to consummate his scheme without ascertaining whether or not the money was in his account. This information was indispensable to complete the execution of the scheme. It could have been obtained by a personal visit to the bank, or by an intrastate telephone call, without violating this law. But it was not. Defendant's call was made in interstate commerce and thus ran afoul of the federal law. . . .

[Conviction affirmed]

Pennsylvania v Root

403 Pa 571, 170 A2d 310 (1961)

Root was challenged to an illegal auto race at night on a public highway. While the challenger was doing 70 to 90 miles an hour in a 50-mile-an-hour no-passing zone, he crossed the dividing line in attempting to pass Root, struck an oncoming truck, and was killed. Root was prosecuted for involuntary manslaughter. From a conviction, Root appealed.

JONES, C.J. . . . While precedent is to be found for application of the tort law concept of "proximate cause" in fixing responsibility for criminal homicide, the want of any rational basis for its use in determining criminal liability can no longer be properly disregarded. When proximate cause was first borrowed from the field of tort law and applied to homicide prosecutions in Pennsylvania, the concept connoted a much more direct causal relation in producing the alleged culpable result than it does

today. Proximate cause, as an essential element of a tort founded in negligence, has undergone in recent times, and is still undergoing, a marked extension. More specifically, this area of civil law has been progressively liberalized in favor of claims for damages for personal injuries to which careless conduct of others can in some way be associated. To persist in applying the tort liability concept of proximate cause to prosecutions for criminal homicide after the marked expansion of *civil* liability of defendants in tort actions for negligence would be to extend possible *criminal* liability to persons chargeable with unlawful or reckless conduct in circumstances not generally considered to present the likelihood of a resultant death. . . .

Legal theory which makes guilt or innocence of criminal homicide depend upon such accidental and fortuitous circumstances as are now embraced by modern tort law's encompassing concept of proximate cause is too harsh to be just. . . .

In this case, the conduct of the defendant was not the proximate cause of the decedent's death as a matter of law. . . .

The deceased was aware of the dangerous condition created by the defendant's reckless conduct in driving his automobile at an excessive rate of speed along the highway but, despite such knowledge, he recklessly chose to swerve his car to the left and into the path of an oncoming truck, thereby bringing about the head-on collision which caused his own death.

To summarize, the tort liability concept of proximate cause has no proper place in prosecutions for criminal homicide and more direct causal connection is required for conviction. . . . In the instant case, the defendant's reckless conduct was not a sufficiently direct cause of the competing driver's death to make him criminally liable therefor. . . .

[Conviction reversed]

EAGEN, J. (dissenting) . . . If the defendant did not engage in the unlawful race and so operate his automobile in such a reckless manner, this accident would never have occurred. He helped create the dangerous event. He was a vital part of it. The victim's acts were a natural reaction to the stimulus of the situation. The race, the attempt to pass the other car and forge ahead, the reckless speed, all of these factors the defendant himself helped create. He was part and parcel of them. That the victim's response was normal under the circumstances, that his reaction should have been expected and was clearly foreseeable, is to me beyond argument. That the defendant's recklessness was a substantial factor is obvious. All of this, in my opinion, makes his unlawful conduct a direct cause of the resulting collision. . . .

Acts should be judged by their tendency under the known circumstances, not by the actual intent which accompanies their performance. Every day of the year, we read that some teenagers, or young adults, somewhere in this country, have been killed or have killed others, while racing their automobiles. Hair-raising, death-defying, law-breaking rides, which encompass "racing," are the rule rather than the exception, and endanger not only the participants, but also every motorist and passenger on the road. To call such . . . [conduct] unlikely to result in death, is to ignore the cold and harsh reality of everyday occurrences. . . .

1 Wharton, Criminal Law and Procedure § 68 [Anderson Edition] (1957), speaking of causal connection, says: "A person is only criminally liable for what he has caused, that is, there must be a causal relationship between his act and harm sustained for which he is prosecuted. It is not essential to the existence of a causal relationship that the ultimate harm which has resulted was foreseen or intended by the actor. It is sufficient that the ultimate harm is one which a reasonable man would foresee as being reasonably related to the acts of the defendant." Section 295, in speaking about manslaughter, says: "When homicide is predicated upon the negligence of the defendant, it must be shown that his negligence was the proximate cause or a contributing cause of the victim's death. It must appear that the death was not the result of misadventure, but the natural and probable result of a reckless or culpably negligent act. To render a person criminally liable for negligent homicide, the duty omitted or improperly performed must have been his personal duty, and the negligent act from which death resulted must have been his personal act, and not the act of another. But he is not excused because the negligence of someone else contributed to the result, when his act was the primary or proximate cause and the negligence of the other did not intervene between his act and the result."

Professor Joseph Beale, late renowned member of the Harvard Law School faculty, in an article entitled, The Proximate Consequence of an Act, 33 HarvLRev 633, 646, said, "Though there is an active force intervening after defendant's act, the result will

nevertheless be proximate if the defendant's act actually caused the intervening force. In such a case the defendant's force is really continuing in active operation *by means of the force it stimulated into activity.*"
. . .

But, says the majority opinion, these are principles of tort law and should not in these days be applied to the criminal law. But such has been the case since the time of Blackstone. . . .

Lund v Virginia

217 Va 688, 232 SE2d 745 (1977)

Lund was a graduate student at a university. In working on his doctoral dissertation he made use of the university computer and was assisted by the personnel of the computer facility. The value of what he thus obtained was about $30,000. Lund had not been authorized to use the computer and he was prosecuted for grand larceny. He was convicted and appealed.

I'ANSON C.J. . . . Defendant, Charles Walter Lund, was charged in an indictment with . . . using "without authority computer operation time and services of Computer Center Personnel at Virginia Polytechnic Institute and State University [V.P.I. or University] . . . with intent to defraud, such . . . services having a value of one hundred dollars or more." Code §§ 18.1-100 and 18.1-118 were referred to in the indictment as the applicable statutes. Defendant pleaded not guilty and waived trial by jury. He was found guilty of grand larceny and sentenced to two years in the State penitentiary. The sentence was suspended, and defendant was placed on probation for five years.

Defendant was a graduate student in statistics and a candidate for a Ph.D. degree at V.P.I. The preparation of his dissertation on the subject assigned to him by his faculty advisor required the use of computer operation time and services of the computer center personnel at the University. His faculty advisor neglected to arrange for defendant's use of the computer, but defendant used it without obtaining the proper authorization.

The computer used by the defendant was leased on an annual basis by V.P.I. from the IBM Corporation. . . .

Defendant testified that he used the computer without specific authority. He stated that he knew he was a large computer user, but, because he was doing work on his doctoral dissertation, he did not consider this use excessive or that "he was doing anything wrong."

Four faculty members testified in defendant's behalf. They all agreed that computer time "probably would have been" or "would have been" assigned to defendant if properly requested. Dr. Hinkleman, who replaced defendant's first advisor, testified that the computer time was essential for the defendant to carry out his assignment. He assumed that a sufficient number of computer hours had been arranged by Lund's prior faculty advisor.

The head of the statistics department, at the time of the trial, agreed with the testimony of the faculty members that Lund would have been assigned computer time if properly requested. He also testified that the committee which recommended the awarding of degrees was aware of the charges pending against the defendant when he was awarded his doctorate by the University.

The defendant contends that his conviction of grand larceny . . . cannot be upheld under the provision of Code §§ 18.1-100 because . . . computer time and services are not the subject of larceny under the provision of Code §§ 18.-1-100 or 18.1-118.

Code §§ 18.1-100 . . . provides as follows: "Any person who: (1) Commits larceny from the person of another of money or other thing of value of five dollars or more, or (2) Commits simple larceny not from the person of another of goods and chattels of the value of one hundred dollars or more, shall be deemed guilty of grand larceny . . . ."

Section 18.1-118 . . . provides as follows: "If any person obtain, by any false pretense or token, from any person, with intent to defraud, money or other property which may be the subject of larceny, he shall be deemed guilty of larceny thereof; . . . ." . . . For one to be guilty of the crime of larceny by false pretense, he must make a false representation of an existing fact with knowledge of its falsity and, on that basis, obtain from another person money or other property which may be the subject of larceny, with the intent to defraud. . . .

At common law, larceny is the taking and carrying away of the goods and chattels of another with intent to deprive the owner of the possession thereof permanently. Code § 18.1-100 defines grand larceny as a taking from the person of another money or other thing of value of five dollars or more, or the taking not from the person of another goods and chattels of the value of $100 or more. The phrase

"goods and chattels" cannot be interpreted to include computer time and services in light of the often repeated mandate that criminal statutes must be strictly construed. . . .

At common law, the labor or services could not be the subject of the crime of false pretense because neither time nor services may be taken and carried away. It has been generally held that, in the absence of a clearly expressed legislative intent, labor or services could not be the subject of the statutory crime of false pretense . . . ; 2 Wharton, *Criminal Law and Procedure* § 604 at 369 (Anderson Edition 1957). Some jurisdictions have amended their criminal codes specifically to make it a crime to obtain labor or services by means of false pretense. E. g., New York Penal Code § 165.15; New Jersey Penal Code ch. 2A:111; and California Criminal Code § 322. We have no such provision in our statutes.

Furthermore, the unauthorized *use* of the computer is not the subject of larceny. Nowhere in Code § 18.1-100 or § 18.1-118 do we find the word "use." The language of the statutes connotes more than just the unauthorized use of the property of another. It refers to a taking and carrying away of a certain concrete article of personal property. *See People v Ashworth,* 220 App.Div. 498, 222 N.Y.S. 24, 27 (1927). There it was held that the unauthorized use of machinery and spinning facilities of another to process wool did not constitute larceny under New York's false pretense statute.

We hold that labor and services and the unauthorized use of the University's computer cannot be construed to be subjects to larceny under the provisions of Code §§ 18.1-100 and 18.1-118. . . .

[Conviction reversed]

California v Randono

32 Cal App 3d 164, 108 Cal Rptr 326 (1973)

Randono and Dreyer were partners. They owned two bars and restaurants—Feliciano's and the Saddleback Inn. Saddleback Inn was headed for bankruptcy. The partners decided to take advantage of this situation by ordering $20,000 worth of liquor on credit to be charged to the Saddleback Inn with the intent of immediately transferring the liquor to Feliciano's without paying for it. This was done and one of the partners was then prosecuted for theft by false pretenses.

KERRIGAN, A.J. . . . The trial court specifically found that the defendant was guilty of theft by false pretenses. To support a false pretenses conviction, it must be shown that the defendant made a false pretense or representation with intent to defraud the owner of his property, and that the owner was in fact defrauded, in that he relied on the false representation in parting with his property. . . .

The Attorney General contends that the evidence also supports conviction of larceny by trick or device. We disagree. Larceny by trick or device is the appropriation of property, the possession of which was fraudulently acquired; obtaining property by false pretenses is the fraudulent or deceitful acquisition of both title and possession. . . . Where one is induced to sell property through another's false representations, if the seller intends to pass only possession at the time of sale, the buyer commits the offense of larceny by trick or device, but if the seller intends to pass title, the buyer commits the offense of obtaining property by false pretenses. . . .

. . . In the absence of evidence to the contrary, we must presume that defendant's suppliers intended . . . to convey title to defendant or the Saddleback on delivery of the liquor. Consequently, the offense, if any, must have been theft by false pretenses. . . .

There is no dispute as to the element of actual fraud. . . .

Nor is there any question about the reliance element. Reliance may be inferred from all the circumstances. . . . The only reasonable inference to be drawn from delivery of 334 cases of liquor under invoices marked with prices and terms of payment is that the dealers expected to be paid, and relied on that expectation in making the deliveries.

The false pretense may consist in any act, word, symbol, or token calculated and intended to deceive. It may be either express or implied from words or conduct. . . . The trial court adopted the prosecution's theory, that the false representations consisted of defendant's implied promise to pay for the ordered liquor, with the intention not to perform. Such a promise is a false or fraudulent representation or pretense within the meaning of . . . the Penal Code. . . .

Defendant ordered the liquor from wholesale suppliers. There is no evidence of any facts or circumstances that would suggest to any of the dealers that the orders were out of the ordinary. When goods are ordered by one dealer from another in the ordinary course of business, the law will imply a promise to pay. . . .

The alternative is to suppose that the dealers intended the $20,000 worth of liquor as gifts. Any such presumption would fly in the face of reason and experience. The invoices, which include both price and terms of payment, contradict any inference of donative intent. . . .

Dreyer testified that he and defendant agreed to order the liquor and not to pay for it; that the liquor was removed from the Saddleback to Feliciano's and hidden behind a wall built for that purpose. His testimony was corroborated by three witnesses. . . .

[Penal Code] Section 484 provides: "Every person . . . who shall knowingly and designedly, by any false or fraudulent representation or pretense, defraud any other person of money, labor or real or personal property, . . . is guilty of theft." . . .

Defendant's position is that to construe the words "representation or pretense" to include silence is counter to the fair import of those words. . . .

But defendant's false representation was not manifested by silence; it was manifested by his conduct in ordering the liquor. Nothing in section 484 requires that the false pretense be expressed in words; conduct is sufficient if it is calculated to mislead. . . .

[Conviction affirmed]

Missouri v Sneed

(MoApp) 549 Sw2d 105 (1977)

Sneed enlisted the assistance of Guffey and Castelli to rob the Weisberg Apartment. They did so. Guffey and Castelli then left the building first and unknown to Sneed held up two men in the parking lot. Later the loot from all three robberies was divided with Sneed but he did not know that any of it had come from any robbery other than the Weisberg robbery. Sneed was prosecuted and convicted for the Weisberg robbery and the two parking lot robberies. He appealed from the conviction for the parking lot robberies.

SMITH, P.J. . . . Guffey, who testified for the State, and two of the Weisbergs identified defendant [as a participant to the Weisbergs robbery]. . . .

Guffey testified that Castelli then left the Weisberg apartment followed by Guffey. In the parking lot they confronted two other men, Clarence Martin and Michael Vitale. Guffey ordered both men onto the ground at gunpoint and took their wallets. These were put into the bag with the loot from the Weisberg apartment. . . .

Guffey testified that at the time of the parking

lot robberies, defendant was still at the apartment or still inside the house. No discussions had been had between Guffey, Castelli and defendant about robbing anyone other than Weisberg. Guffey further stated defendant had nothing to do with the parking lot robberies and was not told about them until the three arrived back at defendant's house. There they divided the money and each took two of the guns obtained from Weisberg. There was no evidence that either Martin or Vitale had money in their wallets or that defendant knowingly received any proceeds of the Martin-Vitale robberies.

On this record we are unable to find sufficient evidence to support the verdicts on Count II, the Vitale robbery, or Count III, the Martin robbery. While there is evidence that Guffey and Castelli committed the parking lot robberies, there is no evidence that defendant did so. His guilt for those offenses must be based upon the rule: "If two or more persons join in a purpose to commit a crime, each of them, if actually or constructively present, is not only guilty as a principal, if the other (or others) commits that particular crime, but he is also guilty of any other crime committed by the other in pursuance of the common purpose, or as a natural or probable consequence thereof." . . .

For this rule to apply there must be knowledge of the intention or purpose to commit the particular crime or of a common purpose as to the particular offense. . . . As was true in State v Brooks, 513 S.W.2d 168 (Mo.App.1973), the rule also applies where the particular offense, while not originally planned, is the natural and probable consequence of the planned offense. . . .

The requisites for application of this rule of law are not found in the evidence here. The robberies on the parking lot were not in furtherance of the robbery of Weisberg, the planned crime nor the natural or probable consequence of that crime. Nor does the evidence show any knowledge by defendant of his cohorts' intention to commit such crimes, or even that he was aware of such crimes until the parties had left the scene. The only evidence was that he had no such knowledge. The parking lot victims were unplanned targets of opportunity by Guffey and Castelli who were, in the language of the civil law, on a "frolic of their own." Since the evidence fails to establish defendant's knowledge or participation in the parking lot robberies we must reverse as to [them].

[Conviction reversed as to parking lot robberies]

QUESTIONS AND CASE PROBLEMS

1. What is the objective of the rule of law that an irrestistible impulse to commit a crime does not excuse criminal liability when the mental instability is not the result of disease?
2. Koonce entered a gas station after it was closed for the night. By means of force, he removed the cash box from a soft drink vending machine. He was prosecuted for burglarizing a "warehouse." Was he guilty? [Koonce v Kentucky, (Ky) 452 SW2d 822; Shumate v Kentucky, (Ky) 433 SW2d 340]
3. Buckley took a credit card from the coat of its owner with the intent to never return it. He then purchased some goods at a department store and paid for them by presenting the credit card to the sales clerk and then signing the credit card slip with the name of the owner of the credit card. How many crimes, if any, did Buckley commit? [See Buckley v Indiana, — IndApp —, 322 NE2d 113]
4. Tauscher was prosecuted for embezzlement. It was shown that while claiming to act as agent, he, without authority, had drawn a check on his employer's bank account and kept the proceeds of the check for his own use. Was he guilty of embezzlement? [Oregon v Tauscher, 227 Ore 1, 360 P2d 764]
5. Morse was convicted of forging the name "Hillyard Motors" as the drawer of a check. He appealed on the ground that signing such a name had no legal effect, and that therefore he was not guilty of forgery. Decide. [Washington v Morse, 38 Wash 2d 927, 234 P2d 478]

6. Wolfe gave some counterfeit money to Ballinger, telling her that the bills were counterfeit and that she should go "downtown" to pass them and that, being New Year's Eve, it was a good time to pass them. Ballinger thereafter spent two of the bills and attempted to destroy the balance. Wolfe was arrested and prosecuted for passing counterfeit obligations of the United States with intent to defraud. He raised the defense that he could not be guilty as Ballinger was told that the money was counterfeit. Decide. [United States v Wolfe (CA7 Ill) 307 F2d 798 cert den 372 US 945]

7. Berman organized the Greatway Travel Ltd. Greatway sold travel consultant franchises and promised that the franchisees would receive various discounts and assistance. None of these promises were ever kept because Greatway lost all its money through mismanagement. Berman was prosecuted for obtaining money by false pretenses. Was he guilty? [Berman v Maryland (MD App) 370 A2d 580]

8. Dumont was prosecuted for obtaining merchandise by using a stolen credit card and signing a sales slip with the name of the card holder. Dumont was prosecuted under a general criminal law statute that classified the offense as a felony. Dumont claimed that this statute had been superseded by a later statute specifically applying to the unlawful use of credit cards, under which the offense was merely a misdemeanor, and that she could not be prosecuted under the earlier forgery statute. Was she correct? [Oregon v Dumont, 3 OreApp 189, 471 P2d 847]

9. Lang and his wife lived in a trailer in a trailer park. Winhoven broke into the trailer in order to steal. He was prosecuted and convicted of breaking and entering "an occupied dwelling" with the intent to commit larceny. He raised the defense that he had not broken into an occupied dwelling but into a trailer. Was he correct? [Michigan v Winhoven, 65 MichApp 522, 237 NW2d 540]

10. Socony Mobil Oil Co. ran a telephone bingo game series. The gasoline station dealers purchased the bingo cards from Socony and gave them free to anyone requesting them, whether a customer or not. It was not possible to play the game without a card. A cash prize was awarded the winner. The State of Texas brought an injunction action against Socony to stop this on the ground that it was a lottery. Socony raised the defense that since no value or consideration was given by the persons participating in the bingo games, it was not a lottery. Decide. [Texas v Socony Mobil Oil Co. (Tex Civ App) 386 SW2d 169]

11. Swanson wanted to procure a loan from the Lincoln Bank. He falsely represented to the bank that he owned 629 head of cattle when in fact he owned only 80. The bank made a loan to him of approximately $3,000 and credited his account with this amount. Before Swanson drew any money from the bank, the bank's agent learned of the falsity of Swanson's representation. Swanson thereafter drew out by check the amount of the loan. Swanson was then prosecuted by the state for obtaining property by false pretenses. He defended on the ground that he had not actually drawn any money from the bank until after the bank, through its agent, knew of the fraud and that since the bank took no steps to prevent the money from going out thereafter, it was in effect the bank's own negligence that made it sustain loss. Was this a valid defense? [Nebraska v Swanson, 179 Neb 693, 140 NW2d 618]

4 The Law of Torts and Business

A *tort* is a private injury or wrong arising from a breach of a duty created by law. It is often defined as a wrong independent of contract. Most torts, although not all, involve moral wrongs, but not all moral wrongs are torts.

A. GENERAL PRINCIPLES

Tort law includes harm to the person, as well as damage to property caused negligently or intentionally. In some instances, liability is imposed merely because the activity of the wrongdoer is so dangerous that it is deemed proper that the wrongdoer should pay for any harm that has been caused.

§ 4:1. Tort, Crime, and Breach of Contract. A *crime* is a wrong arising from a violation of a public duty, whereas a tort is a wrong arising from a violation of a private duty. An act may be both a crime and a tort as in the case of the theft of an automobile.

Although the law regards both crimes and torts as wrongs, it attaches different consequences to them. In the case of a crime, the state brings the action to enforce a prescribed penalty or punishment. On the other hand, when an act or omission is a tort, the state allows an action for damages by the injured party.

The wrongs or injuries caused by a *breach of contract* arise from the violation of an obligation or duty created by consent of the parties. A tort arises from the violation of an obligation or duty created by law. The same act may be both a breach of contract and a tort. For example, when an agent exchanges property instead of selling it as directed by the principal, the agent is liable for breach of contract and for the tort of conversion.

§ 4:2. Basis of Tort Liability. The mere fact that a person is hurt or harmed in some way does not mean that such person can sue and recover damages from the person causing the harm. There must exist a recognized basis for liability.

(a)   Voluntary Act. The defendant must be guilty of a voluntary act or omission. Acts committed or omitted by one who is confronted with sudden peril caused by another are considered involuntary acts.

(b)   Intent. Whether intent to do an unlawful act or intent to cause harm is required as a basis for tort liability depends upon the nature of the act involved. Liability is imposed for some torts even though the person committing the tort acted without any intent to do wrong. Thus, a person going on the land of another is liable for the tort of trespass unless permisson has been obtained.

In the case of other torts, such an assault, slander, malicious prosecution, or interference with contracts, it is necessary for the plaintiff to show that there was an intent on the part of the defendant to cause harm or at least the intent to do an act which a reasonable person would anticipate as likely to cause harm.

(c)   Motive. As a general rule, motive is immaterial except as it may be evidence to show the existence of intent. In most instances, any legal right may be exercised even with bad motives, and an act that is unlawful is not made legal by good motives.

(d)   Proximate Cause. In order to fix legal responsibility upon one as a wrongdoer, it is necessary to show that the injury was the proximate result of the defendant's voluntary act. Whether an act is the proximate cause of an injury is usually a question of fact for the jury to determine.

(e)   Liability for Tort of Employee or Child. A person may be innocent of wrong yet be held liable for the tort committed by another person. As will be discussed later in the chapters on agency, the tort of an employee or agent may in some cases impose liability upon the employer.

A parent is ordinarily not liable for the tort committed by a child. That is, the mere fact that the person sued is the parent of the child committing the wrong does not impose liability on the parent.

There are several instances in which a parent will, however, be held liable. If the parent knows that the child has a dangerous characteristic, such as a disposition toward setting fire to houses, and does not take reasonable steps to prevent this, the parent will be held liable for the harm caused by the child. If the child is a reckless driver and the parent allows the child to use the parent's car, the parent is liable on the theory that the parent was negligent in entrusting the car to the child.[1]

In some states, any person lending an automobile is liable for the harm caused by the negligence of the person borrowing or renting the car. In some states, statutes make a parent liable for willful or malicious property damage of minor children. Such statutes have a maximum limitation for such liability, which limitation is generally either $300 or $1,000.

§ 4:3. Liability-Imposing Conduct. In the more elementary forms, intentional harm involves wrongs such as an assault; a battery; intentionally caused mental distress; and intentional wrongs directed against property, such as stealing another's automobile, cutting timber from another's land, or setting a house on fire. Note that most of these "elementary" torts are also crimes. Somewhat more complex are the torts of fraud, slander and libel, the invasion of privacy, and the intentional interference with contract rights or business relations of others.

§ 4:4. Absolute Liability. In some areas of the law, liability for harm exists without regard to whether there was any negligence or intention to cause harm. For example, in most states when a contractor blasts with dynamite and debris is hurled onto the land of

[1] Markland v B and O RR Co. (DelSuper) 351 A2d 89.

another, the landowner may recover damages from the contractor even though the contractor used due care, and therefore was not negligent, and did not intend to cause the landowner any harm by committing an intentional trespass on the land.

By this concept of absolute liability, society is saying that the activity is so dangerous to the public that liability must be imposed even though no fault is present. Yet society will not go so far as to say that the activity is so dangerous that it must be outlawed. Instead, the compromise is made to allow the activity but make the one who stands to benefit from the activity pay its injured victims regardless of the circumstances under which the injuries were sustained.

(a)   Industrial Activity. Generally there is absolute liability for harm growing out of the storage of inflammable gas and explosives in the middle of a populated city; crop dusting, where the chemical used is dangerous to life and the dusting is likely to be spread by the wind; factories emitting dangerous fumes, smoke, and soot in populated areas.

(b)   Consumer Protection. Pure food statutes may impose absolute liability upon the seller of foods in favor of the ultimate consumer who is harmed by them. Decisions and statutes have imposed a nearly absolute liability on the manufacturer of goods.

(c)   Wild Animals. A person keeping a wild animal is absolutely liable for any harm caused by it. This liability is not affected by the fact that the animal was tame and the owner had no reason to foresee that harm would occur.

§ 4:5. Negligence. The widest range of tort liability today arises in the field of *negligence,* which exists whenever the defendant has acted with less care than would be exercised by a reasonable person under the circumstances. Such negligence must be the proximate cause of harm to a person or property.

(a)   The Imaginary Reasonable Person. The reasonable person whose behavior is made the standard is an imaginary person. In a given case which is tried before a jury, the reasonable person is what appears to the composite or combined minds of the jurors to be a model person.

This reasonable person is not any one of the jurors nor an average of what the jurors would do. The law is not concerned with what the jurors would do in a like situation, for it is possible that they may be more careful or less careful than the abstract reasonable person. Likewise the standard is not what is done in the community, for the community may live above or below the standard of the reasonable person.

(b)   Variable Character of the Standard. By definition, the standard is a variable standard for it does not tell you specifically in any case what should have been done. This flexibility is confusing to everyone, in the sense that you never know the exact answer in any borderline case until after the lawsuit is over. From the standpoint of society, however, this very flexibility is desirable because it is obviously impossible to foresee every possible variation in the facts that might arise and even more impossible to keep such a code of conduct up-to-date. Imagine how differently the reasonable person must act while driving today's automobile on today's superhighways than when driving a Model-T more than a half century ago.

Many states have made an exception to the common-law rule by requiring the landowner to anticipate the presence of trespassing children and a few states have extended that duty to adult trespassers.

(c)   Degree of Care. The degree of care required of a person is that which an ordinarily prudent person would exercise under similar circumstances. It does not mean such a degree of care as would have prevented the harm from occurring, nor is it enough that it is just as much care as everyone else exercises. Nor is it sufficient that one has exercised the degree of care which is customary for persons in the same kind of work or business, or that one has employed the methods customarily used. If one is engaged in services requiring skill, the care, of course, must measure up to a higher standard. The degree of care exercised must be commensurate with the danger that would probably result if such care were lacking. In all cases it is the diligence, care, and skill that can be reasonably expected under the circumstances. Whether one has exercised that degree of care which is required under the circumstances is a question that is determined by the jury.

(d)   Contributory Negligence. Generally, a plaintiff cannot recover for injuries caused by another's negligence if the plaintiff's own negligence has contributed to the injury. The plaintiff's negligence, however, must be a proximate cause of the injury; that is, it must contribute to the injury in order to defeat recovery.

In this connection there has developed a doctrine variously called the *doctrine of last clear chance,* the *humanitarian doctrine,* or the *doctrine of discovered peril.* Under this doctrine, although the plaintiff is negligent, the defendant is held liable if the defendant had the last clear chance to avoid the injury. In such a case the theory is that the plaintiff's negligence is not the proximate cause and therefore does not contribute to the injury.

At common law, a plaintiff guilty of contributory negligence, was ordinarily denied recovery without regard to whether the defendant was more negligent. The common law does not recognize comparative degrees of negligence, nor does it try to apportion the injury to the two parties in terms of the degree of their respective fault. As an exception to these principles, a number of states provide that the plaintiff's negligence does not bar recovery but merely reduces the amount which the plaintiff recovers.

(e)   Comparative Negligence. In some states, the common-law rule of contributory negligence is regarded as unjust because the plaintiff forfeits all rights even when only slightly negligent and although the defendant may have been very negligent. These states therefore provide that there should be a comparing of the negligence of the plaintiff and the negligence of the defendant with the result that negligence of the plaintiff does not bar recovery but only reduces the plaintiff's recovery to the extent that the harm was caused by the plaintiff. For example if the jury decides that the plaintiff has sustained damages of $100,000 but that the plaintiff's own negligence was the cause of one fourth of the damage, the plaintiff would be allowed to recover $75,000. At common law, the plaintiff in such case would recover nothing.

In some states the comparative negligence concept is modified by ignoring the negligence of the plaintiff if it is slight and the negligence of the defendant is great or *gross.* At the other extreme, some states refuse to allow the plaintiff to recover anything if the negligence of the plaintiff was more than 50 percent of the cause of the harm.

(f) Proof of Negligence. The plaintiff ordinarily has the burden of proving that the defendant did not exercise reasonable care. In some instances, however, it is sufficient for the plaintiff to prove that the injury was caused by some thing that was within the control of the defendant. If injury ordinarily results from an object only when there is negligence, the proof of the fact that injury resulted is sufficient proof that the defendant was negligent. This is expressed by the maxim *res ipsa loquitur* (the occurrence or the thing speaks for itself). For example, when a sealed control unit explodes it is proper to infer that there was negligence in the factory because a factory-sealed unit does not ordinarily explode unless someone has been negligent in the factory. This concept does not establish that the defendant was negligent but merely allows the jury to conclude or infer that the defendant was negligent.[2] The defendant is not barred from proving lack of negligence or from explaining that the explosion was caused by some act for which the defendant was not responsible; and the jury, if it believes the defendant's evidence, can refuse to infer negligence from the happening of the event and can conclude that the defendant was not negligent.

The burden of proving that the plaintiff was contributorily negligent is upon the defendant.

(g) Violation of Statute. By the general rule, if harm is sustained while the defendant is violating a statute, the defendant is deemed negligent and is liable for the harm. Many courts are narrowing this concept so that the defendant is liable only if the statute is intended to protect against the kind of harm which was sustained due to violation of the statute. For example, courts which make this distinction will ignore the fact that the defendant was driving an automobile without proper tags in violation of the Automobile Registration Law, as that statute was not intended to protect against negligent driving.

§ 4:6. Division of Liability. In some instances, when two or more defendants have caused harm to the plaintiff, it is difficult or impossible to determine just what damage was done by each of such wrongdoers or tort-feasors. For example, automobile No. 1 strikes automobile No. 2, which is then struck by automobile No. 3. Ordinarily, it is impossible to determne how much of the damage to automobile No. 2 was caused by each of the other cars. Similarly, a tract of farm land down the river may be harmed because two or more factories have dumped industrial wastes into the river. It is not possible to determine how much damage each of the factories has caused the farm land.

By the older view, a plaintiff was denied the right to recover from any of the wrongdoers in these situations. The courts followed the theory that a plaintiff is not entitled to recover from a defendant unless the plaintiff can prove what harm was caused by that defendant. The modern trend of the cases is to hold all of the defendants jointly and severally (collectively and individually) liable for the total harm sustained by the plaintiff. (See p. 59, Maddux v Donaldson)

§ 4:7. Who May Sue. In some torts, the wrongdoer's act gives not only the immediate victim the right to sue but also persons standing in certain relationships to the victim. Thus, under certain circumstances, one spouse can sue for an injury to the other spouse or a parent can sue for an injury to the child. In a wrongful death action, members

---

[2] Gilber v Korvette, Inc., 457 Pa 602, 327 A2d 94.

of the surviving group (typically the spouse, child, and parents of the person who has been killed) have a right to sue the wrongdoer for such death.

§ 4:8. Immunity from Liability.

(a)   **Governments.** Governments are generally immune from tort liability. This rule has been eroded by decision and in some instances by statutes, such as the Federal Tort Claims Act, which, subject to certain exceptions, permits the recovery of damages for property, personal injury, or death action claims arising from the negligent act or omission of any employee of the United States under such circumstances that the United States, "if a private person, would be liable to the claimant in accordance with the law of the place where the act or omission occurred." A fast-growing number of states have abolished governmental immunity.[3]

(b)   **Minors.** All persons are not equally liable for torts. A minor of tender years, generally under 7, cannot be guilty of negligence or contributory negligence. Between the ages of 7 and 14, a minor is presumed to have capacity to commit a tort, although the contrary may be shown. Above 14 years, no distinction is made in terms of age. A minor who drives a motorcycle or an automobile on the public highway must observe the same standard of care as an adult.

(c)   **Family Relationships.** At common law no suit could be brought by a husband against his wife and vice versa. By statute this immunity has been abolished as to torts involving property. The immunity continues in most states with respect to personal torts, whether intentional or negligent, although a substantial number of states now allow personal tort actions between spouses. The trend of judicial decisions rejects the argument that the allowance of such suits would open the door to fraud and collusion between spouses when one of them is insured. A similar immunity exists between parent and child in most states with respect to personal tort claims.

(d)   **Charities.** Charities were once exempt from tort law. For example, a hospital could not be held liable for the negligent harm to a patient caused by its staff or employees. Within the last three decades this immunity has been rejected in nearly all of the states. It is quite likely that in the coming years it will be repudiated generally.

B. SECURITY FROM BUSINESS TORTS

In business dealings several kinds of torts may occur. These business torts include intentional causing of mental distress; false imprisonment; fraud; defamation; disparagement of goods and slander of title; infringement of trademarks, patents, and copyrights; unfair competition; combinations to divert trade; interference with business relations and contracts; violence; and trespass.

§ 4:9. Intentional Causing of Mental Distress.
When the defendant commits an act which by itself is a tort, there is ordinarily recovery for the mental distress which is caused thereby. With the turn of the century, and particularly in the last quarter century,

---

[3] Ayala v Philadelphia Board of Education, 453 Pa 584, 305 A2d 877.

recovery has been allowed in a number of cases in which no ordinary or traditional form of tort was committed and the common element in these cases was that the defendant had willfully subjected the plaintiff to unnecessary emotional disturbance. This result was reached when the common carrier or the hotel insulted a patron; a collection agency used unreasonable means of collection designed to harass the debtor; an outrageous practical joke was played upon the plaintiff; the corpse of a close relative was concealed, mistreated, or interference made with the burial; or the defendant engaged in a steady campaign to intimidate a critic of the defendant's product, including illegal electronic eavesdropping.[4]

Statements made to humiliate the plaintiff because of race, creed, or national origin will impose liability for the emotional distress caused thereby and for any physical illness which results therefrom. Generally the theory on which recovery is allowed in these cases is clouded by efforts to bring the case within the standard patterns of liability. Occasionally a court frankly recognizes that it is imposing liability merely because mental distress was intentionally caused.

§ 4:10. False Imprisonment.

False imprisonment is the intentional, unprivileged detaining of a person without that person's consent. It may take the extreme form of kidnapping. At the other extreme, a shopper who is detained in the store manager's office and questioned as to shoplifting is the victim of false imprisonment where there is no reasonable ground for believing that the shopper was a thief. False imprisonment also includes detention under an official arrest when there is no legal justification for that arrest.

(a)   Detention. Any detention at any place by any means for any duration of time is sufficient. Stone walls are not required to make a false imprisonment. If a bank robber holds a bank teller at gun point for the purpose of preventing the teller from attacking the other robbers or from escaping, there is a detention.

(b)   Consent and Privilege. By definition, no false imprisonment occurs when the person detained consents thereto. For example, when a merchant without any justification detains a person on the suspicion of shoplifting, such detention is not a false imprisonment if the victim consents to it without any protest. If the merchant has reasonable ground for believing that the victim is guilty of shoplifting, the action of the merchant is not false imprisonment even though the victim is detained under protest and does not consent thereto. Statutes in some states give merchants a privilege to detain persons reasonably suspected of shoplifting.

§ 4:11. Fraud.

A person is entitled to be protected from fraud and may recover damages for harm caused by fraud. This protects the plaintiff from false statements made with knowledge of their falsity or with reckless indifference to whether they are false. (See p. 60, Midwest Supply, Inc. v Waters)

In some instances, anti-fraud provisions have been adopted by consumer protection statutes. To illustrate, when the seller of a used car turns the odometer back with the intent to defraud, the seller is liable under the federal Motor Vehicle Information and Cost Savings Act to whoever purchases the automobile, without regard to

---

[4] Nader v General Motors Corp., 25 NY2d 560, 255 NE2d 765.

whether the purchaser bought directly from that dealer or from an intermediate dealer.[5]

§ 4:12. Defamation—Slander. Reputation is injured by *defamation,* which is a publication tending to cause one to lose the esteem of the community. *Slander* is a form of defamation consisting of the publication or communication to another of false, spoken words or gestures. Liability for slander is imposed to provide security of reputation.

   (a)   Privilege. Under certain circumstances, no liability arises when false statements are made and cause damage. This *absolute privilege* exists in the case of publication by a public officer when the publication is within the officer's line of duty. The rule is deemed necessary to encourage public officers in the performance of their public duties.

   Other circumstances may afford a *qualified* or *conditional privilege.* A communication made in good faith upon a subject in which the party communicating has an interest or right is privileged if made to a person having a corresponding interest or right, although it contains matter which, without this privilege, would be slanderous. Thus, the owner of a watch may in good faith charge another person with the theft of the watch. A mercantile agency's credit report is conditionally privileged when made to an interested subscriber in good faith in the regular course of the agency's business. Also, when a client falsely tells an attorney that a customer of the client owes money, such statement does not impose liability for defamation even though it is wrong.

   (b)   Malice. When a public officer or a public figure is defamed by a publisher, broadcaster, or telecaster, there is no liability to the injured person unless the plaintiff can show that the false statements were made with *actual malice;* that is, with knowledge that the statements were false or with reckless disregard of whether they were false. It is not sufficient that the plaintiff shows that the defendant acted out of spite, from illwill, or even with the intention to harm the plaintiff.

   However, if the plaintiff is a private person, liability for defamation may be imposed when the statements were made negligently as well as when they were made maliciously. This is true even when the defamation concerns a matter of public interest.[6]

§ 4:13. Defamation—Libel. Another wrong against the security of business relations takes the form of written defamation. This is known as *libel.* Although usually in writing, it may be in print, picture, or in any other permanent, visual form. For example, to construct a gallows in front of another's residence is libelous.

§ 4:14. Defamation by Computer. A person's credit standing or reputation may be damaged because a computer contains erroneous information. When the computer is part of a data bank system and the erroneous information is supplied to third persons, that could be more than merely annoying; it could be damaging. Will the data bank operator or service company be held liable to the person so harmed? There does not appear to be any reported decision on this point, but it is believed that if the

---

[5] Mataya v Behm Motors, Inc. (DC Wis) 409 FSupp 65.
[6] Gertz v Robert Welch, Inc., 418 US 323; Time, Inc. v Firestone, 424 US 448.

operator or the company has exercised reasonable care to prevent errors and to correct errors, there will not be any liability on either the actual programmer-employee operating the equipment or the management providing the computer-service. Conversely, if negligence or an intent to harm is shown, existing principles of law would sustain the liability of the persons involved for what may be called *defamation by computer*. It might be that liability could be avoided by supplying the person to whom the information relates with a copy of any printout of information which the data bank supplies to third persons, as this would tend to show good faith on the part of the management of the data bank operation and a reasonable effort to keep the information accurate.

Liability for defamation by computer may arise under the federal Fair Credit Reporting Act of 1970 when the person affected is a consumer. The federal Credit Card Act of 1970 further protects from defamation by computer. These acts, which are not limited to situations involving computers, are discussed in Chapter 8 on consumer protection.

§ 4:15. Disparagement of Goods and Slander of Title. In the transaction of business, one is entitled to be free from interference by means of malicious, false claims or statements made by others in respect to the quality or the title to property. Actual damages must be proved by the plaintiff to have proximately resulted from the false communication by the defendant to a third person. The plaintiff must show that in consequence thereof the third person has refrained from dealing with the plaintiff.

§ 4:16. Infringement of Trademarks. A *trademark* is a word, name, device, symbol, or any combination of these, used by a manufacturer or seller to distinguish the goods from those of other persons. When the trademark of a particular person is used or substantially copied by another, it is said that the trademark is infringed. The owner of the trademark may sue for damages and enjoin its wrongful use.

§ 4:17. Infringement of Patents. A grant of a *patent* entitles the patentee to prevent others for a period of 17 years from making, using, or selling the particular inventions. Anyone so doing without the patentee's permission is guilty of a patent infringement. If the inventor does not have any patent or if the patent is invalid, anyone may copy the invention without liability. (See p. 61, Sears, Roebuck & Co. v Stiffel Co.)

An infringement exists, even though all the parts or features of an invention are not copied, if there is a substantial identity of means, operation, and result between the original and new devices. In the case of a process, however, all successive steps or their equivalent must be copied. In the case of a combination of ingredients, the use of the same ingredients with others constitutes an infringement, except when effecting a compound essentially different in nature.

§ 4:18. Infringement of Copyrights. A wrong similar to the infringement of a patent is the infringement of a copyright. A *copyright* is the right given by statute to prevent others for a limited time from printing, copying, or publishing a production resulting from intellectual labor. The right exists for the life of the author and for fifty years thereafter.[7]

---

[7] Copyrights Act of 1976, PL 94–553, 90 Stat. 2541, 2572, § 302, 17 USC § 302.

Infringement of copyright in general consists of copying the form of expression of ideas or conceptions. There is no copyright in the idea or conception itself, but only in the particular way in which it is expressed. In order to constitute an infringement, the production need not be reproduced entirely nor be exactly the same as the original. Reproduction of a substantial part of the original, although paraphrased or otherwise altered, constitutes an infringement; but appropriation of only a word or single line does not.

One guilty of infringement of copyright is liable to the owner for damages and profits, or only damages, which are to be determined by the court. The owner is also entitled to an injunction to restrain further infringement.

§ 4:19. Unfair Competition. Unfair competition is unlawful and the person injured thereby may sue for damages or for an injunction to stop the practice, or may report the matter to a trade commission or other agency.

It is unfair competition to imitate signs, store fronts, advertisements, and packaging of goods of a competitor. Thus, when one adopts a box of distinctive size, shape, and color in which to market candy, and the package is imitated by a competitor, the latter may be enjoined from so doing and in some cases may be liable for damages.

Every similarity to a competitor, however, is not necessarily unfair competition. For example, the term "downtown" is merely descriptive, so the Downtown Motel cannot obtain an injunction against the use of the name Downtown Motor Inn, because a name that is merely descriptive cannot be exclusively appropriated or adopted. As an exception, if the descriptive word has been used by a given business for such a long time as to be identified with the business in the public mind, a competitor cannot use that name.

The goodwill that is related to a trade name is an important business asset; and there is a judicial trend in favor of protecting a trade name from a competitor's use of a similar name, not only when such use is intentionally deceptive but also when it is merely confusing to the public.

Historically the law was only concerned with protecting competitors from unfair competition by their rivals. Under consumer protection statutes most states now give protection to the consumer who is harmed by the unfair competitive practices.

§ 4:20. Combinations to Divert Trade. Business relations may be disturbed by a combination to keep third persons from dealing with another who is the object of attack. Such a combination, resulting in injury, constitutes an actionable wrong known as *conspiracy* if the object is unlawful, or if a lawful object is sought by unlawful means.

If the object of a combination is to further a lawful interest of the combination, no actionable wrong exists so long as lawful means are employed. For example, when employees are united in a strike, they may peacefully persuade others to withhold their patronage from the employer. On the other hand, all combinations to drive or keep away customers or prospective employees by violence, force, threats, or intimidation are actionable wrongs. To illustrate, a combination is usually treated as an unlawful conspiracy for which damages may be recovered when the customers are threatened and for this reason withdraw their patronage.

Labor laws prohibit some combinations as unfair labor practices, while other combinations to divert trade are condemned as illegal trusts.

§ 4:21. Wrongful Interference with Business Relations. One of the fundamental rights of an individual is to earn a living by working or by engaging in trade or business. A wrongful interference with this liberty is a tort for which damages may be recovered and which, in some cases, may be restrained by an injunction.

The right to conduct one's business is, nevertheless, subject to the rights of others. Hence, the injuries suffered by one in business through legitimate competition give no right of redress. Contrary to the general rule, however, it has been considered wrongful interference if one destroys the business of another for a malicious purpose, even though legal means are used.

§ 4:22. Interference with Contract. The tort law relating to interference with contracts and other economic relationships has increased greatly in recent years as a result of the law's seeking to impose upon the marketplace higher ethical standards to prevent the oppression of victims of improper practices. In general terms, when the defendant interferes with and brings about the breach of contract between a third person and the plaintiff, the circumstances may be such that the plaintiff has an action in tort against the defendant for interfering with contractual relations. Likewise, the plaintiff may have such a claim for the defendant's interfering with performance by the plaintiff of an existing contract.

The mere fact that the defendant's voluntary conduct has the effect of interfering with the plaintiff's contract does not establish that the defendant is liable to the plaintiff. For example, when the defendant is acting for what the law regards as a legitimate economic end, the fact that there results a breach of contract between a third person and the plaintiff does not impose liability on the defendant.

(a)   Contracts Terminable at Will. The fact that a contract is terminable at will does not deprive it of the right to protection from interference.

(b)   Prospective Contracts. In addition to protecting existing contracts from intentional interference, tort liability is imposed for acts intentionally committed to prevent the making of a contract.

To illustrate, an action may be brought for slander of title when the malicious false statements of the defendant as to the plaintiff's ownership of property scares a buyer away and prevents the plaintiff from making a sale.

(c)   Requirement of Malice. There is no liability for interference with contractual relations unless such interference is malicious. The term "malicious" is misleading because it may mean either (1) acting with actual malice, that is, the desire to harm for the sheer sake of causing harm, or (2) the infliction of harm only as a consequence of competition intended to advance the actor's personal interest.

§ 4:23. Violence. Statutes in many states impose upon counties and cities liability for harm caused by rioting mobs. Some statutes extend only to property damage, but others impose liability for personal injuries or death. The statute may define the term "mob" although ordinarily it does not do so.

The term "property" in a mob violence statute generally applies only to tangible property and does not authorize recovery for loss of profits or goodwill resulting from business interruption. The fact that the government was unable to prevent the harm or damage is not a defense to liability under such statutes.

§ 4:24. Trespass to the Person. Trespass to the person consists of any contact with the victim's person for which consent was not given. It thus includes what is technically described as a battery. It likewise includes an assault in which the victim apprehends the commission of a battery but is in fact not touched, and includes false imprisonment. There is liability also for intentionally causing mental stress that results in physical harm to or illness of the victim.

In some instances, a person will have a right to use force which would otherwise constitute an unlawful battery. (See p. 62, Simms v School District No. 1)

§ 4:25. Invasion of Privacy. As an aspect of the freedom of the person from unreasonable interference, the law has come to recognize and give protection to a *right of privacy*. This right is most commonly invaded in one of the following ways: (a) invasion of physical privacy, as by planting a microphone in a person's home; (b) giving unnecessary publicity to personal matters of the plaintiff's life, such as financial status or past career; (c) false public association of the plaintiff with some product or principle, such as indicating that the plaintiff endorses a product or is in favor of a particular law, when such is not the fact; or (d) commercially exploiting the plaintiff's name or picture, as using them in advertising without permission.

When a party has a legitimate business interest in making information known, such conduct is generally not regarded as an invasion of privacy and the conduct is protected by a privilege as long as good faith is exercised. (See p. 63, Senogles v Security Benefit Life Insurance Company)

§ 4:26. Trespass to Land. A *trespass to land* consists of any unpermitted entry below, on, across, or above land. This rule is modified to permit the proper flight of aircraft above the land so long as it does not interfere with a proper use of the land.

§ 4:27. Trespass to Personal Property. An illegal invasion of property rights with respect to property other than land constitutes a *trespass to personal property* when done negligently or intentionally, as when one car hits another. When done in good faith and without negligence, there is no liability, in contrast with the case of trespass to land where good faith and absence of negligence is not a defense.

Negligent damage to personal property imposes liability for harm done. Intentional damage to personal property will impose liability for the damage done and also may justify exemplary or punitive damages.

Conversion occurs when personal property is taken by the wrongdoer and kept from its true owner or prior possessor. Thus a bank clerk commits conversion by unlawfully taking money from the bank. Conversion is thus seen to be the civil side of the crimes relating to stealing. The good faith of the converter, however, is not a defense, and an innocent buyer of stolen goods is liable for damages for converting them.

CASES FOR CHAPTER 4

Maddux v Donaldson

362 Mich 425, 108 NW2d 33 (1961)

Maddux was injured when the car in which she was riding was hit by a skidding truck driven by Donaldson, and then by the car following the truck. Maddux sued Donaldson for injuries caused by both collisions. Donaldson claimed that he could only be sued for those injuries which Maddux could show were caused by him and not for the total amount of damages. Because Maddux could not show what part of her injuries were caused by Donaldson, the trial court dismissed the action. Maddux appealed.

SMITH, J. . . . This is one of the most baffling of our current legal problems, critical because of the extensive use of expressways upon which large numbers of cars travel at high speeds in close proximity to one another. . . . What we have is injury to plaintiffs resulting from the independent and tortious acts of two tort-feasors.

There is authority, in this situation, that plaintiff must separate the injuries, ascribing some to one tort-feasor and the balance to the other, much as a housewife separates the colored and the white goods before laundering. Such authority concludes that if plaintiff cannot make such differentiation, he cannot recover from either. This type of decision is well illustrated by the case of Adams v Hall, 1829, 2 Vt 9. In this case an owner of sheep suffered loss to his flock through the depredations of two dogs. The owners he sued jointly. It was shown at the trial, however, that they were not joint owners. In addition, there was no testimony as to which dog killed which sheep. In approving a [dismissal of the action] it was held that neither owner was liable for the actions of the other's dog, merely because they "did the mischief in company."

However defensible such a result may have been in this and cases similar in principle in an agrarian economy shortly after the American Revolution (and even this is open to question), we do not regard it as precedent governing the liability of automobile owners in what are known as "chain collisions" on today's highways. It should be unnecessary to spell out the differences between the social problems presented or the judicial policies involved in their solution. When we impose upon an injured plaintiff the necessity of proving which impact did which harm

in a chain collision situation, what we are actually expressing is a judicial policy that it is better that a plaintiff, injured through no fault of his own, take nothing, than that a tort-feasor pay more than his theoretical share of the damages accruing out of a confused situation which his wrong has helped to create. . . .

It is our conclusion that if there is competent testimony, adduced either by plaintiff or defendant, the injuries are factually and medically separable, and that the liability for all such injuries and damages, or parts thereof, may be allocated with reasonable certainty to the impacts in turn, the jury will be instructed accordingly and mere difficulty in so doing will not relieve the triers of the facts of this responsibility. This merely follows the general rule that "where the independent concurring acts have caused distinct and separate injuries to the plaintiff, or where some reasonable means of apportioning the damages is evident, the courts generally will not hold the tort-feasors jointly and severally liable."

But if, on the other hand, the triers of the facts conclude that they cannot reasonably make the division of liability between the tort-feasors, this is the point where the road of authority divides. Much ancient authority, not in truth precedent, would say that the case is now over, and that plaintiff shall take nothing. Some modern courts, as well, hold that this is merely the case of the marauding dogs and the helpless sheep relitigated in the setting of a modern highway. The conclusion is erroneous. . . .

Here, then, is the essence of the problem—Where is the likelihood of injustice? We think it is in denying the blameless victim of traffic chain collision any recovery whatever. We perceive no reason why his tort-feasors should escape liability because of the very complexity of the injury created by their wrong. . . .

[Judgment reversed and new trial ordered]

BLACK, J. (concurring in reversal). Until now the Michigan rule has been settled. Where two or more wrongdoers separately cause the plaintiff to suffer an unknown or uncertain part or portion of the damages he has shown, each—hitherto—stood responsible to the plaintiff only for the harm caused by his tort, however difficult it may have been to establish the same. . . .

Now we affirm that, where the trier or triers of fact find they cannot ascertain the amount of damages each wrongdoer has inflicted, then such trier or triers are authorized to assess the plaintiff's damages against any one or all of such wrongdoers on the ground that the latter have—in law—participated in the infliction of "a single, indivisible injury.". . .

Midwest Supply, Inc. v Waters

89 Nev 210, 510 P2d 876 (1973)

Waters advertised that he possessed expertise in tax matters. Relying on such advertising, Midwest Supply had Waters prepare its federal income tax return. Waters had a new employee prepare the return. The new employee was not qualified and the tax return was defective. Midwest was required to pay additional taxes and sued Waters for damages. The jury returned a verdict in favor of Midwest for compensatory damages and also for $100,000 of punitive damages. Judgment was entered on this verdict and Waters appealed.

GUNDERSON, J. . . . Attracted by public advertisements, respondents contacted appellants in 1966 to ascertain if they might file amended personal and partnership income tax returns, reallocating to respondents Wallace Waters and Margaret Waters a larger share of an investment tax credit from business equipment purchased in 1964. In February of 1967, appellants prepared for respondents original tax returns for 1966, and nine amended tax returns for 1963, 1964, and 1965. Such returns claimed refunds for taxes previously paid. Although the amended returns showed that the partnership had disposed of the business equipment in 1965, the refund claims were predicated on investment tax credit attributable to that equipment.

At the time, the Internal Revenue Code required repayment of any investment tax credit previously claimed, if the equipment was not retained for the prescribed qualifying period. Hence, after respondents improperly received refunds that appellants erroneously caused them to claim, an Internal Revenue Service audit resulted in assessment to respondents of additional taxes. Enforced collection procedures for these additional taxes, including the filing of tax liens, and numerous levies on wages and bank accounts, caused severe hardship to respondents.

1. Appellants contend the trial court erred in instructing the jury as to fraud because there was no evidence that appellants intentionally misled respondents when undertaking to prepare their tax returns. We disagree. The record contains evidence of willful and wanton misrepresentations, in appellants' advertising and in their internal business practices, specifically aimed at deceiving the members of the public who might rely on appellants for tax expertise.

In their public advertising, appellants "guaranteed accurate tax preparation," stating that they would prepare "complete returns—$5 up." Thereby, appellants suggested their employees' expertise in preparing all types of tax returns. Despite this, they made no effort to hire employees with even rudimentary skill in accounting or in the preparation of tax returns. Appellants sometimes administered to new employees a 72-hour course in tax return preparation, but apparently even this minimal training was not a prerequisite to serving the public. The temporary employee who prepared respondents' tax returns had been employed in construction work for several years prior to his employment with appellants, and had received no formal training in the preparation of tax returns, either prior to or during his employment with appellants.

Appellants' manual instructed their office managers to counter inquiries concerning the qualifications of employees by saying that "[the company] has been preparing taxes for 20 years." The manual further instructed office managers not to refer to an employee as a "specialist or tax expert," but never to correct news reporters or commentators if they referred to employees in this manner.

In our view, such evidence supports a determination of fraud. "The suppression of a material fact which a party is bound in good faith to disclose is equivalent to a false representation, since it constitutes an indirect representation that such fact does not exist.". . .

3. Finally, appellants contend the jury's award of $100,000 punitive damages was actuated by passion and prejudice.

Our law authorizes punitive damages in proper cases to punish and deter culpable conduct. . . . The amount appropriate to these purposes, which lies in the discretion of the court, need bear no fixed relationship to the compensatory damages awarded. . . . At trial, appellants' net worth was established at six million dollars. The jury was properly instructed, and under the circumstances of this case, we do not find the jury's award of punitive damages excessive. . . .

[Judgment affirmed]

Sears, Roebuck & Co. v Stiffel Co.

376 US 225 (1964)

Stiffel manufactured a floor lamp which it patented. After this lamp became popular, Sears, Roebuck & Co. made an identical lamp, which they then sold successfully at a lower price. Stiffel sued Sears for an injunction claiming that his patents had been infringed and that Sears was guilty of unfair competition. The District Court held the patents invalid but granted an injunction. Sears appealed.

BLACK, J. . . . The District Court, after holding the patents invalid for want of invention, went on to find as a fact that Sears' lamp was "a substantially exact copy" of Stiffel's and that the two lamps were so much alike, both in appearance and in functional details, "that confusion between them is likely, and some confusion has already occurred." On these findings the court held Sears guilty of unfair competition, enjoined Sears "from unfairly competing with [Stiffel] by selling or attempting to sell pole lamps identical to or confusingly similar to" Stiffel's lamp, and ordered an accounting to fix profits and damages resulting from Sears' "unfair competition."

The Court of Appeals affirmed. . . . That court held that to make out a case of unfair competition under Illinois law, there was no need to show that Sears had been "palming off" its lamps as Stiffel lamps; Stiffel had only to prove that there was a "likelihood of confusion as to the source of the products"—that the two articles were sufficiently identical that customers could not tell who had made a particular one. . . .

The grant of a patent is the grant of a statutory monopoly. . . .

When the patent expires, the monopoly created by it expires, too, and the right to make the article—including the right to make it in precisely the shape it carried when patented—passes to the public. . . .

Obviously a state could not, consistently with the Supremacy Clause of the Constitution, extend the life of a patent beyond its expiration date or give a patent on an article which lacked the level of invention required for federal patents. To do either would run counter to the policy of Congress of granting patents only to true inventions, and then only for a limited time. Just as a state cannot encroach upon the federal patent laws directly, it cannot, under some other law, such as that forbidding unfair competition, give protection of a kind that clashes with the objects of the federal patent laws.

In the present case the "pole lamp" sold by Stiffel has been held not to be entitled to the protection of either a mechanical or a design patent. An unpatentable article, like an article on which the patent has expired, is in the public domain and may be made and sold by whoever chooses to do so. What Sears did was to copy Stiffel's design and to sell lamps almost identical to those sold by Stiffel. That it had every right to do under the federal patent laws. That Stiffel originated the pole lamp and made it popular is immaterial. . . . To allow a state by use of its law of unfair competition to prevent the copying of an article which represents too slight an advance to be patented would be to permit the state to block off from the public something which federal law has said belongs to the public. The result would be that while federal law grants only . . . 17 years' protection to genuine inventions, . . . states could allow perpetual protection to articles too lacking in novelty to merit any patent at all under federal constitutional standards. This would be too great an encroachment on the federal patent system to be tolerated. . . .

Of course, there could be "confusion" as to who had manufactured these nearly identical articles. But merely inability of the public to tell two identical articles apart is not enough to support an injunction against copying or an award of damages for copying that which the federal patent laws permit to be copied. . . . Because of the federal patent laws a state may not, when the article is unpatented and uncopyrighted, prohibit the copying of the article itself or award damages for such copying. . . . The judgment below did both and in so doing gave Stiffel the equivalent of a patent monopoly on its unpatented lamp. That was error, and Sears is entitled to a judgment in its favor. . . .

[Judgment reversed]

Simms v School District No. 1

13 Ore App 269, 508 P2d 236 (1973)

**Simms was a 14-year old student. He was re-
moved from the classroom by a teacher. Simms
claimed that the teacher wantonly shoved him into
a door. The glass in the door broke and injured
Simms. He sued the School District and the teacher
for damages. The teacher claimed that he was conducting Simms out of the classroom because of the
unruly conduct and vulgar language of Simms; that
he was holding Simms by the arm; that as they approached the door, he released Simms' arm and that
Simms then swung his arm into the door and was
injured. Judgment was entered for the defendants
and Simms appealed.**

FORT, J. . . . Can a teacher use reasonable
force to remove a disruptive child from a classroom? . . .

The annotation at 43 A.L.R.2d 469, 471-72
(1955), discusses at length the teacher's civil liability
for administering corporal punishment to pupils. It
summarizes the rule:

"It is a well-established rule of the law of torts
that a teacher is immune from liability for physical
punishment, reasonable in degree, administered to
a pupil. The teacher is held (and in some jurisdictions
is stated by statute) to . . . share the parent's right
to obtain obedience to reasonable commands by
force.

"But a teacher's right to use physical punishment is a limited one. His immunity from liability
in damages requires that the evidence show that the
punishment administered was reasonable, and such
a showing requires consideration of the nature of
the punishment itself, the nature of the pupil's misconduct which gave rise to the punishment, the age
and physical condition of the pupil, and the teacher's
motive in inflicting the punishment. . . ."

"The general rule for the use of corporal punishment, as developed through judicial decisions, is
that corporal punishment, reasonable in degree and
administered by a teacher to a pupil as a means of
discipline, is privileged in that the administration
of such punishment will not give rise to a cause of
action for damages against the teacher. . . ."

In 1 Wharton, Criminal Law and Procedure
694, § 345 (Anderson Edition 1957), the author
states: "At common law a schoolmaster or teacher
possessed discretionary power to inflict punishment

upon his pupils and was not criminally liable for
assault in so doing unless the punishment was of
such nature as to cause permanent injury to the child
or had been inflicted arbitrarily and without proper
cause or maliciously."

Plaintiff urges that corporal punishment
should be barred under the cruel and inhuman punishment provision of the Eighth Amendment. He
points, however, to no case which holds that the
common law rule set forth above . . . constitutes
a violation of that provision.

. . . We can find nothing . . . which would
hold unconstitutional the physical removal of a disruptive student from the classroom by a teacher who
used only such means as were reasonable and necessary for that purpose. . . . In Ware v Estes, 328
F.Supp. 657 (N.D.Tex.1971), aff'd 458 F.2d 1360
(5th Cir. 1972), the court . . . said: "It is not within
this Court's function, or individual competence, to
pass judgment upon the merits of corporal punishment as an educational tool or a means of discipline.
The wisdom of the policy is not the Court's concern.
The only judgment made is that the evidence has
not shown this policy to be arbitrary, capricious,
unreasoanble or wholly unrelated to the competency
of the state in determining its educational policy." . . .

More recently, in Glaser v Marietta, 351
F.Supp. 555, 558 (W.D.Pa.1972), the court said:
". . . If corporal punishment administered by a parent is not unconstitutional, then a reasonable utilization of the same form of chastisement by a properly
delegated person is not prohibited. The child has
no constitutional grounds to object to such disciplinary methods so long as they are reasonable, properly
administered so as not to cause harm, and are legally
authorized. . . .

. . . Corporal punishment of school children
is not a *per se* cruel and unusual punishment in the
constitutional sense. . . .

We find it persuasive in our analysis of the
Oregon statutory scheme that the 1971 legislature
in adopting the new Criminal Code provided in ORS
161.205, relating to justification:

"The use of physical force upon another person that would otherwise constitute an offense is justifiable and not criminal under any of the following
circumstances:

"(1) A parent, guardian or other person entrusted with the care and supervision of a minor
or an incompetent person may use reasonable physical force upon such minor or incompetent person

when and to the extent he reasonably believes it necessary to maintain discipline or to promote the welfare of the minor or incompetent person. *A teacher may use reasonable physical force upon a student when and to the extent the teacher reasonably believes it necessary to maintain order in the school or classroom. . . ."* (Emphasis supplied.)

[Judgment affirmed]

Senogles v Security Benefit Life Insurance Company

217 Kan 438, 536 P2d 1358 (1975)

The Medical Information Bureau (M.I.B.) was a nonprofit association formed by approximately seven hundred insurance companies. Whenever an application for insurance was made to any of these member companies, it would relay the medical information concerning the applicant to the M.I.B. Any other member could obtain this information from the data bank maintained by M.I.B. Senogles applied to the Security Benefit Life Insurance Company for a policy of health insurance. The medical information which he furnished the company was forwarded to the M.I.B. He sued Security for damages, claiming that his privacy had been invaded by the company's giving the information to M.I.B. From a judgment against Senogles, he appealed.

KAUL, J. . . . The question presented is whether communication to a third party of medical information received by defendant from plaintiff's physicians, under authorization given by plaintiff in connection with an application for life insurance, was made under such circumstances that the transmission thereof was qualifiedly or conditionally privileged.

. . . Right of privacy was defined in Johnson v Boeing Airplane Co., 175 Kan. 275, 262 P.2d 808, wherein we held: "The doctrine of the 'right of privacy' is defined as 'the right to be let alone,' the right to be free from unwarranted publicity, the right to live without unwarranted interference by the public in matters with which the public is not necessarily or legitimately concerned, and the right to be free from unwarranted appropriation or exploitation of one's personality, private affairs and private activities.". . .

". . . Only unwarranted invasions of the right of privacy are actionable. The corollary to this rule is that a 'warranted' invasion of the right of privacy

is not actionable. . . . The right of privacy does not prohibit the communication of any matter though of a private nature, *when the publication is made under circumstances which would render it a privileged communication according to the law of libel and slander . . ."*

In the case of Faber v Byrle, 171 Kan. 38, 229 P.2d 718, [qualifiedly privileged was defined as:] ". . . A communication made in good faith on any subject matter in which the person communicating has an interest, or in reference to which he has a duty, is privileged if made to a person having a corresponding interest or duty, even though it contains matter which, without this privilege, would be actionable, and although the duty is not a legal one, but only a moral or social duty of imperfect obligation. The essential elements of a conditionally privileged communication may accordingly be enumerated as good faith, an interest to be upheld, a statement limited in its scope to this purpose, a proper occasion, and publication in a proper manner and to proper parties only. The privilege arises from the necessity of full and unrestricted communication concerning a matter in which the parties have an interest or duty, and is not restricted within any narrow limits.". . .

We believe the communication and the surrounding circumstances under which it was made in the instant case falls within the boundaries of the definition. Defendant had an interest in the medical information which it forwarded to the M.I.B. by reason of which, through its membership, it would receive information pertaining to other applicants for insurance. Defendant had a duty under its contract of membership with M.I.B. M.I.B. had a duty to furnish the information to other members when the requirements of M.I.B. rules were met. . . .

In the instant case there is no evidence of bad faith on the part of defendant. It is undisputed that the medical information in question was not divulged to the public or to anyone who did not have a legitimate interest in the health of the plaintiff. Our examination of the rules of M.I.B. and affidavits of Joseph C. Wilberding, Executive Director of Medical Information Bureau, indicates the M.I.B. rules are geared to protect against misuse of the information and that it is to be revealed only to home office employees of member companies who directly pass upon the transaction. . . .

In a recently published article appearing in Vol. 4 (1974) Rutgers Journal of Computers And The Law, the author makes a comprehensive analysis of the purposes and activities of M.I.B. He concludes: "The M.I.B. serves an invaluable function in the life insurance industry by meeting underwriters' informational needs. The proved ability to set premiums which result from use of the M.I.B. benefits the policyholders. It is they who bear the burden of increased costs if an applicant is assessed for premiums inadequate to cover the risk of loss he represents." (p. 40.)

We are satisfied there is a valid business interest in the communication in question; it was made in good faith; and M.I.B. and member companies had a corresponding interest; and that the informa-

tion was limited in scope to a proper purpose, published in a proper manner and to proper parties only. In other words, the communication here falls within the definition of qualified privilege. . . .

There is no evidence that the privilege accorded to defendant had been lost by abuse thereof. . . .

We agree with defendant that cases involving agency credit reporting wherein a communication to those with a legitimate business report is generally deemed qualifiedly privileged are analogous in many respects to the case at bar. . . .

[Judgment affirmed]

QUESTIONS AND CASE PROBLEMS

1. What is the objective of each of the following rules of law?
   (a) In some areas of law, liability for harm exists without regard to whether there was any negligence or intention to cause harm.
   (b) Geographical and descriptive names cannot ordinarily be adopted as trademarks.

2. Jessica Sorensen was a minor. She was riding in an automobile driven by her father, Paul. The car collided with another car. Jessica was injured. She sued her father for her injuries. He raised the defense that a child could not sue its father for negligence. Was he correct? [Sorensen v Sorensen (Mass) 339 NE2d 907]

3. Henry Niederman was walking on a center city pavement with his small son. An automobile driven by Brodsky went out of control, ran up on the sidewalk, and struck a fire hydrant, a litter pole and basket, a newsstand, and Niederman's son. The car did not touch Niederman, but the shock and fright caused damage to his heart. He sued Brodsky for the harm that he sustained as the result of Brodsky's negligence. Brodsky defended on the ground that he was not liable because he had not touched Niederman. Was this a valid defense? [Niederman v Brodsky, 436 Pa 401, 261 A2d 84]

4. Catalano ran a gasoline service station which was licensed by the State of New York to conduct inspections of motor vehicles. Capital Cities Broadcasting Corporation prepared and televised a "news special" on the subject of the difficulty of obtaining an automobile inspection. It sent an on-the-spot interviewer and photographer to Catalano's station. Catalano, believing that the interviewer was a customer, told her that he could not inspect her automobile because the space in the station was filled with cars being repaired but that, as soon as one of the car stalls was empty, he would take the interviewer's car. This discussion was recorded by the interviewer by means of a concealed tape recorder; but before it was televised, it was edited by eliminating the explanation given by Catalano and thus merely broadcasted his flat refusal to inspect the car. Catalano claimed that this caused him a loss of business and sued Capital for damages. Was it liable? [Catalano v Capital Cities Broadcasting Corp. 313 NYS2d 52]

5. Carrigan, a district manager of Simples Time Recorder Company, was investigating complaints of mismanagement of the Jackson office of the company. He called at the home of Hooks, the secretary of that office. She expressed the opinion that part of the trouble was caused by stealing of parts and equipment by McCall, another employee. McCall was later discharged and sued Hooks for slander. Was she liable? [Hooks v McCall, (Miss) 272 So2d 925]

6. Giles, a guest at a Pick Hotel, wanted to remove his brief case from the right-hand side of the front seat of his auto. To support himself while so doing, he placed his left hand on the center door pillar of the right-hand side of the car. The hotel bellboy closed the rear door of the car without noticing Giles' hand. One of Giles' fingers was smashed by the closing of the door and thereafter had to be amputated. Giles sued the Pick Hotels Corp. Was he entitled to recover? [Giles v Pick Hotels Corp. (CA6 Mich) 232 F2d 887]

7. Anheuser-Busch holds a trademark registry for the names of Budweiser and Bud as applied to beer which it manufactures and sells under the slogan, "Where there's life . . . there's Bud." It spent millions of dollars advertising with this slogan. Chemical Corporation of American manufactured a combined floor wax and insecticide which is marketed under the slogan of "Where there's life . . . there's bugs." In addition, there was a similarity between the pattern, background, and stage settings of the television commercials employed by both companies. Anheuser-Busch sued for an injunction to prevent the use of such a slogan. The defendant objected on the ground that the parties were not in competing businesses. Should the injunction be issued? [Chemical Corp. v Anheuser-Busch (CA5 Fla) 306 F2d 433, cert den 372 US 965]

8. Burdett repaired a neon sign on the restaurant of Cinquanta. They disagreed whether Cinquanta or his insurance company should pay for the work. Burdett and some friends went to the restaurant and ordered an expensive meal for which they refused to pay. A heated argument followed in which Burdett stated to Cinquanta, "I don't like doing business with crooks. You're a deadbeat. You've owed me $155 for three or four months. You're crooks." Cinquanta sued Burdett for slander but did not show in what way he had been damaged by these remarks. Burdett claimed that he was not liable for slander. Decide. [Cinquanta v Burdett, 154 Colo 37, 388 P2d 779]

9. A statute required that air vent shafts on hotel roofs have parapets at least 30 inches high. Edgar Hotel had parapets only 27 inches high. Nunneley was visiting a registered guest at the Edgar Hotel. She placed a mattress on top of a parapet. When she sat on the mattress, the parapet collapsed and she fell into the air shaft and was injured. She sued the hotel, claiming that its breach of the statute as to the height of the parapets constituted negligence. Decide. [Nunneley v Edgar Hotel, 36 Cal 2d 493, 225 P2d 497]

10. Bialkin borrowed money from the Third National Bank and delivered U.S. Treasury bills to it as security for the loan. The Morgan Guaranty Trust Co. sued the Third National Bank for conversion, claiming that it was the owner of the bills delivered by Bialkin, that the bills had been stolen from it, and that the Third National Bank was guilty of conversion by treating the bills as belonging to Bialkin. Third National Bank raised the defense that if the bills in fact had been stolen the theft had been made possible by the negligent handling of the bills by the Morgan Guaranty Trust Co. and that such negligence barred it from recovering. Was this a valid defense? [Morgan Guaranty Trust Co. v Third National Bank (DC Mass) 400 FSupp 383]

11. *A, B,* and *C* owned land. They did some construction work on their land which prevented the free flow of surface water and caused a flooding of land owned by *D. D* sued *A*

for the damage caused his land by the flooding. *A* claimed that *D* could not hold him liable for any damage since *D* could not prove how much of the total damage had been caused by *A,* and how much by *B* and *C,* and that in any event, *A* could not be liable for more than ⅓ of the total damage sustained by *D.* Decide. [See Thorson v Minot, (ND) 153 NW2d 764]

12. Morris insured his automobile with the South Texas Lloyds. He drove it to a local grocery store and parked on the grocery store lot, leaving the keys in the ignition. While he was in the store, Jones drove the car away without permission and wrecked it. Lloyds paid the loss to Morris and then sued Jones to recover the money which it had paid Morris. Jones denied liability on the grounds that (1) a statute prohibited leaving ignition keys in an unattended vehicle parked on a street, and (2) Morris had been negligent in leaving his keys in the car on the parking lot. Were these defenses valid? [South Texas Lloyds v Jones (La App) 273 So2d 853]

13. The Attorney General of the State of Washington informed the news media that a proceeding had been started by him against a dealer because of alleged violations of the State Consumer Protection Act. The dealer sued the State claiming that this was libelous. Decide. [Gold Seal Chinchillas, Inc. v. Washington, 69 Wash 2d 828, 420 P2d 698]

Part Two • Government, Business, and Society

5 Government Regulations

The wisdom of whether government should regulate business or whether the free forces of competition should be relied upon to solve a problem presents questions which lie within the domain of disciplines in economics, political science, humanities, and related areas. The problems of government regulation today are primarily what to regulate and how to do it.

§ 5:1. Power to Regulate. The states, by virtue of their police power, may regulate business in all of its aspects so long as they do not impose an unreasonable burden on interstate commerce or any activity of the federal government. The federal government may impose any regulation upon any phase of business that is required by "the economic needs of the nation." [1]

For the most part, there are no significant constitutional limitations on the power of government, state or federal, to regulate business. For the most part, regulations of business are valid as long as they apply uniformly to all members within the same class.

§ 5:2. Regulation of Production, Distribution, and Financing. In order to protect the public from harm, government may establish health and purity standards for food, drugs, and cosmetics, and protect consumers from false advertising and labeling. Without regard to the nature of the product, government may regulate business with respect to what materials may be used, the quantity of a product that may be produced or grown, and the price at which the finished product may be sold. Government may also engage in competition with private enterprises or own and operate an industry.

Under its commerce power the federal government may regulate all methods of interstate transportation and communication, and a like power is exercised by each state over its intrastate traffic. The financing of business is directly affected by the national government in creating a national currency and in maintaining a federal

---

[1] American Power & Light Co. v SEC, 329 US 90.

reserve bank system. State and other national laws may also affect financing by regulating the contracts and documents used in financing, such as bills of lading and commercial paper.

The federal government may also establish standards for weights and measures. The Metric Conversion Act of 1975 declares that it is the policy of the United States to convert to the metric system.[2] Various agencies have adopted regulations to execute this policy.

§ 5:3. Regulation of Competition. The federal government, and the states in varying degrees, prohibit unfair methods of competition. Frequently, a commission is established to determine whether a given practice comes within the general class of unfair methods of competition. In other instances, the statutes specifically define the practices condemned.

The Congress has declared "unlawful" all "unfair methods of competition" and has created a Federal Trade Commission to administer the law. The FTC has condemned harassing tactics, coercing by refusing to sell, boycotting, discriminating, disparaging of a competitor's products, enforcing payment wrongfully, cutting off or restricting the market, securing and using confidential information, spying on competitors, and inducing breach of customer contracts. The law also prohibits misrepresentation by appropriating business or corporate names, simulating trade or corporate names, appropriating trademarks, simulating the appearance of a competitor's goods, simulating a competitor's advertising, using deceptive brands or labels, and using false and misleading advertising.

In the current decade, a shift of emphasis is taking place in appraising methods of doing business. Instead of harm to competitors being the sole consideration, the effect upon the consumer is being given increasing recognition. Many practices that were condemned earlier only because they would harm a competitor by diverting customers are now condemned because such practices prevent the customer from getting full value for the money spent.

§ 5:4. Regulation of Prices. Governments, both national and state, may regulate prices. This may be done directly by the lawmaker, that is, the Congress or the state legislature, or the power to do so may be delegated to an administrative officer or agency. This power extends to "prices" in any form. It includes not only what a buyer pays for goods purchased from a store, but also what a borrower pays as interest on a loan and what a tenant pays for rent.[3]

(a)   Price Discrimination Prohibited. The Clayton Act of 1914, applicable to interstate and foreign commerce, prohibits price discrimination between different buyers of commodities "where the effect of such discrimination may be substantially to lessen competition or tend to create a monopoly in any line of commerce."

The federal law prohibits the furnishing of advertising or other services that, when rendered to one purchaser but not another, will have the effect of granting the former a price discrimination or lower rate. It is made illegal for a seller to accept any fee or commission in connection with a sale except for services actually

---

[2] PL 94-168, 89 Stat 1007, 15 USC §205 et seq.
[3] Birkenfeld v City of Berkeley, 17 Cal3d 129, 130 CalRptr 465,550 P2d 1001.

rendered and unless the services are equally available to all on the same terms. The Act makes both the giving and the receiving of any illegal price discrimination a criminal offense.

(b) Permitted Price Discrimination. Price discrimination is expressly permitted when it can be justified on the basis of: (1) difference in grade, quality, or quantity involved; (2) the cost of the transportation involved in making the sale; (3) when the sale is made at the lower price in good faith in order to meet competition; (4) differences in methods or quantities; (5) deterioration of goods; or (6) when the seller in good faith is making a close-out sale of a particular line of goods. The Robinson-Patman Act of 1936 reaffirms the right of a seller to select customers and to refuse to deal with anyone as long as the refusal is in good faith and not for the purpose of restraining trade.

§ 5:5. Prevention of Monopolies and Combinations. To protect competitors and the public from monopolies and combinations in restraint of trade, the federal government and almost all of the states have enacted antitrust statutes.

(a) The Federal Antitrust Act. The federal antitrust act, known as the Sherman Antitrust Act, is applicable to both sellers and buyers.[4] It provides that "[§ 1] Every contract, combination in the form of trust or otherwise, or conspiracy, in restraint of trade or commerce among the several states, or with foreign nations, is declared to be illegal. [§ 2] Every person who shall monopolize, or attempt to monopolize, or combine or conspire with any other person or persons to monopolize any part of the trade or commerce among the several states, or with foreign nations, shall be deemed guilty of a misdemeanor." [5] (See p. 75, Mandeville Island Farms v American Crystal Sugar Co.)

(b) Conduct Prohibited. Section 1 of the Sherman Act applies only when two or more persons agree or conspire to restrain trade. Under Section 2, one person or corporation may violate the law by a monopolizing or attempting to monopolize interstate commerce.

(c) Punishment and Civil Remedy. The punishment fixed for the violation of either of the Sherman Act provisions stated above may be a fine or imprisonment or both. In addition to this criminal penalty, the law provides for an injunction to stop the unlawful practices and permits suing the wrongdoers for damages. The plaintiff in such civil actions may be permitted to recover three times the damages actually sustained (treble damages).

(1) Individual Damage Suit. Any person or enterprise harmed may bring a separate action for treble damages.

(2) Class Action Damage Suit by State Attorney General. When the effect of an antitrust violation is to raise prices, the attorney general of a state may bring a class action to recover damages on behalf of those who have paid the

---

[4] This Act has been amended by the Clayton Act, the Federal Trade Commission Act, the Shipping Act, and other legislation.

[5] 15 United States Code, Ch. 1, §§ 1, 2.

higher prices.[6] This action is called a *parens patriae* action, on the theory that the state is suing as the "parent" of its people.

(d)   The Rule of Reason. The general approach of the Supreme Court of the United States to the trust problem has been that an agreement is not automatically or per se to be condemned as a restraint of interstate commerce merely because it creates a power or a potential to monopolize interstate commerce. It is only when the restraint actually imposed is unreasonable that the practice is unlawful.

(e)   Bigness. The Sherman Antitrust Act does not prohibit bigness.

> *(1)   Mergers.* To some extent the question of bigness, at least when it results from merger, has been met by Congress by amending Section 7 of the Clayton Act to provide that a merger of corporations doing interstate business shall be illegal when the effect of the acquisition by one corporation of all or any part of the assets of the other "may be substantially to lessen competition, or to tend to create a monopoly." [7]

> *(2)   Premerger notification.* When large-size enterprises plan to merge, they must give written notice to the Federal Trade Commission and to the attorney in charge of the Antitrust Division of the Department of Justice and then wait a specified time to see if there is any official objection to the proposed merger.[8]

(f)   Price Fixing. Agreements fixing prices, whether horizontally or vertically, violate the federal antitrust law. Thus manufacturers cannot agree between themselves as to the price at which they will sell (horizontal price fixing); likewise a wholesaler cannot require a buyer to agree not to resell below a stated price (vertical price fixing).[9]

(g)   Stock and Director Control. The Clayton Act prohibits the purchase by a corporation of the stock of another corporation engaged in interstate or foreign commerce when the effect is to lessen competition substantially, or when it restrains commerce or tends to create a monopoly.

The Clayton Act does not prohibit the holding of stock in competing corporations by the same person. Although it prohibits the director of one corporation from being a director of another competing corporation engaged in commerce if either corporation has assets in excess of $1 million, this prohibition is not effective in checking the monopoly potential of interlocking private shareholding.

(h)   Tie-in Sales and Exclusive Dealer Agreements. The Clayton Act of 1914, applicable to interstate and foreign commerce, prohibits the *tie-in sale* or *tie-in lease* by which the person buying or renting goods agrees to use with such goods only other

---

[6] Antitrust Improvement Act of 1976, P.L. 94-435, 90 Stat 1383, Title III; Illinois Brick Co. v. Illinois, (US) 54 LEd2d 164.

[7] 15 USC § 18.

[8] Antitrust Improvements Act of 1976, PL 94-435, 90 Stat 1383, § 201.

[9] Vertical price-maintenance agreements were authorized by statutes in varying degrees from 1931 to 1975 but the Consumer Goods Pricing Act of 1975, PL 94-145, 89 Stat 801, abolished the immunity from the federal antitrust law which had been given to such agreements. Although the states may permit such agreements as long as interstate commerce is not involved, the area of intrastate commerce is so slight that for all practical purposes such agreements are now illegal.

material sold or leased by the other party. The Act also prohibits *exclusive dealer agreements* by which a dealer agrees not to handle a competitor's articles. These tie-in and exclusive dealer arrangements are not absolutely prohibited, but only when their effect "may be substantially to lessen competition or tend to create a monopoly in any line of commerce." By virtue of this qualification, a provision that a person leasing machinery shall use only the materials furnished by the lessor is a lawful restriction if the nature of the materials and the machine are such that the machine will not operate properly with the materials produced or offered by any other person. When the materials furnished by any other competitor would be equally satisfactory, however, the agreement is illegal. Thus, an agreement that the lessee of office machines should use only the paper sold by the lessor of the machines was illegal when it was shown that any other seller could supply paper of suitable quality.

(i) **Refusal to Deal.** A combination of manufacturers, distributors, and retailers, acting in concert to deprive a single merchant of access to goods or access to the market in which such goods are sold is a group boycott which violates the Sherman Antitrust Act.

(j) **Exceptions to the Antitrust Law.** By statute or decision, associations of exporters, marine insurance associations, farmers' and dairymen's cooperatives, and labor unions are exempt from the Sherman Antitrust Act with respect to agreements between their members. Congress has also authorized freight pooling and revenue division agreements between railroad carriers, provided the approval of the Interstate Commerce Commission (ICC) is obtained. By virtue of statutory exemptions, traffic and trust agreements otherwise prohibited by the antitrust law may be made by ocean carriers, and interstate carriers and telegraph companies may consolidate upon obtaining the approval of the government commission having jurisdiction over them. The Newspaper Preservation Act of 1970 grants an antitrust exemption to operating agreements entered into by newspapers to prevent financial collapse.

§ 5:6. Regulation of Employment. Basically the parties are free to make an employment contract on any terms they wish, but by statute employment is subject to certain limitations. Thus, persons under a certain age cannot be employed at certain kinds of labor. Statutes commonly specify minimum wages and maximum hours which the employer must observe. A state may also require employers to pay employees' wages for the time that they are away from work for the purpose of voting.

(a) **Fair Labor Standards Act.** By this statute, which is popularly known as the Wage and Hour Act, Congress provides that, subject to certain exceptions, persons working in interstate commerce or in an industry producing goods for interstate commerce cannot be paid less than a specified minimum wage; and they cannot be employed for more than 40 hours a week unless they are paid time and a half for overtime.[10] The Act prohibits the employment of children under the age of 14 years. It permits the employment of children between the ages of 14 and 16 years in all industries, except mining and manufacturing, under certain prescribed conditions.

---

[10] Fair Labor Standards Amendments of 1977, PL 95-151, 91 Stat 1245.

This Act has been copied by a number of states in regulating those phases of industry not within the reach of the federal statute.

(b)   Fair Employment Practices Acts. With some exceptions, employers of 15 or more persons are forbidden to discriminate as to compensation and other privileges, and conditions of employment against any person because of race, religious creed, color, sex, or national origin, or because of age.[11] (See p. 75, Griggs v Duke Power Co.)

> *(1)   Allowable Distinctions.* The federal law does not require that every employee be treated the same as every other. It does not prohibit the testing or screening of applicants or employees for the purpose of determining whether a person is qualified to be hired, or promoted, or given a wage increase, or given special training. The Civil Rights Act has no effect upon the employer's right to establish compensation scales, to provide bonus pay and incentive pay, or to pay different rates in different geographic areas. The employer may also recognize seniority status, whether voluntarily or as part of a collective bargaining agreement.
>
> *(2)   Sex Discrimination.* An employer cannot discriminate on the basis of sex. An employer may not hire on the basis of a stereotype pattern of what is woman's work and what is man's work. Women, therefore, cannot be excluded from working as bartenders and men cannot be excluded from working as airline flight attendants. Indirect sex discrimination is also prohibited, as when the employer establishes height and weight specifications for job applicants but such requirements have no bearing on the performance of the work and their effect is to exclude women from the job.
>
> The equality of the sexes is literally applied so that a law is unconstitutional when it gives to women a protection or an advantage which it does not give to men performing the same work. (See p. 77, Eslinger v Thomas) Likewise, it is a discriminatory labor practice to allow women seniority rights which are not available to men on the same terms, or to prohibit women from working at jobs which involve the lifting of heavy weights. A standardized "compulsory pregnancy leave" regulation for public school teachers is unconstitutional because no consideration is given the fitness of the individual teacher to continue teaching and there is no proof that pregnant teachers as a class are necessarily and universally unfit to teach.[12]
>
> The Federal Civil Rights Act expressly declares that an employer is not required to readjust the "balance" of employees in order to include any particular percentage of each race, creed, or sex. The only obligation on an employer hiring a new employee is to refrain from discriminating as to each applicant.

---

[11] Federal Civil Rights Act of 1964, Title VII, as amended by the Equal Employment Opportunities Act of 1972. In some states and cities, statutes and ordinances make similar provision. The Federal Anti-Age Discrimination Act prohibits such discrimination only as to persons between 40 and 70 years of age.

[12] Cleveland Board of Education v La Fleur, 414 US 632.

§ 5:7. Labor Representation. Statutes generally declare the right of employees to form a union and require the employer to deal with the union as the bargaining representative of the employees.

(a) **Machinery to Enforce Collective Bargaining.** To protect the rights of workers to unionize and bargain collectively, the federal government created the National Labor Relations Board (NLRB). The NLRB determines the proper collective bargaining unit and eliminates unfair practices by which the employer and the union might interfere with employees' rights.

(b) **Selection of Bargaining Representative.** Generally there is an election by secret ballot to select the bargaining representative of the employees within a particular collective bargaining unit.

(c) **Exclusive and Equal Representation of All Employees.** Any union selected by the majority of the workers within the unit is the exclusive representative of all the employees in the unit for the purpose of bargaining with respect to wages, hours of employment, or other conditions of employment. Whether or not all the workers are members of the representative union is immaterial for, in any case, this union is the exclusive representative of every employee. It is unlawful for any employee, whether a member or nonmember of the union, to attempt to make a contract directly with the employer. Except as to grievances, every worker must act through the representative union with respect to the contract of employment. At the same time, the union is required to represent all workers fairly, nonmembers as well as members. It is unlawful for the union, in bargaining with the employer, to discriminate in any way against any employee. The union cannot use its position as representative of all workers to further its interest as a union.

§ 5:8. Unfair Labor Practices. The National Labor Relations Act prohibits certain practices as unfair and authorizes the NLRB to conduct proceedings to stop such practices.

(a) **Unfair Employer Practices.** The federal law declares that it is an unfair labor practice for an employer to interfere with unionization, to discriminate against any employee because of union activities, or to refuse to bargain collectively.

(b) **Unfair Union Practices.** The federal law declares it to be an unfair labor practice for a union to interfere with employees in forming a union or in refraining from joining a union; to cause an employer to discriminate against an employee for belonging to another union or no union; to refuse to bargain collectively; and under certain circumstances to stop work or refuse to work on materials or to persuade others to stop work.

(c) **Procedure for Enforcement.** Under the National Labor Relations Act, the NLRB issues a complaint whenever it appears that an unfair labor practice has been committed. The complaint informs the party of the charges made and gives notice to appear at a hearing thereon. At the hearing, the General Counsel of the Board acts as a combination of prosecuting attorney and referee, charged with the duty of presenting the case on behalf of the complainant and of seeing that the hearing is properly conducted. After the hearing, the Board makes findings of fact and conclusions of law and either dismisses the complaint or enters an order against the defending party to stop the unfair labor practices "and to take such affirmative action including reinstatement of employees with or without back pay, as will effectuate the policy of the Act. . . "

§ 5:9. Union Organization and Management. In order to insure the honest and democratic administration of unions, Congress adopted the Labor-Management Reporting and Disclosure Act of 1959 to regulate unions operating in or affecting interstate commerce. (See p. 78, United Steelworkers of American v Usery)

The Act protects the rights of union members within their unions by guaranteeing equality, the right to vote on specified matters, and the right to information on union matters and contracts. It also protects members from interference with the enjoyment of these rights.

§ 5:10. Social Security. The federal Social Security Act establishes a single federal program of aid for the needy aged, the blind, and the disabled. This is called the Supplemental Security Income Program (SSI). Payments are administered directly by the Department of Health, Education, and Welfare.[13]

The states also have plans of assistance for the unemployed, aged, and disabled. The federal law encourages the making of payments under state programs in addition to those received under the federal program. Such additional programs are called State Supplemental Payments (SSP). State plans typically establish an administrative board or agency with which claims for assistance are filed by persons coming within the category to be benefited by the statute. If the board approves a claim, assistance is given to the applicant in the amount specified by the statute for the number of weeks or other period of time designated by the statute.

Federal law allows a state which elects to supplement the SSI payments with an SSP program to choose whether it will retain control over the administration of such supplements or will delegate that responsibility to HEW.

Unemployment compensation laws generally deny the payment of benefits when the employee was discharged for good cause, or abandoned work without cause, failed or refused to seek or accept an offer of suitable employment, or when the unemployment was the result of a labor dispute.

§ 5:11. Limitations on State Regulation of Business. The states possess a general power to adopt laws to protect the general welfare, health, safety, and morals. This is called the *police power.* By virtue of this power, the states may regulate business to prevent the sale of harmful products, to protect from fraud, and so on. The power of the states is subject to two important limitations.

(a)   Constitutional Limitations. A state law, although made under the police power, cannot (1) impose an unreasonable burden on or discriminate against interstate commerce, nor (2) invade a right which is protected by the federal Constitution. (See p. 80, Virginia Pharmacy Board v Virginia Consumer Council)

---

[13] This system of centralized and unified federal administration replaces the prior Social Security system under which the federal grovernment made grants to states which administered aid under four different programs.

(b) **Federal Supremacy.** A state law cannot conflict with a federal law or regulation on the same subject matter.

CASES FOR CHAPTER 5

Mandeville Island Farms v American Crystal Sugar Co.

334 US 219 (1948)

Three California sugar refiners agreed among themselves to pay California sugar-beet farmers a uniform price for their crops. The refined sugar would be sold by the refiners in interstate markets. Mandeville Island Farms, a sugar-beet farmer, sued American Crystal Sugar Co., one of the refiners, for treble damages under the Sherman Act. From a judgment for Mandeville, the sugar company appealed.

RUTLEDGE, J. . . . The refiners controlled the seed supply and the only practical market for beets grown in northern California. When the new contracts were offered to the farmers, they had the choice of either signing or abandoning sugar-beet farming. . . . Because beet prices were determined for the three seasons with reference to the combined returns of the three refiners, the prices received by petitioners for those seasons were lower than if respondent, the most efficient of the three, had based its prices on separate returns. . . .

[The respondent claimed that the growing, purchasing, and refining of sugar beets were local activities and not within the reach of the Sherman Act, which applied only to transactions in interstate commerce, and that no illegal practice occurred in the subsequent interstate distribution of the refined sugar.]

. . . The broad form of respondent's argument cannot be accepted. It is a reversion to conceptions formerly held but no longer effective to restrict either Congress' power . . . or the scope of the Sherman Act's coverage. The artificial and mechanical separation of "production" and "manufacturing" from "commerce," without regard to their economic continuity, the effects of the former two upon the latter, and the varying methods by which the several processes are organized, related, and carried on in different industries, or indeed within a single industry, no longer suffices to put either production or manufacturing and refining processes beyond reach of congress' authority or of the statute. . . .

. . . The inquiry whether the restraint occurs in one phase or another, interstate or intrastate, of the total economic process is now merely a preliminary step. . . . The vital question becomes whether the effect is sufficiently substantial and adverse to Congress' paramount policy . . . to constitute a forbidden consequence. If so, the restraint must fall; and the injuries it inflicts upon others become remediable under the act's prescribed methods, including the treble damage provision.

. . . It is clear that the agreement is the sort of combination condemned by the act, even though the price fixing was by purchasers and the persons specially injured under the treble damage claim are sellers, not customers or consumers. . . .

. . . The statute does not confine its protection to consumers, or to purchasers, or to competitors, or to sellers. Nor does it immunize the outlawed acts because they are done by any of these. . . . The act is comprehensive in its terms and coverage, protecting all who are made victims of the forbidden practices by whomever they may be perpetrated. . . .

Nor is the amount of the nation's sugar industry which the California refiners control relevant, so long as control is exercised effectively in the area concerned.

. . . Under the facts characterizing this industry's operation and the tightening of controls in this producing area by the new agreements and understandings, there can be no question that their restrictive consequences were projected substantially into the interstate distribution of the sugar. . . .

[Judgment affirmed]

Griggs v Duke Power Co.

401 US 424 (1971)

Griggs and other blacks were employed in the labor department of the Duke Power Company. They

sought promotion to higher paying departments of their employer but could not obtain promotion because the employer had established promotion standards of (1) high school education, and (2) satisfactory scores on two professionally prepared aptitude tests. The tests were not designed to measure ability to perform the work in the particular department to which they sought promotion. Griggs and other employees brought a class action under Title VII of the Federal Civil Rights Act of 1964, claiming that the promotion criteria discriminated against them because of race. The Court of Appeals held that there was no prohibited discrimination even though white workers apparently obtained better scores on the tests because of having obtained a better public school education. Griggs appealed to the Supreme Court.

BURGER, C.J. . . . In 1955 the Company instituted a policy of requiring a high school education for initial assignment to any department except Labor. . . .

The Company added a further requirement for new employees on July 2, 1965. . . . To qualify for placement in any but the Labor Department it became necessary to register satisfactory scores on two professionally prepared aptitude tests, as well as to have a high school education. . . . In September 1965 the Company began to permit incumbent employees who lacked a high school education to qualify for transfer from Labor or Coal Handling to an "inside" job by passing two tests—the Wonderlic Personnel Test, which purports to measure general intelligence, and the Bennett mechanical Comprehension Test. Neither was directed or intended to measure the ability to learn to perform a particular job or category of jobs. The requisite scores used for both initial hiring and transfer approximated the national median for high school graduates. . . .

. . . The Court of Appeals noted . . . that there was no showing of a racial purpose or invidious intent in the adoption of the high school diploma requirement or general intelligence test and that these standards had been applied fairly to whites and Negroes alike. It held that, in the absence of a discriminatory purpose, use of such requirements was permitted by the Act. In so doing, the Court of Appeals rejected the claim that because these two requirements operated to render ineligible a markedly

disproportionate number of Negroes, they were unlawful under Title VII unless shown to be job related. . . .

The objective of Congress in the enactment of Title VII is plain from the language of the statute. It was to achieve equality of employment opportunities and remove barriers that have operated in the past to favor an identifiable group of white employees over other employees. Under the Act, practices, procedures, or tests neutral on their face, and even neutral in terms of intent, cannot be maintained if they operate to "freeze" the status quo of prior discriminatory employment practices.

The Court of Appeals' opinion . . . agreed that, on the record in the present case, "whites register far better on the Company's alternative requirements" than Negroes. . . . This consequence would appear to be directly traceable to race. . . . Because they are Negroes, petitioners have long received inferior education in segregated schools. . . . What is required by Congress is the removal of artificial, arbitrary, and unnecessary barriers to employment when the barriers operate invidiously to discriminate on the basis of racial or other impermissible classification. . . .

. . . The Act proscribes not only overt discrimination but also practices that are fair in form, but discriminatory in operation. The touchstone is business necessity. If an employment practice which operates to exclude Negroes cannot be shown to be related to job performance, the practice is prohibited.

On the record before us, neither the high school completion requirement nor the general intelligence test is shown to bear a demonstrable relationship to successful performance of the jobs for which it was used. Both were adopted, as the Court of Appeals noted, without meaningful study of their relationship to job-performance ability. Rather, a vice president of the Company testified, the requirements were instituted on the Company's judgment that they generally would improve the overall quality of the work force.

The evidence, however, shows that employees who have not completed high school or taken the tests have continued to perform satisfactorily and make progress in departments for which the high school and test criteria are now used. The promotion record of present employees who would not be able to meet the new criteria thus suggests the possibility that the requirements may not be needed even for the limited purpose of preserving the avowed policy of advancement within the Company. . . .

The Court of Appeals held that the Company had adopted the diploma and test requirements without any "intention to discriminate against Negro employees.". . . But good intent or absence of discriminatory intent does not redeem employment procedures or testing mechanisms that . . . are unrelated to measuring job capability.

The Company's lack of discriminatory intent is suggested by special efforts to help the undereducated employees through Company financing of two-thirds the cost of tuition for high school training. But Congress directed the thrust of the Act to the *consequences* of employment practices, not simply the motivation. More than that, Congress has placed on the employer the burden of showing that any given requirement must have a manifest relationship to the employment in question. . . .

The Company contends that its general intelligence tests are specifically permitted by § 703(h) of the Act. That section authorizes the use of "any professionally developed ability test" that is not "designed, intended *or used* to discriminate because of race. . . ." (Emphasis added.)

The Equal Employment Opportunity Commission, having enforcement responsibility, has issued guidelines interpreting § 703 (h) to permit only the use of job-related tests. . . .

Nothing in the Act precludes the use of testing or measuring procedures; obviously they are useful. What Congress has forbidden is giving these devices and mechanisms controlling force unless they are demonstrably a reasonable measure of job performance. Congress has not commanded that the less qualified be preferred over the better qualified simply because of minority origins. Far from disparaging job qualifications as such, Congress has made such qualifications the controlling factor, so that race, religion, nationality, and sex become irrelevant. What Congress has commanded is that any tests used must measure the person for the job and not the person in the abstract.

[Judgment reversed]

Eslinger v Thomas

(CA4 SC) 476 F2d 225 (1973)

Victoria Eslinger was a student in law school. She applied for a job as a page in the South Carolina Senate. Her application was refused because she was a female. She brought suit claiming that she had been denied her civil rights. The suit was dismissed and she appealed.

WINTER, C.J. . . . The district court found that, at the time plaintiff sought employment, pages were usually college students and a large number were law students at the University of South Carolina Law School. Pages performed various duties assigned by senators, the clerk and other employees of the senate, including running errands, both personal and official, for senators, preparation and distribution of Acts, proofreading, indexing, bookkeeping, obtaining food and drink for the senators, assisting with committee records, relaying messages to senators, attending committee meetings, acting as assistants and helpers to clerks of various committees, and otherwise taking care of senators' needs.

Pages are temporary employees; they work only for the months the senate is in session. The positions are quite attractive to students. Although they are not overpaid, working hours are not long, working hours may be adjusted to suit the convenience of the employee, and pages have the opportunity to view the lawmaking process and to meet state officials.

Suit was filed in February, 1971. Several months thereafter, the South Carolina Senate adopted Resolution S.525, establishing new classifications and duties of part-time employees formerly known as pages. Under this resolution, females may be employed as "clerical assistants" and "committee attendants," but not as "Senate pages." As a condition of employment, a female is also required to furnish a written statement from her parent or guardian assuming responsibility for her transportation, safety and supervision to and from her local residence and the senate and at her local residence. At the time of trial, three women had been employed pursuant to this resolution, but plaintiff did not apply for such employment, insisting on her right to be a "Senate page.". . .

. . . The district court determined that the custom of the South Carolina Senate to deny females positions as pages, prior to the adoption of Resolution S.525, denied plaintiff her "Constitutional right to seek employment and be employed." The district court concluded, however, that the constitutional rights of female citizens were not violated by the superseding provisions of S.525, and that the prohibition against females running personal errands for senators (one practical effect of the resolution) was not shown to be "arbitrary or wanting in rational justification.". . .

A federal cause of action based on sex discrimination has no deep common-law roots; rather, it emerges from recent enlightened approaches to what constitutes equal protection of the laws under the Fourteenth Amendment. . . .

. . . Plaintiff's challenge to the employment practices of the South Carolina Senate is grounded primarily on the equal protection clause of the Fourteenth Amendment. She urges us to find sex a "suspect classification," which would require "close judicial scrutiny" of a governmental action based upon such a classification. . . .

Until recently an argument that a classification based upon sex violated the equal protection clause bore little chance of success. However, in Reed v Reed, 404 US 71 . . . (1971), the Court struck down a classification based upon sex, holding invalid an Idaho statute which gave a mandatory preference to a male over a female for appointment as administrator of an estate when both were equally qualified and within the same entitlement class. . . .

When we apply the test of *Reed,* we are compelled to conclude that S.525 denies equal protection. The "public image" of the South Carolina State and of its members is obviously a proper subject of state concern. Apparently, the South Carolina Senate felt that certain functions performed by pages on behalf of senators, e.g. running personal errands, driving senators about in their autos, packing their bags in hotel rooms, cashing personal checks for senators, etc., were "not suitable under existing circumstances for young ladies and may give rise to the appearance of impropriety." Resolution S.525, n. 2, *supra.* In their brief, defendants argue that "[i]n placing this restriction upon female pages, the Senate is merely attempting to avoid placing one of its employees in a conceivably damaging position, protecting itself from appearing to the public that an innocent relationship is not so innocent, and maintaining as much public confidence while conducting the business of the people of South Carolina as possible."

We find this rationale unconvincing. It rests upon the implied premise, which we think false, that "[o]n the one hand, the female is viewed as a pure, delicate and vulnerable creature who must be protected from exposure to criminal influences; and on the other, as a brazen temptress, from whose seductive blandishments the innocent male must be protected. Every woman is either Eve or Little Eva—and either way, she loses." Johnson and Knapp, Sex Discrimination By Law: A Study in Judicial Perspective, 46 N.Y.U.L.Rev. 675, 704—5 (1971). . . . We have only to look at our own female secretaries and female law clerks to conclude that an intimate business relationship, including traveling on circuit, between persons of different sex presents no "appearance of impropriety" in the current age, graduated as we are from Victorian attitudes. We note also that South Carolina has had female senators. While the record does not reflect their ages, the association of female senator with male page has not given rise to a sufficient "appearance of impropriety" to require legislative regulation which is the reverse of S.525. In short, present societal attitudes reject the notion that, in most forms of business endeavor, free association between the sexes is to be limited, regulated and restricted because of a difference in sex.

The requirements of S.525 of a written statement from the female's parent or guardian assuming responsibility for her transportation, safety and well-being and for her "strict supervision" stand on no firmer ground. Adult females, or nearly adult females, are no longer chattels of their husbands or parents. If they are tendered and accept special protection or special courtesies, there is no violation of right; but unwelcome special protection, especially denial of employment opportunity, foisted upon them is counter to modern law and modern social thinking. . . .

Since we can find no "fair and substantial" relation between the object of S.525 (combatting the "appearance of impropriety") and the ground of difference (sex) upon which the classification rests, we reverse with regard to the denial of declaratory and injunctive relief and remand the case for further proceedings. . . .

[Judgment reversed on the equal protection issue]

United Steelworkers of America v Usery

429 US 305 (1977)

A rule of the steelworkers' union provided that a union member was not eligible to hold office in a local union unless the member had attended at least one half of the regular meetings of the union in the

preceding three years. The application of this rule to Local 3489 made 96.5% of the union members ineligible to hold office. This left only 23 members eligible. Nine of these were already officers of the local union. An election was held in the union. The Secretary of Labor of the United States then brought an action to invalidate the election on the ground that it was illegal because it had been conducted subject to the meeting-attendance rule and that such rule was invalid because it was not a "reasonable qualification" and therefore violated the Labor-Management Reporting and Disclosure Act, § 401(e), 29 USC § 481(e), which declared that "every member in good standing shall be eligible to be a candidate and hold office . . . subject to . . . reasonable qualifications uniformly imposed." The district court sustained the meeting-attendance rule. On appeal, the court of appeals held the rule invalid. The union appealed to the Supreme Court.

BRENNAN, J. . . . LMRDA does not render unions powerless to restrict candidacies for union office. The injunction in § 401(e) that "every member in good standing shall be eligible to be a candidate and to hold office" is made expressly "subject to . . . reasonable qualifications uniformly imposed.". . . But "Congress plainly did not intend that the authorization . . . of 'reasonable qualifications . . .' should be given a broad reach. The contrary is implicit in the legislative history of the section and its wording. . . ." The basic objective of Title IV of LMRDA is to guarantee "free and democratic" union elections modeled on "political elections in the country" where "the assumption is that voters will exercise common sense and judgment in casting their ballots.". . . Thus, Title IV is not designed merely to protect the right of a union member to run for a particular office in a particular election. ". . . Congress emphatically asserted a vital public interest in assuring free and democratic union elections that transcends the narrower interest of the complaining union member." . . . The goal was to "protect the rights of rank-and-file members to participate fully in the operation of their union through processes of democratic self-government, and, through the election process, to keep the union leadership responsive to the membership."

Whether a particular qualification is "reasonable" within the meaning of § 402(e) must therefore "be measured in terms of its consistency with the Act's command to unions to conduct 'free and democratic' union elections." . . . Congress was not concerned only with corrupt union leadership. Congress chose the goal of "free and democratic" union elections as a preventive measure "to curb the possibility of abuse by benevolent as well as malevolent entrenched leadership." [The ability to attain these goals is] seriously impaired by candidacy qualifications which substantially deplete the ranks of those who might run in opposition to incumbents. . . .

. . . The antidemocratic effects of the meeting attendance rule outweigh the interests urged in its support. . . . An attendance requirement that results in the exclusion of 96.5% of the members from candidacy for union office hardly seems to be a "reasonable qualification" consistent with the goal of free and democratic elections. A requirement having that result obviously severely restricts the free choice of the membership in selecting their leaders. . . .

Petitioners next argue that the rule is reasonable within § 401(e) because it encourages attendance at union meetings, and assures more qualified officers by limiting election to those who have demonstrated an interest in union affairs, and are familiar with union problems. But the rule has plainly not served these goals. It has obviously done little to encourage attendance at meetings, which continue to attract only a handful of members. Even as to the more limited goal of encouraging the attendance of potential dissident candidates, very few members, as we have said, are likely to see themselves as such sufficiently far in advance of the election to be spurred to attendance by the rule.

As for assuring the election of knowledgeable and dedicated leaders, the election provisions of LMRDA express a congressional determination that the best means to this end is to leave the choice of leaders to the membership in open democratic elections, unfettered by arbitrary exclusions. Pursuing this goal by excluding the bulk of the membership from eligibility for office, and thus limiting the possibility of dissident candidacies, run directly counter to the basic premise of the statute. We therefore conclude that Congress, in guaranteeing every union member the opportunity to hold office, subject only to "reasonable qualifications," disabled unions from establishing eligibility qualifications as sharply restrictive of the openness of the union political process as is petitioners' attendance rule.

[Judgment affirmed]

Virginia State Board of Pharmacy v Virginia Citizens Consumer Council, Inc.

425 US 748 (1976)

Approximately 95% of all prescriptions filled by druggists require only the dispensing of pills, capsules, or liquid already prepared or packaged by the drug manufacturer. Virginia prohibited druggists from advertising the prices of their prescription drugs. A Virginia resident who was required to take prescription drugs daily and two consumer groups claimed that the anti-advertising law was unconstitutional as it prevented the consumer from learning where the drugs could be purchased at the lowest price. The lower federal court held the statute void as a violation of the free speech guarantee of the First Amendment of the Federal Constitution. The Virginia State Board of Pharmacy appealed.

BLACKMUN, J. . . . The . . . attack on the statute is one made not by one directly subject to its prohibition, that is, a pharmacist, but by prescription drug consumers who claim that they would greatly benefit if the prohibition were lifted and advertising freely allowed. . . . Their claim is that the First Amendment entitles the user of prescription drugs to receive information, that pharmacists wish to communicate to them through advertising and other promotional means, concerning the prices of such drugs.

Certainly that information may be of value. Drug prices in Virginia, for both prescription and nonprescription items, strikingly vary from outlet to outlet even within the same locality. It is stipulated, for example, that in Richmond "the cost of 40 Achromycin tablets ranges from $2.59 to $6.00, . . . and that in the Newport News-Hampton area the cost of tetracycline ranges from $1.20 to $9.00, a difference of 650%. . . .

The question first arises whether, even assuming that First Amendment protection attaches to the flow of drug price information, it is a protection enjoyed by the appellees as recipients of the information, and not solely, if at all, by the advertisers themselves who seek to disseminate that information.

Freedom of speech presupposes a willing speaker. But where a speaker exists, as is the case here, the protection afforded is to be the communication, to its source and to its recipients both. . . .

The appellants contend that the advertisement of prescription drug prices is outside the protection of the First Amendment because it is "commercial speech.". . .

One question is whether speech which does "no more than propose a commercial transaction,". . . is so removed from any "exposition of ideas," . . . and from " 'truth, science, morality, and arts in general, in its diffusion of liberal sentiments on the administration of Government' " . . . that it lacks all protection. Our answer is that it is not. . . .

As to the particular consumer's interest in the free flow of commercial information, that interest may be as keen, if not keener by far, than his interest in the day's most urgent political debate. Appellees' case in this respect is a convincing one. Those whom the suppression of prescription drug price information hits the hardest are the poor, the sick, and particularly the aged. A disproportionate amount of their income tends to be spent on prescription drugs; yet they are the least able to learn, by shopping from pharmacist to pharmacist, where their scarce dollars are best spent. When drug prices vary as strikingly as they do, information as to who is charging what becomes more than a convenience. It could mean the alleviation of physical pain or the enjoyment of basic necessities.

Generalizing, society also may have a strong interest in the free flow of commercial information. Even an individual advertisement, though entirely "commercial," may be of general public interest. . . .

Moreover, there is another consideration that suggests that no line between publicly "interesting" or "important" commercial advertising and the opposite kind could ever be drawn. Advertising, however tasteless and excessive it sometimes may seem, is nonetheless dissemination of information as to who is producing and selling what product, for what reason, and at what price. So long as we preserve a predominantly free enterprise economy, the allocation of our resources in large measure will be made through numerous private economic decisions. It is a matter of public interest that those decisions, in the aggregate, be intelligent and well informed. To this end, the free flow of commercial information is indispensable. . . .

[Judgment affirmed]

QUESTIONS AND CASE PROBLEMS

1. What is the objective of each of the following rules of law?
   (a) Horizontal price-fixing is illegal under the federal law without regard to whether the price fixed is fair and reasonable.
   (b) Farmers' and dairyfarmers' cooperatives are exempt by statute from the operation of the Sherman Antitrust Act.

2. The Delco Cleaners and Dyers did business in Delaware County. The name Delco was a contraction of the name of the county. A suit was brought to enjoin the use of the name "Delco" by another local concern calling itself the "Delco Valet Service." Decide. [Berberian v. Ferm, 166 Pa Super 108, 70 A2d 394]

3. A manufacturer, The White Motor Co., gave each of its dealers an exclusive right to sell its product within a specified territory. The United States claimed that this was an illegal restraint of trade. White replied that the division of territory between its dealers was a marketing necessity because each dealer had to be protected within his or her territory against the competition of the other White dealers so that the dealer would be free to concentrate on competing with the dealers of other companies. Was the White dealership plan a restraint of trade? [The White Motor Co. v United States, 372 US 253]

4. The Winsted Hoisery Co. labeled mixed woolen articles as "natural wool," "Australian wool," and other similar terms that did not indicate the mixed nature of the article. The Federal Trade Commission ordered the company to stop the practice of using a "wool" label to describe a mixed article on the ground that it was an unfair trade practice. The company defended on the ground that all other manufacturers understood that the label was not to be taken as true and that the competitors of the company were not deceived. Was this a valid defense? [Federal Trade Commision v Winsted Hoisery Company, 258 US 483]

5. Ohio statutes required employers to furnish seats in lunchroom facilities for female employees, limited the hours that women could be employed, and prohibited the employment of women in certain specified occupations or at work requiring the frequent or repeated lifting of weights over 25 pounds. The statutes were challenged as invalid on the ground that they violated the Federal Civil Rights Act of 1964 because they did not treat male and female employees alike. Were the statutes valid? [Jones Metal Products Co. v Walker, 29 Ohio 173, 281 NE2d 1, reversing 25 Ohio App 2d 141, 267 NE2d 814]

6. Kinney Shoe Company and the Brown Shoe Company proposed to merge by giving the Kinney stockholders shares of the Brown Shoe Company stock in exchange for their shares. By dollar value, Brown was the third largest seller of shoes in the United States and fourth largest manufacturer. Kinney was the eighth largest seller and owned and operated the largest independent chain of family shoe stores in the nation. It was claimed that the merger would not lessen competition as Kinney manufactured less than ½ percent of shoes in the United States and Brown produced about 4 percent. Decide. [Brown Shoe Company v United States, 370 US 294]

7. A Nevada statute required that at all gas stations a sign should be displayed on each pump setting forth the price of the gasoline and certain other information as to taxes and brand. The sign was to be not less than 7 inches high and 8 inches wide nor larger than 12 inches by 12 inches. The statute prohibited any other signs showing prices on the premises. The Redman Petroleum Corporation maintained proper signs on its pumps but also had large signs near the side of the road. There was no claim

that any fraud or price-cutting was involved. The signs by the road stated information that conformed to the information of the signs on the pumps. Redman claimed that a substantial sum of money had been invested in these signs by the side of the road and that they had been used for over ten years. Redman claimed that the statute was unconstitutional. Was Redman correct? [Nevada v Redman Petroleum Corp., 77 Nev 163, 360 P2d 842]

8. A New Jersey statute provides that no rebates, allowances, concessions, or benefits shall be given, directly or indirectly, so as to permit any person to obtain motor fuel from a retail dealer below the posted price or at a net price lower than the posted price applicable at the time of the sale. An action was brought by Fried, a retail gasoline dealer, to prevent the enforcement of the statute. He claimed that it was invalid because it was discriminatory in that it related only to the sale of gasoline and that it denied due process by regulating the price. Was the law constitutional? [Fried v Kervick, 34 NJ 68, 167 A2d 380]

9. Moore ran a bakery in Santa Rosa, New Mexico. His business was wholly intrastate. Mead's Fine Bread Company, his competitor, engaged in an interstate business. Mead cut the price of bread in half in Santa Rosa but made no price cut in any other place in New Mexico or in any other state. As a result of this price cutting, Moore was driven out of business. Moore then sued Mead for damages for violation of the Clayton and Robinson-Patman Acts. Mead claimed that the price cutting was purely intrastate and therefore did not constitute a violation of federal statutes. Was Mead correct? [Moore v Mead's Fine Bread Co., 348 US 115]

10. The El Paso Natural Gas Company acquired the stock and assets of the Pacific Northwest Pipe Line Company. El Paso, although not a California enterprise, supplied over half of the natural gas used in California; all the other natural gas was supplied by California sources. No gas was sold in California by Pacific Northwest, although it was a strong experienced company within the Northwest area and had attempted several times to enter the California market. United States claimed that the acquisition of Pacific by El Paso constituted a violation of § 7 of the Clayton Act, as amended, because the effect would be to remove competition between the two companies within California. The defense was raised that (a) California was not a "section" of the country within the Clayton Act, and (b) the sale of natural gas was not a line of commerce, and (c) the acquisition did not lessen competition when there had not been any prior sales by Pacific within the area. Decide. [United States v El Paso Natural Gas Co., 376 US 651]

11. Sun Oil sells gasoline retail in its own gas stations, as well as selling gas to independently-owned gas stations. In selling to one independent, it gave that independent a price cut to enable it to meet the competition of other independent gas stations. The Federal Trade Commission claimed this was an unlawful price discrimination. Sun Oil defended on the ground that the price cut was made as authorized by the statute "in good faith to meet an equally low price of a competitor." Was this defense valid? [Federal Trade Commission v Sun Oil Co., 371 US 505]

12. Collier sued Roth for damages for violating a state Unfair Milk Sales Practices Act. He claimed that he was entitled to recover treble damages. The statute declared that, "Any person who is injured in business or property by reason of another person's violation of any provision [of the statute] may intervene in the suit for injunction . . . against the other person or he may bring a separate action and recover three times the actual damages sustained as a result of the violation, together with the cost of the suit, or he may sue to enjoin the violation. . . ." Was Collier entitled to treble damages? [Collier v Roth, (Mo App) 468 SW2d 57]

6 Administrative Agencies

Large areas of the American economy are governed by federal administrative agencies created to carry out the general policies specified by Congress. A contract must be in harmony with public policy not only as declared by Congress and the courts but also as applied by the appropriate administrative agency. For example, a contract to market particular goods might not be prohibited by any statute or court decision but it may still be condemned by the Federal Trade Commission as an unfair method of competition. When the proper commission has made its determination, a contract not in harmony therewith, such as a contract of a carrier charging a higher or a lower rate than that approved by the Interstate Commerce Commission, is illegal. Other federal administrative agencies include the Civil Aeronautics Board, the Federal Communications Commission, the Federal Maritime Commission, the Federal Power Commission, the National Labor Relations Board, and the Securities and Exchange Commission. The law governing these agencies is known as *administrative law*.

State administrative agencies may also affect business and the citizen, because state agencies may have jurisdiction over fair employment practices, workmen's compensation claims, and the renting of homes and apartments.

§ 6:1. Uniqueness of Administrative Agencies. The structure of government common in the states and the national government is a division into three branches—executive, legislative, and judicial—with the lawmaker selected by popular vote and with the judicial branch acting as the superguardian to prevent either the executive or the legislative branch from exceeding the proper spheres of their respective powers. In contrast, members of administrative agencies are ordinarily appointed (in the case of federal agencies, by the President of the United States with the consent of two thirds of Congress); and the major agencies combine legislative, executive, and judicial powers in that they may make the rules, police the community to see that the rules are obeyed, and sit in judgment to determine whether there have been violations of their rules. (See p. 90, Withrow v Larkin)

Although an appeal to the courts may be taken from the action of an administrative agency, the agency is to a large degree not subject to control by the courts. The subject matter involved is ordinarily so technical and the agency is clothed with such discretion that courts will not reverse agency action unless it can be proved arbitrary and capricious. Very few agency decisions are reversed on this ground.

§ 6:2. The Administrator's Powers. The administrator may be an agency or commission of a few or many persons or the head of an executive department of the United States government. The name or size is not important. It is the function of "administering" which is here considered; and for the sake of brevity, the term *administrator* will be used to refer to all these administrators as a general class without indicating the number of persons or the structure of the agency involved.

(a)   Legislative Powers. The modern administrator has power to make the laws that regulate a particular segment of life or industry. (See p. 92, United States v Howard) There once was a great reluctance to accept the fact that the administrator made law, because of our constitutional doctrine that only the lawmaker, the Congress or the state legislature, can make laws. It therefore seemed an improper transfer or delegation of power for the lawmaker to set up a separate body or agency and give to it the power to make the laws.

The same forces that led society initially to create the administrator caused society to clothe the administrator with the power to make the laws. Practical expediency gradually prevailed in favor of the conclusion that if we want the administrator to do a job, we must grant the administrator sufficient power to do so.

In the early days of administrative regulation, the legislative character of the administrative rules was not clearly perceived, largely because the administrator's sphere of power was so narrow that the administrator was, in effect, merely a thermostat. That is, the lawmaker told the administrator when to do what, and all that the administrator did was to act in the manner specified by such program. For example, the cattle inspector was told to take certain steps when it was determined that cattle had hoof-and-mouth disease. Here it was clear that the lawmaker had set the standard, and the administrator merely "swung into action" when the specified fact situation existed.

The next step in the growth of the administrative power was to authorize the cattle inspector to act upon finding that cattle had a contagious disease, leaving it to the inspector to formulate a rule or guide as to what diseases were contagious. Here again, the discretionary and the legislative aspects of the administrator's conduct were obscured by the belief that the field of science would define "contagious," leaving no area of discretionary decision to the administrator.

Today's health commission, an administrator, is authorized to make such rules and regulations for the protection or improvement of the common health as it deems desirable. Its rules thus make the "health law." In regulating various economic aspects of national life, the administrator is truly the lawmaker.

Gradually, the courts have come to recognize, or at least to tolerate, the entrusting of a job to an agency although the lawmaker did nothing more than state the goal or objective to be attained by the agency.

Thus, it has been sufficient for a legislature to authorize an administrator to grant licenses "as public interest, convenience, or necessity requires;" "to prohibit unfair methods of competition;" to regulate prices so that they "in [the administrator's] judgment will be generally fair and equitable;" to prevent "profiteering;" "to prevent the existence of intercorporate holdings, which unduly or unnecessarily complicate the structure [or] unfairly or inequitably distribute voting power among security holders;" and to renegotiate government contracts to prevent "excessive profits."

The authority of an administrator is not limited to the technology existing when the administrator was created. To the contrary, the sphere in which the administrator may act expands with new scientific developments. So it has been held that although community cable television (CATV) was developed after the Federal Communication Commission was created by the Federal Communications Act of 1934, the Commission can regulate CATV. This power to regulate includes both the mechanical aspects of broadcasting and reception and also the content of the broadcast. Thus the Commission may require such systems to originate local programs (cablecasting) in order to serve the local communities, in addition to their activity of transmitting programs from a distance.[1]

(b)   Executive Powers. The modern administrator has executive power to investigate and to require persons to appear as witnesses and to produce relevant papers. Thus the administrator may investigate in order to see if there is any violation of the law or of its rules generally, to determine whether there is need for the adoption of additional rules, to ascertain the facts with respect to a particular suspected or alleged violation, and to determine whether its decisions are being obeyed.

The federal Antitrust Civil Process Act is an example of the extent to which administrative investigation is authorized. The Act authorizes the Attorney General or the Assistant Attorney General in charge of the Antitrust Division of the Department of Justice to make a civil investigative demand (CID) upon any person believed to have knowledge relevant to any civil antitrust investigation, such as an investigation before bringing a suit to enjoin a monopolistic practice or an investigation made upon receiving a premerger notification. The person so notified can be compelled to produce relevant documents, furnish written answers to written questions, or appear in person and give oral testimony.[2] Similar power to require the production of papers is possessed by the Federal Trade Commission, the Federal Maritime Commission, the National Science Foundation, the Treasury Department, the Department of Agriculture, the Department of the Army, the Department of Labor, and the Veterans Administration.

The power to investigate is a continuing power, with the result that the administrative agency can, in effect, put the party on probation and require periodic reports to show whether the party has complied with the law.[3]

(c)   Judicial Powers. The modern administrator may be given power to sit as a court and to determine whether there have been any violations of the law or of its regulations. Thus, the National Labor Relations Board determines whether there has been a prohibited unfair labor practice, the Federal Trade Commission will act as a court to determine whether there is unfair competition, and so on.

---

[1] United States v Midwest Video Corp. 406 US 649 (sustaining a Commission regulation which provided that "no CATV system having 3,500 or more subscribers shall carry the signal of any television broadcast station unless the system also operates to a significant extent as a local outlet by cablecasting and has available facilities for local production and presentation of programs other than automated services.").

[2] Antitrust Civil Process Act of 1962, as amended by the Antitrust Improvement Act of 1976, §§ 101, 102, PL 94-435, 90 Stat 1383, 15 USC § 1311 et seq.

[3] United States v Morton Salt Co. 338 US 632.

At first glance, this is contrary to American tradition. For example, when an administrative agency sits as a judge as to the violation of a regulation that it has made, there is the element that the "judge" is not impartial because it is trying the accused for violating "its" law rather than "the" law. There is also the objection that the administrator is determining important rights but does so without a jury, which seems inconsistent with the long-established emphasis of our history upon the sanctity of trial by jury. In spite of these objections to the administrator's exercise of judicial power, such exercise is now firmly established.

(d)   Decentralization of Administrative Functions. In order to meet the objection that the exercise of executive, legislative, and judicial powers by the same administrator is a potential threat to impartiality, some steps have been taken toward decentralizing the administrative functions. Thus the prosecutorial power of the National Labor Relations Board was severed from the Board and entrusted to an independent General Counsel by the Labor-Management Relations Act of 1947. In a number of agencies, such as the FTC, the judicial function is assigned to Administrative Law Judges.

§ 6:3. Constitutional Limitations on Administrative Investigation. With the exception of the searching of premises, such as a factory building, the Constitution does not impose any significant limitation on the power of an administrator to conduct an investigation.

(a)   Inspection of Premises. In general, a person has the same protection against unreasonable search and seizure by an administrative officer as that person has against unreasonable search and seizure by a police officer. Thus the administrator must have a search warrant in order to inspect a building over the objection of the occupant when the administrator is seeking to see if there have been any violations of the building or fire code.[4]

In contrast, when the danger of concealment is great, a warrantless search is validly made of the premises of a business which is highly regulated, as that of selling liquor or firearms. Similarly, a welfare recipient who claims an allowance for a dependent child can be required to allow a welfare investigator to enter a dwelling without a warrant to determine that there was in fact such a dependent child.

(b)   Production of Papers. For the most part, the constitutional guarantee against unreasonable search and seizure does not afford much protection for papers and records against investigation by an administrator, since that guarantee does not apply in the absence of an actual seizure. That is, a subpoena to testify or to produce records cannot be opposed on the ground that it is a search and seizure, as the constitutional protection is limited to cases of actual search and seizure rather than the obtaining of information by compulsion.

The protection afforded by the guarantee against self-incrimination is likewise narrow. It cannot be invoked (1) when the person compelled to present self-incriminating evidence is given immunity from future prosecution; nor can it be claimed as to

---

[4] This requirement has been greatly relaxed in Marshall v Barlow's, Inc. 56 LEd2d 305 (May 23, 1978), in which job safety inspectors were required to obtain a search warrant but were required only to show good faith rather than probable violation of the law in order to obtain the warrant.

(2) corporate records, even though the officer or employee of the corporation who produces them would be incriminated thereby; nor for (3) records which by law must be kept by the person subject to the administrative investigation. (See p. 92, Shapiro v United States)

§ 6:4. Pattern of Administrative Procedure.

At the beginning of the era of modern regulation of business, the administrator was, to a large extent, a minor executive or police officer charged with the responsibility of enforcing laws applicable to limited fact situations. The health officer empowered to condemn and destroy diseased cattle was typical. In view of the need for prompt action and because of the relative simplicity of the fact determination to be made, it was customary for such administrator to exercise summary powers; that is, upon finding cattle believed to be diseased, the animals would be killed immediately without delaying to find their true owner and without holding a formal hearing to determine whether they were in fact diseased.

Today, the exercise of summary powers is the exceptional case. Concepts of due process generally require that some notice be given those who will be adversely affected and that some form of hearing be held at which they may present their case.

(a) **Preliminary Steps.** It is commonly provided that either a private individual aggrieved by the conduct of another, or the administrator may present a complaint. This complaint is served on the alleged wrongdoer, who is given opportunity to file an answer. There may be other phases of pleading between the parties and the administrator, but eventually the matter comes before the administrator to be heard. After a hearing, the administrator makes a decision and enters an order either dismissing the complaint or directing the adverse party to do or not to do certain acts.

The complaint filing and prehearing stage of the procedure may be more detailed. In many of the modern administrative statutes, provision is made for an examination of the informal complaint by some branch of the administrator to determine whether the case comes within the scope of the administrator's authority. It is also commonly provided that an investigation be made by the administrator to determine whether the facts are such to warrant a hearing of the complaint. If it is decided that the complaint is within the jurisdiction of the administrator and that the facts appear to justify it, a formal complaint is issued and served on the adverse party, and an answer is then filed as above stated.

With the rising complexity of the subjects regulated by administrative agencies, the trend is increasingly in the direction of greater preliminary examination upon the basis of an informal complaint.

(b) **The Administrative Hearing.** In order to satisfy the requirements of due process, it is generally necessary for the administrator to give notice and to hold a hearing. A significant difference between the administrator's hearing and a court hearing is that there is no right of trial by jury before an administrator. For example, a workmen's compensation board may pass on a claim without any jury. The absence of a jury does not constitute a denial of due process. The theory is that a new right unknown to the common law has been created, and the right to a jury trial exists only where it was recognized at the common law. (See p. 93, Atlas Roofing Company, Inc. v Occupational Safety and Health Review Commission)

Another significant difference between an administrative hearing and a judicial determination is that the administrator may be authorized to make an initial determination without holding a hearing. If the administrator's conclusion is challenged, the administrator will then hold a hearing. A court, however, must have a trial before it makes a judgment. This has important practical consequences in that when a hearing is sought after the administrator has acted, the objecting party has the burden of proof and the cost of going forward. The result is that fewer persons go to the trouble of seeking such a hearing. This, in turn, reduces the amount of hearings and litigation in which the administrator becomes involved, with the resultant economy of money and personnel from the government's standpoint.

Cutting across these procedures are the practical devices of informal settlement and consent decrees. In many instances, the alleged wrongdoer is willing to change upon being informally notified that a complaint has been made. It is therefore sound public relations, as well as expeditious handling of the matter, for the administrator to inform the alleged wrongdoer of the charge made prior to the filing of any formal complaint in order to encourage a voluntary settlement. A matter that has already gone into the formal hearing stage may also be terminated by agreement, and a stipulation or consent degree may be filed setting forth the terms of the agreement.

A further modification of this general pattern is made in the case of the Interstate Commerce Commission. Complaints received by the Commission are referred to the Bureau of Informal Cases, which endeavors to secure an amicable adjustment with the carrier. If this cannot be done, the complainant is notified that it will be necessary to file a formal complaint. At this stage of the proceedings, the parties can expedite the matter by agreeing that the case may be heard on the pleadings alone. In this case, the complainant files a pleading or memorandum to which the defendant files an answering memorandum, the plaintiff then filing a reply or rebuttal memorandum. If the parties do not agree to this procedure, a hearing is held after the pleadings have been filed.

§ 6:5. Punishment and Enforcement Powers of Administrators. Originally administrators were powerless to impose any punishment or to enforce their decisions. If the person regulated did not voluntarily comply with the administrator's decision, the administrator could only petition a court to order that person to obey.

Within the last few decades, administrators have been increasingly given the power to impose a penalty and to issue orders which are binding on the regulated person unless an appeal is taken to a court and the administrative decision reversed. As an illustration of the first, the Occupational Safety and Health Act of 1970 provides for the assessment of civil penalties against employers failing to put an end to dangerous working conditions when ordered to do so by the administrative agency created by that statute.[5] Likewise environmental protection statutes adopted by states commonly give the state agency the power to assess a penalty for a violation of the environmental protection regulations. As an illustration of the second type of administrative action, the Federal Trade Commission can issue a cease and desist order to stop a practice which it decides is improper. This order to stop is binding unless reversed on an appeal.

---

[5] Lake Butler Apparel Co. v Secretary of Labor (CA5 OSHA) 519 F2d 84.

§ 6:6. **Finality of Administrative Determination.** Basic to the Anglo-American legal theory is the belief that no one, not even a branch of the government, is above the law. Thus, the growth of powers of the administrative agency was frequently accepted or tolerated on the theory that if the administrative agency went too far the courts would review the administrative action. The typical modern statute provides that an appeal may be taken from the administrative action by any person in interest or by any person aggrieved. When the question which the administrator decides is a question of law, the court on appeal will reverse the administrator if the court disagrees with the decision. But if the controversy turns on a question of fact, a court will generally accept the conclusion of the administrator as final. The net result is that the determination by the administrative agency will, in most cases, be final.

The greatest limitation upon court review of the administrative action is the rule that a decision involving discretion will not be reversed in the absence of an error of law; or a clear abuse of, or the arbitrary or capricious exercise of, discretion. (See p. 94, Moog Industries v Federal Trade Commission)

The courts reason that since the administrator was appointed because of expert ability, it would be absurd for the court that is manifestly unqualified technically to make a decision in the matter to step in and determine whether the administrator made the proper choice. Courts will not do so unless the administrator has clearly acted wrongly, arbitrarily, or capriciously. As a practical matter, the action of the administrator is rarely found to be arbitrary or capricious. As long as the administrator has followed the proper procedure, the fact that the court disagrees with the conclusion reached by the administrator does not make that conclusion arbitrary or capricious. In areas in which economic or technical matters are involved, it is generally sufficient that the administrator had a reasonable basis for the decision made and a court will not attempt to second guess the administrator as to complex criteria with which an administrative agency is intimately familiar. The judicial attitude is that for protection from laws and regulations which are unwise, improvident, or out of harmony with a particular school of thought, the people must resort to the ballot box and not to the court.

§ 6:7. **Publicity and Administrative Activity.**

(a) **Open Meetings.** The Government in the Sunshine Act of 1976 requires most of the meetings of the major administrative agencies to be open to the public.[6] The object of this statute is to enable the public to know what is being done and to prevent administrative misconduct by making the administrator aware that the public is watching.

(b) **Public Participation in Adoption of Regulations.** In some instances, nongovernmental bodies or persons play a part in furnishing information or opinions that may ultimately affect the adoption or nature of the rule adopted by the administrator. This pattern of cooperation with the administrator may be illustrated by the Federal Trade Commission practice begun in 1919, of calling together members of each significant industry so that the members can discuss which practices are fair trade practices

---

[6] PL 94-409, 90 Stat 1241, 5 USC § 552.

and which are not. The conclusions of these conferences are not automatically binding on the Federal Trade Commission, but they serve as a valuable means of bringing to the Commission detailed information respecting the conduct of the particular industry or business in question. Under the Federal Trade Commission practice, the rules of fair practice agreed to at a trade conference may be approved or disapproved by the Commission. When the rules are approved, a further distinction is made between those rules that are "affirmatively approved" by the Commission and those that are merely "accepted as expressions of the trade." In the case of the former, the Commission will enforce compliance by the members of the industry. In the case of the latter, the Commission will accept the practices as fair trade practices but will not enforce compliance by persons not willing to comply.

(c)   Public Knowledge of Regulations. When the administrator adopts a regulation, a practical problem arises as to how to inform the public of its existence. Some regulations will have already attracted such public attention that the news media will give the desired publicity. The great mass of regulations, however, do not attract this attention. In order to provide publicity for all regulations, the Federal Register Act provides that an administrative regulation is not binding until it is printed in the Federal Register. This is a government publication, published five days a week, in which are printed all administrative regulations and all presidential proclamations and executive orders and such other documents and classes of documents as the President or Congress may from time to time direct.

The Federal Register Act provides that the printing of an administrative regulation in the Federal Register is sufficient to give notice of the contents of the regulation to any person subject thereto or affected thereby. This means that no one can claim ignorance of the published regulation as an excuse.

CASES FOR CHAPTER 6

Withrow v Larkin

421 US 35 (1975)

Larkin was a doctor licensed under the laws of Wisconsin. The state medical licensing board conducted an investigation after which it concluded that a hearing should be held by it to determine whether Larkin's license to practice should be suspended. Larkin claimed that his constitutional rights were violated if the same body which had investigated the case against him would also act as judge to determine whether his license should be suspended. He brought a lawsuit against Withrow and the other members of the licensing board to enjoin them from holding the hearing. An injunction was granted and Withrow and the other members of the board appealed.

WHITE, J. . . . Concededly, a "fair trial in a fair tribunal is a basic requirement of due process." . . .

The contention that the combination of investigative and adjudicative functions necessarily creates an unconstitutional risk of bias in administrative adjudication has a . . . difficult burden of persuasion to carry. It must overcome a presumption of honesty and integrity in those serving as adjudicators; and it must convince that, under a realistic appraisal of psychological tendencies and human weakness, conferring investigative and adjudicative powers on the same individuals poses such a risk of actual bias or prejudgment that the practice must be forbidden if the guarantee of due process is to be adequately implemented.

Very similar claims have been squarely rejected in prior decisions of this Court. . . .

More recently we have sustained against due process objection a system in which a Social Security examiner has responsibility for developing the facts and making a decision as to disability claims, and observed that the challenge to this combination of functions "assumes too much and would bring down too many procedures designed, and working well, for a government structure of great and growing complexity." . . .*

That is not to say that there is nothing to the argument that those who have investigated should not then adjudicate. The issue is substantial, it is not new, and legislators and others concerned with the operations of administrative agencies have given much attention to whether and to what extent distinctive administrative functions should be performed by the same persons. No single answer has been reached. Indeed, the growth, variety, and complexity of the administrative processes have made any one solution highly unlikely. Within the Federal Government itself, Congress has addressed the issue in several different ways, providing for varying degrees of separation from complete separation of functions to virtually none at all. For the generality of agencies, Congress has been content with § 5 of the Administrative Procedure Act, 5 USC § 554(d) [5 USCS § 554(d)], which provides that no employee engaged in investigating or prosecuting may also participate or advise in the adjudicating function, but which also expressly exempts from this prohibition

---

* The decisions of the courts of appeals touching upon this question of bias arising from a combination of functions are also instructive. In Pangburn v Civil Aeronautics Board, 311 F2d 349 (CA1 1962), the Board had the responsibility of making an accident report and also reviewing the decision of a trial examiner that the pilot involved in the accident should have his airline transport pilot rating suspended. The pilot claimed that his right to procedural due process had been violated by the fact that the Board was not an impartial tribunal in deciding his appeal from the trial examiner's decision since it had previously issued its accident report finding pilot error to be the probable cause of the crash. The Court of Appeals found the Board's procedures to be constitutionally permissible: "[W]e cannot say that the mere fact that a tribunal has had contact with a particular factual complex in a prior hearing, or indeed has taken a public position on the facts, is enough to place that tribunal under a constitutional inhibition to pass upon the facts in a subsequent hearing. We believe that more is required. Particularly is this so in the instant case where the Board's prior contact with the case resulted from its following the Congressional mandate to investigate and report the probable cause of all civil air accidents." Id., at 358. . . .

"the agency or a member or members of the body comprising the agency."

. . . The case law, both federal and state, generally rejects the idea that the combination [of] judging [and] investigating functions is a denial of due process. . . ." Similarly, our cases . . . offer no support for the bald proposition applied in this case by the District Court that agency members who participate in an investigation are disqualified from adjudicating. . . .

When the Board instituted its investigative procedures, it stated only that it would investigate whether proscribed conduct had occurred. Later in noticing the adversary hearing, it asserted only that it would determine if violations had been committed which would warrant suspension of appellee's license. Without doubt, the Board then anticipated that the proceeding would eventuate in an adjudication of the issue; but there was no more evidence of bias or the risk of bias or prejudgment than inhered in the very fact that the Board had investigated and would now adjudicate. Of course, we should be alert to the possibilities of bias that may lurk in the way particular procedures actually work in practice. The processes utilized by the Board, however, do not in themselves contain an unacceptable risk of bias. The investigative proceeding had been closed to the public, but appellee and his counsel were permitted to be present throughout; counsel actually attended the hearings and knew the facts presented to the Board. No specific foundation has been presented for suspecting that the Board had been prejudiced by its investigation or would be disabled from hearing and deciding on the basis of the evidence to be presented at the contested hearing. The mere exposure to evidence presented in nonadversary investigative procedures is insufficient in itself to impugn the fairness of the board members at a later adversary hearing. Without a showing to the contrary, state administrators, "are assumed to be men of conscience and intellectual discipline, capable of judging a particular controversy fairly on the basis of its own circumstances." . . .

We are of the view, therefore, that the District Court was in error when it entered the restraining order against the Board's contested hearing and when it granted the preliminary injunction based on the untenable view that it would be unconstitutional for the Board to suspend appellee's license "at its own contested hearing on charges evolving from its own investigation. . . ."

[Judgment reversed]

United States v Howard

352 US 212 (1957)

The Congress made it a federal crime to transport fish in interstate commerce from a state if such transportation was "contrary to the law of the state." Howard transported fish from Florida. No Florida statute made it unlawful, but such transportation violated a rule of the Florida Game and Fresh Water Fish Commission. Howard was convicted for violating the federal statute. She claimed that she had not violated the statute because no Florida "law" prohibited such transportation.

REED, J. . . . The sole question presented is whether Rule 14.01 of the Commission's regulations, . . . is a "law" of the State of Florida as that term is used in the Federal Act.

This Court has repeatedly ruled, in other circumstances, that orders of state administrative agencies are the law of the State. . . . In *Grand Trunk R. Co.* v *Indiana R. Comm'n*, 221 U.S. 400, 403, the Court stated that: "the order [of the Indiana Railroad Commission] . . . is a law of the State within the meaning of the contract clause of the Constitution. . . ." And in *Lake Erie & W. R. Co.* v *Public Utilities Comm'n*, 249 U.S. 422, 424, it was said that an order of the state public utilities commission "being legislative in its nature . . . is a state law within the meaning of the Constitution of the United States and the laws of Congress regulating our jurisdiction." A similar statement may be found in *Arkadelphia Co.* v *St. Louis S. W. R. Co.*, 249 U.S. 134, 141. . . .

Appellee argues that the rules of the Florida Commission are so subject to change that they lack sufficient substance and permanence to be the "law" of Florida. We need not decide now whether a state agency could make a rule of such a temporary nature and so unaccompanied by the procedural niceties of rule making that the declaration should not be considered the law of the State for purposes of a statute such as the Black Bass Act. . . .

Accordingly we hold that the phrase "law of the State," as used in this Act, is sufficiently broad to encompass the type of regulation used in Florida. . . .

[Conviction sustained]

Shapiro v United States

335 US 1 (1948)

Shapiro was a wholesaler of fruit and produce. The Price Administrator acting under the federal Emergency Price Control Act subpoenaed him to produce his business records. Under protest of constitutional privilege he furnished the records. He was later prosecuted for making illegal tie-in sales contrary to the Emergency Price Control Regulations. The evidence on which the prosecution was based was obtained from information found in the records that he had been required to produce before the administrator. He claimed that he was entitled to immunity from prosecution for any matter arising out of those records. His claim of privilege was overruled and he was convicted. He appealed from the conviction.

VINSON, C.J. . . . The Circuit Court of Appeals ruled that the records which petitioner was compelled to produce were records required to be kept by a valid regulation under the Price Control Act; that thereby they became public documents, as to which no constitutional privilege against self-incrimination attaches.

. . . The language of the statute and its legislative history, viewed against the background of settled judicial construction of the immunity provision, indicate that Congress required records to be kept as a means of enforcing the statute and did not intend to frustrate the use of those records for enforcement action by granting an immunity bonus to individuals compelled to disclose their required records to the Administrator. . . .

"The physical custody of incriminating documents does not of itself protect the custodian against their compulsory production. The question still remains with respect to the nature of the documents and the capacity in which they are held. It may yet appear that they are of a character which subjects them to the scrutiny demanded and that the custodian has voluntarily assumed a duty which overrides his claim of privilege. . . . The principle applies not only to public documents in public offices, but also to *records required by law to be kept in order that there may be suitable information of transactions which are the appropriate subjects of governmental regulation and the enforcement of restrictions validly established. There the privilege, which exists as to private papers, cannot be maintained."* . . .

[Conviction affirmed]

Atlas Roofing Company, Inc. v Occupational Safety and Health Review Commission

430 US 442 (1977)

Under the Occupational Safety and Health Act of 1970 (OSHA), an employer may be ordered to eliminate or abate an unsafe working condition. On failing to do so, a civil penalty may be assessed against him. Atlas Roofing was ordered to abate a specified working condition and a penalty was assessed against it for failing to do so.

It claimed that the procedure which had been followed violated the guaranty of a jury trial declared by the 7th Amendment of the Federal Constitution: "In suits at common law, where the value in controversy shall exceed twenty dollars, the right of trial by jury shall be preserved, and no fact tried by a jury shall be otherwise re-examined in any court of the United States, than according to the rules of the common law." The lower court decided against Atlas and it appealed.

WHITE, J. . . . The issue in this case is whether, consistent with the Seventh Amendment, Congress may create a new cause of action in the Government for civil penalties enforceable in an administrative agency where there is no jury trial. After extensive investigation, Congress concluded, in 1970, that work-related deaths and injuries had become a "drastic" national problem.

. . . Congress enacted the Occupational Safety and Health Act of 1970, . . . The Act created a new statutory duty to avoid maintaining unsafe or unhealthy working conditions, and empowers the Secretary of Labor to promulgate health and safety standards. Two new remedies were provided—permitting the Federal Government, proceeding before an administrative agency, (1) to obtain abatement orders requiring employers to correct unsafe working conditions and (2) to impose civil penalties on any employer maintaining any unsafe working condition. Each remedy exists whether or not an employee is actually injured or killed as a result of the condition,

and existing state statutory and common law remedies for actual injury and death remain unaffected.

Under the Act, inspectors, representing the Secretary of Labor, are authorized to conduct reasonable safety and health inspections. . . . If a violation is discovered, the inspector, on behalf of the Secretary, issues a citation to the employer fixing a reasonable time for its abatement and, in his discretion, proposing a civil penalty. . . . Such proposed penalties may range from nothing for de minimis and nonserious violations, to not more than $1,000 for serious violations, to a maximum of $10,000 for willful or repeated violations, . . .

If the employer wishes to contest the penalty or the abatement order, he may do so by notifying the Secretary of Labor within 15 days, in which event the abatement order is automatically stayed. . . . An evidentiary hearing is then held before an administrative law judge of the Occupational Safety and Health Review Commission. The Commission consists of three members, appointed for six-year terms, each of whom is qualified to adjudicate contested citations and assess penalties "by reason of training, education or experience." . . . At this hearing the burden is on the Secretary to establish the elements of the alleged violation and the propriety of his proposed abatement order and proposed penalty; and the judge is empowered to affirm, modify, or vacate any or all of these items, giving due consideration in his penalty assessment to "the size of the business of the employer . . . , the gravity of the violation, the good faith of the employer, and the history of previous violations." . . . The judge's decision becomes the Commission's final and appealable order unless within 30 days a Commissioner directs that it be reviewed by the full Commission. . . .

If review is granted, the Commission's subsequent order directing abatement and the payment of any assessed penalty becomes final unless the employer timely petitions for judicial review in the appropriate court of appeals. . . . The Secretary similarly may seek review of Commission orders, . . . but, in either case, "[t]he findings of the Commission with respect to questions of fact, if supported by substantial evidence on the record considered as a whole, shall be conclusive." . . . If the employer fails to pay the assessed penalty, the Secretary may commence a collection action in a federal district court in which neither the fact of the violation nor the propriety of the penalty assessed may be retried.

. . .Thus, the penalty may be collected without the employer ever being entitled to a jury determination of the facts constituting the violation.

Congress has often created new statutory obligations, provided for civil penalties for their violation, and committed exclusively to an administrative agency the function of deciding whether a violation has in fact occurred. These statutory schemes have been sustained by this Court, . . .

. . . It is apparent from the history of jury trial in civil matters that factfinding, which is the essential function of the jury in civil cases . . . was never the exclusive province of the jury under either the English or American legal systems at the time of the adoption of the Seventh Amendment; and the question whether a fact would be found by a jury turned to a considerable degree on the nature of the forum in which a litigant found himself. Critical factfinding was performed without juries in suits in equity, and there were no juries in admiralty . . . neither was there in the military justice system. The jury was the factfinding mode in most suits in the common law courts, but it was not exclusively so: condemnation was a suit at common law but constitutionally could be tried without a jury. . . .

The Seventh Amendment was declaratory of the existing law, for it required only that jury trial in suits at common law was to be "preserved." It thus did not purport to require a jury trial where none was required before. . . .

The point is that the Seventh Amendment was never intended to establish the jury as the exclusive mechanism for factfinding in civil cases. It took the existing legal order as it found it, and there is little or no basis for concluding that the Amendment should now be interpreted to provide an impenetrable barrier to administrative factfinding under otherwise valid federal regulatory statutes. We cannot conclude that the Amendment rendered Congress powerless—when it concluded that remedies available in courts of law were inadequate to cope with a problem within Congress' power to regulate—to create new public rights and remedies by statute and commit their enforcement, if it chose, to a tribunal other than a court of law—such as an administrative agency—in which facts are not found by juries. . . .

Congress found the common law and other existing remedies for work injuries resulting from unsafe working conditions to be inadequate to protect the Nation's working men and women. It created

a new cause of action, and remedies therefore, unknown to the common law, and placed their enforcement in a tribunal supplying speedy and expert resolutions of the issues involved. The Seventh Amendment is no bar to the creation of new rights or to their enforcement outside the regular courts of law.

[Judgment affirmed]

Moog Industries v Federal Trade Commission

355 US 411 (1958)

Moog Industries was ordered to stop certain pricing practices by the Federal Trade Commission. It raised the objection that its competitors were also guilty of the same practices and that Moog would be ruined if it were required to stop the practices without also requiring its competitors to stop such practices. The Commission rejected this argument. Moog appealed.

Opinion by the Court . . . In view of the scope of administrative discretion that Congress has given the Federal Trade Commission, it is ordinarily not for courts to modify ancillary features of a valid Commission order. This is but recognition of the fact that in the shaping of its remedies within the framework of regulatory legislation, an agency is called upon to exercise its specialized, experienced judgment. Thus, the decision as to whether or not an order against one firm to cease and desist from engaging in illegal price discrimination should go into effect before others are similarly prohibited depends on a variety of factors peculiarly within the expert understanding of the Commission. Only the Commission, for example, is competent to make an initial determination as to whether and to what extent there is a relevant "industry" within which the particular respondent competes and whether or not the nature of that competition is such as to indicate identical treatment of the entire industry by an enforcement agency. Moreover, although an allegedly illegal practice may appear to be operative throughout an industry, whether such appearances reflect fact and whether all firms in the industry should be dealt with in a single proceeding or should receive individualized treatment are questions that call for discretionary determination by the administrative agency. It is clearly within the special competence of the Commission to appraise the adverse effect on competition that might result from postponing a particular order prohibiting continued violations of the law. Furthermore, the Commission alone is empowered to develop that enforcement policy best calculated to achieve the ends contemplated by Congress and to allocate its available funds and personnel in such a way as to execute its policy efficiently and economically.

The question, then, of whether orders such as those before us should be held in abeyance until the respondents' competitors are proceeded against is for the Commission to decide. . . . If the Commission has decided the question, its discretionary determination should not be overturned in the absence of a patent abuse of discretion. . . .

[Judgment against Moog]

QUESTIONS AND CASE PROBLEMS

1. Woodham held a license as insurance agent. He was notified to appear in person or by counsel at a hearing to be held by Williams, the State Insurance Commissioner, for the purpose of determining whether Williams should revoke Woodham's license because of improper practices as agent. Woodham appeared at the hearing and testified in his own behalf. He did not make any objection that what he was asked would incriminate him. Williams revoked Woodham's license. Woodham appealed and claimed, among other grounds, that the proceeding before Williams was invalid because Woodham had not been warned that what he would say could be used against him. Were the proceedings valid? [Woodham v Williams, (Fla App) 207 So2d 320]

2. The New York City charter authorizes the New York City Board of Health to adopt a health code and declares that it "shall have the force and effect of law." The Board adopted a Code in 1964 that provided for the fluoridation of the public water supply. A suit was brought to enjoin the carrying out of this program on the ground that it was unconstitutional and that money could not be spent to carry out such a program in the absence of a statute authorizing such expenditure. It was also claimed that the fluoridation program was unconstitutional because there were other means of reducing tooth decay; fluoridation was discriminatory in that it benefited only children; it unlawfully imposed medication on the children without their consent; and fluoridation "is or may be" dangerous to health. Was the Code provision valid? [Paduano v City of New York, 257 NYS2d 531]

3. A federal statute provides that when a contract between the government and a contractor provides for the determination of a dispute by a federal department head or agency, the decision "shall be final and conclusive unless the same is fraudulent or capricious or arbitrary or so grossly erroneous as necessarily to imply bad faith, or is not supported by substantial evidence." Bianchi contracted with the government to build a water tunnel. The contract contained a standard provision for additional compensation in the event of "changed conditions." The contractor claimed that conditions discovered after the work was begun constituted "changed conditions" and claimed additional compensation. In accord with a provision of the contract, he submitted this claim first to the contracting officer and then to the Board of Claims and Appeals of the Corps of Engineers. Both rejected his claim. Six years thereafter Bianchi sued in the Court of Claims claiming that he was entitled to additional compensation and that he was not bound by the decision of the contracting officer and of the Board of Claims because their decisions were "capricious or arbitrary or so grossly erroneous as necessarily to imply bad faith, or were not supported by substantial evidence." In this proceeding, a substantial amount

of new evidence was heard and a decision made in favor of the contractor. The United States appealed. Decide. [United States v Bianchi, 373 US 709]

4. Ordinarily the testimony of a witness at a trial in one case is not admissible as evidence in the trial of a different case involving different parties. Welch, a workman, was injured and filed a workmen's compensation claim. He testified before the compensation board with respect to his injuries. He thereafter died and his widow began a new proceeding before the board to recover damages for his death under the workmen's compensation statute. At the trial of this second case, brought by the widow, the testimony of the deceased husband in the first case was offered as evidence. Should it have been admitted? [Welch v Essex County, 6 NJS 422, 68 A2d 787]

5. The state insurance commissioner was authorized to regulate advertising by insurance companies. A bill was introduced in the legislature affecting insurance companies. One of the companies circulated printed matter in opposition to the proposed law. The state insurance commissioner began to investigate this printed matter on the ground that it was advertising. The insurance company claimed that he did not have jurisdiction to do so. Decide. [See Ex parte Allstate Ins. Co., 248 SC 550, 151 SE2d 849]

6. Rikard was prosecuted for violating the federal Wholesale Meat Act by selling unmarked horsemeat and representing it to be beef. He claimed that the federal statute under which he was prosecuted was unconstitutional because it gave the Secretary of Agriculture "too much prosecutorial discretion" in that the Act expressly gave the Secretary the discretion to determine whether to initiate a criminal prosecution against the violator of the Act or to merely give a violator a written warning when the Secretary of Agriculture believed "that the public interest will be adequately served" by such a notice. Was Rikard correct? [United States v Rikard (CA5 Ga) 552 F2d 153]

7. The practice developed for owners of trucks who drove their loaded trucks from one point to another to hire themselves and their trucks out to a common carrier so that the return trip would not be made with empty trucks. This made it possible for motor freight carriers to meet the needs of their customers with a smaller number of trucks owned by the carriers which in turn reduced the rates charged by carriers to shippers. The Interstate Commerce Commission decided that these one-trip rentals made it possible for the carriers to operate in part without satisfying the requirements otherwise applicable to them. In order to stop this, the Commission adopted a set of rules which provided that trucks could not be rented by a carrier for less than thirty days. This made impossible the one-trip leasing and an action was brought to declare the Commission regulation invalid because (1) by abolishing one-trip leasing it caused financial loss to the truck owners, the carriers, and the public; and (2) the Transportation Act under which the Commission was adopting regulations did not make any provision authorizing the regulation or prohibiting of trip leasing. Was the regulation valid? [American Trucking Associations v United States, 344 US 298]

7 Environmental Law and Community Planning

The term *environmental law* refers to the body of law aimed at preventing damage to the environment. Within recent years society has come to recognize the social importance of the conservation of natural resources and the protection of the environment from pollution.

A. PREVENTION OF POLLUTION

As American society changed from rural and agricultural to urban and industrialized, new laws were needed to prevent the pollution of the environment. Today society accepts the fact that there must be some limitation upon freedom of action if an environment fit for life is to be maintained.

§ 7:1. Statutory Environmental Protection. Beginning with the National Environmental Policy Act of 1969 (NEPA), Congress has adopted a series of laws designed to prevent the pollution of the air and water and to reduce noise.[1] Congress has adopted other statutes designed to reduce the problem of waste disposal by encouraging recycling or reuse of various products.[2]

State legislatures have also been active in this area, and many states have laws which are similar to the federal laws. A state law, however, is invalid if it conflicts with or is inconsistent with a federal statute or if the state law places an unreasonable burden on interstate commerce. (See p. 102, Burbank v Lockheed Air Terminal, Inc.)

§ 7:2. Environmental Impact Statements. Environmental protection legislation typically requires that any activity which might have a significant effect upon the environment be supported by an environmental impact statement. Whenever any bill is proposed in Congress and whenever any federal action significantly affecting the quality of the human environment is considered, a statement must be prepared as to the environmental impact of the action. (See p. 103, Natural Resources Defense Council, Inc. v Morton)

---

[1] For example, see the Clean Air Act, 42 USC § 1857 et seq., the National Motor Vehicles Emissions Standards Act, 42 USC § 1857f-1 et seq., the Noise Control Acts of 1970 and 1972, 42 USC § 4901, the Water Pollution Control Act Amendments of 1972, 33 USC § 1251 et seq. The pollution of navigable waters had already been prohibited by the River and Harbor Appropriations Act of 1899.

[2] For example, see the Solid Waste Disposal Act, 42 USC § 3251 et seq., the Resource Recovery and Material Policy Act of 1970, PL 91-512, 84 Stat 1227, 42 USC § 3251 et seq., the Resource Conservation and Recovery Act of 1976, PL 94-580, 90 Stat 2795, 42 USC § 6901 et seq.

A number of states impose the same requirement on government officials and some require an environmental impact statement for any large private building construction.

§ 7:3. Regulation by Administrative Agencies. For the most part, the law against pollution is a matter of the adoption and enforcement of regulations by administrative agencies, such as the federal EPA (Environmental Protection Agency).[3] Administrative agency control is likely to increase in the future because of the technical nature of the problems involved, and because of the interrelationship of pollution problems and nonpollution problems. It is also likely that there will be increasing cooperation between government and industry to achieve desired goals.

§ 7:4. Litigation. A private person may bring a lawsuit to recover damages or obtain an injunction against a polluter if damages peculiar to such plaintiff can be shown. This requirement of harm to the plaintiff has to some extent been relaxed so that a person may sometimes sue without proving any harm different than that sustained by any other member of the general public. For example, federal statutes authorize a private suit by "any person" in a federal district court to stop a violation of the air, water, and noise pollution standards. Courts have been increasingly willing to recognize the right of organizations to sue on behalf of their members.

A private person does not always have the right to sue for violation of an environmental protection control. In some instances the right to sue is restricted to a particular government agency. Likewise, an action brought for a violation of the Marine Protection, Research, and Sanctuaries Act of 1972 may only be brought by the Attorney General of the United States.[4]

It is reasonable to expect that courts will not take an active part in the solution of pollution problems. It is likely that on these technical problems they will defer to the decisions made or to be made by the appropriate administrative agency.[5]

Courts will be particularly likely to avoid pollution litigation when the matter before them is merely a small segment of the total pollution problem involved so that the exercise of jurisdiction by a court could hamper or disrupt the work of administrative agencies and study groups.[6]

§ 7:5. Criminal Liability. In many states, criminal proceedings may be instituted to punish violations of the environmental protection regulations. Under such statutes, it is no defense that the defendant did not intend to violate the law or was not negligent. (See p. 104, Arizona v Arizona Mines Supply Co.)

The fact that the defendant operated a business in the customary way and did not produce any greater amount of pollution than other similar enterprises is not a defense to a prosecution for polluting the environment.

---

[3] The EPA was established under the Reorganization Plan No. 3 of 1970.

[4] PL 92-532, 86 Stat 1052, § 303(d), 16 USC § 1433(d).

[5] Boomer v Atlantic Cement Co. 26 NY2d 219, 309 NYS2d 312, 257 NE2d 870.

[6] Ohio v Wyandotte Chemicals Corp. 401 US 493 (Ohio sought to enjoin Canadian, Michigan, and Delaware corporations from dumping mercury into tributaries of Lake Erie, which allegedly polluted that lake which was used by parts of Ohio as a water supply. The Supreme Court refused to decide the case.).

B. COMMUNITY PLANNING

In order to provide for the orderly growth of our communities, some planning and control is necessary. Community planning may be classified as private (restrictive covenants) and public (zoning).

§ 7:6. Restrictive Covenants In Private Contracts. In the case of private planning, a real estate developer will take an undeveloped tract or area of land, map out on paper an "ideal" community, and then construct the buildings shown on the plan. These are then sold to private purchasers. The deeds by which the buyers take title will contain *restrictive covenants* that obligate the buyers to observe certain limitations in the use of their property, the nature of buildings that will be maintained or constructed on the land, and so on.

§ 7:7. Public Zoning. Public community planning is generally synonymous with zoning. By *zoning,* a governmental unit, such as a city, adopts an ordinance imposing restrictions upon the use of the land. The object of zoning is to insure an orderly physical development of the regulated area. In effect, zoning is the same as the restrictive covenants with the difference being the source of their authority.

Zoning, however, is based not upon a contract but rather upon a legislative enactment. In most cases, this is an ordinance of a local political subdivision, such as a municipality or a county, and not a statute adopted by a state legislature or by the United States Congress.[7]

A local zoning ordinance may be supplemented or reinforced by a general state statute, such as a statute that makes it a crime to violate a local zoning ordinance. As in the case of all laws, questions arise as to the meaning of a zoning regulation. (See p. 105, Kyritsis v Fenny)

Zoning is to be distinguished from building regulations, although the distinction between the two is not always apparent. For example, a requirement that there be at least four feet of clear space between a building wall and a boundary line is regarded as a zoning requirement, whereas a law requiring that the walls of the building be built of fireproof material is regarded as a building regulation.

(a)   **Validity of Zoning.** In terms of social forces, zoning represents the subordination of the landowner's right to use property to the interest of the community at large. Zoning is held constitutional as an exercise of the police power so long as the zoning regulation bears a reasonable relation to health, morals, safety, or general welfare.

A zoning ordinance may constitutionally exclude gas stations from downtown shopping areas or may seek to limit population density by limiting the number of dwelling units which may be included in a high-rise apartment. A zoning ordinance may also limit community growth in order to preserve the "small town" character of the community.[8]

The fact that the use authorized by zoning is not the most profitable to the owner does not affect the validity of the zoning regulation. That is, the fact that a landowner could make more money if the land were zoned to permit a different use does not render unconstitutional the zoning ordinance which restricts the use.

[7] In some states, the legislative enactment of a local political subdivision is called a "resolution."
[8] Village of Belle Terre v Boraas, 416 US 1.

(b) **Nonconforming Use.** When the use to which the land is already being put when the zoning ordinance goes into effect is in conflict with the zoning ordinance, such use is described as a *nonconforming use*. For example, when a zoning ordinance was adopted which required a setback of 25 feet from the boundary line, an already existing building that was only set back 10 feet was a nonconforming use.

The nonconforming use represents one of the major problems involved in zoning. A nonconforming use has a constitutionally protected right to continue. That is, a business or activity which is in itself lawful cannot be wiped out by a zoning ordinance even though it is in conflict with the zoning pattern. Thus, a grocery store already in existence cannot be ordered away when the area is zoned as residential.

If the nonconforming use is discontinued, it cannot be resumed. The right to make a nonconforming use may thus be lost by abandonment; as when the owner of a garage stops using it for a garage and uses it for storing goods, a return to the use of the property as a garage will be barred by abandonment.

(c) **Variance.** The administrative agency charged with the enforcement of a zoning ordinance may generally grant a *variance*. This permits the owner of the land to use it in a specified manner inconsistent with the zoning ordinance.

When a departure from the zoning plan is authorized for a general area, it is called *rezoning*.

The agency will ordinarily be reluctant to permit a variance when neighboring property owners object because, to the extent that variation is permitted, the basic plan of the zoning ordinance is defeated. Likewise, the allowance of an individual variation may result in such inequality as to be condemned by the courts as *spot zoning*. In addition, there is the consideration of practical expediency that if variances are readily granted, every property owner will request a variance and thus flood the agency with such requests.

§ 7:8. Federal Legislation. Federal legislation in the area of community planning is largely directed toward research and financial aid to cities and housing projects.

The executive branch of the national government has been expanded by the creation of a Department of Housing and Urban Development (HUD).

§ 7:9. Eminent Domain. *Eminent domain* is the power of government to take private property for a public purpose. The power of eminent domain plays an important role in community planning because it is the means by which the land required for housing, redevelopment, and other projects may be acquired. Eminent domain has not become important in the area of environmental protection, although it is always present as a possible alternative on the theory that a government-owned plant would be more concerned with protection of the environment.

When property is taken by government by eminent domain, it must be taken for a public purpose. The taking of property for a private purpose is void as a deprivation of property without due process of law.

Whether the purpose of the taking is public is a question for the courts to determine. The courts are not bound by the declaration in a statute that a particular purpose shall be deemed a public purpose when in fact it is a private purpose. As a practical matter, however, a declaration by the lawmaker, particularly by Congress, that a taking is a public purpose will generally be given great respect by the courts. With the widening of the concept of "public purpose," the possibility of a conflict between the lawmaker and the courts as to whether a particular taking is for a public purpose becomes increasingly unlikely.

CASES FOR CHAPTER 7

American Can Co. v Oregon Liquor Control Commission

15 Ore App 618, 517 P2d 691 (1973)

The state of Oregon adopted a law, commonly called the "bottle bill," which prohibited the use of nonreturnable containers for beverages and required returnable glass bottles. The American Can Company brought an action against the Oregon Liquor Control Board and sought to have the statute declared unconstitutional. From a decision sustaining the law, American Can appealed.

TANZER, J. . . . The primary legislative purpose of the bottle bill is to cause bottlers of carbonated soft drinks and brewers to package their products for distribution in Oregon in returnable, multiple-use deposit bottles toward the goals of reducing litter and solid waste in Oregon and reducing the injuries to people and animals due to discarded "pull tops."

. . . The evidence . . . demonstrated that the consumption of malt beverages and soft drinks had increased greatly in the United States in recent years, and that a large part of this increase could be attributed to the use of convenient "one-way" packages, including both cans and nonreturnable bottles. Plaintiffs assert that nonreturnable containers are essential to the existence of national and regional beer markets, and that nonreturnable containers are also essential to the continued existence of soft drink enterprises. The nonreturnable containers were shown to have provided economies in the packaging and distribution of soft drinks and beer by eliminating the cost of shipping the containers both ways, thus causing an increase in feasible shipping distances and enlarging the market each manufacturer could cover. Among the effects of the bottle bill, plaintiffs' witnesses predicted, would be a substantial reduction in Oregon sales of soft drinks packaged outside Oregon, and impairment of the ability of distant brewers to compete in the Oregon market. The bottle bill would necessitate substantial changes in the structure of the industries involved in the manufacturing and merchandising of beer and soft drinks. . . .

The Oregon legislature was persuaded that the economic benefit to the beverage industry brought with it deleterious consequences to the environment and additional cost to the public. The aggravation of the problems of litter in public places and solid waste disposal and the attendant economic and esthetic burden to the public outweighed the narrower economic benefit to the industry. Thus the legislature enacted the bottle bill. . . .

As with every change of circumstance in the market place, there are gainers and there are losers. Just as there were gainers and losers, with plaintiffs apparently among the gainers, when the industry adapted to the development of nonreturnable containers, there will be new gainers and losers as they adapt to the ban. The economic losses complained of by plaintiffs in this case are essentially the consequences of readjustment of the beverage manufacturing and distribution systems to the older technology in order to compete in the Oregon market. . . .

Economic loss restricted to certain elements of the beverage industry must be viewed in relation to the broader loss to the general public of the state of Oregon which the legislature sought, by enactment of the bottle bill, to avoid. The availability of land and revenues for solid waste disposal, the cost of litter collection on our highways and in our public parks, the depletion of mineral and energy resources, the injuries to humans and animals caused by discarded pull tops, and the esthetic blight on our landscape, are all economic, safety and esthetic burdens of great consequence which must be borne by every member of the public. The legislature attached higher significance to the cost to the public than they did to the cost to the beverage industry and we have no cause to disturb that legislative determination. . . .

We find that the bottle bill in all of its aspects is reasonably calculated to achieve legitimate state objectives under the police power. . . . The ban on pull tops is reasonably calculated to diminish the injuries to people who step on them and to animals who eat them at pasture as well as to reduce the litter which they create. The placing of a monetary value on beverage containers and its attendant encouragement for people to return them instead of discarding them by the roadside or in other public places or throwing them into the garbage is reasonably calculated to diminish the amount of solid waste and the amount of litter with which the state is required to deal. . . .

The fact that other containers may also create litter and solid waste does not invalidate the legislature's intent to deal with this species of solid waste and litter. . . . "It is no requirement of equal protection that all evils of the same genus be eradicated or none at all.". . . "Evils in the same field may be of different dimensions and proportions, requiring different remedies. Or so the legislature may think. Or the reform may take one step at a time, addressing itself to the phase of the problem which seems most acute to the legislative mind. The legislature may select one phase of one field and apply a remedy there, neglecting the others.". . .

. . . We hold the bottle bill to be a valid exercise of Oregon's police power. . . .

[Judgment affirmed]

Burbank v Lockheed Air Terminal, Inc.

411 US 624 (1973)

The City of Burbank, California, adopted an ordinance prohibiting the nighttime takeoffs of jet aircraft between 10 p.m. and 7 a.m. Lockheed Air Terminal owned and operated the Hollywood-Burbank Airport. It sued Burbank to prevent the enforcement of the ordinance.

DOUGLAS, J. . . . The Federal Aviation Act of 1958, . . . as amended by the Noise Control Act . . . and the regulations under it, . . . provides in part, "The United States of America is declared to possess and exercise complete and exclusive national sovereignty in the airspace of the United States. . . ." By § 1348 the Administrator of the Federal Aeronautics Act (FAA) has been given broad authority to regulate the use of the navigable airspace, "in order

to insure the safety of aircraft and the efficient utilization of such airspace . . ." and "for the protection of persons and property on the ground. . . ."

. . . The District Court found: "The imposition of curfew ordinances on a nationwide basis would result in a bunching of flights in those hours immediately preceding the curfew. This bunching of flights during these hours would have the twofold effect of increasing an already serious congestion problem and actually increasing, rather than relieving, the noise problem by increasing flights in the period of greatest annoyance to surrounding communities. Such a result is totally inconsistent with the objectives of the federal statutory and regulatory scheme." It also found "the imposition of curfew ordinances on a nationwide basis would cause a serious loss of efficiency in the use of the navigable airspace.". . .

The Noise Control Act of 1972, . . . amending § 611 of the Federal Aviation Act, also involves the Environmental Protection Agency (EPA) in the comprehensive scheme of federal control of the aircraft noise problem. Under the amended § 611(b)(1) the FAA, after consulting with EPA, shall provide "for the control and abatement of aircraft noise and sonic boom, including the application of such standards and regulations in the issuance, amendment, modification, suspension or revocation of any certificate authorized by this title." Section 611(b)(2) as amended provides that future certificates for aircraft operations shall not issue unless the new aircraft noise requirements are met. . . .

. . . The pervasive nature of the scheme of federal regulation of aircraft noise . . . leads us to conclude that there is preemption. . . . "Federal control is intensive and exclusive. Planes do not wander about in the sky like vagrant clouds. They move only by federal permission, subject to federal inspection, in the hands of federally certified personnel and under an intricate system of federal command. The moment a ship taxis onto a runway it is caught up in an elaborate and detailed system of controls.". . .

. . . Control of noise is of course deep seated in the police power of the States. Yet the pervasive control vested in EPA and in FAA under the 1972 Act seems to us to leave no room for local curfews or other local controls. . . . The ultimate remedy for aircraft noise which plagues many communities and tens of thousands of people is not known. The procedures under the 1972 Act are under way. In addition, the Administrator has imposed a variety of regulations relating to takeoff and landing procedures and runway preferences. The Federal Aviation Act requires a delicate balance between safety and efficiency . . . and the protection of persons on the ground. . . . Any regulations adopted by the Administrator to control noise pollution must be consistent with the "highest degree of safety.". . . The interdependence of these factors requires a uniform and exclusive system of federal regulation if the congressional objectives underlying the Federal Aviation Act are to be fulfilled.

If we were to uphold the Burbank ordinance and a significant number of municipalities followed suit, it is obvious that fractionalized control of the timing of take-offs and landings would severely limit the flexibility of the FAA in controlling air traffic flow. The difficulties of scheduling flights to avoid congestion and the concomitant decrease in safety would be compounded. In 1960 the FAA rejected a proposed restriction on jet operations at the Los Angeles airport between 10 p.m. and 7 a.m. because such restrictions could "create critically serious problems to all air transportation patterns.". . . The complete FAA statement said: "The proposed restriction on the use of the airport by jet aircraft between the hours of 10 p.m. and 7 a.m. under certain surface wind conditions has also been reevaluated and this provision has been omitted from the rule. The practice of prohibiting the use of various airports during certain specific hours could create critically serious problems to all air transportation patterns. The network of airports throughout the United States and the constant availability of these airports are essential to the maintenance of a sound air transportation system. The continuing growth of public acceptance of aviation as a major force in passenger transportation and the increasingly significant role of commercial aviation in the nation's economy are accomplishments which cannot be inhibited if the best interest of the public is to be served. It was concluded therefore that the extent of relief from the noise problem which this provision must have achieved would not have compensated the degree of restriction it would have imposed on domestic and foreign Air Commerce."

This decision, announced in 1960, remains peculiarly within the competence of the FAA, supplemented now by the input of the EPA. We are not at liberty to diffuse the powers given by Congress to FAA and EPA by letting the States or municipalities in on the planning. If that change is to be made,

Congress alone must do it.

[Enforcement of ordinance enjoined]

Natural Resources Defense Council, Inc. v Morton

(CA Dist Col) 458 F2d 827 (1972)

Morton, the U.S. Secretary of the Interior, announced that the United States proposed to sell certain offshore oil lands. The Director of the Bureau of Land Management prepared an environmental impact statement. An injunction against the proposed governmental action was obtained by the Natural Resources Defense Council which claimed that the environmental impact statement was not adequate. The Government moved to dismiss the injunction.

LEVENTHAL, C.J. . . . Oil pollution is the problem most extensively discussed in the Statement and its exposition of unavoidable adverse environmental effects. . . .

. . . The [District] Court found that the Statement failed to provide the "detailed statement" required by NEPA [National Environmental Policy Act] of environmental impact and alternatives. The Court stated:

> . . . The defendants only superficially discussed the alternatives listed in their Final Impact Statement, and they failed to discuss in detail the environmental impacts of the alternatives they listed in the statement. The Court does not wish to give the impression that it believes the alternatives are better than the proposed lease sale, but it believes that these alternatives must be explored and discussed thoroughly in order to comport with the intent and requirements of . . . NEPA.

. . .

Congress contemplated that the Impact Statement would constitute the environmental source material for the information of the Congress as well as the Executive, in connection with the making of relevant decisions, and would be available to enhance enlightenment of—and by—the public. The impact statement provides a basis for (a) evaluation of the benefits of the proposed project in light of its environmental risks, and (b) comparison of the net balance for the proposed project with the environmental risks presented by alternative courses of action. . . .

. . . A sound construction of NEPA . . . requires a presentation of the environmental risks incident to reasonable alternative courses of action. The agency may limit its discussion of environmental impact to a brief statement, when that is the case, that the alternative course involves no effect on the environment, or that their effect, briefly described, is simply not significant. . . .

We think the Secretary's Statement erred in stating that the alternative of elimination of oil import quotas was entirely outside its cognizance. Assuming, as the Statement puts it, that this alternative "involves complex factors and concepts, including national security, which are beyond the scope of this statement," it does not follow that the Statement should not present the environmental effects of that alternative. While the consideration of pertinent alternatives requires a weighing of numerous matters, such as economics, foreign relations, national security, the fact remains that, as to the ingredient of possible adverse environmental impact, it is the essence and thrust of NEPA that the pertinent Statement serve to gather in one place a discussion of the relative environmental impact of alternatives.

The Government also contends that the only "alternatives" required for discussion under NEPA are those which can be adopted and put into effect by the official or agency issuing the statement. The Government seeks to distinguish the kind of impact statement required for a major Federal action from that required with a legislative proposal. . . .

When the proposed action is an integral part of a coordinated plan to deal with a broad problem, the range of alternatives that must be evaluated is broadened. While the Department of the Interior does not have the authority to eliminate or reduce oil import quotas, such action is within the purview of both Congress and the President, to whom the impact statement goes. The impact statement is not only for the exposition of the thinking of the agency, but also for the guidance of these ultimate decisionmakers, and must provide them with the environmental effects of both the proposal and the alternatives, for their consideration along with the various other elements of the public interest. . . .

. . . The discussion of environmental effects of alternatives need not be exhaustive. What is required is information sufficient to permit a reasoned choice of alternatives so far as environmental aspects are concerned. As to alternatives not within the scope of authority of the responsible official, reference may

of course be made to studies of other agencies—including other impact statements. Nor is it appropriate, as Government counsel argues, to disregard alternatives merely because they do not offer a complete solution to the problem. If an alternative would result in supplying only part of the energy that the lease sale would yield, then its use might possibly reduce the scope of the lease sale program and thus alleviate a significant portion of the environmental harm attendant on offshore drilling. . . .

The mere fact that an alternative requires legislative implementation does not automatically establish it as beyond the domain of what is required for discussion, particularly since NEPA was intended to provide a basis for consideration and choice by the decisionmakers in the legislative as well as the executive branch. . . .

. . . In this as in other areas, the functions of courts and agencies, rightly understood, are not in opposition but in collaboration, toward achievement of the end prescribed by Congress. So long as the officials and agencies have taken the "hard look" at environmental consequences mandated by Congress, the court does not seek to impose unreasonable extremes or to interject itself within the area of discretion of the executive as to the choice of the action to be taken.

Informed by our judgment that discussion of alternatives may be required even though the action required lies outside the Interior Department, the Secretary will, we have no doubt, be able without undue delay to provide the kind of reasonable discussion of alternatives and their environmental consequences that Congress contemplated.

[Motion denied]

Arizona v Arizona Mines Supply Co.

107 Ariz 199, 484 P2d 619 (1971)

The Arizona Mines Supply Co. was prosecuted for violating the county air pollution regulations. It raised the defense that it did not intentionally violate the law and offered evidence that it had installed special equipment in order to meet the standards imposed by the law. The prosecution objected to the admission of this evidence on the ground that the absence of any intent to violate the law was not a defense and that accordingly evidence of an attempt to comply with the law was irrelevant. The trial court admitted the evidence and the prosecution

filed a petition with the state Supreme Court to review the ruling of the trial court.

UDALL, J. . . . [The defendant contends] that the State must prove knowledge or intent as a prerequisite to conviction. [The] Maricopa County Air Pollution Control Regulation . . . provides that: "No person shall cause, suffer, allow or permit the discharge into the atmosphere from any single source of emission whatsoever any air contaminants for a period or periods aggregating more than three minutes in any one hour which is:

a. As dark as or darker in shade than that designated as No. 2 on the Ringelmann Chart as published by the U.S. Bureau of Mines, or

b. Of an opacity equal to or greater than an air contaminant designated as No. 2 on the Ringelmann Chart."

Nowhere does this regulation (or the Air Pollution Act, for that matter) provide, either expressly or impliedly, that before the state may convict someone of "air pollution" it must first prove that the air contaminant was discharged knowingly or intentionally. Defendant argues that some degree of knowledge or intent is prerequisite to conviction. The State, on the other hand, contends that it need not prove intent or knowledge since this offense is more in the nature of "malum prohibitum."

After having carefully considered the apparent intent of legislature, . . . and the consequences of unabated air pollution to public health; we find that the state need not prove intent or knowledge on the part of the accused as a prerequisite to conviction. That the legislature may make the doing of an act or the neglect to do something a crime without requiring criminal intent is well-settled. . . .

" 'Whether a criminal intent or guilty knowledge is a necessary element of a statutory offense is a matter of construction to be determined from the language of the statute, *in view of its manifest purpose and design.* There are many instances in recent times where the legislature in the exercise of the police power has prohibited, under penalty, the performance of a specific act. *The doing of the inhibited act constitutes the crime,* and the moral turpitude or *purity of the motive* by which it was prompted *and knowledge or ignorance* of its criminal character *are immaterial circumstances* on the question of guilt. The only fact to be determined in these cases is whether the defendant did the act.' " [Emphasis added.] 17 Ariz 506 at 508, 154 P 1048 at 1049.

With regard to the introduction by a defendant of evidence of expenditures made in installing pollution control equipment and precautions taken to avoid pollution, such will not constitute a defense to prosecution and conviction, and are, therefore, inadmissible at trial. Evidence of "extenuating circumstances" may, however, be presented to the court *after verdict* in mitigation of the penalty to be imposed. ". . . *Although extenuating circumstances would be no legal bar to conviction, they would certainly be important factors in determining a penalty, and might even warrant granting of probation."* [Emphasis added.] . . .

The basic premise of the concept of "strict liability" or "malum prohibitum" offenses is that the mere doing of the act constitutes the offense and the fact that the act was done without intent or in "happy ignorance" will not exonerate the party, nor does this make the prohibited act any less harmful to society. . . .

In accordance with the foregoing, we hold that the state need not prove criminal intent as a prerequisite to conviction. It is therefore ordered that the petitioner's motion . . . be granted without prejudice to defendant's right to introduce evidence *after verdict* of extenuating circumstances, in mitigation of the penalty to be imposed. [Defendant's evidence held improperly admitted on issue of guilt]

Kyritsis v Fenny

320 NYS2d 702 (1971)

The zoning ordinance of the town of Fishkill provided that mobile homes could only be placed in licensed parks. Kyritsis was a co-owner of a lot in the town. He and the other owner wanted to erect a prefabricated or modular home on their lot. They petitioned to the local zoning board for a license to do so. The license was refused on the ground that the proposed home was a mobile home and was therefore restricted to a mobile home park. Kyritsis and the other owner of the lot filed a petition to compel the board, headed by Fenny, to issue the requested license.

GRADY, J. . . . This . . . proceeding presents a question . . . of whether a modular home falls within the definition of "mobile home" as set forth in a Zoning Ordinance requiring mobile homes to be located in mobile home parks. Section 720 of the Zoning Ordinance of the Town of Fishkill defines "mobile home" as follows: "Any vehicle or similar portable structure with or without a foundation or wheels, jacks skirtings, wood or masonry block supports, designed or constructed to be towed, driven or otherwise transported to its resting site and which is further designed to permit occupancy for dwelling or sleeping purposes. The term 'mobile home' shall also include the term 'house trailer'.". . .

The term "dwelling" under § 720 of the Town of Fishkill Zoning Ordinance is defined as follows: "Dwelling: A detached building, designed or used exclusively as living quarters for one or more families: the term shall not be deemed to include automobile court, motel, boarding or rooming house, mobile home trailer, tourist home or tent."

Petitioners contend that a modular home is clearly a "dwelling" and not a "mobile home" within the meaning of the Town Zoning Ordinance. It appears that the modular home under consideration consists of a minimum of two large sections, each of which must be transported to the building site separately. The modular home cannot be moved to a building site in one single unit. The heating system is installed and the siding applied after the modular home has been erected. The Town Zoning Ordinance in question was adopted on December 2, 1962, and revised on December 8, 1965. Modular homes are a new method of construction. It is only within the last two years that modular homes have been constructed in this area. Although the definition of "mobile home" extends to "any vehicle or similar portable structure," the drafters of the Zoning Ordinance could not have intended at the time the Ordinance was adopted to have included modular homes since they were not in existence in this area nor was their presence contemplated.

. . . While a mobile home is now available in expandable and double-wide units which create a more "homelike" appearance, the concept of a mobile home is entirely different than that of a modular home. A mobile home is a single entity which when placed on a building site is completed and needs no further installation of a heating system or materials. A modular home is transported to the construction site in several pieces. Moreover, a modular home is indistinguishable in appearance from conventionally built homes while a mobile home cannot be easily mistaken for a conventional dwelling. It appears that the average cost of a modular home is at least twice that of a mobile home.

Today with the urban housing crisis, it would be unrealistic to exclude from residential zones all modular construction since people are seeking dwelling space which is readily available at a lower cost. With modern technology, modular homes may be constructed more economically and more quickly than conventional homes.

The respondents have erroneously determined that a modular home is classified as a "mobile home" within the meaning of § 720 of the Town Zoning Ordinance.

[Petition granted]

QUESTIONS AND CASE PROBLEMS

1. "Smoke, fumes, and noise from public utilities and power plants are not to be condemned as nuisances merely because some harm is sustained from their activity by a particular plaintiff." Which of the objectives of the law listed in Chapter 2 are operative?

2. Causby owned a chicken farm. The United States Air Force maintained an air base nearby. The flight of heavy bombers and fighter planes frightened the Causbys and the chickens. Although flying at proper altitude, the planes would appear to be so close as to barely miss striking the trees on the farm. The lights of the planes lit up the farm at night. The noise and the lights so disturbed the chickens that Causby abandoned the chicken business. He claimed compensation from the United States. Decide. [United States v Causby, 328 US 256]

3. An action was brought to determine whether a condominium building could be constructed on a particular tract of land. The deed to the land permitted only single-family dwellings and prohibited apartment houses and further declared that the property could only be used by white persons. Did these restrictions bar a condominium building? [Callahan v Weiland, 291 Ala 183, 279 So2d 451]

4. The Urban Redevelopment Law of Oregon authorized the condemning of blighted urban areas and the acquisition of the property by the Housing Authority by eminent domain. Such part of the land condemned as was not needed by the Authority could be resold to private persons. Foeller and others owned well-maintained buildings within the Vaughn Street area that was condemned under this statute by the Portland Housing Authority as "physically substandard and economically deteriorated." The plaintiffs brought an action to have the statute declared unconstitutional. Decide. [Foeller v Housing Authority of Portland, 198 Ore 205, 256 P2d 752]

5. A zoning ordinance of the City of Dallas, Texas, prohibited the use of property in a residential district for gasoline filling stations. Lombardo brought an action against the City to test the validity of the ordinance. He contended that the ordinance violated the rights of the owners of property in such districts. Do you agree with this contention? [Lombardo v City of Dallas, 124 Tex 1, 73 SW2d 475]

6. Shearing was a homeowner in Rochester. The City burned trash on a nearby tract of land. Fires burned continuously on open ground, not in an incinerator, at times within 800 yards of the plaintiff's house. The smoke and dirt from the fires settled on the house of the plaintiff and on those of other persons in the area. The plaintiff sued to stop the continuance of such burning and to recover damages for the harm done to his home. Decide. [Shearing v Rochester, 51 Misc 2d 436, 273 NYS2d 464]

7. The Belmar Drive-In Theatre Co. brought an action against the Illinois State Toll Highway Commission because the bright lights of the toll road station interfered with the showing of motion pictures at the drive-in. Decide. [Belmar Drive-In Theatre Co. v Illinois State Toll Highway Commission, 34 Ill 2d 544, 216 NE2d 788]

8. Mayfield operated an unfenced automobile junkyard. This was a crime under the ordinances of the Town of Clayton. The Town brought an action against Mayfield to stop the operation of the junkyard and to compel him to remove the accumulated junk. The Town presented evidence showing that the junk served as a breeding ground for mosquitoes, that young children were likely to be attracted to the junkyard and be harmed, and that the combustible nature of the junk constituted a fire hazard. Mayfield testified that he intended to burn the old cars. The evidence indicated that this would create a large quantity of smoke. Decide. [Town of Clayton v Mayfield, 82 NM 596, 485 P2d 352]

9. The City of Colby prohibited placing a mobile home within the city limits except in a mobile home park or community. Hurtt owned a mobile home. He requested permission from the city to place this home on a tract of land owned in the city by his father. Permission was refused because of the ordinance. In spite of this refusal, Hurtt placed his home on his father's land. He was then prosecuted and convicted in the police court for violating the ordinance. He claimed that the zoning regulation was invalid because it interfered with the free use of property by its owner. Was he correct? [City of Colby v Hurtt, 212 Kan 113, 509 P2d 1142]

10. The Stallcups lived in a rural section of the state. In front of their house ran a relatively unused unimproved public county road. Wales Trucking Co. transported concrete pipe from the plant where it was made to a lake where the pipe was used to construct a water line to bring water to a nearby city. In the course of four months Wales made 825 trips over the road carrying from 58,000 to 72,000 pounds of pipe per trip and making the same number of empty return trips. The heavy use of the road by Wales cut up the dirt and made it like ashes. The Stallcups sued Wales for damages caused by the deposit of dust on their house and for the physical annoyance and discomfort caused by the dust. Wales defended on the ground that it had not been negligent and that its use of the road was not unlawful. Decide. [Wales Trucking Co. v Stallcup, (Tex Civ App) 465 SE2d 44]

8 Consumer Protection

In the early decades of the Twentieth Century, the law was concerned to a large degree with maintaining fair competition among businesses. This goal was sought by application of general equity principles prohibiting unfair competition; by the statutory prohibition of certain practices, such as trusts and conspiracies in restraint of trade; and by administrative regulation, as by the Federal Trade Commission to prevent unfair competition. In the last decade the law has become increasingly concerned with the practices of businesses with respect to consumers.

§ 8:1. Who Is a Consumer? Many persons are given the protection of a consumer.[1] For example, one does not usually think of a borrower or an investor as a "consumer." The pedestrian run over when a car goes out of control is not ordinarily regarded as a consumer. There is in all these situations, however, a common denominator of protecting someone from a hazard, and the law has extended protection to all these persons whether or not they are strictly consumers. For the sake of brevity, such protected persons will be called "consumers" although they may only be persons affected by the use of a product by a person who is a consumer.

Product safety is discussed in Chapter 26, and pollution in Chapter 7. This chapter deals with protection of the person as a consumer and a borrower.

§ 8:2. Advertising. Statutes commonly prohibit fraudulent advertising, but most advertising regulations are entrusted to an administrative agency, such as the Federal Trade Commission (FTC), which is authorized to issue orders to stop false, misleading advertising.[2]

(a) Deception. Under the Federal Trade Commission Act, deception in advertising, rather than fraud, is the significant element. This is a shift of social point of view. That is, instead of basing the law in terms of fault of the actor, the law is concerned with the problem of the buyer who is likely to be misled by statements made without

---

[1] The National Consumer Act (NCA) defines *consumer* as "a person other than an organization who seeks or acquires business equipment for use in his business, or real or personal property, services, money, or credit for personal, family, household or agricultural purposes." NCA § 1.301 (8). This definition includes a small business sole proprietor and thus goes beyond the ordinary image of a consumer.

Consumer protection is not limited to the protection of persons of limited education or economic means. See Weisz v Parke-Bernet Galleries, Inc. (NYCivCt) 67 Misc2d 1077, 325 NYS2d 576.

Additional protection for consumers who are servicepersons is provided by the Soldiers' and Sailors' Civil Relief Act, 50 United States Code App §§ 501-548.

[2] 15 USC §§ 45, 52.

regard to whether the defendant had any evil intent. (See p. 119, FTC v Colgate-Palmolive Co.)

The good faith of an advertiser or the absence of intent to deceive is immaterial, as the purpose of false advertising legislation is to protect the consumer rather than to punish the advertiser. The sale of an automobile with its odometer set back to show about one half of its actual mileage is a violation of a consumer protection statute even though the salesperson acting for the seller did not know that this had been done.

The FTC requires that an advertiser maintain a file containing the data claimed to support an advertising statement as to safety, performance, efficacy, quality, or comparative price of an advertised product. The FTC can require the advertiser to produce this material. If it is in the interest of the consumer, the Commission can make this information public, except to the extent that it contains trade secrets or matter which is privileged.

(b)   Corrective Advertising. When an enterprise has made false and deceptive statements in advertising, the Federal Trade Commission may require that a new advertising be made in which the former statements are contradicted and the truth stated. This corrective advertising required by the Federal Trade Commission is called *retractive advertising.*

§ 8:3. Seals of Approval. Many commodities are sold or advertised with a sticker or tag stating that the article has been approved or is guaranteed by some association or organization. Ordinarily, when a product is thus sold, it will in fact have been approved by some testing laboratory and will probably have proven adequate to meet ordinary consumer needs. A seller who sells with a seal of approval of a third person makes, in effect, a guarantee that the product has been so approved, so that such a seller is liable, if the product was in fact not approved. In addition, the seller would ordinarily be liable for fraud when the statement is not true.

§ 8:4. Labels and Packaging. Closely related to the regulation of advertising is the regulation of labels and marking of products. Various federal statutes are designed to give the consumer accurate information about the product, while others require warnings as to dangers of use or misuse. Consumer protection regulations prohibit the use of such terms as "jumbo," "giant," "full," which tend to exaggerate and mislead.

Federal statutes that protect the consumer from being misled by labels or by packaging methods include the Fair Packaging and Labeling Act; the Fur Products Labeling Act; the Wool Products Labeling Act; the Cigarette Labeling and Advertising Act; the Food, Drug, and Cosmetic Act; the Wholesome Meat Act; the Wholesome Poultry Products Act; and the Flammable Fabrics Act. The last three statutes seek to protect the consumer from personal harm as well as economic loss.

The Fair Packaging and Labeling Act applies generally to consumer goods and requires that a product bear a label stating (a) the identity of the product; (b) the name and place of business of the manufacturer, packer, or distributor; (c) the net quantity of the contents; and (d) the net quantity of a serving when the number of servings is stated. The Act gives to the FTC and the Department of Health, Education, and Welfare (HEW) authority to add additional requirements with respect to (a) the use of terms describing packages, such as "large"; (b) the use of "cents-off" or "savings" claims; (c) requiring the disclosure of information as to ingredients in the case of nonfoods; [3] and (d) preventing the deceptive partial filling of packages. The disclosure of the name and address of the manufacturer or distributor of the product is initially important to the consumer who may be purchasing in reliance upon the fact that the product came from a particular source. In the event that the consumer has a product liability claim, this information as to the source is important so that the consumer knows against whom suit can be brought in addition to the seller.

§ 8:5. Selling Methods. Consumer protection statutes prohibit the use of improper and deceptive selling methods.[4]

(a) **Disclosure of Transaction Terms.** The federal law requires the disclosure of all interest charges, points for granting loans, and similar charges. (See p. 120, Glaire v LaLanne-Paris Health Spa) These charges must be set forth as an annual percentage rate so that the consumer can see just how much the transaction costs a year.[5]

If sellers advertise that they will sell or lease on credit, they cannot state merely the monthly installments that will be due. They must give the consumer additional information: (1) the total cash price; (2) the amount of the down payment required; (3) the number, amounts, and due dates of payments; and (4) the annual percentage rate of the credit charges.[6] When a consumer protection law requires that certain information be set forth in a certain way, the failure to comply with the law cannot be excused on the ground that the information was set forth in the particular manner so that it could be used in the national computer system with which the defendant-lender was affiliated.[7]

In various ways, consumer protection statutes seek to protect the consumer from surprise or unbargained-for terms and from unwanted contracts.[8]

(1) Four-Installment Rule. Whenever a sale or contract provides for payment in four or more installments, it is subject to the Truth in Lending Act. This is so even though no service or finance charge is expressly added because of the installment pattern of paying. (See p. 121, Mourning v Family Publications Service, Inc.) When consumer credit is advertised as repayable in more than

---

[3] Such disclosure is required with respect to foods by the Food, Drug, and Cosmetic Act.

[4] As to states adopting the Uniform Consumer Credit Code (UCCC) see § 1:3. The Uniform Consumer Sales Practices Act has been adopted in Kansas, Ohio, and Utah; a Uniform Deceptive Trade Practices Act (1966 revision) has been adopted in Colorado, Georgia, Hawaii, Minnesota, Nebraska, New Mexico, Ohio, and Oregon; the 1964 version of the Uniform Deceptive Trade Practices Act was adopted in Delaware, Illinois, Maine, and Oklahoma; and a Uniform Land Sales Practice Act has been adopted in Alaska, Connecticut, Florida, Hawaii, Kansas, Montana, South Carolina, and Utah.

[5] Consumer Credit Protection Act (CCPA), 15 USC §§ 1605, 1606, 1636; Regulation Z adopted by the Federal Reserve Board of Governors, § 226.5. "The avowed purpose of the Consumer Protection Act was to 'assure a meaningful disclosure of credit terms so that the consumer will be able to compare more readily the various credit terms available to him and avoid the uninformed use of credit.' The Act is remedial in nature, designed to remedy what Congressional hearings revealed to be unscrupulous and predatory creditor practices throughout the nation." N. C. Freed Co. Inc. v Board of Governors of Federal Reserve System (CA2 NY) 473 F2d 1210.

[6] Regulation Z § 1210; Consumer Leasing Act of 1976, 15 USC § 1667.

[7] Allen v Beneficial Finance Co. (CA7 Ind) 531 F2d 797.

[8] Uniform Commercial Code § 2-316 is in effect a forerunner of such antisurprise protection in requiring that a disclaimer of certain warranties be conspicuous.

four installments and no financing charge is expressly imposed, the advertisement must "clearly and conspicuously" state that "the cost of credit is included in the price" quoted for the goods and services.[9]

(2)   Contract on Two Sides. In order to be sure that disclosures required by federal law are in fact seen by the consumer, special provision is made for the case when the terms of the transaction are printed on both the front and back of a sheet or contract. In such case, (1) both sides of the sheet must carry the warning: "NOTICE: see other side for important information," and (2) the page must be signed at the end of the second side. Conversely, the requirements of the federal law are not satisfied when there is no warning of "see other side" and the parties sign the contract on the face of the first side of the paper only.

(3)   Particular Sales and Leases. The Federal Real Estate Settlement Procedures Act of 1974 protects consumers purchasing homes by requiring disclosures of charges, prohibiting kickbacks and the splitting of fees except for services actually rendered, and limiting the amount that a borrower must pay into a special or escrow fund for taxes and insurance.[10] The Motor Vehicle Information and Cost Savings Act requires the disclosure to the buyer of various elements in the cost of an automobile. The Act prohibits selling an automobile without informing the buyer that the odometer has been reset below the true mileage. A buyer who is caused actual loss by odometer fraud may recover from the seller 3 times the actual loss or $1500, whichever is greater.[11] The Consumer Leasing Act of 1976 requires that persons leasing automobiles and other durable goods to consumers make a full disclosure to the consumer of the details of the transaction.[12] The Act also regulates advertising and seeks to protect lessees from loss if the property is resold by the lessor upon the expiration of the lease.

(4)   State Laws. In some states, transactions are subject to a state law rather than to the Federal Truth in Lending Act. Under Regulation Z, the Federal Reserve Board may grant a state an exemption from the federal laws when the state law imposes requirements similar to the federal law and makes adequate provision for enforcement.

(b)   Home Solicitation Sales. A sale of goods or services for $25 or more made to a buyer at home may be set aside within 3 days. This right may be exercised merely because the buyer does not want to go through with the contract. There is no requirement of proving any misconduct of the seller nor any defect in the goods or services.[13]

(c)   Referral Sales. The technique of giving the buyer a price reduction for customers referred to the seller is theoretically lawful. In effect, it is merely paying the buyer a "commission" for the promotion of other sales. In actual practice, however, the

[9] PL 93-495, 88 Stat 1500, Title IV.
[10] PL 93-533, PL 94-205, 88 Stat 724, 12 USC § 2601 et seq.
[11] PL 92-513, 86 Stat 947, §§ 403, 409, 15 USC § 1901 et seq.
[12] PL 94-240, 90 Stat 257, 15 USC § 1601 et seq.
[13] Federal Trade Commission Regulation, 16 CFR § 429.1.

referral sales technique is often accompanied by fraud or by exorbitant pricing, so that consumer protection laws variously condemn referral selling. The referral system of selling has been condemned as unconscionable under the UCC,[14] and is expressly prohibited by UCCC.[15]

§ 8:6. Credit Cards. Today's credit card may cover travel and entertainment, as in the case of the cards issued by American Express; or a particular group of commodities, as in the case of a gasoline credit card; or it may be a general-purpose card, covering the purchase of any kind of goods and services, such as Master Charge and Visa (BankAmericard).

(a)   Unsolicited Credit Cards. The unsolicited distribution of credit cards to persons who have not applied for them is prohibited.

(b)   Surcharge Prohibited. A seller cannot add any charge to the purchase price because the buyer uses a credit card instead of paying with cash or a check.[16]

(c)   Unauthorized Use. A cardholder is not liable for more than $50 for the unauthorized use of a credit card. In order to impose liability up to that amount, the issuer of the card must show that (1) the credit card is an accepted card,[17] (2) the issuer has given the holder adequate notice of possible liability in such case, (3) the issuer has furnished the holder with a self-addressed, prestamped notification form to be mailed by the holder in the event of the loss or theft of the credit card, (4) the issuer has provided a method by which the user of the card can be identified as the person authorized to use it,[18] and (5) the unauthorized use of the card has occurred or may occur as a result of loss, theft, or otherwise.

§ 8:7. Contract Terms. Consumer protection legislation does not ordinarily affect the right of the parties to make a contract on such terms as they choose. It is customary, however, to prohibit the use of certain clauses which, it is believed, bear too harshly on the debtor or which have too great a potential for exploitive abuse by a creditor. For example, the UCCC prohibits provisions permitting a creditor to enter a judgment against a debtor without giving the debtor any chance to make a defense.[19]

The federal Warranty Disclosure Act of 1974 establishes disclosure standards for consumer goods warranties in order to make them understood by the consumer.[20]

Methods of computing charges and billing methods are frequently regulated. This is done to prevent the creditor from adding back into the contract an element

---

[14] New York v I.T.M. 52 Misc2d 39, 275 NYS2d 303.
[15] UCCC § 2.411.
[16] Truth in Lending Act Amendment of 1976, 15 USC § 1666f.
[17] A credit card is "accepted" when "the card holder has requested and received or has signed or has used, or authorized another to use [it], for the purpose of obtaining money, property, labor, or services on credit." CCPA § 103(1).
[18] Regulation Z of the Board of Governors of the Federal Reserve § 226.13(d), as amended, provides that the identification may be "signature, photograph, or fingerprint on the credit card or by electronic or mechanical confirmation."
[19] UCCC §§ 2.415, 3.407.
[20] PL 93-637, 88 Stat 2183, 15 USC § 2301.

or a charge that could not have been included in the original contract or from enforcing a contract which was different than that bargained for by the consumer.

(a) Unconscionability. To some extent, consumer protection has been provided under the UCC by those courts which hold that the "unconscionability" provision protects from "excessive" or "exorbitant" prices when goods are sold on credit.

(b) Form of Contract. Consumer protection laws commonly regulate the form of the contract, requiring that certain items be specifically listed, that payments under the contract be itemized, and indicate the allocation to principal, interest, insurance, and so on. Generally certain portions of the contract or all of the contract must be printed in type of a certain size and a copy must be furnished to the buyer. Such statutory requirements are more demanding than the statute of frauds section of the UCC. It is frequently provided that the copy furnished the consumer must be completely filled in. Back-page disclaimers are void if the front page of the contract does not call attention to the presence of such terms.[21]

(c) Limitation of Credit. Various laws may limit the ability to borrow money or purchase on credit. In some states, it is prohibited to make "open end" mortgages by which the mortgage secures a specified debt and such additional loans as may thereafter be made. Consumer protection is also afforded in some states by placing a time limit on smaller loans.[22]

§ 8:8. Payments. Under the UCCC, when a consumer sale or lease is made, the consumer may pay only by check or cash. The consumer cannot be required to sign a promissory note.

(a) Progressive Application of Payments. Consumer legislation may provide that when a consumer makes a payment on an open charge account, the payment must be applied to pay the oldest items. The result is that, should there be a default at a later date, any right of repossession of the creditor is limited to the later unpaid items. This outlaws a contract provision by which, upon the default of the buyer at a later date, the seller could assert the right to repossess all purchases that had been made at any prior time. Such a provision is outlawed by the UCCC [23] and is probably unconscionable under the UCC.[24]

(b) Balloon Payments. Installment contracts sometimes provide for a payment, usually the final payment, which may be substantially larger than the usual or average installment under the contract. Sometimes the purpose of requiring such a payment

---

[21] The same conclusion is reached under the UCC on the ground that such a back page disclaimer of a warranty is not "conspicuous," and therefore does not satisfy the requirements of UCC §§ 2-316(2), 1-201(10). Hunt v Perkins Machine Co. 352 Mass 535, 226 NE2d 228. A front page disclaimer is also invalid if not conspicuous. Woodruff v Clark County Farm Bureau Cooperative Association, 153 IndApp 31, 286 NE2d 188.

[22] Abrams v Commercial Credit Plan, Inc. 120 GaApp 520, 197 SE2d 384.

[23] UCCC § 2.409(1).

[24] Williams v Walker-Thomas Furniture Co. (CA Dist Col) 350 F2d 445.

is to impose on the debtor a greater obligation than can be paid, with the result that the debtor is almost certain to go into default and entitle the creditor to repossess the collateral. The UCCC seeks to outlaw this practice by providing that whenever a payment balloons out to more than double the average of earlier scheduled payments, the debtor has a right to refinance that payment on terms no less favorable than those of the original transaction. That is, the creditor must extend further credit rather than claim that the debt is in default.[25]

Regulation Z of the Federal Reserve Board, adopted under the CCPA, provides that "if any payment is more than twice the amount of an otherwise regularly scheduled equal payment, the creditor shall identify the amount of such payment by the term 'balloon payment' and shall state the conditions, if any, under which that payment may be refinanced if not paid when due." [26]

(c)   Acceleration of Payment. The ability of a creditor to accelerate payment of the balance due upon default has worked great hardship where the default was trivial in nature or where in fact there was no default. Although the right to accelerate payments upon default is permitted under both the UCC and the UCCC, the former seeks to impose some limitation on the power to accelerate by providing that a power of the creditor to accelerate "at will" or "when he deems himself insecure" must be exercised in good faith,[27] and the UCCC requires the refund of unearned credit charges when the due date has been accelerated.

Some debtor protection laws require that the debtor be in default for a minimum period of time or with respect to a minimum number of installment payments before the balance of the debt can be accelerated.[28] Other consumer protection laws make acceleration clauses invalid.

§ 8:9. Preservation of Consumer Defenses. Consumer protection laws generally prohibit a consumer from waiving or giving up any defense provided by law. The consumer is also protected from entering into a transaction of such a nature that defenses would be lost.

In the ordinary contract situation, when goods or services purchased or leased by a consumer are not proper or are defective, the consumer is not required to pay the seller or lessor or is only required to pay a reduced amount. With the modern expansion of credit transactions, sellers and lessors have made use of several techniques for getting paid without regard to whether the consumer had any complaint against them.

To prevent this, the Federal Trade Commission has adopted a regulation which requires that in every sale or lease of goods or services to a consumer, the contract of the consumer contain a clause giving the consumer the right to assert defenses not only against the seller or lessor but also against a third person, such as a bank or finance company, to which the seller or lessor transfers the rights against the

[25] UCCC §§ 2.405, 3.402.
[26] Regulation § 226.8(b)(3).
[27] UCC § 1-208.
[28] UCCC § 2.210(8). "If the maturity is accelerated for any reason and judgment is obtained, the buyer is entitled to the same rebate as if payment had been made on the date judgment is entered."

consumer. The Commission regulation requires that the following notice be included in boldface type at least ten point in size:

NOTICE
ANY HOLDER OF THIS CONSUMER CREDIT CONTRACT IS SUBJECT TO ALL CLAIMS AND DEFENSES WHICH THE DEBTOR COULD ASSERT AGAINST THE SELLER OF GOODS OR SERVICES OBTAINED WITH THE PROCEEDS HEREOF. RECOVERY HEREUNDER BY THE DEBTOR SHALL NOT EXCEED AMOUNTS PAID BY THE DEBTOR HEREUNDER.[29]

§ 8:10. Credit, Collection, and Billing Methods.

(a) **Credit Discrimination.** It is unlawful to discriminate against an applicant for credit on the basis of race, color, religion, national origin, sex, marital status, or age; because all or part of the applicant's income is obtained from a public assistance program; or because the applicant has in good faith exercised any right under the Consumer Credit Protection Act. When a credit application is refused, the applicant must be furnished a written explanation why the application was rejected.[30]

(b) **Correction of errors.** When the consumer believes that an error has been made in billing by the issuer of a credit card, the consumer should send the creditor a written statement and explanation of the error. The creditor or card issuer must investigate and make a prompt written reply to the consumer.[31]

(c) **Improper Collection Methods.** Unreasonable methods of debt collection are often expressly prohibited by statute or are held by courts to constitute an unreasonable invasion of privacy.[32] Statutes generally prohibit sending bills in such form that they give the impression that a lawsuit has been initiated against the consumer and that the bill is legal process or a warrant issued by the court. The CCPA prohibits the use of extortionate methods of loan collection. A creditor may be prohibited from informing the employer of the debtor that the latter owes money.

When the seller made telephone calls to the buyer and the buyer's relatives and made obscene, threatening, and malicious statements which caused the buyer to become physically ill, the seller was liable for the tort of intentional mental disturbance. In order to give rise to such liability, "the conduct must be more than mere insults, indignities, threats, and annoyances and must be so shocking and outrageous as to exceed all reasonable bounds of decency." [33]

(d) **Licensing of Sellers and Lenders.** Consumer protection statutes sometimes provide for the licensing of persons selling on credit and making loans. Sometimes these statutes are limited to particular kinds of goods, such as automobiles, or home improvements and services. When such licensing is required, procedures are established for suspending or revoking the license of a licensee who seriously violates the statute.

---

[29] This notice is here printed in ten point, boldface type.
[30] Equal Credit Opportunity Act, as amended, PL 93-495, PL 94-239, 15 USC § 1691 et seq.
[31] Fair Billing Credit Act, PL 93-495, Title III, 15 USC § 1601.
[32] Fair Debt Collection Practices Act, added as Title VIII to the CCPA, PL 95-109, 91 Stat 874, 15 USC § 1692 et seq.
[33] Callarama v Associates Discount Corp., 69 Misc 2d 287, 329 NYS2d 711.

§ 8:11. Protection of Credit Standing and Reputation. In many instances one party to a transaction wishes to know certain things about the other party. This situation arises when a person purchases on credit or applies for a loan, a job, or a policy of insurance. Between two and three thousand private credit bureaus gather such information on borrowers, buyers, and applicants and sell such information to interested persons.

The Fair Credit Reporting Act (FCRA) of 1970 [34] seeks to protect from various abuses that may arise. FCRA applies only to consumer credit, which is defined as credit for "personal, family, and household" use, and does not apply to business or commercial transactions.

(a)   Privacy. A report on a person based on personal investigation and interviews, called an *investigative consumer report* may not be made without informing the person investigated of the right to discover the results of the investigation.[35] Bureaus are not permitted to disclose information to persons not having a legitimate use for it. It is a federal crime to obtain or to furnish a bureau report for an improper purpose.

On request, a bureau must tell a consumer the names and addresses of persons to whom it has made a credit report during the previous six months. It must also tell, when requested, which employers were given such a report during the previous two years.

Some states require that a copy of a report be furnished to the subject person whenever a bureau sends a report to its customer.

(b)   Protection from False Information. Much of the information obtained by bureaus is based on statements made by persons, such as neighbors, when interviewed by the bureau's investigator. Sometimes the statements are incorrect. Quite often they are hearsay evidence and would not be admissible in a legal proceeding. Nevertheless, they may go on the records of the bureau without further verification and will be furnished to a client of the bureau who will tend to regard them as accurate and true.

A person has a limited right to request an agency to disclose the nature and substance of the information possessed by the bureau. The right to know does not extend to medical information. It is not required that the bureau identify the persons giving information to its investigators. The bureau is required neither to give the applicant a copy of, nor to permit the applicant to see, its file.

(1)   Correction of Error. When a person claims that the information of the bureau is erroneous, the bureau must take steps within a reasonable time to determine the accuracy of the disputed item. It is not required to do so, however, if the bureau has reasonable grounds for believing that the objection is frivolous and irrelevant. If it determines that the information is erroneous, it must give notice of the correction to anyone to whom it had sent a credit report in the preceding six months or for employment in the preceding two years. If the bureau and the applicant do not reach an agreement as to the disputed item, the applicant may give the bureau a written statement of the applicant's version of the matter. The bureau must supply a copy of this statement when it furnishes any subsequent report, and on request must send copies of the statement to

[34] PL 91-508, 15 USC § 1681 et seq. adding Title VI to the Consumer Credit Protection Act.
[35] CCPA § 606, 15 USC § 1681(d).

persons to whom it has already sent a report within the time limitations stated above.

(2)   Elimination of Stale Items. Adverse information obtained by investigation cannot be given to a client after 3 months unless verified to determine that it is still valid. Most legal proceedings cannot be reported by a bureau after 7 years. A bankruptcy proceeding cannot be reported after 14 years.[36] Information based on a public record must be up-to-date, or the applicant must be notified that information based on the public record is being furnished. This is designed to eliminate the danger that the bureau will not have been aware of the latest developments in the matter. In many instances cases are settled out of court without any formal notation being made thereof on the court record, with the consequence that if the bureau or anyone else relied only on the court record, there would appear to be an outstanding claim or unpaid judgment in existence.

(3)   Inadequacy of Prior Law. In some instances the person harmed by false information could sue the informant for damages for the tort of interference with economic relations or defamation. Ordinarily the injured party cannot recover under either theory because as a practical matter it is not possible to prove that the defendant acted with malice, and in the absence of malice the informant is protected from liability by a qualified privilege. (See p. 123, Bartels v Retail Credit Co.)

§ 8:12. Expansion of Consumer Protection.

Various state laws aimed at preventing fraudulent sales of corporate securities, commonly called blue-sky laws, have been adopted. These statutes are discussed in Chapter 48 on corporate stock. Other statutes have been adopted to protect purchasers of real estate and buyers of services.

(a)   Real Estate Development Sales. Anyone promoting the sale of a real estate development which is divided into fifty or more parcels of less than five acres each must file with the Secretary of Housing and Urban Development a *development statement* setting forth significant details of the development required by the federal Land Sales Act.[37]

Anyone buying or renting one of the parcels in the subdivision, must be given a *property report.* This is a condensed version of the development statement filed with the Secretary of HUD. This report must be given to the prospective customer more than 48 hours before signing the contract to buy or lease.

If the development statement is not filed with the Secretary, the sale or renting of the real estate development may not be promoted through the channels of interstate commerce nor by the use of the mail.

If the property report is given to the prospective buyer or tenant less than 48 hours before signing a contract to buy or a lease, or after it has been signed, the contract may be avoided within 48 hours. If the property report is never received,

---

[36] These time limitations do not apply to an application for a loan or for life insurance of $50,000 or more or for employment at a salary of $20,000 a year or more.

[37] PL 91-547, 84 Stat 1413, 15 USC § 77(b),(c), 78(c),(l), 80a-2 et seq.

the contract may be avoided and there is no statutory limitation on the time in which to do so.

(b)   Service Contracts. The UCCC treats a consumer service contract the same as a consumer sale of goods if payment is made in installments or a credit charge is made and the amount financed does not exceed $25,000.[38] It defines "services" broadly as embracing work, specified privileges, and insurance provided by a noninsurer. The inclusion of "privileges" makes the UCCC apply to contracts calling for payment on the installment plan or including a financing charge for transportation, hotel and restaurant accommodations, education, entertainment, recreation, physical culture, hospital accommodations, funerals, and similar accommodations.

Some states have adopted statutes requiring that any present payments for future funeral services or goods must be deposited in a bank account or similar depository to be held for the benefit of the customer. A contract which does not provide for such deposit is void as being against public policy.

Another form of consumer exploitation involves charging for unperformed services. This practice is generally regarded as improper. (See p. 123, New York v Hotel Waldorf-Astoria)

§ 8:13. Consumer Remedies. The theoretical right of the consumer to sue or to assert a defense is often of little practical value to the consumer because of the small size of the amount involved and the high cost of litigation. Consumer protection legislation provides special remedies.

(a)   Government Agency Action. The UCCC provides for an administrator who will, in a sense, police business practices to insure conformity with the law.[39] This is not regarded by some as an improvement and has been criticized because of the danger that the administrator may be creditor-oriented, and that the debtor might, as a consequence, be deprived of protection in many cases when it is a question of policy or discretion as to what action, if any, should be taken by the administrator.[40]

(b)   Action by Attorney General. A number of states provide that the state attorney general may bring an action on behalf of a particular group of consumers to obtain cancellation of their contracts and restitution of whatever they had paid. Many states permit the attorney general to bring an action to enjoin violation of the consumer protection statute.

Consumer protection statutes commonly give the attorney general the authority to seek a voluntary discontinuance of improper practices before seeking to obtain an injunction from a court.

(c)   Action by Consumer. Some consumer protection statutes provide that a consumer who is harmed by a violation of the statutes may sue the wrongdoing enterprise to recover a specified penalty or may bring an action on behalf of consumers as a class. Consumer protection statutes are often designed to rely on private litigation as an

---

[38] UCCC § 2.104(1). Credit card transactions are exempted unless the person selling the services and the consumer expressly agree that the transaction is subject to the UCCC. § 2.104(2)(a).

[39] UCCC § 6.103-6.116.

[40] Furthermore, this opens the door to all the other problems involved in the regulation of business by administrative agencies.

aid to enforcement of the statutory provisions. The Consumer Protection Safety Act of 1972 authorizes "any interested person" to bring a civil action to enforce a consumer product safety rule and certain orders of the Food, Drug, and Consumer Protection Agency.[41] But in some cases the individual consumer cannot bring any action, and enforcement of the law is entrusted exclusively to an administrative agency.

§ 8:14. Civil and Criminal Penalties. The seller or lender engaging in improper consumer practices may be subject to civil penalties and criminal punishment. In some instances the laws in question are the general laws applicable to improper conduct, while in other cases the laws are specifically aimed at the particular consumer practices.

Illustrative of the applicability of the general law, a contractor who falsely stated to a homeowner that certain repairs needed on the roof cost, with labor and materials, $650 when in fact they cost only $200, was guilty of the crime of obtaining money by false pretenses. Illustrative of specific consumer protection statutes, the Truth In Lending Act subjects the creditor to a separate claim for damages for each periodic statement which violates the disclosure requirements. Furthermore, consumer protection statutes of the disclosure type generally provide that the creditor cannot enforce the obligation of the debtor if the specified information is not set forth in the contract.

[41] PL 92-573, 86 Stat 1207, § 23, 15 USC § 2072.

CASES FOR CHAPTER 8

FTC v Colgate-Palmolive Co.

380 US 374 (1965)

The Colgate-Palmolive Company ran a television commercial to show that its shaving cream "Rapid Shave" could soften even the toughness of sandpaper. The commercial showed what was described as the sandpaper test. Actually what was used was a sheet of Plexiglas on which sand had been sprinkled. The FTC claimed that this was a deceptive practice. The advertiser contended that actual sandpaper would merely look like ordinary colored paper and that Plexiglas had been used to give the viewer an accurate visual representation of the test. The FTC issued an order to stop the commercial. The Court of Appeals reversed this order.

WARREN, C.J. . . . The Commission found that the undisclosed use of a plexiglass substitute for sandpaper was [a] material misrepresentation that was a deceptive act separate and distinct from [any] misrepresentation concerning Rapid Shave's underlying qualities. Even if the sandpaper could be shaved just as depicted in the commercials, the Commission

found that viewers had been misled into believing they had seen it done with their own eyes. As a result of these findings the Commission entered a cease-and-desist order against the respondents [Colgate and the advertiser]. . . .

. . . The Commission expressed the view that without this visible proof of Rapid Shave's moisturizing ability some viewers might not have been persuaded to buy the product. . . .

. . . When the Commission was created by Congress in 1914, it was directed by § 5 to prevent "[u]nfair methods of competition in commerce." Congress amended the Act in 1938 to extend the Commission's jurisdiction to include "unfair or deceptive acts or practices in commerce"—a significant amendment showing Congress' concern for consumers as well as for competitors. It is important to note the generality of these standards of illegality. . . .

This statutory scheme necessarily gives the Commission an influential role in interpreting § 5 and in applying it to the facts of particular cases arising out of unprecedented situations. Moreover, as an administrative agency which deals continually with cases in the area, the Commission is often in a better position than are courts to determine when a practice is "deceptive" within the meaning of the Act. . . .

We accept the Commission's determination that the commercials involved in this case contained three representations to the public: (1) that sandpaper could be shaved by Rapid Shave; (2) that an experiment had been conducted which verified this claim; and (3) that the viewer was seeing this experiment for himself. . . . For the purposes of our review, we can assume that the first two representations were true; the focus of our consideration is on the third, which was clearly false. The parties agree that § 5 prohibits the intentional misrepresentation of any fact which would constitute a material factor in a purchaser's decision whether to buy. They differ, however, in their conception of what "facts" constitute a "material factor" in a purchaser's decision to buy. Respondents submit, in effect, that the only material facts are those which deal with the substantive qualities of a product. The Commission, on the other hand, submits that the misrepresentation of *any* fact so long as it materially induces a purchaser's decision to buy is a deception prohibited by § 5.

The Commission's interpretation of what is a deceptive practice seems more in line with the decided cases than that of respondents. . . .

We agree with the Commission . . . that the undisclosed use of plexiglass in the present commercials was a material deceptive practice. . . . Respondents claim that it will be impractical to inform the viewing public that it is not seeing an actual test, experiment or demonstration, but we think it inconceivable that the ingenious advertising world will be unable, if it so desires, to conform to the Commission's insistence that the public be not misinformed. If, however, it becomes impossible or impractical to show simulated demonstrations on television in a truthful manner, this indicates that television is not a medium that lends itself to this type of commercial, not that the commercial must survive at all costs. . . .

[Judgment reversed]

Glaire v La Lanne-Paris Health Spa

12 Cal3d 915, 117 CalRptr 541, 528 P2d 357 (1975)

Glaire purchased a seven-year membership in the La Lanne-Paris Health Spa. The membership for the seven years was $408. It could be paid, at no extra cost, in monthly installments of $17 each, over two years. La Lanne would sell such memberships to the Universal Guardian Acceptance Corporation for $255. Glaire claimed that the Federal Truth in Lending Act was violated because it had not been disclosed to her that a $255 membership was costing her $408 because she was paying on the installment plan. Glaire claimed that this violated the Federal Truth in Lending Act and sued to enjoin the making of such membership contracts by La Lanne. Judgment was entered for the defendants, La Lanne and Universal, and Glaire appealed.

MOSK, J. . . . Plaintiff elected to pay over time, as do most of La Lanne's customers, and accordingly entered into a . . . standard form contract which declared that no "service charge" was made for the extension of credit and provided that any default in installment payments would render the entire balance due. As a matter of course in its business practice, La Lanne thereupon sold plaintiff's contract to Universal at a discount of 37.5 percent. La Lanne thus immediately received $255 in cash and plaintiff became obligated to Universal for the full $408 payable over two years. La Lanne and Universal are interlocking corporations with common ownership and control, and Universal regularly assists La Lanne in its financing by accepting chattel paper at a discount. . . .

In order to encourage the informed use of credit, Truth-in-Lending requires merchants who regularly extend credit to disclose to each consumer certain information relevant to the cost of deferring payment. . . .

Truth-in-Lending requires disclosure by only those merchants who satisfy the statutory meaning of the term "creditor.". . . That term is defined in the act to include "creditors who regularly extend, or arrange for the extension of, credit for which the payment of a finance charge is required, whether in connection with loans, sales of property or services, or otherwise.". . . Thus, the act contemplates the coverage of two types of creditors, socalled "extenders" and "arrangers," and imposes disclosure responsibilities on both in three-party transactions in which a seller, as a matter of course, arranges for his customers to obtain credit from a financer. The regulations elaborate on the concept of an arranger, as distinguished from an extender: " 'Arrange for the extension of credit' means to provide or offer to provide consumer credit which is or will be extended by another person under a business or other relationship pursuant to which the person arranging such credit receives or will receive a fee, compensation, or other consideration for such service or has knowledge of the credit terms and participates in the preparation of the contract documents required in connection with the extension of credit." (12 C.F.R. § 226.2, subd. (f).) . . .

Plaintiff's theory is that because of the continuing business relationship and interlocking ownership of La Lanne and Universal and because of La Lanne's customary practice of systematically discounting its chattel paper to Universal, La Lanne qualifies as an arranger of credit under Truth-in-Lending and Universal in fact extends the credit. According to plaintiff, La Lanne's practice of offering to its customers unitary price contracts, i.e., contracts in which the price payable in cash at the outset would equal the sum to be paid in installments over time, is merely a device to conceal the actual cost of credit of the consumer, which corresponds to the amount of the discount La Lanne regularly allows to Universal. Thus, when La Lanne charges $408 to be paid in installments, it in fact receives only $255 for its services, with Universal ultimately recouping the $255 which it paid at once to La Lanne for the contract and gaining an additional $153 in return for the risk of permitting the consumer to pay over time. It is this differential of $153 between the amount La Lanne receives and the amount the consumer pays for La Lanne's services which plaintiff claims to constitute a finance charge for the extension of credit which must be disclosed under Truth-in-Lending.

Three recent federal court decisions have upheld contentions virtually identical to those advanced by plaintiff in circumstances remarkably similar to the case at bar. . . .

We find persuasive the logic and analysis of these federal decisions. According to the complaint, Universal accepts the vast majority of La Lanne's installment contracts at a fixed discount contemporaneously with their execution. Universal's practice of accepting such contracts is functionally equivalent to extending loans directly to La Lanne's customers at a defined rate of interest: in either case, La Lanne receives a net cash sum and the customer becomes obligated to Universal for a greater amount which includes a charge for the credit risk assumed by Universal. Nevertheless, by employing this method of systematic discounting Universal purports to evade

all liability under Truth-in-Lending, whereas a direct loan would be clearly covered under the act. . . .

Where, as appears here, a finance company assumes so close a relationship with a seller that it becomes an integral part of the seller's financing program, the finance company must bear full responsibility for all disclosures required under Truth-in-Lending. Thus, there comes a point at which, because of its continual dealings with a particular seller, a finance company may be viewed directly as the extender of consumer credit which the seller has merely arranged. (15 U.S.C. § 1602, subd. (f); 12 C.F.R. § 226.2 subd. (f).) . . .

Defendants suggest that plaintiff is in fact attacking their pricing decision not to allow their customers the opportunity to pay a lower cash price equal to the discounted value of the installment contracts, and that such pricing policy is not monitored by Truth-in-Lending. Again, the argument misses its mark. The thrust of plaintiff's complaint is not directed at coercing La Lanne into adopting a particular pricing structure, but rather at exposing a method of financing which operates to conceal the actual cost of credit to the consumer. . . .

It follows from the foregoing analysis that plaintiff has succeeded in stating a cause of action against both La Lanne and Universal . . . under Truth-in-Lending. Accordingly, the trial court erred in sustaining defendants' demurrer to the cause. . . .

[Judgment reversed]

Mourning v Family Publications Service, Inc.

411 US 356 (1973)

Acting under the Truth in Lending Act, the Federal Reserve Board adopted a Regulation Z. Among other things, this Regulation declared that whenever a consumer agreed to pay in more than four installments, the person dealing with him was subject to the Truth in Lending Act. The Family Publications Service sold a magazine to Leila Mourning but failed to disclose the information required by the federal Act although payment was to be made by her in 30 monthly installments. Family Publications claimed that the four-installment rule of Regulation Z was invalid and that the federal Truth in Lending Act could not apply to it because it did not make any extra charge for the making of installment payments. The Court of Appeals held the regulation invalid and Mourning appealed.

BURGER, C.J. . . . Passage of the Truth-in-Lending Act in 1968 culminated several years of congressional study and debate as to the propriety and usefulness of imposing mandatory disclosure requirements on those who extend credit to consumers in the American market. By the time of passage, it had become abundantly clear that the use of consumer credit was expanding at an extremely rapid rate. . . .

The Truth-in-Lending Act was designed to remedy the problems which had developed. . . . This purpose was . . . "to assure a meaningful disclosure of credit terms so that the consumer will be able to compare more readily the various credit terms available to him and avoid the uninformed use of credit.". . .

. . . Congress determined to lay the structure of the Act broadly and to entrust its construction to an agency with the necessary experience and resources to monitor its operation. Section 105 delegated to the Federal Reserve Board broad authority to promulgate regulations necessary to render the Act effective. . . . In addition to granting to the Board the authority normally given to administrative agencies to promulgate regulations designed to "carry out the purposes" of the Act, Congress specifically stated: "These regulations may contain such classifications, differentiations, or other provisions, and may provide for such adjustments and exceptions for any class of transactions, as in the judgment of the Board are necessary or proper . . . to prevent circumvention or evasion [of the Act], or to facilitate compliance therewith." . . .

One means of circumventing the objectives of the Truth-in-Lending Act, as passed by Congress, was that of "burying" the cost of credit in the price of goods sold. Thus in many credit transactions in which creditors claimed that no finance charge had been imposed, the creditor merely assumed the cost of extending credit as an expense of doing business, to be recouped as part of the price charged in the transaction. Congress was well aware, from its extensive studies, of the possibility that merchants could use such devices to evade the disclosure requirements of the Act. The Committee hearings are replete with suggestions that such manipulation would render the Act a futile gesture in the case of goods normally sold by installment contract. Opponents of the bill contended that the reporting provisions would actually encourage merchants who had formerly segregated their credit costs not to do so. They predicted

that the effect of the Act would thus be to reduce the amount of information available to the consumer, a result directly contrary to that which was intended. . . .

. . . The Board's objective in promulgating the [four-installment] rule was to prevent the Act from fulfilling the prophecy which its opponents had forecast. . . .

. . . In delegating rule making authority to the Board, Congress emphasized the Board's authority to prevent such evasion. . . .

. . . We see no reason to doubt the Board's conclusion that the rule will deter creditors from engaging in the conduct which the Board sought to eliminate. The burdens imposed on creditors are not severe, when measured against the evils which are avoided. . . .

The Truth-in-Lending Act reflects a transition in congressional policy from a philosophy of let-the-buyer-beware to one of let-the-seller-disclose. By erecting a barrier between the seller and the prospective purchaser in the form of hard facts, Congress expressly sought "to . . . avoid the uninformed use of credit.". . . The Four-Installment Rule serves to insure that the protective disclosure mechanism chosen by Congress will not be circumvented.

That the approach taken may reflect what respondent views as an undue paternalistic concern for the consumer is beside the point. The statutory scheme is within the power granted to Congress under the Commerce Clause. It is not a function of the courts to speculate as to whether the statute is unwise or whether the evils sought to be remedied could better have been regulated in some other manner.

[Judgment reversed and remanded]

POWELL, J. (dissenting) I would affirm the judgment of the Court of Appeals on the ground that there was no extension of consumer credit within the meaning of the Truth in Lending Act. . . .

Clearly the Act applies only to transactions involving the extension of credit. . . .

The transaction before the Court may well have been a credit transaction, but it was *not respondent* that extended the credit. Petitioner obligated herself to pay in advance for the magazines she was to receive. The contract required petitioner to pay equal installments over a 30-month period, but respondent was obligated only to provide magazines over 60 months. In effect petitioner paid every month for two months' worth of magazines. Until the last magazine had been delivered, petitioner would have paid for more magazines than she received. Thus, the contract called for the extension of credit by petitioner to respondent. For this reason it was not an "extension of consumer credit" within the meaning of the Act. . . .

New York v Hotel Waldorf-Astoria

323 NYS2d 917 (1971)

The New York Waldorf-Astoria Hotel added a 2% charge to the bill of every guest. The charge was described on the bill as "sundries." No further explanation or itemization was made. The Hotel claimed that this charge was justified as covering messenger service. However, only about 77% of the guests used such service. The Attorney General of the state brought an action to enjoin the making of this charge for "sundries" and to cause the Hotel to refund the money which prior guests had paid for such item.

BAER, J. . . . The General Business Law does require every hotel to post "a statement of the charges or rate of charges by the day and for meals furnished and for lodging." It further provides that "No charge or sum shall be collected or received by any such hotel keeper or inn keeper for any service not actually rendered. . . ."

Between December 2, 1969 and May 21, 1970 the [Waldorf] did add to each bill of each customer a 2% charge for Sundries. The respondents contend that this was a proper charge because of the peculiar needs of their clientele, and the capital cost and maintenance cost of their internal communications system. . . .

It was fraudulent and deceitful to add to each billing after the room charge "Sund's" without any explanation, itemization or identification.

[The Waldorf argues] that there was no violation of General Business Law section 206 because that section only prohibits charges "for any service not actually rendered . . ." and that message services in fact were rendered. However, even [Waldorf admits] that all . . . customers did not receive special, costly messenger service. . . . None . . . received any explanation or itemization of the charge for sundries. All of them were charged this 2% during the period in question.

In any event, the practice was fraudulent within the meaning of the Executive Law, section 63(12) wherein fraud is defined as "any device, scheme or artifice to defraud and any deception, misrepresentation, concealment . . . or unconscionable contractual provisions.". . .

The amount of money to be refunded is admitted. The petitioner, by its Bureau of Consumer Frauds and Protection, investigated the records of the respondents and claims that the 2% charge for sundries during the period in question involved 64,338 customers and amounts to $113,202.83. . . .

Refunds are to be made within 60 days of the date of service of the judgment herein with notice of entry. Within 30 days thereafter cancelled vouchers or copies thereof will be exhibited to the petitioner. If payment cannot be made to any customer for any reason, the amounts thereof will be deposited with the petitioner who will deposit same with the Court if restitution cannot be made (Abandoned Property Law section 600). Petitioner may suggest another method of creating a fund to assure restitution upon settlement of judgment, if so advised.

[Judgment for plaintiff]

Bartels v Retail Credit Co.

185 Neb 304, 175 NW2d 292 (1970)

Bartels applied for life insurance to the Northwestern Mutual Life Insurance Company and to the Surety Life Insurance Company. These companies requested information on Bartels from the Retail Credit Company, a merchantile reporting agency. It made a report indicating that Bartels was an excessive drinker. Because of this he was refused life insurance and the Farmers Insurance Group cancelled his automobile insurance. Bartels sued the Retail Credit Company for damages for defamation. From a judgment for Bartels, Retail Credit appealed.

SPENCER, J. . . . The reports were privileged and not subject to an action for defamation. . . .

. . . Reports of mercantile agencies, published in good faith and based upon probable cause, are subject to a qualified or conditional privilege, and ordinarily are not subject to an action for defamation. . . . We are of the opinion that reports made by a mercantile agency to an interested subscriber should be conditionally privileged. A publication loses its character as privileged and is actionable if it is motivated by express or actual malice or if there is such a gross disregard of the rights of the person injured as is equivalent to malice in fact. . . .

The defendant argues: "The reason for the privilege granted in connection with a retail credit report is obvious. It is the necessity of the service of mercantile agencies to the business world and the fact that without the qualified privilege, such agencies would be unable to function properly and business and industry would ultimately suffer the consequences because reports on their proposed customers would either not be obtainable or would be long delayed."

We recognize the need for the services of mercantile agencies, but we must not lose sight also of the need to protect an individual from the secret destruction of his good name and reputation. Users of reports of mercantile agencies usually have utmost confidence in the accuracy of such reports and act accordingly. Consequently, the privilege granted to such agencies must be a qualified one. The privilege

must be predicated upon the premise that the reporting agency will exercise all reasonable care to ascertain the facts. Such reports must be compiled with regard to the effect the report will have upon the rights of the subject of the report. To be privileged, a mercantile agency's representatives must act impartially and in good faith, carefully evaluating all information before disseminating any defamatory statements to its subscribers. This requires them to make a thorough and complete investigation and to fully and accurately report information only from reliable sources. An erroneous or careless report serves no purpose except to substantially damage the subject of the report, and when once the report is published, the damage has been done and very little can be done to correct it. . . .

[Judgment reversed because of improper instructions given by the trial court to the jury on other issues]

QUESTIONS AND CASE PROBLEMS

1. What is the object of each of the following rules of law:
   (a) Back-page disclaimers are void if the front page of the contract does not call attention to the presence of such terms.
   (b) A consumer's waiver of a statute designed for consumer protection is void, but the transaction otherwise binds the consumer.
2. Name the two most common seals of approval established by magazines and what is the extent of the obligation imposed by them?
3. A state statute prohibited false advertising. A bank advertised the "per annum" interest on its loans but did not state that the year to which it referred was a year of 360 days. An action was brought against the bank for false advertising. It raised the defense that in the banking industry it was customary to regard a year as consisting of 360 days and that in doing what all banks did it was clear that there was no intent to defraud anyone. Was this a valid defense? [Chern v Bank of America, 15 Cal3d 866, 127 CalRptr 110, 544 P2d 1310]
4. A debtor borrowed money from a bank to construct a building. The promissory note signed by the debtor called for payments in installments and gave the bank the right to call the entire balance due if any installment were not paid. The debtor missed some payments on the note. The New England Mutual Life Insurance Company which then held the note brought an action for the entire balance of the note against the debtor, the Luxury Home Builders. The debtor raised the defense that it could not be held liable for the entire debt because the acceleration clause was contrary to public policy and that its failure to pay was excused because it did not make payment because of personal and business misfortune. Was Luxury Home liable? [New England Mut. Life Ins. Co. v Luxury Home Builders, Inc. (FlaApp) 311 So2d 160]
5. Clairol is a manufacturer of hair dyes. In order to save packaging costs and for advertising purposes, it sold to jobbers for resale to beauty parlors and beauty schools bottles of

dyes in cartons containing six bottles marked "Professional Use Only." Cody's Cosmetics, a discount retailer, procured and broke the six packs and sold the bottles individually to the general public. Clairol's products would deteriorate with time when exposed to light. Cody's displayed the individual bottles in open bins exposed to bright store lighting and sold some bottles after the product life date placed on the bottles by Clairol had expired. Clairol sought to enjoin as unfair competition the sale of its hair dyes by Cody's in the manner above described. Was it entitled to an injunction? [Clairol v Cody's Cosmetics, 353 Mass 385, 231 NE2d 912]

6. Wilke was contemplating retiring. In response to an advertisement, he purchased from Coinway 30 coin-operated testing machines. He purchased these because Coinway's representative stated that, by placing these machines at different public places, Wilke could obtain supplemental income. This statement was made by the representative although he had no experience as to the cost of servicing such machines or their income-producing potential. The operational costs of the machines by Wilke exceeded the income. Wilke sued Coinway to rescind the contract for fraud. Wilke defended on the ground that the statements made were merely matters of opinion and did not constitute fraud. Was Wilke entitled to rescission? [Wilke v Coinway, Inc., 257 Cal App 2d 126, 64 Cal Rptr 845]

7. On loans made by Test, who ran a pawn shop, he charged 10 percent per month whereas the maximum interest rate allowed was 10 percent per year. Test used the excess charges to defray overhead costs—storage, paper work, and insurance. Test did not make any profit from such charges but made his profit from the resale of pawned articles that were not redeemed by their owners. Miller borrowed money from Test and later claimed that the transactions were usurious because of the "overhead" charges. Was he correct? [Miller v Test, 243 Ark 694, 421 SW2d 345]

8. Greif obtained credit cards from Socony Mobil Oil Co. for himself and his wife. The card specified, "This card is valid unless expired or revoked. Named holder's approval of all purchases is presumed unless written notice of loss or theft is received." Later Greif returned his card to the company, stating that he was canceling it, but that he could not return the card in his wife's possession because they had separated. Subsequently Socony sued Greif for purchases made by the wife on the credit card in her possession. He defended on the ground that he had canceled the credit card contract. Decide. [Socony Mobil Oil Co. v Greif, 10 App Div 2d 119, 197 NYS2d 522]

9. Jordan purchased a stereo from Montgomery Ward & Co. on credit in reliance on the statement in the seller's catalog that the purchase could be charged and no payment would be required until several months later. It was not disclosed that the credit charge was computed by the seller from the date of purchase and not from the later date when payment was due. Jordan claimed that this violated the federal Truth in Lending Act, which requires a disclosure of financing terms in advertising and further provides that "any creditor who fails in connection with any consumer credit transaction to disclose to any person any information required under this Act to be disclosed to that person is liable to that person in an amount equal to . . . twice the amount of the finance charges . . . except that liability under this paragraph shall not be less than $100 nor greater than $1,000." The seller contended that Jordan could not bring suit. Decide. [Jordan v Montgomery Ward & Co., (CA8 Minn) 442 F2d 78]

10. Romain sold educational materials on a house-to-house sales basis, catering to minority groups and persons of limited education and economic means. The materials were sold at a price approximately two and a half times the reasonable market value of the materials if they were fit for their intended purpose, but there was evidence that much of it was practically worthless. Kugler, the Attorney General, brought a class-action suit on behalf

of all customers of Romain to declare their contracts invalid. Decide. [Kugler v Romain, 58 NJ 522, 279 A2d 640]

11. A New York statute authorized a buyer to cancel a home-solicited sale by giving written notice within three days. Becerra went to the office of Nu Dimensions Figure Salons and signed a contract to take a course of 190 weight-reducing sessions. The contract declared that "buyer specifically acknowledges and understands that the sum promised to be paid herein shall be paid whether or not buyer avails herself of the sessions purchased." When Becerra got home she decided that she did not want the course and notified Nu Dimensions that she cancelled her contract. Was she entitled to do so? [Nu Dimensions Figure Salons v Becerra, (NY Civil Court) 340 NYS2d 268]

12. The Consumer Protection Law of 1969 for the city of New York created the office of Commissioner of Consumer Affairs and authorized the Commissioner to adopt regulations outlawing "unconscionable trade practices." He adopted a regulation by which a creditor, or an agency on his behalf, was prohibited from informing a debtor's employer that money was owed by the employee unless a judgment had been obtained by the creditor. This regulation was adopted in the belief that there had been widespread harassment of employees by notifying their employers, with the result that employees frequently paid nonmeritorious claims for fear of losing their jobs. The Commercial Lawyers Conference brought an action against Grant, the Commissioner of Consumer Affairs, to enjoin enforcement of the regulation on the ground that it interfered with a creditor's freedom of speech. Decide. [Commercial Lawyers Conference v Grant, 318 NYS2d 966]

13. Green ran a fraudulent ad for sixty days. He was prosecuted under a false advertising statute which made it "unlawful . . . to cause to be inserted in any newspaper any false . . . advertisement." The maximum fine provided by the statute was $500. Green was charged with 60 violations of the law. He defended on the ground that he had engaged in false advertising once and that each day was not a separate offense. Was he correct? [Green v United States (DistColApp) 312 A2d 788]

Part Three • Contracts

9 Nature and Classes of Contracts

Practically every personal business activity involves a contract—an enrollment in college, the purchase of a color TV on the installment plan, the rental of an apartment. Similarly, in each transaction relating to the acquisition of raw materials, their manufacture, and the distribution of the finished products by businesses, a contract that defines the relationship and the rights and obligations of the parties is involved.

Essential to free enterprise in our economic system is the protection of rights created by contracts. Each party to a contract is legally obligated to observe the terms of the agreement, and government generally cannot impair those obligations.

§ 9:1. Definition of Contract. A contract is a binding agreement.[1] By one definition "a *contract* is a promise or a set of promises for the breach of which the law gives a remedy, or the performance of which the law in some way recognizes as a duty."[2] Contracts arise out of agreements; hence, a contract is often defined as "an agreement creating an obligation."[3]

The substance of the definition of a contract is that by mutual agreement or assent the parties create legally enforceable duties or obligations that had not existed before.

§ 9:2. Essential Elements of a Contract. The requirements of a contract are: (1) an agreement, (2) between competent parties, (3) based upon the genuine assent of the parties, (4) supported by consideration, (5) made for a lawful objective, and (6) in the form required by law, if any. These elements will be considered in the chapters that follow.

---

[1] The Uniform Commercial Code defines "contract" to mean "the total legal obligation which results from the parties' agreement as affected by [the Code] and any other applicable rules of law," UCC § 1-201(11).

[2] Restatement, Contracts, (2d) § 1; Mag Construction Co. v McLean County (ND) 181 NW2d 718.

[3] H. Liebes & Co. v Klengenberg (CA9 Cal) 23 F2d 611.

§ 9:3. Subject Matter of Contracts. The subject matter of a contract may relate to the performance of personal services, such as contracts of employment to work on an assembly line in a factory, to work as a secretary in an office, to sing on television, or to build a house. The contract may provide for the transfer of the ownership of property, such as a house (real property) or an automobile (personal property), from one person to another. A contract may also call for a combination of these things. For example, a builder may contract to supply materials and do the work involved in installing the materials, or a person may contract to build a house and then transfer the house and the land to the buyer.

§ 9:4. Parties to a Contract. A person who makes a promise is the *promisor,* and the person to whom the promise is made is called the *promisee.* If the promise is binding, it imposes upon the promisor a duty or obligation and the promisor may be called the *obligor.* The promisee who can claim the benefit of the obligation is also called the *obligee.* The parties to a contract are said to stand in privity with each other, and the relationship between them is termed *privity of contract.*

In written contracts, parties may be referred to as "party of the first part" and "party of the second part." Frequently, however, they are given special names that serve better to identify each party. For example, the parties to a contract by which one person agrees that another may occupy a house upon the payment of money are called landlord and tenant, or lessor and lessee, and the contract between them is known as a lease. Other parties have their distinctive names, such as vendor and vendee, for the parties of a sales contract; shipper and carrier, for the parties to a transportation contract; insurer and insured, for the parties of an insurance policy.

A party to a contract may be an individual, a partnership, a corporation, or a government. A party to a contract may be an agent acting on behalf of another person. There may be one or more persons on each side of the contract. In some cases there are three-sided contracts, as in the case of a credit card transaction, which involves the company issuing the card, the holder of the card, and the business furnishing goods and services in reliance on the credit card.

In addition to the original parties to the contract, other persons may have rights or duties with respect to it. For example, one party may to some extent assign rights under the contract to a third person. Again, the contract may have been made for the benefit of a third person, as in a life insurance contract, and the third party (the beneficiary) is permitted to enforce the contract.

§ 9:5. How a Contract Arises. A contract is based upon an agreement. An agreement arises when one person, the *offeror,* makes an offer and the person to whom the offer is made, the *offeree,* accepts. There must be both an offer and an acceptance. If either is lacking, there is no contract.[4]

An offeror may make an offer to a particular person or it may be made to the public at large. The latter case arises, for example, when a reward is offered to the public for the return of lost property.

---

[4] Milanko v Jensen, 404 Ill 261, 88 NE2d 857.

THIS AGREEMENT is made on September 6, 1978, between Kenneth D, Shaw,

2628 Dawes Lane, Des Moines, Iowa, the party of the first part, and John W.

Gordon, 788 Ackley Road, Des Moines, Iowa, the party of the second part.

The party of the first part agrees [here state what he agrees to do;

as: to install aluminum triple-track storm windows in the home of the

party of the second part at (address) by (date) in accordance with the

specifications attached hereto.]

The party of the second part agrees [here state what he agrees to do,

as: to pay the party of the first part $ 575.94 upon the satisfactory

completion of the work.]

Kenneth D. Shaw

John W. Gordon

CONTRACT

Note that this contract includes the important items of information: (1) the date, (2) the name and address of each party, (3) the promise or consideration of the seller, (4) the promise or consideration of the buyer, and (5) the signatures of the two parties.

It is frequently said that a meeting of the minds is essential to an agreement or a contract. Modern courts do not stress the meeting of the minds, however, because in some situations the law finds an agreement even though the minds of the parties have not in fact met.

The real test is not whether the minds of the parties met, but whether under the circumstances one party was reasonably entitled to believe that there was an offer and the other to believe that there was an acceptance.

§ 9:6. Intent to Make a Binding Agreement. Because a contract is based on the consent of the parties and is a legally binding agreement, it follows that there must be an intent to enter into an agreement which is binding. Even when an agreement appears on its face to be a final agreement, it may be shown to be "noncontractual" by its own terms or by the subject matter of the agreement and the surrounding circumstances. (See p. 135, Pappas v Hauser)

When the elements of a contract exist there is a binding contract, even though there is no express statement that the parties are making a contract, that a promise is made, or that something is consideration for a promise. Consequently, when the subcontractors on a construction job were threatening to quit work because they were afraid the contractor would not pay them, the owner became bound by a contract to pay them when the owner told the subcontractors, "Don't do that. I'll see that you get your money," and "Don't worry about it"; as against the contention that there was no contract because the owner had not made an express promise to pay the subcontractors.

§ 9:7. Working Arrangements. Working arrangements between parties are sometimes not regarded as "contracts" because it is in fact not the intention of the parties to be so bound thereby that suit could be brought for nonperformance. For example, when a city agreed to provide firefighting protection for an area adjoining the city in order to protect the city from the hazard of the spread of an outlying fire, there was no contract, even though persons in the outlying area made money donations or payments in exchange for such fire protection.

When a working arrangement is part of a clearly contractual relationship, the transaction remains a binding contract because the purpose of the working arrangement is merely to provide flexibility to a contract. Consequently, a contract by which a bank agrees to accept the assignment from a dealer of such contracts as the bank shall deem "acceptable" remains a contract, even though theoretically the bank could refuse to find any contract acceptable. Likewise, a contract to pay commissions to a sales agent on a specified sliding scale on orders under one-quarter million dollars and to pay on larger orders such compensation as shall be agreed to remains a binding contract obligating the employer to pay the agent reasonable compensation for orders over one-quarter million dollars, as against the contention that there was no contract because the parties might never agree to the compensation to be paid on the large orders.

§ 9:8. Statistical Projections. Many transactions contemplate future events or benefits. For example, a person may obtain a life insurance policy which pays a certain amount of income per month upon retirement or a person might take a particular job because of the pension plan benefits offered by that employer. In the course of negotiation or discussion leading up to a contract, one party to a transaction may show the other party various charts, tables, and statistical projections into the future to show the actual dollar value of the particular transaction to the other party. It is a question of intent to what extent such matter is merely illustrative and to what extent it is part of the contract. If it is merely illustrative and there is no element of fraudulent deception, there is no liability when the subsequent facts are different than had been projected or estimated. If it is part of the contract, then if there is a difference between the projection and the subsequent reality, there is breach of contract and liability will be imposed accordingly.

§ 9:9. Enclosed Printed Matter. Frequently a contract is mailed or delivered by one party to the other in an envelope which contains additional printed matter. Similarly, when goods are purchased, the buyer often receives with the goods a manufacturer's manual and various pamphlets. What effect do all these papers have upon the contract?

(a) Incorporation of Other Statement. The contract itself may furnish the answer. Sometimes the contract will expressly refer to and incorporate into the contract the terms of the other writing or printed statement. For example, a warehouse contract may expressly state that it covers the "goods" of the customer, but instead of listing the goods, the contract will continue by following the words "goods of the customer" with the words "as set forth in Schedule A which is delivered to the customer with this contract." Frequently such a schedule will be stapled or otherwise attached to the contract itself. Or the contract may say that the customer will be charged at the rates set forth in the approved tariff schedule posted on the premises of the warehouse, and may continue with the words, "a copy of which is attached hereto and made part of this contract."

(b) Exclusion of Other Statement. As the opposite of incorporation, the contract may declare that there is nothing outside of the contract. This means that either there never was anything else or that any prior agreement was merely a preliminary step which is finally canceled out or erased and the contract in its final form is stated in the writing. For example, the seller of goods may state in the contract that no statements as to the goods have been made to the buyer and that the written contract contains all of the terms of the sale.

In a strict sense an exclusion clause is unnecessary because if there is a written contract, it will ordinarily be regarded as the entire contract and anything outside of that contract will be ignored. As a practical matter, however, the exclusion clause has value in that some situations arise when it is not quite clear whether the writing is the entire contract or whether the situation is to be treated as though the writing had expressly stated that the earlier terms were incorporated into the contract. In order to avoid uncertainty and make clear the intent of the parties, a provision stating that the writing is the total and exclusive contract has practical value.

(c) Reduction of Contract Terms. The effect of accompanying or subsequently delivered printed matter may be to reduce the terms of the written contract. That is, one party may have had a better bargain under the original contract. In this case the accompanying matter will generally be ignored if it is not shown that the party who would be harmed has agreed that it be part of the contract. (See p. 136, Adamick v Ferguson-Florissant School District)

If a contract has already been made and the accompanying matter seeks to reduce the rights of one party, as when the manufacturer's manual reduces the rights which the buyer would otherwise have, such reducing writing has no effect. A contract once made cannot be changed by unilateral action; that is, by the action of one party or one side to the contract without the agreement of the other.

§ 9:10. Formal and Simple Contracts. Contracts are classified in terms of their form as (a) contracts under seal, (b) contracts of record, and (c) simple contracts. The first two classes are formal contracts.

formal k

(a) Contracts Under Seal. A *contract under seal* is executed by affixing a seal or making an impression upon the paper or upon some tenacious substance, such as wax, attached to the instrument. Although at common law an impression was necessary, the courts now treat various signs or marks to be the equivalent of a seal. Most states hold that there is a seal if a person's signature or a corporation's name is followed by a scroll or scrawl, the word "seal," or the letters "L.S."

A contract under seal was binding at common law solely because of its formality. In many states, this has been changed by statute. The Uniform Commercial Code abolishes the law of seals for the sale of goods. In some states the law of seals has been abolished generally without regard to the nature of the transaction involved.

(b) Contracts of Record. One form of *contract of record* arises when one acknowledges before a proper court the obligation to pay a certain sum unless a specified thing is done or not done. For example, a party who has been arrested may be released on a promise to appear in court and may agree to pay a certain sum on failing to do so. An obligation of this kind is known as a *recognizance.*

Similarly, an agreement made with an administrative agency is binding because it has been so made. For example, when a business agrees with the Federal Trade Commission that the enterprise will stop a particular practice which the Commission regards as unlawful, the business is bound by its agreement and cannot thereafter reject it.

(c) Simple Contract. All contracts other than contracts of record and contracts under seal are called *simple contracts* or informal contracts, without regard to whether they are oral or written.

§ 9:11. Express and Implied Contracts. Simple contracts may be classified in terms of the way in which they are created, as express contracts or implied contracts.

(a) Express Contracts. An *express contract* is one in which the parties have made oral or written declarations of their intentions and of the terms of the transaction.

(b) Implied Contracts. An *implied contract* (or, as sometimes stated, a contract implied in fact) is one in which the evidence of the agreement is not shown by words, written or spoken, but by the acts and conduct of the parties.[5] Such a contract arises, for example, when one person renders services under circumstances indicating that payment for them is expected, and the other person, knowing such circumstances, accepts the benefit of those services. (See p. 136, First National Bank v Stoberl)

In terms of effect, there is no difference between an implied contract and an express contract. The difference relates solely to the manner of proving the existence of the contract.

An implied contract cannot arise when there is an existing express contract on the same subject. Likewise, no contract is implied when the relationship of the parties is such that by a reasonable interpretation the performance of services or the supplying of goods was intended as a gift.

---

[5] Capital Warehouse Co. v McGill-Warner Farnham Co. 276 Minn 108, 148 NW2d 31. Contracts of this nature may be more accurately described as contracts "expressed" by conduct, as distinguished from contracts expressed in words. It is more common, however, to refer to these contracts as implied.

§ 9:12. Valid and Voidable Contracts and Void Agreements. Another classification of contracts is in terms of their enforceability or validity.

(a) **Valid Contracts.** A *valid contract* is an agreement that is binding and enforceable.

(b) **Voidable Contracts.** A *voidable contract* is an agreement that is otherwise binding and enforceable but, because of the circumstances surrounding its execution or the lack of capacity of one of the parties, it may be rejected at the option of one of the parties. For example, one who has been forced to sign an agreement involuntarily may in some instances avoid the contract.

(c) **Void Agreements.** A *void agreement* is without legal effect. An agreement that contemplates the performance of an act prohibited by law is usually incapable of enforcement; hence it is void. Likewise, it cannot be made binding by later approval or ratification.[6]

§ 9:13. Executed and Executory Contracts. Contracts may be classified, in terms of the extent to which they have been performed, as executed contracts and executory contracts.

(a) **Executed Contracts.** An *executed contract* is one that has been completely performed. In other words, an executed contract is one under which nothing remains to be done by either party. A contract may be executed at once, as in the case of a cash sale; or it may be executed or performed in the future.

(b) **Executory Contracts.** In an *executory contract*, something remains to be done by one or both parties. For example, if a utility company agrees to furnish electricity to a customer for a specified period of time at a stipulated price, the contract is executory. If the entire price is paid in advance, the contract is still deemed executory; although, strictly speaking, it is executed on one side and executory on the other.

Whether a contract is executory determines in some cases whether it can be set aside by a minor or a trustee in bankruptcy of a party. In some cases, if it is executed, it cannot be set aside; if it is executory, it can.

§ 9:14. Bilateral and Unilateral Contracts. In making an offer, the offeror is in effect extending a promise to do something, such as to pay a sum of money, if the offeree will do what the offeror requests. If the offeror extends a promise and asks for a promise in return and if the offeree accepts the offer by making the promise, the contract is called a *bilateral contract* because one promise is given in exchange for another and each party is bound by the obligation. For example, when the house painter offers to paint the owner's house for $1000 and the owner promises to pay $1000 for the job, there is an exchange of promises and the agreement gives rise to a bilateral contract.

In contrast, the offeror may offer to do something only when something is done by the offeree. As only one party is obligated to perform after the contract has been made, this kind of contract is called a *unilateral contract*. This is illustrated by the case of the reward for the return of lost property because the offeror does

---

[6] See § 15:1. Although the distinction between a void agreement and a voidable contract is clear in principle, there is frequently confusion because some courts describe a given transaction as void while others regard it as merely voidable.

not wish to have promises by members of the public that they will try to return
the property. The offeror wants the property and promises to pay anyone who returns
the property.

§ 9:15. Quasi Contracts.

(a) Prevention of Unjust Enrichment. Under certain circumstances, the law imposes
an obligation to pay for a benefit received as though a contract had actually been
made. This will be done in a limited number of situations in order to attain an
equitable or just result. For example, when a homeowner permits repairs to be made
with the knowledge that they are being made by a stranger who would expect to
be paid for such repairs, there is a quasi-contractual duty to pay for the reasonable
value of the improvements in order to avoid the homeowner's unjust enrichment at
the expense of the person making the repairs. (See p. 137, Continental Forest Products,
Inc. v Chandler Supply Co.) In order to distinguish this type of obligation from a
true contract which is based upon the agreement of the parties, the obligation is
called a *quasi contract*. It is to be distinguished from an implied contract, as a contract
for repairs, in which the homeowner communicates to the repairer the homeowner's
willingness that repairs be made and the circumstances are such that a reasonable
person would expect that compensation would be paid for such repairs.

(b) When Quasi-Contractual Liability Does Not Exist. While the objective of the
quasi contract is to do justice, one must not jump to the conclusion that a quasi
contract will arise every time there is an injustice. The mere fact that someone has
benefitted someone else and has not been paid will not necessarily give rise to a
quasi contract. For example, no quasi contractual obligation arises when the plaintiff
merely confers upon the defendant a benefit to which the defendant was already
entitled.

(1) Unexpected Cost. The fact that performance of a contract proves more
difficult or more expensive than had been expected does not entitle a party to
extra compensation when there was no misrepresentation as to the conditions
that would be encountered or the events that would occur and particularly
when the party complaining is experienced with the particular type of contract
and the problems which are likely to be encountered. That is, the contractor
is not entitled to a quasi-contractual recovery for extra expense on the theory
that the extra work had conferred a greater benefit than had been contemplated.

(2) Disappointed Expectations. If a person wrongly concludes that there is
or will be a binding contract and proceeds to make purchases on that assumption,
there is no right to recover for the loss sustained when the other person refuses
thereafter to enter into a contract which is binding.[7]

(3) Contract With Third Person. When a person has a binding contract with
a third person, only that person is required to pay for the performance made
under the contract. Even though the performance conferred a benefit upon
the defendant, the person cannot sue the defendant for quasi contract when

---

[7] Brighenti v New Britain Shirt Corp., 167 Conn 403, 356 A2d 181.

the third person fails to make payment under the contract. (See p. 139, Haggard Drilling Inc. v Greene) For example, a subcontractor doing work which benefits the homeowner can only sue the contractor on the contract between the subcontractor and the contractor. The subcontractor cannot sue the owner merely because the owner was benefitted by the work done by the subcontractor.[8]

[8] Seegers v Sprague, 70 Wis 2d 997, 236 NW2d 227. Note that state statutes generally give unpaid laborers and suppliers of material a mechanics' lien on the building they construct in order to overcome the inability to sue the owner. § 42:5(b).

CASES FOR CHAPTER 9

Pappas v Hauser *

(Iowa) 197 NW2d 607 (1972)

A movement was organized to build a Charles City College. Hauser and others signed pledges to contribute to the college. The college failed financially and Pappas was appointed receiver to collect and liquidate the assets of the college corporation. He sued Hauser for the amount due on his pledge. Judgment was entered for Pappas and Hauser appealed.

UHLENHIPP, J. . . . The original pledge form stated, "It is my intention to contribute the sum of $——— to the College Founder's Fund." The form also recited, "This is a statement of intention and expectation and shall not constitute a legal obligation and shall not be legally binding in any way.". . .

. . . The college promoters discovered that they could not obtain credit on the original pledge form. After consideration, they redrafted the form by dropping the statement that the pledge was not a legal obligation and by making the form read "I/we intend to subscribe to the College Founder's Fund the sum of ——— Dollars.". . .

. . . Bruno approached . . . Hauser for a pledge. . . . The redrafted pledge form was then in use. Before Hauser signed the pledge form, he and Bruno had a discussion about its meaning. [It was agreed that when Hauser asked]: "What if I should die, have a financial reversal or the College should fail?" Mr. Bruno said, "this is only an intent

*The structure or anatomy of a judicial opinion is considered in § 2:7. See also § 2:8. Checklist for Case Study.

and not binding and if anything like this should happen you just forget it.". . .

Hauser did not pay his pledge and the receiver commenced the present action against him to have the pledge declared obligatory. . . .

. . . A subscription by which a person for a consideration *binds himself to pay* is a contract. . . . The first issue is whether Hauser "bound himself to pay.". . .

[It was agreed that when Hauser] asked what would happen if he died, had a financial reversal, or the college failed, Bruno answered that the pledge was only a letter of intent and not binding and if anything like that happened "just forget it." This . . . indicates that the pledge was not intended to be obligatory.

The receiver is correct that Hauser also stated at trial at the time he signed the pledge he intended to pay. We have no doubt Hauser did intend to pay; the pledge says so. But that conclusion does not answer the question before us. The question is, was that intention to pay *to be obligatory?*

This is not one of those cases in which a writing is intended as a nullity or a sham. The problem here relates to the *meaning* of a writing which was intended to be effective. We have no doubt the participants intended the pledge to be effective. But effective as what—as a legal obligation or as a nonobligatory declaration of what Hauser planned to do? . . . We think the pledge was intended not legally obligatory. . . .

Three possible pledge forms may be considered. The first one is the original pledge. That form was clear and certain that a legal obligation was not intended; the form so stated. The second possible form is on the other extreme. When the college promoters discovered they could not obtain credit on the original pledge form, they could have drafted a form which was clear and certain that a legal obligation was in fact intended: "I hereby subscribe" or "I promise to pay" or an expression of like import. But the promoters did not adopt such a form. Instead, they took a middle course and drafted a third possible form: "I/we intend to subscribe" and "I intend to pay [] Monthly," etc. What does "intend" mean? . . .

. . . "Care should be taken not to attach promissory and contractual effect to what was at the time merely an expression of intention concerning future action"; . . . "The expression of an *intention* to do a thing, is not a *promise* to do it.". . . "A declaration of intention to act in a certain way, which does not show that the party who makes such declaration promises to act in such way, or intends to incur a legal liability obliging him to act in such way, is not an offer which can be accepted so as to make a contract.". . .

We conclude that the pledge is not obligatory . . . [and] deny liability.

[Judgment reversed]

Adamick v Ferguson-Florissant School District

(Mo App) 483 SW2d 629 (1972)

The School District mailed a teaching contract to Adamick. In the same envelope there was a copy of the school calendar. Adamick and other teachers later brought an action against the school to prevent it from holding classes on three specified dates not listed on the calendar. The District defended on the ground that the calendar could be changed by the District.

CLEMENS, J. . . . The critical issue is whether the calendar is part of the teachers' contract and thus not subject to change without the teachers' consent.

For financial reasons school did not start as scheduled and the district issued a revised calendar by which there were several changes in days of school attendance. . . .

. . . The teachers contend the original school calendar is an integral part of their contract which the district could not change unilaterally. Conversely, the district contends the contract itself is the complete agreement, that the original calendar

was merely the announcement of the district's school attendance plan, and changing it by the revised calendar was but a matter of discretionary management.

The general law of contracts applies in the construction of teachers' contracts. . . . Under certain circumstances several documents may be read as a single contract. However, each case the teachers cite involved an actual reference on the face of the contract to a set of rules or an explanatory document which is thereby made a part of the contract. There is no such reference here. Therefore, the cases cited by the teachers are not persuasive.

The intention of the parties must govern the interpretation and construction of a contract. . . . [A contract] "should be interpreted and read in the light of the circumstances of the parties at the time." . . . The contract was mailed at a time when all parties knew there was a substantial possibility the district's voters would not pass a new tax rate and some sort of schedule disruption was likely; the letter of transmittal mentioned the financial crisis. It cannot reasonably be presumed that the school board— well aware of its precarious financial situation—intended to lock itself into a rigid attendance schedule fixed by contract.

Moreover, the contract itself states that the teacher is hired to teach "such number of days as the board of education establishes." If the parties intended to fix the work schedule by contract, this clause is meaningless; the quoted language contemplates unilateral action on the part of the board. We cannot ignore this express language and say the parties intended it to be of no effect.

. . . The calendar did not become a part of the contract. . . .

[Relief denied]

First National Bank v Stoberl

132 Ill App 2d 322, 270 NE2d 493 (1973)

Glenn owned and operated the Seminole Bus Company. The First National Bank held a chattel mortgage on the buses. Stoberl ran a gas and service station. Glenn and Stoberl made an agreement that if Glenn would buy all his gas and have all his repairs made at Stoberl's, he could park his buses at Stoberl's without charge. Because of illness, Glenn stopped running the bus business. He stored the buses at Stoberl's station. Some time thereafter the bank sued Stoberl for possession of the buses. He defended on the ground that he was holding the buses

for storage charges under agreement for storage with the bank.

DEMPSEY, J. . . . Leonard Brody, a vice-president of the bank and the bank's sole witness at the trial, testified that the bank did not receive the October and November mortgage installments due from Glenn, and early in December learned that he was ill and that the vehicles were stored at Stoberl's service station. Brody and another official of the bank visited the station. Stoberl informed them that he needed the space occupied by the buses and wished to have them removed. On December 23, 1966, the bank wrote a letter asking him to prepare the vehicles for winter and saying that it would like to work out an arrangement "wherein we will guarantee payment of reasonable storage charges from this point on." Stoberl winterized the buses and the bank paid him $200.00.

During the succeeding months, the parties conducted discussions concerning a possible agreement for the storage charges. Stoberl demanded $7.50 a day for each bus but later reduced this to $4.50 a day. On March 9, 1967, he served a five-day notice for unpaid rent and followed this up with an eviction action in the Circuit Court. However, he dismissed this action and on March 21, 1967, his attorney received a letter from the bank saying that it would be willing to pay $200.00 a month and would be willing to negotiate a settlement for past due rent. No definite agreement was reached. . . .

. . . Stoberl contends that the evidence was sufficient to establish that the dealings between him and the bank constituted a contract implied in law under which the bank was bound to pay reasonable storage charges for the buses parked on his premises.

An implied contract is an obligation created by law independent of an agreement of the parties. It arises out of the acts and conduct of the parties— out of circumstances from which the intent to contract can be inferred. . . .

Such a contract was found to exist in Shaw v. Blessman, 67 Ill. App. 2d 242, 213 N.E.2d 784 (1966). There, the plaintiff, without any express agreement, permitted the defendants to use her trailer for storage purposes. The defendants accepted the benefits of the trailer under such conditions that its use could not have been presumed to be gratuitous. The court determined that out of such acceptance and use there arose a promise implied in law that the defendants would make reasonable rental payments.

In the present case there was no express agreement between Stoberl and the bank, but the evidence discloses that the bank recognized that some compensation was due for storage. Although Brody testified that the bank felt no obligation to pay storage charges, and although a promise to settle is not necessarily a promise to pay . . . it must have been obvious to officials of the bank either from Stoberl's telephone call in October 1966 or when they called upon him in December, that he expected to be compensated monetarily for keeping the vehicles at his station. While there was no meeting of the minds thereafter as to the amount, the failure to agree on a specific sum cannot relieve the bank of the obligation to pay Stoberl for the use of his premises. The law, therefore, will imply a contract so that he may receive reasonable rental.

It may be argued that inasmuch as Glenn did not pay a specific amount for parking the buses, the bank should not be obliged to do so. However, Stoberl was entitled to rely upon the profits he derived from the continuous sale of gasoline, oil and repair work as rent. From the time the bank asserted authority over the buses, Stoberl received only $200.00—and this for preparing them against cold weather damage. This amount cannot be considered as payment in full for the privilege of using his property for several months.

. . . The case will be remanded so that the court may determine . . . the reasonable compensation due Stoberl for storage of the buses. . . .

[Reversed and action remanded]

Continental Forest Products, Inc. v Chandler Supply Co.

95 Idaho 739, 518 P2d 1201 (1974)

Chandler Supply Company ordered two carloads of lumber from North America Millwork. Continental Forest Products acknowledged the Chandler orders which apparently had been taken to that company when Barker of North America left and went to work for Continental Forest. Chandler assumed that Continental was filling its orders on behalf of North America. Chandler kept the lumber but informed Continental that he had ordered it from North America. North America owed Chandler approximately $6,000 which Chandler expected to set off against the purchase price of its new order. Chandler offered to pay North America the purchase price of the lumber less the $6,000. North America refused to accept payment because the money for the lumber

was owed to Continental. Continental, however, demanded full payment without any deduction for the $6,000 owed by North America. Continental sued Chandler and obtained a judgment against Chandler for the full purchase price of the lumber without any deduction for the $6,000 debt due by North America. Chandler appealed.

BAKES, J. . . . This was Chandler's first order for plywood from North America Millwork, although it had transacted a considerable volume of other lumber business with North America Millwork between December, 1968, and July, 1969. . . .

. . . It is not entirely clear how Continental received Chandler's orders sent to North America. Apparently Ed Barker left his employment with North America and commenced brokering for Continental and gave the orders to Continental. . . .

. . . The trial . . . court discussed the relationship between Continental and Chandler and found that "the very least we have was an implied agreement or quasi contract."

Basically the courts have recognized three types of contractual arrangements. . . . First is the express contract wherein the parties expressly agree regarding a transaction. . . . Secondly, there is the implied in fact contract wherein there is no express agreement but the conduct of the parties implies an agreement from which an obligation in contract exists. . . . The third category is called an implied in law contract, or quasi contract. However, a contract implied in law is not a contract at all, but an obligation imposed by law for the purpose of bringing about justice and equity without reference to the intent or the agreement of the parties and, in some cases, in spite of an agreement between the parties. . . . It is a noncontractual obligation that is to be treated procedurally *as if* it were a contract, and is often referred to as quasi contract, unjust enrichment, implied in law contract or restitution. . . . "The promise is purely fictitious and unintentional, originally implied to circumvent rigid common-law pleading. It was invoked . . . to create one 'for the purpose of bringing about justice without reference to the intention of the parties.' . . .". . .

In this case it is clear that there is neither an express nor an implied in fact contract since there was [no intention] by Chandler . . . to enter into a contract with Continental. . . . However, we agree with the trial court that under the peculiar circumstances of this case, the third type of contract, implied in law or quasi contract, exists obligating Chandler to pay for the materials which he received. However, the problem which arises is determining the amount of recovery to which Continental is entitled.

As the essence of a contract implied in law lies in the fact that the defendant has received a benefit which it would be inequitable for him to retain, it necessarily follows that the measure of recovery in a quasi-contractual action is not the actual amount of the enrichment, but the amount of the enrichment which, as between the two parties it would be unjust for one party to retain. . . . In the instant case we feel that the enrichment which Chandler "unjustly received" was the value of the plywood shipped less the trade set off which Chandler had against North America Millwork and which he would have been entitled to take had the transaction been completed the way Chandler had intended and attempted to complete it. Chandler had a right to deal exclusively with North America and use his trade set off as part of the purchase price. Chandler should not be deprived of this set off in view of the way that Continental became involved in this transaction. . . .

. . . If any party was responsible for the situation present in this case, it was Continental. Although it is not entirely clear from the record, it would appear that Barker breached the fiduciary duty which he owed to his employer North America Millwork by taking the Chandler purchase orders to Continental. Continental then, wittingly or unwittingly, took advantage of that breach of a fiduciary relationship and filled the orders, apparently without inquiry concerning the status of North America Millwork, the existence of a trade debt, the situation behind Barker's taking the purchase orders to Continental, or notifying Chandler that it was attempting to take over the North America transactions. Under these circumstances we feel that it would not be unjust to require Chandler to pay only that amount which he would have had to pay to North America had the transaction gone the way Chandler had intended and attempted to have it go.

Judgment should be entered for Continental against Chandler in the amount of the principal claim less the amount of the North America Millwork trade debt which Chandler had. . . .

[Judgment reversed and remanded]

Haggard Drilling, Inc. v Greene

195 Neb 136, 236 NW2d 841 (1975)

Maddux and his wife owned a track of land. They gave Greene and Lewis the option to purchase part of the land. The buyers agreed that at their expense they would have twelve irrigation wells drilled, seven on the part retained by the sellers and five on the land subject to the option. The agreement further provided that if the buyers exercised the option the purchase price would be reduced by the cost of the seven wells on the part retained by the sellers. The buyers made a contract with the Haggard Drilling Company to drill the wells. Lewis exercised the option to purchase the portion of the tract. Haggard was not paid and sued Greene, Lewis, and Maddux for breach of contract. Maddux raised the defense that he had not made any contract with Haggard. Haggard then claimed that Maddux was liable in quasi contract for the wells. From a decision in favor of Maddux, Haggard appealed.

Colnell, D.J. . . . There was no understanding between any of the parties that the sellers were to pay or underwrite or guarantee the payment for any of the wells drilled; and there is no evidence in the record that sellers at any time represented to the driller or its agent that they would pay for any such service or material. . . .

Beginning on May 1, 1970, and continuing through June 5, 1970, . . . wells were drilled. . . . During this time . . . Maddux was occasionally present observing the drilling work and, at times, he did make suggestions as to the location of some of the wells and the drilling work. He did not assume the role of directing the drilling work and he made no representation contrary to any term of the option. . . .

We next consider plaintiff's theory to recover on quasi contract based upon unjust enrichment flowing to defendants Maddux. There is little controversy in the evidence. . . .

"A quasi contract is a contract implied in law and usually has its origin in the principle that a person shall not be allowed to enrich himself unjustly at the expense of another. . . . Where benefits have been received and retained under such circumstances that it would be inequitable and unconscionable to permit the party receiving the benefits to avoid payment therefore, the law required the party receiving and retaining the benefits to pay the reasonable value of them.". . .

"The mere fact that a third person benefits from a contract between two other persons does not make such third person liable in quasi contract, unjust enrichment, or restitution. Moreover, where a third person benefits from a contract entered into between two other persons, in the absence of some misleading act by the third person, the mere failure of performance by one of the contracting parties does not give rise to a right of restitution against the third person.". . .

The failure of Greene and Lewis to be responsible credit risks cannot be a basis to provide equitable relief absent either fraud, misrepresentation, or wrongful conduct on the part of defendants Maddux; we find none of these present here. Defendants Maddux were not unjustly enriched. . . .

[Judgment affirmed]

QUESTIONS AND CASE PROBLEMS

1. State the specific objective(s) of the law (from the list in Chapter 2, pages 17–21) illustrated by the following quotation: "A person shall not be allowed to enrich himself unjustly at the expense of another."

   Note: *As you study the various rules of law in this chapter and the chapters that follow, consider each rule in relationship to its social, economic, and moral background. Try to determine the particular objective(s) of each important rule. To the extent that you are able to analyze law as the product of society striving for justice, you will have a greater insight into the law itself, the world in which you live, the field of business, and the mind of people.*

2. *A* made a contract to construct a house for *B*. Subsequently, *B* sued *A* for breach of contract. *A* raised the defense that the contract was not binding because it was not sealed. Is this a valid defense? [See Cooper v G.E. Construction Co., 116 Ga App 690, 158 SE2d 305]

3. Tetrauld made a written agreement to sell his land to Bauer. Tetrauld died. Bauer claimed that after agreement for the sale of the land had been made, they had orally agreed that Tetrauld would give the land to Bauer for his past services instead of selling it to him. Monroe, who was administering the estate of Tetrauld, objected to changing the written contract. A Montana statute provided that a "contract in writing may be altered by a contract in writing or by an executed oral agreement, and not otherwise." Was the oral agreement barred by this statute? [Bauer v Monroe, 117 Mont 306, 158 P2d 485]

4. Prior to the death of Emma Center, her nephew's wife, Clara Stewart, rendered various household services to Emma. All of the parties lived in the same house as a family group. During most of the time in question, Clara also had a full-time job. After Emma's death, Clara sued Emma's estate for the value of her household services. Was Clara entitled to recover? [Stewart v Brandenburg (Ky) 383 SW2d 1122]

5. Mrs. Herbert, the owner of an orchard, and Cantor, to whom she had leased the orchard, desired to borrow money so that a crop could be grown by the tenant. Part of the money required by them was loaned by the Pinnacle Packing Co. and the Medford National Bank. The loan agreement stated that the lenders would "furnish" the money and that when the crops were sold, there would be deducted a sufficient amount "to repay the advances made by [the lenders] before any payments would be made to the borrowers." There was no express provision in the agreement that the borrowers would repay the money. No oral agreement to repay was made by either borrower. Pinnacle Packing Co. then sued Herbert to recover the amount of the money advanced. She defended on the ground that she had not expressly agreed to repay the money borrowed. Decide. [Pinnacle Packing Co. v Herbert, 157 Ore 96, 70 P2d 31]

6. Martha Parker reared Louis Twiford as a foster son from the time he was 6 or 7 years of age. He lived with her until he was 27 years of age when he married and moved into another house. During the next few years Martha was very ill, and Louis took care of her. She died; and Louis made a claim against Waterfield, her executor, for the reasonable value of the services he had rendered. Was he entitled to recover? [Twiford v Waterfield, 240 NC 582, 83 SE2d 548]

7. Dozier and his wife, daughter, and grandson lived in the house Dozier owned. At the request of the daughter and grandson, Paschall made some improvements to the house. Dozier did not authorize these, but he knew that the improvements were being made and did not object to them. Paschall sued Dozier for the reasonable value of the improvements. Dozier defended on the ground that he had not made any contract for such improvements. Was he obligated to pay for such improvements? [Paschall's v Dozier, 219 Tenn 45, 407 SW2d 150]

8. A state statute required the County Board of Commissioners to advertise their proceedings in a newspaper. The *Greensburg Times* published the notices for the commissioners. The commissioners later refused to pay the newspaper on the ground that they had not executed a written contract with the newspaper on behalf of the county. Decide. [Board of Commissioners v Greensburg Times, 215 Ind 471, 19 NE2d 459]

9. Lombard insured his car under a theft policy that required the insurer to repair damages to the car when stolen or to pay the money equivalent of the damages. Lombard's car was stolen, and when it was recovered he and the insurance adjuster agreed as to what repairs should be made. The adjuster then took the car to General Auto Service, Inc.

to make the repairs. When the insurance company was unable to pay for the repairs, General Auto Service sued Lombard because he had received the benefit of the contract. Was he liable for the repair bill? [General Auto Service, Inc. v Lombard, (La) 151 So2d 536]

10. *A* sued *B*. *A* claimed that because of certain conduct *B* was under a quasi-contractual liability to pay *A* a sum of money spent by *A* in performing certain work. *B* claimed that he could not be liable because he had never made any agreement with *A* to do the work nor to pay him any sum of money. Was this a valid defense? [See Minnesota Avenue, Inc. v Automatic Packages, Inc., 211 Kan 461, 507 P2d 268]

11. *A* rented a building from *B* under a long-term lease. *A* contracted with *C* for the installation of an air-conditioning unit in such a way that it could not be removed. *B* had no knowledge of the installation. When *A* did not pay for the work, *C* sued *B* on the ground that *C* had improved *B*'s property and that *B* would be unjustly enriched if not required to pay for the benefit he received. Was *C* entitled to recover the reasonable value of the installation from *B*? [See Kemp v Majestic Amusement Co., 427 Pa 429, 234 A2d 846]

12. William was a certified public accountant. He did all the accounting work for his wife, Frances. William and Frances were divorced but remained friendly. William continued to perform the accounting services as before and also for North Star Motors, a business operated by the brother of Frances. When Frances sued William on a promissory note, he counterclaimed for compensation for his accounting services rendered to his ex-wife and her brother on the theory that an implied contract arose to pay him for such services. Was he entitled to recover on the counterclaim? [Ryan v Ryan (Del Super) 298 A2d 343]

13. The State of North Dakota provided by statute for the distribution among the counties of the state of money paid to the state as motor vehicle registration fees. On the basis of wrong advice by the state's attorney general, the fund was distributed among the counties in an improper manner and nothing remained. Stark County, North Dakota, as a result did not receive the full amount to which it was entitled. Part of the money it should have received was paid to other counties. Stark County sued the State of North Dakota, claiming that the state had a quasi-contractual duty to pay the county the amount which it should have been paid. Decide. [Stark County v State of North Dakota, (ND) 160 NW2d 101]

10 The Agreement

As stated in Chapter 9, one of the essential elements of a contract is an agreement. An agreement is formed when an offer is accepted.

A. REQUIREMENTS OF AN OFFER

An *offer* expresses the willingness of the offeror to enter into a contractual agreement regarding a particular subject. It is a promise which is conditional upon an act, a forbearance, or a return promise that is given in exchange for the promise or its performance.

§ 10:1. Contractual Intention. To constitute an offer, the offeror must intend to create a legal obligation or must appear to intend to do so. It is not necessary, however, that the parties expressly state that they are making a contract. (See p. 156, Steinberg v Chicago Medical School) When there is neither the intention nor the appearance of the intention to make a binding agreement, there is no contract. It makes no difference whether the offeree takes any action in reliance on the apparent offer. The following are examples of lack of contractual intention on the part of the apparent offeror:

(a)   Social Invitations. Ordinary invitations to social affairs are not "offers" in the eyes of the law. The acceptance of a social invitation, such as an invitation to go to dinner, does not give rise to a legally binding agreement or contract.

(b)   Offers Made in Jest or Excitement. If an offer is made in obvious jest, the offeree cannot take it seriously, pretend to accept it, and then sue the offeror for breach of the agreement. Here the offeree, as a reasonable person, should realize that no contract is intended and therefore no contract arises even though the offeror speaks words which, if seriously spoken, could be accepted and result in a contract. Likewise an extravagant offer of a reward made in the heat of excitement cannot be acted upon as a valid offer.

It is not always obvious or apparent to the offeree when the offer is made in jest or excitement. If it is reasonable under the circumstances for the offeree to believe that the offer was made seriously, a contract is formed by the offeree's acceptance. (See p. 157, Lucy v Zehmer)

(c)   Invitations to Negotiate. The first statement made by one of two persons is not necessarily an offer. In many instances there may be a preliminary discussion or an *invitation* by one party to the other *to negotiate* or to make an offer.

Ordinarily a seller sending out circulars or catalogs listing prices is not regarded as making an offer to sell at those prices, but as merely indicating a willingness to consider an offer made by a buyer on those terms. The reason for this rule is in part the practical consideration that since a seller does not have an unlimited supply of any commodity, the seller cannot possibly intend to make a contract with everyone who sees the circular. The same principle is applied to merchandise that is displayed with price tags in stores or store windows and to most advertisements. A "for sale" advertisement in a newspaper is merely an invitation to negotiate and is not an offer which can be accepted by a reader of the paper, even though the seller in fact has only one of the particular item advertised.

The circumstances may be such, however, that even a newspaper advertisement constitutes an offer. Thus the seller may make an offer when the advertisement states that specific items will be sold at a clearance sale at the prices listed and adds the words "first come, first served." [1]

Quotations of prices, even when sent on request, are likewise not offers in the absence of previous dealings between the parties or the existence of a trade custom which would give the recipient of the quotation reason to believe that an offer was being made. Whether a price quotation is to be treated as an offer or merely an invitation to negotiate is a question of the intent of the party making such quotations. Although sellers are not bound by quotations and price tags, they will as a matter of goodwill ordinarily make every effort to deliver the merchandise at those prices.[2]

In some instances, it is apparent that an invitation to negotiate and not an offer has been made. When construction work is done for the national government, for a state government, or for a political subdivision, statutes require that a printed statement of the work to be done be published and circulated. Contractors are invited to submit bids on the work, and the statute generally requires that the bid of the lowest responsible bidder be accepted. Such an invitation for bids is clearly an invitation to negotiate, both from its nature and from the fact that it does not specify the price to be paid for the work. The bid of each contractor is an offer, and there is no contract until the government accepts one of these bids. This procedure of advertising for bids is also commonly employed by private persons when a large construction project is involved. (See p. 158, Olson v Beacham)

In some cases the fact that material terms are missing serves to indicate that the parties were merely negotiating and that an oral contract had not been made. When a letter or printed promotional matter of a party leaves many significant details to be worked out later, the letter or printed matter is merely an invitation to negotiate and is not an offer which may be accepted and a contract thereby formed.

(d)   Statement of Intention. In some instances a person may make a statement of intention but not intend to be bound by a contract. For example, when a lease does not expressly allow the tenant to terminate the lease because of a job transfer, the landlord might state that should the tenant be required to leave for that reason, the landlord would try to find a new tenant to take over the lease. This declaration of intention does not give rise to a binding contract, and the landlord cannot be held

---

[1] Lefkowitz v Great Minneapolis Surplus Store, Inc. 251 Minn 188, 86 NW2d 689.
[2] Meridian Star v Kay, 207 Miss 78, 41 So2d 746. Statutes prohibiting false or misleading advertising may also require adherence to advertised prices. See § 10:12(c) in this book.

liable for breach of contract should the landlord fail to obtain a new tenant or not even attempt to obtain a new tenant.

(e)   Agreements to Make a Contract at a Future Date. No contract arises when the parties merely agree that at a future date they shall consider making a contract or shall make a contract on terms to be agreed upon at that time. In such a case, neither party is under any obligation until the future contract is made. Similarly there is no contract between the parties if essential terms are left open for future negotiation.[3] Thus, a promise to pay a bonus or compensation to be decided upon after three months of business operation is not binding.

(f)   Sham Transactions. Sometimes what appears to be a contract is entered into for the purpose of deceiving a third person or a government examiner. For example, when a bank does not hold sufficient assets to meet the deposit reserve ratio established by the Federal Reserve Bank, a friend of the bank may sign a promissory note payable to the bank so that the bank would appear to hold more assets than it actually does. Such a sham transaction cannot be enforced between the parties. That is, the bank cannot enforce the note against the maker because the bank knew that it was never intended to be a binding transaction. However, when a third person, such as the Federal Deposit Insurance Corporation, sues the maker of the sham note, the maker is liable on the note and cannot avoid the obligation on the ground that it was a sham.[4]

§ 10:2. Definiteness. An offer, and the resulting contract, must be definite and certain. If an offer is indefinite or vague or if an essential provision is lacking, no contract arises from an attempt to accept it. The reason is that the courts cannot tell what the parties are to do. Thus, an offer to conduct a business for such time as should be profitable is too vague to be a valid offer. The "acceptance" of such an offer does not result in a contract that can be enforced. Likewise, a promise to give an injured employee "suitable" employment that the employee was "able to do" is too vague to be a binding contract.

(a)   Definite by Incorporation. An offer and the resulting contract which by themselves may appear "too indefinite" may be made definite by reference to another writing. For example, an agreement to lease property which was too vague by itself was made definite because the parties agreed that the lease should follow the standard form with which both were familiar. An agreement may also be made definite by reference to the prior dealings of the parties and to trade practices.

(b)   Implied Terms. Although an offer must be definite and certain, not all of its terms need to be expressed. Some of the omitted terms may be implied by law. For example, an offer "to pay $50 for a watch" does not state the terms of payment. A court, however, would not condemn this provision as too vague but would hold that it required that cash be paid and that the payment be made upon delivery of the watch.

---

[3] Willowood Condominium Ass'n., Inc. v HNC Realty Co. (CA5 Tex) 531 F2d 1249.
[4] Federal Deposit Insurance Corp. v Oehlert (Iowa) 252 NW2d 728.

(c) **Divisible Contracts.** When the agreement consists of two or more parts and calls for corresponding performances of each part by the parties, the agreement is a *divisible contract.* Thus, in a promise to buy several separate articles at different prices at the same time, the agreement may be regarded as separate or divisible promises for the articles. When a contract contains a number of provisions or performances to be rendered, the question thus arises whether the parties intended merely a group of separate, divisible contracts or whether it was to be a "package deal" so that complete performance by each party is essential.

(d) **Unimportant Vague Details Ignored.** If the term of an agreement which is too vague is not important, it may sometimes be ignored. If the balance of the agreement is definite, there can then be a binding contract. For example, where the parties agreed that one of them would manage a motel which was being constructed for the other and it was agreed that the contract would begin to run before the completion of the construction, the management contract did not fail because it did not specify any date on which it was to commence, as it was apparent that the exact date was not essential and could not be determined at the time when the contract was made.[5]

§ 10:3. Exceptions to Definiteness. As exceptions to the requirement of definiteness, the law has come to recognize certain situations where the practical necessity of doing business makes it desirable to have a "contract," yet the situation is such that it is either impossible or undesirable to adopt definite terms in advance. Thus, the law recognizes binding contracts in the following situations, although at the time that the contract is made there is some element which is not definite:

(a) **Cost-Plus Contracts.** Cost-plus contracts are valid as against the contention that the amount to be paid is not definite when the contract is made. Such contracts enable the contractor to enter into a transaction without setting up extraordinary reserves against cost contingencies that may arise.

(b) **Requirements and Output Contracts.** Contracts by which a supplier agrees in advance to sell its entire future output to a particular buyer or by which a buyer agrees to buy all of its needs or requirements from a particular supplier are valid, as discussed in § 23:4(d), even though at the time of contracting the amount of goods to be covered by the contract is not known.

A contract by which the buyer agrees to purchase its fuel oil requirements for its electricity-generating system from the seller is binding, even though the buyer was free to purchase from another seller natural gas which could be used as well in the buyer's system. The contract is valid as against the contention that the contract was not binding and was illusory because there was no obligation on the part of the buyer to purchase any quantity from the seller. A contract to supply "necessary electrical service" is likewise binding as against the objection that it is too indefinite and does not state a price.[6]

(c) **Services as Needed.** An enterprise may desire to be assured that the services of a given person, ordinarily a professional or a specialist, will be available when

---

[5] Innkeepers International, Inc. v McCoy Motels, Ltd. (FlaApp) 324 So2d 676.
[6] Illinois Commerce Commission v Central Illinois Public Service Co., 25 IllApp3d 79, 322 NE2d 520.

needed. It is thus becoming valid to make a contract with the professional to supply such services as in the professional's opinion will be required, although this is indefinite and would appear to give the professional the choice of doing nothing.[7] (See p. 159, Griswold v Heat Incorporated)

(d)   Indefinite Duration Contract. Contracts with no specific time limit are valid. The law meets the objection that there is a lack of definiteness by interpreting the contract as being subject to termination at the election of either party. This type of contract is used most commonly in employment and in sales transactions.

(e)   Open-Term Sales Contracts. Contracts for the sale of goods are valid even though the price or some other term remains open and must be determined at a future date. This is discussed further in § 23:4(c).

(f)   Current Market Price Contracts. An agreement is not too indefinite to enforce because it does not state the exact price to be paid but states the price shall be that prevailing on a recognized market or exchange. Likewise, a provision in a lease is sufficiently definite to be binding when it specifies that if the lease is renewed, the rental should be that of similar properties at the time of renewal.

(g)   First Refusal Contracts. The owner of property may agree to give the other contracting party a first right to buy the property by matching any serious offer made by a third person. A contract conferring such a *preemptive right* or right of first refusal is binding (against the contention that it is not definite because it does not specify the terms of the subsequent sale), for the offer made by a third person will supply those details.

(h)   Joint Venture Participation. When two or more persons or enterprises pool resources in order to obtain a government contract, agreements as to the manner of dividing the work or profits between them may be enforced even though they are dependent upon future negotiation.[8] In effect, the law is influenced by the practical consideration that from the nature of the activity it would be impossible or impractical to make the agreements between the parties more specific until the government contract was awarded.

§ 10:4. Communication of Offer to the Offeree. The offer must be communicated to the offeree by the offeror. Until the offer is made known to the offeree, the offeree does not know that there is something which can be accepted. Sometimes, particularly in the case of unilateral contracts, the offeree performs the act called for by the offeror without knowing of the offer's existence. Thus, without knowing that a reward is offered for the arrest of a particular criminal, a person may arrest the criminal. In most states, if that person learns thereafter that a reward has been offered for the arrest, the reward cannot be recovered.[9]

---

[7] Under such contracts the duty to act in good faith supplies the protection found in most contracts in the "usual rules as to certainty and definiteness." McNussen v Graybeal, 141 Mont 571, 405 P2d 447.

[8] Air Technology Corp. v General Electric Co. 347 Mass 613, 199 NE2d 538.

[9] With respect to the offeror, it should not make any difference as a practical matter whether the services were rendered with or without knowledge of the existence of the offer. Only a small number of states have adopted this view, however.

B. TERMINATION OF OFFER

An offer gives the offeree power to bind the offeror by contract. This power does not last forever, and the law specifies that under certain circumstances the power ends or is terminated.

§ 10:5. Effect and Methods. Once the offer is terminated, the offeree cannot revive it. If an attempt is made to accept the offer after it has been terminated, this attempt is meaningless, unless the original offeror is willing to regard the "late acceptance" as a new offer which the original offeror then accepts.

Offers may be terminated in any one of the following ways: (1) revocation of the offer by the offeror, (2) counteroffer by offeree, (3) rejection of offer by offeree, (4) lapse of time, (5) death or disability of either party, and (6) subsequent illegality.

§ 10:6. Revocation of the Offer by the Offeror. Ordinarily the offeror can revoke the offer before it is accepted. If this is done, the offeree cannot create a contract by accepting the revoked offer. Thus, the bidder at an auction sale may withdraw (revoke) a bid (offer) before it is accepted. The auctioneer cannot thereafter accept that bid.

An ordinary offer may be revoked at any time before it is accepted, even though the offeror had expressly promised that the offer would be good for a stated period and that period had not yet expired, or even though the offeror had expressly promised to the offeree that the offer would not be revoked before a specified later date.

(a)   What Constitutes a Revocation. No particular form of words is required to constitute a revocation. Any words indicating the offeror's termination of the offer is sufficient. A notice sent to the offeree that the property which is the subject of the offer has been sold to a third person is a revocation of the offer. An order for goods by a customer, which is an offer to purchase at certain prices, is revoked by a notice to the seller of the cancellation of the order, provided such notice is communicated before the order is accepted.

(b)   Communication of Revocation. A revocation of an offer is ordinarily effective only when it is made known to the offeree. Until it is communicated to the offeree, directly or indirectly, the offeree has reason to believe that there is still an offer which may be accepted; and the offeree may rely on this belief.

Except in a few states, a letter or telegram revoking an offer made to a particular offeree is not effective until received by the offeree.[10] It is not a revocation at the time it is written by the offeror nor even when it is mailed or dispatched. A written revocation is effective, however, when it is delivered to the offeree's agent, or to the offeree's residence or place of business under such circumstances that the offeree may be reasonably expected to be aware of its receipt.

It is ordinarily held that there is a sufficient "communication" of the revocation when the offeree learns indirectly of the offeror's revocation. This is particularly true in a land sale, when the seller-offeror, after making an offer to sell the land to the offeree, sells the land to a third person, and the offeree indirectly learns of such sale and necessarily realizes that the seller cannot perform the original offer and therefore must be deemed to have revoked it.

---

[10] Hogan v Aluminum Lock Shingle Corp. 214 Ore 218, 329 P2d 271.

If the offeree accepts an offer before it is effectively revoked, a valid contract is created. Thus, there may be a contract when the offeree mails or telegraphs an acceptance without knowing that a letter of revocation has already been mailed.

When an offer is made to the public it may usually be revoked in the same manner in which it was made. For example, an offer of a reward that is made to the general public by an advertisement in a newspaper may be revoked in the same manner. A member of the public cannot recover the amount of the reward by thereafter performing the act for which the reward was originally offered. This exception is made to the rule requiring communication of revocation because it would be impossible for the offeror to communicate the fact that the offer was revoked to every member of the general public who knows of the offer. The public revocation of the public offer is effective even though it is not seen by the person attempting to accept the original offer.

(c)   Option Contracts. An *option contract* is a binding promise to keep an offer open for a stated period of time or until a specified date. This requires that the promisor receive consideration, that is something, such as a sum of money, as the price for the promise to keep the offer open. In other words, the option is a contract to refrain from revoking an offer.

When there is a binding option contract, the offeror cannot revoke the offer. If the owner of a house gives a prospective purchaser a 60-day written option to purchase the property at $50,000 and the customer pays the owner a sum of money, such as $500, the owner cannot revoke the offer within the 60-day period. Even though the owner expressly tells the purchaser within that time that the option contract is revoked, the purchaser may exercise the option; meaning that the purchaser may accept the offer in spite of the attempted revocation.

Under an option contract the offeree is under no obligation to exercise the option. Unless an additional requirement is imposed by the option contract, the optionee can exercise the option by communicating to the optionor that the option is being exercised. (See p. 160, Doolittle v Fruehauf Corporation) If the option is exercised, the money paid to obtain the option is ordinarily, but not necessarily, applied as a down payment. If the option is not exercised, the offeror keeps the money paid by the offeree.

An option exists only when the option holder has the right to demand the performance called for by the option. If the agreement states that the "option" may be exercised only with the consent of the other party, it is not an option even though so called by the agreement.

If a promise is described by the parties as an "option" but no consideration is given, the promise is subject to revocation as though it were not described as an "option." In those jurisdictions in which the seal retains it common-law force, however, the option contract is binding on the offeror if it is set forth in a sealed writing, even though the offeror does not receive any payment for the agreement.

Frequently an option contract is combined with a lease of real estate or personal property. Thus a tenant may rent a building for a number of years by an agreement which gives the tenant the option of purchasing the building for a specified amount during or at the end of the lease.

An option is to be distinguished from a preemptive right or first refusal contract by which a person is given the right to buy if the owner chooses to sell, but the holder of such right cannot require the owner to sell, as is the case in an option contract.

(d)   Firm Offers. As another exception to the rule that an offer can be revoked at any time before acceptance, statutes in some states provide that an offeror cannot revoke an offer prior to its expiration when the offeror makes a *firm offer,* that is, an offer which states that it is to be irrevocable, or irrevocable for a stated period of time. Under the Uniform Commercial Code, this doctrine of firm offers applies to a merchant's signed, written offer to buy or sell goods, but with a maximum of three months on its duration.[11]

(e)   Detrimental Reliance. There is growing authority that when the offeree relies on the offer, the offeror is obligated to keep the offer open for a reasonable time after such action has been taken by the offeree. Thus it has been held that a subcontractor cannot revoke a bid made to the general contractor after the general contractor had used the subcontractor's bid in computing the general bid given to the owner and the contractor's general bid was then accepted by the owner.[12]

(f)   Revocation of Offer of Unilateral Contract. As the offer of a unilateral contract can be accepted only by performing the act called for, it theoretically follows that there is no acceptance until that act is fully performed by the offeree and that the offeror is therefore free to revoke the offer even though the offeree has partly performed and has expended time and money in so doing. To avoid this hardship, a number of courts hold that after the offeree has done some substantial act toward acceptance, the offeror cannot revoke the offer until after the lapse of a reasonable time in which the offeree could have completed performance. Some courts hold that the offeror of a unilateral contract cannot revoke the offer once the offeree begins to perform the called-for act.

§ 10:7. Counteroffer by Offeree. Ordinarily if *A* makes an offer, such as to sell a used automobile to *B* for $1,000, and *B* in reply makes an offer to buy at $750, the original offer is terminated. *B* is in effect saying, "I refuse your original offer, but in its place I make a different offer." Such an offer by the offeree is known as a *counteroffer.*

In substance, the counteroffer presupposes a rejection of the original offer. In some instances, however, circumstances may show that both parties knew and intended that the offeree's response was not to be regarded as a definite rejection of the original offer but merely as further discussion or as a request for further information. In such case, the counteroffer does not terminate the original offer and the original offer may therefore be accepted after the counteroffer is rejected.

Counteroffers are not limited to offers that directly contradict the original offers. Any departure from, or addition to, the original offer is a counteroffer even though the original offer was silent as to the point added by the counteroffer. For example, when the offeree stated that the offer was accepted and added that time was of the essence, the "acceptance" was a counteroffer because the original offer had been silent on that point. Likewise, when a financer made an offer to a business enterprise to obtain a bank loan for the enterprise from "a local bank," the enterprise rejected

---

[11] Uniform Commercial Code § 2–205.
[12] Jenkins and Boller Co., Inc. v Schmidt Iron Works, Inc. 36 IllApp3d 1044, 344 NE2d 275.

the offer when it specified that instead of "a local bank," the transaction should utilize a particular local bank, the Bank of Tacoma.[13]

§ 10:8. Rejection of Offer by Offeree. If the offeree rejects the offer and communicates this rejection to the offeror, the offer is terminated, even though the period for which the offeror agreed to keep the offer open has not yet expired. It may be that the offeror is willing to renew the offer; but unless this is done, there is no longer any offer for the offeree to accept.

The fact that the offeree replies to the offeror without accepting the offer does not constitute a rejection when it is apparent that the failure to accept at that time was not intended as a rejection. For example, when the seller on receiving an order from a customer sent a reply that a "formal confirmation" of the order would be sent as soon as the seller received confirmation from the seller's supplier that the goods were available, the reply of the seller was not a rejection of the offer made by the customer.

§ 10:9. Lapse of Time. When the offer states that it is open until a particular date, the offer terminates on that date if it has not yet been accepted. This is particularly so where the offeror declares that the offer shall be void after the expiration of the specified time. Such limitations are strictly construed. For example, it has been held that the buyer's attempt to exercise an option one day late had no effect.[14]

If the offer does not specify a time, it will terminate after the lapse of a reasonable time. What constitutes a "reasonable" time depends upon the circumstances of each case; that is, upon the nature of the subject matter, the nature of the market in which it is sold, the time of the year, and other factors of supply and demand. If the commodity is perishable in nature or fluctuates greatly in value, the reasonable time will be much shorter than if the subject matter is a staple article. An offer to sell a harvested crop of tomatoes would expire within a very short time. When a seller purports to accept an offer after it has lapsed by the expiration of time, the seller's acceptance is merely a counteroffer and does not create a contract unless that offer is accepted by the buyer.

§ 10:10. Death or Disability of Either Party. If either the offeror or the offeree dies or becomes insane before the offer is accepted, it is automatically terminated.

§ 10:11. Subsequent Illegality. If the performance of the contract becomes illegal after the offer is made, the offer is terminated. Thus, if an offer is made to sell alcoholic liquors but a law prohibiting such sales is enacted before the offer is accepted, the offer is terminated.

C. ACCEPTANCE OF OFFER

Once the offeror expresses or appears to express a willingness to enter into a contractual agreement with the offeree, the latter may accept the offer. An *acceptance*

---

[13] H. M. Johnson v Star Iron and Steel Co. 9 WashApp 202, 511 P2d 1370.

[14] Watts v Teagle, 124 GaApp 726, 185 SE2d 803 (Buyer was given an option on February 19. The option stated that it expired 180 days from its date, when it would "become void and of no force and effect." The buyer attempted to exercise the option on August 19.)

is the assent of the offeree to the terms of the offer. No particular form of words or mode of expression is required, but there must be a clear expression that the offeree agrees to be bound by the terms of the offer.

§ 10:12. Privilege of Offeree. Ordinarily the offeree may refuse to accept an offer. If there is no acceptance, by definition there is no contract.[15]

Certain partial exceptions exist to the privilege of the offeree to refuse to accept an offer.

(a)   Places of Public Accommodation and Public Utilities. These are under a duty to serve any fit person. Consequently, when a fit person offers to register at a hotel, that is, offers to hire a room, the hotel has the obligation to accept the offer and to enter into a contract for the renting of the room. This is a partial exception to the general rule because there is no duty to accept on the part of the hotel unless the person is fit and the hotel has space available.

(b)   Antidiscrimination. When offers are solicited from members of the general public, an offer may generally not be rejected because of the race, nationality, religion, or color of the offeror. If the solicitor of the offer is willing to enter into a contract to rent, sell, or employ, as the case may be, antidiscrimination laws compel the solicitor to accept an offer from any otherwise fit person.

(c)   Consumer Protection. Statutes and regulations designed to protect consumers from false advertising may require a seller to accept an offer from a customer to purchase advertised goods and may impose a penalty for an unjustified refusal.

§ 10:13. Nature of the Acceptance. In the absence of a contrary requirement in the offer, an acceptance may be indicated by an informal "O.K.," by a mere affirmative nod of the head, or, in the case of an offer of a unilateral contract, by performing the act called for. However, while the acceptance of an offer may be shown by conduct, it must be very clear that the offeree intended to accept the offer.

(a)   Unqualified Acceptance. The acceptance must be absolute and unconditional. It must accept just what is offered. If the offeree changes any terms of the offer or adds any new term, there is no acceptance because the offeree does not agree to what was offered.

Where the offeree does not accept the offer exactly as made, the addition of any qualification converts the "acceptance" into a counteroffer and no contract arises unless such counteroffer is accepted by the original offeror.

(b)   Apparent Qualifications. In some cases, the fact that additional terms are stated in the acceptances does not constitute a qualification of the acceptance and therefore the acceptance is effective as such and a contract arises.

(1)   Implied Terms. An acceptance that states that which is implied by law does not add a new term to the acceptance. Thus a provision in an acceptance that payment must be made in cash will usually not be deemed to add a new term, as a cash payment is implied by law in the absence of a contrary provision.

---

[15] A & A Construction Co., Inc. v Corpus Christi (TexCivApp) 527 SW2d 833.

(2) Requests. An acceptance otherwise unconditional is not made conditional by the fact that an additional matter is requested as a favor rather than being stated as a term of or a restriction upon the acceptance. Accordingly an acceptance by a buyer of an offer to sell real estate is effective even though it contains a request that the title be conveyed to a third person.

(3) Clerical Matters. A provision in an acceptance relating to routine or mechanical details of the execution of a written contract will usually not impair the effect of the acceptance.

§ 10:14. Who May Accept. An offer may be accepted only by the person to whom it is directed. If any one else attempts to accept it, no agreement or contract with that person arises.

If the offer is directed not to a specified individual but to a particular class, it may be accepted by anyone within that class. If the offer is made to the public at large, it may be accepted by any member of the public at large who has knowledge of the existence of the offer.

When a person to whom an offer was not made attempts to accept it, the "acceptance" has the effect of an offer. If the original offeror is willing to accept this offer, a binding contract arises. If the offeror does not accept the new offer, there is no contract.

§ 10:15. Manner of Acceptance. The acceptance must conform to any conditions expressed in the offer concerning the manner of acceptance. When the offeror specifies that there must be a written acceptance, no contract arises when the offeree makes an oral acceptance. If the offeror calls for an acceptance by a specified date, a late acceptance has no effect. When an acceptance is required by return mail, it is usually held that the letter of acceptance must be mailed the same day that the offer was received by the offeree. If the offer specifies that the acceptance be made by the performance of an act by the offeree, the latter cannot accept by making a promise to do the act but must actually perform it.

Ordinarily if the offeree departs from the manner of acceptance specified by the offer, there is no acceptance. Some courts avoid this strict rule by holding that the directions of the offeror were not conditions but merely indicated an acceptable alternative.[16] Unless the offer is clear that a specified manner of acceptance is exclusive, a manner of acceptance indicated by the offeror will be interpreted as merely a suggestion and the offeree's entering upon the performance of the contract will be an acceptance when the offeror has knowledge that the offeree is doing so. An order or offer to buy goods from prompt or current shipment may be accepted by the seller either by promptly making the shipment or promising to do so.[17] When shipment of goods is claimed to constitute an acceptance of the buyer's order, the seller must notify the buyer of such acceptance within a reasonable time.[18]

---

[16] University Realty & Development Co. v Omid-Graf, Inc. 19 ArizApp 488, 508 P2d 747 (Lease provided for notice by registered mail of the tenant's exercise of option to renew the lease. It was held that there was a sufficient acceptance of the option offer when the tenant delivered the notice by hand instead of registered mail.)

[17] UCC § 2-206(1)(b).

[18] UCC § 2-206(2).

When a person accepts services offered by another and it reasonably appears that compensation was expected, the acceptance of the services without any protest constitutes an acceptance of the offer and a contract exists for the payment of such services.

(a)   Silence as Acceptance. In most cases, the offeree's silence and failure to act cannot be regarded as an acceptance. Ordinarily the offeror is not permitted to frame an offer in such a way as to make the silence and inaction of the offeree operate as an acceptance.

In the case of prior dealings between the parties, as in a record or book club, the offeree may have a duty to reject an offer expressly and the offeree's silence may be regarded as an acceptance.

(b)   Unordered Goods and Tickets. When a seller writes to a person with whom the seller has not had any prior dealings that, unless notified to the contrary, specified merchandise will be sent to be paid for at stated prices, there is no acceptance if the recipient of the letter ignores the offer and does nothing. The silence of the person receiving the letter is not an acceptance, and the sender as a reasonable person should recognize that none was intended.

This rule applies to all kinds of goods, books, magazines, and tickets sent to a person through the mail when they have not been ordered. The fact that the items are not returned does not mean that they have been accepted; that is, the offeree is neither required to pay for nor return the goods or other items. If desired, the recipient of the unordered goods may write "Return to Sender" on the unopened package and put the package back into the mail without any additional postage. This is not required and the Postal Reorganization Act of 1970 provides that the person who receives unordered mailed merchandise from a commercial (non-charitable) sender has the right "to retain, use, discard, or dispose of it in any manner [the recipient] sees fit without any obligation whatsoever to the sender." [19] It provides further that any unordered merchandise that is mailed must have attached to it a clear and conspicuous statement of the recipient's rights to treat the goods in this manner.

The mailing of unordered merchandise, other than a free sample conspicuously marked as such, or of a bill for its payment, constitutes an unfair method of competition and an unfair trade practice. The distribution of unsolicited goods as part of a scheme to use the mail to defraud violates federal statutes.

(c)   Insurer's Delay in Acting on Application. The delay of an insurance company in acting upon an application for insurance generally does not constitute an acceptance. A few courts have held that an acceptance may be implied from the company's failure to reject the application promptly, that there is accordingly a binding contract and the application cannot be thereafter rejected. Courts are particularly likely to reach this conclusion when the applicant has paid the first premium and the insurer fails to return it. Some decisions attain the same practical result by holding the insurer liable for tort if, through its unjustified delay in rejecting the application, the applicant remains unprotected by insurance and then, in the interval, suffers loss that would have been covered by the insurance which the applicant could have obtained if the insurer had promptly rejected the application.

---

[19] Federal Postal Reorganization Act § 3009.

§ 10:16. Communication of Acceptance. If the offeree accepts the offer, must the offeror be notified? The answer depends upon the nature of the offer. When communication is required, the acceptance must be communicated directly to the offeror or the offeror's agent. A statement made to a third person is not sufficient.

(a)   Bilateral Contract. If the offer pertains to a bilateral contract, an acceptance is not effective unless communicated to the offeror.

(b)   Unilateral Contract. If the offeror makes an offer of a unilateral contract, communication of acceptance is ordinarily not required. In such a case, the offeror calls for a completed or accomplished act. If that act is performed by the offeree with knowledge of the offer, the offer is accepted without any further action by way of notifying the offeror. As a practical matter, there will eventually be some notice to the offeror because the offeree who has performed the act will ask the offeror to pay for the performance which has been rendered.

(c)   Guaranty Contract. The general rule that notification of acceptance is not necessary in cases of an offer requesting the performance of an act is not applied in many states when the act called for is the extension of credit to a buyer in return for which the offeror promises to pay the buyer's debt if it is not paid. To illustrate, a friend may write to a local merchant that if the merchant allows a buyer to purchase goods on credit, the friend will pay the bill if the buyer does not. The friend thus makes an offer of a unilateral contract as the friend has not asked for a promise by the merchant to extend credit, but for the doing of the act of extending credit. If the merchant extends the credit, the merchant does the act which the friend calls for by the offer. If the general rule governing acceptance applied, the performance of this act would be a complete acceptance and would create a contract. In the guaranty case, however, another requirement is added, namely that within a reasonable time after extending credit, the merchant must notify the friend.

(d)   Exercise of an Option. Since an option obligates the offeror to hold an offer open and to refrain from revoking it, the same principles which govern the communication of the acceptance of an offer of a bilateral contract apply to the exercise of an option. There must be a clear and unequivocal expression of the intention to exercise the option. Conduct that is ambiguous or which is as consistent with nonexercise of the option as it is with its exercise is not sufficient.

§ 10:17. Acceptance by Mail or Telegraph. When the offeree conveys an acceptance by mail or telegraph, questions may arise as to the right to use such means of communication and as to the time when the acceptance is effective.

(a)   Right to Use Mail or Telegraph. Express directions of the offeror, prior dealings between the parties, or custom of the trade may make it clear that only one method of acceptance is proper. For example, in negotiations with respect to property of rapidly fluctuating value, such as wheat or corporation stocks, an acceptance sent by mail may be too slow. When there is no indication that mail or telegraph is not a proper method, an acceptance may be made by either of those instrumentalities without regard to the manner in which the offer was made. The trend of the modern decisions supports the following provision of the Uniform Commercial Code relating to sales of personal property: "Unless otherwise unambiguously indicated by the language or circumstances, an offer to make a [sales] contract shall be construed as inviting acceptance in any manner and by any medium reasonable in the circumstances."

(b)   When Acceptance by Mail or Telegraph Is Effective. If the offeror specifies that an acceptance shall not be effective until received, the law will respect the offeror's wish. If there is no such provision and if acceptance by letter is proper, a mailed acceptance takes effect when the acceptance is properly mailed.

The letter must be properly addressed to the offeror, and any other precaution that is ordinarily observed to insure safe transmission must be taken. If it is not mailed in this manner, the acceptance does not take effect when mailed, but only when received by the offeror.

The rule that a properly mailed acceptance takes effect at the time it is mailed is applied strictly. The rule applies even though the acceptance letter never reaches the offeror.

An acceptance sent by telegraph takes effect at the time that the message is handed to the clerk at the telegraph office, unless the offeror specifies otherwise or unless custom or prior dealings indicate that acceptance by telegraph is improper.

(c)   Proof of Acceptance by Mail or Telegraph. How can the time of mailing be established, or even the fact of mailing in the case of a destroyed or lost letter? A similar problem arises in the case of a telegraphic acceptance. In either case, the problem is not one of law but one of fact: a question of proving the case to the jury. The offeror may testify in court that an acceptance was never received or that an acceptance was sent after the offer had been revoked. The offeree or a stenographer may then testify that the acceptance letter was mailed at a particular time and place. The offeree's case will be strengthened if postal receipts for the mailing and delivery of a letter sent to the offeror can be produced, although these of course do not establish the contents of the letter. Ultimately, the case goes to the jury, or to the judge, if a jury trial has been waived, to determine whether the acceptance was made at a certain time and place as claimed by the offeree.

(d)   Payment and Notice by Mail Distinguished from Acceptance. The preceding principles relate to the acceptance of an offer. When a contract exists and the question is whether a notice has been given or a payment has been made under the contract, those principles do not necessarily apply. Thus the mailing of a check is not the payment of a debt as of the time and place of mailing.

Contracts, however, will often extend the "mailed acceptance" rule to payment and giving notice. Thus insurance contracts commonly provide that the mailing of a premium is a sufficient "payment" of the premium to prevent the policy from lapsing for nonpayment of the premium. Likewise, an insurance policy provision requiring that notice of loss be given to the insurer is generally satisfied by a mailing of the notice without actual proof that the notice was received.

§ 10:18. Acceptance by Telephone. Ordinarily acceptance of an offer may be made by telephone unless the circumstances are such that by the intent of the parties or the law of the state no acceptance can be made or contract arise in the absence of a writing.

A telephoned acceptance is effective when and where the acceptance is spoken into the phone. Consequently, where an employee who lived in Kansas applied for a job to work in Missouri and the employer telephoned from Missouri to Kansas accepting the application, the employment contract was a Missouri contract because the acceptance by the employer was spoken into the phone in that state and therefore the Kansas Workmen's Compensation statute did not apply when the employee was subsequently injured.[20]

§ 10:19. Auction Sales. At an auction sale the statements made by the auctioneer to draw forth bids are merely invitations to negotiate. Each bid is an offer, which is not accepted until the auctioneer indicates that a particular offer or bid is accepted. Usually this is done by the fall of the auctioneer's hammer, indicating that the highest bid made has been accepted.[21] As a bid is merely an offer, the bidder may withdraw the bid at any time before it is accepted by the auctioneer.

Ordinarily the auctioneer may withdraw any article or all of the property from the sale if not satisfied with the amounts of the bids that are being made. Once a bid is accepted, however, the auctioneer cannot cancel the sale. In addition, if it had been announced that the sale was to be made "without reserve," the goods must be sold to the person making the highest bid regardless of how low that may be.

---

[20] Neumer v Yellow Freight System, Inc., 220 Kan 607, 556 P2d 202.

[21] "Where a bid is made while the auctioneer's hammer is falling in acceptance of a prior bid, the auctioneer may in his discretion reopen the bidding or declare the goods sold under the bid on which the hammer is falling." UCC § 2-328(2).

CASES FOR CHAPTER 10

Steinberg v Chicago Medical School

4 Ill App 3d 804, 354 NE2d 586 (1976)

The Chicago Medical School stated in its 1974-75 brochure the criteria that would be used in acting on applications for admissions to the Medical School. An applicant was required to send $15 with the application. Steinberg sent an application and $15 to the School. He was rejected. He claimed that the School was not following its published criteria for admission and that applicants were admitted depending on whether they were related to a member of the faculty or the board of trustees or whether the family of the applicant could make a financial contribution to the School. He sued for an injunction to compel the School to stop using unpublished criteria in passing on admission applications. The School raised the defense that there was no contractual obli-

gation on it to adhere to the criteria printed in the brochure. The lower court decided in favor of the School on this issue and Steinberg appealed.

DEMPSEY, J. . . . . The 1974-75 bulletin of the school, which was distributed to prospective students, represented that the following criteria would be used by the school in determining whether applicants would be accepted as first-year medical students: "Students are selected on the basis of scholarship, character, and motivation without regard to race, creed, or sex. The student's potential for the study and practice of medicine will be evaluated on the basis of academic achievement, Medical College Admission Test results, personal appraisals by a pre-professional advisory committee or individual instructors, and the personal interview, if requested by the Committee on Admissions."

Steinberg contends that the Chicago Medical School's informational brochure constituted an invitation to make an offer; that his subsequent application and the submission of his $15 fee to the school amounted to an offer; that the school's voluntary reception of his fee constituted an acceptance and because of these events a contract was created between the school and himself. He contends that the school was duty bound under the terms of the contract to evaluate his application according to its stated standards and that the deviation from these standards . . . breached the contract . . .

The school counters that no contract came into being because informational brochures, such as its bulletin, do not constitute offers, but are construed by the courts to be general proposals to consider, examine and negotiate. The school points out that this doctrine has been specifically applied in Illinois to university informational publications. *People ex rel. Tinkoff v. Northwestern University* (1947), 333 Ill. App. 224, 77 N.E.2d 345. In *Tinkoff,* a rejected applicant sued to force Northwestern to admit him, claiming that the university had violated the contract that arose when he demonstrated that he had met the school's academic entrance requirements and had submitted his application and fee. His primary contention was that the school's brochure was an offer and that his completion of the acts, required by the bulletin for application, constituted his acceptance.

In rejecting this argument, the court stated: "Plaintiffs complain Tinkoff, Jr. was denied the right to contract as guaranteed by the Illinois and United States constitutions. We need only say that he had no right to contract with the University. His right to contract for and pursue an education is limited by the right which the University has under its charter. We see no merit to plaintiff's contention that the rules and regulations were an offer of contract and his compliance therewith an acceptance giving rise to a binding contract. The wording of the bulletin required further action by the University in admitting Tinkoff, Jr. before a contract between them would arise."

The court based its holding on the fact that Northwestern, as a private educational institution, had reserved in its State charter the right to reject any application for any reason it deemed adequate.

Although the facts of the *Tinkoff* case are similar to the present situation, we believe that the defendant's reliance upon it is misplaced. First, Steinberg is not claiming that his submission of the application and the $15 constituted an acceptance

by him; he is merely maintaining that it was an offer, which required the subsequent acceptance of the school to create a contract. Also, it is obvious that his assertion that the bulletin of the school only amounted to an invitation to make an offer, is consistent with the prevailing law and the school's own position.

More importantly, Steinberg is not requesting that the school be ordered to admit him as a student, pursuant to the contract, but only that the school be prohibited from misleading prospective students by stating in its informational literature, evaluation standards that are not subsequently used in the selection of students. Furthermore, the school does not allege, nor did it demonstrate by way of its bulletin or its charter that it had reserved the right to reject any applicant for any reason. It only stated certain narrow standards by which each and every applicant was to be evaluated.

We agree with Steinberg's position. We believe that he and the school entered into an enforceable contract; that the school's obligation under the contract was stated in the school's bulletin in a definitive manner and that by accepting his application fee—a valuable consideration—the school bound itself to fulfill its promises. Steinberg accepted the school's promises in good faith and he was entitled to have his application judged according to the school's stated criteria.

The school argues that he should not be allowed to recover because his complaint did not state a causal connection between the rejection of his application and the school's alleged use of unpublished evaluation criteria. It points out that there is an equal probability that his application was rejected for failing to meet the stated standards, and since the cause of his damages is left to conjecture they may be attributed as easily to a condition for which there is no liability as to one for which there is.

This argument focuses on the wrong point. Once again, Steinberg did not allege that he was damaged when the school rejected his application. He alleged that he was damaged when the school used evaluation criteria other than those published in the school's bulletin. . . .

[Judgment reversed and action remanded]

Lucy v Zehmer

196 Va App 493, 84 SE2d 516 (1954)

Zehmer discussed selling a farm to Lucy. After some discussion of a first draft of a contract, Zehmer

and his wife signed a paper stating: "We hereby agree to sell to W. O. Lucy the Ferguson Farm complete for $50,000.00, title satisfactory to buyer." Lucy agreed to purchase the farm on these terms. Thereafter the Zehmers refused to transfer title to Lucy and claimed that they had made the contract for sale as a joke. Lucy brought an action for specific performance of the contract. From a judgment for the Zehmers, Lucy appealed.

BUCHANAN, J. . . . The defendants insist that the evidence was ample to support their contention that the writing sought to be enforced was prepared as a bluff or dare to force Lucy to admit that he did not have $50,000; that the whole matter was a joke; . . . and no binding contract was ever made between the parties. . . .

The appearance of the contract, the fact that it was under discussion for forty minutes or more before it was signed; Lucy's objection to the first draft because it was written in the singular, and he wanted Mrs. Zehmer to sign it also; the rewriting to meet that objection and the signing by Mrs. Zehmer; the discussion of what was to be included in the sale, the provision for the examination of the title, the completeness of the instrument that was executed, the taking possession of it by Lucy with no request or suggestion by either of the defendants that he give it back, are facts which furnish persuasive evidence that the execution of the contract was a serious business transaction rather than a casual, jesting matter as defendants now contend. . . .

If it be assumed, contrary to what we think the evidence shows, that Zehmer was jesting about selling his farm to Lucy and that the transaction was intended by him to be a joke, nevertheless the evidence shows that Lucy did not so understand it but considered it to be a serious business transaction and the contract to be binding on the Zehmers as well as on himself. The very next day he arranged with his brother to put up half the money and take a half interest in the land. The day after that he employed an attorney to examine the title. The next night, Tuesday, he was back at Zehmer's place and there Zehmer told him for the first time, Lucy said, that he wasn't going to sell and he told Zehmer, "You know you sold that place fair and square." After receiving the report from his attorney that the title was good, he wrote to Zehmer that he was ready to close the deal.

Not only did Lucy actually believe, but the evidence shows he was warranted in believing, that the contract represented a serious business transaction and a good faith sale and purchase of the farm.

In the field of contracts, as generally elsewhere, "We must look to the outward expression of a person as manifesting his intention rather than to his secret and unexpressed intention. 'The law imputes to a person an intention corresponding to the reasonable meaning of his words and acts.' ". . .

The mental assent of the parties is not requisite for the formation of a contract. If the words or other acts of one of the parties have but one reasonable meaning, his undisclosed intention is immaterial. . . .

[Judgment reversed and action remanded]

Olson v Beacham

(ND) 102 NW2d 125 (1960)

Beacham and McElroy advertised for bids for the installation of a cooling system in a building they owned. Olson submitted the lowest bid, but the owners accepted the slightly higher bid of another contractor. Olson sued the owners for breach of contract. From a judgment in favor of the owners, Olson appealed.

SATHRE, C.J. . . . It is the contention of the plaintiff that having submitted the lowest bid . . . a contract resulted between the parties, and that failure on the part of the defendants to accept plaintiff's bid constituted a breach of contract resulting in damages to the plaintiff. . . .

The defendants in advertising for bids stated . . . : "The owner reserves the right to reject any or all bids when such rejection is in the interest of the owner. . . ."

The plaintiff in his bid stipulated: "The undersigned, as bidder, hereby proposes, and if this proposal is accepted, agrees to enter into a contract.". . .

The defendants did not accept the bid of the plaintiff. . . . They clearly had the right under the terms of their advertisement for bids and instruction to bidders to accept or reject any of the bids that might be submitted. The plaintiff recognized the right of the owners and stated . . . he would enter into a contract . . . *if the defendant accepted his bid.* The defendants having rejected the bid of the plaintiff were under no obligation to him and they had the right to determine for themselves which bid submitted would be to their best interest. The plaintiff was aware of this fact when he submitted his bid. The advertisement of the defendants for bids was merely an invitation for offers and was not an offer to accept any particular bid. The advertisement could result in a contract only upon acceptance of a bid submitted by a bidder. . . .

[Judgment affirmed]

Griswold v Heat Incorporated

108 NH 119, 229 A2d 183 (1967)

Heat Incorporated made an agreement with Griswold, an accountant, by which it agreed to pay him $200 a month for rendering such accounting services "as he, in his sole discretion, may render." When the corporation refused to pay on the ground that the agreement was so indefinite that it was not binding, Griswold sued for damages.

LAMPRON, J. . . . When Heat was incorporated in New Hampshire in 1956, its stockholders and directors were Kretschmar, Harris, and the defendant Illig, each holding 500 shares. Its business, the distribution of heating equipment and boilers, was based in Nashua and operated by Kretschmar, as Harris and Illig had businesses of their own, the former in Portland, Maine, the latter in Fitchburg, Massachusetts.

Plaintiff Griswold, a certified public accountant, was associated with Heat from its beginning. He installed its accounting system, kept the stock book records, the records of meetings of the directors and the stockholders, counseled and advised on bookkeeping and accounting procedures, and on the financial operation of the company. The Trial Court found that Griswold is a 78-year old man with a life expectancy in excess of the remainder of the contract in dispute, who is somewhat deaf, has sciatica, but is alert, moves briskly and he presently is still active in his profession as a certified accountant as a member of a large Portland firm of accountants.

When Kretschmar died in May, 1957, the corporation bought his 500 shares of stock. The remaining stockholders, Harris and Illig, because of their own full time interests, agreed to continue Heat only if a manager could be obtained and if Griswold agreed to continue to serve the corporation as he had in the past. This was arranged and thereafter Griswold, who became the holder of one share of stock, served as director, assistant treasurer, clerk, and continued as financial advisor to the corporation.

For these services Griswold received $300 per month, which was reduced to $100 per month in 1960, when Heat had financial reverses, and continued at that rate until January 1, 1964.

Prior to December 2, 1963, Harris notified Illig that he was interested in disposing of his stock in Heat to him. On that date Harris transferred his shares to Illig who became owner of 998 of the 1,000 shares outstanding. Mrs. Illig owning one share and Griswold the other. Illig testified that in connection with this purchase he was desirous that Griswold continue to serve Heat in the same manner as he had in the past and that Griswold agreed to do so for $200 per month which Illig agreed to pay. Both Harris and Griswold, who with Illig then constituted the board of directors of Heat, testified that was the agreement between Illig and Griswold. . . .

Defendants take the position that Griswold's promise by its terms gives the plaintiff such an option in regard to the performance required of him as to render his promise illusory. . . .

Does Griswold's promise or obligation "for such services as he, in his sole discretion, may render" constitute sufficient consideration for Heat's promise to pay him $200 per month for 5 years in accordance with the terms of their agreement?

It has long been the rule in this state that "the proper interpretation of a contract is that which will make it speak the intention of the parties at the time it was made.". . . It follows that in construing the written agreement of these parties, all of its provisions, its subject matter, the situation of the parties at the time, and the object intended to be effected will be considered in arriving at the sense of the words they used. . . .

There was evidence that the nature of the services rendered by Griswold to Heat from its origin in 1956 to December 2, 1963, the date of the agreement, were well known to both Griswold and Illig. The latter testified that on the above date when he purchased Harris' interest, he wanted Griswold to continue to serve the corporation as "he had over the years." He asked Griswold if he was willing to continue in "this fashion," at $200 a month and Griswold said he would. The latter testified that Illig agreed to pay him $200 per month for his "usual services" the nature of which was known to Illig. This insight of the object intended to be effected by the agreement is an important factor in determining the sense of the words used therein by these parties. . . .

The course of conduct of the parties for the first year following their agreement is further evidence "of their common understanding of the meaning of their contract and the result they expected to accomplish thereby.". . . The Trial Court properly found that "the plaintiff during the year 1964 performed approximately the same services as he had previously performed and was paid by the corporation for the entire twelve months." Griswold was paid $200 per month as provided for by the agreement. During that period Illig owned all of the shares of Heat except two, one owned by his wife, the other by Griswold. The three of them constituted the board of directors.

Since this agreement was made by businessmen, it is reasonable to assume that it was made for business reasons and was intended to have business efficacy. . . . It should be so construed. . . . In all such business undertakings an obligation of good faith is implied. . . . An interpretation which makes the agreement fair and reasonable will be preferred to one which leads to harsh and unreasonable results. . . . Similarly "an interpretation that would place one party at the mercy of another should, if at all be possible, be avoided.". . .

Construing the language of the agreement in the light of all the criteria previously mentioned, we hold that the provision "for such services as he (Griswold), in his sole discretion, may render" obligated Griswold to render some services to Heat and imposed on him the duty to exercise good faith in the determination of their amount. . . . We further hold that these obligations . . . were sufficient [to support] Heat's promises in the agreement. . . .

The plaintiff is entitled to recover on the contract.

Doolittle v Fruehauf Corporation

(FlaApp) 332 So2d 107 (1976)

Doolittle leased real estate to the Fruehauf Corporation. The lease gave Fruehauf the option to purchase the property. Thereafter Fruehauf sent Doolittle a letter which it claimed exercised the option. Doolittle claimed that it did not. Fruehauf sued Doolittle to compel Doolittle to sell the property to it. From a judgment for Fruehauf, Doolittle appealed.

MILLS, J. . . . The lease gave Fruehauf an option to purchase the leased premises. The option read as follows:

"Lessee shall have the further right and option to purchase the demised premises after the first year of this lease and during the remainder of the term and any extension or renewal thereof for the sum of $50,000 cash."

The lease ended on 31 October 1973. On 19 September 1973, Fruehauf gave written notice of its desire and intent to purchase the leased premises. Doolittle acknowledged receipt of this notice by letter of 28 September 1973 and enclosed with the letter a proposed form of warranty deed. No further correspondence was had between the parties until 12 December 1973, when Doolittle by letter of that date wrote Fruehauf: "Since you have elected not to exercise the option . . . the option has expired."

On 18 December Fruehauf tendered the $50,000 purchase price and asked for delivery of Doolittle's warranty deed. The $50,000 check was not accepted by Doolittle. She stated that the tender of the purchase price had not been made prior to the termination of the lease.

From the outset, it should be noted that the lease did not specify the manner in which the option was to be exercised nor did it set forth any time or procedure for closing the purchase in the event the option was exercised.

It is not necessary to tender purchase money as a condition precedent to exercising an option, if this condition is not expressly stated in the option. . . .

The two steps which are necessary to exercise an option are: (1) there must be a decision by the optionee to purchase the property under the terms of the option; (2) The optionee must communicate the decision to the optionor within the life of the option. . . .

In the case before us, Fruehauf determined that it wished to purchase the property in accordance with the terms of the option. In other words, for $50,000 cash. Then by letter of 19 September, Fruehauf attempted to communicate this decision to Doolittle. Doolittle contends that the language used in the letter was not sufficient to constitute an acceptance and would not have been binding on Fruehauf had Doolittle chosen to maintain an action for specific performance. The language Doolittle refers to are the phrases "desire to purchase" and "intent to purchase." However, this supposedly conditional language must be read in the context of the letter: "Fruehauf Corporation herewith tenders formal notice of their desire to purchase the property. We are hopeful conveyance can be officially consummated on or about October 31, 1973. We will appreciate acknowledgment from you of this notice of our intent to purchase. Also, we would appreciate your suggestions and comment on what documents you will prepare and/or provide before and at the closing."

In our opinion, this language is not equivocal, ambiguous or conditional. It clearly communicates Fruehauf's decision to purchase the property from Doolittle, and that is all that is required to exercise an option. At this point the option became a bilateral contract, binding on both parties, and susceptible of enforcement by a court of equity in a suit for specific performance.

Doolittle contends that. . . . Fruehauf breached the contract by not paying the purchase price by 31 October when the lease was to be extinguished. There is nothing in the option which indicates that the purchase price had to be paid before 31 October. When there is no time set for the performance of a certain act, it is interpreted to mean that the act must be done within a reasonable time. Here there was no time set for the payment of the purchase money.

[Judgment affirmed]

BOYER, C.J. (dissenting) . . . I am of the view that the language of the letter from Fruehauf Corporation tendering "formal notice" of its *"desire"* to purchase the subject property was not sufficient to turn a unilateral contract (the option) into a binding bilateral contract which would have bound Fruehauf to purchase, had it subsequently refused so to do. Certainly I agree that, absent a provision so requiring, in order to exercise an option to purchase it is not necessary for the exercise to be accompanied by a tender of the purchase price. However, in the absence of a simultaneous tender of the purchase price, the exercise of the option must be unequivocal. A recitation that the optionee "desires" to purchase the subject of the option is not unequivocal. Further, the option clearly provided that Fruehauf Corporation had the option *"to purchase"* the subject property during the term of the lease. The lease term expired on October 31, 1973. Normally an option provides the manner by which it may be exercised, the date thereof, the terms of the purchase and a deadline for consummating the purchase. The option here involved contained no such provisions. In the absence of such provisions I would hold that the language of the option means what it says and that the "purchase" was required to have been accomplished within the prescribed period of time. It was not.

I would reverse.

QUESTIONS AND CASE PROBLEMS

1. What objective of the law (from the list in Chapter 2, page 17–21) is illustrated by each of the following quotations?
   (a) "Economic life would be most uncertain . . . if we did not have the assurance that contracts once made would be binding."
   (b) An offer is terminated by the lapse of a reasonable time when no time has been stated.

2. Why does the law require that an offer be definite?

3. Compare the communication of an offer, the communication of the revocation of an offer, and the communication of the acceptance of an offer.

4. Compare an auction sale, which is announced to be "with reserve" and a sale which is advertised as "will sell to the highest bidder."

5. The Willis Music Co. advertised a television set at $22.50 in the Sunday newspaper. Ehrlich ordered a set, but the company refused to deliver it on the ground that the price in the newspaper ad was a mistake. Ehrlich sued the company. Was it liable? Reason? [Ehrlich v Willis Music Co., 93 Ohio App 246, 113 NE2d 252]

6. Laseter was employed by Pet Dairy Products Co. When he was injured at work, Pet promised to continue to employ him and to give him light work. Pet later discharged

him, and he sued Pet for breach of contract. Was he entitled to recover? [Laseter v Pet Dairy Products Co., (CA4 SC) 246 F2d 747]

7. Berryman signed a paper which he gave to Kmoch. The paper stated "for ten dollars . . . , I hereby grant unto you . . . an option for 120 days after date to purchase" certain specified real estate. The ten dollars was never paid. About a month later, Berryman sold the same land to a third person. Although Kmoch learned of the sale he notified Berryman that he exercised his option to purchase the land. Berryman claimed that the option was void. Was he correct? [Berryman v Kmoch, 221 Kan 304, 559 P2d 790]

8. Brown agreed to give Dobry an option to purchase a tract of land. Brown refused to carry out this agreement and Dobry sued him to enforce it. Was he entitled to do so? [Brown v Dobry (FlaApp) 311 So2d 159]

9. Owen wrote to Tunison asking if Tunison would sell his store for $6,000. Tunison replied, "It would not be possible for me to sell unless I received $16,000 cash." Owen replied, "Accept your offer." Tunison denied that there was a contract. Decide. [Owen v Tunison, 131 Maine 42, 158 A 926]

10. Ranch owned land. Bentzen and Ranch entered into an "agreement for warranty deed" which provided for the sale of the property to Bentzen, with the purchase price to be paid $1,000 down and the balance "payable by future agreement on or before" a specified date. Thereafter Ranch refused to transfer the property to Bentzen. Bentzen then sued Ranch for breach of contract and to enforce the contract. Decide. [Bentzen v Ranch, 78 Wyo 158, 320 P2d 440]

11. A buyer sent an offer in the form of a written contract signed by him to the seller on January 15. The seller signed the contract and delivered it to his attorney on January 17. On January 17 the buyer mailed a letter to the seller revoking his offer. The seller received this letter on January 19 but the seller's lawyer sent the signed contract to the buyer on January 22. The buyer refused to perform the contract and the seller sued for damages for its breach. Was the buyer liable? [Kendel v Pontious, (Fla App) 244 So2d 543]

12. *A* owned land. He signed a contract agreeing to sell the land but reserving the right to take the hay from the land until the following October. He gave the contract form to *B*, a broker. *C*, a prospective buyer, agreed to buy the land and signed the contract but crossed out the provision as to the hay crop. Was there a binding contract between *A* and *C*? [Koller v Flerchinger, 73 Wash 2d 857, 441 P2d 126]

13. The Canonie Construction Company sent Dayhuff a signed paper reading: "Field Purchase Order CANONIE CONSTRUCTION COMPANY . . . To Jack R. Dayhuff . . . Haul sand [for a highway construction project] as required. Approximately 35,000 to 50,000 cubic yards 0.95 per ton scaled." Thereafter Canonie gave the hauling work to the Gibson Coal Company. Dayhuff sued on the grounds that the purchase order form gave him the right to do all the hauling for the specified construction job. Was he correct? [Dayhuff v Canonie Construction Co., 152 Ind App 154, 283 NE2d 425]

14. Feaheny offered to sell Quinn her house. She made an offer to sell on an installment payment basis, but also asked Quinn to make a cash offer. Quinn made a cash offer which Feaheny rejected. Quinn then accepted the installment payment basis. Feaheny refused to perform the contract, and Quinn sued her. Was she liable for breach of contract? [Quinn v Feaheny, 252 Mich 526, 233 NW 403]

15. Soar was a professional football player in the National Football League. He claimed that a commissioner of the league had agreed that he would be included in the league's pension plan "if sufficient funds become available." Soar brought suit against the football league players' association to enforce this promise. Was he entitled to recover? [Soar v National Football League Players' Ass'n (CA1 RI) 550 F2d 1287]

11 Contractual Capacity

All persons do not have the same legal capacity to make a contract. In some cases the legal capacity of a person has no relation to the individual's actual ability. A person who is 17 years old, for example, may have just as much ability to make a contract as an older person. Nevertheless, a 17-year-old is ordinarily under a legal incapacity. In other cases, such as those involving insane persons, the legal incapacity is based upon the inability to understand the consequences of the particular transaction. Persons whose legal capacity is or may be restricted include minors, insane persons, intoxicated persons, convicts, and aliens.

Every party to a contract is presumed to have contractual capacity until the contrary is shown.[1] The fact that a person does not understand a contract does not mean that contractual capacity is lacking.

§ 11:1. Minors.
At common law any person, male or female, under twenty-one years of age was a *minor* (or an infant). At common law, minority ended the day before the 21st birthday. The "day before the birthday" rule is still followed, but the 21 years has been reduced to 18 years in most of the states and to 19 in a few. Some states provide for the termination of minority upon marriage and some specify that the minority of girls shall terminate sooner than that of boys.

§ 11:2. Minor's Power To Avoid Contracts.
With exceptions that will be noted later, a contract made by a minor is voidable [2] at the election of the minor.[3] If the minor so desires, the minor may perform the contract. The adult party to the contract, however, cannot avoid the contract on the ground that the minor could do so.

With the lowering of the age of majority, the importance of the law as to minors has greatly diminished. It has significance, however, as the prototype or precursor of consumer protection legislation.

(a) **Minor's Misrepresentation of Age.** Generally the fact that the minor has misrepresented age does not affect the minor's power to avoid the contract. A few states hold that such fraud of the minor prevents the minor from avoiding the contract.

---

[1] Kruse v Coos Head Timber Co. 248 Ore 294, 432 P2d 1009.

[2] In some jurisdictions the appointment of an agent or an attorney by a minor is void rather than voidable. There is no reason why this exception should be made, and there is a tendency to eliminate it.

[3] If the minor dies, the personal representative of the minor's estate may avoid a contract which the minor could have avoided.

A few states permit the minor to avoid the contract in such case but require the minor to pay for any damage to the property received under the contract.

In any case, the other party to the contract may avoid it because of the minor's fraud.

(b)   Time for Avoidance. A minor's contract, whether executed or not, ordinarily can be disaffirmed or avoided by the minor at any time during minority or for a reasonable time after becoming of age.[4] What is a reasonable time is a question of fact to be determined in the light of all the surrounding circumstances. (See p. 168, Eastern Airlines, Inc. v Stuhl)

The minor can avoid a contract only during minority and for a reasonable time after attaining majority. After the lapse of such reasonable time, the contract is deemed ratified and cannot be avoided by the minor. A few states permit the former minor to avoid a wholly executory contract thereafter in the absence of an express affirmance. If the contract has been executed by the other contracting party, as by delivering property to the minor, the retention of such property by the minor after the minor attains majority will generally be regarded as a ratification or affirmance of the contract by the minor even though the contract is executory as to performance of the minor's obligation.

In some states, statutes declare that a minor's debt is not binding unless there is some act of ratification after attaining majority. This reverses the pattern of the common law under which the burden would be on the minor to disaffirm the obligation.

(c)   Effect of Avoidance. The minor's avoidance of a contract only avoids the contract. It does not wipe out the fact that there was a contract. Hence, the fact that a minor avoids the purchase of an automobile after a collision does not affect the rights of the injured third person nor the liability of the minor's insurer.[5]

§ 11:3. What Constitutes Avoidance. Avoidance or disaffirmance of a contract by a minor may be any expression of an intention to repudiate the contract. Any act inconsistent with the continuing validity of the contract is a disaffirmance. Thus, when a minor conveyed property to *A* and later, on reaching majority, made a conveyance of the same property to *B,* the second conveyance was an avoidance of the first.

§ 11:4. Restitution by Minor upon Avoidance.

(a)   Original Consideration Intact. When a minor still has what was received from the other party, the minor, on avoiding the contract, must return it to the other party or offer to do so. That is, the minor must put things back to the original position, or as it is called, restore the *status quo ante*. If the minor who is able to return the consideration does not do so, the minor cannot avoid the contract. By virtue of this rule, when a contract is avoided, the minor must avoid all of it. The minor cannot keep part of the contract and reject the balance.

(b)   Original Consideration Damaged or Destroyed. What happens if the minor cannot return what has been received because it has been spent, used, damaged, or

---

[4] Mechanics Finance Co. v Paolino, 29 NJSuper 449, 102 A2d 784.
[5] Wise v Truck Insurance Exchange, 11 WashApp 405, 523 P2d 431.

destroyed? The minor's right to avoid the contract is not affected thereby. The minor can still avoid the contract and is only required to return what remains. The fact that nothing remains or that what remains is damaged does not bar the right to avoid the contract. In those states which follow the common-law rule, the minor can thus refuse to pay for what has been received under the contract or can get back what had been paid or given, even though the minor does not have anything to return or returns any property in a damaged condition. There is, however, a trend which would limit this rule.

§ 11:5. Recovery of Property by Minor upon Avoidance. When a minor avoids a contract, the other contracting party must return the money received from the minor. Any property received from the minor must also be returned. If the property has been sold to a third person who did not know of the minority of the original seller, the minor cannot get the property back,[6] but in such cases the minor is entitled to recover the money value of the property or the money received by the other contracting party from the third person.

§ 11:6. Ratification. A minor's voidable contract becomes binding and cannot be avoided if the minor ratifies or approves the contract.

(a)   What Constitutes Ratification. Ratification may consist of any expression that indicates an intention to be bound by the contract. The making of payments after attaining majority may constitute a ratification. Many courts, however, refuse to recognize payment as ratification in the absence of further evidence of an intent to ratify, an express statement of ratification, or an appreciation by the minor that such payment might constitute a ratification.[7]

An acknowledgment by the minor that a contract had been made during minority, without any indication of an intent to be bound thereby, is not a ratification.

(b)   Form of Ratification. Generally no special form is required for ratification of a minor's voidable contract, although in some states a written ratification or declaration of intention is required.

(c)   Time for Ratification. A minor can avoid a contract any time during minority and for a reasonable time thereafter but, of necessity, can only ratify a contract after attaining majority. The minor must have attained majority or the "ratification" would itself be regarded as voidable.

§ 11:7. Contracts for Necessaries. A minor can avoid a contract for necessaries but must pay the reasonable value for furnished necessaries. This duty of the minor is called a quasi-contractual liability.[8] It is a duty which the law imposes upon the minor rather than one created by contract.

Originally necessaries were limited to those things absolutely necessary for the sustenance and shelter of the minor. Thus limited, the term would extend only to the most simple foods, clothing, and lodging. In the course of time, the rule was

---

[6] Uniform Commercial Code § 2-403(1).
[7] Bronx Savings Bank v Conduff, 78 NMex 216, 430 P2d 374.
[8] See § 9:16 as to quasi-contractual liability generally.

relaxed to extend generally to things relating to the health, education, and comfort of the minor. Thus, the rental of a house used by a married minor is a necessary. And services reasonably necessary to obtaining employment by a minor have been held to be necessaries. (See p. 169, Gastonia Personnel Corporation v Rogers)

The rule has also been relaxed to hold that whether an item is a necessary in a particular case depends upon the financial and social status, or station in life, of the minor. The rule as such does not treat all minors equally. To illustrate, college education may be regarded as necessary for one minor but not for another, depending upon their respective stations in life.

Property other than food or clothing acquired by a minor is generally not regarded as a necessary. Although this rule is obviously sound in the case of jewelry and property used for pleasure, the same view is held even though the minor is self-supporting and uses the property in connection with work, as tools of trade, or an automobile used to go to and from work. The more recent decisions, however, hold that property used by a minor to earn a living is a necessary. Thus it has been held that a tractor and farm equipment were necessaries for a married minor who supported the family by farming.

It is likely that necessaries will in time come to mean merely that which is important by contemporary standards.[9]

§ 11:8. Contracts That Minors Cannot Avoid.

Statutes in many states deprive a minor of the right to avoid an education loan, a contract for medical care, a contract made while running a business, a contract approved by a court, a contract made in performance of a legal duty, or relating to bank accounts, insurance policies, or corporate stock. In most states, the contract of a veteran, although a minor, is binding, particularly those for the purchase of a home. In some states, by court decision, a minor who is nearly an adult or who appears to be an adult cannot avoid a contract, particularly when it is made in connection with a business or employment. Some courts take an intermediate position with respect to employment contracts by allowing the minor to avoid the contract but prohibiting the use of any information obtained from the employment. (See p. 170, Pankas v Bell) It is also held that when a minor has settled a claim and received the amount specified in a release, the release is binding upon the minor and cannot be set aside when the minor attains majority.[10]

As an exception to the right to disaffirm a contract during minority, a minor cannot fully avoid a conveyance for the transfer of land until majority is attained.

§ 11:9. Liability of Third Person for Minor's Contract.

(a) **Liability of Parent.** Ordinarily a parent is not liable on a contract made by a minor child. The parent may be liable, however, if the child is acting as the agent of the parent in making the contract.[11] Also, the parent is liable to a seller of necessaries for the reasonable value of the necessaries supplied by the seller to the child if the parent has deserted the child.[12]

---

[9] Chrysler Credit Corp. v Waegele, 29 CalApp3d 681, 105 CalRptr 914.
[10] Frank v Volkswagenwerk (CA3 Pa) 522 F2d 321.
[11] See § 41:5 in this book.
[12] See § 39:11 in this book.

(b)   Liability of Cosigner. When the minor makes a contract, another person, such as a parent or a friend, may sign the contract along with the minor for the purpose of accommodating the minor by making the contract more attractive to the third person.

With respect to the other contracting party, the cosigner is bound equally with the minor. Consequently, when the minor avoids the contract the cosigner remains bound by the contract. If the debt to the creditor is actually paid, or if the minor, on avoiding the contract, makes full restitution, the obligation of the cosigner is discharged. (See p. 170, Allen v Small)

§ 11:10. Insane Persons.

An insane person lacks capacity to make a binding contract. The contract of an insane person is either voidable or void. In order to constitute insanity within the meaning of this rule, the party must be so deranged mentally as to not understand that a contract is being made or does not understand the consequences of what is done. If a party lacks such understanding, the cause of the mental condition is immaterial. It may be idiocy, senile dementia, lunacy, imbecility, or such excessive use of alcoholic beverages or narcotics as to cause mental impairment.

If a person with sufficient capacity to know that a contract is being made, makes a contract, the contract is binding and it is immaterial that the person has delusions or insane intervals, or is eccentric. As long as the contract is made in a lucid interval and is not affected by any delusion, it is valid.

(a)   Effect of Insanity. An insane party may generally avoid a contract in the same manner as a minor.[13] Upon the removal of the disability, that is, upon becoming sane, the former insane person may either ratify or disaffirm the contract. If the insane person dies, a personal representative or heirs may also affirm or disaffirm the contract.

As in the case of minors, the other party to the contract has no right to disaffirm the contract merely because the insane party has the right to do so.

(b)   Appointment of Guardian. If a proper court has appointed a guardian for the insane person, a contract made before that appointment may be ratified or disaffirmed by the guardian. If the insane person makes a contract after a guardian has been appointed, the contract is void and not merely voidable.

§ 11:11. Intoxicated Persons.

The capacity of a party to contract and the validity of the contract are not affected by the party's being drunk at the time of making the contract as long as the party knew that a contract was being made. The fact that the contract was foolish and would not have been made if sober does not make the contract voidable unless it can be shown that the other party purposely caused the person to become drunk in order to induce the making of the contract.

If the degree of intoxication is such that a person does not know that a contract is being made, the contract is voidable. The situation is the same as though the person were so insane at the time as to not know what was being done. Upon becoming sober, the person may avoid or rescind the contract. An unreasonable delay in taking steps to set aside a known contract entered into while intoxicated, however, may bar the intoxicated person from asserting this right.

[13] Davis v Colorado Kenworth Corp. 156 Colo 98, 396 P2d 958.

§ 11:12. Convicts. The capacity to contract of a person convicted of a major offense (a felony or treason) varies from state to state. In some states, the convict may make a valid transfer of property. In others, there is either a partial or total contractual disability. When there is a disability, it generally exists only during the period of imprisonment.[14]

§ 11:13. Aliens. An *alien* is a national or subject of a foreign country. Originally aliens were subject to many disabilities. These have been removed in most instances by treaty between the United States and the foreign country, under which each nation agrees to give certain rights to the citizens of the other. Generally an alien's right to make a contract is recognized.[15]

If this country is at war with a nation of which an alien is a subject, the alien is called an *enemy alien* without regard to whether the alien is actually assisting that country in the prosecution of the war. An enemy alien is denied the right to make new contracts or to sue on existing ones, but if sued on an existing contract, may defend the action. A contract made by an enemy alien, even though made before the war began, will at least be suspended during the war. In some instances, if the contract calls for continuing services or performance, the war terminates the contract.

§ 11:14. Married Women. At common law a married woman could not make a binding contract. Her agreements were void, rather than voidable, even when she lived apart from her husband. Consequently, she could not ratify an agreement after the removal of the disability by the death of her husband.

The common-law disability of a married woman has almost been abolished by statute in practically all the states.[16] There are still a few restrictions in some jurisdictions, mainly in instances where the wife might be unduly influenced by the husband. It is probable that these will disappear in the near future. (See p. 171, Peddy v Montgomery)

---

[14] "Civil death" statutes depriving prisoners of their civil rights have been adopted in one-fourth of the states. Some courts hold these statutes to be unconstitutional. Delmore v Pierce Freightlines Co. (DC Ore) 353 FSupp 258.

[15] A state cannot restrict or prohibit the employment of aliens in private or public employment. Truax v Raich, 239 US 33; Purdy & Fitzpatrick v California, 79 CalRptr 77, 456 P2d 645.

[16] United States v Yazell, 382 US 341.

CASES FOR CHAPTER 11

Eastern Airlines, Inc. v Stuhl

(NY Civil Court) 65 Misc 2d 901, 318 NYS2d 996 (1970) affirmed 68 Misc 2d 269, 327 NYS2d 752

Stuhl was 20 years of age. He gave checks to Eastern Airlines. These checks were not honored by the bank. Eastern Airlines sued him on the checks. In his answer filed in the lawsuit five months after he attained majority,* he disaffirmed the contract for which the checks had been given.

KASSAL, J. . . . Addressing the defense of disaffirmance, the court concludes that the same is not

---

* *Authors' Comment:* At the time the above case and the next two cases arose and were decided, 21 years was the age of majority.

a valid defense herein since it had not been exercised within a reasonable time after the defendant attained his majority. The defendant attained his majority on April 21, 1964, but he did not disaffirm these checks until September 26, 1964, a period more than five months thereafter.

Some of the considerations which lead to the conclusion that this was not a reasonable period are these: The five months hiatus, the said disaffirmance did not occur until asserted as a defense in legal action, the fact that the defendant is not truly an "infant" in the moral or business concept of this principle since he had admittedly been actively involved in various and numerous business enterprises for at least three years prior thereto or from his 17th birthday on.

Obviously, these all add up to a person who had more than sufficient mental capacity and his disaffirmance, five months after attaining his majority, with regard to the issuance of checks in his twentieth year, should not under these circumstances be considered a disaffirmance within a reasonable period. In the court's opinion, some of the elements that should be considered in determining a reasonable period for a disaffirmance are the business experience, awareness and general acumen of the said infant. We have, in this instance, an example of a very world-wise man attempting, by the device of invoking a disaffirmance, to avail himself of a "free ride" both literally and figuratively.

[Judgment for airline]

Gastonia Personnel Corporation v Rogers

276 NC 279, 172 SE2d 19 (1970)

Bobby Rogers, 19, married, quit school, and looked for work. He agreed with the Gastonia Personnel Corporation, an employment agency, that if he obtained employment through it, he would pay a stated commission. Rogers obtained work through the agency but refused to pay the agreed commission of $295 for which he denied liability on the ground of infancy. From a judgment in favor of Rogers, the agency appealed.

BOBBITT, C.J. . . . Under the common law persons, whether male or female, are classified and referred to as *infants* until they attain the age of twenty-one years. . . .

"By the fifteenth century it seems to have been well settled that an infant's bargain was in general void at his election (that is voidable), and also that he was liable for necessaries.". . .

In accordance with this ancient rule of the common law, this Court has held an infant's contract, unless for "necessaries" or unless authorized by statute, is voidable by the infant, at his election, and may be disaffirmed during infancy or upon attaining the age of twenty-one. . . .

"Necessaries . . . embrace boarding; for shelter is as necessary as food and clothing. They have also been extended so as to embrace schooling and nursing. . . . In regard to the quality of the clothes and the kind of food &c., a restriction is added, that it must appear that the articles were suitable to the infant's degree and estate.". . .

[The court noted a number of statutes which had limited the ability of a minor to disaffirm his contracts.]

. . . Without awaiting additional statutory changes, . . . it seems appropriate that this common-law rule, which is rooted in decisions made by judges centuries ago, should be modified at least to the extent set forth below. . . .

In general, our prior decisions are to the effect that the "necessaries" of an infant, his wife, and child, include only such necessities of life as food, clothing, shelter, medical attention, etc. In our view, the concept of "necessaries" should be enlarged to include such articles of property and such services as are reasonably necessary to enable the infant to earn the money required to provide the necessities of life for himself and those who are legally dependent upon him. . . .

The evidence before us tends to show that defendant, when he contracted with plaintiff, was nineteen years of age, . . . married, a high school graduate, within "a quarter or 22 hours" of obtaining his degree in applied science, and capable of holding a job at a starting annual salary of $4,784.00. To hold, as a matter of law, that such a person cannot obligate himself to pay for services rendered him in obtaining employment suitable to his ability, education, and specialized training, enabling him to provide the necessities of life for himself, his wife and his expected child, would place him and others similarly situated under a serious economic handicap.

In the effort to protect "older minors" from improvident or unfair contracts, the law should not deny to them the opportunity and right to obligate themselves for articles of property or services which are reasonably necessary to enable them to provide for the proper support of themselves and their dependents. The minor should be held liable for the reasonable value of articles of property or services received pursuant to such contract. . . .

[Judgment reversed and action remanded]

Pankas v Bell

413 Pa 494, 198 A2d 312 (1964)

Bell, aged 20 years and 7 months, went to work in the beauty parlor of Pankas and agreed that when he left the employment, he would not work in or run a beauty parlor business within a ten-mile radius of downtown Pittsburgh, Pennsylvania, for a period of two years. Contrary to this provision, Bell and another employee of Pankas opened up a beauty shop three blocks from his shop and advertised themselves as former employees of Pankas. Pankas sued Bell to stop the breach of the noncompetition or restrictive covenant. Bell claimed that he was not bound because he was a minor when he had agreed to the covenant. From a decision for Pankas, Bell appealed.

JONES, J. . . . The issue [is] not one of the liability of a minor for a breach of his contract but whether a minor should be . . . permitted to repudiate his contract without restoring what he had received and, if restoration cannot be made, without being enjoined from making use of the information he had gained from his employment by the plaintiff to the latter's damage. The [lower] court held that the minor should be enjoined "from making use of that information, in violation of his agreement made at the time when he desired and obtained employment, and upon the faith of which he obtained the information and acquaintance" and the court further observed: "No man would engage the services of an infant if he could not impose the same condition for his own protection against the use of his formulas, trade secrets, and lists of customers that he could exact of an adult.". . .

In the case at bar, we need not nor do we decide that a contract for the employment of a minor is an exception to the general rule that the contracts of minors are voidable. What we do determine is

that, although this contract is voidable, the minor should not be permitted to utilize any benefits, training, or knowledge derived from such contract to the damage and detriment of his former employer. As a practical matter, to hold otherwise would deter the employment of minors because no person would care to run the risk of employing a person who could not only avoid the contract but also utilize that which he has derived from the contract to compete with his former employer.

Behind the rule rendering voidable the contracts of a minor is the very laudable purpose of the law to protect minors from contracts which may be disadvantageous to them and to protect them "against their own lack of discretion and against the snares of designing persons.". . . This "protective cloak" is to safeguard the interests of the minor; it is not to be employed as a vehicle whereby the minor is enabled to practice unconscionable business methods. It is a shield for defense, not a sword for offense. In enjoining this minor from using to his own benefit and to the detriment of his former employer that which he has gained from his former employment, we declare that, even though the contract is voidable, the minor is prohibited from exploiting that which he gained from the contract and that equity should restrain such exploitation.

There is no evidence of any fraud or overreaching on Pankas' part, the contract as a whole was beneficial to Bell, and Bell should be enjoined from exploiting that which he gained from his employment by Pankas. . . .

[Decree affirmed]

Allen v Small

129 Vt 77, 271 A2d 840 (1970)

Bruce Small, a minor, purchased a used car from Allen's Garage for $225. He paid $100 in cash. He and his mother, as surety, signed a note for the balance. The son paid the balance in weekly installments of $25 and the note was marked paid in full on August 19, 1960. On August 29, 1960, Bruce avoided the sale and returned the car to Allen. After being sued, Allen refunded the $225 to Bruce. Allen then sued Bruce's mother on the note on the theory that as Bruce had avoided his liability, the debt represented by the note was unpaid and therefore the mother was liable for its payment. From a judgment for the mother, Allen appealed.

KEYSER, J. . . . The plaintiff contends that on the facts established by the record, the defendant is liable to the plaintiff on the note to the extent of its face amount. He argues that since Bruce rescinded his contract with plaintiff, the lien note was restored to its former status as far as the defendant was concerned, she being an accommodation maker. Whether or not it was is the sole issue before us.

The plaintiff claims that marking of "Paid in Full" on the note must be classed as a mistake since the minor demanded a refund of the purchase price within ten days after making his final payment. Thus, he says the marking should be deemed a nullity. . . .

There is no question made but the note was fully paid according to its terms and tenor. . . . Payment is the final act which extinguishes a [note] and transmutes it into a cancelled voucher, . . . on which no suit may thereafter be maintained. . . .

The findings establish that the defendant signed the note to insure its payment. When Bruce Small made the final payment of $25.00 on August 19, 1960, the note was fully paid and intentionally discharged by [Allen] and delivered to Bruce. . . .

The debt due as evidenced by the lien note was paid and discharged on August 19, 1960. "(A)ll the authorities agreed that such discharge (of the principal) operates to discharge the surety.". . . Whatever action Bruce Small took on his own behalf concerning his rights as a minor was between him and the plaintiff and could not affect the rights of the defendant.

Moreover, the record establishes that the minor returned the 1949 motor vehicle, together with a transfer of any title he had in it, to the plaintiff. This occurred after full payment of the . . . note by the minor and after he had possessed the vehicle for only around five weeks. There is no claim that the vehicle was not in as good condition when returned as it was when sold. "(W)here restoration of the consideration is made by law a condition of disaffirmance by the infant, and he has disaffirmed and put the other party in the statu quo, the surety on a note given by the infant is discharged.". . .

[Judgment affirmed]

Peddy v Montgomery

(Ala) 345 So2d 631 (1977)

An Alabama statute provided that a married woman could not sell her land without the consent of her husband. Montgomery made a contract to sell to Peddy land owned by her. Montgomery's husband did not consent thereto. Montgomery did not perform the contract and was sued by Peddy. The defense was raised that the contract was void and could not be enforced because of the statute. Peddy claimed that the statute was unconstitutional. The lower court held that it was constitutional, and Peddy appealed.

SHORES, J. . . . Because of this statute, if the wife conveys or mortgages her separate property without the signature of the husband as a co-grantor, the conveyance or mortgage is void.

Contracts made by the wife for the sale of her lands without the concurrence of the husband at the time the contract is made are also void because of this statute.

There is no dispute that [the statute] treats married women differently than married men and unmarried females. The question is whether that difference in treatment is permissible under the Constitution. . . .

The United States Supreme Court has dealt with gender related classifications contained in various statutes within the last few years. In Reed v. Reed, 404 U.S. 71, 92 S.Ct. 251, 30 L.Ed.2d 225 (1972), that court held that an Idaho statute which gave a mandatory preference to males over females to act as administrators of estates violated the equal protection clause of the constitution. In Frontiero v. Richardson, 411 U.S. 677, 93 S.Ct. 1764, 36 L.Ed.2d 583 (1973), the issue was whether the Due Process Clause of the Fifth Amendment prevented requiring a married woman Air Force Officer to show, in fact, that her spouse was dependent on her for over one-half of his support for the purpose of obtaining increased quarters allowance and medical and dental benefits, while a male member of the Air Force is allowed to claim his spouse as a dependent without such proof. The court held that the challenged statute violated the constitution, . . .

In Stanton v Stanton, 421 U.S. 7, 95 S.Ct. 1373, 43 L.Ed.2d 688 (1975), Mr. Justice Blackmun, writing for a majority of the court, held that a Utah [child support] statute establishing that minority for males extended to age twenty-one and for females to age eighteen was a violation of the equal protection clause.

In the instant case, the appellee argues that to hold that the challenged statute violates the Constitution of this state would be to destroy ". . . the basic concepts of the common law ownership of real property and the right and prerogative of our legislature to govern that part of our social and economic life.". . .

[We are not] persuaded that the legislature has the unbridled authority to govern all aspects of our social and economic life. That legislative discretion is limited by the Constitution to the enactment of laws which do not deny to persons of this state the equal protection of the laws. To hold that all conveyances of a wife's land, or any interest therein, must, to be valid, carry the signature of her husband, is to deny to a married woman rights which are freely exercised by every other adult person, male or female, in Alabama. To justify such a holding on the legal presumption that all married women are incapable of dealing with their own land, without the guidance of their husbands, is to ignore the realities of life as we know it.

We hold that [the statute] limiting the freedom of a married woman to alienate or mortgage her lands, or any interest therein, without the assent and concurrence of her husband, violates the provisions of Article 1, [Alabama] Constitution of 1901, in that it denies to that category of adult landowners rights guaranteed to all other adult landowners by the Constitution and laws of this state. . . .

There is no provision of the Constitution which would permit the legislature to deny to married women rights possessed by all other adults. [The legislature's] authority to do so must be found in that document, and cannot rest upon an ancient myth that married women are presumed to be more needful of protection of their own interests than other adults, male or female. . . .

[Judgment reversed and action remanded]

QUESTIONS AND CASE PROBLEMS

1. (a) What is the objective of the rule of law that a minor who avoids a contract usually cannot recover property if the other party has transferred it to a third person who did not know of the minority and purchased the property for value?
   (b) How is the evolutionary nature of the law illustrated by the changes in the definition of a minor's necessaries?

2. Compare the power of a minor to avoid a contract when (a) the minor has said nothing as to age, (b) the minor knowingly misrepresents age, and (c) the minor cannot return the goods which were obtained by the contract.

3. Compare ratification by a minor of a contract when (a) the minor ratifies the contract while still a minor, and (b) the minor ratifies the contract a day after becoming an adult.

4. Compare the avoidance of a minor's contract for (a) a luxury, and (b) a necessary.

5. Saccavino made a contract with Carl Gambardella, then 15 years of age, and Carl's parents, that he would train Carl to be a horse rider and that he would receive in return a share of Carl's earnings from exhibitions and racing. When Saccavino sued on the contract years later, Carl claimed that it was void. Was he correct? [Saccavino v Gambardella, 22 Conn Supp 168, 164 A2d 304]

6. Martinson executed a note payable to Matz. At the time Martinson was drunk. The next day he was told that he had signed the note. Five years later, Martinson's wife told Matz's attorney that Martinson would not pay the note as he was drunk at the time he executed the note. Matz brought suit on the note two years after that. Could he recover? [Matz v Martinson, 127 Minn 262, 149 NW 370]

7. Mary McCoy, a married woman, sold land that she owned to Niblick. Her husband did not sign the contract. Niblick moved onto the property before a deed was delivered and made improvements. Later Mary sought to set the contract aside. A Pennsylvania statute provided that a married woman had the right to sell or dispose of her property

but that she could not execute a deed to the property without having her husband sign the deed. Who was entitled to the property? [McCoy v Niblick, 221 Pa 123, 70 A 577]

8. On February 28, 1958, Alice Sosik signed a note promising to make certain payments to Conlon. She later sued to have the note set aside on the ground that she lacked mental capacity. A letter from a physician was presented which stated that he had examined her on July 3, 1959, and that she "is suffering from a chronic mental illness and is totally incapable of managing her affairs." Was she entitled to set the note aside? [Sosik v Conlon, 91 RI 439, 164 A2d 696]

9. A, who appeared to be over 21 years of age, purchased an automobile from B. He later informed B that he was a minor and avoided the contract. A gave as his explanation that there were certain defects in the car. B claimed that these defects were trivial. Assuming that the defects were trivial, could A avoid the contract? [Rose v Sheehan Buick, (Fla App) 204 So2d 903]

10. In 1936 Palmer was adjudicated incompetent. In 1942 he was adjudicated competent. In 1952 he purchased policies of fire insurance from the Lititz Mutual Insurance Co. The property insured was destroyed by fire. The company refused to pay on the policies on the ground that Palmer was insane when he applied for and obtained the insurance. Was this a valid defense? [Palmer v Lititz Mutual Insurance Co., (DC WD SC) 113 F Supp 857]

11. Gary Muniz, a minor, purchased a dune buggy from Jones. When Gary's father learned of the purchase, he ordered Gary to take the dune buggy back to Jones or dispose of it. While taking the buggy back to Jones, Gary was involved in an accident. The father's insurer denied liability on the basis that Gary was not the owner of the dune buggy at the time of the collision because he had avoided the contract. Was the insurer correct? [St. Paul Fire & Marine Ins. Co. v Muniz, 19 Ariz App 5, 504 P2d 546]

12. Paolino executed a promissory note to pay the Mechanics Finance Co. $960.92. The note was to be paid in weekly installments. Paolino was 3 months under the age of majority. Installments due on the note were not paid, and the finance company sued Paolino. He was then 3 months over majority. Paolino raised the defense that he was a minor when he signed the note. Mechanics Finance claimed that it was too late to avoid the contract. Was Mechanics Finance correct? [Mechanics Finance Co. v Paolino, 29 NJSuper 449, 102 A2d 784]

13. Edward Griffin and his wife were both minors. They contracted with Cogen Properties, Ltd. to build a home for them. They did not pay and when sued for breach of contract, they raised the defense that they were minors and could avoid the contract. A local statute provided that a minor could not avoid a contract to purchase a home. Can they avoid the contract? [Cogen Properties, Ltd. v Griffin, 358 NYS2d 929]

14. Chiara in Texas purchased furniture from Ellard. He sold some to a third person and moved the balance of it to New York. Chiara, who was of unsound mind, later brought an action to set aside the purchase from Ellard. The latter claimed that Chiara must first return all of the property. Was Ellard correct? [Ellard v Chiara (Tex CivApp) 252 SW2d 991]

12 Genuineness of Assent

An agreement is the result of an offer and an acceptance by competent parties. The enforceability of a contract based upon that agreement may be affected, however, because a mistake was made by either or both of the parties or because the assent of one of the parties was obtained through fraud, undue influence, or duress.

The law does not treat all mistakes the same. Some have no effect whatever; others make the agreement voidable or unenforceable. Mistakes may be unilateral or mutual (bilateral).

§ 12:1. Unilateral Mistake. Ordinarily a unilateral mistake regarding a fact does not affect the contract unless the agreement states that it shall be void if the fact is not as believed, or unless the mistake is known to or should be recognized by the other party.

A unilateral mistake of law or as to expectations does not have any effect upon the contract. The courts refuse to recognize ignorance of the law as an excuse. If they did, the unscrupulous could avoid their contracts at will by saying that they did not understand the law. Under the rule that a unilateral mistake of law has no effect, the fact that a signer of a contract would not have signed it if the signer had understood the legal effect of the contract is not a defense.[1]

Contrary to the rule that a unilateral mistake has no effect, an exception is made by some courts in the case of government construction work. Here a contractor who makes a unilateral mistake in the computation of a bid may retract the bid even though it has already been accepted by the government.

If one party knows that the other party has made a mistake, the mistaken party is entitled to rescind the contract. If the wrong offer is within the range of reasonable offers, it is unlikely that a jury will conclude that the offeree knew that the offeror had made a mistake.

(a) Negligent Mistake As to Nature of Paper. When a party makes a negligent mistake as to the nature of a paper, the party is bound according to its terms. For example, when the printed form for applying for a loan to a corporation contained a guaranty by the president of the corporation of the corporate debt, the president signing the application without reading it was bound by this guaranty, even though the president did not know that it was in the application and the application was headed merely "application for credit."

---

[1] Manufacturers and Traders Trust Co. v Commercial Door & Hardware, Inc., 51 AppDiv2d 362, 381 NYS2d 709.

(b)   Mistakes As to Releases. An insurance claimant is bound by the release given to the insurance company when there is a unilateral mistake as to its meaning resulting from carelessness in reading the release. When a release is given and accepted in good faith, it is initially immaterial that the releasor or both of the parties were mistaken as to the seriousness or possible future consequences of a known injury or condition. If the release covers all claims "known or unknown," the courts following the common-law view hold the releasor is bound even though there were other injuries of which the releasor was unaware because the effects of the unknown injuries had not yet appeared. Some courts depart from this and hold the release effective only with respect to the conditions or consequences which were known when the release was given.

(c)   Identity of Other Party. When the parties deal face to face, a contract is not affected by the fact that one party may be mistaken as to the identity of the other. When the mistake as to the identity of a party is induced by trick or deception of that party, however, the contract is voidable and may be set aside by the deceived party.

§ 12:2. Mutual Mistake. When both parties make the same mistake of fact, the agreement is void. When the mutual or bilateral mistake is one of law, the contract generally is binding. Thus, the fact that both parties to a lease mistakenly believed that the leased premises could be used for boarding animals does not give the tenant a right to rescind the lease for mutual mistake of law, the theory being that in the eyes of the law the parties knew what the zoning regulations allowed. A few courts have refused to follow this rule, and in several states statutes provide that a mutual mistake of law shall have the same vitiating effect as a mutual mistake of fact. A bilateral mistake with respect to expectations ordinarily has no effect on the contract unless the realization of those expectations is made a condition of the contract.

(a)   Possibility of Performance. An agreement is void if there is a mutual mistake as to the possibility of performing the agreement. Assume that *A* meets *B* downtown and makes a contract to sell to *B* an automobile, which both believe is in *A's* garage. Actually the automobile was destroyed by fire an hour before the agreement was made. Since this fact is unknown to both parties, there is a mutual mistake as to the possibility of performing the contract, and the agreement is void.

(b)   Identity of Subject Matter. An agreement is void if there is a mutual mistake as to the identity of the subject matter of the contract. (See p. 183, Ouachita Air Conditioning, Inc. v Pierce) For example, if a buyer and seller discuss the sale of an electrical transformer, but one is thinking of a one-phase transformer and the other is thinking of a three-phase transformer, there is no contract.

(c)   Collateral Matters. When a mutual mistake occurs as to a collateral matter, it has no effect on the contract thereafter executed. (See p. 184, Interstate Industrial Uniform Rental, Inc. v Couri Pontiac, Inc.) For example, where the plaintiff asks the fire insurer to issue a policy if there was no existing policy, and both the insured and the insurance company wrongly believed that there was no other policy, the policy which was then issued to the insured was not void because of the mutual mistake that there was no other policy. That mistake was as to a collateral matter;

there was no concealment, as the insured had given the insurer all the information which the insured possessed and the insurer then concluded that the applicant was not already covered by insurance; and the circumstances made it clear that the policy had not been issued on the express condition that it was binding only if there was no other policy protecting the applicant.

§ 12:3. Misrepresentation. Suppose that one party to a contract makes a statement of fact which is false but which is innocently made without intending to deceive the other party. Can the other party set aside the contract on the ground of being misled by the statement? Generally it is held that the contract is binding and cannot be set aside because of the innocent misrepresentation. In some instances, however, the law protects the deceived person by allowing rescission of the contract.

Equity will permit the rescission of the contract when the innocent misstatement of a material fact induces another to make the contract. If the deceived person is a defendant in an action at law, it is generally held that such innocent deception by the plaintiff cannot be asserted as a defense. There is a tendency, however, for the law courts to adopt the rule of equity. For example, it may be possible for an insurance company to avoid its policy because of an innocent misstatement of a material fact by the applicant. Contracts between persons standing in confidential relationships, such as guardian and ward, or parent and child, can be set aside for the same reason.

When a person gives an expert opinion for the purpose of guiding another in a business transaction in which both the expert and the other person are financially interested, there is an ordinary tort duty upon the expert to exercise due care in making statements. Consequently, when the expert negligently, although innocently, makes a false statement, the expert is liable to the other person.

§ 12:4. Concealment.

(a)   General Rule of Non-liability. Ordinarily there is no duty on a party to a contract to volunteer information to the other. If *A* does not ask *B* any questions, *B* is not under any duty to make a full statement of material facts. Consequently, the nondisclosure of information which is not asked for does not impose fraud liability nor impair the validity of a contract. For example, where a seller and a buyer entered into a settlement agreement of their differences, it was not fraudulent for the seller to fail to inform the buyer that the seller would not do any further business with the buyer, the buyer believing that their business relationship would continue if the dispute were put out of the way by the settlement agreement.

(b)   Exceptions. In some instances, the failure to disclose information which was not requested is regarded as fraudulent and the party to whom the information was not disclosed has the same remedies as though a known false statement were intentionally made.

(1)   Unknown Defect or Condition. There is developing in the law a duty on a party who knows of a defect or condition to disclose that information to the other party where the defect or condition is obviously unknown to the other person and is of such a nature that it is unlikely that the other person would discover the truth or inquire about it. To illustrate, where there was a

non-apparent problem with the water supply of a farm, the seller of the farm was under a duty to inform the buyer of that defect. The owner of a house must inform a prospective buyer that several years before there had been a severe fire, even though the house remained structurally sound and had been repaired following the fire so that no signs of fire damage were visible. The manufacturer of wall paneling is liable to a buyer for failing to inform the buyer that the paneling did not satisfy the local fire code, in consequence of which the buyer was required to replace the paneling.[2]

Likewise, in transactions between banks there seems to be a growing concept of a duty to disclose information which one bank should foresee would be desired by another bank even though the latter had not specifically requested the information.[3]

(2) Confidential Relationship. If *A* and *C* stand in a confidential relationship, such as that of attorney and client, *A* has a duty to reveal anything that is material to *C*'s interest when dealing with *C,* and *A*'s silence has the same legal consequence as a knowingly made false statement that there was no material fact to be told to *C.*

(3) Fine Print. An intent to conceal may be present when a printed contract or document contains certain clauses in such fine print that it is reasonable to believe that the other contracting party will never take the time nor be able to read such provisions.

In some instances, legislatures have outlawed certain fine-print contracts. Statutes commonly declare that insurance policies may not be printed in type of smaller size than designated by statute. Consumer protection statutes designed to protect the credit buyer frequently require that particular clauses be set in large type. When a merchant selling goods under a written contract disclaims the obligation that goods be fit for their normal use, the Uniform Commercial Code requires the waiver to be set forth in "conspicuous" writing [4] which is defined as requiring "a term or clause . . . [to be] so written that a reasonable person against whom it is to operate ought to have noticed it. A printed heading in capitals . . . is conspicuous. Language in the body of a form is 'conspicuous' if it is in larger or other contrasting type or color. . . ." [5]

There is a growing trend to treat a fine-print clause as not binding upon the party who would be harmed thereby, without considering whether fraud was involved. This may be justified legalistically on the basis that the person prejudiced by the clause did not know of its existence and could not reasonably be expected to have known of its existence, and therefore the fine-print clause was not one of the terms agreed to by the parties. Moreover, the supplier of the form containing the fine-print clause should have realized that the victim of the clause would not know nor have reason to know of its existence. As a

---

[2] St. Joseph Hospital v Corbetta Constr. Co., Inc., 21 IllApp3d 925, 316 NE2d 51.
[3] Lehigh Valley Trust Co. v Central National Bank (CA5 Fla) 409 F2d 989.
[4] Uniform Commercial Code § 2-316(2).
[5] UCC § 1-201(10).

practical matter, the conclusion is justified by the consideration that the fine-print clause ordinarily appears in a standard printed form of contract prepared by the enterprise and offered to one who has an inferior bargaining position, such as a consumer, and is offered on a "take-it-or-leave-it" basis.

Although the Uniform Commercial Code does not establish any general rule governing all fine-print situations, it is likely that the Code concept of "conspicuous" will be applied by courts increasingly in the future, so that no provision in a contract will be deemed a part of the bargain unless the provision is conspicuous or otherwise called to the attention of the other contracting party. Thus, it will be held that a provision which is in fine print, is under a misleading title or heading, or is buried in many unrelated provisions, was not agreed to by the parties and is not binding upon the party who did not know of its existence.

(4)   Active Concealment. Concealment may be more than the passive failure to volunteer information. It may consist of a positive act of hiding information from the other party by physical concealment, or it may consist of furnishing the wrong information. Such conduct is generally classified and treated as fraud.

§ 12:5. Fraud.
Fraud is the making of a false statement of fact with knowledge of its falsity or with reckless indifference as to its truth, with the intent that the listener rely thereon and the listener does so rely and is harmed thereby. Conduct that is merely unethical does not constitute fraud. (See p. 185, Houston Oilers v Neely) When one party to the contract is guilty of fraud, the contract is voidable and may be set aside by the injured party.

For convenience, this discussion refers to fraudulent statements, but any kind of communication may be involved. The representation may be made by conduct as well as by words.

(a)   Misstatement of Fact. A misstatement of a past or present fact is an essential element of fraud. A statement that a painting is the work of Rembrandt when the speaker knows that it is the work of an art student in a neighboring school is such a misstatement.

An intentional misrepresentation of the nature of the transaction between the parties is fraudulent. A person is guilty of fraud by falsely making another believe that the paper about to be signed, which in fact is a contract, is not a contract, but is a receipt or a petition.

(b)   Mental State. The speaker must intend that the other party rely upon the statement which is false. The speaker must either know or believe that what is said is false or must speak with reckless indifference as to whether it is true or not.

(1)   Misrepresentation of Intention. A misrepresentation of intention can constitute fraud when a promise is made by a person who does not intend to keep it. To illustrate, a customer purchases goods from a merchant on credit and agrees to pay for them in 60 days. If the customer does not intend to pay for the goods and does not do so, the customer is guilty of fraud by misrepresenting intention. Similarly, a misrepresentation by a real estate developer that houses

would be constructed in accordance with FHA standards and specifications constitutes fraud when the developer did not actually so intend.[6]

(2) Misstatement of Opinion or Value. Ordinarily a misstatement of opinion or value is not regarded as fraudulent on the theory that the person hearing the statement recognizes or should recognize that it is merely the speaker's personal view and not a statement of fact.

A promotional or sales talk statement as to future events is not fraud. Thus, a statement by a motion picture distributor to a theater owner that a given picture "should be a 'blockbuster' " does not constitute fraud.[7]

If, however, the defendant, in making a statement as to the future, had knowledge not available to the plaintiff which showed that such expectations could not be realized, the statement as to the future expectations can be held fraudulent. Thus a statement that a business would make a stated profit in the future is actionable when the speaker knows that on the basis of past events such prediction was false.[8]

(3) Misstatement of the Law. A misstatement of law is treated in the same manner as a misstatement of opinion or value. Ordinarily, the listener is regarded as having an opportunity of knowing what the law is, an opportunity equal to that of the speaker, so that the listener is not entitled to rely on what the speaker says. When the speaker has expert knowledge of the law or claims to have such knowledge, however, the misstatement of law can be the basis for fraud liability.

(c) Investigation Before Relying on Statement. If the listener had available the ready means of determining the truth of the statement, as by examining that which was in front of the parties, the listener is not entitled to let that opportunity pass, rely on the false statement, and then recover damages from the speaker. Likewise, the fact that the listener relies on the speaker or is too busy to read a paper before signing it does not protect the listener. The listener takes the risk that the paper will conform to the speaker's statement when the listener signs it without reading it. When an illiterate person or one physically unable to read signs a paper without having it explained or read aloud, such signer is ordinarily bound by its contents.

As a limitation on this rule, however, some courts hold that the negligence of the injured party is not a bar to a claim for damages when the wrongdoer takes active steps to conceal the truth, as by substituting one paper for another and falsely informing the injured party as to the nature of the paper. As a further limitation on the effect of the negligence of the victim of fraud, there is a trend in favor of permitting the inexperienced person to rely on the statements of the expert as to what it is that the inexperienced person is signing, with the result that on seeking to avoid the transaction because of fraud, the inexperienced person is not met by the defense that it was negligent to have signed the paper without closer examination. Thus it has been held that an inexperienced buyer may set aside a deed and mortgage because of the fraud of the builder's agent who had misrepresented the papers in

---

[6] Brennaman v Andes & Roberts Brothers Construction Co. (MoApp) 506 SW2d 462.
[7] Twentieth Century Fox Distributing Corp. v Lakeside Theatres, Inc. (LaApp) 267 So2d 225.
[8] Bissett v Ply-Gem Industries, Inc. (CA5 Fla) 533 F2d 142.

question as being merely papers which had to be signed in order to "get on with the building"; the court holding that the inexperienced buyer was entitled to rely on the statements of the experienced agent.[9]

There is no general duty to investigate to verify the truth of statements made by the other party. Consequently, when a buyer asks the seller questions as to repairs and water leaks and the seller knowingly makes false statements relating thereto, the buyer may recover damages for fraud and is not barred by a failure to examine the building to see if the statements of the seller were true. In any case, if an examination by the plaintiff would not have revealed a particular defect or condition, either because it is not visible, or because of the technical nature of the matter, or if a simple examination could not be made, the injured person may rely on the statements of the other party and raise the issue of fraud on learning that the statements were false. A misrepresentation made to prevent further inquiry also constitutes fraud.

(d)   Use of Assumed Name. The use of an assumed name is not necessarily fraudulent or unlawful. It is only such when the user of the name uses the name of another person or makes up a name for the purpose of concealment to avoid arrest or to avoid creditors or to imitate a competitor and deceive customers.

In the absence of any intent to evade or deceive by the use of the assumed name, it is lawful for a person to go by any name, although other persons may refuse to enter into contracts unless the actual name is used. If a person makes a contract in an assumed or fictitious name or in a trade name, such person is bound by the contract because that name was in fact used to identify that person.[10]

§ 12:6. Undue Influence. An aged parent may entrust all business affairs to a trusted child; an invalid may rely on a nurse; a client may follow implicitly whatever an attorney recommends. The relationship may be such that for practical purposes the one person is helpless in the hands of the other. When such a confidential relationship exists, it is apparent that the parent, the invalid, or the client is not in fact exercising a free will in making a contract suggested by the child, nurse, or attorney, but is merely following the will of the other person. Because of the great possibility that the person dominating the other will take unfair advantage, the law presumes that the dominating person exerts *undue influence* upon the other person whenever the dominating person obtains any benefit from a contract made with the dominated person. The contract is then voidable and may be set aside by the dominated person unless the dominating person can prove that at the time the contract was made no unfair advantage had been taken.

The class of confidential relationships is not well-defined. It includes the relationships of parent and child, guardian and ward, physician and patient, attorney and client, and any other relationship of trust and confidence in which one party exercises a control or influence over another.

In some states, however, the mere fact that there is a close blood relationship, such as parent and child, does not constitute a confidential relationship.[11]

---

[9] Modern American Mortgage Corp. v Nelson, 250 Ark 928, 469 SW2d 124.
[10] Weikert v Logue, 121 GaApp 171, 173 SE2d 268.
[11] Nelson's Estate, 132 IllApp2d 740, 270 NE2d 65.

Whether undue influence exists is a difficult question for the court (ordinarily the jury) to determine. The law does not regard every "influence" as undue. Thus, nagging may drive a person to make a contract, but that is not ordinarily regarded as undue influence. Persuasion and argument are not in themselves undue influence.

An essential element of undue influence is that the person making the contract does not exercise free will. In the absence of a recognized type of confidential relationship, such as that between parent and child, the courts are likely to take the attitude that the person who claims to have been dominated was merely persuaded and consequently there was no undue influence.

(a)   Domination by Seller. In some instances the domination of the market or of the buyer by a particular seller may make the agreement with a buyer illegal as a violation of the federal antitrust law.

(b)   Unequal Bargaining Power. Sometimes the party with the weaker bargaining power has no practical choice although, as far as the rule of law is concerned, the contract is binding as the voluntary act of a free adult person.

Underlying the traditional concept of the law of contracts is the belief that a person can go elsewhere to contract and therefore every contract is necessarily voluntary. But "going elsewhere" may be meaningless when better terms cannot be obtained elsewhere because the entire industry does business on the basis of the terms in question, or when the particular person cannot obtain better terms elsewhere because of inferior economic standing or bargaining position.

When the condition of relative immobility of a party exists, the tendency of the law is to find that that party might be oppressed or exploited and the social forces which oppose such a result come into play.

In some instances, the bargaining scales are sought to be balanced by rules of construction. Thus, an insurance contract is strictly construed against the insurer because it is regarded as a standardized "contract of adhesion" prepared by the insurer to which the insured must adhere in order to obtain any insurance.

In some areas, statutes have been adopted to offset the inequality of bargaining power, such as the Uniform Commercial Code's provision that establishes higher standards for merchants as compared with casual sellers, and the rights given to labor by the labor-management relations statutes. To these may be added the statutes permitting exporters to combine for the purpose of the exporting trade so that they can meet the competition of foreign dealers, such privilege creating an exception to the federal antitrust law under which such combinations in foreign commerce would be prohibited.

§ 12:7. Duress.

(a)   Physical Duress. A person makes a contract under *duress* when there is such violence or threat of violence that the person is deprived of free will and makes the contract to avoid harm. The threatened harm may be directed at a near relative of the contracting party as well as against a contracting party. If a contract is made under duress, it is voidable at the victim's election. (See p. 186, Rhode Island v Rollins)

(b) Economic Duress. The economic pressure on a contracting party may be so great that it will be held to constitute duress. (See p. 186, Austin Instrument Inc. v Loral Corp.) Economic duress occurs when the victim is threatened with irreparable loss for which adequate recovery could not be obtained by suing the wrongdoer. Generally, however, a threat of economic loss or the pressure caused by economic conditions does not constitute duress which makes a contract voidable. For example, it is generally not economic duress to threaten to cut off a contractor's line of credit which the contractor needs to obtain building materials. The fact that a party executed a release only because the money was needed does not constitute duress so as to impair the validity of the release. Likewise the fact that a debtor only borrowed money because of being financially desperate does not constitute economic duress and does not affect the binding character of the contract between the debtor and the lender.[12]

§ 12:8. Remedies. Mistake, fraud, undue influence, and duress may make the agreement voidable or, in some instances, void. The following remedies are then available.

(a) Rescission. If the contract is voidable, it can be rescinded or set aside by the party who has been injured or of whom advantage has been taken. If not avoided, however, the contract is valid and binding. In no case can the other party, the wrong-doer, set aside the contract. If the agreement is void, neither party can enforce it and no act of avoidance is required by either party to set the contract aside.

When a contract is voidable, the right to rescind the contract is lost by any conduct that is inconsistent with an intention to avoid it. For example, when a party realizes that there has been a mistake but continues with the performance of the contract, the right to avoid the contract because of the mistake is lost.[13] Likewise, it is generally held that a contract, although procured by duress, may be ratified by the victim of the duress, as by adhering to the terms of the contract or making claims to benefits arising therefrom. The right to rescind the contract is lost if the injured party, with full knowledge of the facts, affirms the transaction, or when, with such knowledge, the injured party fails to object to the guilty party within a reasonable time. In determining whether a reasonable time has expired, the court considers whether the delay benefited the injured party, whether a late avoidance of the contract would cause unreasonable harm to the guilty person, and whether avoidance would harm intervening rights of third persons acquired after the original transaction.

When the contract has resulted in the transfer of property from the guilty person to the victim, the latter also loses the right to rescind if, with knowledge of the true situation, the victim retains and uses the property, sells it to another, or uses it after the guilty person refuses to take it back.

(b) Damages. If the other party was guilty of a wrong, such as fraud, as distinguished from making an innocent mistake, the injured party may sue for damages caused by such a wrong. In the case of the sale of goods, the aggrieved party may both

---

[12] Puget Sound Power and Light Co. v Shulman, 84 Wash2d 433, 526 P2d 1210.
[13] Dayton v Gibbons & Reed Co. 12 Utah2d 296, 365 P2d 801.

rescind and recover damages; [14] but in other contracts, the victim must choose one of these two remedies. Thus a buyer rescinding a contract for the sale of a house because of fraud cannot also recover damages for the fraud.

(c)   Reformation of Contract by Court. When a written contract does not correctly state the agreement already made by the parties, either party can have the court correct or reform the contract to express the intended meaning. Under modern procedures, a person may generally sue on the contract as though it had been reformed and recover if it is established that reformation of the contract should be made and that there has been a breach of the contract as reformed. Thus, instead of first suing to reform an insurance policy and then bringing a second suit on the policy as reformed, most jurisdictions permit the plaintiff to bring one action in which to prove the case as to reformation and also as to breach of the contract as reformed.

---

[14] UCC § 2-721. See also § 2-720, providing that, unless a contrary intent clearly appears, an expression of "rescission" of a sale contract will not be treated as a renunciation or discharge of a claim in damages for a prior breach.

CASES FOR CHAPTER 12

Ouachita Air Conditioning, Inc. v Pierce

(La App) 270 So2d 595 (1972)

Ouachita Air Conditioning Company installed an Amana condenser in Pierce's home to replace the York condenser of his air conditioning system. Pierce did not pay for the replacement condenser and Ouachita sued him for the purchase price. He raised the defense that he was not liable because of a mutual mistake of fact. From a judgment for Pierce, Ouachita appealed.

HALL, J. . . . Defendant's home was equipped with a four-ton York air conditioning system which had originally been engineered and installed by Ballard's, a York distributor. The unit was not cooling properly so defendant called a Mr. Walters, who had been servicing the unit and who was with Ballard's at the time the unit was installed. Walters said he was no longer in the air conditioning repair business and suggested that defendant contact Mr. Lawler, who is president of Ouachita Air Conditioning, Inc. Defendant checked with Ballard's and was informed that Lawler formerly worked for that company when they were installing air conditioners. Defendant then called Lawler and asked him to come out and check the unit and repair it.

Lawler handled Amana air conditioning units and advertised generally as an Amana dealer but this fact was never communicated by Lawler to defendant.

Upon checking defendant's unit, Lawler found that one of the two two-ton compressors was burned out and needed replacing and the other compressor was not working properly. That night Lawler telephoned defendant and suggested that the two compressors be replaced with one four-ton condensing unit. Lawler quoted defendant a price and in answer to defendant's inquiry, assured defendant that the new unit carried a five-year warranty. Defendant agreed to the price and instructed Lawler to go ahead and install the new unit which Lawler advised was on order and should arrive in a few days. The brand name of the new unit was never mentioned. Defendant never stated that he was expecting a York unit to be installed and Lawler never advised defendant he intended to install an Amana unit.

When the new unit arrived, Lawler installed it at plaintiff's home replacing the two York compressors which he removed from the premises. That evening defendant observed that the new unit installed was an Amana unit and he immediately telephoned Lawler and told him that he was expecting a York unit and did not want any brand other than York. Some discussion and negotiations were had between Lawler and defendant about getting a York unit in place of the Amana but they could not agree on the extra cost, particularly as to who should bear the additional installation expense. Defendant made other arrangements and had a new York unit installed and asked Lawler to pick up the Amana unit which he refused to do. This suit followed.

Plaintiff takes the position that it entered into a contract with defendant for the sale and installation of a four-ton condensing unit of unspecified brand at an agreed price and that plaintiff fulfilled its end of the contract by installing a new unit equivalent to the old one and capable of performing the required mechanical function. Plaintiff contends that if there was error or mistake on the part of defendant as to the brand of unit to be installed such error was unilateral and was unknown to plaintiff and cannot serve as the basis for invalidating the contract. . . .

Defendant contends that there was never a completed contract or sale between the parties because there was never a meeting of the minds as to the object of the sale. . . . Defendant further contends that if there was a completed contract it is subject to rescission for error as to the substance or object. . . .

There is nothing in the evidence to indicate that either party acted other than in complete good faith and the testimony of both Lawler and Pierce was straightforward and frank. The evidence supports a finding that Lawler honestly believed that since no brand was specified the agreement was simply for a four-ton condensing unit which would do a job equivalent to the one being replaced. The evidence equally supports a finding that Pierce honestly believed that since they were discussing replacement of a major component part of a complete York system, then the replacement unit would be of the same brand. This belief on the part of defendant was entirely reasonable in view of the fact that he was put in contact with plaintiff through a York serviceman and a York distributor and Lawler was recommended as being experienced in repairing York units.

. . . In this instance the contract of sale was never perfected because there was no . . . agreement as to the thing or object. Otherwise stated, there was error of fact as to the thing or object which vitiated consent. . . .

. . . There was error of fact as to the quality of the object, that is, the manufacturer of the unit, and that this quality was a principal cause of making the contract from defendant's standpoint. While the seller did not have actual knowledge that this was a principal cause or motive it should be presumed that he knew it from the nature of the transaction.

. . . Although Lawler was in good faith, when he was confronted with a complete York system in which a major component needed replacing he should have been aware that without anything being said to the contrary, the buyer would expect replacement with the same brand of unit. The trial court was correct in setting aside the sale and rejecting plaintiff's demands. . . .

[Judgment affirmed]

Authors' Comment: This case was decided in a non-UCC jurisdiction but it rests on general principles of contract law. These principles would be recognized in a UCC state as they have not been displaced by the UCC (UCC § 1-103) and would be recognized generally in situations not governed by the Uniform Commercial Code.

Interstate Industrial Uniform Rental, Inc. v Couri Pontiac, Inc.

(Me) 355 A2d 913 (1976)

Couri Pontiac made a contract with Interstate Industrial Uniform Rental, Inc. by which the latter agreed to supply Couri with clean uniforms for its personnel. At the time, Couri was already under a contract for the same service with Standard Uniform Rental, Inc. Both Couri and Interstate knew this but both believed that Couri could terminate the contract with Standard whenever it chose to do so. This was a mistake. The contract with Standard obligated Couri to take its service on a year to year basis, with the contract continuing to exist each year unless timely notice was given to terminate the agreement. Couri refused to go through with its contract with Interstate. Interstate sued Couri for breach of the contract. Couri claimed that there was no contract because the parties had made a mutual mistake as to the existence of a binding contract with Standard. From a judgment for Couri, Interstate appealed.

WEATHERBEE, J. . . . The principle that a contract is not legally binding if both parties have entered into it under an actual and good-faith mutual misunderstanding is well-established . . . A mistake of fact occurs if the parties entertain a conception of the facts which differs from the facts as they really exist. . . . The mistake must be mutual, that is, the minds of the parties must fall prey to the same misconception with respect to the bargain. . . . For example, a mistaken assumption about the subject matter of the bargain by one party and ignorance of that mistake by the other party is not a mutual mistake, but two unilateral mistakes; the initial mistake by the first party and a mistake as to the first party's mental state by the second party.

We need not decide whether the present case presents a true mutual mistake or merely two unilateral mistakes; for even if the mistake was mutual to both the plaintiff and defendant, it was not sufficiently material to justify recission of the contract. The doctrine of mutual mistake requires that the mistake touch the subject matter of the bargain and not merely be collateral to it. Only if the mutual mistake relates to a material fact of the essence of the bargain can the injured party avoid the contract. . . . Because the materiality of the mistake depends upon the circumstances of each case, this requirement is necessarily imprecise and is better understood by illustration than through mere recitation. For example, a contract to sell land, "275 acres more or less," will not be enforced where, unknown to the parties, the parcel of land in question was less than 200 acres, . . . nor will a sales agreement requiring the transfer of good and marketable title to land be enforced where neither party knew of a third party's option on the land. . . . In other words, the mutual mistake must so vitally affect the facts upon the basis of which the bargain was struck that the written contract does not express the intent of the parties. The parties must have, in fact, agreed to something other than that established by the writing. . . .

In the present case we believe that if any mutual mistake occurred, it related solely to a collateral issue involving the propriety of wisdom of entering into the contract and does not, therefore, render the contract unenforceable. The basic subject matter of the contract between the plaintiff and defendant is unaffected by their misconceptions although the defendant, had he been aware of the true facts, would doubtlessly have perceived the need for the contract differently. The defendant could legally have executed a score of agreements with different uniform rental companies and each contract would express the correct respective intents of the parties to supply and receive rented uniforms. The contract adequately expresses the bargain agreed to by both parties and we believe that the Justice below erred in rescinding the contract.

[Judgment reversed]

Houston Oilers, Inc. v Neely

(CA10 Okla) 361 F2d 36 (1966)

On December 1, 1964, Neely, a senior in college, made a contract to play the following year for the Houston Oilers professional football team. It was agreed orally that the making of this contract would be kept secret so that Neely would appear to be eligible for a postseason college game. Neely then received a better offer from the Dallas Cowboys and after college went to play for them. Houston sought an injunction against Neely. Neely claimed Houston could not enforce the contract because of its fraud in stating that the contract would be effective on January 2, 1965, and filing the contract with the League Commissioner before that time in violation of the agreement to keep the execution of the contract secret so as to make him appear eligible for the postseason college football game. From a decision in Neely's favor, Houston appealed.

PICKETT, C.J. . . . Neely was over the age of 21 years, and it is stipulated that he had "special, exceptional, unique knowledge, skill, and ability as a football player." He was competent to enter into a valid contract to perform these services exclusively for a designated person or organization, and upon agreeing to so limit his services, he was subject . . . to be enjoined from performing them for anyone else. . . .

. . . The essence of Neely's contentions . . . is that the contracts are unenforceable because Houston falsely represented that the effective date of the agreement would be January 2, 1965, and that Houston's filing of the contract copies with the Commissioner was a violation of its promise to keep the matter secret. The trial court was of the opinion that these alleged misrepresentations constituted fraud in the inducement of the contract which would subject it to rescission. As has been heretofore stated, each contract specifically provides otherwise. Neely does not say that he was so naive that he did not know his eligibility for further intercollegiate football competition would be destroyed when he signed a professional football contract and received the bonus money. . . . The purpose of secrecy surrounding the execution of the contracts was not to preserve Neely's eligibility, but rather to prevent his ineligibility from becoming known. . . .

Neely, a bright young man, ably advised by his father-in-law, knew exactly what he wanted. With commendable foresight, he sought not only a favorable contract, but also a business arrangement extending beyond his football days. Houston, through its president, undertook to meet this requirement. Neely, after consulting his wife and father-in-law, . . . accepted Houston's final proposal, which he characterized as a "fine offer." Unexpectedly Dallas arrived on the scene, and Neely found another bidder for his services. He welcomed this new opportunity, and apparently plans were set in motion designed to convince him that he could ignore the existing agreements with Houston. . . .

There is insufficient evidence to sustain a finding of material misrepresentation on the part of Houston amounting to fraud which would affect the validity of the contracts. It is true that Neely testified that it was his understanding that the contracts were not to become effective until after the game on January 2. The contracts, however, provided otherwise, and we are not at liberty to rewrite them. Furthermore, the letter of employment, . . . and the $25,000 bonus check which was delivered upon the execution of the contracts, were all dated December 1, 1964. . . .

While it is not contended here that Houston did not have a legal right to sign Neely to a professional player's contract, it is urged that when Houston participated in a scheme to conceal that fact for the purpose of permitting an ineligible player to participate in a postseason game, it was such deceit upon others that a court of equity should not intervene to assist in the enforcement of the contract. With this argument we cannot agree. It is neither unlawful nor inequitable for college football players to surrender their amateur status and turn professional at any time. Neely was free to bind himself to such a contract on December 1, 1964, as he would have been after January 2, 1965. Nor was Houston under any legal duty to publicize the contract or to keep it secret. Its agreement to keep secret that which it had a legal right to keep secret cannot be considered inequitable or unconscionable. . . .

[Judgment reversed and action remanded with instructions to grant the injunction]

Rhode Island v Rollins

(RI) 359 A2d 315 (1976)

Rollins was a prisoner in a state prison. There was an uprising of the prisoners accompanied by violence and the holding of prison personnel as hostages. The director of the Department of Corrections promised Rollins and others immunity from prosecution if they would stop. They did so and were later indicted and prosecuted for the crimes committed in the course of the uprising. Rollins and the others raised the defense that a promise of immunity had been made to them. The prosecution claimed that the promise of immunity was not binding because it had been obtained by duress. The trial court refused to enforce the promise of immunity. Rollins and the others were convicted and appealed.

PAOLINO, J. . . . [The appellants argue] that the Attorney General cannot prosecute a defendant after a promise of immunity was given. . . .

We find no merit in any of the arguments made by defendants under this point. Promises extorted through violence and coercion are no promises at all; they are void from the beginning and unenforceable as a matter of public policy.

We conclude our consideration of this issue by stating that even if the director had the power to make the alleged promises, they would be unenforceable as a matter of public policy because they were secured by violence and coercion.

[Conviction affirmed]

Austin Instrument, Inc. v Loral Corporation

29 NY2d 124, 324 NYS2d 22, 272 NE2d 533 (1971)

Loral was awarded a $6 million contract by the United States Navy for the production of radar sets. To perform this contract, Loral required 40 precision-gear component parts. It advertised for bids on these parts and let a subcontract to Austin to supply 23 of the gear parts. In the following year Loral was awarded a second Navy contract. Austin declared that it would not make further deliveries under its subcontract unless Loral agreed to a price increase, both as to parts already delivered and parts to be delivered and also unless Loral gave Austin a subcontract under the second Navy contract for all 40 component gear parts. Loral did not want to increase the prices under the original contract and wished to let subcontracts for parts under the second Navy contract on the basis of individual subcontracts for each part with the lowest bidder thereon. Loral communicated with 10 manufacturers of precision

gears but could find none that could supply gears in time to perform its contract with the Navy. Loral then agreed to the price increase in connection with the first Navy contract and awarded Austin the subcontract for all 40 parts under the second Navy contract. After performance of the contracts was completed, Austin sued Loral for the balance due under the contracts. Loral sued Austin to recover the amount of the price increase on the theory that such increase had been agreed to under economic duress. The lower court dismissed Loral's claim and it appealed.

FULD, C.J. . . . A contract is voidable on the ground of duress when it is established that the party making the claim was forced to agree to it by means of a wrongful threat precluding the exercise of his free will. . . . The existence of economic duress or business compulsion is demonstrated by proof that "immediate possession of needful goods is threatened" . . . or, more particularly, in cases such as the one before us, by proof that one party to a contract has threatened to breach the agreement by withholding goods unless the other party agrees to some further demand. . . . However, a mere threat by one party to breach the contract by not delivering the required items, though wrongful, does not in itself constitute economic duress. It must also appear that the threatened party could not obtain the goods from another source of supply and that the ordinary remedy of an action for breach of contract would not be adequate.

We find without any support in the record the conclusion reached by the courts below that Loral failed to establish that it was the victim of economic duress. On the contrary, the evidence makes out a classic case, as a matter of law, of such duress.

It is manifest that Austin's threat—to stop deliveries unless the prices were increased—deprived Loral of its free will. As bearing on this, Loral's relationship with the Government is most significant. . . . Its contract called for staggered monthly deliveries of the radar sets, with clauses calling for liquidated damages and possible cancellation on default. Because of its production schedule, Loral was, in

July, 1966, concerned with meeting its delivery requirements in September, October and November, and it was for the sets to be delivered in those months that the withheld gears were needed. Loral had to plan ahead, and the substantial liquidated damages for which it would be liable, plus the threat of default, were genuine possibilities. Moreover, Loral did a substantial portion of its business with the Government, and it feared that a failure to deliver as agreed upon would jeopardize its chances for future contracts. . . . It was perfectly reasonable for Loral, or any other party similarly placed, to consider itself in an emergency, duress situation. . . .

Loral . . . also had the burden of demonstrating that it could not obtain the parts elsewhere within a reasonable time, and . . . it met this burden. The 10 manufacturers whom Loral contacted comprised its entire list of "approved vendors" for precision gears, and none was able to commence delivery soon enough. As Loral was producing a highly sophisticated item of military machinery requiring parts made to the strictest engineering standards, it would be unreasonable to hold that Loral should have gone to other vendors, with whom it was either unfamiliar or dissatisfied, to procure the needed parts. . . . Loral "contacted all the manufacturers whom it believed capable of making these parts" . . . and this was all the law requires.

It is hardly necessary to add that Loral's normal legal remedy of accepting Austin's breach of the contract and then suing for damages would have been inadequate under the circumstances, as Loral would still have had to obtain the gears elsewhere. . . . In other words, Loral actually had no choice, when the prices were raised by Austin, except to take the gears at the "coerced" prices and then sue to get the excess back. . . .

In sum, the record before us demonstrates that Loral agreed to the price increases in consequence of the economic duress employed by Austin. Accordingly, the matter should be remanded to the trial court for a computation of its damages. . . .

[Judgment reversed and action remanded]

QUESTIONS AND CASE PROBLEMS

1. What is the objective of each of the following rules of law?
(a) One party generally cannot set aside a contract because the other party failed to

volunteer information which the complaining party would desire to know.

(b) In certain close relationships that are regarded as confidential, it is presumed that a contract which benefits the dominating person was obtained by undue influence, and the dominating person has the burden of proving the contrary.

2. Compare a unilateral and bilateral mistake as to the identity of goods being sold to a buyer.

3. Compare (a) misrepresentation, (b) concealment, and (c) fraud.

4. Compare the remedies for fraud of (a) rescission, and (b) damages.

5. Schottco Corporation ordered paper for wrapping bricks from the Graham Paper Company. Through a mistake of its manager, approximately ten times too much paper was ordered. The paper was not paid for and when Graham sued for the purchase price, Schottco raised the defense that there had been a mistake in the amount ordered. Was this a valid defense? [Graham Paper Co. v Schottco Corp. (DC ED Mo) 419 FSupp 608 aff'd (CA8) 555 F2d 193]

6. Tucker purchased an automobile from Central Motors, relying on the representation that it was the latest model available. The sale was completed on February 9. On February 10, Tucker learned that the representation that the automobile was the latest model was false. He continued to drive the car; and after having driven it in excess of one thousand miles, he demanded on April 7 that the purchase be set aside for fraud. Decide. [Tucker v Central Motors, 220 La 510, 57 So2d 40]

7. Hylton was arrested on the complaint of the Cox Construction Company. The admitted facts showed that there was no legal basis for the arrest. The deputy sheriffs of the county, Phillips and Bay, put Hylton in a jail cell and dressed him in prison clothing. They told him that he could get out if he signed a paper releasing them from any liability for false imprisonment. Hylton signed the paper. He was released. Hylton then sued Phillips and Bay. They defended by proving that Hylton had released them from liability. Hylton claimed the release was void. Was he correct? [Hylton v Phillips, 270 Ore 766, 529 P2d 906]

8. A claimed that he was entitled to payment of a specified sum under a contract which he had with B. B denied this liability. A threatened to sue B if he would not agree to pay the claimed amount. B promised to pay the claimed amount. He failed to keep his promise and A sued B on this later promise for the greater amount. B defended on the ground that the promise was not binding because it was obtained by duress. Was this defense valid? [Eggleston v Humble Pipe Line Co. (Tex Civ App) 482 SW2d 909]

9. DeMeo rented a building from Horn. DeMeo was represented by an attorney who prepared the lease. The terms of the lease showed that DeMeo intended to make a particular use of the building which would require alterations necessitating a building permit. Horn knew that the building permit could not be obtained because the building was located in an urban renewal area and was to be demolished but said nothing to DeMeo. The lease recited that "the agreement was entered into after full investigation, neither party relying upon any statement or representation not embodied in this agreement made by the other." When DeMeo learned that he could not obtain the building permit he sued Horn for (1) rescission of the contract, (2) recovery of the down payment made on the lease, and (3) damages for fraud. What, if any, relief is DeMeo entitled to? [DeMeo v Horn, 70 Misc 2d 339, 334 NYS2d 22]

10. A claimed that B owed him money. A was under the impression that B did not have much money. On the basis of this impression, A made a settlement agreement with B for a nominal amount. When A later learned that B was in fact reasonably wealthy, A sought to set the agreement aside. Was he entitled to do so? [Myers v Bernard, 38 App Div 2d 619, 326 NYS2d 279]

11. A dealer induced a distributor to sell to him on credit by telling the distributor that the dealer expected to inherit money which he would invest in the business. The dealer did not inherit any money. The distributor claimed that the dealer had been guilty of fraud. Was this correct? [United Fire & Cas. Co. v Nissan Motor Corp., 164 Colo 42, 433 P2d 769]

12. An agent of Thor Food Service Corp. was seeking to sell Makofske a combination refrigerator-freezer and food purchase plan. Makofske was married and had three children. After being informed of the eating habits of Makofske and his family, the agent stated that the cost of the freezer and food would be about $95 to $100 a month. Makofske carefully examined the agent's itemized estimate and made some changes to it. Makofske then signed the contract and purchased the refrigerator-freezer. The cost proved to be greater than the estimated $95 to $100 a month, and Makofske claimed that the contract had been obtained by fraud. Decide. [Thor Food Service Corp. v Makofske, 28 Misc 2d 872, 218 NYS2d 93]

13. Jacobs purchased an automobile from Lowell Perkins Agency. She traded in her old car. For some reason she incorrectly believed that she would not be required to pay any sales tax on the purchase of the new car. Lowell asked her to pay $86 to $87 for the tax in addition to the purchase price. She refused to do so and sued to recover her traded-in car. [Lowell Perkins Agency, Inc. v Jacobs, 250 Ark 952, 469 SW2d 89]

14. The highway department of the state of Washington advertised for bids for the construction of a section of highway. J. J. Welcome & Sons Construction Company submitted a bid. Thereafter Welcome sent the highway commission a telegram stating that item (1) in the bid was changed from $210,000 to $295,000. Western Union made a mistake and the telegram as delivered to the highway commission made it a change from 210 to 285 thousand dollars. Welcome was the lowest responsible bidder and its bid was accepted by the highway commission at a total figure of $6,560,049.65. The next lowest bidder was approximately one-quarter million dollars higher. Welcome learned that its bid was accepted and that the correction telegram was erroneous. Welcome requested that the contract be increased by $10,000 to rectify the mistake made by Western Union and pointed out that this would not injure the state nor any other bidder because the next lowest bidder was still so much more than Welcome's bid. Was Welcome entitled to reformation to correct the mistake? [J. J. Welcome & Sons Construction Co. v Washington, 6 Wash App 2d 985, 497 P2d 953]

15. A corporation had forfeited its charter and plans were under way to sell its business to a buyer. *A* was a major stockholder of the corporation and was concerned because he had become liable on leases of equipment used by the corporation and hoped that the leases could be transferred to the new business, which would then assume payment of the rentals. *B* held a judgment against the corporation and was about to use legal process to enforce the judgment against the equipment which had been leased to and was used by the corporation. *A* promised *B* that *A* would pay the judgment to *B* if *B* would drop the execution against the leased equipment and the corporate assets. *A* did not keep his promise. *B* sued *A,* who raised the defense that he had made the promise because of economic duress and therefore was not liable. Was he correct? [Blumenthal v Heron, 261 Md 234, 274 A2d 636]

16. The state of North Dakota, through the Bank of North Dakota, sold county industrial development revenue bonds to the Security State Bank. Thereafter Security State Bank sued to set aside the contract on the ground that it was prohibited by statute from purchasing such bonds in excess of 5% of its capital and the contract to purchase the bonds represented more than 5%. Was it entitled to set aside the contract? [Security State Bank v North Dakota, (ND) 181 NW2d 225]

13   Consideration

Ordinarily a promise is not binding unless there is consideration for the promise. That is, in addition to all the other elements necessary for a contract, the promise of each party must be supported by consideration.

§ 13:1. Definition of Consideration. *Consideration* is what a promisor demands and receives as the price for the promise. Consideration is something to which the promisor is not otherwise entitled and which the promisor specifies as the price for the promise. To be consideration, however, it is not necessary that the promisor expressly use the word "consideration."

Since consideration is the price paid for the promise, it is unimportant who pays that price as long as it has been agreed that it should be paid in that way. For example, consideration may be the extending of credit to a third person, as extending credit to the corporation of which the promisor is a stockholder.[1]

(a) Benefit and Detriment. Some cases define consideration in terms of benefit to the promisor or detriment to the promisee. It is immaterial, however, whether benefit or detriment is present. The essential thing is that the act or thing which is done or promised has been specified by the promisor as the price to be paid in order to obtain the promise. (See p. 199, Baehr v Penn-O-Tex Oil Corporation)

(b) Unspecified Benefit. An unspecified benefit to the promisor does not constitute consideration. Thus there is no consideration although the promisor is benefitted when the benefit was not specified as the price for the promise. For example, the Federal Aviation Administration planned to conduct high altitude tests of supersonic planes. To win public support for the program, the agency declared that it would pay all property damage caused by sonic boom. Some property owners who had commenced actions to enjoin the testing then stopped prosecuting their actions. Other owners did not bring any action. Thereafter the owners of damaged property sued the government claiming that the declaration that damages would be paid constituted a binding contract. It was held that there was no contract because the promise to pay damages was not supported by consideration. The forbearance of the property owners was not consideration for the promise to pay damages even though the promise may in fact have induced such action.[2]

---

[1] State Bank of Arthur v Sentel, 10 IllApp3d 86, 293 NE2d 444.
[2] Kirk v United States (CA10 Okla) 451 F2d 690.

In some cases, the courts will hold that it can be implied that the benefit received was not an unspecified benefit but that the benefit was intended by the parties as the price to be paid to obtain the promise. (See p. 200, Newberger v Rifkind)

(c)   **Nature of Contract.** In a unilateral contract, the consideration for the promise is the doing of the act called for. The doing of the act in such case is also the acceptance of the offer of the promisor.

In a bilateral contract, which is an exchange of promises, each promise is the consideration for the other promise. When a lawsuit is brought for breaking a promise, it is the consideration for that promise on which suit is brought to which attention is directed.

(d)   **Valuable Consideration.** Consideration is sometimes described as "valuable consideration." This is done to distinguish it from the so-called "good consideration," namely, the love and affection existing between near relatives. In most states, good consideration is not consideration at all but is merely a matter of inducement in the making of a promise. Moral obligation is likewise not consideration.

§ 13:2. Effect of Absence of Consideration. The absence of consideration makes a promise not binding. Thus a person sued for breaking a promise will not be held liable when no consideration was received for the promise.

Because of the requirement of consideration, the fact that there is an agreement between competent parties does not necessarily mean that there is a binding contract. The agreement may not be binding because there is no consideration for the promise which is sued upon.

While the absence of consideration ordinarily prevents enforcing a promise, the absence of consideration has no greater effect. That is, the agreement is not illegal because there was no consideration. Consequently, when a person keeps the promise, the performance rendered cannot be thereafter revoked on the ground that there was no consideration. To illustrate, a promise to make a gift cannot be enforced because there is no consideration for the promise, but once the gift is made, the donor cannot take the gift back because there was no consideration.

§ 13:3. A Promise as Consideration. In a bilateral contract, each party makes a promise to the other. The promise which one party makes is consideration for the promise made by the other.

(a)   **Binding Character of Promise.** To constitute consideration, a promise must be binding, that is, it must impose a liability or create a duty. Suppose that a coal company promises to sell to a factory at a specific price all the coal which it orders, and that the factory agrees to pay that price for any coal which it orders from the coal company. The promise of the factory is not consideration because it does not obligate the factory to buy any coal from the coal company. If, however, the factory promises to purchase all the coal it requires for a specific period and the coal dealer agrees to supply it at a specific price per ton, there is a valid contract.

(b)   **Impossibility of Performance.** In some instances when it is obvious that a particular act is impossible to perform, a promise to do that act is not consideration. If there is a possibility that the performance can be made, the consideration is valid.

(c) Cancellation Provision. Although a promise must impose a binding obligation, it may authorize one or either party to terminate or cancel the agreement under certain circumstances or upon giving notice to the other party. The fact that the contract may be terminated in this manner does not make the contract any less binding prior to such termination.

§ 13:4. Promise to Perform Existing Obligation. Ordinarily a promise to do, or the performance of, what one is already under a legal obligation to do is not consideration. It is immaterial whether the legal obligation is based upon a preexisting contract, upon the duties pertaining to an office held by the promisor, or upon statute or general principles of law.[3]

Similarly, a promise to refrain from doing what one has no legal right to do is not consideration.

(a) Completion of Contract. When a contractor refuses to complete a building unless the owner promises a payment or bonus in addition to the sum specified in the original contract, and the owner promises to make that payment, the question arises whether the owner's promise is binding. Most courts hold that the second promise of the owner is without consideration. A few courts hold that the promise is binding on the theory that the first contract was mutually rescinded and that a second contract, including the promise to pay the bonus, was then agreed upon. Some courts hold the promise enforceable on the theory that the contractor has given up the right to elect either to perform or to abandon the contract and pay damages.

If the promise of the contractor is to do something that is neither expressly nor impliedly a part of the first contract, then the promise of the other party is binding. For example, if a bonus of $1,000 is promised in return for the promise of a contractor to complete the building at a date earlier than that specified in the original agreement, the promise to pay the bonus is binding.

(1) Good Faith Adjustment. There is a trend to enforce a second promise to pay a contractor a greater amount for the performance of the original contract when there are extraordinary circumstances caused by unforeseeable difficulties and when the additional amount promised the contractor is reasonable under the circumstances. Some courts sustain this result on the theory that there was an implied condition in the first contract that the circumstances would be or would continue to be as supposed by the parties and that the contract is therefore discharged when the circumstances prove otherwise. If such a condition is implied, the first contract is discharged by the change of circumstances and the parties are then free to make a second contract on any terms.

A growing minority of courts will enforce a promise to pay a promisee for performing an existing duty when there is no element of exploitation or oppression and the additional payment is an adjustment made in good faith to meet circumstances which were not reasonably foreseen. (See p. 201, Angel v Murray) When parties to a contract in a good-faith effort to meet the business realities of a situation agree to a reduction of contract terms, there is some authority that the promise of the one party to accept the lesser performance

---

[3] Davis v Mathews (CA4 WVa) 361 F2d 899.

by the other is binding even though technically the promise to render the lesser performance is not consideration because the obligor was already obligated to render the greater performance. Thus a landlord's promise to reduce the rent was binding when the tenant could not pay the original rent and the landlord preferred to have the building occupied even though receiving a smaller rental. When the contract is for the sale of goods, any modification made by the parties to the contract is binding without regard to the existence of consideration for the modification.

(b) **Compromise and Release of Claims.** The rule that doing or promising to do what one is bound to do is not consideration applies to a part payment made in satisfaction of an admitted debt. For example, if one person owes another $100, the promise of the latter to accept $50 in full payment is not binding and will not prevent the creditor from demanding the remainder later because the part payment made by the debtor was not consideration for the promise to release the balance of the claim.

This rule has been severely criticized because it seems unfair. In some instances, it has been changed by statute or by court decision. Some courts treat the transaction as a binding gift of the remainder on the part of the creditor. Other courts seize the slightest opportunity to find some new consideration.

If the debtor pays before the debt is due, there is, of course, consideration since on the day when payment was made, the creditor was not entitled to demand any payment. Likewise if the creditor accepts some article, even of slight value, in addition to the part payment, the agreement is held to be binding.

If there is a bona fide dispute as to the amount owed or as to whether any amount is owed, a payment by the debtor of less than the amount claimed by the creditor is consideration for the latter's agreement to release or settle the claim. It is generally regarded as sufficient if the claimant believes in the merit of the claim. Conversely, if the claimant knows that the claim does not have any merit and is merely pressing it in order to force the other party to make some payment to buy peace from the annoyance of a lawsuit, the settlement agreement based on the part payment is not binding.

(c) **Part-payment Checks.** The acceptance and cashing of a check for part of a debt releases the entire debt when the check bears a notation that it is intended as final or full payment and the total amount due is disputed or unliquidated. It probably has this same effect even though the debt is not disputed or unliquidated.[4]

In some jurisdictions, this principle is applied without regard to the form of payment or whether the claim is disputed, it being required only that the part payment was in fact received and accepted as discharging the obligation.[5] The California Civil Code § 1541, provides: "An obligation is extinguished by a release therefrom given to the debtor by the creditor upon a new consideration, or in writing, with or without new consideration." If the notation that the acceptance of the check constitutes final payment is in print which the court regards as too small, it may not be binding in

---

[4] Uniform Commercial Code § 3-408. Official Comment, point 2. See also § 1-107, generally, and § 2-209(1) as to the sale of goods.
[5] Rivers v Cole Corp. 209 Ga 406, 73 SE2d 196 (local statutes).

the absence of evidence that the notation was actually seen by the creditor receiving the check.[6]

(d)   Composition of Creditors. In a *composition of creditors,* the various creditors of one debtor mutually agree to accept a fractional part of their claims in full satisfaction thereof. Such agreements are binding and are supported by consideration. When creditors agree to extend the due date of their debts, the promise of each creditor to forbear is likewise consideration for the promise of other creditors to forbear.

§ 13:5. Present Versus Past Consideration. Since consideration is what the promisor states must be received for the promise, it must be given after the promisor states what is demanded. Past consideration is not effective. When one person performs some service for another without the latter's knowledge and without any understanding that compensation is to be paid, a promise made later to pay for such past services is not supported by consideration and is not enforceable. A promise made by an employee to refrain from competing with the employee's employer must be supported by new consideration when the employment relationship already exists and the employee was not subject to any such restriction under that existing contract.

(a)   Moral Obligation. Ordinarily the fact that the promisor is under a moral obligation to the promisee or is under a moral duty to perform the promise does not make the promise binding when there is no consideration for the promise. Some courts, however, hold that when benefits are obtained by fraud or under circumstances that create a moral obligation, a promise to compensate by the person benefited is supported by consideration.

When one promises to pay a debt that was unenforceable because of minority, or that is barred by the statute of limitations, or that has been discharged in bankruptcy, the promise operates as a waiver of the bar or defense to the enforcement of the original obligation. No consideration is required for a waiver but the promisee must produce clear proof that the promise was in fact made.

To constitute a promise to pay a debt discharged by bankruptcy, the promise must be clear and must reasonably identify the discharged debt. Thus, a promise "to pay debts" does not revive a debt barred by a bankruptcy discharge as it was not clear whether this meant such debts as would be incurred after the bankruptcy discharge or embraced the earlier debts which had been discharged.

(b)   Complex Transactions. In applying the rule that past consideration is not consideration, care must be taken to distinguish between the situation in which the consideration is in fact past and the situation in which the earlier consideration and the subsequent promises were all part of one complex transaction.

§ 13:6. Forbearance as Consideration. In most cases consideration consists of the performance of an act or the making of a promise to act. But consideration may also consist of forbearance, which is refraining from doing an act, or a promise of forbearance. In other words, the promisor may desire to buy the inaction of the other party or a promise not to act.

---

[6] Kibler v Frank L. Garrett & Sons, Inc. 73 Wash2d 523, 439 P2d 416.

The waiving or giving up of any right, legal or equitable, can be consideration for the promise of another. Thus, the relinquishment of a right in property, of a right to sue for damages, or of a homestead right will support a promise given in return for it.

When the creditor agrees to extend the time for paying the debt in return for the debtor's promise of a higher return of interest, the agreement to extend is consideration for the promise to pay the higher rate of interest.[7]

When a supplier has the right to terminate the contract with the dealer selling its products, the promise of the supplier to refrain from revoking the contract with the dealer is consideration for the dealer's agreement to reduce the commissions deducted on the resale of the supplier's product.[8]

The right that is surrendered in return for a promise may be a right against a third person, as well as against the promisor.

As under the rule governing compromises, forbearance to assert a claim is consideration when the claim has been asserted in good faith, even though it is without merit. In the absence of such a belief, forbearance with respect to a worthless claim is not consideration.

Forbearance is not consideration unless it is the price for the promise. The mere fact that some act is done, as the giving of a promissory note, and thereafter the creditor does nothing, does not establish that the forbearance was the price for the making of the promissory note. At the same time such an intent may be inferred from the circumstances and it is not necessary that there be an express declaration or a statement that a promise is made in consideration of the forbearance of the creditor.

§ 13:7. Adequacy of Consideration.
Ordinarily the courts do not consider the adequacy of the consideration given for a promise. The fact that the consideration supplied by one party is slight when compared with the burden undertaken by the other party is immaterial, as it is a matter for the parties to decide when they make their contract whether each is getting an adequate return. In the absence of fraud or other misconduct, the courts usually will not interfere to make sure that each side is getting a fair return.[9]

(a) Wisdom of Contract. As a corollary of the concept that the court will not consider the adequacy of consideration, the ordinary rule is that the enforceability of a contract does not depend upon whether it is a wise or sensible contract. As long as the parties have capacity and there has been genuine assent to the terms of the contract, the court is not concerned with the terms of the contract.

(b) Failure of Expectations. The fact that what the party obtains in return for a promise is not as advantageous as had been expected does not mean that there was no consideration for the promise. Consequently, when an investor obtained the desired shares of stock, the contract was fully performed by the seller and the fact that the

---

[7] Bloch v Fedak, 210 Kan 63, 499 P2d 1052.
[8] Mattlage Sales, Inc. v Howard Johnson's Wholesale Division, Inc. 39 AppDiv2d 958, 333 NYS2d 491.
[9] Cook v American States Insurance Co. 150 IndApp 88, 275 NE2d 832.

stock thereafter proved worthless did not mean that there was no consideration for the buyer's promise to pay for the stock.

The fact that a club member does not use the club privileges does not constitute a lack of consideration for the promise to become a member and to pay for the membership.[10]

§ 13:8. Exceptions to Adequacy of Consideration Rule. The courts make some exceptions to the rule that the law will not weigh the consideration.

(a)   Unconscionability. An excessively hard bargain obtained by a seller of goods at the expense of a small buyer with weak purchasing power has been held to constitute unconscionability,[11] although such a conclusion is merely another way of stating that the consideration received by the buyer was not adequate.

(b)   Statutory Exception. In a few states, statutes require that the consideration be adequate, or fair or reasonable, in order to make a contract binding.

Adequacy of the consideration may be questioned in computing tax liability. For example, when it is claimed that the taxable balance of a decedent's estate should be reduced by the amount owed a given creditor, such debt may be deducted only to the extent that the decedent had received an equivalent value from the creditor. Thus, if the decedent owed the creditor $1,000 for property that was worth $200, only the sum of $200 could be deducted in computing the value of the estate. This determination for tax purposes, however, does not affect the validity of the creditor's contract.

(c)   Evidence of Fraud. The smallness of the consideration may be evidence of fraud.[12] Suppose that *R* sells a $50,000 house to *E* for $500. It might be a perfectly innocent transaction in which *R* virtually makes a gift in return for the nominal payment. Since *R,* as the owner of the house, could give it away, nothing prevents "selling" it at such a low figure. The transaction, however, may be of a different nature. It may be that *E* has defrauded *R* into believing that the property is worthless, and *R* therefore sells it for $500. Or there may be collusion between *R* and *E* to transfer the property in order to hide it from creditors of *R*. The smallness of the consideration does not mean that the transaction is necessarily made in bad faith or for a fraudulent purpose; but if other evidence indicates fraud, the smallness of the consideration corroborates that evidence.

(d)   Exchange of Different Quantities of Identical Units. A promise to pay a particular amount of money or to deliver a particular quantity of goods in exchange for a promise to pay or deliver a greater amount or quantity of the same kind of money or goods at the same time and place is not adequate consideration. If I promise to pay you $50 in exchange for your promise to pay me $100 under such circumstances, my promise is not regarded as adequate consideration for your promise, and your promise therefore is not binding upon you.

---

[10] Sorensen Health Studio v McCoy, 261 Iowa 891, 156 NW2d 341.

[11] Toker v Westerman, 113 NJSuper 452, 274 A2d 78. See also American Home Improvement, Inc. v MacIver, 105 NH 435, 201 A2d 886.

[12] Woods v Griffin, 204 Ark 514, 163 SW2d 322.

(e)   **Equitable Relief.** When a plaintiff seeks equitable relief, such as the specific performance of a contract, the courts will generally refuse to assist the plaintiff unless valuable or substantial consideration has been given by the plaintiff.

§ 13:9. Exceptions to Requirement of Consideration.

(a)   **Voluntary Subscriptions.** When charitable enterprises are financed by voluntary subscriptions of a number of persons, the promise of each one is generally enforceable. For example, when a number of people make pledges of subscriptions for the construction of a church, for a charitable institution, or for a college, the subscriptions are binding.

The theories for sustaining such promises vary. The real answer to the question of whether consideration is present is that in these cases consideration is lacking according to the technical standards applied in ordinary contract cases. Nevertheless, the courts enforce such promises as a matter of public policy.

(b)   **Commercial Paper.** The fact that there was no consideration for commercial paper, such as a check or promissory note, may not be raised against persons acquiring the paper in the course of ordinary business transactions. The result is that the commercial paper may be enforceable even though no consideration was given.

(c)   **Sealed Instruments.** At common law, consideration was not necessary to support a promise under seal. In a state which gives the seal its original common-law effect, the gratuitous promise or a promise to make a gift is enforceable when it is set forth in a sealed instrument.

In some states a promise under seal must be supported by consideration, just as though it did not have a seal. Other states take a middle position and hold that the presence of a seal is prima facie proof that there is consideration to support the promise. This means that if nothing more than the existence of the sealed promise is shown, it is deemed supported by consideration. The party making the promise, however, may prove that there was no consideration. In that case, the promise is not binding.

(d)   **Debts of Record.** No consideration is necessary to support obligations of record, such as a court judgment. These obligations are enforceable as a matter of public policy.

(e)   **State Statutes.** Under statutes in some states no consideration is necessary in order to make certain written promises binding. The Model Written Obligations Act, which has been adopted only in Pennsylvania, provides that no release (or promise) made and signed by the person releasing (or promising) shall be "invalid or unenforceable for lack of consideration, if the writing also contains an additional express statement, in any form of language, that the signer intends to be legally bound."

(f)   **Uniform Commercial Code.** Consideration is not required for (1) a merchant's written firm offer as to goods, stated to be irrevocable; (2) a written discharge of a claim for an alleged breach of a commercial contract; or (3) an agreement to modify a contract for the sale of goods.[13]

---

[13] UCC § 2-209(1).

(g) Promissory Estoppel. Many courts enforce promises that are not supported by consideration by applying the doctrine of *promissory estoppel*. By this doctrine, if a person makes a promise to another under such circumstances that the promisor should reasonably foresee that the promisee will be induced to rely thereon and that the promisee will then sustain substantial loss if the promise is not kept, the promise is binding even though there is no consideration for it. In applying the doctrine of promissory estoppel, courts are ignoring the requirement of consideration in order to attain a just result. (See p. 202, Hoffman v Red Owl Stores, Inc.)

Promissory estoppel differs from consideration in that the reliance of the promisee is not the bargained-for response sought by the promisor. To be consideration, it would be necessary that the promisor had specified or requested the particular reliance as the price of making the promise. Under promissory estoppel, it is sufficient that the promisor foresees that there will be such reliance.

(1) Limitations. The doctrine of promissory estoppel applies only when (a) the promisor has reason to foresee the detrimental reliance by the promisee, and (b) the promisee in fact would sustain a substantial loss by such reliance if the promise is not performed.

The doctrine is not applied merely because a promise has been broken. Thus an employer cannot be held liable to an injured employee on the theory of promissory estoppel, even though the employer dissuaded third persons from taking a collection for the employee by stating that this was unnecessary and promising to take care of the employee for life but thereafter failing to do so.[14]

The doctrine of promissory estoppel is not applied when no promise is made and one party merely takes a chance on future developments. Nor does it apply when it is made clear that certain conditions must be met before any obligation will arise and the claimant fails to meet those conditions, such as making payment in advance. Likewise, since promissory estoppel is based on the ground that there has been reliance on a promise, there must be a communication of the promise to the promisee in the same sense that an offer must be communicated to an offeree.

(2) Extended Application. Some courts extend promissory estoppel beyond its function of making a promise binding and apply it to imply a promise that an offer will not be revoked. These courts apply the doctrine to hold that an offer will be kept open for a reasonable time even though there is no consideration to do so and although the firm offer concept is not applicable. Thus, when a subcontractor makes a bid to a general contractor and recognizes that the general contractor will rely thereon in making the bid for the construction job, in some states the subcontractor is barred from revoking the offer until a reasonable time has elapsed in which the contractor may accept the offer of the subcontractor.[15]

§ 13:10. Legality of Consideration. The law will not permit persons to make contracts that violate the law. Accordingly, a promise to do something which the law prohibits or

[14] Overlock v Central Vermont Public Service Corp., 126 Vt 549, 237 A2d 356.
[15] Drennan v Star Paving Co. 51 Cal2d 409, 333 P2d 757.

a promise to refrain from doing something which the law requires is not valid consideration and the contract is illegal. This subject is further discussed in Chapter 14.

§ 13:11. Failure of Consideration. When a promise is given as consideration, the question arises as to whether the promisor will perform the promise. If the promise is not performed, the law describes the default as a "failure of consideration." This is a misnomer since the failure of the promisor is one of performance, not of consideration. (See p. 203, Sanitary Linen Service Co. v Alexander Proudfoot Co.)

The fact that performance of the contract by the other party does not have the result that one hoped for does not mean that there is a failure of consideration. For example, when one buys a store building in a real estate development, the buyer obviously does so in the expectation of obtaining a large volume of trade by virtue of the location. It may be that this will not occur because of the continuing of earlier purchasing patterns of the public. While the buyer of the store building is disappointed, there has not been any failure of consideration with respect to the contract for the purchase of the store building from the owner.

CASES FOR CHAPTER 13

Baehr v Penn-O-Tex Oil Corporation

258 Minn 533, 104 NW2d 661 (1960)

Kemp leased a gas filling station from Baehr. Kemp, who was heavily indebted to the Penn-O-Tex Oil Corporation, transferred to it his right to receive payments on all claims. When Baehr complained that the rent was not paid, he was finally assured by the corporation that the rent would be paid to him. Baehr did not sue Kemp for the overdue rent but later sued the corporation. From a judgment for the defendant, the plaintiff appealed.

LOEVINGER, J. . . . There was an unequivocal assurance given that the rents would be paid. This cannot be anything but a promise.

However, the fact that a promise was given does not necessarily mean that a contract was made. It is clear that not every promise is legally enforceable. Much of the vast body of law in the field of contracts is concerned with determining which promises should be legally enforced. On the one hand, in a civilized community men must be able to assume that those with whom they deal will carry out their undertakings according to reasonable expectations. On the other hand, it is neither practical nor reasonable to expect full performance of every assurance given, whether it be thoughtless, casual, and gratuitous, or deliberately and seriously made.

The test that has been developed by the common law for determining the enforceability of promises is the doctrine of consideration. This is a crude and not altogether successful attempt to generalize the conditions under which promises will be legally enforced. Consideration requires that a contractual promise be the product of a bargain. However, in this usage, "bargain" does not mean an exchange of things of equivalent, or any, value. It means a negotiation resulting in the voluntary assumption of an obligation by one party upon condition of an act or forbearance by the other. Consideration thus insures that the promise enforced as a contract is not accidental, casual, or gratuitous, but has been uttered intentionally as the result of some deliberation, manifested by reciprocal bargaining or negotiation. In this view, the requirement of consideration is not mere technicality, historical anachronism, or arbitrary formality. It is an attempt to be as reasonable as we can in deciding which promises constitute contracts. . . .

Consideration, as essential evidence of the parties' intent to create a legal obligation, must be something adopted and regarded by the parties as such. Thus, the same thing may be consideration or not, as it is dealt with by the parties. In substance, a contractual promise must be of the logical form: "If . . . [consideration is given] . . . then I promise that. . . ." Of course, the substance may be expressed in any form of words, but essentially this is the logical structure of those promises enforced by the law as contracts.

Applying these principles to the present case, it appears that although defendant's agent made a promise to plaintiff, it was not in such circumstances that a contract was created. . . .

There is no evidence that either of the parties took defendant's assurances seriously or acted upon them in any way. There was, therefore, no consideration. . . .

[Judgment affirmed]

Newberger v Rifkind

28 CalApp3d 1070, 104 CalRptr 663 (1972)

Newberger and three others were key employees of Avnet, Inc., an electronic corporation. Robert Avnet was a principal stockholder of the corporation. Avnet, with the approval of the other two principal stockholders, gave Newberger and the other three employees options to purchase stock of the corporation which he owned individually. The option could be exercised in full after five years of employment. If exercised earlier, the option could only be exercised up to 20% of the full amount for each year of employment. Avnet died two years after giving the options. Three years later, Newberger and the others exercised the options. Rifkind, the executor of Avnet, refused to honor the options on the theory that they were not supported by consideration and therefore had been revoked by the death of Avnet. Newberger and the others sued Rifkind. A judgment was entered in Rifkind's favor and they appealed.

KINGSLEY, J. . . . Plaintiffs' argument on appeal is that there was consideration for the options, and therefore the options were not revoked by the death of the optionor.

Defendants argue that they sustained the burden of proving that no consideration was given by plaintiffs for the options.

The record is replete with testimony that plaintiffs gave no property or money of any kind in exchange for the options. Defendants' evidence that no money or property was given by the plaintiffs in exchange for the options, does not show an absence of consideration. Consideration is inherent where stock options are granted to employees and the employee continues employment knowing of the options

. . . and no additional consideration in money or property is required. "[A] bonus is not a gift or gratuity, but a sum paid for services, or upon a consideration or in addition to that which would ordinarily be given.". . . "It is well settled in this state that, where the employer has a pension plan and the employee knows of it, continued employment constitutes consideration for the promise to pay the pension."

Furthermore, in finding consideration for pensions or other benefits, the courts do not distinguish between an inducement to continue employment and an inducement to begin employment. . . . In the instant case plaintiffs testified that they gave their time or effort in reliance on the options, and no other showing of consideration was necessary.

Defendants argue that, although continued employment by plaintiffs might have been consideration *had it been bargained for,* there is no showing in the record that defendants ever requested that plaintiffs continue in employment in exchange for defendants' promise to grant the option. Defendants point out that, in some of the cases relied on by plaintiffs those optionees were specifically requested to remain in employment or asked to increase their efforts, but in the instant case there was no similar request. In essence, defendants are arguing that, since there was no evidence of an express request by the optionor that the optionees either promise to continue employment, or that the optionees do the act of continuing employment, the consideration was not bargained for, and therefore there is an absence of consideration.

No express, formal request for either a promise or for an act is required for us to find a contract supported by consideration. "It is the universal custom of mankind to speak elliptically and to assume the existence and the understanding of things that are not expressed in words."

In the case before us the bargain was implied from the circumstances, and there was an implied request by the optionors that the optionees continue the act of remaining employees in exchange for the granting of the options. No formal bargain or offer was necessary. "The law has outgrown its primitive stage of formalism when the precise word was the sovereign talisman, and every slip was fatal. It takes a broader view today.". . . The realities of the corporate market place lead us to believe that stock options are given to employees as an inducement to continue employment or to put forth greater efforts, and they are not granted as an act of philanthropy or as a magnanimous gesture. . . .

. . . The attitude is to consider the "additional advantages to employees as being in effect offers for a unilateral contract which offer is accepted if the employee continues in the employment, and not as being mere offers of gifts. They make the employees more content and happier in their jobs, cause the employees to forego their rights to seek other employment, assist in avoiding labor turnover, and are considered of advantage to both the employer and the employees.". . . Thus, we hold plaintiffs' act of continuing employment was both acceptance and consideration for the option, even in the absence of a formal bargain.

[Judgment reversed]

Angel v Murray

113 RI 482, 322 A2d 630 (1974)

Murray was director of finance of the City of Newport. A contract was made with Maher to remove trash. Later, Maher requested that the city council increase his compensation because his costs were greater than had been anticipated because 400 new dwelling units had been put into operation. The city council voted to pay Maher an additional $10,000 a year. After two such annual payments had been made, Angel and other citizens of the city sued Murray and Maher for a return of the $20,000, on the theory that Maher was already obligated by his contract to perform the work for the contract sum and there was accordingly no consideration for the payment of the increased compensation. From a decision in favor of the plaintiffs, the City and Maher appealed.

ROBERTS, C.J. It is generally held that a modification of a contract is itself a contract, which is unenforceable unless supported by consideration. . . .

The preexisting duty rule is followed by most jurisdictions, . . .

The primary purpose of the preexisting duty rule is to prevent what has been referred to as the "hold-up game.". . . A classic example of the "hold-up game" is found in Alaska Packers' Ass'n v Domenico, 117 F. 99 (9th Cir. 1902). There 21 seamen entered into a written contract with Domenico to sail from San Francisco to Pyramid Harbor, Alaska. They were to work as sailors and fishermen out of Pyramid Harbor during the fishing season of 1900. The contract specified that each man would be paid $50 plus two cents for each red salmon he caught. Subsequent to their arrival at Pyramid Harbor, the men stopped work and demanded an additional $50. They threatened to return to San Francisco if Domenico did not agree to their demand. Since it was impossible for Domenico to find other men, he agreed to pay the men an additional $50. After they returned to San Francisco, Domenico refused to pay the men an additional $50. The court found that the subsequent agreement to pay the men an additional $50 was not supported by consideration because the men had a preexisting duty to work on the ship under the original contract, and thus the subsequent agreement was unenforceable.

Another example of the "hold-up game" is found in the area of construction contracts. Frequently, a contractor will refuse to complete work under an unprofitable contract unless he is awarded additional compensation. The courts have generally held that a subsequent agreement to award additional compensation is unenforceable if the contractor is only performing work which would have been required of him under the original contract. . . .

These examples clearly illustrate that the courts will not enforce an agreement that has been procured by coercion or duress and will hold the parties to their original contract regardless of whether it is profitable or unprofitable. However, the courts have been reluctant to apply the preexisting duty rule when a party to a contract encounters unanticipated difficulties and the other party, not influenced by coercion or duress, voluntarily agrees to pay additional compensation for work already required to be performed under the contract. For example, the courts have found that the original contract was rescinded, . . . abandoned, . . . or waived. . . .

Although the preexisting duty rule has served a useful purpose insofar as it deters parties from using coercion and duress to obtain additional compensation, it has been widely criticized as a general rule of law. . . . The modern trend appears to recognize the necessity that courts should enforce agreements modifying contracts when unexpected or unanticipated difficulties arise during the course of the performance of a contract, even though there is no consideration for the modification, as long as the parties agree voluntarily.

Under the Uniform Commercial Code, § 2-209(1), which has been adopted by 49 states, "[a]n agreement modifying a contract [for the sale of goods] needs no consideration to be binding.". . . Although at first blush this section appears to validate modifications obtained by coercion and duress, the comments to this section indicate that a modification under this section must meet the test of good faith imposed by the Code, and a modification obtained by extortion without a legitimate commercial reason is unenforceable.

The modern trend away from a rigid application of the preexisting duty rule is reflected by § 89D(a) of the American Law Institute's Restatement Second of the Law of Contracts, which provides: "A promise modifying a duty under a contract not fully performed on either side is binding (a) if the modification is fair and equitable in view of circumstances not anticipated by the parties when the contract was made. . . ."

We believe that § 89D(a) is the proper rule of law and find it applicable to the facts of this case. It not only prohibits modifications obtained by coercion, duress, or extortion but also fulfills society's expectation that agreements entered into voluntarily will be enforced by the courts. . . .

Section 89D(a), of course, does not compel a modification of an unprofitable or unfair contract; it only enforces a modification if the parties voluntarily agree and if (1) the promise modifying the original contract was made before the contract was fully performed on either side, (2) the underlying circumstances which prompted the modification were unanticipated by the parties, and (3) the modification is fair and equitable.

The evidence, which is uncontradicted, reveals that in June of 1968 Maher requested the city council to pay him an additional $10,000 for the year beginning on July 1, 1968, and ending on June 30, 1969. This request was made at a public meeting of the city council, where Maher explained in detail his reasons for making the request. Thereafter, the city council voted to authorize the Mayor to sign an amendment to the 1964 contract which provided that Maher would receive an additional $10,000 per year for the duration of the contract. Under such circumstances we have no doubt that the city voluntarily agreed to modify the 1964 contract.

Having determined the voluntariness of this agreement, we turn our attention to the three criteria delineated above. First, the modification was made

in June of 1968 at a time when the five-year contract which was made in 1964 had not been fully performed by either party. Second, although the 1964 contract provided that Maher collect all refuse generated within the city, it appears this contract was premised on Maher's past experience that the number of refuse-generating units would increase at a rate of 20 to 25 per year. Furthermore, the evidence is uncontradicted that the 1967-1968 increase of 400 units "went beyond any previous expectation." Clearly, the circumstances which prompted the city council to modify the 1964 contract were unanticipated. Third, although the evidence does not indicate what proportion of the total this increase comprised, the evidence does indicate that it was a "substantial" increase. In light of this, we cannot say that the council's agreement to pay Maher the $10,000 increase was not fair and equitable in the circumstances.

[Judgment reversed and action remanded]

Hoffman v Red Owl Stores, Inc.

26 Wis 2d 683, 133 NW2d 267 (1965)

Hoffman wanted to acquire a franchise as a Red Owl Grocery Store, Red Owl being a corporation that maintained a system of chain stores. The agent of Red Owl informed Hoffman and his wife that if they would sell their bakery in Wautoma, acquire a certain tract of land in Chilton, another city, and put up a specified amount of money, they would be given a franchise as desired. Hoffman sold his business, acquired the land in Chilton, but was never granted a franchise. He and his wife sued Red Owl, which raised the defense that there had only been an assurance that Hoffman would receive a franchise but no promise supported by consideration and therefore no binding contract to give him a franchise. From a judgment in the Hoffmans' favor, Red Owl appealed.

CURRIE, C.J. . . . The development of the law of promissory estoppel "is an attempt by the courts to keep remedies abreast of increased moral consciousness of honesty and fair representations in all business dealings.". . .

The Restatement avoids use of the term "promissory estoppel," and there has been criticism of it as an inaccurate term. . . . Use of the word "estoppel" to describe a doctrine upon which a party to a lawsuit may obtain affirmative relief offends the traditional concept that estoppel merely serves as a shield and cannot serve as a sword to create a cause of action. . . .

Because we deem the doctrine of promissory estoppel, as stated in Sec. 90 of Restatement, 1 Contracts, as one which supplies a needed weapon which courts may employ in a proper cause to prevent injustice, we endorse and adopt it.

The record here discloses a number of promises and assurances given to Hoffman by Lukowitz in behalf of Red Owl upon which plaintiffs relied and acted upon to their detriment. . . .

There remains for consideration the question of law raised by defendants that agreement was never reached on essential factors necessary to establish a contract between Hoffman and Red Owl. Among these were the size, cost, design, and layout of the store building; and the terms of the lease with respect to rent, maintenance, renewal, and purchase options. This poses the question of whether the promise necessary to sustain a cause of action for promissory estoppel must embrace all essential details of a proposed transaction between promisor and promisee so as to be the equivalent of an offer that would result in a binding contract between the parties if the promisee were to accept the same.

Originally the doctrine of promissory estoppel was invoked as a substitute for consideration rendering a gratuitous promise enforceable as a contract. . . . In other words, the acts of reliance by the promisee to his detriment provided a substitute for consideration. If promissory estoppel were to be limited to only those situations where the promise giving rise to the cause of action must be so definite with respect to all details that a contract would result were the promise supported by consideration, then the defendants' instant promises to Hoffman would not meet this test. However, Sec. 90 of Restatement, 1 Contracts, does not impose the requirement that the promise giving rise to the cause of action must be so comprehensive in scope as to meet the requirements of an offer that would ripen into a contract if accepted by the promisee. Rather the conditions imposed are:

(1) Was the promise one which the promisor should reasonably expect to induce action or forbearance of a definite and substantial character on the part of the promisee?

(2) Did the promise induce such action or forbearance?

(3) Can injustice be avoided only by enforcement of the promise? . . .

We conclude that injustice would result here if plaintiffs were not granted some relief because of the failure of defendants to keep their promises which induced plaintiffs to act to their detriment. . . .

[Judgment affirmed on this phase of the case]

Sanitary Linen Service Co. v Alexander Proudfoot Co.

(CA5 Fla) 435 F2d 292 (1971)

Alexander Proudfoot Company was in the business of devising efficiency systems for industry. It undertook to devise such a system for the Sanitary Linen Service Company. Sanitary claimed that the system failed to effect the promised savings and sued Alexander to get back the money which it had paid. Judgment was entered for Sanitary; Alexander appealed.

BELL, C.J. . . . Proudfoot was to supply a "worthwhile installation of schedule and method improvements designed to provide greater control over utilization of man and machine hours and to effect operating economies." The purpose of the schedule or system, according to Proudfoot's negotiator, was to ferret out and recover lost time in all phases of production, delivery and office work in Sanitary's operations. The benefit would accrue to Sanitary in the form of reduced manpower thus resulting in payroll savings. . . .

The gathering of the data and development of the schedule fell behind and Sanitary's management became restless to see some results. Proudfoot's man in charge of the project reassured Sanitary that savings were just around the corner and that they were going to recommend very shortly that 26 persons be eliminated in the ironing department of the Miami plant. On June 5, 1964 this installation was actually accomplished and the people discharged. Proudfoot's former employees who were on the job at the time admitted at the trial that at the time they had not really worked out a schedule and that without it, the layoff would not achieve the desired result. Shortly after the layoff the plant had to operate at longer hours to get out the necessary production. Employee complaints followed. With the approval of Proudfoot's employees, the 26 persons were rehired. Similar difficulty occurred at the Orlando plant. In sum, as the district court found, former employees of Proudfoot, witnesses for Sanitary at the trial, testified that they were unable to develop an over-all schedule plan that would develop a continuous flow and eliminate lost time.

In July the installation manager was discharged by Proudfoot and new personnel placed on the job in an effort to develop a workable program or installation. Further studies were made and plans and forms drawn up, but no further "installations" were attempted. On October 9, 1964, after having collected $74,200, and spent the contemplated time on the Sanitary job, Proudfoot discontinued its efforts. Several contracts were made after this in an effort to have Proudfoot perform. The parties, however, broke off negotiations and this suit followed.

Originally Sanitary was suing on a theory of breach of express or implied warranty in that the savings promised by Proudfoot did not occur. The district judge found that there was no express prom-

ise to effect savings and that there is no implied warranty in a contract for services. He did find, albeit in a rather unspecified way, that Sanitary did not receive what they bargained for, i.e., workable system. He then awarded damages to Sanitary in the nature of restitution. According to the court, they paid for a service which they did not get and thus were entitled to have their money back. . . .

In the final analysis, the question presented is whether a scheduling installation was devised for Sanitary and made operative. After a careful study of the record we conclude, as did the district court, that no scheduling installation as contemplated in the agreement was ever devised or furnished to Sanitary. Thus, as Proudfoot did not produce what they contracted to do, there was a failure of consideration. . . .

[Judgment for plaintiff]

QUESTIONS AND CASE PROBLEMS

1. What is the objective of each of the following rules of law?
   (a) An executed gift or a performance that has been rendered without consideration cannot be rescinded for lack of consideration.
   (b) In the absence of fraud, the adequacy of consideration is usually immaterial.

2. Compare (a) adequate consideration, (b) moral consideration, and (c) past consideration.

3. Is promissory estoppel applicable whenever the promisee relies on the promise and sustains substantial loss?

4. How does fraud affect the rule of law as to the adequacy of consideration?

5. Husted made a down payment on a contract to purchase most of the assets of a corporation. He was not able to complete the purchase and forfeited the down payment. Fuller, who in effect owned, controlled, and was the corporation, stated that he felt an obligation to Husted to see that he got his down payment back and promised that he would give him a promissory note covering the amount of the down payment. He failed to do so. Husted sued Fuller for breach of his promise to deliver such a note. Fuller claimed that his promise was not binding on him. Decide. [Husted v Fuller, (CA7Ill) 361 F2d 187]

6. Smith worked for the Stardust Hotel which was owned and operated by Recrion Corporation. He made certain suggestions for recreational facilities adjoining the hotel. After the facilities were constructed, the management promised Smith that he would be paid for his ideas. He was not paid and sued Recrion for breach of this promise. Was Recrion liable? [Smith v Recrion Corp., 91 Nev 666, 541 P2d 663]

7. Morgan was employed by the Management Search Inc., an employment agency. The employer promised to pay a bonus to employees exceeding a specified quota of job placements. Morgan exceeded the quota. Management Search refused to pay him the bonus. Was it required to do so? [Management Search Inc. v Morgan, 136 GaApp 651, 222 SE2d 154]

8. *A* owed money to a bank. *A* had a bank account in the bank, and under the loan agreement the bank could repay itself the amount of the loan from the bank account. When *A* died, his widow was made his executrix. She signed a note individually and, as executrix, promised to pay the bank the amount of *A*'s debt. She did this in return for the bank's promise not to deduct *A*'s debt from his bank account. When the bank sued her on her note, she raised the defense that there was no consideration for it. Was this a valid defense? [Jeter v Citizens National Bank, (Tex Civ App) 419 SW2d 916]

9. Fedun rented a building to Gomer who did business under the name of Mike's Cafe. Later, Gomer was about to sell out the business to Brown and requested Fedun to release him from his liability under the lease. Fedun agreed to do so. Brown sold out shortly thereafter. The balance of the rent due by Gomer was not paid, and Fedun sued Mike's Cafe on the rent claim. Could he collect after having released Gomer? [Fedun v Mike's Cafe, 204 Pa Super 356, 204 A2d 776]

10. *A* was employed by *B* for some time. At *B*'s request *A* signed a paper stating that *A* would not work for any competitor of *B* for 5 years after *A* left *B*'s employ. Was this contract binding on *A*? [Engineering Associates, Inc. v Pankow, 268 NC 137, 150 SE2d 56]

11. Before Youngman went to work for the Nevada Irrigation District, the superintendent promised him that he would receive a specified pay increase in April of each year. When he did not receive the increase he sued the District. He claimed that he had relied on the promise that he would receive such increase and that accordingly the promise was binding. Was he correct? [Youngman v Nevada Irrigation District, 70 Cal 2d 235, 74 Cal Rptr 398, 449 P2d 462]

12. Allen owned land which was being developed. Her brother, Norburn, wrote to the vice-president of Investment Properties of Asheville, Inc., stating that "this is to certify that I will stand personally liable" for the land preparation expenses. When Investment Properties sued him on this guaranty, he raised the defense that he did not receive any consideration for his promise and therefore it was not binding. Was this a valid defense? [Investment Properties of Asheville, Inc. v Norburn, 281 NC 300, 188 SE2d 342]

13. Sears, Roebuck & Co. promised to give Forrer "permanent employment." Forrer sold his farm at a loss in order to take the job. Shortly after commencing work, he was discharged by Sears which claimed that the contract could be terminated at will. Forrer claimed that promissory estoppel prevented Sears from terminating the contract. Was he correct? [Forrer v Sears, Roebuck & Co., 36 Wis 2d 388, 153 NW2d 587]

14. A prospective buyer of a house told the real estate broker to hire a contractor to inspect the building for termites. A contractor agreed to do so for $35, but he made a negligent inspection and failed to detect the presence of termites. The buyer sued the contractor for the loss caused by the contractor's negligence. The contractor defended on the ground that he had not charged much for the job. Was this a valid defense? [Mayes v Emery, 3 Wash App 2d 315, 475 P2d 124]

15. Creswell promised Baruffy and others that they would be the directors of the Interchange, Inc. and the latter promised to serve as directors "for a period of ten years or until their sooner resignation." Creswell did not keep his promise to make Baruffy and the others directors and they sued him for breach of contract. Was he liable? [Interchange Associates v Interchange, Inc., 16 WashApp 359, 557 P2d 357]

14 Legality and Public Policy

Viewed from the standpoint of the parties to the contract, a contract is a matter of the agreement of the parties. But the contract does not exist in a vacuum and therefore it must satisfy certain standards which society imposes. The agreement of the parties must satisfy all the rules relating to a contract and then in addition it must satisfy the standards relating to legality and public policy. Negatively stated, the agreement will not be a valid contract if it is illegal or contrary to public policy.

A. GENERAL PRINCIPLES

An agreement is illegal when either its formation or performance is a crime or a tort, or is contrary to public policy. Ordinarily an illegal agreement is void.

§ 14:1. Effect of Illegality. When an agreement is illegal, the parties are usually regarded as not entitled to the aid of the courts. If the illegal agreement has not been performed, neither party can sue the other to obtain performance or damages. If the agreement has been performed, neither party can sue the other for damages or to set it aside.

(a)   Exceptions. The following are exceptions to the general rule that the court will not aid a party to an unlawful agreement:

(1)   Protection of One Party. When the law which the agreement violates is intended for the protection of one of the parties, that party may seek relief. For example, when, in order to protect the public, the law forbids the issuance of securities or notes by certain classes of corporations, a person who has purchased them may recover the money paid.

(2)   Unequal Guilt. When the parties are not equally guilty or, as it is said, are not *in pari delicto,* the one less guilty is granted relief when public interest is advanced by so doing. For example, when a statute is adopted to protect one of the parties to a transaction, as a usury law adopted to protect borrowers, the person to be protected will not be deemed to be in pari delicto with the wrongdoer when entering into a transaction which is prohibited by the statute.

(3)   Collateral Illegality. An exception may also exist when the illegality is collateral or incidental, as when one of the parties has not obtained a government permit or license necessary for the performance of the contract.

Similarly when a bank makes a prohibited loan, it and its officers become subject to the penalties specified by law but that illegality does not affect the binding character of the loan. The borrower must repay the loan and cannot defend on the ground that the lending of the money was illegal.[1]

(4)   Money Held for Illegal Purpose. When one person has entrusted another with money or property to be used for an illegal purpose, the first person may have a change of mind and usually may recover the money or property, provided it has not been spent for the illegal purpose. Thus, money entrusted to an agent for use as a bribe of a third person may be recovered from the agent before it is so used.

If bets are held by a stakeholder and either of the bettors repudiates the bet, the stakeholder must return the bet and would be liable if the money were paid to the other bettor. When the act of betting is itself made a crime, some states deny the debtor the right to recover a bet from the stakeholder.[2]

§ 14:2. Partial Illegality. An agreement may involve the performance of several promises, some of which are illegal and some legal. The legal parts of the agreement may be enforced, provided that they can be separated from the parts which are illegal. The same rule applies when the consideration is illegal in part. The rule is not applied, however, to situations in which the illegal act or consideration is said to taint and strike down the entire agreement.

When there is an indivisible promise to perform several acts, some of which are illegal, the agreement is void. Also when there is a single promise to do a legal act, supported by several considerations, some of which are illegal, the agreement cannot be enforced.

If a contract is susceptible of two interpretations, one legal and the other illegal, the court will assume that the legal meaning was intended unless the contrary is clearly indicated.

§ 14:3. Crimes and Civil Wrongs. An agreement is illegal and therefore void when it calls for the commission of any act that constitutes a crime. To illustrate, one cannot enforce an agreement by which the other party is to commit an assault, to steal property, to burn a house, to print a libelous article, or to kill a person.

An agreement that calls for the commission of a civil wrong is also illegal and void. Examples are agreements to damage the goods of another; to slander a third person; to defraud another; or to infringe another's patent, trademark, or copyright; or to fix prices.[3]

§ 14:4. Good Faith and Fairness. In addition to the limiting factors of illegality and being contrary to public policy, the law is evolving toward requiring that contracts be fair and be made in good faith. The law is becoming increasingly concerned with whether *A* has utilized a superior bargaining power or superior knowledge to obtain better terms from *B* than *A* would otherwise have obtained.

---

[1] Cooper v Mercantile National Bank, 137 GaApp 605, 224 SE2d 442.
[2] Some courts require that a person repudiating a bet do so before the event which was the subject of the bet has occurred. Other courts permit the recovery of the bet from the stakeholder as long as demand is made prior to payment of the money to the other bettor, even though the event which was the subject of the bet has occurred.
[3] See § 5:5(f), in this book.

In the case of goods, the seller must act in good faith, which is defined as to merchant sellers as "honesty in fact and the observance of reasonable commercial standards of fair dealing in the trade." [4]

§ 14:5. Unconscionable and Oppressive Contracts. Ordinarily a court will not consider whether a contract is fair or unfair, wise or foolish, or operates unequally between the parties.[5] However, in a number of instances the law holds that contracts or contract clauses will not be enforced because they are too harsh or oppressive to one of the two parties. This principle is most commonly applied to invalidate a clause providing for the payment by one party of a large penalty upon breaking the contract or a provision declaring that a party shall not be liable for the consequences of negligence. This principle is extended in connection with the sale of goods to provide that "if the court . . . finds the contract or any clause of the contract to have been unconscionable at the time it was made, the court may refuse to enforce the contract, or it may enforce the remainder of the contract without the unconscionable clause, or it may so limit the application of any unconscionable clause as to avoid any unconscionable result." [6] (See p. 216, Williams v Walker-Thomas Furniture Co.) A provision which gives what the court believes is too much of an advantage over a buyer is likely to be held void as unconscionable.

In order to bring the unconscionability provision into operation, it is not necessary to prove that fraud was practiced. When there is a grossly disproportionate bargaining power between the parties so that the weaker or inexperienced party "cannot afford to risk confrontation" with the stronger party but "just signs on the dotted line," courts will hold that "grossly unfair" terms obtained by the stronger party are void as contrary to public policy.

Under the UCCC a particular clause or an entire agreement relating to a consumer credit sale, a consumer lease, or a consumer loan is void when such provision or agreement is unconscionable.[7] If the debtor waives any rights under the UCCC in making a settlement agreement with the seller or lender, such waiver is likewise subject to the power of the court as to unconscionability.[8]

The fact that a contract is a bad bargain does not make it unconscionable. Moreover, unconscionability is to be determined in the light of the circumstances existing at the time when the contract was made. The fact that later events make the contract unwise or undesirable does not make the contract unconscionable. Hence the fact that there is a sharp rise in the market price of goods after the contract has been made does not make the contract unconscionable.[9]

---

[4] See Uniform Commercial Code § 2-103(1)(b) as to good faith. Higher standards are also imposed on merchant sellers by other provisions of UCC. See § 2-314, as to warranties; § 2-603, as to duties with respect to rightfully rejected goods; and § 2-509(3), as to the transfer of risk of loss. While the provisions of the Code above noted do not apply to contracts generally, there is a growing trend of courts to extend Article 2 of the Code, which relates only to the sale of goods, to contract situations generally, on the theory that it represents the latest restatement of the law of contracts made by expert scholars and the legislators of the land.

[5] Oklahoma ex rel. Derryberry v Kerr-McGee Corp. (Okla) 516 P2d 813.

[6] UCC § 2-302(1). The Code as adopted in California and North Carolina omits the unconscionability section.

[7] Uniform Consumer Credit Code § 5.108.

[8] UCCC § 1.107.

[9] Bradford v Plains Cotton Cooperative Ass'n. (CA10 Okla) 539 F2d 1249.

§ 14:6. Social Consequences of Contracts. The social consequences of a contract are an important element today in determing its validity and the power of government to regulate it. The social consequences of a contract are related to the concept of unconscionability, although the latter concept, would seem to be concerned with the effect of the contract as between the parties, whereas social consequences have a broader concern for the effect of the particular contract and other similar contracts upon society in general.

(a)   The Private Contract in Society. The law of contracts, originally oriented to private relations between private individuals, is moving from the field of bilateral private law to multi-party societal considerations. The Supreme Court has held that private contracts lose their private and "do-not-touch" character when they become such a common part of our way of life that society deems it necessary to regulate them.

The significance of the socioeconomic setting of the contract is seen in the minimum wage law decisions. The Supreme Court at first held such laws unconstitutional as an improper interference with the rights of two adult contracting parties. Thereafter it changed its point of view to sustain such laws because of the consequences of substandard wages upon the welfare of the individual, society, and the nation.

This reevaluation of old standards is part of the general move to make modern law more "just."

(b)   The *n* Factor. With the expansion of the concepts of "against public policy" and "unconscionability" on the one hand, and government regulation of business on the other, the importance of a given contract to society becomes increasingly significant in determining the validity of the contract as between the parties. Less and less are courts considering a contract as only a legal relationship between *A* and *B*. More and more, the modern court is influenced in its decision by the recognition of the fact that the contract before the court is not one *in* a million but is one *of* a million.

For example, *J* Company makes an insurance contract with *K* that is of the same nature as one that *J* makes with *M*. Also these contracts are the same as the one that Company *R* makes with *S*, and so on. A like similarity or industry-wide pattern is seen in the case of the bank loan made by bank *O* to borrower *P*, by bank *Q* to borrower *T*, and so on.

The appreciation that a particular contract is merely one of many has not only influenced the courts in the interpretation of such contracts but has also been held to justify regulation of the contract by government. The view has been adopted that "when a widely diffused public interest has become enmeshed in a network of multitudinous private arrangements, the authority of the state 'to safeguard the vital interests of its people' . . . is not to be gainsaid by abstracting one such agreement from its public context and treating it as though it were an isolated private contract constitutionally immune from impairment." [10]

§ 14:7. Illegality in Performing Contract. When a contract is otherwise legal, the fact that one of the parties in performing the contract commits illegal acts not contemplated by the other party does not ordinarily prevent the wrongdoer from recovering on the contract. In some instances, however, the wrong may be regarded as so serious

---

[10] East New York Savings Bank v Hahn, 326 US 230, 232.

that the wrongdoer is punished by being denied the right to recover on the agreement. (See p. 217, McConnell v Commonwealth Pictures Corp.)

B. AGREEMENTS AFFECTING PUBLIC WELFARE

Agreements that interfere with public service or the duties of public officials, obstruct legal process, or discriminate against members of minority groups are considered detrimental to public welfare, and as such are not enforceable.

§ 14:8. Agreements Injuring Public Service. An agreement that tends to interfere with the proper performance of the duties of a public officer—whether legislative, administrative, or judicial—is contrary to public policy and void. Thus, an agreement to procure the award of a public contract by corrupt means is not enforceable. Other examples are agreements to sell public offices, to procure pardons by corrupt means, or to pay a public officer more or less than legal fees or salary.

One of the most common agreements within this class is the *illegal lobbying agreement.* This term is used to describe an agreement to use unlawful means to procure or prevent the adoption of legislation by a lawmaking body, such as Congress or a state legislature. Such agreements are clearly contrary to the public interest since they interfere with the workings of the democratic process. They are accordingly illegal and void.

Some courts hold illegal all agreements to influence legislation, regardless of the means contemplated or employed. Other courts adopt the better rule that such agreements are valid in the absence of the use of improper influence or the contemplation of using such influence.

§ 14:9. Agreements Involving Conflicts of Interests. Various statutes prohibit government officials from being personally interested, directly or indirectly, in any transaction entered into by such officials on behalf of the government.

§ 14:10. Agreements Obstructing Legal Processes. Any agreement intended to obstruct or pervert legal processes is contrary to public interest and therefore void. Agreements that promise to pay money in return for the abandonment of the prosecution of a criminal case, for the suppression of evidence in any legal proceeding, for initiating litigation, or for the perpetration of any fraud upon the court are therefore void.

An agreement to pay an ordinary witness more than the regular witness fee allowed by law or a promise to pay a greater amount if the promisor wins the lawsuit is void. The danger here is that the witness will lie in order to help win the case.

Contracts providing for the arbitration of disputes are generally recognized as valid by modern decisions and statutes. Earlier cases held such agreements void as interfering with the jurisdiction of the courts.

(a)   Selection of the Court. Contracts representing a substantial obligation will generally contain a provision for dispute settlement and tribunal selection. Sometimes it will be specified that any dispute shall be referred to arbitrators. In some instances it will be specified that any lawsuit must be brought in the courts of a particular state. Such provision will ordinarily be held valid as an aspect of the parties' freedom of contract to agree on such terms as they choose.

(b)   **Unconscionability and Public Policy.** When the obvious purpose of the tribunal designation provision is to erect a hurdle against being sued, the provision will be held void when the parties are not in an equal bargaining position. Thus, it has been held that where the contract of the seller of prefabricated homes specified that any suit brought against the seller by a buyer must be brought in a third state which had no relationship to either the consumer buyer, the seller, or to the performance of the contract, the provision was void as unconscionable because it was clearly aimed at discouraging litigation by the consumer purchaser.

§ 14:11. Sunday Laws. Under the English common law, an agreement or contract could be executed on any day of the week. Today, however, most states have statutes that prohibit to some extent the making or performance of contracts on Sunday. The terms of the statutes vary greatly from state to state. The statutes may expressly declare agreements void if they are made on Sunday or if they call for performance on Sunday, or they may prohibit the sale of merchandise on Sunday.[11] They may prohibit only "servile" or manual labor, prohibit "worldly employment," or prohibit labor or business or one's "ordinary calling."

(a)   **Works of Charity and Necessity.** Sunday laws expressly provide that they do not apply to works of charity or necessity. *Works of charity* include those acts that are involved in religious worship or in aiding persons in distress. In general a work of necessity is an act which must be done at the time in order to be effective in saving life, health, or property.

The "necessity" exception to Sunday laws is generally liberally interpreted so as to permit sales where a contrary conclusion would cause serious economic loss or inconvenience. Thus, it has been held that the necessity exception permitted an auto parts dealer to sell a water pump to a motorist traveling through the state to replace a pump which broke down.

When an offer is made on Sunday but the acceptance is not made until the next day, the agreement is valid because in law it is made on the weekday when it is accepted. When a preliminary oral agreement is made on Sunday but the parties intend that a formal written contract be prepared by their attorneys during the week, the contract so prepared is not a Sunday contract.[12] If a contract is made on Sunday, some courts hold that it can be ratified on another day. Other courts, however hold the contrary on the ground that the contract was illegal when made, and therefore is void and cannot be ratified.

(b)   **Sunday as Termination Date.** When the last day on which payment may be made is a Sunday, it is commonly provided by statute that it may be made on the following business day. In the absence of statute, however, the time is not extended because the day falls on a Sunday.

§ 14:12. Illegal Discrimination Contacts. A contract that a property owner will not sell to a member of a particular race cannot be enforced because it violates the Fourteenth Amendment of the federal Constitution.[13] Hotels and restaurants may not deal with

---

[11] McGowan v Maryland, 366 US 420; Braunfeld v Brown, 366 US 599.
[12] Wasserman v Roach, 336 Mass 564, 146 NE2d 909.
[13] Shelley v Kraemer, 334 US 1.

their customers on terms that discriminate because of race, religion, color, national origin, or sex.[14]

§ 14:13. Wagers and Lotteries. Largely as a result of the adoption of antigambling statutes, wagers or bets are generally illegal. Private lotteries involving the three elements of prize, chance, and consideration, or similar affairs of chance, also are generally held illegal. Raffles are usually regarded as lotteries. Sales promotion schemes calling for the distribution of property according to chance among the purchasers of goods are held illegal as lotteries, without regard to whether the scheme is called a guessing contest, raffle, or gift. (See p. 218, Seattle Times Co. v Tielsch)

Giveaway plans and games are lawful as long as it is not necessary to buy anything or to give anything of value in order to participate.[15] If participation is "free," the element of consideration is lacking and there is no lottery.

In many states public lotteries (lotteries run by a state government) have been legalized by statute.

§ 14:14. Transactions in Futures. A person may contract to deliver goods not owned at the time the agreement is made. The fact that the seller does not have the goods at the time the contract is made does not affect the legality of the transaction.

C. REGULATION OF BUSINESS

Local, state, and national laws regulate a wide variety of business activities and practices. A person violating such regulations may under some statutes be subject to a fine or criminal prosecution or under others to an order to cease and desist by an administrative agency or commission.

Whether an agreement made in connection with business conducted in violation of the law is binding or void depends upon how strongly opposed the public policy is to the prohibited act. Some courts take the view that the agreement is not void unless the statute expressly so specifies. In some instances, as in the case of the failure to register a fictitious name under which the business is done, the statute expressly preserves the validity of the contract by permitting the violator to sue on a contract made while illegally conducting business after the name is registered as required by the statute.

§ 14:15. Statutory Regulation of Contracts. In order to establish uniformity or to protect one of the parties to a contract, statutes frequently provide that contracts of a given class must follow a statutory model or must contain specified provisions. For example, statutes commonly specify that particular clauses must be included in insurance policies in order to protect the persons insured and their beneficiaries. Others require that contracts executed in connection with credit buying and loans contain particular provisions designed to protect the debtor.

Consumer protection legislation gives the consumer the right to rescind the contract in certain situations. Laws relating to truth in lending, installment sales,

---

[14] Federal Civil Rights Act of 1964, 42 United States Code § 2000a et seq.; Katzenback v McClung, 379 US 294; Heart of Atlanta Motel v United States, 379 US 241.

[15] Federal Communications Commission v American Broadcasting Co., 347 US 284.

and home improvement contracts commonly require that an installment sale contract specify the cash price, the down payment, the trade-in value, if any, the cash balance, the insurance costs, the interest and finance charges.

When the statute imposes a fine or imprisonment for violation, the court should not hold that the contract is void since that would increase the penalty which the legislature had imposed. If a statute prohibits the making of certain kinds of contracts or imposes limitations on the contracts that can be made, the attorney general or other government official may generally be able to obtain an injunction or court order to stop the parties from entering into a prohibited kind of contract.

§ 14:16. Licensed Callings or Dealings. Statutes frequently require that a person obtain a license, certificate, or diploma before one can practice certain professions, such as law or medicine, or carry on a particular business or trade, such as that of a real estate broker, peddler, stockbroker, hotelkeeper, or pawnbroker. If the requirement is imposed to protect the public from unqualified persons, an agreement to engage in such a profession or business without having obtained the necessary license or certificate is void. (See p. 219, Schara v Thiede) Thus, an agreement with an unlicensed physician for services cannot be enforced by the physician. The patient of the unlicensed physician, however, may sue for damages if the contract is not properly performed.

In contrast with the protective license, a license may be required solely as a revenue measure by requiring the payment of a fee for the license. In that event, an agreement made in violation of the statute by one not licensed is generally held valid. The contract may also sometimes be held valid when it is shown that no harm has resulted from the failure to obtain a permit to do the work contemplated by the particular contract.[16]

It is likewise frequently held that the absence of a license cannot be raised as to transactions between persons who should all be licensed, such as dealers, when the purpose of the license requirement is not to protect such persons as against each other but to protect the public generally against such persons.

§ 14:17. Fraudulent Sales. Statutes commonly regulate the sale of certain commodities. Scales and measures of grocers and other vendors must be checked periodically, and they must be approved and sealed by the proper official. Certain articles must be inspected before they are sold. Others must be labeled in a particular way to show their contents and to warn the public of the presence of any dangerous or poisonous substance. Since these laws are generally designed for the protection of the public, transactions in violation of such laws are void.

When the aim of the law is to raise revenue by requiring the payment of a fee, the violation merely makes the wrongdoer liable for the penalty imposed by the law but does not make the transaction void.

§ 14:18. Administrative Agencies. Large areas of the American economy are governed by federal administrative agencies created to carry out the general policies specified by Congress. A contract must be in harmony with public policy not only as declared by Congress and the courts but also as applied by the appropriate administrative agency. For

---

[16] Meissner v Caravello, 4 IllApp2d 428, 124 NE2d 615.

example, a particular contract to market goods might not be prohibited by any statute or court decision but may still be condemned by the Federal Trade Commission as an unfair method of competition. When the proper commission has made its determination, a contract not in harmony therewith, such as a contract of a carrier charging a higher or a lower rate than that approved by the Interstate Commerce Commission, is illegal.

§ 14:19. Contracts in Restraint of Trade. An agreement that unreasonably restrains trade is illegal and void on the ground that it is contrary to public policy. Such agreements take many forms, such as a combination to create a monopoly or to obtain a corner on the market, or an association of merchants to increase prices. In addition to the illegality of the agreement based on general principles of law, statutes frequently declare monopolies illegal and subject the parties to such agreements to various civil and criminal penalties.[17]

§ 14:20. Agreements Not to Compete. When a going business is sold, it is commonly stated in the contract that the seller shall not go into the same or a similar business again within a certain geographical area, or for a certain period of time, or both. In early times, such agreements were held void since they deprived the public of the service of the person who agreed not to compete, impaired the latter's means of earning a livelihood, reduced competition, and exposed the public to monopoly. To the modern courts, the question is whether under the circumstances the restriction imposed upon one party is reasonably necessary to protect the other party. If the restriction is reasonable, it is valid.

Restrictions to prevent competition by an employee are held valid when reasonable and necessary to protect the interest of the employer. For example, a provision that a doctor employed by a medical clinic would not practice medicine for one year within a 50-mile radius of the city in which the clinic was located is reasonable and will be enforced.

While the validity of an employee's restrictive covenant is generally determined in terms of whether its restraint is greater than is required for the reasonable protection of the employer, some courts use a broader test of whether the contract is fair to the employer, the employee, and the public.[18]

In the absence of the sale of a business or the making of an employment contract, an agreement not to compete is void as a restraint of trade and a violation of the antitrust law.

When a restriction on competition as agreed to by the parties is held invalid because its scope as to time or geographical area is too great, there is a conflict of authority as to the action taken by the court. Some courts trim the covenant down to a scope which the court deems reasonable and require the parties to abide by that revision.[19] Other courts hold that this is rewriting the contract for the parties,

[17] Sherman Antitrust Act. 15 USC §§ 1-7; Clayton Act, 15 USC §§ 12-27; Federal Trade Commission Act, 15 USC §§ 41 to 58.
[18] E.P.I. of Cleveland v Basler, 12 Ohio App2d 16, 230 NE2d 552 (holding that a covenant not to compete within a 200-mile radius of a city was unreasonable and not binding when the employer generally did business only within a 60-mile radius and did not operate regularly in 91 percent of the territory within the 200-mile radius).
[19] Electronic Data Systems Corp. v Powell (TexCivApp) 524 SW2d 393.

which courts ordinarily cannot do, and refuse to revise the covenant, holding that the covenant is totally void and that the contract is to be applied as though it did not contain any restrictive covenant.

§ 14:21. Usurious Agreements. *Usury* is committed when money is loaned at a greater rate of interest than is allowed by law. In determining whether a transaction is usurious, courts will look through the form of the transaction to determine whether there is in fact a loan on which excess interest is charged.

Service charges and points, a fee for making the loan, are to be added to the interest in determining whether a loan is usurious.

(a)   Contract Rate. Most states prohibit by statute the taking of more than a stated amount of interest. These statutes provide a *maximum contract rate* of interest, commonly 8 or 10%, which is the highest annual rate that can be exacted or demanded under the law of a given state. Usually the creditor can recover this amount only when there is an agreement in writing to pay it. A federal statute limits interest charges to service personnel to 6% a year on obligations incurred before entering the service.[20] The trend of legislation is to raise the maximum contract rate. Under the UCCC, the maximum rate of interest in consumer transactions is 18% and in the case of non-consumer loans is 45%.

(b)   Legal Rate. All states provide for a legal rate of interest. When there is an agreement for the paying of interest but no rate is specified or when the law implies a duty to pay interest, as on judgments, the *legal rate* is applied. In some states, the legal rate of interest is 6% per year.

(c)   Effect of Usury. The effect of an agreement that violates the usury law differs in various states. In some states, the entire amount of interest is forfeited by the lender. In other states, the recovery of only the excess is denied. In still others, the agreement is held to be void.[21]

In some states a special consumer protection statute governs the effect of usury in an installment contract. In contrast with the penalty ordinarily imposed by the usury statutes of permitting the debtor to recover interest or double or treble the amount of interest, some consumer protection statutes declare the original transaction void and permit the debtor to recover both the principal and interest which were paid and bar the creditor from recovering any of the unpaid debt. In many states, corporations are prohibited from raising the defense of usury.

§ 14:22. Credit Sale Contracts. Sales of goods and services on credit are not technically within the scope of the usury laws as the seller does not make an express "loan" to the buyer. When the sale is made on credit, the price which the seller charges is ordinarily not controlled by the usury law.

(a)   Credit Sale Price. A seller may charge one price for cash sales and a higher price for credit or installment sales. The difference between these two prices is called the *time-price differential.* As the usury law is not applicable, the time-price differential

---

[20] Soldiers' and Sailors' Civil Relief Act, § 206, 50 USC App § 526.
[21] Curtis v Securities Acceptance Corp. 166 Neb 815, 91 NW2d 19.

may be greater than the maximum amount of interest which could be charged on a loan equal to the cash price.

A few states, however, hold that the time price differential is subject to the usury law or have amended their usury laws or have adopted statutes to regulate the differential between cash and time prices charged by the seller. Such statutes, however, are sometimes limited to sales by retailers to consumers or apply only to sales under a stated dollar maximum. In any case, the price differential credit sale is held to be a usurious transaction when it is in fact a loan of money that is disguised as a sale for the purpose of avoiding the usury law.

Many states have adopted retail and installment sale laws which apply whenever the sale price is to be paid in installments and the seller retains a security interest in the goods. These laws frequently fix a maximum for the time price differential,[22] thereby remedying the situation created by the fact that the price differential is not subject to the usury laws.

(b)   Revolving Charge Accounts. When a merchant sells on credit and puts the bill on a charge account and then adds a charge to the unpaid balance due by the customer, most courts hold that the amount of such charge is not controlled by the usury law. (See p. 219, Overbeck v Sears, Roebuck and Co.) These courts hold that the charge is not subject to the usury law because it is merely a variation of the time-price differential. These courts also hold that it is immaterial whether the charge account pattern is an in-house program conducted by the seller for the customers of the seller only, or whether there is a central financing agency which handles the accounts for a number of participating merchants.[23] A contrary minority holds that the revolving charge account is subject to the usury law.

---

[22] See, for example, Singer Co. v Gardner, 121 NJ Super 261, 296 A2d 562 (imposing a 10% limitation).

[23] Kass v Central Charge Service, Inc. (DistColApp) 3304 A2d 632.

CASES FOR CHAPTER 14

Williams v Walker-Thomas Furniture Co.

(CA Dist Col) 350 F2d 445 (1965)

The Walker-Thomas Furniture Co. sold furniture on credit under contracts which contained a provision that a customer did not own the purchase as long as any balance on any purchase remained due. It sold goods to Williams. At the time when the balance of her account was $164, Walker-Thomas Furniture Co. sold her a $514 stereo set with knowledge that she was supporting herself and seven children on a government relief check of $218 a month. From 1957 to 1962 Williams had purchased $1,800 worth of goods and made payments of $1,400. When she stopped making payments in 1962, Walker-Thomas sought to take back everything she had purchased since 1957. From a judgment in favor of Walker-Thomas, Williams appealed.

WRIGHT, J. . . . The notion that an unconscionable bargain should not be given full enforcement is by no means novel. In Scott v United States, 79 U.S. (12 Wall) 443, 445 (1870), the Supreme Court stated: "If a contract be unreasonable and unconscionable, but not void for fraud, a court of law will give to the party who sues for its breach damages, not according to its letter, but only such as he is equitably entitled to." . . .

Congress has recently enacted the Uniform Commercial Code, which specifically provides that the court may refuse to enforce a contract which it finds to be unconscionable at the time it was made. 28 D.C. Code § 2–302 (Supp. IV 1965). The enactment of this section, which occurred subsequent to the contracts here in suit, does not mean that the common law of the District of Columbia was otherwise at the time of enactment, nor does it preclude the court from adopting a similar rule in the exercise of its powers to develop the common law for the District of Columbia. In fact, in view of the absence of prior authority on the point, we consider the congressional adoption of § 2–302 persuasive authority for following the rationale of the cases from which the section is explicitly derived. Accordingly, we hold that where the element of unconscionability is present at the time a contract is made, the contract should not be enforced.

Unconscionability has generally been recognized to include an absence of meaningful choice on the part of one of the parties together with contract terms which are unreasonably favorable to the other party. Whether a meaningful choice is present in a particular case can only be determined by consideration of all the circumstances surrounding the transaction. In many cases the meaningfulness of the choice is negated by a gross inequality to bargaining power. The manner in which the contract was entered is also relevant to this consideration. Did each party to the contract, considering his obvious education or lack of it, have a reasonable opportunity to understand the terms of the contract, or were the important terms hidden in a maze of fine print and minimized by deceptive sales practices? Ordinarily, one who signs an agreement without full knowledge of its terms might be held to assume the risk that he has entered a one-sided bargain. But when a party of little bargaining power, and hence little real choice, signs a commercially unreasonable contract with little or no knowledge of its terms, it is hardly likely that his consent, or even an objective manifestation of his consent, was ever given to all the terms. In such a case the usual rule that the terms of the agreement are not to be questioned should be abandoned and the court should consider whether the terms of the contract are so unfair that enforcement should be withheld. . . .

Because the trial court and the appellate court did not feel that enforcement could be refused, no findings were made on the possible unconscionability

of the contracts in [this case]. Since the record is not sufficient for our deciding the issue as a matter of law, the [case is] remanded to the trial court for further proceedings.

So ordered.

McConnell v Commonwealth Pictures Corp.

7 NY2d 465, 166 NE2d 482, 199 NYS2d 483 (1960)

Commonwealth Pictures Corp. agreed to pay McConnell $10,000 and a specified commission if he could persuade Universal Pictures Company to give Commonwealth the distribution rights on its pictures. Without the knowledge of either Universal or Commonwealth, McConnell obtained the distribution rights by bribing an agent of Universal with the $10,000 Commonwealth paid McConnell. McConnell thereafter sued Commonwealth for the agreed commission. From a judgment in favor of McConnell, Commonwealth appealed.

DESMOND, C.J. . . . [The lower court] said that, since the agreement sued upon—between plaintiff and defendant—was not in itself illegal, plaintiff's right to be paid for performing it could not be defeated by a showing that he had misconducted himself in carrying it out. The court found a substantial difference between this and the performance of an illegal contract. We take a different view. Proper and consistent application of a prime and long-settled public policy closes the doors of our courts to those who sue to collect the rewards of corruption.

New York's policy has been frequently and emphatically announced in the decisions. "It is the settled law of this State (and probably of every other State) that a party to an illegal contract cannot ask a court of law to help him carry out his illegal object, nor can such a person plead or prove in any court a case in which he, as a basis for his claim, must show forth his illegal purpose. . . . The money plaintiff sues for was the fruit of an admitted crime and 'no court should be required to serve as paymaster of the wages of crime.' "

. . . It is true that some of the leading decisions . . . were in suits on intrinsically illegal contracts, but the rule fails of its purpose unless it covers a case like the one at bar. . . .

We are not working here with narrow questions of technical law. We are applying fundamental concepts of morality and fair dealing not to be weakened by exceptions. So far as precedent is necessary, we can rely on Sirkin v Fourteenth Street Store, 124 App Div 384, 108 NYS 830 . . . and Reiner v North American Newspaper Alliance, 259 NY 250, 181 NE 564, 83 ALR 23. . . . Sirkin is the case closest to ours and shows that, whatever be the law in other jurisdictions, we in New York deny awards for the corrupt performance of contracts even though in essence the contracts are not illegal. Sirkin had sued for the price of goods sold and delivered to defendant. Held to be good was a defense which charged that plaintiff seller had paid a secret commission to an agent of defendant purchaser. There cannot be any difference in principle between that situation and the present one where plaintiff (it is alleged) contracted to buy motion-picture rights for defendant but performed his covenant only by bribing the seller's agent. In the Reiner case (supra), likewise, the plaintiff had fully performed the services required by his agreement with the defendant but was denied a recovery because his performance had involved and included "fraud and deception" practiced not on defendant but on a third party. . . .

Perhaps this application of the principle represents a distinct step beyond Sirkin and Reiner . . . in the sense that we are here barring recovery under a contract which in itself is entirely legal. But if this be an extension, public policy supports it. We point out that our holding is limited to cases in which the illegal performance of a contract originally valid takes the form of commercial bribery or similar conduct and in which the illegality is central to or a dominant part of the plaintiff's whole course of conduct in performance of the contract. . . .

[Judgment reversed]

Seattle Times Company v Tielsch

80 Wash App 2d 502, 495 P2d 1366 (1972)

The Seattle Times ran a football forecasting contest, called "Guest-Guesser." The Seattle Chief of Police claimed this was illegal as a lottery. The Times brought a declaratory judgment action to determine the legality of the contest. The court held the contest was a lottery and the Seattle Times appealed.

ROSELLINI, J. . . . The result of a football game may depend upon weather, the physical condition of the players and the psychological attitude of the players. It may also be affected by sociological problems between and among the members of a football team. The element of chance is an integral part of the game of football as well as the skill of the players.

The lure of the "Guest-Guesser" contest is partially the participant's love of football, partially the challenge of competition and partially the hope enticingly held out, which is often false or disappointing, that the participant will get something for nothing or a great deal for a very little outlay. . . .

The elements of a lottery are prize, consideration and chance. . . .

The appellant maintains that chance is not a dominant element in football forecasting contests. . . . The trial court found to the contrary upon that evidence, and we think the finding is justified. The appellant's expert statistician who testified at the trial did not state that chance plays no part in the outcome of such a contest or even that it does not play a dominant role. He merely testified that such a contest is not one of "pure chance." Pure chance he defined as a 50-50 chance. He acknowledged that a contestant who consistently predicted the outcome of 14 out of 20 games correctly would be a "highly skilled" contestant. . . .

. . . Where a contest is multiple or serial, and requires the solution of a number of problems to win the prize, the fact that skill alone will bring contestants to a correct solution of a greater part of the problems does not make the contest any the less a lottery if chance enters into the solution of another lesser part of the problems and thereby proximately influences the final result. . . .

Our research has revealed only one case involving a football forecasting game and the game there was a "pool," that is, a gambling game wherein wagers were placed. The Superior Court of Pennsylvania held that it was a lottery. What is most relevant in the case for our consideration here is the court's discussion of the element of chance in forecasting the result of football games. That court said: It is true that for an avid student of the sport of football the chance taken is not so great as for those who have little interest in the game. However, it is common knowledge that the predictions even among these so-called "experts" are far from infallible. Any attempt to forecast the result of a single athletic contest, be it football, baseball, or whatever, is fraught with chance. This hazard is multiplied directly by the number of predictions made. The operators of the scheme involved in this case were all cognizant of this fact for the odds against a correct number of selections were increased from 5 to 1 for three teams picked up to 900 to 1 for fifteen teams. Commonwealth v Laniewski, 173 Pa Super 245, 249, 98 A2d 215, 217 (1953).

The trial court in the instant case recognized the same basic realities attendant upon the enterprise of football game-result forecasting. We are convinced that it correctly held that chance, rather than skill, is the dominant factor in the Times' "Guest-Guesser" contest. The very name of the contest conveys quite accurately the promoter's as well as the participants' true concept of the nature of the contest.

We conclude that the contest, however harmless it may be in the opinion of the participants and the promoters, is a lottery. . . .

[Judgment against Seattle Times]

Schara v Thiede

58 Wis 489, 206 NW2d 129 (1973)

Thiede was a licensed tavern owner. Schara wished to purchase the business but he did not have a license. To enable Schara to run the business under Thiede's license, the parties executed an agreement by which Schara was described as running the business as manager for Thiede for the balance of the period of Thiede's license, after which Thiede was to lease the business to Schara. Thiede refused to execute the lease and Schara brought an action against him for breach of his agreement to lease the business. From a judgment for Schara, Thiede appealed.

HEFFERNAN, J. . . . The contract on its face discloses no illegality. It provides merely for the employment of Schara as the manager of Thiede's tavern until June 30, 1970, with Schara to receive a one year lease of the premises thereafter on the condition that the premises remain licensed to operate as a tavern. Taken literally, the contract was legal, and a breach of its conditions by either party could render the other liable for damages.

Despite the facial legality of an agreement, parol evidence is admissible to show that a writing valid on its face is a mere cover for an illegal transaction. . . .

The evidence adduced at trial established that the written contract had little similarity to the parties' actual agreement as they understood it. Both Schara and Thiede . . . testified that there was never any intention that the operator of the tavern act as "manager" for Thiede. On the contrary, the parties contemplated that . . . Schara would operate the tavern as his own business and that the agreement was a lease and a contract of employment.

While they denied that they knew that the arrangement was illegal, all parties to the contract recognized that the agreement was a subterfuge to cover the fact that . . . Schara [was] operating the tavern without a proper license. The agreement, as understood by the parties, was in violation of secs. 176.04 and 176.05, Stats., insofar as it involved the operation of the tavern . . . without having first obtained a proper license.

Thiede relies upon the illegality of the contract to defeat Schara's claim for damages. . . .

"The general rule is that . . . a court will not aid either party to an illegal agreement, whether executory or executed, but leaves the parties where it finds them." Schara does not deny the illegality of the agreement, but argues that the illegal provisions are severable and that the remainder of the agreement, including Thiede's promise to execute a one-year lease on July 1, 1970, is enforceable. The principle of severability may be applicable even though a portion of a contract may be tainted with illegality. . . .

The rule, however, gives no comfort to the plaintiff in this case, for his right to the one-year lease was expressly conditioned upon his faithful performance as "manager" pursuant to the illegal agreement. Schara clearly relies upon the past performance of an illegal transaction and accordingly, cannot expect relief from the courts.

[Judgment reversed]

Overbeck v Sears, Roebuck and Co.

(IndApp) 349 NE2d 286 (1976)

Sears, Roebuck and Co. issued the credit cards by which the holder of a card could buy on credit and would be billed monthly for purchases. If payment of the balance shown on a monthly statement

was made within thirty days, no service charge was
added. If not so paid, a service charge was added.
This charge was 1.5% a month on the balance but
not less than fifty cents. On an annual basis, this
amounted to 18%. Overbeck made purchases on a
Sears credit card and paid the monthly service
charges. Thereafter he brought suit claiming that
the 18% rate was usurious as the maximum legal
rate was 6% and sought to recover the "excess"
interest on behalf of himself and all other credit
card holders. From a decision in favor of Sears, he
appealed.

SULLIVAN, J. . . . The trial court, adhering
to the logic which compelled our brethren of the
First District to uphold the legality of defendant
American Oil Co.'s revolving charge account scheme
in *Standard Oil Co. (Indiana) v Williams* (1st Dist.
1972), 153 Ind.App. 489, 288 N.E.2d 170 (trans.
den.), granted Sears' motion for summary judgment.

The first pillar upholding the decision in
Standard Oil and the court below was the determination that the "time-price differential" theory, or the
"time-price" doctrine, immunizes revolving charge
account plans like those used by American Oil Co.
and Sears from the usury statutes. ". . . [U]sury
can only attach to a loan of money, or to the forbearance of a debt, and that, on a contract to secure
the price or value of work and labor done, or to
be done, or of property sold, the contracting parties
may agree upon one price if cash be paid, and upon
as large an addition to the cash price as may suit
themselves, if credit be given; and it is wholly immaterial whether the enhanced price be ascertained by
the simple addition of a lumped sum to the cash
price, or by a percentage thereon. In neither case
is the transaction usurious. It is neither a loan nor
the forbearance of a debt, but simply the contract
price of work and labor done and property sold;
and the difference between cash and credit in such
cases, whether 6, 10, or 20 per cent, must be left
exclusively to the contract of the parties, and no
amount of difference fairly agreed upon can be considered illegal. . . ." Plaintiff points out that there
is a certain unreality inherent in the "time-price differential" theory; that it is at worst pure "fiction,"
or at best "mathematical and intellectual impurity,"
to say that Sears' 1.5% monthly finance charge on
the unpaid balance is the differential between a cash

price for the goods and a "time-price," rather than
a "charge . . . for the forbearance to collect the full
cash price, or for the use of money. . . ." *Lloyd v
Gutgsell, supra,* 175 Neb. at 783, 124 N.W.2d at
204. Plaintiff implies that we should not ignore what
we know as men—that a finance charge, which goes
up as the length of time which we put off paying
for goods bought on credit increases, is nothing more
than "interest" for the free use of the seller's goods
and our own cash which we would have otherwise
parted with when the goods were first obtained. . . .

While the "time-price differential" theory may
seem to some a slender reed upon which to rest a
judicial determination, it has been termed the "cor-
nerstone of the sales finance industry." Felsenfeld,
Consumer Interest Rates: A Public Learning Process,
23 Bus.Law. 931, 932 (1968). The reality of which
we must be aware is not the legal nature of the transactions taking place under the terms of the Sears
Revolving Charge Account, but the unreality of conducting consumer credit transactions with strict adherence to an 8% per annum ceiling on interest in
1976. As one writer notes: "It is generally conceded
in the finance industry that extension of consumer
credit is significantly more expensive than extension
of normal business credit. Indeed, one commentator
labels any contrary conclusion 'naive.' If, then, retailers presently availing themselves of the immunizing
effect of the time-price doctrine are forced to reduce
their rates to 'nonusurious' levels, restrictions of
credit would presumably result. In an attempt to
reduce costs by minimizing losses, retailers might
well extend their charge account agreements to only
the most secure risks. Consequently, many middle
and lower income families may be excluded from
what is presently an important avenue of consumer
credit. *See also,* Williams, *The Credit Deficiency of
Retailers in Arkansas,* 3 Ark.Bus. & Econ.Rev. 14
(1970) (commenting upon and studying the adverse
economic effects of the abrogation of the time-price
doctrine in Arkansas by the court in *Sloan v Sears,
Roebuck & Co., supra*): McCallister, *Retail Installment Credit: Growth and Legislation* 109 (1965)
(commenting upon the adverse economic effects of
the Nebraska high court's renunciation of the time-
price differential theory in *Lloyd v Gutgsell, supra*);
If the "time-price differential" theory is indeed a
fiction, it is one not only recommended by case law
but compelled by the realities of our society.

[Judgment affirmed]

QUESTIONS AND CASE PROBLEMS

1. What social forces are affected by the rule that a credit sale price is not usurious although the difference between the credit price and the cash price is greater than the interest which could be charged on a loan in the amount of the cash price?

2. Compare the effect of illegality as to (a) the subject matter of a contract, and (b) the manner of performing a lawful contract.

3. Compare the legality of a prize drawing with winners selected by a random drawing from (a) names in the telephone book, (b) names of persons attending a television show, and (c) names of persons written on entry blanks obtained on purchasing goods from the sponsoring store.

4. Burgess, a salesman for Bowyer, failed to turn over to Bowyer an indefinite amount of money collected by him. In order to avoid a criminal prosecution of Burgess by Bowyer, Burgess and his brother-in-law entered into a contract with the employer by which they agreed to pay Bowyer $5,000 if full restitution was not made. No restitution was made, and Bowyer sued Burgess and his brother-in-law on the contract for $5,000. Was he entitled to recover? [Bowyer v Burgess, 54 Cal 2d 97, 4 Cal Rptr 521, 351 P2d 793]

5. Las Vegas Hacienda, Inc., advertised that it would pay $5,000 to anyone shooting a hole in one on its golf course. Gibson, who paid the fee of 50 cents, made a hole in one. The golf course corporation refused to pay the $5,000. When Gibson sued for breach of contract, it raised the defense that the contract was an illegal gambling contract and could not be enforced even though gambling as such was legalized in the state. Decide. [Las Vegas Hacienda, Inc. v Gibson, 77 Nev 25, 359 P2d 85]

6. The Rhode Island Grocers Association held an annual exhibition to which there was no admission charge. As an added feature to attract public interest, arrangements were made with the Transocean Air Lines for a drawing of a door prize for a free round trip to Hawaii for two. Any spectator attending the exhibition could participate in the drawing by filling out a card with the spectator's name and address. Was this a lottery? [Finch v Rhode Island Grocers Association, 93 RI 323, 175 A2d 177]

7. *A* was employed by *B*. *A* embezzled money from *B*. When his crime was discovered, he promised *B* that he would repay the money which he had taken. He did not do so. *B* sued *A* for breach of his promise. Can *B* recover? [Gallaher Drug Co. v Robinson, 13 Ohio Misc 216, 232 NE2d 668]

8. The Western Cab Company filed an application with the State Taxicab Authority for permission to issue stock. The owner of the business made a contract with Kellar, the former owner of the business, by which it agreed to pay Kellar a specified sum of money and to transfer certain shares of stock to him if he testified before the Authority in the manner suggested by the owner and if the Authority granted the application. The application was granted but the owner of the business did not pay Kellar as he had agreed. Kellar sued the Western Cab Company and its new owner for breach of the contract. Were they liable? [Western Cab Co. v Kellar, 90 Nev 240, 523 P2d 842]

9. A Virginia statute required builders and persons doing construction work to obtain a license and imposed a fine for failing to do so. F. S. Bowen Electric Co. installed equipment in a building being constructed by Foley. Bowen had not obtained a license. When Foley did not pay Bowen, the latter sued Foley for the money due. Could he recover? [F. S. Bowen Electric Co. v Foley, 194 Va 92, 72 SE2d 388]

10. A person borrowed money and executed a promissory note for the loan. The note called for the payment of interest at a usurious rate. Under the local law this made the note void. The lender sued on the note. When the borrower raised the defense that the note was void because of usury, the creditor asserted that he was only claiming the amount of interest which could be lawfully claimed and that therefore the usury aspect was eliminated and he could recover on the note. Was he correct? [Yakutsk v Alfino, 43 App Div 2d 552, 349 NYS2d 718]

11. Smith was employed as a salesman for Borden, Inc., which sold food products in 63 counties in Arkansas, 2 counties in Missouri, 2 counties in Oklahoma, and 1 county in Texas. The contract with Smith prohibited him from competing with Borden after leaving its employ. Smith left Borden and went to work for a competitor, Lady Baltimore Foods. Working for this second employer, Smith sold in three counties of Arkansas. He had sold in two of these counties while he worked for Borden. Borden brought an injunction action against Smith and Lady Baltimore to enforce the anticompetitive covenant in Smith's former contract. Was Borden entitled to the injunction? [Borden, Inc. v Smith, 252 Ark 295, 478 SW2d 744]

12. Colonial Stores was looking for someone to build a store in the city and lease it to Colonial. McArver and Gerukos agreed between themselves that they would obtain options to buy some land for a store site and resell the options to a third person who would build a store and lease it to Colonial. All of this was successfully done, but Gerukos kept all of the profits from the transaction. When McArver sued him for his share of the profits, Gerukos raised the defense that McArver could not recover because a statute required that all real estate brokers and salesmen be licensed and McArver did not have such a real estate license. Was this defense valid? [McArver v Gerukos, 265 NC 413, 144 SE2d 277]

13. Costello held a license as a professional engineer in New York, Maryland, Illinois, and New Mexico, but he was not licensed in New Jersey. He did consulting engineering work for a New Jersey licensed architect in designing a city swimming pool. When Costello was not paid in full for his services, he sued the architect, who claimed that Costello was not allowed to recover because he did not have a license in New Jersey to render the services for which he claimed compensation. Was he entitled to recover? [Costello v Schmidlin, (CA3 NJ) 404 F2d 87]

14. Doherty ran a lounge and bar known as the Orchid Room in California where betting is illegal. Bradley was a patron in the Orchid Room who made bets with Doherty on the scores he could attain on the pinball machine. Bradley lost $70,000 on such bets. He sued Doherty to recover this money. Doherty raised the defense that Bradley was in pari delicto and therefore could not recover. Bradley claimed that this defense did not apply because the pinball machines were fixed by electronic devices and also because he, Bradley, was a compulsive gambler. Was Bradley correct? [Bradley v Doherty, 30 CalApp3d 991, 106 CalRptr 725]

15. Hall made a contract to purchase a tract of land from Montaleone. The contract provided for a down payment and then the payment of the balance with interest. Montaleone refused to perform the contract. When Hall sued him, Montaleone raised the defense that the contract was illegal because the interest which was charged Hall on the unpaid balance was usurious as it exceeded the statutory maximum. Was that a valid defense? [Hall v Montaleone, 38 IllApp2d 591, 348 NE2d 196]

15   Form Of Contract

As a practical matter, every important contract should be written. In the first place, when the agreement is written, each party knows just what is being agreed to. Second, the writing assures both parties that at a future date there will be less chance of disagreement as to what has been agreed upon. Third, it eliminates the possibility that either party to the contract can effectively deny having made the contract.

A. STATUTE OF FRAUDS

In Chapter 9 it was stated that a contract is a binding agreement. Must the agreement be evidenced by a writing?

§ 15:1. Oral Contracts Valid. Generally a contract is valid whether it is written or oral. By statute, however, some contracts must be evidenced by a writing. Such statutes are designed to prevent the use of the courts for the purpose of enforcing certain oral agreements or alleged oral agreements. The statutes do not apply when an oral agreement has been voluntarily performed by both parties.

Apart from statute, the parties may agree that their oral agreement is not to be binding until a formal written contract is executed, or the circumstances of the transaction may show that such was their intention. Conversely, they may agree that their oral contract is binding even though a written contract is to be executed later.

Consequently, the failure to sign and return a written contract does not establish that there is no contract as there may have been an earlier oral contract. If one of the parties, with the knowledge or approval of the other contracting party, undertakes performance of the contract before it is reduced to writing, it is generally held that the parties intended to be bound from the moment the oral contract was made.

In order for the prior oral agreement to be a binding contract, it must satisfy the requirement of definiteness. If it does not, that not only means that there is no binding oral contract, but it also lends support to the view that the oral negotiations were not intended to be a contract and that there should not be any contract until a definite written contract has been signed.

§ 15:2. Contracts That Must Be Evidenced By A Writing. Ordinarily a contract, whether oral or not, is binding if the existence and terms of the contract can be established to the satisfaction of the trier of fact, ordinarily the jury. In some instances a statute, commonly called a statute of frauds,[1] requires that certain kinds of contracts be evidenced by a writing or they cannot be enforced. This means that either (a) the contract itself must be in writing and signed by both parties, or (b) there be a sufficient written memorandum of the oral contract signed by the person being sued for breach of contract.

Ordinarily an offer may be written, oral, or expressed by conduct. Even when the contract must be evidenced by a writing under the statute of frauds, the offer which leads up to the contract may be oral. As an exception, statutes regulating the letting of government contracts may require that bids by contractors, the offers, be written and signed.

σ (a) **An Agreement That Cannot be Performed Within One Year after the Contract is Made.** A writing is required when the contract by its terms or subject matter cannot be performed within one year after the date of the agreement. The year runs from the time of the making of the oral contract rather than from the date when performance is to begin. In computing the year, the day on which the contract was made is excluded. The year begins with the following day and ends at the close of the first anniversary of the day on which the agreement was made.

The statute of frauds does not apply if it is possible under the terms of the agreement to perform the contract within one year. Thus, a writing is not required when no time for performance is specified and the performance will not necessarily take more than a year. In this case the statute is inapplicable without regard to the time when performance is actually begun or completed.

If a contract of indefinite duration is terminable by either party at will, the statute of frauds is not applicable since the contract may be terminated within a year.

A writing claimed to satisfy the statute of frauds as to a contract which cannot be performed within one year must set forth all the material terms of the contract. Consequently, a letter is not sufficient as a writing to evidence an oral contract of employment for more than one year when the letter does not state the salary.[2]

---

[1] The name is derived from the original English Statute of Frauds and Perjuries, which was adopted in 1677 and became the pattern for similar legislation in America. The seventeenth section of that statute governed the sale of goods, and its modern counterpart is § 2-201 of the Uniform Commercial Code, discussed in Chapter 23. The fourth section of the English statute provided the pattern for American legislation with respect to contracts other than for the sale of goods described in this section of the chapter. The English statute was repealed in 1954, except as to land sale and guaranty contracts. The American statutes remain in force, but the liberalization by Uniform Commercial Code § 2-201 of the pre-Code requirements with respect to contracts for the sale of goods may be regarded as a step in the direction of the abandonment of the statute of frauds concept.

When the English Statute of Frauds was adopted, the parties to a lawsuit were not permitted to testify on their own behalf, with the result that a litigant had difficulty in disproving perjured testimony of third persons offered as evidence on behalf of the adverse party. The Statute of Frauds was repealed in England partly because it was felt that it permitted the assertion of a "technical" defense as a means of avoiding just obligations and partly on the ground that with parties in interest now having the right to testify there is no longer the need for a writing to protect the parties from perjured testimony of third persons. Azevedo v Minister, 86 Nev 576, 471 P2d 661.

[2] Olympic Junior, Inc. v David Crystal, Inc. (CA3 NJ) 463 F2d 1141.

(b) An Agreement to Sell or a Sale of Any Interest in Real Property. All contracts to sell and sales of land, buildings or interests in land, such as mortgages which are treated as such an interest, must be evidenced by a writing.

A contract for the sale of sand, coal, or oil without any specification as to its location, such as "ten tons of grade A sand," is merely a contract to sell personal property and not the sale of an interest in land. Such a contract must satisfy the requirements of the Uniform Commercial Code as to a sale of goods.

> *(1) Collateral Contracts.* The statute applies only to the agreement between the owner and purchaser, or between their agents. It does not apply to other or collateral agreements, such as those which the purchaser may make in order to raise the money to pay for the property or to agreements to pay for an examination or search of the title of the property. Similarly, a partnership agreement to deal in real estate is generally not required for that reason to be in writing. The statute ordinarily does not apply to a contract between a real estate agent and one of the parties to the sales contract employing the agent.

(c) A Promise to Answer for the Debt or Default of Another. When *A* promises *C* to pay *B*'s debts to *C* if *B* does not do so, *A* is promising to answer for the debt of another. Such a promise must usually be evidenced by a writing to be enforceable. Thus, the oral promise of the president of a corporation to pay the debts owed by the corporation to its creditors if they will not sue the corporation does not bind the president, even though the president is a major shareholder of the corporation and would be indirectly benefited by the forbearance of the creditors.

If the promise is made directly to the debtor that the promisor will pay the creditor of the debtor what is owed, the statute of frauds is not applicable. In contrast, if the promisor makes the promise to the creditor, it comes within the category of a promise made for the benefit of another and must therefore be evidenced by a writing which satisfies the statute of frauds.

> *(1) Primary Purpose Exception.* The fact that a particular promise is made to the creditor and is a promise to answer for the debt of another does not mean that the statute of frauds will necessarily bar enforcement when the promise is oral. If that promise was made primarily for the benefit of the promisor, rather than for the benefit of the debtor, an exception to the statute of frauds is recognized. In such a case the promise may be enforced even though it is oral. (See p. 232, R. H. Freitag Mfg. Co. v Boeing Airplane Co.)

(d) A Promise by the Executor or Administrator of a Decedent's Estate to Pay a Claim Against the Estate from Personal Funds. The personal representative (executor or administrator) has the duty of winding up the affairs of a deceased person, paying the debts from the proceeds of the estate and distributing any balance remaining. The executor or administrator is not personally liable for the claims against the estate of the decedent. If the personal representative promises to pay the decedent's debts with the representative's own money, the promise cannot be enforced unless it is evidenced by a writing that complies with the terms of the statute.

If the personal representative makes a contract on behalf of the estate in the course of administering the estate, a writing is not required since the representative is then contracting on behalf of the estate. Thus if the personal representative employs an attorney to settle the estate or makes a burial contract with an undertaker, no writing is required.

(e) **A Promise Made in Consideration of Marriage.** If a person makes a promise to pay a sum of money or to give property to another in consideration of marriage or a promise to marry, the agreement must be evidenced by a writing.[3] This provision of the statute of frauds is not applicable to ordinary mutual promises to marry, and it is not affected by the statutes in some states that prohibit the bringing of any action for breach of promise of marriage.

(f) **A Sale of Goods.** When the contract price for goods is $500 or more, the contract must ordinarily be evidenced by a writing. See Chapter 23.

(g) **Miscellaneous Statutes of Frauds.** In a number of states, special statutes require other agreements to be in writing or evidenced by a writing. Thus, a statute may provide that an agreement to name a person as beneficiary in an insurance policy must be evidenced by a writing.

The Uniform Commercial Code contains three statutes of frauds relating to sales of personal property: (1) goods; (2) securities, such as stocks and bonds; and (3) personal property other than goods and securities.

In some states contracts with brokers relating to the sale of land are also subject to the statute of frauds.

§ 15:3. Note or Memorandum. The statute of frauds requires a writing to evidence those contracts which come within its scope. This writing may be a note or memorandum, as distinguished from a contract. It may be in any form because its only purpose is to serve as evidence of the contract. The statutory requirement is, of course, satisfied if there is a complete written contract signed by both parties.

(a) **Contents.** Except in the case of a sale of goods, the note or memorandum must contain all the material terms of the contract so that the court can determine just what was agreed. Thus, it is insufficient if the contract is partly oral and partly written. The subject matter must be identified either within the writing itself or in other writings to which it refers. A writing is not sufficient that does not identify the land which is the subject of the contract.

In some states a description of real estate by street number, city or county, and state, is not sufficient; the writing must show the lot and block numbers of the property as well as name the city or county and state. When the writing does not contain a description which satisfies the statute of frauds, the land may not be identified by the testimony of witnesses. It is not necessary that the writing specifically state a term that would be implied, as that the price therein stated is to be paid in "cash." (See p. 233, Klymyshyn v Szarek) Some states make an exception to the general rule and do not require that the writing set forth the consideration or terms of payment.

A check is ordinarily not a sufficient memorandum to satisfy the statute of frauds because it does not set forth the terms of the contract.[4]

---

[3] Koch v Koch, 95 NJSuper 546, 232 A2d 157; Miller v Greene (Fla) 104 So2d 457.
[4] Southern Industrial Banking Corp. v Delta Properties, Inc., (Tenn) 542 SW2d 815.

The note or memorandum may consist of one writing or instrument or of separate papers, such as letters or telegrams, or of a combination of such papers.

Separate writings cannot be considered together unless they are linked, either by express reference in each writing to the other or by the fact that each writing clearly deals with the same subject matter. Conversely, when the papers go no further than to show that they deal with similar subject matters, the papers cannot be integrated. For example, a signed memorandum relating to the sale of unidentified land and an unsigned deed could not be deemed one writing for the purpose of the statute of frauds because at most each only showed that it related to a real estate transaction and did not show that they both related to the same transaction and neither writing referred to the other.[5]

It is not necessary that the writing be addressed to the other contracting party or to any person, nor is it necessary that the writing be made with the intent to create a writing to satisfy the statute of frauds. When a corporation made an oral contract of employment with an employee, the minutes of the corporation reciting the adoption of the resolution to employ the employee (which minutes were signed by the president of the corporation) together with the salary check paid the employee constituted a sufficient writing to satisfy the statute of frauds.

The memorandum may be made at the time of the original transaction or at a later date. It must, however, ordinarily exist at the time a court action is brought upon the agreement.

(b)   Signing. The note or memorandum must be signed by the party sought to be charged or that person's agent. A letter from an employer setting forth the details of an oral contract of employment satisfies the statute of frauds in a suit brought by the employee against the employer, as the writing was signed by the party "sought to be charged." If the employer had sued the employee in such case, the employer's letter would not satisfy the statute of frauds as it would not be signed by the employee.

It should be noted that a contrary rule exists in some states in regard to contracts for the sale of land. Either because of special language in the statute or because of the rather extraordinary view that "the party to be charged" necessarily means the vendor, these courts hold not only that the vendor must sign the writing regardless of who the defendant is in the suit, but also that the vendor's signature is sufficient to bind the vendee.

Some states require that the authorization of an agent to execute a contract coming within the statute of frauds must also be in writing. In the case of an auction, it is the usual practice for the auctioneer to be the agent of both parties for the purpose of signing the memorandum. If the seller acts as auctioneer, however, the seller cannot sign as agent for the buyer.

The signature may be made at any place on the writing, although in some states it is expressly required that the signature appear at the end of the writing. The signature may be an ordinary one or any symbol that is adopted by the party as a signature. It may consist of initials, figures, or a mark. When a signature consists of a mark made by a person who is illiterate or physically incapacitated, it is commonly required that the name of the person be placed upon the writing by someone else, who may be required to sign the instrument as a witness. A person signing a trade

---

[5] Young v McQuerrey (Hawaii) 508 P2d 1051.

or assumed name is liable to the same extent as though the contract had been signed with the signer's name. In the absence of a local statute that provides otherwise, a signature may be made by pencil, pen, or by typewriter, by print, or by stamp.

§ 15:4. Effect of Noncompliance. The majority of states hold that a contract which does not comply with the statute of frauds is voidable. A small minority of states hold that such an agreement is void. Under either view, if an action is brought to enforce the contract, the defendant can raise the objection that it is not evidenced by a writing. No one other than the defendant, however, can make the objection. Thus, an insurance company cannot refuse to pay on its policy on the ground that the insured did not have any insurable interest in the insured property because there was no writing relating to the property that satisfied the statute of frauds.

(a)   **Part Performance.** In some cases, when a writing is not made as required by the statute, the courts will nevertheless enforce the agreement if there has been a sufficient part performance to make it clear that a contract existed. In other instances the court will not enforce the contract but will permit a party to recover the fair value of work and improvements made in reliance upon the contract. This situation arises when a tenant improves the land while in possession under an oral lease which cannot be enforced because of the statute of frauds. The situation also arises when a buyer of land under an oral agreement enters into possession of the land. If the tenant or purchaser has made valuable improvements to the land, the courts will commonly enforce the oral agreement.

In order for part performance to take an oral contract out of a statute of frauds, the performance must be such as is clearly referable to the terms of the contract. Where this is not so, conduct claimed to be part performance does not establish the oral contract.

Ordinarily the performance of personal services does not constitute such part performance as will take the case out of the statute of frauds except in extraordinary cases when the value of the services cannot be measured by money.[6] In any case, evidence as to part performance must be clear and convincing.

(b)   **Promissory Estoppel.** There is a conflict of authority as to the effect of the fact that the promisee has relied on the oral agreement. Some courts hold that reliance on the promise bars the promisor *(promissory estoppel)* from claiming that the oral agreement was not binding. (See p. 234, McIntosh v Murphy)

(c)   **Recovery of Value Conferred.** In most instances, a person who is prevented from enforcing a contract because of the statute of frauds is nevertheless entitled to recover from the other party the value of any services or property furnished or money given under the oral contract. Recovery is not based upon the terms of the contract but upon the quasi-contractual obligation of the other party to restore to the plaintiff what was received in order to prevent unjust enrichment at the plaintiff's expense. For example, when an oral contract for services cannot be enforced because of the statute of frauds, the person performing the work may recover the reasonable value of the services rendered.[7]

---

[6] Crosby v Strahan's Estate, 78 Wyo 302, 324 P2d 492.
[7] Roaderick v Lull Engineering Co., 296 Minn 385, 208 NW2d 761.

B. PAROL EVIDENCE RULE

When the contract is evidenced by a writing, may the contract terms be changed by the testimony of witnesses? The answer depends upon the circumstances surrounding the execution of the writing and the nature of the writing.

§ 15:5. Exclusion of Parol Evidence. The general rule is that spoken words, that is, *parol evidence,* will not be allowed to modify or contradict the terms of a written contract which is complete on its face unless there is clear proof that because of fraud, accident, or a mistake, the writing is not in fact the contract or the complete or true contract. This is called the *parol evidence rule.* It excludes words spoken before or at the time the contract was made.

To illustrate, assume that *L,* the landlord who is the owner of several new stores in the same vicinity, discusses leasing one of them to *T* (tenant). *L* agrees to give to *T* the exclusive right to sell soft drinks and agrees to stipulate in the leases with the tenants of other stores that they cannot do so. *L* and *T* then execute a detailed written lease for the store. The lease with *T* makes no provision with respect to an exclusive right of *T* to sell soft drinks. Thereafter *L* leases the other stores to *A, B,* and *C,* without restricting them as to the sale of soft drinks, which they then begin to sell, causing *T* to lose money. *T* sues *L,* claiming that the latter has broken the contract by which *T* was to have the exclusive right to sell soft drinks. *L* defends on the ground that there was no prior oral agreement to that effect. Will the court permit *T* to prove that there was such an oral agreement?

On the facts as stated, if nothing more is shown, the court will not permit such parol evidence to be presented. The operation of this principle can be understood more easily if the actual courtroom procedure is followed. When *T* sues *L,* the first step will be to prove that there is a lease between them. Accordingly, *T* will offer in evidence the written lease between *T* and *L. T* will then take the witness stand and begin to testify about an oral agreement giving an exclusive right. At that point *L*'s attorney will object to the admission of the oral testimony by *T* because it would modify the terms of the written lease. The court will then examine the lease to see if it appears to be complete; and if the court decides that it is, the court will refuse to allow *T* to offer evidence of an oral agreement. The only evidence before the court then will be the written lease. *T* will lose because nothing is in the written lease about an exclusive right to sell soft drinks.

If a written contact appears to be complete, the parol evidence rule prohibits its alteration not only by oral testimony but also by proof of other writings or memorandums made before or at the time the written contract was executed. An exception is made when the written contract refers to and identifies other writings or memorandums and states that they are to be regarded as part of the written contract. In such a case, it is said that the other writings are integrated or incorporated by reference.

(a) Reason for the Parol Evidence Rule. The parol evidence rule is based on the theory that either (1) there never was an oral agreement or (2) if there was, the parties purposely abandoned it when they executed their written contract. Some courts enforce the parol evidence rule strictly in order to give stability to commercial transactions.

(b)   Conflict Between Oral and Written Contracts. Initially, when there is a conflict between the prior oral contract and the later written contract, the variation is to be regarded as (1) a mistake, which can be corrected by reformation, or (2) an additional term in the written contract, which is not binding because it was not part of the agreement. Illustrative of the latter, when a customer and a warehouse made a storage contract over the telephone and nothing was said as to the warehouse's limitation of liability, a limitation-of-liability clause appearing in the printed contract mailed to the customer was not binding because it was not part of the contract as already made on the telephone.

In view of the fact that a reasonable person in the twentieth century should anticipate that the formal contract will contain many provisions not mentioned in the brief oral negotiating, as in the case of a life insurance contract, courts are very likely to find that any additional term in the formal written contract has either been authorized because it was anticipated or has been accepted or ratified because the person receiving the printed form has not repudiated the contract or objected to the term in particular or has performed or accepted performance under the contract. To prevent a loss of rights, it is therefore important to read a contract thoroughly and to make prompt objection to any departure from or addition to the original oral contract if such variation is not acceptable.

(c)   Liberalization of Parol Evidence Rule. The strictness of the parol evidence rule has been relaxed in a number of jurisdictions. A trend is beginning to appear which permits parol evidence as to the intention of the parties when the claimed intention is plausible from the face of the contract even though there is no ambiguity. There is likewise authority that parol evidence is admissible as to matters occurring before the execution of the contract in order to give a better understanding of what the parties meant by their written contract.[8]

§ 15:6. When the Parol Evidence Rule Does Not Apply. The parol evidence rule may not apply in certain cases, which are discussed in the following paragraphs.

(a)   Incomplete Contract. The parol evidence rule necessarily requires that the written contract sum up or integrate the entire contract. If the written contract is on its face, or is admittedly, not a complete summation, the parties naturally did not intend to abandon the points upon which they had agreed but which were not noted in the contract; and parol evidence is admissible to show the actual agreement of the parties. (See p. 235, Williams and Associates v Ramsey Products Corporation)

A contract may appear on its face to be complete and yet not include everything the parties agreed upon. It must be remembered that there is no absolute standard by which to determine when a contract is complete. All that the court can do is to consider whether all essential terms of the contract are present, that is, whether the

---

[8] Hohenstein v S.M.H. Trading Corp. (CA5 Ga) 382 F2d 530. This is also the view followed by UCC § 2-202(a) which permits terms in a contract for the sale of goods to be "explained or supplemented by a course of dealing or usage of trade . . . or by course of performance." Such evidence is admissible not because there is an ambiguity but "in order that the true understanding of the parties as to the agreement may be reached." Official Code Comment to § 2-202.

It has also been held that UCC § 1-205 permits proof of trade usage and course of performance with respect to non-Code contracts even though there is no ambiguity. Chase Manhattan Bank v First Marion Bank (CA5 Fla) 437 F2d 1040.

contract is sufficiently definite to be enforceable, and whether it contains all provisions which would ordinarily be included in a contract of that nature.

The fact that a contract is silent as to a particular matter does not mean that it is incomplete, for the law may attach a particular legal result (called *implying a term*) when the contract is silent. In such a case, parol evidence which is inconsistent with the term that would be implied cannot be shown. For example, when the contract is silent as to the time of payment, the obligation of making payment concurrently with performance by the other party is implied, and parol evidence is not admissible to show that there was an oral agreement to make payment at a different time.

(b) Ambiguity. If a written contract is not clear, parol evidence may generally be admitted to clarify the meaning. This is particularly true when the contract contains contradictory measurements or descriptions, or when it employs symbols or abbreviations that have no general meaning known to the court. Parol evidence may also be admitted to show that a word used in a contract has a special trade meaning or a meaning in the particular locality that differs from the common meaning of that word.

The fact that the parties disagree as to the meaning of the contract does not mean that it is ambiguous.[9] Some courts have departed from requiring strict ambiguity and permit parol evidence whenever it is not unreasonably inconsistent with the writing. This is done to throw further light on the intent of the parties and in effect permits parol evidence of anything which is plausible. (See p. 236, Delta Dynamics v Arioto)

(c) Fraud, Accident, or Mistake. A contract apparently complete on its face may have omitted a provision which should have been included. Parol evidence may be admitted to show that a provision was omitted as the result of fraud, accident, or mistake, and to further show what that provision stated.

(d) Conduct of Parties. The parol evidence rule does not prevent a party from showing by parol evidence that the making of the contract was fraudulently induced or that the other party to the contract has not performed an obligation imposed thereby. Thus, parol evidence is admissible to show that the seller never made delivery of the goods covered by the contract.[10]

(e) Existence or Modification of Contract. The parol evidence rule prohibits only the contradiction of a complete written contract. It does not prohibit proof that an obligation under the contract never existed or that the contract was thereafter modified or terminated. Thus, parol evidence may be admitted to show that a construction contract was not to be binding unless and until the contractor procured a 100 percent construction loan.[11]

Written contracts commonly declare that contracts can only be modified by a writing. In the case of construction contracts, it will ordinarily be stated that no payment will be made for extra work unless there is a written order from the owner or architect calling for such extra work. If the parties proceed in disregard of such

---

[9] Modern Construction, Inc. v Barce, Inc. (Alaska) 556 P2d 528.
[10] Associates Discount Corp. v Fitzwater (MoApp) 518 SW2d 574.
[11] Sheldon Builders v Trojan Towers, 225 CalApp2d 781, 63 CalRptr 425.

a clause requiring a writing, it may be shown by parol evidence that they have done so and the contract will be modified accordingly.

(1)   Nonbinding Character of Written Contract. Persons may sign documents which look like binding contracts but parol evidence is admitted by the courts to show that the parties never really intended to be bound. Frequently, there is present an element of high-pressure selling in which one party is reluctant to sign but only does so when assured that the paper is not a binding contract. Parol evidence is admissible to show this background, with the result that the contract is held not to be binding.

(2)   Modification of Contract. To return to the illustration of the store lease by *L* to *T* and the alleged oral agreement of an exclusive right to sell soft drinks, three situations may arise. It may be claimed that the oral agreement was made (a) before the execution of the final written lease; (b) at the same time as the execution of the written lease; or (c) subsequent to the execution of the written lease. The parol evidence rule only prohibits the proof of the oral agreement under (a) and (b). It is not applicable to (c), for it can be shown that subsequent to the execution of the contract the parties modified the contract, even though the original contract was in writing and the subsequent modification was oral. Clear proof of the later agreement is required.

When it is claimed that a contract is modified by a later agreement, consideration must support the modifying agreement except in the case of a contract for the sale of goods.[12] In any case, if the parties have performed the part of the contract that is modified, it is immaterial that there was no consideration for the agreement for such modification.

(f)   Collateral Contract. The parol evidence rule only applies with respect to the written contract of the parties. If they have made two contracts, one written and the other oral, the parol evidence rule does not bar proof of the oral contract. Difficulty arises in determining whether in fact there are two separate contracts or whether there was merely one contract which was written and the existence of a separate oral contract is asserted in order to evade the prohibition of the parol evidence rule and thereby contradict or bypass the written contract.

[12] UCC § 2-209(1).

CASES FOR CHAPTER 15

R. H. Freitag Mfg. Co. v Boeing Airplane Co.

55 Wash 2d 334, 347 P2d 1074 (1959)

Boeing Airplane Co. contracted with Pittsburgh-Des Moines Steel Co. for the latter to construct a supersonic wind tunnel. R. H. Freitag Mfg. Co. sold material to York-Gillespie Co., which subcontracted to do part of the work. In order to persuade Freitag to keep supplying materials on credit,

Boeing and the principal contractor both assured Freitag that he would be paid. Freitag was not paid by the subcontractor and then sued Boeing and the contractor. They defended on the ground that the assurances given Freitag were not written. From a judgment in favor of the defendants, the plaintiff appealed.

ROSELLINI, J. . . . . It is conceded that the Statute of Frauds . . . renders unenforceable any special promise to answer for the debt, default, or misdoings of another. However, this court has recognized and followed the very widely accepted doctrine that, where the leading purpose of the promisor is not to aid the third person in getting credit but to secure a benefit for himself, he will be considered a debtor himself, rather than a surety, and the statute will not apply. . . .

"The purpose of [the statute] was not to effectuate, but to prevent, wrong. It does not apply to promises in respect to debts created at the instance and for the benefit of the promisor, but only to those by which the debt of one party is sought to be charged upon and collected from another. . . .

It is so obviously just that a promisor receiving no benefits should be bound only by the exact terms of his promise, that this statute requiring a memorandum in writing was enacted. Therefore, whenever the alleged promisor is an absolute stranger to the transaction, and without interest in it, courts strictly uphold the obligations of this statute. But cases sometimes arise in which, though a third party is the original obligor, the primary debtor, the promisor has a personal, immediate and pecuniary interest in the transaction, and is therefore himself a party to be benefited by the performance of the promisee. In such cases the reason which underlies and which prompted this statutory provision fails, and the courts will give effect to the promise.". . .

The allegations of the complaint in this instance are ample to support a finding that the assurances of Pittsburgh and Boeing were given to secure a benefit to themselves, a technically satisfactory and expeditious construction of the needed parts, and there is no allegation to show that they had any motive or purpose to benefit York-Gillespie. . . .

[Judgment reversed]

Klymyshyn v Szarek

29 Mich App 638, 185 NW2d 820 (1971)

Szarek orally agreed to sell an apartment building to Klymyshyn. Klymyshyn made a deposit of $500, for which Szarek gave him a receipt. Szarek later claimed that the oral contract was not binding because the receipt did not satisfy the statute of frauds. From a judgment for Klymyshyn, Szarek appealed.

McGregor, J. . . . Plaintiff agreed to purchase the premises, . . . and defendants gave the following document to him:

"May 2, 1969

Received from Mr. Stephan Klymyshyn the sum of $500.00 as deposit to purchase apt. at 20001 Conant, for $94,000.00.

(signed) Alex Szarek and Elsie Szarek"

Defendants claim that a preliminary agreement was to be prepared and executed by the parties which would further define the terms of the transaction, and additional terms not agreed upon when the receipt was executed. Defendants' principal contentions are that the document as described above is insufficient to satisfy the statute of frauds, in that the essential terms, *e.g.,* whether for cash or credit, are not defined, and that the time for performance is not specified. . . .

Our courts have indicated a continuing "disposition 'to liberalize its interpretation of the statute of frauds.' " . . . In the case of Duke v Miller (1959), 355 Mich 540, 542, 543, 94 NW2d 819, a similar action for specific performance was instituted, and the only memorandum of the agreement in plaintiff's bill of complaint was as follows:

"Detroit, Mich., Sept. 24, 1957.

Received of Mr. Newell Duke $150.00 DOLLARS as Down Payment on Lot 109 on Fenkel.

Balance $4,350

$150.00

[s] Ray Miller"

The trial court therein had granted the defendant's motion to dismiss, on the ground that the agreement could not be specifically enforced because the memorandum failed to meet the requirements of the statute of frauds, in that it did not specify the time for payment of the balance and the time for closing the transaction. The Supreme Court was not impressed by the defendant's allegations and reversed the trial court, holding that when a contract is silent as to the time for performance or payment, and absent any expression of a contrary intent, the law will presume a reasonable time.

Furthermore, the Court was not concerned that the contract did not mention the terms of payment of the balance of the purchase price, in that, absent a contrary intention on the face of the instrument, the terms were to be for cash. The Court then went on to say: "Indulgence of that presumption [payment for cash] or inference does not amount to the court's making a new contract for the parties or varying its terms, but merely gives effect to what it is reasonable to assume the parties intended when no contrary intention appears on the face of the instrument.". . .

We find the trial court here was correct in its ruling that the memorandum satisfied the statute of frauds.

[Reversed on other grounds]

McIntosh v Murphy

52 Hawaii 29, 112, 469 P2d 177 (1970)

Murphy owned a Chevrolet-Oldsmobile dealership in Hawaii. He went to California to interview applicants for employment. McIntosh who lived in Los Angeles orally agreed to work for Murphy in a management position for a year. McIntosh then sold or moved his belongings from his residence in Los Angeles to Honolulu, a distance of approximately 2,200 miles. McIntosh began working for Murphy but was discharged 2½ months later. He sued Murphy for breach of contract. Murphy raised the defense that the contract could not be enforced because the statute of frauds barred proving the oral agreement as the oral agreement could not be performed within one year. From a judgment for McIntosh, Murphy appealed.

LEVINSON, J. . . . When courts have enforced an oral contract in spite of the Statute, they have utilized the legal labels of "part performance" or "equitable estoppel" in granting relief. Both doctrines are said to be based on the concept of estoppel, which operates to avoid unconscionable injury. . . .

The doctrine of estoppel to assert the statute of frauds has been consistently applied by the courts of this state to prevent fraud that would result from refusal to enforce oral contracts in certain circumstances. Such fraud may inhere in the unconscionable injury that would result from denying enforcement of the contract after one party has been induced by the other seriously to change his position in reliance on the contract. . . .

In seeking to frame a workable test which is flexible enough to cover diverse factual situations and also provide some reviewable standards, we find very persuasive section 217A of the Second Restatement of Contracts. That section specifically covers those situations where there has been reliance on an oral contract which falls within the Statute of Frauds. Section 217A states:

(1) A promise which the promisor should reasonably expect to induce action or forbearance on the part of the promisee or a third person and which does induce the action or forbearance is enforceable notwithstanding the Statute of Frauds if injustice can be avoided only by enforcement of the promise. The remedy granted for breach is to be limited as justice requires.

(2) In determining whether injustice can be avoided only by enforcement of the promise, the following circumstances are significant: (a) the availability and adequacy of other remedies, particularly cancellation and restitution; (b) the definite and substantial character of the action or forbearance in relation to the remedy sought; (c) the extent to which the action or forbearance corroborates evidence of the making and terms of the promise, or the making and terms are otherwise established by clear and convincing evidence; (d) the reasonableness of the action or forbearance; (e) the extent to which the action or forbearance was forseeable by the promisor.

We think that the approach taken in the Restatement is the proper method of giving the trial court the necessary latitude to relieve a party of the hardships of the Statute of Frauds. . . .

There is no dispute that the action of the plaintiff in moving 2200 miles from Los Angeles to Hawaii was foreseeable by the defendant. In fact, it was required to perform his duties. Injustice can only be avoided by the enforcement of the contract and the granting of money damages. No other remedy is adequate. The plaintiff found himself residing in Hawaii without a job.

It is also clear that a contract of some kind did exist. The plaintiff performed the contract for two and one-half months receiving $3,484.60 for his services. The exact length of the contract, whether terminable at will as urged by the defendant, or for a year from the time when the plaintiff started working, was up to the jury to decide.

In sum, the trial court might have found that enforcement of the contract was warranted by virtue of the plaintiff's reliance on the defendant's promise. Naturally, each case turns on its own facts. Certainly there is considerable discretion for a court to implement the true policy behind the Statute of Frauds, which is to prevent fraud or any other type of unconscionable injury. We therefore affirm the judgment of the trial court on the ground that the plaintiff's reliance was such that injustice could only be avoided by enforcement of the contract.

[Judgment affirmed]

Williams and Associates v Ramsey Products Corporation

19 NCApp 1, 198 SE2d 67 (1973)

Ramsey Products Corporation desired to have a new factory constructed for it. Ramsey made a written contract with Williams and Associates, architects, to design the building. This contract described the project as being a new manufacturing plant and offices but did not specify the maximum cost or any details of construction. Williams prepared plans for a factory which would cost about one half million dollars to build. This was too much for Ramsey and it abandoned the contract. Williams then sued Ramsey for compensation for services. Ramsey claimed that Williams had not performed the contract because, according to Ramsey, Williams had agreed to prepare plans for a building which would have 25,000 square feet and would cost one quarter million dollars, and that as this had not been done, Williams was not entitled to recover compensation for his services. Williams objected to the admission of the parol evidence as to the size and cost of the proposed factory. The trial judge admitted the parol evidence and a judgment was entered against Williams. Williams appealed.

VAUGHN, J. Plaintiffs challenge the admission and consideration of parol evidence of negotiations held prior to the execution of the written agreement concerning size, cost and time of completion of the project. Generally, parol evidence may not be considered if its purpose is to vary, add to or contradict a written agreement on matters intended to be covered by the written agreement.

"A contract not required to be in writing may be partly written and partly oral. However, where the parties have deliberately put their engagements in writing in such terms as import a legal obligation free of uncertainty, it is presumed the writing was intended by the parties to represent all their engagements as to the elements dealt with [in] the writing. Accordingly, all prior and contemporaneous negotiations in respect to those elements are deemed merged in the written agreement. And the rule is that, in the absence of fraud or mistake or allegation thereof,

parol testimony of prior or contemporaneous negotiations or conversations inconsistent with the writing, or which tend to substitute a new and different contract from the one evidenced by the writing, is incompetent."

There has been considerable appellate deliberation on whether parol evidence can be considered in order to prove that the parties to a written contract for an architect's services had agreed that the structure to be designed should be such that it could be erected within a maximum cost limitation. "In the great majority of the cases where the question has been raised the evidence has been held admissible, usually on the ground that the written contract failed to disclose the parties' intention as to the cost of the structure contemplated, and that such contemplated cost was an element which must have entered into the negotiations." . . .

The written agreement executed by the parties in this case provides that the architect shall consult with the owner to ascertain the requirements of the project, confirm these requirements to the owner and that the owner shall provide full information regarding his requirements for the project. An examination of the written agreement shows that, other than the statement that it is the intention of the owner to construct a new manufacturing plant and offices referred to as the project, there is no indication of the size, location, style, material, time of completion or cost requirements of the project. We hold, therefore, that the court properly considered parol evidence to determine what the agreement was with respect to these matters. In Hite v. Aydlett, 192 N.C. 166, 134 S.E. 419, the Supreme Court held that when an architect agreed to furnish plans and specifications for the project which would not exceed a fixed sum, defendant could show the agreement by parol evidence, not to contradict, vary or add to the terms contained in the written contract, but to make certain what plans the architect agreed to furnish so that the jury could determine whether those furnished were in compliance with the contract. In Hite the court held that if the architect agreed to furnish plans for a project not to cost more than $17,000.00 and the cost of doing the work according to the plans proposed by him exceeded $22,000.00, the architect could not recover, for he failed to perform his contract. . . .

. . . The court did not err when it considered the parol evidence, . . .

[Judgment affirmed]

Delta Dynamics, Inc. v Arioto

69 Cal 2d 525, 72 Cal Rptr 785, 446 P2d 785
(1968)

Delta Dynamics developed a trigger lock as a safety device on firearms. It gave Arioto and his partners, doing business as Pixey Distributing Co., the right to distribute the lock for five years; and Pixey agreed to sell a specified number of such locks in each year. The agreement stated: "Should Pixey fail to distribute in any one year the minimum number of devices to be distributed, . . . this agreement shall be subject to termination by Delta on thirty days' notice." The contract also provided that "in the event of breach of this agreement by either party, the party prevailing in any action for damages or enforcement of the terms of this agreement shall be entitled to reasonable attorneys' fees." Pixey failed to order the contract minimum in the first year. Delta sued Arioto and his partners for breach of contract.

The defendants claimed that suit could not be brought for damages for not ordering the quota on the theory that the only remedy for such breach was that Delta could terminate the contract. At the trial Pixey offered testimony to show that the parties had understood that the termination provision was intended as the sole remedy. Counsel for the defendants called one of the partners and asked, "During the negotiations that culminated in the execution of this contract between your company and Delta Dynamics, was there any conversation or discussion as to what would happen as far as Pixey Distributing Co. is concerned if they failed to meet the minimum quota set up in that contract?" Counsel for Delta objected to this question on the ground that it called for the admission of parol evidence. Counsel for the defendants stated that the contract was ambiguous and that the purpose of the testimony was to show the intention of the parties. The trial judge sustained the objection to the parol evidence, and a judgment was entered in favor of Delta. Arioto and his partners appealed.

TRAYNOR, C.J. . . . Pixey contends . . . that the termination clause made Delta's right to terminate the contract Delta's exclusive remedy for Pixey's failure to meet the annual quota and that the trial court erred in refusing to admit extrinsic evidence offered to prove that the termination clause had that meaning.

"The test of admissibility of extrinsic evidence to explain the meaning of a written instrument is not whether it appears to the court to be plain and unambiguous on its face, but whether the offered evidence is relevant to prove a meaning to which the language of the instrument is reasonably susceptible." To determine whether offered evidence is relevant to prove such a meaning, the court must consider all credible evidence offered to prove the intention of the parties. "If the court decides, after considering this evidence, that the language of a contract, in the light of all the circumstances, is 'fairly susceptible of either of the two interpretations contended for . . .' extrinsic evidence to prove either of such meanings is admissible." . . .

In the present case the parties may have included the termination clause to spell out with specificity the condition on which Delta would be excused from further performance under the contract, or to set forth the exclusive remedy for a failure to meet the quota in any year, or for both such purposes. That clause is therefore reasonably susceptible of the meaning contended for by Pixey, namely, that it expresses the parties' determination that Delta's sole remedy for Pixey's failure to meet a quota was to terminate the contract. There is nothing in the rest of the contract to preclude that interpretation. It does not render meaningless the provision for the recovery of attorneys' fees in the event of an action for damages for breach of the contract, for the attorneys' fees provision would still have full effect with respect to other breaches of the contract. Accordingly, the trial court committed prejudicial error by excluding extrinsic evidence offered to prove the meaning of the termination clause contended for by Pixey. The judgment must therefore be reversed. . . .

QUESTIONS AND CASE PROBLEMS

1. What social forces are affected by the following rule of law? "Parol evidence is not admissible for the purpose of modifying a written contract when that evidence relates to an agreement made before or at the time that the written contract was executed."

237

2. What is the difference between stating that (a) a contract must be in writing, and (b) a contract must be evidenced by a writing?

3. How are the statute of frauds and the parol evidence rule (a) alike, and (b) different?

4. When a nephew buys goods for $100 from a merchant, what is the difference between (a) the uncle's promise to the merchant to pay the bill if the nephew does not, and (b) the uncle's instruction to the merchant to charge the purchase to the uncle?

5. Aratari obtained a franchise from the Chrysler Corp. to engage in business as an automobile dealer in Rochester, New York. A written franchise contract was executed between the parties identifying the location of the dealer in the city. Aratari later claimed that when the franchise agreement was being negotiated, it had been agreed that Chrysler Corp. would move him to a better location in the city. Was Chrysler liable for damages for failing to keep this promise? [Aratari v Chrysler Corp., 35 App Div 2d 1077, 316 NYS2d 680]

6. Lawrence loaned money to Moore. Moore died without repaying the loan. Lawrence claimed that when he mentioned the matter to Moore's widow, she promised to pay the debt. She did not do so and Lawrence sued her on her promise. Does she have any defense? [Moore v Lawrence, 252 Ark 759, 480 SW2d 941]

7. Investors Premium Corporation purchased computer equipment from Burroughs Corporation. It made the purchase because of various statements made by the Burroughs sales representative. A written contract was finally executed for the purchase of the system. The contract stated that there were no warranties which were not stated in the contract and that the written contract was the complete statement of the obligation of Burroughs. The system did not work properly and Investors claimed that Burroughs was liable because the system did not perform as the salesman had warranted. Is Burroughs liable for breach of the agent's warranty? [Investors Premium Corp. v Burroughs Corp. (DC SC) 389 FSupp 39]

8. Evans made a written contract to buy property from Borkowski. Under the sales contract the buyer was to make payment in certain installments prior to the delivery of the deed. When the buyer could not make payments on time, the parties entered into a new written agreement, the buyer persuading the seller to do so by orally promising him that he would pay interest on late payments. He was late in making the payments and paid the interest under protest. The buyer later sued the seller to recover the interest payments. Was the buyer entitled to recover the interest [Evans v Borkowski (Fla) 139 So2d 472]

9. Allvend Industries made a written contract to purchase candy vending machines from the Smiles Candy Corporation. Allvend did not pay for the machines because it claimed that they had been misrepresented. Smiles sued Allvend. When Allvend raised the objection of misrepresentation of the machines, Smiles asserted that the parol evidence rule prevented proof of the objection. Was it correct? [Smiles Candy Corp. v Allvend Industries, Inc., 43 AppDiv2d 748, 350 NYS2d 731]

10. Williams promised to give her cousin, Robinson, her home in her will if he would leave his home and take care of her for the balance of her life. He did so but Williams did not give the property to him by her will. He sued for breach of the oral contract to give him the property. Did the statute of frauds bar his claim? [Williams v Robinson, 251 Ark 1002, 476 SW2d 1]

11. Burgess signed a paper which stated that Eastern Michigan University had a 60-day option to purchase Burgess' home. The writing acknowledged receipt of "one dollar" and "other valuable consideration." Thereafter, Burgess revoked the option. The University claimed that the option could not be revoked because of the recital of consideration. It further claimed that the revocation was not effective under the statute of frauds because

it was orally made. It was admitted that in fact Burgess had not received a dollar nor any valuable consideration as recited. Was Burgess bound by a contract? [Board of Control of Eastern Michigan University v Burgess, 45 Mich App 183, 206 NW2d 256]

12. *A* borrowed money from the bank for use by *B*. In obtaining the loan, *A* was required to give the bank a promissory note. *B* told *A* that he would never be required to pay on the note as *B* would pay the balance before the bank could proceed against *A*. When the bank sued *A* on the note, *A* joined *B* as a third party defendant and claimed that *B* had broken his contract by failing to pay the note. *B* defended on the theory that his promise was not binding because of the statute of frauds governing a promise to pay the debt of a third person. Was this a valid defense? [Farmers State Bank v Conrardy, 215 Kan 334, 524 P2d 690]

13. Davis went to work for Monorail, Inc. At the time his employment was discussed, Wenner-Gren promised Davis that if Monorail did not pay his salary to him, Wenner-Gren would see that Alwac International, Inc., a corporation which Wenner-Gren controlled, would pay the salary. After 2½ years of employment, Monorail stopped paying his salary whereupon Davis sued Alwac and Wenner-Gren. Wenner-Gren raised the defense that it was not liable because of the statute of frauds. Was it correct? [David v Alwac International Inc., (Tex Civ App) 369 SW2d 797]

14. Rhodes had an automobile collision and liability policy which was issued by the Southern Guaranty Insurance Company. By an amendment to the policy, an exclusion was made so that it did not apply to any automobile driven by the insured's son, James L. Rhodes. In 1968 the father purchased a 1968 Pontiac for James and sought to obtain liability insurance for him and the new car. The father discussed such insurance with the agent for Southern Guaranty. Thereafter the Southern Guaranty policy was amended to provide liability and collision coverage for the 1968 Pontiac but no change was made to the clause excluding James and the father remained the named insured in the policy. James was in a collision while driving that Pontiac and sued Southern Guaranty. It raised the defense that the policy expressly excluded liability as to James. He replied that he was not suing on the written policy but on a separate and distinct oral contract of insurance which provided liability coverage for him. The insurer asserted that the parol evidence rule prevented proof of any such oral contract because in fact there was no separate contract to cover the son by insurance and the son by suing on an alleged oral contract was merely trying to contradict the exclusion in the written policy, which the parol evidence rule prevented. Was the insurance company correct? [Southern Guaranty Ins. Co. v Rhodes, 46 Ala App 454, 243 So2d 717]

16 Interpretation of Contracts

The terms of a contract should be clearly stated and all important terms should be included. If they are not, the parties might interpret the terms differently. When such differences cannot be resolved satisfactorily by the parties and the issues are brought into court, certain principles of construction and interpretation are applied.

A. RULES OF CONSTRUCTION AND INTERPRETATION

An understanding of the rules discussed in the following paragraphs should help contracting parties to avoid many of the difficulties that may arise when a contract is not drafted carefully.

§ 16:1. Intention of the Parties. A contract is to be enforced according to its terms. The court must examine the contract to determine and must give effect to what the parties intended, provided their objective is lawful. It is the intention of the parties as expressed in the contract that must prevail. (See p. 247, Keyworth v Industrial Sales Co.) The "impression" of one contracting party as to the obligation imposed by the contract has no effect where this impression was not communicated to the other party.[1]

A secret intention of one party that is not expressed in the contract has no effect. A party to a contract will ordinarily not be allowed to state what was secretly meant by the words used, for the test is what a reasonable person would have believed was intended by those words. For example, when a person guaranteed payment, it could not be shown that it was secretly intended not to do so.

A court should not remake a contract for the parties under the guise of interpreting it. Therefore, if the contract is so vague or indefinite that the intended performance cannot be determined, the contract cannot be enforced.

No particular form of words is required and any words manifesting the intent of the parties are sufficient. In the absence of proof that a word has a peculiar meaning or that it was employed by the parties with a particular meaning, a common word is given its ordinary meaning.[2]

A word will not be given its literal meaning when it is clear that the parties did not intend such a meaning. For example, "and" may be substituted for "or," "may" for "shall," and "void" for "voidable," and vice versa, when it is clear that the parties so intended.

---

[1] Dwelley v Chesterfield, 14 WashApp 480, 542 P2d 1261.
[2] Reno Club v Young Investment Co. 64 Nev 312, 182 P2d 1011.

Rules of grammatical construction and punctuation may be employed to throw light on the intention of the parties, but they are ignored when they clearly conflict with the intention of the parties.

§ 16:2. Whole Contract. The provisions of a contract must be construed as a whole.[3] This rule is followed even when the contract is partly written and partly oral, but this principle does not apply when an oral agreement must be excluded according to the parol evidence rule. Every word of a contract is to be given effect if reasonably possible.

The objective of viewing the contract in its entirety is not only to make every term of the contract effective but also to understand the objective of the parties in light of the particular transaction involved.

(a) Divisible Contract. When a contract contains a number of provisions or performances to be rendered, the question arises as to whether the parties intended merely a group of separate contracts or whether they intended a "package deal" so that complete performance of every provision of the contract was essential.

(b) What Constitutes the Whole Contract. The question may arise whether separate papers or particular parts of a paper constitute part of the whole contract. The inclusion of other papers in the contract was discussed in § 9:9.

Terms in a printed letterhead or billhead or on the reverse side of the printed contract form are not part of a contract written thereon unless a reasonable person would regard such terms as part of the contract. An employer's manual that is shown after the signing of an employment contract is not part of that contract. Similarly, provisions in a manufacturer's instruction manual, or in invoices, or on labels that are never seen or called to the attention of a buyer until after a contract of sale has been made are not part of the contract and do not bind the buyer.

§ 16:3. Conditions. In most bilateral contracts the performance of each party is dependent upon the performance by the other party. That is, neither party is required to perform until the other party performs or tenders performance. Frequently the contract will specify or indicate that one person must perform first. For example, in a contract to pay a painter $1,000 for painting a house, the painter must perform the painting work before the owner is required to perform the promise of paying for the work. In other contracts, the occurrence of some event outside of the contract may affect performance under the contract. When the occurrence or non-occurrence of an event affects the obligation of a party to a contract, the event is called a *condition.*

(a) Conditions Precedent. A condition or obligation-triggering event may be described as a *condition precedent* because it precedes the existence of the obligation.

A contract between a contractor and a government may contain a condition precedent that the contract shall not be binding unless the proper fiscal officer of the government indorses on the contract a certification that sufficient money is held to make the payments required by the contract. Similarly, a contract for the sale of a tenant's cotton crop may be made subject to the condition that it shall not be

---

[3] Archibald v Midwest Paper Stock Co. (Iowa) 176 NW2d 761.

binding unless signed by the landlord of the tenant. If the landlord <u>does not sign,</u> the contract is not binding.[4]

(b) Conditions Subsequent. The parties may specify that the contract shall terminate when a particular event occurs or does not occur. Such a <u>provision is a *condition*</u> <u>*subsequent.*</u> If government approval is required, the parties may specify that the con-tract shall not bind them if the government approval cannot be obtained.[5]

      A contract for the purchase of <u>land may contain a condition subsequent</u> which cancels the contract if the buyer is not able to obtain a zoning permit to use a building for a particular purpose.

(c) Guarantee Distinguished. A condition is to be distinguished from a guarantee. When a provision is a condition its occurrence or non-occurrence either discharges or makes the contract operative but there is no personal liability on anyone to achieve or prevent the satisfaction of the condition. In the case of a guarantee, a person promises that a matter will be as guaranteed and is liable for breach of contract if it is not. For example, a provision in a contract declaring the contract to "be null and void" if roof and termite damage exceeded $100 is a condition subsequent that discharges the contract when there is termite damages in excess of $100.[6] In contrast, if the contract stated that the contractor promised that no termite damage would exceed $100 there would be a guarantee.

§ 16:4. Contradictory Terms. When the terms of a contract are contradictory or conflict as to a significant matter, the existence of such conflict prevents there being a binding contract. For example, where one paragraph of the contract stated that the purchase price for 372.12 acres was $110,000 but another paragraph stated that the price was $275 an acre, which would produce a total price of $102,333, <u>there was no</u> <u>contract</u> because <u>the conflict in the terms</u> could not be reconciled in any way.[7]

      In some instances, the conflict between the terms of a contract is eliminated by the introduction of parol evidence or by applying an appropriate rule of construction.

(a) Nature of Writing. When a contract is partly printed or typewritten and partly written and the written part conflicts with the printed or typewritten part, the written part prevails. When there is a conflict between a printed part and a typewritten part, the latter prevails. When there is a conflict between an amount or quantity expressed both in words and figures, as on a check, the amount or quantity expressed in words prevails.

(b) Strict Construction Against Drafting Party. An ambiguous contract is inter-preted more strictly against the party who drafted it. (See p. 248, Grove v Charbonneau Buick-Pontiac, Inc.) Thus, printed forms of a contract, such as <u>insurance policies,</u> which are supplied by one party to the transaction, are interpreted <u>against the supplier</u>

---

      [4] Baccus v Plains Cotton Cooperative (TexCivApp) 515 SW2d 401.
      [5] Security National Life Insurance Co. v Pre-Need Camelback Plan, Inc. 19 ArizApp 580, 509 P2d 652.
          [6] Fraser v Ameling (La) 277 So2d 633.
          [7] Moore v Mohon (TexCivApp) 514 SW2d 508.

and in favor of the other party when two interpretations are reasonably possible. If the contract is clear and unambiguous it will be enforced according to its terms even though this benefits the party who drafted the contract.

(c)   Knowledge of Complaining Party. The rule that an ambiguous contract is interpreted against the party who prepared the contract is not applied when the other party knew what the preparing party intended.

§ 16:5. Implied Terms. In some cases the court will imply a term to cover a situation for which the parties failed to provide or when needed to give the contract a construction or meaning which is reasonable. (See p. 249, Phillips v Rogers) A term will not be implied in a contract when the court concludes that the silence of the contract on the particular point was intentional.

(a)   Details of Performance. The details of performance of a contract which are not expressly regulated by the contract will often be implied. Thus an obligation to pay a specified sum of money is implied to mean payment in legal tender. In a contract to perform work there is an implied promise to use such skill as is necessary for the proper performance of the work. In a "cost-plus" contract there is an implied undertaking that the costs will be reasonable and proper. When a note representing a loan is extended by agreement, an implied promise to pay interest during the extension period arises when nothing about interest is stated by the parties. When payment is made "as a deposit on account," it is implied that if the payment is not used for the purpose designated, the payment will be returned to the person who made the deposit. When the contract for work to be done does not specify the exact amount to be paid for the work, the law will imply an obligation to pay the reasonable value for such work.[8]

A local custom or trade practice, such as that of allowing 30 days' credit to buyers, may form part of the contract when it is clear that the parties intended to be governed by this custom or trade practice or when a reasonable person would believe that they had so intended.

When a written contract does not specify the time for performance, a reasonable time is implied and parol evidence is not admissible to establish a different time for performance.

(b)   Good Faith. In every contract there is an implied covenant that neither party shall do anything which will have the effect of destroying or injuring the right of the other party to receive the fruits of the contract, which means that in every contract there exists an implied covenant of good faith and fair dealing.[9]

(c)   Governmental Approval. In some situations, the ability to perform a contract will depend upon obtaining a governmental permit or approval. When this is so, the failure to obtain such approval or permit may be made an express condition subsequent so that the contract is discharged by such failure. An implied term generally arises that one party to the contract will cooperate with the other in obtaining any necessary governmental permit or approval.[10]

---

[8] New Mexico v Fireman's Fund Indemnity Co. 67 NMex 360, 355 P2d 291.
[9] Davis v Kahn, 7 CalApp3d 868, 86 CalRptr 872.
[10] Western Natural Gas Co. v Cities Service Gas Co. (Okla), 507 P2d 1236.

§ 16:6. Conduct and Custom. The conduct of the parties in carrying out the terms of a contract may be considered in determining just what they meant by the contract. When performance has been repeatedly tendered and accepted without protest, neither party will be permitted to claim that the contract was too indefinite to be binding. For example, when a travel agent made a contract with a hotel to arrange for "junkets" to the hotel, any claim that it was not certain just what was intended must be ignored when some 80 junkets had already been arranged and paid for by the hotel at the contract price without any dispute as to whether the contract obligation was satisfied.[11]

The conduct of parties is admissible to show the meaning of the contract as viewed in the way that the parties perform thereunder. Moreover, when the conduct of the parties is inconsistent with the original written contract, proof of such conduct may justify concluding that the parties had orally modified the original agreement.

§ 16:7. Avoidance of Hardship. When there is ambiguity as to the meaning of a contract, a court will avoid the interpretation that gives one contracting party an unreasonable advantage over the other or which causes a forfeiture of a party's interest. When there is an inequality of bargaining power between the contracting parties, courts will sometimes classify the contract as a *contract of adhesion* in that it was offered on a "take-it-or-leave-it" basis by the stronger party, and the court will interpret the contract as providing what appeared reasonable from the standpoint of the weaker bargaining party.

In some instances, if hardship cannot be avoided in this manner, the court may hold that the contract or a particular provision is not binding because it is unconscionable or contrary to public policy. The extent to which this protection is available is uncertain, and as a general rule a party is bound by a contract even though it proves to be a bad bargain.

When the hardship arises because the contract makes no provision for the situation which has occurred, the court will sometimes imply a term in order to avoid the hardship. (See p. 250, Perkins v Standard Oil Co.)

§ 16:8. The Absent Term. What is the effect of the absence of a provision on a particular matter? It must first be determined whether the silence of the contract is intentional or is an accidental omission. Sometimes it will be obvious that the silence was not accidental. For example, a contract to deliver 10 tons of coal on the first Monday of January, February, and March, would obviously be interpreted as meaning just that and it would not be said that the contract was incomplete or ambiguous because it did not say anything about other months. Here the intent of the parties is clear even though it did not say "January, February, and March only" or "January, February, and March and no other months."

Assume, however, that a coal delivery contract purports to sell 50 tons of coal and then states that 10 tons shall be delivered on the first Monday of January, February, and March. Here it is clear that there are 20 more tons to be delivered but the contract says nothing as to that. In this case, the silence of the contract is not an intentional exclusion but is a defect in the contract.

---

[11] Casino Operations, Inc v Graham, 86 Nev 764, 476 P2d 953; see Uniform Commercial Code § 2-208(1) as to course of performance in the interpretation of contracts for the sale of goods and UCC § 1-105 as to both Code and non-Code transactions.

When it is concluded that the omission of a term is a defect, what is the legal result? Generally the result will be one of the following.

(a)   Implied Terms. In some omission cases the law will imply a term to fill up the omission as discussed in § 16:5. Thus, when there is a promise to pay $100, it will be implied that the $100 must be in cash.

(b)   Parol Evidence. The omission may be regarded as making the contract ambiguous or incomplete and justifying the admission of parol evidence to determine what was actually intended. If the parol evidence shows that the parties have in fact agreed on the matter not covered by the written contract, the obligation of the parties will be interpreted as a blend or composite of the written contract and the oral terms.

(c)   No Contract. If a term is omitted from the contract and the omission is not cured by either the implication of a term under (a) or by the introduction of parol evidence under (b), the court may conclude that there is no contract. In some cases, the statute of frauds may compel the conclusion that there is no contract when a term is omitted.

(d)   Strict Enforcement of Contract. When the terms which are stated are sufficient to constitute a binding contract, the court may conclude that an omission has no effect and instead of concluding that there is no contract under (c), the contract will be enforced according to its exact letter. (See p. 251, Rogers v Rogers)

§ 16:9. Joint, Several, and Joint and Several Contracts. When two or more persons are on either side of a contract, an additional question of interpretation may arise, as it may be necessary to determine whether the contract is (a) joint, (b) several, or (c) joint and several.

(a)   Joint Contracts. A *joint contract* is one in which two or more persons jointly promise to perform an obligation. If *A, B,* and *C* sign a contract stating "we jointly promise" to do a particular act, the obligation is the joint obligation of *A, B,* and *C.* In the absence of an express intent to the contrary, a promise by two or more persons is generally presumed to be joint and not several.

Each of two or more joint promisors is liable for the entire obligation, but an action must be brought against all who are living and within the jurisdiction of the court. If one of the promisors dies, the surviving promisors remain bound to perform the contract unless it was personal in character and required the joint action of all the obligors for its performance. If the deceased obligor had received a benefit from the contract, a court of equity will also hold the obligor's estate liable for the performance of the contract.

Generally the release by the promisee of one or more of the joint obligors releases all.

(b)   Several Contracts. *Several contracts* arise when two or more persons separately agree to perform the same obligation even though the separate agreements are set forth in the same instrument.

If *A, B,* and *C* sign a contract stating "we severally promise" or "each of us promises" to do a particular act or to pay a specified sum of money, the three signers are severally bound to perform or to pay; that is, each signer is individually bound.

In many jurisdictions persons liable on related causes of action can be sued at one time. Since the liability of each obligor of a several contract is by definition separate or distinct, the release of one or more of the obligors by the promisee does not release the others.

(c)   Joint and Several Contracts. A *joint and several contract* is one in which two or more persons are bound both jointly and severally. If *A, B,* and *C* sign a contract stating "we, and each of us, promise" (or "I promise") to pay a specified sum of money, they are jointly and severally bound. The obligee may treat the claim either as a joint claim or as a group of separate claims, and may bring a suit against all at the same time or against one at a time. The plaintiff may also sue any number of the severally liable parties instead of suing them either singly or all at one time.

B. CONFLICT OF LAWS

When a lawsuit is brought, the court will seek to apply the law under which the contract was made. That is, a California court in many cases will not apply California law to a foreign contract. The principles which determine when a court applies the law of its own state, the *law of the forum,* or some foreign law is called *conflict of laws.*

Because there are fifty state court systems and a federal court system, and a high degree of interstate activity, these conflict of laws questions arise frequently.

§ 16:10. State Courts. It is important to distinguish between the state in which the parties are domiciled or have their permanent home, the state in which the contract is made, and the state in which the contract is to be performed. The state in which the contract is made is determined by finding the state in which the last act essential to the formation of the contract was performed. Thus, when an acceptance is mailed in one state to an offeror in another state, the state of formation of the contract is the state in which the acceptance is mailed if the acceptance becomes effective at that time.

If acceptance by telephone is otherwise proper, the acceptance takes effect at the place where the acceptance is spoken into the phone. Thus, an employment contract is made in the state in which the job applicant telephoned an acceptance, and consequently, the law of that state governs a claim to workmen's compensation, even though the injuries were sustained in another state.

If an action on a contract made in one state is brought in a court of another state, an initial question is whether that court will lend its aid to the enforcement of a foreign (out-of-state) contract. Ordinarily suit may be brought on a foreign contract. But, if there is a strong contrary local policy, recovery may be denied even though the contract was valid in the state where it was made.

The capacity of a natural person to make a contract is governed by the place of contracting; a corporation's capacity to do so is determined by the law of the state of incorporation. The law of the state where the contract is made determines whether it is valid in substance and satisfies requirements as to form. Matters relating to the performance of the contract, excuse or liability for nonperformance, and the measure of damages for nonperformance are generally governed by the law of the state where the contract is to be performed.

At times the courts of one jurisdiction refuse to enforce foreign contracts because, although lawful by the law of the jurisdiction where the contract was made or was to be performed, there is a dominant local policy which bars enforcing the foreign claim or a claim based on a foreign transaction. The fact that a contract requires or contemplates the performance of an act in another state which would be illegal if performed in the state where the contract was made does not make the contract illegal in the absence of a dominant, local policy opposed to such a contract.

When a lawsuit is brought on a contract, the law of the forum, determines the procedure and the rules of evidence.[12]

(a)   Center of Gravity. There is a growing acceptance of the rule that, in place of the rigid or mechanical standards described above, a contract should be governed by the law of the state that has the most significant contacts with the transaction, to which state the contract may be said to gravitate.

For example, when the buyer's place of business and the seller's factory are located in state *A* and the buyer is purchasing to resell to customers in state *A,* many courts will hold that this is a contract governed by the law of state *A* in all respects even though it may happen to be a state *B* contract by virtue of some chance circumstance as that the seller's offer was accepted by the buyer in state *B*.

(b)   Specification by the Parties. It is common for the more important contracts to specify that they shall be governed by the law of a particular state. When this is done, it is generally held that if the contract is lawful in the designated state, it will be enforced in another state and interpreted according to the law of the designated state, even though a contrary result would be reached if governed by the law of the state in which the suit is brought. Whenever a transaction is governed by the Uniform Commercial Code, the parties may agree that their rights and duties shall be governed by the law of any state or nation which "bears a reasonable relation" to the transaction.[13]

§ 16:11. Federal Courts. When the parties to a contract reside in different states and an action is brought on the contract in a federal court because of their different citizenship, the federal court must apply the same rules of conflict of laws that would be applied by the courts of the state in which the federal court is sitting.[14] Thus, a federal court in Chicago deciding a case involving parties from Indiana and Wisconsin must apply the same rules of conflict of laws as would be applied by the courts of Illinois. The state law must be followed by the federal court in such a case whether or not the federal court agrees with the state law.

---

[12] In contract actions it is generally held that whether a claim is barred by the statute of limitations is determined by the law of the forum. There is a division of authority as to whether a statute of frauds relates to the substance of the contract, the law of the place of making then governing, or whether it is a question of procedure, the law of the forum then governing.

[13] UCC § 1-105(1).

[14] Erie R.R. Co. v Tompkins, 304 US 64.

CASES FOR CHAPTER 16

Keyworth v Industrial Sales Co.

241 Md 453, 217 A2d 253 (1966)

Keyworth was employed by Industrial Sales Co. In the course of employment, he was injured by Israelson. Industrial Sales made a contract with Keyworth to pay him $100 per week until he was able to return to normal work but specified that such payments would be paid back to Industrial Sales from any recovery that Keyworth would obtain in a lawsuit against Israelson, such payments to be made to Industrial Sales upon the "successful conclusion of the case." Keyworth obtained a recovery in the action against Israelson of $16,600 but refused to make any payment to Industrial Sales because he believed that he had not recovered enough and therefore there was not a "successful conclusion of the case." Industrial Sales sued Keyworth. From a judgment in favor of Industrial Sales, Keyworth appealed.

OPPENHEIMER, J. . . . Keyworth contends that whether or not his personal injury case resulted in a "successful conclusion". . . is a matter to be determined by a jury. . . .

The construction of a written contract . . . is ordinarily for the determination of the court. . . . The questions here are whether the written agreement is susceptible of a clear and definite understanding, and what effect, if any, is to be given to Keyworth's interpretation of it. . . .

"We may note first that the theory of 'objective law' of contracts has been almost universally adopted by this time. The written language embodying the terms of an agreement will govern the rights and liabilities of the parties, irrespective of the intent of the parties at the time they entered into the contract. . . . The test of a true interpretation of an offer or acceptance is not what the party making it thought it meant or intended it to mean, but what a reasonable person in the position of the parties would have thought it meant.". . .

In this case Keyworth's deposition as to what he thought the phrase "successful conclusion" of the litigation meant is not the test, nor does his interpretation cast doubt or create an ambiguity, if the language used is clear and definite. . . . There was "a clear indication that the parties to the agreement looked to the creation of a fund consisting of the proceeds of the verdict or settlement resulting from the third-party action; and that [Keyworth] was to receive the proceeds and was to use them, in part, for the repayment of the advances made by the employer. . . . We think the agreement between the employer and Keyworth, construed in the light of the facts and circumstances, meant that the source of the monies to be refunded would be the monies actually paid by the third party defendants . . . and that these monies were to be held as security for the repayment."

On the undisputed facts, Keyworth, as a result of his litigation, received a total of $16,600. His out-of-pocket expenses and losses came to $10,361.55, but this total included $7,057.15 for loss in salary, which, while a proper item in his claim for damages, was more than covered by the $7,200 which the employer advanced him, on the basis of the salary he had been receiving. As the order of the equity court in connection with the distribution of the fund shows, even after the repayment to the employer's workmen's compensation insurance carrier, . . . the repayment of the $7,200 to the employer, and the payment of $5,000 as counsel fee to Keyworth's attorneys, there was a residue for Keyworth of $686.82. . . .

. . . There was no legal obligation of any kind on the employer to make the advances. Under the agreement, Keyworth received money in lieu of salary to which he was not entitled but which he needed. The employer obviously wished to have Keyworth return to his employment when he was able to do so. Keyworth was placed under no requirement to return the money unless his litigation produced the funds necessary to do so, and the employer was given no right to demand repayment except upon the same condition. There was no reason for Keyworth not to repay, as long as he did not have to do so except through the creation of the fund, and no reason for the employer to waive repayment if Keyworth, through the litigation, received enough to cover the amounts he had gratuitously received. This, under the circumstances, was the obvious meaning of the agreement. The test of whether or not the litigation was successfully concluded on the facts before us is not whether Keyworth was satisfied or dissatisfied with what he received, but whether the net amount which he recovered was enough to cover the advances which the employer had made to him. The amount Keyworth received as a result of the litigation, even after deduction of the amounts of the claims which had priority, was more than sufficient for that purpose. The clear meaning of the agreement, on the facts, is that the litigation was successfully concluded. . . .

[Judgment affirmed]

Grove v Charbonneau Buick-Pontiac, Inc.

(ND) 240 NW2d 853 (1976)

The Dickinson Elks Club conducted an annual Labor Day golf tournament. Charbonneau Buick-Pontiac offered to give a new car as a prize to any one making a hole-in-one on hole No. 8. The golf course of the club was only nine holes so that in order to play 18 holes, the players would go around the course twice, although they would play from different tees or locations for the second nine holes. On the second time round, what was originally the eighth hole became the seventeenth hole. Grove was a contestant in the tournament. On the first day he scored 3 on the No. 8 hole but on approaching it for the second time as the seventeenth hole, he made a hole-in-one. He claimed the prize car from Charbonneau. The latter claimed that Grove had not won the prize because he did not make the hole-in-one on the eighth hole. Groves sued Charbonneau for the value of the prize car. From a judgment in favor of Grove, Charbonneau appealed.

SAND, J. . . . The general rule of the law of contracts which provides that where an offer or promise for an act is made, the only acceptance of the offer that is necessary is the performance of the act, applies to prizewinning contests. When a word is used in an agreement between two parties, . . . such word is to be given its ordinary, popular meaning. The words are given the common prevailing meaning as generally understood among people.

Grove contends that the words of the offer, when used in their ordinary sense, mean that any time in the process of an official play in the tournament a ball is hit into the eight hole in one stroke, from either tee No. 8 or tee No. 17, the conditions of the offer are satisfied. Charbonneau, however, contends that the language of the offer has a technical meaning under the rules of golf and that there cannot be a hole-in-one on hole No. 8 unless the ball, with a single stroke, is hit from tee area No. 8 and lands in hole No. 8.

. . . Where a contract contains ambiguous terms which are in dispute it is the duty of the court to construe them. . . . The ambiguous terms of a contract will be interpreted most strongly against the party who caused the ambiguity. . . .

The rule on ambiguous contracts applies to this case, and therefore any language of this contract which is not clear and definite or in which an uncertainty exists as to its meaning must be interpreted most strongly against Charbonneau.

The crucial or pivotal point in this case rests upon the meaning of the language "a hole-in-one on Hole No. 8," where the 9-hole golf course was converted to or used as an 18-hole course without adding any additional holes. Does this language, "on Hole No. 8," refer to the actual, physical designation of the hole, which is generally identified with the number on the flagstick, or does it refer to the hypothetical number given to the hole because of the sequence in which it is "played"? . . .

The offer does not contain any qualifications, restrictions, or limitations as to what is meant by the phrase "on hole No. 8." Neither does the award or offer make any statement restricting or qualifying that the hole-in-one on hole No. 8 may be accomplished only from tee No. 8. If Charbonneau had in mind to impose limitations, restrictions, or qualifications he could have made this in the offer so that a person with ordinary intelligence would have been fully apprised of the offer in every respect.

The distance from tee No. 17 to hole No. 8 was greater than the distance from tee No. 8 to hole No. 8. Thus an argument cannot be made that a player had an advantage playing from tee No. 17 to hole No. 8, as compared to playing from tee No. 8 to hole No. 8. Actually, it would be a disadvantage.

When good arguments can be made for either of two contrary positions as to the meaning of a term in a document an ambiguity exists. . . . The contending parties have made good arguments, if not convincing arguments, for their positions.

The language in question, "hole-in-one on Hole No. 8," in the offer, . . . is ambiguous.

Having concluded as a matter of law that the offer in this setting is ambiguous, the rule of law providing that the ambiguous terms will be construed and interpreted most strongly against the party who caused the ambiguity applies.

We have no reason to suspect that anyone other than Charbonneau deliberately chose the ambiguous language. We are not suggesting that Charbonneau intended to trifle with the public, but if we do not apply the rule of law on ambiguous contracts, as set out earlier herein, to this situation we would permit promoters to trifle with the public, which we do not believe the law should permit, and in fact, does not permit.

If this rule of law were not applied it would permit the promoter who is so inclined, where there has been a performance, to keep adding requirements or conditions which were not stated in the offer. As an example, such as, "must use a certain club; the ball must be of a certain brand; the play must be accomplished by a person left-handed," to name only a few.

Both of the constructions and interpretations of the language in the offer as contended by the parties are reasonable and each has some strong convincing points, but that does not constitute legal grounds for not applying the rule of law as to how ambiguities in a contract are to be resolved in a situation or setting we have here.

By interpreting and construing the ambiguous provisions of the offer most strongly against the party who caused them . . . we construe it to mean that an entrant in the golf tournament who had paid the fee and who during regular tournament play drives the ball in one stroke into hole No. 8 from either the 8th or 17th tee has made a hole-in-one on hole No. 8, and has met the conditions of the offer and is entitled to the award or the equivalent in money damages. . . .

[Judgment affirmed]

Phillips v Rogers

(WVa) 200 SE2d 676 (1973)

Phillips owned a farm. Rogers wished to buy it. The parties signed a written agreement which stated that if for any reason the land could not be sold the deposit made by Rogers would be returned. Mr. and Mrs. Rogers took possession of the land. Thereafter Phillips sued them to get the land back on the theory that she was entitled to set the contract aside on the theory that the provision for the return of the deposit if the land could not be sold gave her the right to say that the land should not be sold.

From a judgment in favor of the Rogers', Phillips appealed.

NEELY, J. . . . The handwritten instrument dated July 8, 1968 on which the appellees relied . . . read as follows:

"July 8, 1968, we, the undersigned, wish to pay one hundred dollars ($100.00) for an option to buy the L. S. Phillips farm at Ovapa, West Virginia.

"In case the farm for any reason cannot be sold to us the one hundred dollars ($100.00) will be returned.

"Said farm is to be six thousand dollars ($6,000.00) cash. Remainder to be paid when deed is made.

"/s/Dessie Phillips
Ralph Rogers
Pansy Rogers."

While it is obvious that the July 8, 1968 agreement was poorly drafted, . . . mere lack of art in drafting a contract does not necessarily make the contract void for vagueness. . . . Regardless of poor draftsmanship, courts will attempt to give effect to the intent of the parties. . . .

"It must be borne in mind that when the parties entered into this contract they intended to accomplish some purpose by it, and this court will not give to it a construction which will render it void if it can reasonably be interpreted so as to give it effect."

. . . The language in the July 8, 1968 instrument which said: "In case the farm for any reason cannot be sold to us the one hundred dollars will be returned" did not mean that the appellant could refuse to sell the farm for any reason whatsoever. To construe that language to mean that the appellant was in no way bound to perform her part of the bargain, would be to deny that the parties had any agreement at all. . . . Obviously there are factors beyond the control of either party which would preclude passage of clear title to the farm, the most outstanding of which would be the absence of clear title in the appellant, and . . . the last quoted sentence [refers] to these situations beyond the control of either party. Therefore, . . . the appellant could not refuse to sell for reasons over which she had complete control.

[Judgment affirmed]

Perkins v Standard Oil Co.

235 Ore 7, 383 P2d 107 (1963)

Standard Oil made a jobbing or wholesale dealership contract with Perkins which limited him to selling Standard's products and required Perkins to maintain certain minimum prices. Standard Oil had the right to approve or disapprove of Perkins' customers. In order to be able to perform under this contract, Perkins had to make a substantial money investment, and his only income was from the commissions on the sales of Standard's products. Standard Oil made some sales directly to Perkins' customers. When Perkins protested, Standard Oil pointed out that the contract did not contain any provision making his rights exclusive. Perkins sued Standard Oil to compel it to stop dealing with his customers. From a decision in Standard's favor, Perkins appealed.

ROSSMAN, J. . . . The contract authorized the plaintiff [Perkins] to sell without Standard's written consent "on a nonexclusive basis" the products which Standard consigned to him but only to service stations or consuming accounts. Standard's written consent was required before the plaintiff could sell to any other account. The plaintiff promised in the contract to use his "best efforts to promote the sale of products consigned hereunder" and to sell a specified minimum amount during each year. . . . The plaintiff was required to deliver to Standard a complete list of the names and addresses of all his distributors and submit to it the names of any new potential distributors. . . .

The plaintiff claims that the contract by its very nature contains an implied condition that Standard would not solicit business directly from his (plaintiff's) customers. Standard protests that such an implied condition would be contrary to the express terms of the contract since the latter (1) provides that the plaintiff was authorized to sell Standard's products only "on a nonexclusive basis" and (2) reserved to Standard the "right to select its own customers." Plaintiff proposes a more restricted interpretation. . . . He concedes that the contract reserved to Standard the right to sell to any new accounts which it found, and to accept or reject any new accounts which he (the plaintiff) might obtain, but he insists that it does not permit Standard to solicit accounts which it had approved as his customers. . . .

In order to be successful in his business and to comply with the terms of his contract, the plaintiff was obliged to make substantial investments in storage facilities, delivery trucks, and other equipment. He was also obliged to hire employees. He was required to use his "best efforts" to promote the sale of Standard's products. Only if he sold Standard's products exclusively could it be said that he was using his best efforts to promote their sale. It is clear, then, that the contract limited his dealership to Standard products. Plaintiff was also required to sell a minimum quantity of other designated Standard petroleum products. If he at any time failed to sell the minimum quantity, Standard was at liberty to terminate its contract with him. Plaintiff's compensation was based exclusively on the sales he made to customers, which he secured through his own efforts. No compensation was available for the plaintiff if he obtained customers for Standard who bought directly from it. Nor does the contract obligate Standard to compensate him for sales made directly by Standard to plaintiff's customers. . . .

. . . A condition must be implied that Standard would not solicit customers which had been obtained through plaintiff's efforts. The interpretation of the contract for which Standard contends would leave plaintiff and others in a position similar to his completely at the mercy of Standard. . . .

"We cannot accept [Standard's] construction of its meaning. An intention to make so one-sided an agreement is not readily to be inferred. . . .

"In every contract there is an implied covenant that neither party shall do anything that will have the effect of destroying or injuring the right of the other party to receive the fruits of the contract, which means that in every contract there exists a covenant of good faith and fair dealing.". . .

The implication of a condition finds support in many circumstances. . . . Plaintiff's only source of return on his substantial investments in the business was the sales he made to his customers. If Standard was at liberty to solicit as direct customers, as it contends, . . . plaintiff was in a state of economic servility; we do not believe that the parties intended such a result at the time the contract was signed. . . .

The contract before us is obviously a form contract prepared by Standard. It is a contract of "adhesion" in the sense that it is a take-it-or-leave-it whole. Such contracts are regarded by some authorities as anachronistic or inconsistent with real freedom of contract. At least they should be construed with an awareness of the inequality of the bargainers. . . .

[Judgment reversed]

Rogers v Rogers

(Vt) 373 A2d 507 (1977)

Richard and Marcia Rogers obtained a divorce. They agreed that Richard would pay Marcia $2,500 a year "alimony and support" in consideration of her giving up all claim to property of Richard. Five years later Marcia remarried. Richard stopped paying the alimony on the ground that his obligation under the agreement ended when Marcia remarried. Several months later, Marcia had her second marriage annulled for fraud. She then brought an action to determine her right to alimony payments under the agreement with Richard. The court held that her right to payments was not terminated. Richard appealed.

HILL, J. . . . Defendant has argued . . . that . . . the subsequent remarriage of a divorced woman gives rise to an inference that she has chosen to obtain her support elsewhere and has thereby surrendered any right she may have had to support from her prior spouse. However, it appears to us that the instant case is readily distinguished from those cited by defendant. Here we are presented with [a] . . . separation agreement in which the parties sought to settle all property rights and provisions for support. This agreement must be construed in accordance with the clear intention of the parties as evidenced by the language employed in the document itself. . . . Applying this rule of construction to the facts here, the inference is clear that the parties intended an integrated agreement in which the provisions for support and property disposition are an integral and inseparable part of the entire settlement. . . . The agreement here expressly acknowledges its support by mutual consideration and provides for a consensual waiver of all marital and property rights beyond those set out in the agreement. Accordingly, we are confronted not with a statutorily modifiable decree of alimony, but with an integrated contract to whose provisions the parties have freely given their assent. . . . Such agreements are to be enforced as is any other proper contract.

The separation agreement at issue here nowhere provides for termination of support payments upon the remarriage of the wife. In light of our view that the agreement is an integrated, non-severable contract; and in the absence of any showing of fraud, duress or other unconscionable advantage, that document is to be enforced according to its terms.

[Judgment affirmed]

QUESTIONS AND CASE PROBLEMS

1. What social forces are affected by the rule that a secret intention which is not expressed has no effect?

2. Compare (a) a promised condition and (b) a condition precedent or subsequent.

3. Compare the concepts of (a) divisibility of contracts, (b) implied terms, and (c) avoidance of hardship.

4. Compare with respect to contract interpretation, (a) the secret intent of a party and (b) a trade custom.

5. Avril, a Pennsylvania corporation, agreed to sell certain cleaning products to Center Chemical Co. at a discount of 45 percent for 20 years and gave Center the exclusive right to sell such products in Florida. Four years later, Center stopped purchasing from Avril, which then sued it for breach of contract. Did the law of Pennsylvania or the Florida law determine the damages which could be recovered? [Center Chemical Co. v Avril, (CA5 Fla) 392 F2d 289]

6. McGill and his grandson, Malo, made an agreement by which the former would live with the latter and receive support and maintenance in return for deeding to the grandson the house of the former. After a number of years, the grandfather left the house because of the threats and physical violence of the grandson. There was no complaint of lack

of support and maintenance. Had the grandson broken the contract? [McGill v Malo, 23 Conn Supp 447, 184 A2d 517]

7. *A* and *B* signed a printed form of agreement by which it appeared that *A* promised to sell and *B* promised to buy certain land. On the blank lines of the printed form, there was a typewritten provision that *B* had an option to purchase the land. Could *A* sue *B* for breach of contract if *B* did not buy the land? [Welk v Fainbarg, 255 Cal App 2d 269, 63 Cal Rptr 127]

8. Gerson Realty Co. rented an apartment to Casaly. The lease stated that it could be renewed on giving notice but declared that "such notice . . . shall be given or served and shall not be deemed to have been duly given or served unless in writing and forwarded by registered mail." Casaly sent a renewal notice by certified mail. Two years after receiving the notice, Gerson claimed that it was not effective because it had not been sent by registered mail. Was the notice effective? [Gerson Realty Inc. v Casaly, 2 MassApp 875, 316 NE2d 767]

9. Fincher was employed by Belk-Sawyer Co. as fashion coordinator for the latter's retail stores. The contract of employment specified her duties as fashion coordinator and also provided for additional services of Fincher to be thereafter agreed upon in connection with beauty consultation and shopping services to be established at the stores. After Fincher had been employed as fashion coordinator for several months, Belk-Sawyer Co. refused to be bound by the contract on the ground that it was too indefinite. Was it bound? [Fincher v Belk-Sawyer Co. (Fla App) 127 So2d 130]

10. Harwood rented an apartment in an apartment house complex from Lincoln Square Apartments. Air conditioning was among the services to be provided by the landlord. The lease stated that the landlord was not liable for "any interruption or curtailment of any service." The central air conditioning system in the apartment house broke down and would not function for 6 weeks in the summer. Harwood rented an air conditioning unit which he placed in his apartment and then sued the landlord for the cost thereof. The landlord denied liability because of the disclaimer clause. Was the landlord right? [Harwood v Lincoln Square Apartments Section 5, Inc. (NY Civil Court) 359 NYS2d 387]

11. All the shareholders of Continental Title Company signed an agreement giving the Stewart Title Company the option to purchase "all" of their shares for a quarter million dollars. The option contract specified that notice of its exercise was to be given to the chairman of the board of the Continental Title Company. The Stewart Title Company notified one of the Continental stockholders, Herbert, that it exercised the option to purchase his 350 shares, paying for them the prorated portion of a quarter million dollars. Herbert refused to sell. A lawsuit was brought against him and evidence was offered that the executives of Stewart understood that they were obtaining an option to purchase the stock of the Continental shareholders one by one. There was no evidence that this belief was communicated to anyone else. Was Herbert required to sell his shares to Stewart? [Stewart Title Company v Herbert, 6 Cal App 3d 957, 85 Cal Rptr 654]

12. Carolina Plywood Distributors was a corporation. It purchased building materials from Clear Fir Sales Company. The president of Carolina wrote a letter to Clear Fir which in part stated, "Please accept this letter as my personal guarantee for the purchase of Carolina Plywood Distributors through December 31, 1970. If we are continuing to do business at that time, we will be glad to renew this guarantee." The debt of Carolina was not paid and Clear Fir sued Carolina and its president. Clear Fir claimed that the quoted letter guaranteed the debt of the corporation. The president defended on the ground that Clear Fir had never accepted his offer of guaranty and therefore he was not bound. Was this defense valid? [Clear Fir Sales Co. v Carolina Plywood Distributors, Inc., 13 NC App 429, 185 SE2d 737]

13. Physicians Mutual Insurance Company issued a policy covering the life of Ruby Brown. The policy declared that it did not cover any deaths resulting from "mental disorder, alcoholism, or drug addiction." Ruby was killed when she fell while intoxicated. The insurance company refused to pay because of the quoted provision. Her executor, Savage, sued the insurance company. Did the insurance company have a defense? [Physicians Mut. Ins. Co. v Savage, 156 IndApp 283, 296 NE2d 165]

14. Ern-Roc Homes, a builder, guaranteed that its homes would have no seepage of water into the basement "through the foundation walls." Water entered the basement of the home purchased by Gomes by passing through a door installed in the basement wall, level with the ground in back of the house. The water caused extensive damage in the house. Gomes sued Ern-Roc Homes claiming that there was a breach of the builder's guaranty. Was Gomes correct? [Gomes v Ern-Roc Homes, Inc. (NY Civil Court) 72 Misc 2d 410, 339 NYS2d 401]

15. Axford rented land from Shellhart. The lease gave the lessee the option to purchase the leased property "any time during the term of this lease or its extension for the sum of $12,000. This option may be exercised at any time prior to December 1, 1969 by giving the Lessors at least 30 days notice in writing of Lessee's intention to so exercise said option." Could the lessee exercise the option by giving notice without paying the purchase price at the same time? [Shellhart v Axford, (Wyo) 485 P2d 1031]

16. Richard and Ruby Lewis owned separate tracts of land, designated as Section 1 and Section 18, which they leased to Gailey and Sredanovich. The lease specified that the Lewises would convey to the tenants a one-half interest in the land if the tenants or lessees developed water on the land suitable for irrigation. The tenants developed such a water supply on Section 18 but not on Section 1. Arrow Gas Co. acquired the interest of the lessees and claimed that it was entitled to a one-half interest in Section 18. The Lewises contended that Arrow was not entitled to any interest in the land because the lessees had not developed nor made any effort to develop water on Section 1. Were they correct? [Arrow Gas Co. v Lewis, 71 NMex 232, 377 P2d 655]

17. A buyer had been purchasing turkeys from the same seller for ten years. During all this time, the seller had supplied cross breed turkeys. In the eleventh year, the buyer rejected a shipment of turkeys on the ground that they were cross breed. He then sued the seller for breach of contract. Did the seller have a defense? [Amerine Nat. Corp. v Denver Food Co. (CA10 Colo) 493 F2d 1275]

17 Third Persons and Contracts

When two parties make a contract, does an outsider have any rights under that contract? Can the promisor be sued on the contract? This chapter discusses the situations when a third person can assert rights on a contract made by others.

A. THIRD PARTY BENEFICIARY CONTRACTS

A third person who is benefited by the performance of a contract may enforce it against the promisor when such was the intention of the parties to the contract.

§ 17:1. Definition. Ordinarily A and B will make a contract that concerns only them. However, they may make a contract by which B promises A that B will make a payment of money to C. That is, the contracting parties intend to benefit C. Because of this intent, if B fails to perform that promise, C, who is not the original promisee, may enforce the contract against B, the promisor. Such an agreement is a _third party beneficiary contract_.[1]

(a) Modification or Termination of Contract. Can the parties to the contract modify or terminate it so as to destroy the right of the third party beneficiary? If the third party beneficiary had accepted the contract or changed position in reliance on it, the original parties generally cannot thereafter modify or rescind the contract so as to affect or release the obligation to the third party beneficiary. (See p. 260, Bass v Hancock Mutual Life Ins. Co.) However, if the third party beneficiary has not accepted the contract nor acted in reliance thereon, it may be modified or terminated by the contracting parties and thereby change or destroy the rights of the third party beneficiary. Likewise, the contract itself may expressly reserve the power of the original parties to make such modification or rescission,[2] or the third party may consent to such a change.

---

[1] Springer v Powder Power Tool Corp. 220 Ore 102, 348 P2d 1112.

A life insurance contract is a third party beneficiary contract, since the insurance company promises the insured to make payment to the beneficiary. Such a contract entitles the beneficiary to sue the insurance company upon the insured's death even though the insurance company never made any agreement directly with the beneficiary.

[2] A common form of reservation is the life insurance policy provision by which the insured reserves the right to change the beneficiary. § 142 of the 1967 tentative draft Restatement of Contracts 2d provides that the promisor and promisee may modify their contract and affect the right of the third party beneficiary thereby unless the agreement expressly prohibits this or the third party beneficiary has changed position in reliance on the promise or has manifested assent to it.

§ 17:2. Limitations on Third Party Beneficiary. While the third party beneficiary rule gives the third person the right to enforce the contract, it obviously gives no greater rights than the contract provides. Otherwise stated, the third party beneficiary must take the contract as it is. If there is a time limitation or any other restriction in the contract, the third party beneficiary cannot ignore it but is bound thereby.

§ 17:3. Incidental Beneficiary Distinguished. Not everyone who benefits from the performance of a contract between other persons is entitled to sue as a third party beneficiary. A person who is classified as an incidental beneficiary may not recover on a contract made by others.[3] For example, when a private employer makes a contract with the United States government to employ and train disadvantaged unemployed persons, such persons are merely incidental beneficiaries of the contract and therefore cannot sue for damages when the contract with the government is broken by the employer. (See p. 261, McDonald Construction Co. v Murray.)

B. ASSIGNMENTS

The parties to a contract have both rights and duties. Can rights be transferred or sold to another person? Can duties be transferred to another person?

§ 17:4. Definitions. An *assignment* is a transfer of rights. The party making the assignment is the *assignor,* and the person to whom the assignment is made is the *assignee.* An assignee of a contract may generally sue directly on the contract, rather than suing in the name of the assignor.

§ 17:5. Form of Assignment. Generally an assignment may be in any form. Any words, whether written or spoken, that show an intention to transfer or assign will be given the effect of an assignment. Statutes, however, may require that certain kinds of assignments be in writing or be executed in a particular form. This requirement is common in respect to statutes limiting the assignment of claims to wages.

An assignment is a completed transfer, not a contract. It is therefore immaterial whether or not there is any consideration. An assignment may be made as a gift, although it is usually part of a business transaction.

§ 17:6. Assignment of Right to Money. A person entitled to receive money, such as payment for the price of goods or for work done under a contract, may generally assign that right to another person. A claim or cause of action against another person may be assigned. A contractor entitled to receive payment from the owner can assign that right to the bank as security for a loan or can assign it to anyone else.

(a) Future Rights. By the modern rule, future and expected rights may be assigned. Thus the contractor may assign the money which is not yet due under the contract because the building has not yet been constructed. Likewise an author may assign royalties which are expected to be received from contracts which the author expects to enter into in the future. The fact that there is nothing in existence now does not prohibit the assignment of what is expected to be existing in the future.

---

[3] Costanza v Costanza (Ala) 346 So2d 1133.

(b) Prohibition of Assignment of Rights. A contract may prohibit the assignment of any rights arising thereunder. The prohibition may be stated as a condition subsequent which makes the contract void if a prohibited assignment is made, or it may state it merely as a personal agreement by a party to refrain from assigning any rights. In most states, the effect of a prohibited assignment depends upon which of the above provisions is in the contract. If it is the conditional form, the contract is void and the assignee acquires no interest. If it is the personal agreement or covenant form, there is a division of authority as to its effect. In some jurisdictions, if a right to money is otherwise assignable, the right to transfer cannot be restricted by the parties to the contract. Such a restriction is regarded in those states as contrary to public policy because it places a limitation on the assignor's right of property. In other states, such a prohibition is recognized as valid on the theory that the parties to the original contract may include such a provision if they choose to do so.[4] In any event, a prohibition against the assignment must be clearly expressed and any uncertainty is resolved in favor of assignability.

Statutes may prohibit the assignment of rights to money. Contractors who build public works are frequently prohibited from assigning money due or money that will become due under the contract. In some states, wage earners are prohibited from assigning their future wages, or the law limits the percentage of their wages that can be assigned. In some instances, an assignment of wages is lawful, but the assignment must be a separate instrument. The purpose of such a provision is to protect employees from signing printed forms containing "hidden" wage assignment clauses.

(c) Prohibition of Assignment of Contract. When a contract prohibits the assignment of "the contract," it is narrowly interpreted to prohibit only the performance of the contract by an assignee. Such a prohibition does not bar transferring rights under the contract.[5] For example, when a statute states that the contractor to whom a government contract has been awarded may not assign the contract, such provision is to be interpreted as prohibiting a delegation of the duty of performance and as not affecting the right to assign money due or to become due under the contract.

§ 17:7. Assignment of Right to a Performance. When the right of the obligee under the contract is to receive a performance by the other party, the obligee may assign that right, provided the performance required of the other party will not be materially altered or varied by such assignment. In contrast, if a transfer of a right to a performance would materially affect or alter a duty or the rights of the obligor, an assignment of the rights to the performance is not permitted. When an obligee is entitled to assign a right, it may be done by unilateral act. There is no requirement that the obligor consent or agree. Likewise, the act of assigning does not constitute a breach of the contract, unless the contract specifically declares so.

(a) Assignment Increasing Burden of Performance. When the assigning of a right would increase the burden of the obligor in performing, an assignment is ordinarily not permitted. To illustrate, if the assignor has the right to buy a certain quantity

---

[4] UCC § 2-210(2). But compare UCC § 9-318(4).
[5] UCC § 2-210(3).

of a stated article and to take such property from the seller's warehouse, this right can be assigned. If, however, the sales contract stipulated that the seller should deliver to the buyer's premises, and the assignee lived or had a place of business a substantial distance from the assignor's place of business, the assignment would not be given effect. In this case, the seller would be required to give a different performance by providing greater transportation if the assignment were permitted.

(b)   Personal Satisfaction. A similar problem arises when the goods to be furnished must be satisfactory to the personal judgment of the buyer. Since the seller only contracted that the performance would stand or fall according to the buyer's judgment, the buyer may not substitute the judgment of an assignee.

(c)   Personal Services. An employer cannot assign to another the employer's right to have an employee work. The relationship of employer and employee is so personal that the right cannot be assigned. The performance contracted for by the employee was to work for a particular employer at a particular place and at a particular job. To permit an assignee to claim the employee's services would be to change that contract.

(d)   Credit Transactions. When a transaction is based on extending credit, the person to whom credit is extended cannot assign any rights under the contract to another. For example, when land is sold on credit the buyer cannot assign the contract unless the seller consents thereto.[6] The making of an assignment is here prohibited because the assignee is a different credit risk. Whether the assignee is a better or worse credit risk is not considered.

§ 17:8. Delegation of Duties. *A delegation of duties* is a transfer of duties by a party to a contract to another person who is to perform them. Under certain circumstances, a contracting party may obtain someone else to do the work. When the performance is standardized and nonpersonal so that it is not material who performs, the law will permit the delegation of the performance of the contract. In such cases, however, the contracting party remains liable for the default of the person doing the work just as though the contracting party had performed or attempted to perform the job.

If the performance by the promisor requires personal skill or is a performance in which the promisor's credit standing was material in the promisee's selection of the promisor, delegation of performance is prohibited. Whether a contractual duty is so personal that it cannot be delegated is a question of intention of the parties to be ascertained from the contract, its nature, and the surrounding circumstances.[7]

(a)   Intention to Delegate Duties. A question of interpretation arises as to whether an assignment of "the contract" is only an assignment of the rights of the assignor or is both an assignment of those rights and a delegation of duties. The trend of authority is to regard such a general assignment as both a transfer of rights and a delegation of duties. (See p. 262, Radley v Smith)

With respect to contracts for the sale of goods, "An assignment of 'the contract' or of 'all my rights under the contract' or an assignment in similar general terms is

---

[6] Farrell v Evans (TexCivApp) 517 SW2d 585.
[7] Rossetti v New Britain, 163 Conn 283, 303 A2d 714.

an assignment of rights and, unless the language or the circumstances (as in an assignment for security) indicate the contrary, it is a delegation of performance of the duties of the assignor and its acceptance by the promisee constitutes a promise . . . to perform the duties. This promise is enforceable by either the assignor or the other party to the original contract." [8]

(b)   Transfer of Assets Distinguished. When an enterprise sells all of its assets to a buyer, no delegation of any duty takes place. Consequently, the buyer of the assets does not become subject to the debts of the transferor. This rule is followed, even though the debts represent the unpaid balance due for the purchase of the assets which are transferred.

The agreement of the parties, however, will often expressly provide that the transferee of the property of the enterprise will also be responsible for the obligations of the transferor, either generally or with specific reference to the acquisition of the goods which were transferred. In the case of corporate enterprises, statutes will frequently impose liability upon a new corporation which is formed to take over the assets and the business of the former corporation.

(c)   Novation. One who is entitled to receive performance under a contract may agree to release the person who is bound to perform and to permit another person to render the required performance. When this occurs, it is not a question of merely assigning the liability under the contract but is really one of abandoning the old contract and substituting in its place a new contract. This change of contracts is called a *novation.*

§ 17:9. Continuing Liability of Assignor. The making of an assignment does not relieve the assignor of any obligation of the contract. In the absence of a contrary agreement, such as a novation, an assignor continues to be bound by the obligations of the original contract. Thus, the fact that a buyer assigns the right to goods under a contract does not terminate the buyer's liability to make payment to the seller. Likewise, when an independent contractor is hired to perform a party's obligations under a contract, that party is liable if the independent contractor does not properly perform the contract.[9]

§ 17:10. Defenses and Setoffs. The assignee's rights rise no higher than those of the assignor. If the obligor (the other party to the original contract) could successfully defend against a suit brought by the assignor, the obligor will also prevail against the assignee. (See p. 263, Associates Loan Co. v Walkers)

The assigning of a right does not free it from any defense or setoff to which the right would be subject if it were still held by the assignor.[10] The fact that the assignee has given value for the assignment does not give the assignee any immunity from defenses which the other party, the obligor, could have asserted against the assignor. The rights acquired by the assignee remain subject to any limitations imposed by the contract.

---

[8] UCC § 2-210(4).
[9] Weaver v Harmon, (ColoApp), 508 P2d 412.
[10] Walker v Nitzberg, 13 CalApp3d 359, 91 CalRptr 526.

(a)   Waiver of Exemptions and Defenses Against Assignee. Modern contract forms commonly provide that the debtor waives or will not assert against an assignee of the contract exemptions and defenses which could have been raised against the assignor. Except as noted in the following paragraph, such waivers are generally valid.

(b)   Consumer Protection. Statutes designed to protect consumer buyers commonly prohibit such a buyer from agreeing to not assert against the seller's assignee any defense which could have been asserted against the seller. Some statutes take a modified position and permit barring the buyer if, when notified of the assignment, the buyer fails to inform the assignee of the defense against the seller.

§ 17:11. Notice of Assignment. An assignment, if otherwise valid, takes effect the moment it is made. It is not necessary that the assignee or the assignor give notice to the other party to the contract that the assignment has been made. It is highly desirable, however, that the other party be notified as soon as possible after the making of the assignment.

(a)   Effect on Defenses and Setoffs. Notice of an assignment prevents the obligor from asserting against the assignee any defense or setoff arising after such notice with respect to a matter not related to the assigned claim.[11]

(1)   Post-Notice Matters. If the matter of defense relates to the assigned claim, notice does not affect the right of the obligor to assert against the assignee any defense or setoff that would have been available were suit brought by the assignor.

For example, *O* owns two lots of ground, No. 1 and No. 2. *O* makes two separate contracts with *C,* a paving contractor to pave these two lots. *C* assigns to *A* the right to be paid for lot No. 1 before that contract has been performed, and *A* notifies *O* of the assignment. After making the assignment, *C* paves both lots but does a poor job on each. When *A* sues *O* for the contract price for lot No. 1, *O* claims a setoff for the damages suffered because of the poor work on lots No. 1 and No. 2. The poor work defense with respect to lot No. 1 is obviously related to the claim for the contract price for paving lot No. 1. That defense or setoff may therefore be asserted by *O* against *A,* without regard to when the paving was done or when notice of the assignment was given to *O.*

In contrast, the claim of *O* to set off damages because of the poor work done on lot No. 2 is not related to the claim that was assigned to *A.* Consequently, the giving of notice of the assignment to *O* cut off the right of *O* to assert against *A* any claim which would thereafter arise with respect to an unrelated matter. Since *O* knew of the assignment of the lot No. 1 contract claim before there was any breach as to lot No. 2, *O* cannot assert a defense with respect to lot No. 2 against *A.*[12]

(2)   Pre-Notice Matters. The only way in which the assignee can be protected from defenses and setoffs arising before notice of assignment has been given is to ask the obligor whether there is any defense or setoff or counterclaim against

---

[11] Ertel v Radio Corporation of America, (IndApp), 297 NE2d 446.
[12] UCC § 9-318(1); Dickerson v Federal Deposit Insurance Corp., (FlaApp) 244 So2d 748.

the assignor. If the obligor states that there is none or makes a declaration of no setoff, the obligor is estopped (barred) from contradicting that statement and is not permitted to prove a defense, setoff, or counterclaim based on facts existing prior to the time of the statement to the assignee.

(b)   Discharge. Until the obligor knows that there has been an assignment, the obligor is legally entitled to pay to or perform for the assignor just as though there were no assignment. Such payment or performance is a complete discharge of the obligation under the contract; but in such a case the assignee could proceed against the assignor to require the assignor to account for what had been received. If the assignee has given the obligor notice of the assignment, however, the obligor cannot discharge the obligation to the assignee by making a payment to or performance for the assignor.

If the debtor, knowing of the assignment, pays the assignor, the assignee may sue either the assignor or the debtor. The payment by the latter with knowledge of the existence of the assignment does not discharge the debt and the obligor remains liable to the assignee.[13] (See p. 263, American Bank of Commerce v City of McAlester) The assignee may recover the payment from the assignor as the assignor is deemed to have received such payment from the debtor on behalf of the assignee.

The notice here considered must identify the particular claim against the defendant. Thus, knowledge that a business enterprise was obtaining refinancing on the basis of its accounts receivable was not a notice to the debtor of one of the accounts that that account had been assigned to the lending agency.

(c)   Priority. If a person assigns the same right to two different assignees, the question arises as to which assignee has obtained the right. By the American rule, the assignee taking the first assignment prevails over the subsequent assignees.

§ 17:12. Warranties of Assignor. When the assignment is made for a consideration, the assignor is regarded as impliedly warranting that the right assigned is valid, that the assignor is the owner of the claim or right assigned, and that the assignor will not interfere with the assignee's enforcement of the obligation. The assignor does not warrant that the other party will pay or perform as required by the contract.

---

[13] Bank of Commerce v Intermountain Gas Co., 96 Idaho 29, 523 P2d 1375.

CASES FOR CHAPTER 17

Bass v John Hancock Mut. Life Ins. Co.

10 Cal 3d 792, 112 Cal Rptr 195, 518 P2d 1147 (1974)

Pursuant to the Ford Motor Company's contract with the United Automobile Workers (UAW), Ford obtained from John Hancock Mutual Life Insurance Company a group insurance policy in 1964 covering the Ford employees. In 1964 Bass was employed by Ford. He notified Ford that he did not wish to be under the group plan. In 1967, Ford made a new contract with UAW and obtained a new group policy covering all employees. Ford assumed that Bass did not want to be covered by this new group policy and paid no premiums to the insurance company to cover him. Bass was killed in an automobile accident in 1968 and his beneficiary sued the insurance company. It raised the defense that any coverage of Bass by the 1967 policy had been terminated when Ford failed to pay the premiums with respect to Bass. From a judgment for the insurer, the beneficiary of the policy appealed.

BURKE, J. . . . Bass evidently waived coverage under a 1964 group plan offered by his employer, Ford Motor Company, despite the fact that such insurance was offered free of charge to all employees.

In October 1967, the Ford union contract was renegotiated. . . . As part of the new contract, the Hancock plan was amended . . . to provide for increased benefits. Although three years had passed since Bass had refused coverage, neither Ford nor Hancock solicited Bass' desires with respect to the 1967 plan. . . .

It seems evident to us that a waiver which occurred in 1964 is not necessarily controlling with respect to rights under a 1967 insurance program. . . . Bass was a third party beneficiary under the Ford-UAW union contract and the Ford-Hancock group insurance program, and as such he initially acquired valuable rights to insurance coverage. . . . Although the rights of a third party beneficiary may be voluntarily waived or disclaimed . . . the burden is on the party claiming the waiver ". . . to prove it by clear and convincing evidence that does not leave the matter to speculation, and 'doubtful cases will be decided against a waiver. . . .'"

We may assume that the contract rights which Bass acquired under the 1964 insurance program were, as the trial court found, unequivocally and voluntarily waived or disclaimed by him. . . . The record contains no evidence whatever that Bass subsequently relinquished the new rights to coverage which accrued to him in 1967 by reason of the renegotiation of Ford's labor contract and the amendment of the Hancock group plan. . . . Yet in the absence of a renewed rejection or disclaimer from Bass, or other "clear and convincing" indicium of waiver, we must conclude that Bass retained his group insurance rights under the 1967 plan.

Defendant Hancock contends that even if Bass did not waive his rights to coverage, plaintiff's cause of action would be against Ford rather than Hancock, since Ford paid Hancock no premiums on Bass' account. To the contrary, nonpayment of premiums may have constituted a breach of *Ford's* obligations to Hancock, but would not affect the right of Bass

(or plaintiff) to enforce coverage which Hancock agreed to extend to *all* Ford employees. (. . . An employee who otherwise satisfies the conditions of a group plan may maintain an action against the insurer as a third-party beneficiary. . . . The same reasoning would apply, of course, to the employee's beneficiaries.) In a series of recent cases we have held that the employer is the agent of the insurer in performing the duties of administering group insurance policies, including the payment of premiums, and that accordingly the insurer shares responsibility for the employer's mistakes. . . . We see no reason to deviate from this principle in the instant case. Indeed, we note that Hancock's own representative admitted at trial that if a Ford employee were not included in the calculation of premiums by reason of clerical error or mistake, Hancock would nevertheless honor his claim under the group policy and backcharge Ford for the unpaid premiums.

In the instant case, Ford's "mistake" was in assuming that Bass had rejected coverage under the 1967 group plan, without verifying that fact with Bass himself. We think that this kind of mistake is one for which Hancock should share responsibility despite the nonpayment of premiums.

[Judgment reversed and action remanded]

McDonald Construction Co. v Murray

5 Wash App 68, 485 P2d 626 (1971)

Murray owned a building. He contracted with the McDonald Construction Company to make an addition to the building. Queen Anne News, Inc., was to be a tenant in the new addition. The contract required completion of the work within 75 days. It took 239 days to complete. Murray and Queen Anne News sued McDonald for the damages caused by the delay. The lower court entered judgment for Murray but dismissed Queen Anne News from the action. McDonald appealed.

JAMES, J. . . . The trial judge found as a fact that Queen Anne News, Inc. was not a party to the construction contract and that its only relationship to the transaction was as a prospective tenant for the premises McDonald undertook to construct. Consequently, Queen Anne News was dismissed from the action.

Queen Anne News claims that the delay in completion of the premises caused it to lose anticipated profits. It asserts a right to recover from

McDonald upon the legal theory that it was a third-party beneficiary of the construction contract.

A third-party beneficiary is one who, though not a party to the contract, will nevertheless receive direct benefits therefrom. In determining whether or not a third-party beneficiary status is created by a contract, the critical question is whether the benefits flow directly from the contract or whether they are merely incidental, indirect or consequential. . . . An incidental beneficiary acquires no right to recover damages for non-performance of the contract. Restatement of Contracts, § 147 (1932). "It is not sufficient that the performance of the promise may benefit a third person, but that it must have been entered into for his benefit, or at least such benefit must be the direct result of performance and so within the contemplation of the parties.". . . "The question whether a contract is made for the benefit of a third person is one of construction. The intention of the parties in this respect is determined by the terms of the contract as a whole construed in the light of the circumstances under which it was made.". . . Such "intent" is not a desire or purpose to confer a benefit upon the third person, nor a desire to advance his interests, but an intent that the promisor shall assume a direct obligation to him. . . .

Queen Anne News points out that the evidence established that McDonald was aware of the fact that it was to become the Murrays' tenant when the addition to the Murrays' building was completed. Queen Anne News argues that the Murrays' intent, together with McDonald's knowledge thereof, is sufficient to afford the News the status of a third-party beneficiary.

We do not agree. Any benefit which Queen Anne News could assert would be derived from the intervening tenancy agreement which it had with the Murrays. Queen Anne News derived no direct benefit from the construction contract and consequently had no right of action against McDonald because of McDonald's breach of performance. The trial judge did not err in dismissing Queen Anne News' cross-complaint.

[Judgment affirmed as to dismissal of Queen Anne News]

Radley v Smith

6 Utah 2d 314, 313 P2d 465 (1957)

Smith, who owned the Avalon Apartments, sold individual apartments under contracts that re- **quired each purchaser to pay $15 a month extra for hot and cold water, heat, refrigeration, taxes, and fire insurance. Smith assigned his interest in the apartment house and under the various contracts to Roberts. She failed to pay the taxes on the building. Radley and other tenants sued Smith and Roberts to compel them to pay the taxes. The action was dropped as to Smith. From a judgment against Roberts, she appealed.**

CROCKETT, J. . . . The first of defendant's contentions is that the trial court erred in finding she had assumed any of the duties and obligations arising under the contracts between Smith and the plaintiffs. She maintains that in purchasing Smith's interest she was acquiring only the right to collect payments from the plaintiffs and that she had no intention of assuming the burdens of the contracts. While it is no doubt possible for a party to become the assignee of the rights under a contract without becoming responsible for the duties, the question whether a purported assignment of an entire contract includes such assumption depends upon its terms and the intent of the parties. Whenever uncertainty or ambiguity exists with respect thereto, it is proper for the court to consider all the facts and circumstances, including the words and actions of the parties forming the background of the transaction.

It appears that the defendant had available Smith's contracts which set forth the corresponding rights and duties of the parties, and expressly stated that the provisions would bind the "successors and assigns." She, therefore, knew of the services required of the seller and in fact initially accepted and performed those responsibilities, and further, accepted the $15 per month which the contract recited was to pay for them, and for the payment of taxes. Applicable to this situation is the rule of construction stated in § 164 (1) of the Restatement of Contracts:

"Where a party to a bilateral contract, which is at the time wholly or partially executory on both sides, purports to assign the whole contract, his action is interpreted, in the absence of circumstances showing a contrary intention, as an assignment of the assignor's rights under the contract and a delegation of the performance of assignor's duties."

There is nothing in this case to affirmatively indicate anything other than that defendant was to assume the responsibilities of the seller under the contracts and the trial court's finding with respect to that issue must therefore be affirmed. . . .

[Judgment affirmed]

Associates Loan Co. v Walkers

76 NMex 520, 416 P2d 529 (1966)

The Walkers purchased on trial a mechanical water softener from Partin. He represented that the use of the softener would increase the milk production at the Walkers' dairy, and the purchase price could be paid for through such increased production. Partin assigned his contract with the Walkers to Associates Loan Co. When Associates sued the Walkers for the money due under the contract, the Walkers raised the defense that the mechanical water softener did not work as represented. From a judgment for the defendants, Associates appealed.

SPIESS, J. . . . The defense, in substance, is that Partin and Walkers agreed that there would be no sale and the contract would not be effective unless after trial the water softener served to increase Walkers' milk production. This agreement was made orally at the time, or prior to the signing of the written contract. Walkers contend that the oral agreement created a condition precedent to the written contract becoming a valid obligation.

It is further asserted that since the condition failed, the contract did not come into existence. . . .

It is first contended that the transaction falls within the Uniform Commercial Code, and in accordance with its provisions an assignee takes an assigned chose in action subject only to such equities and defenses between the debtor and assignee as are specified in UCC § 9-318(1). . . . It is argued that the equities or defenses so specified do not include the type of defense interposed by Walkers. Therefore, the trial court was in error in permitting Walkers to raise the defense against Associates.

The cited section is as follows: "(1) Unless an account debtor has made an enforceable agreement not to assert defenses or claims arising out of a sale as provided in Section 9-206 . . . the rights of an assignee are subject to (a) all the terms of the contract between the account debtor and assignor and any defense or claim arising therefrom; and (b) any other defense or claim of the account debtor against the assignor which accrues before the account debtor receives notification of the assignment."

The contract involved here does not contain an agreement under which the account debtor[s], Walkers, have precluded themselves from asserting defenses arising out of the sale as against assignee. Consequently, this phase of the Code is not involved.

It is apparent that the section quoted makes no substantial change in the law as it existed prior to the adoption of the Uniform Commercial Code. See Anderson's Uniform Commercial Code, Vol. 2, page 602, and Secured Transactions under the Uniform Commercial Code, Coogan, Hogan and Vagts, Vol. 2, p. 1599.

The fundamental rule of law, unchanged by the quoted section of the Uniform Commercial Code, is that an assignee of a chose in action acquires by virtue of his assignment nothing more than the assignor had, any and all equities and defenses which could have been raised by the debtor against the assignor are available to the debtor against the assignee. . . .

If the contract in Partin's hands was subject to a condition precedent under which it was not to become effective until the happening of a contingency, upon assignment the assignee took the contract subject to the same condition. The trial court correctly held that the defense raised by Walkers was available against the assignee, Associates. . . .

[Judgment affirmed]

American Bank of Commerce v City of McAlester

(Okla), 555 P2d 581 (1976)

Irvine made a construction contract with the City of McAlester. The contract specified that money to be due under the contract could not be assigned without the consent of the City. Irvine borrowed money from the American Bank of Commerce and, as security for the loan, assigned to the bank the money to become due under the contract with the City. The consent of the City was not obtained, but the bank gave the City a copy of the assignment. The City thereafter ignored the assignment and paid Irvine the money due under the contract. The bank then sued the City for paying to Irvine after it had notice of the assignment. From a judgment in favor of the bank, the City appealed.

DAVISON, J. . . . The first issue raised is whether the provisions of [UCC] § 9-318(4) have an effect upon the nonassignment clause in the construction contract.

[It provides:] "A term in any contract between an account debtor and an assignor which prohibits assignment of an account or contract right to which they are parties is ineffective."

"Subsection (4) breaks sharply with the older contract doctrines by denying effectiveness to contractual terms prohibiting assignment of accounts and contract rights—that is, sums due and to become due under contracts of sale, construction contracts and the like. Under the rule as stated an assignment would be effective even if made to an assignee who took with full knowledge that the account debtor had sought to prohibit or restrict assignment of the account or of the money to be earned under the contract."

Therefore, even though the initial construction contract, in and of itself, did not intend to effect a security, the contract is affected by § 318 of Article 9, because the legislative intent, as shown by the language of the provision, was to make accounts and contract rights freely assignable—this being the case, parties by contract should not and are not permitted to circumvent the intent of the statute. Section 9-318 merely codified this prohibition which is necessary to maintain the free assignability of accounts and contract rights.

In adopting § 9-318(4) of the Uniform Commercial Code, the Legislature clearly intended, as a matter of law, to make contract rights and accounts freely assignable. We therefore hold that any contract provisions which prohibit or restrict the assignability of accounts or contract rights to be contra to the law, and thus null and void and of no effect. This being so, contractor Irvine's assignment of his rights under the construction contract with the City of McAlester, to American Bank of Commerce was an effective and valid assignment under the Code.

. . . The appellant urges that the assignment made by the contractor was invalid because the assignment was made in violation of 61 O.S. 1971 § 39 which provides: "No contract awarded to the lowest responsible bidder or the highest responsible bidder, as the case may be, shall be assignable by the successful bidder without written consent of the contracting authority evidenced by resolution. . . ."

We would agree with appellant that, under the above quoted statute, public work contracts affected by the statute cannot be assigned, but we disagree with appellant as to its interpretation of the statute. The question presented is one going to the scope of the prohibition against assignment—does it mean only that the builder shall not delegate performance of his duties, or not only this, but also that he shall not assign his rights to the payments to which he is or will be entitled?

We hold that the intent of the statute was to prohibit delegation of duties under contracts affected, and not to prohibit assignments of rights to payments under the contract. We therefore hold that the assignment by the contractor to the Bank was valid. We will now consider the effect of that assignment on the rights and liabilities of the parties involved.

[UCC] § 9-318(3) establishes a duty upon an account debtor to make payments to the assignee, once the account debtor has received proper notification of the assignment: "The account debtor is authorized to pay the assignor until the account debtor receives notification that the account has been assigned and that payment is to be made to the assignee."

Thus, if the City of McAlester received proper notice of contractor Irvine's assignment to the Bank, the City had a duty to make payments directly to the assignee Bank. . . . The record before the trial court demonstrates that the City of McAlester had received proper notice of the assignment.

A true copy of the assignment was delivered to McAlester's City Manager. . . . We hold that these facts were . . . sufficient to constitute notice. We also hold that, under [UCC] § 9-318(3), . . . such notice gave rise to a duty upon the account debtor to make payments directly to the assignee Bank, and . . . that the duty was breached, when after notice of the assignment, the City continued to make payments to the contractor rather than to the assignee Bank.

Appellant lastly urged that even if the assignment were valid and the notice of it sufficient, the claim of the assignee Bank is a claim against the funds due the contractor which were retained by the City, and the City's liability to the Bank is limited to the amount of those funds. We do not agree with appellant's contention. . . . "The notice of an assignment puts a debtor on guard, and if thereafter he pays any money to the assignor which under the terms of the assignment belongs to the assignee, or if he does anything prejudicial to the rights of the assignee he is liable for the resulting damage." . . .

If we were to embrace the contention that the City's liability to the Bank under the assignment is limited to the amount of retained funds held by the City, we would be allowing the City to reduce its total liability to the Bank by subtracting the amount of the payments wrongfully made to the contractor from the total liability. In so doing, we would, in essence, be allowing appellant to use such payments as a defense against the assignee. . . . We therefore hold that the liability of the City of McAlester to the assignee Bank is not limited to the amount of the funds retained. . . .

[Judgment affirmed]

QUESTIONS AND CASE PROBLEMS

1. What social forces are affected by allowing an obligee to assign his right to obtain payment?

2. Compare a contract and an assignment of a contract right.

3. Compare a third party beneficiary contract and an assignment.

4. Compare a delegation of duties and a novation.

5. Rexroad contracted with the City of Assaria to improve certain streets within the city. The contract specified that "the contractor shall be liable for all damages to buildings . . . located outside the construction limits (and shall) make amicable settlement of such damage claims . . . " Anderson, whose house was damaged by the construction work, sued Rexroad for the damages. The latter defended on the ground that Anderson did not have any agreement with him and had not given him any consideration. Decide. [Anderson v Rexroad, 175 Kan 676, 266 P2d 320]

6. Ewin Engineering Corporation owed money to Girod. The latter borrowed money from the Deposit Guaranty Bank & Trust Co. and assigned to it as security for the loan the claim he held against Ewin. The bank immediately notified Ewin of the assignment. Thereafter Ewin paid Girod the balance due him. Ewin then notified the bank that it had paid Girod in full and that it refused to recognize the assignment. The bank sued Ewin. Could it recover? [Ewin Engineering Corp. v Deposit Guaranty Bank & Trust Co., 216 Miss 410, 62 So2d 572]

7. Enos had a policy of insurance with the Franklin Casualty Insurance Company providing for the payment of all reasonable hospitalization expenses up to $500 for each person injured while a passenger in, or upon entering or leaving, the insured's automobile. Wagner, a guest in the automobile, was injured in a highway accident. She was treated by Dr. Jones, who then sued the insurer to obtain payment. Decide. [Franklin Casualty Insurance Company v Jones, (Okla) 362 P2d 964]

8. Hudgens purchased a used car from Mack, a dealer. Mack falsely informed Hudgens that the car was in good condition when, in fact, it needed extensive repairs. Mack also refused to live up to his 30-day guarantee when the car was brought back within a few days after the sale. The day following the sale Mack had assigned the contract to Universal C.I.T. Credit Corp. When Hudgens refused to pay on the contract, he was sued by Universal. Hudgens claimed the right to set aside the contract for fraud. Was he entitled to do so? [Universal C.I.T. Credit Corp. v Hudgens, 234 Ark 668, 356 SW2d 658]

9. Lone Star Life Insurance Company agreed to make a long-term loan to Five Forty Three Land, Inc. whenever requested to do so by that corporation. Five Forty Three wanted this loan in order to pay off its short-term debts. The loan was never made as it was never requested by Five Forty Three. That corporation owed the Exchange Bank & Trust Company on a short-term debt. Exchange Bank then sued Lone Star for breach of its promise on the theory that the Exchange Bank was a third party beneficiary of the contract to make the loan. Was the Exchange Bank correct? [Exchange Bank & Trust Co. v Loan Star Life Ins. Co., (TexCivApp) 546 SW2d 948]

10. The City of New Rochelle Humane Society made a contract with the City of New Rochelle to capture and impound all dogs running at large. Spiegler, a minor, was bitten by some dogs while in the school yard. She sued the School District of New Rochelle and the Humane Society. With respect to the Humane Society, she claimed that she was a third party beneficiary of the contract that the Society had made with the City and could therefore sue it for its failure to capture the dogs by which she had been bitten. Was she entitled to recover? [Spiegler v School District, 39 Misc 2d 946, 242 NYS2d 430]

11. Hardin County entered into a contract with Pettigrew & Finney Contracting Co. to install air conditioning in a building owned by the county. The contractor, with the New Amsterdam Casualty Co., executed a performance bond and a labor and material bond naming the county as obligee. By the labor and material bond, the contractor and its surety promised to pay for all labor and materials used in performing the contract. The contractor then subcontracted all nonelectrical work in the project to T. O. Morris. Morris obtained equipment and materials from Air Temperature, Inc. The latter was not paid and it brought suit against Morris, the contractor, and the surety. Neither the contractor nor the surety had any direct dealings with Air Temperature. At the time when Air Temperature furnished the goods to Morris, Air Temperature did not know that the contractor and the surety had executed bonds and Air Temperature had not acted in reliance on the existence of any bonds. Were the contractor and the surety liable to Air Temperature? [Air Temperature Inc. v Morris, (Tenn App) 469 SW2d 495]

12. A purchased B's business. A orally agreed to pay the business debts of B. C had sold goods to B for B's store but had not been paid. C sued A. A raised the defense that he was not liable because there was no writing for his promise to pay B's debt and the statute of frauds made an oral promise to pay the debt of another unenforceable. Was this a valid defense? [Campbell v Hickory Farms of Ohio, 258 SC 563, 190 SE2d 26]

13. Tennefos Construction Company did highway construction work for the North Dakota Highway Department. Alexander supplied them with fill for the construction. Alexander owed money to Rheault who supplied him with oil and fuel. Rheault would not supply Alexander further unless payment of his debts was guaranteed. It was finally agreed that when Tennefos paid for the fill, the checks would be made payable to the order of Rheault and Alexander. Was there an assignment to Rheault? [Rheault v Tennefos Constr. Co., (ND) 189 NW2d 626]

14. A buyer purchased goods on credit from a seller. Unknown to the buyer, the seller assigned to a finance company his rights to the purchase price. Thereafter the buyer, without knowledge of the assignment, returned the goods to the seller who accepted them and cancelled the buyer's debt. The finance company sued the buyer for the purchase price which had been assigned to it and claimed that it was not bound by the act of the seller. Was the finance company entitled to recover the purchase price from the buyer? [Peoples Finance & Thrift Co. v Landes, 28 Utah 2d 392, 503 P2d 444]

15. A buyer made a contract with a farmer to buy the next crop of cotton which the farmer would grow. The buyer then assigned his rights under this contract. The farmer objected that the buyer could not assign the contract because it called for personal services. Was this objection valid? [Mitchell-Huntley Cotton Co. v Waldrep, (DC Ala) 377 FSupp 1215]

18 Discharge of Contracts

When two parties enter into a binding agreement, does the contract run on forever? If it does not, when does it end? Generally, a contract may be discharged by performance, mutual agreement of the parties, impossibility of performance, operation of law, or acceptance of breach.

§ 18:1. Discharge by Performance. A contract is usually discharged by the performance of the terms of the agreement. In most cases, the parties perform their promises and the contract ceases to exist or is thereby discharged.

§ 18:2. Nature of Performance.

(a) **Payment.** When payment is required by the contract, performance consists of the payment of money or, if accepted by the other party, the delivery of property or the rendering of services.

Payment by commercial paper, such as a check, is ordinarily a conditional payment. A check merely suspends the debt until the check is presented for payment. If payment is then made, the debt is discharged; if not paid, the suspension terminates and suit may be brought on either the debt or the check.[1]

(1) Application of Payments. If a debtor owes more than one debt to the creditor and pays money, a question may arise as to which debt has been paid. If the debtor specifies the debt to which the payment is to be applied and the creditor accepts the money, the creditor is bound to apply the money as specified. Thus, if the debtor specifies that a payment is to be made for a current purchase, the creditor may not apply the payment to an older balance.

If the debtor does not specify the application to be made, the creditor has the choice of deciding to which debt the payment should be applied. As between secured and unsecured claims, the creditor is free to apply the payment to the unsecured claim. The creditor, however, must apply the payment to a debt that is due as contrasted with one which is not yet due. The creditor cannot apply a payment to a claim that is illegal or invalid; but may apply the payment to a claim which cannot be enforced because it is barred by the statute of limitations and, according to some authorities, to a claim that cannot be enforced for lack of a writing required by the statute of frauds.

---

[1] Uniform Commercial Code § 3-802(1)(b).

(2) *No Application Specified.* If neither the debtor nor the creditor has made any application of the payment, application will be made by the court. There is a division of authority, however, whether the court is to make such application as will be more favorable to the creditor or the debtor. In some instances, the court will apply the payment to the oldest outstanding debt. Consumer protection statutes commonly require such application to the oldest debt.

(b)   Tender of Performance. An offer to perform is known as a *tender.* If performance requires the doing of an act, a tender that is refused will discharge the party offering to perform. If performance requires the payment of a debt, however, a tender that is refused does not discharge the debt. But it stops the running of interest charges and prevents the collection of court costs if the party is sued, providing the tender is kept open and the money is produced in court.

A *valid tender of payment* consists of an unconditional offer of the exact amount due on the date when due or an amount from which the creditor may take what is due without the necessity of making change. The debtor must offer *legal tender* or, in other words, such form of money as the law recognizes as lawful money and declares to be legal tender for the payment of debts. The offer of a check is not a valid tender of payment as a check is not legal tender even when it is certified. A tender of part of the debt is not a valid tender and has no legal effect unless the creditor accepts it. In addition to the amount owed, the debtor must tender all accrued interest and any costs to which the creditor is entitled. If the debtor tenders less than the amount due, the creditor may refuse the offer without affecting the right to collect the amount which is due. If the creditor accepts the smaller amount, the question arises whether it has been accepted as payment on account or as full payment of the balance which was due.

§ 18:3. Time of Performance. When the date or period of time for performance is specified in the contract, performance should be made on that date or within that time period. (See p. 278, Creasy v Tincher)

(a)   When Time Is Essential. If performance of the contract on or within the exact time specified is vital, it is said that "time is of the essence." Time is of the essence when the contract relates to property that is perishable or that is fluctuating rapidly in value.[2]

An express statement in the contract that time is of the essence is not controlling. When it is obvious that time is not important, such a statement will be ignored by the courts. It is the nature of the subject matter of the contract and the surrounding circumstances rather than the declaration of the parties which control. Time may be made essential in a repair contract by imposing a time limitation on performance. For example, where a sign contractor was obligated to repair any damage to the sign within 24 normal working hours after notice of damage, time was of the essence for the making of repairs.

(b)   When Time Is Not Essential. Ordinarily, time is not of the essence, and performance within a reasonable time is sufficient.

In the case of the sale of property, time will not be regarded as of the essence when there has not been any appreciable change in the market value or condition

[2] Mercury Gas & Oil Corp. v Rincon Oil & Gas Corp. 79 N Mex 537, 445 P2d 958.

of the property and when the person who delayed does not appear to have done so for the purpose of speculating on a change in market price.[3]

A provision in a contract that time is of the essence will be ignored when the complaining party does not prove that harm was caused by the delay. (See p. 278, Lane v Crescent Beach Lodge & Resort)

(c) Conditional Time. In some contracts, the time of performance is conditional, that is, it depends upon the happening of a particular event, the failure of a certain event to happen, or the existence of a certain fact. If the condition is not fulfilled, the promisor has no obligation to perform. To illustrate, a fire insurance policy does not impose any duty for performance on the insurance company until there has been a fire loss within the coverage of the contract. Thus, if there is no fire loss there will be no performance by the company during the life of the contract.

(d) No Time Specified. When the time for performance is not specified in the contract, an obligation to perform within a reasonable time will be implied. (See p. 280, Robinson v Commercial Contractors, Inc.) The fact that no time is stated does not impair the contract on the ground that it is indefinite nor does it allow an endless time in which to perform.

§ 18:4. Adequacy of Performance.
When a party renders exactly the performance called for by the contract, no question arises as to whether the contract has been performed. In other cases, there may not have been a perfect performance or a question arises as to whether the performance made satisfies the standard set by the contract.

(a) Substantial Performance. Perfect performance of a contract is not required. A party who in good faith has substantially performed the contract may sue to recover the payment specified in the contract. However, because the performance was not perfect, the performing party is subject to a counterclaim for the damages caused the other party because the performance was not perfect.

This rule of *substantial performance* applies only when departures from the contract or the defects were not made willfully.[4] A contractor who willfully makes a substantial departure from the contract is in default and cannot recover any payment from the other party to the contract. In large construction contracts when the total value of the partial performance is large compared to the damages sustained through incomplete or imperfect performance, the courts tend to ignore whether or not the breach was intentional on the part of the contractor.

In any case, the rule of substantial performance will not be applied unless the contractor has performed enough of the contract so that the subject matter of the contract may be used for its intended purpose.

(b) Satisfaction of Promisee or Third Person. When the agreement requires that the promisor perform an act to the satisfaction, taste, or judgment of the other party on the contract, the courts are divided as to whether the promisor must so perform as to satisfy the promisee or whether it is sufficient that the performance be such as would satisfy a reasonable person under the circumstances. When personal taste is an important element, the courts generally hold that the performance is not sufficient unless the promisee is actually satisfied, although in some instances it is insisted

[3] Cline v Hullum (Okla) 435 P2d 152.
[4] Lautenbach v Meredith, 240 Iowa 166, 35 SW2d 335.

that the dissatisfaction be shown to be in good faith and not merely to avoid paying for the work that has been done.[5] The personal satisfaction of the promisee is generally required under this rule when one promises to make clothes or to paint a portrait to the satisfaction of the other party.

There is a similar division of authority when the subject matter involves the fitness or mechanical utility of the property. With respect to things mechanical and to routine performances, however, the courts are more likely to hold that the promisor has satisfactorily performed if a reasonable person should be satisfied with what was done.

When a building contract requires the contractor to perform the contract to the "satisfaction" of the owner, the owner generally is required to pay if a reasonable person would be satisfied with the work of the contractor.

Similarly, when a building owner makes a contract for painting and paperhanging, and the contract specifies that "work will be completed in the best workmanship manner by union skillful craftsmen," the work is properly performed when it conforms to the standards specified and the owner cannot avoid liability on the ground of not being personally satisfied with the work.

When performance is to be approved by a third person, the tendency is to apply the reasonable-person test of satisfaction, especially when the third person has wrongfully withheld approval or has become incapacitated.

When work is to be done subject to the approval of an architect, engineer, or other expert, the determination of that expert is ordinarily final and binding upon the parties in the absence of fraud.

§ 18:5. Guarantee of Performance. It is common for an obligor to guarantee the performance. Thus, a builder may guarantee for one year that the work will be satisfactory.

The guarantee may be made by a third person. Thus, a surety company may guarantee to the owner that a contractor will perform the contract. In such case, it is clear that the obligation of the surety is in addition to the liability of the contractor and does not take the place of such liability.

§ 18:6. Consumer Protection Rescission. Contrary to the basic principle of contract law that a contract between competent persons is a binding obligation, consumer protection legislation is introducing into the law a new concept of giving the consumer a chance to think things over and to rescind the contract. Thus the federal Consumer Credit Protection Act (CCPA) gives a debtor the right to rescind a credit transaction within three days when the transaction would impose a lien upon the debtor's home.[6]

---

[5] Commercial Mortgage & Finance Corp. v Greenwich Savings Bank, 112 GaApp 388, 145 SE2d 249; American Oil Co. v Carey (DC ED Mich) 246 FSupp 773.

[6] The buyer is given until midnight of the third full business day following the making of the contract in which to rescind. Consumer Credit Protection Act § 125; 15 United States Code § 1635(a), (e), although it would appear that this section has been to a large extent canceled by the regulation of the Federal Reserve Board permitting the debtor to waive his right of rescission. Regulation Z, § 226.9(e), 12 CFR 226. Likewise the statute does not permit a home buyer to avoid a lien created in financing a purchase. If the creditor does not inform the debtor of the right to rescind at the time of the transaction or make the other disclosures required by federal law, the time within which the debtor may rescind is extended until such disclosures are made. § 226.9(a).

A Federal Trade Commission Regulation gives the buyer three days in which to avoid a home-solicited sale of goods or services costing more than $25.00.[7]

§ 18:7. Discharge by Agreement.
A contract may be terminated by the operation of one of its provisions or by a subsequent agreement.

(a) Provision of Original Contract. The contract may provide that it shall terminate upon the happening of a certain event, such as the destruction of a particular building, or upon the existence of a certain fact, even though the intended performance by one or both parties has not been completed. The contract may specify that one party may terminate the contract upon giving notice to the other. A notice to terminate must be clear and definite.

When a contract provides for a continuing performance but does not specify how long it shall continue, it is terminable at the will of either party, with the same consequences as though it had expressly authorized termination upon notice.

(b) Rescission by Agreement. The parties to a contact may agree to undo the contract by returning any property or money that had been delivered or paid. It is said that they agree to rescind the contract or that there is a *mutual rescission.* Ordinarily no formality is required for rescission; and an oral rescission, or conduct evidencing such an intent, may terminate a written contract. An oral rescission is not effective, however, in the case of a sale of an interest in land; for, in such a case, the purpose of the rescission is to retransfer the interest in land. Accordingly, the retransfer or rescission must satisfy the same formalities of the statute of frauds as are applied to an original transfer.

A mutual rescission works a final discharge of the contract in the absence of an express provision in the rescission agreement providing for the later revival of the original contract. Consequently, when there is a mutual rescission of a sales contract following a fire which destroyed the seller's factory, the contract is not revived by the subsequent rebuilding of the factory.[8]

If an agreement is voidable because of the fraud of one of the parties, the aggrieved or complaining party may obtain a decree from the court rescinding the contract. This is distinct, however, from rescission based on the agreement of the parties.

(c) Waiver. A term of contract is discharged by *waiver* when one party fails to demand performance by the other party or to object when the other party fails to perform according to the terms of the contract. Unlike rescission, a waiver does not return the parties to their original positions; it leaves the parties where they are at the time.

(d) Substitution. The parties may decide that their contract is not the one they want. They may then replace it with another contract. If they do so, the original contract is discharged by substitution.

It is not necessary that the parties expressly state that they are making a substitution. Whenever they make a new contract that is clearly inconsistent with a former

---

[7] 16 CFR § 429.1. This displaces state laws making similar provision for rescission, such as UCCC § 2.502.

[8] Goddard v Ishikawajima-Harima Heavy Industries Co. 27 Misc2d 863, 287 NYS2d 901.

contract, the court will conclude that the earlier contract has been superseded by the later. Since the new contract must in itself be a binding agreement, it must be supported by consideration. The agreement modifying the original contract may be expressed in words or by conduct, but in any event, it is essential that an agreement to modify be found.

(e)   **Novation.** In a novation, as explained in Chapter 17, the original contract is discharged by the new contract. When a party's liability under a contract is discharged by a novation, that party cannot thereafter sue to enforce a contract or to recover damages for its breach.

(f)   **Accord and Satisfaction.** In lieu of the performance of an obligation specified by a contract, the parties may agree to a different performance. Such an agreement is called an *accord.* When the accord is performed or executed, there is an *accord and satisfaction,* which discharges the original obligation. An accord is not binding until the satisfaction is made. When an accord specifies that payment shall be made of a specific amount, either party may revoke the accord before the payment has been made.

(g)   **Release.** A person who has a contract claim or any other kind of claim against another may agree to give up or release the claim. This may be done by delivering a writing which states that the claim is released. If supported by consideration, or if it comes within a statutory or common-law exception to the requirement of consideration, the release is effective to discharge the obligor from the contract obligation. If there are joint obligors, a release which is effective to release one obligor will also discharge the other joint obligor. To avoid this result, a releasor will often execute a written promise not to sue the adverse party. Such a *covenant not to sue* is binding and bars suit against the released party but does not bar the one who makes the covenant from suing other persons.

Ordinarily there will be a preliminary agreement to deliver a written release or covenant not to sue for which payment will be made. Generally the preliminary agreement is not a binding contract because it is contemplated that the obligee shall not be bound until the writing has been delivered and payment has been made.

§ 18:8. Discharge by Impossibility.
Impossibility of performance refers to external or extrinsic conditions as contrasted with the obligor's personal inability to perform. Thus, the fact that a debtor does not have the money to pay and cannot pay a debt does not present a case of impossibility.

Riots, shortages of materials, and similar factors, even though external, usually do not excuse the promisor from performing a contract. The fact that a seller cannot obtain from any supplier the goods which the seller has already contracted to sell to the buyer does not excuse the seller from liability to the buyer, unless the inability to procure the goods was made a condition subsequent to the sales contract. The fact that it will prove more costly to perform the contract than originally contemplated, or that the obligor has voluntarily gone out of business, does not constitute impossibility which excuses performance. No distinction is made in this connection between the acts of nature, people, or governments.

Frequently this problem is met by a provision of the contract that expressly excuses a contractor or provides for extra compensation in the event of certain unforeseen or changed conditions. A party seeking to claim the benefit of such a clause has the burden of establishing the facts that justify its application.

Interference with the performance of a contract by fire does not excuse performance. Consequently, when a contractor is constructing a building and it is destroyed by fire, the contractor must rebuild the building and cannot obtain extra compensation for the extra work. The fire does not excuse the contractor from performing the contract. Likewise, the inability to obtain a government license or approval is not an "impossibility" which discharges the contract when the necessity of obtaining the license or approval was foreseeable.[9]

When the condition or event that is claimed to have made performance impossible is the result of foreseeable wartime conditions, a party is not excused because of the occurrence of such condition or event. By failing to have made express provision therefor in the contract, the party must be regarded as having assumed that risk.

(a)   Destruction of Particular Subject Matter. When the parties contract expressly for or with reference to a particular subject matter, the contract is discharged if the subject matter is destroyed through no fault of either party. When a contract calls for the sale of a wheat crop growing on a specific parcel of land, the contract is discharged if that crop is destroyed by blight.

On the other hand, if there is merely a contract to sell a given quantity of a specified grade of wheat, the seller is not discharged when the seller's crop is destroyed by blight. The seller had made an unqualified undertaking to deliver wheat of a specified grade. No restrictions or qualifications were imposed as to the source from which the wheat would be obtained. If the seller does not deliver the goods called for by the contract, the contract is broken and the seller is liable for damages.

(b)   Change of Law. A contract is discharged when its performance is made illegal by a subsequent change in the law of the state or country in which the contract is to be performed. Thus, a contract to construct a nonfireproof building at a particular place is discharged by the adoption of a zoning law prohibiting such a building within that area. Mere inconvenience or temporary delay caused by the new law, however, does not excuse performance.

(c)   Death or Disability. When the contract obligates a party to perform an act that requires personal skill or which contemplates a personal relationship with the obligee or some other person, the death or disability of the obligor, obligee, or other person (as the case may be) discharges the contract, as when a newspaper cartoonist dies before the expiration of the contract. If the act called for by the contract can be performed by others or by the promisor's personal representative, however, this rule does not apply.

The death of the person to whom personal services are to be rendered also terminates the contract when the death of that person makes impossible the rendition of the services contemplated. Thus, a contract to employ a person as the musical director for a singer terminates when the singer dies.

---

[9] Nebaco, Inc. v Riverview Realty Co. 87 Nev 55, 482 P2d 305.

When the contract calls for the payment of money, the death of either party does not affect the obligation. If the obligor dies, the obligation is a liability of the obligor's estate. If the obligee dies, the right to collect the debt is an asset of the obligee's estate. The parties to a contract may agree, however, that the death of either the obligee [10] or the obligor shall terminate the debt. In any case, the creditor can obtain insurance on the life of the debtor.

(d) Act of Other Party. There is in every contract "an implied covenant of good faith and fair dealing" in consequence of which a promisee is under an obligation to do nothing that would interfere with performance by the promisor. When the promisee prevents performance or otherwise makes performance impossible, the promisor is discharged from the contract. Thus a subcontractor is discharged from any obligation when unable to do the work because the principal contractor refuses to deliver the material, equipment, or money required by the subcontract. When the default of the other party consists of failing to supply goods or services, the duty may rest upon the party claiming a discharge of the contract to show that substitute goods or services could not be obtained elsewhere, either because they were not reasonably available or were not acceptable under the terms of the contract.

When the conduct of the other contracting party does not make performance impossible but merely causes delay or renders performance more expensive, the contract is not discharged; but the injured party is entitled to damages for the loss incurred.

A promisor is not excused from performing under the contract when it is the act of the promisor which has made performance impossible. Consequently, when a data service contracted with a bank to keypunch all its daily operations and to process the cards, the bank was not excused from its obligation under the contract by the fact that it converted to magnetic tapes and installed its own computers. Accordingly the bank could not ignore its contract. It could only terminate the contract with the data service by giving the notice required by the contract.

§ 18:9. Economic Frustration. In order to protect from the hardship imposed by the strict principles relating to impossibility, some courts excuse performance on the ground of *economic* or *commercial frustration* as distinguished from impossibility. (See p. 281, Howard v Nicholson)

The effect of the economic frustration concept is to substitute "impracticability" for "impossibility," and to regard performance as impracticable, and therefore excused, when it can only be done at an excessive and unreasonable cost. When property is leased in order to use the building for a particular purpose, some courts hold that the lease is discharged when the building burns down, on the theory that the purpose of the lease has been frustrated.[11] The doctrine of frustration will not be applied to protect a party who has taken a calculated risk and lost.

---

[10] Woods v McQueen, 195 Kan 380, 404 P2d 955.
[11] Jones v Fuller-Garvey Corp. (Alaska) 386 P2d 838. In some jurisdictions, this result is reached by statute authorizing the termination of the lease in such a case. At common law the destruction of the building did not discharge the obligation of the tenant.

§ 18:10. Temporary Impossibility. Ordinarily a temporary impossibility has either no effect on the obligation to perform of the party who is affected thereby, or at most suspends the duty to perform so that the obligation to perform is revived upon the termination of the impossibility. If, however, performance at that later date would impose a substantially greater burden upon the obligor, some courts discharge the obligor from the contract.

(a)   Weather. Acts of God, such as tornadoes, lightning, and sudden floods, usually do not terminate a contract even though they make performance difficult or impossible. Thus, weather conditions constitute a risk that is assumed by a contracting party in the absence of a contrary agreement. Consequently, extra expense sustained by a contractor because of weather conditions is a risk which the contractor assumes in the absence of an express provision for additional compensation in such case.

(b)   Weather Clauses. Modern contracts commonly contain a "weather" clause, which either expressly grants an extension for delays caused by weather conditions or expressly denies the right to any extension of time or additional compensation because of weather condition difficulties. Some courts hold that abnormal weather conditions excuse what would otherwise be a breach of contract. Thus, nondelivery of equipment has been excused when the early melting of a frozen river made it impossible to deliver.

§ 18:11. Discharge by Operation of Law. In certain situations the law provides for the discharge of a contract, such as when the contract has been altered, has been destroyed by the obligee, is subject to bankruptcy proceedings, or is barred by a statute of limitations.

(a)   Alteration. A written contract, whether under seal or not, may be discharged by alteration.[12] To have this effect, (1) it must be a *material alteration,* that is, it must change the nature of the obligation; (2) it must be made by a party to the contract, because alterations made by a stranger have no effect; (3) it must be made intentionally, and not through accident or mistake; and (4) it must be made without the consent of the other party to the contract. For example, when one party to an advertising contract, without the consent of the other party, added "at a monthly payment basis," thus making the rate of payment higher, the advertiser was discharged from any duty under the contract.

There is no discharge of the contract by alteration when the term added is one which the law would imply, for in such a case the change is not material.

(b)   Destruction of the Contract. The physical destruction of a written contract may discharge the contract. When the person entitled to performance under a sealed instrument destroys the writing with the intent to terminate the liability of the obligor, the latter's liability is discharged. In any case, the physical destruction of the writing may be evidence of an intention to discharge the obligation by mutual agreement.

(c)   Merger. In some instances, contract rights are merged into or absorbed by a greater right. When an action is brought upon a contract and a judgment is obtained

---

[12] The definition and effect of alteration in the case of commercial paper has been modified by UCC § 3-407.

by the plaintiff against the defendant, the contract claim is merged into the obligation under the judgment.

(d)   Bankruptcy. Most debtors may voluntarily enter into a federal court of bankruptcy or be compelled to do so by creditors. The trustee in bankruptcy then takes possession of the debtor's property and distributes it as far as it will go among the creditors. After this is done, the court grants the debtor a discharge in bankruptcy if it concludes that the debtor has acted honestly and has not attempted to defraud creditors.

Even though all creditors have not been paid in full, the discharge in bankruptcy is a bar to a subsequent enforcement of ordinary contract claims against the debtor. The cause of action or contract claim is not destroyed, but the bankruptcy discharge bars a proceeding to enforce it. As the obligation is not extinguished, the debtor may waive the defense of discharge in bankruptcy by promising later to pay the debt. Such a waiver is governed by state law. In a few states, such a waiver must be in writing.

(e)   Statutes of Limitations. Statutes provide that after a certain number of years have passed a contract claim is barred. Technically, this is merely a bar of the remedy and does not destroy the right or cause of action. A few states hold that the statute bars the right as well as the remedy and that there is accordingly no contract after the lapse of the statutory period.

The time limitation provided by state statutes of limitations vary widely. The period usually differs with the type of contract—ranging from a relatively short time for open accounts (ordinary customers' charge accounts) and other sales of goods, 4 years;[13] to a somewhat longer period for written contracts, usually 5 to 10 years; to a maximum period for judgments of record, usually 10 to 20 years.

> *(1)   Computation of Statutory Period.* The statute of limitations begins to run from the moment that the cause of action of the plaintiff arises, that is, when the plaintiff is first entitled to bring suit. When the party entitled to sue on the contract is under a disability, such as insanity, at the time the cause of action arises, the period of the statute does not begin to run until the disability is removed. When a condition or act prevents the period of the statute of limitations from running, it is said to *toll the running of the statute.*
>
> Statutes of limitations do not run against governments because it is contrary to public policy that the rights of society generally, as represented by the government, should be prejudiced by the failure of the proper governmental officials to take the necessary action to enforce the claims of the government.
>
> *(2)   Waiver of Statute of Limitations.* The defense of a statute of limitations may be waived by the debtor. The waiver must ordinarily be an express promise to pay or such an acknowledgment of the existence of the debt that the law can imply therefrom a promise to pay the debt. In some states, the promise or acknowledgement must be in writing. Part payment of the principal or interest is also regarded as a waiver of the bar of the statute and revives the debt.

---

[13] UCC § 2-725(1).

(f)   Contractual Limitations. Some contracts, particularly insurance contracts, contain a time limitation within which suit may be brought. This is, in effect, a private statute of limitations created by the agreement of the parties.

A contract may also require that notice of any claim be given within a specified time. A party who fails to give notice within the time specified by the contract is barred from suing thereon and the failure to give notice is not excused because it was wrongly believed that there was not any claim about which to give notice. (See p. 282, State Bank of Viroqua v Capitol Indemnity Corp.)

§ 18:12. Discharge by Acceptance of Breach. There is a *breach of contract* whenever one party or both parties fail to perform the contract. A contract is discharged by breach if, when one party breaks the contract, the other party accepts the contract as ended. When a breach occurs, however, the injured party is not required to treat the contract as discharged. Since the contract bound the defaulting party to perform, the injured party may insist on the observance of the contract and resort to legal remedies. An aggrieved party is not held to have accepted the other party's breach as terminating the contract unless notice has been clearly given that the breach was so accepted.

A breach of a part of a divisible contract is not a breach of the entire contract.

A breach does not result in the discharge of a contract if the term broken is not sufficiently important. A term of a contract that does not go to the root of the contract is a *subsidiary term*. When there is a failure to perform such a term, the agreement is not terminated, but the defaulting party may be liable for damages for its breach.

In addition to the effect of a breach as such, the occurrence of a breach also excuses the injured party from rendering a performance if the defaulter's performance was a condition precedent to the duty of the injured party to perform. For example, when a seller is required to deliver goods and the buyer is required to pay upon delivery of the goods, the seller's failure to deliver is a breach of the duty to deliver and also excuses the buyer from paying under the contract because the delivery of the goods was a condition precedent to the duty to pay. There being no delivery, the buyer is not required to pay.

(a)   Renunciation. When a party to a contract declares in advance of the time for performance that the required performance will not be rendered, the other party may (1) ignore this declaration and insist on performance in accordance with the terms of the contract, (2) accept this declaration as an *anticipatory breach* and sue the promisor for damages, or (3) accept the declaration as a breach of the contract and rescind the contract. It is for the injured party to determine what to do when the other party has made a renunciation.

To constitute a renunciation there must be a clear, absolute, unequivocal refusal to perform the contract according to its terms.[14]

(b)   Incapacitating Self. Another form of anticipatory breach occurs when the promisor makes it impossible to perform the obligation. Under such circumstances, the promisee is entitled to treat the contract as discharged. For example, when one party

---

[14] Golf Cars, Inc. v Mid-Pacific Country Club (Hawaii) 493 P2d 1338.

who is bound by the terms of the contract to deliver specific bonds, stocks, or notes to another party transfers them to a third person instead, the promisee may elect to treat the contract as discharged; or may hold the promisor accountable for nonperformance when the time of performance arrives. The same is true when one agrees to sell specific goods to another person and then sells them to a third person in violation of the original contract.

CASES FOR CHAPTER 18

Creasy v Tincher

154 WVa 18, 173 SE2d 332 (1970)

The Tinchers signed a contract to sell land to Creasy. The contract specified that the sales transaction was to be completed in 90 days. At the end of the 90 days, Creasy requested an extension of time. The Tinchers refused to grant an extension and stated that the contract was terminated. Creasy sued the Tinchers to compel specific performance of the agreement. From a judgment for the Tinchers, Creasy appealed.

CAPLAN, J. . . . Paragraph 4 [of the sales agreement] provides: "This sale shall be completed and all necessary papers executed and delivered within *90 days* from the date of acceptance hereof by Seller, which date is set forth on the reverse side hereof."

The Tinchers accepted the plaintiff's offer by executing the agreement on August 10, 1966. Thereafter, the plaintiff employed an attorney, Walton Shepherd, to examine the title of the subject real estate. As a result of his examination Mrs. Creasy was advised that one-half of the minerals under one of the tracts had been acquired by the Tinchers by a tax deed and that some corrective action should be taken to clear any cloud that might be created by such deed. On a later occasion, Mr. Shepherd referred to this matter as a "minor" defect in the title.

Mrs. Creasy testified that upon learning of the tax deed she related this matter to Mr. Burgess who indicated that he would discuss it with the Tinchers' attorney. Mr. Burgess testified that he was unable to contact their attorney during the ninety-day period referred to in the contract. Nothing further was done by the parties. . . .

. . . The time expressed in the agreement in which the contract shall be consummated is of the

essence of the agreement. The language used is clear and unequivocal. It provides that the sale shall be completed within ninety days from the date of acceptance by the seller. [A] contract need not include the words "time is of the essence." In determining this question the general rules of construction are applied. . . . If the language is clear and unambiguous it is to be applied. . . . Here, we believe, the language clearly shows the intention of the parties. . . .

The plaintiff, although denying that time was of the essence of the agreement, says that her failure to perform within the ninety-day period was prompted by the refusal of the sellers to offer her a good and marketable title as provided in the agreement. She asserts that she was thereby relieved of any obligation to have acted within the prescribed period. Thus, we are presented with the question of whether the plaintiff, in these circumstances, is entitled to an order requiring the defendants to specifically perform under the agreement.

Pertinent to the resolution of this question is Paragraph 8 of the agreement which reads: "Seller will, upon tender of the unpaid balance of the purchase price, convey the said property to purchaser by apt and proper deed. . . ." This provision makes it incumbent upon the buyer, the plaintiff, to make a tender of the unpaid balance of the purchase price before the seller is obligated to deliver the deed. This she did not do, either during or after the ninety-day period. . . .

[Judgment affirmed]

Lane v Crescent Beach Lodge & Resort

(Iowa) 199 NW2d 78 (1972)

Lane sold a resort to the Crescent Beach Lodge & Resort, Inc. on the installment plan. The

contract required Crescent to keep the property insured and specified that the payment of the premiums when due was of the essence. Crescent did not pay the premiums when due but the insurance company extended credit to Crescent and kept the policies in force. Lane sued Crescent to cancel the installment sale contract on the ground that Crescent had breached the contract by failing to pay the insurance on time and that time was of the essence. From a judgment for Lane, Crescent appealed.

MCCORMICK, J. [The sales contract provided:]

"Sellers agree to carry existing insurance until date of possession; thereafter, until final settlement. Buyer agrees to keep the improvements upon said premises insured against loss by fire, tornado, and extended coverage for a sum not less than the balance owing under this contract, with insurance payable to Sellers and Buyer as their interests may appear, and to deliver policies therefor to Sellers. If Buyer fails to perform this agreement in any respect, time being of the essence of this agreement, then Sellers may forfeit this contract as provided by Chapter 656 of the Iowa Code, and all payments made and improvements made on said premises shall be forfeited, it being understood, however, that the Buyer shall have ninety days after said notice of forfeiture to correct any deficiencies or delinquencies; or Sellers may declare the full balance owing due and payable and proceed by suit at law or in equity to foreclose this contract, in which event Buyer agrees to pay costs and attorney fees and any other expense incurred by Sellers."

The parties agree the corporation met its contract obligations prior to October 1969. All payments including $135,250 in reduction in principal had been made. In addition close to $50,000 in improvements had been added. There was a tornado loss in 1968 resulting in $34,000 insurance recovery used to repair damage.

The five casualty insurance policies on the property were underwritten by the Reimers Insurance Agency, a corporation, of Spencer. The broker could and did extend credit to defendant. The total of $6497 in premiums was not paid when billed in 1969.

Richard Reimers, owner of the Reimers agency, told Joseph C. West, defendant's president and resort manager, in December, 1969 that defendant had to pay the premiums because he could not afford to remit to the insurers from his own pocket. Mr. West promised to make every effort to make

at least partial payment and to get in touch with him soon. Mr. Reimers agreed to that. His agency borrowed from a bank and paid the insurers.

The insurers would not cancel the policies unless requested to do so by Mr. Reimers. He made no such request, had not even discussed it with Mr. West, nor was he then planning cancellation.

Lane learned the premiums had not been paid from conversation with a member of the Reimers agency. He quickly confirmed this with Mr. Reimers, made no effort to contact defendant, and paid Mr. Reimers $3497 in cash. He also gave a $3000 90-day six percent note to Mr. Reimers individually. The note was paid shortly after due and proceeds credited to the premium account on May 12, 1970.

Mr. West had held a stockholders' meeting in an unsuccessful effort to raise money for the premiums. Sometime before January 20, 1970, he had told defendant's lawyer he could not pay it, and the lawyer told plaintiff's lawyer the premium had not been paid and he might as well commence legal proceedings.

On January 22, 1970, plaintiffs caused a standard notice of forfeiture of real estate contract to be served on defendant alleging as its sole basis: "The premium on the fire, tornado, and extended coverage insurance which was due December 31, 1969, has not been paid. $6497.00"

The crucial question is whether the contract was breached by defendant's failure to pay the insurance premiums when due. If it was, forfeiture was properly carried out. If it was not, the first attempted forfeiture was void.

There is no dispute the premises were insured to the extent required by the contract at the time Mr. Lane stepped in and paid the premiums. The contract did not expressly obligate defendant to pay the insurance premiums when due. However, plaintiffs argue it made time of the essence and failure to pay the premiums on time was failure to keep the premises insured within the meaning of the contract.

Plaintiffs have the burden of proving the existence of facts which entitle them to forfeiture under the terms of the contract. They base their forfeiture claim upon reading into the contract a requirement that insurance premiums be paid when due with time of the essence. However, "It is well settled that forfeitures by implication or by construction, not compelled by express requirements, are regarded with disfavor, and that contracts involving a forfeiture cannot be extended beyond the strict and literal meaning of the words used. Since forfeitures are not favored . . . provisions for forfeitures are to receive, where the intent is doubtful, a strict construction against those for whose benefit they are introduced. Courts are reluctant to declare and enforce a forfeiture if by reasonable construction it can be avoided. Forfeitures are enforced only where there is the clearest evidence that that was what was meant by the stipulation of the parties. . . ."

Defendant was contractually obliged to purchase the insurance it promised to maintain. Presumably the insurance would have a price which defendant was bound to pay.

But was time of such payment of the essence in the real estate contract? We cannot stretch the implication that far. The timeliness of premium payments would not necessarily affect the covenant to keep the improvements insured. In addition, the timing of such payments was clearly left open to whatever bargain might be negotiated between defendant and the insurer. There is no implied contractual term prohibiting defendant from accepting credit in purchasing insurance. Credit was extended here. Time was not of the essence in the insurance contracts and there is no basis for saying the real estate contract made it so.

In this case cancellation of the insurance had not even been discussed, much less threatened.

[Judgment reversed and action remanded]

Robinson v Commercial Contractors, Inc.

6 Conn Cir 393, 274 A2d 160 (1970)

The Olin Mathieson Company hired commercial contractors to demolish a building. Robinson made a contract with Commercial to purchase the brick from the demolished building. No specific time for the removal of the brick by Robinson was stated. Commercial bulldozed a large quantity of the brick into the basement in order to fill the excavation. Robinson sued Commercial for breach of contract for not giving him sufficient time in which to remove the brick. Judgment was entered for Robinson and Commercial appealed.

CASALE, J. . . . The trial court reached the following conclusions: The parties entered into a contract for the acquisition by the plaintiff of 150 to 200 loads of brick for $4000. No completion date was agreed on by the parties. A reasonable period

of time was necessary to allow the plaintiff to remove the purchased brick from the demolition site. The plaintiff was denied the opportunity of removing the brick purchased. The defendant used much of the brick contracted for to fill the basement, at a great saving to the defendant. The contract was broken by the defendant.

. . . The only conclusion . . . pursued in argument is the conclusion that the plaintiff was denied a reasonable time by the defendant to remove more brick from the demolition site. . . .

It has long been settled law that where no time is specified for the fulfilment of a contract it must be carried out within a reasonable time. . . . The next question is, what constitutes reasonable time?

What is a reasonable time is usually a question of fact under all the circumstances. . . . "What constitutes a reasonable time within which an act is to be performed where a contract is silent upon the subject depends on the subject matter of the contract, the situation of the parties, their intention and what they contemplated at the time the contract was made, and the circumstances attending the performance.". . .

. . . The defendant argues that the plaintiff had approximately sixty days to remove brick from the demolition site and that that period constituted a reasonable time for him to have removed all the brick to which he was entitled. The finding states the plaintiff removed brick from October, 1964, to late December, 1964; on the whole record, it is questionable whether he did in fact have sixty days. Whatever the number of days, however, there is nothing in the finding indicating how many days in that period there was brick on the ground available for removal by the plaintiff; nor is there anything in the finding indicating how many days were unsuitable for brick removal because of weather conditions. The defendant was in charge of the demolition of the building. The progress of the demolition work could determine to a large extent when and in what quantity brick would be available on the ground for removal by the plaintiff.

The subordinate facts found by the trial court indicate that the defendant refused the plaintiff brick; that the defendant had bulldozed good brick into the basement and had used brick for fill purposes; that the plaintiff had complained to the defendant about the lack of brick; and that he was unable to take more than twenty-five loads "because of the action of the defendant."

The trial court was justified in the conclusion that the plaintiff was denied reasonable time to remove the purchased brick from the demolition site. . . .

[Judgment affirmed]

Howard v Nicholson

(MoApp) 556 SW2d 477 (1977)

Nicholson made a contract with Howard to construct a building to meet the specifications of the tenant to whom the building would be rented. The tenant was Honey's International and the building was designed as a bridal salon and could not be used for any other purpose. Honey's went into bankruptcy. When Nicholson found that he had no tenant, he cancelled the construction contract. Howard then sued him for breach of contract. Nicholson claimed that the contract was discharged because of commercial frustration based on the bankruptcy of Honey's. From a judgment in favor of Nicholson, Howard appealed.

McMILLIAN, P. J. . . . Appellant's first argument challenges the validity of the trial court's findings that this was the proper situation for the application of the doctrine of commercial frustration to excuse respondents from performance. Appellant argues that the appropriate rule in Missouri is the doctrine of impossibility of performance: if a party, by his contract, obligates himself to a performance which is possible to be performed, he must make it good unless his performance is rendered impossible by an Act of God, the law, or the other party.

The applicability of the doctrine of commercial frustration presents a question of first impression in Missouri. The doctrine has been followed in other states and in the federal courts . . . and has been applied in the United States in a variety of circumstances, *e.g., Marks Realty Co. v Hotel Hermitage Co.,* 170 App.Div. 484, 156 N.Y.S. 179 (1915) (cancellation of yacht races by war excused nonperformance of advertising contract). Under the doctrine, if the happening of an event not foreseen by the parties and not caused by or under the control of either party has destroyed or nearly destroyed either the value of the performance or the object or purpose of the contract, then the parties are excused from further performance. The doctrine of commercial frustration is close to but distinct from the doctrine of impossibility of performance. Both concern the

effect of supervening circumstances upon the rights and duties of the parties but in cases of commercial frustration "Performance remains possible but the expected value of performance to the party seeking to be excused has been destroyed by a fortuitous event, which supervenes to cause an actual but not literal failure of consideration.". . .

"Where parties enter into a contract on the assumption that some particular thing essential to its performance will continue to exist and be available for the purpose and neither agrees to be responsible for its continued existence and availability, the contract must be regarded as subject to an implied condition that if, without the fault of either party, the particular thing ceases to exist or be available for the purpose, the contract shall be dissolved and the parties excused from performing.". . .

Cases and commentators have approached the doctrine of commercial frustration as the problem of "allocating, in the most generally satisfactory way, the risks of harm and disappointment that result from supervening events. . . . The problem in commercial frustration cases [is] "whether an unanticipated circumstance, the risk of which should not be fairly thrown on the promisor, has made performance vitally different from what was reasonably to be expected.". . . If the event was reasonably foreseeable then the parties should have provided for its occurrence in the contract and its absence indicates an assumption of risk by the promisor.

Courts consider the relation of the parties, the terms of the contract and the circumstances surrounding its formation in determining whether the supervening event was reasonably foreseeable. In *Berline v Waldschmidt,* 159 Kan. 585, 156 P.2d 865 (1945), the court found certain wartime regulations to be reasonably foreseeable by the parties and therefore capable of being covered by the terms of the contract. In *North American Capital Corp. v McCants,* 510 S.W.2d 901 (Tenn. 1974), the court held the failure of government agency officials to approve the site for a proposed savings and loan association as required was reasonably foreseeable and that therefore the defence of commercial frustration was not applicable in an action for rent due.

The doctrine of commercial frustration, like that of impossibility of performance, grew out of the demands of the commercial world to excuse performance in cases of extreme hardship. Sound public policy, while requiring that the doctrine be limited in its application so as to preserve the certainty of contract requires the law to be flexible and equitable in situations where unexpected contingencies operate to make performance valueless and the allocation of contractual risks capricious or fortuitous.

In this case the proposed building could have been built. But in view of the findings by the trial court that the building had been specifically designed for use as a bridal salon by Honey's and for the sale of bridal fashions and accessories and that it was not suited for other uses, the value of the building as such was destroyed by the supervening circumstance of the bankruptcy of Honey's, the proposed tenant. In addition, appellant was at all times aware of respondents' ultimate purpose in purchasing the property and in construction of the building, its use as a Honey's Bridal Salon. In fact, there was some evidence that appellant, interested in construction of Honey's Bridal Salons in this area, had gone to Chicago several times to meet with representatives of Honey's before he ever met the respondents and had obtained plans and specifications directly from Honey's. Both parties to the construction contract contemplated construction of a building to be used as a Honey's Bridal Salon.

The other factor to consider in the application of commercial frustration as an excuse of performance is the foreseeability of the supervening event—was the bankruptcy of Honey's a reasonably foreseeable event that should have been provided for in the construction contract? While the possibility of bankruptcy of businesses in general is a foreseeable and all-too-frequent occurrence, the future bankruptcy of a particular company, the continuing existence of which was essential to complete the entire transaction, was not reasonably within the contemplation of the parties at the time of contracting such that the parties would have made provision for such an event. The bankruptcy of Honey's was a fortuitous and unexpected supervening event over which neither party had any control. . . . The doctrine of commercial frustration "reads into" a contract an implied condition that Honey's would be able to rent the proposed building and use it as a bridal salon. The bankruptcy of Honey's effectively destroyed the value of the building which was suitable only for such use and excused performance by respondents.

In this case it is not inequitable to maintain that appellant had assumed part of the risk in the contract in light of appellant's active participation and knowledge of the entire transaction. Appellant was aware that the construction of the proposed building was for one purpose only, the long-term

lease by Honey's and operation as a bridal salon. Inasmuch as the bankruptcy of Honey's made this objective unattainable and destroyed the value of the performance of the contract, the doctrine of commercial frustration will operate to excuse further performance under the contract. . . .

[Judgment affirmed]

State Bank of Viroqua v Capitol Indemnity Corp.

61 Wis 2d 699, 214 NW2d 42 (1974)

The State Bank of Viroqua obtained a bankers blanket bond from the Capitol Indemnity Corporation to protect it from loss by forgery. The bond required that the bank give the insurer notice of any loss at "the earliest practicable moment." DeLap borrowed money from the bank by means of paper on which he forged the name of Mellem. This was learned in October 1969. In October 1970 an agent of Capitol was discussing the bond with the bank. The bank then realized for the first time that the bond covered the DeLap forgery loss. Fifteen days later the bank notified Capitol of that claim. Capitol denied liability because of the delay. The bank sued Capitol. From a judgment in favor of Capitol, the bank appealed.

HALLOWS, C.J. . . . The trial court held the giving of notice 15 months after discovery of the forgery was too late as a matter of law and constituted noncompliance with the contract unless excusable. . . .

The bank claims error on the theory that the language in the bond requiring notice to be given at "the earliest practicable moment" means within a reasonable time under all the circumstances and such circumstances in this case consist of the uncertainty of coverage, the lack of a forfeiture clause and the lack of prejudice to Capitol Indemnity because of the delay.

. . . Most courts have regarded the notice of loss provision as a condition precedent even though the contract does not expressly say so or contain a forfeiture clause and have held that noncompliance will defeat recovery on the bond. The rationale behind the majority rule is to give the earliest opportunity to the surety to investigate, minimize and recoup losses while the time is ripe for such purpose, and to give the surety a reasonable opportunity to protect its rights. Under this view, the failure to comply with the condition precedent to liability vitiates the insured's claim regardless of whether or not prejudice to the surety resulted from the delay or the relative carelessness of the insured in giving notice or the insured's ignorance of coverage under the bond.

     . . . We hold that where the giving of timely notice is required by the Bankers Blanket Bond prior to the maturity of the liability of the insurer, such requirement is a condition precedent in fact to liability whether or not expressly so stated and is to be enforced as written whether or not its importance is emphasized by further language that noncompliance works a forfeiture or voids the policy.

     Ignorance of policy provisions or a belief that coverage is questionable is no excuse for failure to give notice of loss under the Bankers Blanket Bond.

In case of questionable coverage, notice of loss to the insurance company would start the investigative process in motion and resolve the uncertainty of coverage. As for ignorance of coverage, a bank should know its business and the ordinary terms of standard insurance contracts applying to banking business. The existence of such ignorance on the part of a bank would seem to be inexcusable and unreasonable.

     The fact that Capitol Indemnity was not prejudiced is irrelevant. The contract language requiring timely notice of loss is designed to prevent prejudice or harm to the insurer. It is a fact of life in the insurance field that a timely notice of loss is important. It is a notice of loss that starts the investigation by the insurance company while the evidence is fresh and gatherable. Insurers are entitled to contract for this protection.

     [Judgment affirmed]

QUESTIONS AND CASE PROBLEMS

1. What social forces are affected by the doctrine of economic frustration?

2. Compare (a) the principle that time is generally not of the essence, with (b) the right of a construction contractor to recover for a substantial performance of the contract.

3. Compare (a) an accidental destruction of a written contract with (b) a discharge of a contract by destruction.

4. The death of a third person who is not a party to a contract does not discharge the contract. Appraise this statement.

5. Maze purchased 50 shares of stock in the Union Savings Bank, but he did not pay the full purchase price. Maze was later discharged in bankruptcy. Thereafter he was sued for the balance of the purchase price due. Decide. [Burke v Maze, 10 Cal App 206, 101 P 438]

6. The Powers entered into a home improvement contract with Sims and Levin. The contract declared that the amount due was a lien on the home of the Powers and that they had two days in which to cancel the contract if they changed their mind. Was this cancellation provision valid? [Powers v Sims and Levin (CA4Va) 542 F2d 1216]

7. Hertz Commercial Leasing Corporation sued Phillips on a leasing contract. The contract was signed "Phillips Ceramic Tile Installation & Boziz Tile Co. of Georgia, Bobby James Phillips Pres." and "Bobby James Phillips—as an individual." Phillips claimed that he was not personally liable on the theory that the words "as an individual" had been added by the plaintiff after the contract had been signed by Phillips and that such addition was an alteration that discharged the contract. Was the contract discharged by alteration? [Phillips v Hertz Commercial Leasing Corp., 138 GaApp 441, 226 SE2d 287]

8. Warren and Geraldine Bates, husband and wife, were about to be divorced. They made a written agreement that Warren would pay Geraldine $50 a month until their younger child attained the age of 18 years and that in consideration thereof Geraldine released Warren from all property claims. The agreement did not say that it was binding upon

Warren's estate. Upon his death it was claimed by his second wife that the obligation to make the monthly payments terminated with his death. Decide. [Hutchings v Bates, (Tex Civ App) 393 SW2d 338]

9. Brown loaned money to Halvorson, a relative, with the understanding that if Brown should die before the money was repaid, the loan was canceled. The loan was not paid by the time Brown died and Fabre, the executor of the estate of Brown, sued Halvorson for the amount of the debt. Was he entitled to recover? [Fabre v Halvorson, 250 Ore 238, 441 P2d 640]

10. Dickson contracted to build a house for Moran. When it was approximately 25-40% completed, Moran would not let Dickson work any further because he was not following the building plans and specifications and there were many defects. Moran hired another contractor to correct the defects and finish the building. Dickson sued Moran for breach of contract, claiming that he had substantially performed the contract up to the point when he had been discharged. Was Dickson correct? [Dickson v Moran, (LaApp) 344 So2d 102]

11. A contractor was engaged in open-air sandblasting. The sand caused damage to machinery on neighboring land. A court injunction was obtained against the contractor requiring him to take precautions to prevent such damage. He claimed that it was impossible for him to perform his contract for sandblasting and that he was discharged from his obligation. Was he correct? [Savage v Kiewit, 249 Ore 147, 432 P2d 519]

12. Claterbaugh was the owner and president of the Madison Park Appliance and Furniture, Inc. Acting in his individual capacity and without naming Madison Park or indicating that he was acting as its agent, Claterbaugh borrowed money from Hayes. A few days later Claterbaugh made another loan from Hayes in the same manner and gave Hayes a promissory note of the corporation for the total of both loans. Later a payment was made on the loans by a money order in the name of Madison Park. Later, when Hayes sued Claterbaugh for the loans, the latter claimed that there had been a novation by which the corporation was substituted in his place. Was he correct? [Hayes v Claterbaugh, (LaApp) 140 So2d 737]

13. *A* leased a trailer park to *B*. At the time, sewage was disposed of by a septic tank system which was not connected with the public sewage system. *B* knew this and the lease declared that *B* had examined the premises and that *A* made no representation or guarantee as to the condition of the premises. Some time thereafter, the septic tank system stopped working properly and the county health department notified *B* that he was required to connect the sewage system with the public sewage system or else close the trailer park. *B* did not want to pay the additional cost involved in connecting with the public system. *B* claimed that he was released from the lease and was entitled to a refund of the deposit which he had made. Was he correct? [Glenn R. Sewell Sheet Metal v Loverde, 70 Cal 2d 666, 75 Cal Rptr 889, 451 P2d 721]

14. Miller was a farmer. In October he made a contract to deliver 10,000 bushels of soybeans to the Bunge Corporation in October and November. He was raising the soybeans on land which he owned, land which he rented, and on land which he and his brother jointly owned. The land was flooded when the Mississippi and other rivers rose. Miller could not perform his contract because of the flood. Bunge sued him for damages for nondelivery of the soybeans. Miller raised the defense of impossibility. Was this a valid defense? [Bunge Corp. v Miller, (DC Tenn) 381 FSupp 176]

19 Breach of Contract and Remedies

When a contract obligation is not performed, it is said that the party who failed to perform as agreed has broken or breached the contract. The other party is given certain legal remedies for such breach.

A. REMEDIES FOR BREACH OF CONTRACT

There are several remedies for breach of contract, one or more of which may be available to the injured party. The injured party may bring an action for damages, rescind the contract, bring a suit in equity to obtain specific performance, or commence a proceeding to obtain relief from an administrative agency of the government.

§ 19:1. Damages. Whenever a breach of contract occurs, the injured party is entitled to bring an action for damages to recover such sum of money as will place the injured party in the same position that would have been attained if the contract had been performed. If the defendant has been negligent in performing the contract, the plaintiff may sue for the damages caused by the negligence. Thus, a person contracting to drill a well for drinking water can be sued for the damage caused by negligently drilling the well so as to cause the water to become contaminated. However, damages representing annoyance or mental anguish ordinarily may not be recovered for breach of contract.

(a) Direct and Consequential Damages. The breach of a contract may cause the other party *direct* and *consequential* loss. For example, if the seller breaks the contract to deliver a truck which operates properly, the buyer sustains the damages of receiving a truck that cannot be used. This is the direct loss. Because the truck cannot be used the buyer may lose profits which could have been made if the truck could have been used to haul freight. The loss of profits is a consequential loss.

A direct loss is one which necessarily is caused by the breach of the contract. A consequential loss is one which does not necessarily follow the breach of the contract but happens to do so in the particular case because of the circumstances of the injured party. For example, if the buyer of the truck needed the truck to take a harvest of ripe tomatoes to the cannery but was unable to do so because the truck would not operate, the loss of the crop which could not be transported would be the consequential loss sustained by the farmer-buyer.

In business activities and construction contracts, the contractor's loss of profits is a direct loss while the extra cost incurred by the other contracting party in getting another contractor to finish the job is a consequential loss.

A party breaking the contract is always liable for the direct loss caused by the breach. That party is liable for only those consequential damages which were reasonably foreseeable as resulting from a breach of the contract. That is, the wrongdoer is not liable for everything that may happen but only for those consequential damages which were within the contemplation of the parties at the time of contracting. Thus, an electric power company, which interrupted service without warning for six hours during a summer heat wave, is liable to food stores for the spoiling of perishable food items.[1]

When a contractor delays in completing the performance of a contract, the injured party sustains a direct loss of the cost of renting other premises or goods. For example, when a contractor is late in the construction of a potato cellar, the injured person is entitled to recover the fair rental value of another cellar for the period of the delay, together with the cost of transporting the potatoes to the alternate place of storage.

Because of the contemplation-of-the-parties rule, damages may not be recovered for loss caused by remote injuries unless the plaintiff, at the time the contract was executed, had informed the defendant of facts that would have given the defendant reason to foresee that a breach of the contract would cause such loss. What constitutes remote loss for which there can be no recovery depends largely upon the facts of each case. In any case, recovery is not allowed as to losses that are not clearly related to the defendant's breach.

(b)   Measure of Damages. An injured party who does not sustain an actual loss from the breach of a contract is entitled to a judgment of a small sum, such as $1.00, known as *nominal damages*. A plaintiff who has sustained actual loss is entitled to a sum of money that will, so far as possible, compensate for that loss; such damages are called *compensatory damages*.

The fact that damages cannot be established with mathematical certainty is not a bar to their recovery. All that is required is reasonable certainty and the trier of fact is given a large degree of discretion in determining the damages.

Ordinarily only compensatory damages are recoverable for breach of contract and damages in excess of actual loss will not be imposed for the purpose of punishing or making an example of the defendant; such damages are known as *punitive damages* or *exemplary damages*. In some consumer situations, the recovery of punitive damages is allowed in order to discourage the defendant from breaking the law with others. For example, in cases in which the plaintiff is a consumer and the seller has acted wrongfully and stubbornly, there is an increasing trend to awarding punitive damages in order to prevent a repetition of such conduct.[2]

(c)   Present and Future Damages. The damages recoverable on the breach of a contract may also be analyzed in terms of whether the plaintiff has already sustained the loss in question or will do so in the future. A plaintiff who has been required to buy or rent elsewhere because of the defendant's breach can recover the costs thereof as an element of damages. Damages which the plaintiff will sustain in the future may be recovered to some extent. When damages relate to future loss, such

[1] National Food Stores, Inc. v Union Electric Co. (MoApp) 494 SW2d 379.
[2] Jones v Abriani (IndApp) 350 NE2d 635.

as the loss of future profits, the plaintiff is entitled to recover if the amount of such future loss can be established with reasonable certainty.[3] Mathematical precision is not required in proving future loss; but if the plaintiff cannot establish future loss items with reasonable certainty, they cannot be recovered.

(d)   Interest. The right to recover interest has been considered in Chapter 14 as a term of the contract. Distinct from such interest, the law allows the recovery of interest as an element of damages. Generally interest runs from the date when an obligation is due if the amount at the time is liquidated, meaning definite and specific. If the amount due the plaintiff is not liquidated, interest runs only from the date that judgment is entered in favor of the plaintiff.

(e)   Mitigation of Damages. The injured party is under the duty to *mitigate the damages* if reasonably possible. That is, damages must not be permitted to increase if this can be prevented by reasonable efforts. This means that the injured party must generally stop any performance under the contract in order to avoid running up a larger bill. It may require the injured party to buy or rent elsewhere the goods which the wrongdoer was obligated to deliver under the contract. In the case of the breach of an employment contract by the employer, the employee is required to seek other similar employment and the wages earned or which could have been earned from the other similar employment must be deducted from the damages claimed.

(1)   Effect of Failure to Mitigate Damages. The effect of the requirement of mitigating damages is to limit the recovery by the injured party to the damages which would have been sustained had the injured party mitigated the damages. That is, recovery is limited to the direct loss, and damages for consequential loss are excluded. For example, assume that a commercial hauler makes a contract to buy a truck. Because the seller fails to deliver the truck, the buyer loses a hauling job on which a profit of $500 would have been made. Assume that the hauler could have rented a truck for $50 in time to do the hauling job. The hauler would then be under a duty to rent the truck so that the $500 profit would not be lost. By failing to do this, the hauler permitted the damages to grow from a rental cost of $50 to a loss of profit of $500. When the hauler sues the seller for breach of the sales contract, the rule of mitigation of damages will limit the hauler to recovering only $50 because the additional $450 loss was unnecessarily sustained. If in fact the hauler had rented a truck, the rental of $50 would be recoverable as damages from the seller. Thus the hauler will only receive $50 damages whether or not a truck is rented in order to mitigate the damages.

(2)   Excuse for Failure to Mitigate Damages. If there is nothing which the injured party can reasonably do to reduce damages, there is, by definition, no duty to mitigate damages. For example, when a leasing company broke its contract to supply a specified computer and auxiliary equipment by delivering a less desirable computer and the specified computer and equipment could not be obtained elsewhere by the customer, the customer was entitled to recover full damages.[4]

---

[3] Schafer v Sunset Packing Co. 256 Ore 539, 474 P2d 529.
[4] I.O.A. Leasing Corp. v Merle Thomas Corp., 260 Md 243, 272 A2d 1.

When the cost of mitigating, as by purchasing elsewhere the goods which the seller failed to deliver, is unreasonably great, there is no duty to mitigate damages.

§ 19:2. Liquidated Damages. The parties may stipulate in their contract that a certain amount shall be paid in case of default. This amount is known as *liquidated damages*. Such a provision will be enforced if the amount specified is not excessive and if the contract is of such a nature that it would be difficult to determine the actual damages.[5] For example, it is ordinarily very difficult, if not impossible, to determine what loss the owner of a building under construction suffers when the contractor is late in completing the building. It is therefore customary to include a liquidated damage clause in a building contract, specifying that the contractor is required to pay a stated sum for each day of delay. (When a liquidated damages clause is held valid, the injured party cannot collect more than the amount specified by the clause; and the defaulting party is bound to pay that much damages once the fact is established that there has been a default. (See p. 296, Stein v Bruce))

If the liquidated damages clause calls for the payment of a sum which is clearly unreasonably large and unrelated to the possible actual damages that might be sustained, the clause will be held void as a *penalty*.

§ 19:3. Limitation of Liability. A party to a contract generally may include a provision that there shall be no liability for its breach or that liability shall be limited. Common illustrations of such clauses are the seller's provision of no liability beyond the refund of the purchase price or the replacement of defective parts, or a construction contract provision that the contractor shall not be liable for delays caused by conduct of third persons.

Generally such provisions are valid, particularly between experienced business persons. Thus, a telephone company may limit its liability to a nominal amount for the omission of a customer's name and number from the yellow page directory where the limitation is conspicuous, the customer is experienced in business, and the omission was merely the result of simple negligence.

There is a growing trend, however, to limit such *exculpatory* provisions or to hold them invalid when it is felt that because of the unequal bargaining power of the contracting parties the surrender of a right to damages for breach by the other is oppressive or unconscionable. When the provision is expanded so as to free the contracting party from liability for that party's own negligence, the provision is sometimes held void as contrary to public policy. (See p. 298, Fedor v Mauwehu Council) This is particularly likely to be the result when the party in question is a public utility, which is under the duty to render the performance or to provide the service in question in a nonnegligent way.

The fact that a limitation of liability limits or destroys the liability of one party for performance under the contract does not mean that there is no binding contract between the parties, as against the contention that if one party may break the contract without being liable for damages, that party in fact is not bound by any contract and hence the other party should not be bound either. Thus, there is a binding

---

[5] Massey v Love (Okla) 478 P2d 948; Uniform Commercial Code § 2-718(1); Mellor v Budget Advisors (CA7 Ill) 415 F2d 1218 (recognizing the Code provision in a nonsales transaction).

contract between the supplier of natural gas and its customer even though the supplier declares that while it would make "reasonable provision to insure a continuous supply," it does not insure a continuous supply of gas, will not be responsible for interruptions beyond its control, and "assumes no obligation whatever regarding the quantity and quality of gas delivered . . . or the continuity of service." [6]

§ 19:4. Rescission upon Breach. When one party commits a material breach of the contract, the other party may rescind the contract because of such breach, although in some situations, the right to rescind may be governed or controlled by civil service statutes or similar regulations or by an obligation to submit the matter to arbitration or to a grievance procedure.

An injured party who rescinds after having performed or paid money under the contract may recover the reasonable value of the performance rendered or the money paid. This recovery is not based on the contract which has been rescinded but on a quasi contract which the law implies to prevent the defaulter from keeping the benefit received and thus being unjustly enriched.

The rescinding party must restore the other party to that party's original position. If the rescinding party's own acts make this impossible, the contract cannot be rescinded. Thus a buyer who has placed a mortgage on property purchased cannot rescind the sales contract because the property cannot be returned to the seller in its original, unmortgaged condition.

Care must be exercised in deciding to rescind a contract. If proper ground for rescission does not exist, the party who rescinds is guilty of repudiating the contract and is liable for damages for its breach.

§ 19:5. Specific Performance. Under special circumstances the injured party may seek the equitable remedy of *specific performance* to compel the other party to carry out the terms of a contract. The granting of this relief is discretionary with the court and will be refused (a) when the contract is not definite; (b) when there is an adequate legal remedy; (c) when it works an undue hardship or an injustice on the defaulting party or the consideration is inadequate; (d) when the agreement is illegal, fraudulent, or unconscionable; or (e) when the court is unable to supervise the performance of such acts, as when services of a technical or complicated nature, such as the construction of a building, are to be rendered. The right to specific performance is also lost by unreasonable delay in bringing suit.

As a general rule, contracts for the purchase of land will be specifically enforced. Each parcel of land is unique and the payment of money damages would only enable the injured person to purchase a similar parcel of land but not the particular land specified in the contract. The sale of a business and the franchise held by the business from a third company will be enforced specifically.[7]

---

[6] Texas Gas Utilities Co. v Barrett (Tex) 460 SW2d 409. It would appear that the same consideration of practical expediency that has led the law to sustain output and requirements contract and to trust to the good faith needs of business people for the definition of contract obligations, rather than insisting upon precise contract terms, is tending to favor limitation of liability clauses even though, if given literal effect, they would seem to permit a party to ignore the contract without any legal consequence. This is subject to the qualifications or exceptions noted in the second paragraph of this section, in order to protect a person in an inferior bargaining position.

[7] DeBauge Bros., Inc. v Whitsitt, 212 Kan 758, 512 P2d 487.

Specific performance of a contract to sell personal property generally cannot be obtained. Money damages are deemed adequate on the basis that the plaintiff can purchase identical goods. Specific performance will be granted, however, when the personal property has a unique value to the plaintiff or when the circumstances are such that identical articles cannot be obtained in the market. Thus, specific performance of a contract is granted to sell articles of an unusual age, beauty, unique history, or other distinction, as in the case of heirlooms, original paintings, old editions of books, or relics. Specific performance is also allowed a buyer in the case of a contract to sell shares of stock essential for control of a close corporation [8] when those shares have no fixed or market value and are not quoted in the commercial reports or sold on a stock exchange.

Ordinarily contracts for the performance of personal services will not be specifically ordered, both because of the difficulty of supervision by the court and because of the restriction of the Thirteenth Amendment of the Federal Constitution prohibiting involuntary servitude except as criminal punishment. In some instances, a court will issue a negative injunction which prohibits the defendant from rendering a similar service for anyone else. This may indirectly have the effect of compelling the defendant to work for the plaintiff.

§ 19:6. Waiver of Breach. The fact that one party has broken a contract does not necessarily mean that there will be a lawsuit or a forfeiture of the contract. For practical business reasons, one party may be willing to ignore or *waive* the breach. When it is established that there has been a waiver of a breach, the party waiving the breach cannot take any action on the theory that the contract was broken. The waiver in effect erases the past breach and the contract continues as though the breach had not existed.

(a) Scope of Waiver. The waiver of a breach of contract only extends to the matter waived. It does not show any intent to ignore other provisions of the contract. For example, when a contractor is late in completing the construction of a building but the owner waives objection to the lateness and permits the contractor to continue and finish the construction, such waiver as to time does not waive the obligation of the contractor to complete the building according to the plans and specifications. Only the time of performance requirement is waived.

(b) Reservation of Right. It may be that the party waiving the breach is willing to accept the defective performance or breach but does not wish to surrender any claim for damages for the breach. For example, the buyer of coal may need a shipment of coal so badly as to be forced to accept it although it is defective, yet at the same time, the buyer does not wish to be required to pay the full purchase price for the defective shipment. To the contrary, the buyer wants to claim a deduction for damages because the shipment was defective. In such a case, the buyer should accept the tendered performance with a *reservation of right.* In the above illustration, the buyer would in effect state that the defective coal was accepted but that the right to damages for nonconformity to the contract was reserved.[9] Frequently the buyer will express

---

[8] In a close corporation the stock is owned by a few individuals, and there is no opportunity for the general public to purchase shares.

[9] UCC § 1-207.

the same thought by stating that the coal is accepted without prejudice to a claim for damages for nonconformity or that the shipment is accepted under protest.

The acceptance under reservation described above may be oral. It is preferable for practical reasons that it be in writing. In many cases the practical procedure is to make the declaration orally as soon as possible and then send a confirming letter. When the matter is sufficiently important, it is also desirable to have the wrongdoer countersign or make a written acknowledgement of the reservation letter.

(c) Waiver of Breach as Modification of Contract. When the contract calls for a continuing performance, such as making delivery of goods or the payment of an installment on the first of each month, the acceptance of a late delivery or a late payment may have more significance than merely waiving a claim for damages because of the lateness. Repeated breaches and repeated waivers, may show that the parties had modified their original contract. For example, the contract calling for performance on the first of the month may have been modified to permit performance in the first week of the month. When there is a modification of the contract, neither party can go back to the original contract without the consent of the other.

(d) Anti-Modification Clause. Modern contracts commonly specify that the terms of a contract shall not be deemed modified by waiver as to any breaches. This means that the original contract remains as agreed to and either party may therefore return to and insist upon compliance with the original contract. In order to do this, notice must be given to the other party that in the future the terms of the contract will be insisted upon. For example, where the insurance company followed the pattern of accepting the late payment of insurance premiums, it could not declare a policy lapsed for failure to pay the premiums within the required time without first notifying the insured that it was going to insist on compliance with the terms of the policy contract.

§ 19:7. Reformation of Contract. When a written contract does not correctly state what has been agreed to and its correction cannot be obtained by voluntary cooperation, a court will order the correction of the contract when it is clear that a reforming or *reformation* of the contract should be made. (See p. 299, Interior Elevator Company v Linneroth) In some instances, reforming the contract is the first step in showing that the contract which was actually made has been broken by the defendant. For example, assume that *A* owns two houses at 510 and 512 North Main Street. Assume that a fire policy is obtained to cover 510 but by mistake the policy refers to 512. Thereafter, 510 is detroyed by fire and the insurance company refuses to pay the loss on the theory that it did not insure 510 but insured 512. At this point, *A* would ask the court (a) to reform the insurance contract to show that there was in fact insurance on 510, and (b) to award damages to *A* because of the insurer's breach of its contract as to 510.

B. TORT LIABILITY TO THIRD PERSONS FOR BREACH

Can a third person sue for loss caused by a breach of a contract between other persons?

§ 19:8. Tort Liability to Third Person for Nonperformance. When a party to a contract fails to perform an obligation imposed thereby, a third person may be harmed. In some cases, the third party may recover damages as a third party beneficiary. If this is not possible, the recovery of damages may be sought on a theory of tort liability.

By the general rule, a total failure to perform a contract does not confer upon a third person a right to sue for tort.

(a) Discharge of Obligee's Duty. An exception is made to the general rule when the obligee, that is, the other party to the contract who will receive the benefit of performance, owes a duty to the third person or the general public, and the performance by the contractor would discharge that duty. Here the breach of the duty by the contractor gives rise to a tort liability in favor of the injured third person against the contractor. To illustrate, the operator of an office building owes the duty to third persons of maintaining its elevators in a safe operating condition. In order to discharge this duty, the building management may make a contract with an elevator maintenance contractor. If the latter fails to perform its contract and a third person is injured because of the defective condition of an elevator, the third person may sue the elevator maintenance contractor for the damages sustained.

(b) Partial Performance. Confusion exists in the law as to the classification to be made of conduct involved when the contracting party has entered upon the performance of the contract but omits some act or measure in consequence of which harm is sustained by a third person. The problem is the same as that involved in determining whether the negligent actor who omits a particular precaution has "acted" negligently or has been guilty of a negligent "omission." In many of the older cases, the courts denied recovery on the ground that no tort arose when a third person was injured by the breach of a contract between other persons. A modern trend allows recovery by the third person who is caused economic loss by the breach of a contract between others.

§ 19:9. Tort Liability to Third Person for Improper Performance. When one person contracts to perform a service for another person and a defective or improper performance is rendered which causes harm to a third person, such third person may sue the contractor. This is at least true when the performance of the contract would discharge an obligation or duty which is owed to the injured plaintiff by the person dealing with the contractor. By the older rule of contract law, only the person who had contracted for the services could sue when the services were improperly performed. (See p. 300, A.E. Investment Corp. v Link Builders, Inc.)

When the contractor fails to properly perform a contract for repairs or alterations, there is a conflict of authority as to whether the contractor is liable to a third person who is injured as the result thereof. For example, suppose that an automobile repairer negligently repairs the brakes of an automobile with the result that it does not stop in time when driven by the owner and runs into a pedestrian. Can the pedestrian sue the repairer for tort damages?

By the older view, the injured plaintiff was automatically barred because the plaintiff was not a party to the contract with the repairer. The modern view, however, emphasizes the fact that the person who makes a poor repair of the brakes is launching a dangerous instrumentality on the highway just as much as the manufacturer who manufactures an automobile with defective brakes. Both should recognize that their negligence will expose persons on the highway to an unreasonable risk of foreseeable harm. The modern view accordingly holds the negligent repairer liable to the injured third person.

A party to a contract is, of course, directly liable to a third person injured by negligence in the course of performing the contract. For example, when a contractor used a heavy pile driver close to very old neighboring buildings without taking various precautions to protect them from vibration damages, the contractor was liable to the owners of such houses for the vibration damages caused by such negligence.[10]

C. MALPRACTICE LIABILITY

When is a professional, such as an attorney, a doctor, or an accountant, liable for harm caused by improper performance? Under what circumstances can third persons sue for harm?

§ 19:10. What Constitutes Malpractice. When an accountant, a doctor, or an attorney makes a contract to render services, there is a duty to exercise such skill and care as is common within the community for persons possessing similar skills. If the services are not rendered or not rendered properly there is a breach of contract which is often described as *malpractice.*

In most instances, suit will be brought not for breach of contract but for malpractice on the theory that the breach of the contract was tortious. When suit is brought by the client or patient, a malpractice suit rather than a breach of contract suit is often selected by the plaintiff because of the possibility of recovering larger damages and because the statute of limitations runs on a malpractice claim in most instances from the date when the harm was discovered rather than from the date when there was a breach of contract. When suit is brought by a third person, and not by the patient or client, a malpractice or tort theory claim is naturally followed because the plaintiff is neither a party to the original contract nor a third party beneficiary of that contract. When suit for malpractice is brought by a third person, the principles involved are an extension of the principles discussed under § 19:9 as to tort liability to a third person for the improper performance of a contract.

§ 19:11. Attorneys. An attorney is liable to a client for failing to exercise the care and to apply the knowledge that is reasonably expected of attorneys within the community. If the attorney is a general practitioner, the standard is stated in terms of the skill and knowledge of general practitioners. If the attorney is a specialist, as a patent attorney, a bankruptcy attorney, or a corporate securities attorney, the standard is the care and knowledge of such a specialist.

(a) Particular Applications. An attorney is liable for improperly abandoning a case, failing to give notice to a governmental unit within the time required for making a claim, failing to bring suit before the claim of the client is barred by the statute of

---

[10] Dussell v Kaufman Construction Co., 398 Pa 369, 157 A2d 740.

limitations, and negligently investigating the title to real estate purchased by the client.

(b)   Liability to Third Persons. The majority of states follow the common-law rule that only the client can sue the attorney for malpractice. There is a growing trend which permits third persons harmed by the attorney's negligence to sue the attorney. Courts are most likely to allow such third person recovery where the lawyer's negligence in planning an estate has resulted in greater taxes, where negligence in drafting a will has failed to make proper provision for the third person,[11] or where negligence in making a title search has caused a third person to buy property with a defective title. The fact that in these cases the plaintiff is a person who is more or less within the contemplation of the contracting parties encourages the courts to depart from the privity of contract requirement.

§ 19:12. Medical Doctors. The malpractice liability of a doctor is governed by the same principles as apply to attorneys. The doctor must follow the standards of practice within the local medical community. If the doctor claims special skill, the standard is then elevated to the exercise of the skill of such a specialist.

(a)   Particular Applications. A doctor is liable for malpractice when because of failing to observe the required standards the doctor fails to properly diagnose the patient's condition, fails to prescribe the proper treatment or medicines, or fails to be attentive to dangerous side effects of the medicine prescribed for the patient. A doctor is liable to a patient for failing to inform the patient of the dangers of a particular treatment or operation, to which the patient consents, without being fully informed of the dangers, if the patient then sustains harm because of the undisclosed risks.[12]

(b)   Liability to Third Persons. Ordinarily the negligence of a doctor does not cause harm to a third person, so that the question of liability to a third person does not arise in the ordinary medical malpractice suit.

There are a few instances, however, in which the right of a third person to recover is well-established. If the malpractice of the doctor causes the patient's death, a surviving spouse, child, or parent of the patient may bring an action against the doctor for wrongful death. When the patient does not die but is so seriously invalided that the spouse of the patient has lost the companionship of the patient, at least temporarily, an action may generally be brought by the deprived spouse for the loss of consortium.

A psychotherapist who has reason to believe that a patient will commit a crime against a third person must warn the intended victim and the police and take whatever steps are reasonably necessary to prevent harm.[13]

§ 19:13. Accountants. Accountants are liable to their clients when loss is caused the clients because the accountants failed to observe the standards of sound accounting practices

---

[11] Heyer v Flaig, 70 Cal2d 223, 74 CalRptr 225, 449 P2d 161.
[12] Holt v Nelson, 11 WashApp 230, 523 P2d 211.
[13] Tarasoff v Regents of University of California, 17 CalApp3d 425, 131 CalRptr 14, 551 P2d 334.

and the clients sustain loss or fail to prevent loss because of such malpractice. Basically the concept is the same as is applied to doctors and attorneys.

(a) Particular Applications. An accountant is liable to the client when the accountant negligently fails to detect or fraudulently conceals signs that an employee of the client is embezzling from the client or that the internal audit controls of the client's business are not being observed. An accountant who prepares tax returns and acts as tax manager for the client will be liable when negligently given advice results in additional taxes or penalties being assessed against the client.

(b) Liability to Third Persons.

(1) Common Law. At the beginning of this century, the general American rule was that only the client could sue an accountant for malpractice.[14] In many states, this rule has been abandoned and third persons may sue the accountant when the fraud or negligence of the accountant causes loss to a third party.

When it was foreseen or was within the contemplation of the accountant and the client that a third person would rely on the work of the accountant, there is a greater probability that suit by a third person will be allowed. For example, where the accountant knows that the balance sheet requested by the client is to be shown to a bank from which the client seeks to obtain a loan or to a prospective buyer of the client's business, recovery by the bank or the prospective buyer will probably be allowed because the court does not fear that in allowing such third person to sue it is opening the door to thousands of lawsuits. (See p. 301, Shatterproof Glass Corp. v James)

Even though reliance on the accountant's work by third persons is foreseeable, many courts refuse to allow a malpractice suit to be brought by a third person whose identity was not known to the accountant. For example, it has been held that where the accountant prepared a financial statement for a contemplated sale to *A* but the sale was actually made to an unknown *B*, a malpractice suit could not be brought by *B* against the accountant.[15]

When accountants make a false financial statement for a corporate client with knowledge that it will be used in selling securities of the corporation to third persons, such third persons may sue the accountant for the damages sustained. Thus the accountant has been held liable for disguising the true character of a hoped-for profit from the sale and resale of real estate by describing it as "deferred income," although there was little reason to believe that the transactions could ever be completed; because the buyer, who was obligated to pay $5 million for the property, had assets of only $100,000 and the financial statement would have shown a loss instead of a substantial profit if the true character of the transaction had been disclosed.

(2) Federal Legislation. The malpractice liability of accountants to third persons has been broadened by the federal regulation of the sale of securities. A

---

[14] Ultramares Corp. v Touche, Niven & Co., 255 NY 170, 174 NE 441.
[15] Koch Industries v Bosko, (CA10 Kan) 494 F2d 713.

person purchasing a security on the basis of false information supplied or certified by an accountant may recover damages from the accountant who fraudulently prepared such information.

An accountant fraudulently certifying to non-existing values may be held liable to an investor. The accountant may be held liable for failing to detect false entries in the client's records. Under the federal legislation, the accountant has a duty to protect investors from statements which are misleading even though they are true. Thus liability may be imposed upon an accountant for certifying a statement showing an investment carried at book value when this was much greater than the actual market value. Again, an accountant has been held liable to stockholders for approving information in a statement prepared to show to sellers in which assets were carried at historical or original cost although the current value was greatly in excess. Liability of an accountant to the purchaser of a security may be based on the theory that the accountant aided and abetted the actual perpetrator of a stock fraud.

Liability of an accountant is narrower under the federal law than under state law. Under the federal law, liability cannot be based on negligence. In addition to the falsity of the statements made by the accountant, it must be shown that the accountant acted fraudulently in making the statement or in failing to detect the fraud of others.[16] Because fraudulent intent is required, an accountant is not liable to the purchaser of corporate securities when the accountant was negligent in failing to use appropriate auditing procedures and thereby failed to discover internal accounting practices of the corporate client which prevented the making of an effective audit.[17]

---

[16] An accountant is liable under the federal statutes for making a fraudulent, false, or deceptive statement in a registration statement which is filed with the Securities and Exchange Commission when a new security is issued, Act of 1933 § 11(a), 15 USC § 77k(a). The accountant is also liable for such statements in any document filed with the Securities and Exchange Commission. Securities and Exchange Commission Act of 1934, § 18, 15 USC § 78r.

[17] Ernst & Ernst v Hochfelder, 425 US 185.

CASES FOR CHAPTER 19

Stein v Bruce

(Mo App) 366 SW2d 732 (1963)

Stein, as buyer, and Bruce, as seller, made a contract for the sale of land located in Pennsylvania for $19,000. The contract required an initial down payment of $1,900, which was made. Later Stein paid Bruce $1,000 to extend the final settlement date of the contract until the end of the year. Stein did not go through with the sale, whereupon Bruce resold the land to another person for $19,000 within less than one year. After the final performance date of the original sales contract, Bruce kept the $2,900 paid by Stein, claiming that he was entitled thereto because the contract specified that "time is hereby agreed to be the essence of the agreement" and that "should the buyer fail to make settlement as herein provided, the sum or sums paid on account are to be retained by the seller, either on account of the purchase money, or as compensation for the damages and expenses he has been put to in his behalf, as the seller may elect." Stein sued for the return of the $2,900. From a decision adverse to Stein, she appealed.

CROSS, J. . . . Plaintiff . . . argues that . . . the sum named in the contract as liquidated damages is unreasonably large and that it must therefore be considered as a penalty and void. Under such findings, plaintiff insists, she would be entitled to recover of defendants the entire "downpayment" of $2900. The contract in question was executed in Pennsylvania and the land was located in that state. All the parties to the contract lived in Pennsylvania. Therefore, our determination of the instant question depends upon whether the down payment in issue is held to be liquidated damages or a penalty under law applicable in the State of Pennsylvania. . . .

The term "liquidated damages" signifies the damages, the amount of which the parties to a contract stipulate and agree, when the contract is entered into, shall be paid in case of breach. As distinguished from liquidated damages, a penalty is a sum inserted in a contract, not as a measure of compensation for its breach, but rather as a punishment for default, or by way of security for actual damages which may be sustained by reason of nonperformance, and it involves the idea of punishment. . . .

In determining whether contractual provisions are to be interpreted as providing for liquidated damages or for a penalty, the courts have enumerated various tests, criteria and factors to be considered. . . .

"The name by which such a clause may be called is but of slight weight, and the controlling elements are the intention of the parties and the special circumstances of the case. . . . The question is to be determined 'by the intention of the parties, drawn from the words of the whole contract, examined in the light of its subject matter and its surroundings; and that in this examination we must consider the relation which the sum stipulated bears to the extent of the injury which may be caused by the several breaches provided against, the ease or difficulty of measuring a breach of damages, and such other matters as are legally or necessarily inherent in the transaction.' . . . Real estate transactions, involving breaches in performance, are peculiarly within that class of cases where the measure of damages is difficult to ascertain. It is for that very reason that the practice has developed of inserting in sales agreements a sum certain, agreed to by the parties, as the amount which will be considered as compensation for a breach in performance. This may be the amount of the deposit or hand money, or it may be a sum in a lesser or greater amount, depending upon the consideration involved. Generally, we have held that where a purchaser repudiates an agreement

of sale of real estate containing a provision for liquidated damages, the vendor is entitled to the sum agreed upon as liquidated damages. . . . Where the obligation to purchase has been repudiated, especially where new construction is involved, the vendor usually has the continuing obligation of paying interest on any construction loan, insurance, taxes, broker's commission, maintenance charges, and utilities until the property is actually sold.". . .

The clear language of the contract and the circumstances surrounding the transaction import that the parties intended to stipulate for the retention of the down payment sum as liquidated damages and not as a penalty. That they so intended is strongly supported by the fact that the sale of real estate was the subject matter of the contract. "Damages rising from a breach of a contract for the purchase or sale of real estate are usually so uncertain and difficult of ascertainment that the tendency of the courts generally has been to sustain covenants of the parties liquidating the damages in such cases, unless they are unconscionable or grossly disproportionate to the injury provided against.". . .

"Of all facts difficult to establish, however, the value of land is one of the most difficult; in many neighborhoods sales of land are not frequent and no two persons will precisely agree as to the value thereof. Covenants of the parties liquidating the damages in such cases, when not unconscionable, will be enforced by the courts." Under the foregoing principles of law which govern our deliberations, we must assume that the actual damages resulting from the breach of the real estate sales contract in this case are uncertain in amount and difficult to ascertain or prove, particularly since there is nothing in the contract that furnishes a guide for the determination of damages. Therefore, it will be our duty to hold that the stipulated sum is for liquidated damages *unless we determine it to be unreasonable in amount as a forecast of probable damages and disproportionate to the amount of damages that could probably result from the breach.* We next consider that question.

The amount stipulated in the contract as liquidated damages to be forfeited in event of its breach is the sum of $1,900—exactly 10 percent of the purchase price. It is not, as plaintiff assumes, the sum of $2,900. The sum of $1,000 paid . . . three months after the contract was executed did not represent a stipulated down payment nor was it stipulated to be a sum representing liquidated damages. That sum was paid to defendants as consideration for the extension of time granted for performing the contract—the price of forbearance on the part of defendants from declaring a forfeiture on the part of the purchaser at the termination of the original three month contract period.

We do not believe that an amount representing 10 percent of the total purchase price is an unreasonable provision for liquidated damages in this case, or that it is disproportionate to the probable damages defendants suffered by the breach of the contract. It is apparent from the record that defendants had engaged real estate agents to sell the property and that the sale was effected through them. It is a reasonable inference that defendants were obligated by contract to pay those agents a commission for selling the real estate, that the commission was in fact paid, and further, that it represented a substantial portion of the 10 percent down payment retained after the breach. Furthermore, defendants were burdened by the contract for almost four months. During that interim their property was necessarily "off the market." They were constrained by the contract to reject all other offers of purchase, and forego any opportunity presented to sell it for a higher price. Meanwhile, they were subject to the outlay of money for maintenance of the property and for any continuing obligation such as interest, insurance, taxes, maintenance charges, and utilities. Additionally, defendants were deprived of the use of their money and the opportunity of its investment.

We find ample precedent in Pennsylvania cases for ruling that 10 percent of the purchase price is a reasonable stipulation of liquidated damages. . . . Plaintiff cites certain sections of . . . Pennsylvania's Uniform Commercial Code which applies only to the sale of personal property. We reject them as authority on the issue in this case arising from the sale of real estate. . . .

[Judgment affirmed]

Fedor v Mauwehu Council

21 Conn Supp 38, 143 A2d 466 (1958)

Charles Fedor, a minor, went to a summer camp. His father signed an agreement as a condition to his being admitted to the camp that the minor would not make any claim against the camp for any injury. When Charles was injured at the camp, he sued the camp claiming that the injury was caused by the camp's negligence. It raised the defense that the waiver agreement barred the suit. From a decision for the camp, Charles appealed.

McDONALD, J. . . . Generally speaking, agreements exempting parties from liability for their own negligence are not favored by the law and, if possible, are construed so as not to confer immunity from liability. . . . This general policy against construing agreements of the type involved here so as to confer immunity from liability for negligence is especially desirable in cases where a relationship once entered upon involves a status requiring of one party greater responsibility than that of the ordinary person and where the parties have not equal bargaining power and one party must either accept what is offered or be deprived of the relation. Certain language in defendant's [brief] . . . would appear to a certain extent to indicate the applicability of the foregoing language to the facts of this case—notably where defendant argues: "If this meritorious function [summer camp] is to be kept within the financial means of the greatest number of boys, some concession must be made. The concession in this case was the waiver of liability provision in the camp contract for which has been substituted a personal accident insurance policy to protect the boys and their parents from unfortunate casualties. These were the only terms available to the plaintiff and his parents and they accepted them readily."

In other words, low-income families desiring to take advantage of the opportunity to give their sons the advantages of a Boy Scout camp have no choice other than to sign a waiver absolving the camp from liability for acts of negligence of those responsible for the safety and lives of their sons. In this situation, the language of the court in Parillo v Housing Authority . . . seems particularly in point, where it is stated (16 Conn Supp at page 107): "It can hardly be said to be in the public interest to countenance a policy which would deprive families of low income, otherwise eligible, of the opportunity to obtain dwelling accommodations expressly made available for them by the use of public funds unless they consented to assume the risks flowing from the negligence of the authority in carrying on its operations."

We must bear in mind this general public policy against agreements exempting parties from liability for their own negligence when we consider whether the alleged waiver is binding. . . .

It is doubtful that either the mother or father of this minor plaintiff had the power or authority to waive his rights against the defendant arising out of acts of negligence on the part of the defendant. . . .

[Judgment reversed]

Interior Elevator Company v Limmeroth

278 Ore 589, 565 P2d 1074 (1977)

Limmeroth, a farmer, made a contract to sell wheat to the Interior Elevator Company. It was contemplated that the farmer would sell all the wheat which he owned. This was actually approximately 121 thousand bushels but the parties wrongly estimated it was approximately 126 thousand bushels. The written contract they signed specified that Limmeroth was selling 125,801 bushels. He delivered 120,663 bushels. Interior Elevator sued him for the value of the difference of 5,138 bushels. Limmeroth claimed that the contract was wrong and asked the court to reform the contract. The court reformed the contract so that the obligation of Limmeroth was to sell only 120,663 bushels. Interior Elevator appealed.

CAMPBELL, J. . . . The trial court . . . said: [I]t is clear from the testimony that both parties intended that Limmeroth would sell all of his stored wheat to Interior. . . ."

Thus, that court reformed the instrument of October 10, 1972, to read "120,663 bushels." The trial court never in its decision or findings directly classified the mistake as a "mutual mistake."

Assuming that this was mutual mistake, then the question becomes: Is this the type of mutual mistake for which a court of equity will grant reformation?

. . . To obtain reformation, the evidence of mutual mistake must be clear, convincing and unambiguous. . . . There must be proof of a valid antecedent agreement. . . .

"The purpose of reformation . . . is to make an erroneous instrument express correctly the real agreement between the parties; no court can make a new contract for them. Where a written instrument is merely intended to record a prior, definite, and specific oral understanding of the parties, but, because of a mutual mistake, that instrument fails to set out the prior agreement correctly in some material respect, a court . . . will ordinarily reform it. In

other words, in order for a written instrument to be reformed, . . . it is necessary that the parties thereto shall have previously reached a complete mutual understanding with respect to all of the essential terms of their agreement, for otherwise there would be no standard by which the writing could be reformed. 'It is not enough to justify reformation that the court is satisfied that the parties would have come to a certain agreement had they been aware of the actual facts.' . . .

Thus, to warrant reformation for mutual mistake, the error must have been in the drafting of the instrument and not in the making of the contract. . . . "An instrument will not be reformed on the ground of a mere misunderstanding of the facts, or a mistake as to an extrinsic fact which, if known, would probably have induced the making of a different contract or no contract at all. If there has been any misunderstanding between the parties, or a misapprehension by one or both, . . . no contract has been entered into, and the court will not make for them a contract which they did not make."

. . . It is clear that when the figure of 125,801 bushels appeared in "confirmation of sale" it was not a drafting mistake. Adams [who negotiated the contract] put in the document the exact figures the parties had in mind at the time of their agreement.

The trial court reformed the confirmation agreement to the number of bushels actually delivered, 120,633. This figure of 120,633 bushels was not known to anyone until the defendant's last truck was weighed at the plaintiff's elevator on June 13, 1973, more than eight months after Limmeroth and Adams had negotiated the sale of the wheat.

It could be argued that the contract was for the sale of "all of the wheat owned and in storage by Limmeroth on October 10, 1972," and that the volume was merely descriptive and not controlling. This argument must fail on the facts in this case. It was the undisputed testimony of Adams that because of the nature of [resale transactions], the plaintiff had to have a definite volume amount. Adams also testified that the grain companies, . . . would not accept "over and under" contracts.

The text writers and cases in dealing with the question of mutual mistake draw a distinction between the availability of the remedy of rescission and the remedy of reformation. . . .

"If two parties are caused to enter into a contract by reason of their common ignorance or common mistake as to some fact, but for which they would have not agreed, this may be ground for rescission, but it is not ground for reformation. Proof of such a mistake as this does not show that the parties have ever expressed assent, orally or otherwise, to any contract other than the one that is written. That writing truly expresses the only terms on which they have ever agreed. It may be subject to rescission for mistake; but there is no other agreement in accordance with which it can be 'reformed.' ". . .

The leading case on the classification of mutual mistakes seems to be *Harley v. Magnolia Petroleum Co.,* [37 NE2d 760]:

"Mistakes are generally divided into two groups, first, those fundamental in character, relating to an essential element of the contract . . . so no agreement is made. These generally have to do with such matters as the existence and identity of the subject matter, errors as to price, quantity, and the like. In the other class of mistakes an actual good-faith understanding is reached but through some error, not expressed, the agreement reduced to writing is not the actual agreement. The former of these classes constitutes ground for rescission but not reformation, while the latter may be reformed. . . .

The mutual mistake of Limmeroth and Adams in arriving at the volume of 125,801 bushels is not the type of mistake for which the law will allow reformation.

[Judgment reversed and action remanded]

A. E. Investment Corp. v Link Builders, Inc.

62 Wis 2d 479, 214 NW2d 764 (1974)

The More-Way Development Company contracted with Link to construct a building. DeQuardo, Robinson, Crouch & Associates, Inc., were the architects who designed the building. After the building was constructed, A. E. Investment Corporation rented a part of the building. Because of the negligence of the architects, the building settled. A. E. Investment Corporation was forced to leave the building because of this condition. It then sued the architects for the economic loss sustained thereby. The architects filed a demurrer to the complaint. The lower court overruled the demurrer. The defendant architects appealed.

HEFFERNAN, J. . . . It was alleged that the architect was negligent in its failure to adequately supervise the construction, in that it failed to determine the nature and condition of the subsoil prior to and during construction. It was also alleged that, in view of the subsoil conditions, the plans were negligently drawn because they did not provide for the construction of a floor that was necessary to accommodate the plaintiff's business enterprise.

It was alleged that the defendant knew that the building would be used as a commercial store and the plaintiff would therein operate a supermarket. It was alleged that, as the direct and proximate result of the negligence, the floor space leased to the plaintiff began to settle, damage was caused to the walls, the floor became uneven, and eventually the premises became untenantable. . . .

. . . The defendant defines the question . . . as being whether the defendant had a "duty to protect the subtenant plaintiff's future economic interests from loss allegedly resulting from a condition of the building." It responds to that question only by attempting to show that an architect owes no duty to a person with whom he is not in privity of contract. As a consequence, the defendant relies on the narrow argument that it has no responsibility for any economic loss to the plaintiff because it has no duty to the plaintiff at all and no responsibility to be answerable for any damages, irrespective of the nature of the loss. . . .

We believe that the narrow concept of duty relied on by the defendant architect has long been discarded in Wisconsin law. The duty of any person is the obligation of due care to refrain from any act which will cause foreseeable harm to others even though the nature of that harm and the identity of the harmed person or harmed interest is unknown at the time of the act. . . . ". . . Once an act has been found to be negligent, we no longer look to see if there was a duty to the one who was in fact injured.". . .

In the instant case . . . the defendant's alleged failure to properly take into account the condition of the subsoil when designing and supervising the construction of the building was an act or omission that would foreseeably cause some harm to someone. The duty was to refrain from such act or omission. Where, as here, it is alleged that the architect knew the purpose for which the building was being constructed, it was clearly foreseeable that a future tenant of the building was within the ambit of the harm. Hence, the harm to the particular plaintiff was foreseeable, although under the methodology of this court, it is not necessary that either the person harmed or the type of harm that would result be foreseeable. The act or omission in the face of foreseeable harm was negligence. . . .

Under Wisconsin negligence law, architects may be liable to third parties with whom they are not in privity of contract. The lack of privity does not constitute a policy reason for not imposing liability where negligence is shown to be a substantial factor in occasioning the harm.

The defendant also argues that, since an architect is a professional, his paramount duty is to his client, and that, if no duty is breached in connection with the architect-client relationship, there is no responsibility to third parties. We disagree with the argument that a professional can exonerate himself from liability for a negligent act which will foreseeably cause harm to third parties, merely because his client does not object. The very essence of a profession is that the services are rendered with the understanding that the duties of the profession cannot be undertaken on behalf of a client without an awareness and a responsibility to the public welfare. The entire ambit of state regulations as they apply to the profession of architecture is intended, not solely for the protection of the person with whom the architect deals, but for the protection of the world at large. Professionalism is the very antithesis to irresponsibility to all interests other than those of an immediate employer.

In the instant case, however, if, as it is alleged, the defendant architect negligently designed or permitted the erection of an unsuitable or unstable structure, it was hardly acting in the interests of its client, whether that client has seen fit to complain or not. . . .

[Judgment affirmed]

Shatterproof Glass Corporation v James

(TexCivApp) 466 SW2d 873 (1971)

A certified public accounting partnership of James, Guinn and Head prepared a certified audit report of four corporations, known as the Paschal Enterprises, with knowledge that their report would be used to induce Shatterproof Glass Corporation to lend money to those corporations. The report showed the corporations to be solvent when in fact they were insolvent. Shatterproof relied upon the audit report and loaned approximately one half million dollars to the four corporations and lost almost all of it because the liabilities of the companies were in excess of their assets. Shatterproof claimed that James and the other accountants had been negligent in preparing the report and sued them to recover the loss on the loan. From a judgment for the accountants, Shatterproof appealed.

LANGDON, J. . . . Appellees, according to their testimony, utilized the standards and procedures of the Committee on Auditing Procedures of the American Institute of Certified Public Accountants in the preparation of the audits in question, and admitted that, while it is recognized that the general rules may be subject to exceptions, the burden of justifying departures from the American Institute of Accountants' recommendations must be assumed by those who adopted other practices.

Appellee Guinn, the partner who did most of the work on the audit reports in question, testified that he was familiar with the publication "Auditing Standards and Procedures" published by the Committee on Auditing Procedures of the American Institute of Certified Public Accountants and that such publication was recognized as an authoritative source with respect to auditing. Appellant introduced in evidence the Rules of Professional Conduct promulgated by the Texas State Board of Public Accountancy pursuant to the Public Accountancy Act of 1945. An accountant violates these rules if he expresses an opinion on representations in financial statements which he has examined and (a) fails to disclose a material fact known to him, (b) fails to report any material misstatement known to him to appear in the financial statement, (c) fails to acquire sufficient information to warrant expression of an opinion, or (d) fails to direct attention to any material departure from generally accepted accounting principles, or to disclose any material omission of generally accepted auditing procedures.

The evidence offered by the appellant on the trial of this cause raised fact issues as to whether the appellees violated in a number of ways the above . . . rules and the Auditing Standards and Procedures of the American Institute of Certified Public Accountants in the preparation and publication of the unqualified audit reports concerning the financial condition of the Paschal Enterprises.

Among other matters the evidence presented issues of fact as to whether appellees violated accounting standards by failing to disclose a material fact known to them which was not disclosed in the financial statements to wit: that Buddy Paschal denied owing any part of the $31,000 receivable shown by the Audit Reports to be owed by him to Auto Glass. Second, appellees knew that the financial statement of Auto Glass contained a representation that Buddy Paschal owed Auto Glass $31,000 and Buddy Paschal, President of Auto Glass, denied any such debt. Third, the corporate books and financial records of the Paschal Enterprises were in such a condition that it was impossible for the appellees to acquire sufficient information to warrant expression of an opinion but in spite of such fact, appellees gave an unqualified opinion as to the financial conditions of such companies. Fourth, the appellees wholly failed to make any written evaluation of internal control and relied upon a number of facts which were not contained in their work papers.

The appellees in the audit prepared by them failed to direct attention to alleged material departures from generally accepted accounting principles.

. . . The principal question to be resolved on this appeal is whether the appellees were under a duty to exercise due care to protect the appellant from injury and were liable for damages caused the appellant by their negligence even though they were not in privity of contract. . . . We hold that the appellees were under a duty to exercise due care. Glanzer v Shepard, 233 NY 236, 135 NE 275, 23 ALR 1425 (NY Ct of App, 1922).

In Glanzer a professional weigher contracted with a bean seller to weigh a shipment of beans and certify the weight to the bean buyer. The plaintiff bean buyer paid his seller for the beans in accordance with their weight as represented by the defendant's certificate. When it turned out that the weigher had overweighed, and hence that the buyer had overpaid, the Court allowed the buyer to recover the difference from the misrepresenting weigher." The Court stated at 233 NY 329-340 and 135 NE 276:

"In such circumstances, assumption of the task of weighing was the assumption of a duty to weigh carefully for the benefit of all whose conduct was to be governed. We do not need to state the duty in terms of contract or of privity. Growing out of a contract, it has nonetheless an origin not exclusively contractual. Given the contract and the relation, the duty is imposed by law. . . .

"In fact, the Glanzer principle has been applied to accountants. The tentative drafts of the Re-

statement (Second) of Torts § 552 states the rule of law as follows:

"(1) One who, in the course of his business, profession or employment, or in a transaction in which he has a pecuniary interest, supplies false information for the guidance of others in their business transactions, is subject to liability for pecuniary loss caused to them by their justifiable reliance upon the information, if he fails to exercise reasonable care or competence in obtaining or communicating the information.

"(2) Except as stated in subsection (3), the liability stated in subsection (1) is limited to loss suffered (a) by the person or one of the persons for whose benefit and guidance he intends to supply the information, or knows that the recipient intends to supply it; and (b) through reliance upon it in a transaction which he intends the information to influence, or knows that the recipient so intends, or in a substantially similar transaction.

"(3) The liability of one who is under a public duty to give the information extends to loss suffered by any of the class of persons for whose benefit the duty is created, in any of the transactions in which it is intended to protect them.

"The same tentative draft includes the following hypothetical illustration of the above-stated rule of law:

"A is negotiating with a bank for a credit of $50,000. The bank requires an audit by certified public accountants. A employs B & Company, a firm of accountants, to make the audit, telling them he is going to negotiate a bank loan. A does not get his loan from the first bank but does negotiate a loan with another bank, which relies upon B & Company's certified statements. The audit carelessly overstates the financial resources of A, and in consequence the second bank suffers pecuniary loss. B & Company is subject to liability to the second bank. . . .

We believe that the Restatement (Second), Torts, § 552 (Tent Draft No. 12, 1966) should be adopted in Texas for application to cases of this nature.

We find and hold that within the scope defined in Restatement, Second, Torts, § 552 (Tent Draft No. 12, 1966), an accountant may be held liable to third parties who rely upon financial statements, audits, etc., prepared by the accountant in cases where the latter fails to exercise ordinary care in the preparation of such statements, audits, etc., and the third party because of such reliance suffers financial loss or damage. . . .

The very crux of the entire cause of action was whether the appellees failed to prepare the audit reports in accordance with generally accepted auditing standards including those of the American Institute of Certified Public Accountants. It would be important for the trier of the facts to know if the appellees were familiar with such standards. . . .

[Judgment reversed and action remanded]

QUESTIONS AND CASE PROBLEMS

1. What social forces are affected by the rule as to the mitigation of damages?
2. Compare (a) the third party beneficiary concept and (b) the right of a third person to sue for breach of a contract.
3. Compare the malpractice liability of accountants and doctors.
4. Compare (a) the right to limit liability and (b) the right to liquidate damages.
5. What is the objective of each of the following rules of law?
   (a) A party injured by a breach of contract is under a duty to mitigate the damages as far as is reasonably possible.
   (b) Specific performance of certain contracts is granted as an equitable remedy.
6. Dankowski contracted with Cremona to perform construction work on a house for $5,060 and to make a down payment of $2,500. When the work was about 80 percent completed, Dankowski refused to permit Cremona to do any further work because the work done was defective. Cremona brought suit for breach of contract. It was found that the defects in the work could be remedied at a cost of $500 and that Cremona had spent $4,167.26 in performance of the contract. He was awarded damages of $4,167.26 less the $500 necessary for repairs and less the down payment of $2,500 making damages of $1,167.26. The owner appealed. Decide. [Dankowski v Cremona, (Tex Civ App) 352 SW2d 334]
7. Puga agreed to assign his interest in a cable television enterprise if he was paid $20,000 by June 20, 1967. Harrison made partial payments of $5,000 on March 27 and $2,500 on July 30, 1967. On December 13, 1967, Puga notified Harrison that the agreement was terminated for failing to meet the June 20, 1967 deadline. Was he entitled to terminate the contract? [Harrison v Puga, 4 WashApp 52, 480 P2d 247]
8. *A*, who had contracted to build a house for *B*, departed from the specifications at a number of points. It would cost approximately $1,000 to put the house in the condition called for by the contract. *B* sued *A* for $5,000 for breach of contract and emotional disturbance caused by the breach. Decide. [Jankowski v Mazzotta, 7 Mich App 483, 152 NW2d 49]
9. Protein Blenders, Inc. made a contract with Gingerich to buy from him the shares of stock of a small corporation. When the buyer refused to take and pay for the stock, Gingerich sued for specific performance of the contract on the ground that the value of the stock was unknown and could not be readily ascertained because it was not sold on the general market. Was he entitled to specific performance? [Gingerich v Protein Blenders, Inc., 250 Iowa 646, 95 NW2d 522]
10. The buyer of real estate made a down payment. In the contract it was stated that the buyer would be liable for damages in an amount equal to the down payment if the buyer broke the contract. The buyer refused to go through with the contract and demanded his down payment back. The seller refused to return it and claimed that he was entitled to additional damages from the buyer because the damages which he had suffered were

greater than the amount of the down payment. Decide. [See Waters v Key Colony East, Inc. (FlaApp) 345 So2d 367]

11. Kuznicki made a contract for the installation of a fire detection system by Security Safety Corp. for $498. The contract was made one night and canceled at 9:00 a.m. the next morning. Security then claimed one third of the purchase price from Kuznicki by virtue of a provision in the contract that "in the event of cancellation of this agreement . . . the owner agrees to pay 33 1/3 percent of the contract price, as liquidated damages." Was Security Safety entitled to recover the amount claimed? [Security Safety Corp. v Kuznicki, 350 Mass 157, 213 NE2d 866]

12. Avril agreed to sell certain cleaning products to Center Chemical Co. at a 45 percent discount for 20 years and gave Center an exclusive franchise to sell such products in Florida. If Center did not make specified monthly minimum purchases, Arvil could restrict or terminate Center's exclusive rights. The contract provided for periodic readjustment of prices to meet market conditions. Four years later Center stopped purchasing from Avril, which then sued for breach of contract, claiming that it was entitled to recover for the loss of profits which it would have received in the remaining 16 years of the contract. It offered evidence of what the sales and profits had been the first 4 years. Was it entitled to recover profits for the remaining 16 years? [Center Chemical Co. v Avril, (CA5 Fla) 392 F2d 289]

13. Stabler was under contract to play professional football for Alabama Football, Inc. The corporation was not able to pay Stabler the amount due him under the contract. He sued for rescission. The club defended on the theory that nonpayment was not a sufficiently substantial breach of the contract to justify rescission. Was the club correct? [Alabama Football, Inc. v Stabler, 294 Ala 551, 319 So2d 678]

14. Brewer, who operated a lounge, contracted to give Roberts the right to place amusement machines therein. When Brewer sought to exclude the machines, Roberts sued for specific performance, which Brewer opposed on the ground that specific performance would require the court to supervise the lounge to see that the machines were allowed in it. Decide. [Roberts v Brewer, (Tex Civ App) 371 SW2d 424]

15. Melodee Lane Lingerie Co. was a tenant in a building that was protected against fire by a sprinkler and alarm system maintained by the American District Telegraph Co. Because of the latter's fault, the controls on the system were defective and allowed the discharge of water into the building, which damaged Melodee's property. When Melodee sued A.D.T., it raised the defense that its service contract limited its liability to 10 percent of the annual service charge made to the customer. Was this limitation valid? [Melodee Lane Lingerie Co. v American District Telegraph Co., 18 NY2d 57, 271 NYS2d 937, 218 NE2d 661]

16. The Oregon Highway Commission made a contract with the DeLong Corporation for the construction of the major components of a bridge across the Columbia River. The contract specified that $2,000 would be paid for each day's delay. DeLong abandoned the contract. The Highway Commission then had a second contractor finish the work. This was finished 476 days after the original completion date. The State then sued DeLong for damages for breach of the contract and for $2,000 for each day's delay. The State claimed that because of the delay, it lost approximately $1.4 million in bridge tolls, ferry operations, and a bridge subsidy. Judgment was entered in favor of the state for breach of the contract and for liquidated damages of $2,000 × 476 days of delay. DeLong appealed and claimed that a liquidated damages assessment of $952,000 was a penalty. Was it correct? [Oregon v DeLong Corporation, 9 OreApp 550, 495 P2d 1215]

Part Four • Personal Property and Bailments

20 Personal Property

Property includes the rights of any person to possess, use, enjoy, and dispose of a thing. It is not necessary that all of these rights be held by the same person at one time.

A. GENERAL PRINCIPLES

Property means the rights and interests which one has in anything subject to ownership, whether that thing be movable or immovable, tangible or intangible, visible or invisible. As a legal concept, "property" refers to rights. In common usage, it refers to the thing or object that is subject to the rights.[1] A right in a thing is property, without regard to whether such right is absolute or conditional, perfect or imperfect, legal or equitable.

§ 20:1. Personal Property. *Personal property* consists of (a) things which are tangible and movable, such as furniture and books, and (b) claims and debts, which are called *choses in action.* Common forms of choses in action are insurance policies, stock certificates, bills of lading, and evidences of indebtedness, such as notes.

Personal property can be defined indirectly as including all property that is neither real property nor a lease of real property. *Real property* means all rights and interests of indefinite duration in land and things closely pertaining to land, such as trees and buildings.

(a) Expanding Concept of Personal Property. New types of personal property have developed. Thus, gas and water are generally regarded by courts as "property" for the purpose of criminally prosecuting persons who tap water mains and gas pipes and thus obtain water and gas without paying.

---

[1] Virginia Marine Resources Commission v Forbes, 214 Va 109, 197 SE2d 195.

The modern techniques of sound and image recording have led to the necessity of giving protection against copying and competition. Federal and state statutes provide for the copyright protection of musical compositions and create new crimes of record and tape piracy.[2]

The theft of papers on which computer programs are written is larceny or "theft of property" under a statute which defines "property" as including "all writings, of every description, provided such property possesses any ascertainable value," even though the exact value of such programs cannot be determined.

§ 20:2. Limitations on Ownership. A person who has all possible rights in and over a thing is said to have *absolute ownership* of it. The term "absolute," however, is somewhat misleading, for one's rights in respect to the use, enjoyment, and disposal of things are subject to certain restrictions.

(a) Rights of Government. All property is subject to the *power to tax.* By another power, called the *police power,* the government can adopt reasonable rules and regulations in respect to the use and enjoyment of property for the protection of the safety, health, morals, and general welfare of the community. This police power is in substance the power to govern for the common good. Zoning laws that restrict the use of property within specified areas may be adopted under this power.

Private property is also subject to the right of the government to take it for public purposes. This right of *eminent domain* may also be exercised by certain corporations, such as railroads and public utilities. Constitutional provisions require that fair compensation be paid to the owner when property is taken by eminent domain. Such provisions do not apply when there is merely a loss of value caused by the use of the police power.

(b) Rights of Creditors. Property is subject to the rights of one's creditors. It may be taken by judicial proceedings to satisfy claims against its owner. A person cannot dispose of property in any way so as to defeat the rights of creditors.

(c) Rights of Others. The law restricts the use and enjoyment of property in that the owner is not allowed to use it in a way that will unreasonably injure other members of society. What is a reasonable or unreasonable use of property by the owner depends upon the circumstances in a particular situation. (See p. 318, Fountainbleau Hotel Corp. v Forty-five Twenty-five, Inc.)

B. ACQUIRING TITLE TO PERSONAL PROPERTY

Title to personal property may be acquired in different ways. In this chapter the following methods will be discussed: copyrights, patents, and trademarks; accession; confusion; gifts; lost property; transfer by nonowner; occupation; escheat; and judgments.

§ 20:3. Copyrights. A *copyright* is the exclusive right given by federal statute to the creator of a literary or artistic work to use, reproduce, or display the work. By international

---

[2] PL 92-140, 85 Stat 391, 17 United States Code §§ 1, 5, 20, 101; Pennsylvania, Act of January 10, 1972, PL 872, 18 PS § 1878.1.

treaties, copyrights given under the laws of one nation are generally recognized in another. Works produced in this country for export to foreign countries that have ratified the Universal Copyright Convention may use the internationally accepted copyright symbol © in place of or in addition to the word "copyright" or its abbreviation. Note the form of the copyright notice on the back of the title page of this book.

A copyright does not prevent the copying of an idea but only the copying of the way the idea is expressed. That is, the copyright is violated when there is a duplicating of the words or the pictures of the creator but not when there is merely a copying of the idea which those words or pictures express.

(a)   What is Copyrightable. Copyrights protect literary, musical, dramatic, and artistic work. Protected are books and periodicals; musical and dramatic compositions; choreographic works; maps; works of art, such as paintings, sculptures, and photographs; motion pictures and other audiovisual works; and sound recordings.

(b)   Unpublished Work. As long as a work is not made public, it has the same protection as though it had been copyrighted.[3] But once it is made public, anyone can use or copy it if it has not been copyrighted.

(c)   Duration of Copyright. A copyright lasts for the life of the creator of the work and for fifty years after the creator's death.[4] Special provision is made with respect to works copyrighted before January, 1978, or which were both unpublished and uncopyrighted on that date. After a copyright has expired, the work is in the public domain and may be used by anyone without cost.

(d)   Limitations on Exclusive Character of Copyright. To a limited extent, a free use without permission may be made of copyrighted material in connection with criticism, news reporting, teaching, and research. Copyrighted phonograph records may be played on the radio, on television, and in jukeboxes without permission by paying a specified royalty to the copyright holder.

§ 20:4. Patents. A *patent* is the exclusive right which the inventor of a device can obtain by filing an application under federal law. The patent gives the inventor an exclusive right to make, use, and sell the thing invented for 17 years. The patent then expires and cannot be renewed.

If a patent is not obtained or if the patent has expired, anyone may make, use, or sell the invention without the permission of the inventor and without making any payment therefor.

(a)   What is Patentable. In order to be patentable, the invention must be something which is new and useful and must be something which would not have been obvious to a person of ordinary skill or knowledge in the art or technology to which the invention is related.[5]

It is the thing which is patented: whether it be a machine, a process, or a particular chemical composition of matter. The idea or inspiration, ways of doing

---

[3] Copyrights Act of 1976, § 104(a), 17 USC § 104(a).
[4] Copyrights Act of 1976, § 302(a), 17 USC § 302(a).
[5] 35 USC §§ 101, 102, 103. Graham v John Deere Co., 383 US 1.

business, and scientific principles cannot be patented unless there is some physical thing which is based upon them.

(b)   Computer Programs. The patentability of computer programs is one of the open frontiers of the law. The difficulty is in stating the law in such a way as to protect programs without at the same time making any idea patentable. To date, patent protection has been denied on the theory that a program merely represented "thinking." The commercial necessity of protecting programs will undoubtedly lead to the adoption of a view that a program may be patented, at least when something more than mere "thinking" is shown. It has been held that a patent cannot be obtained for a computer program for programming any type of general purpose digital computer to convert binary-coded-decimal numerals into pure binary numerals, as such a conversion method is not a "process" within the patent law but is merely an idea and can be performed with other existing equipment or without any equipment.[6]

(c)   Contractual Protection of Inventions. Frequently an employee will invent a patentable device during working hours or using the employer's equipment and materials. To protect the employer in such situations, employment contracts commonly provide that any invention relating to the employer's business which is discovered by the employee while still an employee or during the first one or two years after leaving the employment shall be assigned to the employer. Such provisions are generally held valid, although a provision requiring the assignment of all inventions whether or not related to the employer's business has been held contrary to public policy and therefore invalid.[7]

§ 20:5.   Trademarks and Servicemarks. A *mark* is any word, symbol or design, or a combination of these used to identify a product or a service.[8] If the mark identifies a product, such as an automobile or soap, it is also called a *trademark*. If it identifies a service, such as a restaurant or clothes cleaner, it is also called a *servicemark*.

The user of such a mark may obtain protection from its use by others by registering the mark in accordance with federal law.[9] Under the federal statute, two files or registers, a Principal Register and a Supplemental Register, are maintained for the registration of trade and servicemarks. The classification of the mark determines which register can be used. The effect of registering is different for each of the two registers, as discussed in (c) and (d) of this section.

(a)   Descriptive Mark. A trade or servicemark may describe a product or service in some way but yet not identify the particular enterprise producing the product or supplying the service. In such case, the mark is called a *weak mark*. Thus, "Cough Calmers" was held to be a weak mark because it was merely descriptive as applied to cough drops as the term did not distinguish the cough drops in question from those made by other manufacturers of cough drops.[10]

---

[6] Gottschalk v Benson, 409 US 63.
[7] Guth v Minn. Mining & Manufacturing Co. (CA7 Wis) 72 F2d 385.
[8] 15 USC § 1127.
[9] Lanham Act, 15 USC §§ 1050-1127.
[10] In re A. H. Robbins Co., 157 USPQ 590.

(b)   Exclusively-Identifying Mark. When a mark identifies the goods or services of a particular maker or supplier so clearly that they are distinguished from goods and services of anyone else, the mark is described as a *strong mark*. A mark is strong either because (1) it is the name of the user of the mark, as Kodak, Xerox, or Exxon; or (2) through continued use a weak mark has come to be so associated in the mind of the public with a particular supplier or manufacturer that the mark has become a strong mark which has a restricted or secondary meaning which serves to identify the particular products or services and distinguish them from those of others.[11] As an illustration of a secondary meaning converting a weak mark into a strong mark, the geographic term "Philadelphia" as applied to cream cheese now identifies a particular brand, rather than any cheese made in Philadelphia.

(c)   Principal Register. Only a strong or exclusively-identifying mark may be filed in the Principal Register. This registering creates a presumption that the mark is valid, that it is owned by the registrant and that the registrant has the exclusive right to use that mark. Any lawsuit to challenge the right of the registrant must be brought within five years after registration. After the expiration of five years, the right of the registrant is incontestable.

(d)   Supplemental Register. A weak or merely descriptive mark which does not identify the registrant exclusively can only be recorded in the Supplemental Register. This recording does not give the registrant any protection but it provides a source to which other persons designing a mark can go to make sure that they are not duplicating an existing mark.

(e)   Injunction Against Improper Use of Mark. A person who has the right to use a mark may enjoin a competitor from imitating or duplicating the mark. The basic question in such litigation is whether the general public is likely to be confused by the mark of the defendant and to wrongly believe that it identifies the plaintiff. If there is this danger of confusion, the court will enjoin the defendant from using the particular mark.

In some cases, the fact that the products of the plaintiff and the defendant do not compete in the same market was held to entitle the defendant to use a mark which would have been prohibited as confusingly similar if the defendant manufactured the same product as the plaintiff. For example, it has been held that Cadillac as applied to boats is not confusingly similar to Cadillac as applied to automobiles and therefore its use cannot be enjoined.[12]

(f)   Abandonment of Exclusive Right to Mark. An owner who has an exclusive right to use a mark may lose that right. If other persons are permitted to use the mark, it loses its exclusive character and is said to pass into the English language and become generic. Examples of formerly-enforceable marks which have made this transition into the general language are aspirin, thermos, cellophane, and shredded wheat.

---

[11] 15 USC § 1052(f).
[12] General Motors Corporation v Cadillac Marine and Boat Co., 140 USPQ 447.

§ 20:6. Secret Business Information. A business may have developed a fund of information which is not generally known but which cannot be patented or copyrighted under federal law. As long as such information is kept secret it will be protected under state law relating to trade secrets and common-law copyrights.

(a)   Trade Secrets. A trade secret may consist of any formula, patent, device, or compilation of information which is used in one's business, which is of such a nature that it gives an advantage over competitors who do not have such information. It may be a formula for a chemical compound, a process of manufacturing, treating, or preserving materials, or a list of customers.[13]

(b)   Common-Law Copyright. Anything which is put in writing or on paper and is kept secret is protected by a common-law copyright. By this right, the compiler of data or information which has not been made public has a right that no one else use it without permission.

(c)   Protection of Information. When information is a trade secret or is protected by a common-law copyright, the original possessor of the information may obtain an injunction or court order which prohibits anyone else from using that information. In addition, the original possessor of the information may obtain damages for improper use of the information. (See p. 319, Data General Corporation v Digital Computer Controls, Inc.)

An injunction may also be obtained to prevent someone from learning the secret information, as well as from making improper use of it. For example, when a new factory is being constructed to carry out a secret process, a court will enjoin a commercial photographer from taking aerial photographs of the plant construction when such photographs would reveal the steps in the process.

(d)   Loss of Protection by Publication. When secret business information is made public it loses the protection it had while secret. Such loss of protection by publication occurs when the information is made known without any restrictions. In contrast, there is no loss of protection when secret information is shared or communicated for a special purpose and the person receiving the information knows that it is not to be made public.

§ 20:7. Accession. Property may be acquired by *accession,* that is, by means of an addition to or an increase of the thing that is owned, as in the case of produce of land or the young of animals. As a general rule, repairs and additions become a part of the article that is repaired or modified. (See p. 320, Texas Hydraulic & Equipment Co. v Associates Discount Corp.) Likewise, when materials are furnished to another to be manufactured into an article, title to the finished article is in the owner of the materials. If the manufacturer, however, adds a large proportion of other materials, title will then usually vest in him.

A difficult problem arises when a change in property is made by a non-owner against the wishes or at least without the consent of the owner. To illustrate, when a stolen car is retaken on behalf of the owner, the car owner is entitled to keep a

---

[13] Restatement of Torts § 757, comment b; Kewanee Oil Co. v Bicron Corp., 416 US 470.

new engine which has been put into the car by a good faith purchaser, on the basis that the engine had become part of the car by accession.

§ 20:8. Confusion. Title to personal property may be acquired when the property of two persons becomes intermingled under such circumstances that the owner forfeits all right to the property. Under this doctrine of *confusion,* if a person willfully and wrongfully mixes personal property with the personal property of another so as to make it impossible to distinguish which property belonged to which person, the person mixing the property loses all right in the mass and the other party acquires title to the total mass.

The doctrine of confusion does not apply (a) when the mixture is made by the consent of the parties; (b) when the mixture is made innocently without fraudulent intent, as by mistake or accident; or (c) when the goods that have been mixed are of equal kind and grade, as in the case of oil, tea, and wheat. In these cases, each owner is entitled to a proportionate share of the mixture.

§ 20:9. Gifts. Title to personal property may be transferred by the voluntary act of the owner without receiving anything in exchange, that is, by *gift.* The person making the gift, the *donor,* may do so because of things which the recipient of the gift, the *donee,* has done in the past or which the donee is expected to do in the future, but such matters of inducement are not deemed consideration so as to alter the "free" character of the gift.

(a)   Inter Vivos Gifts. The ordinary gift that is made between two living persons is an *inter vivos gift.* For practical purposes, such a gift takes effect upon the donor's expressing an intent to transfer title and making delivery, subject to the right of the donee to disclaim the gift within a reasonable time after learning that it has been made. As there is no consideration for a gift, an intended donee cannot sue for breach of contract if the donor fails to complete the gift.

The fact that a donee is willing to return the gift if needed by the donor does not destroy the character of the transaction as a gift, where such return would be at the option or choice of the donee and the donor did not have any right to compel the return of the property.

(1)   Intent. The intent "to make" a gift requires an intent to transfer title at that time. In contrast, an intent to confer a benefit at a future date is not a sufficient intent to create any right in the intended donee. The absence of an intent to make a gift may be shown to contradict what otherwise would appear to be a gift. Thus, it may be shown that the owner of shares of stock retains such control over the stock that there was no gift even though the shares were registered in the name of the owner's spouse and the dividends were received and kept by the spouse, the owner proving that the transfer was made to the spouse for convenience and that there was no intention that the spouse should receive or keep anything more than the dividends.

(2)   Delivery. Ordinarily the delivery required to make a gift will be an actual handing over to the donee of the thing which is given.

The delivery of a gift may also be made by a *symbolic delivery,* as by the delivery of means of control of property, such as keys to a lock or ignition keys to an automobile, or by the delivery of papers that are essential to or closely associated with the ownership of the property, such as documents of title or a ship's papers. The delivery of a symbol is effective as a gift if the intent to make a gift is established; this is in contrast to merely giving the recipient of the token temporary access to the property, as for example, until the deliveror comes back from the hospital.

A gift may be made by depositing money in the bank account of an intended donee. If the account is a joint account in the names of two persons, a deposit of money in the account by one person may or may not be a gift to the other. Parol evidence is generally admissible to show whether there was an intention to make a gift.

When a savings account passbook is essential to the withdrawal of money from a savings account, parents do not make a gift to a minor child when they open a savings account in the child's name but keep possession of the passbook.[14]

A gift may be made by delivering a deed or an assignment to the donee. Thus, *A* may give a television set to *B* by delivering to *B* a signed and sealed writing which declares that *A* gives the set to *B*. This sealed writing is called a deed and would be used when the subject of the gift is a thing. If the subject of a gift is a claim, an assignment would be used. For example, if *C* was owed $100 by *D, C,* could make a gift of that claim to *E* by giving *E* a writing saying that *C* assigned to *E* the claim of *C* against *D*. The fact that a deed is used instead of an assignment, or vice versa, is unimportant as the courts will carry out the intent of making a gift regardless of what the document is called.

The essential element of delivery is the relinquishment of control over the property. If the owner retains control, there is no delivery. Hence, the fact that property is placed in a jointly-owned safe deposit box does not make the sharer of the box a co-owner of the property. Consequently, upon the death of the person depositing the property, the other person does not become the owner merely because the box was rented by them as "joint tenants with the right of survivorship." This term is narrowly construed to relate only to the use of the box and not to the ownership of its contents.

(3)   Donor's Death. If the donor dies before doing what is needed to make an effective gift, the gift fails. An agent or the executor or administrator of the donor cannot thereafter perform the missing step on behalf of the donor. For example, in a state where a transfer of title to a motor vehicle could not be made without a transfer of the title certificate, that transfer must be made while the donor is living and cannot be made after the donor's death by the executor of the donor.[15]

(b)   Gifts Causa Mortis. A *gift causa mortis* is made when the donor, contemplating imminent and impending death, delivers personal property to the donee with the intent that the donee shall own it if the donor dies. This is a conditional gift and the donor is entitled to take the property back (1) if the donor does not die; (2) if the donor revokes the gift before dying; or (3) if the donee dies before the donor.

---

[14] Ruffalo v Savage. 252 Wis 175, 31 NW2d 175.
[15] Estes v Gibson (Ky) 257 SW2d 604.

(c)   Uniform Gifts to Minors Act. The Uniform Gifts to Minors Act,[16] provides an additional method for making gifts to minors of money and of registered and unregistered securities. Under the Act, a gift of money may be made by an adult to a minor by depositing it with a broker or a bank in an account in the name of the donor or another adult or a bank with trust powers "as custodian for [*name of minor*] under the [*name of state*] Uniform Gifts to Minors Act." If the gift is a registered security, the donor registers the security in a similar manner. If the security is unregistered, it must be delivered by the donor to another adult or a trust company accompanied by a written statement signed by the donor and the custodian acknowledges receipt of the security.[17]

Under the Uniform Act, the custodian is in effect a guardian of the property for the minor but the custodian may use the property more freely and is not subject to many restrictions applicable to true guardians. When property is held by a custodian for the benefit of a minor under the Uniform Gifts to Minors Act, the custodian has discretionary power to use the property for the "support, maintenance, education, and benefit" of the minor but the custodian may not use the custodial property for the custodian's own personal benefit. The gift is final and irrevocable for tax and all other purposes upon complying with the procedure of the Act. The property can be transferred by the custodian to a third person free from the possibility that a minor donee might avoid the transfer.

(d)   Conditional Gifts. A gift may be made on condition, such as "This car is yours when you graduate" or "This car is yours unless you drop out of school." The former gift is subject to a *condition precedent,* and the latter to a *condition subsequent.* That is, the condition to the first gift must be satisfied before any gift or transfer takes place, while the satisfaction of the second condition operates to destroy or divest a title that had already been transferred. Ordinarily, no condition is recognized unless it is expressly stated; but some courts regard an engagement ring as a conditional gift, particularly if the woman breaks or causes the breaking of the engagement.[18] Other gifts made by the man or by friends in contemplation of marriage are not regarded as conditional.

(e)   Anatomical Gifts. The Uniform Anatomical Gift Act [19] permits persons eighteen years or older to make a gift of their body or any part or organ to take effect upon their death. The gift may be made to a school, a hospital, or organ bank, or to a named patient. Such a gift may also be made, subject to certain restrictions, by the spouse, adult child, parent, adult brother or sister, or guardian of a deceased person.[20] Independently of the Act a living person may make a gift, while living, of part of the person's body, as in the case of a blood transfusion or a kidney transplant.

§ 20:10. Lost Property. Personal property is *lost* when the owner does not know where it is located but intends to retain title or ownership to it. The person finding lost property

---

[16] The Uniform Gifts to Minors Act (UGMA) was originally proposed in 1956. It was revised in 1965 and again in 1966. One of these versions, often with minor variations, has been adopted in every state except Georgia. It has been adopted for the Virgin Islands and the District of Columbia.

[17] UGMA § 2.

[18] Goldstein v Rosenthal (NYCivCt) 56 Misc2d 311, 288 NYS2d 503.

[19] This Act has been adopted in every state.

[20] Uniform Anatomical Gift Act (UAGA) §§ 2, 3.

does not acquire title but only possession. Ordinarily the finder of lost property is required to surrender the property to the true owner when the latter establishes ownership. Meanwhile the finder is entitled to retain possession as against everyone else.

Without a contract with the owner or a statute so providing, the finder of lost property is not entitled to a reward or to compensation for finding or caring for the property.

(a) Finding in Public Place. If the lost property is found in a public place, such as a hotel, under such circumstances that to a reasonable person it would appear that the property had been intentionally placed there by the owner and that the owner would be likely to recall where the property had been left and to return for it, the finder is not entitled to possession of the property but must give it to the proprietor or manager of the public place to keep it for the owner.[21] This exception does not apply if it appears that the property was not intentionally placed where it was found, because it is not likely that the owner will recall having left it there.

(b) Statutory Change. In some states, statutes have been adopted permitting the finder to sell the property or keep it if the owner does not appear within a stated period of time. In such a case, the finder is required to give notice, as by newspaper publication, in order to attempt to reach the owner.

§ 20:11. Transfer by Nonowner. Ordinarily a sale or other transfer by one who does not own the property will pass no title. No title is acquired by theft. The thief acquires possession only; and if the thief makes a sale or gift of the property to another, the latter only acquires possession of the property. The true owner may reclaim the property from the thief or from the thief's transferee.[22]

(a) Automobiles. In some states the general rule stated above is fortified by statutes which declare that the title to an automobile cannot be transferred, even by the true owner, without a delivery of a properly indorsed title certificate. The states that follow the common law do not make the holding of a title certificate essential to the ownership of an automobile, although as a matter of police regulation, the owner must obtain such a certificate.

(b) Exceptions. As an exception to the rule that a nonowner cannot transfer title, an agent, who does not own the property, but who is authorized to sell it, may transfer the title of the agent's principal. Likewise, certain relationships create a power to sell and to transfer title, such as a pledge or an entrustment. Likewise an owner of property may be barred or estopped from claiming ownership when the owner has acted to deceive an innocent buyer into believing that someone else was the owner or had authority to sell.

§ 20:12. Occupation of Personal Property. Title to personal property may be acquired by *occupation,* that is, by taking and retaining possession of the property.

---

[21] Jackson v Steinberg, 186 Ore 129, 200 P2d 376.
[22] As to the right of the owner to sue for money damages see § 20:15 of this book.

(a) Wild Animals. Wild animals, living in a state of nature, are not owned by any individual. Title to them is held by the state, as sovereign, in a trustee-like capacity for the public. In the absence of restrictions imposed by game laws, the person who acquires dominion or control over a wild animal becomes its owner. What constitutes sufficient dominion or control varies with the nature of the animal and all the surrounding circumstances. If the animal is killed, tied, imprisoned, or otherwise prevented from going at its will, the hunter exercises sufficient dominion or control over the animal and becomes its owner.

If the wild animal, subsequent to its capture, should escape and return to its natural state, it resumes the status of a wild animal. The first captor thereby loses title, and a new hunter can acquire title to the animal by a subsequent capture.

As a qualification to the ordinary rule, the exception developed that if an animal is killed or captured on the land of another while the hunter is guilty of trespassing, that is, the hunter is upon the land without the permission of the landowner, the animal, when killed or captured, does not belong to the hunter but to the landowner.

(1) Game Laws. Generally state game laws narrow the common-law rights by establishing closed seasons during which the hunter is not permitted to capture the game. A federal statute similarly protects migratory birds which fly across national boundaries. Violation of these statutes is punishable by fine or imprisonment or both.

(2) Pollution Damage to Wild Animals. When a business enterprise pollutes the environment and such pollution causes the death of wildlife, some courts allow the state to bring a suit against the polluter to recover damages for destruction of the wildlife. Other courts deny recovery by the state. (See p. 321, North Dakota v Dickinson Cheese Co.)

(b) Abandoned Personal Property. Personal property is deemed abandoned when the owner relinquishes possession of it with the intention to disclaim title to it. Yesterday's newspaper which is thrown out in the trash is abandoned personal property. Title to abandoned property may be acquired by the first person who obtains possession and control of it. A person becomes the owner at the moment of taking possession of the abandoned personal property.

When the owner of property flees in the face an approaching peril, property left behind is not abandoned, as an abandonment occurs only when the leaving of the property is the voluntary act of the owner.[23]

§ 20:13. Escheat. Difficult questions arise in connection with unclaimed property. In the case of personal property, the practical answer is that the property will probably "disappear" after a period of time, or it may be sold for unpaid charges, as by a carrier, hotel, or warehouse. A growing problem arises with respect to unclaimed corporate dividends, bank deposits, insurance payments, and refunds. Most states have a statute providing for the transfer of title of such unclaimed property to the state government. This transfer of ownership to the government is often called by its feudal name of

---

[23] Menzel v List, 49 Misc2d 300, 267 NYS2d 804.

escheat. Many states have adopted the Uniform Disposition of Unclaimed Property Act.[24]

§ 20:14. Remedies for Violation of Property Rights. The remedy most commonly used by the owner of personal property for violations of property rights is an action for money damages when the property is negligently or willfully harmed, taken, or destroyed by the act of another. When the owner's property is taken under circumstances that would constitute larceny, the owner may sue for the wrong, called *conversion,* and will recover the money value of the property at the time of the unlawful taking, or may recover the property itself by an action at law.

The owner's right to recover damages for conversion may also be asserted against an innocent wrongdoer; that is, a person who in good faith has exercised dominion over the property of the plaintiff. For example, although the buyer of a stolen television set gave value and acted in good faith in the belief that the seller was the owner of the set, the conduct of the innocent buyer in taking possession of the set and exercising control over it is a conversion for which the innocent buyer is liable to the true owner.

If the defendant has infringed copyrights, patents, or marks of the plaintiff, the plaintiff may obtain an injunction ordering the defendant to stop such practices. If the infringement was intentional, the plaintiff may also recover from the defendant any profits obtained by the defendant from such infringement. If the infringement conduct is such as to constitute an unfair trade practice, the plaintiff may obtain a cease and desist order against the defendant from the Federal Trade Commission.

C. MULTIPLE OWNERSHIP OF PERSONAL PROPERTY

When all rights in a particular object of property are held by one person, that property is held in *severalty.* However, two or more persons may hold concurrent rights and interests in the same property. In that case, the property is said to be held in *cotenancy.* The various forms of cotenancy include (1) tenancy in common, (2) joint tenancy, (3) tenancy by entirety, and (4) community property.

§ 20:15. Tenancy in Common. *A tenancy in common* is a form of ownership by two or more persons. The interest of a tenant in common may be transferred or inherited, in which case the taker becomes a tenant in common with the others. This tenancy is terminated only when there is a partition or division, giving each a specific portion, or when one person acquires all of the interest of the co-owners.

§ 20:16. Joint Tenancy. A *joint tenancy* is another form of ownership by two or more persons. A joint tenant's interest may be transferred to a third person, but this destroys the joint tenancy. In such a case, the remaining joint tenant becomes a tenant in common with the third person who has acquired the interest of the other joint tenant.

---

[24] The 1954 version of the Act has been adopted in Arizona, Florida, Idaho, Maryland, New Hampshire, Oregon, Utah, Vermont, Virginia, and West Virginia. A 1969 version of the Act has been adopted in Alabama, Georgia, Illinois, Indiana, Iowa, Louisiana, Minnesota, Montana, New Mexico, Oklahoma, Rhode Island, South Carolina, South Dakota, and Wisconsin.

Upon the death of a joint tenant, the remaining tenants take the share of the deceased tenant, and finally the last surviving joint tenant takes the property as a holder in severalty.

(a)   Statutory Change. Statutes in many states have modified the common law by adding a formal requirement to the creation of a joint tenancy with survivorship. At common law, such an estate would be created by a transfer of property to "*A* and *B* as joint tenants." Under these statutes, it is necessary to add the words "with right of survivorship," or other similar words, if it is desired to create a right of survivorship. If no words of survivorship are used, the transfer of property to two or more persons will be construed as creating a tenancy in common. Under such a statute, a certificate of deposit issued only in the name of "*A* or *B*" does not create a joint tenancy because it does not add words of survivorship. Conversely, when words of survivorship are used, there is a strong presumption that a joint tenancy was created. (See p. 322, Coddington v Coddington)

(b)   Bank Accounts. The deposit of money in a joint account constitutes a gift of a joint ownership interest in the deposit of money when that is the intent of the depositor. The mere fact that money is deposited in a joint account does not in itself establish that there was such a gift, particularly when it can be shown by clear and convincing evidence that the deposits were made in the joint account "solely for the convenience of enabling either of the parties to draw therefrom for family purposes." When the joint account is merely an agency device, the account agent is not entitled to use any part of the account for personal purposes.

In many states, the common law as to joint tenants has been abolished with respect to joint bank accounts and these accounts are governed by the agreement between the parties. Under such a statute they may contract with the bank at the time the account is opened that there shall be the right of survivorship between the account owners.[25]

§ 20:17. Tenancy by Entirety. At common law a *tenancy by entirety* or *tenancy by the entireties* was created when property was transferred to husband and wife in such a manner that it would create a joint tenancy if transferred to other persons, not husband and wife. It differs from joint tenancy, however, in that the right of survivorship cannot be extinguished and one spouse's interest cannot be transferred to a third person, although in some jurisdictions a spouse's right to share the possession and the profits may be transferred. This form of property holding is popular in common-law jurisdictions because creditors of one of the spouses cannot reach the property while both are living. Only a creditor of both the husband and the wife under the same obligation can obtain execution against the property. Moreover, the tenancy by entirety is in effect a substitute for a will since the surviving spouse acquires the complete property interest upon the death of the other. There are usually other reasons, however, why each spouse should make a will.

If property is given to two persons as tenants by the entireties but they are not lawfully married to each other, no tenancy by the entireties can arise. The fact that a tenancy by the entireties was intended, however, is often held a sufficient

---

[25] Commercial Banking Co. v V. B. Spurlock, 238 Ga 123, 231 SE2d 748.

indication that there was to be survivorship, with the result that on the death of one of the co-owner's the share of that co-owner passes to the other by survivorship.[26]

§ 20:18. Community Property. In some states, property acquired during the period of marriage is the *community property* of the husband and wife. Some statutes provide for the right of survivorship, others provide that half of the property of the deceased husband or wife shall go to the heirs or permit such half to be disposed of by will. It is commonly provided that property acquired by either spouse during the marriage is prima facie community property, even though title is taken in a spouse's individual name, unless it can be shown that it was obtained with property possessed by that spouse prior to the marriage.

---

[26] Lopez v Lopez, 250 Md 491, 243 A2d 588.

CASES FOR CHAPTER 20

Fontainebleau Hotel Corp. v Forty-Five Twenty-Five, Inc.

(Fla) 114 So2d 357 (1959)

The Eden Roc and the Fontainebleau are neighboring hotels in Miami Beach, Florida. Fontainebleau proposed to construct a 14-story annex to its building on its land. This construction would block the view of the Atlantic Ocean for persons in the Eden Roc Hotel. The Forty-Five Twenty-Five, Inc., which was the owner of Eden Roc, brought an action against the Fontainebleau Hotel Corp. to prevent the construction of the annex. From a decision against the construction, Fontainebleau appealed.

PER CURIAM. . . . This is indeed a novel application of the maxim *sic utere tuo ut alienum non laedas.* This maxim does not mean that one must never use his own property in such a way as to do any injury to his neighbor. . . . It means only that one must use his property so as not to injure the lawful *rights* of another. . . . "It is well settled that a property owner may put his own property to any reasonable and lawful use, so long as he does not thereby deprive the adjoining landowner of any right of enjoyment of his property *which is recognized and protected by law, and so long as his use is not such a one as the law will pronounce a nuisance.*"[Emphasis supplied.]

No American decision has been cited . . . in which it has been held that—in the absence of some contractual or statutory obligation—a landowner has a legal right to the free flow of light and air across the adjoining land of his neighbor. Even at common law, the landowner has no legal right, in the absence of an easement or uninterrupted use and enjoyment for a period of 20 years, to unobstructed light and air from the adjoining land. . . .

There being, then, no legal right to the free flow of light and air from the adjoining land, it is universally held that where a structure serves a useful and beneficial purpose, it does not give rise to a cause of action, either for damages or for an injunction under the maxim *sic utere tuo ut alienum non laedas,* even though it causes injury to another by cutting off the light and air and interfering with the view that would otherwise be available over adjoining land in its natural state, regardless of the fact that the structure may have been erected partly for spite. . . .

We see no reason for departing from this universal rule. If, as contended on behalf of plaintiff, public policy demands that a landowner in the Miami Beach area refrain from constructing buildings on his premises that will cast a shadow on the adjoining premises, an amendment of its comprehensive planning and zoning ordinance, applicable to the public as a whole, is the means by which such purpose should be achieved. (No opinion is expressed here as to the validity of such an ordinance, if one should be enacted pursuant to the requirements of law.) . . . But to change the universal rule—and the custom followed in this state since its inception—that adjoining landowners have an equal right under the law to build to the line of their respective tracts and to such a height as is desired by them (in the absence, of course, of building restrictions or regulations) amounts, in our opinion, to judicial legislation. . . .

[Judgment reversed]

Data General Corporation v Digital Computer Controls Inc.

(Del Ch) 357 A2d 105 (1975)

Data General Corporation developed a minicomputer, the Nova 1200. Its competitor, Digital Computer Controls, purchased a Nova 1200 from an intermediate dealer. From the drawings and information set forth in the manufacturer's manual given to customers, Digital was able to copy the Nova 1200 and manufactured its own computer which it sold as the D-116. Data General then sued Digital to enjoin or stop it from copying the Nova 1200 on the ground that the information in the manufacturer's manual was secret information and could not be used by anyone for the building of a rival minicomputer and that the plans of the Nova 1200 were protected as a trade secret. Digital defended on the ground that the federal patent law excluded the law of trade secrets and that in any event this protection could not be claimed for the Nova 1200 because the plans had been made public.

MARVEL, V.C. . . . Plaintiff and defendant compete in the business of designing, manufacturing and marketing compact digital computers, commonly known as minicomputers, . . .

Plaintiff complains that . . . defendant, . . . wrongfully made use of drawings which disclosed the design of the Nova 1200, which drawings were intended to be used solely by plaintiff's customers, vendors, licensees, and trainees for the general maintenance, as opposed to the manufacture, of such machine. Defendant having allegedly copied such maintenance drawings, plaintiff goes on to claim that defendant then used them for the improper purpose of designing and making a substantially identical computer, which it named the D-116. . . .

The stated purpose behind the furnishing of such drawings [in the customer's manual] by plaintiff [is] to enable a purchaser to perform his own maintenance of a Nova 1200 in lieu of being required to return such device to plaintiff for repair or to become dependent on a special outside maintenance crew,

prompt repair of a computer, as in a hospital, being often a necessity. . . .

Such drawings bore a proprietary notice or legend,* and the machine itself was accompanied by a standard form of contract which incorporated by reference a confidentiality agreement limiting the use of such drawings to maintenance, as opposed to manufacture, which was stated to be forbidden without plaintiff's consent in writing.

Accordingly, the basic issues to be decided are whether or not the logic design of the Nova 1200 found in plaintiff's maintenance documentation constitutes trade secrets, and, if so, whether or not plaintiff took adequate steps to keep such secrets from becoming public property and thus free as air by failing properly to restrict and restrain their distribution. . . .

First of all, I am satisfied that plaintiff has developed and recorded in its logic drawings of the Nova 1200 concepts of a sufficiently novel nature to entitle each such design drawing to have been a trade secret as of the time of its conception, which property right, if shown to have been adequately withheld from general circulation and thus not freely published may be, upon a proper showing, protected from unauthorized duplication and use, although, of course, an imitator is always entitled to copy a device containing alleged trade secrets through a process of reverse engineering in which the use of protected design drawings are not employed, . . .

Upon the sale and delivery of a Nova 1200, plaintiff's practice has been to deliver with each such machine, whether the buyer be an original equipment manufacturer or an end-user, a complete set of maintenance drawings containing the Nova 1200's logic design. And while other documents, such as a user's and a maintenance manual, promotional articles and brochures of a technical nature as well as advertising have been made generally available by plaintiff to its various established and would-be customers, trainees and vendors, and fallen into the hands of others, I am satisfied that such other documents do not contain sufficient logic design of the Nova 1200 to permit their being successfully used for the purpose of either duplicating such machine or in assembling a computer sustantially identical to the Nova

---

* "This drawing and specifications, herein, are the property of Data General Corporation and shall not be reproduced or copied or used in whole or in part as the basis for manufacture or sale of the items without written permission.". . .

1200. In other words, use of the complete design of such device, which is found in plaintiff's maintenance documentation, is necessary in order for a person to recreate a simulacrum of the Nova 1200 from its existing documentation rather than through reverse engineering. However, each logic diagram made available to Data General's customers and others, including vendors and trainees, bears a legend as noted above, clearly stating that such drawings are not to be used for manufacture or sale of the items disclosed without written permission. . . . Other precautionary measures of Data General designed to protect its alleged proprietary interest in its logic drawings of the Nova 1200 involved the use of standard forms of sales agreements, one being applicable to sales to original equipment manufacturers and the other to sales to end-users. Both forms of such contract, as well as special contracts, contain a provision to the effect that plaintiff's standard terms and conditions, as amended by the sales agreement itself, shall apply to any order filled in response to such an agreement, and a form of such standard terms and conditions, which contains a statement of the proprietary nature of the data furnished with a Nova 1200, including information as to their stated restriction of being used for the installation, testing, operation, and maintenance of the Nova 1200, is furnished to each customer entering into a sales agreement as a prerequisite to obtaining a Nova 1200. In fact, maintenance documentation containing logic diagrams is not furnished to a buyer until he has agreed, under the provisions of the sales agreement, to abide by the provisions of the proprietary legends. . . . Indirect customers not bound by specific contract against the use of plaintiff's documentation, except for maintenance, are, of course, on notice as to the prohibition against the proposed use of such drawings for competitive manufacturing of an identical device by reason of the aforesaid legend or notice affixed to each such document. . . .

Having concluded that plaintiff has trade secrets reposing in the logic design of its Nova 1200, the next matter to be considered is whether or not such secrets are subject to protection by a state court of equity through the granting of injunctive relief and the award of damages . . . In . . . *Kewanee Oil Co. v. Bicron Co.,* 416 U.S. 470, 94 S.Ct. 1879, 40 L.Ed. 2d 315 (1974) . . . the Court made it clear that the field of state trade secret law is not preempted by federal law pertaining to patents in a case in which the majority of the Court protected

a product under the law of trade secrets although it was probably patentable, . . . Secrecy is not lost . . . if the holder of the trade secret reveals the trade secret to another "in confidence, and under an implied obligation not to use or disclose it.". . . Often the recipient of confidential knowledge of the subject of a trade secret is a licensee of its holder. . . .

"The maintenance of standards of commercial ethics and the encouragement of invention are the broadly stated policies behind trade secret law. The necessity of good faith and honest, fair dealing, is the very life and spirit of the commercial world." . . . Even though a discovery may not be patentable, that does not "destroy the value of the discovery to one who makes it, or advantage the competitor who by unfair means, or as the beneficiary of a broken faith, obtains the desired knowledge without himself paying the price in labor, money, or machines expended by the discoverer.". . .

"Trade secret law and patent law have coexisted in this country for over one hundred years. Each has its particular role to play, and the operation of one does not take away from the need for the other. Trade secret law encourages the development and exploitation of those items of lesser or different invention than might be accorded protection under the patent laws, but which items still have an important part to play in the technological and scientific advancement of the Nation. Trade secret law promotes the sharing of knowledge, and the efficient operation of industry; it permits the individual inventor to reap the rewards of his labor by contracting with a company large enough to develop and exploit it. Congress, by its silence over these many years, has seen the wisdom of allowing the States to enforce trade secret protection. Until Congress takes affirmative action to the contrary, States should be free to grant protection to trade secrets."

[Order entered directing trial of issue of damages for violation of trade secrets]

Texas Hydraulic & Equipment Co. v Associates Discount Corp.

(Tex Civ App) 414 SW2d 199 (1967)

Lane bought a dump truck on credit. The Texas Hydraulic replaced the body and hoist on the truck. Lane failed to make the payments for the truck and Associates Discount sought to foreclose on the truck. Texas Hydraulic objected that it owned

the hoist and dump body which it had added to the truck. The lower court held that ownership of the body and hoist had passed to Lane and was subject to the claim of the finance company. Texas Hydraulic appealed.

PHILLIPS, C.J. . . . . Appellant contends that the dump body and hoist had not become a part of the truck by accession. In this connection he points to testimony to the effect that the body and hoist, although welded to the body of the truck, can be cut off with a torch, leaving no damage to the body. On the other hand, appellee calls our attention to testimony that the dump truck had a body or hoist at the time it was originally sold, that it was not a dump truck without a dump bed and that the new dump body had been welded, and in addition bolted, to the bed of the truck.

There was ample evidence for the trial court to find that the dump body and hoist had become part of the truck by accession. . . .

It is undisputed that appellant, in making the transaction with C. H. Lane whereby the dump body and hoist were attached to the truck by welding, did not have any character of written contract with Lane, a chattel mortgage, or any other agreement which in any way purported to make the sale conditional. Nor was there any attempt to retain title to the dump body and hoist in appellant Texas Hydraulics. . . .

Appellant relied on and accepted the promise of a third party . . . for payment before making delivery of the truck, dump body and hoist to Lane, and that, coupled with delivery and the complete absence of any attempt by appellant to enter into a written conditional sales contract, or to retain a chattel mortgage lien on the chattels sold by it clearly indicate that appellant considered the sale to be complete at the time of delivery. . . .

[Judgment affirmed]

North Dakota v Dickinson Cheese Company, Inc.

(ND) 200 NW2d 59 (1972)

In the process of manufacturing cheese, the Dickinson Cheese Company discharged whey into the Heart River in North Dakota. This violated the North Dakota Antipollution Act. It caused the death of some 36,000 pounds of fish. North Dakota sued Dickinson and its plant manager for the damage.

Judgment was entered for the defendants. The State appealed.

STRUTZ, C.J. . . . . The sole question before us on this appeal is whether the State of North Dakota, as represented by the State Game and Fish Department, has such property rights in fish, while they are in the river in a free state, that the invasion of those property rights by the defendants will support an action for damages.

Fish swimming in streams of the State are *ferae naturae*. . . .

Ownership of and title to fish while they are in such state of freedom is in the State for the purpose of regulating the enjoyment, use, possession, disposition, and conservation thereof for the benefit of the people. . . .

The regulatory power of the State extends not only to the taking of its fish but also over the waters inhabited by the fish. . . .

It has been held that the power to protect fish and game is an inherent attribute of the State's sovereign power. . . .

It has been held that although the law provides that the ownership of fish, while they are in a state of freedom, is in the State for the purposes of regulation of their taking and conservation, the interest of the State in fish running wild in the streams of the State is that of a sovereign, and not that of an owner. . . .

As sovereign, the State has the power to determine when and under what conditions fish running wild may be taken and thus reduced to ownership, but it does not have such property interest in the fish while they are in a wild state sufficient to support a civil action for damages for the destruction of those fish which have not been reduced to possession. . . .

Did the . . . "Antipollution Act" bestow upon the State of North Dakota the power to maintain an action for monetary damages for the unlawful killing of fish in the wild state? We think not. That [law] was enacted to give to the State the power to control, prevent, and abate the pollution of surface waters in the State. It gives to the State of North Dakota, through its Water Pollution Control Board, acting jointly with the State Health Council, the authority to adopt, amend, or repeal rules, regulations, and standards of quality of the waters of the State, and it fixes penalties for the violation thereof. It does not give to the State ownership sufficient to support a civil action for damages against one who unlawfully pollutes a stream and thus causes the destruction

of fish while they are running wild in such water. . . .

[Judgment affirmed]

Coddington v Coddington

56 AppDiv2d 697, 391 NYS2d 760 (1977)

The New York Banking Law provides that a
presumption arises that a joint tenancy has been
created when a bank account is opened in the names
of two persons "payable to either or the survivor."
While he was still single, Richard opened a savings
account with his mother Amelia. The signature card
they signed stated that the account was owned by
them as joint tenants with the right of survivorship.
No statement as to survivorship was made on the
passbook. Richard later married Margaret. On his
death, Margaret claimed a share of the account on
the ground that it was not a joint tenancy because
the passbook did not contain words of survivorship
and because the statutory presumption of a joint
tenancy was overcome by the fact that Richard had
withdrawn substantial sums from the account during
his life. The court awarded the entire account to
the mother and Margaret appealed.

PER CURIAM. . . . Appellant urges that the
absence of the words "payable to either or the survivor" on the passbook and some of the ledger cards
prevents the operation of the presumption because
no joint tenancy was created. While appellant is correct in maintaining that a joint tenancy cannot be
created without words of survivorship . . . what is
controlling is the form in which the initial deposit

was made. . . . In the case at bar, the signature
card contained the agreement of the bank and the
depositor and provided as follows:

> Joint Account-Payable to Either or Survivor
> We agree and declare that all funds now, or
> hereafter, deposited in this account are, and
> shall be, our joint property and owned by us
> as joint tenants with right of survivorship, and
> not as tenants in common; and upon the death
> of either of us any balance in said account
> shall become the absolute property of the
> survivor.

The deposit was clearly in the statutory form and
the prima facie presumption of subdivision (b) of
. . . the Banking Law applies.

Addressing our attention to the . . . assertion
of the appellant . . . that the facts adduced at trial
were sufficient to overcome the presumption, we
must again disagree. The heavy burden of rebutting
the presumption rests upon the challenger . . . and
for the appellant to prevail there must be direct proof
or substantial circumstantial proof, clear and convincing and sufficient to support an inference that
the joint account had been opened in that form as
a matter of convenience only. . . . We find no such
proof here. It is true that the appellant was able to
demonstrate that Richard Coddington had, in fact
at one time withdrawn most of the money in the
account. It is true, too, that withdrawal by one depositor of the whole fund or more than his share is
some evidence that no true joint tenancy was intended. . . . However, such action, standing alone,
is insufficient to overcome the presumption. . . .

[Judgment affirmed]

QUESTIONS AND CASE PROBLEMS

1. What social forces are affected by the rule of law requiring that there be an actual or
   symbolic delivery in order to make a gift?
2. Real property consists of actual rights in things as distinct from claims or rights which
   have not been covered by a patent or copyright. Appraise this statement.
3. Compare the protection afforded by a patent and the protection afforded by a trademark
   registration.
4. How does (a) capturing a wild game animal during the hunting season compare with
   (b) finding lost property?
5. Lyons and his wife had a savings account in a bank in the names of "E. L. Lyons or
   Mrs. E. L. Lyons." Both husband and wife signed a signature card agreeing to the
   rules and regulations of the bank. Did this create a tenancy by the entireties? [Lyons'
   Estate, (Fla) 90 So2d 39]

6. Carol and Robert, both over 21, became engaged. Robert gave Carol an engagement ring. He was killed in an automobile crash before they were married. His estate demanded that Carol return the ring. Was she entitled to keep it? [Cohen v Bayside Federal Savings and Loan Ass'n, 62 Misc2d 738, 309 NYS2d 980]

7. Henry Larson delivered a check to his son, Clifford, for $8,500. The check bore the notation "As Loan." Some time later the son asked the father what he should do about the loan. Henry wrote Clifford a note in broken English saying "Keep it No Return." Henry died and the cancelled check with the notation "As Loan" was found among his papers. Henry's administratrix sued Clifford for repayment of the loan. Did he have any defense? [Larson's Estate, 71 Wash 2d 349, 428 P2d 558]

8. International Paper Company desired to register the name "Data-Speed" as the trademark for paper which it sold in bulk reams for conversion into business forms. This was opposed by Valley Paper Company which already had registered the name "Data" for paper. The registration was sufficiently broad to cover paper for business forms although in fact Valley Paper had been manufacturing paper only for writing, typewriting, and printing. International Paper claimed that the objection of Valley Paper had no merit because the Valley Paper Company did not make paper for business forms and therefore the two companies did not sell in the same channel of trade. Was the name "Data-Speed" entitled to registration? [International Paper Co. v Valley Paper Co. (Ct Cust Pat App) 468 F2d 937]

9. Mrs. Weaver opened a joint bank account with right of survivorship in her name and the name of her daughter Mary Lock. Mrs. Weaver later converted the account to a joint tenancy with her son Bill, advising him that it was for her convenience to allow him to pay her bills when she was ill. Bill did not believe he was receiving a gift of an interest in the account. Months later she converted the account back to a joint account with Mary Lock, never telling Mary that the money would be hers on her death. Upon the death of Mrs. Weaver, Mary claimed the balance of the account as the sole owner by survivorship. Is she correct? [Weaver's Estate v Lock, 75 Ill2d 227, 220 NE2d 321]

10. Atomic Oil Company sold an oil product for automobiles under the name of SAVMOTOR. It registered the name under the Lanham Trademark Act of 1946. Bardahl Oil Company sold an oil additive under the name of SAVOIL. Atomic Oil sued Bardahl for an injunction and damages, claiming that SAVOIL infringed the registration of SAVMOTOR. Bardahl defended on the ground that the registration of SAVMOTOR under the Act was improper and that the public did not associate the mark with Atomic Oil. Was Atomic Oil Correct? [Bardahl Oil Co. v Atomic Oil Co. (CA10 Okla) 351 F2d 148]

11. The plaintiff, Herbert Rosenthal Jewelry Corporation, and the defendant, Kalpakian, manufactured jewelry. The plaintiff obtained a copyright registration of a jeweled pin in the shape of a bee. Kalpakian made a similar pin. Rosenthal sued Kalpakian for infringement of copyright registration. Kalpakian raised the defense that he was only copying the idea and not the way the idea was expressed. Was he liable for infringement of the plaintiff's copyright? [Herbert Rosenthal Jewelry Corp. v Kalpakian (CA9 Cal) 446 F2d 738]

12. Brogden acquired a biblical manuscript in 1945. In 1952 he told his sister Lucy that he wanted Texas A. & M. College to have this manuscript. He dictated a note so stating and placed it with the manuscript. He made some effort to have an officer of the college come for the manuscript. In 1956 he delivered the manuscript to his sister, stating that he was afraid that someone would steal it. Later in the year he told a third person that he was going to give the manuscript to the college. In 1957 he was declared incompetent. In 1959 the sister delivered the manuscript to the college. In April, 1960, Brogden died, and his heirs, Bailey and others, sued Harrington and other officers of the college

to have the title to the manuscript determined. Decide. [Harrington v Bailey (Tex CivApp) 351 SW2d 946]

13.   The owner of an investment account certificate issued by a savings and loan association directed the association to name him and the church of which he was a member "as joint tenants with right of survivorship." When the owner opened the account he had signed a signature card. The association did not require a new signature card after being told to add the church as co-owner, and no representative of the church ever signed any card or other document. Interest payments on the certificate were made to the original owner until his death and the church never knew of the transaction until the original owner died. The executor of the original owner then brought action against the church to determine ownership of the certificate. Was the church the owner? [Wantuck v United States Savings and Loan Association (Mo) 461 SW2d 692]

14.   Frank Stamets opened a savings account in the First National Bank. The account stood in the name of "Frank Stamets or Lena Stamets," Lena being his sister. The signature card, which was signed by Frank only, stated that the account was owned by Frank and Lena as joint tenants with the right of survivorship. All the money deposited was Frank's. The signature card was never signed by Lena. On Frank's death, Lena claimed the bank account. The estate of Frank claimed it on the ground that Lena had never signed the signature card. Decide. [Stamets' Estate, 260 Iowa 93, 148 NW2d 468]

21 Bailments

Many instances arise in which the owner of personal property entrusts it to another. A person checks a coat at a restaurant or loans a car to a friend, delivers a watch to a jeweler for repairs, takes furniture to a warehouse for storage, or delivers goods to an airline for shipment. The delivery of property under such circumstances is a bailment.

A. GENERAL PRINCIPLES

A *bailment* is the legal relation that arises whenever one person delivers possession of personal property to another under an agreement, express or implied, by which the latter is under a duty to return the identical property to the former or to deliver it or dispose of it as agreed. The person who turns over the possession of the property is the *bailor*. The person to whom the bailor gives possession is the *bailee.*

§ 21:1 Elements of Bailment.

(a)   Agreement. The bailment is based upon an agreement. Technically the bailment is the act of delivering the property to the bailee and the relationship existing thereafter. The agreement that precedes this delivery is an agreement to make a bailment rather than the actual bailment. Generally this agreement will contain all the elements of a contract so that the bailment transaction in fact consists of (1) a contract to bail and (2) the actual bailing of the property. Ordinarily there is no requirement that the contract of bailment be in writing.

The statute of frauds does not apply to a bailment agreement. If there is a written agreement, the parol evidence rule is applicable to the agreement if the writing is complete. If the written agreement is not complete, the missing terms may be proven by parol evidence.[1]

(b)   Personal Property. The subject of a bailment may be any personal property of which possession may be given. Real property cannot be bailed.

(c)   Bailor's Interest. The bailor is usually the owner, but ownership by the bailor is not required. It is sufficient that the bailor have physical possession. Thus, an

---

[1] In some states, a writing or recording of the bailment agreement may be necessary to protect the interest of the bailor as against third persons.

employee may be a bailor in leaving the employer's truck at a garage. Whether possession is lawful or not is immaterial. A thief, for example, may be a bailor.

(d)   Bailee's Interest. The bailee has only possession of the property. Title to the property does not pass to the bailee and the bailee cannot sell the property to a third person unless the bailee is also an agent authorized to make such a sale. If the bailee attempts to sell the property, such sale only transfers possession and the owner may recover the property from the buyer.

The bailor may cause third persons to believe that the bailee is the owner of the bailed property. If the bailor does so, the bailor is estopped to deny that the bailee is the owner as against persons who have relied on the bailor's representations. As a further exception, if the bailee is a dealer in goods of the kinds entrusted to the bailee by the bailor, a sale by the bailee to a buyer in the ordinary course of business will pass the bailor's title to the buyer.

(e)   Delivery and Acceptance. The bailment arises when, pursuant to the agreement of the parties, the property is delivered to the bailee and accepted by the bailee as subject to the bailment agreement. No bailment arises when personal property is left in a building without the knowledge of the owner of the building. (See p. 334, Berglund v Roosevelt University) Likewise no bailment arises when an employee leaves tools on a workbench overnight, particularly when the employee has been informed by the employer that the latter will not be responsible for any loss of tools. In contrast, if the employer takes possession or exercises control over the personal property of its employees with their consent, express or implied, a bailment arises.

Delivery may be actual as when the bailor physically hands a book to the bailee, or it may be a *constructive delivery,* as when the bailor points out a package to the bailee who then takes possession of it.

(f)   Return of Specific Property. A bailment places a duty upon the bailee to return the specific property that was bailed or to deliver or dispose of it in the manner directed by the bailment agreement. If a person has an option of paying money or of returning property other than that which was delivered by the bailor, there is generally no bailment. Thus, when a farmer delivers wheat to a grain elevator that gives the farmer a receipt which promises to return either the wheat or a certain amount of money upon presentation of the receipt, the relationship is not a bailment.[2]

(1)   Bailment of Fungible Goods. In the case of the bailment of *fungible goods,* such as grain and oil, where any unit or quantity is exactly the same as any other unit or quantity, the law treats the transaction as a bailment when there is only an obligation to return an equal quantity of goods of the same description as the goods originally delivered. Thus an agreement by a grain elevator receiving 1,000 bushels of Grade A wheat from a farmer to return to the farmer on demand 1,000 bushels of Grade A wheat gives rise to a bailment even though there is no agreement that the identical wheat delivered to the elevator will be returned to the farmer.

---

[2] In some states, however, statutes declare that the relationship between farmer and the grain elevator is a bailment and not a sale. United States v Haddix & Sons, Inc. (CA6 Mich) 415 F2d 584.

An "identical return" bailment might be made in some cases, as when a farmer has developed some experimental seed and desires that that very seed be returned by the elevator. Ordinarily, however, the grain that a farmer delivers to the elevator will be of a recognized commercial variety so that the elevator is likely to have or is likely to receive thereafter identically similar grain from other farmers. In that case, the warehouse will not ordinarily undertake to return to any one customer the identical grain delivered by that customer to the elevator but merely an equivalent quantity of grain.

(2)   Option to Purchase. If the bailee has an option to purchase, the transaction is a bailment, with the rights and liabilities of the parties being determined on that basis, until the bailee exercises the option. Theoretically this is inconsistent with the definition of bailment because it contradicts the obligation of the bailee to return the identical property. The bailment with an option to purchase may sometimes be used in connection with credit sales. In such case, the "rental" payments by the bailee (who is actually the buyer) will be calculated in terms of the amount due on the balance of the purchase price. On exercising the option to purchase, the bailee-buyer will be required to pay any unpaid balance of the purchase price.

§ 21:2. Classification of Bailments. Bailments are classified as ordinary and extraordinary. *Extraordinary bailments* are those in which the bailee is under unusual duties and liabilities by law, as in the case of bailments in which a motel or a common carrier is involved. *Ordinary bailments* include all other bailments.

Bailments may or may not provide for compensation to the bailee. Upon that basis they may be classified as *contract bailments* and *gratuitous bailments.*

The fact that no charge is made by the bailor does not necessarily make the transaction a gratuitous bailment. If the bailment is made to further a business interest of the bailor, as when something is loaned "free" to a customer, the bailment is not gratuitous.[3]

Bailments may also be classified in terms of benefit as for the (a) sole benefit of the bailor, as when a farmer gratuitously transports another's produce to the city; (b) sole benefit of the bailee, as when a person borrows the automobile of a friend; or (c) benefit of both parties (mutual-benefit bailment), as when one rents a power tool. A mutual-benefit bailment also arises when a prospective buyer of an automobile leaves the automobile to be traded in with the dealer so that the latter may test it and appraise it.[4]

§ 21:3. Constructive Bailments. When one person comes into possession of personal property of another without the owner's consent, the law treats the possessor as a bailee and calls the relationship a *constructive bailment.* It is thus held that the finder of lost property is a bailee of that property.

---

[3] Coe Oil Service, Inc. v Hair (La) 283 So2d 734.
[4] Sampson v Birkeland, 63 IllApp2d 178, 211 NE2d 139.

When a city impounds an automobile, a bailment arises as to the vehicle and its contents.[5] A seller who has not yet delivered the goods to the buyer is treated as bailee of the goods if title has passed to the buyer. Similarly, a buyer who is in possession of goods, the title to which has not yet passed from the seller, is a bailee.

§ 21:4. Renting of Space Distinguished. When a person rents space in a locker or building under an agreement which gives the renter the exclusive right to use that space, the placing of goods by the renter in that space does not create a bailment. In such a case, putting property into the space does not constitute a delivery of goods into the possession of the owner of the space. On this basis, there is no bailment in a self-service parking lot when the owner of a car parks it, retains the key, and the owner's only contact with any parking lot employee is upon making a payment when leaving the lot. In such situations, the car owner merely rents the space for parking. (See p. 335, Rhodes v Pioneer Parking Lot, Inc.)

The practical consequence of this conclusion is that if the car is damaged or stolen, the car owner cannot recover damages from the parking lot management unless the owner can show some fault on the part of the parking lot. If the transaction were a bailment, the owner of the car would establish a prima facie right to recover by proving the fact of the bailment and that there was a loss.

If the parking lot is a locked enclosure with a guard to whom the patron must surrender a parking ticket received on entering the lot and pay any parking fee that is not yet paid, a modern trend regards the transaction as a bailment. The theoretical objection to this view is that the lot does not have full dominion and control over the car since it cannot move the car because the patron has retained possession of the keys. At the same time, as the lot has the power to exclude others from the car, it is "realistic" to treat the parking lot as a bailee and hold it to a bailee's standard of care.

§ 21:5. Bailment of Contents of Container. It is a question of the intention of the parties, as that appears to a reasonable person, whether the bailing of a container also constitutes a bailment of articles contained in it; that is, whether a bailment of a coat is a bailment of articles in the coat, and so on. When the contained articles are of a class that is reasonably or normally to be found in the container, they may be regarded as bailed in the absence of an express disclaimer. If the articles are not of such a nature and their presence in the container is unknown to the bailee, there is no bailment of such articles. Consequently, although the circumstances were such that the parking of a car constituted a bailment, there was no bailment of valuable drawings and sporting equipment that were on the back seat but which were not visible from the outside of the car.[6]

B. DUTIES AND LIABILITIES

A bailment creates certain rights and imposes certain duties and liabilities upon each party. These may be increased or modified by statute, by custom, or by the express agreement of the parties.

[5] St. Paul v Myles, 298 Minn 298, 218 NW2d 697.
[6] Cerreta v Kinney Corp. 50 NJ Super 514, 142 A2d 917.

§ 21:6. Duties and Liabilities of the Bailee.

(a) Performance. If the bailment is based upon a contract, the bailee must perform the bailee's part of the contract and is liable to the bailor for ordinary contract damages arising out of the failure to perform the contract. Thus, if the bailment is for repair, the bailee is under the duty to make the repairs properly. The fact that the bailee used due care in attempting to perform the contract does not excuse the bailee from liability for failing to perform the contract. (See p. 336, Baena Brothers v Welge)

When a repairer undertakes to repair property, some courts find an implied warranty that the repairs will be effective. Should the repairer fail to repair properly, the bailor who uses the property with knowledge that it has not been effectively repaired, will be barred from claiming for damages sustained through injury arising from such use. For example, when the bailor was aware of the fact that the automobile repairer had failed to repair the brakes, the bailor was barred from recovering damages from the repairer for an injury sustained when the automobile could not be stopped because of the defective brakes and struck a utility pole.[7]

(b) Care of Property. The bailee is under a duty to care for the bailed property. If the property is damaged or destroyed, the bailee is liable for the loss (1) if the harm was caused in whole or in part by the bailee's failure to use reasonable care under the circumstances, or (2) if the harm was sustained during the unauthorized use of the property by the bailee. Otherwise the bailor bears the loss. Thus, if the bailee was exercising due care and was making an authorized use of the property, the bailor must bear the loss of or damage to the property caused by an act of a third person, whether willful or negligent; by an accident or occurrence for which no one is at fault; or by an act of God. In this connection, the term, *act of God,* means a natural phenomenon that is not reasonably foreseeable, such as a sudden flood or lightning.

(1) Standard of Care. The standard for ordinary bailments is reasonable care under the circumstances, that is, the degree of care which a reasonable person would exercise in the situation in order to prevent the realization of reasonably foreseeable harm. The significant factors in determining what constitutes reasonable care in a bailment are the time and place of making the bailment, the facilities for taking care of the bailed property, the nature of the bailed property, the bailee's knowledge of its nature, and the extent of the bailee's skill and experience in taking care of goods of that kind.

Many courts state the standard of care in terms of the benefit characteristic of the bailment, holding the bailee liable for the slightest negligence when the bailment is for the sole benefit of the bailee and for ordinary negligence when the bailment is for the mutual benefit of the parties. In contrast, if the benefit is for the sole benefit of the bailor, it is said that the bailee is only required to exercise slight care and will only be liable for gross negligence.

A bailee is not an insurer of the safety of the property, even though the bailee assures the bailor that good care will be taken of the property.

---

[7] Bereman v Burdolski, 204 Kan 162, 460 P2d 567.

Some courts hold that in the automobile parking lot situation the operator of the lot has the duty to exercise ordinary care for the protection of the automobile regardless of whether the relationship is a bailment or some other relationship, such as a leasing of space or the granting of a license to use the parking lot.

(2)   Contract Modification of Liability. A bailee's liability may be expanded by contract. A provision that the bailor assumes absolute liability for the property is binding, but there is a difference of opinion as to whether a stipulation to return the property "in good condition" or "in as good condition as received" has the effect of imposing such absolute liability. An ordinary bailee may limit liability, except for willful misconduct, by agreement or contract; but modern cases hold that a specialized commercial bailee, such as an auto parking garage, cannot limit its liability for either its willful or negligent conduct.[8]

By definition, a limitation of liability must be a term of the bailment contract before any question arises as to whether it is binding. Thus a bailor is not bound by a limitation of liability which was not known at the time the bailment was made. (See p. 337, Allright, Inc. v Schroeder) Likewise, a limitation contained in a receipt mailed by a bailee after receiving a coat for storage is not effective to alter the terms of the bailment as originally made.

(3)   Insurance. In the absence of a statute or contract provision, a bailee is not under any duty to insure for the benefit of the bailor the property entrusted to the bailee.

(c)   Unauthorized Use. The bailee is liable for conversion, just as though the bailee stole the property, if the bailee uses the property without authority or uses it in any manner to which the bailor had not agreed. Ordinarily the bailee will be required to pay compensatory damages, although punitive damages may be imposed when the improper use was deliberate and the bailee was recklessly indifferent to the effect of the use upon the property.

(d)   Return of Property. The bailee is under a duty to return the identical property which is the subject of the bailment or to deliver it as directed by the bailment agreement. The redelivery to the bailor or delivery to a third person must be made in accordance with the terms of the bailment contract as to time, place, and manner. When the agreement between the parties does not control these matters, the customs of the community govern.

Special statutes may protect the lessor of personal property, as by making it a special criminal offense for the lessee to convert rented property. The statute may create a presumption or inference to aid in the prosecution of the wrongdoer. For example, a statute may declare that it is prima facie evidence of intent to defraud for a person renting property to sign the rental agreement or lease with someone else's name or to fail to return the property to its owner within ten days after being personally served with a written demand for the property. In some states, it is a crime to abandon or conceal rented goods, such as an automobile.

---

[8] In some states, statutes expressly prohibit certain kinds of paid bailees from limiting their liability. Universal Cigar Corp. v The Hertz Corp., 55 Misc 2d 84, 284 NYS2d 337.

The bailee is excused from delivery when the goods are lost, stolen, or destroyed through no fault of the bailee at a time when no unauthorized use of the property was being made. If the fault or neglect of the bailee has caused or contributed to the loss, however, the bailee is liable. To illustrate, certain goods are destroyed by a flood while in the possession of the bailee. If the bailee could have protected the goods from the flood by taking reasonable precautions, the bailee is liable for having failed to do so. The bailee is excused from the duty to return the goods to the bailor when the goods have been taken from the bailee under process of law.

(1) Bailee's Lien. By common law or statute, a bailee is given a *lien* or the right to retain possession of the bailed property until the bailee has been paid for any charges for storage or repairs. If the bailee has a lien on the property, the bailee is entitled to keep possession of the property until payment has been made for the claim on which the lien is based.

A bailee who is authorized by statute to sell the bailed property to enforce a charge or claim against the bailor must give such notice as is required by the statute. A bailee who sells without giving the required notice is liable for conversion of the property.[9]

(2) Constitutionality of Bailee's Lien. Historically, the bailee's lien was merely a right to retain the goods until paid and a statute which goes no further than to authorize such retention is constitutional. There is authority, however, that when the statute goes beyond this common-law pattern and authorizes a sale of the goods, the statute is unconstitutional if it permits the sale of the property without prior notice and hearing as to the existence of the amount alleged to be due.[10]

§ 21:7. Burden of Proof. When the bailor sues the bailee for damages to the bailed property, as distinguished from a suit for breach of contract, the bailor has the burden of proving that the bailee was at fault and that such fault was the proximate cause of the loss. A prima facie right of the bailor to recover is established, however, by proof that the property was delivered by the bailor to the bailee and thereafter could not be returned or was returned in a damaged condition. When this is done, the bailee has the burden to prove that the loss or damage was not caused by the bailee's failure to exercise the care required by law or by an unauthorized use of the property.

When the loss was caused by fire or theft, a minority rule holds that the bailee is required to prove only that the cause of the loss was fire or theft and that the bailor must then prove that the fire or theft occurred because of the bailee's negligence. Most courts do not make this exception to the general rule that the bailee must produce evidence to establish that due care had been exercised.[11]

§ 21:8. Rights of the Bailor. The typical commercial bailment is a mutual benefit bailment. Under such a bailment, the bailor has the right to compensation, commonly called rent, for the use of the bailed property. If the bailor is obligated to render a service

---

[9] Lewis v Ehrlich, 14 OklaApp 529, 513 P2d 153.
[10] Hernandez v European Auto Collision, Inc. (CA2 NY) 487 F2d 378; Whitmore v New Jersey Division of Motor Vehicles, 137 NJSuper 492, 349 A2d 560.
[11] Classified Parking Systems v Dansereau (TexCivApp) 535 SW2d 14.

to the bailee, such as repairing the rented property, the bailor's failure to do so will ordinarily bar the bailor from recovering compensation from the bailee.

(a) Rights Against the Bailee. The bailor may sue the bailee for breach of contract if the goods are not redelivered to the bailor or delivered to a third person as specified by the bailment agreement. The bailor may also maintain actions for negligence, willful destruction, and unlawful retention or conversion of the goods. Actions for unlawful retention or conversion can be brought only after the bailor is entitled to possession. That is, after the time period of the bailment has expired.

When the bailee obtains possession of the goods by fraudulently inducing the bailor to make a bailment, the bailee is guilty of conversion. For example, when a television technician took a set from a customer's home under the pretext of showing the technician's employer how badly prior repairs had been made by another employee of the employer but the actual purpose was to obtain and keep possession of the set until the customer paid improper service charges, the conduct of the technician constituted a conversion and the customer could recover from the employer the value of the set and also punitive damages for such improper taking.

The fact that the bailment contract states that the bailee shall return the property in good condition, reasonable wear and tear excepted, is generally regarded as not changing the rules as to risk of loss. Thus, the bailor, as in the ordinary case, bears the risk of loss from fire of unknown origin; and the bailee is not made an insurer against fire by the inclusion of such terms in the bailment contract.

(b) Rights Against Third Persons. The bailor may sue third persons damaging or taking the bailed property from the bailee's possession, even though the bailment is for a fixed period that has not yet expired. In such a case, the bailor is said to recover damages for injury to the bailor's *reversionary interest,* that is, the right which the bailor has to regain the property upon the expiration of the period of the bailment.

§ 21:9. Duties and Liabilities of Bailor.

(a) Condition of the Property. In a mutual-benefit bailment, as a bailment for hire, the bailor is under a duty to furnish goods reasonably fit for the purpose contemplated by the parties. If the bailee is injured or the bailee's property is damaged because of the defective condition of the bailed property, the bailor may be held liable. If the bailment is for the sole benefit of the bailee, the bailor is under a duty to inform the bailee of known defects. If the bailee is harmed by a defect that was known by the bailor, the bailor is liable for damages. If the bailor receives a benefit from the bailment, the bailor must not only inform the bailee of known defects, but must also make a reasonable investigation to discover defects. The bailor is liable for the harm resulting from those defects which would have been disclosed had the bailor made such an examination, in addition to those defects which were known to the bailor.

If the defect would not have been revealed by a reasonable examination, the bailor, regardless of classification of the bailment, is not liable for the harm which results.

In any case, the bailee, if aware of the defective condition of the bailed property, is barred by contributory negligence or assumption of risk if, in spite of that knowledge, the bailee makes use of the property and sustains injury because of its condition.

(1) Harm to Bailee's Employee. When the harm is caused a bailee's employee because of the negligence of the bailor, the latter is liable to the employee of the bailee, even though the employee did not have any direct dealings or contractual relationship with the bailor.

(2) Bailor's Implied Warranty. In many cases, the duty of the bailor is described as an implied warranty that the goods will be reasonably fit for their intended use. Apart from an implied warranty, the bailor may expressly warrant the condition of the property, in which event the bailor will be liable for breach of the warranty to the same extent as though the bailor had made a sale rather than a bailment of the property.

With the increase in car and equipment leasing, there is beginning to appear a new trend in the cases that extends to the bailee and third persons the benefit of an implied warranty by the bailor that the article is fit for its intended use and will remain so, as distinguished from merely that it was reasonably fit, or that it was fit at the beginning of the bailment, or that the property was free from defects known to the bailor or which a reasonable investigation would disclose. (See p. 338, Cintrone v Hertz Truck Leasing & Rental Service)

The significance of an analysis on the basis of warranty lies in the fact that warranty liability may exist even though the bailor was not negligent.[12]

When a used car is loaned to a prospective buyer to "test drive," there is no implied warranty that it is fit for use although the dealer as bailor will be liable for negligence if the dealer fails to exercise reasonable care to discover any defect in the car, or fails to disclose to the buyer any defect of which the dealer had knowledge. When the bailee has reason to know that the bailor has purchased, rather than manufactured, the equipment that the bailor is renting to the bailee, and that the bailor has no special knowledge with respect to the equipment, a warranty of fitness for purpose may be disclaimed by the bailment agreement.[13]

(b) Repair of the Property. Under a rental contract, the bailor has no duty to make repairs that are ordinary and incidental to the use of the goods bailed. The bailee must bear the expense of such repairs, in the absence of a contrary contract provision. If, however, the repairs required are of an unusual nature or if the bailment is for a short period of time, the bailor is required to make the repairs unless the need for the repairs arose from the negligence or fault of the bailee.

§ 21:10. Liability to Third Persons.

(a) Liability of Bailee. When the bailee injures a third person with the bailed property, as when the bailee runs into a third person while driving a rented automobile,

---

[12] United Airlines, Inc. v Johnson Equipment Co. (FlaApp) 227 So2d 528 (sustaining right of plaintiff to a new trial on the warranty theory, although the first trial on the theory of negligence had ended with a verdict in favor of the defendant, that is, with the conclusion that the defendant was not negligent. The commercial lessor may also be liable on the strict tort theory).

[13] Northwest Collectors, Inc. v Gerritsen, 74 Wash2d 690, 446 P2d 197. (The lessee selected the supplier, and the particular goods were then purchased from that supplier by the bailor under an agreement that the bailor would rent the goods to the bailee.) Note that if the bailment is actually a plan of selling on installment payments to the bailee, a disclaimer of warranties must satisfy the requirements of a disclaimer provision in a sales contract under Article 2 of the Uniform Commercial Code. § 2-316.

the bailee is liable to the third person to the same extent as though the bailee were the owner of the property. When the bailee repairs bailed property, the bailee is liable to a third person who is injured in consequence of the negligent way in which the repairs were made. Conversely, the bailee is not liable to a third person who is injured by a thief who steals the bailed property from the bailee, even though the theft was possible because the bailee was negligent.

(b)   Liability of Bailor. The bailor is ordinarily not liable to a third person injured by the bailee while using the bailed property. In states which follow the common law, a person lending an automobile to another is not liable to the third person injured by such other person when the lender did not know or have reason to know that such other person was not a fit driver.

The bailor is liable, however, to the injured third person; (a) if the bailor has entrusted a dangerous instrumentality to one known to the bailor to be ignorant of its dangerous character; (b) if the bailor has entrusted an instrumentality, such as an automobile, to one known to the bailor to be so incompetent or reckless that injury of third persons is a foreseeable consequence; (c) if the bailor has entrusted property with a defect that causes harm to the third person when the circumstances are such that the bailor would be liable to the bailee if the latter were injured by the defect; or (d) if the bailee is using the bailed article, such as driving an automobile, as the bailor's employee in the course of employment.

(c)   Statutory Change. A number of states have enacted statutes by which an automobile owner granting permission to another to use the automobile automatically becomes liable for any negligent harm caused by the person to whom the automobile has been entrusted. That is, permissive use imposes liability on the owner or provider for the permittee's negligence. In some states, the statute is limited to cases where the permittee is under a specified age, such as 16 years. Under some statutes, the owner is only liable with respect to harm sustained while the permittee is using the automobile for the specific purpose for which permission was granted.

(d)   Family Purpose Doctrine. Under what is called the *family purpose doctrine,* some courts hold that when the bailor supplies a car for the use of members of the bailor's family, the bailor is liable for harm caused by a member of the family while negligently driving the car. Other jurisdictions reject this doctrine and refuse to impose liability on the bailor of the automobile unless there is an agency relationship between the bailor and the driver.

CASES FOR CHAPTER 21

Berglund v Roosevelt University

18 IllApp3d 842, 310 NE2d 773 (1974)

Berglund was a full-time student at Roosevelt University. He was also the editor and photographer of the student newspaper. He kept his own photographic equipment in the rooms which the University had assigned to the newspaper. One night this equip-

ment was apparently stolen from the newspaper office. Berglund sued the University on the theory that it had breached its duty as a bailee. The University denied that it was a bailee. Judgment was entered in favor of Berglund and the University appealed.

McNAMARA, J. . . . The characteristics common to every bailment are the intent to create a bailment, delivery of possession of the bailed items, and the acceptance of the items by the bailee. . . . A bailment can be established by express contract or by implication. . . . In determining the existence of an implied-in-fact bailment, one must analyze the facts surrounding the transaction, such as the benefits to be received by the parties, their intentions, the kind of property involved, and the opportunity of each to exercise control over the property. . . .

In the present case, plaintiff attempted to show that an implied-in-fact bailment had arisen between the parties. It is clear, however, that the failure of the plaintiff to prove any knowledge on the part of the defendant of the storage of the items doomed this attempt.

Knowledge on the part of the bailee is essential to prove proper delivery and acceptance. Physical control over the property allegedly bailed and an intention to exercise that control are needed to show that one is in possession of the bailed item. . . . And before acceptance can be inferred on the part of the alleged bailee of the goods purportedly bailed, there must be evidence to show notice or knowledge on the part of the bailee that the goods are in fact in his possession. . . . Yet in the present case defendant's consistent denial of having any knowledge that plaintiff had stored his camera equipment on the premises is supported by plaintiff's own testimony. Although normal procedure required plaintiff to seek permission of certain agents of defendant to store his property on the premises, plaintiff never bothered to do so. . . . Nor does the fact that prior student paper photographers may have similarly stored their equipment in the darkroom, without more, prove knowledge on the part of defendant. The record also reveals that defendant's security officers never exercised any degree of intentional control over plaintiff's goods. We conclude that plaintiff's failure to prove knowledge on the part of defendant of the goods stored resulted in his inability to prove a valid delivery of the camera equipment and a true acceptance of the goods by defendant. . . . Our holding on this issue obviates the necessity of considering whether defendant was negligent in its capacity as bailee.

[Judgment reversed]

Rhodes v Pioneer Parking Lot, Inc.

(Tenn) 501 SW2d 569 (1973)

Rhodes parked his car on the self-service, park-and-lock lot of Pioneer Parking Lot, Inc. The car was later stolen from the lot by an unknown thief. Rhodes sued the parking lot on the theory that it had breached its duty as a bailee. The parking lot defended on the ground that it was not a bailee. Judgment was entered for the plaintiff, and Pioneer Parking Lot appealed.

LEECH, S.J. . . . The ticket received by appellee when he parked his car contained the following language: "NOTICE THIS CONTRACT LIMITS OUR LIABILITY—READ IT, WE RENT SPACE ONLY. No bailment is created and we are not responsible for loss of or damage to, car or contents. This ticket is sold subject to space being available and is not transferable." A sign posted on the lot [stated] "CARS WITHOUT VALIDATED TICKET WILL BE TOWED AWAY."

There are no restrictions or controls over entry or departure of vehicles or people to and from the parking lot. Moreover, there has never been any attendant to service or look after this lot. Although there is but one entrance which is also the exit, there are no cashiers on this lot.

On October 8, 1969 at about 12:00 o'clock noon, the plaintiff drove his 1968 Chevrolet Camaro onto the defendant's parking lot. At the entrance to this parking lot there is a ticket meter. Plaintiff placed fifty cents in the meter and the meter returned to him the previously set out ticket. Plaintiff then drove his car further into the lot and without any direction or supervision parked it himself; removed the keys from the ignition; placed his ticket on the dash in accordance with the instructions; and locked his car and left the lot keeping his keys himself. Subsequently, plaintiff returned to the parking lot to find that his car had been stolen. His car was later found in a stripped condition and as a result he brought this suit to recover the value of his car.

The trial judge found that the stipulated facts made out a bailor-bailee relationship between plaintiff and defendant and that plaintiff was entitled to recover the value of the car.

The only issue before this Court is whether the relationship between plaintiff and defendant constituted a bailment, so as to permit plaintiff to recover damages for the failure of defendant to redeliver plaintiff's car on demand.

A bailment is the delivery of personalty to another for a particular purpose or on mere deposit, on a contract express or implied, that after the purpose has been fulfilled, it shall be redelivered to the person who delivered it, or otherwise dealt with according to this direction or kept until he reclaims it. . . .

The creation of a bailment in the absence of an express contract requires that possession and control over the subject matter pass from the bailor to the bailee. In order to constitute a sufficient delivery of the subject matter there must be a full transfer, either actual or constructive, of the property to the bailee so as to exclude it from the possession of the owner and all other persons and give to the bailee, for the time being, the sole custody and control thereof. . . .

In parking lot and parking garage situations, a bailment is created where the operator of the lot or garage has knowingly and voluntarily assumed control, possession, or custody of the motor vehicle; if he has not done so, there may be a mere license to park or a lease of parking space. . . . [Courts have] found a bailment where possession of the vehicle was actually surrendered to an attendant. Another factor used to determine whether the operator of the lot has assumed control is the surrender of the keys by the motorist to the operator. . . . Moreover, in [some cases] the necessary possession and control were found where the car could not be taken from the parking garage without the presentation of a parking ticket and payment of the parking fee to an attendant-cashier. . . .

In the case at bar, however, we find no evidence to justify a finding that the plaintiff delivered his car into the custody of the defendant, nor do we find any act or conduct upon the defendant's part which would justify a reasonable person believing that an obligation of bailment had been assumed by the defendant. To the contrary, the facts show that the plaintiff at no time left his car in defendant's possession and control. Plaintiff paid the designated parking fee by depositing the money in the ticket meter. He drove his car into the parking lot, undirected and unsupervised by defendant, and chose a parking space within a lot suitable to himself. Plaintiff then parked and locked the car, retaining the key. At no time did plaintiff come into contact with any of defendant's employees, nor was plaintiff required to contact an employee of the defendant on taking his car from the parking lot. It necessarily follows, therefore, that there was no bailor-bailee relationship established between the plaintiff and the defendant.

However, plaintiff argues that the statement "CARS WITHOUT VALIDATED TICKETS WILL BE TOWED AWAY" would lead the average person to believe that there would be some supervision of the vehicle while it was parked in the lot, and that such was sufficient to create an implied contract of bailment. We disagree. The clear meaning of the statement is that cars in the parking lot would be checked for the sole purpose of enforcing payment of the parking fee and not that the parking lot operator was exercising dominion over all vehicles parked on the lot, especially where as in the case at bar the parking fee was paid. . . .

[Judgment reversed]

Baena Brothers v Welge

3 Conn Cir 67, 207 A2d 749 (1964)

Welge owned a sofa and chair which Baena Brothers agreed to reupholster and to reduce the size of the arms. The work was not done according to the agreement, and the furniture when finished had no value to Welge and was not accepted by him. Baena then sued him for the contract price. Welge counterclaimed for the value of the furniture. From a judgment in favor of Welge on both issues, Baena appealed.

PRUYN, J. . . . The arms on the sofa and chair had been slimmed to such an extent that the overhang of the arms which the defendant desired—and an overhang appeared on the floor sample—had been entirely eliminated, thereby altering the style of the furniture from colonial to modern. The plaintiff knew the purposes for which the furniture, when reupholstered and slimmed, was intended. The furniture as delivered was not reasonably fit for the purposes for which it was intended, did not conform to the contract, and had no value to the defendant. . . .

The facts in the case before us bring it within the doctrine of . . . "a bailment where work and labor, care and pains, are to be performed or bestowed upon the thing delivered to the bailee. The parties to a bailment of this character—one for their mutual benefit—enter into a contract, express or implied or both, by which the bailee engages to perform the agreed services and return the thing bailed in its altered or repaired form and the bailor in return for the services of the bailee agrees to pay him the agreed upon compensation. In a contract of this character there are certain implied obligations of the bailee which the law attaches to the contract in the absence of express provision in the contract to the contrary: One, that the thing which the bailee agrees to alter or repair, when so altered or repaired, shall be reasonably fit for the purpose intended, or capable of the use intended, and of which purpose or use the bailee shall know. . . . Another, that the bailee shall exercise ordinary care in the performance of the service he agrees to do in relation to the thing bailed." . . . The plaintiff broke the contract of bailment: the alterations were not in accordance with the contract; the furniture was not reasonably fit for the purpose intended, of which the plaintiff was aware. The defendant . . . was under no obligation to pay for it.

Where the bailee has deviated from the bailor's instructions in altering the thing bailed, with the result that it has lost its value to the bailor and is worthless to him, as in the instant case, and has been abandoned to the bailee, the bailor may sue . . . for the value of the property. . . . "In determining this value, it is generally sufficient to show the money value of the goods in the market at that time. . . . Where an article does not, however, have a market value, or in the case of goods having a special and peculiar value to the owner, then full compensation requires that he recover 'the value to him based on his actual money loss, all the circumstances and conditions considered, resulting from his being deprived of the property, not including, however, any sentimental or fanciful value he may for any reason place upon it.' " . . .

[Judgment affirmed]

Allright, Inc. v. Schroeder

(TexCivApp) 551 SW2d 745 (1977)

Schroeder parked his car on a parking lot operated by Allright, Inc. It was stolen from the lot. The lot denied liability to Schroeder on the ground that the parking ticket given him stated there was no liability for theft and that the parking lot closed at 6 p.m. and that a sign stated that after 6 p.m. patrons of the lot could obtain the keys to their cars at another location. From a judgment for Schroeder, Allright appealed.

COLEMAN, C.J. On September 8, 1969, at approximately 1:30 p.m. plaintiff drove his automobile into defendant's parking lot in downtown Houston. He turned possession of the automobile over to one of the defendant's employees, who proceeded to park the automobile, and received a claim ticket from another employee. The words "We close at 6 o'clock

p.m." were printed on the ticket in heavy type. A copy of the ticket is attached as an appendix. It can be seen that the provision limiting liability would not be so readily noticed.

Signs were located throughout the parking lot which stated that the lot closed at 6 o'clock p.m. and that anyone returning after that time could pick up their keys at another parking lot operated by defendant at a specified location. Plaintiff had parked his automobile at this lot previously. He was aware at the time he left the car at the station on the occasion in question that the signs and the claim ticket said the lot closed at 6 o'clock.

When the plaintiff returned to the lot around midnight his car was missing. He inquired at defendant's parking lot at 503 Fannin as to the whereabouts of his car. The attendant did not have his keys and knew nothing about the car. Plaintiff filed an offense report with the Houston police reporting the theft of his automobile, and the car was recovered on September 10 by the Harris County Sheriff's Department. It had been partially "stripped" and suffered other damage. . . .

The defendant contends that the fact issues submitted were designed to establish that the plaintiff knew the lot closed at 6 o'clock p.m. and that the plaintiff had impliedly agreed to the limitation of liability provision printed on the stub of the parking ticket. The defendant further asserts that once it is established that the defendant knew of the closing time a finding that the automobile was stolen after that time would establish a defense to the suit in that the operator of a parking lot would have no duty to protect the patron's automobile after the time of closing. The defendant also contends that where a patron of a public parking lot is aware of a statement limiting liability which appears on the parking stub given him at the time he leaves his automobile in the lot, he impliedly agrees to this limitation as a provision of the contract of bailment.

Where parking lot owners attempt to limit liability by posting notices on the wall or by printing such a limitation on the claim check, the limitation must be called to the attention of the bailor before it may become part of the bailment contract. . . . These provisions are strictly construed against the bailee. . . . In *Elledge* the Supreme Court of Texas held that a provision limiting liability of the parking lot owner to a maximum of $100.00 for loss of the bailor's automobile due to theft occasioned by the ordinary negligence of the parking lot owner was enforceable where this provision was inserted in a written contract signed by the bailor.

In this case the limitation provision printed on the claim check was not specifically called to the attention of the bailor at the time he left his automobile at the parking lot. Plaintiff testified that at the time he left his automobile with the defendant he knew that the claim check stated that the lot closed at 6 o'clock. The defendant asserts that this evidence also raises an issue of fact as to whether or not the plaintiff had read the provision limiting liability printed on the claim check.

There is no evidence that the plaintiff read the material appearing on the claim check which was given him on September 8. . . .

Notice that a lot will "close at 6 o'clock p.m." does not give notice that cars left after such time will be at the owner's risk. Such a sign might be construed to mean that no automobiles would be accepted after 6 o'clock p.m. The fact that the closing time of the lot was posted on signs and was printed on the claim ticket does not exempt the operator of the lot from the exercise of ordinary care with respect to the safety of the property. . . .

The evidence does not establish whether the automobile was stolen before or after the lot had closed for the day on September 8, 1969. There was testimony that on special occasions the lot stayed open to a later hour. The plaintiff testified that he knew that the lot had been open after the 6 o'clock closing time on previous occasions and that he inquired of the attendant whether or not the lot would be open later on this night. He testified that he was told that it would be open later. There was testimony that it closed at 6:00 p.m. on September 8, 1969. When his car was recovered the trunk was open, his spare tire was missing, and the keys were found in the trunk. The defendant represented that the keys to the car would be in its custody until returned to the owner.

The requested issue related to an immaterial fact. The operator had a duty to remove the keys from the car at closing time and to transport them to the place mentioned in their sign. The trial court submitted a general negligence issue and the jury found that the defendant's negligence proximately caused plaintiff's automobile to be stolen. . . .

Here the sign clearly represented to the patrons that some degree of care would be exercised for the safety of their automobiles after the closing

time by reason of the notice that the car keys could be picked up after closing time at another location. No agreement that the bailment would expire at 6 o'clock p.m. will be implied from the fact that the plaintiff knew the signs stated that the lot would close at 6 o'clock p.m. under these circumstances.

APPENDIX

ALLRIGHT, INC.
320 TRAVIS
WE CLOSE AT 6:00 P.M.
IMPORTANT — READ CAREFULLY

In consideration of low rates charged for parking, customer agrees that parking operator won't be responsible for loss by fire, misdelivery or theft, except such loss be occasioned by negligence of operator, and then only up to a maximum value of $100. Proportionately greater rates must be paid in advance if customer sets larger limits of liability.

Articles Left In Car At Own Risk

ALLRIGHT AUTO PARKS

191

[Judgment affirmed]

Cintrone v Hertz Truck Leasing & Rental Service

45 NJ 434, 212 A2d 769 (1965)

Contract Packers rented a truck from Hertz Truck Leasing. Packers' employee, Cintrone, was injured while riding in the truck, being driven by his helper, when the brakes of the truck did not function properly and the truck crashed. Cintrone sued Hertz. From a judgment in favor of Hertz, Cintrone appealed.

FRANCIS, J. . . . Under the lease the trucks were kept at Contract Packers' premises but Hertz agreed to service, repair, and maintain them. . . .

The failure of the brakes at the time of the accident was not chargeable to negligence on defendant's part. Plaintiff seeks a reversal of the adverse judgment, however, on the ground that the contractual relationship between Hertz and his employer gave rise to an implied continuing promissory warranty by Hertz that the truck in question was fit for the purposes for which plaintiff's employer rented it, *i.e.,* operation and transportation of goods on the public highways. . . .

If the relationship in the present case between Contract Packers and Hertz were manufacturer or dealer and purchaser, an implied warranty of fitness for operation on the public highway would have come into existence at the time of the sale. . . .

There is no good reason for restricting such warranties to sales. Warranties of fitness are regarded by law as an incident of a transaction because one party to the relationship is in a better position than the other to know and control the condition of the chattel transferred and to distribute the losses which may occur because of a dangerous condition the chattel possesses. These factors make it likely that the party acquiring possession of the article will assume it is in a safe condition for use and therefore refrain from taking precautionary measures himself. . . .

In this connection it may be observed also that the comment to the warranty section of the Uniform Commercial Code speaks out against confining warranties to sales transactions. The comment says: "Although this section is limited in its scope and direct purpose to warranties made by the seller to the buyer as part of a contract of sale, the warranty sections of this Article are not designed in any way to disturb those lines of case law growth which have recognized that warranties need not be confined either to sales contracts or to the direct parties to such a contract. They may arise in other appropriate circumstances such as in the case of bailments for hire, whether such bailment is itself the main contract or is merely a supplying of containers under a contract for the sale of their contents. . . ." See Comment, [UCC §] 2-313. . . .

"The expansion of enterprises engaged solely in bailment for hire seems to justify increasing imposition of absolute warranties, at least to the extent that they would be imposed upon a seller of similarly used goods. In addition, reliance is greater than in the typical sale, for it is generally true that the bailee for hire spends less time shopping for the article than he would in selecting like goods to be purchased, and since the item is not one he expects to own, he will usually be less competent in judging its quality."

A sale transfers ownership and possession of the article in exchange for the price; a bailment for hire transfers possession in exchange for the rental and contemplates eventual return of the article to the owner. By means of a bailment parties can often reach the same business ends that can be achieved by selling and buying. The goods come to the user for the time being, and he benefits by their use and enjoyment without the burdens of becoming and remaining the owner. The owner-lessor benefits by receiving the rent for the temporary use. . . .

We may take judicial notice of the growth of the business of renting motor vehicles, trucks and pleasure cars. . . . The offering to the public of trucks and pleasure vehicles for hire necessarily carries with it a representation that they are fit for operation. This representation is of major significance because both new and used cars and trucks are rented. In fact, . . . the rental rates are the same whether a new or used vehicle is supplied. In other words, the lessor in effect says to the customer that the representation of fitness for use is the same whether the vehicle supplied is new or old. From the standpoint of service to the customer, therefore, the law cannot justly accept any distinction between the obligation assumed by a U-drive-it company whether the vehicle is new or old when rented. The nature of the business is such that the customer is expected to, and in fact must, rely ordinarily on the express or implied representation of fitness for immediate use. . . . To illustrate, if a traveler comes into an airport and needs a car for a short period and rents one from a U-drive-it agency, when he is "put in the driver's seat," his reliance on the fitness of the car assigned to him for the rental period whether new or used usually is absolute. In such circumstances the relationship between the parties fairly calls for an implied warranty of fitness for use, at least equal to that assumed by a new car manufacturer. The content of such warranty must be that the car will not fail mechanically during the rental period.

In the case before us, it is just as obvious that when a company like Contract Packers rents trucks for limited or extended periods for use in its occupation of transportation of goods, it too relies on the express or implied representation of the person in the business of supplying vehicles for hire, that they are fit for such use. . . .

When the implied warranty or representation of fitness arises, . . . it continues for the agreed rental period. The public interests involved are justly served only by treating an obligation of that nature as an incident of the business enterprise. The operator of the rental business must be regarded as possessing expertise with respect to the service life and fitness of his vehicles for use. That expertise ought to put him in a better position than the bailee to detect or to anticipate flaws or defects or fatigue in his vehicles. Moreover, as between bailor for hire and bailee, the liability for flaws or defects not discoverable by ordinary care in inspecting or testing ought to rest with the bailor just as it rests with a manufacturer who buys components containing latent defects from another maker, and installs them in the completed product, or just as it rests with a retailer at the point of sale to the consumer. . . .

The warranty or representation of fitness is not dependent upon existence of Hertz' additional undertaking to service and maintain the trucks while they were leased. That undertaking serves particularly to instill reliance in Contract Packers upon mechanical operability of the trucks throughout the rental period. But the warranty or representation

that the vehicles will not fail for that period sprang into existence on the making of the agreement to rent the trucks, and was an incident thereof, irrespective of the service and maintenance undertaking. . . .

In this developing area of the law, we perceive no sound reason why a distinction in principle should be made between the sale of a truck to plaintiff's employer by a manufacturer, and a lease for hire of the character established by the evidence. . . .

[Judgment reversed and new trial ordered]

Authors' Note. California and a growing number of states have imposed strict tort liability (see p. 49) on the commercial lessors of motor vehicles, thereby achieving independently of the warranty concept a result similar to that reached in the Cintrone case on the basis of a warranty concept. [Price v Shell Oil Co., 2 Cal 3d 245, 85 Cal Rptr 178, 466 P2d 722]

QUESTIONS AND CASE PROBLEMS

1. What social forces are affected by the recognition of a bailment relationship?
2. Compare a bailment with a constructive bailment.
3. Compare a gift with a bailment.
4. When the possessor of property injures a third person, can the third person recover damages from the owner of the property?
5. The Hawkeye Specialty Co. had a contract to supply the United States with bolts that were heat-chemically treated to protect against corrosion. Hawkeye sent a quantity of untreated bolts to Bendix Corporation under a contract by which Bendix was to treat the bolts as required by Hawkeye's contract with the United States. What was the relationship between Hawkeye and Bendix with respect to the bolts thus delivered? [Hawkeye Specialty Co. v Bendix Corporation, (Iowa) 160 NW2d 341]
6. King owned a credit card issued by the Air Travel Company. It was lost or stolen and King reported it. Thereafter Jackson presented the credit card to the Hertz Corporation office at the Newark, New Jersey, airport. By impersonating King and forging his name, Jackson rented a car from Hertz. Jackson failed to return the car and sometime thereafter had a collision with Zuppa. Zuppa sued Hertz under a statute which had the effect of imposing liability on Hertz for harm to third persons by any bailee of a Hertz automobile. Was Jackson a bailee? [Zuppa v Hertz Corp., 111 NJ Super 419, 268 A2d 364]
7. Osell, who held a private pilot's license, rented an airplane from Hall. While attempting to land the plane, he flew through a cloud formation, although he could have avoided doing so. In turning out of the clouds, he struck a hillside and wrecked the plane. Flying through clouds under these circumstances was a violation of the federal civil air regulations. Hall sued Osell for the destruction of the plane. Decide. [Hall v Osell, 102 Cal App 2d 849, 228 P2d 293]

8. Sky Aviation Corporation rented an airplane to Colt. In flying to his destination, Colt did not make use of weather reports. When he arrived at the destination, there were high winds. He landed, instead of turning back to his point of origin where there were no high winds. In landing, he did not make use of a ground crew man who sought to hold down a wing of the plane while he was taxiing to the tie-down area. The wind flipped the plane over. Sky Aviation sued Colt for the damage to the plane. He defended on the ground that it was an act of God. Was this a valid defense? [Sky Aviation Corp. v Colt (Wyo) 475 P2d 301]

9. Harris, who owned a commercial fishing boat, contracted with Deveau to install radar equipment in the boat. Deveau temporarily loaned Harris some radar equipment, and Harris put out to sea on a fishing trip. When he returned, the borrowed radar was found ruined by salt water. Apparently the sea water had entered when heavy seas broke a window. Deveau sued Harris for the damage to the equipment. Was Harris liable for the damage? [Harris v Deveau, (Alaska) 385 P2d 283]

10. Taylor parked his automobile in a garage operated by the Philadelphia Parking Authority and paid a regular monthly charge therefor. There was a written agreement between them which provided: "The Authority shall have the right to move the applicant's automobile to such location as it may deem necessary in order to facilitate the most effective use of the parking space on the roof. Ignition keys must be left in the automobile at all times." It was thereafter agreed between the parties that Taylor could retain the ignition key at all times and lock the auto in order to protect the valuable merchandise which he carried in his car. Taylor brought the car into the garage, locked it, and left with the keys. The car was missing when he returned. He sued the parking Authority on the theory that it had breached a duty as bailee. The Authority claimed that it was not a bailee. Was the Authority correct? [Taylor v Philadelphia Parking Authority, 398 Pa 9, 156 A2d 525]

11. The State of New York loaned without charge a sand loading machine to the Village of Catskill. Hood was employed by the Village and, while using the loader as part of his work, was injured because the drive chain, which was worn and out of alignment, caught his leg. He sued the State of New York for the damages he sustained. The State produced evidence that the machine had been serviced shortly before the accident and that it was then in good working order. Was Hood entitled to recover? [Hood v New York, (Court of Claims of New York) 48 Misc 2d 43, 264 NYS2d 134]

12. Anders was interested in purchasing a used car from Glover Motors. He was trying out one of the cars when, in consequence of a defect in the brakes, he collided with the car driven by Wilcox. The latter sued Glover Motors, claiming that there was liability because Glover Motors knew or should have known that the brakes were defective. Was Glover Motors liable? [Wilcox v Glover Motors, 269 NC 473, 153 SE2d 76]

13. Gregg sold his motorcycle. The buyer loaned it back to him. When the buyer later requested the motorcycle, Gregg sold it to a third person. Was Gregg guilty of a crime? [New Mexico v Gregg, 83 NMex 397, 492 P2d 1260]

14. Lewis put a paper bag containing $3,000 in cash in a railroad station coinoperated locker. After the period of the coin rental expired, a locker company employee opened the locker, removed the money, and because of the amount, surrendered it to the police authorities, as was required by the local law. When Lewis demanded the return of the money from Aderholdt, the police property clerk, the latter required Lewis to prove his ownership to the funds because there were circumstances leading to the belief that the money had been stolen by Lewis. He sued the police property clerk and the locker company. Was the locker company liable for breach of duty as a bailee? [Lewis v Aderholdt, (CA Dist Col App) 203 A2d 919]

15. Axelrod took draperies to Wardrobe Cleaners to be dry cleaned. The head of the drapery department examined the draperies to determine if they were strong enough to be cleaned. He accepted the drapes from Axelrod. The colors of the drapes were ruined in the process of dry cleaning and Axelrod sued Wardrobe Cleaners for the damages. The head of the drapery department of Wardrobe Cleaners testified that, because of new imported dyes, it could not be determined whether colors would stand cleaning without pretesting, and that Wardrobe was not equipped to chemically test fabrics for color fastness. Was this a valid defense? [Axelrod v Wardrobe Cleaners, Inc. (LaApp) 289 So2d 847]

16. Joan took driving lessons at the A-North Shore Driving School. Later the school loaned her an automobile and took her for her state driving test. Crowley was the state examiner. Joan drove into a signal box on the side of the road. Crowley was seriously injured. He sued the driving school. Was it liable? [Crowley v A-North Shore Driving School, 19 Ill App 3d 1035, 313 NE2d 200]

17. Gilchrist took an automobile to a dealer, Winmar J. Ford, Inc., to have the tires rotated. Gilchrist was a refrigerator mechanic and had a special set of tools in the trunk of the car. He did not inform Ford that the tools were in the car. The car was stolen. Ford was sued for the value of the tools. Ford defended on the ground that it was not liable for the value of the tools and that it had never been informed of their value and therefore was not alerted to take special precautions. Was this a valid defense? [Gilchrist v Winmar J. Ford, Inc. 355 NYS2d 261]

22 Special Bailments and Documents of Title

A special bailment relation, rather than an ordinary bailment, arises when goods are stored in a warehouse, or delivered to a merchant to sell for the owner, or delivered to a carrier to be transported. In some instances a hotelkeeper may have a bailee's liability. Some of these special bailees issue a document of title, such as a warehouse receipt or bill of lading, on receiving goods from the bailor.

A. WAREHOUSERS

In contrast with the short-term or casual leaving of property typical of most bailments, some leaving of property is on a longer basis and on a larger scale and has become known as warehousing.

§ 22:1. Definitions. A *warehouser* is engaged in the business of storing the goods of others for compensation. *Public warehousers* hold themselves out to serve the public generally without discrimination.

A building is not essential to warehousing. Thus an enterprise which stores boats outdoors on land is engaged in warehousing, since it is "engaged in the business of storing goods for hire," as against the contention that the storage is out-of-doors and not in a warehouse or similar structure.

§ 22:2. Rights and Duties of Warehousers. The common-law rights and duties of a warehouser, in the absence of modification by statute, are for the most part the same as those of a bailee in an ordinary mutual-benefit bailment.[1] (See p. 352, Brace v Salem Cold Storage, Inc.)

(a) Statutory Regulation. Most states have passed warehouse acts defining the rights and duties of warehousers and imposing regulations as to charges and liens, bonds for the protection of patrons, and maintenance of storage facilities in a suitable and safe condition, inspections, and general methods of transacting business.

(b) Lien of Warehouser. The public warehouser has a lien against the goods for reasonable storage charges.[2] It is a *specific lien* in that it attaches only to the property

---

[1] Uniform Commercial Code § 7-204; Belland v American Auto Insurance Co. (DistColApp) 101 A2d 517. The UCC does not change the prior rule by which when loss by fire is shown, the burden is upon the warehouser to disprove negligence. Canty v. Wyatt Storage Corp. 208 Va 161, 156 SE2d 582.

[2] UCC § 7-209(1). The warehouser's lien provision of the UCC is constitutional as a continuation of the common-law lien, but there is authority that the provision authorizing the warehouser to sell stored property without any hearing as to the amount due by the customer is unconstitutional.

with respect to which the charges arose and cannot be asserted against any other property of the same owner in the possession of the warehouser. The warehouser, however, may make a lien carry over to other goods by noting on the receipt for one lot of goods that a lien is also claimed thereon for charges as to the other goods.[3] The warehouser's lien for storage charges may be enforced by sale after due notice has been given to all persons who claim any interest in the property stored. When a person holding the goods of another is not a warehouser, the possessor may not assert a warehouser's lien against the goods.

A warehouser's lien is lost when the goods are voluntarily returned to the customer or when the warehouser makes any improper charge against the customer. The fact that the lien is lost does not cancel the underlying debt of the customer to the warehouser. (See p. 353, Associated Bean Growers v Chester B. Brown Company)

§ 22:3. Warehouse Receipts. A *warehouse receipt* is a written acknowledgment by a warehouser that certain property has been received for storage from a named person. It also sets forth the terms of the contract for storage and some details describing the transaction, but beyond this no particular form for a warehouse receipt is required. The warehouse receipt is a document of title because the person lawfully holding the receipt is entitled to the goods or property represented by the receipt.

§ 22:4. Rights of Holders of Warehouse Receipts. A warehouse receipt in which it is stated that the goods received will be delivered to the depositor, or to any other named person, is a *nonnegotiable warehouse receipt;* but a receipt in which it is stated that the goods received will be delivered to a bearer, or to the order of any person named in such receipt, is a *negotiable warehouse receipt.*[4]

The transfer of negotiable warehouse receipts is made by delivery or by indorsement and delivery. It is the duty of the warehouser to deliver the goods to the holder of a negotiable receipt and to cancel such receipt before making delivery of the goods. The surrender of a nonnegotiable receipt is not required.

If the person who deposited the goods with the warehouse did not own the goods or did not have the power to transfer title to them, the holder of the warehouse receipt is subject to the title of the true owner.[5] Accordingly, when goods are stolen and delivered to a warehouse and a receipt is issued for them, the owner prevails over the holder of the receipt.[6]

The transfer of a warehouse receipt makes certain implied warranties for the protection of the transferee; namely, that the receipt is genuine, that its transfer is rightful and effective, and that the transferor has no knowledge of any facts that impair the validity or worth of the receipt.[7]

§ 22:5. Field Warehousing. Ordinarily, stored goods are placed in a warehouse belonging to the warehouser. The owner of goods, such as a manufacturer, may keep the goods

---

[3] UCC § 7-209(1).
[4] UCC § 7-104.
[5] UCC § 7-503(1).
[6] UCC § 7-503(1).
[7] UCC § 7-507. These warranties are in addition to any that may arise between the parties by virtue of the fact that the transferor is selling the goods represented by the receipt to the transferee. See Chapter 26 as to sellers' warranties.

in the owner's own storage room or building. The warehouser may then take exclusive control over the room or the area in which the goods are stored and issue a receipt for the goods just as though they were in the warehouse. Such a transaction has the same legal effect with respect to other persons and purchasers of the warehouse receipts as though the property were in fact in the warehouse of the warehouser. This practice is called *field warehousing* since the goods are not taken to the warehouse but remain "in the field."

The purpose of field warehousing is to create warehouse receipts which the owner of the goods is able to pledge as security for loans. The owner could, of course, have done this by actually placing the goods in a warehouse, but this would have involved the expense of transportation and storage.

§ 22:6. Limitation of Liability of Warehouser. A warehouser may limit liability by a provision in the warehouse receipt specifying the maximum amount for which the warehouser can be held liable. This privilege is subject to two qualifications: (a) the customer must be given the choice of storing the goods without such limitation if the customer pays a higher storage rate, and (b) the limitation must be stated as to each item or as to each unit of weight. A limitation is proper when it states that the maximum liability for a piano is $1,000 or that the maximum liability per bushel of wheat is a stated amount. Conversely, there cannot be a blanket limitation of liability, such as "maximum liability $50," when the receipt covers two or more items.

General contract law determines whether a limitation clause is a part of the contract between the warehouser and the customer. (See p. 353, Birmingham Television Corp. v Water Works) A limitation in a warehouse receipt is not part of the contract when the receipt is delivered to the customer a substantial period of time after the goods have been left for storage.

B. FACTORS

Some selling agents are called factors. A *factor* is a special type of bailee who sells goods consigned to the factor as though the factor were the owner of the goods.

§ 22:7. Definitions. The device of entrusting a person with the possession of property for the purpose of sale is commonly called *selling on consignment.* The owner who consigns the goods for sale is the *consignor.* The person or agent to whom they are consigned is the *consignee;* the consignee may also be known as a commission merchant. A consignee's compensation is known as a *commission* or *factorage.* In a sale on consignment, the property remains the property of the owner or consignor, and the consignee acts as the agent of the owner to pass the owner's title to the buyer.

Factoring as defined above has to a large degree been displaced, except with respect to the sale of livestock, by other methods of doing business. Today one is more likely to find the seller selling the goods on credit to a retail merchant with the latter having the right to return any goods which are not sold, the seller then assigning the debt or account receivable owed by the merchant. Or the seller may store the goods in a warehouse or place them on board a carrier and then effect a sale by delivering the warehouse receipts or bills of lading rather than by sending the goods to a factor.

§ 22:8. Effect of Factor Transaction. As a factor is by definition authorized by the consignor to sell the goods entrusted to the factor, such a sale will pass the title of the consignor to the purchaser. Before the factor makes the sale, the goods belong to the consignor; but in some instances, creditors of the factor may ignore the consignor and treat the goods as though they belonged to the consignee.[8] If the consignor is not the owner, as when a thief delivers stolen goods to the factor, a sale by the factor is an unlawful conversion. It is constitutional, however, to provide that the factor who sells in good faith in ignorance of the rights of other persons in the goods is protected from liability and cannot be treated as a converter of the goods,[9] as would be the case in the absence of such a statutory immunity.[10]

C. COMMON CARRIERS

The purpose of a bailment may be transportation and not storage. In such case, the bailee may be a common carrier.

§ 22:9. Definitions. A *carrier* of goods is one who undertakes the transportation of goods, regardless of the method of transportation or the distance covered. The *consignor* or shipper is the person who delivers goods to the carrier for shipment. The *consignee* is the person to whom the goods are shipped and to whom the carrier should deliver the goods.

A carrier may be classified as (a) a *common carrier,* which holds itself out as willing to furnish transportation for compensation without discrimination to all members of the public who apply, assuming that the goods to be carried are proper and that facilities of the carrier are available; (b) a *contract carrier,* which transports goods under individual contracts; or (c) a *private carrier,* such as a truck fleet owned and operated by an industrial firm. The common carrier law applies to the first, the bailment law to the second, and the law of employment to the third.

§ 22:10. Freight Forwarders. A *freight forwarder* accepts freight from shippers, ordinarily in less-than-carload lots, combines such freight into carloads, and delivers it as carloads to a carrier for shipment to a particular point where the carload lots are separated and the items carried to their respective destinations. A freight forwarder does not own or operate any of the transportation facilities. Freight forwarders are generally subject to the same government regulations as common carriers.

§ 22:11. Bills of Lading. When the carrier accepts goods for shipment or forwarding, it ordinarily issues to the shipper a *bill of lading*[11] in the case of land or marine transportation or an *airbill*[12] for air transportation. This instrument, which is a document of title, is both a receipt for the goods and a contract stating the terms of carriage. Title to

---

[8] UCC § 2-326.

[9] Montana Meat Co. v Missoula Livestock Auction Co. 125 Mont 66, 230 P2d 955.

[10] Sig Ellington & Co. v De Vries (CA8 Minn) 199 F2d 677.

[11] In order to avoid the delay of waiting for a bill of lading mailed to the destination point from the point where the goods were received by the carrier, UCC § 7-305(1) authorizes the carrier at the request of the consignor to provide for the issuance of the bill at the destination rather than the receipt point.

[12] UCC § 1-201(6).

the goods may be transferred by a transfer of the bill of lading made with that intention.

With respect to intrastate shipments, bills of lading are governed by the Uniform Commercial Code.[13] Interstate transportation is regulated by the federal Bills of Lading Act.[14]

A bill of lading is a *negotiable bill of lading* when by its terms the goods are to be delivered to bearer or to the order of a named person.[15] Any other bill of lading, such as one that consigns the goods to a named person is a nonnegotiable or *straight bill of lading.*

(a)   Contents of Bill of Lading. The form of the bill of lading is regulated in varying degrees by administrative agencies.[16]

As against the bona fide transferee of the bill of lading, a carrier is bound by the recitals in the bill as to the contents, quantity, or weight of goods.[17] This means that the carrier must produce the goods which are described, even though they had not existed, or pay damages for failing to do so. This rule is not applied if facts appear on the face of the bill that should keep the transferee from relying on the recital.

(b)   Negotiability. The holder of a bill of lading has the direct obligation of the carrier to hold possession of the goods for such person according to the terms of the bill of lading just as though the carrier had contracted directly with such holder. The holder of the bill ordinarily also acquires the title to the bill and the goods represented by it. The rights of the holder of a negotiable bill are not affected by the fact (1) that the former owner of the bill had been deprived of it by misrepresentation, fraud, accident, mistake, duress, undue influence, loss, theft, or conversion; or (2) that the goods had already been surrendered by the carrier or had been stopped in transit.[18]

The rights of the holder of a bill of lading are subject to the title of a true owner of the goods who did not authorize the delivery of the goods to the carrier. For example, when a thief delivers the goods to the carrier and then negotiates the bill of lading, the title of the owner of the goods prevails over the claim of the holder of the bill.[19]

(c)   Warranties. By transferring for value a bill of lading, whether negotiable or nonnegotiable, the transferor makes certain implied warranties to the transferee. The transferor impliedly warrants that (1) the bill of lading is genuine, (2) its transfer is rightful and is effective to transfer the goods represented thereby, and (3) the transferor has no knowledge of facts that would impair the validity or worth of the bill of lading.[20]

---

[13] UCC, Article 7.
[14] Title 49, United States Code § 81 et seq.
[15] UCC § 7-104(1)(a).
[16] The UCC contains no provision regulating the form of the bill of lading.
[17] UCC § 7-301(1).
[18] UCC § 7-502(2).
[19] UCC § 7-503(1).
[20] UCC § 7-507; Federal Bill of Lading Act (FBLA), 49 USC §§ 114, 116. When the transfer of the bill of lading is part of a transaction by which the transferor sells the goods represented thereby to the transferee, there will also arise the warranties that are found in other sales of goods.

§ 22:12. **Rights of Common Carrier.** A common carrier of goods has the right to make reasonable and necessary rules for the conduct of its business. It has the right to charge such rates for its services as yield it a fair return on the property devoted to the business of transportation, but the exact rates charged are regulated by the Interstate Commerce Commission in the case of interstate carriers and by state commissions in the case of intrastate carriers. As an incident of the right to charge for its services, a carrier may charge *demurrage:* a charge for the detention of its cars or equipment for an unreasonable length of time by either the consignor or consignee.

As security for unpaid transportation and service charges, a common carrier has a lien on goods that it transports. The carrier's lien also secures demurrage charges, the costs of preservation of the goods, and the costs of sale to enforce the lien.[21] The lien of a carrier is a specific lien. It attaches only to goods shipped under the particular contract, but includes all of the shipment even though it is sent in installments. Thus, when part of the shipment is delivered to the consignee, the lien attaches to the portion remaining in possession of the carrier.

§ 22:13. **Duties of Common Carrier.** A common carrier is generally required (a) to receive and carry proper and lawful goods of all persons who offer them for shipment; (b) to furnish facilities that are adequate for the transportation of freight in the usual course of business, and to furnish proper storage facilities for goods awaiting shipment or awaiting delivery after shipment; (c) to follow the directions given by the shipper; (d) to load and unload goods delivered to it for shipment (in less-than-carload lots in the case of railroads), but the shipper or consignee may assume this duty by contract or custom; (e) to deliver the goods in accordance with the shipment contract.

Goods must be delivered at the usual place of delivery at the specified destination. When goods are shipped under a negotiable bill of lading, the carrier must not deliver the goods without obtaining possession of the bill properly indorsed. When goods are shipped under a straight bill of lading, the carrier is justified in delivering the goods to the consignee or the consignee's agent without receiving the bill of lading, unless notified by the shipper to deliver the goods to someone else. If the carrier delivers the goods to the wrong person, the carrier is liable for breach of contract and for the tort of conversion.

§ 22:14. **Liabilities of Common Carrier.** When goods are delivered to a common carrier for immediate shipment and while they are in transit, the carrier is absolutely liable for any loss or damage to the goods unless it can prove that it was due solely to one or more of the following excepted causes: (a) act of God, meaning a natural phenomenon that is not reasonably foreseeable; (b) act of public enemy, such as the military forces of an opposing government, as distinguished from ordinary robbers; (c) act of public authority, such as a health officer removing goods from a truck; (d) act of the shipper, such as fraudulent labeling or defective packing; or (e) inherent nature of the goods, such as those naturally tending to spoil or deteriorate.

Unusually heavy rains do not constitute an act of God, for the reason that rains and even heavy rains are not unexpectable. Consequently, a common carrier is liable for loss caused by delay resulting from such heavy rain conditions.

---

[21] UCC § 7-307(1); FBLA, 49 USC § 105.

When a carrier claims the benefit of an excepted cause, it must show that the excepted cause was the sole cause of the harm. A common carrier cannot exonerate itself by showing that all transportation services were performed without negligence but it must go further and establish that the loss or damage was caused solely by one of the excepted perils.[22]

(a) Carrier's Liability for Delay. A carrier is liable for losses caused by its failure to deliver goods within a reasonable time. Thus, the carrier is liable for losses arising from a fall in price or a deterioration of the goods caused by its unreasonable delay. The carrier, however, is not liable for every delay. The risk of ordinary delays incidental to transporting goods is assumed by the shipper.

(b) Liability of Initial and Connecting Carriers. When goods are carried over the lines of several carriers, the initial and the final carrier, as well as the carrier on whose lines the loss is sustained, may be liable to the shipper or the owner of the goods; but only one payment may be obtained.

(c) C.O.D. Shipment. A common carrier transporting goods under a C.O.D. shipment may not make delivery of the goods without first receiving payment. If it does so, it is liable to the shipper for any loss resulting therefrom. (See p. 354, American Machinery & Motor Co. v United Parcel Service) If the carrier accepts a check from the consignee and the check is not honored by the bank on which it is drawn, the carrier is liable to the shipper for the amount thereof.[23]

(d) Limitation of Liability of Carrier. In the absence of a constitutional or statutory prohibition, a carrier generally has the right to limit its liability by contract. A clause limiting the liability of the carrier is not enforceable unless consideration is given for it, usually in the form of a reduced rate, and provided further that the shipper is allowed to ship without limitation of liability if the shipper chooses to pay the higher or ordinary rate.[24]

A carrier may by contract exempt itself from liability for losses not arising from its own negligence, but may not exempt itself from liability for loss due to its own negligence. Thus, a provision which purports to exempt an air carrier from liability for its own negligence in the carriage of live animals as baggage has been held invalid.

A common carrier may make an agreement with the shipper as to the value of the property. If the amount is reasonable, such an agreement will usually bind the shipper.

Limitation of liability is governed by the Carriage of Goods by Sea Act in the case of water carriers, and by the Warsaw Convention in the case of international air transportation. By the Warsaw Convention, liability is limited to a stated amount. Its provisions apply to both the regular commercial flights and charter flights.

(e) Notice of Claim. The bill of lading and applicable government regulations may require that a carrier be given notice of any claim for damages or loss of goods within a specified time, generally not less than 9 months. A provision in a tariff

[22] Boyd v McCleskey (Tex Civ App) 515 SW2d 25.
[23] National Van Lines, Inc. v Rich Plan Corp. (CA5 Tex) 385 F2d 800.
[24] UCC § 7-309(2).

limiting the time for such notice is not binding on a consignee who has not received a copy of the bill of lading.

(f)   Liability for Baggage. A common carrier of passengers is required to receive a reasonable amount of baggage. With respect to baggage over which the carrier takes control, the carrier has the same liability as the carrier of goods. If a passenger retains custody of baggage, the carrier is liable only for a lack of reasonable care or willful misconduct on the part of its agent and employees. Limitations on baggage liability are commonly authorized by law and are binding upon passengers even though unknown to them.

D. HOTELKEEPERS

A hotelkeeper has a bailee's liability with respect to property specifically entrusted to the hotelkeeper's care. With respect to property in the possession of the guest, the hotelkeeper has supervisory liability.

§ 22:15. Definitions.

(a)   Hotelkeeper. The term *hotelkeeper* is used by law to refer to an operator of a hotel, motel, tourist home, or to anyone who is regularly engaged in the business of offering living accommodations to all transient persons.[25] In the early law, the hotelkeeper was called an innkeeper or a tavernkeeper.

(b)   Guest. The essential element in the definition of a *guest* is that the guest is a transient. The guest need not be a traveler nor come from a distance. A person living within a short distance of a hotel who engages a room at the hotel and remains there overnight is a guest.

A person who enters a hotel at the invitation of a guest or attends a dance or a banquet given at the hotel is not a guest. Similarly, the guest of a registered occupant of a motel room who shares the room with the occupant without the knowledge or consent of the management is not a guest of the motel, since there is no relationship between that person and the motel.

§ 22:16. Discrimination. Since a hotel is by definition an enterprise holding itself out to serve the public, it follows that members of the public, otherwise fit, must be accepted as guests. If the hotel refuses accommodations for an improper reason, it is liable for damages, including exemplary damages. A guest has been held entitled to recover such punitive damages when improperly ejected under circumstances indicating an intentional and willful disregard of the guest's rights.

(a)   Civil Rights Legislation. A hotel may also be liable under a civil rights or similar statutory provision and it may also be guilty of a crime when it discriminates improperly. By virtue of the federal Civil Rights Act of 1964, neither a hotel nor its concessionaire can discriminate against patrons or segregate them on the basis

---

[25] A person furnishing the services of a hotelkeeper has the status of such even though the word "hotel" is not used in the business name. Lackman v Department of Labor and Industries, 78 Wash2d 212, 471 P2d 82.

of race, color, religion, or national origin. The federal Act is limited to discrimination for the stated reasons and does not in any way interfere with the right of the hotel to exclude a person who is drunk or criminally violent, or is not dressed in the manner required by reasonable hotel regulations applied to all persons. When there has been improper discrimination or segregation or it is reasonably believed that such acts may occur, the federal statute authorizes the institution of proceedings in the federal courts for an order to stop such prohibited practices.

(b)   Non-Guest. A hotelkeeper has no duty to admit non-guests who do not apply for accommodations. The hotelkeeper may exclude non-guests from soliciting business from hotel guests. If a non-guest is told to leave the premises but returns, the non-guest will be guilty of the crime of unlawful entry [26] or some similar offense.

§ 22:17. Duration of Guest Relationship. The relationship of guest and hotelkeeper does not begin until a person is received as a guest by the hotelkeeper. The relationship terminates when the guest leaves or when the guest ceases to be a transient, as when the guest arranges for a more or less permanent residence at the hotel. The transition from the status of guest to the status of boarder or lodger must be clearly indicated. It is not established by the mere fact that one remains at the hotel for a long period, even though it runs into months.

§ 22:18. Hotelkeeper's Liability for Guest's Property. As to property expressly entrusted to the hotelkeeper's care, the hotelkeeper has a bailee's liability. As to other property of the guest, the hotelkeeper is ordinarily an insurer as to its safety.[27] As exceptions, the hotelkeeper is not liable for loss caused by an act of God, a public enemy, act of public authority, the inherent nature of the property, or the fault of the guest.

In most states, statutes limit or provide a method of limiting the liability of a hotelkeeper. The statutes may limit the extent of liability, reduce the liability of the hotelkeeper to that of an ordinary bailee, or permit the hotelkeeper to limit liability by contract or by posting a notice of the limitation. Some statutes relieve the hotelkeeper from liability when directions for depositing valuables with the hotelkeeper are posted on the doors of the rooms occupied and the guest fails to comply with the directions. When a statute permits a hotel receiving valuables for deposit in its safe deposit box to limit its liability to the amount specified in the agreement signed by the guest, such limitation binds the guest even though the loss was caused by negligence on the part of the hotel.[28]

Even when there is no limitation on the liability of a hotel, it is not liable for more than the value of the guest's property and is not liable for the consequential harm that may flow from the loss of that property. (See p. 355, Morse v Piedmont Hotel Co.)

When the guest has checked a coat in the hotel checkroom, it is no defense to the hotel that the checkroom was operated by a concessionaire when there is nothing to call that fact to the attention of the guest.[29]

---

[26] Kelly v United States (DistColApp) 348 A2d 884.
[27] Zurich Fire Insurance Co. v Weil (Ky) 259 SW2d 54.
[28] Kalpakian v Oklahoma Sheraton Corp. (CA10 Okla) 398 F2d 243.
[29] Aldrich v Waldorf Astoria Hotel (NY CivCt) 343 NYS2d 830.

§ 22:19. Hotelkeeper's Lien. The hotelkeeper has a lien on the baggage of guests for the agreed charges, or if no express agreement was made, for the reasonable value of the accommodations furnished. Statutes permit the hotelkeeper to enforce this lien by selling the goods of the guests at a public sale.[30] The lien of the hotelkeeper is terminated by (a) the guest's payment of the hotel charges, (b) any conversion of the guest's goods by the hotelkeeper, and (c) surrender of the goods to the guest. In the last situation, an exception is made when the goods are given to the guest for temporary use.

§ 22:20. Boarders or Lodgers. To those persons who are permanent boarders or lodgers, rather than transient guests, the hotelkeeper owes only the duty of an ordinary bailee of personal property under a mutual-benefit bailment.

A hotelkeeper has no common-law right of lien on property of boarders or lodgers, as distinguished from guests, in the absence of an express agreement creating such a lien. In a number of states, however, legislation giving a lien to a boarding house or a lodging housekeeper has been adopted.

---

[30] There is authority that the hotelkeeper's lien may not be exercised unless the guest is given an impartial hearing and that it is unconstitutional as a denial of due process to permit the hotelkeeper to hold or sell the guest's property without such a hearing. Klim v Jones (DC ND Cal) 315 FSupp 109. A hotel cannot seize the goods of a guest under a statutory lien law without first affording the guest a hearing as to liability, and the failure to do so deprives the guest of the due process guaranteed by the federal Constitution. New York v Skinner, 33 NYS2d 23, 300 NE2d 716.

CASES FOR CHAPTER 22

Brace v Salem Cold Storage, Inc.

146 WVa 180, 118 SE2d 799 (1961)

Brace and his brother delivered cabbage to the Salem Cold Storage Company for refrigerated storage. The cabbage was later returned to them in a damaged condition. They sued Salem on the ground that through its negligence it had failed to keep the cabbage at a proper temperature. The jury returned a verdict in favor of the plaintiffs, but the trial judge set the verdict aside on the ground that the negligence of the warehouser had not been established and that therefore the verdict in favor of the plaintiffs was not proper. The plaintiffs appealed from this action.

CALHOUN, J. . . . The liability of a warehouseman for negligence is stated in Code, 1931, 47-5-21, as follows: "A warehouseman shall be liable for any loss or injury to the goods caused by his failure to exercise such care in regard to them as a reasonably careful owner of similar goods would exercise; but he shall not be liable, in the absence of an agreement to the contrary, for any loss or injury

to the goods which could not have been avoided by the exercise of such care." Statutes of this nature are merely declaratory of the common law. . . .

The defendant was not an insurer of the cabbage stored in its cold storage warehouse but was required to exercise only ordinary care. It was, nevertheless, required to employ the skill and peculiar knowledge requisite to the operation of the business in which it was engaged. In order to recover in this action, it was incumbent upon the plaintiffs to establish negligence on the part of the defendant, and that such negligence caused the damage to the cabbage. In a case such as this, if the owner of the goods proves that the goods when placed in the cold storage warehouse were in good condition and that, when demanded within a reasonable time, they were in a damaged condition, there may be cast upon the defendant warehouseman thereby a burden of going forward with the evidence, in accordance with principles previously stated herein; but the ultimate burden of proof remains upon the plaintiff throughout the trial to establish his case by a preponderance of the evidence. . . .

"When the evidence is conflicting, or when the facts, though undisputed, are such that reasonable men may draw different conclusions from them, the question of negligence is for the jury." . . . "As in other cases, the question whether the damage to or loss of perishable property in a cold-storage warehouse is due to the negligence of the warehouseman is one for determination by the jury, where there is substantial evidence on which to submit such issue." . . . [The Court then considered the conflicting testimony as to the warehouseman's negligence.] On the whole case, we feel that the facts bearing both upon the right to recover and upon the amount of the verdict were peculiarly for jury determination; and that the trial court would not have been warranted in setting aside the verdict on the ground of insufficiency of evidence to support such verdict. . . .

The judgment . . . is reversed, the verdict of the jury is reinstated, and judgment for the plaintiffs . . . is rendered in this court.

Code Comment: The provision of the West Virginia Statute cited in the opinion is virtually identical with UCC Sec. 7-204 stating the duty of care of a warehouseman. The same result would be reached under the Code.

Associated Bean Growers v Chester B. Brown Company

198 Neb 775, 255 NW2d 425 (1977)

When beans are brought to a warehouse for storage they are cleaned and bagged. The warehouse makes a charge for this processing. Associated Bean Growers was a farmers cooperative. It brought beans to Chester B. Brown Company for storage. When Associated later attempted to withdraw the beans, Brown demanded that it pay a processing fee of $8.00 per one hundred pounds of beans. Associated claimed that this was unreasonable and sued Brown for a declaratory judgment to determine that Associated was entitled to the full value of the beans which had been stored. Brown claimed that it was entitled to a setoff for the amount of storage and processing. From a judgment for Associated for the full amount of the beans, Brown appealed.

WHITE, C.J. . . . It is not disputed by the plaintiff that a public warehouseman is entitled to assess a reasonable charge for processing dry, edible beans. . . .

The question to be decided . . . is whether or not a processing charge of $8 per cwt. was reasonable under the circumstances. We have reviewed the record and find no evidence in support of this charge as a reasonable one. . . .

The defendant's sole reason for refusing to deliver the plaintiff's beans . . . was its insistence upon payment of an unreasonable and unjustifiable processing charge. This not being a lawful excuse for nondelivery, the defendant was liable to the plaintiff for conversion of the plaintiff's property as of that date. The measure of damages for conversion is the market value of the converted property on the date of conversion. . . . The District Court found the value of the beans in question to be $32 per cwt. . . .

The District Court also allowed the defendant a set-off against the amount due the plaintiff for charges for storage, insurance, and receiving in and loading out. The plaintiff contends the defendant is not entitled to this set-off, citing section 7-209(4), of the Uniform Commercial Code, which provides: "A warehouseman loses his lien on any goods which he voluntarily delivers or which he unjustifiably refuses to deliver."

The District Court properly allowed the set-off. A lien is merely a method by which to enforce an underlying claim. A warehouseman's right to compensation, generally secured by a warehouseman's lien on the property, survives a loss of the lien. . . . While the defendant lost its ability to enforce these charges through the use of the warehouseman's lien, the underlying claim remains valid.

As previously stated, the defendant was entitled to a reasonable charge for processing. The charge it attempted to impose was clearly unreasonable. There is no evidence in the record as to what a reasonable charge would be for processing dry edible beans . . . and therefore we remand the cause to the District Court to ascertain what was a reasonable charge for processing on that date. Once determined, the defendant will be allowed a set-off for this against the amount due the plaintiff. . . .

[Affirmed as modified and action remanded]

Birmingham Television Corp. v Water Works

292 Ala 147, 290 So2d 636 (1974)

The Birmingham Television Corporation stored some equipment with Harris Warehouse Company. A water main in the city burst. The warehouse

was flooded. The television corporation sued the water works and the warehouse. The warehouse raised the defense that the action was not commenced within nine months after notice was given of the damage, as was expressly required by the terms of the warehouse receipt. The television corporation claimed that the provision was not binding because it was on the back of the receipt. Summary judgment was entered in favor of the warehouse. The television corporation appealed.

BLOODWORTH, J. . . . The sole issue on this appeal is whether or not the trial court was correct in granting a motion for summary judgment in favor of the appellees based upon the warehouse receipt provision limiting the time within which action may be maintained by the appellant against the appellees for damages to the bailed goods. We conclude that the trial court erred herein and reverse and remand. . . .

. . . (The nine-month limitation appears at the bottom of the copy hereinabove set forth under the heading "NOTICE OF CLAIM AND FILING OF SUIT—Sec. 12.") Motion for summary judgment was granted, whereupon appellant appealed. The Water Works is not a party to this appeal.

Appellant [argues that] nine months is unreasonable as a matter of law, . . . that the trial court erred in holding appellant to be bound by the nine-month limitation because there was no evidence that the provision was specifically called to appellant's attention, [and] that appellant cannot be charged with knowledge of the contract terms. . . .

. . . We think there existed for the jury's determination a genuine issue of fact as to whether the conditions of bailment set forth on the reverse side of the warehouse receipt were accepted by the appellant-bailor so as to become part of the bailment contract. . . .

"*Such special provision* in a contract of bailment *limiting bailee's liability,* to be effective, *must be known to, or brought to the notice of, the bailor, and be assented to by him.* . . . A disclaimer of liability can only become effective if brought to the bailor's knowledge. . . .

"More specifically, to the case at bar, the rule of modern authorities is that the bailor is not chargeable with notice of special provisions diminishing liability of the bailee which appear upon something not apparently related to the bailment contract itself

or given to the bailor ostensibly as a ticket of identification of the bailed property, unless called to his attention or known to him. . . .

Reviewing the facts in the instant case in light of the above stated principles, we find that a genuine issue of fact exists as to whether the terms on the reverse side of the warehouse receipt were accepted by the appellant-bailor and thereby became a part of the contract of bailment. Neither the motion for summary judgment nor appellees' pleas state whether the terms set forth on the reverse side of the warehouse receipt (which purport to materially modify both the common-law rights and obligations of bailor and bailee as well as the statutory provisions respecting limitation of actions) were called to the appellant's attention and were accepted by it.

Nor do we think that such knowledge on appellant's part can be presumed from the issuance of the warehouse receipt itself. The front of the warehouse receipt appears to be just that—a receipt identifying the bailed goods and listing charges—nothing more. No part of the contract appears on the face of the receipt. No notation appears on the face of the receipt advising the bailor to "see reverse side." Nothing on the face of the receipt in any way gives notice that the receipt is a contract of bailment which materially alters the rights of the parties. . . .

Having concluded that there exists at least one genuine issue of fact for the jury's determination, we find it unnecessary to consider the other issues argued on this appeal.

We . . . conclude that the trial court erred in granting the motion for summary judgment in favor of appellees. . . .

[Judgment reversed and action remanded]

American Machinery & Motor Co., Inc. v United Parcel Service

383 NYS2d 1010 (1976)

American Machinery & Motor Co. sent goods by United Parcel Service to a buyer. The shipment was C.O.D. for approximately $1,000. United Parcel delivered the goods to the consignee in return for a check which was a year old and which was visibly altered. The bank on which the check was drawn refused to pay the check because there was no account in the name of the drawer. Neither the consignee nor the goods could be located. American

Machinery sued United Parcel for the amount of the check.

RYP, J. . . . What's in a "C." in C.O.D.? "Cash" say the consignor-shipper and the English. "Check" say the carrier and its tariff. 'Collect,' say Americans. . . .

In this commercial non-jury action, the basically uncontroverted facts are that: plaintiff ("shipper") originally commenced two (2) concurrent causes of action, each for damages to recover the sum of $983.82 (exact amount of shipper's invoice total & tendered consignee's check) from defendant ("carrier") in accepting an allegedly "stale and altered check in payment for a C.O.D. shipment on or about the 7th day of February, 1974." Carrier collected, on delivery, a check, dated February 7, 1973; with the bottom, below the signature line & including the computerized account number, clearly and unevenly cut off and the account number typed in above; and consignee-drawer's address typed in as "P.O. BOX 9251, Pomona, Calif." instead of the invoiced "344 N. Azusa Ave., West Pomona Calif. 91751." . . . This check was returned to shipper, which accepted same from carrier and deposited for collection, as "unable to locate account." Equally unlocatable was the consignee with the C.O.D. shipment, after receipt from carrier.

The first cause of action for negligence was tried by this Court, without a jury. The second cause of action for breach of contract was discontinued, with prejudice, upon shipper's motion, at the outset of trial, granted by this Court without any opposition from carrier. In its answer, carrier interposed a general denial and two (2) complete affirmative defenses: [1] delivery of subject shipment in compliance with its agreement with shipper; and [2] ratification of carrier's act by acceptance of consignee's check for payment. At trial, carrier rested after completion of shipper's case, when the parties made the usual trial motions and waived findings of facts and conclusions of law.

It is clear that current New York law would have precluded shipper's recovery for breach of contract for its ratification of carrier's act by acceptance and deposit for collection of consignee's year old check, apparently altered, and returned as "unable to locate account." . . . However, plaintiff-shipper's tried cause of action is based upon negligence and not barred by any subsequent ratification by acceptance of a check, visibly and patently stale (U.C.C. § 4-404) and altered on its face so, in effect, a worthless piece of paper, not fiscally revivable and collecting nothing. . . . Modern technology in February, 1974, imposed a duty upon defendant, a well-known and highly regarded interstate motor carrier, with national facilities to contact shipper before acceptance of a patently stale and altered check and delivery of subject C.O.D. shipment. It was only carrier (not shipper) who had sole custody and control to relinquish possession of subject C.O.D. shipment at the moment of unauthorized acceptance of such check that was, *on its face,* stale & altered. The risk reasonably to be perceived defines the duty to be obeyed, and risk imports relation. . . . While the parties' original relation was conceived in contract, whose duties are based upon intention, American Courts have extended tort liability for *misfeasance,* as herein, to virtually every type of contact where defective performance injures the promisee, i.e., an agent collecting upon a note. . . . A carrier receiving a C.O.D. shipment is not only a bailee to transport goods but also an agent to receive or collect the price. . . .

[Judgment for plaintiff]

Morse v Piedmont Hotel Co.

110 Ga App 509, 139 SE2d 133 (1964)

Morse, a jewelry salesman, was a guest in the Piedmont Hotel. He entrusted a sample case to a bellboy of the hotel to place on the airport bus of an independent taxicab company. At some point between the hotel and the airport the sample case disappeared. The guest's employer was paid for the loss by his insurer, but the insurer then canceled the policy as to Morse and Morse was then fired by the employer. No other insurance company would cover him as a jewelry salesman, with the result that he was unable to get another job as such, although he had been a jewelry salesman for 40 years. This shock induced a heart attack that confined him at home for several months. Morse then sued both the hotel and the taxicab company for the earnings that he had lost, claiming $100,000; and damages for pain and suffering, claiming $25,000. From a judgment for the defendants, Morse appealed.

HALL, J. . . . The plaintiff relies on the decision in G. C. G. Jewelry Manufacturing Corp. v

Atlanta Baggage & Cab Co., 109 Ga App 469, 136 SE 419, another case which arose out of the loss of the jewelry sample case which allegedly caused the damages the plaintiff sues for in the present case. There the plaintiff's employer sued the defendant cab company as a bailee for the loss of the sample case, and this court held the petition set forth a cause of action. That was an action for property damages caused by the bailee's negligence, for which a bailee is clearly liable. . . . The decision does not support the present action against allegedly negligent bailees, which seeks damages for the plaintiff's inability, resulting from the theft of the jewelry sample case, to obtain insurance covering him as a jewelry salesman and the consequent loss of his employment and earning capacity in this occupation and physical and mental pain and suffering.

In this petition the only duty allegedly owed to the plaintiff and breached by the defendants is the duty to protect the property the plaintiff entrusted to the defendants. The only damages that the plaintiff claims to have resulted to him from this alleged breach of duty are consequent to the loss of an insurance company which had to compensate the plaintiff's employer for its loss of the stolen jewelry case. For such indirect damages the law does not allow recovery. . . .

Generally a person is not liable for the unintentional invasion of the interest of another in his contractual or employment relationships with third persons. The rights or interests of the plaintiff which he alleges have been damaged—the interest in retaining insurance protection and the interest in his employment—he had by virtue of relations with others than the defendants in this case. The petition does not show that the plaintiff had property rights in his relationships with the insurance company, or his employer, but such interests of the plaintiff as were damaged inhered in these relationships. The law does not place upon these defendants the duty to protect these interests of the plaintiff against unintentional invasion. . . .

[Judgment affirmed]

QUESTIONS AND CASE PROBLEMS

1. What social forces are involved in the rule of law governing the liability of a common carrier for loss of freight?

2. Compare the limitation of liability of a warehouser and a hotel.

3. Compare the liens of carriers, warehousers, and hotels in terms of being (a) possessory, and (b) specific.

4. Compare warehouse receipts and bills of lading as to negotiability.

5. Evers owned and operated a warehouse. De Cecchis phoned and inquired as to the rates and then brought furniture in for storage. Nothing was said at any time about any limitation of the liability of Evers as a warehouser. A warehouse receipt was mailed to De Cecchis several days later. The receipt contained a clause that limited liability to $50 per package stored. Was the limitation of liability binding on De Cecchis? [De Cecchis v Evers, 54 Del 99, 174 A2d 463]

6. The Utah Public Service Commission granted a contract carrier permit to the Salt Lake Transportation Company to transport passengers between the Salt Lake airport for four principal airlines and the three leading hotels in the city. The Realty Purchasing Company and various hotels and taxicab companies objected to the granting of the permit on the ground that the company performed a taxicab service and was therefore a common carrier. Decide. [Realty Purchasing Co. v Public Service Commission, 9 Utah 2d 375, 345 P2d 606]

7. Johnston, a guest in a hotel operated by the Mobile Hotel Co., entrusted his property to the hotel. During the night the property was stolen from the hotel in spite of the careful protection given the property by the hotel. Johnston sued the hotel, which claimed it was not liable because the robbers were public enemies and that fact excused the hotel. Was this defense valid? [Johnston v Mobile Hotel Co., 27 Ala App 145, 167 So 595; cert den 232 Ala 175, 167 So 596]

8. The J. C. Trucking Co., Inc., was engaged under contracts to transport dress material from New York City to dressmaking establishments in New Haven, Hartford, and Bridgeport, Connecticut, and then to transport the finished dresses back to New York City. Dresses that were being carried to Ace-High Dresses, Inc., were stolen from the trucking company. Ace-High Dresses sued the trucking company and claimed that the latter was liable for the loss as a common carrier. Was it a common carrier? [Ace-High Dresses v J. C. Trucking Co., 122 Conn 578, 191 A 536]

9. Vanguard Transfer Co. ran a moving and storage business. It obtained an insurance policy from the St. Paul Fire & Marine Insurance Co. covering goods which it had "accepted at the warehouse for storage." Dahl rented a room in Vanguard's building. Both Dahl and Vanguard had keys to the room. Dahl was charged a flat monthly rental for the room and could keep any property there which he desired. Vanguard did not make any record of the goods which Dahl brought to the warehouse. There was a fire in the warehouse and Dahl's property was destroyed. He sued the insurance company. Was it liable? [Dahl v St. Paul Fire & Marine Insurance Co., 36 Wis 2d 420, 153 NW2d 624]

10. Dovax Fabrics, Inc. had been shipping goods by a common carrier, G & A Delivery Corp., for over a year, during which all of G & A's bills to Dovax bore the notation, "Liability limited to $50 unless greater value is declared and paid for. . . ." Dovax gave G & A three lots of goods, having a total value of $1,799.95. A truck containing all three was stolen that night, without negligence on the part of G & A. Should Dovax recover from G & A (a) $1,799.95, (b) $150 for three shipments, or (c) nothing? [Dovax Fabrics, Inc. v G & A Delivery Corp., (NY Civil Ct) 4 UCCRS 492]

11. The guest in a motel opened the bedroom window at night and went to sleep. During the night a prowler pried open the screen, entered the room and stole property of the guest. The guest sued the motel. The motel raised the contentions that it was not responsible for property in the possession of the guest and that the guest had been contributorily negligent in opening the window. Could the guest recover damages? [Buck v Hankin, 217 Pa Super 262, 269 A2d 344]

12. Olson stored a Persian rug with Security Van Lines. Nothing was said to her as to liability for moth damage. Ten days thereafter, Security Van Lines sent her a warehouse receipt for the rug. The receipt contained a provision stating that the warehouseman was not liable for moth damage. While in the possession of Security, the rug was damaged greatly by moths. Olson sued Security for the value of the rug. It raised the defense that it was not liable because of the warehouse receipt provision. Was this provision a valid defense? [Olson v Security Van Lines, Inc., (La App) 297 So 2d 647]

13. Irwin sold to Wells & Coverly merchandise that was shipped to the buyer by Red Star Express, a motor carrier. The goods never arrived. Red Star notified Irwin that the goods were lost. Wells & Coverly sued Red Star, which raised the defense that it had not been given notice of the loss within nine months as required by the tariff or regulations on file with the appropriate governmental agency and as required by the bill of lading that Red Star had issued on receiving the goods. Wells & Coverly proved

that they had never received a copy of the bill of lading and had no prior knowledge of the time limitation. Was Wells & Coverly bound by the time limitation? [Wells & Coverly v Red Star Express, 62 Misc2d 269, 306 NYS2d 710]

14. The Whitney National Bank obtained a banker's blanket bond from Transamerica Insurance Company to protect it from loss from having extended credit on "counterfeit" instruments. The bank loaned money to Allied Crude Vegetable Oil Refining Corp. on the strength of warehouse receipts issued by companies which were owned by the American Express Company. Each of the receipts stated that a specified large quantity of crude soy bean oil was stored and held by the issuing warehouse. Allied failed to repay the loan. It was then discovered that the warehouse did not have the quantity of oil specified in the receipts. This had occurred because of the fraud of Allied and the cooperation or mistakes of warehouse employees. The bank sought to recover its loss by suing on the blanket bond on the theory that the warehouse receipts were "counterfeit." Was it correct? [Whitney Nat. Bank v Transamerica Ins. Co. (CA3 NJ) 476 F2d 632]

15. David Crystal sent merchandise by Ehrlich-Newmark Trucking Co. The truck with Crystal's shipment of goods was hijacked in New York City. Crystal sued Ehrlich-Newmark for the loss. It defended on the ground that it was not liable because the loss had been caused by a public enemy. Was this defense valid? [David Crystal, Inc. v Ehrlich-Newmark Trucking Co., Inc., (NY Civil Ct) 314 NYS2d 559]

Part Five • Sales

23 | Nature and Form of Sales

The most common business transactions involve the sale and purchase of goods, that is, items of tangible personal property, such as food, clothing, and books. The law of sales is a fusion of the law merchant, the common law of England, and former statutes as modified and codified by Article 2 of the Uniform Commercial Code.

A. NATURE AND LEGALITY

A *sale of goods* is a present transfer of title to movable personal property in consideration of a payment of money, an exchange of other property, or the performance of services. The consideration in a sale, regardless of its nature, is known as the *price;* it need not be money. The parties to a sale are the person who owns the goods and the person to whom the title is transferred. The transferor is the seller or vendor, and the transferee is the buyer or vendee. If the price is payable wholly or partly in goods, each party is a seller insofar as those goods are concerned.

A transaction may be held a sale although the parties have not so regarded it. For example, when a "subcontractor" was obligated to deliver ready mix concrete to the "general contractor" by pouring the concrete into forms at the construction site, the relationship between the parties was actually that of seller and buyer.[1]

When a free item is given with the purchase of other goods, it is the purchasing of the other goods which is the price for the "free" goods and hence the transaction as to the free goods is a sale.

§ 23:1 Subject Matter of Sales. The subject matter of a sale is anything that is movable when it is identified as the subject of the transaction.[2] The subject matter may not be (a) investment securities, such as stocks and bonds, the sale of which is regulated by

---

[1] Wilson v Daniel International Corp., 260 SC 548, 197 SE2d 686.
[2] UCC § 2-105(1). It may also include things which are attached to the land, such as those consisting of (a) timber or minerals or buildings or materials forming part of buildings if they are to be removed or severed by the seller, (b) other things attached to land to be removed by either party. § 2-107.

Article 8 of the UCC; (b) choses in action, such as insurance policies and promissory notes, since they are assigned or negotiated rather than sold, or which, because of their personal nature, are not transferable in any case; or (c) real estate, such as a house, factory, or farm.

(a)   Nature of Goods. Most goods are tangible and solid, such as an automobile or a chair. But goods may also be fluid, as oil or gasoline. Goods may also be intangible, as natural gas and electricity. The Code is also applicable to used and secondhand goods.[3]

(b)   Nonexistent and Future Goods. Generally a person cannot make a present sale of nonexistent or future goods or goods not then owned. A person can make a contract to sell such goods at a future date; but not having the title now, there can be no transfer of title now, and hence no sale. For example, an agreement made today that all fish caught on a fishing trip tomorrow shall belong to a particular person does not make that person the owner of those fish today.

When the parties purport to effect a present sale of future goods, the agreement operates only as a contract to sell the goods. Thus a farmer purporting to transfer the title today to a future crop would be held subject to a duty to transfer that crop when it came into existence. If the farmer did not keep the promise, suit could be brought for breach of contract; but the contract would not operate to vest the title in the buyer automatically.

§ 23:2. Sale Distinguished. A sale is an actual present transfer of title. If there is a transfer of a lesser interest than ownership or title, the transaction is not a sale.

(a)   Bailment. A bailment is not a sale because only possession is transferred to the bailee. The bailor remains the owner.

Since a bailment is distinct from a sale, the common practice of leasing equipment and automobiles on a long-term basis would have the effect of making bailment law applicable to many transactions that would otherwise be governed by the law of sales. There is a trend in the law, however, to hold the commercial bailor to the same responsibilities as a seller. Likewise, statutes applicable to "owners" may define that term to include lessees under long-term leases.[4]

(b)   Gift. There can be no sale without consideration, or a price. A gift is a gratuitous transfer of the title to property.

(c)   Contract to Sell. When the parties intend that title to goods will pass at a future time and they make a contract providing for that event, a *contract to sell* is created.[5]

(d)   Option to Purchase. A sale, a present transfer of title, differs from an *option to purchase*. The latter is neither a transfer of title nor a contract to transfer title but a power to require a sale to be made at a future time.

---

[3] Rose v Epley Motor Sales, 288 NC 53, 215 SE2d 573.

[4] The New York Vehicle and Traffic Law defines "owner" to include a lessee renting an automobile for more than 30 days. Aetna Casualty & Surety Co. v. World Wide Rent-A-Car, Inc. 28 AppDiv2d 286, 284 NYS2d 807.

[5] UCC § 2-106(1).

(e)   Conditional Sale. A *conditional sale* customarily refers to a "condition precedent" transaction by which title does not vest in the purchaser until payment in full has been made for the property purchased. This was formerly a common type of sale used when personal property was purchased on credit and payment was to be made in installments. This transaction is now classified as a secured transaction under Article 9 of the UCC.

(f)   Furnishing of Labor or Services. A contract for personal services is to be distinguished from a sale of goods even when some transfer of personal property is involved in the performing of the services. For example, the contract of a repairer is a contract for services, even though in making the repairs, parts are supplied to perform the task. The supplying of such parts is not regarded as a sale because it is merely incidental to the primary contract of making repairs, as contrasted with the purchase of goods, such as a television set, with the incidental service of installation. (See p. 370, Meyers v Henderson Construction Co.)

Similarly, when a surgical pin is inserted in a bone as part of hospitalization, the transaction as to the pin cannot be isolated and treated as a sale but is merely part of a broad contract for services. And an agreement by an artist to make a painting on a television program and donate the painting as part of a charitable drive is an agreement to render services and not a contract for the sale of goods. A contract to build a house is a contract for services and not a contract for the sale of goods even though the contractor supplies the building materials.

When there is a contract only to install and maintain a burglar alarm system but there is no sale of the equipment to the customer, the Code does not apply. However, there is a trend to treat the sale and installation of a system, such as an incinerator, computer, or emergency electrical system, as a sale of "goods." [6]

(g)   Crimes. The word "sale" is often broadly defined by criminal law to include "negotiation" and "solicitation" and other transactions not involving a transfer of title. The Uniform Narcotic Drug Act defines "sale" to include "barter, exchange, or gift, or offer thereof, and each such transaction made by any person, whether as principal, proprietor, agent, servant, or employee." [7]

§ 23:3. Law of Contracts Applicable. A sale is a voluntary transaction between two persons. Accordingly, most of the principles that apply to contractual agreements in general are equally applicable to a sale of goods. Modern marketing practices, however, have modified the strict principles of contract law, and this approach to the problem is carried into the UCC. Thus not only can a sale be made in any manner; but it is sufficient that the parties by their conduct recognize the existence of a contract, even though it cannot be determined when the contract was made, and generally, even though one or more terms are left open. [8]

In some instances, the UCC treats all buyers and sellers alike. In others, it treats merchants differently than it does the occasional or casual buyer or seller; in

---

[6] Regents of University of Colorado v Pacific Pump and Supply, Inc., (ColoApp), 528 P2d 941.
[7] Kansas v Woods 214 Kan 739, 522 P2d 967.
[8] UCC § 2-204. This provision of the UCC is limited by requiring that there be "a reasonably certain basis for giving an appropriate remedy."

this way, the UCC recognizes that the merchant is experienced and has a specialized knowledge of the relevant commercial practices.[9]

(a)   Offer. Contract law as to offers is applicable to sales except that an offer by a merchant cannot be revoked, even though there is no consideration to keep the offer open if (1) the offer expresses an intention that it will not be revoked, and is (2) in a writing, (3) signed by the merchant.[10] The expressed period of irrevocability, however, cannot exceed three months. If nothing is said as to the duration of the offer, this irrevocability continues only for a reasonable time.

(b)   Acceptance. The UCC redeclares the general principle of contract law that an offer to buy or sell goods may be accepted in any manner and by any medium which is reasonable under the circumstances, unless a specific manner or medium is clearly indicated by the terms of the offer or the circumstances of the case.[11]

> *(1)   Acceptance by Shipment.* Unless otherwise clearly indicated, an order or other offer to buy goods that are to be sent out promptly or currently can be accepted by the seller either by actually shipping the goods, as though a unilateral contract offer had been made; or by promptly promising to make shipment, as though a bilateral contract, that is, an exchange of promises, had been offered. If acceptance is made by shipping the goods, the seller must notify the buyer within a reasonable time that the offer has been accepted in this manner.[12]

> *(2)   Additional Terms in Acceptance.* Unless it is expressly specified that an offer to buy or sell goods must be accepted just as made, the offeree may accept a contract but at the same time propose an additional term. This new term, however, does not become binding unless the offeror thereafter consents to it. Consequently, when the buyer sends an order which the seller acknowledges on a printed form, any additional material term in the seller's printed form that is not in the buyer's order form or which is not implied by custom or prior dealings is regarded merely as an additional term that may or may not be accepted by the buyer. That is, the order is deemed "accepted" in spite of the addition of this new material term, but the new term does not become part of the contract unless and until it is accepted by the buyer.

> The acceptance by the buyer may be found either in an express statement, oral or in writing, that the additional term is accepted, or it may be deduced from conduct, as when the goods are accepted with knowledge that the additional term has been added.

> When the form used by the seller to acknowledge the buyer's order contains a provision limiting the seller's liability, but such provision was not in the buyer's order form, and the buyer never expressly agreed to the limitation in the seller's form, the limitation provision is not part of the contract between the parties and does not bind the buyer.[13]

> In a transaction between merchants, the additional term becomes part of the contract if that term does not materially alter the offer and no objection

---

[9] UCC § 2-104(1).
[10] UCC § 2-205.
[11] UCC § 2-206(1)(a).
[12] UCC § 2-206(2).
[13] Air Products and Chemicals, Inc. v Fairbanks Morse, Inc. 58 Wis2d 193, 206 NW2d 414.

is made to it.[14] If such an additional term in the seller's form of acknowledgment operates solely to the seller's advantage, however, it is a material term and must be accepted to be effective.

(c)   Determination of Price. The price for the goods may be expressly fixed by the contract, or the parties may merely indicate the manner of determining price at a later time.[15] A sales contract is binding even though it calls for a specified price "plus extras" but does not define the extras, which it leaves for future negotiation and agreement.

When persons experienced in a particular industry make a contract without specifying the price to be paid, the price will be determined by the manner which is customary in the industry.

Ordinarily, if nothing is said as to price, the buyer is required to pay the reasonable value of the goods. The reasonable price is generally the market price, but not necessarily, as when the market price is under the control of the seller.

In recent years there has been an increase in use of the "cost plus" formula for determining price. Under this form of agreement the buyer pays the seller a sum equal to the cost to the seller of obtaining the goods plus a specified percentage of that cost.

The contract may expressly provide that one of the parties may determine the price, in which case that party must act in good faith in so doing.[16] Likewise, the contract may specify that the price shall be determined by some standard or by a third person. If for any reason other than the fault of one of the parties the price cannot be fixed in the manner specified, the buyer is required to pay the reasonable value for the goods unless it is clear that the parties intended that if the price were not determined in the manner specified, there would be no contract. In the latter case the buyer must return the goods and the seller refund any payment made on account. If the buyer is unable to return such goods, the buyer must pay their reasonable value at the time of delivery.

(d)   Output and Requirement Contracts. Somewhat related to the open-term concept concerning price is that involved in the output and requirements contracts in which the quantity which is to be sold or purchased is not a specific quantity but is such amount as the seller should produce or the buyer should require. Although this introduces an element of uncertainty, such sales contracts are valid. To prevent oppression, they are subject to two limitations: (1) the parties must act in good faith; and (2) the quantity offered or demanded must not be unreasonably disproportionate to prior output or requirements or to a stated estimate.[17] (See p. 371, Romine, Inc. v Savannah Steel Co.)

When the sales contract is a continuing contract, as one calling for periodic delivery of fuel, but no time is set for the life of the contract, the contract runs for a reasonable time but may be terminated on notice by either party.[18]

---

[14] UCC § 2-207; Application of Doughboy Industries, Inc. 17 AppDiv2d 216, 233 NYS2d 488.

[15] UCC § 2-305.

[16] Good faith requires that the party in fact act honestly and, in the case of a merchant, also requires the party to follow reasonable commercial standards of fair dealing which are recognized in the trade. UCC § 1-201(19), 2-103(b).

[17] UCC § 2-306(1).

[18] UCC § 2-309(2); Sinkoff Beverage Co. v Schlitz Brewing Co. 51 Misc2d 446, 273 NYS2d 364.

(e) Seals. A seal on a contract or on an offer of sale has no effect. Thus, in determining whether there is consideration or if the statute of limitations is applicable, the fact that there is a seal on the contract is ignored.[19]

(f) Usage of Trade and Course of Dealing. Established usages or customs of trade and prior course of conduct or dealings between the parties are to be considered in connection with any sales transaction. In the absence of an express term excluding or "overruling" the prior pattern of dealings between the parties and the usages of the trade, it is to be concluded that the parties contracted on the basis of the continuation of those patterns of doing business. More specifically, the patterns of doing business as shown by the prior dealings of the parties and usages of the trade enter into and form part of their contract and may be looked to in order to find what was intended by the express provisions and to supply otherwise missing terms. (See p. 372, in re Boone Livestock Co.)

(g) Implied Conditions. The field of implied conditions under contract law is broadened by the UCC to permit the release of a party from any obligation under a sales contract when performance has been made commercially impracticable, as distinguished from impossible: (1) by the occurrence of a contingency, the nonoccurrence of which was a basic assumption on which the contract was made; or (2) by compliance in good faith with any applicable domestic or foreign governmental regulation or order, whether or not it is later held valid by the courts.[20] "A severe shortage of raw materials or of supplies due to a contingency such as war, embargo, local crop failure, unforeseen shutdown of major sources of supply, or the like, which either causes a marked increase in cost or altogether prevents the seller from securing supplies necessary to his performance, is within the contemplation" of this provision of the UCC.[21]

(h) Modification of Contract. A departure is made from the general principles of contract law in that an agreement to modify a contract for the sale of goods is binding even though the modification is not supported by consideration.[22]

(i) Parol Evidence Rule. The parol evidence rule applies to the sale of goods with the slight modification that a writing is not presumed or assumed to represent the entire contract of the parties unless the court specifically decides that it does. If the court so decides, parol evidence is admissible to show what the parties meant by their words but cannot add additional terms to the writing. If the court decides that the writing was not intended to represent the entire contract, the writing may be supplemented by parol proof of additional terms so long as such terms are not inconsistent with the original written terms. The writing may show from its terms that it was not intended as a final statement of the complete contract as when the writing stated "we confirm the purchase from you, as per our conversation . . ."[23]

---

[19] UCC § 2-203.
[20] UCC § 2-615(a). If under the circumstances indicated in the text the seller is totally disabled from performing, the seller is discharged from the contract. A seller who is able to produce some goods, must allocate them among customers, but any customer may reject the contract and such fractional offer. § 2-615(b), § 2-616.
[21] UCC § 2-615, Official Comment, point 4.
[22] UCC § 2-209(1).
[23] Paymaster Oil Mill Co. v Mitchell, (Miss), 319 So2d 652.

When a written contract is ambiguous, parol evidence is admissible. Accordingly when the seller contracted to sell an entire cotton crop for a price specified as to a particular quality of cotton, the contract was ambiguous as to whether that was the price for cotton of a higher quality as well or whether the price for the higher quality was an open term, and therefore parol evidence was properly admitted to show the intent of the parties.[24]

A sales contract, although written, may be modified by an oral agreement except to the extent that a writing is required by the statute of frauds. Even when the sales contract specifies that there cannot be an oral modification, the conduct of the parties may be such that there is a waiver of such prohibition and an oral modification is then binding.

(j) Fraud and Other Defenses. The defenses that may be raised in a suit on a sales contract are in general the same as those that may be raised in a suit on any other contract. A defrauded party may cancel the transaction and recover what was paid or the goods that were delivered, together with damages for any loss sustained. If title was obtained by the buyer by means of fraud, the title is voidable by an innocent seller while the goods are still owned by the buyer, and the sale may be set aside.

If the sales contract or any clause in it was unconscionable when made, a court may refuse to enforce it, as discussed in Chapter 14.

§ 23:4. Illegal Sales. Certain conditions must exist for a sale to be considered illegal.

(a) Illegality at Common Law. At common law a sale is illegal if the subject matter is itself wrong. The transaction may also be illegal even though the subject matter of the sale may be unobjectionable in itself, as when the agreement provides that the goods that are sold shall be employed for some unlawful purpose or when the seller assists in the unlawful act. To illustrate, when the seller falsely labels domestic goods, representing them to be imported, to assist the buyer in perpetrating a fraud upon customers, the sale is illegal. The mere fact, however, that the seller has knowledge of the buyer's unlawful purpose does not, under the general rule, make the sale illegal unless the purpose is the commission of a serious crime.

(b) Illegality under Statutes. Practically every state has legislation prohibiting certain sales when they are not conducted according to the requirements of the statutes. Thus, a statute may require that a particular class of goods, such as meat, be inspected before a legal sale can be made. In addition to statutes which invalidate the sale, a number of statutes make it a criminal act or impose a penalty for making a sale under certain circumstances. Statutes commonly regulate sales by establishing standards as to grading, size, weight, and measure, and by prohibiting adulteration.

In addition to the restrictive state statutes, federal legislation regulates the sale of goods in interstate commerce. The federal Food, Drug, and Cosmetic Act, for example, prohibits the interstate shipment of misbranded or adulterated foods, drugs, cosmetics, and therapeutic devices. A product which does not carry adequate use instructions and warnings is deemed "misbranded" for the purpose of the statutes.

---

[24] Esteve Cotton Co. v Hancock (TexCivApp) 539 SW2d 145.

Other statutes, such as those designed to regulate competition, further protect the consumer.

States may prohibit the making of sales on Sunday either generally or as to particular commodities or classes of stores. Such laws do not violate any guarantee of religious freedom nor deprive persons of the equal protection of the laws. In some instances, however, a Sunday closing law may be unconstitutional because it is too vague.

Statutes may regulate the sale of "secondhand" goods. Such a statute does not apply to a casual seller, but only applies to one whose regular business consists of selling goods of the kind covered by the statute.[25]

(c) **Effect of Illegal Sale.** An illegal sale or contract to sell cannot be enforced. This rule is based on public policy. As a general rule, courts will not aid either party in recovering money or property transferred pursuant to an illegal agreement. Relief is sometimes given, however, to an innocent party to an unlawful agreement. For example, if one party is the victim of a fraudulent transaction, recovery may be obtained of what was transferred to the other party even though the agreements between them arose out of some illegal scheme.

When a sale is made illegal by statute, a seller who violates the law may be held liable for the damage caused.

§ 23:5. Bulk Transfer. Whenever a merchant is about to transfer a major part of the merchant's materials, supplies, merchandise, or other inventory, not in the ordinary course of business, advance notice of the transfer must be given to creditors in accordance with Article 6 of the Uniform Commercial Code. The essential characteristic of businesses subject to Article 6 is that they sell from inventory or a stock of goods, as contrasted with businesses which render services. If the required notice is not given, the creditors may reach the sold property in the hands of the transferee and also in the hands of any subsequent transferee who knew that there had not been compliance with the UCC or who did not pay value.[26] This is designed to protect the creditors of a merchant from the danger of the merchant's selling all the inventory, pocketing the money, and then disappearing, leaving the creditors unpaid. The protection given to creditors by the bulk transfer legislation is in addition to the protection which they have against their debtor for fraudulent transfers or conveyances, and the remedies that can be employed in bankruptcy proceedings.

Ordinarily the transferee who receives the goods does not become liable for the debts of the transferor merely because the requirements of Article 6 have not been satisfied. In contrast, if the transferee has mixed the transferred goods with other goods so that it is not possible to identify the transferred goods, the transferee is personally liable for the debts of the transferor. (See p. 373, Cornelius v J & R Motor Supply Corp.)

The fact that there has been noncompliance with Article 6 of the UCC regulating bulk transfers, however, does not affect the validity of a bulk sale of goods as between the immediate parties to the transfer since Article 6 is operative only with respect to the rights of creditors of the seller.

---

[25] Michigan v E. L. Rice & Co. 33 MichApp2d 699, 190 NW2d 309.
[26] UCC § 6-101 et seq.

B. FORMALITY OF THE SALES CONTRACT

As in the case of contracts generally, an oral contract for the sale of goods is valid. However, for the purpose of protecting from false claims, certain sales of goods must be evidenced by a writing in order to be enforceable in court.

§ 23:6. Amount. The statute of frauds provision of the Uniform Commercial Code applies whenever the sales price is $500 or more.[27] If the total contract price equals or exceeds this amount, the law applies even though the contract covers several articles, the individual amounts of which are less than $500, provided the parties intended to make a single contract rather than a series of separate or divisible contracts. In the latter case, if each contract is for less than $500, no writing is required.

§ 23:7. Nature of the Writing Required. The writing evidencing the sales contracts must meet certain requirements. As under contract law generally the writing may be either a complete written contract signed by both parties or a memorandum signed by the defendant. There is no requirement that the writing must be a contract signed by both parties.

(a) Terms. The writing need only give assurance that there was a transaction. Specifically it need only indicate that a sale or a contract to sell has been made and state the quantity of goods involved. Any other missing terms may be shown by parol evidence in the event of a dispute.

If the writing does not state a quantity of goods or does not indicate that a sale or a contract has been made, the writing does not satisfy the statute of frauds. Consequently, when the writing merely shows that there was a continuing buy-sell relationship between the parties but does not specify any quantity, the writing is not sufficient to satisfy the statute of frauds. A writing which is merely an offer is not sufficient to satisfy the statute of frauds as it does not indicate that there has been a completed transaction as to goods.[28]

(b) Signature. The writing must be signed by the person who is being sued or by the authorized agent of that person. The signature must be placed on the writing with the intention of authenticating the writing. It may consist of initials or be printed, stamped, or typewritten as long as made with the necessary intent.

When the transaction is between merchants, an exception is made to the requirement of signing. The failure of a merchant to repudiate a confirming letter sent by another merchant binds just as though the receiving merchant had signed the letter or other writing.[29] This ends the evil of a one-sided writing under which the sender of the letter was bound, but the receiver could wait to see what the market did and then could either ignore the transaction or hold the sender to the terms of the writing.

The provision as to merchants makes it necessary for a merchant-buyer or merchant-seller to watch the mail and to act promptly upon receiving a mailed confirmation.

---

[27] UCC § 2-201.
[28] Alice v Robett Mfg. Co. (DC Ga) 328 FSupp 1377, affd (CA5 Ga) 445 F2d 316.
[29] UCC § 2-201(2).

(c) Time of Execution. The writing required may be made at or after the making of the sale. It may even be made after the contract has been broken or a suit brought on it, as the essential element is the existence of written proof of the transaction when the trial is held.

(d) Purpose of Execution. A writing can satisfy the statute of frauds although it was not made for that purpose. Accordingly, when the buyer writes in reply to the seller, after a 45-day delay, and merely criticizes the quality of the goods, the letter of the buyer satisfies the statute.

(e) Particular Writings. Formal contracts, bills of sale, letters, and telegrams are common forms of writing that satisfy the requirement. Purchase orders, cash register receipts, sales tickets, invoices, and similar papers generally do not satisfy the requirement as to a signature, and sometimes they do not specify any quantity or commodity.

Two or more writings may constitute the "writing" which satisfies the statute of frauds. For example, an unsigned written contract could be combined with an advance payment check from the buyer which the seller indorsed; the unsigned contract providing the necessary content for the writing and the seller's indorsement on the check constituting the necessary signature.[30]

§ 23:8. Effect of Noncompliance. A sales agreement that does not comply with the statute of frauds is not enforceable. The fact that a party to the oral sales contract relies on its being performed does not make the contract binding.[31] However, the oral contract itself is not unlawful and may be voluntarily performed by the parties.

When the question is whether there has been a sale or a bailment, the fact that there is a writing under the statute of frauds is evidence indicating that the transaction was a sale. Conversely, the fact that an automobile dealer did not execute either a bill of sale or a memorandum satisfying the requirement of a writing was evidence which confirmed the contention of the car owner that an automobile had not been sold by the latter to the dealer but had been entrusted to the dealer for resale. The result was that the dealer was the owner's agent or bailee and the dealer was therefore guilty of embezzlement upon failing to account to the owner for the proceeds from the resale of the car.

§ 23:9. When Proof of Oral Contract is Permitted. The absence of a writing does not always bar proof of a sales contract.

(a) Receipt and Acceptance. An oral sales contract may be enforced if it can be shown that the goods were delivered by the seller and were received and accepted by the buyer. Consequently, when the buyer purchases and receives goods on credit, the seller may sue for the purchase price even though the total is $500 and there is no writing, for the reason that the receipt and acceptance of the goods by the buyer took the contract out of the statute of frauds. Both a receipt and an acceptance by the buyer must be shown. If only part of the goods have been received and accepted, the contract may be enforced only insofar as it relates to those goods received and accepted.[32]

---

[30] Cargill, Inc. v Wilson (Mont) 532 P2d 988.
[31] UCC § 2-201(1).
[32] UCC § 2-201(3)(c).

The buyer's receipt of the goods may be symbolic, as in the case of the seller's transfer of a covering bill of lading to the buyer.

When the goods are delivered at the buyer's direction to a third person who accepts the goods, the oral contract of the buyer is taken out of the statute of frauds. Consequently, a buying broker's oral contract is taken out of the statute when, following instructions, the goods are delivered to and accepted by the broker's customer.

(b)   Payment. An oral contract may be enforced if the buyer has made full payment. In the case of part payment for divisible units of goods, a contract may be enforced only with respect to goods for which payment has been made and accepted.[33] When the goods are not divisible, as in the case of an automobile, the part payment takes the entire contract out of the statute of frauds.

There is some uncertainty as to the effectiveness of "payment" by check or a promissory note executed by the buyer. Under the law of commercial paper a check or note is conditional payment when delivered, and does not become absolute until the instrument is paid. The earlier decisions held that the delivery of a negotiable instrument was not such a payment as would make the oral contract enforceable unless it was agreed at that time that the instrument was to be accepted as absolute, and not conditional, payment. A modern contrary view, which is influenced by the fact that business persons ordinarily regard the delivery of a check or note as "payment," holds that the delivery of such an instrument is sufficient to make the oral contract enforceable.[34]

When the buyer has negotiated or assigned to the seller a commercial paper that was executed by a third person and the seller has accepted the instrument, a payment has been made within the meaning of the statute of frauds.

(c)   Nonresellable Goods. No writing is required when the goods are specifically made for the buyer and are of such an unusual nature that they are not suitable for sale in the ordinary course of the seller's business. (See p. 374, LTV Aerospace Corp. v Bateman) For example, when 14 steel doors were tailor-made by the seller for the buyer's building, and were not suitable for sale to anyone else in the ordinary course of the seller's business, and could only be sold as scrap, the oral contract of sale was enforceable.

In order for the nonresellable goods exception to apply, however, the seller must have made a substantial beginning in manufacturing the goods or, if a distributor, in procuring them, before notice of repudiation by the buyer is received.[35]

(d)   Judicial Admission. No writing is required when the defendant in a legal proceeding admits the making of the oral contract. When the seller sues on an oral contract, there is an admission which takes the contract out of the statute of frauds when the defendant admits the existence of the contract but claims that payment was not due until the goods were resold.[36]

§ 23:10. Non-Code Local Requirements. In addition to the UCC requirement as to a writing, other statutes may impose requirements. For example, consumer protection legislation

---

[33] UCC § 2-201(3)(c).
[34] Kaufman v Solomon (CA3 Pa) 524 F2d 501.
[35] UCC § 2-201(3)(a).
[36] Giant Peanut Co. v Carolina Chemicals, Inc., 129 GaApp 718, 200 SE2d 918.

commonly requires the execution of a detailed contract and the giving of a copy thereof to the consumer. The result is that even though the Code requirements have been satisfied, the buyer may still be able to avoid the transaction for noncompliance with some other statutory requirement.

§ 23:11. Bill of Sale. Regardless of the requirement of the statute of frauds, the parties may wish to execute a writing as evidence or proof of the sale. Through custom this writing has become known as a *bill of sale;* but it is neither a bill nor a contract. It is merely a receipt or writing signed by the seller reciting the transfer to the buyer of the title to the described property.

In some states, provision is made for the public recording of bills of sale when goods are left in the seller's possession. In the case of the sale of certain types of property, a bill of sale may be required in order to show that the purchaser is the lawful owner. Thus in some states, the purchaser of a new automobile is required to carry the bill of sale for a two-day period.[37] Some states require the production of the bill of sale before the title to any automobile will be registered in the name of the purchaser.

---

[37] Massachusetts v Brady (Mass) 351 NE2d 199.

CASES FOR CHAPTER 23

Meyers v Henderson Construction Co.

147 NJ Super 77, 370 A2d 547 (1977)

Meyers was under contract with the Henderson Construction Company to install overhead doors in a factory which Henderson was building. Meyers obtained the prefabricated but disassembled doors from the manufacturer. His contract with Henderson required Meyers to "furnish all labor, materials, tools and equipment to satisfactorily complete the installation of all overhead doors." Five years later, when Meyers sued Henderson for breach of the contract, Henderson raised the defense that the contract was for the sale of goods, in which case it would be barred by the Code's four-year statute of limitations. Meyers claimed that it was a contract for services, in which case the Code's statute of limitation was not applicable and suit could be brought within six years.

WEISS, J.D.C. . . . Which statute properly applies depends upon how the contract may be most accurately characterized—as one for the sale of goods (as defined in [UCC§] 2-105(1)) plus incidental services, or as one for construction services with the

subcontractor furnishing materials as well as labor. . . .

[UCC§] 2-105 requires that, in order to be classified as goods, the subject matter of a contract must be "movable at the time of identification to the contract." This definitional section continues, excluding some "things" from UCC coverage. But there is no exception for goods which require servicing before they can be used. . . . Some courts have characterized contracts as involving primarily services, with the transfer of materials being so incidental to the services as to exclude coverage by the UCC. . . .

It is apparent that at some point the service element may so dominate the subject matter of a contract as to bring it outside UCC coverage. An agreement to paint a house is a classic example of this situation. In *Bonebrake v Cox,* [(CA 8 Iowa) 499 F2d 951] the Eighth Circuit was faced with the task of enunciating a test to cover borderline cases. There the issue was whether the four-year UCC limitation period barred an action on allegedly defective used bowling equipment which had been supplied and installed by defendant. . . .

As is the case here, *Bonebrake* involved the purchase of manufactured goods which were useless without a substantial amount of labor. One lump sum was charged for the equipment and its installation.

The cases presenting mixed contracts of this type are legion. The test for inclusion or exclusion is not whether they are mixed, but, granting that they are mixed, whether their predominant factor, their thrust, their purpose, reasonably stated, is the rendition of service, with goods incidentally involved (e.g., contract with artist for painting) or is a transaction of sale, with labor incidentally involved (e.g., installation of a water heater in a bathroom). . . .

It cannot be denied that the overhead doors were useless without the performance of installation services. . . .

When presented with two elements of a contract, each absolutely necessary if the subject matter is to be of any significant value to the purchaser, it is a futile task to attempt to determine which component is "more necessary." Thus the Bonebrake test looks to the predominant purpose, the thrust of the contract as it would exist in the minds of reasonable parties. There is no surer way to provide for predictable results in the face of a highly artificial classification system.

Applying the test here, we find the predominant reason for the agreement to have been the procurement of overhead doors, with the installation services being incidental. The contract is, therefore, governed by the UCC, and the four-year limitation period of [UCC§] 2-725 is properly applicable. . . .

[Judgment for defendant]

Romine, Inc. v Savannah Steel Co.

117 Ga App 353, 160 SE2d 659 (1968)

Romine, a contractor, had a construction contract with the government. Savannah Steel Co. contracted to supply Romine with the steel required for the construction. Because of an error in the government specifications, the amount of steel actually needed was less than one tenth of the amount of the estimate on which Romine and Savannah had relied. Savannah sued Romine for breach of the requirements contract. The trial judge entered a summary judgment in favor of Savannah Steel, from which Romine appealed.

JORDAN, P.J. . . . Savannah Steel Co., Inc. brought suit against Romine, Inc. to recover an alleged balance due of $3,788.04 on a contract to supply the defendant with its steel requirements in performing a contract with the United States Government. The defendant, Romine, Inc., admitted a portion of the indebtedness, but contends that the amount of $2,725 on a purchase order submitted to the plaintiff as the cost of all reinforcing steel for concrete paving, is not alone determinative of the amount due for such steel requirements, and claims a credit of $2,474 for steel not required, shipped, or delivered. The trial judge considered the pleadings and depositions, granted a summary judgment for the plaintiff in the full amount sought, and simultaneously denied the motion of the defendant for a summary judgment. The defendant appeals from this order.

. . . If a court determines as a matter of law that a provision of a contract is unconscionable when made, it may, among other things, so limit the application of any unconscionable provision to avoid an unconscionable result. [UCC Sec.] 2-302. See discussion, Anderson's Uniform Commercial Code, Vol. 1, pp. 146-150. This provision is not designed, however, merely to relieve a party of a bad bargain. Ibid., p. 148.

. . . Where a term is used in a contract which is intended to cover the requirements of the buyer as may occur in good faith, no quantity unreasonably disproportionate to any stated estimate may be tendered or demanded. [UCC Sec.] 2-306. The agreed estimate is to be regarded as a center around which the parties intend the variation to occur. See Uniform Commercial Code, 1962 Official Text with Comments, published by The American Law Institute and Uniform Conference of Commissioners on Uniform State Laws, p. 75, Comment 4. The cited provision is applicable regardless of the character of the seller or buyer. See Anderson, supra. Vol. 1, p. 164. It would seem to follow logically that where the quantity actually delivered and accepted to meet the requirements of the buyer is unreasonably disproportionate to the estimated requirements, the lot price for the estimated total requirements is not a lot price for the actual requirements, although it may serve to establish a unit price therefor. . . .

. . . Applying the foregoing principles to the case at bar, where a contractor furnishes a steel supplier with the drawings and specifications on a proposed construction contract with the United States

Government, and the supplier estimates the steel requirements, and furnishes the contractor with a written proposal to furnish, among other items, the necessary reinforcing steel for "concrete paving (15½ tons)—$2,725," and the contractor, upon the award of the construction contract, submits a purchase order to the supplier for "all reinforcing required for concrete pavement, except for dowel pins, including support accessories 2725," which the supplier purports to fulfill, the intent of the parties is to be gathered from a consideration of both documents, and the order for "all" at the stated price of "$2,725" is to be construed as conditioned upon the recognized estimate of 15½ tons, in the absence of anything to the contrary appearing in the documents, or otherwise. In brief, that part of the proposal showing "15½ tons" is not without meaning in construing the contract. Actually, both the purchase order and the proposal are deficient in many respects unless explained by the requirements of the government contract on which the proposal and order are based. Construed in this manner, the amount of $2,725 is the "quid pro quo" for "all" of the steel required in terms centering around "15½ tons" and the intent of the parties cannot be enlarged upon to the extent of limiting the total price to $2,725 if the amount of steel, as required and delivered, is grossly disproportionate to 15½ tons, either above or below such stated amount. Under such circumstances the monetary consideration due the supplier under the contract is for determination based on all the steel actually furnished in terms of the price per ton at the rate of 15½ tons for $2,725.

. . . It is obvious from the record before this court that the estimate of steel requirements as shown in the contract is grossly disproportionate to the actual requirements, and that this situation arose as the result of a mistake without fault of either party. The drawings and specifications prepared by the government made it appear that reinforcing steel would be required for 3,438 square yards of concrete paving, but the government informed the contractor and the contractor notified the supplier that this was not true, as only 316 square yards required reinforcing steel. In fact, the remainder was unacceptable if constructed with reinforcing steel. The supplier apparently delivered the steel as required for 316 square yards of paving and the claimed credit of $2,474 by the defendant for 3,122 square yards not requiring steel appears to be an apportionment on this basis. But there is no evidence to show what steel was

actually delivered by the supplier in terms of actual weight to support a computation of the amount due on a price per ton basis as the true consideration under the construction placed on the contract in the preceding division of this opinion. Thus, while the result may be substantially the same when there is proof of the amount of steel actually delivered, this issue is not resolved by the record before this court.

. . . Under these circumstances the amount actually due the plaintiff is still in issue even though the plaintiff is entitled to judgment in some amount, and it was error for the trial judge to grant a summary judgment for the plaintiff in the full amount claimed, but he did not err in refusing to grant a summary judgment for the defendant.

[Judgment affirmed on the refusal of a summary judgment for the defendant; reversed on the grant of a summary judgment for the plaintiff]

In re Boone Livestock Co.

US Dept of Agriculture, 27 AD 475, 5 UCCRS 498 (1968)

Boone Livestock Co. was in the business of buying and selling cattle. It purchased cattle and resold them, specifying to its customers that the cattle weighed certain amounts, whereas these amounts were the weights at which the cattle had been purchased by Boone from its suppliers increased by arbitrary amounts. It was claimed that these weights were false, and a proceeding was brought against Boone.

FLAVIN, Judicial Officer. This is a disciplinary proceeding under the Packers and Stockyards Act, 1921, as amended and supplemented (7 USC § 181 et seq.), instituted by a complaint filed November 17, 1965, by the Director, Packers and Stockyards Division (presently the Packers and Stockyards Administration), Consumer and Marketing Service, United States Department of Agriculture. . . .

The complaint filed herein alleges, in part, that respondent "during the period from, on, or about January 14, 1965, through, on, or about June 5, 1965, purchased livestock for its own account in Alabama, Florida, Mississippi, and Texas" at listed or stated weights "and, on the dates of said purchases or within a few days thereafter, knowingly sold such livestock for its own account on a weight basis, in commerce, to various persons, at false and incorrect weights which respondent obtained by adding an arbitrary number of pounds to the purchase weights." Specific instances of such practice are then set forth in the complaint. . . .

It is clear from the record that the weight of the livestock involved herein sold by respondent and listed on its invoices to the purchasers thereof was comprised of, and resulted from, the addition of an arbitrary figure or number of pounds, usually a total of 1,000 pounds or more per sale, to the weight at which respondent purchased such live stock. . . .

Respondent makes much of the fact that it made no affirmative statements or representations during negotiations with its customers or on the invoices that the stated or listed weight in each transaction was its purchase weight. However, in view of the prevailing custom, practice or "usage of trade," no affirmative representation was needed to make respondent's purchase weights a part or term of the contracts involved. See § 1-205 of Uniform Commercial Code. . . . On the contrary, it would be incumbent upon respondent expressly to provide otherwise in its sales contracts with its customers. In other words, respondent had a duty to speak or to alter the prevailing custom by specific contract terms if it wished to sell the livestock involved at other than its purchase weights. Rather than doing so, respondent sold the cattle at other than its purchase weights without contracting to do so or so informing its customers while aware that such customers assumed and believed that they were purchasing the livestock on the basis of respondent's purchase weights. Also, no other assumption would be reasonable in view of the circumstances of the sales, that is, purchase of the livestock while they were in transit with no additional weighing to determine contract weight. Respondent's contentions that the sale weight in each of the transactions involved was an agreed arbitrary weight between respondent and the buyer, or merely a weight at which respondent was willing to sell the livestock or a reasonable weight subject to the buyer's approval are all without foundation and negatived by the custom in the industry, the testimony of respondent's customers, and the statements of respondent's president. . . .

[Disciplinary order entered against Boone]

Cornelius v J & R Motor Supply Corp.

(Ky) 468 SW2d 781 (1971)

Costello owned an automobile accessory and appliance business. He purchased goods for his inventory from J & R Motor Supply Corporation. Cos-tello sold his business to Cornelius before paying for the purchases from J & R. Cornelius mixed the Costello inventory with his own so that the two could not be identified. J & R and another creditor claimed that Cornelius was liable for the amount of the bills owed by Costello because the sale of the business had been made without complying with Article 6 of the Uniform Commercial Code. The court held that Cornelius was personally liable for plaintiffs' claims. Cornelius appealed.

STEINFELD, J. . . . The questions before us are whether personal judgments were proper, the amounts for which judgments should have been entered if plaintiffs below prevail and whether filing of the claims in the bankruptcy proceeding precluded the creditors from prosecuting the suits.

[UCC §] 6-104 declares that ". . . a bulk transfer subject to this article is ineffective against any creditor . . . unless: (a) The transferee requires the transferor to furnish a list of his existing creditors . . ." prepared as statutorily required. [UCC §] 6-105 provides:

". . . any bulk transfer subject to this article . . . is ineffective against any creditor of the transferor unless at least ten days before he takes possession of the goods or pays for them, whichever happens first, the transferee gives notice of the transfer in the manner and to the persons hereafter provided [UCC §] 6-107. . . ."

The intent of the Bulk Sales Law is to protect the rights of all creditors existing at the time of the transfer. . . .

We now approach the question of whether a personal judgment was authorized. We believe the act did not so contemplate except under special circumstances. . . . The ordinary bulk sales statute ". . . merely makes it (the sale) voidable against both parties for the benefit of creditors." With respect to section 6-104 the Official Code Comments state: "Any such creditor or creditors may therefore disregard the transfer and levy on the goods as still belonging to the transferor, or a receiver representing them can take them by whatever procedure the local law provides." The status of the buyer is as a trustee or receiver for the benefit of creditors of the seller existing at the time of the sale. The rule is well expressed in Southwestern Drug Corp. v McKesson & Robbins, 141 Tex 284, 172 SW2d 485, 155 ALR 1056 (1943):

"Failure of the purchaser to comply with the Bulk Sales Law fixes his liability as that of a receiver, and he becomes bound to see that the property, or its value, is applied to the satisfaction of claims of the creditors of the seller. In other words, he becomes a trustee, charged with the duties and liabilities of a trustee. Under the law he is charged with liability only to the extent of the value of the property received by him, and his liability is to all of the creditors pro rata. . . . However, if a purchaser or receiver disposes of or converts to his own use property acquired in violation of the Bulk Sales Law, placing it beyond the reach of creditors, he will be held personally liable for the value thereof. . . .

. . . Since the purchasers so commingled the merchandise that it could not be segregated personal liability ensued. . . .

The Bulk Sales Law is not new in the state. The provisions of the present act are quite similar to our earlier one. Therefore the teachings of cases decided before the enactment of the Uniform Commercial Code are helpful. . . .

"Stated generally a purchaser in violation of the Bulk Sales Act acquires no rights in the property purchased as against the creditors of the seller.

His status is generally considered, the statute sometimes expressly so providing, to be that of a trustee or receiver for the benefit of all the creditors of the seller, existing at the time of transfer. . . .

The liability as a trustee or receiver is to all the creditors pro rata. . . ."

. . . The appellees were entitled to judgment merely for their pro rata share determined on the basis of the creditors existing when the sale was consummated. . . . Also see 2 Anderson's Uniform Commercial Code, page 199 which points out that the existing, as distinguished from future creditors, are to share. . . .

The judgment is reversed for proceedings consistent herewith.

LTV Aerospace Corp. v Bateman

(Tex Civ App) 492 SW2d 703 (1973)

The LTV Aerospace Corporation manufactured all-terrain vehicles for use in South-east Asia. LTV made an oral contract with Bateman under which it would supply the packing cases needed for overseas shipment. Bateman made substantial beginnings in the production of packing cases following LTV's specifications. LTV thereafter stopped production of its vehicles and refused to take delivery of the cases. When sued for breach of contract, LTV raised the defense that there was no writing to satisfy the statute of frauds. From a judgment for Bateman, LTV appealed.

McKAY, J. . . . In December, 1969, appellant circulated a detailed invitation to bid so as to find a local supplier who could manufacture the shipping containers or crates to specifications and in quantities to 8,000 containers. The containers were to be delivered on a periodic basis to be specified by appellant to fit its production schedule.

Appellee in December, 1969, received from a third party a copy of the invitation to bid, and later in that month submitted a detailed written bid to appellant. Negotiations between appellee and representatives of appellant followed and after some oral changes on both specifications and price an agreement was reached and the bid was accepted by appellant. The exact terms of the agreement were disputed at the trial.

Appellee in January, 1970, employed workmen, purchased raw materials, plant equipment and facilities and began building shipping containers or crates, the first being delivered about January 20, 1970.

In March, 1970, appellee received a written purchase order from appellant, dated January 7, 1970, requesting delivery of 900 containers of the type and at the price previously agreed. Some crates had already been delivered and accepted by appellant before the purchase order was received by appellee about March 17, 1970.

In September, 1970, appellee received an amended or revised purchase order changing and reducing the quantity of containers from 900 to 653, the number 653 being the number of containers which had already been delivered and paid for. The new purchase order also requested production of 450 container bottoms only at a price then specially agreed upon. These bottoms were manufactured, delivered and paid for.

No additional containers or bottoms were ordered or built, and appellant's Tyler plant subsequently ceased operations.

The record shows that appellant did not sign appellee's written bid, which was amended and later orally changed, and appellee did not sign either of appellant's purchase orders. . . .

The contract which appellee seeks to enforce involves sale and purchase of shipping containers of the value of substantially more than $500. Appellant did not sign appellee's written bid. Therefore, it must be determined whether the contract here is governed by Subsection (c) (1) of sec 2-201, UCC, as specially manufactured goods for appellant and not suitable for sale to others in the ordinary course of appellee's business. We hold that the contract is so governed.

These shipping crates or containers were manufactured by appellee to detailed specifications required by appellant, and they were to be used for shipping overseas an all-terrain vehicle manufactured by appellant. They were not suitable for sale to others in the ordinary course of appellee's business. The record discloses that appellee had made a substantial beginning in manufacture of the goods, and it was done for appellant's benefit before any notice of repudiation was given or received. The contract was not rendered unenforceable by the statute because it falls under an exception under which the statute of frauds

need not be complied with. Appellant's first three points are overruled. Rose Acre Farms, Inc. v L. P. Cavett Co. of Indiana, 279 NE2d 280 (Ind App 1st Dist, 1972); 1 Anderson, Uniform Comm. Code, sec. 2-201.46; Ann Statute of Frauds—Manufactured Goods, 25 ALR2d 692.

Appellant claims that there is a writing which satisfies the requirements of subsection (a), and that it is the purchase order, and therefore subsection (c) (1) cannot apply. Subsection (a) requires "some writing sufficient to indicate that a contract for sale has been made between the parties and *signed by the party against whom enforcement is sought. . . .*" Emphasis ours. The issuing of a purchase order for 900 crates or containers, unsigned by appellee against whom it is sought to be enforced, is not such a writing as will satisfy subsection (a). . . .

[Judgment affirmed]

QUESTIONS AND CASE PROBLEMS

1. What social forces are affected by the rule that consideration is not required by a modification of a contract for the sale of goods?

2. Compare the liability of (a) a transferee of a bulk transfer when the requirements of the Uniform Commercial Code are not satisfied, (b) a person buying goods on credit, and (c) a person buying out an existing business and promising to pay the creditors of the original business.

3. Compare the content of the writing required to satisfy the statute of frauds in the case of a sale of goods with a contract which comes under the general statute of frauds.

4. Compare the effect of (a) payment by check, and (b) payment by cash, for goods purchased under an oral contract for a purchase price of $500 or more.

5. Raymond International, Inc., was a highway contractor. Blue Rock Industries sold Raymond large quantities of sand for use in the construction of highways. Raymond did not pay for the sand. Was the liability of Raymond governed by the Uniform Commercial Code? [Blue Rock Industries v Raymond International, Inc., (Me), 325 A2d 66]

6. The Tober Foreign Motors, Inc., sold an airplane to Skinner on installments. Later it was agreed that the monthly installments should be reduced in half. Thereafter Tober claimed that the reduction agreement was not binding because it was not supported by consideration. Was this claim correct? [Skinner v Tober Foreign Motors, Inc., 345 Mass 429, 187 NE2d 669]

7. Suburban Gas Heat of Kennewick sold propane gas for domestic consumption. As the result of its negligence in supplying propane gas mixed with water, there was an explosion which caused damage to Kasey. When Kasey sued to enforce the liability of Suburban Gas Heat as a seller, Suburban raised the defense that it was engaged in furnishing a public service and not in the sale of personal property within the meaning of the Uniform Sales Act. Was Suburban correct? [Kasey v Suburban Gas Heat of Kennewick, Inc., 60 Wash 2d 468, 374 P2d 549]

8. Gallick sold sugar to Castiglione with knowledge that the latter intended to use it in the illegal manufacture of liquor. The buyer did not pay the purchase price. Gallick then sued him for the purchase price. Castiglione defended on the ground that the contract was illegal. Decide. [Gallick v Castiglione, 2 Cal App 2d 716, 38 P2d 858]

9. Berger did business under the name of Warren Freezer Food Co. A consumer named Vernon made a contract for the purchase of a large quantity of freezer items, under which it was agreed that Warren Freezer would keep Vernon's food in its freezer, Vernon would take a portion of the order each week and would make a weekly installment payment, which would be applied to the note that Vernon had signed for the total bill. When Vernon would call for a part of the order of food, each item was individually wrapped in plain paper. When Vernon requested delivery, the individual packages were put into cardboard boxes on the exterior of which was a statement of the gross and net weight of the total contents and the defendant's name and place of business. Berger was prosecuted for violating the Michigan statute against "misbranding," which statute declared that an article was misbranded "if in package form" and the package did not show the true net weight. Was Berger guilty of violating this statute? [Michigan v Berger, 7 Mich App 695, 153 NW2d 161]

10. A farmer made a written contract to sell "all cotton produced in 400 acres." The buyer claimed that this required a solid planting of the 400 acres. The seller claimed that it was the custom to plant by "skip row" method in which every two planted rows would be separated by an idle row. The seller claimed that parol evidence was admissible to show that there was a custom to plant in this manner. The buyer claimed that the parol evidence could not be allowed to contradict the writing. Was the parol evidence admissible? [See Leob & Co. v Martin, 295 Ala 262, 327 So2d 711]

11. Crocker printed and distributed Christmas cards. At certain intervals such cards which could not be sold would be destroyed. Crocker's employees took a large quantity of Christmas cards for that purpose to McFaddin who ran a dump and salvage operation. Persons bringing material to McFaddin would pay one fee for material that could be salvaged by him and a higher fee if instructions were given to destroy the material. When Crocker's employees took the Christmas cards to McFaddin, nothing was said as to the disposition to be made of them and only a salvage fee was paid. Later, Crocker learned that McFaddin had resold the cards. He sued McFaddin, claiming that McFaddin could not make such a sale because the transaction between Crocker and McFaddin was a bailment. McFaddin defended on the ground that the transaction was a sale, an abandonment, or a gift, and that in any instance McFaddin could sell the property and otherwise treat it as his own. Decide. [H. S. Crocker Co. v McFaddin, 148 Cal App 2d 639, 307 P2d 429]

12. Members of the Colonial Club purchased beer from outside the state and ordered it sent to the Colonial Club. The club then kept it in the club refrigerator and served the beer to its respective owners upon demand. The club received no compensation or profit from the transaction. The club was indicted for selling liquor unlawfully. Decide. [North Carolina v Colonial Club, 154 NC 177, 69 SE 771]

13. Hess entered into a contract to supply Hazle Township with "100 tons more or less" of crushed gravel. Hess delivered 6,000 tons and claimed that the Township was required to pay for that amount by virtue of the language quoted above. Was Hess correct? [J. A. & W. A. Hess, Inc. v Hazle Township, 9 Pa Commonwealth Ct 409, 305 A2d 404]

14. A letter signed by the seller stated that the seller sold "all the cotton" produced on a specified tract of land to the buyer. The seller later claimed that this letter did not satisfy the statute of frauds because it did not state a quantity of goods. Was the seller correct? [See Harris v Hine, 232 Fla 183, 205 SE2d 847]

15. Hy-Grade Construction and Materials took equipment from the possession of Nelson. He sued it for the conversion of his property. The corporation raised the defense that it had purchased the equipment from Nelson under an oral contract of sale and that the corporation could prove the oral contract because it had possession of the goods. Was the corporation correct? [Nelson v Hy-Grade Construction and Materials, Inc. (Kan) 527 P2d 1059]

16. A merchant made an oral contract to sell $1,000 worth of goods to another merchant. The buyer broke the contract and the seller sued for breach of the contract. The buyer raised the defense that suit could not be brought on the oral contract because there was no writing satisfying UCC § 2-201. The seller offered evidence showing that it was customary for merchants in the trade to deal on the basis of oral contracts. Was the seller entitled to recover on the oral contract? [See Dangerfield v Market (ND) 222 NW2d 373]

17. A customer purchased furniture from a dealer. The furniture selected by the customer was not in stock, and the dealer loaned the customer some furniture to use until the selected furniture was delivered. An item of the loaned furniture collapsed and injured the customer. The customer sued the dealer three years and four months later. The dealer defended on the ground that the non-Code two-year statute of limitations had expired. The customer claimed that there was a sale and that accordingly suit could be brought within the four-year period authorized by the UCC § 2-725. Decide. [Garfield v Furniture Fair-Hanover, 113 NJ Super 509, 274 A2d 325]

18. Fallis farmed about 550 acres. He made an oral contract to sell and deliver to Grains 5,000 bushels of soybeans at $2.54 per bushel. Shortly thereafter, Grains sent Fallis a written contract signed by Grains. Fallis did not sign the contract and did not return it. When he failed to deliver the soybeans under the contract, he was sued for the breach thereof by Grains. He raised the defense of the statute of frauds. Grains claimed that the statute of frauds was not applicable because Fallis had not rejected the written contract that had been sent to him. Decide. [Grains v Fallis, 239 Ark 962, 395 SW2d 555]

19. Crown Central Petroleum Corporation, a refinery, orally agreed to supply Davis, an independent dealer, with 1.2 million gallons of gas a month. Because of the oil shortage Crown refused to deliver the gas as promised. Davis sued Crown. Was Crown liable? [Davis v Crown Central Petroleum Corp., (CA4 NC) 483 F2d 1014]

24 Risk and Property Rights

In most sales transactions the buyer receives the proper goods, makes payment, and the transaction is thus completed; however, several types of problems may arise—(a) problems pertaining to damage to goods, (b) those resulting from creditors' claims, and (c) problems relating to insurance. These problems usually can be avoided if the parties make express provisions concerning them in their sales contract. When the parties have not specified by their contract what results they desire, however, the rules stated in this chapter are applied by the law.

§ 24:1. Types of Problems.

(a) **Damage to Goods.** If the goods are damaged or totally destroyed without any fault of either the buyer or the seller, must the seller bear the loss and supply new goods to the buyer; or is it the buyer's loss, so that the buyer must pay the seller the purchase price even though the goods are damaged or destroyed?[1] The fact that there may be insurance does not diminish the importance of this question, for the answer to it determines whose insurer is liable and the extent of that insurer's liability.

(b) **Creditors' Claims.** Creditors of a delinquent seller may seize the goods as belonging to the seller, or the buyer's creditors may seize them on the theory that they belong to the buyer. In such cases the question arises whether the creditors are correct as to who owns the goods. The question of ownership is also important in connection with the consequence of a resale by the buyer, or the liability for or the computation of certain kinds of taxes, and the liability under certain registration and criminal law statutes.[2]

(c) **Insurance.** Until the buyer has received the goods and the seller has been paid, both the seller and buyer have an economic interest in the sales transaction.[3] The question arises as to whether either or both have enough interest to entitle them to insure the property involved; that is, whether they have an insurable interest.[4]

---

[1] UCC § 2-509.

[2] UCC § 2-401.

[3] See UCC § 2-501(1)(a), and note also that the seller may have a security interest by virtue of the nature of the shipment or the agreement of the parties. The buyer also acquires a special property right in the goods that entitles the buyer to reclaim the goods on the seller's insolvency if payment of all or part of the purchase price has been made in advance. § 2-502

[4] In order to insure property, a person must have such a right or interest in the property that its damage or destruction would cause financial loss. This is called an insurable interest in the property. The ownership of personal property for the purpose of insurance is determined by the UCC. Motors Insurance Corp. v Safeco Insurance Co. (Ky) 412 SW2d 584.

§ 24:2. Nature of the Transaction. The answer to be given to each of the questions noted in the preceding section depends upon the nature of the transaction between the seller and the buyer. Sales transactions may be classified according to (a) the nature of the goods and (b) the terms of the transaction.

(a)   Nature of Goods. The goods may be (1) existing and identified goods or (2) future goods.

(1)   Existing and Identified Goods. Existing goods are (a) physically in existence and (b) owned by the seller. When particular goods have been selected by either the buyer or seller, or both of them, as being the goods called for by the sales contract, the goods are described as *identified goods.* If the goods are existing and identified, it is immaterial whether the seller must do some act or must complete the manufacture of the goods before they satisfy the terms of the contract.

(2)   ·Future Goods. If the goods are not both existing and identified at the time of the sales transaction, they are *future goods.* Thus, goods are future goods when they are not yet owned by the seller, when they are not yet in existence, or when they have not been identified to the contract.

(b)   Terms of the Transaction. Ordinarily, the seller is only required to make the goods available to the buyer. If transportation is provided, the seller is normally only required to make shipment and the seller's part of the contract is performed by handing the goods over to a carrier for shipment to the buyer. The terms of the contract, however, may obligate the seller to deliver the goods at a particular place, for example, to make delivery at the destination. The seller's part of the contract is then not completed until the goods are brought to the destination point and there tendered to the buyer. If the transaction calls for sending the goods to the buyer, it is ordinarily required that the seller deliver the goods to a carrier under a proper *contract for shipment* to the buyer. Actual physical *delivery at destination* is only required when the contract expressly so states.

Instead of calling for the actual delivery of goods, the sales transaction may relate to a transfer of the document of title representing the goods. For example, the goods may be stored in a warehouse, and the seller and the buyer have no intention of moving the goods, but intend that there shall be a sale and a delivery of the warehouse receipt that stands for the goods. Here the obligation of the seller is to produce the proper paper as distinguished from the goods themselves. The same is true when the goods are represented by any other document of title, such as a bill of lading issued by a carrier.

As a third situation, the goods may be stored with, or held by a third person who has not issued any document of title for the goods, but the seller and the buyer intend that the goods shall remain in the bailee's hands, the transaction being completed without any delivery of the goods themselves or of any document of title.

§ 24:3. Risk, Rights, and Insurable Interest in Particular Transactions. The various kinds of goods and terms may be combined in a number of ways. Only the six more common types of transactions will be considered in relationship to the time when risk, rights, and insurable interest are acquired by the buyer. The first three types relate to existing and identified goods; the last three, to future goods.

Keep in mind that the following rules of law apply only in the absence of a contrary agreement by the parties concerning these matters. Title to the goods cannot pass to the buyer before the parties so intend.

(a)   Existing Goods Identified at Time of Contracting.

(1)   No Documents of Title. If the seller is a merchant, the risk of loss passes to the buyer on receiving the goods from the merchant; if a nonmerchant seller, the risk passes when the seller makes the goods available to the buyer. Thus the risk of loss remains longer on the merchant seller, a distinction which is made on the ground that the merchant seller, being in business, can more readily obtain protection against such continued risk.

The title to existing goods identified at the time of contracting, when no document of title, such as a warehouse receipt or a bill of lading, is involved, passes to the buyer at the time and place of contracting regardless of whether delivery and payment are to be made at a later date. The agreement of the parties may alter this rule of law as by providing that title will not pass to the buyer until a particular debt of the seller is assumed by the buyer. Likewise, when the contract for the sale of existing identified goods specifies that title will not pass until the buyer takes the goods from the seller's premises, the transfer of title will not take place until that time, although otherwise it would have taken place at the time the contract was made.

When the goods are in the possession of the buyer before the contract of sale has been made, title passes to the buyer as soon as it is agreed that the buyer will buy the goods.

When the buyer becomes the owner of the goods in the situation here considered, the buyer has an insurable interest in them. In contrast the seller has an insurable interest in the goods before title passes to the buyer. The insurable interest of the seller terminates when title passes to the buyer unless the seller has reserved a security interest to protect any unpaid balance due on the contract.

(2)   Goods Represented by Negotiable Document of Title. Here the buyer has an insurable interest in the goods at the time and place of contracting but does not ordinarily become subject to the risk of loss nor acquire the title until delivery of the document is made.[5]

(3)   Goods Held as Bailee Without Document of Title. Here the goods owned by the seller are held by a repairer, or other bailee, but there is no document of title and the sales contract does not call for a physical delivery of goods; the parties intending that the goods should remain where they are. In such a case, the answers to the various problems are the same as in situation (1), § 24:3(a)(1), except that the risk of loss does not pass to the buyer, but remains with the seller, until the bailee acknowledges holding the goods in question for the buyer.

---

[5] Express provision is made for the case of a nonnegotiable document and other factual variations. UCC § 2-509(2)(c), § 2-503(4). When delivery of a document is to be made, the seller may send the document through customary banking channels as well as make a tender in person or by an agent. § 2-503(5)(b). Even though the form of the document of title is such that title is retained by the seller for security purposes, the risk of loss nevertheless passes to the buyer.

(b)   Future Goods.

(1)   Marking for Buyer. If the buyer sends an order for goods to be manufactured by the seller or to be filled from inventory or by purchases from third persons, one step in the process of filling the order is the seller's act of marking, tagging, labeling, or in some way doing an act for the benefit of the shipping department to indicate that certain goods are the ones to be sent or delivered to the buyer under the order. This act of unilateral identification of the goods is enough to give the buyer a property interest in the goods which entitles the buyer to insure them.[6] Neither risk of loss nor title passes to the buyer at that time, however, but remains with the seller, who, as the continuing owner, also has an insurable interest in the goods. Thus, neither title nor risk of loss passes to the buyer until some later event, such as a shipment or delivery, occurs.

The parties may by their agreement delay the transfer of title until a later date, as by specifying that title shall not pass until payment is made or until the goods arrive at their destination. This retention of title by the seller is for the purpose of security only and the buyer nevertheless acquires an insurable interest upon identification.

(2)   Contract for Shipment to Buyer. In this situation, the buyer has placed an order for future goods to be shipped to the buyer, and the contract is performed by the seller by delivering the goods to a carrier for shipment to the buyer. Under such a contract, the risk of loss and the title pass to the buyer when the goods are delivered to the carrier, that is, at the time and place of shipment. After that happens, the seller has no insurable interest unless the seller has reserved a security interest in the goods.[7]

The fact that a shipment of goods is represented by a bill of lading or an airbill issued by the carrier, and that in order to complete the transaction it will be necessary to transfer that bill to the buyer, does not affect these rules or bring the transaction within situation (2) of § 24:3(a).

A provision for the inspection or testing of the goods by the buyer or by a third person at the buyer's place of business, at a building site, or at a place where the goods are to be installed may have the effect of delaying the transfer of the risk of loss to the buyer until the time when the goods are inspected or tested and approved as conforming. (See p. 390, Wilke v Cummins Diesel Engines)

(3)   Contract for Delivery at Destination. When the contract requires the seller to make delivery of future goods at a particular destination point, the buyer acquires a property right and an insurable interest in the goods at the time and place they are marked or shipped; but the risk of loss and the title do not pass until the carrier tenders or makes the goods available at the destination point. The seller retains an insurable interest until that time; and a security interest of the seller in the goods continues until the purchase price has been paid.

---

[6] UCC § 2-501(1)(b). Special provision is made as to crops and unborn animals. § 2-501(1)(c).

[7] The reservation of a security interest by the seller does not affect the transfer of the risk to the buyer.

Risk and Property Rights in Sales Contracts

Nature of Goods	Terms of Transaction	Transfer of Risk of Loss to Buyer	Transfer of Title to Buyer	Acquisition of Insurable Interest by Buyer *
Existing Goods Identified at Time of Contracting	1. Without document of title	Buyer's receipt of goods from merchant seller; tender of delivery by nonmerchant seller § 2-509(3)	Time and place of contracting § 2-401(3)(b)	Time and place of contracting § 2-501(1)(a)
	2. Delivery of document of title only	Buyer's receipt of negotiable document of title § 2-509(2)(a)	Time and place of delivery of documents by seller § 2-401(3)(a)	Time and place of contracting § 2-501(1)(a)
	3. Goods held by bailee, without document of title	Time of bailee's acknowledgment of buyer's right to possession § 2-509(2)(b)	Time and place of contracting § 2-401(3)(b)	Time and place of contracting § 2-501(1)(a)
	4. Marking for buyer	No transfer	No transfer	At time of marking § 2-501(1)(b)
Future Goods	5. Contract for shipment to buyer	Delivery of goods to carrier § 2-509(1)(a)	Time and place of delivery of goods to carrier § 2-401(2)(a)	Time and place of delivery to carrier or of marking for buyer § 2-501(1)(b)
	6. Contract for delivery at destination	Tender of goods at destination § 2-509(1)(b)	Tender of goods at destination § 2-401(2)(b)	Time and place of delivery to carrier or of marking for buyer § 2-501(1)(b)

* The seller retains an insurable interest in the goods as long as the seller has a security interest in them. When the buyer acquires an insurable interest, the buyer also acquires a special property in the goods, less than title, which entitles the buyer to assert certain remedies against the seller.

A provision in the contract directing the seller to "ship to" the buyer does not convert the contract into a contract calling for delivery at destination.[8]

§ 24:4. Self-Service Stores. In the case of goods in a self-service store, the reasonable interpretation of the circumstances is that the store by its act of putting the goods on display on the shelves makes an offer to sell such goods for cash and confers upon a prospective customer a license to carry the goods to the cashier in order to make payment. Most courts hold that there is no transfer of title until the buyer makes payment to the cashier and therefore hold that no warranty liability of the store arises prior to the buyer's payment.

A contrary rule accepts the view that "a contract to sell" is formed when the customer "accepts" the seller's offer by taking the item from the shelf, but then holds that the buyer has warranty protection although there has not yet been a transfer of title to the buyer. (See p. 392, Fender v Colonial Stores, Inc.) By another contrary view, a sale actually occurs when the buyer takes the item from the shelf. That is, title passes at that moment to the buyer even though the goods have not yet been paid for. The fact that the buyer can return the item to the shelf is merely a "return" by the buyer by which the buyer transfers back to the seller the title which had already passed to the buyer when the item was removed from the shelf.

§ 24:5 Automobiles. Most states provide for the registration of the title to automobiles. These ordinarily provide for the transfer of the title certificate upon the making of a sale of a registered automobile. As between the seller and a buyer, however, the transfer of such a title certificate is not essential. That is, title passes from the seller to the buyer in accordance with the provisions of the Uniform Commercial Code. After it has so passed, the new owner is entitled to obtain a title certificate showing such ownership.

In states which follow the rule that the title certificate is not controlling, there is accordingly a transfer of title to the buyer when possession of the car is given to the buyer with the intent that title should pass, even though there has not been any indorsement and delivery of the title certificate as required by law. (See p. 393, Waggoner v Wilson) In such a state, a transfer of title may occur when the parties agree that the automobile "belongs" to the other party even though nothing has been done with respect to the title certificate.[9] Likewise when the purchased automobile has been delivered to the buyer on a cash and trade-in sale, the ownership passes to the buyer for the purpose of insurance coverage at the time of delivery, even though the title papers are to be executed and the cash balance paid on the following day. Consequently an automobile is no longer covered by a dealer's insurance policy as being "owned" or "held for sale" by the dealer after it has been bought and driven away by the buyer.

In contrast to the view that the transfer of title to an automobile is governed by the UCC, some states by statute have declared that the title to an automobile cannot be transferred without an indorsement and delivery of the certificate of title. In those states, the parties must satisfy the requirement of such a statute and it is immaterial that title would otherwise pass under the Uniform Commercial Code.

---

[8] Eberhard Mfg. Co. v Brown, 61 MichApp 268, 232 NW2d 378.
[9] UCC § 2-401; Metropolitan Auto Sales Corp. v Koheski, 252 Md 145, 249 A2d 141.

In most states, the pre-Code motor vehicle statute remains in force to determine the location of "ownership" for the purpose of imposing tort liability or determining the coverage of liability insurance.

§ 24:6. Damage or Destruction of Goods. In absence of a contrary agreement,[10] damage to or destruction of the goods affects the transaction as follows:

(a) Damage to Identified Goods Before Risk of Loss Passes. When goods that were identified at the time the contract was made are damaged or destroyed without the fault of either party before the risk of loss has passed, the contract is avoided if the loss is total. If the loss is partial or if the goods have so deteriorated that they do not conform to the contract, the buyer has the option, after inspection of the goods, (1) to treat the contract as avoided, or (2) to accept the goods subject to an allowance or deduction from the contract price. In either case, the buyer cannot assert any claim against the seller for breach of contract.[11]

When the buyer makes an effective rejection of nonconforming goods and the goods are then stolen before the seller has come for them, the buyer is not liable for the value of the stolen goods, unless the seller can establish that the buyer was negligent in caring for the goods after their rejection. (See p. 394, Graybar Electric Co. v Shook)

A provision in a credit sale agreement that the buyer will at all times keep the goods fully insured against loss is not a "contrary agreement" within the UCC so as to shift the loss to the buyer at an earlier time.

(b) Damage to Identified Goods After Risk of Loss Passes. If partial damage or total destruction occurs after the risk of loss has passed to the buyer, it is the buyer's loss. It may be, however, that the buyer will be able to recover the amount of the damages from the person in possession of the goods or from a third person causing the loss.

(c) Damage to Unidentified Goods. A long as the goods are unidentified, no risk of loss has passed to the buyer. If any goods are damaged or destroyed during this period, the loss is the seller's. The buyer is still entitled to receive the goods covered by the contract. The seller is therefore liable for breach of contract if the proper goods are not delivered.

The only exception arises when the parties have expressly provided in the contract that the destruction of the seller's supply shall release the seller from liability or when it is clear that the parties contracted for the purchase and sale of part of the seller's supply to the exclusion of any other possible source of such goods. In such case, the destruction of or damage to the seller's supply is a condition subsequent which discharges the contract.

(d) Reservation of Title or Possession. When the seller reserves title or possession solely as security to make certain that the buyer will pay the purchase price, the risk of loss is borne by the buyer if the circumstances are such that the loss would be on the buyer in the absence of such a reservation.

---

[10] UCC § 2-303.
[11] UCC § 2-613.

§ 24:7. Sales on Approval and with Right to Return. A sales transaction may give the buyer the privilege of returning the goods. In a *sale on approval,* the sale is not complete, that is, there is no transfer of title, until the buyer approves. A *sale or return* is a completed sale with the right of the buyer to return the goods and thereby set aside the sale. The agreement of the parties determines whether conforming goods can be returned and whether the sale is on approval or with return. If there is no agreement that conforming goods can be returned, the buyer cannot return them. If a "return" has been agreed to but the parties do not specify on what basis, it is a sale on approval if the goods are purchased for use, that is, by a consumer, and a sale or return if purchased for resale, that is, by a merchant.[12]

(a)   Sale on Approval. In the absence of a contrary agreement, title and risk of loss remain with the seller under a sale on approval until there is an approval. Approval by the buyer may be shown by the express words of the buyer or by conduct of the buyer. Use of the goods by the buyer consistent with the purpose of trial is not an election or approval. There is an approval shown by conduct, however, if the buyer acts in a manner that is not consistent with merely trying the goods, or if the buyer fails to express a choice within the time specified for approval or within a reasonable time if no time is specified. Notice of disapproval to the seller prevents the lapse of time from constituting an approval. If the goods are actually returned by the buyer, the seller bears the risk and the expense involved in making the return.[13] As the buyer is not the "owner" of the goods while they are on approval, the buyer's creditors cannot reach the goods.[14]

(b)   Sale or Return. In a sale or return, title and risk of loss pass to the buyer as in the case of an ordinary or absolute sale. In the absence of a contrary agreement, the buyer under a sale or return may return all of the goods or any commercial unit thereof. A *commercial unit* is any article, group of articles, or quantity which commercially is regarded as a separate unit or item, such as a particular machine, a suite of furniture, or a carload lot.[15] In order to exercise the right to return the goods, they must be substantially in their original condition, and the option to return must be exercised within the time specified by the contract or within a reasonable time if none is specified. The return under such a contract is at the buyer's risk and expense.[16] Until the actual return of the goods is made, the risk of loss remains on the buyer. As long as the goods are in the buyer's possession under a sale or return contract, the buyer's creditors may treat the goods as belonging to the buyer.[17]

The delivery of goods to an agent for sale is not a sale and return. Therefore, when the owner of an automobile leaves it with a dealer to obtain an offer of purchase which the owner would then be required to approve in order to effect the sale, there is no "sale or return" and the creditors of the dealer cannot make any claim against the automobile.

---

[12] UCC § 2-326(1). An "or return" provision is treated as a sales contract for the purpose of applying the statute of frauds, and cannot be established by parol evidence when it would contradict a sales contract indicating an absolute sale. § 2-326(4).

[13] UCC § 2-327(1).

[14] UCC § 2-326(2).

[15] UCC § 2-105(6).

[16] UCC § 2-327(2).

[17] UCC § 2-326(2); Guardian Discount Co. v. Settles, 114 GaApp 418, 151 SE2d 530.

(c)   Consignment Sale. A consignment or a sale on consignment is merely an authorization or agency to sell. It is neither a sale on approval nor a sale with right to return. As the relationship is merely an agency, the consignor, in the absence of some contrary contract restriction, may revoke the agency at will and retake possession of the property by any lawful means. If such repossession of the goods constitutes a breach of the contract with the consignee, the consignor is liable to the consignee for the damages. Whether goods are sent to a person as buyer, either on approval or with right to return, or on consignment to sell for the seller is a question of the intention of the parties. In some instances, the creditors of the consignee may treat the goods held by the consignee on consignment as though they belonged to the consignee, thereby ignoring and destroying the consignor's ownership.

§ 24:8. Sale of Fungible Goods. *Fungible goods* are of a homogeneous nature that may be sold by weight or measure. They are goods of which any unit is from its nature or by commercial usage treated as the same as or the equivalent of any other unit.[18] Wheat, oil, coal, and similar bulk commodities are fungible goods since, given a mass of the same grade or uniformity, any one bushel or other unit of the mass will be exactly the same as any other bushel or similar unit.

Title to an undivided share or quantity of an identified mass of fungible goods may pass to the buyer at the time of the transaction, making the buyer an owner in common with the seller.[19] For example, when a person sells to another 600 bushels of wheat from a bin which contains 1,000 bushels, title to 600 bushels passes to the buyer at the time of the transaction, giving the buyer a 6/10ths undivided interest in the mass as an owner in common.[20] The courts in some states, however, have held that title does not pass until a separation of the purchased share has been made.

§ 24:9. Auction Sales. When goods are sold at an auction in separate lots, each lot is a separate transaction, and title to each passes independently of the other lots.[21] Title to each lot passes when the auctioneer announces by the fall of the hammer or in any other customary manner that the auction is completed as to that lot,[22] that is, the lot in question has been sold to the bidder.

§ 24:10. Reservation of a Security Interest. The seller may fear that the buyer will not pay for the goods. The seller could protect against this danger by insisting that the buyer pay cash immediately. This may not be practical for geographic or business reasons. The seller may then give credit to the buyer but can obtain protection by retaining a security interest in the goods.

(a)   Bill of Lading. The seller may retain varying degrees of control over the goods by the method of shipment. Thus the seller may ship the goods to the seller's agent in the buyer's city, receiving from the carrier the bill of lading for the goods.[23] In such a case, the buyer cannot obtain the goods from the carrier as the shipment is

---

[18] UCC § 1-201(17).
[19] UCC § 2-105(4).
[20] UCC § 2-403(1).
[21] UCC § 2-328(1).
[22] UCC § 2-328(2).
[23] UCC § 2-505.

not directed to the buyer, in the case of a straight bill of lading; or because the buyer does not hold the bill of lading, if it is a negotiable or order bill. The seller's agent in the buyer's city can then arrange for or obtain payment from the buyer after which the agent gives the buyer the bill of lading to enable the buyer to obtain the goods from the carrier.

If the goods are sent by a carrier under a negotiable bill of lading to the order of the buyer or the buyer's agent, the seller may also retain the right of possession of the goods by keeping possession of the bill of lading until payment is received or assured.[24]

(b) C.O.D. Shipment. In the absence of an extension of credit, a seller has the right to keep the goods until paid but loses this right by delivering possession of the goods to anyone for the buyer. Hence the right is lost when the seller delivers the goods to a carrier under a straight bill of lading and does not make any reservation of a security interest by means of the bill of lading. However, on delivering the goods to a carrier, the seller may preserve the right to possession by making the shipment C.O.D., or by the addition of any other terms indicating an intention that the carrier should not surrender the goods to the buyer until the buyer has made payment. Such a provision has no effect other than to keep the buyer from obtaining possession until payment has been made. The C.O.D. provision does not affect the problem of determining whether title or risk of loss has passed.

(c) Secured Transactions. The security interest under a bill of lading or a C.O.D. shipment is only temporary, because it is related to the period of the transportation of the goods to the buyer. The seller may obtain a permanent or continuing security interest by entering into a secured transaction with the buyer. This is the typical pattern for selling large appliances and automobiles on credit. This type of transaction is governed by Article 9 of the Uniform Commercial Code and is discussed in Chapters 34 and 35.

§ 24:11. Effect of Sale on Title. As a general rule, a seller can only sell such interest or title in the goods as the seller possesses. If the property is subject to a rental bailment, a sale by the bailor is therefore subject to the bailment. Likewise, the bailee can only transfer a bailee's right under the bailment, assuming that the bailment agreement permits that right to be assigned or transferred. The fact that the bailee is in possession of the property does not give the bailee the right to transfer the title to the property. Similarly, a thief or finder generally cannot transfer the title to property since the thief or finder can only pass that which the thief or finder has, namely the possession but not the title. In fact, the purchaser from a thief or finder not only fails to obtain title but also becomes liable to the owner of the property as a converter of the property even though such purchaser made the purchase in good faith.

A thief cannot pass good title to a stolen automobile. The owner may recover the automobile from the subpurchaser although the latter buys in good faith and pays value. The fact that the negligence or the act of the owner contributed to or facilitated the theft does not stop the true owner from asserting title. Thus the owner of a stolen automobile remained its owner even though the owner had signed a title

---

[24] UCC § 2-505(1)(a).

certificate in blank and left it in the glove compartment of the car and left the keys in the car, apparently with the intent that should the owner die, a child of the owner would be able to take the car readily.[25]

The buyer of stolen goods must surrender them to the true owner even though such buyer had acted in good faith.

There are certain instances, however, when either because of the conduct of the owner or the desire of society to protect the bona fide purchaser for value, the law permits a greater title to be transferred than the seller possessed.

(a)   Sale by Entrustee. If the owner entrusts goods to a merchant who deals in goods of that kind, the latter has the power to transfer the entruster's title to anyone who buys from the entrustee in the ordinary course of business. (See p. 395, Medico Leasing Co. v Smith)

It is immaterial why the goods were entrusted to the merchant. Hence the leaving of a watch for repair with a jeweler who sells new and secondhand watches gives the jeweler the power to pass the title of the repair customer to a buyer in the ordinary course of business.[26] Goods in inventory thus have a degree of "negotiability" so that the ordinary buyer, whether a consumer or another merchant, buys the goods free of the ownership interest of the person entrusting the goods to the seller.[27] The entrustee is, of course, liable to the owner for damages caused by the entrustee's sale of the goods and is guilty of some form of statutory offense of embezzlement.

If the entrustee is not a merchant, such as a prospective customer trying out an automobile, there is no transfer of title to the buyer from the entrustee. Likewise, there is no transfer of title when a mere bailee, such as a repairer, who is not the seller of goods of that kind, sells the property of a customer.

(b)   Consignment Sale. A manufacturer or distributor may send goods to a dealer for sale to the public with the understanding that the manufacturer or distributor is to remain the owner, and the dealer in effect is to act as selling agent. When the dealer maintains a place of business at which the dealer sells goods of the kind in question under a name other than that of the consigning manufacturer or distributor, the creditors of the dealer may reach the goods as though they were owned by the dealer.[28]

(c)   Estoppel. The owner of property may be estopped from asserting ownership and thus be barred from denying the right of another person to sell the property. A person may purchase something and have the bill of sale made out in the name of a friend to whom possession of the property and the bill of sale are given. This might be done in order to deceive creditors of the true owner or to keep other persons from knowing that the purchase was made. If the friend should sell the property to a bona fide purchaser who relied on the bill of sale as showing that the friend was

[25] Stohr v Randle, 81 Wash2d 881, 505 P2d 1281.
[26] UCC § 2-403(2),(3). There is authority that, for this section to apply, the merchant status of the entrustee must be known both to the entruster and the purchaser. Atlas Auto Rental Corp. v Weisber, 54 Misc2d 168, 281 NYS2d 400.
[27] UCC § 2-403(1); Mattek v Malofsky, 42 Wis2d 16, 165 NW2d 406.
[28] UCC § 2-326(3). The manufacturer or dealer may be protected by complying with Article 9 of the Code or, in some cases, with a local statute.

the owner, the true owner is estopped or barred from denying the friend's apparent ownership and right to sell. Likewise where a buyer allowed the seller to retain possession of the goods for a number of years, the seller was clothed with such apparent authority that the original buyer was estopped to claim the title when the seller resold the goods to another buyer.[29]

(d)   Powers. In certain circumstances, persons in possession of someone else's property may sell the property. This arises in the case of pledges, lienholders, and some finders who, by statute, may have authority to sell the property to enforce their claim or when the owner cannot be found.

(e)   Negotiable Documents of Title. By statute, certain documents of title, such as bills of lading and warehouse receipts have been clothed with a degree of negotiability when executed in proper form.[30] By virtue of such provisions, the holder of a negotiable document of title may transfer to a purchaser, for value and acting in good faith, such title as was possessed by the person leaving the property with the issuer of the document. In such cases, it is immaterial that the holder had not acquired the document in a lawful manner.

(f)   Recording and Filing Statutes. In order to protect subsequent purchasers and creditors, statutes may require that certain transactions be recorded or filed and may provide that if that is not done, the transaction has no effect against a purchaser who thereafter buys the goods in good faith from the person who appears to be the owner or against the execution creditors of such an apparent owner. Thus, if a seller retains a security interest in the goods sold to the buyer by entering into an Article 9 secured transaction but fails to file a financing statement in the required manner, the purchaser appears to be the owner of the goods free from any security interest and subsequent bona fide purchasers or creditors of the buyer can acquire title from the buyer free of the seller's security interest.

(g)   Voidable Title. If the buyer has a voidable title, as when the buyer obtained the goods by fraud, the seller can rescind the sale while the buyer is still the owner. If, however, the buyer resells the property to a bona fide purchaser before the seller has rescinded the transaction, the subsequent purchaser acquires valid title.[31] It is immaterial whether the buyer having the voidable title had obtained title by fraud as to identity, or by larceny by trick or by payment for the goods with a bad check; or that the transaction was a cash sale and the purchase price had not been paid.[32]

(h)   Goods Retained by Seller. When the seller after making the sale is permitted by the buyer to retain possession of the goods, the seller has the power to transfer the title to a buyer in the ordinary course of business. Such permitted retention is an entrusting within the sale by entrustee rule described in § 24:12(a). The purpose of this rule of law is to protect the second purchaser, on the basis that the second purchaser had the right to rely on the apparent ownership of the seller.

---

[29] Tumber v Automation Design & Mfg. Corp., 130 NJ Super 5, 324 A2d 602.
[30] UCC § 7-502(2).
[31] UCC § 2-403(1).
[32] UCC § 2-403(1)(a) to (d).

(i)   **Protection of Seller.** As will be discussed in connection with the remedies of the parties, a seller who is lawfully in possession of property that has already been sold may resell it to a second purchaser if the first purchaser is in default in the payment of the purchase price. Here the object of the statute is not to protect the second purchaser but to enable the seller to remedy the situation created by the first purchaser's default.

(j)   **Protection of Creditors of Seller.** The continued possession of goods by the seller after their sale is generally deemed evidence that the sale was a fraud upon creditors, that is, that the sale was not a bona fide actual transfer of title but was merely a device to place the title out of the reach of the creditors of the seller. When the sale is fraudulent by local law, creditors of the seller may treat the sale as void and may have the property put up for sale on execution as though the property still belonged to the seller. The retention of possession by a merchant seller is declared not fraudulent, however, when made in good faith in the current course of business and when it does not exceed a period of time which is commercially reasonable.[33] For example, the fact that the merchant retains possession until transportation of the goods is arranged is not fraudulent as to creditors.

---

[33] UCC § 2-402(2).

CASES FOR CHAPTER 24

Wilke v Cummins Diesel Engines

252 Md 611, 250 A2d 886 (1969)

Wilke purchased a generator from Cummins Diesel Engines, subject to field tests after delivery and installation at a job site where Wilke was engaged in construction work as a subcontractor on certain facilities. Cummins delivered the generator in August, long before needed. The next spring, in hooking it up, Wilke found it severely damaged from water frozen in its cooling system. He notified Cummins, who removed and repaired it and billed Wilke for the repairs. Wilke sued Cummins to recover possession. Judgment was rendered for Cummins. Wilke appealed.

SINGLEY, J. . . . William F. Wilke, Inc. (Wilke), the appellant here and plaintiff below, is a mechanical contractor who was a subcontractor on a job involving the construction of certain facilities for the United States Government at Aberdeen Proving Ground. The performance of the contract required, among other things, that Wilke supply and install an emergency diesel-powered generator in

conformance with government specifications. After a discussion with representatives of Cummins Diesel Engines, Inc. (Cummins), the appellee here and defendant below, Wilke received a quotation from them dated 14 July 1965. On 3 August 1965, Wilke issued a purchase order for an emergency diesel generator "in strict compliance with plans and specifications . . . $13,300. *This price includes all requirements as set forth in paragraph 39.22* [the portion of the government specifications which dealt with the emergency diesel generator] *except subparagraphs k and l*" [which dealt with the fuel oil storage tank, the cleaning and painting of such tanks, and oil pipe and fittings]. (Emphasis added)

The job progressed with agonizing slowness, and by August, 1966, was only 50 percent complete. Although it was far too early to install the generator, Cummins was anxious to deliver it to the job site and did so on 17 August 1966. It was delivered by Cummins' truck, unloaded by Wilke's crane, and placed on a permanent base which had been prepared for it. At the time of delivery, the generator was lacking two starting batteries. When asked how Cummins' representative explained the absence of the batteries, Wilke's foreman at the job answered:

"He said the batteries were not in the machine because he did not want us to start it or fool with it. His statement was, 'This is my baby until I start it and turn it over to you.'" This testimony was not challenged by Cummins. Also missing were the maintenance and operating instruction manuals that were included in the specifications. . . .

The job continued to move at a snail's pace, and until the spring of 1967 the generator sat on its base enclosed in a housing intended to protect it from the weather since it was designed to operate out of doors. When Wilke started to hook up the generator, it was discovered that the water in its cooling system had frozen during the previous winter and that the engine had been severely damaged.

Wilke notified Cummins of the damage, and Cummins, after an investigation, decided that repairs could not be made on the job site. The generator was picked up by Cummins and taken away to be repaired. There were no discussions between the parties as to the responsibility for the repairs prior to their completion. On 9 June, Cummins sent Wilke a bill for $2,231.20 for the work and conditioned return of the generator on the payment of the bill. On 19 June, Wilke instituted an action of replevin, and on the same day, Cummins sent Wilke a corrected bill in the amount of $2,798.27. The generator was returned to the job site where Cummins supervised the electrical installation, start-up, and field tests. In April of 1968, the replevin action was tried without a jury by the Superior Court of Baltimore City which, on 8 April 1968, entered judgment absolute in favor of Cummins for the return of the property or, alternatively, for $2,798.27, one cent damages, and costs. It is from this judgment that Wilke has appealed.

The court below concluded the "title did pass at the time of delivery of the machine, and that the tests which were to be made thereafter were not a condition to the passing of title" and that "the implication is that when someone in this kind of business (Cummins) is told that it is necessary that [the generator] be put into operation, these circumstances justify Cummins' conclusion that they have an implied order to repair . . . [which] carries with it the responsibility of payment for the repairs before the machine can be released from the custody of the repairman." . . .

One of the more startling differences between the UCC and the [Uniform] Sales Act is the UCC's adoption of the flexible contractual approach instead of following the more rigid concept of title to which the Sales Act adhered. . . .

The Official Comment to UCC § 2-101 . . . puts it this way:

"The arrangement of the present Subtitle is in terms of contract for sale and the various steps of its performance. The legal consequences are stated as following directly from the contract and action taken under it without resorting to the idea of when property or title passed or was to pass as being the determining factor. *The purpose is to avoid making practical issues between practical men turn upon the location of an intangible something, the passing of which no man can prove by evidence and to substitute for such abstractions proof of words and actions of a tangible character.*" . . . (Emphasis added)

. . . In the absence of a delivery of conforming goods, the risk of damage remained with Cummins, the seller, notwithstanding the delivery of the generator to the job site, the receipt of payment from Wilke, and some eight months' delay in start-up. . . .

The narrow issue here is, whether Cummins made a "delivery" of goods which conformed to the contract. . . . Wilke's purchase order specifically incorporated the government specifications, which consisted of two and a half pages of single-spaced typescript which detailed the field tests to be performed prior to acceptance by the government. . . .

The delivery of the generator to the job site, while identifying the goods to the contract, did not amount to a delivery of goods or the performance of obligations conforming to the contract. It could not constitute such a delivery and performance until the generator had been installed, started up, and field tests completed to the satisfaction of the government. Until then, risk of loss remained with Cummins regardless of where title may have stood.

While it is conceivable that a negligent act could be postulated which would have made it possible to hold Wilke responsible for the cost of repairing the damage, such a course of conduct is absent here. The generator, when delivered, was completely enclosed and had been delivered in an inoperable condition so that no one could "start it or fool with it" until it was "turned over" to Wilke. On these facts, the judgment in Cummins' favor was clearly erroneous.

[Judgment reversed]

Fender v Colonial Stores, Inc.

138 GaApp 138, 225 SE2d 691 (1976)

Fender was a customer in the Big Star self-service store owned by Colonial Stores, Inc. She placed her selections on the cashier's counter. While lifting a six-pack of Coca Cola from her cart to the counter, one of the bottles exploded and she was injured by the flying glass. She sued Colonial Stores. She claimed that the defendant was liable for breach of warranty. The defendant denied this liability on the ground that there could be no warranty liability until there was a sale and that the Coca Cola had not been sold to Fender because she had not yet paid for the six-pack. From a judgment for Colonial, Fender appealed.

DEEN, P.J. . . . An action based on breach of warranty necessitates a showing of the existence of the warranty, the fact that the warranty was broken and that the breach of the warranty was the proximate cause of the loss sustained. . . . The defendant-retailer contends that the plaintiff's evidence failed to establish the existence of a warranty. [UCC§] 2-314(1) provides . . . a warranty that the goods shall be merchantable is implied in a *contract for their sale* if the seller is a merchant with respect to goods of that kind . . ." (Emphasis supplied.) The retailer urges there was no warranty because at the moment of explosion the plaintiff had as yet not paid for the bottle.

The retailer argues that no title had passed on the goods; this ignores, however, the clear language of [UCC§] 2-314 that a warranty is implied upon a contract for sale and not solely upon the execution of the sale itself. [UCC§] 2-106(1) defines "contract for sale" as "both a present sale of goods and a contract to sell goods at a future time . . ." We therefore see this issue as not one of title passing from the retailer to the consumer but one of the existence of a contract between the parties to sell goods at a future time. A contract is of course "an agreement between two or more parties for the doing or not doing of some specified thing" and requires "parties able to contract, a consideration moving to the contract, the assent of the parties to the terms of the contract, and a subject-matter upon which it can operate." . . . The plaintiff has the burden of showing the existence of the warranty by establishing that at the time the bottle exploded there was a contract for its sale existing between herself and the retailer.

The plaintiff's evidence in this case showed that the retailer's store was of the usual "self-service" type, in which customers were supplied with carts and allowed to roam the aisles at will, selecting items from the shelves and cases and then negotiating the check-out line where the purchases are rung up on the register and the total price is paid. The plaintiff testified that she had finished her shopping and was in the physical act of placing the bottles on the counter for payment when the explosion occurred; she further testified that she was at the check-out counter to pay for her purchases.

We think this evidence sufficient to show that the retailer's act of placing the bottles on the shelf with the price stamped upon them manifested an intent to offer them for sale, the terms of the offer being that it would pass title to the customer when they were presented at the check-out counter and paid for. Likewise we think that the evidence shows that the plaintiff's act of taking physical possession of the goods with the intent to purchase them manifested an intent to accept the offer and a promise to take them to the check-out counter and to there pay for them. . . . Placing the goods on the shelf for customer inspection and selection was clearly an offer to sell them at the stated price; the retailer did not indicate by language or circumstances that acceptance of this offer could not be accomplished by taking possession of the goods with an implied *promise* to pay for them upon check-out rather than by the actual act of exchanging money. It is equally reasonable under the terms of the offer that acceptance could occur in any one of three ways: (1) by delivering the goods to the check-out counter and paying for them; (2) by the promise to pay for the goods as evidenced by their physical delivery to the check-out counter; and (3) by the promise to deliver the goods to the check-out counter and to pay for them there as evidenced by taking physical possession of the goods by their removal from the shelf. Under the circumstances surrounding this transaction we believe reasonable men could conclude that the plaintiff's act of taking physical possession of the goods with the intent to pay for them constituted a reasonable mode of acceptance; that by taking physical possession and delivering to the check-out counter the plaintiff promised to pay for them at the stated price and that this promise is sufficient consideration to support a contract . . . ; that a contract for the sale of the goods came into being when the plaintiff accepted the offer by taking physical possession thereof with the intent to pay for them;

and that from that moment forward the implied warranties of [UCC§] 2-314 were applicable. . . . "A contract for sale of goods may be made in any manner sufficient to show agreement, including conduct by both parties which recognizes the existence of such a contract. An agreement sufficient to constitute a contract for sale may be found even though the moment of its making is undetermined." . . .

Nor do we believe that the fact that the customer in a "self-service" store has the right to return merchandise to the shelves at any time before payment is made militates against a finding that a contract for the sale of goods has come into being before such payment. " 'Termination' occurs when either party pursuant to a power created by agreement or law puts an end to the contract otherwise than for its breach . . ." [UCC§] 2-106(3). We believe that the fact that the retailer permits the customer to "change his mind" indicates only an agreement between the parties to allow the customer to end his contract with the retailer irrespective of a breach of the agreement by the retailer. . . .

In reaching this decision that in the context of a self-service store a contract for sale of goods may arise before payment is actually made for the goods, we are not unaware of decisions in other jurisdictions to the contrary. *Loch v Confair,* 361 Pa. 158, 63 A2d 24; *Lasky v Economy Grocery Stores,* 319 Mass. 224, 65 N.E2d 305; *Day v Grand Union Co.,* 280 App.Div. 253, 113 N.Y.S.2d 436. These cases were all decided prior to the adoption in their jurisdictions of the Uniform Commercial Code with its liberalized concept of contract formation and at a time when passage of "title" was the relevant legal prerequisite to a warranty action. It is true that the Court of Appeals of our sister state of North Carolina by discussion of the "passage of title" in a recent decision reached a similar result to that we have reached here. *Gillispie v The Great Atlantic and Pacific Tea Co.,* 14 N.C. App. 1, 187 S.E.2d 441. While we agree with the result reached in the *Gillispie* decision we do not agree that the question of whether a contract for sale exists is dependent upon the passage of title. We embrace rather the well-reasoned opinions of *Seigel v Giant Foods, Inc.,* [20 Md.App 611, 318 A2d 874]; and *Giant Food, Inc. v Washington Coca-Cola Bottling Co., Inc.,* 273 Md. 592, 332 A.2d 1, 16 UCC 340 (1975) to the effect that a contract of sale of goods in the self-service supermarket context may arise before payment is actually made for the goods and title passes.

The retailer urges that even if we find a warranty has arisen in this case, as we have in fact so found, that the plaintiff's evidence fails to show a breach thereof. The testimony was that the goods selected were normal in appearance, that the bottles had not struck or touched the carton or any of the bottles against any object at any time after they were removed from the shelf, but that the bottle exploded as it was being placed on the counter for check-out and that the plaintiff was injured by flying glass. "It is obvious that Coca Cola bottles which would break under normal handling are not fit for the ordinary use for which they were intended and that the relinquishment of physical control of such a defective bottle to a consumer constitutes a breach of warranty. Thus the evidence was sufficient to show that when the bottles left the retailer's control they did not conform to the representations of the warranty of merchantability, and that this breach of the warranty was the cause of the loss sustained. Having made this *prima facie* showing appellant was entitled to have the jury pass upon the questions of whether the warranty was breached, and if so, whether the breach caused his injury." . . .

[Judgment reversed]

Waggoner v Wilson

(ColoApp) 507 P2d 482 (1973)

State Farm Insurance Company issued an automobile liability policy to Wilson. The policy covered a specified automobile and any non-owned automobile driven by Wilson. While driving a 1961 Ford Thunderbird, Wilson was involved in a collision with Waggoner. This 1961 Ford was not the car described in Wilson's policy. It was a car which Wilson had originally owned but which she had sold to Beucker. Waggoner obtained a judgment against Wilson for approximately $40,000 and then claimed that State Farm was liable under the non-owned automobile coverage. State Farm claimed that the automobile was still owned by Wilson on the theory that the sale to Beucker had not been effective and therefore the automobile was not within the non-owned coverage, and that as it was not the automobile described in the policy there was no coverage by the policy. From a judgment for State Farm, Waggoner appealed.

SMITH, J. . . . Charles Beucker was purchasing the automobile in question from defendant . . . , pursuant to an oral sales agreement entered into on

June 10, 1969. Beucker had made payments to defendant . . . , but neither the license plates nor the certificate of title had been transferred to him. Defendant . . . delivered possession of the automobile to Beucker and retained the title as security for the balance of the purchase price.

The oral sales agreement was a sales contract covered by the Uniform Commercial Code. [UCC§] 2-106(1). Although the certificate of title was not transferred to Beucker, delivery of possession of the car to Beucker constituted a transfer of its ownership to him. [UCC§] 2-401(2). Notwithstanding the provision of C.R.S.1963, 13-6-8, that no purchaser "shall acquire any right, title or interest in and to a motor vehicle purchased by him unless and until he shall obtain . . . the certificate of title thereto," non-delivery of the certificate of title does not prevent change of ownership as between the parties to the transaction. . . . Thus, as a matter of law, the automobile in question was not owned by defendant [Wilson] . . .

Having determined the automobile in question was not owned by . . . defendant, it follows that, in the terms of the policy, the automobile in question was a "non-owned automobile." Therefore, defendant was entitled to coverage under her insurance policy with State Farm.

[Judgment reversed and action remanded]

Graybar Electric Co. v Shook

283 NC 213, 195 SE2d 514 (1973)

Shook ordered three reels of burial cable from Graybar Company for use in construction work. By mistake, two of the three reels which were sent were aerial cable, although each carton was marked "burial cable." Shook accepted the one reel of proper cable and rejected the two nonconforming reels. Because of their size they were left on the ground at the construction site and Graybar was notified of the rejection. Graybar did not collect the cable. Shook attempted to return the cable but could not do so because there was a strike of truck drivers. About four months later the two reels of cable were stolen by unidentified persons. Graybar sued Shook for the purchase price. Graybar claimed that after the rejection was made by Shook, it had been agreed that Shook would return the nonconforming reels to Graybar. From a judgment for Shook, Graybar appealed.

HIGGINS, J. . . . The parties admitted the following: (1) The defendant placed an order with the plaintiff for three reels of burial (underground) cable to be delivered at Six Run Grocery Store, a rural community sixteen miles south of Clinton. (2) On April 6 the plaintiff delivered one reel of burial cable and, by mistake, delivered two reels of aerial cable. The aerial cable was totally unsuited to the defendant's use. Defendant notified the plaintiff of the mistake and received a request that the nonconforming reels be returned. Here the parties disagree. The plaintiff contends the defendant contracted to make the return. The defendant contends he agreed to contact a trucking company and request that it pick up and return the nonconforming reels. The defendant's request was turned down by three different trucking concerns on account of a strike in the trucking industry.

As the defendant's underground cable work progressed beyond the Six Run Grocery Store, the defendant left the nonconforming cable at the store and so notified the plaintiff. The evidence discloses that the cable was stored directly beside the grocery store building near the owner's dwelling in a space which the defendant rented for storage purposes. "The area where the cable was stored was well lighted at all times."

On July 20, 1970, the defendant discovered that one of the reels had been stolen and the following day notified the plaintiff. On that day, also, the defendant contacted a garage operator who promised to pick up the remaining reel and store it in his garage some distance from Six Run. However, before the transfer, the second reel was stolen. The defendant so notified the plaintiff.

The court, upon the disputed facts, found the defendant had not entered into a contract to return the nonconforming cable. A finding supported by evidence "must be accepted as final truth upon the appeal to the Supreme Court." . . . When findings of fact sufficient to determine the entire controversy are made by the court, failure to find other facts is not error. . . . The plaintiff's claim, therefore, that it was prejudiced by the court's failure to make requested findings is not error. The court's actual findings determined the entire controversy.

The plaintiff, having made the error of delivering the nonconforming goods on a moving job in the country, was entitled to notice of the nonconformity sufficient to enable it to repossess the nonconforming goods. The plaintiff was given prompt notice but delayed action for more than three months. The cable was stolen from the defendant's regular storage space where the plaintiff had delivered it. Evidence is lacking that a safer storage space was available. The defendant's workmen moved on, leaving the cable and the responsibility for its safety on the owner.

The plaintiff, failing in its efforts to establish a contract on the part of the defendant to return the shipment, however, contends in the alternative that [UCC §] 2-602(2)(b) . . . required the defendant to exercise reasonable care in holding the rejected goods pending the plaintiff's repossession and removal and that the defendant failed to exercise the required care in storage.

Actually, the plaintiff made an on the spot delivery at a store and dwelling in the country. The defendant's work force was stringing underground cable along the highway and the crew was in continual movement. Obviously the crew could not be expected to carry with it two thousand pounds of useless cable and was within its rights placing the cable in its regular storage space and notifying the plaintiff of the place of storage. Both parties realized that cable weighing almost a ton would require men and a truck to remove it. Also both parties assumed that the danger of theft from a well lighted store area was a minimal risk. The property itself was a poor candidate for larceny. The cable was permitted to remain where the plaintiff knew it was located for more than three months. The plaintiff, therefore, had ample opportunity to repossess its property.

The Uniform Commercial Code emphasizes promptness and good faith. The prospective purchaser may exercise a valid right to reject and even if he takes possession, responsibility expires after a reasonable time in which the owner has opportunity to repossess. "Where a tender or delivery of goods so fails to conform to the contract as to give a right of rejection the risk of their loss remains on the seller until cure or acceptance." [UCC §] 2-510(1). The defendant did not accept the aerial cable. According to the evidence and the court's findings, the defendant acted in accordance with the request of the owner in attempting to facilitate the return of that which the defendant rejected. The plaintiff with full notice of the place of storage which was at the place of delivery did nothing but sleep on its rights for more than three months.

The superior court was fully justified in the findings of fact, conclusions of law, and in the judgment dismissing the action. The judgment of the Court of Appeals affirming the superior court was correct. . . .

[Judgment affirmed]

Medico Leasing Co. v Smith

(Okla) 457 P2d 548 (1969)

Medico Leasing Co. owned a used Buick automobile which it delivered to Smith, a used car dealer, to find a buyer. Smith sold it to Wessel Buick Co., which sold it to Country Cousins Motors, which sold it to the Carters. When Smith failed to pay Medico, the latter brought an action of replevin against the Carters in which the other dealers were made additional defendants. The claim of Medico was dismissed, and damages were awarded the Carters and Country Cousins on cross-petitions. Medico appealed.

HODGES, J. . . . The principal issue presented by this appeal is the trial court's ruling that the defendant, Wessel Buick Co., was a "buyer in the ordinary course of business" in good faith as defined by Sections 1-201(9) and 2-403(2) of the Oklahoma Uniform Commercial Code when they . . . purchased the automobile from defendant Smith, a used car dealer, to whom plaintiff had entrusted possession of the car. The trial court found that Wessel Buick acquired sufficient legal title even though the sale was made without the actual transfer of the automobile's Certificate of Title, and therefore the defendants, Carters and Country Cousins Motors, were entitled to damages for the wrongful taking.

The evidence shows substantially the following facts: Plaintiff corporation was engaged in the business of leasing various items of equipment and had leased a 1962 Buick automobile for a period of two years. Subsequent to the termination of the lease, the car was offered for sale by means of advertising in the newspaper. In answer to the ad, the defendant Smith telephoned the treasurer of the corporation, hereinafter referred to as Raskin, who had placed the ad and informed him that he could sell the car. Raskin informed Smith that he could have the car to show to a prospect; however, he did not give Smith the certificate of title. Smith, testifying for the plaintiff, contradicted the testimony of Raskin in that he stated that the only instructions he got from Raskin was that he wanted $2,200.00 for the car. Raskin was later warned by the president of plaintiff corporation to be careful of Smith. Smith was engaged in the used car business and had been for some time prior to this transaction. This fact was known to both the president of the corporation and to Raskin. In addition to showing the car to the prospect, Smith took the car to defendant Wessel Buick Co., sold it to them, and retained the money himself. Some three weeks following the sale, Smith gave Raskin a check for $600.00 with the notation thereon, "Partial payment 62 Buick, hold for cashiers check." Raskin testified that he accepted this check on the date that it bears. This check was never cashed, however, as there were insufficient funds deposited in the bank to cover it.

Some time following the sale of the car to defendant Wessel, an employee of Wessel, designated as the title clerk, called Smith for the certificate of title and was informed by him that the certificate had been left with her previously. Subsequent to that conversation, the clerk again contacted Smith and was informed that he did not have the certificate but that he would try to get it. Not receiving the certificate, the clerk made application to the Tax Commission for a lost certificate of title and in time received it. Prior to making application for lost title, defendant Wessel sold the Buick to the defendant Country Cousins Motors, who subsequently sold the car to defendants W. C. and Dorene Carter.

Meanwhile, plaintiff had not received any money for its car and, further, could not find the car. Through the Tax Commission it traced the ownership registration of the car and found it to be in the possession of W. C. and Dorene Carter. Plaintiff then filed a suit in replevin, posted bond, took possession of the car from the Carters and sold it to a third party.

Plaintiff does not contest the fact that Smith is their agent, but they maintain that he . . . did not have title to the automobile or authority to convey title. They assert that Smith could not convey any better title than he had, and as he had no title, none was conveyed. It is further asserted by plaintiff that defendant Wessel was not a buyer in good faith as required by our Uniform Commercial Code, because they purchased the car without a certificate of title under facts and circumstances which would have put an ordinarily prudent businessman on inquiry.

The provisions of the Code pertinent to the issues in this case are in part set out:

"[UCC §] 2-403(2) Any entrusting of possession of goods to a merchant who deals in goods of that kind gives him power to transfer all rights of the entruster to a buyer in the ordinary course of business.

"[UCC §] 1-201(9) "Buyer in ordinary course of business means a person who in good faith and without knowledge that the sale to him is in violation of the ownership rights or security interest of a third party in the goods buys in ordinary course from a person in the business of selling goods of that kind but does not include a pawnbroker. 'Buying' may be for cash or by exchange of other property or on secured or unsecured credit and includes receiving goods or documents of title under a preexisting contract for sale but does not include transfer in bulk or as security for or in total or partial satisfaction of a money debt."

The "entruster" in the instant case, the plaintiff, had good title to the Buick, which was a used car. The one to whom the automobile was entrusted, Smith, as a used car dealer, is a "merchant who deals in goods of that kind" within the meaning of the statute. Smith was known by the plaintiff to be a used car dealer. . . .

. . . The question then arises as to whether Wessel was a buyer in good faith when they purchased the car without a certificate of title.

It has long been held by this court that a certificate of title to an automobile issued under the motor vehicle act is not a muniment of title which establishes ownership, but is merely intended to protect the public against theft and to facilitate recovery of stolen automobiles and otherwise aid the state in enforcement of its regulation of motor vehicles. . . . This rule was not changed with the passage of the Uniform Commercial Code. Under Sec. 1-201(15) the certificate of title of an automobile is not listed as a "document of title." It was not necessary for the defendant Smith to deliver the certificate of title before he conveyed ownership of the Buick automobile, and the absence of a certificate does not invalidate the sale or prevent title from passing. . . .

. . . There was no proof that any defendant knew of any limitation of title or should have known prior to or at the time of purchase of the Buick automobile. We find the action of the trial court in sustaining the demurrers was proper.

[Judgment affirmed]

QUESTIONS AND CASE PROBLEMS

1. What social forces are affected by the rule that the buyer has an insurable interest when future goods are marked for shipment to the buyer?

2. Compare the legal classification of (a) goods physically existing and owned by the seller at the time of contracting, (b) goods physically existing but not owned by the seller at the time of contracting, and (c) goods not physically existing at the time of contracting.

3. Compare the time when risk of loss passes from a merchant seller to a buyer when the goods (a) are being transported to the buyer's address in the seller's own delivery trucks, and (b) have been delivered by the seller's supplier to an independent carrier for delivery to the buyer.

4. Compare (1) a sale on approval, (2) a sale and return, and (3) a consignment sale, with respect to (a) transfer of title, and (b) transfer of risk of loss.

5. Gerber purchased on approval draperies which were cut to measure for his home. Two months passed and Gerber had not notified the seller whether he approved or not. A dispute arose between the Valley Bank, Gerber, and others as to whether Gerber was the. owner of the draperies at that time. Was he the owner? [Valley Bank and Trust Co. v Gerber (Utah) 526 P2d 1121]

6. *O* owned a television set. *T* stole the set and sold it to *A* who purchased for value and in good faith. *A* resold the set to *B* who also purchased in good faith and for value. *O* sued *B* for the set. *B* raised the defense that he had purchased it in good faith from a seller who had sold in good faith. Was this defense valid? [See Johnny Dell, Inc. v New York State Police, 84 Misc 2d 360, 375 NYS2d 545.]

7. Burke fraudulently induced Cavanaugh Bros. to sell him a horse. Three months later Burke sold the horse to Porell, a bona fide purchaser. Cavanaugh sued Porell to obtain the horse on the theory that because of Burke's fraud he never obtained title and Cavanaugh Bros. still owned the horse. Decide. [Porell v Cavanaugh Bros., 69 NH 364, 41 A 860]

8. A buyer purchased furniture on credit and made a number of payments thereafter. When he stopped making payments, the seller claimed the right to repossess the furniture on the theory that it had been sold on approval and that the buyer had never manifested his approval. Was the seller correct? [Gantman v Paul, 203 Pa Super 158, 199 A2d 519]

9. *B* purchased a used automobile from *A* with a bad check. *B* then took the automobile to an auction in which the automobile was sold to *C,* who had no knowledge of the prior history of the automobile. When *B*'s check was dishonored, *A* brought suit against *C* to reclaim the automobile. Was he entitled to do so? [Greater Louisville Auto Auction, Inc. v Ogle Buick, Inc., (Ky) 387 SW2d 17]

10. Coppola collected coins. He joined a coin club, First Coinvestors, Inc. The club would send coins to its members who were to pay for them or return them within ten days. What was the nature of the transaction? [First Coinvestors, Inc. v Coppola, 88 Misc 2d 495, 388 NYS2d 833]

11. A seller sold goods to a buyer which were to be delivered to the buyer's warehouse. The written contract required the seller to execute any necessary document required to make the sale effective. Was the transaction a sale of documents? [See Puamier v Barge BT 1973, (DC Va) 395 FSupp 1019]

12. Eastern Supply Co. purchased lawn mowers from the Turf Man Sales Corp. The purchase order stated on its face "Ship direct to 30th & Harcum Way, Pitts., Pa." Turf Man

delivered the goods to Helm's Express, Inc. for shipment and delivery to Eastern at the address in question. Did title pass on delivery of the goods to Helm or upon their arrival at the specified address? [In re Eastern Supply Co., 21 (Pa) D&C 2d 128, 107 Pitts Leg J 451]

13. Atlas Auto Rental Corp., which rented automobiles to the public, would sell its used cars from time to time. It permitted Schwartzman, a prospective buyer, to test drive a two-year old station wagon. Before Schwartzman left with the car, he gave Atlas a check which was later returned by the drawee bank marked "No funds." Schwartzman and the car disappeared. Schwartzman apparently sold the car to Weisberg, a licensed automobile wrecker and junk dealer for $300. Weisberg did not obtain a bill of sale or a title certificate from Schwartzman. Weisberg resold the automobile on the same day for $1,200. Atlas sued Weisberg for converting the automobile. Weisberg raised the defense that he was protected by the UCC. Was he correct? [Atlas Auto Rental Corp. v Weisberg, (NY Civil Court) 54 Misc 2d 168, 281 NYS2d 400]

14. Smith operated a marina and sold and repaired boats. Gallagher rented a stall at the marina at which he kept his vessel, the River Queen. Without any authorization, Smith sold the vessel to Courtesy Ford. Gallagher sued Courtesy Ford for the vessel. Was Courtesy Ford liable to Gallagher? [Gallagher v Unenrolled Motor Vessel River Queen (CA5 Tex) 475 F2d 117]

15. A manufacturer of knitwear loaded a trailer with goods ordered by the buyer. The loaded trailer was to be hauled away by a carrier. After the trailer was loaded but before it was taken away, it was damaged by fire. The manufacturer claimed that the buyer must bear the risk of loss because the goods were future goods covered by a shipment contract. Was the manufacturer correct? [See A. M. Knitwear Corp. v All America Export-Import Corp., 50 AppDiv2d 558, 375 NYS2d 23]

16. Di Lorenzo had possession of certain goods that belonged to Wolf, a dealer in household furniture. The goods were destroyed by fire. Not knowing of this, the parties made an agreement for the sale of the goods. Was Di Lorenzo liable for the purchase price of the goods? [Wolf v Di Lorenzo, 22 Misc 323, 49 NYS 191]

17. The Auburn Motor Co. sold five automobiles to Levasseur of Rhode Island to be shipped C.O.D. via the Adams Express Co. from Indiana to Providence, Rhode Island. While the goods were in transit, Levasseur borrowed money from the New England Auto Insurance Co. to pay for the cars and executed a mortgage on the cars to secure payment of the loan. On the day the cars were received, Levasseur transferred one of them to the Whitten Motor Vehicle Co. The Whitten company sold the car to Andrews. In an action brought by the New England Auto Investment Co. against Andrews, the defendant alleged that the mortgage was invalid and contended that the Auburn Motor Co. had retained title and right of possession. Do you agree with this contention? [New England Auto Investment Co. v Andrews, 47 RI 299, 132 A 883]

18. An automobile dealer had a used Cadillac on its sales lot. The title certificate was in the front office of the automobile dealer. The assignment on the title certificate was signed by the owner but the name of the transferee had been left blank. The title certificate and the Cadillac were both stolen from the dealer and sold to a buyer who purchased in good faith. The automobile dealer sued the buyer for the Cadillac. Was the automobile dealer entitled to recover it? [See Chapman Motors, Inc. v Taylor (TexCivApp) 506 SW2d 724]

25 Obligations and Performance

Each party to a sales contract is bound to perform according to its terms. Each is likewise under the duty to exercise good faith in its performance and to do nothing that would impair the expectation of the other party that the contract will be duly performed.

A. GENERAL PRINCIPLES

Contracts for the sale of goods impose certain obligations on the parties to the contracts.

§ 25:1. Basic Obligations

(a) Good Faith. "Every contract or duty . . . imposes an obligation of good faith in its performance or enforcement." [1] The UCC defines good faith as meaning "honesty in fact in the conduct or transaction concerned." [2] In the case of the merchant seller or buyer of goods, the Code carries the concept of good faith further and imposes the additional requirement that the merchant seller or buyer observe "reasonable commercial standards of fair dealing in the trade." [3] (See p. 407, Umlas v Acey Oldsmobile, Inc.)

(b) Insurance of Property. The seller is not under any duty to insure the goods for the benefit of the buyer. The Code gives a buyer an insurable interest at the earliest possible date in order to enable the buyer to obtain insurance if it is so desired.

The seller may, however, expressly agree, as a term of the sales contract, to obtain insurance for the benefit of the buyer. If the seller so agrees but fails to obtain the promised insurance, the seller is liable to the buyer for the amount of any loss which would have been covered by the insurance which the seller promised to obtain.[4]

§ 25:2. Conditions Precedent to Performance. In the case of a cash sale not requiring the physical moving of the goods, the duties of the seller and buyer are concurrent. Each one has the right to demand that the other perform at the same time. That

---

[1] UCC § 1-203.
[2] UCC § 1-201(19).
[3] UCC § 2-103(1)(b).
[4] Jones v Adkins, (ColoApp), 526 P2d 153.

is, as the seller hands over the goods, the buyer theoretically must hand over the purchase money. If either party refuses to act, the other party has the right to withhold performance.[5] In the case of a shipment contract, there is a time interval between the performance of the parties; the seller will have performed by delivering the goods to the carrier, but the buyer's obligation will not arise until the goods have been received and accepted by the buyer.

The duty of a party to a sales contract to perform under the contract may be subject to a *condition precedent,* that is, by the terms of the contract the party is not required to perform until some event occurs or until some act is performed. Quite commonly, the condition precedent is performance by the other party. Thus, a contract may provide that the seller shall deliver the merchandise but that the buyer must first pay for it in full. Under this contract, the duty of the seller to deliver the merchandise is subject to the condition precedent of payment in full by the buyer. If the buyer never performs, the duty of the seller under that contract never arises.

If there is a promise that the condition precedent shall happen or be performed, the promisee may treat nonperformance as a breach of contract and claim damages from the other party for failing to bring about the fulfillment of the condition.

§ 25:3. Anticipatory Repudiation. Prior to the time specified by the contract for performance, the seller or the buyer may inform the other party that the required performance will never be performed. This is an *anticipatory repudiation.*

The mere fact that a party fails to perform, as that the buyer does not make a required payment, does not constitute an anticipatory repudiation.

(a) Action of Aggrieved Party. If there is a clear repudiation of the contract and the loss of the repudiated performance substantially impairs the value of the contract to the other party, that other party, the aggrieved party, may request the repudiating party to retract or take back the repudiation. While waiting to see what happens, the aggrieved party may hold up rendering any further performance under the contract. In any case, the aggrieved party may assert that the contract has been broken and utilize any of the remedies available for breach.[6]

If the aggrieved party has acted without sufficient justification, that is, if in fact there was no anticipatory repudiation, the aggrieved party who withholds performance will be the one who is breaking the contract and will be liable for damages for breach. (See p. 408, Teeman v Jurek)

(b) Retraction of Repudiation. Prior to the time when performance is required, the repudiating party may retract or take back the repudiation. This cannot be done, however, if the aggrieved party has cancelled the contract because of the repudiation or materially changed position, as by making other sales or purchases, or otherwise indicated that the repudiation was accepted as final.[7]

§ 25:4. Adequate Assurance of Performance. Whenever a party to the sales transaction has reason to believe that the other party may not perform the contract, a written demand

---

[5] UCC §§ 2-507, 2-511.
[6] UCC § 2-610.
[7] UCC § 2-611.

may be made upon the other party for adequate assurance that the contract will be performed. For example, when goods are to be delivered at a future date or in installments over a period, the buyer may become fearful that the seller will not be able to make the future deliveries required. The buyer may in such case require assurance from the seller that the contract will be performed.[8]

(a) Form of Assurance. The person upon whom demand for assurance is made must give "such assurance of due performance as is adequate under the circumstances of the particular case."[9] The exact form of assurance is not specified by the Code. If the party on whom demand is made has an established reputation, a reaffirmation of the contract obligation and a statement that it will be performed may be sufficient to assure a reasonable person that it will be performed. In contrast, the person's reputation or economic position at the time may be such that there is no assurance that there will be a proper performance in the absence of a guarantee by a third person or the furnishing of security by way of a pledge or other device to protect the demanding party against default.[10]

(b) Failure to Give Assurance. The party on whom demand is made may state that it will not be performed, that is, that the contract is repudiated. In contrast with a flat repudiation, the party upon whom demand is made may fail to reply or may give only a feeble answer that is not sufficient to assure a reasonable person that performance will in fact be made. The failure to provide adequate assurance within 30 days after receiving the demand, or a lesser time when 30 days would be unreasonable, constitutes a repudiation of the contract.[11]

B. DUTIES OF THE PARTIES

The obligations and performance of the parties to a sales contract may be grouped as follows: (1) seller's duty to deliver the goods, (2) buyer's duty to accept the goods, (3) buyer's duty to pay for the goods, and (4) duties of the parties under particular contract terms pertaining to the transportation of the goods.

§ 25.5 Seller's Duty to Deliver. It is the seller's duty to make "delivery," which does not refer to a physical transportation but merely means that the seller must permit the transfer of possession of the goods to the buyer. That is, the seller makes the goods available to the buyer. The delivery must be made in accordance with the terms of the sale or contract to sell.

(a) Place, Time, and Manner of Delivery. The terms of the contract determine whether the seller is to send the goods or the buyer is to call for them, or whether the goods must be transported by the seller to the buyer, or whether the transaction is to be completed by the delivery of documents without the movement of the goods.

---

[8] UCC § 2-609(1). Between merchants the reasonableness of the grounds for insecurity is determined according to commercial standards. § 2-609(2).

[9] UCC § 2-609(4).

[10] Between merchants the adequacy of any assurance is determined according to commercial standards. UCC § 2-609(2).

[11] UCC § 2-609(4). This enables the adverse party to take steps at an earlier date to protect against the default of the other party, as by making a substitute contract to replace the repudiated contract.

In the absence of a provision in the contract or a contrary course of performance or usage of trade, the place of delivery is the seller's place of business, if the seller has one; otherwise it is the seller's residence. If, however, the subject matter of the contract consists of identified goods that are known by the parties to be in some other place, that place is the place of delivery. Documents of title may be delivered through customary banking channels.[12]

When a method of transportation called for by the contract becomes unavailable or commercially unreasonable, the seller must make delivery by means of a commercially reasonable substitute if available and the buyer must accept such substitute.[13] This provision is applicable when a shipping strike makes impossible the use of the specified method of transportation.

(b)   Quantity Delivered. The buyer has the right to insist that all the goods be delivered at one time. If the seller delivers a smaller quantity than that stipulated in the contract, the buyer may refuse to accept the goods. In the case of a divisible contract, if the buyer accepts or retains part of the goods with knowledge of the seller's intention to deliver no more, the buyer must pay the proportionate price representing the items or units which have been received; if the contract is not divisible, the full contract price must be paid. If the goods are used or disposed of by the buyer before learning of the seller's intention, the buyer is only required to pay the fair value of the goods that were received.

(1)   Delivery in Installments. The buyer is under no obligation or duty to accept delivery of goods by installments unless the contract contemplates such deliveries [14] or unless the circumstances are such as to give rise to the right to make delivery in lots.[15]

If payment is to be made for each installment, the delivery of each installment and the payment for each installment are conditions precedent to the respective duties of the buyer to accept and of the seller to deliver subsequent installments.

(c)   Delivery to Carrier. When the seller is required to or may send the goods to the buyer but the contract does not require delivery at a particular destination, the seller, in the absence of a contrary agreement, must put the goods in the possession of a proper carrier and make such contract for their transportation as is reasonable in view of the nature of the goods and other circumstances of the case. For example, if the goods require refrigeration and the risk of loss passes to the buyer on delivery to the carrier, the seller must contract with the carrier to provide the necessary refrigeration.

(d)   Delivery at Destination. If the contract requires the seller to make delivery at a destination point, the seller must make a proper tender of the goods at that point. If any documents that are necessary to obtain possession of the goods are issued by a carrier, the seller must also tender such documents.[16]

---

[12] UCC § 2-308.
[13] UCC § 2-514(1).
[14] UCC § 2-307.
[15] UCC § 2-307. This situation would arise whenever it is physically impossible because of the buyer's limited facilities or commercially impractical for any reason for the seller to make complete delivery.
[16] UCC § 2-503(3).

(e) **Cure of Defective Tender.** The seller has the right to *cure,* or remedy, a defective tender by making a second tender or *curative tender* or delivery after the first has been properly rejected by the buyer because it did not conform to the contract. If the time for making delivery under the contract has not expired, the seller need only give the buyer seasonable (timely) notice of the intention to make a proper delivery within the time allowed by the contract, and the seller may then do so. If the time for making the delivery has expired, the seller is given an additional reasonable time in which to make a substitute conforming tender if (1) the seller so notifies the buyer and (2) the seller had acted reasonably in making the original tender, believing that it would be acceptable to the buyer.[17]

§ 25:6. Buyer's Duty to Accept Goods. It is the duty of the buyer to accept the delivery of proper goods.

(a) **Right to Examine Goods.** Unless otherwise agreed, the buyer, when tender of goods is made, has the right before payment for or acceptance of the goods to inspect them at any reasonable place or time and in any reasonable manner to determine whether the goods conform to the requirements of the contract.[18] A C.O.D. term, however, bars inspection before payment unless there is an agreement to the contrary.

(b) **What Constitutes Acceptance of Goods.** Acceptance ordinarily is an express statement by the buyer that the goods are accepted or approved as conforming to the contract. It may also consist of conduct which expresses such an intent, such as the failure to object within a reasonable period of time or a use of the goods in such a way as would be inconsistent with a rejection of them by the buyer and with the continued ownership of the goods by the seller.[19] Thus, a buyer accepts the goods by making continued use of them and by not attempting to return the goods until after 14 months. A buyer, of course, accepts the goods by modifying them because such action is inconsistent with a rejection or the continued ownership of the goods by the seller. Consequently, when the purchaser of a truck installed a hoist and a dump bed on it, such action constituted an acceptance by conduct and the buyer therefore became liable for the contract price of the truck.[20] (See p. 409, United States for the use of Fram Corp. v Crawford)

Likewise there is an acceptance when a dealer puts price tags on goods received from a supplier and puts the goods on public display where customers of the dealer can buy them.[21]

(c) **Effect of Acceptance on Breach.** Acceptance of the goods by the buyer does not discharge the seller from liability in damages or other legal remedy for breach of any promise or warranty in the contract to sell or the sale. But the seller is not liable if, after acceptance of the goods, the buyer fails to give notice of the breach of any promise or warranty within a reasonable time after the buyer knows or ought to know of the breach.[22]

---

[17] UCC § 2-508.
[18] UCC § 2-513(1).
[19] UCC § 2-606(1).
[20] Park County Implement Co. v Craig (Wyo) 397 P2d 800.
[21] Chrysler Corp. v Adamatic, Inc. 59 Wis 2d 219, 208 NW2d 97.
[22] UCC § 2-607(2), (3). This section rejects the view that acceptance of the goods is a waiver of any claim for damages.

§ 25:7. Buyer's Duty to Pay. The buyer is under a duty to pay for the goods at the contract rate for any goods accepted.[23] In the absence of a contrary provision, payment must be made in cash and must be made concurrently with receipt of the goods; and, conversely, payment cannot be required before that time.[24]

A buyer is not required to pay for partial or installment deliveries unless the contract expressly so requires. (See p. 409, Cameras for Industry v I. D. Precision Components Corp.)

If delivery by lots is proper and the price can be apportioned, however, the buyer must pay for each lot as delivered.[25]

The parties may agree to a sale on credit. This may be done for each sale individually or for sales generally, as in the case of a charge account in a department store. When a sale is made on credit, the parties may include special provisions to protect the seller.

Tender or offer of the purchase price has the same effect as actual payment in imposing upon the seller the duty to make delivery. If the seller fails to make delivery when a proper tender of payment is made, the seller is in default under the contract. It must also be remembered that if the seller is in default, the buyer may cancel the contract.

(a)   Payment with Commercial Paper. The seller may accept a commercial paper, such as a check, in payment of the purchase price. This form of payment, unless the parties expressly agree otherwise, is merely a conditional payment, that is, conditional upon the instrument's being honored and paid. If the instrument is not paid, it ceases to be payment of the purchase price and the seller is then an unpaid seller.[26] Refusal of payment by check does not affect the rights of the parties under the sales contract as long as the seller gives the buyer a reasonable time in which to procure the legal tender with which to make payment.

(b)   Escrow Payment. When money is deposited with a bank or other third person under an agreement, it is commonly called an *escrow deposit* and the fund so deposited must be maintained as a separate or distinct fund. The escrow payment provides a form of security. This technique can be employed where one party is unwilling to act until the other party pays while the payor is unwilling to pay until the other party acts. For example, the goods which the seller is selling to the buyer may be in the warehouse of a supplier in a distant city. If the buyer would pay the seller in advance, the buyer would then be taking a number of risks. The same would be true if the seller would obtain and deliver the goods before being paid. In such a case the parties could agree that the buyer would deposit the purchase price in an escrow account in a bank, with instructions to the bank to pay the money to the seller when proper papers were submitted by the seller to the bank showing that the goods had been sent to the buyer, or to return the money to the buyer if the seller had not performed within a specified time.

---

[23] UCC §§ 2-301, 2-607(1).

[24] UCC § 2-310(a). If delivery under the contract is to be made by a delivery of document of title, payment is due at the time and place at which the buyer is to receive the document regardless of where the goods are to be received. § 2-310(c).

[25] UCC § 2-307.

[26] UCC § 2-511.

(c)   Electronic Fund Transfer. The consumer will sometimes pay for the goods by a debit card in an electronic fund transfer system. This in effect makes an immediate cash payment from the consumer's bank account. This places the consumer at a disadvantage if there is some defect in the goods. In contrast, if the consumer had made the purchase on credit or with a credit card, and there was a defect in the goods, the consumer would have the practical weapon of refusing to pay for the goods. This is so because when the buyer buys on credit or with a credit card the buyer can raise against a suit by the seller for the purchase price or against the suit by the credit card issuer any defense which is given to a buyer by the Uniform Commercial Code.

§ 25:8. Duties Under Particular Terms. A sale may be as simple as a face-to-face exchange of money and goods, but it frequently involves a more complicated pattern, with some element of transportation, generally by a common carrier. This, in turn, generally results in the addition of certain special terms to the sales transaction.

(a)   F.O.B. The term f.o.b. or "free on board," may be used with reference to the seller's city, or the buyer's city, or an intermediate city, as in the case of a transshipment. It may also be used with reference to a named carrier, such as f.o.b. a specified vessel, car, or other vehicle. In general, an f.o.b. term is to be construed as requiring delivery to be made at the f.o.b. point, as contrasted with merely a shipment to that point,[27] and as imposing upon the seller the risk and expense involved in getting the goods to the designated place or on board the specified carrier.[28] (See p. 410, Custom Built Homes Co. v Kansas State Commission of Revenue)

(b)   C.I.F. The term C.I.F. indicates that the payment by the buyer is a lump sum covering the cost (selling price) of the goods, insurance on them, and freight to the specified destination of the goods. The C.I.F. term imposes upon the seller the obligation of putting the goods in the possession of a proper carrier, of loading and paying for the freight, of procuring the proper insurance, of preparing an invoice of the goods and any other document needed for shipment, and of forwarding all documents to the buyer with commercial promptness.[29]

Under a C.I.F. contract, the buyer bears the risk of loss after the goods have been delivered to the carrier.[30] The buyer must pay for the goods when proper documents representing them are tendered, which in turn means that the buyer is not entitled to inspect the goods before paying for them, unless the contract expressly provides for payment on or after the arrival of the goods.[31]

---

[27] See § 25:5(c) in this book. When a port is selected as the f.o.b. point for an imported article, the price is frequently described as the price p.o.e. or "port of entry."

[28] UCC § 2-319(1).

[29] UCC § 2-320(1), (2). The term c. & f. or c.f. imposes the same obligations and risks as a c.i.f. term with the exception of the obligation as to insurance. Under a c.f. contract, the seller completes performance by delivery of the goods to the carrier and by proper payment of the freight charges on the shipment, whereupon title and risk of loss pass to the buyer.

[30] UCC § 2-320(2)(c). The c.i.f. and c.f. contracts may be modified to place the risk of deterioration during shipment on the seller by specifying that the price shall be based on the arrival or "out turn" quality, or by having the seller warrant the condition or quality of the goods on their arrival. § 2-321(2).

[31] UCC § 2-320(4), 2-321(2).

(c)   **Ex-ship.** If the contract provides for delivery ex-ship, the seller bears the risk of loss until the goods have left the ship's tackle or have otherwise been properly unloaded. The seller must discharge all liens arising from the transportation of the goods and must furnish the buyer with such documents or instructions as enable the buyer to obtain the goods from the carrier.[32]

(d)   **No Arrival, No Sale.** When goods are sent under such a term, the seller bears the risk of loss during transportation; but if the goods do not arrive, the seller is not responsible to the buyer, for in such case there is no sale. The buyer is protected by being required to pay for the goods only if they arrive.

The "no arrival, no sale" contract requires the seller to ship proper conforming goods and to tender them on their arrival if they arrive. The seller must, of course, refrain from interfering with the arrival of the goods.[33]

C. ASSIGNMENT OF SALES CONTRACTS

The assignment of a sales contract by either party ordinarily does not affect the obligations of the original seller and buyer. The seller and the buyer are each bound by the same obligations as before.

§ 25:9. Effect of Assignment. If the buyer is the assignor, there may be a modification of the original contract as by specifying that the seller is to deliver the goods to the buyer's assignee. The printed form used by the seller usually will specify that if the seller assigns the contract, the buyer agrees to pay the assignee.

When, as is generally the case, the seller and a finance company have an agreement that the seller's contracts with buyers shall be assigned to the finance company, the printed form of the seller will commonly name the finance company as assignee. Such a form is often supplied to the seller by the finance company. It may be provided, however, that the individual buyers shall continue to make payments to the seller with the latter making periodic payments of lump sums to the finance company.

§ 25:10. Obligation of Seller's Assignee as to Performance. Ordinarily an assignment by a seller is merely a way of converting the seller's account receivable or contract rights into immediate cash and does not represent an undertaking by the assignee to perform the contract. When the seller has more contracts than can be handled or is going out of business, however, the assignment of a contract may be intended to delegate to the assignee the performance of the contract.

An assignee of the seller is not liable to the buyer for a breach of the assigned contract by the original seller, particularly when the assignee is not bound to render any performance. For example, the finance company to which the seller has assigned a credit contract is not liable for breach of warranty.[34]

§ 25:11. Defenses of Buyer Against Seller's Assignee. Ordinarily the assignee of the seller is subject to any defense which the buyer would have against the seller. Credit sales

---

[32] UCC § 2-322(2).
[33] UCC § 2-324(a).
[34] Pendarvis v General Motors Corp., (NY) 6 UCCRS 457.

contracts commonly provide, however, that the buyer agrees not to assert against the seller's assignee any claim which could be asserted against the seller. This makes the contract much more attractive to the assignee by, in effect, making it "negotiable" and giving the assignee greater assurance of being able to collect the amount due under the contract. Such provisions are valid,[35] although greatly restricted in the case of consumer goods.[36]

---

[35] UCC § 9-206(1).
[36] See § 31:17 of this book.

CASES FOR CHAPTER 25

Umlas v Acey Oldsmobile, Inc.

(NY Civil Court) 62 Misc 2d 819, 310 NYS2d 147 (1970)

Umlas made a contract to buy a new automobile from Acey Oldsmobile. He was allowed to keep his old car until the new car was delivered. The sales contract gave him a trade-in value on the old car of $650, but specified that it would be reappraised when it was actually brought in to the dealer. When Umlas brought the trade-in to the dealer, an employee of Acey took it for a test drive and told Acey that it was worth from $300 to $400. Acey stated to Umlas that the trade-in would be appraised at $50. Umlas refused to buy from Acey and purchased from another dealer who appraised the trade-in at $400. Umlas sued Acey for breach of contract. Acey defended on the ground that its conduct was authorized by the reappraisal clause.

SANDLER, J. . . . Underlying plaintiff's lawsuit is the charge . . . that the reappraisal was not done in good faith.

The defendant interposed a counterclaim for an amount just in excess of $300.00 that is totally without any semblance of merit, and that was obviously designed to harass the plaintiff by removing the case from the Small Claims Part of this Court.

I find as a fact that defendant's employee did state to plaintiff that he had reappraised plaintiff's car in the amount of $50.00 . . . and that this valuation was not made in good faith.

The critical legal question thus becomes whether the provision of the form order, under which defendant reserved the right to reappraise the used car allowance at the time of delivery where delivery is deferred, implies that the right of reappraisal is

to be exercised in good faith. I conclude as a matter of law that good faith is an essential implied condition for the exercise of the right of reappraisal. See Uniform Commercial Code, 1-201, 2-103; c.f. 2-305.

To hold otherwise would mean that the order agreement, and the promises exchanged therein, was intended to be wholly illusory until delivery had been completed. Such a construction would make a travesty of an agreement that evoked from the plaintiff, as it was intended to, the following substantial reliance: a down payment, suspension for a period of his right to acquire a car elsewhere, and the securing of a bank loan. . . .

In reaching the above conclusion, I do not wish to be understood as doubting the legitimate considerations prompting the provision in question when the delivery of the car is to be deferred. Obviously, the buyer's car may suffer some deterioration during the intervening period. . . .

But the fact that the clause represents a reasonable response to a practical problem does not obscure the reality that it is open to, and indeed lends itself to, serious and recurrent abuse. In the presence of a potential buyer, searching for the optimum price for his used car, a dealer may well be disposed to place a generous value on the used car, realizing that he could later renegotiate the figure when his bargaining position was immensely strengthened.

For it is surely clear that when a buyer has signed an order for a particular car of a certain color and with special accessories, has made a cash down-payment, has secured a bank loan, and has arrived in his somewhat worn old car ready to receive a resplendent new vehicle, his ability to resist a new less-favorable deal is at a very low ebb indeed.

Surely, it is no surprise that defendant's witness acknowledged that used car allowances are often lowered at the delivery date. And although no testimony was presented directly, it is surely a fair surmise that instances in which used cars are found to have a higher value at the delivery date would represent extraordinary phenomena in the annals of any car dealer.

In evaluating the appropriate remedy for the kind of breach presented, I have considered that the arrangement of circumstances in this very common situation presents car dealers with a powerful inducement to place high values on used cars when attempting to land the order and low values when the physical presence of the new car after an intervening period has substantially reduced the purchasers' resistance. Car dealers should be encouraged to withstand this temptation. . . .

The plaintiff, like any purchaser under the circumstances, was entitled to a good faith valuation of his car on the delivery date.

In the absence of any good faith reappraisal by the defendant, the only valuation by the defendant is that fixed at the time of the original order, and I find that to be controlling.

Accordingly, I find for the plaintiff in the sum of $270.00 with interest from December 1, 1969.

Teeman v Jurek

(Minn) 251 NW2d 698 (1977)

Teeman made a contract to sell 48,000 bushels of corn to Jurek with knowledge that Jurek would resell the corn to the Farmers Union Grain Terminal Association (GTA). The price Jurek was to pay Teeman depended on the resale price to GTA. Teeman claimed that GTA was underweighing the deliveries of corn. To end the dispute, GTA agreed that Teeman could have the corn weighed at any one of three other grain elevators. Thereafter Jurek received a payment from GTA for corn which had been delivered. Instead of using this check to pay Teeman, Jurek kept it for himself. Teeman stopped making delivery of corn. Teeman later sued Jurek on another contract and Jurek counterclaimed against Teeman for damages sustained because of the breach of the corn contract. The court held that Teeman was not justified in withholding delivery of corn and entered judgment for Jurek for the damages sustained by the breach of the corn contract. Teeman appealed.

WINTON, J. . . . In mid-August 1973, GTA delivered a check in part payment in accordance with its commitment to Jurek, who in turn indorsed and gave it to Teeman. The defendant subsequently received from GTA a second check, but instead of indorsing and delivering that check to the plaintiff, the defendant held and ultimately cashed it.

Notwithstanding GTA's commitments, Teeman withheld delivery of corn in August. Under date of September 14, 1973, he wrote a letter to GTA with a copy to defendant in which he stated in part:

> "In my previous letter to you on August 8th, I stated that I would not deliver any more corn to Superior and take the losses I have taken on every load that had a check weight on it. This still stands with me, if there is not going to be any other adjustments than what has been made, there is not going to be any more corn. In fact the 18,000 bu. is now gone and there is also another contract for 20,000 bu. for February 1974 delivery that will not be delivered either under the conditions I have experienced with delivery of corn to Superior up to this time." . . .

The contract between plaintiff and defendant was one for the sale of goods and, therefore, is governed by the Uniform Commercial Code. . . . Plaintiff contends that under the facts and the applicable law he was entitled to withhold delivery of the corn. The trial court specifically concluded that he was not justified in doing so. Plaintiff's second contention is that the trial court erred in implicitly finding that defendant did not repudiate the contract by retaining GTA's second . . . check. . . .

1. Is the evidence sufficient to sustain the trial court's finding that plaintiff was not entitled to withhold delivery under [UCC §] 2-609? . . .

That Teeman as seller had reasonable grounds for insecurity seems by no means clear from the evidence. To be sure, he complained about short weight and grading discounts, but whatever the merit of those complaints the evidence more than sufficiently shows that he received adequate assurance that his complaints would be remedied. He was promised reimbursement for the grading discounts and was given the option of directing future deliveries at another elevator. Moreover, nothing can be found in the transcript of the evidence to indicate that Teeman ever in writing demanded adequate assurance of due performance from Jurek. This court concludes that the evidence amply sustains the trial court's finding that the plaintiff was not entitled to withhold delivery of the corn under [UCC §] 2-609.

2. Plaintiff contends on appeal that the trial court by implication must have found that defendant did not repudiate the contract by failing to indorse and transmit GTA's second reimbursement check to him and that such a finding was erroneous. Apparently plaintiff contends that defendant's withholding of the second check constituted a repudiation of the contract and cites *Jurek v Thompson,* Minn., 241 N.W.2d 788 (1976). That contention has no merit. It does not clearly appear that Jurek had received the second check from GTA before Teeman wrote the letter of September 14, 1973, a fact that would seem basic to plaintiff's position. Nor is there any evidence of defendant's having informed plaintiff either that he had received the check or that he intended to withhold it. In short, there is no evidence surrounding the second check sufficient to support a finding that defendant's conduct with respect to it justified withholding delivery under [UCC §] 2-610.

Jurek v Thompson, supra, affords no support to defendant's contentions here. In that case the buyer communicated to the seller his intention to withhold payment for 4,000 bushels of corn to be sold under one contract as a setoff against damages he claimed for alleged breach of a second contract. This court held that since [UCC §] 2-717 makes the right of setoff available only when the claimed damages result from a breach of the same contract under which any part of the purchase price still is due, the seller could properly interpret the seller's declared intention as a wrongful refusal to pay on the contract and thus justification for withholding delivery. In the instant case, by contrast, withholding the second check could quite properly be viewed as a setoff against damages incurred because of plaintiff's refusal to perform the balance of his part of the contract.

[Judgment affirmed]

United States for the Use of Fram Corp. v Crawford

(CA5 Ga) 443 F2d 611 (1971)

Crawford, who was constructing a building for the United States Navy, purchased fuel equipment from Fram Corp. and installed the equipment in the building. Fram sued for the purchase price. Crawford claimed that he had not accepted the equipment because it was defective. From a judgment for Crawford, Fram appealed.

AINSWORTH, C.J. . . . . The contract price for the fuel filter/separator units was $55,564.20. Floyd Crawford admitted at the trial that of that sum, $6,298.50 had not been paid. There was no testimony to the contrary. The appellees maintain that they are excused from further payment by the deficiencies in Fram's performance on the contract. Fram contends, to the contrary, that the Trial Judge should have directed a verdict in its favor on its claim for the $6,298.50. We sustain Fram's contention.

It is undisputed that Fram furnished the eighteen fuel filter/separator units called for by the contract, and that Crawford received and installed all eighteen units. Section 2-607 of the Uniform Commercial Code . . . provides . . . : "The buyer must pay at the contract rate for any goods accepted." Acceptance of goods occurs when the buyer "does any act inconsistent with the seller's ownership." Georgia UCC § 2-606(1)(c). No case is reported in which the Georgia courts have had occasion to interpret section 2-606(1)(c). Courts in other jurisdictions, interpreting the same section of the Uniform Commercial Code, have held that installation by the buyer of heavy equipment supplied by the seller is an act inconsistent with the seller's ownership. See Marbelite Company v City of Philadelphia, 1966, 208 Pa Super 256, 222 A2d 443 (traffic signal equipment); Park County Implement Co. v Craig, Wyo. 1964, 397 P2d 800 (hoist and dump bed on vehicle). We believe that the Georgia courts, confronted with the same issue in the instant case, would give section 2-606(1)(c) the same construction. A buyer who has accepted goods may under certain conditions revoke his acceptance. Georgia UCC § 2-608. However, once Crawford had accepted and installed the units supplied in place on the Albany site, any subsequent attempt at revocation was ineffective. . . .

[Judgment reversed and action remanded]

Cameras for Industry v I. D. Precision Components Corp.

49 Misc 2d 1044, 268 NYS2d 860 (1966)

Cameras for Industry made a contract to purchase component parts from Precision Components Corp. for use in the manufacture of security camera systems. When full deliveries were not made under the purchase orders, Cameras brought suit against Precision. The case, by agreement of the parties, was referred to a special referee to determine if there had been a breach of the contract.

MAZUR, Special Referee . . . By purchase orders dated March 1, 1963, and March 19, 1963, certain specified parts were ordered. The March 1 purchase order provided for an April 10, 1963, delivery date, while the March 19 purchase order provided for a delivery date of five to six weeks, or before, with a promise of partial shipment during the week of April 8. Both orders provided that time was of the essence and that partial shipments would be accepted. It is conceded that these orders were placed by plaintiff and were accepted by the defendant.

Apparently on April 9, 1963, and at various dates thereafter, up to and including April 26, 1963, partial shipments were made, with a total invoice value of $1,748.73. After that date, however, no further deliveries were made by the defendant to the plaintiff.

Plaintiff's insistence on timely delivery appears to have been occasioned by the fact that it had schedules to meet in its own production.

According to plaintiff's version of the facts, when it appeared that there would not be timely fulfillment of its orders, one of its representatives visited defendant's plant and discovered that plaintiff's work had been taken off the machines in favor of other jobs. However, so frantic was he for delivery, that he requested shipment of anything available, whether in finished or unfinished state, so that plaintiff could utilize whatever parts were usable. There appears to be some indication that at least part of the shipments were not usable.

Defendant's version of what happened is in direct contravention to plaintiff's testimony. According to defendant, it refused to fulfill the balance of the orders because plaintiff failed to pay for the partial shipments, and because plaintiff had been complaining that the tolerances and finishes were not in strict accordance with its specifications. It is defendant's contention that it was justified in halting production by plaintiff's attempt to vary its previously submitted specifications by requiring tolerances and finishes out of line with the original price estimates. . . .

Since the transaction herein took place prior to September 27, 1964, the effective date of the Uniform Commercial Code, it is governed by the appropriate provisions of Article 5 of the Personal Property Law, (Uniform Sales Act) now repealed. . . . Naturally, the seller is excused from performance if its failure is due to the acts of the buyer, or a refusal by the buyer to perform on his part. . . .

Partial deliveries do not obligate a buyer to make partial payments. The fact that the contracts herein provided that partial deliveries would be accepted merely obligated the buyer to accept shipments in a manner he would not otherwise be bound to do . . . but did not, without more, obligate it to make advance payments. . . .

It is obvious that the refusal by the seller herein to further perform the contracts was occasioned not as a result of anything the buyer did or omitted to do, but rather as a result of seller's realization either that it had made an unprofitable bargain or that it could use its machines more profitably. A buyer is entitled to expect full performance of a deal as made, and this is what the plaintiff herein did not get. Plaintiff is, therefore, entitled to recover for damages ensuing by defendant's delay in performing and refusing to complete deliveries. . . .

Code Comment: The same decision would be made under the Code as there was no evidence that the sales contract provided for delivery by lots and that the price could be apportioned to the respective lots. The general rule under the Code, by which a buyer is not required to pay for partial or installment deliveries when the contract does not so require, would therefore apply. UCC § 2-307.

Custom Built Homes Co. v Kansas State Commission of Revenue

184 Kan 31, 334 P2d 808 (1959)

Custom Built Homes purchased unassembled prefabricated houses from Page-Hill in Minnesota to be delivered by the seller "F.O.B. building site . . . Kansas." The seller brought the houses to the building site in sections by tractor-trailer, where he would unhitch the trailer and unload the shipment. Kansas taxed Custom Built on the sale. Custom Built raised the defense that there was no sale within the state of Kansas. From a judgment in favor of Kansas, Custom Built appealed.

SCHROEDER, J. . . . When did title pass? The parties recognize this to be the determinative question in this lawsuit.

Appellant seizes upon the finding of the trial court that title to the prefabricated exterior and interior sections passed to the appellant at the time the hooks of the Page-Hill crane were removed from such sections. . . . The sections were nailed to the foundation at the time the hooks were removed and had thus become permanently affixed to and had become a part of the real estate prior to the passing of title to the appellant.

Further argument by the appellant inferentially proceeds on the theory that title to a prefabricated house unit cannot pass in parts at different times, but of necessity under the contract must pass *in toto* at a specific time in accordance with the intention of the parties. Appellant argues that title to the prefabricated roof and ceiling sections did not pass until such sections had become permanently affixed to and had become a part of the real estate. This is based upon testimony that initially these sections were unloaded by a separate stationary crane furnished by Page-Hill in much the same fashion as the exterior and interior wall panels. . . .

Appellant also contends that the trial court erred as to the time title passed to the loose materials since it failed to amplify such finding by stating what percentage these loose items bore to the entire unit, and further in failing to make a finding as to the time title to all of these units of a prefabricated house as a whole was contemplated to pass from Page-Hill to the appellant under the sales contract. . . .

The initial letters, "F.O.B." frequently found in contracts for goods to be shipped stand for the words "free on board." In commercial practice these words have a well-defined meaning, and, as applied to the sale of merchandise destined for shipment, mean that such goods are to be put into the hands of the carrier at the point of shipment free of expense to the buyer. . . .

" 'Where the contract provides for a sale f.o.b. the point of destination, the title is generally held not to pass, in the absence of a contrary intention between the parties, until the goods have been delivered at the point designated.' " . . .

In our opinion "F.O.B. building site in Wyandotte County, Kansas," has a clear and unambiguous meaning. Applied to the facts in this case as to each prefabricated house unit under the contract it means free on board the semi-trailer at the building site in Stony Point Heights Addition, Wyandotte County, Kansas. No contrary intention between the parties to the sales contract appearing from the face of the instrument, title to the merchandise passed upon delivery to the appellant (buyer) free on board the semi-trailer at the building site in Wyandotte County, Kansas. . . .

. . . As to each prefabricated house unit under the contract title passed upon delivery to the appellant—the time at which the tractor was unhooked from the semi-trailer loaded with the merchandise parked at the building site. On the issues here this is practically equivalent to the trial court's conclusion that title to portions of the merchandise passed when it was unloaded from the semi-trailer. The ultimate conclusion of the trial court that the merchandise occupied the status of tangible personal property at the time title passed to the appellant resulted in a correct decision.

[Judgment affirmed]

Code Comment: This case was decided under the prior Uniform Sales Act but the same decision would be made under UCC §2-319(1).

QUESTIONS AND CASE PROBLEMS

1. What social forces are involved in the rule of law governing the substitution of a different method of transportation to replace the method specified in the contract of sale?

2. Compare the making of a curative tender (a) before the expiration of the time for performance, and (b) after the expiration of the time for performance.

3. Compare the buyer's right to inspect goods tendered by the seller (a) under an ordinary sale, and (b) under a C.O.D. sale.

4. Compare (a) a telephoned demand made by a buyer to a seller for assurance that the seller will perform the contract, and (b) a written demand made by a buyer to a seller for assurance that the seller will perform the contract.

5. Price agreed to purchase two barge-loads of coal from Brown. The coal was delivered on barges of the buyer on the Green River at or near Mining City, Kentucky, in accordance with the agreement. The buyer, after being given an opportunity to inspect the coal, hooked onto the barges and transported them up the river to Bowling Green, several

miles away. During subsequent litigation the buyer contended that he had not accepted the coal. Do you agree? [Brown v Price, 207 Ky 8, 268 SW 590]

6. International Minerals and Metals Corporation contracted to sell Weinstein scrap metal to be delivered within 30 days. Later the seller informed the buyer that it could not make delivery within that time. The buyer agreed to an extension of time, but no limiting date was set. Within what time must the seller perform? [International Minerals and Metals Corp. v Weinstein, 236 NC 558, 73 SE2d 472]

7. The Spaulding & Kimball Co. ordered from the Aetna Chemical Co. 75 cartons of window washers. The buyer received them and sold about a third to its customers. The buyer later refused to pay for them, claiming that the quality was poor. The seller sued for the price, claiming that the goods had been accepted. Decide. [Aetna Chemical Co. v Spaulding & Kimball Co., 98 Vt 51, 126 A 582]

8. George A. Ohl & Co. made a contract "to sell to A. J. Ellis a No. 5 press . . . for the sum of $680." The press was known by both parties to be stored in the factory of another company. The agreement contained no stipulation as to the place of delivery, and there was no usage of the trade governing the question. In an action brought by Gruen, assignee of Ellis, against the Ohl company, the place of delivery was a point of contention. Decide. [Gruen v George A. Ohl & Co., 81 NJL 626, 80 A 547]

9. A computer manufacturer promoted the sale of a digital computer as a "revolutionary breakthrough." It made a contract to deliver one of these computers to a buyer. It failed to deliver the computer and explained that its failure was caused by unanticipated technological difficulties. Was this an excuse for nonperformance by the seller? [United States v Wegematic Corp., (CA2 NY) 360 F2d 674]

10. The Tri-Bullion Smelting & Development Co. agreed to sell, and Jacobsen to buy, the seller's output of zinc concentrates for a two-year period. A year and a half later, the Tri-Bullion Co. closed its mine and notified Jacobsen that it would make no further deliveries. Jacobsen refused to pay for the last shipment. Jacobsen sued the Tri-Bullion Co. The defendant contended that the plaintiff had breached the contract by failure to pay for the goods delivered. Do you agree? [Tri-Bullion Smelting & Development Co. v Jacobsen, 147 CCA 454, 233 F 646]

11. Mexican Produce Company sold goods to Sonny Mohamed. The contract was C.I.F. Trinidad. Mexican Produce delivered the goods to a carrier in Trinidad, Sea-Land Service, Inc. Subsequently, the goods were damaged in transit. Mexican Produce sued Sea-Land Service, Inc. for the damage. Was it liable to Mexican Produce Company? [Mexican Produce Co. v Sea-Land Service, Inc. (DC Puerto Rico) 429 FSupp 552]

12. A buyer made a contract for equipment which was to be installed in a new building which was being constructed. When the equipment was delivered to the buyer, the buyer refused to accept it on the ground that the architect had made a mistake and the tendered goods could not be used in the new building. The seller sued the buyer for breach of contract. Was the buyer entitled to reject the goods? [See R. R. Waites Co. v E. H. Thrift Air Conditioning, Inc., (MoApp), 510 SW2d 759]

13. The Rock Glen Salt Co. agreed to sell to Segal of Massachusetts some bags of salt. It obtained from the Watkins Salt Co., New York, the bags of salt ordered by Segal and 15 barrels of salt ordered by another customer. The bags and barrels of salt were placed in a car and shipped to Boston. The bill of lading for the entire shipment was made out to the seller, and indorsed and sent to Segal, who was notified by the carrier of the arrival of the car. In an action brought by the salt company against Segal to recover the purchase price, he contended that (a) he could accept the salt in the bags and reject the salt in the barrels or (b) reject the entire shipment. What is your opinion? [Rock Glen Salt Co. v Segal, 229 Mass 115, 118 NE 239]

14. The seller sold goods to a township. Under the state law governing townships, it was not possible for the township to make immediate payment of any bill presented to it. To the contrary, it was necessery that a bill be presented to the township auditor and approved by him before payment could be made. The seller claimed that the township was obligated to pay for the goods upon delivery. Decide. [J. C. Georg Service Corp. v Summit, 28 App Div 2d 578, 279 NYS2d 674]

15. Fleet purchased an ice cream freezer and compressor unit from Lang. Thereafter Fleet disconnected the compressor and used it to operate an air conditioner. When sued for the purchase price of the freezer and compressor unit, Fleet claimed that he had not accepted the goods. Was he correct? [Lang v Fleet, 193 Pa Super 365, 165 A2d 258]

16. A seller was required to deliver a specific kind of goods not later than the tenth of the month. On the second day of the month, the seller delivered goods which he knew were not the right goods. The buyer rejected the goods. Three days later, the seller returned with other goods. The buyer refused to accept the second delivery. The seller claimed that the buyer could not reject the second delivery because it conformed to the contract. Was the seller correct? [See Hayes v Hettinga, Iowa, 228 NW2d 181; Meads v Davis, 22 NC App 479, 206 SE2d 868]

26 Warranties and Other Product Liabilities

When goods that are purchased do not conform to the contract, what rights does the buyer have? This chapter discusses the principles of warranties and problems related to product liability.

A. GENERAL PRINCIPLES

When goods prove defective or cause harm, a question arises as to whether anyone is liable to the person harmed for the loss sustained. The answer in some instances is based on general common-law rules. In other instances, it is based upon the Uniform Commercial Code or new liability concepts.

§ 26:1. Introduction. When a product is defective, harm may be caused to (1) person, (2) property, or (3) economic or commercial interests. Under (1), the buyer of a truck may be injured when it goes out of control and plunges down the side of a hill. Third persons may also be injured, such as passengers in the truck, bystanders, or the driver of another car. The defective truck may also cause injury to a total stranger who seeks to rescue one of the victims. Property damage under (2) is sustained when the buyer's truck is damaged when it plunges down the slope. The car of the other driver may be damaged or a building into which the runaway truck careens may be damaged. Under (3), commercial and economic interests of the buyer are affected by the fact that the truck is defective. Even if no physical harm is sustained, the fact remains that the truck is not as valuable as it would have been, and the buyer who has paid for the truck on the basis of the value it should have had has sustained an economic loss.

If the buyer is required to rent a truck from someone else or loses an opportunity to haul freight for compensation, the fact that the truck was defective causes economic or commercial loss.

When there is a loss as above described, product liability may often arise on the basis of any of six theories of product liability: negligence, fraud, strict tort, express guarantee, express warranty, and implied warranty. Statutes may create product liability.

(a) Consumer Protection. The Consumer Product Safety Act of 1972 [1] created an independent federal agency with broad power to establish safety regulations for all

---

[1] PL 92-573, 86 Stat 1207, 15 United States Code § 2051 et seq.

food, drugs, and common household products. The purpose of this agency, the Food, Drug, and Consumer Protection Agency (FDCPA), is to protect the consumer from physical injury, adulteration, misbranding, and illegal distribution of products.

(b) Employee Protection. The federal Occupational Safety and Health Act [2] authorizes the Secretary of Labor to establish job standards and creates an agency known as the Occupational Safety and Health Administration (OSHA). This protects employees from dangerous things at work as well as dangerous working conditions.

§ 26:2. Who May Sue and Be Sued. Down to the early part of this century, only the parties to the sales contract could sue each other. Thus a seller could be sued by the buyer but other persons were excluded by the concept that they were not parties to the sales contract. That is, they could not sue because they were not in *privity of contract.*

This requirement of privity of contract has been widely rejected and the law is moving toward the conclusion that anyone harmed because of an "improper" product may sue whoever is in any way responsible.

(a) The Plaintiff. By the modern view, not only the buyer, but also customers and employees of the buyer and even third persons or bystanders may sue because of harm caused by an improper product. (See p. 429, Nobility Homes of Texas, Inc. v Shivers) The UCC expressly abolishes the requirement of privity when the plaintiff is a member of the buyer's family or household or a guest of the buyer and has sustained personal injury because of the product.[3]

Some states require privity of contract when the plaintiff does not sustain personal injury or property damage and seeks to recover only economic loss. However, a manufacturer making an express warranty as to a consumer product costing over $15 which was manufactured after July 4, 1975, may be sued for the economic loss sustained by the buyer.

(b) The Defendant. The plaintiff who is entitled to sue may sue the seller, a remote seller, a manufacturer, and generally even the manufacturer of the component part of the product which caused the harm. For example, when a person is struck by an automobile because of its defective brakes, the victim may sue the seller and the manufacturer of the car and the maker of the brake assembly or system which the car manufacturer had installed in the car.

(c) Advertising. The fact that the defendant advertised the particular product through mass media has been significant in extending the right to sue to members of the public relying on such advertising. However, the fact that a defendant has not advertised does not protect from liability to a member of the public who is harmed by the product.[4]

(d) Direct Sales Contact. In many instances recovery is allowed by a buyer against a remote manufacturer because there have been direct dealings between them which justify regarding the buyer and the manufacturer as being in privity, as against the contention that the buyer was only in privity with the local dealer from whom the

---

[2] 29 USC § 651 et seq.
[3] UCC § 2-318.
[4] Lonzrick v Republic Steel Corp. 6 Ohio2d 227, 35 OO2d 404, 218 NE2d 185.

product was bought. When the manufacturer enters into direct negotiations with the ultimate buyer with respect to any phase of the manufacturing or financing of the transaction, the sale will probably be treated as though it were made directly by the manufacturer to the ultimate purchaser even though, for the purpose of record keeping, the transaction is treated as a sale by the manufacturer to the dealer and by that dealer to the ultimate purchaser.[5] Likewise, recovery may be allowed when the consumer mails to the manufacturer a warranty registration card which the manufacturer had packed with the manufactured article.

B. EXPRESS WARRANTIES

A warranty may be express or implied. Both have the same legal effect and operate as though the seller had made an express guarantee. An express guarantee is governed by general principles of contract law. Express and implied warranties are governed by the UCC.

§ 26:3. Definition of Express Warranty. An *express warranty* is a statement which is part of the basis for the sale; that is, the buyer has purchased the goods on the reasonable assumption that they were as stated by the seller. (See p. 431, Werner v Montana) Thus, a statement by the seller with respect to the quality, capacity, or other characteristic of the goods is an express warranty. To illustrate, the seller may say: "This cloth is all wool," "This paint is for household woodwork," or "This engine can produce 50 horsepower."

A representation that an airplane is a 1969 model is an express warranty. A statement that a product was particularly developed for a special purpose is an express warranty that it will achieve that purpose.[6]

There is no requirement of reliance upon an express warranty as the question is merely whether the statement of the seller became part of the bargain of the parties.

§ 26:4. Form of Express Warranty. No particular form of words is necessary to constitute an express warranty. A seller need not state that a warranty is being made nor that one is intended. It is sufficient that the seller assert a fact that becomes a part or term of the bargain or transaction between the parties.

It is not necessary that the seller make an express statement, for the express warranty may be found in conduct. Accordingly, if the buyer asks for a can of outside house paint and the seller hands over a can of paint, the seller's conduct expresses a warranty that the can contains outside house paint.

The seller's statement may be written or printed, as well as oral. The words on the label of a can and in a newspaper ad for "boned chicken" constitute an express warranty that the can contains chicken that is free of bones.

The illustrations in a seller's catalogue are descriptions of the goods and therefore an express warranty arises that the goods will conform to a catalogue illustration.

A manufacturer's warranty does not bind a subsequent seller unless the seller has in some way adopted the manufacturer's warranty.

---

[5] Marion Power Shovel v Huntsman, 246 Ark 149, 437 SW2d 784.
[6] Swenson v Chevron Chemical Co. (SD) 234 NW2d 38 (insecticide for use against corn root worm larvae).

§ 26:5. Federal Regulation. A seller who makes an express warranty as to a consumer product costing more than $15 must conform to certain standards imposed by federal statute [7] and by regulations of the Federal Trade Commission.[8] Initially, the seller is not required to make any express warranty but if one is made, it must be stated in ordinary understandable language and must be made available for inspection before purchasing so that the consumer may "comparison shop."

(a) Full Warranties. If the seller or the label states that a *full warranty* is made, the seller is obligated to fix or replace a defective product within a reasonable time, without cost to the buyer. If the product cannot be fixed or if a reasonable number of repair attempts are unsuccessful, the buyer has the choice of a cash refund or a free replacement. No unreasonable burden may be placed on a buyer seeking to obtain warranty service. A full warranty runs for its specified life without regard to the ownership of the product.

(b) Limited Warranties. Any warranty which does not provide the complete protection of a full warranty is a *limited warranty* and must be so described by the seller. For example, a warranty is limited if the buyer must pay any cost, or if only the first buyer is covered by the warranty, or if the warranty only covers part of the product. A warrantor making a full warranty cannot require that the buyer pay the cost of sending the product to or from a warranty service point, or to return the product to such a point if it weighs over 35 pounds, or to return a built-in product for service unless it can be easily removed, or to fill and return a warranty registration card shortly after purchase in order to make the warranty effective. If the warrantor imposes any of these burdens the warranty must be called a limited warranty.

§ 26:6. Time of Making Express Warranty. It is immaterial whether the express warranty is made at the time of or after the sale. No separate consideration is required for the warranty when it is part of a sale. If a warranty is made after the sale, no consideration is required since it is regarded as a modification of the sales contract.[9]

§ 26:7. Seller's Opinion or Statement of Value. "An affirmation of the value of goods or a statement purporting to be merely the seller's opinion or commendation of the goods does not create a warranty." [10] A purchaser, as a reasonable person, should not believe such statements implicitly, and therefore cannot hold the seller to them should they prove false. Thus, "sales talk" by a seller that "this is the best piece of cloth in the market" or that glassware "is as good as anyone else's" is merely an opinion which the buyer cannot ordinarily treat as a warranty.

It is probable, however, that the UCC will permit an exception to be made, as under the prior law, when the circumstances are such that a reasonable person would rely on such a statement. If the buyer has reason to believe that the seller is possessed of expert knowledge of the conditions of the market and the buyer requests the seller's opinion as an expert, the buyer would be entitled to accept as a fact the

---

[7] PL 93-636, 15 USC § 2301 et seq.
[8] 16 CFR § 700.1 et seq.
[9] UCC § 2-313. Official Comment, point 7.
[10] UCC § 2-313(2).

seller's statement as to whether a given article was the best obtainable. The statement could be reasonably regarded as forming part of the basis of the bargain. Thus, a statement by a florist that bulbs are of first-grade quality may be a warranty.

C. IMPLIED WARRANTIES

Whenever a sale of goods is made, certain warranties are implied unless they are expressly excluded. The scope of these warranties may differ in terms of whether the seller is a merchant or a casual seller.

§ 26:8. Definition. An *implied warranty* is one that was not made by the seller but which is implied by the law. In certain instances the law implies or reads a warranty into a sale although the seller did not make it. That is, the implied warranty arises automatically from the fact that a sale has been made; as compared with express warranties, which arise because they form part of the basis on which the sale has been made.

The fact that express warranties are made does not exclude implied warranties; and when both express and implied warranties exist, they should be construed as consistent with each other and as cumulative if such construction is reasonable. In case it is unreasonable to construe them as consistent and cumulative, an express warranty prevails over an implied warranty as to the same subject matter, except in the case of an implied warranty of fitness for a particular purpose. When there is an express warranty as to a particular matter, it is unnecessary to find an implied warranty relating thereto.

§ 26:9. Implied Warranties of All Sellers. A distinction is made between a merchant seller and the casual seller. There is a greater range of warranties in the case of the merchant seller.

(a)   Warranty of Title. Every seller, by the mere act of selling, makes a warranty that the seller's title is good and that the transfer is rightful.[11]

A warranty of title may be specifically excluded, or the circumstances may be such as to prevent the warranty from arising. The latter situation is found when the buyer has reason to know that the seller does not claim to hold the title or that the seller is purporting to sell only such right or title as the seller or a third person may have. For example, no warranty of title arises when the seller makes the sale in a representative capacity, such as a sheriff, an auctioneer, or an administrator of a decedent's estate. Likewise, no warranty arises when the seller makes the sale as a pledgee or mortgagee.

(b)   Warranty Against Encumbrances. Every seller by the mere act of selling makes a warranty that the goods shall be delivered free from any security interest or any other lien or encumbrance of which the buyer at the time of the sales transaction had no knowledge.[12] Thus, there is a breach of warranty if the automobile sold to the buyer is delivered subject to an outstanding encumbrance that had been placed

---

[11] UCC § 2-312(1)(a). A warranty of title, as well as a warranty of freedom from encumbrances, which arises when a sale is made, is not classified as an implied warranty by the UCC even though it is in the nature of an implied warranty.

[12] Fields v Sugar, 251 Ark 1062, 476 SW2d 814.

on it by the original owner and which was unknown to the buyer at the time of the sale.

This warranty refers to the goods only at the time they are delivered to the buyer and is not concerned with an encumbrance which existed before or at the time the sale was made. For example, a seller may not have paid in full for the goods and the original supplier may have a lien on them. The seller may resell the goods while that lien is still on them and the seller's only duty is to pay off the lien before delivering the goods to the buyer.

(c)   Warranty of Conformity to Description, Sample, or Model. When the contract is based in part on the understanding that the seller will supply goods according to a particular description or that the goods will be the same as the sample or a model, the seller is bound by an express warranty that the goods shall conform to the description, sample, or model.[13] Ordinarily a *sample* is a portion of a whole mass that is the subject of the transaction, while a *model* is a replica of the article in question. The mere fact that a sample is exhibited in the course of negotiations does not make the sale a sale by sample, as there must be an intent manifested that the sample be part of the basis of contracting. Likewise, when a piece of the material from which the goods are made is shown to the buyer, such specimen of the material does not constitute a sale by sample as a sample must be a part drawn from the total bulk of goods.

(d)   Warranty of Fitness for a Particular Purpose. If the buyer intends to use the goods for a particular or unusual purpose, as contrasted with the ordinary use for which they are customarily sold, the seller makes an implied warranty that the goods will be fit for the purpose when the buyer relies on the seller's skill or judgment to select or furnish suitable goods, and when the seller at the time of contracting knows or has reason to know the buyer's particular purpose and the buyer's reliance on the seller's judgment.[14] For example, where a farmer relied on the sales representative in purchasing feed for cattle, a particular purpose warranty arose. Where a government representative inquired of the seller whether the seller had a tape suitable for use in the government's NCR 304 computer system, there arose an implied warranty, unless otherwise excluded, that the tape furnished by the seller was fit for that purpose. When the seller knows that the buyer is purchasing an accounting machine in order to produce a payroll on time and with reduced work hours, an implied warranty arises that the machine will perform as desired by the buyer and there is a breach of that warranty when the machine malfunctions continuously and cannot be repaired by the seller.[15]

A warranty for a particular purpose frequently arises when a customer shows the seller a sample and requests something to meet the customer's needs. For example, where the seller was asked to supply bricks of the color and texture of a sample

---

[13] UCC § 2-313(1)(b),(c).
[14] UCC § 2-315. This warranty applies to every seller, but as a matter of fact it will probably always be a merchant seller who has such skill and judgment so that the Code provision would be applicable. In contrast, when a seller of coal has had no experience in the selection of coal for the manufacture of coke, no implied warranty of fitness for that purpose arises. Sylvia Coal Co. v Mercury Coal & Coke Co. 151 WVa 818, 156 SE2d 1.
[15] National Cash Register Co. v Adell Industries Inc., 57 MichApp 413, 225 NW2d 785.

brick which would be suitable for the construction of retaining walls and walks, an implied warranty of fitness for that particular purpose arose.

When the buyer makes the purchase without relying on the seller's skill and judgment, no warranty of fitness for a particular purpose arises. (See p. 432, Lewis and Sims, Inc. v Key Industries, Inc.)

§ 26:10. Additional Implied Warranties of Merchant Seller. A seller who deals in goods of the kind in question is classified as a *merchant* by the UCC and is held to a higher degree of responsibility for the product than one who is merely making a casual sale.

(a)   Warranty Against Infringement. Unless otherwise agreed, every merchant seller warrants that the goods shall be delivered free of the rightful claim of any third person by way of patent or trademark infringement or the like.

(b)   Warranty of Merchantability or Fitness for Normal Use. A merchant seller makes an implied warranty of the merchantability of the goods sold.[16] This warranty is in fact a group of warranties, the most important of which is that the goods are fit for the ordinary purposes for which they are sold. Also included are implied warranties as to the general or average quality of the goods, and their packaging and labeling.[17]

A merchant is not protected from warranty liability by the fact that every possible step was taken to make the product safe. Similarly, it is no defense that the defendant could not have known of or discovered the dangerous character of the product, for warranty liability is not merely an assurance that the defendant has exercised due care but is an undertaking or guarantee that the product is fit for use. (See p. 433, Sams v Ezy-Way Foodliner Company)

The implied warranty of merchantability relates to the condition of the goods at the time the seller is to perform under the contract. Once the risk of loss has passed to the buyer, there is no warranty as to the continuing merchantability of the goods unless such subsequent deterioration or condition is proof that the goods were in fact not merchantable when the seller made delivery.

When a merchant sells goods, the warranty of merchantability arises without regard to whether the buyer is a consumer or is another merchant purchasing for resale.[18]

§ 26:11. Warranties in Particular Sales. Particular types of sales may involve special considerations.

(a)   Sale of Food or Drink. The sale of food or drink, whether to be consumed on or off the seller's premises, is a sale and, when made by a merchant, carries the implied warranty that the food is fit for its ordinary purpose, that is, human consumption.[19]

---

[16] This includes the seller of food or drink to be consumed on the premises or to be taken out. UCC § 2-314(1).

[17] UCC § 2-314(2). Other implied warranties on the part of a merchant may also arise from a course of dealing or usage of trade. § 2-314(3).

[18] Ambassador Steel Co. v Ewald Steel Co., 33 MichApp 495, 190 NW2d 275.

[19] UCC § 2-314(1), (2)(c).

The UCC does not end the conflict between courts applying the foreign-natural test and those applying the reasonable-expectation test. The significance of the two is that in the first test a buyer cannot recover as a matter of law when injured by a "natural" substance in the food, such as a cherry pit in a cherry pie; whereas under the reasonable-expectation test, it is necessary to make a determination of fact, ordinarily by the jury, concerning whether the buyer could reasonably expect to find such an object in the food. It is, of course, necessary to distinguish the foregoing situations from those in which the preparation of the food contemplates the continued presence of some element that is not removed, such as prune stones in cooked prunes. The reasonable-expectation test has been applied in determining whether a restaurant is liable to a patron who broke a tooth on an olive pit.

The buyer of food that is unwholesome, as in the case of a customer purchasing a spoiled sandwich, may recover either on strict tort or breach of warranty theory.

(b)   Sale of Article under Patent or Trade Name. The sale of a patented or trade name article is treated with respect to warranties in the same way as any other sale. If the seller is a merchant selling goods of the kind in question, the ordinary merchant's warranty of merchantability arises even though the parties have described the goods by a patent number or trade name. The fact that the sale is made on the basis of the patent or trade name does not bar the existence of a warranty of fitness for a particular purpose when the circumstances giving rise to such a warranty exist.

(c)   Sale on Buyer's Specifications. When the buyer furnishes the seller with exact specifications for the preparation or manufacture of such goods, the same warranties arise as in the case of any other sale of such goods by the particular seller. No warranty of fitness for a particular purpose can arise, however, since it is clear that the buyer is purchasing on the basis of the buyer's own decision and is not relying on the seller's skill and judgment.

In sales made upon the buyer's specifications, no warranty against infringement is impliedly made by the merchant seller; and conversely, the buyer in substance makes a warranty to protect the seller from liability should the seller be held liable for patent violation by following the specifications of the buyer.[20]

(d)   Sale of Secondhand or Used Goods. No warranty arises as to fitness of used property for ordinary use when the sale is made by a casual seller. If made by a merchant seller, such a warranty may sometimes be implied. Prior to the UCC a number of states followed the rule that no warranty arose in connection with used or secondhand goods, particularly automobiles and machinery; whereas some courts found a warranty of fitness for ordinary use in the sale of secondhand goods, particularly airplanes and heavy farm equipment. It is likely that this conflict will continue under the UCC.[21]

D. DISCLAIMER OF WARRANTIES

The seller and the buyer may agree that there shall be no warranties. In some states this is limited in terms of public policy or consumer protection.

---

[20] UCC § 2-312(3).
[21] See UCC § 2-314, Official Comment, point 3.

§ 26:12. Validity of Disclaimer. Warranties may be disclaimed by agreement of the parties,[22] subject to the limitation that such a provision must not be unconscionable.[23]

If a warranty of fitness [24] is excluded or if it is modified in writing, it must be conspicuous in order to make certain that the buyer will be aware of its presence. If the implied warranty of merchantability is excluded, the exclusion clause must expressly mention the word "merchantability" and it must be conspicuous.

(a) Conspicuousness. A disclaimer provision is made conspicuous by printing it under a conspicuous heading, but in such case the heading must indicate that there is an exclusion or modification of warranties. Conversely, a heading cannot be relied upon to make such a provision "conspicuous" when the heading is misleading and wrongfully gives the impression that there is a warranty, as a heading stating "Vehicle Warranty," when in fact the provision that follows contains a limitation of warranties. And a disclaimer that is hidden in a mass of printed material handed to the buyer is not conspicuous and is not effective to exclude warranties. Similarly, an inconspicuous disclaimer of warranties under a heading of "notice to retail buyers" has no effect.

When a waiver of warranties fails to be effective because it is not conspicuous, the implied warranties which would arise in the absence of any waiver are operative.

(b) Unconscionability and Public Policy. An exclusion of warranties made in the manner specified by the Code is not unconscionable.[25] But there is also authority that when the breach of warranty was the result of negligence of the seller, the disclaimer of warranty liability and a limitation of remedies to refunding of purchase price is not binding because such a limitation is unreasonable, unconscionable, and against sound public policy. In some states, warranty disclaimers are invalid as contrary to public policy or because they are prohibited by consumer protection laws.[26]

If a seller makes any written warranty of a consumer product costing more than $15, the seller is barred from excluding any implied warranty that would be implied under the law of sales.

§ 26:13. Particular Provisions. Such a statement as "there are no warranties which extend beyond the description on the face hereof" excludes all implied warranties of fitness.[27] Implied warranties are excluded by the statement of "as is," "with all faults," or other language which in normal common speech calls attention to the warranty exclusion and makes

---

[22] The term *disclaimer* refers to the consensual agreement of the parties which constitutes an express term of their contract. *Exclusion of warranties* may refer to any conduct which excludes warranties, and embraces not only disclaimers but also exclusion by examination and by custom or course of dealing. *Modification of warranties* is often misused to refer to a partial disclaimer.

[23] UCC §§ 2-316(1), 2-302(1). A distinction must be made between holding that the circumstances do not give rise to a warranty, thus precluding warranty liability, and holding that the warranty which would otherwise arise was excluded or surrendered by the contract of the parties.

[24] By the letter of the Code, the text statement is applicable to any warranty of fitness, see UCC § 2-316(2), although by the Official Comment to § 2-316, point 4, it would appear to be only the warranty of fitness for a particular purpose.

[25] Avery v Aladdin Products Division, National Service Industries, Inc. 128 GaApp 266, 196 SE2d 357.

[26] Geo. G. Christopher & Son, Inc. v Kansas Paint & Color Co., 215 Kan 185, 523 P2d 709.

[27] UCC § 2-316(2).

it clear that there is no implied warranty.[28] (See p. 434, Robinson v Branch Moving & Storage Company, Inc.)

In order for a disclaimer of warranties to be a binding part of an oral sales contract, the disclaimer must be called to the attention of the buyer.

These provisions as to exclusions of warranties apply to leases of personal property that in substance are sales.

§ 26:14. Exclusion of Warranties by Examination of Goods.
There is no implied warranty with respect to defects in goods that an examination should have revealed when the buyer before making the final contract has examined the goods, or model or sample, or has refused to make such examination.[29]

The examination of the goods by the buyer does not exclude the existence of an express warranty unless it can be concluded that the buyer thereby learned of the falsity of the statement claimed to be a warranty, with the consequence that such statement did not in fact form part of the bargain.

§ 26:15. Post-Sale Disclaimer.
Frequently the statement excluding or modifying warranties appears for the first time in a written contract sent to confirm or memorialize the oral contract made earlier; or it appears in an invoice, a bill, or an instruction manual delivered to the buyer at or after the time the goods are received. Such post-sale disclaimers have no effect on warranties that arose at the time of the sale. Likewise, an oral express warranty made by the seller's agent is not excluded by a disclaimer of oral warranties appearing on the back of a printed credit form which was subsequently executed without the disclaimer being called to the buyer's attention.

An exclusion of warranties in a manufacturer's manual given to the buyer after the sale is not binding on a buyer because it is not a term of the sales contract.[30]

If the buyer would assent to the post-sale disclaimer, however, it would be effective as a modification of the sales contract.

E. PARTICULAR PROBLEMS OF PRODUCT LIABILITY

Particular problems and situations in product liability law occur frequently and a definite body of law is growing up to deal with these situations.

§ 26:16. Other Theories of Product Liability.
In addition to suit for breach of an express guarantee, an express warranty, or an implied warranty, a plaintiff in a given product liability case may be able to sue for negligence, fraud, or strict tort.

(a)   Negligence. Independently of the UCC, a person injured because of the defective condition of goods may be entitled to sue the seller or manufacturer for the damages sustained when the defendant was negligent in the preparation or manufacture of the article or in failing to provide proper instructions and warnings as to dangers. A manufacturer is responsible for having the knowledge of an expert and must therefore

---

[28] UCC § 2-316(3)(a).
[29] UCC § 2-316(3)(b).
[30] Karczewski v Ford Motor Co. (DC Ind) 382 FSupp 1346.

take reasonable steps to guard against the dangers that would be apparent to an expert.

(1)   *Testing and Inspection.* A manufacturer of a product is liable for negligence if due care is not exercised in the making of tests and inspections during the course of and after the manufacture of the product.[31] In contrast, there is no duty on a distributor or retailer to test or inspect in the absence of any reason to believe that a particular product is defective. Statutes, however, sometimes impose upon dealers, as in the case of automobiles, the duty to make tests.

The fact that proper tests have been made or that testing is not required merely protects a defendant from negligence liability. If the product is defective, a given defendant may still be liable for breach of warranty and possibly strict tort, even though the defendant was not negligent.

(2)   *Violation of Governmental Safety Regulation.* If the manufacturer or the seller violates a statute or an applicable administrative regulation, such violation is often held to be evidence of negligence or to constitute negligence in itself (negligence per se). The consequence is that when such breach is the cause of the harm, negligence liability may be enforced.

(b)   **Fraud.** The UCC expressly preserves the pre-Code law as to fraud, with the consequence that a person defrauded by false statements as to a product made by the seller or the manufacturer will generally be able to recover damages for the harm sustained because of such misrepresentations when they were made with knowledge that they were false or with reckless indifference as to whether they were true.

(c)   **Strict Tort Liability.** Independently of the UCC, a manufacturer, distributor, or seller of a defective product is liable to a person injured by the product when, because of the defect, the product is dangerous to the user to a degree more than the user would ordinarily expect. The fact that the defendant merely assembles component parts manufactured by others does not shield the defendant from strict tort liability, because the defendant is still in the chain of distribution and produces and supplies products to others for their use and consumption.[32]

The strict tort concept is not one of absolute liability; that is, it must first be shown that there was a defect in the product. It is like warranty liability in that the defendant is liable because the defective product caused harm, and it is no defense that there was no negligence.[33]

Strict tort liability is not imposed upon a casual seller making an isolated single sale of the goods.

---

[31] Kross v Kelsey Hayes Co. 29 AppDiv2d 901, 287 NYS2d 926.

[32] Foster v Day & Zimmerman, K Inc. (CA8 Tex) 502 F2d 867.

[33] The concept of strict tort liability was judicially declared in Greenman v Yuba Power Products, 59 Cal2d 57, 27 CalRptr 697, 377 P2d 897. This concept was restated by and is often identified as Restatement of Torts 2d § 402A. In some jurisdictions the term "products liability" is used to refer to the strict tort theory of liability. Willeford v Mayrath, 7 IllApp3d 357, 287 NE2d 502.

"The doctrine of strict liability is hardly more than what exists under implied warranty when stripped of the contract doctrines of privity, disclaimer, requirements of notice of defect, and limitations through inconsistencies with express warranties." Shepard v Alexian Brothers Hospital, Inc. 33 CalApp3d 606, 109 CalRptr 132. By this view, it is sufficient that the product be "defective." Other courts adhere to the Restatement's requirement that the product be "dangerously defective."

(d)   Cumulative Liabilities. The theories of product liability are not mutually exclusive. Thus, a given set of facts may give rise to two or more theories of liability. For example, where a rock-crushing machine was dangerous to workers because an unguarded rotating axle projected from the machine, it was held that there was (a) liability for breach of the express warranty that the machine was safe, (b) liability for breach of the implied warranty of fitness for the particular purpose of crushing rock, and (c) liability for strict tort.

In many instances it will not make any difference to anyone whether there is only one basis of product liability or several. In some instances it may be important. For example, a warranty liability is barred if injury is sustained in the fifth year after the delivery of the goods for the reason that the statute of limitations as to warranty claims runs from the date of delivery of the goods and not from the later date when injury is sustained. In contrast, the statute of limitations applicable to strict tort generally runs from the date of the injury so that an injured plaintiff probably would have two years after the date of injury in which to sue.

It is to be remembered that any seller or manufacturer, by the express terms of the sales contract, may assume a liability broader than would arise without such an express undertaking.

§ 26:17. Nature of the Transaction. Warranty liability arises only when there has been a sale or a commercial leasing of goods. Fraud liability and negligence liability may arise without regard to the nature of the transaction involving the plaintiff or the defendant.

The strict tort liability concept may be applied whenever there is any transfer of possession of goods, whether the transaction is a sale, a free distribution of samples, or a commercial leasing of goods.

Neither the strict tort liability concept nor the UCC warranties apply to transactions that are regarded as the sale of services, although a modern trend appears to extend the sale-of-goods concepts to service transactions. Likewise, consumer protection laws frequently treat contracts for services the same as contracts for the sale of goods. If one views the situation from the standpoint of the buyer, many of the reasons which give rise to the modern law of product liability also urge the extension of those concepts to service contracts. It is probable that this will occur in time. Contracts for computer services have sometimes been interpreted as sales contracts.

§ 26:18. Improper Product.

(a)   Defect. The mere fact that harm is sustained by using the defendant's product does not impose liability under any theory. There must be some defect in the product which was caused or not removed by the defendant. If the product is defective when it leaves the control of the defendant, this element of product liability is satisfied.

(b)   Design. Is a product defective because it could have been designed better? At present neither negligence nor warranty liability can be based on the fact that the product could have been designed so that it would have been safer, whether this would have prevented the occurrence of any harm or would have reduced the extent of injury when harm occurred. The law does not require that a product be "accident-proof" or "crash-proof." At the same time, a product must be designed so that undue harm will not be caused when the product is involved in a collision or accident.

Moreover, if the design of a product is imperfect the making of the product in that manner may impose negligence liability on the manufacturer for harm or constitute a breach of the warranty of merchantability by rendering the product not fit for its normal use. Moreover, if the design is such as to constitute a danger because the user is not likely to be aware of the danger, liability may be imposed. Thus warranty and strict tort liability have been imposed because the absence of safety devices made the product unreasonably dangerous. Hence, the manufacturer of an auto camper is liable when the porous construction of the floor permitted carbon monoxide fumes to penetrate the camper and kill the occupants.[34]

(c) **Malfunction.** The fact that the product doesn't work or does not work properly may constitute a breach of an implied warranty of fitness for ordinary use or for a particular purpose or an express warranty as to performance.

A malfunction of the product is not sufficient to impose liability for negligence or strict tort. However, when the product is destroyed so that it is impossible to make a post-accident examination to determine whether there was a defect, there is an increasing tendency of the courts to find that malfunction before or at the time of the accident is sufficient evidence of a defect or that the mere fact of malfunctioning was a sufficient basis for a recovery, although the plaintiff could not prove that there was a defect. For example, when the evidence establishes a malfunctioning of the steering wheel of an automobile which caused the automobile to cross into the other lane and strike the oncoming plaintiff, it will generally be held that the "defect" element is satisfied when the lane-crossing car is destroyed by a fire following the collision or is so badly damaged that an examination of the steering mechanism is useless. In many instances it is sufficient to establish that the malfunctioning of the product was the cause of the harm, without specifically establishing why the product malfunctioned.

(d) **Foreseeable Misuse.** A product is "defective" for the purpose of the product liability principles when it is not safe to use in either the way the product was intended to be used or when used for a purpose not intended by the defendant but which was reasonably foreseeable.

§ 26:19. Instructions and Warnings. When the proper manner of use is part of the common knowledge of the community and the dangers are obvious, there is ordinarily no duty to furnish instructions as to use or to furnish with warnings as to any dangers. If the product is not a common object, instructions may be essential to enable the user to know how to use it. In such case the product alone without the necessary instructions would not satisfy the warranty of fitness for normal use embraced within the warranty of merchantability nor the warranty of fitness for a particular purpose. Furthermore, if use of the product without instructions would expose the user or bystanders to an unreasonable risk of harm, the absence of instructions would make the product defective so as to impose liability for negligence or strict tort upon the defendant.

---

[34] Gardner v General Motors Corp. (CA10 Colo) 507 F2d 525.

The duty to warn of dangers is not discharged by directions which explain the manner of operating the product, but which do not specifically identify the dangers inherent in deviating from those directions.[35] When the failure to follow instructions would expose the user to a danger that might not be anticipated, a manufacturer has the duty to warn of such danger. For example when violating instructions as to proper use could cause a fire, the manufacturer is liable for a fire resulting from a failure to warn of such danger. Consequently, where placing a stereo receiver on a soft or yielding surface would block the bottom vents of the unit and cause overheating which could result in a fire, the manufacturer was negligent even though stating that the unit should not be placed on a soft or yielding surface when not specifically warning that fire could result from so doing. A mere warning to keep a product away from fire is not a sufficient warning that fumes from the product could ignite and explode with terrific force several hours after the product had been used. When the injured person ignored the warning on the product, it is immaterial whether the warning was adequate.

Various state and federal statutes regulate the subject of instructions and warnings as to certain kinds of products, such as drugs, explosives, and inflammable products. A defendant who fails to furnish the proper instructions and warnings may be liable for violation of such a statute as well as subject to product liability for the harm caused. If a seller knows that a buyer is purchasing for resale and the product is not "packaged" in the manner required by law for a lawful resale, the seller would be guilty of a breach of the implied warranty of merchantability.[36]

§ 26:20. Cause of Harm. The harm sustained by the product liability plaintiff must have been "caused" by the defendant. Here the concepts are the same as in the case of "proximate" in tort liability, discussed in § 4:2(d), without regard to whether suit is brought for negligence or on the theory of strict tort liability or breach of warranty. Consequently the mere fact that the plaintiff has sustained harm does not impose liability. The plaintiff must establish that it was the product manufactured or sold by the defendant which caused the plaintiff's harm. Thus it has been held that the fact that the plaintiff became ill after eating food did not establish that there was a breach of warranty with respect to such food.[37]

§ 26:21. Intervention of Dealer or Processor. In many product liability situations, the product is distributed or resold by a dealer. The question then arises whether a defendant manufacturer is shielded from liability to the ultimate purchaser or to a third person if it is the act or omission of the dealer which makes the product defective.

If the negligence of the dealer makes the product defective, the manufacturer is not liable when there is no reason to foresee such negligence. To illustrate, if the

---

[35] Good v A. B. Chance Co., (ColoApp), 565 P2d 217.

[36] Frequently the reselling buyer will require a seller to make an express warranty as to compliance of the product with government regulations, so that any violation of the government regulation constitutes a breach of the express warranty. The breach of the government standard is often sufficient to establish negligence liability of the defendant and to establish the defective character of the product both for negligence and strict tort liability.

[37] Minder v Cielito Lindo Restaurant, 67 CalApp3d 972, 136 CalRptr 915.

mechanic of the car dealer tightens the steering mechanism of an automobile but does so in an improper way which causes a cable to snap and this makes the car go out of control, the manufacturer is not liable for this intervening act.

A more difficult problem arises when the manufacturer expects or depends upon the dealer or other intervening processor to make the product safe for its ultimate use. In such cases, the manufacturer may be protected from negligence liability but is not protected from strict tort liability. For example, if the manufacturer expects or depends upon the dealer to make the car safe for use, the manufacturer is not liable for negligence when the dealer fails to make the car safe if the manufacturer had no reason to foresee that there would be such failure. In contrast, if the manufacturer would be liable to the injured person for strict tort liability because of a defect in the car, that liability cannot be avoided by delegating the function of checking or repairing to a distributor or dealer. That is, the manufacturer's duty to put a "safe" car into the channels of commerce cannot be delegated to another.

§ 26:22. Accident and Misconduct of Plaintiff. A seller or manufacturer is not liable for damages when the harm to the plaintiff is caused not by a defect in the goods but by an accident or by the conduct of the plaintiff. Consequently, there is no product liability when the buyer removed a protective guard from the product and was injured by tripping on some other object and falling into the unguarded part of the product.

The defendant is generally not liable on any theory of product liability when the harm was caused by the plaintiff's misuse of the product or unreasonable voluntary use of the product with knowledge that it was defective.

Use of a product without following directions bars recovery from the manufacturer where the product would not have caused harm if the directions had been followed. For example, a manufacturer sold a cleaning fluid. The label stated that it was "heavy concentrated" and stated how much water should be added before using. A purchaser who failed to add the required amount of water could not recover from the manufacturer when she was burned by the undiluted cleaner because it was not the product but her failure to follow instructions which caused the harm.[38]

§ 26:23. Notice of Defect.

(a)   Breach of Warranty. A buyer cannot recover for breach of warranty unless the buyer gave the seller notice of the defect constituting the breach of warranty within a reasonable time after the defect was discovered or should have been discovered.[39] This notice requirement does not apply when the buyer sues a remote defendant and not the seller from whom the buyer purchased the goods. The giving of notice of the defect is sufficient. The buyer is not required to return the goods at the same time.

(1)   Form of Notice. The notice of the defect may be oral or written. The Code does not set any formal requirement for the notice.[40]

---

[38] Evershine Products, Inc. v Schmitt, 132 GaApp 34, 202 SE2d 228.
[39] UCC § 2-607(3); Ford v Barnard, Sumner & Putnam Co., 1 MassApp 192, 294 NE2d 467.
[40] Lynx, Inc. v Ordnance Products, Inc., 273 Md 1, 327 A2d 502.

As the buyer must be able to prove that the required notice was given, it is desirable to send a written notice of defects or a letter confirming a prior oral notification. Moreover, it may be necessary to give a written statement of defects or deceptive practices in order to establish the basis for proceeding under a state consumer protection statute.

(2) Content of Notice. A notice of defects is sufficient when it informs the seller that there is something wrong. The buyer is not required to specify the exact cause of the trouble or to identify the defect. The notice is not required to threaten litigation nor make any claim for money damages.

(b) Tort Liabilities. When the product liability plaintiff sues for fraud, negligence, or strict tort, there is no requirement that notice was given to the defendant of the existence of the defect.

Ordinarily, the facts are such that the strict tort liability plaintiff is generally a subpurchaser or a third person so that no notice could have been given of any defect prior to the injury. For example, the buyer of an automobile could be required to give notice to the seller that the brakes of the car were defective; but it is obvious that a bystander who is run over when the brakes failed to hold would not know in advance of being run over that there was any defect, or the identity of the car which would be involved, or the identity of the manufacturer who should be notified.

§ 26:24. Disclaimer of Liability. With some exceptions, a party may disclaim warranty liability under a sale or commercial leasing if the requirements of UCC § 2-316 are satisfied. When the defendant is negligent, a disclaimer of liability will often be held invalid as contrary to public policy, particularly when the sale relates to consumer goods which the buyer is purchasing for consumer use, as contrasted with a merchant purchasing for resale. When the defendant would otherwise be liable for strict tort, a disclaimer of liability made by the buyer does not bind the buyer nor any third person injured by the product.

In any case, a disclaimer included in a contract by the defendant will be strictly interpreted against the defendant and not given wider application than is required by its terms. For example, when a sales contract disclaims the seller's liability for breach of warranty, it will not have any effect on product liability based on theories other than warranty. That is, a disclaimer of warranty liability does not disclaim product liability based on fraud, negligence, or strict tort.[41]

---

[41] Sterner Aero AB v Page Airmotive, Inc. (CA10 Okla) 499 F2d 709.

CASES FOR CHAPTER 26

Nobility Homes of Texas, Inc. v. Shivers

(TexCivApp) 539 SW2d 190 (1976)

Shivers and his wife purchased a mobile home from Hurley. Because of many defects, the home had a market value of approximately $9,000 less than the contract price. The buyers sued the manufacturer, Nobility Homes of Texas, for this amount. From a judgment in favor of the plaintiffs, Nobility Homes appealed.

DIES, C.J. . . . Hurley had previously purchased this unit from the defendant, the manufacturer thereof. Hurley was not an agent for the defendant. . . .

Defendant . . . asserts that it could not be liable for any damages to plaintiffs because there was no privity of contract between them, and plaintiffs are only seeking economic loss. . . . The generally recognized landmark case for support of the principle that privity is not required in pure economic loss cases is *Santor v A & M Karagheusian, Inc.,* 44 N.J. 52, 207 A.2d 305 (1965). There, Santor brought suit against the manufacturer of a carpet which he had purchased from one of its distributors. The only contract was between Santor and the distributor, which had subsequently gone out of business. Santor sought recovery only for the loss of value of the carpeting.

After a thorough discussion of the positions of the various states and the concomitant rationale of the divergent views, the New Jersey Supreme Court held that privity was not necessary to maintain an action by a consumer against the manufacturer for redress of an economic loss. The Court restated the holdings which do not require privity for recovery in instances of personal injury and said:

> "But we see no just cause for recognition of the existence of an implied warranty of merchantability and a right to recovery for breach thereof regardless of lack of privity of the claimant in the one case [as in personal injury] and the exclusion of recovery in the other simply because loss of value of the article sold is the only damage resulting from the breach. . . .
>
> "From the standpoint of principle, we perceive no sound reason why the implication of reasonable fitness should be attached to the transaction and be actionable against the manufacturer where the defectively made product has caused personal injury, and not actionable when inadequate manufacture has put a worthless article in the hands of an innocent purchaser who has paid the required price for it. In such situations considerations of justice require a court to interest itself in originating causes and to apply the principle of implied warranty on that basis, rather than to test its application by whether personal injury or simply loss of bargain resulted from the breach

of the warranty. True, the rule of implied warranty had its gestative stirrings because of the greater appeal of personal injury claim. But, once in existence, the field of operation of the remedy should not be fenced in by such a factor." *Santor v A and M Karagheusian, Inc.,* supra at 309.

The court accepted these logical principles of equity and incorporated with them the substantive law of strict liability in tort. It again refused to accept the personal injury/economic loss dichotomy and held that only through tort liability would the burden of the injury be placed where it should be—on the maker of the product. This is because, though the breach arose initially from the sales contract, it was a " 'tortious wrong suable by a noncontracting party . . .' ".

It is our opinion that the interests of equity and justice will best be served by accepting the view that privity in cases now under consideration should not be required. Matters of public policy dictate that no different treatment should be accorded in instances where a consumer suffers personal injury or damage to other property, and situations where the harm is the diminution of value of the product itself and the resulting economic loss. In both circumstances there is an "injury" to the public sector, whose only action in the commercial transaction is to purchase goods placed in the stream of commerce by the manufacturer. To insulate the maker of the goods under these conditions can result only by resort to reasoning which is no longer viable in our current economic practices and present sense of justice. . . .

A practical consideration also supports the position advanced by this Court today; the problem of wasteful litigation. In quoting from *Randy Knitwear, Inc. v American Cyanamid Company,* supra (226 N.Y.S.2d 363, 181 N.E.2d 399) the Court in Santor restated: "It is true that in many cases the manufacturer will ultimately be held accountable for the falsity of his representations, but only after an unduly wasteful process of litigation. Thus, if the consumer or ultimate business user sues and recovers, for breach of warranty, from his immediate seller and if the latter, in turn, sues and recovers against his supplier in recoupment of his damages and costs, eventually, after several separate actions by those in the chain of distribution, the manufacturer may finally be obliged to shoulder the responsibility which should have been his in the first instance." . . . The pursuit of such wasteful litigation which is often inadequate should not be required in this State.

This jurisdication should refrain from the "narrow legalistic view" that privity is necessary before the public may recover for damages suffered when the product diminishes in value and/or becomes worthless because of the defective workmanship of the manufacturer. . . .

[Judgment affirmed]

Werner v Montana

(NH) 378 A2d 1130 (1977)

Werner purchased the White Eagle, a wooden sailing sloop, from Montana. The sloop leaked and Werner brought an action to cancel the sale on the ground that there had been an express oral warranty that it would not leak. Montana contended that no warranty was stated in any of the writings involved in the transaction and that the parol evidence rule prevented proof of statements made in the course of negotiations and that accordingly there was no express warranty. The case was heard by a master who recommended that judgment be entered for Werner. Montana appealed.

LAMPRON, J. . . . Plaintiff put the White Eagle into the water. After allowing ordinarily sufficient time for the planking to swell, or "make up," to form a watertight hull, plaintiff found that the White Eagle still leaked and could not be sailed. Plaintiff then discovered that there was extensive dry rot in the hull and that the cost of repairs would be substantial. After some discussions with defendant in the course of the summer concerning the problem, on September 8, 1972, plaintiff wrote defendant a letter complaining about the dry rot and unseaworthiness of the White Eagle and demanding that defendant take back the White Eagle and refund the purchase price. Defendant refused and plaintiff brought this action.

The basis for plaintiff's action is that there was a breach of an express warranty. [UCC §] 2-313. Plaintiff alleged that defendant, in the course of negotiations prior to sale, made certain statements to the effect that the White Eagle would "make up" when placed in the water and become watertight, and that such statements amounted to an express

warranty as to the sloop's condition. Defendant argues that any statements made by the defendant prior to sale could not be admitted or considered as constituting an express warranty by virtue of [UCC §] 2-202 (Parol or extrinsic Evidence Rule). . . .

Under the Uniform Commercial Code an express warranty may be created by a seller who makes "any affirmation of fact or promise . . . to the buyer which relates to the goods and becomes part of the basis of the bargain." [UCC §] 2-313(1)(a). In addition, "any description of the goods which is made part of the basis of the bargain creates an express warranty that the goods shall conform to the description." [UCC §] 2-313(1)(b).

In general, affirmations of fact made by a seller about the goods being sold are considered a part of the description of the goods and are regarded as forming a part of the sales agreement. Uniform Laws Comment 3 to [UCC §]2-313; 1 R. Anderson, Uniform Commercial Code § 2-313:45 (2d ed. 1970). There was evidence that during the course of negotiations the parties had discussed the ship's watertightness and that defendant had told plaintiff that the White Eagle would become watertight once placed in water and allowed sufficient time to "make up." Considering the negotiations of the parties as a whole, particularly plaintiff's concern with whether the White Eagle was watertight, and considering the importance of watertightness for a ship, these assurances by defendant regarding the condition of the White Eagle could properly be considered as making part of the basis of the bargain. See 1 R. Anderson, *supra* § 2-313:7. Therefore, . . . the master did not err in ruling that these affirmations or descriptions of the White Eagle by the defendant created an express warranty under both [UCC §] 2-313(1)(a) and (b).

[UCC §] 2-202 excludes evidence of any additional oral agreement or terms when a written agreement is intended by the parties to be a final expression of their agreement. However, unless the writing was intended as a complete and exclusive statement of the terms of the agreement, evidence of consistent additional terms are admissible. [UCC §] 2-202(b). There was no evidence that the writings in this case, the notice of intent to purchase, the bill of sale, and the advertisement incorporated therein by reference, were intended by the parties as constituting a complete and exclusive statement of the terms of their agreement. The master therefore could properly find defendant's statements regarding the White Eagle's watertightness as being an express warranty which was a consistent additional term of the agreement . . . 1 R. Anderson, Uniform Commercial Code § 2-313:22; R. Nordstrom, Sales § 53 (1970). . . .

Defendant argues that plaintiff failed to prove a breach of warranty because the evidence did not establish that the leaking of the White Eagle was caused by the dry rot, or by any other cause, and therefore did not establish that the leaking constituted a breach of the alleged warranty. It is true that the master found there was no evidence to connect the leaking with the dry rot in the hull. However, the master did not find that defendant had made any warranty that the White Eagle was free from dry rot. Rather, the master found that defendant had told plaintiff that the White Eagle was suitable for sailing, and that defendant's statements which created the warranty were to the effect that the White Eagle had not leaked and would not leak after a sufficient swelling period was allowed. The master found that the White Eagle's "inability to 'make up' " created a breach of this warranty. While it is true that there was no evidence to establish the cause of the leaking, such evidence was not necessary. The plaintiff was required only to establish the existence of an express warranty and to establish that the White Eagle was defective in that its condition did not comply with the condition warranted by defendant . . . The evidence was undisputed that the White Eagle continued to leak and was not seaworthy despite being allowed to soak for over six weeks. Plaintiff therefore met his burden establishing the boat's defective condition.

Defendant also argues that any warranty made related only to the condition of the White Eagle at the time of sale and that plaintiff failed to prove that the White Eagle was not as warranted at that time. While an express warranty generally related only to the condition of the goods at the time of sale, a warranty may relate to another point in time if so specified. 1 R. Anderson, supra § 2-313:12. The warranty found by the master to have been made by defendant was that the White Eagle would not leak; that it would be tight after a two-week swelling period. The discussions between the parties prior to sale occurred after September 1, 1971, and the bill of sale was dated January 1, 1972. It would not be until the following spring or summer that plaintiff would have the first occasion to put the White Eagle in the water and allow for the swelling defendant indicated would occur. The warranty as to tightness

therefore did not relate simply to the condition of the White Eagle as of the date of sale, but necessarily related to the time when the boat would be put in the water and prepared for sailing. Under these circumstances defendant's statement amounted to an express warranty . . . See R. Anderson, Uniform Commercial Code § 2-313:12.1 (1970-1974 Cumulative Supp.). . . .

Although reliance on the part of the buyer is not necessary for the creation of an express warranty, the master properly found that plaintiff did in fact rely on defendant's affirmation that the boat would not leak and it became part of the bargain. . . .

[Judgment affirmed]

Lewis and Sims, Inc. v Key Industries, Inc.

16 Wash App 619, 557 P2d 1318 (1976)

Lewis and Sims, a contracting corporation, was installing a water and sewer system in the town of North Pole, Alaska. It ordered pipe stating only the size and quantity of the pipe and that the pipe be "coal tar enamel lined." The pipe could not withstand the intense cold and before the pipe lines could be constructed, the enamel lining had pulled away from the pipe. Because of this it was rejected and Lewis and Sims were required to purchase other pipe. It then sued the suppliers of the original pipe for damages for breach of a warranty of fitness for a particular purpose. From a judgment in favor of Lewis and Sims, the defendants appealed.

SWANSON, J. . . . In order to invoke the provisions of the Section 2-315 warranty, the evidence must be sufficient to show that (1) the seller at the time of contracting had reason to know the particular purpose for which the goods were required, and (2) that the buyer relied upon the seller's skill or judgment in selecting or furnishing suitable goods. . . . 1 R. Anderson, *Uniform Commercial Code*, § 2-315:4 (1970). In marked contrast to other commercial code warranties, it is imperative to the existence of a warranty of fitness for a particular purpose that the buyer relied upon the seller's skill or judgment in selecting the appropriate goods. In so relying, the buyer generally is ignorant of the fitness of the article offered by the seller and thus relies on the superior skill, information or judgment the seller possesses and not on his own judgment.

In *Frisken v Art Strand Floor Coverings, Inc.,* 47 Wash.2d 587, 288 P.2d 1087 (1955),* the owner of a commercial building entered into an agreement with a corporation engaged in the business of selling and laying floor coverings whereby the latter contracted [to] furnish and install asphalt tile on the floor of the premises. The building's floor was concrete covered with magnesite. The corporation's agent, after viewing the premises, recommended a certain tile suitable for the building owner's needs. The tile, as it turned out, was incompatible with the magnesite underflooring such that the tile floor became uneven and buckled. Our Supreme Court held that the seller impliedly warranted that the floor would be fit for the intended use regardless of the structure of the underflooring. In so holding, the court found that the buyer was ignorant of the risk involved in covering magnesite with tile and that she relied on the seller's knowledge and judgment in the matter. . . . *Accord, Catania v Brown,* 4 Conn. Cir. 344, 231 A.2d 668 (1967); . . . In similar fashion, the Catania case involved a fairly typical situation where application of the implied warranty of fitness for a particular purpose is deemed appropriate. In Catania, the buyer asked the seller, who was engaged in the retail paint business, to recommend a paint to cover the exterior stucco walls of the buyer's house. The seller was told that the stucco was in a chalky or powdery condition. Based on this information, the seller recommended a particular brand name product and also provided instructions on its use. Subsequent to its application, the paint began to flake and blister. The Connecticut Supreme Court found that the implied warranty liability existed since the buyer justifiably relied on the superior information, skill, and judgment of the seller.

If, as has been shown, liability for the implied warranty for fitness for a particular purpose flows from the existence of: (1) reliance by the buyer on the judgment of the seller and (2) the fact that the seller had reason to know the buyer's particular purpose, . . . then it conversely follows that no warranty of fitness for a particular purpose arises when it is clear that the buyer orders goods according to his own specifications. As stated in 1 R. Anderson, *Uniform Commercial Code,* §2-315:21 at 666 (1970), a buyer does not rely upon the seller's judgment,

skill, or experience where an article, although intended for a disclosed purpose, is to be made or manufactured or furnished by the seller in accordance with plans and specifications furnished by the purchaser; there is in such case no implied warranty that the article, if in accordance with the specifications, will answer the intended purpose, or in other words, no warranty against unfitness arising out of defects in the plans and specifications. . . .

We turn now from the abstract legal aspects of the warranty of fitness for purpose to a discussion of that warranty as it applies to the facts before us. In order to prevail in the instant action, the respondent-buyer was under an obligation to show that he relied on the seller's judgment in choosing a pipe that best suited the needs of an underground water-sewer system in North Pole, Alaska. While the trial court apparently believed such reliance existed, we are at a loss to find substantial evidence within the record to sustain the trial court. On the contrary, after carefully reviewing the record, we find ample evidence to conclude that Lewis and Sims ordered a specific size and type of pipe and that any deviation from the coal tar enamel lined pipe that was manufactured would not have been accepted by Lewis and Sims. In short, neither supplier was asked for its recommendations, nor did either select the pipe or lining to be used. The warranty for fitness for a particular purpose was not meant to be applied in a situation such as we face today. The central tenet—reliance upon the skill, judgment, or experience of the seller—is not manifested. What is apparent is the fact that both parties to this action knew what was desired, and that desire was fulfilled. It is also important to note that the pipe itself was not negligently manufactured; rather, the lining was susceptible to cracking upon exposure to extreme cold. . . .

In summary then, we find no breach of an implied warranty of fitness for purpose owed to Lewis and Sims . . .

[Judgment reversed]

Sams v Ezy-Way Foodliner Company

157 Maine 10, 170 A2d 160 (1961)

Sams purchased some frankfurts at Ezy-Way's Self Service Food supermarket. They were contained in a sealed plastic bag labeled "Jordan's Hot Dogs." The manufacturer had a good reputation and there was no evidence of any negligence. In eating one of the hot dogs, Sams was cut by pieces of glass

---

* This case arose before the enactment of the present-day Uniform Commercial Code; however, the same principles are still applicable.

which it contained. He sued Ezy-Way for his damages. From a judgment in favor of the supermarket, Sams appealed.

WILLIAMSON, C.J. . . . The controlling issue in this action of a plaintiff purchaser-consumer against a defendant-retailer is whether there is a "sealed container exception" from the implied warranty of merchantability. . . .

A "hot dog" containing glass is, of course, not fit to eat and is therefore not of merchantable quality. . . .

The fact that the frankfurts were sold in a self-service market does not affect the result. The sign, or label, effectively described the goods in the market and in the package. The printed word was the silent salesman. . . . Compare Mead v Coca Cola Bottling Co., [329 Mass. 440, 108 NE2d 757] holding a warranty of merchantability . . . attached to the sale of coca cola in an automatic vending machine. . . .

We come to the issue of whether the retailer of food in a sealed container is insulated from an implied warranty of merchantability. . . . We make no distinction between [a] can of asparagus . . . , [a] package of macaroni . . . , bread wrapped in paper and sealed [referring to cases involving such containers], and the "hot dogs" in the sealed plastic bag. In each instance we have a sealed container or an original package effectively preventing inspection by the retailer at any time and by the purchaser until the container is opened. The basis of the "sealed container exception" is that the purchaser could not have placed reliance upon the retailer's skill or judgment in determining that the contents were fit to eat. . . .

Vast changes have taken place in the manufacture and distribution of food products. . . . The purchase of food in a can, jar, package, or sealed bag under brand or trade name is commonplace. The pantry shelf, the refrigerator, and the "deep freeze" evidence the fact. Sales are made over the counter, at self-service markets, and by vending machines. Inspection of such products which will uncover the defect within the container, as the defective asparagus, or the pin in the bread, is impossible as a practical matter until at least the container is opened, or in many instances, as here, until the product is eaten. . . .

If the frankfurts here had not been sold in the sealed bag, inspection would not have disclosed the glass within the edible casing. . . .

[Judgment for defendant reversed and action remanded]

Code Comment: The same conclusion would be made under the UCC. The considerations which persuaded the court in the Sams case would be equally persuasive under the UCC.

Robinson v Branch Moving & Storage Company, Inc.

28 NC App 244, 221 SE2d 81 (1976)

Robinson was employed by the Branch Moving & Storage Company. It sold one of its trucks to him. He was eager to purchase the truck and agreed to purchase it "as it was" without inspecting the truck. When a number of repairs were thereafter required because of defects in the truck, Robinson sued Branch Moving for breach of warranty. From a judgment in his favor, Branch Moving appealed.

MORRIS, J. . . . Plaintiff buyer stated that the truck was purchased "as it was" at the time of sale and he must bear the loss. Throughout this transaction the defendant seller diligently and repeatedly advised the plaintiff of the risk he was taking by purchasing the unit without an inspection. There is, of course, some question as to whether an inspection would or could have revealed any defects in the truck, but notwithstanding that issue, we hold that where a buyer insists on closing the sale he should not later be allowed to shift the unfortunate results of his own shortsightedness onto his defendant seller. The Uniform Commercial Code is designed to structure the course of sales transactions efficiently and fairly and foster ". . . greater flexibility[,] . . . [provide] relief from unconscionable provisions and . . . [engender] some degree of protection from the hardship resulting from the failure of conditions which it had been assumed would continue to exist." 1 Anderson, Uniform Commercial Code, § 2-101:3, p. 200 (1970). The Code, however, is not a law which guarantees every buyer and every seller a "good deal."

Under the Uniform Commercial Code . . . an implied warranty can . . . be excluded or modified. . . . Moreover, the fact that this exclusion, . . . is oral does not vitiate its utility or relevance.

"In view of the fact that a writing is not desired merely for the sake of having a writing but in order to assure that the buyer is adequately protected against surprise disclaimers, it would seem that a court if faced with the issue of whether a disclaimer had to be in writing, would readily conclude that where the oral waiver was in fact bargained for and was not a surprise term that the buyer is bound by it. In view of the fact that the prime objective of the section of the Code relating to the exclusion or modification of warranties is the prevention of unbargained-for disclaimers, it is probable that if the circumstances are such that the buyer has consciously made an oral waiver of warranties, the court will give effect to such waiver even though it is an oral, and not a written waiver." 1 Anderson, supra, § 2-316:21, at 691-692.

Furthermore, "[i]f there is writing . . . and such a writing does not contain the oral clause relied on by the seller as a waiver or limitation of warranties, a question [then] arises under UCC § 2-202 as to whether parol evidence is admissible to establish the existence of such an alleged oral term of the contract." . . . Parol evidence . . . may be used in order to help explain and supplement this particular lease-purchase agreement. When so supplemented, it is clear that this buyer purchased this truck "as is" and cannot raise an implied warranty claim against his seller. . . .

[Judgment reversed and action remanded]

QUESTIONS AND CASE PROBLEMS

1. What social forces are affected by the abolition of the requirement of privity in product liability suits?

2. Compare (a) an express guarantee, (b) an express warranty, and (c) an implied warranty.

3. Compare (1) warranty liability, (2) strict tort liability, and (3) negligence liability, with respect to (a) fault of the defendant, and (b) disclaimer of liability.

4. Compare (a) a merchant seller, and (b) a casual seller, with respect to implied warranty liability.

5. An automobile manufacturer was sued for negligence in the construction of the automobile which injured the plaintiff. The manufacturer raised the defense that it had sold the automobile "as is." Was this a good defense? [Fleming v Stoddard Wendle Motor Co., 70 Wash 2d 465, 423 P2d 926]

6. A buyer purchased a new automobile car wash from a dealer. It washed the cars effectively but it would knock off external accessories such as mirrors and radio antennas. When the buyer complained, the seller stated that the contract made no provision with respect to such matters. Was this a valid defense? [See Auto-Teria, Inc. v Ahern, (Ind App), 352 NE2d 774]

7. *A* purchased a refrigerator from the *B* store. The written contract stated that the refrigerator was sold "as is" and that the warranty of merchantability and all warranties of fitness were excluded. This was stated in large capital letters printed just above the line on which *A* signed his name. The refrigerator worked properly for a few weeks and then stopped. *B* refused to do anything about it because of the exclusion of the warranties made by the contract. *A* claimed that this exclusion was not binding because it was unconscionable. Was *A* correct? [See Avery v Aladdin Products Div., Nat. Service Industries, Inc., 128 GaApp 266, 196 SE2d 357]

8. Frank purchased a used automobile from the McCafferty Ford Co. The person who sold the auto to McCafferty was not the owner, and the true owner successfully reclaimed it from Frank. Frank then sued McCafferty although McCafferty had said nothing about the title of the automobile. Was McCafferty liable to Frank? [Frank v McCafferty Ford Co., 192 Pa Super 435, 161 A2d 896]

9. Page purchased a camper from Camper City. While driving in the camper, the seat broke and Page was injured. She went immediately to Camper City and reported what had happened. After several years, she sued Camper City. It asserted that it was not

liable because written notice of the defect had not been given to it. Was this a valid defense? [Page v Camper City & Mobile Home Sales, 292 Ala 562, 297 So2d 810]

10. A manufacturer advertised its product in national magazines. The advertisement induced a buyer to purchase the product. The product did not live up to the statements in the advertisement. The buyer claimed that there was a breach of warranty. The manufacturer contended that the statements in the advertisement were obviously sales talk and therefore could not constitute a warranty. Was this a valid defense? [See Westric Battery Co. v Standard Electric Co. (CA10 Colo) 482 F2d 1307]

11. Alden Leeds purchased dry organic chlorine from Monsanto Company. The chemical was stored in the Leeds Terminal, Inc. Because of a defect in the chemicals, a fire started which destroyed the warehouse. When Monsanto sued Alden Leeds for the purchase price, Leeds Terminal intervened to assert a claim in strict tort for the destruction of its warehouse. The objection was raised that the warehouse was not a buyer or user of the product and that the loss sustained was economic. Was Leeds Terminal entitled to recover in strict tort? [Monsanto Co. v Alden Leeds, Inc., 130 NJSuper 245, 326 A2d 90]

12. Lowe purchased a lawnmower from Sears and Roebuck. It had been manufactured by the American Machine & Foundry Company. Lowe was cut while using the mower. He sued the manufacturer and Sears. He claimed that Sears was liable for negligence on the ground that there was a latent defect and that Sears had failed to test the product to discover the defect. Was Sears liable for negligence? [Lowe v American Machine & Foundry Co., 132 GaApp 572, 208 SE2d 585]

13. The defendant, Zogarts, manufactured and sold a practice device for beginning golfers. The statements on the package stated that the device was completely safe and that a player could never be struck by the golf ball of the device. Hauter was hit by the ball when practicing with the device. He sued Zogarts for fraud, breach of warranty, and strict tort. Zogarts denied liability on the ground that the statements were merely matters of opinion and therefore liability could not be based on them. Was this a valid defense? [Hauter v Zogarts, 14 Cal 104, 120 CalRptr 681, 534 P2d 377]

14. A manufacturer sold a machine to the buyer. The written contract stated that the manufacturer's warranty ran for one year. Two years later, the buyer was injured because of a defect which was in the machine when made but which had not been detected by the manufacturer because of negligence in testing. The buyer sued the manufacturer for the injuries the buyer sustained. The manufacturer raised the defense that warranty liability was limited to one year. The buyer claimed that he was not barred because of this limitation as he was suing for negligence for failure to test and for strict tort for a defective product, and that the statute of limitations applicable to such tort actions was six years. Was the buyer barred by one-year limitation in the contract? [See Green v Los Angeles, 40 CalApp3d 819, 115 CalRptr 685]

15. Queen ordered goods by sample from Loomis Bros. Corp., a dealer in that kind of goods. The goods that were delivered conformed to the sample but were not fit for the normal intended use. Loomis claimed that it had fully performed its contract since it was only required to deliver goods that conformed to the sample. Was it correct? [Loomis Bros. Corp. v Queen, (Pa) 17 D&C 2d 482, 46 Del County 79]

16. Filler was a member of the high school baseball team. The coach had purchased sunglasses manufactured by Rayex Corp. for use by the team members. The glasses were advertised and the package described them as "professional" glasses for baseball as "sports-world's finest sunglasses" and that they gave "instant eye protection." Unknown to everyone, the glasses were very thin, with the lens ranging from 1.2 to 1.5 millimeters. Because of this thinness, the glasses, when struck by a baseball, shattered into fine splinters

and injured Filler's right eye. He sued Rayex Corp., claiming that there was a breach of implied warranty of fitness for a particular purpose. Rayex denied liability and raised the defense of lack of privity. Decide. [Filler v Rayex Corp., (CA7 Ind) 435 F2d 336]

17. The buyer purchased an engine to operate an irrigation pump. The buyer selected the engine from a large number that were standing on the floor of the seller's stockroom. A label on the engine stated that it would produce one hundred horsepower. The buyer needed an engine which would generate at least eighty horsepower. In actual use in the buyer's irrigation system, the pump only generated sixty horsepower. The buyer sued the seller for damages. The seller raised the defense that no warranty of fitness for the buyer's particular purpose of operating an irrigation pump had arisen because the seller did not know of the use to which the buyer intended to put the pump and the buyer had not relied on the seller's skill and judgment in selecting the particular pump. Was the seller liable? [See Potter v Ryndall, 22 NC App 129, 205 SE2d 808, cert den 285 NC 661, 207 SE2d 762]

18. McCarty purchased automobile tires from Korvette. The tires were expressly guaranteed against blowouts for the first 36,000 miles. One of the tires blew out at about 7,000 miles and caused McCarty's car to roll over several times. He sued Korvette for the damage. It raised the defense that there was no proof of a defect in the tire. Was this a valid defense? [McCarty v E. J. Korvette, Inc., 28 MdApp 421, 347 A2d 253]

19. Farrior purchased a Ford automobile from Courtesy Ford Sales, Inc. She received a copy of the manufacturer's warranty. When the car proved defective, she brought suit against Courtesy Ford and the Ford Motor Company claiming that they were jointly liable for the breach of the manufacturer's warranty. Was she correct? [Courtesy Ford Sales, Inc. v Farrior, 53 AlaCivApp 94, 298 So2d 26]

20. Eli Lilly manufactured a weed killer called Treflan. Casey purchased some Treflan from a local dealer. It did not kill the weeds. Casey sued Lilly for the damage to his crops resulting from the weeds. Was he entitled to recover? [Eli Lilly & Co. v Casey, (Tex Civ App) 472 SW2d 598]

21. The Yamaha Motor Co. sold a motorcycle to a dealer, Harley Davidson of Essex, New Jersey. The motorcycle was partly assembled, and Yamaha depended upon Harley Davidson to assemble it and make it ready to use. Sabloff purchased a motorcycle made by Yamaha from Harley Davidson. He was injured while riding when the front wheel locked for no apparent reason. He sued Yamaha. It raised the defense that Sabloff had been harmed because Harley Davidson had not assembled the motorcycle in a proper manner. Decide. [Sabloff v Yamaha Motor Co., 113 NJ Super 270, 273 A2d 606]

27 Remedies for Breach of Sales Contract

If one of the parties to a sale fails to perform the contract duties, the law makes several remedies available to the other party. In addition, the parties may have included certain provisions pertaining to remedies in their contract.

A. STATUTE OF LIMITATIONS

Judicial remedies are ordinarily subject to a time limitation which bars resort to the courts after the expiration of a particular period of time. The Uniform Commercial Code supplies the statute of limitations for sales of goods except when suit is brought on a theory of tort, such as negligence, fraud, or strict tort.

§ 27:1. Code Claim. An action for a breach of a sales contract must be commenced within four years after the cause of action arises, regardless of when the aggrieved party learned that there was a cause of action.[1] In the case of a warranty, the breach occurs when tender of delivery is made to the buyer even though no defect then appears and no harm is sustained until a later date. No distinction is made as to the nature of the harm sustained. That is, a claim for personal injury or for property damage resulting from a breach of a sales contract is governed by the four-year statute of limitations.

(a) Future Performance Warranty. When a warranty relates to performance that is to begin in the future, the statute of limitations does not begin to run at the time of the sale but only when the time for the performance would begin. The result is that when a heating system was installed in midsummer under a warranty that it would heat to a certain degree in subzero weather, the cause of action for the breach of warranty did not arise until subzero weather existed. Hence, the statute of limitations did not begin to run in the summer when the heater was sold or installed but later in the winter when the heating system was found to be inadequate.

Where a burial vault was sold under the warranty to give "satisfactory service at all times" the warranty explicitly extended to future performance and from the nature of the goods implied performance over an extended period of time; with the result that the statute of limitations ran from the date the defect was discovered and not from the date of the sale which was made 12 years earlier.

---

[1] UCC § 2-725(1), (2).

(b) Notice of Defect. In addition to bringing suit within four years under the UCC statute of limitations, the plaintiff who sues the person from whom the goods were purchased for damages claimed because of a breach of the sales contract must have given the seller notice of such breach within a reasonable time after the plaintiff discovered or should have discovered the defect.[2]

§ 27:2. Non-Code Claims. When the plaintiff sues on a non-Code theory, even though it relates to goods, the UCC statute of limitations does not apply. Thus, when the plaintiff sues a remote manufacturer on the basis of strict tort liability, the action is subject to the general tort statute of limitations and not the UCC four-year statute.

When the issuer of a credit card sues the credit card holder for the balance due on the credit card account, the suit is merely an ordinary action on a contract and is governed by the contract action statute of limitations and is not subject to the four-year limitation of the Code merely because the original transactions that gave rise to the credit card debt were purchases of goods made by the credit card holder.[3]

B. REMEDIES OF THE SELLER

When a sales contract is broken by the buyer, the seller has a number of remedies available.

§ 27:3. Seller's Lien. In the absence of an agreement for the extension of credit to the purchaser, the seller has a lien on the goods, that is, the right to retain possession of the goods until the seller is paid for them. Even when the goods are sold on credit, the seller has a lien on the goods if the buyer becomes insolvent or if the credit period expires while the goods are in the seller's possession.

The seller's lien may be lost by (a) waiver, as by a later extension of credit, (b) delivery of the goods to a carrier or other bailee, without a reservation of title or possession, for the purpose of delivery to the buyer, (c) acquisition of the property by the buyer or an agent by lawful means, or (d) payment or tender of the price by the buyer.

§ 27:4. Completion or Salvage of Repudiated Contract. It may be that the buyer repudiates or otherwise breaches the contract while the seller has some or all of the goods in either a finished or ready-to-deliver stage or in a partially manufactured stage. If the seller has goods that satisfy or conform to the contract with the buyer, the seller may identify those goods to the contract which the buyer has broken. This will enable the seller to sue the buyer for the purchase price and to make a resale of the goods, holding the buyer responsible for any loss thereon.

If the goods intended for the buyer are in an unfinished state, the seller must exercise reasonable commercial judgment to determine whether (a) to sell them for scrap or salvage, or (b) to complete their manufacture, then identify them to the buyer's contract, and resell them. In any case, the buyer is liable for the loss sustained

---

[2] UCC § 2-607(3)(a).
[3] Harris Trust & Sav. Bank v McCray, 21 IllApp3d 605, 316 NE2d 209.

by the seller if the latter has acted properly. (See p. 450, Detroit Power Screwdriver Co. v Ladney)

§ 27:5. Stopping Delivery by Carrier or Other Bailee.

The goods may be in transit on their way to the buyer. They also may be in the hands of a noncarrier bailee who is to surrender them to the buyer. The seller may stop delivery of the goods to the buyer, without regard to the quantity involved, if the buyer is insolvent. In addition, the seller may stop delivery if the quantity involved is a carload, truckload, or planeload, or more, whenever the buyer has repudiated the contract or failed to make a payment due before delivery or if for any reason the seller would have the right to retain or reclaim the goods.[4]

After the seller regains possession of the goods by stopping delivery, the seller is in the same legal position as though the goods had not been delivered to the carrier or to the bailee and the seller may therefore assert a lien against the goods. When the seller reserves title or the right to possession, the seller need not invoke the right to stop delivery as the seller can withhold the property from the buyer by virtue of such reservation.

(a) Exercise of the Right. The seller exercises the right to stop delivery by notifying the carrier or bailee that the goods are to be returned to or held for the seller. If the seller gives the carrier or bailee proper notice in sufficient time so that through the exercise of due diligence it can stop delivery, the carrier or bailee must obey the seller's order. Any additional cost involved must be borne by the seller. If the carrier or bailee fails to act, it is liable to the seller for any loss sustained.

After proper notice has been given to it, the carrier or bailee must follow the instructions of the seller as to the subsequent disposition of the goods. When a negotiable document of title for the goods is outstanding, however, the carrier or bailee cannot be required to surrender the goods until the document is surrendered to it.

(b) Termination of Right to Stop Delivery. The seller's right to stop delivery is terminated or lost, even though a proper notification is given when (1) the goods have already been delivered to the buyer, (2) a carrier acknowledges the right of the buyer by reshipping at the buyer's direction or by agreeing to hold for the buyer as a warehouser, (3) a bailee in possession acknowledges holding the goods for the buyer, or (4) a negotiable document of title covering the goods is outstanding and is not surrendered to the carrier or bailee.

§ 27:6. Reclamation of Goods Received by Insolvent Buyer.

The buyer may have obtained goods from the seller on credit when, unknown to the seller, the buyer was insolvent. If the buyer made a false written statement to the seller that the buyer was solvent and received the goods within three months after that time, the seller may at any time demand and reclaim the goods sold to the buyer on credit. If the buyer never made a false written statement of insolvency, or made it more than three months before receiving the goods, the seller in order to reclaim the goods, must demand the return of the goods within ten days after they were received by the buyer.

---

[4] UCC § 2-705(1).

§ 27:7. Resale by Seller. When the buyer has broken the contract by wrongfully rejecting the goods, wrongfully revoking acceptance, failing to pay, or repudiating the contract, the seller may resell the goods or the balance of them remaining in the seller's possession, or the goods of which possession has been reacquired as by stopping delivery. After the resale, the seller is not liable to the original buyer upon the contract or for any profit obtained on the resale. On the other hand, if the proceeds are less than the contract price, the seller may recover the loss from the original buyer.[5]

Reasonable notice must be given to the original buyer of the intention to make a private sale. Such notice must also be given of a public sale unless the goods are perishable in nature or threaten to decline rapidly in value. Notice of a public sale must also be given to the general public in such manner as is commercially reasonable under the circumstances.

§ 27:8. Cancellation by Seller. When the buyer wrongfully rejects the goods, wrongfully revokes an acceptance of the goods, repudiates the contract, or fails to make a payment due on or before delivery, the seller may cancel the contract. Such action puts an end to the contract, discharging all obligations on both sides that are still unperformed but the seller retains any remedy with respect to the breach by the buyer.[6] Cancellation revests the seller with title to the goods.

A seller may only cancel the contract if the buyer's breach substantially impairs the value of the contract to the seller. If the seller cancels without such justification, the seller has broken the contract and is liable to the buyer for damages. Consequently, when the buyer's breach did not justify cancellation by the seller, the seller who proceeded to cancel could be held liable to the buyer for damages for nondelivery of the goods.[7]

§ 27:9. Seller's Action for Damages. If the buyer wrongfully refuses to accept the goods or repudiates the contract, the seller may sue for the damages that the seller sustains. In the ordinary case, the amount of damages is to be measured by the difference between the market price at the time and place of the tender of the goods and the contract price.[8]

If this measure of damages does not place the seller in the position in which the seller would have been placed by the buyer's performance, recovery may be permitted of lost profits, together with an allowance for overhead. The seller may in any case recover, as incidental damages, any commercially reasonable charges, expenses, or commissions, incurred in enforcing that remedy, such as those sustained in stopping delivery; in the transportation, care, and custody of the goods after the buyer's breach; and in the return or resale of the goods.[9] Such additional damages are recovered in addition to any other damages that may be recovered by the seller.

The seller is not entitled to recover the contract or purchase price except as stated in § 27:10. Thus a tailor was only allowed to recover costs and lost profit

---

[5] UCC § 2-706(1),(6).

[6] UCC § 2-106(4).

[7] Gulf Chemical and Metallurgical Corp. v Sylvan Chemical Corp. 122 NJSuper 499, 300 A2d 878.

[8] UCC § 2-708(1); Iverson v Schnack, 263 Wis 266, 57 NW2d 400.

[9] UCC § 2-710.

when the customer of the tailor broke the contract after the tailor had cut the cloth for the customer's suit. The tailor could not recover the contract price of the finished suit.

§ 27:10. Seller's Action for the Purchase Price. The seller may bring an action to recover the purchase price, together with incidental damages as described in connection with the action for damages, if (a) the goods have been accepted and there has not been any rightful revocation of acceptance; (b) conforming goods were damaged or destroyed after the risk of loss passed to the buyer; or (c) the seller has identified proper goods to the contract but, after the buyer's breach, has been or will be unable to resell them at a reasonable price.[10] In consequence of these limitations, the right to sue for the contract price, as distinguished from a suit for damages for breach of contract, is a remedy that is not ordinarily available to the seller.

§ 27:11. Repossession of Goods by Seller. The fact that the seller has not been paid does not confer any right to take back or repossess the goods. In modern commercial practice, however, when major items of goods are sold on credit, a provision will ordinarily be included in the contract expressly giving the seller the right to repossess the goods if the buyer defaults in payment,[11] but the mere fact that a sale is made on credit or is an installment sale does not confer any right of repossession.

C. REMEDIES OF THE BUYER

When a sales contract is broken by the seller, the buyer has a number of remedies provided by Article 2 of the Uniform Commercial Code.

§ 27:12. Rejection of Improper Delivery. If the goods or the tender made by the seller do not conform to the contract in any respect, the buyer may reject the goods. For example, the buyer may reject a mobile home when it does not contain the capacity of air conditioner specified by the contract.

When the goods tendered consist of different units some of which conform to the contract, the buyer has the choice of (a) rejecting the entire quantity tendered, (b) accepting the entire tender, or (c) accepting any one or more commercial units and rejecting the rest.[12]

The rejection must be made within a reasonable time after the delivery or tender, and the buyer must notify the seller of the choice made.[13]

After rejecting the goods, the buyer may not exercise any right of ownership as to the goods but must hold them awaiting instructions from the seller.

§ 27:13. Revocation of Acceptance. The buyer may revoke acceptance of the goods when they do not conform to the contract to such an extent that the defect substantially impairs

---

[10] UCC § 2-709(1).
[11] In addition, a security agreement will ordinarily be executed by the buyer, thus giving rise to a secured transaction. See Chapter 34.
[12] UCC § 2-601.
[13] UCC § 2-602(1). The failure to specify the particular ground for rejection may bar the buyer from proving it in a subsequent action. § 2-605. As to the right of the seller to cure the default, see § 2-508.

the value of the contract to the buyer, provided (a) the goods were accepted without knowledge of the nonconformity, because it could not be reasonably discovered, or because the seller assured the buyer that the goods were conforming; or (b) the buyer accepted the goods with knowledge of the nonconformity but reasonably believed that the defect would be cured by the seller.[14] (See p.451, Asciolla v Manter Oldsmobile-Pontiac, Inc.) The buyer may not revoke the acceptance merely because the goods do not conform to the contract unless such nonconformity substantially impairs their value to the buyer. However, proof of substantial impairment is all that is required. It is not necessary that the buyer show that the goods are "worthless." [15] Revocation of acceptance may be made not only with respect to the entire quantity of goods but also with respect to any lot or commercial unit that is nonconforming. A buyer revoking acceptance stands in the same position as though the buyer had rejected the goods when they were originally tendered.

(a)   Notice of Revocation. The acceptance of goods cannot be revoked unless the buyer gives the seller a notice of revocation. The revocation of acceptance is effective when the buyer notifies the seller. It is not necessary that the buyer make an actual return of the goods in order to make the revocation effective.

(b)   Time for Revocation. The notice of revocation must be given within a reasonable time after the buyer discovers that the goods do not conform or after the buyer should have discovered such nonconformity. A buyer is not required to notify the seller of the revocation of acceptance until the buyer is reasonably certain that the nonconformity of the goods substantially impairs the value of the contract. Thus, the mere fact that the buyer suspects that the goods do not conform and that such nonconformity may substantially impair the value of the contract does not in itself require that the buyer immediately give notice.

A buyer is not barred from revoking acceptance of the goods because the buyer has delayed until attempts of the seller to correct the defects proved unsuccessful. For example, the lapse of even a year does not bar revocation of acceptance where the goods are of a complex nature, such as a computer, and the seller was continuously experimenting and assuring the buyer that the goods would be made to work.[16]

(c)   Disposition of Goods After Revocation. After making a revocation of acceptance, the buyer must hold the goods awaiting instructions from the seller. If the buyer has paid the seller in advance, the buyer may retain possession of the goods after revoking acceptance as security for the refund of the money which has been paid.

Ordinarily the revocation of acceptance is cancelled if the buyer, after giving notice of revocation, makes any use of the goods which is inconsistent with the ownership by the seller. This rule is not applied when the non-use of the goods would impose a substantial hardship on the buyer. (See p. 452, Mobile Home Sales Management, Inc. v Brown)

§ 27:14. Reclamation of Goods on Seller's Insolvency.

The buyer may have paid in advance for the goods that are still in the seller's possession. Assuming that the seller then

---

[14] UCC § 2-608(1).
[15] Jacobs v Metro Chrysler-Plymouth, Inc., 125 GaApp 462, 188 SE2d 250.
[16] Carl Beasley Ford, Inc. v Burroughs Corp. (DC Pa) 361 FSupp 325.

becomes insolvent, can the buyer claim the goods from the possession of the seller or is the buyer limited to making a general claim for the refund of the amount paid for them? If the goods have been identified to the contract by either or both the buyer and seller, and the seller becomes insolvent within ten days after payment of the price, the buyer is entitled to recover the goods. The buyer who makes a partial payment has a similar right of reclamation if the seller becomes insolvent within ten days after the first payment is made, but the buyer must pay the balance due.[17]

§ 27:15. Buyer's Action for Damages for Nondelivery. If the seller fails to deliver as required by the contract or repudiates the contract, or if the buyer properly rejects tendered goods or revokes acceptance as to such goods, the buyer is entitled to sue the seller for damages for breach of contract. The buyer is entitled to recover the difference between the market price at the time the buyer learned of the breach and the contract price.[18]

Within a reasonable time after the seller's breach, the buyer may *cover,* that is, procure the same or similar goods elsewhere. If the buyer acts in good faith, the measure of damages for the seller's nondelivery or repudiation is then the difference between the cost of cover and the contract price.[19]

The buyer is not under any duty to cover as far as direct damages are concerned. In contrast, the buyer who does not cover and sustains consequential damages may not recover for those consequential damages that could have been avoided by reasonably effecting cover.[20] For example, when a trucker cannot haul freight for customers because the truck purchased from the seller is defective, the trucker may recover damages equal to the difference between the value of the truck as it was and as it should have been. When the trucker does not cover by purchasing or renting a truck from another source, the trucker is barred from recovering the lost profits that could have been obtained had the original truck been fit for hauling freight. Recovery is denied because the trucker could have prevented this loss by effecting cover.

§ 27:16. Action for Breach of Warranty.

(a)   Notice of Breach. If the buyer has accepted goods that do not conform to the contract or as to which there is a breach of warranty, the buyer must notify the seller of the breach within a reasonable time after the breach is discovered or should have been discovered. Otherwise the buyer is not entitled to complain.

(b)   Measure of Damages. If the buyer has given the necessary notice of breach, the buyer may recover damages measured by the loss resulting in the normal course of events from the breach. If suit is brought for breach of warranty, the measure of damages is the difference between the value of the goods as they were when accepted and the value that they would have had if they had been as warranted.

---

[17] UCC § 2-502.
[18] UCC § 2-713(1). In the case of anticipatory breach, as a repudiation by the seller in advance of the delivery date, the buyer has the option of waiting until the performance date or of treating such repudiation as a breach fixing damages as of that time, unless the buyer effects cover. § 2-610.
[19] UCC § 2-712(2).
[20] UCC § 2-712(3).

The buyer may recover the difference between the contract price and the actual value of the goods.

The buyer may also recover as damages for breach of warranty the loss directly and naturally resulting from that breach. In other words, the buyer may recover for the loss proximately resulting from the failure to deliver the goods as warranted. Thus a buyer may recover the cost of renting other equipment when the equipment sold by the defendant did not work because of its defective condition.[21] When the buyer resells the goods and then, because of their defective condition, is required to indemnify customers of the buyer and the purchasers from those customers, the original buyer may recover such loss from the original seller as consequential damages.[22]

A buyer who is entitled to recover damages from the seller may deduct the amount of such damages from any balance remaining due on the purchase price, provided the seller is notified of the buyer's intention to do so.[23] A buyer sued for the contract price of accepted goods may counterclaim for damages for breach of warranty even though the time for revoking the acceptance or rejecting the goods has passed.

(c)   Notice of Third Party Action Against Buyer. The buyer may be sued in consequence of the seller's breach of warranty, as when the buyer's customers sue because of the condition of the goods which the buyer has resold to them. In such a case, it is optional with the buyer whether or not to give the seller notice of the action and to request the seller to defend that action.[24]

The buyer may also be sued by a third person because of patent infringement. In this case, however, the buyer must give notice of the action to the seller. Moreover, the seller can demand control over the defense of that action.[25]

When the seller is given notice of a suit against the buyer but fails to defend the buyer, the seller cannot dispute the facts shown in that action when the buyer thereafter sues the seller for indemnity.

§ 27:17. Cancellation by Buyer. The buyer may cancel or rescind the contract if the seller fails to deliver the goods or repudiates the contract or if the buyer has rightfully rejected tender of the goods or rightfully revoked acceptance of them. A buyer who cancels the contract is entitled to recover as much of the purchase price as has been paid, including the value of any property given as a trade-in as part of the purchase price. The fact that the buyer cancels the contract does not destroy the buyer's cause of action against the seller for breach of that contract. The buyer may therefore recover from the seller not only any payment made on the purchase price [26] but, in addition, damages for the breach of the contract. The damages represent the difference between the contract price and the cost of cover if the buyer has purchased other goods.[27]

---

[21] Wagner v Dan Unfug Motors, Inc., (ColoApp), 529 P2d 656.

[22] Ambassador Steel Co. v Ewald Steel Co., 33 MichApp 495, 190 NW2d 275.

[23] UCC § 2-717.

[24] UCC § 2-607(5)(a).

[25] UCC § 2-607(3)(b), (5)(b).

[26] Lanners v Whitney, 247 Ore 223, 428 P2d 398.

[27] UCC § 2-712(1), (2). If the buyer has not covered, it is the difference between contract and market price. In any case, the buyer is entitled to recover incidental damages.

The right of the buyer to cancel or rescind the sales contract may be lost by a delay in exercising the right. A buyer loses the right by refusing to permit the seller to attempt to make normal adjustments to remedy the defect. A buyer who with full knowledge of the defects in the goods makes partial payments or performs acts of dominion inconsistent with any intent to cancel cannot thereafter cancel the contract.

The mere fact that a written sales contract was not filled in before signing does not entitle a buyer who has received delivery of the goods to cancel the contract, although consumer protection legislation may prohibit the signing of a sales contract in blank and may give the buyer the right to cancel the sale when this has been done or when the goods have not been delivered.

The fact that the buyer cancels the sale does not destroy liability of the buyer on a check or promissory note given by the buyer in payment.

§ 27:18. Buyer's Resale of Goods. When the buyer has possession of the goods after rightfully rejecting them or after rightfully revoking acceptance, the buyer is treated the same as a seller in possession of goods after the default of a buyer. That is, the aggrieved buyer has a security interest in the goods to protect the claim against the seller and may resell the goods as though the aggrieved buyer were a seller. From the proceeds of the sale, the aggrieved buyer is entitled to deduct any payments made on the price and any expenses reasonably incurred in the inspection, receipt, transportation, care and custody, and resale of the goods.[28]

§ 27:19. Action for Conversion or Recovery of Goods. When, as a result of the sales agreement, ownership passes to the buyer and the seller wrongfully refuses or neglects to deliver the goods, the buyer may maintain any action allowed by law to the owner of goods wrongfully converted or withheld. The obligation of the seller to deliver proper goods may be enforced by an order for specific performance when the goods are "unique or in other proper circumstances."[29] Distributors have been granted specific performance against suppliers to deliver the goods covered by supply contracts.[30] Specific performance will not be granted, however, merely because the price of the goods purchased from the seller has gone up. The buyer can still purchase the goods in the open market and the fact that it will cost more to cover can be compensated for by allowing the buyer to recover greater damages from the seller.

§ 27:20. Remedies for Fraud of Seller. Independently of the preceding remedies, the buyer has the right to sue the seller for damages for the latter's fraud or to cancel the transaction on that ground. As these remedies for fraud exist independently of the provisions of the UCC, the buyer may assert such remedies even though barred by the UCC from exercising any remedy for a breach of warranty. Likewise a limitation on remedies or exclusion of warranty liability has no effect on the buyer's claim for damages for fraud.[31]

[28] UCC § 2-715(1).
[29] UCC § 2-716(1).
[30] Laclede Gas Co. v Amoco Oil Co. (CA8 Mo) 522 F2d 33, later app (CA8 Mo) 531 F2d 942 (propane gas).
[31] Lamb v Bangart (Utah) 525 P2d 602.

When the seller of an automobile fraudulently turns back the odometer, the defrauded buyer may recover damages either under the Federal Motor Vehicle Information and Cost Savings Act, or under the applicable state law governing liability for fraud. Under the federal statute, the buyer recovers three times the actual damages sustained or $1,500, whichever is greater. Under state law, the buyer may recover damages for the loss actually sustained and may also recover punitive damages.

Suit for fraud is generally not a satisfactory solution for the consumer because of the difficulty of proving the existence of fraud. Furthermore, some courts require clear and convincing proof of fraud. Hence, it is not sufficient in those courts to prove the existence of fraud by a mere preponderance of evidence, although that ordinarily is a sufficient degree of proof in civil litigation.

D. CONTRACT PROVISIONS ON REMEDIES

The UCC permits the parties to modify or limit by the terms of their contract the remedies which they otherwise possess.

§ 27:21. Limitation of Damages. The parties to the sales contract may seek to limit or exclude the recovery of damages in case of breach.

(a) Liquidation of Damages. The parties may specify the exact amount of damages which may be recovered in case of breach. Such a *liquidation of damages* is valid if the amount so specified is reasonable in the light of the actual harm that would be caused by the breach, the difficulty of proving the amount of such loss, and the inconvenience and impracticality of suing for damages or enforcing other remedies for breach.[32]

(b) Exclusion of Damages. The sales contract may provide that in case of breach no damages may be recovered or that no consequential damages may be recovered. Such total exclusions are prima facie unconscionable and therefore prima facie not binding, when goods are sold for consumer use and personal injuries are sustained.[33] Thus, a defendant, in such a case, cannot rely on the contract limitation unless the defendant is able to prove that the limitation of liability was commercially reasonable and fair, rather than oppressive and surprising. Moreover, when the seller would be liable to the buyer for damages, the seller cannot exclude liability for personal injuries to members of the buyer's family or household, or to guests of the buyer.[34] In cases not involving consumer goods and personal injuries, the plaintiff has the burden of proving that a limitation on damages is not binding because unconscionable. When the seller knows that the failure of the product, such as a harvester, to perform will cause serious economic loss, a limitation of damages for breach to the return of the purchase price is void as unconscionable.[35]

Whether the exclusion of consequential damages or of all damages is valid when no consumer use or when personal injuries are not involved depends upon a

---

[32] UCC § 2-718(1).

[33] UCC § 2-719(3).

[34] UCC § 2-318.

[35] Steele v Case Co. 197 Kan 554, 419 P2d 902 (pre-Code but citing UCC § 2-719(3) "as evidencing a trend of modern thought").

consideration of all the surrounding circumstances. A court will not determine the validity of such a provision as an abstract question of law. (See p. 455, J. A. Jones Construction Company v Dover)

§ 27:22. Down Payments and Deposits. The buyer may have made a deposit with the seller or an initial or down payment at the time of making the contract. If the contract contains a valid liquidation-of-damages provision and the buyer defaults, the seller must return any part of the down payment or deposit in excess of the amount specified by the liquidated damages clause. In the absence of such a clause, and in the absence of proof of greater damages sustained, the seller's damages are computed as 20 percent of the purchase price or $500, whichever is the smaller. The extent to which the down payment exceeds such amount must be returned to the buyer.

The rule just stated applies to payments made by the buyer in goods as well as in cash as, for example, by making a trade-in. Such goods given in payment are assigned a dollar value for the purpose of determining the payment made by the buyer. If the goods have been resold, their value is the proceeds of the resale; if not, it is the reasonable value of such goods.

§ 27:23. Limitation of Remedies. The parties may validly limit the remedies that are provided by the Code in the case of breach of contract. (See p. 453, Dow Corning Corp. v Capitol Aviation Inc.) Thus a seller may specify that the only remedy of the buyer for breach of warranty shall be the repair or replacement of the goods or that the buyer shall be limited to returning the goods and obtaining a refund of the purchase price. How much further the restrictions may go is not clear, but the limitation is not binding if it is unconscionable.

(a)   Construction Favoring Cumulative Remedies. When the sales contract specifies a remedy to which a party will be entitled, a question arises whether the parties intended that that should be the sole or exclusive remedy. It must be clearly stated that the remedy was to be the exclusive remedy. If it is not clearly stated, the remedy stated will be regarded as being in addition or cumulative to the remedies already existing under the Code.

(b)   Failure of Limited Remedy. A provision limiting the seller's obligation to the repair of the goods or the replacement of defective parts fails of its essential purpose and is not binding when the seller is unable or refuses to make the goods function properly within a reasonable time; because the buyer is entitled to goods which will be fit to the extent required by the particular warranties which have been made expressly or which are implied.[36]

The fact that a product requires more repair service than the buyer expected does not mean that there is a failure of a limitation of remedy to repair or replace where the seller made every repair when requested and corrected every defect.

There is a failure of an exclusive remedy limiting the obligation of the seller to that of repairing the goods when the seller refuses or is unable to repair the goods.[37] When there is such a failure, the buyer may use any remedy authorized by the Code, just as though the contract had not contained any limitation on remedies.

---

[36] Kohlenberger, Inc. v Tyson's Foods, Inc. (Ark) 510 SW2d 555.
[37] National Cash Register Co. v Adell Industries, Inc., 57 MichApp 413, 225 NW2d 785.

§ 27:24. Waiver of Defenses. A buyer may be barred from objecting to a breach of the contract by the seller because the buyer has waived the right to do so.

    (a)   Express Waiver. When sales are made on credit, the seller will ordinarily plan to assign the sales contract to a bank or other financer and thereby convert into immediate cash the customer's obligation to pay in the future. To make the transaction more attractive to banks and financers, the credit seller will generally include in the sales contract with each buyer a *waiver of defense* clause. By this clause, the buyer agrees not to assert against the seller's assignee any defense held against the seller. For example, if the television set does not work properly, the buyer agrees to complain only to the seller. The buyer agrees not to complain to the seller's assignee but will continue to pay the assignee just as though everything were satisfactory.

    (b)   Implied Waiver. When the buyer executes a promissory note as part of the credit transaction described above, the buyer automatically waives with respect to the seller's assignee any defense which could not be raised against a holder in due course of the note. This will be considered in greater detail in Chapter 31. What it means in the ordinary situation is that when the buyer signs a promissory note for the balance due, the buyer cannot assert against the finance company or the bank the defense that the buyer never got the goods called for by the contract, that the goods were defective and did not work, or that the contract had been entered into because of the fraudulent misstatements of the seller.

§ 27:25. Preservation of Defenses. Consumer protection laws and regulations seek to protect consumers by preserving defenses. If the basis for the defense to a home-solicited sale becomes apparent within time to cancel the sale, it is possible that the consumer may assert the defense by exercising the right of cancellation.[38]

    (a)   Preservation Notice. Consumer defenses will be preserved by the Federal Trade Commission regulation requiring that the papers signed by a consumer contain a provision which expressly states that the consumer is reserving any defense arising from the transaction.[39] A third person acquiring such paper is necessarily charged with knowledge of such provision and a defense of the consumer arising from the original transaction may therefore be asserted against such third person.

    (b)   Prohibition of Waiver. When the Federal Trade Commission preservation notice is included in the paper which is received by the third person, it is unnecessary to consider whether a waiver of defenses could be validly made. If the preservation notice is not included, the seller has committed an unfair trade practice but the question then arises of whether the buyer may assert against an assignee a defense

---

    [38] See § 18:5, in this book.

    [39] 16 CFR § 433.1. It is an unfair or deceptive trade practice to take or receive a consumer credit contract which fails to contain the following provision in at least ten point, bold face, type:

NOTICE

ANY HOLDER OF THIS CONSUMER CREDIT CONTRACT IS SUBJECT TO ALL CLAIMS AND DEFENSES WHICH THE DEBTOR COULD ASSERT AGAINST THE SELLER OF GOODS OR SERVICES OBTAINED PURSUANT HERETO OR WITH THE PROCEEDS HEREOF. RECOVERY HEREUNDER BY THE DEBTOR SHALL NOT EXCEED AMOUNTS PAID BY THE DEBTOR HEREUNDER.

which could have been asserted against the seller. The answer to this question depends upon state law. In many states, consumer protection statutes nullify a waiver of defenses by expressly providing that the buyer may assert against the seller's transferee any defense which might have been raised against the seller. Under some statutes, the buyer must give notice of any defense within a specified number of days after being notified of the assignment. Some courts extend consumer protection beyond the scope of the statute by ignoring a time limitation on the giving of notice of defenses and allowing consumers to give late notice of defenses.[40]

---

[40] Star Credit Corp. v Molina, 59 Misc 2d 290, 298 NYS2d 570.

CASES FOR CHAPTER 27

Detroit Power Screwdriver Co. v Ladney

25 Mich App 478, 181 NW2d 848 (1970)

The Detroit Power Screwdriver Company made a contract to manufacture a very complicated stud-driving machine for Ladney. The machine was to be made to Ladney's specifications and was not like the machines made by Detroit. When the manufacturing of the machine was nearly completed, Ladney notified Detroit that he would not take the machine. Detroit stopped production and sued Ladney. From a judgment for Ladney, Detroit appealed.

LESENSKI, J. . . . The trial court held that a contract existed and that defendant breached the contract. The court also held, however, that plaintiff had failed to prove damages with sufficient certainty to permit a recovery. . . .

The disposition of the instant case is clearly governed by the Uniform Commercial Code. However, due to the differences between various sections providing remedies to sellers, it is necessary to make a preliminary determination of which sections of the Code control the final outcome.

The Code is, of course, a highly integrated statute, the sections of which must be read together. Accurate application of the Code rarely involves reference to only one section.

. . . Plaintiff places principal reliance on [UCC § 2-709(1)]. . . . Since the machine was not completed, § 2-709(1) is inapplicable. . . .

Since plaintiff is not entitled to the price under § 2-709(1), its right to recovery is controlled by § 2-708.

The measure of damages under § 2-708(1) is: "[T]he measure of damages for nonacceptance or repudiation by the buyer is the difference between the market price at the time and place for tender and the unpaid contract price together with any incidental damages . . . but less expenses saved in consequence of the buyer's breach."

However, § 2-708(2) provides: "If the measure of damages provided in subsection (1) is inadequate to put the seller in as good a position as performance would have done then the measure of damages is the profit (including reasonable overhead) which the seller would have made from full performance by the buyer, together with any incidental damages . . . , due allowance for costs reasonably incurred and due credit for payments or proceeds of resale." . . .

. . . A formula basing damages on the difference between market price and contract price is without meaning in the context of a contract for a specialty item which has no market.

Thus, the question of whether or not the machine in the instant case is a specialty item within the meaning of the Code must be determined in order to know which measure of damages applies. The question, however, also has significance in the instant case beyond the correct measure of damages.

[UCC § 2-610] provides in part: "When either party repudiates the contract with respect to a performance not yet due the loss of which will substantially impair the value of the contract to the other, the aggrieved party may . . . (b) resort to any remedy for breach . . . even though he has notified the repudiating party that he would await the latter's performance and has urged retraction; and (c) in either case suspend his own performance or proceed in accordance with the provisions of this article on the seller's right to identify goods to the contract notwithstanding breach or to salvage unfinished goods. . . ."

The right to suspend performance . . . , however, must be read in light of [UCC § 2-704(2)] . . . which states: "Where the goods are unfinished an aggrieved seller may in the exercise of reasonable commercial judgment for the purposes of avoiding loss and of effective realization either complete the manufacture and wholly identify the goods to the contract or cease manufacture and resell for scrap or salvage value or proceed in any other reasonable manner."

Whether plaintiff's decision not to complete the machine in the instant case was the result of the "exercise of reasonable commercial judgment" thus also depends, at least in part, on whether a market exists for the finished product.

We now return to the initial question of whether the trial court erred in ruling that plaintiff failed to prove damages under the Code.

The record below includes plaintiff's invoice in the amount of $12,017 dated May 11, 1967 for work completed up to April 11th, the date of defendant's stop order. Evidence was also introduced to show that the scrap salvage value of the machine was $1,500.

. . . Plaintiff's invoice was clearly intended to cover expected profits and costs incurred during the work done. That amount would then be reduced by the salvage value of $1,500.

Yet, § 2-708(2) applies only "if the measure of damages provided in subsection (1) is inadequate to put the seller in as good a position as performance would have done." As noted above, however, § 2-708(1) does not apply where the contract is found to involve a specialty item without a reasonably accessible market. Such a finding is crucial since it determines whether § 2-708(1) or § 2-708(2) controls the measure of damages. The determination of which paragraph of § 2-708 controls is, in turn, important since plaintiff has proven its loss under paragraph (2) but has not proven the amount of its loss under paragraph (1).

The ruling of the court below did not include a factual determination of whether the machine here involved is a specialty item without a reasonably accessible market. . . .

We therefore remand the case for further findings. If the trial court finds that the machine is a specialty item without a reasonably accessible market, then it shall award damages pursuant to § 2-708(2). If it does not so hold, the trial court shall dismiss the action due to plaintiff's failure of proof under § 2-708(1). . . .

[Action remanded]

Asciolla v Manter Oldsmobile-Pontiac, Inc.

8 NH 91, 370 A2d 270 (1977)

Asciolla purchased a new automobile in December. The car was waterproofed and then delivered to the buyer. He drove it to Wisconsin in the following January. The car stood outside overnight. The next day the car would not run because the transmission was inoperable. There was ice in the transmission and substantial rust which seemed to confirm the statement that was later made to the buyer that the car had been flooded before it had been sold to him. The dealer offered to repair the car. The buyer refused to accept repairs and insisted that he could revoke his acceptance and demanded a new car. He sued the dealer and the manufacturer. The case was referred to a master who recommended that damages be awarded to the buyer but decided that the buyer should not be allowed to revoke the acceptance because a reasonable person would have been satisfied with the repairs that were offered by the seller. From this judgment, the plaintiff appealed.

DOUGLAS, J. . . . The question . . . is whether the inoperable transmission of the plaintiff's car was a defect that substantially impaired the value of the product to him. [UCC§] 2-608, Comment 2 states that the test of "substantial impairment" is "whether the non-conformity is such as will *in fact* cause a substantial impairment of value *to the buyer* . . . ." (Emphasis added). This section, therefore, creates a subjective test in the sense that the needs and circumstances of the particular buyer must be examined. . . . The trier of fact must make an objective determination that the value of the goods to the buyer has in fact been substantially impaired.

We find . . . that the value of the subject automobile to [the buyer] was substantially impaired. In purchasing a new car the plaintiff was making a major investment. Few items which are considered necessities occupy such a significant portion of an individual consumer's income as does a new automobile. Few purchases are made with more care and deliberation. The record indicates that the plaintiff was a particularly prudent and painstaking car buyer and that he had indeed once before refused to accept an automobile from the defendants which merely had a dented fender which had been repaired. Within three weeks of the purchase of the car at issue in this case he found it to be totally inoperable. He was informed by franchised representatives of the manufacturer that the car had been flooded or submerged. While the master found that the evidence presented at the hearing did not support such a conclusion, no satisfactory reason was ever presented to the plaintiff to otherwise explain the presence of ice in his transmission. Nor was [the buyer] offered any guarantees concerning other deficiencies, caused by the same mysterious condition, which he very reasonably apprehended might arise in the future.

Under these facts, we think it clear that the plaintiff's confidence in the reliability and integrity of his new automobile was severely undermined. He had bargained for a new car, expecting to receive a vehicle upon whose dependability and safety he could comfortably rely. Instead he received a product which he understandably feared was what is known in popular parlance as "a lemon." The plaintiff is correct in his assertion that a new automobile is more than the sum of its various components. It is the integrity of the vehicle as a whole which is the essence of the consumer's bargain. As the Superior Court of New Jersey said in a markedly similar case concerning a new car with a defective transmission, "[the buyer] assumed what every new car buyer has a right to assume and, indeed, has been led to assume by the high powered advertising techniques of the auto industry—that his new car, with the exception of very minor adjustments, would be mechanically new and factory-furnished, operate perfectly, and be free of substantial defects." *Zabriskie Chevrolet, Inc. v Smith*, 99 N.J.Super.441, 452, 240 A.2d 195, 201-02 (1968). The plaintiff's situation cannot be accurately compared to cases . . . in which the cars presented defects which were trivial and readily repaired. The new car in the instant case was rendered wholly inoperable by a defective condition which permeated one of its most essential systems. Under such circumstances, his revocation of acceptance is justified. . . .

The defendants contend that they are entitled to cure the nonconformity in the tendered goods. Although a seller is given the right to cure under [UCC§] 2-508 in the context of rejection of goods, no such right is granted by [UCC§] 2-608(1)(b) when acceptance is being revoked. Whether a seller's right to cure may be implied under this section has been

the subject of considerable dispute. . . . We need not decide the question in this case, however. For the reasons set forth above, any cure other than replacement of the automobile with a new one would, under the facts of this case, be insufficient to accomplish a conforming tender. *See Zabriskie Chevrolet, Inc. v Smith, supra;* 2 R. Anderson, Uniform Commercial Code § 2-608:10 (2d ed. 1971). . . .

[Judgment reversed and action remanded]

Mobile Home Sales Management Incorporated v Brown

115 ArizApp 11, 562 P2d 1378 (1977)

Brown and his wife purchased a mobile home from Mobile Home Sales Management. There were many defects in the home and six weeks after delivery of the home to Brown, he wrote Mobile Home that he revoked acceptance of the home and cancelled the contract. Mobile Home refused to return the purchase price. The Browns then sued Mobile Home to cancel the contract and recover the purchase price and damages. Mobile Home raised the defense that the Browns were not entitled to the relief sought because they had not returned the mobile home and that their continued use of the home while the lawsuit was pending waived any objection that they might have had. The trial court held that the issues should be submitted to a jury. This was done and a verdict was returned for the Browns. From a judgment for the Browns, Mobile Home appealed.

DONOFRIO, J. . . . Defendant contends that plaintiffs' suit is one of rescission and being such a suit that a tender back of the goods, in this case the mobile home, was a prerequisite to recovery. Defendant also argued that plaintiffs' use of the merchandise (mobile home) for so long a period of time as plaintiffs had it in their possession, i.e., during pendency of law suit, was a waiver as a matter of law of their right to revoke the acceptance of the mobile home. We do not agree with these contentions. . . .

The law, prior to our adoption of the UCC, may have required a tender back in a similar situation, but we are of the opinion that the tender back requirement has now been eliminated by the adoption of the UCC.

Based upon the breach, plaintiffs . . . had a security interest in the home for the purchase monies they had paid to the seller. The question then arises as to what should be done insofar as tendering back of the home and protecting his security interest is concerned when a buyer justifiably revokes acceptance . . .

Assuming the absence of a security interest, . . . if a buyer wishes to revoke his acceptance of goods that he had physically accepted then he has an obligation to hold the goods with reasonable care ready for the seller's disposition. In other words, if the seller asks for the goods back then the buyer must be in a position to make those goods available to him. The next question which is crucial to this case is: What then must a buyer do when he has a security interest and has not been given any direction or request of what to do by the seller? A sensible interpretation of the rule would be that if no request is made by the seller then the buyer should not be penalized by denying said buyer rights that are given to him under the other sections of the code. Particularly the right given to him under the section which provides that he may hold the goods and resell them . . .

In this case, it is clear that the Code provides that when purchase money has been paid for goods this creates a security interest in the goods in favor of the buyer for the purchase money, and that the buyer has not only the right to retain the goods, but under certain circumstances has a right, after having given notice of revocation of acceptance and no response having been received, to hold them with reasonable care and to sell those goods if necessary in order to acquire the money to get back his purchase price. . . .

We . . . therefore hold that tender back is not a legal prerequisite to the Browns' (buyers') action for cancellation in this case. The observation can be made at this point that plaintiffs by living in the home and maintaining it to the best of their ability were also preserving it for the benefit of the seller as well as holding it for their own security.

We do not pass upon the issues that might be involved had plaintiffs in this case brought an action for rescission under the common law rules of equity.

Defendant contends that plaintiffs by staying in the mobile home during all the time through the pendency of the suit was a waiver of their right to revoke their acceptance of the unit. . . . Defendant also claims that these issues were matters for the trial court and not the jury. . . .

In opposition to defendant's contentions plaintiffs argue that under the issues joined these were proper questions for the jury. We agree.

The following excerpts taken from Anderson, Uniform Commercial Code (2nd Ed. 1971) on the UCC are pertinent, . . . "The use of goods by the buyer does not necessarily bar his revocation of acceptance. This is particularly so where the defect did not become apparent until use was made of the goods." Anderson, § 2-608:26, p. 250. "Where the buyer makes use of the goods because it was the commercially reasonable thing to do, it is likely that the Code courts will not hold that he is barred or has waived his right to cancel, where the use of the goods reasonably appear to hold the prospect of less harm or loss than would be sustained by not attempting to use them. A Code court which is unwilling to give literal effect to the 'inconsistent with the ownership' provision has pre-Code authority under the Sales Act in support of its position, it having been held that although the Sales Act similarly provided 'that a buyer is deemed to have accepted the goods when he does any act inconsistent with the ownership of the seller', the use of the goods by the buyer did not bar the buyer from rescinding where he gave prompt notice of his objection and only made a trial use of the goods because there was no other escape from the predicament caused by the seller's breach." Anderson, § 2-711:27, p. 424.

We hold that the staying in the mobile home pending the lawsuit cannot be, as a matter of law in this case, considered a waiver of the buyers' right to revoke the prior acceptance of the home.

[Judgment affirmed]

Dow Corning Corp. v Capitol Aviation, Inc.

(CA7 Ill) 411 F2d 622 (1969)

Dow Corning contracted to purchase an airplane from Capitol Aviation with delivery to be made in August, 1965. Both parties knew that the plane was being developed experimentally by Aero-Commander, Inc., and Capitol contracted to purchase the plane from Aero. Delivery of the plane was not made to Dow; and when Dow sued Capitol for breach of contract, Capitol sued Aero for breach of its contract with Aero. Aero defended on the ground that this latter contract limited its liability for nondelivery to a return of any payment made by Capitol on the purchase price. Capitol claimed that such limitation was void under the Code. The trial court held

that the limitation was not binding and entered judgment for Capitol against Aero. Aero appealed.

DUFFY, J. . . . The District Court entered judgment for Dow against Capitol for $64,000, [and] ruled Aero should reimburse Capitol for the $64,000, and further found Capitol should recover an additional sum of $43,865 for lost profits, making a total judgment for Capitol against Aero of $107,865. . . .

In the fall of 1964, at an aircraft industry convention in Miami which was attended by personnel from Dow and Capitol, Aero announced it would offer for sale a twin-engine turbine-powered executive-type passenger aircraft which it hoped to have available in about a year. . . .

On November 17, 1964, Capitol placed its written order with Aero for one of these new type aircraft at wholesale price of $260,000 with standard equipment. In an appropriate blank on the order with reference to a delivery date was a typewritten insertion TBD (to be determined). Also typed on the order was the recital "Specifications to be supplied at a later date." On February 19, 1965, Aero accepted Capitol's order.

On February 10, 1965, Capitol ordered from Aero two more Turbo-Commanders and a conventional piston type aircraft. As to delivery dates, these three orders also contained the letters TBD (to be determined). These three orders were accepted on February 18 and 19, 1965.

On February 25, 1965, Capitol's sales manager, at Dow's request and without prior consultation with Aero, wrote to Dow's Administrative Service Manager, Coultrip, advising that Aero's "target delivery date" for Turbo-Commander 1552-12 was "the end of August, 1965," and enclosed several alternative purchase orders. No delivery date was set. Dow took the information from one of the orders and placed it upon its own order form and submitted it to Capitol. However, Dow, without consultation with Aero, and although a delivery date had not been fixed between Aero and Capitol, inserted August, 1965, as the date of shipment. Capitol executed the order committing itself to the August, 1965, date. Later, Aero was informed by Capitol that it had sold a plane to Dow but no details were given. . . .

Consistent with industry custom and practice, there were valid reasons for the contract to provide for an open delivery date. All parties concerned knew that the aircraft which Aero proposed to construct was in an experimental stage of development; that

on November 17, 1964, the date of Capitol's order, a prototype of that aircraft had not been flown; and further, that the plane had not been type certified, and no airworthiness certification had been issued for a turbo-commander type aircraft. Both certificates were necessary prerequisites to the delivery of aircraft to a distributor for redelivery to a customer.

Furthermore, it was well known by all concerned in the transaction before us, that Aero was dependent on other suppliers for engines, brakes, landing gear and avionics.

Certain it is that Capitol, at no time, indicated any objection to the open delivery date. . . .

There is no breach of promise here because Aero undertook the obligation of delivery of a plane then in experimental stages, at such time as it could be flown safely. Aero could not furnish and would not be permitted by the Federal Aviation [Administration] to deliver a plane that would not fly safely.

Our conclusion in this respect is, in itself, a reason for a reversal but in the alternative, it is our view that the trial court erred in holding that Paragraph 4 of the purchase order signed by Capitol was not an exclusive remedy and that it was unconscionable and an unreasonable attempt to limit liability under the Uniform Commercial Code. . . .

The trial court pointed out that Section 2-719(1)(b) of the Code provides that a remedy as provided is optional unless it is "expressly agreed to be exclusive." It is true that nowhere does the clause use the word exclusive, but the clear import is that there shall be no remedy other than the return of the deposit. The clause speaks in terms of liability rather than remedies, but it is clear that the parties expressly agreed that this was to be the only recourse. To hold otherwise would be to introduce a new requirement that certain words be used to express the intent of the parties lest they later be found not to have limited their remedies.

As an affirmative defense of the cross claim of Capitol, Aero relied on Paragraph 4 of the purchase order signed by Capitol, to-wit: "Aero Commander, Inc. shall not be liable for failure or delay in making delivery for any cause whatsoever. If delivery of the products covered by this order is not made within thirty (30) days of the 'Specified Delivery Date,' or of the 'Revised Specified Delivery Date,' Purchaser may cancel this order and have the full deposit refunded, provided that such nondelivery is not caused by act of God, war, riot, strikes, or unavoidable casualty." . . .

The case before us is not one where a seller wantonly disregards his obligations to the buyer and sells to another simply for his financial advantage. Here, Aero was desperately trying to construct a new type of aircraft that would be safe to fly. Furthermore, it had been careful not to commit itself to any penalty for late delivery. Under the circumstances of this case, such a provision was reasonable.

The trial court alternatively relied upon Section 2-718 combined with Section 2-302. Section 2-718 provides that an unreasonably large liquidated damage is void as a penalty, and the Comment speculates than an unreasonably small amount might be stricken under the section on unconscionable contracts or clauses. Although it is something of a misnomer to call the return of a deposit a liquidated damage, we will assume the section is available to the appellee.

Section 2-302 makes clear that the unconscionability of a clause is to be judged not in the abstract, but rather in its commercial setting. Here, Aero was constructing what was at least for itself a new type of airplane construction. The plane was to be turbine powered rather than piston powered. Capitol was aware of this. Aero began by making a prototype. This was successful but later effort with production engines proved hazardous. There was an account of a hair-raising trip which revealed substantial difficulty. Aero points out that it is common to the industry not to promise delivery dates, and to obtain a release from liability in the event of failure to deliver. In fact, Aero pointed out that when Dow bought another plane from Aero's competitor, it accepted the same terms as it now claims are unconscionable.

We hold that under the circumstances of this case, Paragraph 4 was not unreasonable or unconscionable. . . .

We hold that Aero, at no time, promised to deliver an aircraft to Capitol on a specified date. We further hold that in any event Aero successfully limited its liability by including Paragraph 4. Therefore, we reverse the judgment Capitol has obtained against Aero.

J. A. Jones Construction Company v Dover

(DelSuper) 372 A2d 540 (1977)

J. A. Jones Construction Company was the general contractor in building an addition to the electric generating plant of the city of Dover. When the contractor sued the city for the contract price, the city sought damages from the equipment suppliers, General Electric Company and Westinghouse Electric Corporation. They defended on the ground that there were clauses in their contracts which stated that they should not be held for breach. The city claimed that the limitation clauses were invalid as a matter of law and moved for summary judgment.

TAYLOR, J. . . . The draftsmen of the Sales Article of the UCC were unwilling to leave the subject of contractual limitation of liability exclusively in the hands of the contracting parties. They permitted contractual limitation upon warranty and liability [UCC§] 2-719 but they provided certain restraints which must be satisfied. One is that a limitation of liability or remedy will not be enforced where the circumstances cause the contractual remedy . . . "to fail of its essential purpose." [UCC§] 2-719(2). . . .

. . . In determining whether the contract limitation fails of its essential purpose, the facts and circumstances surrounding the contract, the nature of the basic obligations of the party, the nature of the goods involved, the uniqueness or experimental nature of the items, the general availability of the items, and the good faith and reasonableness of the provision are factors which should be considered. *2 Anderson on Uniform Commercial Code,* pp. 506-512, §§ 2-719:9-22. . . . Underlying the concept of contractual limitation of liability is the presumption that there will be good faith effort by the contracting party to perform its contractual obligations. [UCC§] 1-203; *2 Anderson on Uniform Commercial Code,* pp. 508-9, § 2-719:14. Performance involves kind, quantity, quality and time.

To the extent that quality of items is not specified in the contract the supplier of goods shall comply with the standards prevailing in the industry. [UCC§] 1-205; *1 Anderson on Uniform Commercial Code,* p. 387, § 2-301:4. Hence, when the supplier undertakes to provide materials of specified dimension or of specified quality or material, the items supplied must meet the traditional standards of compliance. Obviously, parts supplied by the supplier which are intended to be used together must be of such dimension as to reasonably work together. Implicit in the limitation of remedy provision is the expectation that the supplier will reasonably comply with the specific terms of the contract. . . . The applicability of this test may depend upon the nature of the item being supplied and whether it is unique or experimental.

Time of performance is often an important contractual item. Where the buyer is entitled to segmented performance the significance of time of performance specified in the contract may be less clear. Time may have particular significance where the work of various contractors or suppliers is interdependent. Where a time of delivery is specified without being made of the essence, it is contemplated that there shall be reasonable compliance therewith in accordance with the standards of the industry. [UCC§] 1-204, § 1-309; *1 Anderson on Uniform Commercial Code,* p. 447, § 2-309:4. . . .

This case involves charges of unreasonable delay and hence the issue is whether defendants are protected from liability for delays which do not qualify as reasonable delays. Insofar as a liability limitation clause undertakes to limit liability to the cost of replacement from an outside source if a defendant fails to replace within a reasonable time, the clause may be contrary to a basic objective of the contract, which is that delivery and repair or replacement of defective items will have been effected within a reasonable time. . . . While the delay might be slight in the case of goods available on the open market, substantial delay may be involved if the goods must await production after order. An essential contractual purpose may be that the item or services be received within a reasonable time.

In *Beal v General Motors Corporation,* D.Del., 354 F.Supp. 423 (1973), Judge Stapleton considered the disqualification of a limitation of liability provision because it failed of its essential purpose. He found that the provision which limited the buyers' remedy to replacement or repair of defective parts was founded upon the premise that the buyer would receive goods that conformed to the contract within a reasonable time after the defect was discovered. Hence, where the seller failed to correct the defect as promised within a reasonable time, the limitation if applied would cause failure of its essential contractual purpose and the seller was held liable in damages for breach of warranty notwithstanding the contractual limitation. . . .

Subject to any pertinent showing concerning the contract negotiations indicating that the parties intended the provision to have a different effect here, the reasonable time test applied in *Beal* . . . is strongly persuasive and should be applied. . . .

General Electric contends that its liability limitation clause cannot make the remedy fail of its essential purpose because the buyer is assured of obtaining the contract items at the expense of the seller even if the buyer has to purchase them elsewhere. Assuming that clause, which is found in a contract section entitled "Defective Material and Workmanship," applies to all instances of seller's failure to comply with the contract and overrides the seller's more protective and conflicting language in the section entitled "Limitation of Liability," it becomes operative only after the seller has had a reasonable time to repair or replace. Hence that clause requires the buyer to assume the financial burdens for the reasonable repair or replacement time afforded seller and also for the time required to find an alternate supplier and the waiting time until that supplier can perform.

To give the liability limitation clause the full effect sought by defendants would be to convert the contract into an optional contract in which the sole determination of whether the contract would be performed would rest upon defendants' choice and the buyer would assume all of the expense and inconvenience of delay.

Contracts are entered into based upon the premise that each party will in good faith make reasonable effort to meet its obligations under the contract. Hence, contract terms will ordinarily be read to incorporate that premise. It has been noted above that liability limitation provisions must meet the test of reasonableness if it is to be given effect. *2 Anderson on Uniform Commercial Code,* p. 501, § 2-719:1, p. 507, § 2-719:12.

I conclude that if a liability limitation provision is relied upon to protect a party from the results of its violation of the premise stated above, to that extent the provision may not pass the test of reasonableness and there may be failure of essential purpose. In making this determination it may be appropriate that the contract negotiations be considered to determine whether they placed the contractual relationship of the parties upon a different basis. . . .

The issue of whether limitation provisions are enforceable under the contractual relations of the parties and the nature of the contractual performance are matters which generally should not be decided on the pleadings or on summary judgment. . . .

[Defendants' motions for summary judgment are denied]

QUESTIONS AND CASE PROBLEMS

1.   What social forces are affected by the rule of law governing the seller's choice of conduct when the buyer repudiates a contract for goods which are then partially manufactured?

2.   Compare (a) the seller's action for damages and (b) the seller's action for the purchase price.

3.   Compare (a) the seller's lien, (b) the stopping of delivery of goods, and (c) repossession of goods by the seller.

4.   Compare a buyer's rejection of nonconforming goods with the buyer's revocation of acceptance of goods.

5   The buyer of a truck noticed on the first day he drove it that the speed control was defective and that the truck used excessive oil. He continued to use the truck and made several payments. Five months later he demanded that the seller take the truck back. Decide. [Hudspeth Motors, Inc. v Wilkinson, 238 Ark 410, 382 SW2d 191; Marbelite Co. v Philadelphia, 208 Pa Super 256, 222 A2d 443]

6.   Carta bought from Barker, a dealer, a bicycle that was manufactured by the Union Cycle Co. He took it home for his minor daughter. Sandra, a guest at the Carta home, was injured while using the bicycle. Suit was brought against the town of Cheshire, claiming that it had defectively maintained the road, and against the manufacturer, claiming that the bicycle was defectively constructed. The manufacturer, Union Cycle, defended on the ground that Sandra had not given it notice of the defect in the bicycle as required by UCC § 2-607. Decide. [Tomczuk v Town of Cheshire, 26 Conn Supp 219, 217 A2d 71]

7.   Skopes Rubber Corp. purchased skin-diving suits from the United States Rubber Co. The sale was made on the basis of a sample on which the vinyl coating on the suits had been hand applied and was smooth. The suits that were delivered were wrinkled because the vinyl had been machine applied. In use, the suits split at the wrinkle lines. Skopes returned the first installment of the suits because of this defect. He then sued United States Rubber Co. for breach of warranty. It raised the defense that by returning the first installment, Skopes had rescinded the contract and could not thereafter sue for damages. Was this correct? [Skopes Rubber Corp. v United States Rubber Co., (CA1 Mass) 299 F2d 584]

8.   A seller sold goods to a buyer on credit. The buyer did not pay for the goods. The seller claimed that the title to the goods revested in him because of the buyer's default. Was he correct? [Jordan v Butler, 182 Neb 626, 156 NW2d 778]

9.   The goods purchased by the buyer were defective. The seller made repeated attempts to correct the defect. It became apparent that it was impossible to correct the defect. The buyer notified the seller that the buyer was revoking acceptance of the goods. The seller offered to try again to repair the goods. The buyer rejected this offer and repeated that acceptance of the goods was being revoked. The seller claimed that the buyer could not revoke acceptance as long as the seller offered to repair the goods. Was the seller correct? [See Fenton v Contemporary Development Co., 12 WashApp 345, 529 P2d 883]

10. After a sales contract was made, the seller's factory was destroyed by fire. The seller and the buyer then agreed to cancel the contract. Thereafter the seller's factory was rebuilt, and the buyer demanded that the seller perform the contract. Was the seller required to do so? [Goddard v Ishikawajima-Harima Heavy Industries Co., 29 App Div 2d 754, 287 NYS2d 901]

11. The buyer of goods at an auction sale did not pay for and take the goods. The auctioneer sued the buyer for the amount of the buyer's bid. Was the buyer liable for that amount? [French v Sotheby & Co., (Okla) 470 P2d 318]

12. Wolosin purchased a vegetable and dairy refrigerator case from the Evans Manufacturing Corp. Evans sued Wolosin for the purchase price. Wolosin raised as a defense a claim for damages for breach of warranty. The sales contract provided that Evans would replace defective parts free of charge for one year and that "this warranty is in lieu of any and all other warranties stated or inferred, and of all other obligations on the part of the manufacturer, which neither assumes nor authorizes anyone to assume for it any other obligations or liability in connection with the sale of its products." Evans claimed that it was only liable for replacement of parts. Wolosin claimed that the quoted clause was not sufficiently specific to satisfy the requirement of UCC § 2-719. Decide. [Evans Mfg. Corp. v Wolosin, (Pa) 47 Luzerne County Leg Reg 238]

13. McInnis purchased a tractor and scraper as new equipment of current model from the Western Tractor & Equipment Co. The written contract stated that the seller disclaimed all warranties and that no warranties existed except as were stated in the contract. Actually, the equipment was not the current model but that of the prior year. Likewise, the equipment was not new but had been used for 68 hours as a demonstrator model and then the hour meter had been reset to zero. The buyer sued the seller for damages. The latter defended on the ground that all liability for warranties had been disclaimed. Was this defense valid? [McInnis v Western Tractor & Equipment Co., 63 Wash 2d 652, 388 P2d 562]

14. Bosway Tube & Steel Corporation purchased a machine for making tubes from McKay Machine Company. The machine did not work properly and McKay was unable to repair the machine. Bosway sued for damages. McKay claimed that it was only liable for the cost of repairs, as the contract specified that it had no liability "beyond repairing or replacing it." Was McKay correct? [Bosway Tube & Steel Corp. v McKay Machine Co., 65 MichApp 426, 237 NW2d 488]

15. Chaplin purchased a walk-in hardening box from Bessire & Co. for approximately $7,000. In effect, it was an insulated room for the storage of ice cream and similar products. It was especially manufactured for Chaplin and installed in the fall of 1957. It developed leaks at once, and Bessire made repairs and guaranteed that it would work properly, which it did during that winter, but in the summer of 1958 it developed other defects which required a modification of the corrective repairs that had been made the fall before. The box worked through the cold months of 1958 and 1959, but in the spring it developed leaks again. In May, 1959, a fuse blew, and within a few hours the temperature of the box rose 30 degrees causing the contents to spoil. Bessire refused to take the box back. Chaplin sued Bessire for breach of warranty, claiming the right to rescind the contract, to recover payments paid on the contract, and to recover special damages for lost merchandise. During the course of the lawsuit, Chaplin made unsuccessful attempts to sell the box. Bessire defended on the ground that Chaplin had delayed too long before seeking to rescind and that, by attempting to sell the box, he lost any right of rescission. Decide. [Chaplin v Bessire & Co., (Ky App) 361 SW2d 293]

Part Six • Commercial Paper

28 Kinds of Paper, Parties, and Negotiability

Under the law of contracts a promise, when supported by consideration, creates certain legal rights that may be assigned to another person. Even before these common-law rules relating to contracts were developing, another body of law, the law merchant, was creating principles relating to a different type of obligation and the transfer of rights arising therefrom. In the course of time this obligation became the bill of exchange, which today we also know as a draft, a trade acceptance, or, with certain modification, a check. In time, another type of instrument, the promissory note, appeared. Both drafts and promissory notes may have the quality of negotiability. As a group, they are known today as commercial paper or negotiable instruments.

A. KINDS OF COMMERCIAL PAPER AND PARTIES

Commercial paper, such as checks and promissory notes, provide a substitute for money and can be used as a means of providing credit.

§ 28:1. Definition. *Commercial paper* includes written promises (such as promissory notes) or orders (such as checks or drafts) to pay money that may be transferred by the process of negotiation. Much of the importance of commercial paper lies in the fact that it is more readily transferred than ordinary contract rights and that the transferee of commercial paper may acquire greater rights than would an ordinary assignee. A person who acquires a commercial paper may therefore be subject to less risk.

§ 28:2. Kinds of Commercial Paper. Commercial paper falls into four categories: (a) promissory notes, (b) drafts or bills of exchange, (c) checks, and (d) certificates of deposit.

(a) Promissory Notes. A *negotiable promissory note* is an unconditional promise in writing made by one person to another, signed by the maker, engaging to pay on demand or at a definite time a sum certain in money to order or to bearer.[1]

---

[1] UCC § 3-104(1).

> $ *200* .00   Albany, New York *July 6,*   19 *79*
>
> *One year*   after date *I* promise to pay to
>
> the order of *Ronald Adams*
>
> *Two hundred.* ————————————————— Dollars
>
> Payable at *First Union Bank*
>
> with interest at *6* %.
>
> No. *21* Due *July 6, 1980*   *John Clark*

Promissory Note
Parties: maker (buyer, borrower, or debtor)—John Clark;
payee (seller, lender, or creditor)—Ronald Adams.

(b)   Drafts. A *negotiable draft* or *bill of exchange* is an unconditional order in writing addressed by one person to another, signed by the person giving it, requiring the person to whom it is addressed to pay on demand, or at a definite time a sum certain in money to order or to bearer.[2] In effect, it is an order by one person upon a second person to pay a sum of money. The person who gives the order is called the *drawer* and is said to draw the bill. The person on whom the order to pay is drawn is the *drawee*. The person to whom payment is to be made is the *payee*. The drawer may also be named as the payee.

The drawee who is ordered to pay the paper is not bound to do so. The drawee, however, may agree to pay the paper, in which case the drawee is called an *acceptor.*

> $ *400.00*   Des Moines, Iowa *September 8,*   19 *79*
>
> *Thirty days after date*   PAY TO THE
>
> ORDER OF *Freedom National Bank*
>
> *Four hundred* ——————————————— DOLLARS
>
> VALUE RECEIVED AND CHARGE TO ACCOUNT OF
>
> TO *Harold Monroe*
>
> No. *12*   *Iowa City, Iowa*   *Jean Jefferson*

Draft (Bill of Exchange)
Drawer (seller or creditor)—Jefferson; drawee (buyer or debtor)—Monroe;
payee (seller's or creditor's bank)—Freedom National Bank.

(c)   Checks. A *check* is a draft drawn on a bank payable on demand.[3] It is an order by a depositor (the drawer) upon a bank (the drawee) to pay a sum of money

---

[2] UCC § 3-104(1).
[3] UCC § 3-104(2)(b).

to the order of another person (the payee). A check is always drawn upon a bank as drawee and is always payable upon demand.

(d)   Certificates of Deposit. A *certificate of deposit* is an instrument issued by a bank that acknowledges the deposit of a specific sum of money and promises to pay the holder of the certificate that amount, usually with interest, when the certificate is surrendered.[4]

§ 28:3. Parties to Commercial Paper. A note has two original parties—the maker and the payee; and a draft or a check has three original parties—the drawer, the drawee, and the payee. In addition to these original parties, a commercial paper may have one or more of the parties described under (d) through (i) of this section.

(a)   Maker. The *maker* is the person who writes out and creates a promissory note. If the paper is not a promissory note, this person has a different name, as the drawer of a check.

(b)   Drawer. The *drawer* is the person who writes out and creates a draft. This includes bills of exchange, trade acceptances, and checks. It is essential to bear in mind the distinction between a maker and a drawer for the reason that the liability of the maker is primary while that of a drawer is secondary.

(c)   Payee. The *payee* is the person named on the face of the paper to receive payment. In "pay to the order of John Jones," the named person, John Jones, is the payee.

A payee has no rights in the paper until it has been delivered by the drawer or the maker. Likewise, the payee is not liable on the paper in any way until the payee transfers the paper to someone else or receives payment of it.

(d)   Indorser.[5] The owner of commercial paper who signs on the back of the paper is an *indorser*. Thus, if a check is made payable to the order of *P, P* may indorse it to *E* to pay a debt that *P* owes *E.* In such a case, *P,* who is the payee of the check is now also an indorser.

(e)   Indorsee. The person to whom an indorsement is made payable is called an *indorsee.* The indorsee may in turn indorse the instrument; and then is also an indorser.

(f)   Bearer. The person in physical possession of a commercial paper which is payable to bearer is called a *bearer.*

(g)   Holder. A *holder* is a person in possession of commercial paper which is payable at that time either to such person, as payee or indorsee, or to bearer. A holder may be (1) a holder for value, or (2) a holder in due course.

(1)   Holder for Value. Ordinarily a commercial paper is given to a person in the course of business in return for or in payment for something. If the holder gives consideration for the instrument or takes it in payment of a debt, such

---

[4] A certificate of deposit "is an acknowledgment by a bank of receipt of money with an engagement to repay it," as distinguished from a note, which "is a promise other than a certificate of deposit." UCC § 3-104(2)(c), (d).

[5] The spelling *endorse* is commonly used in business. The spelling *indorse* is used in the UCC.

holder is a *holder for value*. Thus, if an employee is paid wages by check, the employee is a holder for value of the check, as the check was received in payment of wages earned and due. If such employee indorses the check to a landlord to pay the rent, the landlord becomes a holder for value.

A person may receive a commercial paper without giving anything for it. Thus, when an aunt gives her niece a check for $100 as a birthday present, the niece becomes the owner or holder, but she has not given anything for the check and she is not a holder for value.

(2)   Holder in Due Course. A person who becomes a holder of the paper in the regular course of ordinary business is called a *holder in due course* and is immune from certain defenses when such favored holder brings suit on the paper. A person becoming the holder of an instrument at any time after it was once held by a holder in due course is described as a *holder through a holder in due course,* and is ordinarily given the same special rights as a holder in due course.

(h)   Accommodation Party. A person who becomes a party to a commercial paper in order to add strength to the paper for the benefit of another party to the paper is called an *accommodation party.* (See p. 470, Pioneer Insurance Company v Gelt) For example, *M* applies to a bank for a loan and is willing to give the bank a promissory note naming it as payee. The bank may be unwilling to lend money to *M* on the strength of *M*'s own promise. It may be that *C,* who has a satisfactory credit standing, will sign the note as a comaker with *M.* If *C* does this for the purpose of bolstering *M*'s credit, *C* signs for accommodation and is an accommodation maker.

Parol evidence is admissible to determine whether a party is an accommodation party, as this is not determined by the manner of signing.

(i)   Guarantor. A *guarantor* is a person who signs a commercial paper and adds a promise to pay the instrument under certain circumstances. Ordinarily this is done by merely adding "payment guaranteed" or "collection guaranteed" to the signature of the guarantor on the paper.

The addition of "payment guaranteed" or similar words means that the guarantor will pay the instrument when due. "Collection guaranteed" or similar words means that the guarantor will not pay the paper until after the holder has sought to collect payment from the maker or acceptor and has been unable to do so.

If the meaning of the guaranty is not clear, it is construed as a guaranty of payment. For example, when an indorser adds a statement that the paper is "guaranteed" or adds the word "guarantor" to the indorsement without specifying whether it is payment or collection which is guaranteed, the indorser is deemed to be a guarantor of payment, with the consequence that the holder of the paper may proceed directly against such guarantor without first proceeding against any other party on the paper.

The liability of a guarantor is as extensive as that of the original debtor.

§ 28:4. Liability of Parties. A person who by the terms of the instrument is absolutely required to pay is primarily liable. For a note, the maker is primarily liable; for a draft, the acceptor (the drawee who has accepted) is primarily liable. A guarantor of payment is primarily liable in any case. Other parties are either secondarily or conditionally liable, as in the case of an indorser, or they are not liable in any capacity. A person who transfers the paper but does not sign it is not liable for its payment.[6]

Each party liable on commercial paper may be sued individually by the holder. Modern procedure generally permits the plaintiff-holder to sue in one action all or any of the parties liable on the paper. A defendant who is sued cannot object that the plaintiff has omitted other persons who could also have been sued.

(a) Accommodation Parties. An accommodation party is liable for payment of the paper regardless of whether the paper is signed merely as a matter of friendship or in return for payment. When suit is brought against an accommodation party by a plaintiff who acquired the paper before it was due and who gave value for it, the accommodation party cannot avoid liability on the ground that the plaintiff knew of the accommodation character.

The accommodation party is not liable to the party accommodated.[7] If the accommodation party is required to pay the paper, that party may recover the payment from the person accommodated.

(b) Guarantors. A *guarantor of payment* has primary liability. The guarantor of payment is liable for payment of the paper even though the holder has not sought to obtain payment from any other party and it is immaterial that payment was not demanded from the primary party or that the primary party had sufficient assets to pay the paper.

The *guarantor of collection* is not required to pay the paper until collection has been attempted and has failed, or an attempt to collect would obviously be useless. This means that the holder must first obtain a judgment against the maker or acceptor of the paper, which judgment remains unpaid because the sheriff cannot find sufficient property of the debtor in question to pay it; or the debtor must be insolvent.[8] Not until then is the guarantor of collection liable.

B. NEGOTIABILITY

In order to be classified as commercial paper, instruments must satisfy the requirements of negotiability.

§ 28:5. Requirements of Negotiability. In order to be negotiable, an instrument must be (a) in writing and (b) signed by the maker or drawer; it must contain (c) a promise or order (d) of an unconditional character (e) to pay in money (f) a sum certain; (g) it must be payable on demand or at a definite time; (h) it must be payable to order or bearer; [9] and (i) a party who is a drawee must be identified with reasonable certainty.

In addition to these formal requirements, the instrument usually must be delivered or issued by the maker or drawer to the payee or the latter's agent with the intent that it be effective and create a legal obligation.

---

[6] UCC § 3-401(1). Such a person, however, may be bound by certain warranties that bind any person who transfers commercial paper.

[7] UCC § 3-415(5). United Refrigerator Co. v Applebaum, 410 Pa 210, 189 A2d 253.

[8] UCC § 3-416(1)(2). The guaranty written on the commercial paper is binding without regard to the requirements of a local statute of frauds. § 3-416(6).

[9] UCC § 3-104(1).

If an instrument is not negotiable, the rights of the parties are governed by the general body of contract law.[10] (See p. 470, Frank v Hershey Nat. Bank) If there is any uncertainty as to whether a paper is negotiable it is deemed nonnegotiable.

§ 28:6. Writing. A commercial paper must be in writing. "Writing" includes handwriting, typing, printing, and any other method of setting words down in a permanent form. The use of a pencil is not wise because such writing is not as durable as ink and the instrument may be more easily altered. A commercial paper may be partly printed and partly typewritten with a handwritten signature.

(a)   Parol Evidence. As the commercial paper is a writing, the parol evidence rule applies. This rule prohibits modifying the instrument by proving the existence of a conflicting oral agreement alleged to have been made before or at the time of the execution of the commercial paper.

§ 28:7. Signature. The instrument must be signed by the maker or drawer. The signature usually appears at the lower right-hand corner of the face of the instrument, but it is immaterial whether the signature is so placed. However, if the signature is placed on the instrument in such a manner that it does not in itself clearly indicate that the signer was the maker, drawer, or acceptor, the signer is held to be only an indorser.

In the absence of a local statute that provides otherwise, the signature may be made by pen or pencil, by typewriter, by print, or by stamp.

The signature itself may consist of the full name or of any symbol adopted for that purpose. It may consist of initials, figures, or a mark.[11] A person signing a trade or an assumed name is liable to the same extent as though the signer's own name had been used.[12]

(a)   Agent. A signature may be made by a person or by an authorized agent.[13] No particular form of authorization to an agent to execute or sign a commercial paper is required.

An agent signing commercial paper should disclose on the paper (1) the identity of the principal, and (2) the fact that the signing is made in a representative capacity. When both are done, an authorized agent is not liable on the paper.[14] The representative capacity of an officer of an organization is sufficiently shown by the signature of the officer preceded or followed by the title of the office and the organization name.

---

[10] Business Aircraft Corp. v Electronic Communications (TexCivApp) 391 SW2d 70. Note however, that if the nonnegotiability results from the fact that the instrument is not payable to order or bearer, it is governed by Article 3 of the Code with the limitation that there cannot be a holder in due course of such paper. UCC § 3-805.

[11] When a signature consists of a mark made by a person who is illiterate or physically incapacitated, it is commonly required that the name of the person be placed upon the instrument by someone else, who may be required to sign the instrument as a witness. Any form of signature is sufficient in consequence of the definition of "signed" as including any symbol executed or adopted by a party with the present intention to authenticate a writing. UCC § 1-201(39).

[12] UCC § 3-401(2).

[13] UCC § 3-403(1).

[14] UCC § 3-403; Childs v Hampton, 80 GaApp 748, 57 SE2d 291.

(b)   Nondisclosure of Agency or Principal. If a person who signs a commercial paper in a representative capacity, such as an agent or an officer of a corporation, executes the paper without disclosing both the identity of the principal and the existence of the representative capacity, the agent appears to be signing the paper as a personal obligation, and the agent is personally bound by the paper with respect to subsequent holders, regardless of whether the agent had intended to be personally bound or to act in a representative capacity. (See p. 471, Griffin v Ellinger)

As to subsequent holders, parol evidence is not admissible to show that it was not intended that the representative or agent be bound or to show that it was intended to bind the undisclosed principal. Such evidence is admissible, however, against the person with whom the officer or agent had dealt.

A representative who is personally bound as the result of failing to disclose representative capacity is jointly and severally liable with the principal. For example, when the name of the corporation appears as maker with the name of its treasurer signed immediately below but without any notation indicating a representative capacity, the treasurer is jointly and severally liable with the corporation.

(c)   Partial Disclosure of Agency. The instrument may read or the agent may sign in a way that either identifies the principal or discloses the agent's representative capacity but both are not done. In such a case, the agent is personally liable on the paper to third persons acquiring it; but if sued by the person with whom the agent dealt, it may be proven that it was intended that the principal should be bound.[15]

§ 28:8. Promise or Order to Pay. A promissory note must contain a promise to pay money.[16] No particular form of promise is required; the intention as gathered from the face of the instrument controls. If the maker uses such a phrase as "I certify to pay" a promise is implied; but a mere acknowledgment of a debt, such as a writing stating "I.O.U." is not a commercial paper.

A draft or check must contain an order or command to pay money.[17] As in the case of a promise in a note, no particular form of order or command is required.

§ 28:9. Unconditional Order or Promise. The promise or order to pay must be unconditional. For example, when an instrument makes the duty to pay dependent upon the completion of the construction of a building or upon the placement of the building at a particular location, the promise is conditional and the instrument is nonnegotiable. A promise to pay "when able" is generally interpreted as being conditional.[18]

The use of a term of politeness, such as "please," before an otherwise unconditional order to pay does not destroy the effect of the order within the meaning of the requirements for negotiability. But if the effect of the provision is only to seek payment of money or to request it if certain facts are true, the "order" to pay is conditional and the instrument is nonnegotiable.

---

[15] UCC § 3-403(2)(b).
[16] UCC § 3-104(1)(b).
[17] UCC § 3-104(1)(b).
[18] A minority of states regard such a promise as requiring payment within a reasonable time and as therefore being an absolute promise. Mock v First Baptist Church, 252 Ky 243, 67 SW2d 9.

An order for the payment of money out of a particular fund, such as ten dollars from next week's salary, is conditional.[19] If, however, the instrument is based upon the general credit of the drawer and the reference to a particular fund is merely to indicate a source of reimbursement for the drawee, such as "charge my expense account" the order is considered absolute.[20]

An exception is made in the case of paper issued by a government, a trust, or by certain business organizations. Thus a promise or order is not made conditional by the fact that it "is limited to payment out of a particular fund or the proceeds of a particular source, if the instrument is issued by a government or governmental agency or unit; or is limited to payment out of the entire assets of a partnership, unincorporated association, trust, or estate by or on behalf of which the instrument is issued." [21]

§ 28:10. Payment in Money. A commercial paper must call for payment in *money*, that is, any circulating medium of exchange which is legal tender at the place of payment. It is immaterial, as far as negotiability is concerned whether it calls for payment in a particular kind of current money.

If the order or promise is not for money, the instrument is not negotiable. For example, an instrument which requires the holder to take stock or goods in place of money is nonnegotiable.

An instrument is also nonnegotiable when the promise or order to pay money is coupled with an agreement by the maker or drawer to do something else, unless that agreement will make it easier for the holder of the instrument to collect the money due on the instrument. A provision of the latter type does not impair negotiability because the effect of its inclusion is to make the paper more attractive to a purchaser and thus it encourages the exchange or transfer of the commercial paper.

§ 28:11. Sum Certain. This means an exact amount. The instrument must not only call for payment in money but also for an exact amount of money. (See p. 472, Universal C.I.T. Credit Corp. v Ingel) Unless the instrument is definite on its face as to how much is to be paid, there is no way of determining how much the instrument is worth.

The fact that the instrument may require certain payments in addition to the amount specified as due does not make the instrument nonnegotiable when such additional amounts come within any of the following categories:

(a)   Interest. A provision for the payment of interest does not affect the certainty of the sum, even though the interest rate increases upon default in payment.[22] In contrast, a note payable "with interest at bank rates" is not for a sum certain because bank rates of interest are not constant, and a paper calling for payment at bank rate interest is therefore not negotiable.

(b)   Installments. A provision for payment in installments does not affect certainty. Nor is certainty affected when the installment provision is coupled with a provision

---

[19] UCC § 3-105(2)(b).
[20] UCC § 3-105(1)(f).
[21] UCC § 3-105(1)(g),(h).
[22] UCC § 3-106(1)(b).

for acceleration of the date of payment for the total amount upon default in any payment.

(c)   Exchange. A provision for the addition of exchange charges does not affect the certainty of the sum payable since its object is in effect to preserve the constancy of the value involved. In this connection, the fact that the money due on the instrument is stated in a foreign currency does not make the instrument nonnegotiable.[23]

(d)   Collection Costs and Attorney's Fees. The certainty of the sum is not affected by a provision adding collection costs and attorney's fees to the amount due, although general principles of law may place a limit upon the amount that can be recovered for such items.

(e)   Discount and Addition. The certainty of the sum and the negotiability of the instrument are not affected by a provision that allows a discount if earlier payment is made or which increases the amount due if late payment is made.[24]

§ 28:12. Time of Payment. A commercial paper must be payable on demand or at a definite time. If it is payable "when convenient" the instrument is nonnegotiable because the day of payment may never arrive. An instrument payable only upon the happening of a particular event that may never happen is not negotiable. For example, a provision to pay when a person marries is not payable at a definite time since that particular event may never occur. It is immaterial whether the contingency in fact has happened, because from an examination of the instrument alone it still appears to be subject to a condition that may never happen.

(a)   Demand. An instrument is payable on *demand* when it is expressly specified to be payable "on demand," or at sight or upon presentation, that is, whenever the holder tenders the instrument to the party required to pay and demands payment; or when no time for payment is specified.[25]

(b)   Definite time. The time of payment is *definite* if it can be determined from the face of the instrument. An instrument satisfies this requirement when it is payable (a) on or before a stated date, (See p. 472, Ferri v Sylvia), (b) at a fixed period after a stated date, (c) at a fixed period after sight, (d) at a definite time subject to any acceleration, (e) at a definite time subject to extension at the option of the holder, (f) at a definite time subject to extension to a further definite date at the option of the maker of acceptor, or (g) at a definite time subject to an extension to a further definite date automatically upon or after the occurrence of a specified act or event.[26]

An instrument payable in relation to an event which though certain to happen will happen on an uncertain date, such as a specified time after death, is not negotiable.[27]

§ 28:13. Order or Bearer. A commercial paper must be payable to order or bearer. This requirement is met by such expressions as "Pay to the order of John Jones," "Pay to

---

[23] UCC § 3-107(2).
[24] UCC § 3-106(1)(c).
[25] UCC § 3-108.
[26] UCC § 3-109(1).
[27] UCC § 3-109(2).

John Jones or order," "Pay to bearer," and "Pay to John Jones or bearer." [28] The use of the phrase "to the order of John Jones" or to "John Jones or order" is important in showing that the person executing the instrument is indicating that there is no intention to restrict payment of the instrument to John Jones only and that there is no objection to paying anyone to whom John Jones orders the paper to be paid. Similarly, if the person executing the instrument originally states that it will be paid to "bearer" or "to John Jones or bearer," there is no restricting of payment of the paper to the original payee. If the instrument is payable on its face "to John Jones," however, the instrument is not negotiable.

(a) **Order paper.** An instrument is payable to *order* when by its terms it is payable to the order or assigns of any person specified therein with reasonable certainty (pay to the order of K. Read), or to a person so described or order (pay to K. Read or order).[29]

(b) **Bearer Paper.** An instrument is *payble to bearer* when by its terms it is payable (a) to bearer or the order of bearer, (b) to a specified person or bearer, or (c) to "cash," or "the order of cash," or any other designation that does not purport to identify a person.[30]

An instrument payable to order and indorsed in blank becomes payable to bearer and may be negotiated by transfer of possession until specially indorsed.[31]

§ 28:14. Drawee. In the case of a draft or check, the drawee must be named or described in the instrument with reasonable certainty.[32] This requirement which is based upon practical expediency, is designed to enable the holder of the instrument to know by whom payment is to be made.

When there are two or more drawees, they may be either joint drawees (*A* and *B*) or alternative drawees (*A* or *B*).[33]

§ 28:15. Effect of Provisions for Additional Powers or Benefits. Certain provisions in an instrument that give the holder certain additional powers and benefits may or may not affect negotiability.[34]

(a) **Collateral.** The inclusion of a power to sell collateral security, such as corporate stocks and bonds, upon default does not impair negotiability. An instrument secured by collateral contains as absolute a promise or order as an unsecured instrument. Negotiability is not affected by a promise or power to maintain or protect collateral

---

[28] It is not necessary that the instrument actually use the word "order" or "bearer." Any other words indicating the same intention are sufficient. It has been held that the words "pay to holder" could be used in place of "bearer" without affecting the negotiability of the instrument. UCC §§ 3-110, 3-111.

[29] An instrument is also payable to order when it is conspicuously designated on its face as "exchange" or the like, and names a payee. UCC § 3-110(1).

[30] UCC § 3-111.

[31] UCC § 3-204(2).

[32] UCC § 3-102(1)(b).

[33] UCC § 3-102(1)(b). The instrument is nonnegotiable if there are successive drawees. *Successive drawees* exist when, if one drawee fails to pay, the holder is required to go to the next drawee for payment rather than proceed at once against secondary parties.

[34] UCC § 3-112.

or to give additional collateral,[35] or to make the entire debt due, if the additional collateral is not supplied.

(b) Acceleration. A power to accelerate the due date of an instrument upon a default in the payment of interest or of any installment of the principal, or upon the failure to maintain or provide collateral does not affect the negotiability of an instrument. However, a power to accelerate "at will" or when a person "deems himself insecure" must be exercised in good faith.[36]

(c) Confession of Judgment. Negotiability is not affected by a provision authorizing the entry of a judgment by confession upon a default. If the holder of the instrument is authorized to confess judgment at any time, whether before maturity or not, however, the instrument is generally nonnegotiable.

(d) Waiver of Statutory Benefit. State statutes commonly provide that when a person is sued for a debt, a certain amount or kind of property is exempt from the claim. If the party who executes a commercial paper promises to waive those rights under such a statute in order that it will be a little easier to collect the amount due, negotiability is ordinarily not affected. A waiver of this kind is void in some states, however.

(e) Requirement of Another Act. A provision authorizing the holder to require an act other than the payment of money, such as the delivery of goods, makes the instrument nonnegotiable.[37]

§ 28:16. Additional Documents. The fact that a separate document is executed that gives the creditor additional protection, as a mortgage on real estate, or the right to repossess goods sold to the maker of the instrument, does not impair the negotiability of the commercial paper.

As between the parties to the original transaction, the liability on the paper will be controlled by the terms of any other documents. In contrast, subsequent holders of the commercial paper can rely on the face of the paper and are not affected by the terms of any additional separate document.

§ 28:17. Immaterial Provisions. The addition or omission of certain other provisions has no effect upon the negotiability of a commercial paper that is otherwise negotiable.

A commercial paper is not affected by the omission of the date. In such case it is regarded as carrying the date of the day on which it was executed and delivered to the payee. If the date is essential to the operation of the instrument, as when the instrument is payable a stated number of days or months "after date," any holder who knows the true date may insert that date.

When a commercial paper is dated, the date is deemed prima facie to be the true date, whether the date was originally inserted or was thereafter added.[38] A

---

[35] UCC § 3-112(1)(c).
[36] UCC § 1-208.
[37] UCC § 3-104(1)(b).
[38] UCC § 3-114(3). If the wrong date is inserted, the true date can be proved unless the holder is a holder in due course or a holder through a holder in due course, in which case the date, even though wrong, cannot be contradicted.

commercial paper may be antedated or postdated, provided that is not done to defraud anyone. The holder acquires title as of the date of delivery without regard to whether this is the date stated in the instrument.

It is immaterial so far as negotiability is concerned (a) whether an instrument bears a seal; (b) whether it fails to state that value has been given; or (c) whether it recites the giving of value without stating its nature or amount, although local law may require such a recital.

Negotiability is not affected by a provision that by indorsing or cashing the instrument, the person receiving it takes it in full settlement of a specified claim or all claims against the drawer.[39]

---

[39] UCC § 3-112(1)(f).

CASES FOR CHAPTER 28

Pioneer Insurance Company v Gelt

(CA8 Neb) 558 F2d 1303 (1977)

Sack applied for a loan to the Educators Security Insurance Company. In order to induce the company to make the loan, Gelt as maker executed a promissory note for the amount of the loan and named Educators as the payee of the note. The note was not signed by Sack. When the note became due, the claim was held by the Pioneer Insurance Company and Gelt as maker executed a renewal note naming Pioneer as payee. When Pioneer thereafter sued Gelt on the renewal note he claimed that he was not liable because he was an accommodation party. From a judgment in favor of Pioneer, Gelt appealed.

HENLEY, C. J. . . . The defendant . . . simply contended that he was an "accommodation maker" of the notes and for that reason was not liable to Pioneer on the renewal note.

Under the Uniform Commercial Code . . . an accommodation party is not liable to the accommodated party, and if the accommodating party discharges the obligation, he has a right of recourse on the instrument against the accommodated party. . . . [UCC] § 3-415(5). Section 3-415(1) defines an accommodation party as one who signs an instrument in any capacity for the purpose of "lending his name to another party to it." And § 3-415(2) provides that when an instrument has been taken for value before it is due, an accommodation party

is liable in the capacity in which he has signed even though the taker knows of the accommodation.

Both the original note and the renewal note were executed by Gelt as maker and the respective insurance companies appeared as payees. There were no other parties to the instruments. Thus, Gelt did not "lend his name" to any other parties to the instrument and was not an "accommodation maker." Additionally, Educators took the first note for value before it was due, and Pioneer gave value when it took the renewal note.

While there is no doubt that Gelt executed the instruments as an accommodation to Sack, that did not make him an "accommodation party" within the meaning of § 3-415(1) and (5).

[Judgment affirmed]

Frank v Hershey National Bank

269 Md App 138, 306 A2d 207 (1973)

The East Penn Broadcasting Company borrowed money from the Hershey National Bank. A promissory note representing the loan was executed "payable to the Hershey National Bank." The note authorized the confession of judgment at any time. The note was signed with the typewritten name of the borrowing corporation and the handwritten signatures of three individuals. One of these was Frank. When the loan was not paid, the bank sued him and the others on the note. They raised certain defenses under the Uniform Commercial Code. The bank claimed that the UCC was not applicable. From a

judgment for the bank, Frank and the others appealed.

DIGGES, J. . . . The parties have proceeded . . . on the assumption that these notes were negotiable and therefore governed by the provisions of the UCC. We find the notes to be nonnegotiable and the UCC to be inapplicable. Therefore, the liability of the parties is determined as a matter of simple contract law. . . .

. . . To be negotiable, an instrument must, among other requirements, "be payable to order or to bearer." (§ 3-104(1)(d)) The absence of these magic words renders a note nonnegotiable. Here, the notes in question contain just a "promise to pay to the Hershey National Bank" the amount due. However, § 3-805 entitled "instruments not payable to order or to bearer" specifies that: "This subtitle *applies* to any instrument whose terms do not preclude transfer and *which is otherwise negotiable within this subtitle* but which is not payable to order or to bearer, except that there can be no holder in due course of such an instrument." . . . The official comments to this section indicate that: "This section covers the 'nonnegotiable instrument.' As it has been used by most courts, this term has been a technical one of art. It does not refer to a writing, such as a note containing an express condition, which is not negotiable and is entirely outside of the scope of this Subtitle and to be treated as a simple contract. It refers to a particular type of instrument which meets all requirements as to form of a negotiable instrument except that it is not payable to order or to bearer."

Thus, while these notes could still be governed by the Code even though they lack words of negotiability, they must meet all other "requirements as to form of a negotiable instrument" except for that. The notes here do not conform to this standard. The UCC § 3-112(1)(d) provides that the negotiability of an instrument is not affected by "a term authorizing confession of judgment on the instrument if it is not paid when due." We held in Stankovich v Lehman, 230 Md 426, 187 A2d 309 (1963), a case decided under the Negotiable Instruments Act, that the authorization to confess judgment "as of any term" permitted entry of judgment at any time prior to the maturity of the note and therefore destroyed negotiability. . . . "It would seem logical that if the statute, as it does, preserves negotiability only if the confession of judgment is at or after maturity, the warrant to confess must expressly, or by necessary implication, restrict its exercise to that time if the note is to be negotiable, and that if the warrant is silent as to the time when it can be exercised, the reasonable implication must be that it can be done at any time. Most of the cases involving this general area of the law have arisen in Pennsylvania, and the Courts of that State have held that notes containing stipulations for confession of judgment without specification or limitation as to time are, like those expressly authorizing judgment prior to maturity, nonnegotiable." . . . .

Since these nonnegotiable notes are not governed by the UCC, their effect is, as already noted, determined under principles of simple contract law.

[Judgment affirmed]

Griffin v Ellinger

(Tex) 538 SW2d 97 (1976)

Greenway Building Company was the prime contractor on a construction job. Ellinger supplied it with some labor and materials needed for the construction. Ellinger was paid with drafts drawn on the Northeast Bank and signed by Griffin, an officer of Greenway. Griffin signed only his name. The name of the Greenway Corporation appeared at two places on each draft. It was printed at the top of each draft. Each draft was stamped with a protector and the protector imprinted both the amount of the draft and the name Greenway. The drafts were dishonored and Griffin was sued as drawer of the drafts. He claimed that when he signed as drawer he was acting in a representative capacity and was therefore not personally liable on the drafts. From a judgment for Ellinger, Griffin appealed.

DOUGHTY, J. . . . The first question is whether the draft shows on its face that Griffin signed in a representative capacity only. Although the draft clearly names the person represented, it does not show that Griffin signed only in his capacity as president of Greenway. Griffin contends, however, that considering the instrument as a whole, and taking into account the normal business usage of personalized checks, it should be apparent from the instrument itself that Griffin signed only as an authorized agent of Greenway. We disagree. . . . We can find nothing on the face of the checks in the present case to show that Griffin intended to sign only in a representative capacity. Petitioner points out that each check is stamped by a "check protector," which imprinted not only the amount of the draft but also the company's name. Although the stamp clearly reveals the name of the principal, it does not aid petitioner [Griffin] because it gives no information as to the capacity in which he signed the instrument.

The fact that the name of the corporation appears on the check indicates that the account drawn upon is that of the corporation and that the funds in the account are the corporation's. While the drawer of a check is ordinarily the owner of the funds in the account drawn upon, the Code does not require that this be so. Under [UCC§] 3-413, *any person* who signs a draft engages that, upon dishonor, he will pay the amount thereof to the holder. Indeed, under [UCC§] 3-404, the signer of a draft who has no authority to draw upon the account is nevertheless liable upon his contract as drawer to any person who takes the instrument in good faith for value. Petitioner points out that, since a corporation can only act through its agents, a personal signature is always required to authorize withdrawal of funds from a corporate account. Under [UCC§] 3-403, however, one signing an instrument is personally liable thereon even though he is authorized to and does in fact bind his principal, if he does not disclose that he is signing only in a representative capacity. In short, the burden is on the signer to relieve himself of personal liability by disclosing his agency. The fact that the instrument is an authorized draft drawn on a corporate account is not enough to disclose the representative character of the signature thereon. [UCC§] 3-403(c) expressly provides that the signer of an instrument may avoid personal liability by disclosing both the name of the organization of which he is an agent and the office he holds with the organization. Absent such a disclosure or its equivalent, the signer is personally liable on the instrument according to its terms, unless "otherwise established between the immediate parties" under subsection (b)(2). We hold that the checks in question do not show on their face that Griffin signed only in a representative capacity.

[Judgment affirmed]

Universal C.I.T. Credit Corp. v Ingel

347 Mass 119, 196 NE2d 847 (1964)

Ingel made a contract with Allied Aluminum Associates for the installation of aluminum siding on his home. He signed a promissory note which stated that group credit life insurance would be obtained by the holder of the note without additional charge to the customer. Later the note was transferred to a finance company, Universal C.I.T. Credit Corp. When it brought suit against Ingel, he claimed that the note was nonnegotiable because of the above insurance provision and also because the note provided for the payment of "interest after maturity at the highest lawful rate." From a judgment in favor of Universal, Ingel appealed.

SPIEGEL, J. . . . The defendants contend that the note was nonnegotiable as a matter of law and, therefore, any defense which could be raised against Allied may also be raised against the plaintiff. They argue that the note contained a promise other than the promise to pay, [and] failed to state a sum certain. . . .

It appears that the note was a form note drafted by the plaintiff. . . . We are . . . satisfied that the insurance clause in the note does not affect negotiability under [UCC] § 3-104(1) (b) since it is clear that the "no other promise" provision refers only to promises by the maker.

The provision in the note for "interest after maturity at the highest lawful" rate does not render the note nonnegotiable for failure to state a sum certain as required by [UCC] § 3-104(1)(b). We are of [the] opinion that after maturity the interest rate is that indicated [by general statute] since in this case there is no agreement in writing for any other rate after default. This being the case, we do not treat this note differently from one payable "with interest." The latter note would clearly be negotiable under . . . [UCC] § 3-118(d). . . .

[Judgment affirmed]

Ferri v Sylvia

100 RI 270, 214 A2d 470 (1965)

Ferri made a note payable to the order of Sylvia "within ten years after date." Within less than that time Sylvia sued for the money due, claiming that the note was uncertain and therefore parol evidence could be admitted to show that she could have the money any time she needed it. From a judgment in Sylvia's favor, Ferri appealed.

JOSLIN, J. . . . The payment provisions of the note are not uncertain nor are they incomplete.

At the law merchant it was generally settled that a promissory note or a bill of exchange payable "on or before" a specified date fixed with certainty the time of payment. . . . The same rule has been fixed by statute first under the negotiable instruments law . . . and now pursuant to the Uniform Commercial Code. The Code in § 3-109(1) reads as follows: "An instrument is payable at a definite time if by its terms it is payable (a) on or before a stated date or at a fixed period after a stated date. . . ."

" 'Within' a certain period, 'on or before' a day named, and 'at or before' a certain day are equivalent terms, and the rules of construction apply to each alike."

We . . . equate the word "within" with the phrase "on or before." So construed, it fixes both the beginning and the end of a period, and insofar as it means the former it is applicable to the right of a maker to prepay, and insofar as it means the latter it is referable to the date the instrument matures. We hold that the payment provision of a negotiable instrument payable "within" a stated period is certain as well as complete on its face and that such an instrument does not mature until the time fixed arrives.

For the foregoing reasons it is clear that the parties unequivocally agreed that the plaintiff could not demand payment of the note until the expiration of the ten-year period. It is likewise clear that any prior or contemporaneous oral agreements of the parties relevant to its due date were so merged and integrated within the writing as to prevent its being explained or supplemented by parol evidence. . . .

[Judgment reversed]

QUESTIONS AND CASE PROBLEMS

1. What social forces are affected by the rule of law governing the nature of a signature on commercial paper?

2. Compare the obligation of a party to a contract and the obligation of a party to commercial paper.

3. The requirement that commercial paper be for a sum certain requires that the paper state on its face the exact amount to a penny which must be paid. Appraise this statement.

4. Compare a check payable "to the order of Jones" and a check payable "to Jones."

5. A contractor signed a note promising to pay to the order of the holder $10,000 payable from "jobs now under construction." Was the note negotiable? [Webb & Sons, Inc. v. Hamilton, 30 App Div 2d 597, 290 NYS2d 122]

6. Nation-Wide Check Corp. sold money orders through local agents. A customer would purchase a money order by paying an agent the amount of the desired money order plus a fee. The customer would then sign his or her name on the money order as the remitter or sender and would fill in the name of the person who was to receive the money following the printed words "Payable to." In a lawsuit between Nation-Wide and Banks, a payee on some of these orders, the question was raised whether these money orders were negotiable. Decide. [Nation-Wide Check Corp. v Banks, (Dist Col App) 260 A2d 367]

7. The Texas Export Development Corporation borrowed money from Schleder. The note representing the loan was signed by the corporation and individually by two of its stockholders, Rodgerson and Wise. The loan was obtained in order to finance a business transaction relating to oil. The oil transaction failed and suit was brought by Schleder on the note against the corporation and the two signing stockholders. They raised the defense that they had signed only because it had been agreed that the note would be repaid from the profits from the oil transaction and that they would not be held individually liable for payment. Can Schleder recover on the note? [Texas Export Development Corp. v Schleder (TexCivApp) 519 SW2d 134]

8. Goodwin purchased goods on credit. He signed a "retail installment contract and security agreement" for the amount due. The seller assigned this to a finance company, the

Pacific Finance Loans. Pacific demanded payment. Goodwin raised the defenses of breach of warranty and failure of consideration. Pacific Finance Loans then claimed that the defenses could not be raised because the paper signed by Goodwin was a negotiable instrument. Pacific Finance Loans was correct if the paper was negotiable. Looking at the paper it was doubtful whether it was or was not a negotiable instrument. Pacific Finance claimed that the doubt should be decided in favor of saying it was negotiable. Goodwin claimed that the doubt should be decided in favor of saying that it was not negotiable. Who is correct? [Pacific Finance Loans v Goodwin, 41 OhioApp2d 141, 324 NE2d 578]

9. Money was borrowed from a bank by a corporation. The president of the corporation negotiated the loan and signed the promissory note. On the first line he wrote the name of the corporation. On the second line he signed his own name. The note was negotiated by the lending bank to the Federal Reserve Bank. The note was not paid when due, and the Federal Reserve Bank sued the corporation and the president. The president raised the defense that he was not bound on the note because he did not intend to bind himself and because the money obtained by the loan was used by the corporation. Is the president liable on the note? [See Talley v Blake (LaApp) 322 So2d 877 (non-Code); Geer v Farquhar, 270 Or 642, 528 P2d 1335.]

10. B wished to pay a bill that he owed to C but did not have sufficient money in his bank. He drew a postdated check on his bank account and gave it to A. A then gave B a check drawn on A's bank account for the amount of B's check. When A was sued on his check by C, A claimed that he was an accommodation party. Was he correct? [Midtown Commercial Corp. v Kelner, 29 App Div 2d 349, 288 NYS2d 122]

11. A seller offered to sell a house to a buyer. The offer stated that $2,000 was to be paid on "acceptance of this contract." The buyer gave the seller a postdated check. Thereafter the seller claimed there was no contract because the giving of the postdated check was a qualified acceptance of the offer and therefore was not an acceptance. Was the seller correct? [See How v Fulkerson, 22 ArizApp 467, 528 P2d 853]

12. David Lane Motors, a corporation, was indebted to the Phoenix-Girard Bank. The debt was evidenced by a series of promissory notes. When the notes became due, the bank extended the loan and new notes were executed. Franklin who was a stockholder of the corporation signed the renewal notes as a comaker. He did not receive anything for so doing and was persuaded to sign because it was orally agreed that he would not be personally liable on the notes. Blake guaranteed the payment of the notes by a separate contract of guaranty executed with the bank. When the notes were not paid when due, Blake paid the bank on the notes, the bank assigned the notes to Blake, and he then sued Franklin and the corporation. Franklin raised the defense of lack of consideration for his promise and the agreement that he would never be held liable on the paper. Were these defenses valid? [Blake v Coates (Ala) 294 So2d 433]

13. A note was made by the Mid-South Building & Improvement Co., Inc. Cotten indorsed the note as an accommodation indorser. Later suit was brought on the note by Parker, the holder, against Mid-South Building and Cotten. Cotten raised the defense that when he indorsed the note he was not aware that he could be required to pay the note if it was not paid by Mid-South Building. Was this a valid defense? [Parker v Mid-South Building & Improvement Co., Inc. (AlaCivApp) 326 So2d 763]

14. A wrote a check payable to the order of B but did not send it to him. Who was the holder of the check? [See Silvian's Estate (FlaApp) 347 So2d 632]

15. Ruth Laudati obtained a loan from Brown University and signed a promissory note for the repayment of the loan. Her mother, Josephine, guaranteed payment of the note. When the note was not paid, Brown University sued Josephine. She raised the defense

that Brown had not sued Ruth. Was this a valid defense? [Brown University v Laudati, 113 RI 299, 320 A2d 609]

16. The NMD Realty Company borrowed money from the Bank of Delaware. The loan was evidenced by a note bearing 9% interest. 6% was the legal maximum rate of interest but corporations were not permitted to raise the defense of usury. The note was indorsed by Weiner individually as an accommodation indorser. The bank sued the corporation and Weiner. He raised the defense that the note was usurious. Could he raise this defense? [Bank of Delaware v NMD Realty Co. (DelSuper) 325 A2d 103]

17. James G. Dornan was the treasurer and vice-president of Chet B. Earle, Inc. On behalf of the corporation he executed a promissory note that was signed in the following manner:

| Corporate | Chet B. Earle, Inc. | (Seal) |
| Seal | James G. Dornan | (Seal) |

The holder of the note, an indorsee, sued Dornan on the ground that he was personally liable as a comaker. He defended on the ground that he was merely an agent for the corporation and was not personally liable. Was this defense valid? [Bell v Dornan, 203 Pa Super 562, 201 A2d 324]

18. Herdlicka and Thieda executed a promissory note as makers. The latter was in fact, an accommodation party. Subsequently Kratovil, the holder of the note, agreed with Herdlicka to extend the time for paying the note and to reduce the monthly payments that were to be made. When the note was not paid in full, Kratovil sued Thieda who claimed that he was released by the fact that the obligation of Herdlicka had been changed by the extension of time, which was made without Thieda's consent. Decide. [Kratovil v Thieda, 62 Ill App 2d 234, 210 NE2d 819]

29 Transfer of Commercial Paper

Commercial paper may be transferred by negotiation or assignment. When the transfer is made by negotiation, the rights of the transferee may rise higher than those of the transferor, depending upon the circumstances attending the negotiation. When the transfer is made by assignment, the assignee has only those rights which the assignor possessed.

A. KINDS OF INDORSEMENTS

There are a number of different kinds of indorsements which can be made on commercial paper.

§ 29:1. Introduction. Some commercial paper may be transferred without an indorsement. An indorsement is required in other cases. If the transfer is made in the manner required by the Uniform Commercial Code, the transfer is called a negotiation and the transferee becomes a holder. If there is no negotiation, the transferee is merely an assignee.

The person to whom an instrument is payable either on its face or by indorsement or the person in possession of bearer paper may indorse it for the purpose of negotiating it by merely signing it, or may add certain words or statements as part of the indorsement. By definition, an indorsement is written on the back of an instrument.

An indorsement must be written on the commercial paper itself, or, if necessary, on a paper attached to it, called an *allonge*,[1] provided it is so firmly attached to the commercial paper that it becomes part of it. A signature on a separate piece of paper which is pinned or clipped to the commercial paper is not effective as an indorsement.

§ 29:2. Blank Indorsement. When the indorser merely signs the paper, the indorsement is called a *blank indorsement* since it does not indicate the person to whom the instrument is to be paid, that is the indorsee. A person who is in possession of paper on which the last indorsement is blank is the holder and may sue thereon without proving ownership of the paper. This is the most common form of indorsement because it is the simplest and the easiest to write. It may be a dangerous form, however, since it has the effect of making the instrument payable to bearer and it thereafter can be negotiated by delivery by anyone, even a finder or a thief. Such an indorsement

---

[1] UCC § 3-202(2).

usually may be made with safety on a check when the holder is in a bank where the check is to be cashed or deposited.

The holder of an instrument on which the last indorsement is blank may write above the signature of the blank indorsement a statement that the instrument is payable to that particular holder.[2] This is called "completing" the indorsement or "converting" the blank indorsement to a special indorsement by specifying the identity of the indorsee. It protects the holder because the paper cannot be negotiated thereafter without the indorsement and delivery of such holder.

Unless they otherwise agree, indorsers are liable to each other in the order in which they indorse, which is presumed to be the order in which their signatures appear on the paper.

Negotiation by a blank indorsement does three things: (1) it passes the ownership of the instrument; (2) it makes certain warranties; and (3) it imposes upon the indorser a secondary liability to pay the amount of the instrument if the maker or drawee fails to do so and certain conditions are then satisfied by the holder.

§ 29:3. Special Indorsement. A *special indorsement* consists of the signature of the indorser and words specifying the person to whom the indorser makes the instrument payable, that is, the indorsee. Common forms of this type of indorsement are "Pay to the order of Robert Hicks, E. S. Flynn" and "Pay to Robert Hicks or order, E. S. Flynn." It is not necessary that the indorsement contain the words "order" or "bearer." Thus, a commercial paper indorsed in the form "Pay to Robert Hicks, E. S. Flynn" continues to be negotiable and may be negotiated further. In contrast, an instrument which on its face reads "Pay to E. S. Flynn" is not negotiable.

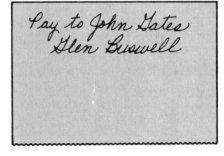

Blank Indorsement   Special Indorsement

When the last indorsement on the instrument is special, both an indorsement and a delivery by or on behalf of the last indorsee is required for further negotiation.[3]

As in the case of the blank indorsement, a special indorsement transfers title to the instrument and results in the making of certain warranties and in imposing a secondary liability upon the indorser to pay the amount of the instrument under certain conditions.

---

[2] UCC § 3-204(3).
[3] UCC § 3-204(1).

§ 29:4. Qualified Indorsement. A *qualified indorsement* is one that qualifies the effect of a blank or a special indorsement by disclaiming or destroying the liability of the indorser to answer for the default of the maker or drawee. This may be done by including the words "without recourse" in the body of the indorsement or by using any other words that indicate an intention to destroy the indorser's secondary liability for the default of the maker or drawee.[4]

The qualification of an indorsement does not affect the passage of title or the negotiable character of the paper. It merely limits the indorser's liability to the extent of the qualification.

This form of indorsement is most commonly used when the qualified indorser is known to be a person who has no personal interest in the transaction, as in the case of an agent or an attorney who is merely indorsing to a principal or client a check of a third person made payable to the agent or attorney. Here the transferee recognizes that the transferor is not a party to the transaction and therefore should not be asked to vouch for the payment of the paper.

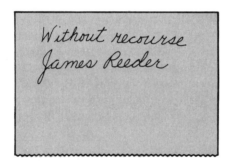

Qualified Indorsement   Restrictive Indorsement

§ 29:5. Restrictive Indorsements. A *restrictive indorsement* specifies the purpose of the indorsement or the use to be made of the paper. An indorsement "without recourse" is a qualified and not a restrictive indorsement.

(a)   **Terms.**

(1)   Indorsement for Deposit. This indorsement indicates an intent that the instrument be deposited, such as "For deposit only," "For deposit only to the account of Joan Sacuto" and "Pay to the Springfield National Bank for deposit only."[5]

(2)   Indorsement for Collection. This indorsement indicates an intention that the instrument be received by the indorsee, usually for the purpose of effecting the collection of the instrument. "For collection only" or "Pay to any bank or banker"[6] are examples of this type of indorsement.

---

[4] UCC § 3-414(1).
[5] UCC § 3-205(c).
[6] UCC § 3-205(c).

(3) Indorsement Prohibiting Further Negotiation. The indorsement, "Pay to Harold Singer only," indicates an intent that no further negotiation should occur and is therefore restrictive.[7]

(4) Agency or Trust Indorsement. An indorsement that makes the indorsee the agent of the indorser, such as "Pay to (indorsee, agent) on account of (indorser, principal)," or which makes the indorsee the owner subject to a trust for another person, such as "Pay to (indorsee, mother) to hold for use of (third person, son)," are restrictive indorsements in that they state that the indorsement is for the benefit of the indorser or another person.[8]

(5) Condition as a Part of the Indorsement. An indorsement which indicates that it is effective only upon the satisfaction of a condition, such as "Pay to Carol Nash upon completion of Contract #83," is a restrictive indorsement.[9]

(b) Effect of Restrictive Indorsement. A restrictive indorsement does not have the effect of prohibiting further negotiation even though it expressly attempts to do so.[10] In all cases, the transferee may therefore be a holder, just as is true under a nonrestrictive indorsement. A bank may ignore and is not affected by the restrictive indorsement of any person except the holder transferring the instrument to the bank or the person presenting it to the bank for payment. However, a *depositary bank,* that is, the one in which the customer deposits the item, and persons not in the bank collection process must recognize the restrictive indorsement to the extent of applying any value given in a manner consistent with the indorsement.[11]

§ 29:6. Irregular Kinds of Indorsements.

The indorser may make an indorsement that does not fall into any of the standard categories of indorsements. For example, an indorser may write "I hereby assign all my right, title, and interest in the within note," and then sign. The signature in such case is effective as an indorsement in spite of the added words, on the theory that the indorser actually intended to indorse and was merely endeavoring to make certain that total ownership was transferred.[12]

§ 29:7. Correction of Name by Indorsement.

Sometimes the name of the payee or indorsee of a commercial paper is improperly spelled. Thus, H. A. Price may receive a paycheck which improperly is payable to the order of "H. O. Price." If this was a clerical error and the check was intended for H. A. Price, the employee may ask the employer to write a new check payable in the proper name.

Instead of doing this, the payee or indorsee whose name is misspelled may indorse the wrong name, the correct name, or both. A person giving or paying value for the instrument may require both.[13]

---

[7] UCC § 3-205(b).
[8] UCC § 3-205(d).
[9] UCC § 3-205(a).
[10] UCC § 3-206(1). As to effect of the indorsement, "Pay any bank" or "For deposit," see § 4-201(2).
[11] UCC § 3-206(2). Additional limitations are imposed in the case of collection and conditional indorsements. § 3-206(3), and trust indorsements, § 3-206(4).
[12] UCC § 3-202(4).
[13] UCC § 3-203.

This correction of name by indorsement may only be used when it was intended that the indorsement should be payable to the person making the corrective indorsement. If there were in fact two employees, one named H. A. Price and the other H. O. Price, it would be illegal as a forgery for one to take the check intended for the other and by indorsing it obtain the benefit of the proceeds of the check.

§ 29:8. Bank Indorsements. In order to simplify the transfer of commercial paper from one bank to another in the process of collecting items, "any agreed method which identifies the transferor bank is sufficient for the item's further transfer to another bank." [14] Thus, a bank may indorse with its Federal Reserve System number instead of using its name.

Likewise, when a customer has deposited an instrument with a bank but has failed to indorse it, the bank may make an indorsement for the customer unless the instrument expressly requires the payee's personal indorsement. Furthermore, the mere stamping or marking on the item of any notation showing that it was deposited by the customer or credited to the customer's account is declared to be as effective as an indorsement by the customer would have been. [15]

B. NEGOTIATION OF COMMERCIAL PAPER

The way in which commercial paper is negotiated depends upon whether it is order paper or bearer paper.

§ 29:9. Definition. *Negotiation* is the transferring of commercial paper in such a way as to make the transferee the holder of the paper. This in turn is controlled by whether the paper is order paper or bearer paper.

A negotiation is a final or definitive act. Once the holder has made an effective negotiation of the paper, the negotiation cannot be cancelled without the consent of the transferee.

§ 29:10. Time for Determining Order or Bearer Character of Paper. The order or bearer character of the paper is determined as of the time when the negotiation is about to take place, without regard to what it was originally or at any intermediate time. Accordingly, when the last indorsement is special, the paper is order paper without regard to whether it was bearer paper originally or at any intermediate time, and the holder cannot ignore or strike out intervening indorsements, or otherwise treat the paper as bearer paper because it had once been bearer paper.

§ 29:11. Negotiation of Order Paper. An instrument payable to order may be negotiated only by indorsement by the person to whom it is payable at that time and the delivery of the paper by such person. Indorsement and delivery may also be made by an authorized agent of the person to whom the paper is then payable.

---

[14] UCC § 4-206.
[15] UCC § 4-205(1).

(a)   Multiple Payees and Indorsees. Ordinarily one person is named as the payee in the instrument, but two or more payees may be named. In that case, the instrument may specify that it is payable to any one or more of them or that it is payable to all jointly. If nothing is specified, the instrument is payable to all of the payees and they are *joint payees.* For example, if the instrument is made payable "to the order of *A* and *B,*" the two persons named are joint payees.

The importance of this kind of designation is that it requires the indorsement of both *A* and *B* to negotiate the instrument further. (See p. 486, State National Bank v Sumco Engineering, Inc.) This protects *A* against the action of *B,* and vice versa. Each knows that the other cannot secretly negotiate the instrument and pocket the proceeds. This rule does not apply, however, when the payees are partners or when one person is authorized to act for all and indorses for all.

Joint payees or joint indorsees who indorse are deemed to indorse jointly and severally. If the instrument is payable to *alternate payees* or if it has been negotiated to alternate indorsees, as *A* or *B,* it may be indorsed and delivered by either of them.

The UCC declares the rights of joint payees only with respect to the paper. Non-Code principles will determine the rights of the joint payees as between themselves. Thus, a check payable to husband and wife is initially "their" property but when it is a check for a refund of income taxes for a year in which the husband alone produced the income on which the tax was paid, the husband is entitled to the proceeds of the check to the exclusion of the wife.

(b)   Agent or Officer as Payee. The instrument may be made payable to the order of an officeholder. For example, a check may read "Pay to the order of Receiver of Taxes." Such a check may be received and negotiated by the person who at the time is the Receiver of Taxes. This is a matter of convenience since the person writing the check is not required to find out the actual name of the Receiver of Taxes at that time.

If the instrument is drawn in favor of a person as "Cashier" or some other fiscal officer of a bank or corporation, it is prima facie payable to the bank or corporation of which such person is an officer, and may be negotiated by the indorsement of either the bank or the corporation, or of the named officer. If drawn in favor of an agent, it may similarly be negotiated by the agent or the agent's principal.[16]

(c)   Partial Negotiation. A negotiation of part of the amount due on the paper cannot be made.[17] The entire instrument must be negotiated to one person or to the same persons. If the instrument has been partly paid, however, the unpaid balance may be transferred by indorsement. This is proper as the entire amount then due, although it is only a portion of the original amount due, is being transferred.

(d)   Missing Indorsement. Although order paper cannot be negotiated without indorsement, it can be assigned to another without indorsement. In such a case, the transferee has the same rights as the transferor; and if the transferee gave value for

---

[16] UCC § 3-117.
[17] UCC § 3-202(3). The partial negotiation is not a nullity but is given the effect of a partial assignment.

the paper, the transferee also has the right to require that the transferor indorse the instrument unqualifiedly and thereby effect a negotiation of the instrument.

When the transferor fails to indorse, the transferee may bring suit as an assignee and it is no defense to the obligor that there was no indorsement.

§ 29:12. Negotiation of Bearer Paper. Any commercial paper payable to bearer may be negotiated by a mere transfer of possession.[18] Thus bearer paper is negotiated to a person taking possession of it, without regard to whether this was done with the consent of the owner of the paper.

The paper may be negotiated by a mere transfer of possession not only when the instrument expressly states that it is payable to bearer, but also when the law interprets it as being payable to bearer, as in the case of a check payable to the order of "Cash."

Although bearer paper may be negotiated by such transfer, the one to whom it is delivered may insist that the bearer indorse the paper so as to impose the liability of an indorser. This situation most commonly arises when a check payable to "Cash" is presented to a bank for payment.

§ 29:13. Government Checks. The regulations of the United States Treasury govern the payment and indorsement of government checks. These regulations require a party presenting a Treasury check to the government to guarantee that all prior indorsements on the check are genuine, and grant the Treasurer the right to demand a refund if that guarantee is breached. Consequently, a bank presenting a government check to the government for payment is liable to the government when it is established that the payee was dead and an indorsement had been forged, as against the contention that UCC § 3-406 should apply and estop the United States because of its negligence in issuing a check to a deceased payee.[19]

§ 29:14. Forged and Unauthorized Indorsements. A forged or unathorized indorsement is by definition no indorsement of the person by whom it appears to have been made and, accordingly, the possessor of the paper is not the holder when the indorsement of that person was necessary for effective negotiation of the paper to the possessor.

If payment of commercial paper is made to one claiming under or through a forged indorsement, the payor is ordinarily liable to the person who is the rightful owner of the paper (See p. 487, Gast v American Casualty Co.), unless such person is estopped or barred by negligence or other conduct from asserting any claim against the payor.

§ 29:15. Forged Payee Impostor Exceptions. Ordinarily when the name of the payee is forged on commercial paper there is no effective negotiation of the paper to the person to whom it is delivered thereafter: the paper has not been indorsed and delivered by the person to whom it was then payable, namely, the payee.

The Code makes exceptions to this general rule in three situations. In these situations, the forged character of the payee's signature is ignored as far as negotiation

---

[18] UCC § 3-202(1).
[19] United States v City National Bank & Trust Co. (CA8 Mo) 491 F2d 851.

of the paper is concerned and the forged signature is given the same effect as though it had been authorized by the named payee: (a) an impostor has induced the maker or drawer to issue the instrument to the person whose identity has been assumed by the impostor, or to a confederate in the name of that payee; (b) the person signing as, or on behalf of, the drawer intends that the named payee shall have no interest in the paper, or (c) an agent or employee of the drawer has given the drawer the name used as the payee, intending that the latter should not have any interest in the paper.

The first situation is present when a person impersonates the holder of a savings account and, by presenting a forged withdrawal slip to the savings bank, gets the bank to issue a check payable to the bank's customer but which it hands to the impersonator in the belief that the impersonator is the customer. The second situation arises when the owner of a checking account, who wishes to conceal the true purpose of taking money from the bank, makes out a check purportedly in payment of a debt which in fact does not exist.

The last situation is illustrated by the case of the employee who fraudulently causes the employer to sign a check made to a customer or another person, whether existing or not, but the employee does not intend to send it to that person but rather intends to forge the latter's indorsement, to cash the check, and to keep the money.

These forged payee exceptions are known as the *impostor rule*[20] although it in fact covers situations which might be better described as (a) impersonations, (b) dummy payees, and (c) dummy payees-fraudulent employees.

The impostor rule applies when the person whose name is forged is a copayee of the paper as well as when that person is the sole payee.

The impostor rule does not apply when there is a valid check to an actual creditor for a correct amount owed by the drawer and someone thereafter forges the payee's name, even though the forger is an employee of the drawer.

Even when the unauthorized indorsement of the payee's name is effective by virtue of the impostor rule, a person forging the payee's name is subject to civil and criminal liability for making such indorsement.

§ 29:16. Effect of Incapacity or Misconduct on Negotiation. A negotiation is effective even though (1) it is made by a minor or any other person lacking capacity; (2) it is an act beyond the powers of a corporation; (3) it is obtained by fraud, duress, or mistake of any kind; (4) or the negotiation is part of an illegal transaction or was made in breach of duty. Under general principles of law apart from the UCC, the transferor in such cases may be able to set aside the negotiation or to obtain some other form of legal relief. If, however, the instrument has in the meantime been acquired by a holder in due course, the negotiation can no longer be set aside.[21]

§ 29:17. Lost Paper. The effect of losing commercial paper depends upon who is suing or demanding payment from whom and whether the paper was order paper or bearer paper when it was lost. If the paper is order paper, the finder does not become the holder because the paper, by definition, is not indorsed and delivered by the person to whom

---

[20] UCC § 3-405.
[21] UCC § 3-207.

it was then payable. The former holder who lost it is still the rightful owner of the paper, although technically not the holder because not in possession of the paper.

When a commercial paper is lost, it may be possible to have a new paper issued in its place. Thus an employer may issue a new pay check to replace the check lost by the employee. If the lost paper is a promissory note, it is less likely that the maker will oblige by executing a new promissory note. In any event, the owner of the lost paper may bring suit on it against any party liable thereon. (See p. 488, Kraft v Sommer) There is, of course, the practical difficulty of proving just what the lost paper provided and explaining the loss of the paper. The court may also require that the plaintiff suing on the lost instrument furnish the defendant with security to indemnify the defendant against loss by reason of any claim which might thereafter be made on the lost instrument.[22]

If the paper is in bearer form when it is lost, the finder, as the possessor of bearer paper, is the holder, and is entitled to enforce payment.

C. ASSIGNMENT OF COMMERCIAL PAPER

Although commercial paper may be negotiated, it may also be assigned. The assignment may result from the act of the parties or by operation of law.

§ 29:18. Assignment by Act of the Parties. Commercial paper may be assigned in the same manner as any other contract right by the express act of the holder. A commercial paper is also regarded as assigned when a person whose indorsement is required on the instrument transfers it without indorsing it. (See p. 488, Waters v Waters)

When a necessary indorsement is missing, the transferee has only the rights of an assignee. If the transferee acquires the paper for value, the transferee is entitled, however, to require that the transferor indorse the instrument.[23] If the indorsement is obtained, then the transferee is deemed a holder but only as of the time when the indorsement is made.

§ 29:19. Assignment by Operation of Law. An assignment by operation of law occurs when by virtue of the law the title of one person to commercial paper is vested in another. If the holder of a commercial paper becomes a bankrupt or dies, the title to the instrument vests automatically in the trustee in bankruptcy or in the personal representative of the decedent's estate.

D. WARRANTIES OF TRANSFEROR

When commercial paper is transferred, the transferor ordinarily makes certain implied warranties.

§ 29:20. Introduction. The transferor of commercial paper may make an express guarantee. In any case, certain warranties are implied. The transferor, by the act of making the transfer, warrants the existence of certain facts. The warranties of the transferor

---

[22] UCC § 3-804.
[23] UCC § 3-201(3).

are not always the same but vary according to the nature of the indorsement and whether the instrument is transferred with or without an indorsement. A distinction is made between the warranties arising in connection with acceptance or payment and those arising in connection with transfer. In the case of transfer by indorsement, the warranty may run to a subsequent holder; in the case of transfer by delivery only, the warranty runs only to the immediate transferee.

§ 29:21. Warranties of Unqualified Indorser. When the holder of a commercial paper negotiates it by an unqualified indorsement, and receives consideration, the transferor warrants:

(1) Ownership of good title, which includes the genuineness of all indorsements necessary to title to the instrument, or authorization to act for one who has such good title.[24]

(2) The act of transferring the instrument is rightful, independent of the question of title or authority to act.[25]

(3) The signatures on the instrument are genuine or executed by authorized agents.[26]

(4) The instrument has not been materially altered.[27]

(5) The indorser has no knowledge of the existence or commencement of any insolvency proceeding against the maker or acceptor of the instrument, or against the drawer of an unaccepted draft or bill of exchange.[28]

(6) No defense of any party is good as against the indorser.[29]

These warranties made by the unqualified indorser pass to the transferee and to any subsequent holder who acquires the instrument in good faith.[30]

When the holder presents a check to the drawee bank for payment, an indorsement of the check does not give rise to any warranty that the account of the drawer in the drawee bank is sufficient to cover the check.

When an item has been paid to the possessor on the basis of a forged indorsement, a collecting bank which sustains loss by being required to pay the true owner of the paper or prior collecting bank may recover its loss from its customer because of the customer's warranty of the genuineness of prior signatures when the customer indorsed the item in the course of depositing it with the collecting bank. This right of recovery may be enforced in an ordinary lawsuit or by charging back the account of the customer or of a collecting bank to which the proceeds of the item had been paid. When the bank claiming the right to recover and to charge back has delayed unreasonably under the circumstances, its right to recover or charge back is barred by such delay if the other party has sustained loss because of the delay. (See p. 489, First Federal Savings & Loan Ass'n. v Branch Banking & Trust Co.)

§ 29:22. Warranties of Other Parties.

(a) Qualified Indorser. The qualified indorser makes the same warranties as an unqualified indorser except that the warranty as to "no defenses" (6) is limited to a

---

[24] UCC § 3-417(2)(a).
[25] UCC § 3-417(2)(a).
[26] UCC § 3-417(2)(b).
[27] UCC § 3-417(2)(c).
[28] UCC § 3-417(2)(e).
[29] UCC § 3-417(2)(d).
[30] UCC § 3-417(2).

warranty that the indorser does not have knowledge of any defense, rather than that no such defense exists.[31] The warranties of a qualified indorser run to the same persons as those of an unqualified indorser.

(b)   Transferor by Delivery. The warranties made by one who transfers a commercial paper by delivery are the same as those made by an unqualified indorser except that they run only to the immediate transferee and then only if consideration has been given for the transfer.[32] Subsequent holders cannot enforce such warranties against this prior transferor by delivery regardless of the character of such holders.

(c)   Selling Agent or Broker. A selling agent or broker who discloses such representative capacity warrants only good faith and authority to act. One who does not disclose such capacity is subject to the warranties of an ordinary transferor who transfers in the manner employed.[33]

---

[31] UCC § 3-417(3). The qualified indorsement does not exclude other warranties unless it is specified to be "without warranties."
[32] UCC § 3-417(2).
[33] UCC § 3-417(4).

CASES FOR CHAPTER 29

State National Bank v Sumco Engineering

46 Ala App 244, 240 So2d 366 (1970)

A check was drawn by Calument and Hecla, Inc. on the State National Bank payable to Sumco Engineering and Madison Construction and Supply Company. Madison presented the check to the drawee bank for payment. The bank paid Madison the full amount of the check although it had not been indorsed by Sumco. Suit was then brought against the drawee bank by Sumco. From a judgment in Sumco's favor the bank appealed.

PER CURIAM . . . The issue, as we see it, is whether the appellant drawee bank was obligated to the drawer of the check to pay the face amount of it to the two payees listed thereon or not.

". . . The contract of the bank with each depositor is to pay the money deposited on demand made at its banking house, in such sums, at such times, and to such persons as the depositor may direct. Under such contract, the bank is not warranted in paying out the money of its depositor except in strict accordance with his order, and it has an absolute obligation in this respect which is not fulfilled merely by the exercise of reasonable diligence." . . .

". . . Where a check is payable to two or more persons as payees, or to their order, the amount of the check must be paid to both payees or upon the order of both. Payment to one of the payees or to the order of one payee without the authority of the other payee does not discharge the drawee bank of its liability for the amount of the check, unless the payees are partners."

In the case at bar the drawer made the check payable to two joint payees, and the payees had a right to believe that they possessed a valuable instrument with such commercial character that title thereto could not pass or that payment thereof could not be made by the drawee without the indorsements of both of them appearing thereon.

But in this case payment was made by the drawee bank with the indorsement of only one of the two payees appearing thereon. Obviously then, the drawee did not pay the face amount of the check to the two payees whose names also appeared on the face of the check, which is contrary to the directions given to the drawee bank by the drawer as embodied in the terms of the instrument explicitly set out on the face thereof.

The rule requiring the drawee bank to strictly abide by the directions of the drawer as set out on the face of the check is based on sound principles. . . .

. . . In a situation such as the one now before us, the unpaid payee should be allowed to recover as against the drawee for the face amount of the check absent any effort to allege and prove a lesser interest in the face amount of said check. . . .

To hold otherwise, would have the effect of thwarting the expressed intent of the drawer—as spelled out on the face of the check—communicated to the drawee bank, to pay to the order of the joint payees, Madison Construction and Supply Company and Sumco Engineering, Inc., the amount of $5,907.74.

The drawer had a right to expect the drawee bank to carry out his instructions to the letter, and the payees designated on the check had a right to expect that payment would be made to both of them in the absence of a direction by one of them to the contrary.

[Judgment affirmed]

Code Comment: This case was decided under the pre-Code law—the Uniform Negotiable Instruments Law (NIL). The same decision would be made under the Code.

Gast v American Casualty Co.

99 NJ Super 538, 240 A2d 682 (1968)

The Gasts owned a building which they contracted to sell to the Hannas. The building was insured against fire with the American Casualty Co. Thereafter, when the house was damaged by fire, a settlement was reached with the insurance company through Sidney Rosenbaum, a public fire adjuster. In order to make payment for the loss, the insurance company drew a draft on itself payable to the Hannas, the Gasts, and to Sidney Rosenbaum. Apparently the Hannas indorsed the draft, forged the names of the other payees as indorsers, cashed the draft, and then disappeared. Thereafter the Gasts sued the American Casualty Co. From a judgment in favor of the insurance company, the Gasts appealed.

GARTON, J.A.D. . . . Defendant [American Casualty Co.] denied that it had any liability by reason of the forgery of the indorsements on the draft and, in addition, alleged that plaintiffs [Gasts] had contributed to the forgery by their negligence and were thus precluded from recovery. . . . The trial judge instructed the jury that . . . "A drawee is liable for payment to a person whose name had been forged unless the person was subsequently negligent in contributing to the forgery. *Therefore, the factual problem, members of the jury, in this problem reduces itself to one of alleged negligence on the part of the defendant, in their manner of payment and, too, the alleged contributory negligence on the part of the plaintiffs under the facts of this case, and these factual issues, of course, will be for your determination. . . .*" (emphasis supplied)

We conclude that the charge as given was erroneous, both on the issue of defendant's liability as drawer-drawee to plaintiffs on the forged indorsements and on the issue of plaintiffs' contributory negligence.

The [italicized] language is a misconception of the law regarding the elements of defendant's liability. The draft was drawn upon defendant and was executed by defendant. As both drawer and drawee, defendant had the responsibility to make payment to the named payees on the instrument. . . .

The nature of defendant's obligation is set forth in the statute. It is not grounded upon negligence. [UCC §] 3-419 provides in pertinent part:

"(1) An instrument is converted when . . . (c) It is paid on a forged indorsement.

"(2) In an action against a drawee under subsection (1) the measure of the drawee's liability is the face amount of the instrument. In any other action under subsection (1) the measure of liability is presumed to be the face amount of the instrument."

The statute created an absolute right to recover in favor of plaintiffs (absent negligence on their part) upon proof that the draft was paid on the forged indorsements. Plaintiffs' indorsements were concededly forged. It follows that defendant, having paid the draft, was rendered liable for the conversion in the face amount.

Comment 3 to [UCC §] 3-419, by the draftsmen of the Uniform Commercial Code, makes it clear that the above analysis is correct. That comment states: "Subsection (1) (c) is new. It adopts the prevailing view of decisions holding that payment on a forged indorsement is not an acceptance, but that *even though made in good faith, it is an exercise of dominion and control over the instrument* inconsistent with the rights of the owner, *and results in liability for conversion.*" (emphasis added)

. . . It was therefore error to instruct the jury that plaintiffs were required to show that defendant was negligent.

[Judgment reversed and action remanded]

Kraft v Sommer

54 AD 2d 598, 387 NYS2d 318 (1976)

Sommer delivered a check to Kraft. The bank on which the check was drawn refused to pay it and Kraft sued Sommer. The check had apparently been lost. Sommer offered in evidence a copy of the check. The lower court entered judgment for Kraft because Sommer could not produce the original check. Sommer appealed.

MEMORANDUM * . . . Plaintiff alleges . . . that she "is the owner and holder of (a) check, no part of which has been paid" and she seeks payment of the check. It is undisputed that the check was delivered to her by the [drawer] and that the bank in which she deposited the check refused to honor it because payment had been stopped by defendant Sommer, one of the executors of the deceased [drawer]. [The] plaintiff claims [the original check] was not returned to her by the bank to which she had presented it. The bank's affidavit states that it was its standard practice to photograph such a check, to mark it "payment stopped" and to return it by regular mail to the depositor. . . . Plaintiff's inability to produce the original check [does not] require the dismissal of the causes of action relating to the check.

Section 3-804 of the Uniform Commerical Code makes manifest that a suit may be brought by the "owner" of a lost instrument. Although requirements of "proof" as to the ownership of the check, circumstances of the loss and its terms are required, these matters go to the evidence necessary at trial and not to the sufficiency of the pleadings. "The fact that a negotiable instrument is lost, stolen or destroyed does not defeat the right of the holder or discharge his interest. The holder may bring suit upon the instrument in his own name just as if the instrument were available for production in court. It is, of course, necessary for him to prove the terms of the missing instrument, and this requires that there be sufficient evidence produced of his ownership of the instrument and of the facts which prevent its production in court." (1 Anderson, Uniform Commercial Code, § 3-804:3).

---

* [Authors' note] Ordinarily an opinion of the court is filed under the name of the judge who wrote the opinion. When a case is perfectly clear and obvious, the opinion will frequently be filed without naming the writing judge and will then have a heading of "memorandum" or "per curiam" [by the court].

. . . The parties should proceed to trial . . .

[Judgment reversed and action remanded]

Waters v Waters

(Tex Civ App) 498 SW2d 236 (1973)

Jerry Waters and his wife Patsy entered into a property settlement agreement as part of a divorce proceeding. By the agreement, it was agreed that a demand note which had been signed by Jerry payable to the order of Jim Still, who was Patsy's father, should be "transferred to Patsy . . . in the future." Jim delivered the note to Patsy without any indorsement or writing. Jim thereafter died. Patsy sued Jerry on the note. He raised the defense that she was not entitled to sue on the note because she was not the owner of the note. Judgment was entered in favor of Patsy. Jerry appealed.

DUNAGAN, C.J. . . . Appellant [Jerry] contends that there was no evidence . . . that the appellee [Patsy] is the owner of said note. The note does not bear the indorsement of Jim Still. However, the appellee . . . testified that her father gave her the note with the statement that it was hers and she could collect same. The evidence shows that she was in possession of the note.

This evidence is . . . undisputed. This evidence shows a fulfillment of the provisions of the settlement contract "that the note is presently payable to Jim Still, but will be transferred to Patsy A. Waters (appellee) in the future." The settlement contract did not set out or provide in what manner the note was to be transferred to the appellee. . . .

A promissory note can lawfully be transferred without a written assignment or an indorsement of the legal owner and holder thereof. . . . [The Official Code Comment to UCC § 3-201 on the transfer of paper states that] "the section applies to any transfer, whether by a holder or not. Any person who transfers an instrument transfers whatever rights he has in it. The transferee acquires those rights even though they do not amount to 'title.' The transfer of rights is not limited to transfers for value. An instrument may be transferred as a gift, and the donee acquires whatever rights the donor had." . . .

Delivery by a donor to donee of a promissory note payable to donor with intent to invest the donee with ownership is an effective gift of the note and transfer thereof. The gift to appellee from her father did not require a written transfer. Appellant by the settlement agreement and contract agreed for the note to be transferred to appellee and knew that such transfer was to be made and that no particular method for such transfer was provided. Title passes by oral gift. . . .

In Anderson's Uniform Commercial Code, Vol. 2, sec. 3.201:10, p. 752, . . . we find these statements: "Under the pre-Code law there was uncertainty as to the nature of the title received by the transferee of a negotiable instrument without indorsement; that is, as to whether he received a legal title or merely the equitable title to the paper. It is believed that, although the Code does not make any express determination of this issue, the transferee acquires legal title because the 'transfer of an instrument vests in the transferee such rights as the transferor has therein. . . . [UCC § 3-201(1)]. The fact that the transferee for value is given a specifically enforceable right to obtain the missing indorsement should not lead to the conclusion that prior to that time the transferee necessarily has merely equitable title. The only conclusion that must necessarily be drawn from the right to obtain the indorsement is that prior to obtaining the indorsement the transferee is not the 'holder,' for, as stated, 'negotiation takes effect only when the indorsement is made and until that time there is no presumption that the transferee is the owner.' This statement is merely that the transferee is not the holder and must affirmatively prove that he is the 'owner.' There is no statement that he is not the owner nor that he is not the owner of the rights of the transferor, namely, ownership of the legal title to the paper."

Sec. 201:12 reads as follows: "The fact that a transferee lacking a necessary indorsement is not the holder does not mean that the transferee cannot establish his right as assignee and enforce the obligation. To the contrary, a transferee although he has neglected to obtain the indorsement necessary to make him a holder may enforce a note, foreclose on collateral, and obtain a deficiency judgment against the debtor."

Upon a careful review of the entire record, we find ample, competent and legal evidence which supports the trial court's . . . judgment. . . .

[Judgment affirmed]

First Federal Savings & Loan Ass'n v Branch Banking & Trust Co.

282 NC 44, 191 SE2d 683 (1972)

Hanover Insurance Company drew a draft payable to Geraldine Stallings and Winter Park Fed- **eral Savings & Loan Association. The draft bearing the forged indorsement of Winter Park was deposited by Stallings with First Federal Savings & Loan Association. First Federal then sent it to Branch Banking and Trust Company which sent it to Chase Manhattan Bank which presented the draft to and was paid by Hanover. When the forgery was discovered, Hanover paid Winter Park the amount of the draft and that amount was then charged back against Chase which charged it back against Branch Banking which charged it against First Federal. This was done approximately 27 months after the draft had originally been paid by Hanover. Meanwhile Stallings had already withdrawn from her First Federal account all of the proceeds of the draft. First Federal sued Branch Banking for the amount of the draft. The lower court entered judgment for Branch Banking and First Federal appealed.**

LAKE, J. . . . The plaintiff took the draft upon the indorsement of one of the payees and the forged indorsement of the other. Such transfer conferred upon the plaintiff the interest of Geraldine M. Stallings in the draft, and no more. . . .

The plaintiff alleges and Hanover admits that, thereafter, Hanover caused Branch to charge back to the plaintiff's account the full amount so paid by Hanover on the draft when it was presented for payment. If, as the plaintiff alleges, Geraldine M. Stallings, at the time of her indorsement to the plaintiff, was entitled to any part of the proceeds of the draft, this right passed to the plaintiff, and the plaintiff was entitled to retain that portion of the proceeds so paid by Hanover upon the presentment of the draft for payment. If, on the other hand, Winter Park was entitled to the full amount of the draft, as Hanover seems to imply in its allegation that, since the discovery of the forgery of the indorsement, it has paid the full amount to Winter Park, then the plaintiff, who succeeded to none of the rights of Winter Park, would have no right to retain any portion of the proceeds of the draft. . . .

Assuming . . . that Geraldine M. Stallings had no right to retain any portion of the proceeds of the draft at the time of her indorsement to the plaintiff, we turn to the right of the drawee, Hanover, to charge the draft back to the collecting bank, and, through it, to the plaintiff, approximately 27 months after the draft was paid by Hanover. [UCC §] 3-417 provides that any person who obtains payment of an instrument, and any prior transferor thereof, warrants to a person who pays it in good faith that he has a good title to the instrument or is authorized to obtain payment on behalf of one who has a good title to it. This warranty is broken if such person claims through the forged instrument of a joint payee having any interest in the proceeds of the paper.

Article 4 of the Uniform Commercial Code, Chapter 25 of the General Statutes, is applicable to drafts forwarded for collection through a bank or banks. [UCC §] 4-207(1) provides that each customer or collecting bank who obtains payment of such paper, and each prior customer and collecting bank, "warrants to the payor bank *or other payor*," who in good faith pays the paper, that he has a good title to it or is authorized to obtain payment on behalf of one who has a good title thereto. With reference to the transaction involved in this action, Hanover is such "other payor," Chase was the collecting bank who obtained payment, Branch was such prior collecting bank and the plaintiff was such prior customer. Paragraph (4) of [UCC §] 4-207 provides: "Unless a claim for breach of warranty under this section is made within a reasonable time after the person claiming learns of the breach, the person liable is discharged to the extent of any loss caused by the delay in making claim." If, under [the UCC], Hanover was entitled to proceed directly against the plaintiff for reimbursement of the amount paid by Hanover upon the draft, Hanover would not be liable to the plaintiff in this action for having caused Branch to make the chargeback against the plaintiff's account with Branch.

[UCC §] 4-406, relating to the duty of a customer of a bank to discover and report to his bank unauthorized signatures and alterations, has no application to the right of Hanover to proceed against the plaintiff for the recovery of the amount paid by Hanover upon this draft. . . .

"It is generally recognized that the right of a maker or drawee to recover a payment made on a forged indorsement may be lost if he is guilty of negligence or laches whereby the position of the person receiving payment is changed to the damage of such person. Thus, it is held that a drawee may recover if, after discovery of the forgery, he is guilty of no negligence that is injurious to the person receiving payment. But delay in discovering a forged indorsement ordinarily is not negligence and does not preclude recovery, particularly where no injury to the holder results.

"In order for a drawee or other person to recover a payment made upon a forged indorsement it is a general requisite that he give timely notice after discovery of the forgery. Prompt notice of the discovery of the forgery is not a condition precedent to suit, but if it is shown that the drawee or other payor on learning that an indorsement was forged did not give prompt notice of it, and that damage resulted, recovery of the payment by such person is barred. . . . But the damage occasioned by the delay must be established, and not left to conjecture."

The drawee of a draft is not held to know the signature of an indorser, whether the payee or an intermediate indorser. He is under no duty to examine the draft to determine the genuineness of an indorsement, but may rely upon the warranty made to him by the person receiving payment that such person has title to the instrument. When, however, the drawee learns that an indorsement, necessary to the title of the person who has received payment, is forged, the drawee must then act with reasonable promptness or his right to recover from the person receiving payment, or a prior indorser, will be barred, to the extent of any loss which such person sustains by reason of the drawee's delay. . . .

. . . There is no rule of law establishing the time within which the drawee must notify the person receiving payment, or a prior indorser, that such person's title to the draft was defective by reason of a forged indorsement. A reasonable time for such action depends upon the circumstances in each case.

[Judgment reversed and action remanded]

QUESTIONS AND CASE PROBLEMS

1. What social forces are affected by the law as to qualified indorsements?
2. Compare the status of the finder of a lost watch and the finder of a lost check.
3. A check payable to a dummy payee is treated the same as bearer paper. Appraise this statement.

4. Compare the warranty liability of an unqualified indorser, a qualified indorser, and a non-indorsing transferor.

5. A check given in settlement of a lawsuit was drawn to the order of "*A*, attorney for *B*." Could *A* negotiate the check? [Maber, Inc. v Factor Cab Corp., 19 App Div 2d 500, 244 NYS2d 768]

6. Benton, as agent for Savidge, received an insurance settlement check from the Metropolitan Life Insurance Co. He indorsed it "For deposit" and deposited it in the Bryn Mawr Trust Company in the account of Savidge. What was the nature and effect of this indorsement? [Savidge v Metropolitan Life Insurance Co., 380 Pa 205, 110 A2d 730]

7. The Feldman Construction Company made a contract with Interstate Steel Corporation for construction work. General Pipe & Supply furnished building materials to Interstate. Feldman drew a check on its bank, the Union Bank payable to the order of "Interstate Steel Corp. General Pipe & Supply." Interstate indorsed the check and Union Bank then paid the check. Feldman sued Union Bank for the amount of the check because it had not been properly indorsed. Union Bank claimed that the check was payable in the alternative and therefore the indorsement of one of the payees was sufficient. Was the bank correct? [Feldman Constr. Co. v Union Bank, 28 Cal App 3d 731, 104 Cal Rptr 912]

8. Humphrey drew a check for $100. It was stolen and the payee's name forged as an indorser. The check was then negotiated to Miller who had no knowledge of these facts. Miller indorsed the check to the Citizens Bank. Payment of the check was voided on the ground of the forgery. The Citizens Bank then sued Miller as indorser. Decide. [Citizens Bank of Hattiesburg v Miller, 194 Miss 557, 11 So2d 457]

9. Searcy executed and delivered a promissory note payable to the order of the Bank of Ensley. A later holder, the First National Bank of Birmingham, sued Searcy on the note. A dispute arose as to whether the First National Bank was the holder of the instrument on January 10, before the closing of the Ensley Bank on January 11. The First National Bank proved that on January 10 the note was indorsed to it by the Ensley Bank. Did this prove that the First National Bank was the holder on January 10? [First National Bank of Birmingham v Searcy, 31 Ala App 553, 19 So2d 559]

10. When claims filed with the insurance company were approved for payment, they were given to the claims clerk who would prepare checks to pay these claims and then give the checks to the treasurer to sign. The claims clerk of the insurance company made a number of checks payable to persons who did not have any claims, gave them to the treasurer together with the checks for valid claims, and the treasurer signed all the checks. The claims clerk then removed the false checks, indorsed them with the names of their respective payees, and cashed them at the bank where the insurance company had its account. The bank debited the account of the insurance company with the amount of these checks. The insurance company claimed that the bank could not do this because the indorsements on the checks were forgeries. Is the insurance company correct? [See General Acci. Fire & Life Assur. Corp. v Citizens Fidelity Bank & Trust Co. (Ky) 519 SW2d 817.]

11. A corporate check was required to be signed by two officers, *A* and *B*. A check was signed by *A* but the signature of *B* was forged. The check was delivered to the payee *C* and negotiated by him to *D* who indorsed and delivered it for deposit to the *E* bank. The check was dishonored and when *E* bank lost its lawsuit against *B* it sued *D* on his implied warranty that signatures were genuine. *D* raised the defense that the implied warranty extended only to signatures necessary to the title of the holder. Was he correct? [See Davis Aircraft Products Co. v Bankers Trust Co., 36 AppDiv2d 705, 319 NYS2d 379.]

12. Fred Klomann held three notes of Sol K. Graff & Sons. He specially indorsed the notes to his daughter, Candace, and delivered the notes to her. She handed them back to Fred so that he could collect them. Thereafter, Fred crossed out Candace's name and substituted the name of his wife, Georgia. Georgia demanded payment from Sol K. Graff & Sons. They refused to pay on the ground that Georgia had no interest in or right to enforce the notes. She brought suit against Sol K. Graff & Sons. Is she entitled to recover? [Klomann v Sol K. Graff & Sons, — Ill App —, 317 NE2d 608]

13. The Snug Harbor Realty Co. had a checking account in the First National Bank. When construction work was obtained by the Snug Harbor Realty Co., its superintendent, Magee, would examine the bills submitted for labor and materials. He would instruct the bookkeeper as to what bills were approved, and checks were then prepared by the bookkeeper in accordance with such instructions. After the checks were signed by the proper official of Snug Harbor, they were picked up by Magee for delivery. Instead of delivering certain checks, he forged the signatures of the respective payees as indorsers and cashed the checks. The drawee bank then debited the Snug Harbor account with the amount of these checks. Snug Harbor claimed that this was improper and sued the bank for the amount of such checks. Was Snug Harbor entitled to recover such amount? [Snug Harbor Realty Co. v First National Bank, 105 NJ Super 572, 253 A2d 581, affirmed 54 NJ 95, 253 A2d 545]

14. The New Mexico Pipe Trades Welfare Trust Fund had a checking account in the Albuquerque National Bank. The signature card specified that two signatures were required on all checks and stated that the officers of the fund named on the card were authorized to sign checks and to indorse checks for deposit. In an action brought against the bank by Cooper and other trustees of the Welfare Fund, the question arose as to the validity of indorsements made on certain checks. They had been indorsed with two rubber stamps, one reading "New Mexico Pipe Trades Welfare Trust Fund" and the other, "Pay to the order of Albuquerque National Bank . . . For deposit only." No signature of any authorized officer appeared thereon, although the stamps had in fact been put on by one of the named officers. Were the indorsements valid? [Cooper v Albuquerque National Bank, 75 NMex 295, 404 P2d 125]

30 Presentment of Paper for Payment and Acceptance

A promissory note is a two-party commercial paper, which means that originally there are only a maker and a payee. The maker is liable for payment on the due date specified in the note or on demand if the note is a demand instrument. If the maker dishonors the note when it is presented for payment, the indorsers, if there are any, may become liable for payment of the paper. This chapter considers the rules of law that must be followed in order to enforce the liability of a party to a note. It must be remembered that even though these rules have been satisfied, the plaintiff may lose in a given case if the plaintiff is not the holder, as discussed in Chapter 29, or if the defendant has a defense that may be asserted against the plaintiff, as discussed in Chapter 31.

A. PRESENTMENT OF NOTES FOR PAYMENT

There are specific procedures for presenting a note for payment and for giving notice of dishonor. The procedures for presenting a promissory note for payment and for giving notice of dishonor, which are explained in this chapter, apply also to other types of commercial paper, that is, drafts and checks.

§ 30:1. Liability of Maker. The liability of a maker of a promissory note is primary. This means that payment may be demanded of the maker and a maker may be sued by the holder as soon as the debt is due, but not before that time. (See p. 503, Bertolet v Burke) The maker is under the duty to pay the note at the time and at the place named, if any place is specified in the note, unless a defense can be set up that is valid against the holder.

By the very act of signing the promissory note, the maker gives up two possible defenses. The maker thereby admits (1) the existence of the payee named in the instrument, and (2) the payee's capacity at that time to indorse the paper.[1] Thus, even though the payee of a note is a minor or a bankrupt, the maker cannot deny the validity of the title of a subsequent holder of the paper on the ground that the payee lacked capacity to transfer title to the paper.

When a note is issued in payment of a debt, the original obligation is suspended until the instrument is due or until presentment for payment in the case of demand

---

[1] UCC § 3-413(3).

paper. If the note is dishonored by nonpayment, the holder may sue either on the note or on the underlying obligation.[2]

§ 30:2. Need for Presentment for Payment. The holder of a promissory note need not present the paper to the maker for payment in order to hold the latter liable on the note. If the note is payable at a definite time, the maker is under a duty to pay the holder the amount due on the instrument as soon as that date is reached. The liability of the maker continues until barred by the statute of limitations.

If the note is demand paper, no special demand for payment is required. The holder may even begin a lawsuit against the maker without first making a demand for payment as the act of bringing suit is regarded as the making of a demand. If the note is payable at a definite time, the holder may bring suit on the day after the due date without making a prior demand upon the maker.

An unqualified indorser is secondarily liable for the payment of the instrument, which means that the indorser must pay the amount of the instrument to the holder under certain circumstances. Generally, this duty arises only if (1) the instrument was presented for payment to the primary party on the due date or at maturity, (2) the primary party defaulted by failing to pay the amount of the instrument to the holder, and (3) the secondary party in question was given proper notice of the primary party's default.

A qualified indorser or a former holder of bearer paper who negotiates the instrument without indorsing it is not liable for payment of the paper. However, such parties, as well as an unqualified indorser, who does have a secondary liability, may be liable for a breach of warranty.

§ 30:3. Presentment for Payment. When presentment for payment of notes or other commercial paper is required, the following rules apply:

(a) Person Making Presentment. Presentment for payment must be made by the holder of the paper or by one authorized to act and receive payment on behalf of the holder.

(b) Manner of Presentment. Demand for payment in any manner is a sufficient presentment. An actual physical presenting of the paper is not required. The party to whom the demand for payment is made may require, however, that greater formality be observed, such as by requiring (1) reasonable identification of the person making presentment and evidence of authority if that person acts for another; (2) production of the instrument for payment at a place specified in it or, if there be none, at any place reasonable under the circumstances; and (3) a signed receipt on the instrument for any partial or full payment and its surrender upon full payment. If the party presenting the instrument does not comply with such requests at the time of making presentment, the presenting party is allowed a reasonable time within which to do so. If the presenting party does not comply with such reasonable request, the presentment that was made has no effect.[3]

The presentment must make a clear demand for payment and a mere inquiry as to whether payment would be made in the future is not sufficient.

[2] UCC § 3-802(1)(b).
[3] UCC § 3-505.

In addition to a presentment for payment made directly upon the primary party, presentment may be made by sending the paper through the mail to the debtor, or by sending it through a clearinghouse.[4] A collecting bank may also make presentment for payment by sending merely a notice to the nonbank party to whom the demand for payment is made.[5] If the party so notified fails to act within a specified time, such inaction is treated as a dishonor of the note.[6]

(c)   On Whom Presentment Is Made. Presentment for payment must be made to the party primarily liable, that is, the maker of the promissory note, or to a person who is authorized to make or refuse payment on behalf of the maker.[7]

(d)   Place of Making Presentment. Presentment for payment is properly made at the place that is specified in the paper. When a place of payment is not specified, presentment of the instrument is to be made at the place of business or the residence of the person from whom payment is to be demanded.[8]

§ 30:4. Time of Making Presentment. A note payable at a stated date must be presented for payment on that date. If the time for paying the balance due on the note has been accelerated, presentment must be made within a reasonable time after the default in a scheduled payment of principal or interest. For the purpose of determining the secondary liability of any party, presentment for payment must be made within a reasonable time after such person became liable on the instrument.

Presentment must be made at a reasonable time, and if made at a bank, must be made during its banking day.

(a)   Computation of Time. In determining the date of maturity of an instrument, the starting day is excluded and the day of payment is included. Thus, an instrument dated July 3 (which leaves 28 days in July) and payable thirty days from date is due on August 2.

(b)   Instrument Due on Legal or Business Holiday. When the presentment of the paper is due on a day that is not a full business day, presentment is due on the following full business day. This rule is applied when the due day is not a full business day either because it is a legal holiday or merely because the bank or other person required to make payment on the instrument, as a matter of its business practice, is closed all day or for half a day.

This rule is also applied when the due date is a business holiday for either party, that is, if either the person required to present the instrument or the person who is required to pay upon presentment is not open for a full business day on the due date, the day for presentment is extended to the first day thereafter that is a full business day for both of them.[9]

(c)   Excuse for Delay in Making Presentment. Failure of the holder to present an instrument for payment at the proper time will be excused when the delay is

---

[4] UCC § 3-504(2)(a), (b).
[5] UCC § 4-210(1). This provision is not applicable if the paper is payable by, through, or at a bank.
[6] UCC § 4-210(2).
[7] UCC § 3-504(3).
[8] UCC § 3-504(2)(c).
[9] UCC § 3-503(3).

caused by circumstances beyond the control of the holder. It must not, however, be caused by that person's misconduct, negligence, or fault. Mere inconvenience, such as that arising from inclement weather, is not a valid excuse for delay. When the circumstances that excuse the delay are removed, presentment must be made within a reasonable time thereafter.[10]

(d) Effect of Delay in Making Presentment. An unexcused delay in making any necessary presentment for payment discharges an indorser's liability for payment of the paper. If the note is *domiciled,* that is, payable at a bank, the delay may also operate to discharge the maker. The UCC provides as to such paper that "any . . . maker of a note payable at a bank who because the . . . payor bank becomes insolvent during the delay is deprived of funds maintained with the . . . payor bank to cover the instrument may discharge his liability by written assignment to the holder of his rights against the . . . payor bank in respect of such funds, but such . . . maker is not otherwise discharged." [11]

§ 30:5. When Presentment for Payment is Excused or Unnecessary.

(a) Waiver. Presentment for payment is not required if it has been waived by an express or implied agreement of the secondary party in question. A waiver of presentment is binding upon all parties if it appears on the face of the original note. If the waiver is part of an indorsement, however, it binds only that indorser.

(b) Inability. Presentment for payment is not required if it cannot be made in spite of the exercise of due diligence, as when presentment is attempted at the place where payment is to be made but neither the person who is to make payment nor anyone authorized to act can be found at that place.[12]

(c) Death or Insolvency. Presentment for payment is not required if the maker of the note has died or has gone into insolvency proceedings after issuing the note.

(d) Refusal to Pay. The holder is not required to make presentment upon a maker who has already refused to pay the note for any reason other than an objection that proper presentment had not been made.

(e) Belief or Conduct of Secondary Party. A secondary party cannot demand that presentment be made if that party has no reason to expect that the instrument will be paid and no right to require that payment be made.

§ 30:6. Dishonor of Note.
If the maker fails or refuses to pay the note when it is properly presented, the note has been dishonored by nonpayment. The fact that the maker does not make immediate payment of the note when it is presented does not necessarily dishonor the note. The maker has the right to withhold making a payment until a reasonable examination has been made to determine that the note is properly payable to the holder. This examination process, however, cannot delay payment beyond the close of business on the day of presentment.[13]

---

[10] UCC § 3-511(1). Delay is also excused when the holder does not know that the instrument is due, UCC § 3-511(1), as could occur if the due date had been accelerated by a prior holder.
[11] UCC § 3-502(1)(b).
[12] UCC §§ 3-504(2), 3-511(2)(c).
[13] UCC § 3-506(2).

§ 30:7. Notice of Dishonor. If commercial paper is dishonored by nonpayment, any secondary party who is not given proper notice thereof is released from liability, (see p. 504, Hane v Exten) unless the giving of notice is excused.[14] It is only necessary that a party be given notice once because a notice operates for the benefit of all parties who have rights against the party notified.

(a)   Who May Give Notice. The notice of dishonor is ordinarily given by the holder who has been refused payment or the holder's agent. An agent making presentment for payment may give notice of the dishonor to the principal, who in turn may give it to the secondary party in question. When any person who is liable on the paper receives notice of its dishonor, that person may in turn give notice to other secondary parties.

(b)   Person Notified. The notice of dishonor may be given to any party who is liable on the paper. Notice to one partner is notice to all, even though the firm has been dissolved. When the party to be notified is dead or incompetent, notice may be sent to the last known address or be given to the personal representative of such person.

(c)   Form of Notice. Notice may be given in any reasonable manner. It may be oral[15] or written, and it may be sent by mail. It may have any terms as long as it identifies the instrument and states that it has been dishonored. A misdescription that does not mislead the party notified does not nullify or vitiate the notice. Notice may be effected by sending the instrument itself, with a stamp, ticket, or writing attached thereto, stating that payment has been refused or by sending a notice of debit with respect to the paper.

(d)   Place of Notice. The UCC does not specify a place to which notice is to be given, but it provides that notice generally shall be deemed given whenever such steps have been taken as may be reasonably required to inform the other person, whether or not that person actually comes to know of it. Furthermore, a person is deemed to receive notice or notification when the notice is delivered at the place of business through which the contract was made or at any other place held out by that person as the place for the receipt of such communications.

(e)   Time of Notice. Notice must be given before midnight of the third business day after dishonor. If the notice is given following the receipt of notice of dishonor from another party, it must be given before midnight of the third business day after receiving such notice. When required of a bank, notice of dishonor must be given before midnight of the banking day following the banking day on which the note is dishonored or the bank receives notice of such dishonor.[16] A written notice of dishonor is effective when sent. Hence, a notice sent by mail is sufficient even though it is never received, provided it was properly addressed, bore the necessary postage, and was properly mailed.[17]

---

[14] UCC § 3-501(2)(a). In the case of a "domiciled" note payable at a bank, the maker must be given notice that the note was not paid when presented at the bank and, if notice is not so given, the maker is released to the same extent already noted in connection with the effect of failure to present at the bank. UCC § 3-501(2)(b).

[15] Laurel Bank & Trust Co. v Sahadi, 32 Conn Supp 172, 345 A2d 53 (telephone notice).

[16] UCC §§ 3-508(2), 4-105(1)(h).

[17] UCC § 3-504(4).

If notice is not given within the required time and the delay in or the absence of notice is not excused, the person entitled to notice cannot be held liable for the payment of the paper. The fact that the holder was not personally the cause of the delay in giving notice of dishonor does not prevent the discharge of the person not notified. (See p. 505, Nevada State Bank v Fischer)

§ 30:8. Excuse for Delay or Absence of Notice of Dishonor.

Delay in giving notice of dishonor is excused under the same circumstances as delay in making presentment for payment.[18]

The absence of any notice of dishonor is excused for three of the reasons considered as excusing the absence of presentment; namely (1) waiver, (2) inability to give notice in spite of due diligence, and (3) the fact that the party not notified did not have any reason to believe that the instrument would be paid nor any right to require payment.[19] When an indorser has such knowledge or so participates in the affairs of the primary party that the indorser knows that the commercial paper will not be honored by the primary party, it is not required that the holder go through the useless gesture of making a presentment and of notifying the secondary party.

Delay by a bank in returning a dishonored item is excused by equipment failure. (See p. 506, Port City State Bank v American National Bank)

§ 30:9. Proof of Dishonor.

As the liability of the secondary party depends upon whether certain steps were taken within the proper time, it is important for the holder to be able to prove compliance with the requirements of the law. In order to aid in proving such essential facts, certain documents and records are considered evidence of dishonor and of any notice recited therein. The trier of fact must accept such evidence in the absence of proof to the contrary.[20] These documents and records include (1) protests, (2) bank stamps and memorandums, and (3) bank records.

(a) **Protests.** A *protest* is a memorandum or certificate executed by a notary public, or certain other public officers, upon satisfactory information, which sets forth that the particular identified instrument has been dishonored. It may also recite that notice of dishonor was given to all parties or to specified parties.

(b) **Bank Stamps and Memorandums.** If the stamp put on the paper by a bank or the memorandum attached to the note by the bank is consistent with or suggests a dishonor, it is evidence of that fact. For example, a notation "not sufficient funds" or "payment stopped" indicates a dishonor or nonpayment of the instrument and therefore comes within this rule. On the other hand, a notation of "indorsement missing" is not consistent with dishonor and is therefore not admissible as evidence of a dishonor.

(c) **Bank Records.** Bank records kept in the usual course of business are admissible as evidence of dishonor even though it cannot be shown who made the entry in the books.

---

[18] UCC § 3-511.
[19] UCC § 3-511(2).
[20] UCC §§ 3-510, 1-201(31).

B. PRESENTMENT OF DRAFTS

This part considers the rules of law that must be followed in order to enforce the liability of a party to a draft. It must be remembered that even though these rules have been satisfied, a plaintiff will lose in a given case if not the holder as discussed in Chapter 29 or if the defendant has a defense which may be asserted against the plaintiff as discussed in Chapter 31.

A note must be presented for payment in order to hold secondary parties liable; under certain circumstances, a draft must be presented for acceptance as well as for payment.

If the drawer is also named as drawee, the paper has the effect of a promissory note.[21] In such a case, the drawer is the primary party and the procedures peculiar to drafts, such as presentment for acceptance, are eliminated.

§ 30:10. Liability of Drawee.

(a) Before Acceptance. An *acceptance* is the written assent of the drawee to the order of the drawer. A drawee is not liable for payment of a draft before acceptance. In the absence of a prior contract to accept the draft, the drawee is not under any duty to do so. The act of refusing to accept the draft does not give the holder any right to sue the drawee on the paper, even though the refusal breaks the contract with the drawer or some other person which obligated the drawee to accept the draft. Neither does the draft operate as an assignment of money, even though the drawee has possession of funds of the drawer.[22]

(b) After Acceptance. After the drawee accepts a draft, the drawee is an *acceptor* and is primarily liable for payment of the draft. By the acceptance, the acceptor also admits (1) the existence of the payee, and (2) the payee's capacity at the time to indorse the draft.[23]

If the drawee pays the instrument to a person who claims it through a forged instrument, the drawee must bear the loss of such payment.

§ 30:11. Liability of Drawer.
The drawer has a secondary liability. By executing the draft, the drawer undertakes to pay the amount of the draft to the holder if, when the instrument is presented to the drawee for acceptance or payment, it is dishonored and proper proceedings are then taken by the holder.

The drawer, however, may insert in the draft a provision to exclude or limit liability as by adding "without recourse."

The drawer admits two things by the act of drawing the draft: (1) the existence of the payee, and (2) the payee's capacity at the time to transfer the instrument. The effect of these statutory admissions is the same as in the case of the maker of a promissory note or the acceptor of a draft.[24]

When the drawer executes and delivers to the payee a draft in payment of a debt, the original obligation is suspended until the draft is due, or until presentment

---

[21] UCC § 3-118(a).
[22] UCC § 3-409(1); Aiken Bag Corp. v McLeod, 89 GaApp 737, 81 SE2d 215.
[23] UCC § 3-413(3).
[24] UCC § 3-413(3).

for payment if it is demand paper. If the paper is dishonored, the holder may sue either on the paper or on the underlying obligation.[25]

§ 30:12. Liability of Indorser. The liability of an unqualified indorser of a draft is broader than that of an unqualified indorser of a promissory note. Any unqualified indorser is under a secondary liability for the nonpayment of the instrument when due. In addition, the unqualified indorser of a draft is under a secondary liability for the refusal of the drawee to accept the instrument when it is presented for acceptance.

In order to charge the unqualified indorser of the draft for either nonacceptance or nonpayment, it is necessary to prove that a presentment to the drawee had been properly made and that due notice was given to the indorser of the drawee's failure to accept or pay.

§ 30:13. Necessity of Presentment for Acceptance. The best way for the holder to find out whether the drawee will pay a time draft when it becomes due is to present it to the drawee for acceptance. If the drawee is not willing to pay the instrument according to its terms, the drawee will reject it, that is, dishonor it by nonacceptance. If willing to pay the draft when it becomes due, the drawee will accept it.[26]

Any draft may be presented by the drawee for acceptance. A presentment for acceptance must be made if (1) it is necessary in order to fix the date of maturity of the draft, such as when the instrument is payable a specified number of days after sight; (2) the draft expressly states that it must be presented for acceptance; or (3) the draft is made payable elsewhere than at the residence or place of business of the drawee.[27]

§ 30:14. Manner of Presenting for Acceptance. Presentment of a draft for acceptance is made in the same manner as the presentment of a note for payment,[28] with the obvious difference that the presentment is made upon the drawee rather than upon the maker.

(a) Time for Presentment for Acceptance. Unless a different time is specified in the draft, presentment for acceptance must be made on or before the date on which the instrument is payable by its express provisions. If it is payable after sight; it must be presented for acceptance or negotiated within a reasonable time after its date or issue, whichever is later. With respect to the liability of any secondary party on any other form of instrument, presentment for acceptance must be made within a reasonable time after that party became liable for it.[29]

The time for presentment of a draft for acceptance with respect to the hour and day or the effect of holidays is the same as in the case of presentment of a note for payment.

(b) Delay or Absence of Presentment for Acceptance. Delay in a necessary presentment of a draft for acceptance and the failure to make any presentment are excused under the same circumstances as in the case of the presentment of a note for payment.

[25] UCC § 3-802(1)(b). Special provisions apply when a bank is the drawer. UCC § 3-802(1)(a).
[26] UCC § 3-410(1).
[27] UCC § 3-501(1)(a).
[28] UCC § 3-504.
[29] UCC § 3-503(1)(a), (b), (e).

An unexcused delay in making any necessary presentment for acceptance discharges an indorser's liability for payment of the paper. If the draft is domiciled, that is, payable at a bank, the drawer or acceptor is discharged under the circumstances that discharge the maker of a note for dishonor by nonpayment.[30]

(c)   Time Allowed for Acceptance. It is not necessary that the drawee accept or dishonor the draft immediately upon its presentment. In order to afford an opportunity of determining from records whether the draft should be accepted, the drawee may postpone making a decision, without thereby dishonoring the draft, until the close of the next business day following the presentment of the draft. Likewise, the holder may allow the postponement of acceptance for one additional business day when the holder acts in good faith in the hope of obtaining an acceptance. If the holder agrees to such additional postponement, the liability of the secondary parties is not affected and the draft is not thereby dishonored.[31]

§ 30:15. Kinds of Acceptances.

(a)   General Acceptance. A *general acceptance* (or simply an "acceptance") is one in which the acceptor agrees without qualification to pay according to the order of the drawer.

(b)   Draft-Varying Acceptance. A *draft-varying acceptance* is one in which the acceptor agrees to pay but not exactly in conformity with the order of the draft. An acceptance varies the draft when it changes the time or place of payment, when it agrees to pay only a part of the amount of the draft, or when it sets up a condition that must be satisfied before the acceptance is effective.

An acceptance to pay at a particular bank or place in the United States is a general acceptance, unless the draft expressly states that it is to be paid there only and not elsewhere. In the latter case the acceptance varies the draft.[32]

A holder who does not wish to take the varying acceptance, may reject it and treat the draft as dishonored by nonacceptance. After giving due notice, the holder can then proceed at once against secondary parties.

If the holder assents to the draft-varying acceptance, however, the holder in effect consents to the execution of a new instrument; and each drawer and indorser is released from liability unless such other party affirmatively assents to the draft-varying acceptance. The fact that a secondary party fails to object is not sufficient to prevent this release from liability.

§ 30:16. Form of Acceptance.
An acceptance is the drawee's notation on the draft itself that payment will be made as directed thereby. It may be merely a signature, but customarily it will be the word "accepted" and a signature, and generally the date. In any case, however, the acceptance must be written on the draft itself. Usually it is written across the face of the instrument.

---

[30] UCC § 3-502(1)(b). See § 30:5(d) in this book.
[31] UCC § 3-506(1). The time allowed the drawee to determine whether to accept is distinct from any right of representment after dishonor when authorized by the paper. UCC § 3-507(4).
[32] UCC § 3-412(2).

An acceptance cannot be oral, nor can it be contained in some other writing. Thus a bank is not bound by its oral promise to pay a draft drawn upon it. The fact that the drawee is not liable on a draft which it has not accepted means only that it is not liable on the draft. The drawee may still be liable to the holder on other contracts or on the basis of other principles of law. (See p. 507, Home Savings Bank v General Finance Corp.)

There can be no acceptance by misconduct. The refusal to return the draft or its destruction by the drawee does not constitute an "acceptance." If the drawee retains the draft and refuses to return it, such conduct is not an acceptance but a conversion.[33] The measure of damages is the face amount of the instrument.

§ 30:17. Dishonor by Nonacceptance.

When a draft that is presented for acceptance is not accepted within the allowed time, the person presenting it must treat the draft as dishonored by nonacceptance.[34] The failure to do so releases the secondary parties from liability.

When a draft is dishonored by nonacceptance, the holder must give the same notice of dishonor as in the case of dishonor of paper by non-payment. If the draft on its face appears to be drawn or payable outside of the United States, its territories, and the District of Columbia, it is also necessary to protest the dishonor in order to charge the drawer and the indorsers.

§ 30:18. Presentment of Draft for Payment.

The requirements and limitations upon the necessity of presentment of a draft for payment are the same as in the case of a promissory note, with the circumstances excusing delays or failure to make presentment of a note likewise excusing delay or failure to make presentment of a draft for payment. The failure to present for payment is likewise excused with respect to a party who has countermanded payment of the draft.

Furthermore, when a draft has been dishonored by nonacceptance, a later presentment for payment is excused unless the instrument has since been accepted.[35]

The provisions governing notice of dishonor of a draft by nonpayment are the same as those for a note.[36]

§ 30:19. Protest of Dishonor.

A protest of dishonor of a draft by nonacceptance or nonpayment is not necessary unless the draft appears on its face to be drawn or payable outside of the United States, its territories, or the District of Columbia. The holder, however, may protest the dishonor of any instrument. Delay in protesting dishonor or the absence of a protest are excused under the same circumstances that apply in the case of a note dishonored by nonpayment.

(a) **Waiver of Protest.** A *waiver of protest* is effective to excuse the absence of an otherwise required protest. Protest is commonly waived, particularly in the case of out-of-town instruments, because protest does involve an additional cost and some inconvenience. Frequently, therefore, the instrument will contain a clause stating

[33] UCC § 3-419(1)(a).
[34] UCC § 3-507(1)(a).
[35] UCC § 3-511(4).
[36] UCC §§ 3-501(2), 3-508. See § 30:7 of this chapter.

that protest is waived, or it may be stamped with the words "Protest Waived" or "No Protest." A waiver of protest is a waiver of the requirement of presentment and notice of dishonor as well as of the protest itself even though the protest is not required.

(b)   Effect of Guaranty. When words of guaranty, such as "payment guaranteed" or "collection guaranteed," are used, presentment, notice of dishonor, and protest are not necessary to charge the person using such language.[37]

---

[37] UCC § 3-416(5).

CASES FOR CHAPTER 30

Bertolet v Burke

(DC Virgin Islands) 295 F Supp 1176 (1969)

Burke executed a promissory note. He later informed Bertolet, the holder of the note, that he would not make payment on the note when it became due. Bertolet immediately sued Burke. The defendant moved for summary judgment.

STALEY, C.J. . . . The issue presented by this motion for summary judgment is whether a cause of action can be sustained on a promissory note before maturity if it appears that the maker has declared his intention not to pay.

Plaintiff, W. M. Bertolet, brought this action against Frank G. Burke, . . . alleging that Burke informed him in writing that he does not intend to make good on a promissory note, payable to plaintiff, which is due to mature on October 1, 1969. The note was executed on October 1, 1966, and bears the face amount of $18,729, with interest at the rate of 6 percent per annum. At this point in time, the contract for the payment of money represented by the promissory note is a unilateral one, since plaintiff has fully performed, and he asks only that he be paid now or be otherwise secured for that which is owed him.

According to [UCC] § 3-122(1)(a), a cause of action against the maker of a time instrument does not accrue until the day after maturity. We are aware of no provision under Article 3 of . . . (Uniform Commercial Code), entitled "Commercial Paper," which permits an action on a promissory note for anticipatory breach. Nor are we aware of any other statute or Virgin Islands case law which would support such an action. This being the case,

we must refer to the Restatement, since V.I.C. § 4 provides: "The rules of the common law, as expressed in the restatements of the law approved by the American Law Institute, and to the extent not so expressed, as generally understood and applied in the United States, shall be the rules of decision in the courts of the Virgin Islands in cases to which they apply, in the absence of local laws to the contrary."

Restatement of Contracts § 318 (1932) covers those situations constituting an anticipatory repudiation and a total breach of contract. Comment *e* of § 318 states that: "The doctrine of anticipatory breach is not extended to unilateral contracts unless the promisor's duty is conditional on some future performance by the promisee. It is immaterial whether the contract was originally thus unconditionally unilateral or has become so by the performance of one party. In neither case can a breach arise before the time fixed in the contract for the performance. There must be some dependency of performances in order to make anticipatory breach possible."

Illustration 10 of § 318 presents a factual situation quite analogous to the instant case. There it is said: "*A*, in consideration of $10,000 then paid to him by *B*, promises *B* to transfer Blackacre to *B* on the first day of the following May. Before that day *A* tells *B* that he will not transfer the land as promised. Since the contract is unilateral, *A* has not committed an anticipatory breach of contract."

Our research reveals that the case law is in overwhelming concurrence with the position adopted by the Restatement. . . . In view of the great weight of authority on this issue, we are of the opinion that plaintiff's action cannot be sustained.

[Plaintiff's complaint dismissed]

Hane v Exten

255 Md 668, 259 A2d 290 (1969)

Theta Electronic Laboratories executed a promissory note payable to Thomson and his wife, which was indorsed by Exten, O'Neil, and James Hane and their wives. The Thomsons assigned it to John Hane. The note was not paid when due. John Hane took judgment by confession against Theta and the prior indorsers. The judgment against the Extens was vacated, and John Hane appealed.

SINGLEY, J. . . . . John B. Hane is the assignee of the note of Theta Electronic Laboratories, Inc. (Theta) in the stated amount of $15,377.07, with interest at 6 percent per annum. The note was dated 10 August 1964; stipulated that the first monthly payment of $320.47 would be due five months from date, or on 10 January 1965; and that "In the event of the failure to pay the interest or principal, as the same becomes due on this Note, the entire debt represented hereby shall at the end of thirty (30) days become due and demandable. . . . ." The note was assigned without recourse to Hane by George B. and Marguerite F. Thomson, the original payees, on 26 November 1965. A default having occurred in the making of the monthly payments, Hane took judgments by confession in the Circuit Court for Montgomery County on 7 June 1967 against Theta and three individuals, Gerald M. Exten, Emil L. O'Neil, and James W. Hane, and their wives, who had indorsed Theta's note. On motion of the Extens, the judgment was vacated as to them and the case came on for trial on the merits before the court without a jury. From a judgment for the Extens for costs. Hane has appealed.

This case raises the familiar question: Must Hane show that the Extens were given notice of presentment and dishonor before he can hold them on their indorsement?

The court below, in finding for the Extens, relied on the provisions of Uniform Commercial Code. . . . § 3-414(1) provides:

"Unless the indorsement otherwise specifies (as by such words as 'without recourse') every indorser engages that upon dishonor and any necessary notice of dishonor and protest he will pay the instrument according to its tenor at the time of his indorsement to the holder or to any subsequent indorser who takes it up, even though the indorser who takes it up was not obligated to do so."

§ 3-501(1)(b) provides that "Presentment for payment is necessary to charge any indorser" and § 3-501(2)(a) that "Notice of any dishonor is necessary to charge any indorser," in each case subject, however, to the provisions of § 3-511 which recite the circumstances under which notice of dishonor may be waived or excused, none of which is here present. § 3-502 (1)(a) makes it clear that unless presentment or notice of dishonor is waived or excused, unreasonable delay will discharge an indorser. . . .

There was testimony from which the trier of facts could find as he did that presentment and notice of dishonor were unduly delayed.

It is clear that Hane held the note from November, 1965, until some time in April, 1967, before he made demand for payment. UCC § 3-503(1)(d) provides that "Where an instrument is accelerated, presentment for payment is due within a reasonable time after the acceleration." "Reasonable time" is not defined in § 3-503, except that § 3-503(2) provides, "A reasonable time for presentment is determined by the nature of the instrument, any usage of banking or trade, and the facts of the particular case." But § 1-204(2) characterizes it: "What is a reasonable time for taking any action depends on the nature, purpose, and circumstances of such action."

Reasonableness is primarily a question for the fact finder. Vanderberg & Sons, N. V. v Siter, 204 Pa Super 392, 204 A2d 494 (1964); . . . 1 Anderson's Uniform Commercial Code, Commentary, § 1-204:3. . . . We see no reason to disturb the lower court's finding that Hane's delay of almost 18 months in presenting the note "was unreasonable from any viewpoint." . . .

As regards notice of dishonor, § 3-508(2) requires that notice be given by persons other than banks "before midnight of the third business day after dishonor or receipt of notice of dishonor." Exten, called as an adverse witness by Hane, testified that his first notice that the note had not been paid was the entry of the confessed judgment on 7 June 1967. Hane's brother testified that demand had been made about 15 April 1967. He was uncertain as to when he had given Exten notice of dishonor, but finally conceded that it was "within a week." The lower court found that the ambiguity of this testimony, coupled with Exten's denial that he had received *any* notice before 7 June fell short of meeting the three-day notice requirement of the UCC. The date of giving notice of dishonor is a question of fact, solely for determination by the trier of facts. . . . We cannot say that the court erred in its finding.

In the absence of evidence that presentment and notice of dishonor were waived or excused, Hane's unreasonable delay discharged the Extens, § 3-502(1)(a). . . .

[Judgment affirmed, costs to be paid by appellant]

Nevada State Bank v Fischer

(Nev) 565 P2d 332 (1977)

A check was drawn on the Clayton Bank of Clayton, Missouri. Lucile Fischer indorsed the check and cashed it at the Nevada State Bank. That bank sent it on the next day to the Valley Bank of Nevada for collection from the Clayton Bank. Almost 90 days later, Valley Bank informed Nevada State Bank that the check had been dishonored by the Clayton Bank. On the next day, the Nevada Bank notified Fischer and debited her bank account with the amount of the dishonored check. She sued the bank to have this amount recredited to her account. From a judgment in her favor, the bank appealed.

THOMPSON, J. . . . The facts are not disputed. On May 1, 1970, Mrs. Fischer indorsed a $2,000 check payable to the drawer and drawn on the Clayton Bank of Clayton, Missouri. She did this as an accommodation to the payee-drawer. The Nevada State Bank cashed the check for the payee-drawer and initiated collection through Valley Bank of Nevada that same day.

On July 28, 1970, the Valley Bank of Nevada notified Nevada State Bank that the check had been dishonored stating "original lost in transit—account closed." On July 29, 1970, the Nevada State Bank debited Mrs. Fischer's account for $2,000 and notified her in writing of the payor bank's dishonor of the check.

The record does not disclose which of the several banks involved in the collection process either lost the check or delayed action with regard to it. It is clear, however, that Nevada State Bank acted promptly upon receiving notice of dishonor. Whether it was permissible in these circumstances for that bank to charge its innocent depositor rather than to look to one of the other banks involved is the issue for our decision.

Lucile Fischer indorsed the check as an accommodation party and is liable in the capacity in which she signed. [UCC § 3-415] By indorsing the check she engaged that upon dishonor and any necessary notice of dishonor and protest, she would pay the instrument according to the tenor at the time of her indorsement. [UCC § 3-414(1)]

An indorser is a secondary party, . . . whose liability is subject to the preconditions of presentment . . . and proper notice of dishonor. . . . Where, without excuse, any necessary presentment or notice of dishonor is delayed beyond the time it is due, an indorser is discharged. [UCC § 3-502(1)]

It is the contention of Nevada State Bank that since it initiated collection within one day of the indorsement and notified the indorser of dishonor within one day of receipt of such notice by it, "delay" does not exist and Mrs. Fischer, as indorser, is not discharged from liability. . . . Nevada State Bank initiated collection within one day after cashing the check. Consequently, bank collection was timely initiated.

In our view, however, the . . . precondition to liability of the indorser [of] timely notice of dishonor, was not met. Although the Nevada State Bank notified Mrs. Fischer within its midnight deadline, . . . after receipt of notice of dishonor from Valley Bank of Nevada, this fact, alone, does not resolve the timeliness issue.

The record does not disclose at what point in time the check first was dishonored. We know only that almost ninety days elapsed between Mrs. Fischer's indorsement of the check and her receipt of notice of its dishonor. It is apparent that one of the several banks involved in the collection process violated its midnight deadline in giving notice of dishonor. Had such bank given timely notice, Mrs. Fischer would have learned within a reasonable time that the check had been dishonored.

Prompt action by all parties to the transaction is contemplated before an indorser may be held liable. As stated in the official comment to [UCC §]3-503. . . . "The indorser who has normally merely received the check and passed it on and does not expect to have to pay it, is entitled to know more promptly whether it is dishonored, in order that he may have recourse against the person with whom he has dealt."

As already expressed, at some time in the chain of collection a midnight deadline was violated. Notwithstanding such violation, we are asked to conclude that notice of dishonor given ninety days after initiation of bank collection was timely. We decline to so conclude. Mrs. Fischer's liability as an indorser was discharged when the violation of the midnight deadline by a bank, identity unknown, resulted in unreasonable delay in notice of dishonor. The Nevada State Bank may look to the violator for its recovery. . . . Its customer-indorser should not be held responsible for a violation of law committed by another bank involved in the chain of collection.

[Judgment affirmed]

Port City State Bank v American National Bank

(CA10 Okla) 486 F2d 196 (1973)

Port City State Bank received two checks for collection. It sent them to American National Bank, the drawee bank. The drawee bank returned the checks as dishonored for insufficient funds after the midnight deadline. Port City sued American National, basing liability on the late return. American National raised the defense that its computer had broken down. Judgment was entered for American National and Port City Bank appealed.

HILL, C.J. . . . It was stipulated that [the] check was [not] dishonored before the applicable deadline.

These facts establish a prima facie case for the application of 12 C.F.R. 210.12 and [UCC §] 4-302(a), both concerning the necessity of fulfilling the midnight deadline, and thus it became the obligation of appellee at the trial to prove an excuse from these provisions under 12 C.F.R. 210.14 and [UCC §] 4-108(2) [which] prevent the operation of the midnight deadline in cases when the delay by the payor bank is caused by the interruption of communication facilities, suspension of payments by another bank, war, emergency condition or other circumstances beyond the control of the bank provided it exercises such diligence as the circumstances require.

In furtherance of its contention, American National presented evidence that prior to December 1, 1969, it had performed its bookkeeping functions by machine posting, a so-called manual system. During 1969, however, a decision was made to implement a computer bookkeeping operation, and a rental agreement was entered into with a large computer company. That lease provided that all repairs and maintenance were the obligation of the computer firm, and American National was not authorized to undertake any such tasks. After the installation of the computer, American National paralleled its manual system with computer operations for approximately two weeks. Finally the decision was made to change over to computer processing beginning on December 1. A last manual posting was made on Saturday, November 29, and the manual bookkeeping equipment was removed from the bank during that weekend.

At approximately 10:00 a.m. on December 1, the first day for use of computer operations, the American National computer developed a "memory error" which rendered it unusable. Though the computer manufacturer indicated repairs would not take "too long," they lasted until late Monday night and the testing procedure extended into the early hours of Tuesday, December 2.

In reliance upon the belief that the computer would be repaired without prolonged delay, American National took no extraordinary steps to process Monday's business during the business day. However, when it became apparent that evening that the computer was not going to be ready immediately, American National decided to utilize an identical computer in a bank which was a trip of some 2½ hours away, in accord with a backup agreement they had made with the other banking institution. Thus at about 11:30 p.m. personnel from American National and the computer company began processing Monday's business on the backup computer and continued processing through the night. This work had proceeded to the point of capturing the items on discs when, because the backup computer was required by its owner and because they were informed their own computer was operational, the American National personnel returned to their bank to complete the work on their own machine. After returning to American National, the work was processed to the point of completing the printing of the trial balances when another memory error developed which again rendered the computer unusable. No further use could be made of the appellee's computer until a new memory module was installed on Thursday, December 4.

Because of the second failure, American National was forced to utilize the backup computer both Wednesday and Thursday during times it was not required by its owner. Monday's business was completed and work was begun on Tuesday's items the evening of Tuesday, December 2. Tuesday's items were not completed until either Wednesday, the third, or Thursday, the fourth. When the second check arrived in Tuesday's business, it was held to determine if a later deposit had balanced the account. Through the use of the backup computer and then its own computer during the next weekend, American National was fully "caught up" by Monday, December 8.

Based upon this evidence, the trial court held that the computer malfunction suffered by American National was the cause of its failure to meet its required midnight deadline on the checks, and that such malfunction constituted both an emergency condition and a circumstance beyond the control of the bank as outlined in 12 C.F.R. 210.14 and [UCC §] 4-108(2). The court further held that the reaction to the situation by American National fulfilled the requirements of diligence imposed by those regulations, and therefore the court entered judgment for American National. . . .

. . . Appellant contends that a computer failure, as a matter of law, is not an event which [requires] the application of [UCC §] 4-108(2). In our opinion, such a determination is a mixed question of fact and law; however, neither treatment justifies the reversal of the trial court's determination in this case. Factually, it was in no way erroneous to conclude that the malfunction created an emergency condition in the bank and was also a condition beyond the control of the bank. Appellant's argument that in law this malfunction is not included within the prescribed contingencies of § 4-108(2) is without foundation. The statute is clear and unambiguous on its face. . . .

Port City next alleges that the trial court erred in its determination that American National exercised "such diligence" as the circumstances required. Basically, appellant asserts [there were] alternative procedures that American National could have employed, and asserts that if any of these alternatives would have resulted in meeting the deadline, then appellee did not exercise diligence under the circumstances. As the trial court correctly concluded, the statute does not require perfection on the part of appellee, and American National's performance should not be judged on the basis of 20-20 hindsight.

It must first be noted that appellee quickly notified the computer firm of the breakdown, and that company began an immediate repair effort. Further, there was evidence to indicate that such computer breakdowns are generally repaired very quickly. Thus it would appear that appellee was justified in its initial delay in adopting emergency procedures based on its belief such measures would prove unnecessary. Additionally, we must agree with the trial court that appellee's duty under these circumstances was much broader than one requiring merely that it meet its midnight deadline. It was further obligated to keep the bank open and to serve its customers. To abandon the orderly day by day process of bookkeeping to adopt radical emergency measures would have likely prolonged the delay in returning the bank to normal operations.

As to appellant's assertion that appellee should have returned to manual posting, it was shown that the equipment for this procedure was no longer in the bank. Further, no clear evidence was presented to indicate such a procedure would have allowed appellee to fulfill its deadlines if the procedure had been implemented. Any decision to return to manual posting would have to have been made very soon after the discovery of the initial failure. At that time, because of their own experience with computers and the industry history, and also because the manufacturer did not foresee the serious nature of the repairs, American National was justified in believing its computer would be back in service soon. Their delay in commencing emergency operations was reasonable, and these facts prevented a return to manual posting in time to fulfill the deadlines.

As to the possibility of utilizing another backup computer at the regional headquarters of the computer leasing firm, we must agree with the trial court that there was no evidence that this alternative would have proved any more successful than the method actually employed by appellee. . . .

[Judgment affirmed]

Home Savings Bank v General Finance Corp.

10 Wis 2d 417, 103 NW2d 117 (1960)

Schenk's Motor Sales had a checking account in the Home Savings Bank. The bank certified a check drawn by Schenk in reliance on the oral promise of the General Finance Corp. to accept a draft drawn on General by Schenk that had just been deposited in Schenk's account. The certified check was paid by the bank, but General refused to pay the draft on the ground that its oral acceptance was not binding. The bank sued General for the amount of the certified check. From a judgment in favor of General, the Bank appealed.

FAIRCHILD, J. . . . Plaintiff bank points out that it is not attempting to recover from General

Finance upon an accepted bill of exchange. . . . "The acceptance must be in writing and signed by the drawee." . . . Plaintiff bank does claim, however, that General Finance orally promised to accept the draft if the bank would certify the $9,700 check payable to General Finance; that the bank did so, and thereby accepted the offer and furnished consideration for the promise. . . .

The essential elements of quasi contract are a benefit conferred upon the defendant by the plaintiff, appreciation by the defendant of such benefit, and acceptance and retention by the defendant of such benefit under circumstances such that it would be inequitable to retain the benefit without payment of the value thereof. . . . The conferring of the benefit and appreciation by defendant are clear.

It also seems clear that at least as to a part of the money, retention by General Finance is inequitable. It is beyond belief that General Finance could have obtained cash for the $9,700 check in any way except by persuading the bank president that the draft would be honored. No matter how gullible or careless it may have been for the president to rely upon an oral acceptance, the retention of the bank's money after refusal to honor the draft as promised cannot be considered equitable.

$3,080.56 was the balance in Schenk's account when the check was certified. The record does not disclose the payment of any checks by the bank after that except the one for $9,700. We think the amount which General Finance cannot equitably retain is the difference between $9,700 and $3,080.56, or $6,619.44. . . .

It has been suggested that since an acceptance of a bill must be in writing in order to be enforceable, it is against public policy to grant restitution in the situation here present. This question is considered in Restatement, Contracts, sec. 355. In comment *a* of subsec. 1, it is said: "The parties to a contract that is rendered unenforceable by the Statute of Frauds or some similar statute very frequently act in reliance on it by rendering the agreed performance, in part or in whole, or making improvements on land that is the subject matter of the contract. In such cases, the refusal of all judicial remedy would result in harm to one party and unjust enrichment of the other. Therefore, restitution is enforced even though the Statute makes other remedies unavailable." . . .

[Judgment for defendant reversed]

Code Comment: The same decision would be made under the Uniform Commercial Code because the principles on which the case was decided are general principles that are not displaced by the Code. UCC § 1-103.

QUESTIONS AND CASE PROBLEMS

1. What social forces are affected by the rule that giving notice of dishonor to a secondary party before midnight of the third business day following dishonor is sufficient?

2. Compare the liability of a drawee on the paper before and after acceptance of a draft.

3. Compare a note and draft both payable at a definite time with respect to the need of presentment for payment with respect to (a) the maker, (b) an acceptor, and (c) an unqualified indorser.

4. A presentment is not effective unless the holder of the paper physically presents or shows it to the party obligated to make payment. Appraise this statement.

5. Four promissory notes were executed by Continental Diamond Mines, Inc. payable to the order of M. Kopp. The notes were thereafter indorsed to M. Kopp, Inc. and then to Rafkin. Rafkin was the holder on the due date. Was it necessary for him to make a presentment of the notes to Continental Diamond Mines in order to hold it liable on the notes? [Rafkin v Continental Diamond Mines, Inc., 33 Misc 2d 156, 228 NYS2d 317]

6. In an action brought by Hughes against a corporation that had indorsed a promissory note, the latter claimed that notice of protest had not been properly given. It was shown that the notice had been left at the company's office during business hours after the holder was unable to find any of the officers of the corporation. Was sufficient notice given? [Hughes v Rankin Realty Co., 108 NJL 185, 158 A 487]

7. *A* was the president of the *X* Corporation. The *X* Corporation was near bankruptcy. The Corporation borrowed money from *B* bank. The *X* Corporation signed a promissory note which was signed by *A* as accommodation indorser. The bank presented the note to the *X* Corporation on the due date. Payment was not made on the note. This was not unexpected because the corporation was still on the verge of bankruptcy. The bank did not give notice of the corporate default to *A*. The bank later sued *A* as accommodation indorser. He defended on the ground that he had not been given notice of the dishonor of the note. Was this a valid defense? [See Schenectady Trust Co. v Estate of Sciocchetti, 82 Misc 2d 1075, 371 NYS2d 36]

8. *A* signed a promissory note as maker. The face of the note stated that protest was waived. *B* signed the note as an accommodation indorser. The note was presented to *A* when due but he defaulted. Notice thereof was not given to *B*. When the holder sued *B*, *B* raised the defense that notice was required in order to hold him liable and that the waiver of protest on the face of the paper did not bind him because he was an accommodation indorser. Was this a valid defense? [See Bank of Delaware v NMD Realty Co. (Del) 325 A2d 108]

9. Lowe & Myers were contractors doing construction work for the Druid Realty Co. In order to pay for their materials they drew a draft on the realty company directing it to pay $2,000 to the order of the Crane Co. The realty company, through its president, wrote on the instrument that it accepted the instrument and agreed to pay it within 30 days after the completion of the work, provided Crane Company continued to furnish materials to Lowe & Myers. What was the effect of the action by the realty company? [Crane Co. v Druid Realty Co., 137 Md 324, 112 A 621]

10. *A* indorsed a promissory note on the back. At the top of the back, above all indorsements, there were printed the words "Notice of protest waived." The note was not paid when due. The holder sent *A* notice that the note was not paid, but *A* did not receive the notice because it was sent to a former address at which he no longer lived. *A* denied liability because he had not been properly notified. Decide. [Lizza Asphalt Construction Co. v Greenvale Construction Co., (NY Sup Ct) 4 UCCRS 954]

11. Cotton States Mutual Insurance Company made a draft payable to the order of Baum. The draft was payable on acceptance and was drawn on the First National Bank. When Baum presented the draft to First National Bank it refused to accept it. He then sued Cotton States. It raised the defense that it was not liable because the draft was payable on acceptance and the draft had not been accepted. Was this defense valid? [Baum v Cotton States Mut. Ins. Co., 141 GaApp 635, 234 SE2d 178]

12. *H* was the holder of a note on which *M* was the maker. *H* owed money to *I* and indorsed *M*'s note to *I* in payment of his debt. Thereafter *M* failed to pay his note to *I*. When *I* demanded that *H* pay his original debt to *I*, *H* raised the defense that *I* had taken *M*'s note in payment of that debt so that it no longer existed. Decide. [Central Stone Co. v John Ruggiero, Inc., 49 Misc 2d 622, 268 NYS2d 172]

13. Fuller Brothers, as the holder, brought an action against Bovay, as indorser. It was shown that the notice of default of the primary party was given to Bovay by a letter addressed "Jonesboro Rice Mill Co., Jonesboro, Ark., Attention Mr. Bovay." Was this a proper notice? [Bovay v Fuller, (CA8 Ark) 63 F2d 280]

14. The *X* Bank sold money orders in which it was the drawer and by which it ordered itself to pay the amount of the money order through the *Z* Bank to the person designated by the purchaser of the money order. (a) Assuming that the instruments were negotiable, what kind of commercial paper were the money orders? (b) Was the *X* Bank or the *Z* Bank the drawee? [Comet Check Cashing Service v Hanover Insurance Group, (NY Civ Ct) 5 UCCRS 852]

31   Rights of Holders and Defenses

When a contract right is assigned, the assignee's right is subject to any defenses existing between the original parties. For example, when the seller assigns the right to collect the purchase price, the buyer may assert against the seller's assignee the defense that the buyer never received the goods. It is immaterial through how many successive assignees the right has been transferred and whether or not the assignees acted in good faith, in ignorance of the original defenses, and gave value for their assignments. Such a principle of law should make a prospective assignee of a contract right extremely cautious. The prospective assignee should make inquiry as to the existence of defenses, particularly of the original obligor.

If holders of commercial paper were required to conduct such an investigation in every instance in order to protect themselves, the utility of commercial paper would be greatly impaired. First the law merchant, then the Uniform Negotiable Instruments Law, and now the Uniform Commercial Code have met this problem by giving certain holders of commercial paper a preferred standing by protecting them from the operation of certain defenses. Such a favored holder may be either a holder in due course or a holder through a holder in due course. If the holder is not one of these favored holders, then the holder has only the same standing as an ordinary assignee and is subject to all defenses to which an ordinary assignee would be subject.

A. KINDS OF HOLDERS

When a commercial paper is negotiated to a person, that person is the holder; either an ordinary holder or a favored holder.

§ 31:1. Ordinary Holders and Assignees.

(a)   **Ordinary Holders.** The ordinary holder has all the rights relating to the paper. The holder, although an ordinary holder, is the only person who may demand payment, or bring suit for the collection of the paper, or give a discharge or release from liability on the paper, or cancel the liability of another party to the paper.

The holder may generally sue any one or more prior parties on the paper without regard to the order in which such persons signed the paper or the order in which such persons may be liable to each other.

The fact that the holder is merely an ordinary holder has no significance if the defendant does not have any defense.[1]

(b)   Assignees. The assignee of a commercial paper is in the same position and has the same rights as an ordinary holder. It is immaterial whether the person is an assignee by express assignment, by operation of law, or in consequence of the omission of an essential indorsement.

§ 31:2. Favored Holders. The law gives certain holders of commercial paper a preferred standing by protecting them from the operation of certain defenses in lawsuits to collect payment. This protection is given in order to make commercial paper more attractive by giving the favored holder an immunity not possessed by an assignee. The favored holders are known as the *holder in due course,* and a *holder through a holder in due course.*

B. HOLDERS IN DUE COURSE

In order to have the preferred status of a holder in due course, a person must first be a holder. This means that the possessor of the paper must have acquired it by proper negotiation. That is, the person in question must be the possessor of bearer paper or must be the possessor of order paper which is then payable to such person as payee or indorsee.

The concept may be better understood if modern terminology is substituted and "due course" is thought of as a regular, normal business routine. That is, the law protects persons taking the commercial paper as part of a regular, normal business routine—in due course.

§ 31:3. Who May be a Holder in Due Course. Any person may be a holder in due course. This includes the payee of the paper provided the necessary elements are satisfied. Ordinarily the payee would deal directly with the drawer, and therefore would have knowledge of any defense that the latter might raise which would disqualify the payee from being a holder in due course. But the payee may be a holder in due course by acting through an intermediary so that in fact the payee did not deal with the drawer or maker but acquired the paper from the intermediary. The net result is the same as though the maker or drawer had made the paper payable to the intermediary who in turn indorsed it to the payee, even though the paper was in fact made payable to the order of the payee and merely transmitted to the payee.

(a)   Excluded Transactions. Certain types of purchases of commercial paper do not make the purchaser a holder in due course even though all the elements of being such a holder have been satisfied. Such sales are not of an ordinary commercial nature, and therefore the buyer need not be given the protection afforded a holder in due course. Thus, a person is not a holder in due course when the paper was acquired by means of a judicial sale, a sale of the assets of an estate, or a bulk sale not in the regular course of business of the transferor.[2]

---

[1] Hensley v Jones (TexCivApp) 492 SW2d 283.
[2] UCC § 3-302(3).

(b) Participating Transferee. The seller of goods on credit frequently assigns the sales contract and buyer's promissory note to the manufacturer who made the goods, or to a finance company or a bank. In such a case, the assignee of the seller will be a holder in due course of the buyer's commercial paper if the paper is properly negotiated and the transferee satisfies all the elements of being a holder in due course. The transferee, however, may take such an active part in the sale to the seller's customer or may be so related to the seller that it is proper to conclude that the transferee was in fact a party to the original transaction and had notice or knowledge of any defense of the buyer against the seller, which conclusion automatically bars holding that the transferee is a holder in due course.

In what may be regarded a form of "participant liability," many cases hold that it may be shown that there was such a close working arrangement between the seller and the finance company that the transfer of the buyer's note to the finance company was merely a device to bar defenses. In these circumstances, it can be concluded that the finance company is not a holder in due course.[3]

§ 31:4. Proof of Status as Holder in Due Course. The status of the holder does not become important until the person sued by the holder raises a defense that can be asserted against an ordinary holder but not against a holder in due course or a holder through a holder in due course. Initially, the plaintiff in the action is entitled to recover as soon as the commercial paper is put in evidence and the signatures on it are admitted to be genuine. If the genuine character of any signature is specifically denied, the burden is then on the plaintiff to prove the signature is genuine.[4] Once the signatures are admitted or established, the plaintiff-holder is entitled to recover unless the defendant establishes a defense. In the latter situation, the plaintiff has the burden of qualifying as a holder in due course, or a holder through a holder in due course in order to avoid such defense.[5]

§ 31:5. Holder Through a Holder in Due Course. Those persons who become holders of the instrument after a holder in due course are given the same protection as the holder in due course provided they are not parties to fraud or illegality that would affect the instrument.

This means that if an instrument is indorsed from *A* to *B* to *C* to *D* and that if *B* is a holder in due course, both *C* and *D* will enjoy the same rights as *B*. If *C* received the instrument as a gift or with knowledge of failure of consideration or other defense, or if *D* took the instrument after maturity, they could not themselves be holders in due course. Nevertheless, they are given the same protection as a holder in due course because they took the instrument through such a holder, namely, *B*. It is not only *C*, the person taking directly from *B*, but also *D*, who takes indirectly through *B*, who is given this extra protection.

---

[3] Avco Security Corp. v Post, 42 AppDiv2d 395, 348 NYS2d 409.

[4] UCC § 3-307(1). The plaintiff is aided by a presumption that the signature is genuine or authorized except where the action is to enforce the obligation of a signer who has died or become incompetent. § 3-307(1)(b). Carr Estate, 436 Pa 47, 258 A2d 628.

[5] UCC § 3-307(3). If the defense is one that may be asserted against any holder, it is immaterial whether the plaintiff is a holder in due course.

C. ELEMENTS OF A HOLDER IN DUE COURSE

In addition to being a holder, the holder in due course must meet certain conditions that pertain to (a) value, (b) good faith, (c) ignorance of paper overdue or dishonored, and (d) ignorance of defenses and adverse claims.

§ 31:6. Value. Since the law of commercial paper is fundamentally a merchant's or business person's law, it favors only the holders who have given value for the paper. For example, since a legatee under a will does not give value, a person receiving bonds as a legacy is not a holder in due course. When value is given, the courts do not measure or appraise the value given.

A person takes an instrument for value (1) by performing the act for which the instrument was given, such as delivering the goods for which the check was sent in payment; (2) by acquiring a security interest in the paper, as when it has been pledged as security for another obligation; or (3) by taking the instrument in payment of, or as security for a debt.[6]

A promise not yet performed, although sufficient as consideration for a contract, ordinarily does not constitute value to satisfy this requirement for a holder in due course.

A bank does not give value for a deposited check when it credits the depositor's account with the amount of the deposit. The bank gives value to the extent that the depositor withdraws money against that credit.[7]

§ 31:7. Good Faith. The element of good faith requires that the taker of commercial paper act honestly in the acquisition of the instrument. Bad faith may sometimes be indicated by the small value given. This does not mean that the transferee must give full value but that a gross inadequacy of consideration may be evidence of bad faith. Bad faith is established by proof that the transferee had knowledge of such facts as rendered it improper to acquire the instrument under the circumstances.

The fact that a prior indorsement has been crossed out does not require a subsequent taker of the paper to inquire as to the cancellation and therefore the failure to make an inquiry with respect thereto does not constitute bad faith.[8]

If the transferee takes the instrument in good faith, it is immaterial whether the transferor acted in good faith. The fact that a transferee bank is negligent and fails to conform to industry standards or to its own house rules does not establish that the transferee did not act in good faith, as good faith requires only that the transferee acted with honesty and not that it acted with due care or in a commercially reasonable manner.

§ 31:8. Ignorance of Paper Overdue or Dishonored. Commercial paper may be negotiated even though (1) it has been dishonored, whether by nonacceptance or nonpayment;

---

[6] UCC § 3-303. It is also provided that there is a taking for value when another commercial paper is given in exchange or when the taker makes an irrevocable commitment to a third person as by providing a letter of credit, UCC § 3-303(c).

[7] Rockland Trust Co. v South Shore Nat. Bank, 336 Mass 74, 314 NE2d 438.

[8] Handley v Horak, 82 Misc 2d 692, 370 NYS2d 313.

or (2) the paper is overdue, whether because of lapse of time or the acceleration of the due date; or (3) it is demand paper that has been outstanding more than a reasonable time. In other words, ownership may still be transferred. Nevertheless, the fact that the paper is circulating at a late date or after it has been dishonored is a suspicious circumstance that is deemed to put the person acquiring the paper on notice that there is some adverse claim or defense. A person who acquires title to the paper under such circumstances therefore cannot be a holder in due course.

§ 31:9. Ignorance of Defenses and Adverse Claims.
Prior parties on the paper may have defenses which they could raise if sued by the person with whom they dealt. For example, the drawer of a check, if sued by the payee, might have the defense that the merchandise delivered by the payee was defective. In addition to defenses, third persons, whether prior parties or not, may be able to assert that the instrument belongs to them and not to the possessor. A person who acquires the commercial paper with notice or knowledge that any party might have a defense or that there is any adverse claim to the ownership of the instrument cannot be a holder in due course. Thus the holder of commercial paper cannot be a holder in due course when the holder acquired the paper with knowledge that there had been a failure of consideration with respect to the contract for which the paper had been given.

Knowledge acquired by the taker after acquiring the paper does not prevent the taker from being a holder in due course. Consequently, the fact that the payee, subsequent to the paying of value, learns of a defense, does not operate retroactively to destroy the payee's character as a holder in due course. When the transferee makes payment for the transfer of the paper in installments and learns of a defense after making part payment, the transferee can be a holder in due course as to the payments made before, but not as to payments made after, learning of the existence of the defense.

(a) Notice. Knowledge of certain facts constitutes notice to the person acquiring a commercial paper that there is a defense or an adverse claim. The holder or purchaser of the paper is deemed to have notice of a claim or defense (1) if the instrument is so incomplete, bears such visible evidence of forgery or alteration, or is otherwise so irregular as to call into question its validity, terms, or ownership, or to create an ambiguity as to the party who is required to pay; or (2) if the purchaser has notice that the obligation of any party is voidable in whole or in part, or that all parties to the paper have been discharged. For example, if the subsequent holder knows that a note given for home improvement work in fact covers both the improvements and a loan and that the transaction is usurious because excessive costs were charged for the work to conceal the usurious interest, the subsequent holder is not a holder in due course. The purchaser has notice of a claim of ownership of another person to the instrument if the transferee has knowledge that a fiduciary has negotiated the paper in breach of trust.[9]

In general, a holder who has knowledge of such facts as would put a reasonable person upon inquiry is deemed to have knowledge of the facts which would be learned if such inquiry were made.

---

[9] UCC § 3-304(2).

(b)   What Does Not Constitute Notice. The taker of commercial paper does not have notice of a defense which bars being a holder in due course merely because the taker knows that the payee has financial difficulties; that there is a close working relationship between the seller and its assignee; [10] that the person negotiating the paper to the holder is an employee or a fiduciary; or that the check is a business check which has already been indorsed. (See p. 521, McCook County National Bank v Compton)

(c)   Consumer Paper. The duty of inquiry is greater when consumer transactions are involved and the payee has followed a known general pattern of exploitation and deception. Where lenders facilitate consumer credit financing, the courts hold them to a high standard of inquiry to make certain their services are not being misused by unscrupulous merchandisers. Thus, it has been held that the transferee of commercial paper of a home improvement company did not take in good faith and was not a holder in due course when the transferee knew that the improvement company was taking advantage of persons of limited economic means and education and that the company did not make any inquiries as to defenses even though it took a substantial quantity of paper from the improvement company and knew that the broker who dealt with the public was in fact acting for the home improvement company although pretending to the individual home owners to be acting for them.[11]

D. DEFENSES

The importance of being a holder in due course or a holder through a holder in due course is that those holders are not subject to certain defenses when they demand payment or bring suit upon a commercial paper. These may be described as *limited defenses.* Another class of defenses, *universal defenses,* may be asserted against any plaintiff, whether the party is an assignee, an ordinary holder, a holder in due course, or holder through a holder in due course. A holder who is neither a holder in due course nor a holder through a holder in due course is subject to every defense just as though the instrument were not negotiable.

The defenses that cannot be raised against a holder in due course as to an original commercial paper are likewise barred with respect to any instrument which is executed to renew or extend the original instrument.

§ 31:10.   Defenses Available Against an Assignee. An assignee of commercial paper is subject to all the defenses to which an assignee of an ordinary contract right is subject. It is immaterial whether the assignment is by voluntary act of a former holder of the paper or whether the assignment occurs by operation of law.

§ 31:11.   Defenses Available Against an Ordinary Holder. An ordinary holder is subject to every defense that the defendant may possess against the person with whom the defendant dealt. For example, when the finance company sues the buyer on the promissory note the buyer gave the seller, the buyer may raise against the finance company

---

[10] Talcott v Shulman, 82 NJSuper 438, 198 A2d 98.
[11] As to the protection given consumers even when the holder is a holder in due course, see § 31:15 in this book.

a defense which the buyer has against the seller as long as the finance company is not a favored holder.

An ordinary holder is also subject to any defense of the defendant against the holder. For example, the buyer can show that payments had been made to the finance company and that the amount claimed by the finance company was in fact not due.

§ 31:12. Limited Defenses not Available Against a Holder in Due Course. Neither a holder in due course nor one having the rights of such a holder is subject to any of the following defenses.[12] They are limited defenses. These defenses are also barred with respect to any instrument that is executed to renew or extend the original instrument.

(a)   Ordinary Contract Defenses. In general terms, the defenses that could be raised against a suit on an ordinary contract cannot be raised against a holder in due course. Such a holder is not subject to defenses based on defects in the underlying contract. Accordingly, the defendant cannot assert against the holder in due course the defense of lack, failure,[13] or illegality of consideration with respect to the transaction between the defendant and the person with whom the defendant dealt. (See p. 522, Illinois Valley Acceptance Corp. v Woodard)

(b)   Incapacity of Defendant. The incapacity of the defendant may not be raised against a holder in due course unless by general principles of law that incapacity, such as insanity of a person for whom a guardian has been appointed by a court, makes the instrument a nullity.[14]

(c)   Fraud in the Inducement. When a person knowingly executes commercial paper and knows its essential terms but is persuaded or induced to execute it because of false statements or representations, such fraud cannot be raised against a holder in due course nor a holder through a holder in due course. As an illustration, *M* is persuaded to purchase an automobile because of *P*'s statements concerning its condition. *M* gives *P* a note, which is negotiated until it reaches *H,* who is a holder in due course. *M* meanwhile learns that the car is not as represented and that *P*'s statements were fraudulent. When *H* demands payment of the note, *M* cannot refuse to pay on the ground of *P*'s fraud. *M* must pay the instrument and then recover the loss from *P.*

Likewise, the buyer of goods which are in fact stolen cannot claim as against the holder in due course of the check which the buyer gave in payment for the goods that the buyer had been defrauded in the sale, as such fraud was fraud as to the inducement and cannot be raised against a holder in due course.

(d)   Prior Payment or Cancellation. When a commercial paper is paid before maturity, the person making the payment should demand the surrender of the instrument. If this is not done, it is possible for the holder to continue to negotiate it. Another person may thus become the holder of the instrument. When the new holder demands payment of the instrument, the defense cannot be raised that payment had been made to a former holder, if the new holder is a holder in due course. The fact that

---

[12] UCC § 3-305.
[13] Federal Factors, Inc. v Wellbanks, 241 Ark 44, 406 SW2d 712.
[14] UCC § 3-305(2)(b).

the person making the payment obtained a receipt from the former holder does not affect the application of this principle.

When the holder and the party primarily liable have agreed to cancel the instrument but the face of the instrument does not show any sign of cancellation, the defense of cancellation cannot be asserted against a holder in due course. Similarly, an order to stop payment of a check cannot be raised as a defense by the drawer of a check against a holder in due course.

(1)   Overpayment. The fact that the maker or the drawer of the paper has overpaid the payee is a simple contract defense. Thus, it may not be asserted against a holder in due course but may be asserted against anyone who does not have the rights of a holder in due course. To illustrate the latter, an employer is required by law to deduct from the pay of employees a specified percentage which is remitted by the employer to the federal government as an advance payment on the federal income tax of the employees. If the employer by mistake makes out a note or check for the gross amount of an employee's wages, the employer may assert the federal tax as a setoff when sued by the employee for the face of the paper. That is, the employee cannot recover the full face of the paper but only the net amount which should have been received after federal taxes were deducted from the gross amount.[15] In contrast, if suit were brought by a holder in due course, the employer would be liable for the face of the note or check.

(e)   Nondelivery of an Instrument. A person may write out a commercial paper or indorse an existing paper and leave it on a desk for future delivery. At that moment, the instrument or the indorsement is not effective because there has been no delivery.

Assume that through the negligence of an employee or through the theft of the instrument, it comes into the hands of another person. If the instrument is in such form that it can be negotiated, as when it is payable to bearer, a subsequent receiver of the instrument may be a holder in due course or a holder through a holder in due course. As against that holder, the person who wrote the instrument or indorsed it cannot defend on the ground that there had been no delivery.

(f)   Conditional or Specified Purpose Delivery. As against a favored holder, a person who would be liable on the instrument cannot show that the instrument which is absolute on its face was in fact delivered subject to a condition that had not been performed, or that it was delivered for a particular purpose but was not so used. Assume *A* makes out a check to the order of *B* and hands it to *C* with the understanding that *C* shall not deliver the check to *B* until *B* delivers certain merchandise. If *C* should deliver the check to *B* before the condition is satisfied and *B* then negotiates the check, a holder in due course or a holder through a holder in due course may enforce the instrument.

(g)   Duress Consisting of Threats. The defense that a person signed or executed a commercial paper under threats of harm or violence may not be raised as a defense against a holder in due course when the effect of such duress is merely to make the contract voidable at the election of the victim of the duress.

---

[15] Lukens v Goit (Wyo) 430 P2d 607.

(h)   Unauthorized Completion. If a maker or drawer signs a commercial paper and leaves blank the name of the payee, or the amount, or any other term, and then hands the instrument to another to be completed, the defense of an improper completion cannot be raised when payment is demanded or suit brought by a subsequent holder in due course or a holder through a holder in due course. That is, the instrument may be enforced as completed.[16]

This situation arises when an employer gives a signed blank check to an employee with instructions to make certain purchases and to fill in the name of the seller and the amount when these are determined. If the employee fills in the name of a friend and a large amount and then the employee and the friend negotiate the check, the employer cannot defend against a subsequent holder in due course or a holder through a holder in due course on the ground that the completion had been without the authority of the employer. Moreover, the defendant has the burden of proving that the commercial paper was completed in an unauthorized manner.[17]

(i)   Theft. As a matter of definition, a holder in due course will not have acquired the paper through theft and any defense of theft therefore must relate to the conduct of a prior party. Assuming that the theft of the paper does not result in a defect in the chain of necessary indorsements, the defense that the instrument has been stolen cannot be raised against a holder in due course.[18]

§ 31:13. Universal Defenses Available Against all Holders. Certain defenses are regarded as so basic that the social interest in preserving them outweighs the social interest of giving commercial paper the freepassing qualities of money. Accordingly, such defenses are given universal effect and may be raised against all holders, whether ordinary holders, holders in due course, or holders through a holder in due course. Such defenses are therefore appropriately called universal defenses.

(a)   Fraud as to the Nature or Essential Terms of the Paper. The fact that a person signs a commercial paper because fraudulently deceived as to its nature or essential terms is a defense available against all holders. (See p. 524, Schaeffer v United Bank and Trust Company) This is the situation when an experienced business person induces an illiterate person to sign a note by falsely representing that it is a contract for repairs. This defense, however, cannot be raised when it is the negligence of the defending party that prevented learning the true nature and terms of the instrument.

(b)   Forgery or Lack of Authority. The defense that a signature was forged or signed without authority may be raised against any holder unless the person whose name was signed has ratified it or is estopped by conduct or negligence from denying it.[19]

The fact that the drawer may have been lax and unbusinesslike in issuing the check to a named payee does not constitute negligence which under UCC § 3-406 bars the assertion that the signature of the payee was a forgery.

---

[16] UCC § 3-407(3).
[17] Charter Finance Co. v Henderson, 15 IllApp3d 1065, 305 NE2d 338.
[18] UCC § 3-305(1).
[19] UCC § 3-404(1); Cohen v Lincoln Savings Bank, 275 NY 399, 10 NE2d 475.

(c) Duress Depriving Control. When a person executes or indorses a commercial paper in response to a force of such a nature that under general principles of law there is duress which makes the transaction a nullity, rather than merely voidable, such duress may be raised as a defense against any holder.

(d) Incapacity. The fact that the defendant is a minor, who under general principles of contract law may avoid the obligation, is a matter that may be raised against any kind of holder. Other kinds of incapacity may only be raised as a defense if the effect of the incapacity is to make the instrument a nullity.

(e) Illegality. If the law declares that an instrument is void when executed in connection with certain conduct, such as gambling or usury, that defense may be raised against any holder. Similarly, when contracts of a corporate seller are a nullity because its charter has been forfeited for nonpayment of taxes, a promissory note given to it by a buyer is void and that defense may be raised as against a holder in due course. If the law merely makes the transaction illegal but does not make the instrument void, the defense cannot be asserted against a holder in due course or a holder through a holder in due course.[20] (See p. 525, New Jersey Mortgage and Investment Corporation v Berenyi)

(f) Alteration.

(1) What Constitutes an Alteration. An alteration is a change to an instrument which is both material and fraudulently made. An alteration is material when it changes the contract of any party in any way, as by changing the date, place of payment, rate of interest, or any other term. It also includes any modification that changes the number or the relationship of the parties to the paper, by adding new terms, or by cutting off a part of the paper itself.

An alteration must be made to the instrument itself. An oral or a collateral written agreement between the holder and one of the parties that modifies the obligation of the party is not an "alteration" within the sense just discussed, even though the obligation of a party is changed or altered thereby.

(2) Person Making Alteration. By definition, an alteration is a change made by a party to the instrument. A change of the instrument made by a non-party has no effect, and recovery may be had on the instrument as though the change had not been made, provided it can be proved what the instrument had been in its original form.

(3) Effect of Alteration. The fact that an instrument has been altered may be raised against any holder. Unlike other defenses, however, it is only a partial defense as against a holder in due course. That is, the latter holder may enforce the instrument according to its original terms prior to its alteration.[21] Moreover, if the person sued by the holder in due course has by negligence substantially contributed to making the alteration possible, that defendant is precluded or barred from asserting the defense of alteration.

[20] UCC § 3-305(2)(b).
[21] UCC § 3-407(3).

§ 31:14. Adverse Claims to the Paper.

(a) What Constitutes an Adverse Claim. Distinct from a defense which a defendant may raise against the plaintiff as a reason against paying the instrument is a claim of a third person to be the owner of the paper. Assume that a check was made payable to the order of *B;* that thereafter blank indorsements are made by *B, C,* and *D;* and that *E* in possession of the check appears to be the holder. *B* might then claim and show, if such be the case, that *C* had fraudulently deceived *B* into indorsing the check; and that *B* therefore avoids the indorsement because of such fraud; and that accordingly the check still belongs to *B. B* in such case is making an adverse claim to the instrument.

(b) Effect of Adverse Claim. A holder in due course holds commercial paper free and clear from all adverse claims of any other person to the paper, including both equitable and legal interests of third persons, and the right of a former holder to rescind negotiation.[22]

In contrast, such adverse claims may be asserted against a holder who is not a holder in due course, which means that the adverse claimant may bring an action against the holder to obtain the paper as the law generally provides for the recovery of property by the owner from anyone else.

(c) Defendant's Assertion of Adverse Claim. Ordinarily a defendant when sued by a holder cannot raise against the holder the defense that the holder's ownership is subject to an adverse claim. This may be done only when the adverse claimant has also become a party to the action or is defending the action on behalf of the defendant.[23]

This limitation is imposed to protect the adverse claimant from a decision in an action to which the adverse claimant was not a party and to prevent opening the door to perjury by giving any defendant the opportunity of beclouding the issues by raising a false claim that a third person has an adverse interest.

§ 31:15. Consumer Protection.
Consumer protection legislation frequently provides that when the debtor executes a commercial paper which is negotiated thereafter by the creditor, the transferee cannot be a holder in due course or remains subject to the defenses which could be asserted against the transferor. This protects the debtor who may then raise against the transferee, such as the seller's finance company, the same defenses that the debtor could raise against the original creditor, the seller.[24]

Some consumer protection reform prohibits the use of promissory notes in consumer transactions.[25] A Federal Trade Commission regulation requires that papers signed by a consumer contain a statement that defenses of the consumer are preserved

---

[22] UCC §§ 3-305(1), 3-207(2).

[23] UCC § 3-306(d).

[24] Randolph National Bank v Vail, 131 Vt 390, 308 A2d 588. The Uniform Consumer Credit Code proposes two alternative rules: one which would abolish the holder in due course protection of the creditor's transferee in practically all cases; the other which would preserve it to the extent of barring the consumer from asserting against a good faith assignee not related to the assignor a defense which was not raised within three months after being notified of the assignment. UCCC § 2.404.

[25] UCCC § 2.403.

against transferees.[26] Such forms of regulation provide only limited protection for a consumer. A consumer is not protected when commercial paper is executed which does not show on its face its consumer-transaction origin nor contain any reservation of defenses and such paper is acquired by a holder in due course. In such case, the ordinary holder in due course law applies and the consumer may not assert any limited defense against such holder. (See p. 526, Circle v Jim Walter Homes, Inc.)

---

[26] See § 8:9 of this book.

CASES FOR CHAPTER 31

McCook County National Bank v Compton

(CA8 SD) 558 F2d 871 (1977)

Compton drew a check on the Northwestern National Bank payable to the order of Tabke to pay for cattle feeding. The check printer incorrectly printed the amount as $3,430. The handwritten amounts were for $13,430. Tabke indorsed the check and gave it to his wife to take to cash at the McCook County National Bank. The Tabkes did not have an account in the bank but they were known at the bank. Because of the conflict in the amounts, an officer of the bank contacted the Northwestern Bank and was assured that the account was sufficient to cover the larger amount. McCook Bank then cashed the check for the larger amount and Mrs. Tabke obtained six bank money orders payable to six of their creditors with the proceeds from this check. After this was done, Mrs. Tabke chatted with the bank officer in the McCook Bank and made a remark which indicated that other creditors might have a superior right to the money represented by the cashed check. Thereafter Compton stopped payment on the check. The check was dishonored by the drawee bank and McCook National Bank then sued Compton as drawer. Compton claimed that the McCook Bank was not a holder in due course because of the irregularity on the face of the check, its being presented already indorsed, the check was obviously a business expense check and the information as to the claims of other creditors which had been given to the bank. From a judgment against McCook, it appealed.

Ross, C. J. . . . The check in question, drawn on the Northwestern National Bank of Sioux City,

Iowa (Northwestern), for $13,340.00, was payable to Dean Tabke as payment for a cattle feeding contract between Tabke and Compton. The Tabke cattle feeding operation was financed by the United National bank of Sioux Falls, South Dakota (United) . . .

Compton . . . asserts that McCook bank had notice of an irregularity or defense to the instrument from the instrument itself, pointing out four irregularities: first, the check was drawn on a farm account, payable to Dean Tabke, Beef Lodge and obviously, therefore, a business check; second, the indorsement "In Final Settlement of Feeding Contract" also indicated that it was a business account; third, there was a $10,000 discrepancy on the face of it; and fourth, the check was presented already indorsed.

In regard to the fact that the check was already indorsed, we find this to be of no importance; it would not be so unusual for a spouse to handle such a transaction and in addition, McCook bank was familiar with both Dean Tabke and Mrs. Tabke. In regard to the $10,000 discrepancy, as will be discussed below, McCook bank prudently verified the correct amount before proceeding. We need only consider the assertion that the check was obviously a business check.

The indorsement here was not a restrictive endorsement nor was it indorsed by anyone other than the payee. Indeed, this check was indorsed by the payee and was fully negotiable on its face. Compton argues that the fact that the check appeared to be a fully negotiable business check was sufficient to alert McCook bank that this check represented . . . proceeds and in addition, that Tabke had no right to disburse such proceeds to his creditors. We do not agree.

This is not a case of patent irregularity on the face of the instrument. For instance, in *First National Bank of Linton v Otto Huber and Sons, Inc.,* 394 F.Supp. 1284, 1287 (D.S.D. 1975) a note was improperly executed leaving the due date of the note unclear. The court considered this irregularity sufficient to destroy holder in due course status. However in *Eldon's Super Fresh Stores, Inc. v Merrill Lynch, Pierce, Fenner & Smith, Inc.,* 296 Minn. 130, 207 N.W.2d 282(1973) an attorney used a check of a corporate client to buy stock for his personal account. Even though it was drawn on a corporate account, made payable to Merrill Lynch and signed by the corporate president, when it was negotiated by the corporate attorney for a personal stock purchase, the court found that Merrill Lynch had no notice and was still a holder in due course. The court did not require Merrill Lynch to impute bad faith to the attorney who negotiated the check which is what Compton urges this court to do. We fail to find any notice from the instrument or duty to inquire further. . . .

Compton finally asserts that McCook bank had "notice" from the conversations at the bank between Eichinger and Mrs. Tabke on February 3, 1975. The district court found that after the check had been cashed, Mrs. Tabke again spoke with Mr. Eichinger and "made some remark to the effect that she had brought the check to plaintiff bank because her husband wanted six of his creditors to be paid and had they taken the check to the bank where they normally did business, United National Bank in Canistota, that bank would 'grab it.'" Though the testimony concerning this conversation is quite ambiguous, it is quite clear that this conversation occurred after the check had been cashed and is, in this court's opinion, irrelevant to the issue of notice. . . . To be effective notice must be received at such time and in such manner as to give a reasonable opportunity to act on it. It seems logically impossible for a conversation which takes place after a check is cashed to provide effective notice of reasons why the check should not be cashed, thus enabling the bank to act on that knowledge. . . .

In addition to the requirement that the instrument be taken without notice, [the Code] requires that the instrument be taken in good faith. . . . Since it is a statutory requirement to show that a person claiming to be a holder in due course acted in good faith, this court must examine the record and judge the transaction not from hindsight but on the basis of the facts known to McCook bank at the time Compton's check was negotiated. We feel the record is clear that McCook bank had no actual or constructive knowledge that the check represented secured proceeds at the time it was presented. . . . The fact that the Bank might have exercised better credit judgment with respect to the collateral is of no occasion. . . .

McCook bank was presented with a check that had an obvious $10,000 discrepancy on its face. As any prudent bank would, McCook contacted the Northwestern bank to ascertain the correct amount and whether adequate funds existed to cover the check. Assured by the bank and indirectly by Compton, who issued the check, that the check was "okay," McCook proceeded to cash the check and issue money orders. There was no remaining irregularities in the instrument itself. Since this court has found no actual notice and insufficient constructive notice from the reporting service, and no other notice at the time the check was cashed, we can find no bad faith or dishonesty on the part of McCook bank in cashing the check.

In sum, while a better judgment concerning the negotiability of the check *might* have been made we can not find the requisite notice or bad faith that would deprive McCook bank of its status as holder in due course. . . .

[Judgment reversed and action remanded]

Illinois Valley Acceptance Corp. v Woodard

(Ind App) 304 NE2d 859 (1973)

At various times Woodard purchased goods from the Moody Manufacturing Company. In 1968 he made a purchase and arranged for its payment by accepting a trade acceptance drawn on him. He accepted it although the amount was blank because it had not yet been determined what goods he would be purchasing from Moody. An amount was later filled in and thereafter Moody assigned the acceptance to Illinois Valley Acceptance Corp. Illinois sued Woodard on the trade acceptance. He raised the defenses that there had been fraud, that he had never received the goods, and that the trade acceptance had been accepted with the amount in blank. Judgment was entered for Woodard and Illinois Valley appealed.

ROBERTSON, P. J. . . . Whether the trial court erred . . . is tied to Acceptance's classification as a holder in due course of the questioned trade acceptance. . . .

Acceptance's acknowledged status as a holder was not sufficient for it to recover because Woodard raised the defenses of fraud and failure of consideration, each a valid defense under [UCC §] 3-306. . . . These defenses, however, may have been cut off if Acceptance was a holder in due course. The holder in due course takes the instrument "free from all defenses of any party to the instrument with whom the holder has not dealt," subject to several exceptions. [UCC §] 3-305(2) . . . To avail itself of this "super-plaintiff" status, Acceptance had the burden of establishing by a preponderance of the evidence that it was "in all respects a holder in due course." [UCC §] 3-307(3). . . . "In all respects" means that Acceptance had to establish the existence of each of the elements set forth in IC 1971, 26-1-3-302, Ind.Ann.Stat. § 19-3-302 (Burns 1964). It provides: "(1) A holder in due course is a holder who takes the instrument (a) for value; and (b) in good faith; and (c) without notice that it is overdue or has been dishonored or of any defense against or claim to it on the part of any person."

The evidence, when examined with the foregoing requisites in mind, establishes Acceptance as a holder in due course. Briefly summarized that evidence shows the trade acceptance being endorsed over to Acceptance by Moody. Moody in turn received a draft for 85% of the face value of the trade acceptance. There was nothing irregular with the appearance of the trade acceptance and the transaction was similar to other prior transactions between the parties. At that time Acceptance had no knowledge that the trade acceptance had been signed in blank and that the goods had not been delivered.

A portion of Woodard's arguments appears to be directed to the questions of good faith and notice. Both are statutorily defined: "(19) 'Good faith' means honesty in fact in the conduct or transaction concerned." [UCC §] 26-1-1-201, Ind.Ann.Stat. § 19-1-201 (Burns 1964) Notice, insofar as applicable, is defined as: "(1) The purchaser has notice of a claim or defense if (a) the instrument is so incomplete, bears such visible evidence of forgery or alteration, or is otherwise so irregular as to call into question its validity, terms or ownership or to create an ambiguity as to the party to pay; or (b) the purchaser has notice that the obligation of any party is voidable in whole or in part, or that all parties

have been discharged." [UCC §] 3-304. . . .

The gist of Woodard's cross examination of Acceptance's vice-president was directed to when Acceptance became aware of Moody's bankruptcy and to the Finance Agreement between Moody and Acceptance. We believe that the bankruptcy has no relevancy because of its nonexistence at the time the trade acceptance was indorsed over to Acceptance. The Finance Agreement, introduced into evidence by Woodard, may have been an attempt to establish something akin to the doctrine of close connectedness, characterized by Woodard as the lack of an arms-length transaction, for the purpose of showing that Acceptance was so closely related to Moody commercially that it knew, or should have known, either Moody was in poor financial shape or that it had not delivered the goods represented by the trade acceptance. Acceptance's summary judgment affidavit as well as the testimony given at the trial belies such a relationship.

Woodard further argues that there was no value given for the trade acceptance and that the Finance Agreement between Moody and Acceptance was merely a borrowing agreement. The evidence shows that Acceptance paid Moody 85% of the face value of trade acceptance and held the remainder in reserve. There can be little question that the value concept was satisfied. [UCC §] 3-303. . . . Nor does the designation of the Finance Agreement as a borrowing arrangement standing alone serve to frustrate the taking of value. The issuance of the draft by Acceptance and the holding in reserve of the remaining 15% eliminates any question regarding unused credit. . . .

Woodard's affirmative defense of want of consideration is not available against a holder in due course. [UCC §] 3-408. . . .

Turning next to the question of fraud [UCC §] 3-305(2)(c) . . . allows a defense against a holder in due course based upon "such misrepresentation as has induced the party to sign the instrument with neither knowledge nor reasonable opportunity to obtain knowledge of its character or its essential terms." The comments subsequent to this statute state that fraud in the essence or fraud in the factum is a valid defense against a holder in due course with the theory being that the "signature is ineffective because he did not intend to sign such an instrument at all." Woodard's past conduct in signing blank trade acceptances for Moody negates a defense based on the foregoing. Woodard testified he was familiar with the forms and knew they constituted a promise to pay. . . .

It is our conclusion that the evidence conclusively demonstrated Acceptance to be a holder in due course. We, accordingly, reverse and remand for judgment to be entered for the plaintiff-appellant Illinois Valley Acceptance Corp., and against the defendant-appellee Robert Woodard.

[Judgment reversed and remanded]

Schaeffer v United Bank and Trust Company

32 MdApp 339, 360 A2d 461 (1976)

Estepp borrowed money from the United Bank and Trust Company. He signed a promissory note and in order to induce the bank to make the loan, Estepp had Schaeffer sign as an accommodation maker. Estepp was Schaeffer's supervisor at the country club where they both worked. They were friends. Schaeffer could not read and Estepp told him that the note which Schaeffer was signing was a "character reference." When the note was not paid, the bank sued Schaeffer who raised the defense of fraud. The lower court held that the bank had not been guilty of any fraud and entered a judgment in favor of the bank. Schaeffer appealed.

MOORE, J. . . . [The lower court stated] *I do not think that the United Bank did anything wrong in this case in its dealings and I have not seen any evidence here today that it committed any kind of fraud on this particular defendant. . . .*

It is manifest that the court overlooked evidence of fraud on the part of the maker, James Estepp, and herein resides reversible error. . . .

The evidence . . . would establish (1) that [Schaeffer] was almost illiterate, (2) that the nature of the transaction was not explained to him by the bank, (3) that he did not understand that he was assuming any financial responsibility when he signed the note and (4) that Mr. Estepp falsely and fraudulently misrepresented the document. This evidence mounts up to fraud in the *factum.*

Fraud in the *factum,* unaccompanied by negligence, is one of the most potent defenses in the realm of commercial law. When it is successfully interposed it bars recovery not only by the promisee on a simple contract . . . , but also by a holder in due course. . . .

In discussing the elements of fraud in the *factum,* official comment 7 to § 3-305 of the Commercial Law Article is instructive:

"The test of the defense here stated is that of excusable ignorance of the contents of the writing signed. The party must not only have been in ignorance, but must also have had no reasonable opportunity to obtain knowledge. In determining what is a reasonable opportunity all relevant factors are to be taken into account, including the age and sex of the party, his intelligence, education and business experience; his ability to read or to understand English, the representations made to him and his reason to rely on them or to have confidence in the person making them; the presence or absence of any third person who might read or explain the instrument to him, or any other possibility of obtaining independent information; and the apparent necessity, or lack of it, for acting without delay."

Here appellant was a man of limited intelligence, little education, and virtually no ability to read English. His supervisor at work, who had assisted him in the funeral of his wife, and in whom he "had complete confidence in what he said" at the time the note was signed, misrepresented the very essence of the transaction.

In a strikingly similar case, a New Jersey court observed:

"The evidence supports the trial court's finding that De Paul signed the note in issue in reliance upon the false representation made to him by the maker Ronald Perkowsky, that he was signing only a 'character reference' which Perkowsky needed in connection with the purchase of merchandise from Bushberg Brothers of Union City, the payee of the instrument. Because of his subnormal mentality, his only schooling having been in a 'special class' of the public school, De Paul was not able to read, except small words, and then he needed reading glasses for this purpose. When he signed this note, he did not read it; he had no reading glasses with him, and the note was not read to him by Perkowsky or the representative of Bushberg Brothers who witnessed his signature. It seems clear, therefore, that the district court was correct in finding that De Paul's signature was obtained as the result of fraud in the *factum,* without any negligence on his part. . . .

"The rationale of the defense is the fundamental of contract law that one cannot be bound on an obligation he does not know he is entering into. Restatement, Contracts, § 475." *Amsterdam v De Paul,* 70 N.J.Super. 196, 175 A.2d 219,220 (App.Div.1961). *See also, Kearney v Commerce Investment Co.,* 262 A.2d 804 (D.C.App. 1970).

Here, . . . the same considerations lead us to the conclusion that appellant was a victim of fraud in the *factum.*

In *Amsterdam* the plaintiff holder in due course argued that since the fraud was perpetrated by a maker upon a co-maker rather than by the payee, "the defense was not available as against the payee or its transferee, the plaintiff." 175 A.2d at 221. In the instant case the bank correctly argues that "there was no testimony or evidence of fraud perpetrated by the appellee [Bank] on the appellant" [Schaeffer]. This argument is, however, irrelevant. When the individual charged on a note successfully interposes the defense of fraud in the *factum* it is immaterial *who* perpetrated the fraud. . . .

[Judgment reversed]

New Jersey Mortgage and Investment Corporation v Berenyi

140 NJSuper 406, 356 A2d 421 (1976)

Kroyden Industries manufactured and sold carpeting. It sold on the referral plan by which customers were told that they could obtain carpeting free by making required referrals of other customers. Acting under the authority of a state consumer protection statute, the attorney general of the state obtained an injunction prohibiting Kroyden from selling in this manner. Thereafter Kroyden sold carpeting to Berenyi for $1100 with the understanding that the carpeting would not cost anything if referrals were made. This was in violation of the court injunction. Berenyi executed a note for the purchase price of the carpet. The note was negotiated to the New Jersey Mortgage and Investment Corporation. The corporation was a holder in due course and did not know of the injunction against Kroyden. When the corporation sued Berenyi, he claimed that the note was not binding because of the illegality of the sale to him. From a judgment for the corporation, Berenyi appealed.

PER CURIAM * . . . The trial judge ruled that the fact that the note was obtained as part of a transaction entered into . . . in violation of the injuctive order was not a defense in an action brought by plaintiff, whose status as a holder in due course, with no knowledge or notice of the injunctive order, was admitted.

The controlling issue presented is whether the defense here asserted is a "[universal]" defense or a "[limited]" defense. [Universal] defenses are available against even a holder in due course of a negotiable instrument; [limited] defenses are not available against such a holder. We affirm since we are satisfied that the defense presented is [a limited] defense.

Defendant argues that since the transaction which resulted in the execution and delivery of defendant's note was engaged in by Kroyden in violation of the injunctive order, the transaction was "illegal and thus a nullity under [UCC §] 3-305," which provides . . . as follows: To the extent that a holder is a holder in due course he takes the instrument free from . . . (2) all defenses of any party to the instrument with whom the holder has not dealt except . . . (b) such other incapacity, or duress, or illegality of the transaction, as renders the obligation of the party a nullity; . . ."

The fact that it was illegal for Kroyden to enter into the transaction did not by reason of that fact render defendant's obligation under the note she executed a nullity.

A holder in due course takes free and clear of the defense of illegality, unless the statute which declares the act illegal also indicates that payment thereunder is void. . . . Where no such statute is involved, it has been held that a negotiable instrument which is rooted in an illegal transaction or stems from a transaction prohibited by statute or public policy is no reason for refusing to enforce the instrument in the hands of a holder in due course. . . .

There being no statute ordaining that a note obtained in violation of an injunction is void and unenforceable, the illegality involved is not a [universal] defense; the note is enforceable in the hands of

---

* [Authors' note: Ordinarily an opinion of the court is filed under the name of the judge who wrote the opinion. When a case is perfectly clear and obvious, the opinion will frequently be filed without naming the writing judge and will then have a heading of "memorandum" or "per curiam" (by the court).]

a holder in due course who had no knowledge or notice of the injunction.

[Judgment affirmed]

Circle v Jim Walter Homes, Inc.

(CA10 Okla) 535 F2d 583 (1976)

Circle and other home buyers purchased homes from Jim Walter Homes. They paid some cash down and the balance was to be paid in installments. Each buyer executed a promissory note for the balance which was secured by a mortgage on the house which was purchased. This violated the Uniform Consumer Credit Code (UCCC) under which a creditor could only take a check from a consumer and could not take any other kind of negotiable commercial paper. The UCCC authorizes consumers to recover certain refunds and penalties from creditors violating this prohibition. Thereafter Circle and other buyers brought an action to recover the refunds and penalties authorized by the Uniform Consumer Credit Code. Jim Walter raised the defense that the fact that anything other than a check was prohibited by the UCCC made the promissory notes that had been given nonnegotiable and therefore there was no violation of the UCCC because negotiable paper other than a check had not been taken from consumers. From a decision in favor of Jim Walter, Circle and the others appealed.

DOYLE, C. J. . . . The Uniform Consumer Credit Code (UCCC), . . . makes it unlawful for a seller to "take a negotiable instrument other than a check as evidence of the obligation of the buyer" in a consumer credit transaction. [UCCC §] 2-403. Plaintiffs claim that they are entitled to relief under the provision of the UCCC Section 5-202, . . . which provides that (1) If a creditor has violated the provisions of this Act applying to certain negotiable instruments (Section 2-403) . . . the debtor is not obligated to pay the credit service charge or loan finance charge and has a right to recover from the person violating this Act or from an assignee of that person's rights who undertakes direct collection of payments or enforcement of rights arising from the debt a penalty in any amount determined by the court not in excess of three times the amount of the credit service charge or loan finance charge. . . .

We must consider . . . whether the notes are negotiable within the meaning of the UCC, taking into account that the UCCC makes it unlawful

for a seller to accept a negotiable instrument other than a check as evidence of the obligation of the buyer. . . .

The notes in question are *on their face negotiable* meeting all requirements of the UCC, . . . Section 3-104. They contain an unconditional promise to pay a sum certain at a specific time to the order of defendant. . . . The contention of defendant reduces itself to the issue whether the statute providing for the rebate of unearned interest itself creates uncertainty as to amount of the note within the meaning of the UCC or whether [UCCC §] 2-403 prohibiting use of a promissory note itself constitutes a [universal] defense even as to a holder in due course and thus expresses a policy which in effect renders the instrument a nullity as negotiable paper.

. . . No reason exists for holding that the note is non-negotiable and unenforceable in the hands of a holder in due course.

A. *Whether the Prohibition in the UCCC, . . . Section 2-403, Against Use of a Negotiable Instrument in a Consumer Transaction Itself Causes the Note to Be Non-Negotiable.*

We determine this by analyzing the relevant consumer and commercial statutes, the first of which is . . . Section 3-305(2)(a), (b)(UCC). This section states in effect that a holder in due course takes the instrument free from "all claims to it on the part of any person and all defenses of any party to the instrument with whom the holder has not dealt." Exceptions are what might be termed [universal] defenses such as infancy, incapacity, duress or illegality "as renders the obligation of the party a nullity." The question then becomes: Does the above mentioned provision of the UCCC prohibiting use of negotiable instruments in consumer transactions render the obligation of the party (maker) a nullity, for it is only the illegality of this extreme nature which is capable of bringing about the conclusion that the instrument is unenforceable even in the hands of a holder in due course. Though this is not exactly equal to rendering the instrument non-negotiable, it is arguably similar to it.

Turning now to the prohibition against use of negotiable instruments in consumer transactions, Section 2-403 of the UCCC provides:

"In a consumer credit sale or consumer lease, other than a sale or lease primarily for an agricultural purpose, the seller or lessor may not take a negotiable instrument other than a check as evidence of the obligation of the buyer or lessee. A holder is not in good faith if he takes a negotiable instrument with notice that it is issued in violation of this section. A holder in due course is not subject to the liabilities set forth in the provisions on the effect of violations on rights of parties (Section 5-202) and the provisions on civil actions by Administrator (Section 6-113)."

It is clear from a reading of this section that it only prohibits use of the negotiable instrument— it does not undertake to render the instrument a nullity so that it will be the subject of a real defense, nor does it outlaw such an instrument. Instead it displays plainly an intent not to render the note non-negotiable. This is apparent from the statement contained in it that a holder is not a holder in good faith if he takes a negotiable instrument with notice that it is issued in violation of the statute, and so this is the sanction as imposed in connection with the use of negotiable instruments in a consumer transaction. It would follow that if a holder took without notice that it is issued in violation of the statute, he would be a holder in due course and would take free of equities, including that which would arise from its having been issued in violation of the UCCC. An added evidence that the framers consider the note negotiable is to be inferred from the statement that a holder in due course is not subject to other statutory liabilities resulting from violations described in other sections. Therefore, the legislature did not intend that the use of a negotiable instrument in a consumer transaction serves to render the instrument a nullity or to destroy its negotiability. Its recognition that a holder in due course can cut off equities, including violation of the prohibition against the use of negotiable instruments, manifests an intent that their negotiability is not impaired.

Finally, the sole sanction flowing from violation of the consumer act by use of a negotiable instrument is that the debtor is not obligated to pay the credit service charge or loan finance charge and has a right to recover from the violator in not only the amount of the finance charge, but possibly three times the amount of the finance charge in addition, [UCCC §] 5-202(1). On refusal to refund the finance charge within a reasonable time, the court is empowered to impose a penalty not exceeding the greater of the amount of the finance charge or ten times the amount of the excess charge, [UCCC §] 5-202(4). Since these are the sole remedies or sanctions provided in the statutes which have been analyzed, it becomes even more plain that it was not intended that the ostensible promissory note was per se null and void or invalid as contrary to public policy.

B. Comparison with Other Statutes.

An examination of the other statutes furnishes additional evidence that Oklahoma did not intend to outlaw the purported negotiable instrument in a consumer transaction. Vermont Stat.Ann., Title 9, Section 2455 (1971), spells out the breadth of the defense as against one who has taken the instrument. It provides that any person taking an instrument made by a consumer in connection with a contract holds it subject to the defenses that "would be available to the consumer in an action on a simple contract."

Also, the model act proposed by the National Consumer Law Center uses a similar approach in that it forbids a seller to use a negotiable note in a consumer transaction, and then goes on to provide that the holder taking such a note takes it subject to all the consumer's defenses. *See* National Consumer Act, Section 2.405. If the UCCC draftsmen in Oklahoma had intended to eliminate negotiability of consumer paper in addition to prohibiting its use, they could have done so by adopting language such as that shown in the Vermont Statute or the model measure.

[Judgment reversed and action remanded]

QUESTIONS AND CASE PROBLEMS

1. What social forces are affected by the holder in due course rule?
2. Is a check given to a house painter before the house is painted as promised (a) supported by consideration, (b) taken for value?
3. Compare (a) an assignee, (b) a holder, (c) a holder in due course, and (d) a holder

through a holder in due course with respect to the defense that the defendant is seventeen years of age.

4. Compare the effect of the alteration of a contract with the alteration of commercial paper.

5. *A* was the holder of a promissory note made by *C.* In a lawsuit brought against *C* three months after the due date of the paper, the question arose whether *A* was a holder in due course. There was no evidence as to the date on which *A* acquired the paper. Can *A* be a holder in due course? [See College Park Credit Corp. v Carver, 132 Vt 524, 322 A2d 305]

6. Vanella sold his automobile to Blackburn Motors by falsely representing that there were no liens on the car. Blackburn paid Vanella with a check that was cashed by the Marine Midland Trust Co. When Blackburn learned of Vanella's fraud, it stopped payment on the check. Midland then sued Blackburn to enforce its secondary liability as drawer. Blackburn raised the defense of Vanella's fraud. Was this defense available to it? [Marine Midland Trust Co. v Blackburn, 50 Misc 2d 954, 271 NYS2d 388]

7. *D* drew a check to the order of *P.* It was later claimed that *P* was not a holder in due course because the check was postdated and because *P* knew that *D* was having financial difficulties and that the particular checking account on which this check was drawn had been frequently overdrawn. Do these circumstances prevent *P* from being a holder in due course? [Citizens Bank, Booneville v National Bank of Commerce, (CA Okla) 334 F2d 257; Franklin National Bank v Sidney Gotowner, (NY Sup Ct) 4 UCCRS 953]

8. *A* and *B* were negotiating for the sale of land. *A* paid *B* in advance with a postdated check. When *A* and *B* could not agree on a final contract, *A* stopped payment of the check. Was *B* a holder in due course? [Briand v Wild, 110 NH 373, 268 A2d 896]

9. Rocchio executed and delivered a note payable to the order of Berta. When Berta sued Rocchio on the note, the latter offered parol evidence to show that the note had been given as payment for a business and its inventory and that less inventory had been delivered than had been agreed upon. Berta claimed that the obligation of the instrument could not be modified by parol evidence. Was he correct? [Berta v Rocchio, 149 Colo 325, 369 P2d 51]

10. *H* acquired a check by indorsement. At the time that *H* acquired the check he knew of all the circumstances surrounding the original issue of the check. If *H* knew the legal significance of those circumstances, he would have realized that the drawer of the check had a valid defense. Because *H* did not know the law, he did not realize that he had a defense and took the check in good faith believing that everything was proper. In a subsequent lawsuit on the check, the question arose whether *H* was a holder in due course. The defendant claimed that *H* was not because *H* knew of the defense based on the surrounding circumstances and *H*'s ignorance of the law did not excuse him from the consequence of that knowledge, because ignorance of the law is no excuse. Is *H* barred from being a holder in due course? [See Hartford Life Ins. Co. v Title Guarantee Co., 172 App DC 156, 520 F2d 1170.]

11. A customer of a bank purchased a bank money order and paid for it with a forged check. The money order was negotiable and was acquired by *N* who was a holder in due course. When *N* sued the bank on the money order, it raised the defense that its customer had paid with a bad check. Could this defense be raised against *N*? [See Bank of Niles v American State Bank, 14 IllApp3d 729, 303 NE2d 186.]

12. *H* was the holder of a promissory note. When he sued *M,* the maker of the note, *M* raised as a defense the objection that *H* was not a holder in due course. Can *H* recover? [Brock v Adams, 79 NMex 17, 439 P2d 234]

13. Henry executed and delivered a check to Jesse Farley in payment of an automobile. On the face of the check was written "Car to be free and clear of liens." The check

was indorsed and delivered by Farley to the Zachry Company. When the latter sued Henry, Henry raised the defense of fraud in the inducement and failure of consideration, and claimed that Zachry was not a holder in due course because the words "Car to be free and clear of liens" gave notice of defenses. Was Henry correct? [C. D. Henry v A. L. Zachry Co., 93 Ga App 536, 92 SE2d 225]

14. Statham drew a check. The payee indorsed it to the Kemp Motor Sales. Statham then stopped payment on the check on the ground that there was a failure of consideration for the check. Kemp sued Statham on the check. When Statham raised the defense of failure of consideration, Kemp replied that it was a holder in due course. Statham claimed that Kemp could not recover because it learned of his defense before it deposited the check in its bank account. Decide. [Kemp Motor Sales v Statham, 120 Ga App 515, 171 SE2d 389]

15. In an action on a promissory note it was claimed that there had been a material change of the note. Was this a sufficient defense? [Mandel v Sedrish, (NY) 3 UCCRS 526]

16. *B* held a promissory note executed by *A* by which *A* promised to pay to the order of *B* the sum of $1,000. *B* indorsed and delivered the note to *C* for $800. *C* sued *A* for $1,000. *A* raised the defense that the most that *C* could recover was $800 as that was the only value which *C* had given for the note. Was this a valid defense? [See Cantrell v Cafourek (MoApp) 513 SW2d 690.]

17. Kavlick hired Rothman to do construction work and paid him by a note. Rothman indorsed the note "without recourse" to the Eastern Acceptance Corp. The corporation sued Kavlick on the note. He defended on the ground that the consideration for the note had failed and that this defense was available against the corporation because it could not be a holder in due course on account of the form of the indorsement. Decide. [Eastern Acceptance Corp. v Kavlick, 10 NJ Super 253, 77 A2d 49]

32

Discharge of Commercial Paper

A party to a commercial paper who would otherwise be liable on it may be discharged either individually or by some act that has discharged all parties to the paper at one time. The nature of the transaction or occurrence determines which takes place.

A. DISCHARGE OF INDIVIDUAL PARTIES

A party to a commercial paper, like a party to an ordinary contract, is usually discharged from liability by making payment to the proper person; but the discharge from liability may be effected in a number of other ways.

§ 32:1. Manner of Discharge. A party is discharged from liability to any other party (a) with whom an express agreement for discharge is made, or (b) with whom a transaction is entered into which under the law of contracts is effective to discharge liability on an ordinary contract for the payment of money.[1] Accordingly, there may be a discharge by accord and satisfaction, a novation, a covenant not to sue, rescission, or the substitution of another instrument. The liability may also be barred by operation of the law as in the case of a discharge in bankruptcy, the operation of the statute of limitations, or by the merger of liability into a judgment in favor of the holder when an action has been brought on the instrument.

§ 32:2. Discharge by Payment. The obligation of a particular party on commercial paper is discharged by paying the amount of the instrument to the holder or the latter's authorized agent. Payment to anyone else, even though in physical possession of the instrument, is not effective to discharge the liability of the payor. (See p. 535, First National Bank v Gorman)

If the holder consents, payment may be made by a third person, even a total stranger to the paper; and surrender of the paper to such a person gives that person the rights of a transferee of the instrument.[2]

By definition, a commercial paper provides for the payment of a sum of money. Any party liable on the instrument and the holder thereof may, however, agree that the transfer or delivery of other kinds of property shall operate as payment. Sometimes

---

[1] UCC § 3-601(2)
[2] UCC § 3-603.

a new instrument may be executed or delivered to the holder of the original instrument. In the absence of proof of an agreement to the contrary, the delivery of a subsequent instrument, without the destruction or other act to discharge the first, is regarded as merely giving additional security for the payment of the original instrument but not as being a payment or discharge of it.

(a)   Knowledge of Adverse Claim to the Paper. When the payment of the amount of the paper is made to the holder, the party making payment may know that some other person claims an interest in or ownership of the paper. The knowledge that there is an adverse claimant does not prevent making a payment to the holder, and such payment is still a discharge of the obligation of the party making payment. Specifically, an adverse claim may thus be disregarded unless (1) the adverse claimant furnishes the payor with indemnity to protect the payor should payment be made to the adverse claimant but the adverse claim thereafter be proven worthless or (2) the adverse claimant obtains a court injunction against making payment.[3]

The purpose of this provision is to give commercial paper greater acceptance since the person writing such paper knows that the instrument may be discharged by making payment in the ordinary case to the holder without the risk of deciding whether an adverse claim is valid.

(b)   Satisfaction. The principles governing payment apply to a satisfaction entered into with the holder of the instrument.[4] Instead of paying the holder in full in money, a payment of less than all is accepted as full payment or some service is rendered or property is given by the party discharged.

(c)   Tender of Payment. A party who is liable may offer to the holder the full payment when or after the instrument is due. If the holder refuses such payment, the party making the tender of payment is not discharged from liability for the amount then due; but the holder cannot thereafter hold that party liable for any interest that accrues after the date of the rejected tender. Likewise if the holder sues the person making the tender, the holder cannot recover legal costs nor attorney's fees.

If the holder refuses a proper tender, such refusal may discharge a third person even though it does not affect the liability of the person making the tender. Specifically, any party to the paper who would have a right on making payment to recover that amount from the person making the tender is discharged if the tender is not accepted.[5] For example, if the paper is negotiated through the unqualified indorsers, *A, B,* and *C,* to the holder *D,* and if *B* or *C* is required to pay *D,* the party making such payment would have the right to sue *A,* the prior indorser, to recover the amount paid to holder *D.* In such a case, if *A* makes a proper tender of payment which *D* refuses, *B* and *C* are discharged from any liability to *D.*

(d)   Payment by Secondary Party. When a party secondarily liable pays, such payment does not discharge the paper or prior parties but merely transfers the rights of the holder to the party making the payment. This is so even though there is no

---

[3] UCC § 3-603(1). Certain exceptions are made to this rule when payment is made in bad faith on a stolen instrument or when the instrument is restrictively indorsed.

[4] UCC § 3-601(1).

[5] UCC § 3-604(2).

assignment or transfer of the paper from the paid holder to the secondary party making payment.

§ 32:3. Cancellation.

(a)   What Constitutes Cancellation. The holder of an instrument, with or without consideration, may discharge the liability of a particular party by cancellation by a notation on the paper which makes that intent apparent, or by destroying, mutilating, or striking out the party's signature on the paper. Even though this cancels an indorsement necessary to the chain of title of the holder, the holder's title to the paper is not affected,[6] as the paper had already been properly negotiated.

There is no cancellation when the paper is physically destroyed by accident or mistake. In all cases, the party claiming that an apparent cancellation should not take effect has the burden of proof.

(b)   Who May Cancel. The owner of the paper or the owner's agent may make the cancellation or may surrender the paper for cancellation to a party liable thereon. A cancellation is not effective if it is made by a person who is not the owner or the owner's agent. Thus the surrender of a check to the drawer for cancellation has no effect when not made by the payee or the payee's agent. If the paper has not been issued to the payee, it may be canceled or surrendered by the person who prepared it or who caused it to be prepared. (See p. 536, Gillespie v Riley Management Corp.)

§ 32:4. Renunciation.

(a)   What Constitutes Renunciation. The holder of an instrument, with or without consideration, may discharge the liability of a particular party by renunciation. This is done either (1) by surrendering the instrument to the party to be discharged, or (2) by executing a signed written renunciation which is then delivered to the party to be discharged.[7] There is no renunciation when the written renunciation is not delivered but is retained by the holder. (See p. 537, Greene v Cotton)

A holder who surrenders the instrument in effecting a discharge ceases to be the holder and thereafter cannot hold any party liable on the paper, although such other parties are not themselves discharged with respect to the person to whom the paper was surrendered or any other subsequent holder.

(b)   Who May Renounce. A renunciation may only be made by the owner of the paper or the owner's authorized agent. When made by any other person, the renunciation has no effect and the person making the renunciation may be liable for the tort of conversion of the paper to any person whose joinder in the renunciation was required.

(c)   Accounting Methods. If the requirements of the Code are not satisfied there is no renunciation. It is immaterial how the commercial paper is treated by the holder for accounting and record-keeping purposes. (See p. 538, White System v Lehmann)

---

[6] UCC § 3-605.
[7] UCC § 3-605(1).

§ 32:5. Impairment of Right of Recourse. In most instances, there is at least one party to commercial paper who, if required to pay, will have a right of recourse, or a right to obtain indemnity from some other party. For example, in the least complicated situation, the payee of a note has indorsed it without qualification to the present holder. If the holder obtains payment from the indorsing payee, the latter has a right of recourse against the maker of the note. If the holder, without the indorser's consent, discharges the liability of the maker, extends the time for payment, or agrees not to sue, the indorser is also discharged unless that indorser consented thereto, because the right of recourse held by the indorser has been impaired thereby.[8]

A creditor may prevent a release from discharging another party by making an express reservation of the right to proceed against such other party. (See p. 538, Hallowell v Turner)

§ 32:6. Impairment of Collateral. When commercial paper is executed, the maker may give the holder property, such as stocks or bonds, to hold as security for the payment of the instrument. Likewise, any other party liable on the instrument may give collateral as security to the holder for the same purpose. This collateral security benefits all parties who might be liable on the paper because to the extent that payment is obtained from the security, they are not required to make payment. Conversely, if the collateral security is impaired or harmed in any way that reduces its value, the parties who are liable are harmed since the possibility that they will be required to pay increases. Accordingly, a particular party is discharged if the holder unjustifiably impairs collateral security provided by that party or by any person against whom such party has a right of recourse.[9]

§ 32:7. Reacquisition of Paper by Intermediate Party. Commercial paper is sometimes reacquired by a party who has been an earlier holder. This occurs most commonly when that earlier party pays the then existing holder the amount due, thereby in effect purchasing the paper from the holder. When this occurs, the prior party may cancel all indorsements subsequent to the indorsement which such prior party had made on first indorsing the paper, and then may reissue or further negotiate the paper. Those subsequent indorsers whose indorsements have been cancelled are discharged as to the reacquirer and all subsequent holders.[10]

§ 32:8. Alteration. When an instrument is materially and fraudulently altered by the holder, any party whose obligation on the paper is changed thereby is discharged, unless such party has assented to the alteration or is barred by conduct from asserting a discharge. The effect of the discharge by alteration is limited, however, for a holder in due course may enforce the paper according to its original terms.[11]

§ 32:9. Discharge for Miscellaneous Causes. In addition to the discharge of a party as discussed in the preceding sections, the conduct of certain parties with respect to the commercial

---

[8] UCC § 3-606(1)(a). Note that this is similar to the situation where a holder refuses to accept a proper tender of payment from the maker, in which case an indorser is discharged.

[9] UCC § 3-606(1)(b).

[10] UCC § 3-208.

[11] UCC § 3-407.

paper or the enforcement of rights thereunder may release some of the parties to the paper. This occurs (a) when a check has been certified on the application of the holder; (b) when the holder accepts an acceptance that varies the terms of the draft; and (c) when a presentment, notice of dishonor, or protest, when required, is delayed beyond the time permitted or is absent and such delay or absence is not excused.

In addition, federal or local statutes may provide for the discharge of a party by bankruptcy proceedings or by local laws declaring certain obligations not enforceable because they violate particular statutes.

B. DISCHARGE OF ALL PARTIES

In contrast with conduct which discharges individual parties to paper, some types of conduct release everyone from liability.

§ 32:10. Discharge of Party Primarily Liable. The primary party on an instrument, that is, the maker of a note or the acceptor of a draft,[12] has no right of recourse against any party to the paper. Conversely, every other party who may be held liable on the paper has a right of recourse against the person primarily liable. If the holder discharges in any way a party who is primarily liable, all parties to the instrument are discharged, as the discharge of the primary party discharges the persons who had a right of recourse against the primary party.[13]

§ 32:11. Primary Party's Reacquisition of Paper. When a party primarily liable on the paper reacquires it as owner at any time, whether before or after it is due, the instrument is then held by one who has no right to sue any other party on the paper. Such reacquisition therefore discharges the liability of all intervening parties to the instrument.[14]

C. EFFECT OF DISCHARGE ON HOLDER IN DUE COURSE

An ordinary holder or assignee of paper is subject to any discharge. A holder in due course may or may not be subject to a prior discharge.

§ 32:12. Discharge of Individual Party. The fact that a party has been discharged of liability, and even that a new holder of the paper knows of it, does not prevent the new holder from being a holder in due course as to any party remaining liable on the paper.[15] If the holder in due course does not have notice or knowledge of the discharge of a party before acquiring the paper, the holder in due course is not bound by that discharge and may enforce the obligation of the discharged party as though there had been no discharge.[16] To avoid being sued by such a holder in due course,

---

[12] An accommodated payee is in effect also a primary party since the accommodating party, if required to pay an indorsee, has a right of recourse against such payee.

[13] UCC § 3-601(3). In some instances this rule is modified by § 3-606.

[14] UCC § 3-208.

[15] UCC § 3-305(2)(e).

[16] UCC § 3-602. As an exception to this rule, the holder in due course is bound by a prior discharge in insolvency proceedings, such as bankruptcy, whether the holder had notice thereof or not. UCC § 3-305(2)(d).

a party obtaining a discharge should have a notation of it made on the paper so that any subsequent holder would necessarily have notice of that fact.

§ 32:13. Discharge of All Parties. The fact that the liabilities of all parties to a commercial paper have been discharged does not destroy the negotiable character nor the existence of the commercial paper. If it should thereafter be negotiated to a person who qualifies as a holder in due course, the latter may enforce the liability of any party on the paper, although otherwise discharged, of whose discharge the holder in due course had no notice or knowledge.

CASES FOR CHAPTER 32

First National Bank v Gorman

45 Wyo 519, 21 P2d 549 (1933)

Gorman executed and delivered a promissory note to the First National Bank. After several payments, the note was stolen from the bank. Subsequently, Gorman paid the remainder to one representing himself to be Richardson, who previously had been connected with the payee bank. In an action brought by the bank to collect the remainder of the note from Gorman, the latter pleaded payment and produced the note marked paid by the impostor. From a judgment for the plaintiff, the defendant appealed.

BLUME, J. . . . Counsel for the appellant [defendant] claims that defendant's possession of the note raises a presumption that it has been paid; that this presumption has not been overcome; that the plaintiff should have been more careful in not letting the note in question get out of its possession; that that carelessness made it possible for someone to hold himself out as the agent of the defendant; and that it is now estopped to claim that payment was made to one not authorized. Counsel relies partially upon cases which hold that where two innocent parties must suffer, that one should suffer who has made the loss possible. . . . There is some slight authority to sustain the position that mere possession of a note, though not indorsed, entitles the holder to collect the money due thereon. . . . Daniel on Negotiable Instruments . . . in commenting on the point under consideration . . . says:

"If the instrument be payable to a particular party or order, and unindorsed by him, it has been held that a payment to any person in actual possession will still be valid because, although he may have

no legal title, he may be the agent of the actual owner. But this doctrine, it seems to us, goes too far. Such person in actual possession may perhaps be presumed to be agent of the holder prima facie. But even this is doubtful, and to us seems wrong, for nothing is more common than to indorse negotiable instruments to agents for collection; and if the bill or note be unindorsed . . . it might be that the owner had withheld his indorsement for the very purpose of preventing collection by a person not entitled to receive the money; and if this were so, the presumption of agency (if, indeed, it be at all admitted) would be rebutted. The contrary doctrine destroys a great and salutary safeguard to the rights of proprietors of negotiable instruments and to a large degree breaks down the distinction between those payable to order and those payable to bearer." The authorities generally are in full accord with this statement. . . .

In the case of Anderson v Wm. H. Moore Dry Goods Company, . . . payment was made of an unindorsed note to one without authority to collect. Instead of contending in that case that the person who received payment was the apparent agent of the owner, counsel claimed that he was the holder of the note within the meaning of the Negotiable Instruments Law . . . , reading that "payment is made in due course when it is made at or after the maturity of the instrument to the holder thereof in good faith and without notice that his title is defective." The court, however, held that the term "holder" means the person who is legally in possession of the instrument, either by indorsement or delivery or both, and who is entitled to receive payment from the drawer or acceptor or maker of the note, and does not include a person in actual possession who has no right to such possession. . . . Thus we have arrived at the same conclusion by two different methods of reasoning. When the note was presented for payment by a stranger without a legal transfer, the presumption was that it was lost or purloined or otherwise improperly got into circulation. . . . The defendant took the risk of making payment to him, without being able to show that he had authority to collect. Moreover, he had other ample means by which he could have fully protected himself, namely, by obtaining a draft or check payable to the plaintiff bank. . . .

[Judgment for plaintiff affirmed]

Code Comment: The same decision would be made under the Uniform Commercial Code since the requirements of the Uniform Negotiable Instruments Law as to who is the holder of an instrument and the necessity for proper indorsements are continued under the UCC.

Gillespie v Riley Management Corp.

59 Ill 2d 211, 319 NE2d 753 (1974)

As part of a sales transaction Riley Management obtained a cashier's check payable to the order of it and Gillespie, the other party to the transaction. The transaction was abandoned and William Riley, the president of the corporation, took the cashier's check to the National City Bank, indorsed it "not used for purpose issued" and surrendered it in return for two other checks payable to the order of Riley Management. Gillespie then sued Riley Management and the bank for conversion of the cashier's check on the theory that Gillespie as copayee had an ownership interest in the cashier's check which had been destroyed by Riley's intentionally surrendering the check without Gillespie's indorsement. Judgment was entered for Riley and Gillespie appealed. The intermediate appellate court reversed the lower court and Riley appealed.

DAVIS, J. . . . . The plaintiff contends that the cashier's check was issued when the defendant bank signed and delivered it to Riley, and that since the Corporation was named as a co-payee thereon, there was delivery of the cashier's check to the Corporation when Riley, its president, picked it up from the bank; and that thereafter, under section 3-116 of the Uniform Commercial Code, it could be negotiated, discharged, or enforced only by both payees. . . .

The defendant bank urges that under section 3-605(1)(b) of the Uniform Commercial Code Riley Management was a holder and as such it renounced

its rights by writing the notation on the check "not used for purpose issued.". . .

The critical question in this case is in what capacity was the Corporation acting when it returned the check to the bank for cancellation. Was it acting as a purchaser or as one of two joint payees?

In the case at bar, it can be said that since the cashier's check never entered into the stream of commerce, it remained an evidence of a debtor-creditor relationship between the bank and the purchaser. However, the purchaser of a cashier's check remains the "owner" thereof until such time as he delivers or negotiates it to the payee. Until such delivery, the purchaser retains the right to cancel. . . .

Absent any unusual circumstances sufficient to raise a duty of inquiry or knowledge of delivery or wrongdoing, the bank was justified in relying on a presumption of continued ownership by the Corporation. Aside from the legal basis for such a rule, the practical reasons therefor are obvious. One acquires a cashier's check for the purpose of assuring the payee that there are the necessary funds contemplated by a transaction, and that the check, like the money it represents, cannot be countermanded or revoked after the payee has received it. However, often a contemplated transaction does not materialize. The purchaser may then be left with a cashier's check purchased by him, but payable to someone with whom he no longer is commercially involved. It would impose an unwarranted commercial burden to require the purchaser to obtain the indorsement of such a payee to have the cashier's check honored or cancelled. Until the purchaser places such a check in the stream of commerce, he must, of practical, commercial necessity, be able to cancel the check upon its surrender to the bank.

There is little doubt that, in the factual setting of this case, had the purchaser named only the Corporation—purchaser—as payee, the purchaser would have been able to cancel the check upon its retention of possession of the check and surrender to the bank. The bank would have been justified in relying upon a presumption of continued ownership by the purchaser. . . .

We do not believe that the fact that the purchaser of the cashier's check had itself named as a co-payee alters the foregoing presumptions, absent unusual circumstances sufficient to raise a duty of inquiry or knowledge of delivery or wrongdoing.

In the case at bar, however, there were unusual circumstances sufficient to raise a duty of inquiry or knowledge of delivery or wrongdoing by the Corporation. [The Court then held that unusual circumstances were present which justified a departure from the general rule above stated and then sustained the decision of the intermediate appellate court in favor of the plaintiff.]

[Judgment affirmed]

Greene v Cotton

(Ky) 457 SW2d 493 (1970)

Cotton executed a promissory note promising to pay Jones a sum of money. Jones died; Greene and Foree were appointed his executors. Among the papers of Jones was found a writing stating that if Cotton was alive at the time of Jones' death and if any balance on the note remained unpaid, such balance should be released. The note was partly paid at the time of Jones' death. Cotton brought an action against the executors to obtain a declaration that the balance of the note was discharged. From a judgment in Cotton's favor, an appeal was taken by Greene and Foree.

DAVIS, C. . . . On August 17, 1955, the Cottons executed and delivered to S. R. Jones their promissory note in the sum of $72,000 bearing 5% interest and secured by mortgage on real estate in Grant County owned by the Cottons. Various payments on the note had reduced the principal due to $38,400 at the date of the death of Jones on May 2, 1967.

The appellants, executors of the will of Jones, found among Jones' effects a key to a lockbox at Citizens Bank of Dry Ridge. Upon inspecting the contents of that lockbox, they found an envelope bearing the typewritten address:

"To admrs. of my estate
"S. R. Jones"

Within the envelope was found a typewritten paper signed by S. R. Jones, which recited:

"I, S. R. Jones hereby request that if B. C. Cotton be living at the time of my death and if there is an unpaid balance on his note and mortgage to me that same be released and the note and mortgage returned to him marked paid.
Dated July 7, 1966.

/s/ S. R. Jones"

B. C. Cotton was president of Citizens Bank of Dry Ridge, and there was evidence that Cotton knew that Jones had executed a paper purporting to cancel the note. However, Cotton never received physical possession of the paper, nor did he (or anyone other than Jones) have a key to Jones' lockbox. It appears that the last credit on the note was made on July 7, 1966, the date of the purported release. It also appears that Jones kept the typed release in his own office until Tuesday, April 28, 1967, on which date he placed it in the lockbox at Dry Ridge. His death ensued on Saturday, May 2, 1967.

Pursuant to a finding by an advisory jury, and in overruling appellants' motion to set aside the findings reported by the jury, the trial judge recited as one finding of fact:

"S. R. Jones intended to renounce the note and his right, title and interest therein, without the necessity of actually relinquishing control of the note itself."

That finding, so far as it is considered as a *factual* finding, is obviously not clearly erroneous, so it will not be disturbed. . . .

But, that finding of fact does not lead to the trial court's conclusion of law that the *intended* release legally accomplished its purpose. It is manifest that the release was an "iffy" thing. By its own terms it noted its applicability only "if" B. C. Cotton were alive at the time of Jones' death and "if" there then remained an unpaid balance due to Jones on the note. It is not contended, as it could not be, that the release was executed with the formality required for a will.

Patently, Jones was mindful when the release was typed that Cotton might make further payments on the note—indeed that it might be fully paid. Clearly, he did not purport to remit the debt except on the contingency that Jones should die before the death of B. C. Cotton. Most importantly, Jones never delivered the release to Cotton and never parted with dominion over it. Nobody but Jones, or his qualified personal representatives at his death, had any right to enter the lockbox. If Jones had elected to sue on the note, Cotton could not have interposed the release as a defense. If Jones had changed his mind, he could have destroyed the release or modified it, and Cotton would have had no recourse. In short, we agree with the trial judge that Jones thought he had done all that was legally required but that fact, without more, did not accomplish the intended result.

[UCC §] 3-605(1)(b), in treating the legal requirements for cancellation and renunciation of a note, provides that the result may be achieved: "(b) by renouncing his rights by a writing signed *and delivered* or by surrender of the instrument to the party to be discharged.". . .

. . . Since there is no claim of a contract to release supported by consideration, the release must stand or fall as a gift. It falls.

. . . "It may be stated as a general rule that a mere statement, declaration, or memorandum by the creditor to the effect that he gives, has given, or intends to give the debt to the debtor, that he does not desire or intend that the debt shall be paid or collected or that the amount remaining unpaid at his death is to be forgiven, is ineffectual for such purpose." . . .

Despite the *intention* of a donor to effect a transfer of a bank account, the failure to comply with legal requirements cannot be supplied merely by noting the abortive attempt to carry out an intention. . . .

The judgment is reversed for proceedings consistent with the opinion.

White System v Lehmann

(La App) 144 So2d 122 (1962)

White System sued Lehmann on a promissory note which he had executed as maker. Lehmann defended on the ground that the holder had renounced or canceled the obligation when, after Lehmann's default, it carried the note in its profit and loss account. From a judgment in favor of White System, Lehmann appealed.

MILLER, J. pro tem. . . . The primary defense is that the plaintiff, by transferring the obligation to the Profit & Loss Account in his bookeeping records, has in effect renounced or canceled the debt and therefore the obligation is fully discharged. This defense is untenable. In order to renounce his rights, the holder must so expressly state in writing or must surrender or deliver the instrument to the person primarily liable thereon. . . . There is no evidence whatever to establish that the plaintiff executed such a written renouncement, and the fact that the note was attached to his petition clearly refutes that he surrendered or delivered it to the defendant. Obviously there was no renouncement of the debt.

Counsel for defendant in support of his contention that the transfer of the defendant's obligation to the Profit & Loss Account by the plaintiff constituted a discharge of the instrument, cites (LSA) R.S. 7:119 (Pars. 3, 4) which respectively provide that a negotiable instrument is discharged by the intentional cancellation by the holder or by any other act which will discharge a simple contract for the payment of money.

The sections of the Statutes cited . . . are not applicable to the facts of this case. The action of the plaintiff in placing the obligation in the Profit & Loss Account, after its default, is merely an internal bookkeeping entry, utilized by the holder, who was apparently motivated by either recognized accounting principles or for income tax purposes. Unquestionably he could have transferred the defendant's indebtedness to any other account if he so desired, no approval of, nor communication to, the debtor being required. The fact that he carried the account on his books, even though in a substandard classification, clearly negatived any intentional cancellation of the obligation; otherwise his action would have been useless and in vain. The modes of discharging a negotiable instrument, as set forth above, could only be interpreted as meaning that the action of the holder is of such a definite or certain nature that there could be no question of his intention to discharge the obligation arising out of the negotiable instrument. Such were not the facts in this matter. . . .

[Judgment affirmed]

Code Comment: The same decision would be made under the Uniform Commercial Code. There was no act done to the face or back of the paper itself, it was not surrendered to the party claiming that he was discharged, nor was any written renunciation delivered to him. In the absence of any of these, there could be no cancellation or renunciation. UCC § 3-605.

Hallowell v Turner

95 Idaho 392, 509 P2d 1313 (1973)

Kohntopp and Turner signed a promissory note as makers. Hallowell held the note. In consideration of a payment of $2,500 to him made by Kohntopp, Hallowell executed an agreement not "to execute" against Kohntopp. This agreement expressly reserved Hallowell's rights against Turner.

Turner did not know of the existence of this agreement and thus did not consent to it. Later Hallowell sued Turner on the note. The defense was raised that the agreement not to execute against Kohntopp operated as a discharge of Turner. From a judgment for Turner, an appeal was taken by Hallowell.

McQUADE, J. . . . [UCC §] 3-606 provides: *"Impairment of recourse or of collateral.*

(1) The holder discharges any party to the instrument to the extent that without such party's consent the holder

(a) without express reservation of rights releases or agrees not to sue any person against whom the party has to the knowledge of the holder a right of recourse or agrees to suspend the right to enforce against such person the instrument or collateral or otherwise discharges such person, except that failure or delay in effecting any required presentment, protest or notice of dishonor with respect to any such person does not discharge any party as to whom presentment, protest or notice of dishonor is effective or unnecessary; or
(b) unjustifiably impairs any collateral for the instrument given by or on behalf of the party or any person against whom he has a right of recourse.

"(2) By express reservation of rights against a party with a right of recourse the holder preserves

(a) all his rights against such party as of the time when the instrument was originally due; and
(b) the right of the party to pay the instrument as of that time; and
(c) all rights of such party to recourse against others."

Under the above cited provisions, the requirements for a discharge were not met.

Notification to the party against whom rights are reserved is not a prerequisite to the validity of a reservation of rights. Respondent [Turner] cites paragraph 4 of the official comment to [UCC §] 3-606 as indicative of the need for notice. This comment is misleading in its allusion to a requirement of notice, since it refers to a subsection (3). There is no subsection (3) in [UCC §] 3-606 as finally adopted by the Commissioners on Uniform State Laws and enacted in Idaho. The part of paragraph

4 of the official comment to [UCC §] 3-606 referring to subsection (3) should be disregarded.

The express reservation of rights by appellant in the "agreement not to execute" was valid. Under [UCC §] 3-606 there must be consent *or* an express reservation of rights to prevent a discharge. Thus, consent is not necessary where the obligee makes an express reservation of rights.

Both appellant [Hallowell] and respondent discuss whether there was a right of recourse by respondent against Kohntopp. No evidence to support a finding that appellant Hallowell knew of Noble Turner's role of surety, if indeed he was a surety, appears in the record. Paragraph 3 of the official comment to [UCC §] 3-606 reads as follows: "The words 'to the knowledge of the holder' exclude the latent surety, as for example the accommodation maker where there is nothing on the instrument to show that he has signed for accommodation and the holder is ignorant of that fact. In such a case the holder is entitled to proceed according to what is shown by the face of the paper or what he otherwise knows, and does not discharge the surety when he acts in ignorance of the relation."

In this case Ralph Kohntopp and Noble Turner appear on the face of the note to be co-makers. Under [UCC §] 3-118,* this would mean their liability on the face of the note would be joint and several. Even if respondent does have a right of recourse against Kohntopp, appellant still would have avoided discharging respondent by making the express reservation of rights.

It is not necessary on this appeal to decide what effect the "agreement not to execute" has on the obligations of Ralph Kohntopp. However, (2)(c) of [UCC §] 3-606 should be noted in relation to such obligations, reading as follows: "(2) By express reservation of rights against a party with a right of recourse the holder preserves . . . (c) all rights of such party to recourse against others." As already noted, the reservation of rights was effective and [Turner's] obligation to [Hallowell] was not discharged by the "agreement not to execute.". . .

[Judgment reversed]

---

* [UCC §] 3-118 provides in part: *"Ambiguous terms and rules of construction.*—The following rules apply to every instrument: . . . (e) Unless the instrument otherwise specifies two (2) or more persons who sign as maker, acceptor or drawer or indorser and as a part of the same transaction, are jointly and severally liable even though the instrument contains such words as 'I promise to pay.' "

QUESTIONS AND CASE PROBLEMS

1. What social forces are affected by the rule of law that permits the holder of commercial paper to discharge selected parties without discharging the other parties to the paper?

2. Compare the effect of payment of a note by (a) the maker, and (b) an indorser.

3. Compare discharge by (a) renunciation and (b) cancellation.

4. Can the holder of paper safely release a party to commercial paper by releasing that party and doing nothing more?

5. Twombly, who owned negotiable bonds of the Muskogee Electric Traction Co., was advised by her financial agent, the State Street Trust Co., that the bonds had no value. Acting on this belief, Twombly burned the bonds. Some years later it was found that the bonds had some value, and the trust company, on behalf of Twombly, demanded payment on the bonds. Was it entitled to payment? [State Street Trust Co. v. Muskogee Electric Traction Co., (CA10 Okla) 204 F2d 920]

6. Burg executed and delivered a promissory note for $1,060 payable to Liesemer. When the note was due, Burg paid $893 and demanded credit for the remainder of the amount due because of the boarding expense incurred by Liesemer's daughter. Liesemer gave Burg the note so that he could compute the amount due. Burg refused to give credit for Liesemer's claim and kept the note. When Liesemer brought an action to recover the remainder of the note, it appeared that Burg had written across the face of the note, "Paid February 9th." It was contended that the note had been discharged by cancellation. Do you agree? [Liesemer v Burg, 106 Mich 124, 63 NW 999]

7. As part of a business plan Schwald executed and delivered a note to Montgomery. The parties then made a new business arrangement, and Montgomery intentionally tore up the note and threw it into the wastebasket. It was subsequently contended that this note had been canceled. Do you agree? [Montgomery v Schwald, 117 Mo App 75, 166 SW 831]

8. C. Neal executed and delivered a promissory note payable to the order of A. Neal, who indorsed the instrument to his wife, Mary Neal, a holder in due course. Before maturity, the maker paid the amount of the note to the payee. After maturity, Mary, who had divorced A. Neal and resumed her maiden name of Fogarty, brought an action against C. Neal to recover on the note. Neal contended that the note had been discharged by payment. Do you agree with this contention? [Fogarty v Neal, 201 Ky 85, 255 SW 1049]

9. *H* was the holder of a promissory note made by *M*. The note was payable in 12 months. After preliminary discussion between the parties in the eleventh month with respect to refinancing, *H* telephoned *M* that he "canceled" the note. The next day, *H* changed his mind and negotiated the note to *C* who satisfied the requirements of being a holder in due course. When *C* demanded payment of *M*, *M* asserted that he was not liable because he had been discharged when *H* canceled the note. Was he correct? [Citizens Fidelity Bank & Trust Co. v Stark, (Ky) 431 SW2d 722; Bihlmire v Hahn, (DC Wis) 43 FRD 503]

10. Henry and Herbert Mordecai were partners doing business under the name of the Southern Cigar Co. They indorsed a promissory note executed by the firm to Henry Mordecai and delivered it to the District National Bank. They also delivered as security a certificate for certain stock in the Monumental Cigar Co. After maturity of the note, the indorsers made an assignment of a claim against the United States to the bank, which accepted it in satisfaction of its rights on the note. Was the note discharged? [District National Bank v Mordecai, 133 Md 419, 105 A 586]

11. Satek authorized his agent to execute a mortgage with Fortuna as mortgagor. Fortuna executed a note secured by the mortgage. Later Fortuna made a part payment on the note to the agent. This payment was made before maturity, and the agent at the time did not have possession of the note. Satek later sued to foreclose the mortgage. The court refused to allow Fortuna credit for the payment made to the agent. Why? [Satek v Fortuna, 324 Ill App 523, 58 NE2d 464]

12. *A* was the maker of a promissory note held by *B*. *B* telephoned *A* that *A* was released from all liability on the note and that *B* would never try to collect the note from him. Contrary to the foregoing, *B* later sued *A*. *A* is able to prove by reliable witnesses that *B* had made the statements that *A* would not be held liable. Is *A* liable on the note? [See Brunswick Corp. v Briscoe (MoApp) 523 SW2d 115.]

13. The Citizens State Bank issued a cashier's check payable to the order of Donovan. Donovan indorsed it to Denny, who did business as the Houston Aircraft Co., and included in the indorsement a recital that it was "in full [payment of] any and all claims of any character whatever." Denny crossed out this quoted phrase and wrote Donovan and the bank that he had done so. The Houston Aircraft Co. sued the Citizens State Bank on the check. Was the bank liable? [Houston Aircraft Co. v Citizens State Bank, (Tex Civ App) 184 SW2d 335]

33 Checks and Bank Collections

Of the various types of commercial paper in use today, by far the most common is the check. By means of checks it is possible to make payment safely and conveniently without the need of safeguarding a shipment of money. The checkbook stub and the canceled check make a written record which may be used at a later date to show that a payment was made.

A. CHECKS

Checks are one of the four kinds of commercial paper regulated by the Uniform Commercial Code.

§ 33:1. Nature of a Check. A check is a particular kind of draft. The first three of the following features of a check distinguish it from other drafts or bills of exchange: [1]

(1) The drawee of a check is always a bank.

(2) As a practical matter, the check is drawn on the assumption that the bank has on deposit in the drawer's account an amount sufficient to pay the check. In the case of a draft, there is no assumption that the drawee has any of the drawer's money with which to pay the instrument. Actually, the rights of the parties are not affected by the fact that the depositor does not have funds on deposit with the bank sufficient to pay the check.

If a draft is dishonored, the drawer is civilly liable; but if a check is drawn with intent to defraud the person to whom it is delivered, the drawer is also subject to criminal prosecution in most states under what are known as *bad check laws.* Most states provide that if the check is not made good within a stated period, such as 10 days, it will be presumed that the check was originally issued with the intent to defraud.

(3) A check is demand paper. A draft may be payable either on demand or at a future date. The standard form of check does not specify when it is payable, and it is therefore automatically payable on demand. This eliminates the need for an acceptance since the holder of the check will merely present it for payment.

One exception arises when a check is postdated, that is, when the check shows a date later than the actual date of execution and delivery. Here the check is not

---

[1] Checks are governed by both Article 3 of the Uniform Commercial Code relating to commercial paper and Article 4 governing bank deposits and collections.

payable until the date arrives. This, in effect, changes the check to time paper without expressly stating so.

While it is customary for banks to supply depositors with printed forms of checks, a check may be any writing.[2] A card given to a computer terminal located away from a bank for the purpose of withdrawing money from the bank, or making a repayment on a loan, is also a check.[3]

(4) The delivery of a check is not regarded as an assignment of the money on deposit. It therefore does not automatically transfer the rights of the depositor against the bank to the holder of the check, and there is no duty on the part of the drawee bank to the holder to pay the holder the amount of the check.[4]

§ 33:2. Certified Checks. The drawee bank may certify a check drawn on it, which has the same legal consequence as the acceptance of a draft. The certification must be written on the check and signed by an authorized representative of the bank. (See p. 550, Menke v Board of Education) The effect of the certification is to set aside in a special account maintained by the bank as much of the depositor's account as is needed to pay the certified check. With respect to the holder of the check, the certification is an undertaking by the bank that when the check is presented for payment, it will make payment according to the terms of the check without regard to the standing of the depositor's account at that time.

A check may be certified by a bank upon the request of the drawer or the holder. In the latter case all prior indorsers and the drawer are automatically released from liability.[5] Since the holder could have received payment, as the bank was willing to certify the check, and since the holder did not take the payment but chose to take the certification, the prior secondary parties are released from liability. When the certification is obtained by the drawer, there is no release of the secondary parties.

While, as a practical matter, the certification of a check by a bank makes it "as good as money," it must be remembered that the check is still a check, and that even a certified check is not money.

§ 33:3. Liability of Drawer. If the check is presented for payment and paid, no liability of the drawer arises. If the bank refuses to make payment, the drawer is then subject to the same liability as in the case of the nonpayment of an ordinary draft. If proper notice of dishonor is not given the drawer of the check,[6] the drawer will be discharged from liability to the same extent as the drawer of an ordinary draft.

§ 33:4. Duties of Drawee Bank. It is necessary to distinguish between the status of the drawer with respect to a check and the drawer's relationship with the bank on the contract of deposit.

---

[2] The printed bank check is preferable because it generally carries magnetic ink figures which facilitate sorting and posting.

[3] Illinois v Continental Illinois National Bank (CA7 Ill) 536 F2d 176.

[4] UCC § 3-409(1).

[5] UCC § 3-411(1).

[6] Under federal reserve regulations notice of dishonor may be given by telephone. Security Bank and Trust Co. v Federal National Bank (OklaApp) 554 P2d 119.

(a)   Privacy. The bank owes the depositor the duty of maintaining secrecy concerning information which the bank acquires in connection with the depositor-bank relationship. As an exception, certain agents of the federal government can require a bank to disclose information relating to a depositor's account. (See p. 551, United States v Miller)

(b)   Payment. A bank is under a general contractual duty to its depositor to pay on demand all checks to the extent of the funds in the depositor's account. When the bank breaches this contract, the bank is liable to the drawer for damages. As in the case of an unaccepted draft, there is ordinarily no duty owed the holder to accept or pay a check.

(c)   Stale Checks. A bank acting in good faith may pay a check presented more than six months after its date (commonly known as a *stale check*); but, unless the check is certified, it is not required to do so.[7] The fact that a bank may refuse to pay a check which is more than six months old does not mean that it must pay a check which is less than six months old or that it is not required to exercise reasonable care in making payment of any check.

(d)   Payment After Depositor's Death. The effectiveness of a check ordinarily ceases with the death of the drawer. The death of the drawer, however, does not revoke the agency of the bank until it has knowledge of the death and has had reasonable opportunity to act. Even with such knowledge, the bank may continue for ten days to pay or certify checks drawn by the drawer unless ordered to stop payment by a person claiming an interest in the account.[8] Even when the bank has the right to make payment after the death of the depositor, it may refuse to do so and its dishonor of the check in such case is not wrongful.[9]

(e)   Setoff of Bank Loan Against Deposit. When a depositor borrows money from a bank, the loan agreement generally specifies that the bank may deduct the amount due on the loan from the customer's deposit account. This right of setoff may be exercised without first giving notice to the depositor.[10] The loan agreement may specify that the bank may make such a setoff even though the loan is not yet due. In effect, this is a form of acceleration of the loan or of acceleration when the holder is insecure. In the absence of an express provision permitting the bank to set off a loan before it is due, however, no such right exists.

§ 33.5. Stopping Payment of Check. The drawer has the power of stopping payment of a check by notifying the drawee bank not to pay it when it is presented for payment. This is a useful device when a check is lost or mislaid. A duplicate check can be written, and, to make sure that the payee does not receive payment twice or that an improper person does not receive payment on the first check, payment on the first check can be stopped. Likewise, if payment is made by check and then the payee defaults on the contract so that the drawer would have a claim for breach of

---

[7] UCC § 4-404.
[8] UCC § 4-405.
[9] Norris' Estate (ColoApp) 532 P2d 981.
[10] Kruger v Wells Fargo Bank, 11 Cal3d 352, 113 CalRptr 449, 521 P2d 441.

contract, payment on the check can be stopped, assuming that the payee has not already cashed it.

It is to the advantage of the payee to require either a certified check or a cashier's check, for with respect to either check, the other party to the transaction cannot stop payment.

(a)   Form of Stop Payment Order. The stop payment order may be either oral or written. If oral, however, it is only binding on the bank for 14 calendar days unless confirmed in writing within that time. A written stop payment order or confirmation is effective for six months.

(b)   Communication of Stop Payment Order. When the depositor does not give the bank the stop payment notice in person but makes use of a means of communication, such as the telegraph, the depositor cannot hold the bank liable if the notice is delayed in reaching the bank and the bank makes payment before receiving the notice. If negligence on the part of the telegraph company can be established, however, the depositor can sue that company.

(c)   Liability to Holder for Stopping Payment. The act of stopping payment may in some cases make the depositor liable to the holder of the check. If the depositor has no proper ground for stopping payment, the depositor is liable to the holder of the check. In any case, the depositor is liable for stopping payment with respect to any holder in due course or other party having the rights of a holder in due course, unless payment was stopped for a reason that may be asserted against such a holder as a defense. The fact that payment of a check has been stopped does not affect its negotiable character.[11]

§ 33:6. Time of Presentment of Check for Payment. In order to charge a secondary party to demand paper, presentment for payment must generally be made upon the primary party to the instrument within a reasonable time after that secondary party has signed it. Reasonable time is determined by the nature of the instrument, by commercial usage, and by the facts of the particular case.[12]

Failure to make timely presentment discharges all prior indorsers of the instrument. It also discharges the drawer, if the draft was payable at a bank to the extent that the drawer has lost, through the bank's failure, money which was on deposit at the bank to meet the payment of the instrument.[13]

The UCC establishes two presumptions as to what is reasonable time in which to present a check for payment.[14] If the check is not certified and is both drawn and payable within the United States, it is presumed as to the drawer that thirty days after the date of the check or the date of its issuance, whichever is later, is the reasonable period in which to make presentment for payment. In the case of an indorser, it is presumed to be seven days after indorsing.[15]

---

[11] Bigbee v Indiana (IndApp) 364 NE2d 149.
[12] UCC § 3-503(1)(e), (2).
[13] UCC § 3-502(1).
[14] A presumption means that the trier of fact is bound by the presumption in the absence of evidence that supports a contrary conclusion. UCC § 1-201(31).
[15] UCC § 3-503(2).

§ 33:7. Dishonor of Check.

When a check is dishonored by nonpayment, the holder must follow the same procedure of notice to each of the secondary parties as in the case of a draft or bill of exchange in order to hold them liable for payment. As in the case of any drawer of a draft or bill of exchange who countermands payment, notice of dishonor need not be given to the drawer who has stopped payment on a check. Notice is also excused under any circumstances that would excuse notice in the case of a promissory note. For example, no notice need be given a drawer or an indorser who knows that sufficient funds to cover the check are not on deposit, since such party has no reason to expect that the check will be paid by the bank.[16]

A check that is dishonored by nonpayment may be presented to the drawee bank at a later time in the hope that by the later date there will be sufficient funds in the account of the drawer so that the drawee bank will be able to make payment. Although there is this right to make a subsequent presentation for payment, it is essential that notice be given secondary parties after the dishonor of the instrument upon the first presentation. If they are not duly notified at that time, they are discharged and no new rights can be acquired against them by making a subsequent presentment and then notifying the secondary parties of the second dishonor.

When a check is sent in the course of the collection process to the bank on which it is drawn, that bank must either pay or promptly return the check as unpaid, or send notice of its dishonor, as by returning the check unpaid for "insufficient funds." If the drawee bank does not act before the midnight of the business day on which it received the check, it automatically becomes liable for the face of the instrument.[17] Oral notice of dishonor is sufficient.

(a)   Bank's Liability to Drawer of Check. The contract between the depositor (drawer) and the bank (drawee) obligates the latter to pay in accordance with the orders of its depositor as long as there is sufficient money on deposit to make such payment. If the bank improperly refuses to make payment, it is liable to the drawer for damages sustained by the drawer in consequence of such dishonor. (See p. 503, Allison v First National Bank)

(b)   Bank's Liability to Holder. If the check has not been certified, the holder has no claim against the bank for the dishonor of the check, regardless of the fact that the bank had acted in breach of its contract with its depositor. If the bank had certified the check, it is liable to the holder when it dishonors the check as the certification imposes upon the bank a primary liability to pay the face amount of the check.

Regardless of whether the holder has any right against the bank, the holder may proceed against the secondary parties, the drawer, and any unqualified indorsers.

§ 33:8. Agency Status of Collecting Bank.

When a person deposits a commercial paper in a bank, the bank is ordinarily thereby made an agent to collect or obtain the payment of the paper. Unless the contrary intent clearly appears, a bank receiving an item is deemed to take it as agent for the depositor rather than as becoming the purchaser

---

[16] UCC § 3-511(2)(b).

[17] UCC §§ 4-302, 4-104(1)(h); Rock Island Auction Sales v Empire Packing, 32 Ill2d 269, 204 NE2d 721.

of the paper. This presumption is not affected by the form of the indorsement nor by the absence of any indorsement. The bank is also regarded as being merely an agent even though the depositor has the right to make immediate withdrawals against the deposited item.[18] In consequence of the agency status, the depositor remains the owner of the item and is therefore subject to the risks of ownership involved in its collection, in the absence of fault on the part of any collecting bank.[19]

When a bank cashes a check deposited by its customer or cashes the customer's check drawn on the strength of a deposited check, it is a holder of the customer's check and may sue the parties thereon, even though as between the customer and the bank the latter is an agent for collection and has the right to charge back the amount of the deposited check if it cannot be collected. When the bank receives final settlement for an item taken for collection, the agency status ends and the bank is merely a debtor of its customer just as though the customer had made an ordinary cash deposit in the bank.[20]

B. LIABILITY OF BANK FOR IMPROPER PAYMENT AND COLLECTION

The drawee bank may be liable for paying a check contrary to a stop payment order or when there has been a forgery or alteration.

§ 33:9. Payment Over Stop Payment Order. If the bank makes payment of a check after it has been properly notified to stop payment, it is liable to the depositor for the loss the depositor sustains, in the absence of a valid limitation of the bank's liability. The burden of establishing the loss resulting in such case rests upon the depositor.[21] (See p. 554, Tusso v Security National Bank) Thus, the bank does not become automatically liable for the amount of the check paid in violation of the stop payment order. The bank is only liable to the extent that it is shown that the payment has caused loss to the depositor through the making of a payment on a claim which the depositor was not legally obligated to pay.[22]

§ 33:10. Payment on Forged Signature of Drawer. A *forgery* of the signature occurs when the name of the depositor has been signed by another person without authority to do so and with the intent to defraud by making it appear that the check was signed by the depositor.[23] The bank is liable to the depositor (drawer) if it pays a check on which the drawer's signature has been forged since a forgery ordinarily has no effect as a signature.[24] The burden of knowing the signature of all its depositors is thus placed on the bank.

---

[18] UCC § 4-201(1).

[19] UCC § 4-202.

[20] Cooper v Union Bank, 9 Cal3d 123, 107 CalRptr 1, 507 P2d 609; UCC Official Code Comment to § 4-213, point 9.

[21] UCC § 4-403(3).

[22] Cicci v Lincoln National Bank and Trust Co., 46 Misc2d 465, 260 NYS2d 100.

[23] A forgery, as thus defined, is to be distinguished from a changing of the instrument as originally executed, which constitutes an alteration when done by a party to the instrument and a spoliation when done by a stranger to the instrument. See § 31:13(f) of this book.

[24] UCC § 3-404(1).

Although the bank has no right to pay a check on which the drawer's signature is forged, the drawer may be barred from objecting that the signature was a forgery. If the drawer's negligence contributed substantially to the forging of the signature, the drawer cannot assert that it was forged when the drawee bank makes payment of the check while acting in good faith and conforming to reasonable commercial standards.[25] For example, if the drawer signs checks with a mechanical writer, reasonable care must be exercised to prevent unauthorized persons from making use of it to forge or "sign" the drawer's name with such device. If the depositor's negligence enables a third person to make such improper use of it, the depositor is barred from objecting to the payment of the check by the bank.

When a check is presented to the drawee bank for payment, it alone is responsible for determining whether the signature of the drawer, its customer, is a forgery. Prior indorsers do not warrant that the signature of the drawer is genuine; and, if the bank pays money or gives a cashier's check in payment of the depositor's check, it cannot thereafter recover the money paid or defend against payment on the cashier's check on the ground that the drawer's signature had been forged.

§ 33:11. Payment on Forged Indorsement. A bank that pays a check on a forged indorsement may be liable for conversion.[26] The true owner of the check collected on a forged indorsement may recover in a direct suit against any bank. The true owner may recover from the drawee bank or any intermediate collecting bank making payment on a forged indorsement.

When suit is brought by the drawer of the check which was paid on the forged indorsement, it is necessary to distinguish between a collecting bank and the drawee bank. By the better view, an intermediate collecting bank may not be sued by the drawer because the drawer was not the owner of the check which was converted by the bank. (See p. 555, Jett v Lewis State Bank) When the drawee bank makes payment on a forged indorsement, however, it has broken its contract with the drawer to pay to the payee of the check or to the person ordered by the payee. Consequently, the drawee bank may be held liable to the drawer for breach of contract. When the drawee bank pays a check on a forged indorsement, it has no right to charge the drawer's account, because it did not make payment to the order of the drawer's check. If the bank deducts the amount of such check from the drawer's account, it must recredit the account with that amount. The drawee bank may then recover this loss from prior indorsers who, by indorsing, warranted that title to the check was held by the particular indorser.[27]

A collecting bank that has dealt with a check or the proceeds of it on the basis of a forged indorsement is only partly liable to the true owner if the bank has acted in good faith and in accordance with reasonable commercial standards applicable to a bank. In the latter case, the liability of the bank is limited to surrendering the instrument or the proceeds of it to the true owner if the bank still has either in its possession.[28]

---

[25] UCC § 3-404(1), 4-406.
[26] UCC § 3-419(1)(c).
[27] Perini Corporation v First National Bank (CA5 Ga) 553 F2d 398.
[28] UCC § 3-419(3).

The failure to make an inquiry may constitute a failure to act in accordance with reasonable commercial standards, as where the employee's bank was charged with notice of a breach of fiduciary duty from the fact that a check payable to the order of the employer was indorsed by the employee and deposited in the employee's personal bank account but the employee's bank made no inquiry; the court holding that as a matter of law the failure to make inquiry under these circumstances constituted a failure to act in accordance with reasonable commercial standards.

§ 33:12. Payment on Missing Indorsement. A drawee bank is liable for the loss when it pays a check that lacks an essential indorsement. In such a case, the instrument has not been properly presented; and by definition the person presenting the check for payment is not the holder of the instrument and is not entitled to demand or receive payment. It is a defense to the bank, however, that although the person to whom payment was made was not the holder of the instrument, that person was in fact the one whom the drawer or the last holder of the check intended should be paid.

When a person deposits a check but neglects to indorse it, the depositor's bank may make an indorsement on behalf of the depositor unless the check contains a statement that it must be signed personally by that person. Even if the bank does not indorse the check, there is an effective negotiation from the customer to the bank when the check is stamped by the bank to indicate that it was deposited by the customer or credited to the account of the customer.[29]

§ 33:13. Alteration of Check. If the face of the check has been altered so that the amount to be paid has been increased, the bank is liable to the drawer for the amount of the increase when it makes payment for the greater amount. The bank has the opportunity of examining the check when it is presented for payment and, if it fails to detect the alteration, it is liable for the loss.

The drawer may be barred from claiming that there was an alteration by virtue of conduct with respect to writing the check or conduct after receiving the cancelled check from the bank. As to the former, the drawer is barred if the check was carelessly written and that negligence substantially contributed to the making of the material alteration and the bank honored the check in good faith and observed reasonable commercial standards in so doing.[30] For example, the drawer is barred when the check was written with blank spaces so that it was readily possible to change "four" to "four hundred," and the drawee bank paid out the latter sum without any cause to know that there was an alteration. A careful person will therefore write figures and words close together and run a line through or cross out any blank spaces.

§ 33:14. Unauthorized Collection of Check. Although a bank acts as agent for its customer in obtaining payment of a check deposited with it by its customer, it may be liable to a third person when the act of its customer is unauthorized or unlawful with respect to the third person. That is, if the customer has no authority to deposit the check, the bank, in obtaining payment from the drawee of the check and thereafter

---

[29] UCC § 4-205(1).
[30] UCC § 3-406.

depositing the proceeds of the check in the account of its customer, may be liable for conversion of the check to the person lawfully entitled to the check and its proceeds.

§ 33:15. Indemnity Right of Bank. When a bank is held liable to a drawer or a depositor for a payment or collection which is improper because a signature on the check is a forgery, the bank will in many instances be able to recover its loss from a prior party to the paper who has made either an express or implied warranty that signatures are genuine.

It is also to be remembered that in some instances the operation of the impostor rule [31] makes a forgery effective as a negotiation of the check. In that case, the action of the bank with respect to the check is proper and the law governing forged checks and indorsements is not applicable.

§ 33:16. Time Limitations.

(a)   Non-Code Statute of Limitations. A local non-Code statute of limitations will fix the maximum time for asserting a claim against a bank for the breach of the customer-bank deposit contract, an action against any bank for conversion of an item of commercial paper, or an action by one bank against another bank or party to paper to obtain indemnity or contribution.

(b)   Forgery and Alteration Reporting Time. On receiving canceled checks or a bank statement, the customer of a bank must examine the returned items with reasonable promptness and reasonable care to determine if any signature has been forged or if the checks have been altered, and must notify the bank promptly on discovering any such irregularity.[32]

If the customer delays more than one year, the Code bars the customer from holding the bank liable for paying on a check which has been altered or on which the drawer's signature was forged. The maximum time allowed is three years in the case of a forged indorsement.

---

[31] See § 29:15 in this book.

[32] UCC § 4-406(1). Special time limitations are imposed when there is a series of items forged or altered by the same wrongdoer. UCC § 4-406(2)(b).

CASES FOR CHAPTER 33

Menke v Board of Education

(Iowa) 211 NW2d 601 (1973)

Menke submitted a bid to do construction work for the Board of Education of West Burlington. With his bid he submitted a check which had been certified by the State Central Savings Bank. The Board of Education claimed that the check was improperly certified and rejected Menke's bid. He then sued the Board for improperly rejecting his bid and

the bank for improperly certifying his check. The court dismissed Menke's action against the Board of Education and both Menke and the bank appealed.

REES, J. . . . The principal issue presented by the Bank's appeal is whether a check stamped as was the check in the case here is properly certified as a matter of law. The Bank claims the stamp placed upon the check by it is adequate to constitute a certification. The lower court held, and plaintiff Menke and defendant Board assert in this appeal that the stamped words indicating certification without the signature of a bank official do not as a matter of law suffice to effect proper certification of the check. We are persuaded the trial court was correct in its ruling, and agree with plaintiff and defendant Board.

We are unable to find precedent holding that there is any specified form essential to the certification of a check. . . . "The usual practice is to stamp or write on the check the word 'certified', 'good', 'accepted', or an equivalent expression, *with the signature* of the certifying officer." [UCC §] 3-411(1) defines certification of a check to be acceptance. "Acceptance" consists of "the drawee's *signed* engagement to honor the draft as presented. It must be written on the draft, and may consist of his signature alone.". . .

From the foregoing provisions of the Uniform Commercial Code, the following inferences are presented: (1) Certification must be in writing, at least as opposed to parol acceptance. We find other jurisdictions have had occasion to deal with similar provisions and have generally upheld the principle in the interests of commercial certainty and reasonable reliance by third parties. . . . True, we have no parol acceptance issue here, but the underlying rationale against parol certification is relevant. (2) If an acceptance can consist of a signature alone, the logical conclusion would seem to be that a certification consists of no less than a signature and possibly other words indicating acceptance.

Defendant Bank seeks to avoid the above by contending that the stamped words on the Menke check are sufficient to constitute its (the Bank's) signature, and relies upon [UCC § 3-401(2)], the Code, which, . . . provides: "(2) A signature is made by use of any name, including any trade or assumed name, upon an instrument, or by any word or mark used in lieu of a written signature." The Official UCC Comment to the foregoing section is: "(2) A signature may be handwritten, typed, printed or made in any other manner. It need not be subscribed, and may appear in the body of the instrument, as in the case of 'I, John Doe, promise to pay—' without any other signature."

Defendant Bank would have the above settle the question, but we are not so persuaded.

We note the definition of the word "signed" in [UCC § 1-201(39)], the Code, includes "any symbol executed or adopted by a party *with present intention to authenticate a writing.*" (Emphasis supplied). Authentication must be discernable when viewed in the light of commercial reasonableness. The defendant Bank here affixed a stamp bearing words of certification with a blank line for a bank official's signature to assure the holder or third parties that the check was certified by the bank and that the certification was authentic. Rubber-stamps may be easily copied and secured with facility, and fraudulent certification accomplished by the use thereof would be detrimental to the interests of a bank. We therefore feel it is consistent with customary certification practice, as hereinabove referred to, to conclude that defendant Bank had adopted the stamp, but that a "present intention to authenticate" a check required the script signature of a bank official to indicate certification. . . .

We hold, therefore, that a check stamped with words of certification and a signature line, but without any written, printed, stamped or facsimile signature thereon, does not provide sufficient evidence of intent to authenticate certification by a bank to a holder in a commercial transaction, and as a matter of law does not comply with the statutory requirements for certification.

[Judgment affirmed]

United States v Miller

425 US 435 (1976)

Miller was prosecuted for not paying federal taxes. In order to establish the case against him, the government served subpoenas on two banks in which Miller had checking accounts. In obedience to the subpoenas, officers of the banks produced microfilm records of books, deposit slips, and other papers relating to Miller's accounts, which records had been kept by the banks in compliance with the command of the federal Bank Secrecy Act of 1970. Miller moved the court to suppress the information obtained from the banks on the ground that it constituted an unreasonable search and seizure for which no search warrant had been issued and therefore Miller's rights under the Fourth Amendment of the federal Constitution had been violated. The trial court rejected this claim. The Court of Appeals reversed, and the United States appealed to the Supreme Court.

POWELL, J. . . . "No interest legitimately protected by the Fourth Amendment" is implicated by governmental investigative activities unless there is an intrusion into a zone of privacy, into "the security a man relies upon when he places himself or his property within a constitutionally protected area." The Court of Appeals, as noted above, assumed that respondent had the necessary Fourth Amendment interest, pointing to the language in Boyd v United States, 116 US, at 622, . . . which describes that Amendment's protection against the "compulsory production of a man's private papers." We think that the Court of Appeals erred in finding the subpoenaed documents to fall within a protected zone of privacy.

On their face, the documents subpoenaed here are not respondent's "private papers." Unlike the claimant in Boyd, respondent can assert neither ownership nor possession. Instead, these are the business records of the banks. As we said in California Bankers Assn. v Shultz, 416 US at 48-49. "Banks are . . . not . . . neutrals in transactions involving negotiable instruments, but parties to the instruments with a substantial stake in their continued availability and acceptance." The records of respondent's accounts, like "all of the records [which are required to be kept pursuant to the Bank Secrecy Act,] pertain to transactions to which the bank was itself a party.". . .

Respondent argues, however, that the Bank Secrecy Act introduces a factor that makes the subpoena in this case the functional equivalent of a search and seizure of the depositor's "private papers.". . . The mere maintenance of records pursuant to the requirements of the Act "invade[s] no Fourth Amendment right of any depositor." But respondent contends that the combination of the record-keeping requirements of the Act and the issuance of a subpoena to obtain those records permits the Government to circumvent the requirements of the Fourth Amendment by allowing it to obtain a depositor's private records without complying with the legal requirements that would be applicable had it proceeded against him directly. Therefore, we must address the question whether the compulsion embodied in the Bank Secrecy Act as exercised in this case creates a Fourth Amendment interest in the depositor where none existed before. . . .

Respondent urges that he has a Fourth Amendment interest in the records kept by the banks because they are merely copies of personal records that were made available to the banks for a limited purpose and in which he has a reasonable expectation of privacy. He relies on this Court's statement in

Katz v United States . . . that "We have . . . departed from the narrow view" that " 'property interests control the right of the Government to search and seize,' " and that a "search and seizure" become unreasonable when the Government's activities violate "the privacy upon which [a person] justifiably relie[s]." But in Katz the Court also stressed that "[w]hat a person knowingly exposes to the public . . . is not a subject of Fourth Amendment protection.". . . We must examine the nature of the particular documents sought to be protected in order to determine whether there is a legitimate "expectation of privacy" concerning their contents. . . .

Even if we direct our attention to the original checks and deposit slips, rather than to the microfilm copies actually viewed and obtained by means of the subpoena, we perceive no legitimate "expectation of privacy" in their contents. The checks are not confidential communications but negotiable instruments to be used in commercial transactions. All of the documents obtained, including financial statements and deposit slips, contain only information voluntarily conveyed to the banks and exposed to their employees in the ordinary course of business. The lack of any legitimate expectation of privacy concerning the information kept in bank records was assumed by Congress in enacting the Bank Secrecy Act, the expressed purpose of which is to require records to be maintained because they "have a high degree of usefulness in criminal, tax, and regulatory investigations and proceedings.". . .

The depositor takes the risk, in revealing his affairs to another, that the information will be conveyed by that person to the government. . . . The Fourth Amendment does not prohibit the obtaining of information revealed to a third party and conveyed by him to government authorities, even if the information is revealed on the assumption that it will be used only for a limited purpose and the confidence placed in the third party will not be betrayed. . . .

This analysis is not changed by the mandate of the Bank Secrecy Act that records of depositors' transactions be maintained by banks. . . .

Since no Fourth Amendment interests of the depositor are implicated here, this case is governed by the general rule that the issuance of a subpoena to a third party to obtain the records of that party does not violate the rights of a defendant, even if a criminal prosecution is contemplated at the time the subpoena is issued. . . . It was firmly settled, before the passage of the Bank Secrecy Act, that an Internal Revenue Service summons directed to a third-party bank does not violate the Fourth Amendment rights of a depositor under investigation. . . .

Many banks traditionally kept permanent records of their depositors' accounts, although not all banks did so and the practice was declining in recent years. By requiring that such records be kept by all banks, the Bank Secrecy Act is not a novel means designed to circumvent established Fourth Amendment rights. It is merely an attempt to facilitate the use of a proper and longstanding law enforcement technique by insuring that records are available when they are needed.

. . . The District Court correctly denied respondent's motion to suppress, since he possessed no Fourth Amendment interest that could be vindicated by a challenge to the subpoenas. . . .

[Judgment reversed]

Allison v First National Bank

85 NMex 283, 511 P2d 769 (1973)

Allison obtained cashier's checks from the First National Bank which he sent to a bank in Mexico. First National notified the Mexican bank that the cashier's checks would not be paid and that it had requested the return of the checks for cancellation. First National refused to honor the cashier's checks when presented thereafter for payment. Because of this, assets of Allison were seized by legal process in order to satisfy his debt to the Mexican bank, his reputation was damaged, and he was threatened with criminal prosecution. He sued First National for damages for wrongful dishonor. The bank denied liability for the harm which followed the dishonor of the checks. The lower court entered judgment for Allison but refused to award damages for the consequences which followed the dishonor. The bank appealed on the issue of liability for dishonor. Allison filed a cross-appeal on the issue of consequential damages.

SUTIN, J. . . . *Plaintiff was entitled to damages for defendant's wrongful dishonor of plaintiff's checks.* The trial court made the following findings of fact: That on September 30, 1968, defendant bank refused to honor the above numbered cashier's checks.

That defendant's dishonor of said checks was *wrongful* in that the checks had not been paid and were not void. . . .

The plaintiff has not shown any consequential loss or damage resulting to him by reason of the refusal of First National Bank in Albuquerque to pay in 1968 the cashier's checks issued to him in March, 1953, and is entitled to actual damages of $5,000.00.

[UCC §] 4-402, . . . is entitled "Bank's liability to customer for wrongful dishonor."

A payor bank is liable to its customer for damages proximately caused by the wrongful dishonor of an item. When the dishonor occurs through mistake, liability is limited to actual damages proved. *If so, proximately caused and proved damages may include* damages for an arrest or prosecution of the customer or other *consequential damages.* Whether any consequential damages are proximately caused by the wrongful dishonor is a question of fact to be determined in each case. . . .

"Wrongful dishonor" has not been defined by the Code. Official comment states that the above ". . . section does not attempt to specify a theory. . . ." It is different from ". . . failure to exercise ordinary care in handling an item . . ." It ". . . excludes any permitted or justified dishonor. . . ." Uniform Commercial Code, § 4-402, Comments 2, 3 and 4.

Wrongful dishonor means a dishonor done in a wrong manner, unjustly, unfair, in a manner contrary to justice. . . . It excludes negligence or permitted or justified dishonor.

"Mistaken dishonor" means a dishonor done erroneously, unintentionally, a state of mind that is not in accord with the facts. . . .

This section does not deal with "intentional or wilful or malicious dishonor." This type of dishonor permits an award of punitive damages. . . .

In the instant case, on three separate occasions, from September 30, 1968 through January 6, 1969, the defendant dishonored the checks (1) by informing a Mexico bank that the checks were not outstanding; (2) that the checks had been paid by reissuance of new cashier's checks and requested the cashier's checks held by plaintiff be returned for cancellation; (3) against returning the checks unpaid. The bank failed to prove the reasons for its dishonor. This dishonor was not permitted or justified. . . . The trial court correctly found the dishonor was wrongful.

"Consequential damages" are not defined in terms in the Uniform Commercial Code, but are used in the sense given them by the leading cases on the subject. 1 Anderson, Uniform Commercial Code, 2nd Ed., p. 48.

In 3 Anderson, Uniform Commercial Code, 2nd Ed., p. 306, the author makes this comment with reference to § 50A-4-402:

Damages for Wrongful Dishonor. A payor bank is liable to its customer for the damages proximately caused by the wrongful dishonor of an item. The damages may include consequential damages (such as those sustained in connection with an arrest and prosecution), provided they are proximate damages. Whether the consequential damages are proximately related to the wrongful dishonor is a question of fact and not of law.

" 'Consequential damage' is defined in Black's Law Dictionary, Third Edition, as: 'Such damage, loss or injury as does not flow directly and immediately from the act of the party, but only from the consequences or results of such act.' ". . . "Consequential damage" includes injuries to credit as a result of wrongful dishonor. . . . It includes ". . . *any* . . . consequential harm, loss or injury proximately caused by a wrongful dishonor. . . ." . . .

As a consequence of the dishonor (1) An attachment lien was filed against 54 items of personalty of the plaintiff in Mexico seizing all his personal assets for purposes of satisfying his debts owed to the Mexican bank. (2) Plaintiff was personally threatened with imprisonment if the checks were invalid. (3) His credit standing was ruined. (4) He was placed under a cloud of suspicion in his Mexican community. Plaintiff had an excellent professional reputation.

Plaintiff is entitled to reasonable and temperate damages determined by the sound discretion and dispassionate judgment of the trial court. . . .

Plaintiff's judgment is affirmed. Plaintiff's cross-appeal is sustained. This cause is remanded to the trial court solely to determine the amount of consequential damages plaintiff is entitled to. . . .

Authors' Comment: The Allison case was reversed on appeal on the ground that the statute of limitations had run. 85 NMex 511, 514 P2d 30. This does not impair the opinion of the Court of Appeals as to the damages otherwise recoverable.

Tusso v Security National Bank

349 NYS2d 914 (1973)

Tusso sent a check for $600 drawn on the Security National Bank to the Adamson Construction Company. He then realized that he had already paid Adamson. At 9:00 a.m. the next morning he notified the bank to stop payment. Later that morning the check was brought to the bank and at 10:40 a.m. the bank certified the check and charged it to Tusso's account. Tusso sued the bank to recover the amount so charged. The bank claimed that he was required to prove that the bank had been negligent.

COLANERI, J. . . . The bank's . . . defense is incorrect. [UCC §] 4-403(1) entitles a bank customer to stop payment on his check by giving notice to that effect "at such time and in such manner as to afford the bank a reasonable opportunity to act on it prior to any action by the bank with respect to the item . . ." The statute does not place any other affirmative burden of proof upon the plaintiff with respect to the stop payment order other than the "burden of establishing the fact and amount of loss resulting from the payment of an item contrary to a binding stop payment order . . ." (UCC § 4-403(3)). . . .

To read into this statute the additional requirement that the drawer prove the commission of a negligent act by the bank in order to recover would, in effect, alter the statute in a manner not intended by the legislature. . . . In the absence of a contractual provision limiting the bank's liability, a valid stop payment order received by the bank prior to payment or certification renders subsequent payment wrongful, whether or not the bank was shown to be negligent in making such payments. . . .

The plaintiff in this case has the burden of proving that the stop payment order was received by the bank at such time as to afford it a reasonable opportunity to act on such order . . . . The facts as presented support this contention and therefore the court finds in favor of the plaintiff and against the defendant bank.

It has been held that a bank which improperly paid a check on which payment had been stopped may recover from the one who received payment, if such payee was not a holder for value. . . . The facts developed in this case indicate that the defendant construction corporation was already fully paid for its services. Therefore the construction corporation has no right to retain the additional funds improperly paid by the bank, and the court finds that the bank is entitled to judgment against the third party defendant for the amount of the improperly certified check.

Accordingly, judgment for the plaintiff against the defendant (Security National Bank) in the sum of $600.00 with interest thereon from July 25, 1972, together with the costs and disbursements of this action, and, further, the defendant and third-party plaintiff (Security National Bank) may have judgment over and against the third party defendant (Adamson Construction Corporation) in the sum of $600.00 with interest thereon from July 25, 1972, together with the costs and disbursements of this action.

Jett v Lewis State Bank

(Fla App) 277 So2d 37 (1973)

Jett wrote a check for $12,000 as a loan payable to the order of a newly-formed corporation, National Giant Portable Fun Slide, Inc. The three officers and sole stockholders of the corporation took the check to another bank, Lewis State Bank, to open a corporate account. The check was indorsed "for deposit only to account of within named payee." In spite of this, the Lewis Bank was directed to credit only $7,000 to the account of the corporation and to pay $5,000 cash to one of the three officers. National Giant went out of business and Jett sued Lewis Bank for diverting $5,000 from the corporate account. From a judgment for Lewis, Jett appealed.

JOHNSON, J. . . . The drawer or maker of a check has no right of direct action against banks, other than the drawee bank, which honor the check on a forged or unauthorized endorsement. The theory behind this rule is that, in an action for conversion against a collecting bank, the essential elements of conversion would be lacking in that the drawer does not have the right to immediate possession of the check because the beneficial ownership of the check is in the payee, not in the drawer. . . .

In an action sounding in both contract and in tort, for conversion, the drawer of a check has been denied recovery against the collecting bank upon the grounds that the collecting bank had no money in its hands which belonged to the drawer, that the drawer had no right in the proceeds of its own check payable to the payee, and that, not being a holder in due course or an agent for such holder, the drawer could not have presented its check to the drawee bank for payment. The value of the drawer's rights in the check is limited to the physical paper on which it is written and is not measured by its payable amount. The amounts a collecting bank receives from a drawee bank for the check cashed by the collecting bank are the drawee bank's funds and not those of the drawer; and whether the drawer is rightfully or wrongfully deprived of a credit is a matter between the drawer and the drawee bank. In short, the drawer's recourse is limited to an action against the drawee bank, for the only harm which befalls the drawer is the charging of its account by the drawee bank. . . .

It has also been held that a drawer of a check cannot recover against a collecting bank which honors a check bearing a faulty indorsement upon the contractual theory of warranty of prior indorsements. A guaranty of prior indorsements is only for the benefit of subsequent holders in due course, and not for the drawer of a check. There is no privity of contract between the drawer of a check and a collecting bank. . . . Once again, the drawer's recourse is against the drawee bank which may be entitled to recover from the collecting bank on the basis of its warranty of prior indorsements.*

We recognize that there have been other cases adopting different theories than those set out above. See 99 ALR2d 638-651. Nevertheless, we feel that the better rule is that the drawer of a check, in this case the appellant, has no right of direct action against a collecting bank, in this case the appellee, which honors a check even if the check bore a faulty indorsement. We note with interest that many of the cases allowing recovery were cases in which the drawer of the check was also the drawee; the drawer was suing the drawee bank; the plaintiff in the case was the payee, rather than the drawer, of the check, or the collecting bank was put on notice because the unauthorized indorser immediately deposited the funds in his own personal account. . . .

[Judgment affirmed]

---

* For a contrary holding on the theory of warranty of prior indorsements, see Allied Concord F. Corp. v Bank of Amer. Nat. T & S Ass'n, 275 Cal App 2d 1, 80 Cal Rptr 622 (1969), though this case also recognizes that drawer has no right of action for conversion against a collecting bank.

QUESTIONS AND CASE PROBLEMS

1. What social forces are involved in the common statutory provision that it will be presumed that a check was issued with intent to defraud if the drawer does not pay the amount of the check within ten days after its dishonor?

2. Compare the duty of the drawee bank to make payment on a certified check (a) when the drawer orders the bank to stop payment, and (b) the drawer dies.

3. Compare the liability of a bank when it pays a check on which (a) the signature of its depositor has been forged, (b) the signature of an indorser has been forged, and (c) the signature of an indorser is missing.

4. Compare (a) an assignment by a depositor of the amount in the depositor's bank account, with (b) a check drawn by a depositor for the full amount of the bank account.

5. Norwood was prosecuted for the crime of "forging a check." The evidence showed that he had forged county warrants which purported to be signed by the county commissioners and which stated that the treasurer of the county would pay a stated amount to the bearer of the warrant. Was Norwood guilty of the crime charged? [See California v Norwood, 26 CalApp3d 148, 103 CalRptr 7.]

6. The General Electric Credit Corporation repossessed a trailer owned by Sandoz. When Sandoz failed to pay the amount due, General Electric caused the trailer to be sold at a sheriff's sale. The statute required that a buyer pay in full for property sold at a sheriff's sale and the sheriff had advertised the sale as a "cash sale." Charles Mobile Homes, Inc., purchased the trailer and gave a check to the sheriff in payment of the purchase price. Thereafter the check was honored by the bank on which it was drawn but General Electric claimed that the foreclosure sale was not valid because the sheriff had not required payment of the full purchase price in cash. Was General Electric correct? [General Electric Credit Corp. v Tardo (LaApp) 304 So2d 89]

7. A drew a check payable to the order of B. The bank on which it was drawn refused to pay the check. B sued A for the amount of the check. A raised the defense that B had not shown that he sustained any damages by reason of the refusal of the bank to pay. Was this defense valid? [Duncan v Baskin, 8 Mich App 509, 154 NW2d 617]

8. A depositor drew a check and delivered it to the payee. Fourteen months later the check was presented to the drawee bank for payment. The bank did not have any knowledge that anything was wrong and paid the check. The depositor then sued the person receiving the money and the bank. The depositor claimed that the bank could not pay a stale check without asking the depositor whether payment should be made. Was the depositor correct? [Advanced Alloys, Inc. v Sergeant Steel Corp., 340 NYS2d 266]

9. A homeowner bought goods from a salesperson and allowed the salesperson to fill out a check for the purchase price of $1.26. The homeowner signed the check although there were large blank spaces to the left of the words and numerals showing the amount of the check. Unknown to the homeowner, the salesperson later increased the check from $1.26 to $6841.26 and then cashed the check at the homeowner's bank. The homeowner claimed that the check had been altered. Could this claim be made against the bank? [See Williams v Montana Nat. Bank, 167 Mont 24, 534 P2d 1247]

10. Siniscalchi drew a check on his account in the Valley Bank of New York. About a week later, the holder cashed the check at the bank on a Saturday morning. The following Monday morning, Siniscalchi gave the bank a stop payment order on the check. The Saturday morning transactions had not yet been recorded and neither the bank nor Siniscalchi knew that the check had been cashed. When that fact was learned, the bank debited Siniscalchi's account with the amount of the check. He claimed the bank was

liable because the stop payment order had been violated. Was the bank liable? [Siniscalchi v Valley Bank of New York, 359 NYS2d 173]

11. Pflaum mailed a check for $5,000 to the Laura Baker School and stated in the accompanying letter that it was a gift to the school which it could use for any purpose. Before the check was presented to the bank for payment, Pflaum stopped payment on it. The school then sued Pflaum on the check. Decide. [Laura Baker School v Pflaum, 225 Minn 181, 30 NW2d 290]

12. The Virginia Salvage Co. drew a check on the National Mechanics Bank and had the bank certify the check. The check was indorsed by the payee, and a subsequent holder. Schmelz National Bank, demanded payment of the check from the National Mechanics Bank. The latter defended on the ground that the salvage company by that time owed the bank more than the amount of the certified check. Was this a valid defense? [National Mechanics Bank v Schmelz National Bank, 136 Va 33, 116 SE 380]

13. *A* left his car with garage *B* for repairs. When the repairs were finished *B* refused to surrender the car until paid by *A*. *A* paid *B* with a check; took the car away; and then immediately stopped payment on the check. *B* claimed that he was entitled to retake the car and to keep it until the repair bill was paid. *A* claimed that *B* had lost his repair lien when he surrendered possession of the car to *A*. Was *A* correct? [See Leavitt v Charles R. Hearn, Inc., 19 IllApp3d 980, 312 NE2d 806]

14. A check was made payable to the order of *A* and *B*. *A* signed his own name and forged *B*'s name and then deposited the check in his own bank *C* which collected the check from the bank on which it was drawn. *B* sued *C* bank for one-half of the face of the check. Was the bank liable? [See White v Crocker-Citizens Nat. Bank, 253 CalApp2d 368, 61 CalRptr 381]

15. Stone & Webster drew a check on the First National Bank of Boston payable to the order of Westinghouse in payment of a debt. Before the check could be mailed to Westinghouse, an employee of Stone & Webster forged the indorsement of Westinghouse and cashed the check at the First National Bank & Trust Company of Greenfield. The Greenfield bank then presented the check for payment to the drawee bank, the First National Bank of Boston. The latter paid the Greenfield bank the amount of the check and then debited the account of Stone & Webster with the amount of the check. Stone & Webster then sued the Greenfield bank for the amount of the check. Was the plaintiff entitled to recover? [Stone & Webster Eng. Co. v First National Bank of Greenfield, 345 Mass 1, 184 NE2d 358]

16. Berg, who had a checking account in the Central National Bank, drew a check on that bank payable to the order of Anschutz. Colucci obtained the check from Berg by fraudulent misrepresentation and forged the name of Anschutz as an indorsement. The check was subsequently negotiated several times and then presented by a subsequent holder to the Central National Bank for payment. The bank, without knowing that the payee's indorsement was a forgery, paid the amount of the check to the apparent holder. Thereafter Anschutz sued the bank for the amount of the check. Was the bank liable? [Anschutz v Central National Bank, 173 Neb 60, 112 NW2d 545]

17. Pratt had an automobile repaired by Kilborn Motors. He paid for the repairs by check. The repairs were not properly made and Pratt stopped payment on the check. Pratt was prosecuted for deceptive practices. Was he guilty of obtaining property by false pretenses or deceptive practices? [Pratt v Kilborn Motors Inc., 48 IllApp3d 932, 363 NE2d 452]

18. Silver, an attorney, had an account labeled "special account" in the Commonwealth Trust Co. Part of the fund on deposit was money belonging to his client, Goldstein. Silver drew a check on this account for his own use. Goldstein sued the bank, claiming that it had no right to honor the check because the bank should have known that the account included the money of third persons and that the attorney was making improper use of the money. Decide. [Goldstein v Commonwealth Trust Co., 19 NJ Super 39, 87 A2d 555]

19. Bogash drew a check on the National Safety Bank and Trust Co. payable to the order of the Fiss Corp. At the request of the corporation, the bank certified the check. The bank later refused to make payment on the check because there was a dispute between Bogash and the corporation as to the amount due the corporation. The corporation sued the bank on the check. Decide. [Fiss Corp. v National Safety Bank and Trust Co., 191 Misc 397, 77 NYS2d 293]

20. Steinbaum executed and delivered a check payable to the order of the White Way Motors, the name under which DiFranco was doing business. Before the check was paid, Steinbaum stopped payment on the check. DiFranco sued Steinbaum on the check. Decide. [DiFranco v Steinbaum, (Mo App) 177 SW2d 697]

21. Goldsmith told his employee to draw a check on the Atlantic National Bank to the employee's order for $10.10. The employee wrote the check in his own hand, leaving space to the left of the amount. After Goldsmith signed the check, the employee filled in the spaces to the left of the amount, thus raising the check to $2,110.10. The employee presented the check to the bank, which made payment of the raised amount. Goldsmith sued the bank for the raised amount. Decide. [Goldsmith v Atlantic National Bank, (Fla) 55 So2D 804]

Part Seven • Creditors' Rights and Secured Transactions

34 Secured Consumer Credit Sales

Various devices have been developed to provide the credit seller of goods with protection beyond the right to sue the buyer for the purchase price. Today such devices, and others discussed in Chapter 35, are known as *secured transactions* and are governed by Article 9 of the UCC.[1]

A. GENERAL PRINCIPLES

The basic concept of the secured credit sale is that the seller is not made to rely solely on the buyer for payment but has a right or security interest in the goods sold to the buyer, even when possession and title have been transferred to the buyer.

§ 34:1. Nature of Secured Credit Sales. A *secured credit sale* is a sale in which the possession and the risk of loss pass to the buyer, but the seller retains a security interest in the goods until paid in full. In some instances, the seller retains the title until paid, but this is not essential. The seller's security interest entitles the seller to repossess the goods when the buyer fails to make payment as required or when the buyer commits a breach of the purchase contract in any other way. This right is in addition to the right to sue for the purchase price.

Forerunners of this credit device include: (1) a *conditional sale,* where the seller retained title until the condition of payment in full had been satisfied; (2) a *bailment lease,* under which transaction the buyer rented the property and, after the payment of sufficient rentals to equal the purchase price, could elect to take title to the property;

---

[1] This book is based on the 1972 version of the Uniform Commercial Code which is set forth in the Code Appendix. For the benefit of readers in states which are still under the former 1962 version of the Code, significant variations between the two versions are set forth in footnotes. The changes made by the 1972 version are confined mainly to Article 9 on secured transactions. The 1972 version has been adopted in Arizona, Arkansas, California, Colorado, Connecticut, Illinois, Iowa, Kansas, Maine, Minnesota, Mississippi, Nebraska, Nevada, New York, North Carolina, North Dakota, Oregon, Texas, Utah, Virginia, West Virginia, and Wisconsin.

and (3) a *chattel mortgage,* by which the buyer, upon taking title from the seller, in turn gave the seller a mortgage on the property for the amount of the unpaid balance of the purchase price. The laws pertaining to these three types of transactions have been replaced by the secured transaction provisions of the UCC.[2]

The Uniform Commercial Code is not designed solely to aid sellers. The provisions of Article 9 increase the protection given the buyers over that available to them under the former law. Special consumer protection statutes designed to protect buyers, in addition to the UCC, may also be in force within a given state.[3]

§ 34:2. Consumer Goods. *Consumer goods* are those which are used or bought for use primarily for personal, family, or household purposes.[4] It is the intended use, rather than the nature of the article which determines its character. For example, goods purchased by a buyer for resale to ultimate consumers are not consumer goods in the hands of such dealer but constitute inventory.

A mobile home in the possession of the person making use thereof is a consumer good. An automobile is a consumer good when purchased by the buyer to go to and from work. Equipment used in business is not a consumer good. Hence, a tractor purchased by a construction contractor is not a consumer good, but equipment. Likewise, a musical instrument used by a nightclub entertainer is equipment.

In this chapter, secured credit sales relating to consumer goods are considered. In Chapter 35, attention will be given to secured credit sales of inventory and equipment, and to secured loan transactions.

In many states security interests in automobiles in the hands of the ultimate consumer are governed by special installment sale or consumer protection statutes. As to automobiles which constitute a dealer's inventory, security interests are governed by Article 9 of the Uniform Commercial Code.

§ 34:3. Creation of Security Interest. A security interest for the protection of the seller of goods to a buyer arises or *attaches* as soon as the seller and buyer agree that the buyer shall have property rights in particular goods and that the seller shall have a security interest in them.[5] It is immaterial whether or not the sales agreement provides for the seller's retaining title until the buyer has paid for the goods in full, as the location of title to the property involved, called *collateral,* is immaterial.[6]

(a)   Security Agreement. The agreement of the seller and buyer that the seller shall have a security interest in the goods must be evidenced by a written *security agreement*

---

[2] The UCC, however, has not abolished these transactions nor made them illegal. The parties may still enter into a conditional sale, bailment lease, or chattel mortgage; but if they do, the transaction must satisfy the requirements of the secured transaction under the Code. Thus, the UCC establishes certain minimum requirements applicable to all types of security devices employed by the credit seller. An instrument that is called a "chattel mortgage" will be interpreted as a "security agreement." Strevell-Patterson Finance Co. v. May, 77 NMex 331, 422 P2d 366.

[3] Such laws continue in effect under UCC §§ 9-201, 9-203(2) and supplement its provisions. Consumer protection statutes may limit the kind of property which may be used as collateral in a secured transaction by a consumer and declare void a contract which violates the statute. First Nat. Bank v La Joie (Okla) 537 P2d 1207.

[4] UCC § 9-109(1).

[5] UCC § 9-204(1).

[6] UCC § 9-202.

which is signed by the buyer and which describes the collateral.[7] This description need only reasonably identify the collateral. It is not necessary that the goods be described specifically, as by serial number or by manufacturer's model.[8] A description is sufficient when it would enable a third person aided by inquiries made to others to determine what goods are involved.

The description in the security agreement must be sufficiently broad to include all property which the parties intended to include. The creditor does not have any security interest in property which is not included in the description of the collateral in the security agreement. This concept applies to all collateral, whether consumer goods, farm products, inventory, or equipment.

Whether the agreement between the parties is a security agreement depends upon its construction or interpretation. Hence, a buyer cannot claim that an outright sale was made when the contract is conspicuously entitled as a "conditional sales contract" and states that the sale is made "subject to the terms and conditions set forth below and upon the reverse side hereof," and the conditional sale provisions were specified on the reverse side but the buyer apparently neglected to read the reverse side. The fact that a financing statement has been filed does not eliminate the requirement of a security agreement.

(b) Future Transactions. The security agreement may contemplate future action by extending to goods that are to be acquired and delivered to the buyer at a future date. In general, the security interest does not attach to future goods until the buyer has rights in such goods.[9]

In order to protect consumers, a limit is placed upon the extent to which after-acquired property may be bound by a security interest. In order to be collateral for a consumer obligation, the consumer must acquire the latter property within ten days after the creditor gave value to the consumer. That is, the creditor cannot bind all property acquired at any time in the future but only such as is acquired within the ten days after the creditor sells the goods or loans the money to the consumer.[10]

(c) Perfection. When a security interest in property is superior to other interests and claims to the property, it is said to be *perfected* or superior. Whether a security interest is perfected is immaterial when the question is only the effect of the security agreement between the creditor and the debtor. The perfection of a security interest is important only when rival creditors claim the same collateral.

B. RIGHTS OF PARTIES INDEPENDENT OF DEFAULT

In a secured credit sale of consumer goods, both the seller and the buyer have rights independent of default by either party.

§ 34:4. Rights of the Seller of Consumer Goods Independent of Default. The seller stands in a dual position of being both a seller, having rights under Article 2 of the UCC

---

[7] UCC § 9-203(1)(a). No writing is necessary where the security interest is possessory.
[8] UCC § 9-110.
[9] UCC § 9-204(1), (2).
[10] Irvin v Public Finance Co. (AlaCivApp) 340 So2d 811.

governing sales, and a secured creditor, having rights under Article 9 of the UCC regulating secured transactions.[11]

The seller may transfer or assign the seller's interest under the sales contract and under the security agreement to a third person, and the assignee acquires all the rights and interest of the seller. The rights of the assignee may rise higher than those of the seller to the extent that there is a defense or claim valid against the seller which is not effective against the assignee because the buyer has waived such a right as against an assignee.

The secured credit seller of consumer goods has rights that are effective not only against the buyer but also against purchasers of the property from the buyer as soon as the security agreement is executed with respect to goods in which the buyer has acquired an interest. From that moment on, the seller's interest is generally effective against third persons [12] and is described as a *perfected security interest.* Whether a security interest is perfected is immaterial, however, when the question is the effect of the security agreement as between the creditor and the debtor.

(a) Filing Not Required. In an ordinary sale of consumer goods under a secured transaction, no filing in any government office is required in order to perfect the secured seller's interest. Such a seller is protected against creditors of the buyer and from third persons who thereafter buy the property from the buyer.[13]

As an exception to the rule that the seller of such goods has a perfected security interest as soon as the agreement is executed and the buyer has an interest in the property, the seller's security interest is not perfected, and filing is required to perfect it, if the goods purchased are to be attached to buildings or land as a fixture, or if they consist of farm equipment sold for a purchase price of over $2,500. A security interest in a motor vehicle required to be licensed is not perfected unless the vehicle is licensed with a notation of the security interest made in the title certificate, if such is required by law, or if not so required, unless there is a filing under the UCC.[14]

(b) Interstate Security Interests. The UCC regulates not only transactions within the state but also the effect to be given security interests in property brought into the state from another state. If the interest of the secured party was perfected in the other state, that interest will be regarded as perfected by the state into which the property is brought. Within the second state, however, it is necessary to file within four months in order to keep the security interest continuously perfected.

If the secured party's interest in the goods was unperfected when they were brought into the second state, that interest may be perfected in the second state, in

---

[11] UCC § 9-113. No civil liability rests upon the seller for harm sustained by third persons as a result of acts or omissions of the debtor or in consequence of the existence of the secured transaction. UCC § 9-317.

[12] UCC § 9-201.

[13] UCC § 9-302(1)(d). The UCC makes detailed provisions as to the priority of conflicting security interests with respect to fixtures, accessions, and commingled and processed goods. UCC § 9-313 et seq. A good faith subpurchaser will, in some cases, be protected from the security interest, See § 35:7 of this book.

[14] UCC § 9-302(1)(c), (d), (3), (4).

which case the perfection of the security interest dates from the time of such perfection in the second state.[15]

If title to the property, such as an automobile, is represented by a title certificate, the law of the state which issued the certificate determines whether an interest is perfected. Accordingly, if the law of the certificate-issuing state requires that a security interest be noted on the title certificate in order to be perfected, that requirement is the exclusive means of perfecting the interest of the secured creditor.[16]

(c) Repair and Storage Lien. In most states, persons making repairs to or storing property have a right to assert a lien against the property for the amount of their charges. A question of priority arises when the customer bringing the goods for repair or storage is not the absolute owner and there is an outstanding security interest in the goods. In such a case, the lien for repairs or storage charges prevails over the outstanding security interest.[17] (See p. 568, National Bank v Bergeron Cadillac, Inc.)

§ 34:5. Rights of the Buyer of Consumer Goods Independent of Default. The buyer in a secured transaction, like the seller, has a double status under the UCC. By virtue of Article 2, the buyer has certain rights as a buyer, and by virtue of Article 9, the buyer has certain rights as a debtor in a secured transaction.

(a) Rights as a Buyer. The secured credit sale of consumer goods remains fundamentally a sale that is governed by Article 2, and therefore the debtor-buyer has the same rights as an ordinary buyer under that article.[18]

The buyer has certain rights of ownership in the collateral. It is not material whether technically the buyer is the owner of the title. The buyer may voluntarily transfer whatever interest is owned by the buyer, and the creditors of the buyer may reach that interest by the process of law as fully as though there were no security agreement. Such third person generally cannot acquire any greater rights than the buyer, and therefore they hold the property subject to the security interest of the seller.

It is common practice for credit sellers to seek to protect themselves by prohibiting the buyer from reselling the property. Such a provision has no effect and does not prevent an effective resale, even though the security agreement in addition to prohibiting such resale also makes it a default or breach of the contract to make a resale.[19]

(b) Rights as a Debtor. The secured transaction buyer is a debtor to the extent that there is a balance due on the purchase price. In order for the buyer to know just how much is owed and to check what the seller claims to be due, the buyer has the right to compel the seller to state what balance is owed and also to specify in which collateral the seller claims a security interest. This is done by the buyer's sending the seller a statement of the amount believed to be due, or a statement of

---

[15] UCC § 9-103(3).
[16] UCC § 9-103(4).
[17] UCC § 9-310; Gulf Coast State Bank v Nelms (Tex) 525 SW2d 866.
[18] UCC § 9-206(2).
[19] UCC § 9-311.

the collateral believed to be subject to the security agreement, with the request that the seller approve or correct the statement. The seller must so indicate; and if there has been an assignment of the contract and the security interest to a third person, the seller must furnish the buyer with the name and address of such successor in interest.[20]

Independently of the UCC, any person, such as a purchaser from the buyer or a creditor of the buyer, may inquire of the original seller what interest is claimed in the collateral. (See p. 569, Ayers v Yancy Brothers Company)

The demand for a statement of accounts must be made in writing. If made by telephone, the creditor may ignore the request.

(c) Waiver of Defenses. It is common for finance companies and banks that have standing agreements to purchase sales contracts from a credit seller to supply forms to be signed by the buyer. These forms generally specify that a buyer waives, as against the assignee of the sales contract and of the security agreement, any rights that could be asserted against the seller. In addition to this express agreement waiving defenses, a buyer who, as a part of the purchase transaction, signs both a commercial paper and a security agreement is deemed as a matter of law to waive such defenses, even though nothing is said as to any waiver.

(1) Preservation of Defenses. Consumer protection laws may restrict the use of waiver clauses. Thus a Federal Trade Commission regulation requires that the contract signed by the buyer contain an express provision that the buyer retains the right to raise against the assignee of the contract any defense which could be raised against the seller.[21] Some statutes allow the use of waiver clauses and hold them effective if the assignee gives the buyer notice of the assignment and allows the buyer a specified number of days in which to inform the assignee of any defense existing against the seller.

(2) Validity of Waiver of Defenses. The universal defenses which may be raised against a holder in due course cannot be waived by a credit buyer in a secured transaction. Consumer protection laws further restrict the waiver of defenses as just noted. (See p. 570, Household Finance Corp. v Mowdy) With these two exceptions, both express and implied waivers of defenses are valid and bind the buyer if the assignee takes the assignment for value, in good faith, and without notice or knowledge of any claim or defense of the buyer.

A provision in a credit sales contract that the buyer will not assert any defense against the assignee of the seller and will hold only the seller responsible for the performance of the contract is not unconscionable.[22]

§ 34:6 Defined Default. A *default* by the debtor is merely the failure to pay the money as due. In order to provide greater protection to the creditor, the modern financing agreement will expand the definition of default to include matters which are not directly related to nonpayment. Thus, it will be specified that if the debtor moves away without notifying the creditor, such conduct is a default. This is merely a shorthand way of

[20] UCC § 9-208.
[21] See § 8:9 of this book.
[22] Westinghouse Credit Corp. v Chapman, 129 GaApp 830, 201 SE2d 686.

saying that although moving away is not a default as to payment, the creditor shall be entitled to exercise the same remedies when the debtor moves away as though the debtor had defaulted in payment of the debt. When a security agreement states that the debtor's bankruptcy shall constitute a default, such bankruptcy is given the effect of a default within the meaning of Uniform Commercial Code § 9-504(1), so that upon the debtor's bankruptcy the creditor may exercise the rights which the UCC states may be exercised upon default.

§ 34:7 Protection of Subpurchaser. When the seller of consumer goods sells on credit, a security interest in the goods is perfected even though the seller gives the buyer possession of the goods and does not file a financing statement. When no financing statement is filed, however, a resale by the consumer to another consumer will destroy the seller's security interest if the second buyer does not have knowledge of the security interest of the original seller and buys for personal, family, or household use.[23] (See p. 572, Balon v Cadillac Automobile Co.)

In order for sale to destroy a security interest, the security interest must have been created by the seller who has sold the goods to the consumer who has resold them to another consumer. The security interest is not destroyed if it was created by the person who sold the goods to the seller who resold them to the consumer.

When the consumer sells the collateral to a dealer as a trade-in on a new purchase from the dealer, the latter is not a consumer purchasing for a consumer use and therefore takes the collateral subject to the original creditor's security interest in the goods.[24]

C. RIGHTS OF PARTIES AFTER DEFAULT

When the buyer defaults by committing a breach of contract, the secured creditor and the buyer have additional rights.

§ 34:8. Secured Seller's Repossession and Resale of Collateral. Upon the buyer's default, the secured party is entitled to take the collateral or purchased property from the buyer. If this can be done without causing a breach of the peace, the seller may repossess the property without legal proceedings. When the credit seller repossesses in a peaceful, open manner, the seller does not commit larceny or any other crime. In any case, a seller may use legal proceedings if desired.[25]

The seller who has repossessed the goods may resell them at a private or public sale at any time and place and on any terms, provided this is done in good faith in a manner that is commercially reasonable.[26] The seller must give the buyer reasonable advance notice of a resale unless the goods are perishable, or unless they threaten to decline speedily in value, or unless they are a type customarily sold on a recognized market.[27] The seller's resale destroys all interest of the buyer in the goods.

---

[23] UCC § 9-307(2). The same provision applies to farm equipment other than fixtures having an original purchase price not in excess of $2,500 when the purchase by the subpurchaser is for the farming operations of the subpurchaser.

[24] Bennett v W. T. Grant Company (CA4 Va) 481 F2d 664.

[25] UCC § 9-503.

[26] UCC § 9-504(1)(3).

[27] UCC § 9-504(3).

If the secured creditor is the highest bidder or the only bidder at a public sale, the creditor may purchase the collateral even though such a sale is conducted in the creditor's office.

(a) Compulsory Resale. If the buyer has paid 60 percent or more of the cash price of the consumer goods, the seller must resell them within 90 days after repossession, unless the buyer, after default, has signed a written statement surrendering the right to require the resale. If the seller does not resell within the time specified, the buyer may sue for conversion of the collateral or proceed under the UCC provision applicable to failure to comply with the UCC.[28]

(b) Notice. Ordinarily notice must be given of the sale of collateral. The UCC does not specify the form of notice, and any form of notice that is reasonable is sufficient. A letter to the debtor can satisfy this requirement. If a public sale is made, the notice must give the time and place of the sale. If a private sale is made, it is sufficient to give reasonable notice of the time after which the private sale will be made. No notice is required when the collateral is perishable or is threatening to decline rapidly in value or is sold on a recognized market or exchange.[29] Notice must be given of the resale of an automobile that is collateral because there is no "recognized market" for the sale of used cars.

When notice is given to the public, it should be sufficiently explicit to enable a third person to form a basis for evaluating the collateral so that such third person can determine whether to bid at the sale. A warning that if payments are not made, the collateral will be put up for public sale is not a sufficient notice of the sale to satisfy the requirement of the UCC, because there is no notice of the time and place of the sale. Likewise, a declaration by the creditor after repossession that the collateral will be sold to the highest bidder is not sufficient notice of sale when there is no statement as to the time or place of the sale.

A debtor may waive notice of the sale of the collateral after there has been a default but a waiver which is made in advance of a default is invalid. Thus the security agreement cannot contain a waiver of notice.

(c) Redemption of Collateral. If the buyer acts in time, the buyer may redeem or obtain the return of the goods by tendering to the secured party the amount that is owed, including expenses and any legal costs that have been incurred. The right to redeem is destroyed if the seller has made a resale or entered into a binding contract for resale.[30]

(d) Manner of Resale. Upon the debtor's default, the creditor may sell the collateral at public or private sale or may lease it to a third person, as long as the creditor acts in a manner that is commercially reasonable.[31] The UCC does not require any particular kind of sale but only that the disposition be "commercially reasonable." The fact that higher offers are received after the making of a contract for resale of the collateral does not show that the contract was not "commercially reasonable."

---

[28] UCC § 9-507(1).
[29] UCC § 9-504(3).
[30] UCC § 9-506.
[31] UCC § 9-504(1).

(e)   Accounting after Resale. When the secured party makes a resale of the goods, the proceeds of the sale are applied in the following order to pay (1) reasonable costs of repossession, storage, and resale of the goods; (2) the balance due, including interest and any proper additions such as attorney's fees; and (3) subsequent security interests in the property that are discharged by the sale.[32]

If any balance remains after the payment of these claims, the buyer is entitled to the surplus. Conversely, if the net proceeds of sale are insufficient to pay the costs and the debt due the seller, the buyer is liable to the seller for such deficiency unless it has been otherwise agreed by the parties.[33]

In computing a deficiency judgment, a trade-in must be taken at its actual value and not at the amount allowed by the seller for the trade-in.[34]

(f)   Priority as to Other Creditors. A creditor holding a perfected security interest is entitled to priority with respect to the collateral as against (1) a creditor having an unperfected security interest, (2) a general creditor having no security interest, and (3) the debtor's trustee in bankruptcy. If the collateral is claimed by another creditor having a perfected security interest in the same collateral and both creditors have perfected by filing, the one first filing prevails over the other creditor.[35]

§ 34:9. Secured Seller's Retention of Collateral to Discharge Obligation. If a compulsory disposition of the collateral is not required, the secured party may propose in writing to keep the collateral in payment of the debt. If the buyer does not object to this proposal, the secured party may do so and the secured obligation is automatically discharged. If written objection to the retention of the collateral by the secured party is made within 30 days, the secured party must then proceed to dispose of it by resale or other reasonable manner.[36]

§ 34:10. Buyer's Remedies for Violation of UCC by Secured Party. The UCC authorizes both injunctive and money-damage relief against the secured party who violates the provisions of the UCC applicable upon default. The remedies provided by the UCC are not exclusive, and the buyer may also invoke any remedies authorized by any other statute applicable to the particular transaction.

When the sales contract is not executed in the manner required by a statute relating to installment sales, the contract is generally voidable at the election of the buyer and the seller is subject to some form of penalty, such as a criminal fine or loss of financing charges.

Local statutes, such as motor vehicle retail installment sales acts, may impose notice requirements upon a creditor repossessing collateral and provide a penalty for failing to give the required notice.

The buyer is entitled to recover the damages caused by the secured party's failure to comply with the UCC. In the absence of proof of a greater amount of damages, the buyer is entitled to recover not less than the credit service charge together

---

[32] UCC § 9-504(1).
[33] UCC § 9-504(2); Emmons v Easter, 62 MichApp 226, 233 NW2d 239.
[34] Webster v General Motors Acceptance Corp. 267 Ore 304, 516 P2d 1275.
[35] UCC § 9-312(5)(a). Other provisions regulate priorities in other circumstances.
[36] UCC § 9-505(2).

with 10 percent of the principal amount of the debt or the time price differential plus 10 percent of the cash price.[37]

If a resale has not yet been made nor a binding contract for resale entered into, the buyer may obtain a court order or injunction requiring the seller to comply with the UCC provisions.

If the creditor repossesses the collateral when the debtor is not in default or takes other property in which the creditor has no security interest, the creditor commits a conversion. The debtor may recover damages from the creditor for the conversion representing the value of the debtor's interest in the goods. If the creditor has acted recklessly and with willful indifference to the rights of the debtor, the latter may also recover punitive damages.

When the creditor makes a sale of the collateral without giving the debtor notice, the creditor deprives the debtor of the opportunity to bid at the sale. Consequently, the creditor will not be allowed to recover from the debtor any loss sustained or expenses incurred at such sale. Thus, the creditor who has not given the debtor sufficient notice of the sale of the collateral is barred from obtaining a deficiency judgment against the debtor when the collateral is resold for less than the amount due to the creditor.[38] (See p. 574, Turk v St. Petersburg Bank and Trust Co.)

---

[37] UCC § 9-507(1).

[38] Some courts hold that the failure to give notice does not bar the creditor but merely raises a presumption that the collateral was actually of the value of the balance of the debt and that unless the creditor can show otherwise there is no liability for a deficiency judgment. In most cases this presumption has the same effect as a flat prohibition of a deficiency judgment.

CASES FOR CHAPTER 34

National Bank v Bergeron Cadillac, Inc.

66 Ill2d 140, 361 NE2d 1116 (1977)

In order to finance the purchase of a new automobile, Gladys Schmidt obtained a loan from the National Bank and gave the bank a security interest in the new automobile to protect its loan. The bank perfected the security interest in accordance with the Uniform Commercial Code. Gladys later took the automobile to Bergeron Cadillac for repairs. Thereafter she stopped paying installments to the bank and the bank sought to repossess the automobile from Bergeron Cadillac. The latter refused to surrender the automobile until paid for the repairs. The bank claimed that it was entitled to the automobile because it had perfected its security interest and brought an action of replevin against Bergeron to recover the automobile. From a decision in favor of Bergeron, National Bank appealed.

WARD, C. J. . . . The trial court entered judgment for the defendant, holding that its common law possessory lien based on repairs it had made on the auto had priority over the plaintiff's prior security interest under section 9-310 of the Uniform Commercial Code. . . .

In February of 1973 the plaintiff loaned Gladys Schmidt $4,120 to enable her to purchase the automobile, taking a security interest in the automobile to secure the loan. This security interest was perfected by filing in the office of the Secretary of State. . . . In August of 1973 Schmidt brought the auto to the defendant's shop for repairs. The cost of the materials and service was approximately $2,000, and, when Schmidt failed to pay, the defendant, through an inquiry to the Secretary of State, learned of the plaintiff's security interest. The defendant exercised its right of lien for the unpaid charges and retained possession of the auto. In September, Schmidt defaulted on her loan payments, and in October the plaintiff ascertained that the Cadillac was in the defendant's possession. The plaintiff's demand on the defendant for the Cadillac under its security interest was refused, and the plaintiff filed the action in replevin.

The plaintiff contends that the right to a common law possessory lien has been superseded in Illinois by two statutes which provide for repairmen's liens. Ill.Rev.Stat. 1973, ch. 82, pars. 40 through 47 and 47a through 47f.

Section 9-310 of the Uniform Commercial Code . . . provides:

> "When a person in the ordinary course of his business furnishes services or materials with respect to goods subject to a security interest, a lien upon goods in the possession of such person given by statute or rule of law for such materials or services takes priority over a perfected security interest unless the lien is statutory and the statute expressly provided otherwise.". . .

The plain language of section 9-310 gives the lien of persons furnishing services or materials upon goods in their possession priority over a perfected security interest unless the lien is created by statute and the statute expressly provides otherwise.

The comment of Anderson (Anderson, Uniform Commercial Code) is:

> "Code section 9-310 declares the priority of the lien of persons furnishing services or materials with respect to goods in their possession. Such a lien is, basically, the artisan's lien of the common law. Whether such a lien is based upon decision or statute law, Code section 9-310 gives it priority, with one exception, over a preexisting security interest in the goods. . . .
>
> The single exception relates to a lien created by statute; such a lien does not have such priority if the statute expressly provides otherwise. Accordingly, the lien has priority when it is based upon the common law or decision, or when it is based upon a statute which is silent as to priorities or which gives the lien priority. The lien is subordinated to the security interest only when the lien statute expressly so declares." 4 Anderson, Uniform Commercial Code sec. 9-310, at 341-42(2d ed. 1971). . . .

The artisan's possessory lien of the common law is recognized in Illinois. . . .

We cannot accept the plaintiff's contention that the General Assembly's enactment of the two statutes creating liens in favor of repairmen with respect to personal property . . . evidenced an intent to supersede the artisan's common law lien. Both of the statutes expressly provide that the liens created shall be in addition to, and shall not exclude, any lien existing by virtue of the common law. . . .

As the defendant had a common law possessory lien for services and materials in connection with the repairs it made, its lien takes priority over the plaintiff's earlier perfected security interest under the provisions of section 9-310 of the Uniform Commercial Code. . . .

[Judgment affirmed]

Ayers v Yancey Brothers Company

141 GaApp 358, 233 SE2d 471 (1977)

Yancey Brothers sold goods to Dew-Moore on credit. The parties entered into a secured transaction to cover the unpaid balance of the purchase price. Thereafter Dew-Moore sold the collateral to Ayers. A dispute arose as to the balance due on the debt. Yancey brought an action against Ayers to foreclose on the collateral for the amount it claimed to be due. The lower court found that Dew-Moore had never requested Yancey to supply a statement of the balance due and entered judgment in favor of Yancey for the amount it claimed to be due. Ayers appealed.

QUILLIAN, P. J. [The trial judge wrongly decided that because Yancey had never been requested to furnish a statement of the amount due, Ayers could not dispute the amount that was due.]

There was a conflict as to whether Ayers took any steps to check with Yancey regarding the amount owed at the time the property was transferred. An employee of Yancey denied that Yancey was contacted about this. However, Ayers testified that prior to the transfer of the property from Dew-Moore she contacted Yancey about the status of the account, talked with "book-keeping" and got confirmation of the payments due and the amount due; as she at one time stated "all was confirmed." She admitted she did not know the name of the person with whom she conversed.

After taking over the equipment, Ayers made 17 monthly payments to Yancey. Then, just prior to the last payment, Yancey informed Ayers that a balance of $2,408.44, carried on the open account was still due. Thus, when Ayers tendered the last payment "in full satisfaction" and requested a termination statement, Yancey refused to accept it or issue the statement, contending that the last payment of $1,037.39 plus $2,408.44 was due it.

Yancey brought action to foreclose based on an indebtedness of $3,445.83. Ayers tendered the last payment of $1,037.39 into court, leaving the balance of $2,408.44 as the amount in dispute. . . .

. . . The trial judge confined himself to finding that no request was made under . . . UCC § 9-208. . . . However, we do not construe this law as all inclusive. What it does is to provide a means to obtain information but it is not the sole method. We adopt a clear statement of this principle found in 4 Anderson UCC 220, § 9-208.5: "The fact that Code § 9-208 provides for a request for information by the debtor does not preclude a request being made by a third person directly to the creditor . . . Ordinarily the secured party will furnish the information requested by a third person. Should he refuse or fail to do so, the third person should require the debtor to obtain the information from the secured party and may refuse to complete the transaction with the debtor until such information is obtained and is satisfactory to the subsequent party."

Here, Yancey could have refused to supply the information requested by Ayers. Then, if Ayers had proceeded with the transaction without obtaining such information, she would now be in no position to complain. But Yancey, according to her testimony, did verify the figures, omitting any reference to the $2,408.44 which she now claims is owed. Having induced Ayers to act in reliance thereupon, can Yancey now assume a different posture? The Uniform Commercial Code seeks to expedite and facilitate business practices, not stifle them.

The trial judge should not have limited his finding purely to whether there had been compliance with the Georgia Uniform Commercial Code. In making our ruling, we do not intimate what the trial judge's finding should be. Based on the evidence here he could have found that Ayers did not make an inquiry (or on the other hand he could have found that she did do so). Further, he might find that the information given to Ayers on a casual inquiry could not be considered in any way as binding on Yancey. But in any case he must make a finding in this regard; for, the mere fact that the defendant Ayers did not

follow the procedure prescribed in Georgia [UCC §] 9-208 is not the sole determinative factor involved here.

The case therefore must be reversed and remanded with the direction that the trial judge make a finding of fact and conclusion of law addressed to this issue.

[Judgment reversed and action remanded]

Household Finance Corp. v Mowdy

13 Ill App 3d 822, 300 NE2d 863 (1973)

The Mowdys made a contract with Diversified Industries for the installation of a swimming pool, made a down payment of $500, and executed a promissory note for the balance. Diversified sold the note and contract to Household Finance Corporation. The Mowdys stopped paying on the contract. HFC sued them for the balance due. They raised the defenses that the contract had been obtained by fraud and improper practices, that they had defenses valid against Diversified, that all such defenses could be raised against HFC by virtue of the Illinois Consumer Fraud Act, Section 2D, and demanded the return of their deposit of $500 by HFC. Judgment was entered in favor of HFC. The Mowdys appealed.

SEIDENFELD, J. . . . Plaintiff relies on its status as a holder in due course, and contends that section 2D of the Consumer Fraud Act was satisfied by a notice provision in the contract. . . .

Section 2D . . . provides: If a consumer in a retail installment sales transaction gives the seller a negotiable instrument in part or full payment for the merchandise which is the subject of a purchase order, retail charge agreement or retail installment sales contract before that merchandise is delivered or furnished to him, the assignment of that agreement or contract or the transfer of that negotiable instrument does not bar that consumer from asserting against the assignee or transferee any defense or right of action he may have against the seller unless (1) the contract or agreement contains, in at least 10-point bold type, the following notice:

"NOTICE TO BUYER
You have the right to give the assignee named (or if no assignee is named, to give the seller) written notice of any defense or right of action which you may have against the seller within 5 days of delivery of the merchandise described herein. If a notice is not received within that time, you may not assert

such defense or right of action against the assignee."; and (2) such a notice is not given within the time period stated. Notice is received with the meaning of this Section if the seller or assignee has refused to accept delivery by certified or registered mail of such a notice. . . .

HFC relies upon a notice contained in the contract which provides that the buyer may cancel the agreement if it has been signed at a place other than the seller's place of business by giving a notice within three days after the signing of the agreement. However, this notice is pursuant to another statute (Ill Rev Stat 1971, ch. 121½, par. 262B), is designed for a different purpose, and does not fulfill the requirements of section 2D.

Section 2D is unequivocal in its requirement. The statute is designed to combat a specific evil and is remediable in nature. It therefore should be liberally construed to effect its purpose of providing aggrieved buyers in explicit terms a method whereby they may communicate their complaints following delivery of purchased merchandise so as to preserve their claims and defenses against an assignee to whom payments will have to be made. Assuming that defendants did not advise HFC of possible defenses within a reasonable time by waiting 60 days following installation before giving written notice of cancellation, such fact would not obviate the requirement of inserting proper notice in the contract so that defendants would be informed of their rights under the Consumer Fraud Act.

While we hold that section 2D of the Consumer Fraud Act was not complied with in the installment contract assigned to HFC, we must also consider whether or not an express or implied clause in the contract which in substance purports to waive the buyer's defenses and claims against an assignee prevents the purchasers from asserting defenses against the assignee, HFC, even though they did not receive the notice required under section 2D.

UCC § 9-206(1) makes waiver of defense clauses valid subject to any statute or decision which establishes a different rule. Section 17 of the Retail Installment Sales Act . . . specifically validates agreements between buyer and seller not to assert against the assignee of retail installment contracts who takes for value, in good faith and without notice of defenses, any claim or defense the buyer may have against the seller.

Whether the language of paragraph four on the reverse side of the contract stating, "Assignee shall not be chargeable with any obligations or liabilities of seller" operates to waive the buyers' right to assert defenses against HFC need not be decided here. Even in the absence of an express waiver clause UCC § 9-206(1) implies an agreement not to assert defenses, if as part of one transaction, the buyer signs both a negotiable instrument and security agreement. . . . The implied waiver would thus operate in the transaction before us, unless there is an overriding consideration of public policy as expressed in section 2D of the Consumer Fraud Act.

We have held, prior to the enactment of section 2D, that a contractual waiver of certain defenses, such as are involved here, will be given effect, regardless of whether a negotiable note is taken in connection with the installment contract sale. . . . However, giving primacy to a waiver of defense clause would circumvent the remedy provided in section 2D so that dissatisfied consumer-buyers would not be able to preserve their claims and defenses against assignees to whom payments will have to be made. To avoid the operation of section 2D sellers would need merely to insert a waiver clause in their form contracts, which the average consumer-buyer may not read or understand. . . . The circumvention becomes even more blatant, when, as in the instant case, the waiver of defense clause is implied by UCC § 9-206(1) without need for mention of it in the contract itself.

Second, the use of a waiver of defense clause has the effect of imparting the attributes of negotiability to an otherwise nonnegotiable document. . . . In transactions in which either a negotiable note or a contract containing a waiver of defense clause evidences the buyer's obligation, the practical effect on the buyer is much the same. He is deprived of his ability to assert defenses he has on the contract against the seller's assignee. Thus the reasons for enacting section 2D to apply in consumer installment transactions in which a negotiable instrument is taken in payment are equally applicable to contracts which contain a waiver of defense clause, express or implied.

We therefore hold the waiver of defense clause implied in the instant installment contract does not nullify the requirements of section 2D. By our holding, the validity of waiver of defense clauses allowed by statute . . . is not destroyed, but only limited as is required by section 2D of the Consumer Fraud Act. If the notice provision as specified is complied with, and no claims or defenses are brought to the seller's or assignee's attention within the time and in the manner designated, then a waiver of defense clause would be effective to cut off later claims or defenses the buyer might seek to assert against an assignee.

We therefore conclude that the trial court erred in holding that the plaintiff took the contract free of defenses defendants may have had against the original seller. Since the trial court did not pass upon the sufficiency of defendants' grounds for relief, the extent of the damage, if any, or the appropriateness of rescission or revocation of acceptance, the case will be remanded. . . .

[An] issue which might have to be considered on remand if any of defendants' claims or defenses are sustained is whether section 2D authorizes recovery from HFC of moneys paid to Diversified as down payment before the assignment. Defendants rely on the language of section 2D which states that "any defense or *right of action*" that the consumer has against the seller may be asserted against the assignee if the required notice to buyer is not inserted in the contract. Plaintiff argues that such an operation of section 2D would be inequitable.

We believe the buyer's ability to assert "rights of action" against the assignee provided by section 2D is limited by the amount of the debt assigned as indicated by the negotiable instrument or instruments taken by the assignee. The statute is designed only to operate in the context of an assignment of a negotiable instrument which was given as payment by a consumer on a retail installment sales contract. As such it is really the debt assigned which is subject to the buyer's defenses and rights of action, although it is against the assignee who holds the instrument acknowledging the debt that the buyer must assert his claims.

Moreover, in our view, the rights of the buyers in the instant case under section 2D are similar to those provided buyers by virtue of UCC § 3-306, which describes the rights of one not a holder in due course. A reasonable reading of UCC § 3-306 indicates the buyer's rights against the holder are limited by the amount of the note or instrument transferred. Thus the authority of buyers to assert defenses and rights of action should be construed as a right to set off these claims against the assignee's right to collect on the note he is holding. Such a construction of section 2D is in accord with the law generally regarding assignments of contract rights. . . .

[Judgment reversed and action remanded]

Balon v Cadillac Automobile Co.

113 NH 108, 303 A2d 194 (1973)

Balon and Gibert each purchased a Cadillac for personal use from Saia, a private owner. They did not know that each car was subject to an unfiled security interest in favor of the original seller, the Cadillac Automobile Company of Boston. Balon and Gibert claimed that they owned their cars free of the security interest of Cadillac. Cadillac contended that Balon and Gibert did not believe that they were purchasing a clear title and were subject to its unfiled security interests. Cadillac repossessed the cars. Balon and Gibert sued Cadillac. From judgment in their favor, Cadillac appealed.

LAMPRON, J. . . . The issue to be decided is whether the trial court properly found and ruled that Balon and Gibert each had clear title to his automobile by virtue of § 9-307 of the [UCC]. . . .

On September 28, 1965, Charles Pernokas was a salesman for Cadillac Automobile in Boston, Massachusetts. He had previously worked for another employer as a car salesman with Russell Saia. On that day Saia came to Cadillac Automobile looking for a convertible for a customer. Pernokas showed him two cars and Saia said he would hear from him shortly. He telephoned soon thereafter saying that his customer, Peter J. Russell, would take one of the Cadillac convertibles and gave the required credit information and references. On the next day, Saia telephoned Pernokas again and told him another customer, Joseph P. DeLuca, would take the other convertible and gave credit information on him.

Pernokas testified that in each instance he delivered the car to Saia's place and that Saia and another person, supposedly Russell in one instance and DeLuca in the other, identified himself and signed the security agreements. The selling price, $5300 for each car, was paid by a $1000 cash down payment on each and the balance financed on a conditional sale agreement.

At about that time, an individual named Arthur Freije told Balon in Manchester that "somebody" had a "friend" who could get a good deal on Cadillacs. "Somebody" was Fred Sarno who had accompanied Saia on his visit to the Cadillac garage after which the two cars in question were bought. The "friend" was Russell Saia. Balon passed the information along to his stepfather, Gibert, and eventually both Balon and Gibert purchased a Cadillac convertible through Freije for $4300 each.

The October and November payments on these Cadillacs were not made to Cadillac Automobile. As a result of these defaults, Simons, its credit manager, made an investigation and concluded that Peter J. Russell and Joseph P. DeLuca, the apparent purchasers, did not exist and decided that "both of these were two straw deals." There was evidence that payments on these cars were made at the garage in December by Russell Saia or with his knowledge. After the cars were repossessed from Balon and Gibert a meeting was arranged at the Cadillac garage to straighten out the matter. When they had waited there about two hours for someone to come, Simon made a telephone call and a man arrived who was overheard to say he was Peter Russell. In a later conversation with Balon and Gibert the man identified himself as Russell Peters. When asked for credentials by Simon, this same person showed him a license made out to Russell Saia and said that Peter Russell was an alias he used. There was evidence that the address given as that of Peter Russell on the credit statement and security agreement in conjunction with the car purchased in his name was listed in the city directory as the residence of "Mrs. Jean Saia." The trial court properly found on the evidence that the two Cadillac automobiles in question were purchased by Russell Saia and that he was the principal in their sale to Balon and Gibert.

[UCC §] 9-307 . . . reads as follows: (1) "A buyer in the ordinary course of business . . . takes free of a security interest created by his seller even though the security interest is perfected and even though the buyer knows of its existence. (2) In the case of consumer goods . . . a buyer takes free of a security interest even though perfected if he buys without knowledge of the security interest, for value and for his own personal, family or household purposes . . . unless prior to the purchase the secured party has filed a financing statement covering such goods." . . . The secured interest of Cadillac Automobile was perfected when the agreement of the parties was executed. . . . However the security agreements covering these two automobiles were never filed. . . .

The buyer protected by § 9-307(1) is one who purchases in the ordinary course of business from a person in the business of selling goods of the kind involved. § 1-201(9). Hence § 9-307(1) applies primarily to purchases from the inventory of a dealer in the type of goods sold. 4 Anderson, Uniform Commercial Code 323:24 (2d ed. 1971); *see* National Shawmut Bank v Jones, 108 NH 386, 236 A2d 484

(1967). The buyer protected under § 9-307(2) is one who purchases goods for consumer use, that is, for personal, family or household purposes, from a consumer seller. In order to fall within the protection of this section the goods must be consumer goods in the hands of both the buyer and the seller. . . .

The categorization of these automobiles at the time of the execution of the security agreement with Cadillac Automobile is an important factor in determining whether they were inventory or consumer goods in the hands of Saia when he sold them. . . . This classification of the goods remains unchanged in the controversy between Balon, Gibert, and Cadillac Automobile when it seeks to enforce its security agreement. Simon, Cadillac's credit manager, testified that it is company policy to record security agreements except when the buyer is an individual consumer as determined by the contract. Their security agreement provides that if the car is purchased for business purposes the address of the buyer's place of business must appear as the address on the front of the contract. There was evidence that the address on the front of the Peter Russell contract was listed in the Boston directory as the residence of Mrs. Jean Saia. Simon also testified that as far as the seller was concerned these sales were made to two private consumers for their personal, family and household use. Accordingly, following its policy with respect to consumer purchasers, the security agreements were not filed.

We hold that the trial court properly found and ruled that Russell Saia was a dishonest consumer purchaser of these automobiles. We further hold that these cars remained consumer goods in his hands at the time of the sales to Balon and Gibert who are protected by [UCC §] 9-307(2) if they were good faith consumer buyers for value without knowledge of Cadillac's security interest.

The company maintains, however, that the only conclusion which can be reached on the evidence is that Balon and Gibert "could not have conceivably held honest convictions that these transactions were legitimate." In support it cites § 1-201(19) which provides: " 'Good faith' means honesty in fact in the conduct or transaction concerned." By its terms this is a subjective standard of good faith, that is, whether the particular purchaser believed he was in good faith, not whether anyone else would have held the same belief. The test is what the particular person did or thought in the given situation and whether or not he was honest in what he did. . . .

There was evidence that Gibert had known Freije, who made the approaches which culminated in these sales, in a social way for about fifteen years. His wife had known him all her life. Balon knew him also and had purchased a 1963 Cadillac from him without any untoward incidents. Balon and Gibert learned from inquiries made to dealers known to them that the asking price of $4300 was consistent with prices at which such cars could be bought. The explanation advanced that these convertibles sold in September, when the new models were due, could be found by them plausible reasons for the price quoted. Simon testified that when Balon and Gibert came to Boston after their cars were taken they seemed genuinely concerned [in] trying to figure out what happened. There was no evidence that they had actual knowledge of the status of the title to these cars. The fact that others might have acted differently, made more inquiries, or been more suspicious does not require a conclusion that they lacked good faith when they purchased these cars. . . . The evidence is clear that they paid value and bought for personal, family, or household purposes.

We hold that the trial court properly found and ruled that Balon and Gibert were good faith consumer buyers for value from a consumer seller without knowledge of Cadillac Automobile's security interest which had not been filed. . . . Consequently they were entitled to the protection of [UCC §] 9-307(2). . . .

[Judgment affirmed]

Turk v St. Petersburg Bank and Trust Co.

(Fla App) 281 So2d 534 (1973)

Turk was president of Bob King, Inc., which sold automobiles. In order to finance the obtaining of inventory for Bob King, Turk borrowed money from the St. Petersburg Bank. The loan was represented by a note which was secured by the inventory of Bob King. The bank repossessed the collateral and resold it without giving notice of the sale to Turk. The amount obtained by the sale was substantially less than the balance due on the debt and the bank sued Turk for that deficiency. Judgment was entered for the bank and Turk appealed.

LILES, J. . . We believe that the verdict should be reversed. . . .

. . . This transaction was governed by the Uniform Commercial Code, and particularly [§ 9-

504(3)] which reads as follows: "(3) Disposition of the collateral may be by public or private proceedings and may be made by way of one or more contracts. Sale or other disposition may be as a unit or in parcels and at any time and place and on any terms but every aspect of the disposition including the method, manner, time, place and terms must be commercially reasonable. Unless collateral is perishable or threatens to decline speedily in value or is of a type customarily sold on a recognized market, reasonable notification of the time and place of any public sale or reasonable notification of the time after which any private sale or other intended disposition is to be made shall be sent by the secured party to the debtor, and except in the case of consumer goods to any other person who has a security interest in the collateral and who has duly filed a financing statement indexed in the name of the debtor in this state or who is known by the secured party to have a security interest in the collateral. The secured party may buy at any public sale and if the collateral is of a type customarily sold in a recognized market or is of a type which is the subject of widely distributed standard price quotations he may buy at private sale."

. . . Before a secured party (in this instance the bank) can obtain a deficiency against a debtor (in this instance Turk) the debtor must be given notice of what is about to occur. This is as it should be because the debtor in this instance, Turk, could have done many things. He could have purchased the automobiles himself; he could have paid the extent of the liability, i.e., $20,000; he could have secured purchasers for the automobiles. He was not afforded the opportunity to do anything. If the bank in this instance wanted to dispose of the collateral without judicial process or notice to the debtor as the statute provides, it may do so; but it is not then entitled to a deficiency against any debtor not so notified. The record reflects that notice was given to Bob King, Inc., but the statute prevents the bank from securing a deficiency against Irving Turk.

There are exceptions to the rule as will be noted in the statute. However, automobile auctions should not be construed as a "recognized market" under [UCC § 9-504(3)]. Although such auctions do not present some of the evils intended to be prevented by the statute, it seems reasonable to limit the definition of "recognized market" to widely recognized stock and commodity exchanges which are regulated in some substantial way. This will prevent nearly all of the evils while imposing only a slight notice burden on creditors in order to obtain their deficiency judgments.

In the absence of a required notice by the secured creditor . . . the creditor forfeits his right to any deficiency against any debtor not so notified. We hereby adopt the reasoning of the New York Court in Leasco Data Processing Equipment Corporation v Atlas Shirt Company, Inc., 66 Misc2d 1089, 323 NYS2d 13 (NYCiv 1971) to the effect that since deficiency judgments after repossession of collateral are in derogation of the common law, any right to a deficiency accrues only after strict compliance with the relevant statutes. . . .

[Judgment reversed]

QUESTION AND CASE PROBLEMS

1. What social forces are affected by the destruction of a security interest in consumer goods when a consumer-debtor resells the goods to another consumer who does not know of the security interest?

2. Compare the notice requirements for (a) a private sale of repossessed collateral, (b) a public sale of repossessed collateral, and (c) a sale of repossessed collateral which is customarily sold on a recognized market.

3. Compare the right to a surplus and liability for a deficit (a) after a sale of goods upon the buyer's default, and (b) after the sale of repossessed collateral held under a secured transaction.

4. Compare the repossession of collateral with the retention of collateral to discharge the debtor's obligation.

5. Sam's Furniture & Appliance Stores sold furniture and home appliances to the public. Sam went bankrupt. At that time, Sam had in his store various items that had been repossessed from customers. Were such goods inventory or consumer goods? [In re Sam's Furniture & Appliance Stores, (DC WD Pa Ref Bankruptcy) 1 UCCRS 422]

6. Little Brown Jug, Inc., purchased goods from L. & N. Sales Co. Little Brown Jug later claimed that it was not bound by the conditional sales contract because its representative had been too busy to read it and thought that he was merely signing an order form. Was that a valid defense? [L. & N. Sales Co. v Little Brown Jug, Inc., (Pa) 12 D&C 2d 469]

7. Hull-Dobbs sold an automobile to Mallicoat and then assigned the sales contract to the Volunteer Finance & Loan Corp. Later Volunteer repossessed the automobile and sold it. When Volunteer sued Mallicoat for the deficiency between the contract price and the proceeds on resale, Mallicoat raised the defense that he had not been properly notified of the resale. The loan manager of the finance company testified that Mallicoat had been sent a registered letter stating that the car would be sold. He did not state whether the letter merely declared in general terms that the car would be sold or specified a date for its resale. He admitted that the letter never was delivered to Mallicoat and was returned to the finance company "unclaimed." The loan manager also testified that the sale was advertised by posters, but on cross examination he admitted that he was not able to state when or where it was thus advertised. It was shown that Volunteer knew where Mallicoat and his father lived and where Mallicoat was employed. Mallicoat claimed that he had not been properly notified. Volunteer asserted that sufficient notice had been given. Was the notice of the resale sufficient? [Mallicoat v Volunteer Finance & Loan Corp., 57 Tenn App 106, 415 SW2d 347]

8. Allen, who operated a trailer park, rented a trailer, which at all times remained in the park, to Cady under a lease which gave Cady the option to purchase the trailer. The

lease stated that the cash price of the trailer plus various charges was $5,800, of which the down payment was $1,934, and specified that $17 of each weekly payment of $32 was to be applied to the down payment. The lease was for 25 months so that the total payments, if the trailer was not purchased, would be $3,578, or 62 percent of the price of the trailer. Cady became bankrupt and Cohen, his trustee in bankruptcy, claimed that the interest of Allen in the trailer was void because the transaction was a conditional sale and there had not been any recording of the sales contract. Was Allen's claim to the trailer binding? [Allen v Cohen, (CA2 NY) 310 F2d 312]

9. A security agreement described the collateral as "All Olivetti Corporation of American copying machines which have been delivered but not paid in full . . . " it was claimed that this was so broad a description that it was no description and that the security agreement was therefore defective. Is this contention valid? [See First Nat. Bank & Trust Co. v Olivetti Corp. of America, 130 GaApp 896, 204 SE2d 781]

10. Bailey purchased a freezer-and-food plan from Pen Del Farms on the installment plan. The latter sold its rights under the contract to the Associated Acceptance Corp. and gave it a copy of the original contract. When Associated sued Bailey, he claimed that the transaction was void under the Maryland Retail Installment Sales Act because the copy of the contract that had been given him had not been fully signed on behalf of the seller. Associated replied that the copy which it had received had been fully executed and that it contained the statement of Bailey that "purchaser acknowledges receipt of true, executed copy of this contract at time of execution hereof." Was Bailey's defense valid? [Associated Acceptance Corp. v Bailey, 226 Md 550, 174 A2d 440]

11. Cook sold to Martin a new tractor truck for approximately $13,000 with a down payment of approximately $3,000 and the balance to be paid in 30 monthly installments. The sales agreement provided that upon default in any payment Cook could take "immediate possession of the property . . . without notice or demand. For this purpose vendor may enter upon any premises the property may be." Martin failed to pay the installments when due, and Cook notified him that the truck would be repossessed. Martin had the tractor truck, attached to a loaded trailer, locked on the premises of a company in Memphis. Martin intended to drive to the West Coast as soon as the trailer was loaded. When Cook located the tractor truck, no one was around. In order to disconnect the trailer from the truck, as Cook had no right to the trailer, Cook removed the wire screen over a ventilator hole by unscrewing it from the outside with his penknife. He next reached through the ventilator hole with a stick and unlocked the door of the tractor truck. He then disconnected the trailer and had the truck towed away. Martin sued Cook for unlawfully repossessing the truck by committing a breach of the peace. Decide. [Martin v Cook, 237 Miss 267, 114 So2d 669]

12. Hileman purchased a washer from the Maytag Rice Co. on credit and executed a chattel mortgage. The mortgage gave the seller authority "to make use of such force as may be necessary to enter upon, with or without breaking into any premises, where the [goods] may be found." Maytag assigned the contract and mortgage to the Harter Bank & Trust Company. When Hileman failed to pay the installment due, Harter Bank had its employees remove a screen in Hileman's house and enter through a window for the purpose of removing the mortgaged washer. Hileman sued the Harter Bank for unlawfully trespassing upon his property. Was he entitled to damages? [Hileman v Harter Bank & Trust Co., 174 Ohio 95, 186 NE2d 853]

35

Other Secured Transactions, Suretyship, and Letters of Credit

Subject to certain exceptions, Article 9 of the Uniform Commercial Code regulates all secured transactions dealing with personal property. The secured transaction relating to consumer goods sold on credit was discussed in Chapter 34. This chapter considers other common forms of secured transactions.

A. SECURED CREDIT SALES OF INVENTORY

In contrast with one who buys goods for personal use, the buyer may be a merchant or dealer who intends to resell the goods. The goods which such a merchant or dealer buys are classified as *inventory*. The financing of the purchase of inventory may involve a third person, rather than the seller, as creditor. For example, a third person, such as a bank or finance company, may loan the dealer the money with which to make the purchase and to pay the seller in full. In such a case the security interest in the goods may be given by the buyer to the third person and not to the seller.[1] Accordingly, the terms "creditor" and "secured party" as used in this chapter may refer to a seller who sells on credit or to a third person who finances the purchase of goods.

In general, the provisions regulating a secured transaction in inventory follow the same pattern as is applicable to the secured credit sale of consumer goods. Variations recognize the differences in the commercial settings of the two transactions.

Initially there must be a security agreement to give rise to the security interest. (See p. 588, Mosley v Dallas Entertainment Co.) If perfection of the interest is desired, there must also be a filing of a financing statement or the creditor must hold possession of the collateral.

§ 35:1. Use of Property and Extent of Security Interest. A secured transaction relating to inventory will generally give the buyer full freedom to deal with the collateral goods as though the buyer were the absolute owner and the goods were not subject to a security interest. Thus, the parties may agree that the buyer-dealer may mingle the goods with existing inventory, resell the goods, take goods back and make exchanges, and so on, without being required to keep any records of just what became of the

---

[1] Prior to the adoption of the Uniform Commercial Code, security was frequently provided the person financing the purchase of inventory by the device of a trust receipt, under which the purchaser-merchant would declare that the inventory was held in trust for the creditor. This device was regulated by the Uniform Trust Receipts Act (UTRA).

goods covered by the security agreement, or to replace the goods sold with other goods, or to account for the proceeds from the resale of the original goods.

(a)   After-Acquired Property. The security agreement may expressly provide that the security interest of the creditor shall bind after-acquired property, that is, other goods, whether inventory or equipment, thereafter acquired by the buyer. The combination of the buyer's freedom to use and dispose of the collateral and the subjecting of after-acquired goods to the interest of the secured creditor permits the latter to have a *floating lien* on a changing or shifting stock of goods of the buyer. Conversely stated, the UCC rejects the common-law concept that the security interest was lost if the collateral was not maintained and accounted for separately and that a floating lien upon the buyer's property was void as a fraud against the latter's creditors. (See p. 589, Galleon Industries, Inc. v Lewyn Machinery Co., Inc.)

The security interest in inventory covered as after-acquired property has priority over claims of subsequent creditors and third persons, except buyers in the ordinary course of business and sellers to the debtor holding perfected purchase money security interests in the goods sold to the debtor. It is generally held that the perfection of a security interest in after-acquired items dates from the time when the security interest was originally perfected, rather than there being a series of perfection dates as each new item of property is acquired. In consequence of this view, the creditor's security interest in after-acquired property which was perfected more than four months before the debtor's bankruptcy is superior to the debtor's trustee in bankruptcy, even though some items of property were acquired within the four-month period preceding bankruptcy.[2]

(b)   Proceeds of Collateral. The secured transaction covers proceeds from the collateral unless such interest is expressly excluded.[3] Proceeds includes cash, checks, and accounts receivable arising on a sale of the collateral and also money paid to the debtor by an insurance company to indemnify for damage to or destruction of the collateral.[4]

§ 35:2. Filing of Financing Statement. Filing is usually required to perfect the creditor's interest in inventory or the proceeds therefrom. An exception is made when a statute requires the security interest to be noted on the title certificate issued for the property.[5] A security interest in a motor vehicle that is inventory is perfected by filing under the Code; but if it is an individual vehicle owned by a private owner, there must be a notation of the interest on the title registration certificate.[6]

An unperfected security interest is valid as against anyone standing in the position of the debtor or whose rights rise no higher than those of the debtor.

(a)   Financing Statement. The paper that is filed is a financing statement and is distinct from the security agreement which was executed by the parties to give rise

---

[2] Biggins v Southwest Bank (CA9 Cal) 490 F2d 1304.
[3] UCC § 9-203(1)(b), § 9-306(2). Under the 1962 version of the Code, the creditor has only a ten-day perfection in proceeds if a security interest in proceeds is not expressly declared in the security agreement.
[4] UCC § 9-306(1). Under the 1962 version of the Code, the secured creditor has no interest in insurance proceeds.
[5] UCC § 9-302(1), (3), (4).
[6] Apeco Corp. v Bishop Mobile Homes, Inc. (TexCivApp) 506 SW2d 711.

to the secured transaction.[7] The *financing statement* must be signed by the debtor; it must give an address of the secured party from which information concerning the security interest may be obtained; it must give a mailing address of the debtor; and it must contain a statement indicating the types, or describing the items, of collateral.[8]

The financing statement does not set forth the terms of the agreement between the parties. This is done in the security agreement. All that the financing statement does is give notice to the world that the debtor has financed; that is, that the secured creditor who has filed may have a security interest in the collateral described in the statement.

Errors in the financing statement have no effect unless they are seriously misleading. If they are seriously misleading, the filing has no effect and does not perfect the security interest. For example, a description of the collateral in the financing statement as "all personal property" is not sufficient and therefore the filing of the statement does not perfect the security interest.

(b)   Place of Filing. The Code gives each state the option to provide for the filing of the financing statement under (1) *local filing,* as in the county of residence or place of business of the debtor, (2) *central filing,* as in a particular office in the state capitol, or (3) *dual filing,* a combination of both local and central filing.

(c)   Defective Filing. When the filing of the statement is defective either because the statement is so erroneous as to be seriously misleading or the filing is made in a wrong county or office, the filing fails to perfect the security interest.[9] This means that other creditors who have liens on the collateral and the trustee in bankruptcy of the debtor have a right to the collateral superior to that of the original secured creditor.

When a filing is required for perfection, there must be such filing as is required by the Code. The mere fact that the debtor acknowledges in writing that the creditor has a security interest in designated property does not perfect the security interest of the creditor even though the collateral is an automobile and the acknowledgement is written by the debtor on the title certificate.[10]

§ 35:3. Duration and Continuation of Filing. The filing of the financing statement is effective for 5 years. At the expiration thereof, the perfection of the security interest terminates unless a continuation statement has been filed prior thereto.[11] The *continuation statement* is merely a written declaration by the secured party which identifies the

---

[7] UCC § 9-402. However, the security agreement may be filed as a financing statement if it contains the required information and is signed by both parties.

[8] UCC § 9-402(1). The financing statement is insufficient when it does not contain the address of the creditor. Strevell-Patterson Finance Co. v May, 77 NMex 331, 422 P2d 366. The financing statement may be signed only by the secured creditor if the collateral is subject to a security interest arising in a foreign state and the creditor makes a filing in the state into which the collateral is thereafter taken. Likewise, a signing by the secured creditor alone is sufficient if the filing is made to perfect a security interest in proceeds. In states adopting the 1972 version of the Code, a signature by the creditor only is sufficient when an out-of-state debtor has moved into the state, when a filing is made to reperfect a security interest as to which a prior filing had lapsed, or when the debtor has acquired collateral after a change of name, identity, or corporate structure.

[9] In re Thrift Shoe Co. (CA9 Cal) 502 F2d 1211.

[10] National Bank & Trust Co. v Moody Ford, Inc., 149 IndApp 479, 273 NE2d 757.

[11] UCC § 9-403(2).

original filing statement by its file number and declares that it is still effective. The filing of the continuation statement continues perfection of the security for a period of 5 years after the last date on which the original filing was effective. The filing of successive continuation statements will continue the perfection indefinitely.[12]

(a)   Termination Statement. A buyer who has paid the debt in full may make a written demand on the secured party, or the latter's assignee if the security interest has been assigned, to send the buyer a *termination statement* that a security interest is no longer claimed under the specified financing statement. The buyer may then present this statement to the filing officer who marks the record "terminated" and returns to the secured party the various papers which had been filed.

(b)   Assignments. The secured party may have assigned the security interest either before the filing of the financing statement or thereafter. If the assignment was made prior to its filing, the financing statement may include a recital of the assignment and state the name and address of the assignee, or a copy of the assignment may be attached thereto. If the assignment is made subsequent to the filing of the financing statement, a separate written statement of assignment may be filed in the same office.[13]

§ 35:4. Protection of Customer of the Buyer. The customer of the dealer selling from inventory takes the goods free from the security interest of the dealer's supplier. That is, one who buys in the ordinary course of business items of property taken from the original buyer's inventory is free of the secured party's interest, even though that interest was perfected and even though such ultimate customer knew of the secured party's interest.[14] (See p. 591, Taylor Motor Rental Inc. v Associates Discount Corp.)

The sale to a buyer in ordinary course when not authorized by the secured party does not destroy a security interest, whether perfected or not, which was created by a debtor prior to acquisition of the goods by the buyer's seller.

A security interest created by a manufacturer is destroyed by a resale of the goods by the dealer to the buyer on the theory that such sale, which was obviously contemplated by the manufacturer, was authorized, and the destruction of the security interest was likewise authorized.

The buyer of consumer goods or of farm equipment not having an original purchase price in excess of $2,500 is subject to a security interest created by a former owner or that owner's seller if it has been perfected by filing prior to the ultimate sale to the buyer. If it has been perfected without filing, the ultimate buyer is not subject to a security interest created by the original seller, if the ultimate buyer purchased without knowledge of the existence of the security interest and purchased for value intending to use the property for personal, family, or household purposes, or for farming operations.[15]

§ 35:5. Rights and Remedies After Default. The rights and remedies of the secured party and the buyer of inventory after a default on the part of the latter are the same as in the case of a secured credit sale of consumer goods. As a partial modification of

---

[12] UCC § 9-403(3).
[13] UCC § 9-405.
[14] UCC § 9-307(1).
[15] UCC § 9-307(2).

that pattern, the creditor taking possession of inventory on the buyer's default is not required to make a sale of the goods but may retain them in full discharge of the debt due, unless an objection is made by the buyer to such retention. In the latter case the creditor must then make a sale.[16]

B. SECURED CREDIT SALES OF EQUIPMENT

In general, secured credit sales of equipment are treated the same as secured transactions as to inventory, except that the various provisions relating to resale by the buyer and the creditor's rights in proceeds have no practical application because the buyer does not resell the property but makes the purchase with the intention of keeping and using or operating it.

§ 35:6. Use of Collateral. For the purpose of secured transactions, a distinction is made as to the purpose for which the buyer procures the goods. If an ultimate consumer purchases primarily for personal, family, or household use, the goods are described as *consumer goods.* The consumer's purchase, however, is described as *equipment* if used or purchased for use primarily in a business, in farming, or in a profession.[17]

§ 35:7. Filing. In the ordinary sale of consumer goods, filing of a financing statement is not required. In contrast, filing is required to perfect a purchase money security interest in equipment, with the exception of farm equipment having a purchase price not in excess of $2,500, and motor vehicles which must be licensed under a specific licensing statute.[18] If the equipment becomes a fixture as discussed in § 50:6, the priority between the creditors holding security interests therein and other creditors is determined by UCC § 9-313. Whether equipment becomes a fixture so as to come within the scope of this section is determined by the local non-Code law governing fixtures.

C. SECURED LOAN TRANSACTIONS

A secured transaction may be employed to protect one who lends on credit apart from a sale, as well as protecting sellers and the persons financing the sale of goods. In the former situation, the secured transaction may be one in which the collateral is delivered to or pledged with the creditor, or it may be one in which the borrower retains possession of the collateral.

§ 35:8. Pledge. A *pledge* is a secured transaction in which the lender is given possession of the personal property or collateral subject to the security interest. More specifically, a pledge is a bailment created as security for the payment of a debt. Under a pledge, specific property is delivered into the possession of a bailee-creditor with the authority, express or implied, that in the event that the debt is not paid, the property may be sold and the proceeds of the sale applied to discharge the debt secured by the pledge.

---

[16] UCC § 9-505(22). In this situation the secured creditor must give notice not only to the debtor but also to any other party who has an interest in the goods and who has properly filed a financing statement.

[17] UCC § 9-109(2).

[18] UCC § 9-302(1), (c), (3).

For example, a person borrowing $1,000 may give the creditor property worth $1,000 or more to hold as security. In contrast, the mere recital that a debt is "secured by a pledge" of specified property, does not create a pledge when the creditor does not have possession of that property.[19]

If the borrower repays the loan, the property which is pledged is returned by the creditor. If the loan is not repaid, the creditor may sell the property and reduce the debt by the amount of the net proceeds of the sale. Notice of the sale must be given. The notice of a sale must be specific enough to identify the nature of the property to be sold so as to alert persons possibly interested in purchasing.

Upon default, the pledgee does not become the owner of the pledge but has merely the right to expose it to sale. If a fictitious sale of the property is made by the pledgee and then the pledgee actually does resell the property to a third person at a profit, the pledgor is entitled to damages for the loss caused thereby.

In general terms, the rights of the debtor (the *pledgor*) and the creditor (the *pledgee*) under a pledge relationship are the same as the rights of a buyer and seller under a secured credit sale of consumer goods. A distinction arises from the fact that the pledgee is given possession from the commencement of the secured transaction, whereas under a secured credit sale the secured party obtains possession only upon default. After a default occurs, the two transactions may be regarded as the same.

(a)   Creation and Perfection. The pledge relation arises as soon as it is agreed that the pledgee shall have a security interest in the property which is delivered to the pledgee and on the basis thereof the pledgee gives value, such as lending money.[20]

A contract of pledge provides for (1) possession of the pledged property passing from the pledgor to the pledgee; (2) legal title of the pledged property remaining in the pledgor; (3) the pledgee having a lien on the property for the payment of the debt; (4) the pledgor having a right of redemption of the property.

Perfection arises from the fact that the collateral is in the possession of the creditor and filing is not required.[21]

If the creditor returns the pledged property to the debtor, the pledge is terminated.

(b)   Duties of Pledgee. Because the secured party or pledgee is in possession of the property or collateral, reasonable care must be exercised in preserving the property and the creditor is liable for damage which results from failing to do so.[22] The pledgee must keep the collateral separate and identified, although fungible goods of the same kind and quality may be commingled. If money, such as dividends, is received by the pledgee by virtue of holding the collateral, such money must be applied to the reduction of the debt or sent to the debtor.

Commercial paper may be transferred by way of pledge.[23]

---

[19] New Iberia National Bank v Teeter Mobile Home Sales, Inc. (La App) 300 So2d 635.

[20] UCC § 9-204(1).

[21] UCC §§ 9-302(1)(a), 9-305.

[22] UCC § 9-207(1), (3). The reasonable expenses of caring for the collateral, including insurance and taxes, are charged to the debtor and are secured by the collateral. UCC § 9-207(2)(a).

[23] Salem Development Co. v Ross, 251 CalApp2d 53, 59 CalRptr 548. The collection rights of the creditor as respects parties on the paper are defined by UCC § 9-502. As the pledge will ordinarily be accompanied by an indorsing of the paper, the creditor will be a holder of the commercial paper and will have the rights of such.

§ 35:9. Pawn. The term *pawn* is often used to indicate a pledge of tangible personal property, rather than documents representing property rights. A person engaged in the business of lending money at interest, in which a pawn is required as security, is known as a *pawnbroker.* In order to avoid usurious loan practices and trafficking in stolen goods, the business of professional pawnbroking is generally regulated by statute. State and municipal regulations commonly require the licensing of pawnbrokers, and regulate the general conduct of the business and the charges that may be made for loans. In most states pawnbrokers are permitted to charge a higher rate of interest on small loans than would otherwise be legal.

§ 35:10. Securing of Debt Without Change of Possession. This situation is illustrated by the owner of a television set who borrows money from the bank and, to protect the latter, gives the bank a security interest in the television. In general terms, the relation between the lender and the borrower is regulated in the same manner as in the case of a secured credit sale of inventory goods. Filing is required whether or not the collateral constitutes consumer goods. When there is a default in the payment of the debt, the lender has the same choice of remedies under such a secured transaction as does the secured credit seller of inventory.

§ 35:11. Security Interest in Goods Being Manufactured. A manufacturer may borrow and use as collateral goods that are partly finished or goods not yet manufactured. In such a case, the financing party and the manufacturer execute a security agreement giving the lender a security interest in existing goods and in goods to be manufactured thereafter, and the proceeds of all such goods. In general, this security transaction follows the same pattern as a secured credit sale of inventory.

D. SURETYSHIP AND GUARANTY

The relationship by which one person becomes responsible for the debt or undertaking of another person is used most commonly to insure that a debt will be paid or that a contractor will perform the work called for by the contract. A distinction may be made between the two kinds of such agreements. One kind is called a contract or undertaking of *suretyship,* and the third person is called a *surety.* The other kind is called a contract or undertaking of *guaranty,* and the third person is called a *guarantor.* In both cases the person who owes the money or is under the original obligation to pay or perform is called the *principal,* the principal debtor, or debtor, and the person to whom the debt or obligation is owed is known as the *creditor.*[24]

Suretyship and guaranty undertakings have the common feature of a promise to answer for the debt or default of another; but they have a basic difference. The surety is primarily liable for the debt or obligation of the principal; ordinarily the guarantor is only secondarily liable. This means that the moment the principal is in default, the creditor may demand performance or payment of the surety. The creditor generally cannot do so in the case of the guarantor and must first attempt to collect

---

[24] Unless otherwise stated, "surety" as used in the text includes guarantor as well as surety, and "guaranty" is limited to a conditional guaranty. The word "principal" is also used by the law to identify the person who employs an agent. The "principal" in suretyship must be distinguished from the agent's "principal."

from the principal. An exception is an "absolute guaranty" which creates the same obligation as a suretyship. A guaranty of payment creates an absolute guaranty.

There is frequently confusion in the use of the terms suretyship and guaranty, and it becomes a question of construction to determine what the parties really intended by their contract. In some states a statute provides that an undertaking to answer for the debt of another is to be interpreted as a suretyship agreement in the absence of an express statement that only a guaranty agreement was intended. In some states the distinction is in effect abolished.

§ 35:12. Indemnity Contract. Both suretyship and guaranty differ from an *indemnity contract,* which is an undertaking by one person for a consideration to pay another person a sum of money in the event that the other person sustains a specified loss. A fire insurance policy is a typical example of an indemnity contract.

§ 35:13. Creation of the Relation. The suretyship and guaranty relationships are ordinarily based upon contract, express or implied. All of the principles applicable to the capacity, formation, validity, and interpretation of contracts are therefore generally applicable.

Generally the ordinary rules of offer and acceptance apply. Notice of the acceptance, however, must sometimes be given by the creditor to the guarantor.

In most states, the statute of frauds requires that contracts of guaranty be in writing in order to be enforceable, subject to the exception that no writing is required when the promise is made primarily for the promisor's benefit.

In the absence of a special statute, no writing is required for contracts of suretyship or indemnity, because they impose primary liability, and not a secondary liability to answer for the debt or default of another. Special statutes or sound business practice, however, commonly require the use of written contracts for both suretyship and indemnity.

When the contract of guaranty is made at the same time as the original transaction, the consideration for the original promise which is covered by the guaranty is also consideration for the performance of the guarantor. When the guaranty contract is entered into subsequent to the original transaction, it is necessary that there be a new consideration for the promise of the guarantor.[25]

§ 35:14. Rights of Surety. Sureties have a number of rights to protect them from sustaining loss, to obtain their discharge because of the conduct of others that would be harmful to them, or to recover money that they were required to pay because of the debtor's breach.

(a)   Exoneration. If the surety finds its position threatened with danger, as when the debtor is about to leave the state, the surety may call upon the creditor to take action against the debtor. If at that time, the creditor could proceed against the debtor and fails to do so, the surety is released or exonerated from liability to the extent that the surety has been harmed by such failure.

(b)   Subrogation. When a surety pays a debt that it is obligated to pay, it automatically acquires the claim and the rights of the creditor. This is known as *subrogation.* That

---

[25] Union National Bank v Schimke (ND) 210 NW2d 176.

is, once the creditor is paid in full, the surety stands in the same position as the creditor and may sue the debtor or enforce any security that was available to the creditor in order to recover the amount it has paid. The effect is the same as if the creditor, on being paid, made an express assignment of all rights to the surety.

The right of subrogation, which arises when a surety on a contractor's labor and material bond pays labor and material claimants is not a security interest and the surety is therefore entitled to recover the payments made even though no filing was made under the UCC.[26]

(c) Indemnity. A surety that has made payment of a claim for which it was liable as surety is entitled to indemnity from the principal, that is, it is entitled to demand from the principal reimbursement of the amount which it has paid.

(d) Contribution. If there are two or more sureties, each is liable to the creditor for the full amount of the debt, until the creditor has been paid in full. As between themselves, however, each is only liable for a proportionate share of the debt. Accordingly, if the surety has paid more than its share of the debt, it is entitled to demand that its co-sureties contribute to it in order to share the burden, which in the absence of a contrary agreement, must be borne equally.

§ 35:15. Defenses of the Surety. The surety's defenses include not only those that may be raised by a party to any contract but also the special defenses that are peculiar to the suretyship relation.

(a) Ordinary Defenses. Since the relationship of suretyship is based upon a contract, the surety may raise any defense that a party to an ordinary contract may raise, such as lack of capacity of parties, absence of consideration, fraud, or mistake.

Fraud and concealment are common defenses. Since the risk of the principal's default is thrown upon the surety, it is unfair for the creditor to conceal from the surety facts that are material to the surety's risk.

Fraud on the part of the principal that is unknown to the creditor and in which the creditor has not taken part does not ordinarily release the surety.

(1) Disclosure. By common law the creditor was not required to volunteer information to the surety and was not required to disclose that the principal was insolvent. There is a growing modern view which requires the creditor to inform the surety of matters material to the risk when the creditor has reason to believe that the surety does not possess such information. (See p. 591, Sumitomo Bank v Iwasaki) Thus, the creditor is under a duty to inform the surety when there is reason to believe that the surety is in effect walking into a trap of which it is not aware. That is, the creditor is required to volunteer information it possesses about the principal when (a) the creditor has reason to believe that those facts materially increase risk beyond that which surety intends to assume; (b) the creditor has reason to believe that the facts are unknown to surety; and (c) the creditor has reasonable opportunity to communicate the facts to the surety.

---

[26] Jacobs v Northeastern Corp. 416 Pa 417, 206 A2d 49.

(b)   Suretyship Defenses. In addition to the ordinary defenses that can be raised against any contract, the following defenses are peculiar to the suretyship relation:

(1) Invalidity of original obligation.

(2) Discharge of principal by payment or any other means.

(3) Material modification of the original contract to which the surety does not consent, as by a binding extension of time for performance.

The compensated surety of a building contractor is not discharged when the owner makes payments to the contractor earlier than called for by the contract, unless it can show that it was prejudiced thereby and then it is only discharged to the extent of such prejudice.

To discharge a surety by the granting of an extension, there must be a binding contract to forebear. The fact that the creditor accepts two late payments does not establish such a contract to forebear and hence does not discharge the surety.

(4) Loss of securities that had been given the creditor to hold as additional security for the performance of the original contract, to the extent that such loss is caused by the misconduct or negligence of the creditor. For example, a surety, whether compensated or not, is discharged when the creditor fails to perfect the security interest which secures the debt for which the surety is obligated, because this means that collateral is impaired or destroyed which would have been available for the reimbursement of a surety if the interest had been perfected.[27]

E. LETTERS OF CREDIT

A letter of credit is a form of agreement that the issuer of the letter will pay drafts drawn by the creditor. It is thus a form of advance arranging of financing in that it is known in advance how much money may be obtained from the issuer of the letter. It is likewise a security device because the creditor knows that the drafts which the creditor draws will be accepted or paid by the issuer of the letter.

The use of letters of credit arose in international trade. While this continues to be the primary area of use, there is a growing use of letters in domestic sales and in transactions in which the letter of credit takes the place of a surety bond. Thus a letter of credit has been used to assure that a borrower would repay a loan, that a tenant would pay the rent due under a lease, and that a contractor would properly perform a construction contract.[28]

Article 5 of the Uniform Commercial Code establishes certain minimum requirements for letters of credit but for the most part they are governed in international trade by Rules of the International Chamber of Commerce.[29]

§ 35:16. Definition, Parties, and Duration.

(a)   Definition. A letter of credit is an engagement by its issuer that it will pay or accept drafts when the conditions specified in the letter are satisfied. The issuer is usually a bank.

---

[27] Ramsey Nat. Bank & Trust Co. v Suburban Sales & Service, Inc. (ND) 231 NW2d 732.

[28] When so used, it is commonly called a *standby* letter of credit.

[29] "Uniform Customs and Practice for Documentary Credits, fixed by the Thirteenth Congress of the International Chamber of Commerce . . . is the standard reference for banks dealing with letters of credit." Barclays Bank D.C.O. v The Mercantile National Bank (CA5 Ga) 481 F2d 1224.

Three contracts are involved in most letter-of-credit transactions: (1) the contract between the issuer and the account party for the issuance of the credit; (2) the letter of credit itself; and (3) the underlying agreement, often a contract of sale, between the beneficiary and the account party. The letter of credit is completely independent from the other two contracts.[30]

The issuer of the letter of credit is not a surety that is underwriting payment by its customer. (See p. 592, Travelers Indemnity Co. v Flushing National Bank) The issuer of the letter is in effect the obligor on a third party beneficiary contract made for the benefit of the beneficiary of the letter.[31]

(b)   Parties. The parties to a letter of credit are (1) the issuer, (2) the customer who makes the arrangements with the issuer, and (3) the beneficiary who will be the drawer of the drafts which will be drawn under the letter of credit. There may also be (4) an advising bank.[32] This will occur when the local issuer of the letter of credit requests its correspondent bank where the beneficiary is located to notify or advise the beneficiary that the letter has been issued.

As an illustration of the above definitions, an American merchant may buy goods from a Spanish merchant. There may be a prior course of dealings between the parties so that the seller is willing to accept the buyer's commercial paper as payment or to accept trade acceptances drawn on the buyer. If the foreign seller is not willing to do this, the American buyer, as customer, may go to a bank, the issuer, and obtain a letter of credit naming the Spanish seller as beneficiary. The American bank's correspondent or advising bank in Spain notifies the Spanish seller that this has been done. The Spanish seller will then draw drafts on the American buyer. By the letter of credit, the issuer is required to accept or pay these drafts.

(c)   Duration. A letter of credit continues for any time specified in the letter. Generally a maximum amount is stated in the letter so that the letter is exhausted or used up when drafts aggregating that maximum amount have been accepted or paid by the issuer. A letter of credit may be used in installments as the beneficiary chooses. A letter of credit cannot be revoked or modified by the issuer or the customer without the consent of the beneficiary unless that right is expressly reserved in the letter.

§ 35:17. Form. A letter of credit must be in writing and signed by the issuer. Other than this, any form is sufficient. Consideration is not required to establish or to modify a letter of credit.

§ 35:18. Duty of Issuer. The issuer is obligated to honor drafts drawn under the letter of credit if the conditions specified in the letter have been satisfied. Generally this means that the bank must assure itself that all specified papers have been submitted. The issuer has no duty to verify that the papers are properly supported by facts or that the underlying transaction has been performed. It is thus immaterial that the goods sold by the seller in fact do not conform to the contract as long as the seller tenders the documents specified by the letter of credit.[33]

---

[30] Barclays Bank D.C.O. v The Mercantile National Bank (CA5 Ga) 481 F2d 1224.
[31] Courtaulds North America, Inc. v North Carolina Nat. Bank, (DC NC) 387 FSupp 92 revd on other grounds (CA4 NC) 528 F2d 802.
[32] UCC § 5-103(e).
[33] Intraworld Industries, Inc. v Girard Trust Bank, 461 Pa 343, 336 A2d 316.

(a)   Liability of Issuer for Wrongful Dishonor. If the issuer dishonors a draft without justification, it is liable to its customer for breach of contract. The issuer is also liable to the beneficiary, as though the issuer had accepted the draft and then dishonored it.

The fact that the beneficiary of the letter of credit may be guilty of a breach of contract or of fraud with respect to the customer of the bank cannot be raised as a defense when the drafts have been negotiated to a third person who is not a party to any misconduct.[34]

§ 35:19. Liability of Beneficiary. The beneficiary of a letter of credit is a drawer and therefore has a drawer's liability with respect to the paper drawn under the letter. When the beneficiary-drawer presents the paper for acceptance or payment, the beneficiary-drawer becomes subject to the ordinary warranty liabilities specified by Article 3 of the UCC. In addition, the beneficiary-drawer warrants that all necessary conditions specified in the letter of credit have been satisfied.[35]

---

[34] United Bank, Ltd. v Cambridge Sporting Goods Corp., 49 AppDiv2d 868, 374 NYS2d 639.
[35] UCC § 5-111(1).

CASES FOR CHAPTER 35

Mosley v Dallas Entertainment Co., Inc.

(Tex Civ App) 496 SW2d 237 (1973)

The Dallas Entertainment Company operated a club, the Music Box, which it sold to Follies Buffet. A cash register was included in the property which was sold. Dallas and Follies Buffet orally agreed that Dallas was to have a security interest in the property which was sold by Dallas and a financing statement was filed covering all property and equipment. The statement did not specifically describe the cash register. No security agreement was executed. Follies Buffet later sold the cash register to Mosley who resold it to another person. Dallas Entertainment sued Mosley for conversion on the theory that Dallas had a security interest in the cash register which was converted by the act of selling the cash register without its consent. Judgment was entered for Dallas. Mosley appealed.

MOORE, J. . . . Appellant, Bill Mosley, was in the business of buying and selling used cash registers and does not dispute the fact that he purchased the cash register from Follies Buffet in December, 1970, and that he subsequently sold the cash register to a customer in the course of his business. It is not contended that appellant had actual knowledge

of appellee's alleged security interests in the cash register.

[UCC § 9-203(c)] provides that subject to certain exceptions not applicable here, ". . . a security interest is not enforceable against the debtor or third parties unless . . . (2) the debtor has signed a security agreement which contains a description of the collateral. . . ."

By his first four points appellant attacks the judgment on the ground that there is no evidence or alternatively that the evidence is insufficient to show appellee was a secured party under a Security Agreement executed by the debtor because appellee failed to produce a written security agreement. Appellee does not deny that it was required to prove that it had a written security agreement signed by the debtor describing the cash register and that no such security agreement was introduced in evidence. In reply appellee contends first that there is competent oral testimony to prove the existence of a security agreement and secondly that the financing statement itself amounts to a security agreement.

The only evidence of a security agreement is to be found in the oral testimony of Peggy Foley, appellee's president. When viewed in a light most favorable to the judgment her testimony shows that Dallas Entertainment Company received a note and a security agreement at the time the Music Box was sold to Follies Buffet which was signed by a Dr. Cullen. During the course of her testimony she identified an instrument as the security agreement but when the instrument was offered in evidence counsel for appellant objected on the ground the instrument was not signed. The court sustained the objection and the instrument does not appear in the record. Upon being asked whether she had "an independent recollection that Dallas Entertainment Company, Inc. obtained a security interest in a cash register," she replied "Yes. I do." She was not asked nor did she testify that the cash register involved in this suit was described in the security agreement.

The first question for our determination is whether the judgment of the trial court can be sustained on the theory that a security agreement may be established by parol evidence.

We have been unable to find any Texas case interpreting the applicable provisions of the Uniform Commercial Code and therefore must make our own interpretation of the statute aided by authorities from other jurisdictions having similar statutes.

A "security interest" in personal property means an interest which secures payment or performance of an obligation. § 1-201(37). "Security Agreement" is defined in § 9-105(8) as being the bargain of the parties in fact. The requirement that there must be an agreement, not only in connection with § 1-201(3), but also in connection with § 9-203(a)(2) which requires that security agreements be written.

In paragraph 5 of the Uniform Commercial Code Comment following § 9-203, supra, we find this statement: "The formal requisites stated in this Section are not only conditions to the enforceability of a security interest against third parties. They are in the nature of a Statute of Frauds. Unless the secured party is in possession of the collateral, his security interest, absent a writing which satisfies [the UCC,] is not enforceable even against the debtor, and cannot be made so on any theory of equitable mortgage or the like. . . ."

In American Card Company, Inc. v H. M. H. Co., 196 A2d 150 (RI Sup Ct, 1966), the court specifically rejected the argument that the security agreement could be established by parol, stating that oral assertions were without probative force to supply the absence of a required security agreement in writing. . . .

Since the foregoing statute requires the secured party to show that the debtor has signed a security agreement containing a description of the collateral, we hold that the oral testimony of the secured party is without probative force to establish a security interest for the simple reason that it fails to satisfy the statutory requirement that the security agreement be in writing and signed by the debtor.

This brings us to the question of whether the judgment may be sustained on the theory that the financing statement amounts to a security agreement. The financing statement in this case appears to have been written on the Secretary of State's standard form. As noted above, it recites a general description of the collateral in which a security interest is claimed. It is signed by the creditor, appellee, and by a party alleged to be the agent of Follies, though the character of that signature was never established in the trial of this case. Nowhere in the instrument does it grant the creditor a security interest in the collateral nor does it identify the obligation owed to the creditor.

The code makes no provision for a naked financing statement to be enforced as a security agreement. It merely gives notice of the existence of a security interest but in itself does not create a security interest. Anderson, Uniform Commercial Code, 2d Ed. § 9-402:4. A financing statement cannot serve as a security agreement where it does not grant the creditor an interest in the collateral and does not identify the obligation owed to the creditor. . . . Since the financing statement offered by appellee fails to contain any language showing the alleged debtor granted the creditor (appellee) an interest in the collateral and since appellee was unable to produce a written security agreement signed by appellant, appellee failed to establish a cause of action. . . .

[Judgment reversed]

Galleon Industries, Inc. v Lewyn Machinery Co., Inc.

50 Ala App 334, 279 So2d 137 (1973)

In 1969 Galleon borrowed money from the Central Bank and Trust Company. As security for the loan, Galleon gave Central a security interest in the equipment and inventory owned or thereafter acquired by Galleon. Central filed a financing statement and perfected this security interest. Thereafter, in 1970, Lewyn sold equipment to Galleon. The equipment was made by Lancaster and the sale was to be made for cash but, through a mistake, the goods were sent by Lancaster directly to Galleon before

it paid for the goods. Lewyn then sent Galleon an invoice stating that payment was to be made "net 30 days." Galleon failed to pay the loan to Central Bank and Trust Company and it took possession of the equipment sold by Lewyn, claiming such equipment under the authority of the after-acquired property clause. Lewyn then sued Galleon and Central Bank to obtain possession of the equipment. From a judgment for Lewyn, Central Bank appealed.

WRIGHT, J. . . . Plaintiff, Lewyn, presented his case on the theory that title to the machine did not pass to Galleon until it had been paid for and since Galleon never paid, the title, and thus the right to possession, remained in Lewyn. We consider that the vesting of rights, as required under § 9-204 of the Uniform Commercial Code, and not the passing of title (§ 2-401) is the question to be determined on this appeal. The provisions of § 2-401 are explicitly subject to the provisions of Article 9—therefore, the question being the effect of Central's after-acquired property clause, we will limit our discussion to whether or not sufficient rights did in fact vest in the buyer Galleon, for Central's perfected security interest to attach.

It is without dispute in the evidence that the machine was shipped by the manufacturer to the buyer, Galleon. Lewyn stated that such shipment was by mistake, and that it was orally agreed between Galleon and Lewyn that delivery was not to be made except upon payment. However, after receiving notice of the shipment Lewyn sent to Galleon an invoice requiring payment "net in 30 days." Thus any prior agreement as to delivery and payment was modified or waived by Lewyn and Galleon became a credit buyer. We do not decide here the application of § 2-201, the Statute of Frauds, to the sales agreement. The effect of delivery, together with the invoice, was to limit any retention of rights or title to an explicit security agreement subject to the provisions of Article 9 of the Uniform Commercial Code as to perfection and priority. . . .

§ 9-202 states "Each provision of this Article with regards to rights, obligations or remedies applies whether title to collateral is in the secured party or in the debtor." It is stated in Anderson, Uniform Commercial Code, 2d Edition, Volume 2, page 26: "If it is the desire of the parties to effect a reservation of title until the purchase price be paid, a secured transaction should be entered into and a proper filing

made if required to protect the creditor's interest as against third persons."

§ 9-204 provides for a security agreement covering after-acquired property such as that held by Central. This section also provides the manner in which such security interest shall attach. In the case of the security interest of Central, it attached when the debtor, Galleon, acquired "rights" in the collateral covered by the security agreement. As we have previously stated, the delivery of the machine and the forwarding of the invoice stating "net 30 days" made Galleon a credit buyer. A credit buyer acquires "rights" in the property when possession is received from the seller. . . .

Lewyn, if retaining title until payment, by delivery to a credit buyer reserved only a purchase money security interest, such security interest was never perfected by filing as required by § 9-302. Lewyn could have perfected its purchase money security interest and received priority over the perfected security interest of Central by filing a financing statement at the time of delivery, or within 10 days thereafter. § 9-312(4). According to the evidence, Lewyn learned of the foreclosure and taking of possession by Central eight days after delivery to Galleon. There still remained two days for perfection of its security interest by filing a financing statement. Such filing would have given it priority over the perfected security interest of Central. § 9-312(4).

Since sufficient "rights" had passed to Galleon by delivery and the sending of the invoice, the requirements of § 9-204 were satisfied and the security interest of Central attached to the machine. The failure of Lewyn to perfect its security interest by filing within 10 days after delivery gave Central priority. Thus at the time of the filing of the suit. . . , Central had a superior right to possession.

We reject the argument of appellee that use of the term "equipment" in the after-acquired property clause of Central's security agreement is insufficient to include the machine involved. Under the evidence there is no question that the machine involved was to be used in the business of Galleon, and was placed within the premises as equipment. The sufficiency of a description in a financing statement is measured in terms of notice. Does the designation of "equipment now owned or hereafter acquired" give notice to a seller of a machine to be installed on the premises of an operating business and used in production that it is subject or likely to be subject to a perfected security interest? We hold it does. . . .

. . . Central Bank and Trust Company had a superior right to possession to the property sued for. . . .

[Judgment reversed and action remanded]

Taylor Motor Rental, Inc. v Associates Discount Corp.

196 Pa Super 182, 173 A2d 688 (1961)

Associates Discount Corp. held a perfected security interest in an automobile owned by McCurry Motors, Inc. The latter corporation sold the automobile to Taylor Motor Rental, Inc. When payments were not made of the installments due Associates, it repossessed the automobile. Taylor then sued it to recover the automobile. Associates showed that McCurry Motors and Taylor were two corporations that were both managed by Fred McCurry, that the two corporations had common officers, shareholders, and employees, and that Fred McCurry had applied for the state certificate of title in the name of Taylor. From a judgment in favor of Associates, Taylor appealed.

WOODSIDE, J. . . . [Quoting from the opinion of the lower court:] "The precise question in this case is which of the parties was entitled to possession of the automobile. Plaintiff claimed its right to possession by virtue of its purported purchase from McCurry, and the defendant claimed its right to possession of the automobile by virtue of its secured interest.

"There can be no question that the defendant had a valid and perfected security interest in the automobile under the provisions of the Uniform Commercial Code. . . .It gave value for the automobile by its payment of the purchase price to the Studebaker factory, it obtained a security agreement which described the automobile by serial number and it had on file in appropriate offices a properly executed financing statement which described the type of property it was financing for McCurry Motors. . . .

"Defendant's security interest in the automobile was enforceable against everyone, except as otherwise provided in the Commercial Code. . . . Plaintiff claims to be a buyer in the ordinary course of business and relies on (§ 9-307). . . .

"It is clear that plaintiff was not a buyer in the ordinary course of business as defined by the Commercial Code. Both the relationship of plaintiff and McCurry, with their interlocking officers, shareholders, and employees and the fact that both plaintiff corporation and McCurry Motors, Inc., were managed by Fred McCurry negates this. Moreover, Fred McCurry acted for both plaintiff and McCurry Motors, Inc., in applying for the certificate of title in the name of the plaintiff. . . . The purported sale by McCurry Motors, Inc., to the plaintiff was merely a paper transaction for the benefit of Fred McCurry [to obtain] the automobile for which defendant has never been paid.". . .

Only if the appellant were "a buyer in ordinary course of business" would it take free of the appellee's security interest. The facts set forth above clearly support the trial court's finding that the transaction was not in the ordinary course of business. . . .

[Judgment affirmed]

Code Comment: UCC § 9-307(1) provides "a buyer in ordinary course of business. . . . other than a person buying farm products from a person engaged in farming operations, takes free of a security interest created by his seller even though the security interest is perfected and even though the buyer knows of its existence." A buyer in ordinary course of business is defined as "a person who in good faith and without knowledge that the sale to him is in violation of the ownership rights or security interest of a third party in the goods buys in ordinary course from a person in the business of selling goods of that kind. . . ." UCC § 1-201(9).

Sumitomo Bank v Iwasaki

70 Cal 2d 81, 73 Cal Rptr 564, 447 P2d 956 (1968)

Frank Iwasaki sued the Sumitomo Bank to recover the loans which he had made to the Nagayamas and which the bank had guaranteed. The court held that the bank was not liable as to a "third loan" because Frank had not notified the bank that the loan was made to the Nagayamas in order for them to pay their federal taxes. Frank appealed.

TOBRINER, A. J. . . . This appeal presents an issue of first impression: whether a creditor owes a duty of disclosure to a surety on a continuing guaranty during the course, as well as at the inception, of the suretyship relationship, and if so, the nature and extent of that duty. We shall explain why we adopt the Restatement rule. That rule provides that each time the creditor accepts the continuing offer of a surety on a continuing guaranty by extending further credit to the principal debtor, the creditor owes a duty to the surety to disclose facts known by the creditor if the creditor has reason to believe that those facts materially increase the risk beyond that which the surety intended to assume and that those facts are unknown to the surety. (Rest., Security, § 124, subd. (1), com. *c.* pp. 327-328, 330.) . . .

In all suretyship relations, the creditor owes to the surety a duty of continuous good faith and fair dealing. . . . Thus, the creditor must not misrepresent or conceal facts so as to induce or permit the surety to enter or continue in the relationship in reliance on a false impression as to the nature of the risk. As with other contracts, a creditor's fraud, which may consist of intentional or negligent misrepresentation or active suppression of the truth, will discharge the surety as to any subsequently incurred liability. . . .

Section 124, subdivision (1), of the Restatement of Security prescribes three conditions prerequisite to imposition of a duty on a creditor to disclose facts it knows about the debtor to the surety. Those conditions are: (a) "the creditor has reason to believe" that those facts materially increase the risk "beyond that which the surety intends to assume"; (b) the creditor "has reason to believe that the facts are unknown to the surety"; and (c) the creditor "has a reasonable opportunity to communicate" the facts to the surety. . . . The creditor's failure to disclose such facts to the surety prior to an extension of further credit to the debtor will discharge the surety from liability on the subsequent loan only if all three conditions are satisfied. . . . If the evidence fails to establish any one of the three factors, a judgment discharging a surety from liability because of a breach of a duty of disclosure governed by section 124, subdivision (1), cannot stand. . . .

Although the evidence establishes that plaintiff knew about the Nagayamas' inability to pay their federal taxes without a loan, the evidence cannot establish that (a) plaintiff had reason to believe that this fact materially increased the risk beyond that which defendant intended to assume. The evidence cannot establish condition (a) because no evidence discloses the financial condition of the Nagayamas in July, 1961, when defendant executed the guaranty. As a result, no evidence describes the risk defendant intended to assume, or tells us whether plaintiff had reason to know what risk defendant intended to assume. Thus the evidence cannot support a finding that the Nagayamas' inability to pay their taxes without a loan materially increased defendant's risk. *A fortiori*, it cannot support a finding that *plaintiff had reason to believe* this fact materially increased defendant's risk. Indeed, the practice of borrowing funds to pay taxes and the resort to financial assistance for that purpose is so frequent in American life that its presence here surely does not establish that the creditor had reason to believe that this circumstance materially increased the risk beyond that which the surety intended to assume.

The evidence cannot support a finding that a necessary condition of section 124, subdivision (1), of the Restatement was satisfied.

The judgment, insofar as it rests upon the trial court's conclusion that defendant's performance as obligor on the third loan was excused, and insofar as it denies recovery to plaintiff on said third loan, is reversed. The cause is remanded to the trial court with directions to retry the issue of defendant's liability on said third loan. . . .

Travelers Indemnity Company v Flushing National Bank

396 NYS2d 754 (1977)

Berley was a party to a lawsuit. The court required him to file a $40,000 bond. The Travelers Indemnity Company issued the bond but required him to give it a certified check for $40,000 as security. Subsequently Berley obtained a letter of credit for $40,000 from the Flushing National Bank by which the bank agreed to honor drafts drawn upon it by the indemnity company when it incurred liability on the Berley bond. Berley gave this letter of credit to the indemnity company and took back his certified check. Thereafter a claim was made on the Berley bond. The indemnity company then drew a draft upon the bank pursuant to the letter of credit. The bank refused to pay the draft on the ground that the indemnity company had not given any consideration for the letter of credit and that the bank was released from liability because the indemnity company's release of the certified check constituted an impairment of collateral which released the bank as a surety.

FINZ, J. . . . The defendant bank now claims that it should be released from the terms of the letter of credit. . . .

It claims, first of all, that there was no consideration for the issuance of the letter of credit. . . . In addition, it asserts that the credit is unenforceable by reason of the fact that the plaintiff, having in its hands a certified check in the sum of $40,000, released the check and thereby released the defendant since the defendant was, in effect, a guarantor or a surety to the plaintiff. Lastly, the defendant bank alleges that it was the plaintiff's fraud and concealment of facts which have rendered the letter of credit unenforceable.

Before proceeding in any direction it is necessary to make clear the nature of a letter of credit.

" 'Credit' or 'letter of credit' means an engagement by a bank or other person made at the request of a customer and of a kind within the scope of this Article (Section 5-102) that the issuer will honor drafts or other demands for payment upon compliance with the conditions specified in the credit.". . .

"A letter of credit is a contract. It is distinguished by the fact that it is inevitably linked to another understanding, usually also a contract, but is independent of that other understanding or contract. Appreciation of these two simple concepts: that a letter of credit is a contract, and that the letter of credit contract stands alone to be construed within its own four corners, is sufficient to provide understanding of most complex letter of credit transactions. Such appreciation and continuing awareness, however, is not only sufficient to provide understanding, it is indispensable to avoid confusion.

Confining ourselves, as noted above, to bank letters of credit, the first fundamental is that the bank engage itself as a principal in the letter of credit transaction but is neither engaged in nor . . . in any way concerned with the understanding, contract, or transaction which may have made the letter of credit necessary or convenient.

The purpose of the letter of credit is to provide a method of payment, through banking channels, which defines the terms and conditions upon which *and only upon which the payment will be made,* and which, within the strict limits of those terms and conditions, engages the full *primary* responsibility of the bank to make the payment, in addition to whatever obligation may lie upon the party for whose account the bank has issued or confirmed the letter of credit. This is the only role which the bank undertakes, and its only engagement, legal, commercial, or moral. This is, in short, the limitation of the letter

of credit. If the limitation is recognized at all times by all interested parties, there is room neither for dispute nor for disappointment. Disappointment, disputes, and litigation arise only when one or another of the parties overlooks the functional limitation and takes the bank's letter of credit to be a guaranty of performance of some related but separate mercantile contract.". . . (McKinney's Consolidated Laws Uniform Commercial Code, Practice Commentary p. 642.)

The letter of credit, probably because of its simple structure and its unqualified agreement to pay, notwithstanding any condition outside of its own terms, has become a principal instrument of international trade and, increasingly, of domestic transactions. It is in this framework that the defenses raised by the defendant should be considered.

The fact that plaintiff did not rely on the letter of credit when it issued its bond is not relevant to the question of consideration for the issuance of the letter of credit. If this were an issue at all, the question of consideration only arises as between the issuer of the credit and its customer. The beneficiary . . . would not in any event give consideration to the issuer.

The problem of consideration does not arise, however, in view of UCC § 5-105, which states: "No consideration is necessary to establish a credit or to enlarge or otherwise modify its terms.". . .

A letter of credit, insofar as it is a contract, partakes of the rules of construction generally applicable to contracts. . . . Since there were no special rules adopted with regard to interpretation of the terms of a letter of credit, the ordinary rules of law apply (UCC § 1-103). "The same general principles which apply to other contracts in writing govern letters of credit. . . . Moreover, as between the beneficiary of a letter of credit and the issuer . . . if ambiguity exists, the words are taken as strongly against the issuer as a reasonable reading will justify. . . .

In addition, the beneficiary, when it presents a demand for payment or a draft, warrants that there has been compliance with the necessary conditions of the letter of credit (UCC § 5-111[1]).

The claim that the release of the collateral without knowledge or consent of the defendant, discharged the defendant's obligation as a surety, depends upon the relationship of the defendant and plaintiff.

"The issuer of a letter of credit does not have the status of a surety or guarantor. A surety is generally not liable on his undertaking unless his principal is liable and in default on the underlying liability. The defenses of the principal are available to the surety and, if the underlying debt is canceled, the surety's obligation ceases. (*Associacion de Azucareros de Guatemala v United States Nat. Bank* (CA9 Or) 423 F.2d 638). The letter of credit, unlike the classic surety undertaking, is a primary obligation between the issuer and the beneficiary. (See UCC § 5-114:1, pt 1,)" (Anderson Uniform Commercial Code, Second Edition, § 5-114:7.)

Undoubtedly, a guarantor or a surety has the right to expect that the terms upon which the guarantee was made would remain unchanged, absent the knowledge and consent to such change by the guarantor. A release of collateral or a change in the terms would certainly operate to release the surety or guarantor. . . .

In this case, the letter was not issued on the strength of any collateral held by the plaintiff. It is admitted in the affidavit in opposition that defendant had no knowledge that the bond was issued or how it was collateralized. It offered no guarantee to the plaintiff. It dealt entirely with its own customer. It had dealt with him on previous occasions and it knew that he had obligations which "were very substantial" and "the Bank was becoming concerned about Berley's ability to pay the loans . . . Berley owed the Bank nearly $300,000. when the letter of credit was issued." They had nearly five weeks, after being informed of all the circumstances, to inquire of the defendant as to the status of the bond. They questioned Berley as to the wording of the letter of credit and then, finally, accepted it, issuing the letter in the form suggested.

[Judgment for Travelers Indemnity Company]

QUESTIONS AND CASE PROBLEMS

1. What social forces are affected by permitting a floating lien?
2. Compare a security agreement and a financing statement.
3. When goods are sold by a manufacturer to a dealer who then resells them to the present owner, compare the right of the secured creditor of the manufacturer to repossess the goods with the right of the secured creditor of the dealer to repossess the goods.
4. Compare the liability of (a) a maker of a note, (b) the acceptor of a draft, and (c) the issuer of a letter of credit.
5. Henry Platt, who did business under the name of Platt Fur Co., owed money to The Finance Company of America. The financing statements filed by the latter to protect its interests described the debtor as Platt Fur Co. When Henry Platt went into bankruptcy, it was claimed that this financing statement was not sufficient because it was not in the name of Henry Platt. Decide. [In re Platt, (DC ED Pa) 257 F Supp 478]
6. Tiernan Building Corporation contracted with a builder, American Structures, Inc., for the construction of a building. A performance bond was executed by the Equitable Fire & Marine Insurance Company. The contract between the owner and the contractor stated that the building plans could not be changed without Equitable's consent. The contract specified that General Electric air conditioning units were to be installed. The contractor installed a different brand of units. This was done with Tiernan's consent but without the consent of Equitable. The substitute equipment was not satisfactory and had to be replaced. Tiernan sued Equitable for the cost of substituting new replacement units. Was Equitable liable? [Equitable Fire & Marine Ins. Co. v Tiernan Building Corp., (Fla App) 190 So2d 197]
7. Lambert loaned Heaton $25,000 for six months. Heaton gave a promissory note, payable at the end of six months, in the face amount of $30,000, thereby concealing the fact that usurious interest was charged. Under the local statute, the loan contract was, in

fact, void, because of the usury. Heaton obtained a bond from the United Bonding Insurance Co., which guaranteed to Lambert that the promissory note would be paid when due. When the note was not paid, Lambert sued Heaton and the bonding company. The latter raised the defense that its obligation was voided because the usurious character of the transaction had not been disclosed to it. Decide. [Lambert v Heaton, (Fla App) 134 So2d 536]

8. A. D. Runnels purchased goods from J. R. Watkins Co. He asked Hinds Runnels to sign a paper. This paper was, in fact, an agreement to guarantee that Hinds would pay for whatever A. D. Runnels would purchase from Watkins. When sued on this promise by Watkins, Hinds raised the defense that he signed some paper but did not know what he was signing. Was this a valid defense? [J. R. Watkins Co. v A. D. Runnels, 252 Miss 87, 172 So2d 567]

9. Are any of the following statements sufficient for a description of the collateral subject to a security interest:

(a) "Passenger and commercial automobiles financed by Girard Trust Corn Exchange Bank?" [Girard Trust Corn Exchange Bank v Warren Lepley Ford, Inc., No. 2, (Pa) 13 D&C 2d 119]

(b) "All present and future accounts receivable?" [Industrial Packaging Products Co. v Fort Pitt Packaging International, Inc., 399 Pa 643, 161 A2d 19]

(c) A description of an automobile that does not contain a serial number? [Girard Trust Corn Exchange Bank v Warren Lepley Ford, Inc., No. 2. (Pa) 13 D&C 2d 119]

10. Ranalli Construction Co. purchased on credit a construction machine, known as a John Deere Crawler Loader, from Melvin Tractor Equipment, Inc. Melvin filed a financing statement to perfect its security interest in the loader. In the statement, the name of the buyer was misspelled as "Ranelli." Ranalli thereafter sold the loader to Anklin, who resold it to Pahl. Melvin assigned the contract to John Deere Co. When Deere sought to recover possession of the loader from Pahl, it was claimed that Deere could not recover possession on the theory that the filing of the financing statement by Melvin had been fatally defective because of the misspelling of the buyer's name. Was the filing effective to protect Melvin's security interest? [John Deere Co. v Pahl, 59 Misc 2d 872, 300 NYS2d 701]

11. *A* borrowed money from *B*. He orally agreed that *B* should have a security interest in certain equipment that was standing in *A*'s yard. There was nothing in writing to show this and no filing of any kind was made. Nine days later, *B* took possession of the equipment. What kind of interest did *B* have in the equipment? [See Transport Equipment Co. v Guaranty State Bank (CA10 Kan) 518 F2d 377]

12. King was the president of Magnolia Swift Homes, Inc., a construction company. The corporation purchased building materials from John A. Denies Sons Co. King personally guaranteed that payment would be made for the purchases of Magnolia. Later Magnolia went through bankruptcy and was discharged. John A. Denies then sued King on his guaranty. King claimed that since the debt which he guaranteed had been discharged in bankruptcy, there was nothing for which he was liable. Decide. [King v John A. Denies Sons Co., 56 Tenn App 39, 404 SW2d 580]

13. Bank *B* loaned money to luncheonette *L*. *B* and *L* executed a security agreement giving *B* a security interest in "all of the contents of the luncheonette including equipment." *B* filed in the proper office a financing statement in which the collateral was described in the same manner as in the security agreement. Thereafter *S* sold *L* a cash register on credit and delivered it on the first of the month. When *L* did not pay the monthly installment on its loan from *B*, *B* took possession of the luncheonette equipment including the cash register. *S* claimed that it was entitled to the cash register. Decide. [National Cash Register Co. v Firestone & Co., 346 Mass 255, 191 NE2d 47]

14. *A* made a contract to purchase goods from *B*. In order to assure *B* that he would be paid, *A* obtained a letter of credit from the *C* bank. The letter was irrevocable and provided that *C* would honor drafts for the purchase price of goods shipped to *A* upon presentment to the bank of the drafts, the bill of lading showing shipment to *A*, and the invoice showing the nature and price of the goods shipped. Because of financial difficulties. *A* did not want to receive the goods under the contract and made an agreement with *C* that no drafts would be honored pursuant to the letter of credit. *B* shipped goods to *A* under the contract and presented drafts, and the proper bills of lading, and invoices to *C*. *C* refused to honor the drafts. *B* sued *C*. It claimed that it was not liable because the letter of credit which had obligated it to accept the drafts had been terminated by the agreement of its customer. Was this a valid defense? [See Zeevi & Sons, Ltd. v Grindlays Bank (Uganda), Ltd., 37 NY2d 220, 371 NYS2d 892, 333 NE2d, 168, cert den 423 US 866.]

15. Hesser purchased an automobile on credit. The purchase was financed through the Schenectady Discount Corporation which had a security interest in the car. Hesser sold the car to NuTrend, Inc. It resold the car to Welch. Schenectady was not paid the installments that were due and it repossessed the car from Welch acting under the authority of its security interest. Welch claimed that Schenectady's security interest had been destroyed by the successive sales of the car. He claimed that UCC § 9-307 destroyed the security interest. Was Schenectady entitled to possession? [Black v Schenectady Discount Corp., 31 ConnSupp 521, 324 A2d 921]

16. A security agreement identified items *A, B,* and *C* as the collateral. A financing statement was filed which identified the collateral as items *B, C,* and *D*. The trustee in bankruptcy of the debtor claimed that because of the conflict in descriptions between the financing statement and the security agreement there was no valid secured transaction. Was he correct? [See Mitchell v Shepherd Mall State Bank (DC Okla) 324 FSupp 1029, affd (CA10 Okla) 458 F2d 700]

17. *A* owned a store. He borrowed from the *B* Bank and gave the Bank a security interest in the "inventory" of the store. The security agreement described the collateral as inventory but did not contain any provision as to after-acquired property. *A* later went bankrupt and his trustee in bankruptcy claimed the secured transaction did not bind after-acquired property because the security agreement did not expressly state that it did. Was the trustee correct? [See Re Fibre Glass Boat Corp. (DC Fla) 324 FSupp 1054, affd (CA5 Fla) 448 F2d 781]

18. The Girard Trust Corn Exchange Bank financed the purchase of new cars by Warren Lepley Ford, Inc., an automobile dealer. A security agreement was executed between the bank and the dealer, and proper filing was made. Thereafter, the dealer sold the cars that had been purchased as the result of this transaction with the bank and then purchased other cars with the proceeds of the money. Warren Lepley later became insolvent. Girard Trust claimed that it was entitled to a security interest in the subsequently-purchased cars in the hands of the receiver. The receiver contended that the right of the bank did not go beyond the cash proceeds and was lost once the cash proceeds were spent in any way. Decide. [Girard Trust Corn Exchange Bank v Warren Lepley Ford, Inc., No 3. (Pa) 25 D&C 2d 395]

36 Insurance

Insurance is a contract by which a promise is made to pay another a sum of money if the latter sustains a specified loss. Insurance is basically a plan of security against risk by charging losses against a fund created by the *premiums* or payments made by many individuals.

§ 36:1. The Parties. The promisor in an insurance contract is called the *insurer,* sometimes the underwriter. The person to whom the promise is made is the *insured,* the assured, or the policyholder. The promise of the insurer is generally set forth in a written contract called a *policy.*

As a result of statutory regulation, virtually all insurance policies today are written by corporations, fraternal or benefit societies, and national or state governments.

The insured must have the capacity to make a contract. At common law, a minor's insurance contract could be avoided. Statutes increasingly change this and make the minor's contract of insurance as binding as though the minor were an adult.

Insurance contracts are ordinarily made through an agent or a broker. The *insurance agent* is an agent of the insurance company, generally working exclusively for one company. For the most part, the ordinary rules of agency law govern the dealings between this agent and the applicant for insurance.

The *insurance broker* is generally an independent contractor who is not employed by any one insurance company. In some situations, the broker is the agent of the applicant. Under some statutes, the broker is made an agent of the insurer with respect to payments made by the applicant for transmission to the insurer.

§ 36:2. Insurable Interest. The insured must have an insurable interest in the subject matter insured. If not, the insurance contract cannot be enforced.

(a)   Insurable Interest in Property. A person has an insurable interest in property whenever the destruction of the property will cause a direct pecuniary or money loss to that person.

A partner has an insurable interest in property owned by the partnership, as its destruction would cause the partner an actual and substantial economic loss. This is so, even though with respect to "ownership," it is the partnership which owns the property.

It is immaterial whether the insured is the owner of the legal or equitable title, a lienholder, or a person in possession of the property. Thus, a person who is merely a possessor, such as the innocent purchaser of a stolen automobile, has an insurable interest therein. Likewise, a contractor remodeling a building has an insurable interest in the building to the extent of the money that will be paid under the contract; because the contractor would not be able to receive that money if the building were destroyed by fire.

In the case of property insurance, the insurable interest must exist at the time the loss occurs.[1] (See p. 603, Universal C.I.T. Credit Corp. v Foundation Reserve Insurance Co.) Except when expressly required by statute, it is not necessary that the interest exist at the time when the policy or contract of insurance was made.

(b)   Insurable Interest in Life. A person who obtains life insurance can generally name anyone as beneficiary regardless of whether that beneficiary has an insurable interest in the life of the insured. If the beneficiary obtains the policy, the beneficiary must have an insurable interest in the life of the insured. Such an interest exists if the beneficiary can reasonably expect to receive pecuniary gain from the continued life of the other person and, conversely, would suffer financial loss from the latter's death. Thus, it is held that a creditor has an insurable interest in the life of the debtor since the death of the debtor may mean that the creditor will not be paid the amount owed. The creditor may take out insurance in excess of the amount of the debt; but if the amount of the insurance is unreasonably greater than the debt, the policy will generally be void.

A partnership has an insurable interest in the life of each of the partners, for the death of any one of them will dissolve the firm and cause some degree of loss to the partnership. A business enterprise has an insurable interest in the life of an executive or a key employee because that person's death would inflict a financial loss upon the business to the extent that a replacement was not readily available or could not be found.

In the case of life insurance the insurable interest must exist at the time the policy is obtained. It is immaterial that the interest no longer exists when the loss is actually sustained. Thus, the fact that the insured husband and wife beneficiary are divorced after the life insurance policy was procured does not affect the validity of the policy.

Whether a person has an insurable interest is a matter to be raised by the insurance company. It cannot be raised by one beneficiary seeking to disqualify another beneficiary.

Where an insurer issues a policy to a beneficiary who has no insurable interest in the insured's life and particularly when it does so without the consent of the insured, it has been held that the insurer is liable for tort damages to the estate of the insured when the beneficiary thereafter kills the insured in order to collect on the insurance.[2]

---

[1] In some jurisdictions this rule is declared by statute. Fenter v General Accident Fire and Life Assurance Corp., 258 Ore 545, 484 P2d 310.

[2] Ramay v Carolina Life Insurance Co. 244 SC 16, 135 SE2d 362.

§ 36:3. The Insurance Contract. The formation of the contract of insurance is governed by the general principles applicable to contracts. Frequently a question arises as to whether advertising material, estimates, and statistical projections constitute a part of the contract.

By statute it is now commonly provided that an insurance policy must be written. In order to avoid deception, many statutes also specify the content of certain policies, in whole or in part, and some specify the size and style of type to be used in printing them. Provisions in a policy in conflict with a statute are generally void.

In the absence of statute or government regulation, an insurer may enter into a contract of insurance on such terms and upon such examination as it deems fit. An insurer that sold air flight insurance through a vending machine was held not liable to surviving heirs of other passengers killed when the insured caused the plane to crash. The fact that the insurer did not screen persons purchasing flight insurance to determine the existence of any suicide or murder potential did not make the insurer liable for negligence.

(a) The Application as Part of the Contract. The application for insurance is generally attached to the policy when issued and is made part of the contract of insurance by express stipulation of the policy.

The insured must examine the policy and an attached application. Any false statement in the application binds the insured if the policy and the attached application are retained without objection to such statement.[3]

§ 36:4. When the Insurance Contract is Effective.

(a) Preliminary Insurance. An applicant for insurance may or may not be protected by insurance before the written policy is issued. Four situations may arise:

(1) When the applicant tells a broker to obtain property or liability insurance, the applicant is merely employing the broker as agent. If the broker procures a policy, the customer is insured. If the broker fails to do so, the customer does not have any insurance, but the broker may be personally liable to the customer for the loss.

(2) The person seeking insurance and the insurer or its agent may orally agree that the applicant will be protected by insurance during the interval between the time the application is received and the time when the insurer either rejects the application, or accepts it and issues a policy. This agreement to protect the applicant by insurance during such an interval is binding even though it is oral.[4] Generally, however, when such a preliminary contract is made, the agent will sign a memorandum stating the essential terms of the policy to be executed. This oral contract and the written memorandum are called *binders*.[5]

An "oral binder" of insurance is a temporary contract which terminates when the written policy contemplated by it is issued. (See p. 603, Flester v Ohio Casualty Insurance Company) In some states, a maximum duration for an oral contract of insurance is set by statute.

---

[3] Galanis v Mercury International Insurance Underwriters, 247 CalApp2d 690, 55 CalRptr 890.
[4] Overton v Washington National Insurance Co. 106 RI 387, 260 A2d 444.
[5] Altrocchi v Hammond, 17 IllApp2d 192, 149 NE2d 646.

(3) The parties may agree that at a later time a policy will be issued and delivered. In that case the insurance contract is not in effect until the policy is delivered or sent to the applicant. Accordingly, loss sustained after the transaction between the applicant and the insurance agent but before the delivery of the policy is not covered by the policy thereafter delivered.

(4) The parties may agree that a policy of life insurance shall be binding upon the payment of the first premium even though the applicant has not been examined, provided the applicant passes an examination. If death occurs before the examination, it is generally held that the applicant's death is covered by insurance if a fair examination would have been passed.

When the application clearly states that the policy is not in force until the applicant is approved as a risk by an authorized officer of the insurer, coverage is not effective at the time of paying the first premium and submitting the application to the soliciting agent, even though the latter wrongly informs the applicant that the policy is effective.

(b)   Delivery of Policy. Ordinarily delivery of the policy is not essential to the existence of a contract of insurance. As an exception, delivery of the policy may be made an express condition to coverage.

(c)   Prepayment of Premiums. Ordinarily a contract of property insurance exists even though the premium due has not been paid. Thus, it is possible to effect property and liability insurance in most cases by an oral binder or agreement, as by a telephone call. In the case of life insurance policies, it is common to require both delivery of the policy to the insured while in a condition of good health and the prepayment of the first premium on the policy.

(d)   When Coverage is Effective. Distinct from the question of when is there a contract of insurance is the question of when does the coverage of the risk commence under a contract of insurance. Some policies of insurance do not cover the specified risk until after a certain period of time has elapsed after the policy becomes binding. That is, there is a waiting period before the contract of insurance provides protection. In most kinds of insurance, the coverage is immediately effective so that there is no waiting period once the insurer has accepted the application and there is a contract of insurance. (See p. 604, Metts v Central Standard Life Ins. Co.)

(e)   Machine-vended Insurance. When insurance is sold by a vending machine, as in the case of air flight insurance, it becomes effective when the applicant places the application and the premium in the machine and receives a receipt.

§ 36:5. Modification of Contract. In order to make changes or corrections to the policy, it is not necessary to issue a new policy. An indorsement on the policy or the execution of a separate *rider* is effective for the purpose of changing the policy.

When a provision of an indorsement conflicts with a provision of the policy, the indorsement controls because it is the later document.

§ 36:6. Interpretation of Insurance Contract. The contract of insurance is interpreted by the same rules that govern the interpretation of ordinary contracts. Words are to be given their ordinary meaning and interpreted in the light of the nature of the coverage intended. (See p. 605, ProTransCo, Inc. v Oceanus Mutual Underwriting Ass'n.) Thus, an employee who had been killed was not regarded as "disabled" within the meaning of a group policy covering employees.[6]

The courts are increasingly recognizing the fact that most persons obtaining insurance are not specially trained, and therefore the contract of insurance is to be read as it would be understood by the average person or by the average person in business, rather than by one with technical knowledge of the law or of insurance.

If there is an ambiguity in the policy, the provision is interpreted against the insurer.[7] In some instances courts will give a liberal interpretation to the policy terms in order to favor the insured or the beneficiary, on the basis that the insured did not in fact have a free choice.

When there is any uncertainty as to whether a contract of insurance exists before the delivery of the written policy, the uncertainty will be determined against the insurer and it will be concluded that the policy was effective immediately.

§ 36:7. Antidiscrimination. A number of state statutes prohibit insurers from refusing to write or renew policies of insurance because of the age, residence, occupation, national origin, or race of the applicant or insured and prohibit the cancellation of a policy except for nonpayment of premiums or, in the case of automobile insurance, the insured's loss of a required motor vehicle license or registration.[8]

Statutes also commonly prohibit insurance companies from making premium discriminations among members of the same risk class and from making rebates or refunds to particular individuals only.

§ 36:8. Premiums. Premiums may be paid by check. If the check is not paid, however, the instrument loses its character as payment.

If the premiums are not paid, the policy will ordinarily lapse because of nonpayment, subject to anti-lapse statutes or provisions.

(a)   Return of Unearned Premiums. When an insurance policy is canceled according to the terms of the policy before the expiration of the term for which premiums have been paid, the insurer is required to return such part of the premiums as has not been earned.

(b)   Nonforfeiture and Anti-lapse Provisions. As to the payment of premiums due on life insurance policies subsequent to the first premium, the policies now in general use provide or a statute may specify that the policy shall not automatically lapse upon the date the next premium is due if payment is not then made. By policy provision or statute, the insured is also allowed a *grace period* of 30 to 31 days, in which to make payment of the premium due. When there is a default in the payment of a premium by the insured, the insurer may be required by statute (1) to issue a paid-up policy in a smaller amount, (2) to provide extended insurance for a period of time, or (3) to pay the cash surrender value of the policy.

---

[6] Marriot v Pacific National Life Assurance Co. 24 Utah2d 182, 467 P2d 981.

[7] Murray v Western Pacific Insurance Co. 2 WashApp 985, 472 P2d 611. This principle is not applied if the provision in question is in the policy because it is required by statute.

[8] Pennsylvania, 40 PS § 1008.1 et seq.

§ 36:9. Extent of Insurer's Liability. In the case of life and disability insurance, the insurer is required to pay the amount called for by the contract of insurance. When the policy is one to indemnify against loss, the liability of the insurer is to pay only to the extent that the insured sustains loss, subject to a maximum amount stated in the contract. Thus, a fire insurer is liable for only $1,000, even though it has written a $20,000 policy, when the fire loss sustained by the insured is in fact only $1,000. If the loss were $22,000, the liability of the insurer would be limited by the face amount of the policy to only $20,000.

§ 36:10. Cancellation. The contract of insurance may expressly declare that it may or may not be canceled by the insurer's unilateral act. By statute or policy provision, the insurer is commonly required to give a specific number of days' written notice of a cancellation.

Property and liability policies generally reserve to the insurer the right to cancel the policy upon giving a specified number of days' notice. In some states antidiscrimination statutes restrict the right of insurers to cancel. An insurance company may not exercise its right to cancel the policy when it does so to punish the insured for having appeared as a witness in a case against it.

Only the insured is entitled to notice of cancellation unless the policy or an indorsement expressly declares otherwise. The mere fact that a creditor is entitled to the proceeds of the insurance policy in the case of loss does not in itself entitle the creditor to notice of a cancellation of the policy.[9]

§ 36:11. Coverage of Policy. When an insurance claim is disputed by the insurer, the person bringing suit has the burden of proving that there was a loss, that it occurred while the policy was in force, and that the loss was of a kind which was within the coverage or scope of the policy.

A policy will contain *exceptions* to the coverage. This means that the policy is not applicable when an exception applies to the situation. Exceptions to coverage are generally strictly interpreted against the insurer. There is also a modern trend which holds that although an exception is literally applicable to the situation it will be ignored and coverage sustained when there is no cause and effect relationship between the loss and the conduct which constituted the exception. (See p. 606, South Carolina Ins. Co. v Collins)

In any case, the insurer has the burden of proving that there is no coverage because one of the contract exceptions is applicable, or of proving that there is a defense to the claim of liability on the policy.

§ 36:12. Defenses of the Insurer. The insurer may raise any defense that would be valid in an action upon a contract. Some defenses that do not apply to an action on an ordinary contract may also be raised.

---

[9] Ford Motor Credit Co. v Commonwealth County Mutual Insurance Co. (TexCivApp) 420 SW2d 732.

CASES FOR CHAPTER 36

Universal C.I.T. Credit Corp. v Foundation Reserve Insurance Co.

79 NMex 785, 450 P2d 194 (1969)

Norman Bowman purchased an automobile on credit for use by his cousin, Jimmy, but took title in his own name. The Foundation Reserve Insurance Co. issued a policy covering destruction of the car and naming Jimmy as the insured with a clause providing for payment to the finance company. The car was destroyed some time later and the finance company, the Universal C.I.T., sued the insurance company which raised the defense of lack of insurable interest. From a judgment in favor of the insurance company, the finance company appealed.

COMPTON, J. . . . Norman Bowman had purchased the automobile for the benefit of Jimmy Don Bowman, his seventeen-year-old cousin, a student, living with him during the school year 1965-1966, as a means of transportation to and from school and to his work after school. Norman Bowman purchased the vehicle and took title in his name. He alone was liable on the note securing the conditional sales agreement on the automobile.

Appellee's agent with full knowledge that Norman Bowman was the owner of the automobile issued its policy to Jimmy Don Bowman. The agent also knew that Jimmy Don Bowman had no pecuniary interest in the vehicle. A condition of the policy, however, provided that knowledge possessed by the agent would not estop the company from asserting a lack of insurable interest in the named insured.

In May or June, 1966, the school year having ended, Jimmy Don Bowman no longer used the vehicle. He turned it back to Norman Bowman and returned to the State of Washington to live with his father. He had no intention of ever using the automobile again. In July, 1966, the automobile was totally wrecked in a one-car accident while being driven by a party who had possession of the vehicle with the permission of Norman Bowman for the purpose of "trying it out" as a prospective buyer. . . .

The court concluded that Jimmy Don Bowman had no insurable interest in the automobile. It is argued that Jimmy Don Bowman, the named insured, had an insurable interest in the automobile

by virtue of the fact that he might incur liability because of his operation or use of it. . . .

When the insured voluntarily abandoned the use of the vehicle, his insurable interest, if any, ceased to exist. An insurable interest must exist at the time of loss. . . . There was no contractual obligation between Jimmy Don Bowman with anyone. He could not have suffered loss by its destruction. He had no interest in the vehicle and he lost nothing. . . .

[Judgment affirmed]

Flester v Ohio Casualty Ins. Co.

(Md App) 307 A2d 663 (1973)

In 1969, Flester obtained an automobile liability policy from the Ohio Casualty Insurance Company covering a 1962 Ford Fairlane and a 1956 Thunderbird. By subsequent indorsement the Thunderbird was removed from the policy and was replaced by a 1967 Mercury Cougar. Three days later the Cougar was damaged and Flester used the Thunderbird in its place. Flester consulted Marton, his insurance broker, and an agreement was reached on August 11, 1969, for temporary insurance covering the Thunderbird. In the following April, 1970, a renewal policy was mailed to Flester covering the Fairlane and the Cougar but saying nothing as to the Thunderbird. No one noticed the identity of the automobiles covered. Flester paid the premium due on the renewal policy and on May 10, 1970, was in a collision with the Thunderbird. He claimed that Ohio Casualty was liable for the damage to the Thunderbird by virtue of the oral contract of insurance which modified the coverage of the original written policy. The insurer denied liability on the oral contract covering the Thunderbird on the ground that the contract had terminated when the renewal policy was issued in April, 1970, and therefore did not provide coverage at the time of the May 10 collision. Judgment was entered for the insurer and Flester appealed.

LEVINE, J. . . . The conversation of August 11, 1969, between Flester and Marton, resulted in a commitment on behalf of Ohio Casualty which, in the parlance of the insurance world, is called a binder. . . . "The term 'binder' has a well-known significance in the parlance of insurance contracts, and a binder or a binding slip is merely a written memorandum of the most important terms of a preliminary contract of insurance intended to give temporary protection pending the investigation of the risk of insurer, or *until the issuance of a formal policy;* a contract is insurance in praesenti, *temporary in its nature,* intended to take the place of an ordinary policy until one can be issued. . . ." . . .

"Frequently, for the purpose of convenience or expediency so that the owner of an automobile may operate it before obtaining the formal policy of insurance, an oral contract of insurance is entered into, or a binding slip, also called a 'binder,' is issued, for the purpose of insuring the vehicle *until the actual issuance and delivery of the policy* to the insured. As in the case of other types of insurance, it is settled generally that such a contract is valid and binds the insurer *until the issuance and delivery of the policy agreed upon.*" . . .

Clearly, what occurred in this case differs from the commonly-accepted situation outlined above. The underlying thrust of Flester's appeal is the contention that the parties—on August 11, 1969—entered into a separate oral contract, not one which was to terminate upon the issuance of a written policy, but rather upon the replacement of a vehicle which was, itself, not covered by the oral agreement. . . .

By its very definition, a binder is intended to be temporary; and some states have even enacted statutes restricting the length of time during which a binder may remain in force. . . . No such statutory period exists in Maryland; nor did the binder in question here specify a termination date. In such situations elsewhere, the binder's coverage has been held to extend until issuance of the formal policy, . . . or until the passage of a reasonable time to investigate the risk and communicate a rejection to the applicant. . . . In 9 Couch on Insurance 2d, [Anderson Edition] § 39:207 (1962), it is stated: "Since parol contracts of insurance *usually cover the time necessarily elapsing between the placing of the insurance and the issuing of the policy,* the duration is ordinarily for such period of time as is a reasonable one under the circumstances for the issuance of a formal policy. The preliminary or temporary contract is therefore effective *until either superseded by a policy,* when issued, or terminated by a rejection of the application, and notice thereof to the insured, or by the expiration of the time specified in the preliminary

or temporary contract, or of a reasonable time, when none is specified.". . .

As we have stressed, the outcome of the August 11 discussion between Flester and Marton does not reflect the concept of a typical automobile insurance binder, i.e., temporary insurance designed to afford protection for a relatively brief time span. This period usually covers the interval between the application for the insurance and the issuance of a formal policy. It is in this context that binders are normally regarded as expiring "upon the issuance of the policy." While the agreement in this case may not fit into one of the conventional molds, it is no less a binder. The thread that runs through the various definitions of this term is the *temporary* coverage that is provided by the insurer.

Here, the issuance of a new policy covering the Thunderbird was never intended; the binder was only given "with respect to" the policy already in existence. In other words, the binder was intended by the parties to be effective, as Judge McCullough said, during "a period of time when either the Cougar would have been replaced or repaired." With the passage of the relatively short time period intended for either eventuality, however, and without any word from Flester, the binder's existence terminated upon the expiration of the policy which it had *temporarily* modified. At that point, it was "superseded" by the formal policy issued on April 21, 1970. That Flester failed to note what automobiles were listed in that policy does not defeat its operativeness, and he is bound by its description of the insured vehicles. . . .

Under the view we adopt here, there could not have been an independent insurance contract covering the Thunderbird, to expire on some future date when the *Cougar* was ultimately replaced. That argument is contrary to the concept of temporary coverage inherent in the binder, and would, in effect, establish an oral policy of indefinite duration. As Judge McCullough so aptly observed, under this view "the binder goes on and on and on, it would, in effect, still be in force today.". . .

[Judgment affirmed]

Metts v Central Standard Life Insurance Co.

142 Cal App 2d 445, 298 P2d 621 (1956)

Metts filled out a printed application form for polio insurance distributed by the Central Standard Life Insurance Co. He mailed the application to the

company on May 15. It was received by the company on May 23. On May 21, Metts' son was stricken with polio, of which the insurer was notified on May 28. The company refused to pay on the ground that it had not accepted the application. Metts sued the insurer. From a judgment in favor of Metts, the insurer appealed.

BRAY, J. . . . The application form, on its reverse side, stated: "Infantile Paralysis. Immediate First Day Coverage Automatically Covers Entire Family." "No Waiting Period." "Pays from *First Day* that poliomyelitis manifests itself and thereafter, as provided. . . ."

Plaintiff contends that the application form itself was an offer to contract which was accepted by him; that the above mentioned wording on the back of the form caused him to believe that when he mailed the completed form and premium payment, the contract was then in effect and that he was immediately covered.

Defendant contends that there was no representation that the policy would take effect as of the date of the application, and that the application was an offer by the insured not accepted until a policy was issued. . . .

"Because contracts of insurance are not the result of negotiation and are generally drawn by the insurer, any uncertainties or ambiguities therein are resolved most strongly in favor of the insured. . . ."

Our first task is to determine, then, whether there is any uncertainty or ambiguity in the language of the application. . . . The only language [of the application form] important here is that above quoted appearing on the reverse side: "*Immediate* First Day Coverage *Automatically* Covers Entire Family." (Emphasis added.) The use of the words "immediate" and "automatically" in these phrases is difficult to explain as having any meaning other than that the coverage commences from the date of the application. At least, a reasonable conclusion is, that did these phrases apply to the first day of sickness rather than the first day of coverage, there would be no need for the words "immediate" and "automatically." The policy when issued would state that it covered illness from the first day of illness and covered the entire family. The form further states: "Pays from *First Day* that poliomyelitis manifests itself. . . ." In view of that statement, what is the meaning of the words "immediate First Day Coverage" if not coverage immediately upon signing?

Under the rule above mentioned such words are fairly capable of an interpretation which would afford the greater measure of protection to the insured. A layman could hardly be expected to give any other interpretation. . . . We are therefore required to hold that the application form constituted an offer by defendant of coverage to take effect immediately upon the signing and posting of the application. . . .

[Judgment affirmed]

ProTransCo, Inc. v Oceanus Mutual Underwriting Ass'n

(AlaCivApp) 349 So2d 585 (1977)

ProTransCo carried insurance with the American Casualty Company on its tugboat, the Defiance, covering liability for collision with any structure or integral part of a structure. The tug was moving barges on the river. The hooking device of one of the barges caught on a cable that connected pilings which were in the river. The barge could not be disconnected and pulled the pilings out. The owner of the pilings claimed that ProTransCo was liable. It brought suit to determine whether this liability was covered by the American policy or by a second policy which ProTransCo had obtained from Oceanus Mutual. It was agreed that if the American policy covered the loss, there was no liability under the Oceanus policy. From a decision that the American policy covered the loss, ProTransCo appealed.

WRIGHT, P.J. . . . We have before us the anomalous situation of an insured contending against coverage under the terms of his policy. ProTransCo urges that the terms of the American policy be construed most favorably to the insured. ProTransCo actually means that it wishes us to construe the policy so as to favor its present interest—that is that there is no coverage under the American policy so that it can recover under the more advantageous Oceanus policy.

The principle of construction urged by ProTransCo is well known, but it is based upon the proposition that the contract of insurance is written by the insurer and if there is any reasonable uncertainty as to its meaning which requires construction by the court, that uncertainty should be resolved in favor of coverage. . . . ProTransCo is not invoking the principle in this case to secure coverage, but to defeat coverage which the insurer admits is provided by the policy. This is not a case for the principle of liberal construction in favor of an insured.

There can be little reasonable insistance that the pilings were not "structures, floating or otherwise" under a normal and reasonable construction of the term. There is little logic or reason in contending that the steel cable attached to each piling and extending to all of them and used in conjunction with them in mooring or unmooring barges was not an appendage of and a part of the "structure." They are as much a part as would be a fender attached to the piling or a catwalk between the pilings. Such reasonable and practical application is most favorable to the insured seeking coverage. . . . Words of an insurance contract are to be given their natural and usual meaning so as to produce a rational and practical interpretation. . . . We find that the pilings were structures or collectively was a structure and the cable attached was an integral part of the structure. Our finding is supported by Webster's Third New International Dictionary which defines "structure" as something "built or constructed."

The remaining aspect of the issue is whether the hooking of the cable by the bit on the barge and the subsequent pulling was a collision with a structure.

Collision by connotation and definition is the violent or forceful striking together of things opposed. Webster's Third New International Dictionary. In maritime law, collision has come to mean the violent contact of a vessel with another vessel though one vessel is not in motion. . . . Express terms of insurance policies have broadened the meaning of collision to include contact by a vessel with any moving or stationary object. . . .

The problem arises in this case not with the vessel and/or structure involved, but in applying the broad definition of collision with the facts as stipulated. A collision must be considered as the result of the act of colliding. There is no authority to be found that does not include in the definition of collision terms of force or violence, such as "violent encounter," "forceful striking together," a "clashing meeting," "violent impact," or a "meeting in sharp direct opposition."

The factual event, occurring in that case is underlined in the quoted stipulation. These undisputed facts connote no violent encounter nor forceful impact. There was no more collision by definition than if the damage had been done by the tug pulling away without casting off the mooring line of the barge from the pile. The facts stated indicate no forceful coming together of the cable and the bit of the barge. They merely became hung up while the tug was preparing to pull away. There was no collision. . . .

[Judgment reversed and action remanded]

South Carolina Insurance Company v Collins

(SC) 237 SE2d 358 (1977)

Collins owned a Piper Colt airplane. He obtained a liability policy covering the plane from the South Carolina Insurance Company. The policy provided that it did not cover loss sustained while the plane was piloted by a person who did not have a valid pilot's certificate and a valid medical examination certificate. Collins was piloting the plane. He held a valid pilot's certificate but his medical examination certificate had expired three months before. The plane crashed and Collins was killed. His estate claimed that the insurer was liable. The insurer denied liability because Collins did not have a valid medical certificate. The insurer brought an action to have the court declare that it was not liable on its policy. It was stipulated by the parties that the crash was in no way caused by the absence of the medical certificate. From a decision that the insurer was liable to the estate, the insurer appealed.

RHODES, J. . . . A line of South Carolina cases involving contracts of automobile liability and life insurance are, in our judgment, dispositive of the issues raised on this appeal.

The first in this series of cases was decided by this Court in 1932. In *Reynolds v Life & Casualty Ins. Co. of Tennessee,* 166 S.C. 214, 164 S.E. 602, the mother of the insured brought suit in her capacity as beneficiary under two (2) policies of life insurance issued by the defendant company to her son. The contract of insurance involved in the first cause of action contained the following provision: "This policy does not cover . . . loss sustained by the insured . . . while committing some act in violation of law." The contract involved in the second cause of action provided that "[w]ithin two years from date of issuance of this policy, the liability of the company under same shall be limited, under the following conditions, to the return of the premium paid thereon: . . . (2) If the insured shall die . . . as a result of acts committed by him while in the commission of . . . some act in violation of law."

During the effective period of these contracts of insurance, an ordinance of the City of Greenville, the place of residence of the insured, provided that "[n]o person shall be allowed to ride upon the running board of any motor vehicle . . .." The defendant company moved for a directed verdict at the close of the testimony in the trial of the case upon the ground that at the time of the accident, in which fatal injuries were sustained, the insured was riding on the running board of a truck in violation of the ordinance. The trial judge overruled the defendant's motion and the jury found for the plaintiff in the entire policy amounts sued for. The defendant appealed from the denial of its motion and also from the court's charge to the jury that the insurer must establish a causal connection between the insured's loss or death and his violation of the ordinance.

In *Reynolds*, this Court stated that under the evidence and the particular facts adduced at the trial, it could not be held as a matter of law, as defendant contended, that the insured's death was proximately caused by his riding upon the running board of the truck or that his death was the necessary or natural consequence of his act. The Court ruled that these questions had been properly submitted to the jury for determination.

In discussing the issue of causal connection, the Court stated the following:

It is clear that the court properly refused defendant's motion, for, even if it should be admitted that the insured was violating the ordinance at the time he was injured, this alone would not be sufficient ground for direction of a verdict. In order to defeat recovery under policies excluding or limiting liability where death or injury results from an unlawful act on the part of the insured, there must be shown, in addition to the violation of the law, some causative connection between such act and the death or injury.

In *Insurance Co. v Bennett*, 90 Tenn. [256], 267, 16 S.W. 723, 725, 25 Am.St. Rep. 685, the Tennessee court, construing a provision of this kind in an insurance policy, said: "In order to defeat a recovery because of such provision, there must appear a connecting link between the unlawful act and the death. It is not sufficient that there was an unlawful act committed by the insured, and that death occurred during the time he was engaged in its commission. There must be some causative connection between the act which constituted a violation of the law and the death of the insured. . . . The provision of the policy excluding liability for injury received by the insured while committing an unlawful act refers to such injuries as may happen as the necessary or natural consequence of the act." *Reynolds,* supra, 166 S.C. at 217, 218, 164 S.E. at 603.

Approximately two years after the decision in *Reynolds* this Court again had occasion to rule with respect to the necessity on the part of an insurer to show causal connection. In the case of *McGee v Globe Indemnity Co.,* 173 S.C. 380, 175 S.E. 849 (1934), the insured instituted an action on a policy of insurance whereby the insurer had agreed to indemnify the plaintiff against loss or damage to his automobile occasioned by accidental means. The insurer sought to escape liability by alleging that the policy contained a provision that it should not apply "in respect of any automobile . . . (2) while used or maintained by any person in violation of law as to age or by any person under the age of sixteen (16) years." The undisputed facts showed that at the time the automobile was damaged it was being operated by the insured's son who was under 16 years of age. In overruling a demurrer to the insured's reply which alleged that there existed no causal connection between the age of the driver and the collision, the trial judge relied upon *Reynolds v Life & Casualty Ins. Co. of Tennessee, supra.*

On appeal, the insurer attempted to distinguish the *Reynolds* case from the *McGee* case, contending that in *Reynolds* the court was dealing with a provision limiting liability of the insurance company on account of some act of the insured (in other words, an exclusion), while in *McGee* the provision of the policy relied upon to defeat recovery related to a condition. The appellant urged that while it was logical to hold that it is necessary to show some causative connection between the act or acts named in the limiting provision of a policy and the accident involved, a policy which limits liability under a certain condition *absolutely excludes* liability under the named condition, even though the condition might have no causative connection with the accident and resulting loss.

In rejecting this theory advanced by the insurer, this Court held: We are of the opinion that the distinction advanced between the excluded act and condition is without any logical basis. . . . The rule established by the *Reynolds* Case is obviously found upon the reasonable view that, *when the parties made the contract of insurance, they were not inserting a mere arbitrary provision, but that it was the purpose of the insurance company to relieve itself of liability from accidents caused by the excluded condition.* And there is no more reason that the parties to the contract of insurance would arbitrarily exclude liability under a certain condition than they would arbitrarily exclude liability in the commission of a certain act. This case is controlled by the *Reynolds* Case. *McGee, supra,* 173 S.C. at 384, 175 S.E. at 850. (emphasis added)

Subsequent decisions of this Court in the *Reynolds-McGee* line affirm the requirement on the part of the insurer to show causal connection. . . .

The appellant cites cases from other jurisdictions holding that under circumstances virtually identical, or closely related, to those in the instant case, the insurer need not show a causal connection between damages and injuries sustained in the crash of the aircraft and the insured's failure to comply with certain terms of the policy. These decisions hold essentially that the purpose of the exclusionary language of such policies is not that the risk is excluded if damage to the aircraft is *caused* by the failure of the pilot to be properly certificated, but that the risk

is excluded absolutely if loss *occurs while* the aircraft is being flown by a pilot not properly certificated. . . .

In some of these cited cases the courts have referred to the certification provisions sometimes as "conditions" and, at other times, as "exclusions." However, the language quoted above from the *McGee* case resolves adversely to the appellant its contention that the trial judge in the instant case erred in characterizing the policy provisions as an exclusion rather than a condition subsequent or a promissory warranty. While there is a recognized distinction among these various terms, such a difference is immaterial in this case. We rely upon *McGee* in so holding.

After examination of the decisions cited by the appellant, we find them unpersuasive. Only their number, not their reasoning, lends support to a reversal here. . . .

[Judgment affirmed]

QUESTIONS AND CASE PROBLEMS

1. What social forces are affected by imposing the requirement of insurable interest?
2. Compare (a) the reluctance of the courts to hold that time is of the essence in a contract, and (b) a provision for a grace period for the payment on life insurance.
3. Compare (a) a contract of insurance, and (b) an ordinary contract.
4. A contract of insurance is a contract to pay the amount specified by the policy in the event of loss conferred by the policy. Appraise this statement.
5. Hatcher and his wife made an oral contract to purchase a house. They moved into the house and it was agreed that they would receive a deed as soon as they made final payment. The Hatchers were waiting for a check from a loan which had already been approved. They insured the property against fire with Harleysville Mutual Insurance Company. The house was damaged by fire before the Hatchers paid the final balance and received a deed. Harleysville refused to pay under the policy on the ground that the oral contract of the Hatchers for the purchase of land could not be enforced because of the statute of frauds and therefore the Hatchers had no insurable interest in the property insured. Was this a valid defense? [Hatcher v Harleysville Mutual Insurance Company, 226 SC 559, 225 SE2d 181]
6. Lisle applied for life insurance with the Federal Life & Casualty Co. Both Lisle and his wife made false, fraudulent statements to the insurer in connection with the application. The insurer's physician examined Lisle twice but did not ascertain anything that revealed the falsity of those statements. After the insured's death about a year later, the insurer denied liability on the ground of fraud. Lisle's widow claimed that the insurer could not raise the question of fraud since it had examined the insured before accepting his application. Was the insurer liable? [Federal Life & Casualty Co. v Lisle, 140 OhioSt2d 269, 172 NE2d 919]

7. Einhorn held warehouse receipts as collateral security for a loan that he had made to the prior holder of the receipts. Einhorn obtained a fire insurance policy from the Firemen's Insurance Co., which insured him against loss of the property by fire to the extent of his interest in the collateral. The property represented by the receipts was destroyed by fire. Einhorn assigned his claim on the policy to Flint Frozen Foods, which then sued the insurer. Was the policy obtained by Einhorn valid? [Flint Frozen Foods v Firemen's Insurance Co., 8 NJ 606, 86 A2d 673]

8. On October 29, Griffin sent an application for life insurance and the first premium to the Insurance Company of North America. In the application, her son, Carlisle Moore, was named as beneficiary. On November 25 of the same year, Griffin died. On November 26, the company rejected the application and notified the broker who took the application, who in turn notified Moore by letter dated November 30. Moore sued the company for breach of contract. Decide. [Moore v Insurance Co. of North America, 49 Ill App 2d 287, 200 NE2d 1]

9. Rebecca Foster obtained a policy of life insurance from the United Insurance Co. insuring the life of Lucille McClurkin and naming herself as beneficiary. Lucille did not live with Rebecca, and Rebecca did not inform Lucille of the existence of the policy. Rebecca paid the premiums on the policy, and on the death of Lucille sued the United Insurance Co. for the amount of the insurance. At the trial, Rebecca testified vaguely that her father had told her that Lucille was her second cousin on his side of the family. Was Rebecca entitled to recover on the policy? [Foster v United Insurance Co., 250 SC 423, 158 SE2d 201]

10. Moore's wife applied for accident insurance on her husband. She paid the premium due. Unknown to her, the application was rejected. However, when she inquired of the agent as to the status of the application, the agent said that he had had no word. When she inquired some time later, the agent said he thought that the policy had come in and, if it had not, she would be notified in a few days. She heard nothing. Two weeks later her husband was killed accidentally. After his death the insurance company informed her that the application had been rejected. She sued the insurance company. Decide. [Moore v Palmetto State Life Insurance Co., 222 SC 492, 73 SE2d 688]

11. A policy of insurance had the words "double indemnity" across the top imprinted with a rubber stamp. Nothing was said in the policy about double indemnity. When a loss was sustained, the insured claimed that he was entitled to double indemnity. Was he correct? [Niewoehner v Western Life Insurance Co., 149 Mont 57, 422 P2d 644]

12. Bondurant obtained a public liability insurance policy from the United States Fidelity and Guarantee Co. Johnson sustained an injury that came within the coverage of the policy and brought suit against Bondurant and U.S.F.&G. Co. While the action was pending, Bondurant was declared a bankrupt and received his discharge in bankruptcy. Because of such discharge, Johnson could not hold Bondurant liable. U.S.F.&G. Co. thereupon claimed that since Bondurant was not liable to Johnson, it was not liable either since its liability was no greater than that of its insured. Decide. [Johnson v Bondurant, (Kan) 359 P2d 861]

13. Hicks obtained an automobile collision policy from the Alabama Farm Bureau Mutual Casualty Insurance Co. The policy provided that there was no coverage of loss during the period between the expiration of the term of the policy and the date of the actual payment of a renewal premium. Hicks did not pay the renewal premium until several months after the expiration of the policy. During the noncovered period, he was in a collision. He paid the renewal premium to the agent-manager at the insurer's local office and then filed a proof of loss for the damage sustained in the collision. The insurer refused to pay the loss. The insured sued the insurer. Decide. [Alabama Farm Bureau Mutual Cas. Ins. Co. v Hicks, 41 Ala App 143, 133 So2d 217]

37 Kinds of Insurance

Today many different kinds of insurance are available. They tend, however, to group themselves into a few categories in terms of the nature of the interest protected. Fire, automobile, and life insurance will be considered in this chapter.

A. FIRE INSURANCE

A *fire insurance policy* is a contract to indemnify the insured for destruction of or damage to property caused by fire. In almost every state the New York standard fire insurance form is the standard policy.

§ 37:1. Nature of Contract.

(a) Actual, Hostile Fire. In order for fire loss to be covered by fire insurance, there must be an actual flame or burning, and the fire must be hostile. The hostile character is easily determined when the fire is caused by accident, such as a short circuit in electric wiring; but it is often difficult to determine if the fire is intentional, as when it is being used for heating or cooking. A *hostile fire* in the latter case is one which to some extent becomes uncontrollable or escapes from the place where it is intended to be. To illustrate, when soot is ignited and causes a fire in the chimney, the fire is hostile. On the other hand, a loss caused by the smoke or heat of a fire in its ordinary container, which has not broken out or become uncontrollable, results from a *friendly fire,* and is not covered by the policy.

By indorsement, the coverage may be and frequently is extended to include loss by a friendly fire.

Damage by heat alone is not covered, but damage from heat or smoke caused by a hostile fire is covered.

(b) Immediate or Proximate Cause. The fire must be the immediate or proximate cause of the loss. In addition to direct destruction or damage by fire, a fire may set in motion a chain of events that damages property. When there is a reasonable connection between a fire and the ultimate loss sustained, the insurer is liable for the loss.

The New York standard form of fire insurance policy excludes loss or damage caused directly or indirectly by enemy attack by armed forces, invasion, insurrection, rebellion, revolution, civil war, or usurped power, or by order of any civil authority; or by neglect of the insured to use all reasonable means to save and preserve the property at and after a fire or when the property is endangered by fire in neighboring premises; or by theft.

Damage by explosion is also excluded unless fire follows, and then the insurer is liable only for that part of the damage caused by the fire. The standard form of fire insurance policy includes protection from lightning damage even though no fire is caused thereby.

§ 37:2. Determination of Insurer's Liability. Basically the insurer is liable for the actual amount of the loss sustained. This liability is limited, however, by the maximum amount stated in the policy or the amount of damages sustained by total destruction of the property, whichever is less.

(a)   Amount of Loss. The amount of the loss, in the absence of statute or agreement to the contrary, is the actual cash value at the time of the loss. If the insurer and the insured cannot agree, policies commonly provide for the determination of the amount of loss by appraisers or arbitrators.[1]

(b)   Total Loss. A *total loss* does not necessarily mean that the property has been completely destroyed. The loss is regarded as being total if the unconsumed portion is of no value for the purposes for which the property was utilized at the time of the insurance. Consequently, the mere fact that some of the walls and the roof remained after the fire did not prove that the loss was not total.

(c)   Replacement by Insurer. Frequently the insurer will stipulate in the policy that it has the right to replace or restore the property to its former condition in lieu of paying the insured the cash value of the loss.

(d)   Coinsurance. A *coinsurance clause* requires the insured to maintain insurance on the covered property up to a certain amount or a certain percent of the value, generally 80%. Under such a provision, if the policyholder insures the property for less than the required amount, the insurer is liable only for the proportionate share of the amount of insurance required to be carried. To illustrate, suppose the owner of a building with a value of $40,000 insures it against loss to the extent of $24,000, and the policy contains a coinsurance clause requiring that insurance of 80% of the value of the property be carried. Assume that a $16,000 loss is then sustained. The insured would not receive $16,000 from the insurer but only $12,000 because the amount of the insurance carried ($24,000) is only three fourths of the amount required ($32,000, that is 80% of $40,000).

The use of a coinsurance clause is not permitted in all states. In some states, it is prohibited or is permitted only with the consent of the insured.

§ 37:3. Assignment of Fire Insurance Policy. Fire insurance is a personal contract, and in the absence of statute or contractual authorization it cannot be assigned before a loss is sustained without the consent of the insurer.[2] In addition, it is commonly provided that the policy shall be void if an assignment to give a purchaser of the property the protection of the policy is attempted. Such a forfeiture clause applies only when the insured attempts to transfer total ownership of the policy. It does not apply to an assignment as security for a loan to the insured.

---

[1] Saba v Homeland Insurance Co. 159 Ohio 237, 112 NE2d 1.
[2] Shadid v American Druggist Fire Insurance Co. (Okla) 386 P2d 311.

§ 37:4. Mortgage Clause. If the insured property is subject to a mortgage, either or both the mortgagor and mortgagee may take out policies of fire insurance to protect their respective interests in the property. Each has an insurable interest therein. In the absence of a contrary stipulation, the policy taken out by either covers only that insured's own interest. That is, the mortgagor's policy protects only the value of the mortgagor's right to redemption or the value of the property in excess of the mortgage, while the policy of the mortgagee covers only the debt. Neither can claim the benefit of insurance money paid to the other.

It is common, however, for the mortgagee to insist as a condition of making the loan that the mortgagor obtain and pay the premiums on a policy covering the full value of the property and providing that in case of loss the insurance money shall be paid to the mortgagor and the mortgagee as their respective interests may appear. As the amount of the mortgage debt is reduced, the interest of the mortgagee in the property becomes less and the share of insurance proceeds that the mortgagee would receive accordingly becomes less. Such a mortgage clause has the advantage of protecting both the mortgagor and mortgagee by one policy and of providing a flexible method of insuring each of them.

§ 37:5. Extended Coverage. The term *extended coverage* generally refers to protection of property against loss from windstorm, hail, riot, civil commotion, aircraft damage, vehicle damage, and smoke damage, and explosions other than those within steam boilers on the premises.

(a)   Vandalism. A special form of extended coverage may be obtained to protect property from vandalism. Generally this protects from damage to property which breaks or defaces. If vandals burn a building, fire insurance would provide coverage. Likewise, if the harm occurs as part of a riot, standard extended coverage would afford protection.

§ 37:6. Other Provisions. Fire insurance policies commonly prohibit the insured from doing certain acts that will or may increase the hazard or risk involved and provide that the policy is void if the insured commits the prohibited acts.

It is commonly provided that false statements made by the insured when they are known to be false shall avoid the policy. Under such a provision a fraudulent misstatement of the value of the property avoids the policy.

The insured may take out more than one policy on the same property, in the absence of a provision in any of the policies to the contrary; but in the event of loss, recovery cannot be greater than the total loss sustained. Such a loss is prorated among the insurers.

An insurer is not liable when the damage or destruction of the property was intentionally caused by the insured. The fact that the insured negligently caused a fire is not a defense to the insurer, even when there is a stipulation that the insured shall not change or increase the hazard insured against.

§ 37:7. Cancellation. It is common to provide by statute or by the terms of the policy that under certain circumstances the policy may be terminated or canceled by the act of one party alone. When this is done, the provisions of the statute and the policy must be strictly followed in order to make the cancellation effective.[3]

The provision governing a cancellation of a policy may be waived. Thus, when a policy requires five days' notice by the insurer but it gives only three days notice, the insured waives the notice requirement if the insured surrenders the policy for cancellation without objection.

B. AUTOMOBILE INSURANCE.

Associations of insurers, such as the National Bureau of Casualty Underwriters and the National Automobile Underwriters Association, have proposed standard forms of automobile insurance policies that have been approved by their members in virtually all the states.

§ 37:8. Nature of Contract. In the case of insurance to compensate the insured driver or car owner for damages to the insured's own car *(collision insurance)* it is immaterial whether the insured's negligence caused or contributed to the harm sustained. In the case of insurance that protects the insured driver or owner from claims of others *(liability insurance),* no liability of the insurer for a claim arises unless the insured was negligent in the operation of the automobile. To some extent this has been altered by *no-fault insurance* as discussed in § 37:13.

§ 37:9. Financial Responsibility Laws. In a few states and under some no-fault insurance statutes, liability insurance must be obtained before a driver's license will be issued. In most states *financial responsibility* laws require that if a driver is involved in an accident, proof of financial responsibility must be furnished. Under some laws this means that the driver must deposit security sufficient to pay any judgment that may be entered with respect to that accident. Under other statutes, it is sufficient that the driver produce a liability policy in a specified amount as to future accidents.

The security form of statute may not protect the victim of the first accident. If the driver is unwilling or unable to deposit the required security, the driver's license is forfeited; but this does not provide any payment to the victim of the first accident. By definition, the second type of law does not protect the victim of the first accident. Moreover, the efficiency of financial responsibility laws has been reduced by the decision that the United States Constitution requires that there be a hearing to establish the probable liability of a driver to the victim before the driver's license can be suspended or revoked.[4] The requirement of such a hearing has the effect of delaying and making cumbersome what was formerly a relatively simple and swift administrative remedy.

§ 37:10. Liability Insurance. The owner or operator of a motor vehicle may obtain *liability insurance* for protection from claims made by third persons for damage to their property (property damage liability) or person (bodily injury liability) arising from

---

[3] Mobile Fire & Marine Insurance Co. v Kraft, 36 AlaApp 684, 63 So2d 34.
[4] Bell v Burson, 402 US 535.

the use or operation of an automobile. When the insurer pays under such a policy, it makes the payment directly to the third person and is liable to pay for the same items as the insured would be required to pay, but for not more than the maximum amount stated in the policy.

If the insurer is liable for the damage caused a third person or such person's property, it is likewise liable for cost of repairs, loss by destruction of the property, loss of services, and other damages for which the insured would be liable, subject to the policy maximum.

In case of a collision with an insured driver, the plaintiff will recover for the harm sustained if negligence of the driver can be shown or if there is a loss which comes within the scope of a no-fault insurance coverage. Some or all of the plaintiff's damages may not be covered by virtue of no-fault insurance. In that case, the plaintiff does not recover anything unless the negligence of the other driver is established. If the plaintiff was also negligent, that negligence may limit or bar recovery. It is therefore desirable for everyone to carry personal insurance so that payment can be obtained without regard to negligence and even though no-fault coverage is not applicable.

The insured does not cease to be liable merely because there is insurance. If for any reason, the policy does not cover the full loss or the insurance company is not solvent or in business, the insured is liable for any amount not paid, assuming there would be such liability had there been no insurance.

(a)   Ownership of Automobile. Basically, liability insurance protects the insured with respect to an "owned" automobile. Whether a given automobile is owned by the insured is determined by Article 2 of the Uniform Commercial Code, and it is immaterial whether the steps required by a motor vehicle statute have been taken to transfer the title.

(b)   Use and Operation. The terms "use" and "operation" as found in a liability policy are liberally interpreted to include events in which there is some involvement of the automobile even though not for the purpose of transportation. For example, the insured "uses" the automobile when packages are being loaded into it.

(c)   Person Operating. Liability policies ordinarily protect the owner of the auto from liability when it is operated by another person with the permission of the insured, as in the case of an employee or agent of the owner.

Liability insurance may also protect an insured individual or the insured's spouse against liability incurred while operating another person's automobile. This is referred to as *D.O.C.* (drive-other-car) *coverage,* or *temporary replacement coverage.* (See p. 622, State Farm Mutual Auto Ins. Co. v Johnston)

(1)   Members of Household of Insured. Automobile liability policies variously extend coverage to members of the insured's household or residence. Such terms are generally liberally construed to reach the conclusion that a given relative is a member of the insured's "household" or "residence."

(2)   Other Driver. The automobile liability policy protects the insured when driving. If someone else is driving with the insured's permission, the policy protects both the original insured and such other driver. This *omnibus* or *other-driver clause* is generally liberally interpreted so that permission is often found

in acquiescence in the other driver's use or in the insured's failing to object or to prevent such use. In the absence of an express prohibition by the insured against the permittee's lending the car to another, a permission by *A* given to *B* to use the car generally includes an implied permission to *B* to permit *C* to drive, in which case the liability of the insurer is the same as though *A* or *B* were driving.[5]

The buyer of an automobile does not come within the scope of an omnibus clause because the buyer's operation of the automobile is not based upon the permission of the seller but upon the buyer's ownership of the automobile. To avoid litigation, policies commonly expressly exclude buyers from the scope of the omnibus clause. (See p. 624, DeRubbo v Aetna Ins. Co)

(d)   Exclusions. A liability policy does not cover every harm sustained. Such policies may exclude claims of employees of the owner or claims under the workmen's compensation laws, or liability for claims when the insured admits to the injured third person that the insured is liable and agrees to pay the claim.

In the case of commercial vehicles the insurer may stipulate that it shall only be bound by the policy "provided: (a) the regular and frequent use of the automobile is confined to the area within a fifty mile radius of the limits of the city or town where the automobile is principally garaged . . . , (b) no regular or frequent trips are made by the automobile to any locations beyond such radius."

(e)   Notice and Cooperation. A liability policy generally provides that the insurer is not liable unless the insured (a) gives the insurer prompt notice of any serious accident or claim or lawsuit brought against the insured, (b) furnishes the insurance company with all details of the occurrence, and (c) cooperates with the insurer in the preparation of the defense against a lawsuit brought on the policy and participates at the trial. Notice and cooperation under such a policy are conditions precedent to the liability of the insurer.

These requirements are subject to modification in terms of "reasonableness." Thus, the insured is not required to report a trivial accident when there was no reason to believe that the injured person was going to proceed further with the matter. The notice to the insurer need only be given within a reasonable time after the occurrence, and "reasonable" is determined in the light of all the surrounding circumstances.

(f)   Duty to defend. A liability insurer has the duty to defend any suit brought against its insured on a claim which, if valid, would come within the policy coverage. The liability insurer cannot refuse to defend the insured on the grounds that it does not believe the claim of the third person. Consequently, when the third person's complaint against the insured states a claim within the coverage of the policy, a liability insurer cannot refuse to defend on the ground that its investigation shows that the claim is without merit.

If the insurer wrongly refuses to defend and the third person recovers a judgment against the insured in excess of the policy maximum, the insurer is liable to the

---

[5] Some courts interpret the omnibus clause more strictly and refuse to recognize a second permittee when the original insured did not expressly authorize such relending or where the use made by the second permittee was not the same use which the insured contemplated would be made by the first permittee. Hanegan v Horace Mann Mutual Insurance Co. 77 Ill2d 142, 221 NE2d 669; St. Paul Insurance Co. v Carlyle (MoApp) 428 SW2d 753.

insured for the full amount of the judgment. Under statutes in some states, the insurer may also be required to pay the insured the litigation costs and attorney's fees when the insurer refuses in bad faith to settle or defend the action.[6]

§ 37:11. Collision and Upset Insurance. Liability insurance does not indemnify the owner for damage to the insured's own property. In order to obtain this protection for an auto, its owner must obtain property insurance to cover damage from collision and upset.

The term "collision" is generally liberally interpreted so that there is insurance coverage whenever there is an unintended striking of another object even though the object is not an automobile or is not moving. For example, there is a collision when a wheel comes off of the automobile and the automobile falls to the ground.

The phrase "struck by automobile" is likewise liberally interpreted so that there is coverage when the insured ran a motor scooter into an automobile, as against the contention that "struck by automobile" required that the automobile run into the insured.[7]

The term "upset" is likewise liberally construed and covers any event which destroys the normal balance of the automobile even though it does not turn over. Thus it has been held that there is an "upset" when a front wheel of a dump truck slips into a rut and the resulting stress causes the frame and hoist of the truck to twist out of shape.

(a) Exclusions. The insurer against collision is not required to pay in every case. It is commonly provided that the insurer is not liable when the automobile is used by a person who is violating the law. It may also be stipulated that liability is avoided if the auto is subject to a lien or encumbrance that has not been disclosed. It is common to exclude damages, resulting from collision, for the loss of the use of the auto, depreciation, or for loss of personal property in the auto. (See p. 625, Stephan v Allstate Insurance Company)

(b) Notice and Cooperation. As in the case of public liability insurance, the auto owner is under a duty to give notice, to inform, and to cooperate with the insurer. The owner must also give the insurer an opportunity to examine the automobile to determine the extent of damage before making repairs.

§ 37:12. Uninsured Motorist. Statutes and liability policies commonly provide for special coverage when the insured sustains loss because of an uninsured motorist. Since the *uninsured motorist coverage* is a liability coverage, there is no liability of the insurer in the absence of establishing that the uninsured motorist was negligent and would be held liable if sued by the insured. Consequently, collision and accident insurance provide greater protection in that under such coverage the insurer is bound by its contract without regard to whether anyone could be held liable to the insured.

Uninsured motorist coverage generally includes the hit-and-run driver who leaves the scene of the collision before being identified. Policies commonly require that the collision be reported to the police or other appropriate authorities within 24

---

[6] Pendlebury v Western Causalty & Surety Co. 89 Idaho 456, 406 P2d 129.
[7] Foundation Reserve Insurance Co. v McCarthy, 77 NMex 118, 419 P2d 963.

hours and that diligent effort be made to locate the hit-and-run driver. These restrictions are imposed in order to guard against the fraud of reporting the other car as "unknown" when its driver was in fact known, or against the fraud of having a one-car accident and then falsely claiming that the damage was the result of a collision with a hit-and-run driver.

This coverage differs from other insurance that the insured could obtain in that only personal injury claims are covered and generally only up to $10,000. Contact with the uninsured or unidentified vehicle is required, so that there is no uninsured motorist coverage when the insured runs off the road to avoid a collision and sustains injury thereby, or when the insured is injured upon striking oil or an object dropped from the uninsured vehicle.[8]

§ 37:13. No-Fault Insurance. A state statute may require that every automobile liability policy provide for *no-fault coverage.*

(a)   Harm to the Insured. No-fault coverage means that when the insured is injured while using the insured automobile, the insurer will make a payment without regard to whether the other driver was legally liable for the harm. In effect, this is insurance for medical expense and loss of wages that runs in favor of the holder of the liability policy and is in addition to or in lieu of the coverage which the policy provides with respect to liability to other persons.

The no-fault insurance statutes generally do not provide for payment for pain and suffering. Under some statutes recovery is allowed for pain and suffering if the medical expenses exceed $500 or if certain specified injuries have been sustained by the insured.[9]

(b)   Other Party Injury. If another person is harmed, such as a pedestrian or other driver, no-fault insurance statutes generally provide for a similar kind of payment to such third person by that person's auto insurer or by the insurer of the car inflicting the injury.

(c)   Suit Against Party at Fault. No-fault insurance laws bar the claimant from suing the party at fault for ordinary claims. If the automobile collision results in a permanent serious disablement or disfigurement, or death, or if the medical bills and lost wages of the plaintiff exceed a specified amount, suit may be brought against the party who was at fault. A person who is entitled to sue the at-fault party may collect the maximum amount of no-fault insurance and then sue the at-fault party for the total damages, just as though no payment had been received from the insurer. However, if the injured party recovers the total amount from the at-fault party, the injured party must ordinarily repay the insurance company the amount which had been received from it under the no-fault coverage.

(d)   Arbitration. Disputes under no-fault insurance are sometimes determined by arbitration. In addition, some states require the arbitration of small claims of any nature.

---

[8] Wynn v Doe, 255 SC 509, 180 SE2d 95.
[9] Manzanares v Bell, 214 Kan 289, 522 P2d 1291.

(e) **Constitutionality.** No-fault insurance is generally held constitutional, as against the contention that it violates the guarantees of equal protection and due process. It has been sustained as a carefully studied plan to provide a new remedy to meet the problems caused by the automobile: rising cost of insurance, overloading of courts, and delay in making payment to the injured person.[10]

§ 37:14. Theft Insurance. The owner of an automobile can secure theft insurance which will protect from loss through the theft and from a damage to the auto caused by a theft. The standard form of policy covers loss from larceny, robbery, and pilferage as well as theft.

An automobile theft policy does not ordinarily protect against loss of contents. It is common to exclude liability for equipment or personal property taken from the auto, but additional insurance protecting from such theft can be secured. It is common also to exclude liability for loss sustained while a passenger auto is used for commercial transportation or is rented to another.

§ 37:15. Fire, Lightning, and Transportation Insurance. In this type of insurance the insurer agrees to pay for any loss arising out of damage to or the destruction of a motor vehicle or its equipment caused by fire originating in any manner, by lightning, or by the stranding, sinking, burning, collision, or derailment of any conveyance in or upon which the automobile or the truck is being transported. This type of policy is commonly combined with a policy against theft and pilferage and is usually subject to the same exclusions.

§ 37:16. Comprehensive Insurance. In many automobile insurance policies, comprehensive material damage coverage, which protects the policyholder against virtually all such risks except collision or upset, replaces fire and theft insurance. The exclusions for this kind of insurance include wear and tear, freezing, mechanical breakdown, and loss of personal effects.

C. LIFE INSURANCE

A contract of *life insurance* requires the insurer to pay a stipulated sum of money upon the death of the insured. It is not a contract of indemnity since the insurer does not undertake to indemnify the beneficiary for the financial loss sustained as the result of the death of the insured.

§ 37:17. Kinds of Life Insurance Policies.

(a) **Ordinary Life Insurance.** Ordinary life insurance may be subclassified as (1) *straight life insurance,* which requires payments of premiums throughout the life of the insured; (2) *limited payment insurance,* requiring the payment of premiums during a limited period, such as ten, twenty, or thirty years, or until the death of the insured if that should occur before the end of the specified period; (3) *endowment insurance,* under which the insurer undertakes to pay a stipulated sum when the insured reaches

---

[10] Pinnick v Cleary, 271 Mass 592, 271 NE2d 592.

a specified age, or upon death if that occurs sooner; and (4) *term insurance,* under which the insurer undertakes to pay a stipulated sum only in the event of the death of the insured during a specified period, such as one, two, five, or ten years.

Somewhat similar to policies of endowment insurance are *annuity policies* and *retirement income insurance* under which the insured either pays a lump sum to the insurer and thereafter receives fixed annual payments, or pays periodic premiums to the insurer until a certain date and then receives fixed annual payments.

(b)   Group Insurance. *Group life insurance* is insurance of the lives of employees of a particular employer or persons engaged in a particular business or profession. Such policies are usually either term policies or straight life insurance.

(c)   Double Indemnity. Many life insurance companies undertake to pay double the amount of the policy, called *double indemnity,* if death is caused by an accident and occurs within ninety days after the accident. A comparatively small, additional premium is charged for this special protection.

(d)   Disability Insurance. In consideration of the payment of an additional premium, many life insurance companies also provide insurance against total permanent disability of the insured. *Disability* is usually defined in a life insurance policy as any "incapacity resulting from bodily injury or disease to engage in any occupation for remuneration or profit." The policy generally provides that a disability which has continued for a stated minimum period, such as four to six months, will be regarded as a *total permanent disability.*

(e)   Exclusions. Life insurance policies frequently provide that death shall not be within the protection of the policy or that a double indemnity provision shall not be applicable when death is due or caused by (1) suicide, (2) narcotics, (3) violation of the law, (4) execution for a crime, (5) war activities,[11] or (6) operation of aircraft. For such exclusions to operate to relieve the insurer from liability on the policy, there must be a proximate relationship between the prohibited conduct or condition and the harm sustained.

§ 37:18. The Beneficiary. The person to whom the proceeds of a life insurance policy are payable upon the death of the insured is called the *beneficiary.* The beneficiary may be a third person, or the estate of the insured. There may be more than one beneficiary.

The beneficiary named in the policy may be barred from claiming the proceeds of the policy. There may be a prior settlement agreement by which it was agreed that the beneficiary would not claim the insurance. Likewise, it is generally provided by statute or stated by court decision that a beneficiary who has feloniously killed the insured is not entitled to receive the proceeds of the policy.[12]

(a)   Primary and Contingent Beneficiaries. It is desirable to name a primary and a contingent beneficiary. Thus, *A* may make insurance payable to *B,* but provide that if *B* dies before *A,* the insurance shall be payable to *C.* In such case, *B* is the

---

[11] The activity of the United States in Vietnam was a "war" for the purpose of a policy exclusion clause. Bergera v Ideal National Life Ins. Co. (Utah2d) 524 P2d 599.

[12] State Farm Life Insurance Company v Smith, 66 Ill2d 591, 363 NE2d 785.

primary beneficiary, and *C* is the *contingent beneficiary* because *C* takes the proceeds as beneficiary only upon the contingency that *B* dies before *A*.

(b) Change of Beneficiary. The customary policy provides that the insured reserves the right to change the beneficiary without the latter's consent. When the policy contains such a provision, the beneficiary cannot object to a change that destroys all of that beneficiary's rights under the policy and that names another person as beneficiary.[13]

In the absence of a provision in the policy authorizing a change of beneficiary, the original beneficiary acquires a vested interest, even though the beneficiary gave no consideration. The insured therefore cannot thereafter change the beneficiary even with the consent of the insurer. The interest of the beneficiary, however, may still be defeated by the insured if the insured allows the policy to lapse and then obtains a new policy naming a different beneficiary.

The insurance policy will ordinarily state that in order to change the beneficiary, the insurer must be so instructed in writing by the insured and the policy must then be endorsed by the company with the change of the beneficiary. These provisions are generally liberally construed. If the insured has notified the insurer but dies before the endorsement of the change by the company, the change of beneficiary is effective. If, however, the insured has not taken any steps to comply with the policy requirements, a change of beneficiary is not effective, even though a change was intended. (See p. 626, Pena v Salinas)

§ 37:19. Incontestable Clause. Statutes commonly require the inclusion of an incontestable clause in life insurance policies. Ordinarily this clause states that after the lapse of two years the policy cannot be contested by the insurance company. The insurer is free to contest the validity of the policy at any time during the contestable period; but once the period has expired, it must pay the stipulated sum upon the death of the insured and cannot claim that in obtaining the policy the insured had been guilty of misrepresentation, fraud, or any other conduct that would entitle it to avoid the contract of insurance. (See p. 627, Hulme v Springfield Life Insurance Company, Inc.)

The incontestable clause, however, does not bar matters of defense that arise subsequent to the sustaining of loss and does not bar proof that the loss sustained was not covered by the policy.

Generally the incontestable clause is not applicable to double indemnity or disability provisions of a policy.

§ 37:20. Surrender of Policy and Alternatives. The insured may give up or *surrender* the policy of insurance or may use it to raise money in several ways.

(a) Cash Surrender Value. By modern statute or policy provision, it is commonly provided that if the life insurance policy has been in force a stated number of years, usually two or three, the insured may surrender the policy and the insurer will then make a payment of the cash value of the policy to the insured. Term policies do not have a cash surrender value.

---

[13] Reliance Life Insurance Co. v Jaffe, 121 CalApp2d 241, 263 P2d 82.

Each year a certain percentage of the premiums is set aside by the insurer to hold as a reserve against the date when payment must be made under the policy. If the policy is surrendered or canceled, the potential liability of the reserve fund is removed and part of the fund can then be released as a payment to the insured. The longer the policy has been in existence, the larger is the cash surrender value.

(b) **Loan on Policy.** The insured can generally obtain funds by borrowing from the insurer. The modern policy contains a definite scale of maximum amounts that can be borrowed depending upon the age of the policy. The insurer is able to make such loans because it has the security of the cash surrender value if the loan is not repaid; or if the insured dies without making repayment, it may deduct the debt from the proceeds payable to the beneficiary.

The loan value of a policy is usually the same amount as the cash surrender value. The policyholder, as a borrower, must pay interest to the insurance company on the loan.

(c) **Paid-Up Policy.** Under modern statutes or common forms of policies, an insured who can no longer afford the expense of insurance, may request the insurer to issue a new policy of paid-up insurance. The insured in effect takes out a new but smaller paid-up policy through the transfer of the reserve value of the old policy. In some states, when a policy lapses for nonpayment of premiums, the insurer must automatically issue a paid-up policy on the basis of the reserve value of the lapsed policy.

(d) **Extended Insurance.** Instead of a paid-up policy for a smaller amount, it is generally possible under modern statutes and policies for the insured to obtain term insurance that provides the original amount of protection. This remains effective until the reserve value of the original policy has been consumed.

(e) **Reinstatement of Lapsed Policy.** When a premium on a policy is not paid within the required period or within the grace period, the insured generally may reinstate the policy within a reasonable time thereafter as long as the insured is still an insurable risk and provided all premiums that were in arrears are paid.

§ 37:21. Settlement Options. Although an ordinary life insurance policy will provide for the payment of a specified amount upon the death of the insured, the insured generally may designate one or several plans of distribution of this fund. These plans of distribution are called *settlement options*. When the insured has designated a particular option, the beneficiary generally cannot change it after the insured's death. Sometimes the policy reserves to the beneficiary the right to change the settlement option.

§ 37:22. Rights of Creditors. Can creditors complain when a debtor obtains a policy of life insurance? To the extent that the debtor is paying premiums to the insurance company, there is less money with which to pay the creditors. Can the creditors reach the cash surrender value of the policy during the insured's life or the proceeds of the policy upon the insured's death?

If the insured makes the policy payable to the estate of the insured, the proceeds become part of the general assets of the insured's estate upon death, and, in the absence of statute, are subject to claims of the insured's creditors. If the insured is solvent at all times when premiums are paid, the creditors cannot reach the policy in payment of their claims, and the beneficiary is entitled to the entire proceeds of the policy.

Between these two extremes are a variety of situations. The insured may have been insolvent during part or all of the life of the policy; or the obtaining of the insurance policy or the assignment of it or the changing of the beneficiary may have been done to defraud the creditors.

If the policy is originally payable to the estate of the insured, an assignment of the policy by the insured when made in fraud of creditors will not defeat the rights of the insured's creditors.

If the policy is made payable to a third person as beneficiary but the insured is insolvent, courts differ as to the rights of the insured's creditors.

CASES FOR CHAPTER 37

State Farm Mut. Auto Ins. Co. v Johnston

9 Cal 3d 270, 107 Cal Rptr 149, 507 P2d 1357 (1973)

Johnston purchased a 1957 automobile for use by his son Billy, who was under eighteen years of age. Johnston registered the car in his own name and insured it with the State Farm Mutual Automobile Insurance Company. Some time later the car would not run and Billy bought a 1964 car which he registered in his own name. He later sold the 1957 car. He did not insure the 1964 car. When the 1964 car was involved in an accident, he claimed State Farm was liable on the policy obtained by his father on the theory that the 1964 car was within the "temporary substitute automobile" clause of that policy. State Farm denied liability on the ground that the 1964 automobile was a permanent replacement. State Farm brought a declaratory judgment action to determine whether it was liable. The court held that the 1964 car was a "temporary substitute automobile," and that State Farm was liable on its policy. State Farm appealed.

McCOMB, J. . . . [The State Farm] policy provided coverage for the "owned automobile"—meaning the described vehicle and including a "temporary substitute automobile," which was defined as "an automobile not owned by the named insured or his spouse while temporarily used with the permission of the owner as a substitute for the described automobile when withdrawn from normal use because of its breakdown, repair, servicing, loss or destruction." This clause commonly found in automobile liability

insurance policies is primarily designed for the benefit of the insured. The purpose is not to defeat liability but reasonably to define coverage by limiting the insurer's risk to one operating vehicle at a time for a single premium. (12 Couch on Insurance (2d ed. 1964) [Anderson Edition] § 45.219, p. 261.)

. . . As commonly accepted, "temporary" is an antonym of "permanent.". . . Here, it is unclear whether plaintiff, in its use of the word "temporary," was attempting to put a time limitation on the use of the substitute automobile. Any doubt as to its meaning must be resolved in accord with settled rules for interpreting an insurance contract. . . .

Plaintiff argues that since Billy purchased the 1964 car to use in place of the inoperable 1957 car, and then sold the 1957 car, his use of the 1964 car was not a "temporary substitute" but rather a "permanent replacement." In this regard, plaintiff would limit the coverage of the policy to operation of the substituted automobile during the period of repair until the automobile named in the policy is restored to use. But this argument adds a requirement not found in plaintiff's policy and relates the word "temporarily" to the insured car rather than to use of the substitute car. Certainly, plaintiff's policy contemplated that the insured car might never be restored to use during the term of the policy, for it provided for a "temporary substitute" when the insured car should be withdrawn from normal use because of "breakdown . . . loss or destruction." Here, the breakdown of the 1957 car apparently was such that it did not warrant repair but rather replacement for the remainder of the policy period. The important consideration for coverage under this provision of the policy was not the length of time of use but, rather, the purpose of the substitution and the substantial similarity between the use of the originally insured automobile and its substitute. In short, it is contemplated between the insurer and the insured that the *same* use of the *substitute vehicle* will be made as the one originally insured. . . . Here, Billy used the 1964 car substitute for the same driving needs that he had used the 1957 car; Milton, his father, knew of the substitution and approved of its use for the same purposes as had applied with the 1957 car . . . ; and the sale of the inoperable 1957 car would not preclude coverage for the 1964 car as a "temporary substitute automobile" for the remainder of the policy period. . . .

In Nelson v St. Paul Mercury Insurance Company, 83 SD 32, 153 NW2d 397, at page 400, where substantially the same "temporary substitute automobile" provision was considered, the Supreme Court of South Dakota said: "The word 'temporarily' relates to and is a restriction on the use of the substitute vehicle. The policy does not similarly require that the insured vehicle be 'temporarily' withdrawn from normal use. This phase of the insurance contract is without time limit. . . . Furthermore, the policy does not require the replacement, or an intention to replace, the insured vehicle in use after being withdrawn from normal use. A breakdown, repair, loss or destruction might be permanent in nature. Obviously, there would never be an intention to replace in use an automobile damaged beyond repair, as in the present case, or one that has been lost or destroyed. Nevertheless, the substitute automobile clause is clearly designed to extend coverage to an insured in those cases during the remainder of the policy period. The insured is thereby afforded protection paid for and the insurer's risk is confined to one operating vehicle at a time."

Here, if plaintiff's policy, for which a premium was paid, be held to apply to any risk at all, it could apply only to the operation of the 1964 car operated by Billy when the accident occurred. No other risk existed at that time. Plaintiff's risk with respect to the use and operation of the 1957 car ceased with its breakdown and sale. . . . An insurer charges a premium for assuming a risk covered by the policy. An insurer earns a premium only when there is a risk involved. . . . The risk to plaintiff under the policy was the same whether Billy operated the 1957 car or the later substituted 1964 car for the same basic purposes—only one operating vehicle was cov-

ered at the given time. The policy makes clear that its purpose was to extend coverage, without payment of additional premium, to a "temporary substitute automobile" used in place of the insured automobile withdrawn from normal use for reasons stated in the policy. . . .

. . . "In the replacement-automobile cases the courts are usually willing to allow coverage under the policy as long as there is only one operable car. It makes no difference that the replacement car is purchased before the replaced car is sold as long as the replaced car is sold or is not operable at the time of the accident. In this way other users of the highways are protected and the insurance company's liability is limited to the operation of one car by the insured.". . .

While plaintiff's introduction of the word "temporary" into its "substitute automobile" provision appears to have created an ambiguity, it is the plaintiff's language; and plaintiff cannot avoid the effect of its choice of terminology. . . . "The provision for coverage of a substituted vehicle 'is for the insured's benefit' and is to be 'construed liberally in favor of the insured, if any construction is necessary.' ". . . Here, it must be concluded that Billy was using the 1964 car as a "temporary substitute automobile" under the terms of plaintiff's policy.

An argument has been made that the 1964 Chevrolet cannot be regarded as a temporary substitute automobile, because the requirement that the automobile be "temporarily used with the permission of the owner" suggests that the automobile must belong to someone other than the person using it; and Billy owned the 1964 Chevrolet and was using it. Since, however, we must give the policy provisions a liberal interpretation in favor of the insured . . . we find this factor not determinative. Had the 1964 Chevrolet been purchased by Billy's father, the named insured, or the father's spouse, it would clearly have been a newly acquired automobile * and could not be regarded as a temporary substitute automobile, the policy specifically providing that a tem-

---

* Under the policy, "Owned Automobile" includes a newly acquired automobile, which is defined as "an automobile, ownership of which is acquired by the named insured or his spouse, if a resident of the same household, if (1) it replaces an automobile owned by either and covered by this policy . . . and (2) the named insured within 30 days following such delivery date applies to the company for insurance on such newly acquired automobile. . . ."

porary substitute automobile may not be one owned by the named insured or his spouse. But the 1964 car was not acquired by Billy's father or the father's spouse, as a result of which the provisions regarding a newly acquired automobile are inapplicable. At the same time, since the 1964 Chevrolet was owned by someone other than the named insured or his spouse, it can qualify as a temporary substitute automobile.

Billy was unquestionably given unrestricted permission to use the 1957 Chevrolet in order to go to work and run errands; and, as hereinabove pointed out, the 1964 Chevrolet was acquired for use as a temporary substitute for the 1957 Chevrolet after breakdown of the latter. Under the circumstances, since Billy was using the 1964 Chevrolet for the same purposes for which he had been given permission to use the 1957 Chevrolet, he must be regarded as a permissive user of the 1964 Chevrolet and hence covered as an insured under plaintiff's policy.

[Judgment affirmed]

DeRubbo v Aetna Ins. Co.

16 Conn 388, 288 A2d 430 (1971)

Erardi was an automobile dealer. He obtained a liability insurance policy from the Aetna Insurance Company. Joseph Cannatelli, Jr., purchased an automobile from Erardi and paid for it in cash. Over a month later his father, Joseph Cannatelli, Sr., was driving the automobile and was involved in a collision in which DeRubbo and others were injured. At the time the automobile was still registered in the name of Erardi as dealer because he had not given Cannatelli, Jr., a certificate of title in spite of the latter's repeated demands. DeRubbo and the other persons injured obtained a judgment against Cannatelli and then sued Aetna on the theory that Cannatelli, Sr., was an additional insured under the omnibus clause of Aetna's policy issued to Erardi. Aetna denied liability because Cannatelli, Sr., was using the automobile with the permission of a buyer to whom possession and title had been transferred. A judgment was entered in favor of the plaintiffs and Aetna appealed.

THIM, A.J. . . . The basic issue in this case is whether the policy issued by the defendant to Erardi covered the operation of the vehicle by Cannatelli, Sr. . . .

. . . The plaintiffs claimed that there was coverage under the policy because Cannatelli, Sr., was operating the vehicle with the permission of Erardi. The defendant, however, claimed that Cannatelli, Sr., was not an insured under the provisions of the policy because Erardi had transferred possession of the vehicle to Cannatelli, Jr., pursuant to an agreement. The policy specifically states: "[A]ny person or organization other than the named insured with respect to any automobile . . . possession of which has been transferred to another by the named insured pursuant to an agreement of sale" is not an insured within the terms of the policy. . . .

. . . There is nothing ambiguous about the meaning of the language appearing in the disputed provision of this policy. Erardi transferred physical possession of the car to Cannatelli, Jr., pursuant to an agreement of sale. None of the parties contends to the contrary. The plaintiffs concede that Cannatelli, Jr., paid the full price, together with a sum of money to pay taxes and the registration fee, and he received in return a bill of sale for the car. The only part of the transaction to be completed was delivery of a certificate of title. If "agreement of sale" were construed to mean "fully performed agreement of sale," not only would the language of the policy be distorted but the clause would become a nullity. It would be unjust and inequitable to hold the defendant liable for damages inflicted by a motor vehicle which had been sold by the insured and had completely and irrevocably passed from his right of possession and control, simply because the insured had neglected to comply with a provision of the motor vehicle title and registration law by failing to execute and deliver a [proof] of title prior to the occurrence of the accident although the sale and transfer had been completed in every other respect. . . .

Not only had possession been transferred but title had also passed pursuant to the Uniform Commercial Code. "Unless otherwise explicitly agreed title passes to the buyer at the time and place at which the seller completes his performance with reference to the physical delivery of the goods, despite any reservation of a security interest and even though a document of title is to be delivered at a different time or place." [UCC § 2-401(2)]. . . .

In view of the fact that the policy plainly speaks of possession, and since it is uncontested that Cannatelli, Jr., had obtained possession of the car four to six weeks before the accident, the court erred in not charging the jury, as a matter of law, that Cannatelli, Sr., was not an insured under the policy. Further, even if a passing of title were required, which it was not, title had passed under the provisions of the Uniform Commercial Code.

. . . Since, however, this policy ceases to apply to vehicles once there is a transfer of possession, even if the jury found Erardi to be the owner of the vehicle, the policy would not apply, possession having been transferred. . . .

There is no merit to the plaintiffs' claim that the car was being operated, with permission, for garage purposes. Cannatelli, Jr.'s father was using the car to deliver produce for his employer. Assuming, arguendo, that Cannatelli, Sr., had permission from Erardi to use the car, there was still no coverage because possession of and title to the car had been transferred by Erardi to Cannatelli, Jr., pursuant to the agreement of sale. . . .

[Judgment reversed and action remanded]

Stephan v Allstate Insurance Co.

26 ArizApp 367, 548 P2d 1179 (1976)

Stephan obtained a policy from Allstate Insurance Company insuring his car against collision. He was in a collision and the insurance company had the car repaired. During the week that the car was being repaired, Stephan rented another car. He sued Allstate to recover the rental he had paid. From a judgment for the insurance company, he appealed.

HAIRE, C.J. . . . Stephan's claim was based solely on the contention that the policy itself provided *coverage* for such loss of use for the period during which he was deprived of the use of the automobile while being repaired. . . .

. . . He claims that coverage is afforded under the general provisions of Coverage D:

"Automobile Collision Insurance"
"When collision damages your car "Allstate will pay for loss to the owned automobile or non-owned automobile, caused by collision, less the deductible amount stated on the Supplement Page, but the deductible amount shall not be deducted with respect to a collision involving the owned automobile and another automobile insured by Allstate."

Stephan's claim is based upon the language ". . . for loss to the automobile . . . caused by collision. . . ."

. . . The term "loss" is defined as follows: " 'loss' means direct and accidental loss of or damage to (a) the automobile, including its equipment, or (b) other insured property." It should further be noted that Allstate's liability . . . is clearly limited by the precise wording of the policy itself as follows:

"The limit of Allstate's liability is the actual cash value of the property, *or if the loss is of a part its actual cash value at the time of loss, but not to exceed what it would then cost to repair or replace the property or part with other of like kind and quality;* provided, however, the limit of liability for loss to any trailer is $500." (Emphasis added).

Notwithstanding the clear language of the collision provision and the limitation of liability provisions, Stephan contends that the use of the words "loss of" in the definition section could be interpreted to include the "loss of use" of his automobile while undergoing repairs, and thus an ambiguity is created which should be construed in his favor. We disagree.

We recognize that ambiguous provisions in insurance policies must be construed against the insurer. However, this principle becomes applicable only when, after considering all the provisions of the policy, it is not possible for the Court to ascertain the meaning of the language used when applied to the facts before the Court. . . . Here, when all of the provisions of the policy are considered, there is no ambiguity. The collision provisions are clearly limited, . . .

When the provisions of a policy are plain and unambiguous upon its face, as in this case, those provisions must be applied as written, and . . . the Court will not pervert or do violence to the language used, or expand it beyond its plain and ordinary meaning, or add something to the contract which the parties have not put there. . . .

In a further attempt to raise an ambiguity, Stephan places reliance upon an advertising brochure. . . . Stephan does not contend that he placed any reliance on, or was in any way misled, by the brochure provisions. Stephan's contention in this regard is that somehow the brochure indicates that Allstate itself has interpreted its policy collision provision to include coverage for loss of use or cost of a rental replacement while the vehicle is being repaired. Even if we assume that the brochure would be admissible despite the unambiguous language of the parties' contract, a review of its language provides no support for Stephan's contention. The brochure language upon which Stephan bases his contention reads as follows:

> "Collision insurance is really protection for your bank account. If your car is damaged in a collision and it would cut a big chunk out of your savings to get it repaired or replaced—then you need collision insurance.
>
> "You can't count on the 'other guy' to pay. It could take months before the court decides the accident is his fault. Meanwhile, you'll have to pay for your repairs, go without a car or beg, borrow or rent one."

This language, read in its context, is a far cry from a showing that Allstate itself interpreted the collision coverage to include cost of a rental replacement in the brochure. It would require considerable straining on our part to twist this language into the meaning urged by Stephan.

In summary, considering all pertinent provisions of the policy, we find no ambiguity. It simply does not provide coverage for loss of use while an insured automobile is being repaired for collision damage.

[Judgment affirmed]

Pena v Salinas

(TexCivApp) 536 SW2d 671 (1976)

Pena had three insurance policies on his life. He wrote a will in which he specified that the proceeds from the insurance policies should go to his children instead of to Salinas and the other beneficiaries named in the policies. He died the next day. The insurance companies paid the proceeds of the policies to the named beneficiaries. The executor of Pena's estate sued Salinas and the other beneficiaries for the insurance money. From a judgment in favor of the beneficiaries, the executor appealed.

BISSETT, J. . . . Appellant relies solely on the statements contained in the affidavit by his attorney and in the fact that Amador Pena died within 24 hours after he signed the will. The applicable portion of the affidavit reads, as follows:

"Before the death of the said Amador Pena, I was doing some probate work for him in the sale of some property left to him and his children by his deceased wife. A few days before his death, he asked me to look at a will whereby he had left [his] daughter, Leticia Pena Salinas as the sole executrix

of his will. However, at that time, the said Leticia Pena Salinas was having some [marital] problems and had other personal problems and Amador Pena wanted me to change that will which he tore up in my presence. During that time, Amador Pena had been in and out of the Doctor's Hospital with a diagnosis of cancer. Two days before his death [he] called me by telephone and asked me to please expedite the writing of the will so that he could sign it. On the afternoon before his death, the will was finally completed and taken to Amador Pena at the Doctor's Hospital for his review and execution. The will was signed at about 9:00 o'clock that night. The following day, at about 7:00 o'clock in the evening, the said Pedro P. Garcia was informed that earlier in the day, Amador Pena had died. During my conversations with Amador Pena, he could not remember who the named beneficiaries were in his wills but had indicated that he wanted all of his children to share equally in the proceeds of the life insurance policies."

<u>/s/ Pedro P. Garcia</u>
PEDRO P. GARCIA, AFFIANT

The proceeds from the insurance policy to be paid to a designated beneficiary upon the death of the insured becomes a vested right upon the death of the insured and should be paid to the beneficiary unless from some contingency the beneficiary is not entitled to recover the same. . . . In this case, when the insured took out each policy, a contract was formed and all provisions contained within the policy became binding upon the parties to the contract. The two insurance policies involved herein both contained language specifically providing for the manner and method of changing beneficiaries. Such provisions have been upheld by our Courts as valid and binding. . . .

The test for determining whether the requirements of a life insurance policy to change the beneficiary have been met is not strict compliance but "substantial compliance.". . . In essence, this means the policy defines the method by which the insured may change the beneficiary and the insured must substantially comply with that method in order to change the beneficiary. . . .

"Substantial compliance" in terms of its application to the change of a beneficiary provided for in the policy means the "insured' has done all that he reasonably could have done to effect the change. . . .

In making our determination on whether the insured has substantially complied with insurance company requirements, there is no hard and fast rule. Each case must be decided on its own set of facts as to what was done or caused to be done by the insured. . . .

In Creighton v Barnes, 152 Tex. 309, 257 S.W.2d 101 (1953), the testator, B. B. Barnes took out several life insurance policies which named his mother, a daughter and a sister as beneficiaries. The policies contained "change of beneficiary" provisions similar to those present in this case. B. B. Barnes, subsequent to the issuance of the policies, by a will which was duly probated, purported to change the beneficiaries from those persons originally designated by him to his wife. The will provided: "Each of these three policies is being made payable solely to my wife." It was stipulated that B. B. Barnes never forwarded any request for a change of beneficiaries to the Insurance Company. The Supreme Court held that the named beneficiaries in the policies were entitled to the proceeds from the policies. The Court noted that there was no doubt but that B. B. Barnes knew what was necessary to be done in order to change beneficiaries since he had, prior to the making of the will, changed beneficiaries originally named in some of the policies. The Court said: "To permit a change of beneficiary by a will in disregard of provisions in a policy which have the same or similar requirements as to method of change, as these two policies of insurance here, would bring about much uncertainty and litigation as to payment of life insurance policies. Prompt payment of life insurance to those who are the beneficiaries is of inestimable importance to those who are left behind at the death of an insured. Delay and confusion resulting in unnecessary hardship should be avoided.". . .

Neither the decedent (Amador Pena) nor his attorney complied with the provision in each policy that would have effectuated a change of beneficiaries. . . .

Here, the . . . proof shows that the testator was conscious and wanted to change his will in a particular and vital area, and indicated that he wanted all of his children to share equally in the proceeds of the policies. He discussed the matters with his attorney. The new will was drawn and executed within a matter of hours after his conference with his attorney. There is no showing . . . that any effort was made by either the decedent or his attorney to change the name of the beneficiary in

any of the three policies except by the directions and provisions in the will itself. Such is not sufficient. . . . The test of "substantial compliance" was not met in this case. . . .

[Judgment affirmed]

Hulme v Springfield Life Insurance Company, Inc.

(Okla) 565 P2d 666 (1977)

The Springfield Life Insurance Company issued a group policy on the lives of the employees of the Chickasha Transit Mixed Concrete, Inc. Kamm was included in the list of employees and a certificate of insurance was issued to him. Hulme was named in the certificate as the beneficiary. The master contract between the insurer and the employer stated "this contract shall be incontestable after two years from date of issue, except for nonpayment of premiums." Kamm died four years later. The insurer refused to pay the death benefit on the theory that Kamm was not an employee and therefore was not covered by the policy. Hulme claimed that the incontestable clause prevented raising this issue. From a judgment for the beneficiary, the insurer appealed.

LAVENDER, V.C.J. . . . The incontestable clause of the master contract reads: . . . "This contract shall be incontestable after two years from the date of issue, except for nonpayment of premiums. . . ."

Insurer argues Kamm was not covered by the group policy for he was not an employee or partner of the policyholder, Chickasha Transit Mixed Concrete, Inc.; and that defense was not precluded by the incontestable clause. . . .

Appellee Hulme argues the incontestable clause does preclude the issue as to whether Kamm qualified for coverage. . . . Insurer says there was no contract of insurance on the life of Kamm for Kamm did not qualify as a member of the eligible group. An attack on validity is admitted to be precluded by the incontestable clause. It is argued that this is not an attack on the original validity of the contract. This court has rejected that position in *Baum v Massachusetts Mutual Life Insurance Co.,* Okl., 357 P.2d 960, 964 (1960). . . .

The incontestable clause estops the insurer from denying that the insured was an employee at the time of the issuance of the policy. In *Baum, supra,* the deceased regularly did tax work for employer but the evidence failed to show he was, in a technical sense, an employee and as such a member of the class covered under the group policy. On the purpose of the incontestable clause, the opinion quotes from *Metropolitan Life Ins. Co. v Peeler,* 122 Okl. 135, 176 P. 939, 940, 6 A.L.R. 441 (1918), saying: . . . "The meaning of the provision is that, if the premiums are paid, the liability shall be absolute under the policy, and that *no question shall be made of its original validity.* The language admits of no reasonable construction other than that *the company reserves to itself the right to ascertain all the* matter and *facts material to its risk and the validity of its contract* for one (present case, two) year; and that *if within that time it does not ascertain all the facts, and does not cancel and rescind the contract, it may not do so afterwards upon any ground then in existence.* (Citing cases.)" (Explanation and emphasis added.)

Here, whether Kamm qualified as a member of the eligible group goes to the question of original validity. Under the incontestable clause, the insurer reserved the right to ascertain all facts material to the validity of its contract, including the eligibility of Kamm to enroll as a member of the covered group. If within that two year time period, the insurer did not ascertain all the facts, and did not cancel or rescind the contract, it may not do so afterwards upon grounds then in existence. . . .

36 [Oklahoma Statutes] 1971, § 4015 provides: "A clause in any policy of life insurance providing that such policy shall be incontestable after a specified period shall preclude only a contest of the validity of the policy, and shall not preclude the assertion at any time of defenses based upon provisions in the policy which exclude or restrict coverage, whether or not such restrictions or exclusions are excepted in such clause; nor shall it be construed to preclude adjustment at any time of the amount payable or benefits accruing under the policy for misstatement of age, whether or not such age adjustment provision is excepted in such clause." We have heretofore found the present case to be a contest of the validity of the policy. Further language of the section does not allow the incontestable clause to preclude a defence based on policy provisions which exclude or restrict coverage. Those restrictions or exclusions need not be excepted in the incontestable clause.

Insurer contends Section 1 of the master contract is a policy provision excluding or restricting coverage, and a defense based thereunder is excluded from the incontestable clause. That section of the contract defines an "insured person" as an employee of the policyholder and sets up conditions one must meet to be an employee, i.e. be a partner; policyholder treats one as employee by withholding income tax, covering him with workmen's compensation insurance and unemployment compensation insurance; and work at least thirty hours per week at a fixed salary. We do not agree with this position of the insurer.

Section 1 of the master contract relates to original coverage provided in the group policy. It does not include an exclusion or restriction to that original coverage so offered. Defenses, excluded from the operation of the incontestable clause under § 4015 and based on policy provisions of exclusion or restriction, are limited to exclusions from or restrictions on the coverage after it is originally provided and set forth. Here that type of policy provision is found in Section 2 of the master contract. There the class of persons covered is shown to be "All full-time Employees of the Policyholder," with the following classes excluded from coverage shown as "None."

The incontestable clause found in the master contract, here, precludes a defense that Kamm was not an employee. That defense is not excluded from the incontestable clause by operation of § 4015.

[Judgment affirmed]

QUESTIONS AND CASE PROBLEMS

1.   What social forces are affected by the concept of no-fault insurance?
2.   Compare the nature of and extent of coverage of (a) life insurance, (b) fire insurance, and (c) automobile liability insurance.
3.   Compare (a) uninsured motorist coverage and (b) no-fault insurance.

4. Compare the coverage of a fire insurance policy with respect to
   (a) damage sustained when a hot water boiler explodes and a fire results;
   (b) damage caused by fire which was caused by lightning;
   (c) damaged caused to surrounding furniture when a kitchen oven overheats because its thermostat did not shut the oven off; and
   (d) fire caused by the negligence of the insured.

5. Leibold obtained a policy of automobile liability insurance from Security Mutual Insurance Company. He became irate when informed that property damage was not covered and immediately obtained a policy from Providence Washington Insurance Company. Leibold, however, did nothing more about the Security Mutual policy. Some time later, Leibold's son was involved in a collision. Providence claimed that Security should share the loss. Security asserted that its policy had been cancelled when Leibold obtained the Providence policy. Was Security correct? [Providence Washington Ins. Co. v Security Mutual Ins. Co., 35 NY2d 583, 324 NE2d 134]

6. The Hess-Mace Trucking Co. was delivering sand to a contractor, A. Teichert & Son. One of the sand trucks got stuck in a soft ramp. A water truck owned by Marion's Trucking Co. tried to tow the stuck truck. In arranging the tow line, the driver of the sand truck was injured. The insurer of the water truck claimed that the insurer of the sand truck was required to pay for the injury on the theory that the latter's policy covered accidents arising out of the "use" of the sand truck. Decide. [St. Paul Fire & Marine Ins. Co. v Hartford Accident & Indemnity Co., 244 Cal App 2d 826, 53 Cal Rptr 650]

7. Turner had a policy of life insurance issued by the Equitable Life Assurance Society. His wife was the benficiary. When she died, Turner changed the beneficiary to Olsen. Thereafter he began drinking heavily and was committed two times to institutions for alcoholism. About two years after he was released the second time, he changed the beneficiary of the policy to Hawkins. When Turner died, Olsen sued Hawkins and the insurance company for the proceeds of the policy, claiming that the change of beneficiary was not valid on the theory that Turner lacked capacity to change the beneficiary. In addition to Turner's confinement to institutions for alcoholism, it was shown that on a number of instances he had been arrested for minor offenses committed while intoxicated, and there was evidence that he was childish and forgetful. Was Olsen entitled to the proceeds of the policy? [Olsen v Hawkins, 90 Idaho 28, 408 P2d 462]

8. Marshall Produce Co. insured its milk and egg processing plant against fire with the St. Paul Fire & Marine Insurance Co. Smoke from a fire near its plant was absorbed by its egg powder. Cans of the powder delivered to the United States Government were rejected as contaminated. Marshall Produce sued the insurance company for a total loss. The insurer contended that there had been no fire involving the insured property and no total loss. Decide. [Marshall Produce Co. v St. Paul Fire & Marine Insurance Co., 256 Minn 404, 98 NW2d 280]

9. George Rogers insured his life with the National Producers Life Insurance Company. Ten years later he committed suicide. The insurance company denied liability because the policy stated that death by suicide was excepted. The beneficiary of the policy claimed that the insurer could not raise this defense because the two years specified by the two-year incontestability clause had expired. She sued the insurance company. Was she entitled to recover? [National Producers Life Ins. Co. v Rogers, 8 ArizApp 53, 442 P2d 876]

10. A father told his son that the son could have the father's car but that the son must not drive it. The son had a friend drive the car. The friend ran into another car. The insurer denied liability on the ground that the father had not given permission to the

friend to drive the car and that therefore the friend was not an "other driver" within the protection of the omnibus clause. Decide [Esmond v Liscio, 209 Pa Super 200, 224 A2d 793]

11.   A father owned an automobile. He insured it under a policy which also covered temporary substitute and newly-acquired vehicles. Thereafter, when the finance company repossessed the father's car, his son bought a new automobile. Was the son's automobile covered by the father's policy? [Hays v Robertson, 20 Utah 2d 816, 435 P2d 925]

12.   Walker obtained a policy of life insurance from the National Life and Accident Insurance Company. The policy reserved the right to change the beneficiary. Walker named his wife as beneficiary, and she paid the premiums on the policy. Later Walker's wife sued the insurance company and claimed that the insured could not change the beneficiary because she had paid the premiums on the policy. Decide. [National Life and Accident Insurance Co. v Walker, (Ky) 246 SW2d 139]

13.   Harsha had a policy of automobile liability insurance issued by the Fidelity General Insurance Co. that provided coverage as to personal injuries by an "uninsured motorist" to the extent of $10,000. Harsha's son was injured while a passenger when Harsha's automobile collided with Leffard's automobile. The insurance policy carried by Leffard had a liability maximum of $10,000, and his insurer paid $9,500 to Harsha on behalf of her son. Harsha, claiming that her son's injuries were $50,000, sued Fidelity on the theory that Leffard was an uninsured motorist with respect to the $40,000 not covered by his policy. Was she correct? [Harsha v Fidelity General Insurance Co., 11 Ariz App 438, 465 P2d 377]

14.   Allen's tank truck was insured against "explosion" with the Manhattan Fire and Marine Insurance Company. For an unknown reason, the sides of the tank collapsed inward. Allen claimed that this was an explosion within the protection of the policy. Was he correct? [Allen v Manhattan Fire and Marine Ins. Co. (TexCivApp) 519 SW2d 706]

15.   Sackett insured his automobile with the Farmer's Insurance Exchange against loss by accidental means. A gas station attendant improperly fastened the radiator cap with the result that the water boiled out of the radiator and damaged the engine. The Farmers Insurance Exchange claimed that it was not liable because the harm came within the exception of "mechanical breakdown and failure." Was the insurer correct? [Sackett v Farmers Insurance Exchange, 237 Cal App 2d 899, 47 Cal Rptr 350]

16.   Fountain was a passenger in the automobile of Williams. As an "occupant" of the Williams car, Fountain was protected by the no-fault insurance coverage of Williams. When Williams stopped at a service station, Fountain got out to watch the service attendant put water in the radiator. The water contained gasoline and exploded when it touched the radiator. Fountain was injured and sued Williams, seeking to recover under the no-fault insurance of Williams. The insurer denied liability because Fountain was not an "occupant" of the Williams car. Was this a valid defense? [Newcomb Hospital v Fountain, 141 NJSuper 291, 357 A2d 836]

38 Bankruptcy

Our society has provided a system by which the honest debtor can, in substance, pay into court whatever property the debtor possesses, be relieved of all unpaid debts, and start economic life anew. This is achieved by the bankruptcy law in the case of the federal government and, to a limited degree, by insolvency law in the case of the states.

A. GENERAL PRINCIPLES

Historically the bankruptcy and insolvency laws were not concerned with benefiting the debtor, as much as they were with benefiting creditors. In their origin, such laws were designed to enable creditors to compel fraudulent debtors to bring their property into court and to pay it to their creditors, thus preventing them from concealing their property or from paying it to only some of their creditors. Today, bankruptcy and insolvency proceedings have both features, as can be seen from the fact that such proceedings may be started by the debtors or by creditors.

§ 38:1. Classification of Bankrupts.

(a)   Voluntary Bankrupts. A *voluntary bankrupt* is a debtor who voluntarily goes into bankruptcy and requests that the court make an adjudication of bankruptcy. Any person, and in most instances any corporation or association, may become a voluntary bankrupt. The filing of a voluntary petition automatically operates as an adjudication or determination that the petitioner is bankrupt.

Municipal, railroad, insurance, and banking corporations, and savings and loan associations cannot be voluntary bankrupts.[1]

(b)   Involuntary Bankrupts. An *involuntary bankrupt* is one who has been subjected to the bankruptcy law upon the petition of creditors. If the necessary conditions are satisfied, most natural persons, partnerships, and corporations owing debts that amount to the sum of $1,000 or more may be forced by creditors into bankruptcy. Wage earners[2] and farmers; municipal, railroad, insurance, and banking corporations; and building and loan associations cannot be adjudicated involuntary bankrupts.[3]

---

[1] 11 United States Code § 22(a).

[2] A "wage earner" for this purpose is defined as an individual who works for wages, salary, or hire, and whose compensation does not exceed $1,500 a year. 11 USC § 1(32).

[3] Special statutory provision is made for the reorganization and liquidation of such corporations because of the nature of the enterprise and in order to protect the public.

§ 38:2. Involuntary Proceedings. If there are 12 or more creditors, 3 or more of them must join in the petition. If there are less than 12 creditors, one of them may file the petition. (See p. 640, In re Okamoto)

The petitioning creditor or creditors must have provable claims [4] against the debtor totaling $500 or more. The amount of the claims must be in excess of the value of pledged securities held by the creditors.

The debtor against whom the petition is filed may appear and oppose the petition. If there are more than 11 creditors when less than 3 filed the petition, the creditors who have not joined in the petition are given an opportunity to join. If the statutory number of creditors do not join in the petition, it will be dismissed.

§ 38:3. Acts of Bankruptcy. An involuntary petition may not be filed unless the debtor has committed an act of bankruptcy within 4 months prior to the filing of the petition.

A debtor commits an act of bankruptcy under federal statute (1) by concealing, removing, or permitting to be concealed or removed, any property with intent to hinder, delay, or defraud any creditor; (2) by transferring, while insolvent, any property to one or more creditors with intent to prefer such creditor or creditors over other creditors; (3) by permitting, while insolvent, any creditor to obtain a lien upon any property through legal proceedings and failing to vacate or discharge such lien within 30 days from the date thereof or at least 5 days before the date that was set for any sale or other disposition of such property; (4) by making a general assignment for the benefit of creditors; (5) while insolvent, by permitting or being forced to put a receiver or a trustee in charge of the debtor's property; or (6) by admitting in writing an inability to pay debts and the willingness to be adjudged a bankrupt. [5]

§ 38:4. Insolvency. Insolvency is a necessary element of the second, third, and fifth acts of bankruptcy, but not of the others. The Bankruptcy Act declares that a person is deemed to be *insolvent* when the aggregate of the person's property, exclusive of any property conveyed, transferred, concealed, removed, or permitted to be concealed or removed, with intent to defraud, hinder, or delay creditors, shall not at a fair valuation be sufficient in amount to pay debts.

A debtor is insolvent under the bankruptcy act when the debtor's assets, fairly valued, are not sufficient to pay all debts. This contrasts with the equity concept of insolvency, which is the inability to pay debts as they become due. [6]

§ 38:5. Bankruptcy Officials. The actual bankruptcy proceeding, apart from that which takes place in court, is under the control of certain officials: (a) the referee, (b) the receiver, and (c) the trustee.

(a)   Referee. A *referee* is appointed for a 6-year term to hear the evidence in bankruptcy cases and act as a special bankruptcy court. A referee may impose fines for contempt up to $250.

---

[4] See § 38:13 of this chapter. A claim may be unliquidated as to amount, although the unliquidated claim may be disqualified if a maximum value cannot be estimated. 11 USC § 95(b).

[5] The filing of a voluntary petition in bankruptcy is in itself an act of bankruptcy since the debtor admits in writing the inability to pay debts and the willingness to be adjudged a bankrupt.

[6] Note that under the Uniform Commercial Code both criteria for insolvency are employed. UCC § 1-201(23).

(b)   Receiver. On the petition of creditors who fear that the assets of the debtor will be lost, a *receiver* may be appointed as custodian to preserve the assets and turn them over to the trustee when appointed.

(c)   Trustee. The creditors of the debtor elect, or if they fail to do so, the court appoints, a trustee. The *trustee* has a double role as owner of the property of the debtor and as holder of the rights of a most favored creditor.

§ 38:6. The Bankruptcy Trustee as Successor to the Debtor.

The trustee in bankruptcy automatically becomes by operation of the law the owner of all property of the bankrupt in excess of such property as the bankrupt is entitled to under local state exemption laws.

As the statutory owner or successor to the bankrupt's property, the trustee has only the status of an assignee. That is, the trustee will not be a holder in due course of paper as to which the bankrupt was merely an ordinary holder.

(a)   Payment of Bankrupt's Outstanding Checks. The rule that the title to the property of the bankrupt passes to the trustee in bankruptcy is subject to an exception that a drawee bank in which the bankrupt has a checking account may make payment on a bankrupt's check when it has had no notice or knowledge of the bankruptcy.

§ 38:7. The Bankruptcy Trustee as a Favored Creditor.

The bankruptcy trustee possesses the rights that are possessed by the most favored creditor of the bankrupt. Specifically, this means that the trustee can avoid certain preferences gained by a judgment against the bankrupt or by a transfer of property, of which a recording or registering is required, within 4 months prior to the filing of the petition or after the filing thereof and before adjudication.[7] The trustee is required by the terms of the Bankruptcy Act to recover for the benefit of the creditors any of the bankrupt's property that has been transferred within 4 months prior to the filing of the petition, with the intent to hinder, delay, or defraud any creditors, or that is in the hands of a person under a transfer that is void by the laws of any state or that was received by such person with knowledge or reason to know that the debtor was insolvent.[8]

§ 38:8. Voidable Preferences.

To constitute a voidable preference, with the consequence that the transfer or payment may be avoided by the debtor's trustee in bankruptcy, there must be (1) a transfer of property, (2) within the four months preceding bankruptcy, (3) to or for the benefit of a creditor, (4) for or on account of an antecedent debt, (5) which pays that creditor a greater percentage of the debt owed than is paid to other creditors of the same class, and which is made (6) when the debtor is insolvent, and (7) the creditor knows or has reason to know that the debtor is insolvent.[9] (See p. 641, Arst v First National Bank)

§ 38:9. Avoidance of Liens.

The mere adjudication of bankruptcy does not automatically avoid or vacate a lien created within the 4-month period, and the lien remains in force unless avoided by the trustee as a preferential transfer. If the lien is not avoided in

---

[7] 11 USC § 96(b).
[8] 11 USC §§ 107(d), 110(e).
[9] Bankruptcy Act § 60, 11 USC § 96.

the bankruptcy proceeding and if the trustee in bankruptcy sells assets of the bankrupt that are subject to a judicial lien, the purchaser from the trustee in bankruptcy, in an action in a state court, may avoid the creditor's lien to the same extent as could the trustee in bankruptcy.

When a creditor has an unperfected security interest in personal property of the bankrupt, such security interest cannot be asserted against the trustee in bankruptcy of the debtor, without regard to whether it would otherwise be preferential within the meaning of the Bankruptcy Act. If the security interest has been perfected and is not preferential in character, the trustee in bankruptcy and any purchaser of the debtor's assets from the trustee holds such assets subject to the interest of the creditor.[10]

As Article 9 of the UCC has eliminated the significance of title in transactions involving personal property, the determination of whether the creditor prevails over the bankrupt debtor's trustee in bankruptcy is not controlled by the name of the transaction between the creditor and the debtor nor by whether the creditor has or has not reserved title to the collateral. The same conclusion is to be reached when a mortgage of real estate is involved since even in title theory states, the mortgage is merely a lien with respect to third persons even though it purports to transfer title to the mortgagee.

B. ADMINISTRATION OF BANKRUPT'S ESTATE

Federal statutes regulate in detail the manner in which claims against the bankrupt are to be determined and how the assets are to be distributed in payment of the claims.

§ 38:10. Meetings of Creditors. At various times in the administration of the bankruptcy, a meeting of the creditors is held, such as the initial meeting to appoint a trustee, subsequent meetings to pass on particular matters authorized by the Bankruptcy Act, and a final meeting when the estate is to be closed.[11]

A majority in number and in the amount of claims of all creditors who are present and whose claims have been allowed is required for any decision by the creditors. Creditors who have priority or security are not entitled to vote, nor are their claims counted in computing the number of creditors or the amounts of their claims, unless their claims exceed the values of such priority or security, and then only for such excess.[12]

§ 38:11. Interrogation of Persons. Provision is made for the examination of the bankrupt and other persons as to the bankrupt's property and conduct relating thereto.

---

[10] When a security interest in personal property is involved, perfection is governed by Article 9 of the Uniform Commercial Code. If land is involved, the perfection of a security interest therein, such as a mortgage, is governed by non-Code law of the state where the land is located.

[11] 11 USC § 91(d), (e).

[12] 11 USC § 92(a), (b).

§ 38:12. Claims Against the Bankrupt.

(a) **Claims That Are Provable.** In general, any debt of the bankrupt may be proved in bankruptcy. Ordinarily this means any claim to money which can be proved in a law court or before an administrative board can be proved in bankruptcy. Taxes are provable in bankruptcy although they are not strictly "debts" of the bankrupt.

Stating that a debt is provable in bankruptcy merely means that the creditor is permitted to present proof of the claim. Whether the claim will be allowed and the effect of a discharge in bankruptcy upon the claim are controlled by other provisions of the bankruptcy law.

(1) Immature and Contingent Claims. A claim which is not yet due, an immature claim, and a claim which may never be due, a contingent claim, may be proved in bankruptcy although such a claim could not be presented in a court of law because such court requires that a plaintiff have a present definite right.

(2) Unliquidated Claims. The fact that the amount of a claim is unliquidated (uncertain or disputed), as contrasted with a claim for a specific number of dollars, does not prevent its being proved in bankruptcy provided there is a reasonable basis for estimating the maximum amount of the claim. Claims for anticipatory breach of contracts and leases are provable in bankruptcy.[13]

(b) **Claims That Are Not Provable.** The claims which are not provable in bankruptcy may be classified as to the inability to prove the facts or the existence of security for the claim. If a claim is so vague or uncertain that there is no reasonable basis for holding that it is a liability of the bankrupt or for determining the amount of the claim, the claim cannot be proved.

If the creditor has security for the claim, the claim cannot be proven in bankruptcy. If the claim exceeds the value of the security, the creditor may prove the excess of the claim in bankruptcy. If the creditor should release the security to the trustee in bankruptcy, thereby converting the claim into an unsecured claim, the entire claim may be proved in bankruptcy.

§ 38:13. Proof and Allowance of Claims.
Each creditor is required to file a sworn statement setting forth any claim made against the bankrupt and the basis thereof. These claims are ordinarily examined by a referee. The claim is then allowed or disallowed as in any other lawsuit. A claim must ordinarily be disallowed if not presented within six months after the first meeting of creditors.[14]

The six-months time limitation on the filing of claims is mandatory and a creditor is not excused from filing within that time even though the trustee in bankruptcy in fact knew of the existence of the creditor's claim. (See p. 642, In re Vega Baja Lumber Yard)

A creditor who receives some preferential payment or transfer of property within four months prior to the filing of the petition in bankruptcy cannot prove any claim

---

[13] 11 USC § 103(a)(9).
[14] 11 USC § 93(n).

without first surrendering to the trustee the payment or property transferred by the debtor.

§ 38:14. Sale of Bankrupt's Assets. In order to pay the debts of the bankrupt, it is necessary to convert the bankrupt's assets into cash and the trustee is accordingly authorized to sell property. The sale in general may be made in any manner that is in the best interests of the estate. Such sales are under the supervision of the bankruptcy court.

§ 38:15. Distribution of Estate. After all of the bankrupt's debts are determined, the assets that have been collected by the trustee are distributed first to those creditors with priorities; then to the general creditors without priorities; and, should any balance remain after all creditors have been paid, the balance to the bankrupt. These payments to creditors, called *dividends,* are made in installments.

The Bankruptcy Act confers a prior right of payment to (1) costs of administration and expenses necessary to preserve the estate, filing fees paid by creditors in involuntary proceedings, expenses of creditors in recovering property transferred or concealed by the bankrupt, and the reasonable expenses of creditors in opposing a composition that is refused or set aside; (2) wages due employees, clerks, sales personnel, or servants, earned within 3 months preceding the petition, but not to exceed $600 to each person; (3) expenses of creditors in opposing an arrangement or a plan for the discharge of a bankrupt, or in convicting a person of violating the bankruptcy law; (4) taxes owed by the bankrupt, except taxes against property over and above the value of the interest of the bankrupt therein; and (5) debts owed persons, including the United States, who by law are entitled to priority.

Payments due by an employer to a trust for employees are not "wages" within the priority provision where payments from the trust can only be made upon retirement, disability, or death.

C. STATUS OF BANKRUPT

When a debtor is adjudicated a bankrupt, an important change takes place in the debtor's legal status. When thereafter granted a discharge, the debtor is released from ordinary debts.

§ 38:16. Rights and Duties of Bankrupt. The Bankruptcy Act confers certain rights upon and imposes certain duties on the bankrupt.[15] If the debtor fails to cooperate or deceives the court, the law provides specific penalties in addition to denying the bankrupt the benefits of the statute.

(a)   Rights. The debtor has the right to object to being declared or adjudicated a bankrupt. If so adjudicated, the debtor may request a discharge in bankruptcy, and is protected generally from arrest on civil process while within the court district on matters relating to the bankruptcy proceeding. The debtor is given an immunity from criminal prosecution based on the testimony at meetings other than at the hearing on the application for a discharge and other than in a prosecution for perjury.

---

[15] 11 USC §25.

(b)   Duties. The debtor is required to file a statement showing the property possessed; any claims to an exemption; and the names of all creditors, with detailed information as to their claims. The debtor must attend meetings of creditors and hearings before the referee and the court, and must answer all proper questions relating to the property. The debtor must examine the proofs of claims filed to see if there is any question about any of them and must obey the orders of the bankruptcy court.

§ 38:17. Discharge in Bankruptcy. The decree terminating the bankruptcy proceeding is generally a discharge or release of the debtor from debts.

(a)   Application for Discharge. The adjudication of any individual to be a bankrupt operates automatically as an application for a discharge in bankruptcy. A corporation may file an application for a discharge within six months after it is adjudged a bankrupt.[16]

(b)   Denial of Discharge. The application for discharge will be denied if the bankrupt has: (1) committed certain offenses punishable by imprisonment as provided in the Act; (2) unjustifiably destroyed, mutilated, falsified, concealed, or failed to keep books of accounts or records from which the bankrupt's financial status and business transactions might be ascertained; (3) within a year previous to the filing of the petition, did remove, transfer, conceal, or destroy any property with the intent to hinder, delay, or defraud creditors, or did permit others to do so; (4) was granted a discharge in bankruptcy within 6 years; (5) refused, during the proceedings, to answer any material question approved by the court, or to obey any lawful order of the court; (6) failed to explain satisfactorily the loss of any assets, or the deficiency of assets to pay debts; or (7) failed to pay in full the filing fees required by the Bankruptcy Act.[17] A bankrupt who is in business may also be refused a discharge if money or property was obtained by a false representation in writing concerning financial condition.

If a ground for refusing a discharge appears to exist, the bankrupt must be given a reasonable opportunity to explain. Thus it is improper to refuse a discharge for lack of records where the debtor could prove that they had been lost because of accident or fault of third persons.[18]

A discharge in bankruptcy cannot be refused for any ground not stated in the Bankruptcy Act. Consequently, a discharge cannot be refused because the bankrupt was a gambler.

(1)   False Financial Statement. When the debtor has obtained credit by making a false written statement as to financial condition, the claim of the creditor who extended credit in reliance on that statement is not affected by the debtor's discharge in bankruptcy if the misstatement was material and was fraudulently made.

When a debtor has obtained an additional loan on the basis of a fraudulent written misrepresentation as to financial condition, there is a conflict of authority

---

[16] 11 USC § 32(a).
[17] 11 USC § 32(c).
[18] In re Martin (CA2 NY) 554 F2d 55.

whether the total loan or only the additional loan obtained by the false representation is not discharged by the bankruptcy discharge.[19]

If the bankrupt is a nonbusiness debtor, such as an ordinary consumer, the false financial statement does not bar a discharge in bankruptcy but merely prevents the discharge in bankruptcy from barring the claim of the particular creditor who had extended credit.

(2)   False Financial Statement as a Bar to Discharge. The obtaining of credit by means of a false financial statement is a bar to a discharge when the bankrupt was engaged in business.[20]

In addition, it is necessary to show that the creditor had relied on the false financial statement and had acted reasonably in so doing. If the surrounding circumstances indicated to a reasonable person that the statement might be false and that further inquiry should have been made, a creditor who merely relies or claims to have relied on the statement without making any further inquiry cannot raise the falsity of the statement as a bar to the debtor's discharge and the debtor will not be denied a discharge merely because the false financial statement had been made. (See p. 643, Kentile Floors, Inc. v Winham)

§ 38:18.   Effect of Discharge. With certain exceptions, the discharge in bankruptcy releases the bankrupt from all provable debts.

When a claim is discharged in bankruptcy, it must be ignored for all purposes. For example, when a collision damage judgment entered against the bankrupt is discharged, the judgment ceases to exist, even though in fact it has not been paid.

The discharge in bankruptcy does not discharge the debts but merely gives the debtor a protection from their enforcement. The order discharging the bankrupt, however, expressly declares that a judgment obtained in any other court upon a discharged claim is "null and void" and enjoins all creditors of the bankrupt from bringing suit on such obligations.[21]

After a debtor has been discharged in bankruptcy, there are no restrictions upon the debtor's activities or use of property. If necessary capital can be obtained, the bankrupt can reengage in any business, including the business in which the bankrupt had engaged prior to bankruptcy. Property acquired after the discharge in bankruptcy cannot be reached by prebankruptcy creditors even though their claims had not been paid in full. It is immaterial in what manner the postbankruptcy property is acquired, whether as earnings, gifts, inheritance, or investment gains.

A state cannot in any way penalize a person for going through bankruptcy.

(a)   Unscheduled Debts. A debt which is not included in the schedule of debts filed in the bankruptcy proceeding is not discharged by the bankruptcy discharge. It is immaterial why the debt was omitted from the schedule.

(b)   Nondischargeable Debts. Certain debts are not affected by the bankruptcy discharge. Thus any amount remaining unpaid after the bankruptcy may still be collected

---

[19] In re Danns (CA2 NY) 558 F2d 114.
[20] 11 USC § 32(c)(3).
[21] 11 USC § 32(f)(2).

from the bankrupt. The debts which are not discharged are debts that: (a) are due as taxes which became due and owing within the 3 years preceding bankruptcy; (b) are liabilities (1) for obtaining property by false pretenses or false representation, (2) for a loan of property obtained on credit or an extension of credit obtained by a materially false written statement by the debtor as to financial condition, (3) for willful and malicious injuries to the person or the property of another; [22] (4) for alimony for support, (5) for seduction of an unmarried female, (6) for breach of promise accompanied by seduction, and (7) for criminal conversation; (c) have not been listed by the bankrupt in time to be proved, unless the creditor had notice or actual knowledge of the proceedings; (d) are created by the bankrupt's fraud, embezzlement, misappropriation, or defalcation while acting as an officer or in any fiduciary position; (e) are wages due to employees, clerks, sales personnel, or servants, which have been earned within 3 months preceding the petition; or (f) are due for moneys of an employee received or retained by the bankrupt to secure the faithful performance by such employee of the provisions of the contract of employment. (See p. 644, Romero v Allen)

§ 38:19. Liability of Third Persons and Collateral. The fact that a debtor obtains a discharge in bankruptcy does not ordinarily bar a claimant or creditor with respect to third persons or collateral. For example, the bankruptcy of the maker of a promissory note does not discharge the liability of an indorser. Similarly, when an automobile public liability insurer is liable directly to the injured third person, that liability is not affected by the fact that the insured driver has been discharged in bankruptcy. Similarly, if a creditor has a valid security interest in collateral that was perfected more than four months before the filing of the bankruptcy petition, the creditor's security interest is not affected by the debtor's discharge in bankruptcy. Likewise, a tax lien on the bankrupt's property is not affected by the debtor's discharge.

D. BANKRUPTCY COMPOSITIONS

In addition to the traditional liquidation in bankruptcy, twentieth century amendments to the bankruptcy law permit the parties by agreement to make various reorganizations and compositions.

§ 38:20. Corporate Reorganizations. The provisions for corporate reorganization [23] permit a corporation, a trustee acting under a deed of trust, or 3 or more creditors of the corporation with certain claims amounting in the aggregate to $5,000 or over, to file a petition for a reorganization. The petition must show among other things that the corporation is insolvent or is unable to pay its debts as they mature and that relief is necessary under the statute. It may also include a proposed scheme of reorganization. The statute directs the court to confirm a plan of reorganization, provided that it is fair and that all payments made or promised are approved as reasonable.

---

[22] A judgment based on a claim for willful and wanton negligence is within the bankruptcy exception as to "willful and malicious" claims. Bice v Jones, 45 AlaApp 709, 236 So2d 718. It is generally held that conduct which is "intentional" is "willful and malicious," although a minority of courts require proof of actual willfulness and malice. Robinson v Early, 248 CalApp2d 19, 56 CalRptr 183.

[23] 11 USCA §§ 501 to 676, inclusive.

§ 38:21. Arrangements. The provisions for arrangements permit any debtor who could become a bankrupt to file a petition for the acceptance of a plan for the settlement, satisfaction, or extension of the time of payment of unsecured debts. The statute directs the court to confirm the plan if it is satisfied that the plan is fair, equitable, and feasible, that the debtor has done no act which would bar a discharge in bankruptcy, and that the proposal and the acceptance are made in good faith.

§ 38:22. Real Property Arrangements. The provisions for real property arrangements permit any debtor who could become a bankrupt, except a corporation, to file a petition for the acceptance of a plan for the alteration or the modification of the rights of creditors holding debts secured by real property or a leasehold interest of which the debtor is the legal or equitable owner. The statute stipulates that the court shall confirm a plan that is accepted by the creditors in good faith.

§ 38:23. Wage Earners' Plans. The provisions for wage earner's plans permit an individual who is insolvent or is unable to pay debts as they mature and whose principal income is derived from salary, wages, or commissions to file a petition for the acceptance of a composition or an extension of time, or both, in view of future earnings or salary. The statute directs the court to confirm a plan that is proposed and accepted by the creditors in good faith.

CASES FOR CHAPTER 38

In re Okamoto

(CA9 Cal) 491 F2d 496 (1974)

Okamoto owed money to Hornblower & Weeks-Hemphill, Noyes. Hornblower filed a petition to have Okamoto declared an involuntary bankrupt. Okamoto moved to dismiss the petition on the ground that he had more than twelve creditors and therefore the petition could not be filed by only one. Hornblower replied that the claims of the other creditors were too small to count and therefore Okamoto did not have more than twelve creditors and the petition could accordingly be filed by one creditor. The lower court held that every creditor was to be counted and dismissed Hornblower's petition. Hornblower appealed.

ELY, J. . . . Hornblower attempted to proceed as the sole petitioning creditor, pursuant to § 59(b) of the Bankruptcy Act, 11 U.S.C. § 95(b). Okamoto's answer alleged that he was indebted to more than eleven creditors, and the answer was accompanied by a schedule listing twenty-one creditors. The Referee in Bankruptcy conducted a hearing under § 59(d) and found that Okamoto had nineteen unse-

cured creditors which must be counted. Since a single creditor cannot proceed under § 59(b) unless the total number of claimants is less than twelve, the Referee dismissed Hornblower's petition. On review, the District Court affirmed the Referee's Order of dismissal.

. . . Hornblower attacks the finding of the Bankruptcy Court that Okamoto had more than eleven creditors. Hornblower principally asserts that creditors for relatively small current expenses should be excluded in computing the total number of creditors under § 59(b). Section 59(b) provides in part: "Three or more creditors who have provable claims not contingent as to liability against a person, amounting in the aggregate to $500 in excess of the value of any securities held by them, or, if all of the creditors of the person are less than twelve in number, then one or more of the creditors whose claim or claims equal that amount, may file a petition to have him adjudged a bankrupt. . . ." If less than three creditors join in the petition, § 59(e) furnishes the guidelines for computing the total number of claimants. Although § 59(e) does not provide for the exclusion of creditors with small claims. Hornblower contends that the doctrine of *de minimis non curat lex* [the law does not bother with trifles] should be applied. Since eight of the debts here involved were for amounts less than sixty-five dollars, Hornblower argues that the total number of creditors meets the statutory limit.

In support of its contention, Hornblower cites several early District Court decisions, including In re Blount, 142 F. 263 (E.D. Ark. 1906). At the time of filing its petition, Hornblower recognized that the more recent decisions had disapproved the *Blount* rationale. *See, e.g.,* Grigsby-Grunow Co. v Hieb Radio Supply Co., 71 F2d 113 (8th Cir 1934); In re Colorado Lime Co., 298 F Supp 1053 (D Colo 1969). Subsequent to the decision by the Bankruptcy Court, however, the Fifth Circuit issued its opinion in Denham v Shellman Grain Elevator, Inc., 444 F2d 1376 (5th Cir 1971). In *Denham* the Court adopted a similar contention to that here advanced, holding that creditors claiming insignificant amounts are not to be included in determining the total number of creditors for the purposes of § 59(b). The Court explained: "It is our belief that whether or not a scheme was involved, it was not the intent of Congress to allow recurring bills such as utility bills and the like to create a situation which, by refusal of these small creditors to join in an involuntary petition, can defeat the use of the Bankruptcy Act by a large creditor, as in the subject case. This would be grossly inequitable, and for this reason this Court refuses to follow the *Colorado Lime* decision.". . .

We are not persuaded by *Denham,* for it appears to us that the *Denham* court ignored unambiguous Congressional direction. The Congress has explicitly prescribed the procedure that must be followed when less than three creditors join in the petition. In such circumstances the Act provides that the alleged bankrupt *must* have less than twelve creditors and expressly excludes certain types of creditors from the required computation. Since Congress made no distinction between large and small claims, we cannot arrogate unto ourselves the power to do so and thereby engraft an additional exception to the Act. Hornblower's argument properly should be addressed to the Congress. Our conclusion is reinforced by the fact that Congress has clearly and expressly excluded small claims when it has intended to do so. *See* Bankruptcy Act § 56(c), 11 USC § 92(c).*. . .

---

* Bankruptcy Act § 56(c), 11 USC § 92(c), provides: "Claims of $50 or less shall not be counted in computing the number of creditors voting or present at creditors' meetings, but shall be counted in computing the amount."

Since Okamoto was indebted to more than eleven creditors and only one claimant filed the petition, the petition was properly dismissed.

Arst v First National Bank and Trust Co.

211 Kan 758, 508 P2d 520 (1973)

Wilmoth Construction, Inc. was declared a bankrupt. Arst was elected trustee and sued the First National Bank, claiming that a payment made by Wilmoth to the bank was a preferential transfer. The trustee did not produce any evidence that the corporation was insolvent but showed that the bank had been advised that the corporation did not have funds with which to pay maturing obligations. The court held that the trustee did not prove a preferential transfer. The trustee appealed.

FONTRON, J. . . . The position taken by the trustee in this lawsuit is that Wilmoth, Inc., while insolvent, transferred all its assets to the bank; that the value of the assets transferred was $89,687.14 while the indebtedness due the bank was only $79,041.19; that the value of the property turned over to the bank exceeded the balance due the bank by $10,645.95, and to this extent, . . . the transfer constituted a voidable preference under the federal bankruptcy laws; and that the bank is liable to the trustee for such excess. . . .

The defendant argues with great vigor that no evidence whatsoever was offered to prove the insolvency of Wilmoth, Inc. on the transfer date, April 1, 1967, or that the bank had reasonable cause to believe the corporation was then insolvent. Both of these elements had to be established before the trustee could prevail, and the burden of proving the same rested with him.

We find the term "insolvency", as used in the Bankruptcy Act, defined in 11 U.S.C. § 1(19):

"A person shall be deemed insolvent within the provisions of this title whenever the aggregate of his property, exclusive of any property which he may have conveyed, transferred, concealed, removed, or permitted to be concealed or removed, with intent to defraud, hinder, or delay his creditors, shall not at a fair valuation be sufficient in amount to pay his debts;" (p. 44.)

This definition is frequently referred to as the "balance sheet definition", and it denotes a test which requires that assets be weighed against liabilities. The test thus differs from that which is customarily used to determine insolvency, i.e., the inability to meet pecuniary obligations as they come due either through the means of available assets or by the honest use of credit. . . .

Under the "balance sheet test" of the Bankruptcy Act, "insolvency" results when the aggregate of a debtor's property is not sufficient at a fair valuation to pay his debts, which means a fair market price that can be available for payment of debts within a reasonable period of time, and "fair market value" implies a willing seller and a willing buyer. . . .

No evidence was offered by the trustee to establish that, on April 1, 1967, Wilmoth, Inc. was insolvent in the sense the term is used in the Bankruptcy Act. . . . The record in this respect is entirely blank, even though it might be presumed the trustee was in possession of the facts concerning both.

The trustee, it is true, calls attention to a stipulation that on the critical date, April 1, 1967, the bank was advised that Wilmoth, Inc. did not have funds with which to pay maturing obligations. Such, however, is not the test of insolvency spelled out in the Bankruptcy Act. . . . The test for 'insolvency' under § 1(19) of the Bankruptcy Act is not the inability to meet current obligations but is the state of having liabilities exceed assets. . .

We are also aware of the additional stipulation that officers of the bank understood the bankrupt was in serious financial difficulty, although they were never advised it had a negative net worth on a balance sheet basis. This stipulation is not conclusive on the issue of Wilmoth Inc.'s insolvency on a *balance sheet basis.*

Mr. Arst, the trustee bore the burden of proving that Wilmoth, Inc. was insolvent on the date the transfer was made. . . .

As in the other elements of a preference, the burden of proof is on the trustee to show insolvency at the time of the transfer. . . .

One having the burden of proof is required to sustain the same by a preponderance of the evidence. This legal principle is just as binding on a trustee in bankruptcy as on any other party litigant. . . . We are unable to say from the record before us that the trial court erred in finding that the trustee had failed to sustain the burden which was his. . . .

We are constrained to hold that error on the part of the court below has not been established and that judgment in favor of the defendant must be affirmed.

It is so ordered.

In re Vega Baja Lumber Yard, Inc.

(DC D Puerto Rico) 285 F Supp 143 (1968)

The Vega Baja Lumber Yard owed money to the First City National Bank. The bank sued the lumber yard and attached some of its property. Thereafter bankruptcy proceedings were begun and the lumber yard was adjudicated a bankrupt. The bank filed a claim in bankruptcy. The referee rejected the bank's claim because it had been filed more than six months after the debtor had been adjudicated a bankrupt. The bank claimed that the six-months limitation did not bar it because the trustee knew of its claim.

FERNANDEZ-BADILLO, D.J. . . . The weight of authority considers the six month period . . . as peremptory and immutable. . . .

. . . The Court has no discretion to accept an untimely filing of a claim.

It has been equally established that if there is upon the record in the bankruptcy proceedings, within the six months . . . , anything to show the existence, nature and amount of a claim, it may be amended even after expiration of the period. . . . Courts have been watchful in departing from the general rule of strict interpretation of the statute, and amendments offered after the six months period are closely scrutinized to avoid the filing of an untimely new claim under the guise of an amendment. . . .

The creditor must have shown in some form that he had a demand against the estate and intended to hold the estate liable. The substance of a claim must have been made in some form before the statutory period expired. . . .

There are many cases where the dilatory creditor has done some positive act which was considered tantamount to an assertion or demand against the bankrupt's estate. See, for example: Fyne v Atlas Supply Co. (4th Cir 1957) 245 F2d 107 (amendment allowed where there was a letter from claimant's counsel to trustee, attorney participated in the first meeting of creditors, and the claim in question gave rise to the involuntary petition in bankruptcy, which claim had been reduced to judgment): In re Fant (D.C.S.C. 1927) 21 F2d 182 (creditor's claim was fully set up in the petition for bankruptcy, admission in part by the bankrupt that claim was correct, claimant's action in state court brought into the bankruptcy court a considerable fund); 55 F Supp 532, affirmed in Public Operating Corp. v Schneider, 2 Cir, 145 F2d 830 (attorney's letter to the referee stating client was a creditor of bankrupt, that a claim would be filed as soon as an examination of the records of creditor was completed and asking that the letter be accepted as a notice of claim against the estate to be subsequently amended.) . . .

Regardless of how liberal an approach is had as to what is sufficient to constitute a basis for amendment, the courts have consistently searched the record for an assertion or claim, no matter how informal, that would permit amendment. . . .

. . . Pendency of litigation, in and of itself, is not sufficient basis to permit an amendment. . . . Mere knowledge on the part of the trustee or of the referee in bankruptcy as to the existence of a claim is not sufficient basis for allowing the filing of an amended claim. . . .

There is no claim in the files, informal, defective or inarticulately drawn, by or on behalf of the creditor, that could amount to an original proof of claim.

It is therefore ordered that the denial of the petition for approval of claim be affirmed.

Kentile Floors, Inc. v Winham

(CA9 Ariz) 440 F2d 1128 (1971)

Kentile sold goods over an extended period to Winham. The credit relationship began without Winham's being required to furnish any financial statement. After some time, payments were not regularly made. Kentile requested a financial statement. Winham submitted a statement for the year which had then just ended. Thereafter Kentile requested a second statement. The second statement was false. Kentile continued to extend credit to Winham. Winham was later adjudicated bankrupt. Kentile objected to Winham's discharge in bankruptcy because of the false financial statement. The objection of Kentile was dismissed, the discharge of Winham was granted, and Kentile appealed.

HAMLEY, C.J. . . . Kentile also objected to a general discharge because Winham's Floor Covering obtained extensions of credit by publishing materially false financial statements. . . . Both the referee and the district court found materially false financial statements were published by the bankrupts as sole proprietors of Winham's Floor Coverings. The ref-

eree found that Kentile relied on the statements when it subsequently extended credit. The district court found that Kentile did not rely on the statements, and that Kentile had no right to rely on them.

The record discloses that Mr. Winham intentionally modified the true figures on his statement of financial condition for the purpose of showing a good statement. He acknowledged that he felt that if a correct statement were submitted, his credit would be curtailed. After receiving the statements, Kentile did extend further credit to Mr. Winham. While the law favors discharges in bankruptcy, it will not ordinarily tolerate the bankrupt's intentional departure from honest business practices where there is a reasonable likelihood of prejudice. A bankrupt who admits that he prepared false financial statements in an effort to obtain or retain credit standing, and who thereafter achieves that goal, has a heavy burden to carry in trying to show that the false statement was not, or should not have been, instrumental in the subsequent extensions of credit.

Reliance on the financial statements is necessary to preclude discharge for violation of § 14(c)(3). . . . Notwithstanding the bankrupts' heavy burden of proof, referred to above, we agree with the district court that whatever reliance Kentile placed upon these statements was not reasonable reliance, that Kentile therefore had no right to rely upon the statements in this situation, and that the bankrupts should not, on this ground, be denied a general discharge.

A recitation of the facts surrounding the submission of the financial statements and subsequent extensions of credit is necessary to illustrate why Kentile should have been alerted to the actual financial condition of Winham's Floor Coverings and why Kentile should not have relied upon the financial statements without further investigation.

As noted above, the bankrupts had been dealing with Kentile, through its distributor, for a period of time before the arrangement for direct purchases from Kentile was consummated early in 1964. The arrangement corresponded somewhat with the bankrupts' entrance into the field of commercial floor coverings. Kentile acknowledged the bankrupts' history of prompt payment prior to 1965. Kentile further acknowledged representatives had been calling on the bankrupts from time to time for the purpose of reviewing the bankrupts' business records. When Kentile began extending credit to the bankrupts, it did not require publication of a statement of financial condition as a prerequisite.

In the spring of 1965 the bankrupts' payments on the account had become sporadic. Kentile's credit manager stated that the payments were "not satisfactory." The record indicates that Kentile was then seriously considering curtailment of Winhams' credit. Kentile was also aware of Winhams' credit. Kentile was also aware of Winhams' sporadic payments on the account with Kentile's distributor. Kentile was, in fact, aware of many of the difficulties with which the bankrupts were beset in early 1965.

By March 1965, Kentile had begun to insist that the bankrupts supply a statement of financial condition. Before having received any financial statement from the bankrupts, however, Kentile had extended approximately $96,000 in credit. This was the amount due Kentile from the bankrupts when the first financial statement was submitted in April 1965. The statement purported to reflect the financial condition of Winham's Floor Coverings as of December 31, 1964. Kentile was aware of the financial problems the bankrupts had experienced in the interim. Kentile also knew that the total of all Winhams' accounts payable on December 31, 1964, as reflected in the financial statement, was substantially less than the amount Winhams owed Kentile and its distributor when the statement was received in April 1965.

Kentile's credit manager was somewhat equivocal when asked the significance that could be placed on a financial statement such as this. The financial condition reported in the statement seemed, to the credit manager, inconsistent with the manner in which the bankrupts were making payments on the account.

The second financial statement submitted by Winham was received by Kentile in June 1965, and purported to reflect the financial condition as of March 31, 1965. This statement, compared with the first statement, showed an improvement during the first quarter of 1965, contrary to all other information available to Kentile. Credit was curtailed shortly after its receipt. Credit was not curtailed because Kentile discovered the bankrupts' true financial condition, but because the payments on the account were not satisfactory.

Given the lengthy and apparently fairly close business relationship of Kentile and Winham's Floor Coverings, we do not think further investigation by Kentile would have damaged that relationship had Winham's been a going concern. We therefore think Kentile acted unreasonably if it relied upon the first statement in extending credit without any further

investigation of the bankrupts' then existing financial condition. While a financial statement is not necessarily unreliable because it reflects the condition as it existed three or four months earlier, Kentile's knowledge of what occurred in the interim was sufficient to require further inquiry. Reliance on the second statement, showing an improvement of condition in the interim, was similarly unjustified.

[Judgment affirmed]

Romero v Allen

(CA10 NMex) 535 F2d 618 (1976)

Romero was a contractor building houses for Allen. Allen agreed to advance Romero money to pay for the labor and material used in the construction. Allen paid Romero the money but Romero did not use it to pay the labor and material bills and did not refund the money to Allen. Romero went into bankruptcy. Allen made claim for the money which had been advanced to Romero. The court held that Allen's claim against Romero was not dischargeable on the basis that the claim was for fraud committed while acting in a fiduciary capacity. Romero appealed.

BARRETT, C.J. . . . We deem it necessary to consider only whether the debt is nondischargeable under § 17(a)(4) of the Bankruptcy Act. . . . In order to hold the debt nondischargeable under § 17(a)(4), . . . we must be convinced that the conduct of Romero constituted fraud and that the fraud was perpetrated while Romero was acting in a fiduciary capacity.

"Fiduciary capacity" as used in § 17(a)(4) . . . has been held to connote the idea of trust or confidence, which relationship arises whenever one's property is placed in the custody of another. . . . It is also generally recognized that the exception under § 17(a)(4) applies only to technical trusts and not those which the law implies from a contract. . . . Further, the fiduciary relationship must be shown to exist prior to the creation of the debt in controversy. . . .

We shall proceed to determine, from the record before us, whether Romero acted in a fiduciary capacity in his dealings as a general contractor with Allen. New Mexico has enacted a comprehensive scheme for the issuance of licenses to those engaged in the construction industry. §§ 67-35-1 through 67-35-67 N.M.S.A.(1953). § 67-35-26 provides for the revocation or suspension of a license on the ground of: "diversion of funds or property received for prosecution or completion of a specific contract, or for a specified purpose in the prosecution or completion of any contract, obligation or purpose."

The Supreme Court of New Mexico has stated that the purpose of the Act is to provide "a comprehensive method for the licensing and control of contractors in order to protect the public from either irresponsible or incompetent contractors". *Peck v Ives,* 84 N.M. 62, 499 P.2d 684 (1972). In our view, § 67-35-26, *supra,* clearly imposes a fiduciary duty upon contractors who have been advanced money pursuant to construction contracts.

It is undisputed that Romero was advanced $49,950 by Allen. By virtue thereof, Romero stood in a fiduciary capacity toward Allen. Romero was under a duty to assure that money advanced to him was applied in payment for materials and labor relating to the four-plexes. That Romero was acting in a fiduciary capacity imposed by law, rather than one implied by law, is evidenced by the fact that his obligation not to divert advances is imposed by statute. The fiduciary capacity in which Romero was acting accordingly existed independent of any express understanding he had with Allen governing the same obligation. Obtaining a state license by a contractor is a prerequisite to entering the construction industry in New Mexico; accordingly, the obligation and duties imposed under § 67-35-26, . . . were binding upon Romero prior to any dealings he had with Allen. We hold that the Bankruptcy Court's finding that Romero was acting in a fiduciary capac-

ity within the meaning of § 17(a)(4), . . . is not clearly erroneous. . . .

One issue remains involving § 17(a)(4), . . . i.e., whether the debt involved herein was created by fraud, embezzlement, misappropriation or defalcation on the part of Romero. We hold that the debt was created by Romero's fraud.

In order to maintain an action for fraud these elements must be established: that there was a false misrepresentation of a material fact, knowledge of its falsity when made, intent to deceive and reliance thereon with resulting damages. . . . The following facts reflected by the record demonstrate that these elements were met: that the money advanced by Allen was to be used to pay for all work, labor and materials and that at the time the advances were made all materialmen, laborers and subcontractors were not paid; that Romero knew these representations were false when made inasmuch as he subsequently admitted that there were numerous unpaid bills on the Allen four-plexes; that the representations were made for the sole purpose of obtaining additional funds from Allen; and that Allen advanced money to Romero on the representations that the funds advanced were being used to pay materialmen, laborers, and subcontractors on the Allen four-plexes.

We hold that there is substantial evidence in support of the finding of the Bankruptcy Court that the debt in this case was created by the fraud of Romero. . . .

[Judgment affirmed as to nondischarge of claim]

QUESTIONS AND CASE PROBLEMS

1. What social forces are affected by permitting a debtor to avoid paying his debts by going into bankruptcy?
2. Compare a release of claims given by a creditor with a discharge in bankruptcy.
3. Compare voluntary and involuntary bankruptcy.
4. Compare the concepts of (a) provable claims; (b) allowance of claims; and (c) the discharge of claims.
5. At the instigation of Perry, trustee in bankruptcy of Martin, the court directed a referee to decide the validity of claims made by several claimants to a gas and oil leasehold in which the bankrupt had some interest. Chandler and other claimants opposed the proceeding on the ground that the referee did not have power to hear and decide such a question and that it was for a bankruptcy court to decide. Was this contention sound? [Chandler v Perry, (CA5 Tex) 74 F2d 371]

6. Putman, as executrix of the estate of Fred Putman, obtained a judgment for $10,000 against the Ocean Shore Railway Co. for negligently causing the death of Putman. She and two others filed a petition in bankruptcy against Folger, who had a statutory liability for the debts of the railway corporation. In opposing the petition, he contended that the claim of Mrs. Putman was not a provable debt in bankruptcy. Do you agree? [In re Putman, (DC Cal) 193 F 464]

7. An involuntary petition in bankruptcy was filed against a merchant doing business in a building leased from Abbott. On the same day a receiver was appointed, and he took possession of the store and the stock of goods. In an action brought by Abbott upon a claim connected with the possession of the building by the receiver, a question arose as to whether the receiver was vested with title to the bankrupt's assets. What is your opinion? [In re Rubel, (DC Wis) 166 F 131]

8. Certain creditors filed a petition in bankruptcy against the Percy Ford Co. An adjudication of bankruptcy followed. At the time of the filing of the petition, the National Shawmut Bank held four notes upon which the bankrupt was absolutely liable, but the notes were not then due and payable. The bank contended that the notes constituted provable debts. Do you agree? [In re Percy Ford Co., (DC Mass) 199 F 334]

9. Shelton owed money to Winthrop Sales. Shelton went into bankruptcy and was granted a discharge. Later Winthrop Sales sued Shelton although its claim against him had been discharged in bankruptcy. Shelton did not raise any defense with respect to the bankruptcy discharge. A judgment was entered against him. Shelton, on appeal, claimed that the bankruptcy discharge prevented the suit against him. Decide. [Winthrop Sales Corp. v Shelton, (Mo App) 389 SW2d 70]

10. DeAngio owed L & L Leasing approximately $1,000 for the rental of equipment. Pulasko Media was negotiating with DeAngio to purchase his business from him. Pulasko Media paid L & L the $1,000 which was owed by DeAngio. Creditors of DeAngio then filed a petition to declare him an involuntary bankrupt and claimed that the payment made to L & L was a voidable preference and an act of bankruptcy. Were they correct? [Creditors of DeAngio v DeAngio (CA8 Mo) 554 F2d 863]

11. Day was a debtor against whom the East Tennessee National Bank filed a petition in bankruptcy. In the petition the bank alleged that it had made a loan to Day which was secured by stock as collateral, that upon default it sold the stock, and that there was a deficiency which it claimed as a creditor. Day objected by stating that a secured creditor cannot establish any claim in bankruptcy proceedings. Was he correct? [East Tennessee National Bank v Day, (DC Fla) 5 FSupp 473]

12. Star Electric Supply, Inc. owed money to Tru-Lite, Inc. Tru-Lite sued Star and obtained a judgment against it, and then caused the sheriff to seize and sell the inventory of Star to pay the judgment. Star was declared bankrupt and Brown was elected trustee in bankruptcy. Brown claimed that the seizure of Star's inventory under the judgment of Tru-Lite was a voidable preference and could be set aside by him. Was he correct? [Brown v Tru-Lite (DC La) 398 FSupp 800]

13. A California statute provided that the license of a contractor could be revoked if he failed to pay his debts in full by obtaining a discharge in bankruptcy. Grimes was a licensed contractor. He was adjudicated a bankrupt. Thereafter the state licensing board revoked his contractor's license. He brought an action against the registrar of the board to compel the reissuance of such license. Was he entitled to the license? [Grimes v Hoschler, 12 Cal3d 305, 115 CalRptr 625, 525 P2d 65]

Part Eight • Agency and Employment

39   Agency—Creation and Termination

One of the most common legal relationships is that of agency. When it exists, one person can act for and stand in the place of another. By virtue of the agency device, one person can make contracts at numerous different places with many different parties at the same time.

A. NATURE OF THE AGENCY RELATIONSHIP

Agency is a relation based upon an express or implied agreement by which one person, the *agent,* is authorized to act under the control of and for another, the *principal,* in negotiating and making contracts with third persons.[1] The acts of the agent obligate the principal to third persons and give the principal rights against third persons.

Agency is based upon the consent of the parties and, for that reason, is called a consensual relation. If consideration is present, the relationship is also contractual. The law sometimes imposes an agency relationship.

The term "agency" is frequently used with other meanings. It is sometimes used to denote the fact that one has the right to sell certain products, such as when a dealer is said to possess an automobile agency. In other instances, the term is used to mean an exclusive right to sell certain articles within a given territory. In these cases, however, the dealer is not an agent in the sense of representing the manufacturer.[2]

---

[1] Restatement, Agency, 2d § 1; Rule v Jones, 256 Wis 102, 40 NW2d 580. When the question is the tax liability of an enterprise (see Boise Cascade Corp. v Washington, 3 WashApp 78, 473 P2d 429), the definition of agency may be different than when the question is contract or tort liability, which are the areas of law considered in this part.

[2] Pioneer Hi-Bred International, Inc. v Talley (TexCivApp) 493 SW2d 602.

§ 39:1. Agent Distinguished.

(a)   Employees and Independent Contractors.

(1)   Employees. An agent is distinguished from an ordinary employee, who is not hired to represent the employer in dealings with third persons. It is possible, however, for the same person to be both an agent and an employee. For example, the driver of a milk delivery truck is an agent, as well as an employee,[3] in making contracts between the milk company and its customers, but is only an employee with respect to the work of delivering milk.

(2)   Independent Contractors. An agent or employee differs from an *independent contractor* in that the principal or employer has control over and can direct the agent or an employee but does not have control over the performance of the work by an independent contractor.

A person who appears to be an independent contractor may in fact be so controlled by the other party that the contractor is regarded as an agent of or employee of the controlling person. (See p. 656, Hill v Newman). However, the mere reservation of a right to inspect and determine if work has been properly done does not constitute such control of the contractor.[4]

A person may be an independent contractor generally but an agent with respect to a particular transaction. Thus, an "agency" or a "broker" rendering personal services to customers is ordinarily an independent contractor, but will be the agent of a customer when the rendition of a service involves making a contract on behalf of the customer with a third person.

(3)   Name Immaterial. The fact that an agreement does not call a person an agent or an independent contractor is ignored in determining whether the person is an agent or an independent contractor.

(4)   Full-Time Status Immaterial. It is immaterial whether the person is a full-time agent for the particular principal. The controlling question is whether the person was the agent at the time of the transaction between the agent and the third person. For example, when the owner of an automobile which is wrecked in a collision tells the state trooper to have it removed, the state trooper is the owner's agent for the purpose of entering into a contract with a third person.[5]

Not only can an independent contractor, such as an insurance broker, be an agent for different persons, but an employer can be the agent of the employer's own employees. For example, where a group policy of insurance covered the employees of an employer, the employer was the "agent" of the insurer with respect to the handling of applications for group insurance and the sending of premiums, although the ordinary status was that of employer with respect to the employees.[6]

---

[3] In business practice, all employed persons, regardless of the nature of the work performed or the services rendered, are considered as employees.

[4] Lipka v United States (CA2 NY) 369 F2d 288.

[5] Fair v Hamersmith Distributing Co., 214 Va 552, 203 SE2d 120.

[6] Weeks v Pilot Life Ins. Co. (SC) 180 SE2d 875.

(b)   Real Estate Brokers. A real estate broker is generally not an agent with authority to make a contract with a third person which will bind the broker's client. Typically, the broker's authority is limited to locating a seller or buyer and bringing the parties together but does not extend to making a contract. Even when the third person and the broker sign a "contract," it is generally only an offer by the third person which does not become a binding contract until accepted by the client of the broker.

(c)   Bailees. When personal property is delivered to another under an agreement that the property will be returned to the deliveror or transferred to a third person, a bailment arises. The person to whom the property is delivered, the bailee, is not an agent because the bailee has no authority to act for or make any contract on behalf of the bailor.

Situations commonly arise, however, in which the same person is both an agent and a bailee. A salesperson who is loaned a company car, is a bailee with respect to the car; but with respect to making sales contracts, is an agent.

(d)   Required Act. The mere fact that one person requires another person to do an act does not make the latter person the agent of the former. For example, when a bank directs a borrower to obtain the signature of another person in order to obtain a bank loan, the borrower is not the agent of the bank in contacting the other person and procuring the required signature.[7]

§ 39:2. Purpose of Agency. Usually an agency may be created to perform any act which the principal could lawfully do. The object of the agency must not be criminal, nor may it be contrary to public policy. However, some acts must be performed in person and cannot be entrusted or delegated to an agent. Voting, swearing to the truth of documents, testifying in court, and making a will are instances where personal action is required. In the preparation of a document, however, it is proper to employ someone else to prepare the paper which is then signed or sworn to by the employing party. Various forms that are required by statute, such as applications for licenses and tax returns, will in some instances expressly authorize the execution of such forms by an agent as long as the identities of both principal and agent and the latter's representative capacity are clearly shown.

§ 39:3. Who May Be a Principal. Any person who is competent to act may act through an agent. The appointment of an agent by a person lacking capacity is generally void or voidable to the same extent that a contract made by such person would be. Thus, a minor may act through an agent, and a resulting contract will be voidable to the same extent as though made by the minor.

Groups of persons may also appoint agents to act for them.

§ 39:4. Who May Be an Agent. Since a contract made by an agent is in law the contract of the principal, it is immaterial whether or not the agent has legal capacity to make a contract. It is therefore permissible to employ as agents persons who are aliens, minors, and others who are under a natural or legal disability.

[7] First National Bank v Caro Construction Co., Inc. 211 Kan 678, 508 P2d 516.

While ordinarily an agent is one person acting for another, an agent may be a partnership or a corporation.

§ 39:5. Classification of Agents.
A *general agent* is authorized by the principal to transact all affairs in connection with a particular kind of business or trade, or to transact all business at a certain place. To illustrate, a person who is appointed as manager by the owner of a store is a general agent.

A *special agent* is authorized by the principal to handle a definite business transaction or to do a specific act. One who is authorized by another to purchase a particular house is a special agent.

A *universal agent* is authorized by the principal to do all acts that can be delegated lawfully to a representative. This form of agency arises when a person absent in the military service gives another person a "blanket" power of attorney to do anything that must be done during such absence.

§ 39:6. Agency Coupled with an Interest.
An agent has an *interest in the authority* when consideration has been given or paid for the right to exercise the authority. To illustrate, when a lender, in return for making a loan of money, is given, as security, authority to collect rents due to the borrower and to apply those rents to the payment of the debt, the lender becomes the borrower's agent with an interest in the authority given to collect the rents.[8]

An agent has an *interest in the subject matter* when for a consideration the agent is given an interest in the property with which the agent is dealing. Hence, when the agent is authorized to sell property of the principal and is given a lien on such property as security for a debt owed to the agent by the principal, the agent has an interest in the subject matter.

B. CREATING THE AGENCY

An agency may arise by appointment, conduct, ratification, or operation of law.

§ 39:7. Authorization by Appointment.
The usual method of creating an agency is by express authorization; that is, a person is appointed to act for and on behalf of another.

In most instances the authorization of the agent may be oral. Some appointments, however, must be made in a particular way. A majority of the states, by statute, require the appointment of an agent to be in writing when the agency is created to acquire or dispose of any interest in land. (See p. 657, Heinrich v Martin) A written authorization of agency is called a *power of attorney*.

Ordinarily no agency arises from the fact of co-ownership of property or of relationship of the parties. Consequently, when a check was made payable to the order of husband and wife, it was necessary for each to indorse the check because there was no agency by which the husband could indorse the wife's name and deposit the money in the husband's own account.

---

[8] Halloran-Judge Trust Co. v Heath, 70 Utah 124, 258 P 342. When personal property or rights to money are involved, the creditor should require the creation of a secured transaction, as Article 9 of the Uniform Commercial Code will then give the creditor greater protection.

§ 39:8. Authorization by Conduct.

(a) Principal's Conduct as to Agent. Since agency is created by the consent of the parties, any conduct of the principal, including words, that gives a person reason to believe that the principal consents to that person's acting as agent for the principal is sufficient to create an agency. Likewise, if one person, knowingly and without objection, permits another to act as agent, the law will find in such conduct an expression of authorization to the agent, and the principal will not be permitted to deny that the agent was in fact authorized. Thus if the owner of a hotel allows another person to assume the duties of hotel clerk, that person may infer from the owner's conduct an authority to act as the hotel clerk.

(b) Principal's Conduct as to Third Persons. The principal may have such dealings with third persons as to cause them to believe that the "agent" has authority. Thus, if the owner of a store places another person in charge, third persons may assume that the person in charge is the agent for the owner in that respect. The "agent" then appears to be authorized and is said to have *apparent authority,* and the principal is estopped or prevented from contradicting the appearance that has been created.

When a franchisor permits the franchisee to do business under the name of the franchisor, the latter is estopped from denying that the franchisee has authority to make customary contracts, such as a contract for advertising, and to bind the franchisor by such contracts.

The term "apparent authority" is used when there is only the appearance of authority but no actual authority and that appearance of authority was created by the principal. This apparent authority extends to all acts that a person of ordinary prudence, familiar with business usages, and the particular business, would be justified in assuming that the agent has authority to perform. (See p. 658, Walker v Pacific Mobile Homes)

The mere placing of property in the possession of another does not give that person either actual or apparent authority to sell the property.[9]

It is essential to the concept of apparent authority that the third person reasonably believe that the agent has authority. If the basis for such belief is not reasonable, no apparent authority arises.

Any person may be clothed with apparent authority. Not only an existing employee or agent who exceeds actual authority but also a third person who is independent of the alleged principal and has no authority at all.

(c) Acquiescence by Principal. The conduct of the principal that gives rise to the agent's authority may be acquiescence in or failing to object to acts done by the purported or apparent agent over a period of time. For example, a person collecting payments on a note and remitting the proper amounts to the holder of the note will be regarded as the latter's agent for collection when this conduct has been followed over a period of years without objection.[10]

---

[9] Brunette v Idaho Veneer Co. 86 Idaho 193, 384 P2d 233. Note that under Uniform Commercial Code, § 2-403, an entrustee who deals in goods of that kind has the power but not the right to transfer title to a person buying in good faith in the ordinary course of business.

[10] Holsclaw v Catalina Savings & Loan Association, 13 ArizApp 362, 476 P2d 883.

Where the drawer's employee drew checks to herself for fourteen months which were debited to the drawer's account and no complaint was made by the drawer, this lack of objection was in effect a communication to the bank that the employee had the authority to draw the checks in question.

No question can be raised as to whether a person signing a contract as agent was authorized to do so when the parties have been following the contract for six years after its signing by the apparent agent.[11]

§ 39:9. Agency by Ratification. An agent may attempt on behalf of the principal to do an act which was not authorized. Or a person who is not the agent of another may attempt to act as such an agent. Generally, in such case, the principal for whom the agent claimed to act has the choice of ignoring the transaction or of ratifying it. Ordinarily any unauthorized act may be ratified.

(a)   Intention to Ratify. Initially, ratification is a question of intention. Just as in the case of authorization, where there is a question of whether or not the principal authorized the agent, so there is a question whether or not the principal intended to approve or ratify the action of the unauthorized agent.

The intention to ratify may be expressed in words or it may be found in conduct indicating an intention to ratify, such as paying for goods ordered by the agent [12] or performing the contract which the agent had made and accepting payments for such performance. (See p. 658, Melancon v A & M Pest Control Service Co., Inc.)

Ratification of an earlier loan transaction is shown when the principal executes a renewal note and papers which make an extension of the earlier loan.

If the other requirements of ratification are satisfied, a principal ratifies an agent's acts when, with knowledge of the act, the principal accepts or retains the benefit of the act, or brings an action to enforce legal rights based upon the act or defends an action by asserting the existence of a right based on the unauthorized transaction, or fails to repudiate the agent's act within a reasonable time. The receipt, acceptance, and deposit of a check by the principal with knowledge that it arises from an unauthorized transaction is a common illustration of ratification of the unauthorized transaction by conduct.

(b)   Conditions for Ratification. In addition to the intent to ratify, expressed in some instances with certain formality, the following conditions must be satisfied in order that the intention take effect as a ratification:

(1) The agent must have purported to act on behalf of or as agent for the identified principal.[13]

(2) The principal must have been capable of authorizing the act both at the time of the act and at the time when it was ratified.

(3) A principal must ratify the entire act of the agent.

(4) The principal must ratify the act before the third person withdraws. If the third person brings an action against the agent because of lack of authority to make the contract, the bringing of the action is equivalent to a withdrawal that prevents the principal from thereafter ratifying the contract.

---

[11] Feary v Aaron Burglar Alarm, Inc. 32 CalApp3d 553, 108 CalRptr 242.

[12] Southwestern Portland Cement v Beavers, 82 NMex 218, 478 P2d 546.

[13] State ex rel Olsen v Sundling, 128 Mont 596, 281 P2d 499.

(5) The act to be ratified must generally be legal.

(6) The principal must have full knowledge of all material facts.[14] If the agent conceals a material fact, the ratification of the principal that is made in ignorance of such facts is not binding. Of course, there can be no ratification when the principal does not know of the making of the contract by the alleged agent. Consequently, when the owner's agent and a contractor make unauthorized major changes to an installation contract without the knowledge of the owner, the fact that the owner had no knowledge of the matter barred any claim of ratification of the agent's act.

It is not always necessary, however, to show that the principal had actual knowledge; for knowledge will be imputed to a principal who knows of such other facts as would put a prudent person on inquiry, or if that knowledge can be inferred from the knowledge of other facts or from a course of business. Knowledge is likewise not an essential factor when the principal does not care to know the details and is willing to ratify the contract regardless of such lack of knowledge.

(c)   Effect of Ratification. When an unauthorized act is ratified, the effect is the same as though the act had been originally authorized. Ordinarily this means that the principal and the third party are bound by the contract made by the agent. Conversely, when the principal ratifies the act of the unauthorized person, such ratification releases that person from the liability which would otherwise be imposed for having acted without authority.

§ 39:10.   Agency by Operation of Law. In certain instances, the courts, influenced by necessity or social desirability, create or find an agency when there is none. For example, a wife may purchase necessaries and charge them to her husband's account when the husband does not supply them. Here the social policy is the furtherance of the welfare of the neglected wife.

As another example of agency by operation of law, a minor may purchase necessaries upon the father's credit when the latter fails to supply them. If the minor is already adequately supplied by the father, the mother cannot make additional purchases or contracts and charge the father, even though this could have been done if the minor had not been already adequately provided for by the father.

An emergency power of an agent to act under unusual circumstances not covered by the agent's authority is recognized when the agent is unable to communicate with the principal and failure to act would cause the principal substantial loss.

§ 39:11.   Proving the Agency Relationship. The burden of proving the existence of an agency relationship rests upon the person who seeks to benefit by such proof. The third person who desires to bind the principal because of the act of an alleged agent has the burden of proving that the latter person was in fact the authorized agent of the principal and possessed the authority to do the act in question. For example, when the buyer asserts that there has been a breach of an express warranty made by the seller's agent, the buyer must establish that there was an actual or apparent authority to make the warranty. In the absence of sufficient proof, the jury must find that there is no agency. The authority of the agent may be established by circumstantial evidence.

---

[14] Pacific Trading Co. v Sun Insurance Office, 140 Ore 314, 13 P2d 616.

C. TERMINATION OF AGENCY

An agency may be terminated by the act of one or both of the parties to the agency agreement, or by operation of law. When the authority of an agent is terminated, the agent loses all right to act for the principal.

§ 39:12. Termination by Act of Parties.

(a) Expiration of Agency Contract. The ordinary agency may expire by the terms of the contract creating it. Thus, the contract may provide that it shall last for a stated period, as five years, or until a particular date arrives, or until the happening of a particular event, such as the sale of certain property. In such a case, the agency is automatically terminated when the specified date arrives or the event on which it is to end occurs.

When it is provided that the agency shall last for a stated period of time, it terminates upon the expiration of that period without regard to whether the acts contemplated by the creation of the agency have been performed. If no period is stated, the agency continues for a reasonable time, but it may be terminated at the will of either party.

(b) Agreement. Since the agency relation is based upon consent, it can be terminated by the consent of the principal and agent.

(c) Option of a Party. An agency agreement may provide that upon the giving of notice or the payment of a specified sum of money, one party may terminate the relationship.

(d) Revocation by Principal. The relationship between principal and agent is terminated whenever the principal discharges the agent even though the agency was stated to be "irrevocable." [15] If the agency was not created for a specified time but was to exist only at will, or if the agent has been guilty of misconduct, the principal may discharge the agent without liability.

Expressions of dissatisfaction with the work of an agent do not constitute a revocation of the agent's authority. The intent to revoke must be clearly and unequivocally expressed. (See p. 659, Kinmon v J. P. King Auction Co.)

Any conduct which manifests an intent to revoke the authority is sufficient, as when the principal takes back from the agent the property which had been entrusted to the agent for the purpose of the agency or retains another agent to do what the original agent had been authorized to do. When the agency is based upon a contract to employ the agent for a specified period of time, the principal is liable to the agent for damages if the principal wrongfully discharges the agent. The fact that the principal is liable for damages does not, however, prevent the principal from terminating the agency by discharging the agent. In such case, it is said that the principal has the power to terminate the agency by discharging the agent but does not have the right to do so.

(e) Renunciation by Agent. The agency relationship is terminated if the agent refuses to continue to act as agent or when the agent abandons the object of the agency and acts in self-interest in committing a fraud upon the principal.

---

[15] Shumaker v Hazen (Okla) 372 P2d 873.

If the relationship is an agency at will, the agent has the right, as well as the power, to renounce or abandon the agency at any time. In addition, the agent has the right of renunciation of the relationship in any case if the principal was guilty of making wrongful demands or of other misconduct.

If, however, the agency is based upon a contract calling for the continuation of the relationship for a specified or determinable period, that is, until a particular date arrives or a certain event occurs, the agent has no right to abandon or renounce the relationship when the principal is not guilty of wrong.

When the renunciation by the agent is wrongful, the agent is liable to the principal for the damages that the principal sustains.

(f)   Rescission. The agency contract may be terminated by rescission to the same extent that any other contract may be so terminated.[16]

§ 39:13. Termination by Operation of Law.

(a)   Death. The death of either the principal or agent ordinarily terminates the authority of an agent automatically, even though the death is unknown to the other. Some state statutes provide that the death of the principal is not a revocation until the agent has notice nor as to third persons who deal with the agent in good faith and are ignorant of the death. Generally, however, these statutes are limited to principals who are members of the armed forces.

The fact that a contract of agency is terminated by death does not impose any liability for damages even though the contract has not been completed. In an attorney-client relationship the death of the client does not terminate the agency if the client had expressly agreed that the attorney should conduct the proceeding to its conclusion.[17]

(b)   Insanity. The insanity of either the principal or agent ordinarily terminates the agent's authority. If the incapacity of the principal is only temporary, the agent's authority may be merely suspended rather than terminated.

(c)   Bankruptcy. Bankruptcy of the principal or agent usually terminates the relationship. It is generally held, however, that the bankruptcy of an agent does not terminate the agent's power to deal with goods of the principal held by the agent.

Insolvency, as distinguished from a formal adjudication of bankruptcy, usually does not terminate the agency. In most states, accordingly, the authority of an agent is not terminated by the appointment of a receiver for the principal.[18]

(d)   Impossibility. The authority of an agent is terminated when it is impossible to perform the agency for any reason, such as the destruction of the subject matter of the agency, the death or loss of capacity of the third person with whom the agent is to contract, or a change in law that makes it impossible to perform the agency lawfully.

(e)   War. When the country of the principal and that of the agent are at war, the authority of the agent is usually terminated or at least suspended until peace is restored.

---

[16] Cutcliffe v Chestnut, 122 GaApp 195, 176 SE2d 607.
[17] Jones v Miller (CA3 Pa) 203 F2d 131.
[18] Chilletti v Missouri, Kansas & Texas Railway Co. 102 Kan 297, 171 P 14.

When the war has the effect of making performance impossible, the agency is, of course, terminated. For example, the authority of an agent who is a nonresident enemy alien to sue is terminated, because such an alien is not permitted to sue.

(f)   Unusual Events or Changes of Circumstances. The authority of an agent is also terminated by the occurrence of an unusual event or a change in value or business conditions of such a nature that the agent should reasonably infer that the principal would not desire the agent to continue to act under the changed circumstances. For example, an agent employed to sell land at a specified price should regard the authority to sell at that price as terminated when the value of the land increases greatly because of the discovery of oil on the land.

§ 39:14. Termination of Agency Coupled with an Interest. An agency coupled with an interest is an exception to the general rule as to the termination of an agency. Such an agency cannot be revoked by the principal before the expiration of the interest and is not terminated by the death or insanity of either the principal or the agent.

§ 39:15. Effect of Termination of Authority. If the agency is revoked by the principal, the authority to act for the principal is not terminated until notice of revocation is given to or received by the agent. As between the principal and the agent, the right of the agent to bind the principal to third persons generally ends immediately upon the termination of the agent's authority. Such termination is effective without the giving of notice to third persons.

When the agency is terminated by the act of the principal, notice must be given to third persons. If such notice is not given, the agent may have the power to make contracts that will bind the principal and third persons. This rule is predicated on the theory that a known agent will have the appearance of still being the agent unless notice to the contrary is given to third persons.

When the law requires the giving of notice in order to end the power of the agent to bind the principal, individual notice must be given or mailed to all persons who had prior dealings with the agent or the principal. Notice to the general public can be given by publishing a statement that the agency had been terminated in a newspaper of general circulation in the affected geographical area.

If a notice is actually received, the power of the agent is terminated without regard to whether the method of giving notice was proper. Conversely, if proper notice is given, it is immaterial that it does not actually come to the attention of the party notified. Thus, a member of the general public cannot claim that the principal is bound on the ground that the third person did not see the newspaper notice stating that the agent's authority had been terminated.

CASES FOR CHAPTER 39

Hill v Newman

126 NJ Super 557, 316 A2d 8 (1973)

Hill purchased furniture from Grant Furniture. When she complained that it was damaged, she was told that they would send someone to fix the damage. An independent contractor, Newman, was sent to fix the furniture. He identified himself as the man from Grant's. The lacquer he put on the furniture exploded and caused serious fire injury to Hill. She sued Newman and Grant. A verdict was returned in favor of the plaintiff against both defendants.

PER CURIAM . . . Grant first argues that Newman was an independent contractor and it was not vicariously liable for his negligence. . . .

New Jersey has recognized the general rule that one who engages a contractor to do work not in itself a nuisance, is not liable for his negligent acts in the performance of the contract. Certain exceptions have been recognized: (1) where the work is in itself a nuisance or inherently dangerous, or (2) where the landowner in fact retains or exercises control over the manner and means of the work, or (3) where he engages an incompetent contractor. . . . The cases cited in defendant's argument support no more than these principles. The "inherently dangerous" exception was ruled out of the case.

Neither the general rule nor the exceptions relate to a situation in which the independent contractor is allowed to become the apparent agent of the employer. There is nothing in the record to show that Grant retained or exercised control of Newman in the work that he did, or that Newman was an incompetent contractor.

There was enough here to establish an apparent agency: Grant's assurance that they would send somebody to repair the furniture when plaintiff phoned to complain of its condition, the phone call for an appointment that she received from Newman who said he was from Grant's, and his identifying himself when he arrived at her apartment that he was the man from Grant's who had come to fix the furniture. . . .

"One who employs an independent contractor to perform services for another which are accepted in the reasonable belief that the services are being rendered by the employer or by his servants, is subject to liability for physical harm caused by the negligence of the contractor in supplying such services, to the same extent as though the employer were supplying them himself or by his servants."

There is no question under the facts that plaintiff relied upon the manifestation of authority in Newman, thereby constituting an invitation to deal with him and enter into relations with him such as were consistent with the apparent authority.

[Judgment affirmed]

Heinrich v Martin

(ND) 134 NW2d 786 (1965)

Martin and his wife owned land which he listed for sale with Schneider, a real estate broker. Schneider agreed to sell the land to Heinrich. Heinrich sued the Martins for specific performance, claiming that the latter failed to perform the contract for the sale of the land. From a judgment in favor of the Martins, Heinrich appealed.

STRUTZ, J. . . . The listing agreement, which the defendant Martin admits signing, was dated, and it listed, among other things, the total acreage, the number of acres under cultivation, the sale price per acre, the required down payment, and the manner in which the balance due should be paid. Nowhere in the listing agreement was the broker given any authority to enter into a contract of sale of the land with any prospective buyer.

After such listing, the broker sought a buyer and, almost one year after the date on the listing agreement, he interested the plaintiff in the defendants' land. It is agreed that the defendant Gottlieb Martin did not sign any memorandum or other writing by which he contracted to sell the land to the plaintiff, but he did write a letter to the plaintiff, agreeing to sell the land to him under certain definite terms and conditions. He also orally told the broker to get the plaintiff to issue a check to the broker and one to the defendant for a part of the down payment to "close the deal." It is the listing agreement which the defendant signed, the defendant's letter to the plaintiff offering to sell the land, and the request for and delivery of such check, that form the basis for the plaintiff's cause of action.

[By statute] . . . certain contracts are invalid unless the contract, or some note or memorandum thereof, is in writing, signed by the party to be charged, or by his agent. Among the contracts that are thus declared to be invalid are agreements for the sale of real property. This section further provides that, if such agreement is made by an agent of the party to be charged, the authority of the agent must be in writing, signed by the party sought to be charged.

Thus a real estate broker, with whom lands are listed for sale by an owner, has no authority to make a contract for sale which is binding on the owner in the absence of written authority, signed by the owner. Any writing which plaintiff might have received from the broker, as defendants' agent, would not be binding on the defendants since the broker had no such written authority.

The listing agreement, which . . . Martin admits having signed and delivered to the broker, is not an agreement to sell the land to the plaintiff. It is merely a written memorandum, signed by the owner, authorizing the broker to secure a buyer for the land. As this court has held, a real estate broker with whom land is listed does not have the power to make a binding contract for sale of such land unless the broker has written authority to make such contract. . . . A writing, signed by an owner, which merely lists the land for sale is not sufficient to satisfy the provision of the Statute of Frauds and empower the prospective buyer to force the owner to convey the property to him. . . .

[Judgment affirmed]

Reasons only

Walker v Pacific Mobile Homes

68 Wash 2d 347, 413 P2d 3 (1966)

Walker owned a trailer that he wished to sell. He took it to the business premises of Pacific Mobile Homes. The only person on the premises at that time and several other times when Walker was there was Stewart, who identified himself as a salesman of Pacific and who agreed to take possession of Walker's trailer and to attempt to sell it for him. Stewart made out some forms of Pacific Mobile Homes and thereafter wrote some letters on the letterhead of Pacific to Walker. Walker's trailer was sold, but the salesman disappeared with most of the money. Walker sued Pacific for the proceeds of the sale. It denied liability on the ground that Stewart lacked authority to make any sales agreement and that all salesmen of Pacific were expressly forbidden to take used trailers to try to sell them for their owners. From a decision in favor of Walker, Pacific appealed.

HALE, J. . . . The evidence warranted findings and conclusions that Pacific Mobile Homes had clothed Stewart . . . with apparent or ostensible authority to take the trailer onto the lot for sale . . . and to collect the purchase money therefor. The salesman's solitary presence in the company office and about the lot on several occasions, among numerous trailers on display, beneath a sign conspicuously proclaiming the whole to be an enterprise of Pacific Mobile Homes, Inc., and his towing plaintiff's trailer to the trailer lot and putting it on display there, allowed a person of ordinary business prudence to reasonably assume that the salesman had authority from Pacific Mobile Homes, Inc., to buy, sell, receive, and deliver trailers for cash, on credit, consignment, or in exchange. Then, too, the salesman's untrammeled access to and use of his principal's letterhead, stationery, and business forms, and his seeming control of the office and lot, fortify the idea of apparent authority.

Authority to perform particular services for a principal carries with it the implied authority to perform the usual and necessary acts essential to carry out the authorized services. . . . One dealing in good faith with an agent who appears to be acting within the scope of his authority is not bound by undisclosed limitations on the agent's power. . . .

A corporation may be bound by the contracts or agreements of its agent if within the apparent scope of the agent's authority, although the contract may be beyond the scope of his actual authority. . . .

It is also the well-established rule that the apparent or ostensible authority of an agent can be inferred only from acts and conduct of the principal. . . . The extent of an agent's authority cannot be established by his own acts and declarations. . . .

The burden of establishing agency rests upon the one who asserts it. Facts and circumstances are sufficient to establish apparent authority only when a person exercising ordinary prudence, acting in good faith and conversant with business practices and customs, would be misled thereby, and such person has given due regard to such other circumstances as would cause a person of ordinary prudence to make further inquiry. . . .

A principal may be estopped to deny that his agent possesses the authority he assumes to exercise, where the principal knowingly causes or permits him so to act as to justify a third person of ordinarily careful and prudent business habits to believe that he possesses the authority exercised and avails himself of the benefit of the agent's acts. . . .

[Judgment affirmed]

Melancon v A & M Pest Control Service Co., Inc.,

(LaApp) 325 So2d 391 (1976)

Melancon made a contract with A & M Pest Control Service, Inc. to protect his house against termites. The contract contained a warranty which stated "this warranty agreement is personal to the customer named above [Melancon] and may not be assigned or transferred by any means whatever by the person to whom it is issued." Melancon sold his house to Ruiz in 1970. In 1972, a representative of A & M told Ruiz that he could keep the contract in force by paying the renewal fee. Ruiz did this and thereafter A & M made inspections and repairs to the premises. Ruiz claimed that greater repairs should have been made, whereupon A & M claimed that Ruiz could not enforce the warranty because it was limited to Melancon. Ruiz replied that A & M had ratified the action of its representative and was therefore bound by the renewal contract. Melancon and Ruiz jointly sued A & M. From a judgment in their favor, A & M appealed.

LEMMON, J. . . . Although the contract and warranty were issued to Melancon, Ruiz testified that A & M's representative with apparent authority to do so told him the contract could be kept in effect by paying the renewal fee. A & M not only did not deny this statement, but also accepted the renewal fee from Ruiz and contacted him to arrange the annual inspection and treatment pursuant to the contract. We therefore conclude that A & M ratified its agent's agreement to allow Ruiz to take over its contract with Melancon by providing service and accepting payment under the contract, and Ruiz therefore had a right of action to enforce the terms of the contract. . . .

[Judgment affirmed]

Kinmon v J. P. King Auction Co., Inc.

290 Ala 323, 276 So2d 569 (1973)

Kinmon owned a summer home which he wanted to sell at auction. He employed the J. P. King Auction Company to make the sale. King sold the property to the highest bidder for $35,000. Kinmon had expected twice that much and refused to convey title to the buyer or to pay commissions to King. King sued Kinmon to collect the commissions. Kinmon raised the defense that he had revoked King's authority to sell the property. From a judgment for King, Kinmon appealed.

FAULKNER, J. . . . "Bittersweet" is a home in Perdido Beach, Alabama. . . .

On July 29, 1971, George H. Kinmon, the owner, signed a contract with J. P. King Auction Company (King) to sell the property "for the highest price obtainable." Kinmon testified to having "conveyed" to the representatives of King that he expected to realize $103,500 for the property. The latter told Kinmon that Bittersweet would bring what it was worth the day of the sale. The written contract did not incorporate any guaranteed minimum price, referring merely to "the highest price obtainable."

King prepared and distributed a brochure announcing the "absolute auction" of Bittersweet: "This is the place for your Vacation Home or Company Lodge, plenty of room for sleeping and entertaining on Beautiful Soldier Creek just a few minutes by boat to Alabama Point and on out into the Gulf for some of the best fishing in the world. Enjoy swimming and skiing just from your own boathouse or just plain fishing from the pier. There is everything to enjoy at 'Bittersweet.'

Let Today's Investment Be Tomorrow's Security."

"YOUR PRICE IS OUR PRICE."

Kinmon, concerned about the possibility of not realizing an adequate price for his property, protested against the inclusion of the terms "Your Price is Our Price" and "absolute auction." However, preparations for the auction continued. Signs announcing the forthcoming auction and stating "Your Price is Our Price" remained undisturbed by Kinmon.

On August 21, 1971, the day of the auction, Kinmon was "upset." He told King's secretary that he wasn't signing anything. At one point during the bidding, Kinmon went up to King and stated that if Bittersweet did not bring $70,000, "I will take you to Supreme Court." King went ahead with the bidding and sold the property to the highest bidder for $35,000. Kinmon subsequently refused to convey the property or pay King's commission. King sued, and the Circuit Court of Baldwin County held that he was entitled to his commission. Kinmon appealed from this decree.

. . . There is no doubt Kinmon and King could have written a $50,000, $70,000, or $100,000 minimum price for Bittersweet into their auction sale contract. They did not do so. The contract recites that Bittersweet would be sold "for the highest price obtainable." Kinmon may have wished or hoped that the sale would realize $100,000. However, it is elementary that it is the terms of the written contract, not the mental operations of one of the parties, that control its interpretation. . . .

Contracting parties are free to modify their contract by mutual assent. . . . After expressing discontent with the advertised slogan "Your Price is Our Price," Kinmon could have asked King to insert a minimum price guarantee into the contract. He did not do so. Unilateral grumbling cannot modify bilateral contract.

It is the general rule that the agency to sell at auction, whether such auction be "with reserve" or "absolute," may be withdrawn at any time prior to the opening of bids. . . . This withdrawal of authority must be clear and unequivocal. Nowhere in the record is there evidence that Kinmon clearly and unequivocally stated that he no longer wished King to sell his property, that he was revoking King's authority, that he was withdrawing Bittersweet from sale. Being "upset" is not enough; threatening to take King to court if $70,000 were not realized is not enough. . . .

[Judgment affirmed]

QUESTIONS AND CASE PROBLEMS

1. What social forces are affected by allowing an agent to make a contract which will bind the agent's principal and a third person?
2. Compare (a) an agent, (b) an independent contractor, and (c) a real estate broker.
3. Compare authorization of an agent by (a) appointment and (b) ratification.
4. Compare (a) the termination of an agency with (b) the discharge of a contract.
5. A husband and wife owned a house as tenants in common without the right of survivorship. They insured the building against fire. The property was destroyed by fire. The insurance company paid the full amount of the proceeds to the husband on the basis of a release which he signed with his name and the name of the wife. She had not expressly authorized him to do this. Thereafter the wife sued the insurance company for one half of the amount paid by the insurer. It raised the defense that it had made full payment to the husband. Was this a valid defense? [See Gray v Holyoke Mutual Fire Ins. Co., 293 Ala 291, 302 So2d 104
6. An automobile was owned by Peterson. He gave possession of the car to his son, Edward, and Edwards's wife, Gloria, but retained the title to the car. Edward's daughter, Christine, was sixteen and was driving the car to the city at Gloria's direction in order to buy her younger sister a pair of shoes. Because of Christine's negligent driving, the car struck Johnson who was riding a motorcycle. He sued Christine's mother. He claimed that Christine was the agent of the mother. Could the mother raise the defense that Christine was a minor? [Johnson v Peterson, 38 Cal App 3d 619, 113 Cal Rptr 445]
7. Through his agent, Davis, Fieschko executed a written agreement to sell his real estate to Herlich. The agreement had been negotiated by Dykstra as Herlich's agent. The contract for the purchase of the land was signed by Dykstra as the agent for Herlich. Thereafter Herlich sent a check for the down payment to Davis. The check did not contain any reference to the sale or the terms of the sale. Herlich did not go through with the sale and, when sued for breach of the contract, he argued that he was not bound by the contract since he had not signed it and Dykstra had not been authorized in writing to sign it. Fieschko claimed that Herlich had ratified the contract when he sent the check for the down payment. Decide. [Fieschko v Herlich, 32 Ill App 2d 280, 177 NE2d 376]
8. Perry was a building contractor. Rothrock made a contract with Perry to build a house for Rothrock on his land. Perry contracted with Maxwell to provide labor and materials for flooring and walls of the house. Maxwell was not paid. He sued Perry and Rothrock for the amount due him. Maxwell claimed that Rothrock was liable because Perry was his agent. Was Maxwell correct? [Maxwell v Perry, 22 NC 58, 205 SE2d 350]

9. Fishbaugh employed Scheibenberger to run a farm for him. Scheibenberger was authorized to rent the farm, to collect the rent, to superintend and direct repairs, and to allow the tenant to sell corn for the payment of taxes and fencing. The agent leased the farm to Hinsley, who sold certain crops to Spunaugle. Fishbaugh sued Spunaugle for the value of these crops. The decision turned on whether Scheibenberger was a general agent. What is your opinion? [Fishbaugh v Spunaugle, 118 Iowa 337, 92 NW 58]

10. Whitehead had a policy of hospital insurance. The authority of the agent who had "sold" him the policy and to whom Whitehead paid premiums was terminated by the insurance company, but Whitehead was never notified of this fact. He continued to pay premiums to the former agent. When Whitehead told a hospital that he had an insurance policy, the company confirmed this statement and admitted that the policy was in force. Thereafter the insurer refused to pay any hospital bills on the ground that the former agent to whom premium payments were made had no authority to receive the payments. Was the insurer liable? [American Casualty Co. v Whitehead, (Miss) 206 So2d 838]

11. Joanne Zak had a policy of automobile liability insurance issued by the Metropolitan Casualty Insurance Co. Zak was involved in an accident and was sued by the person injured. Metropolitan refused to defend Zak in the action as required by the policy, on the ground that the policy had been cancelled for nonpayment of premiums. A judgment was entered against Zak. Then Zak sued Metropolitan for the alleged breach of the obligation of the policy by failing to defend Zak in the earlier action. Fidelity-Phenix Insurance Co., which had taken over the business of Metropolitan, defended in the latter action. Zak showed that she had made payment of the premium to a subagent of Agres, who was an authorized agent of Metropolitan. The subagent misappropriated the money and Agres notified Metropolitan to cancel the policy for nonpayment of premiums. Zak relied on an Illinois statute which provided that "any [insurance] company which directly or through its agent delivers in this State to any insurance broker a policy or contract for insurance pursuant to the application or request of such broker, acting for an insured other than himself, shall be deemed to have authorized such broker to receive on its behalf payment of any premium which is due on such policy or contract for insurance at the time of its issuance or delivery or which becomes due thereon not more than ninety (90) days thereafter." Was the insurer liable? [Zak v Fidelity-Phenix Ins. Co. 58 IllApp2d 341, 208 NE2d 29]

12. A daughter was using the family car to buy sweet corn for the family from a roadside stand. When she collided with another driver, the latter claimed that the former was the father's agent and that the father was liable for her tort. Was she the agent of her father? [Grimes v Labreck, 108 NH 26, 226 A2d 787]

13. Coffin had a liability and property damage insurance policy on his automobile issued by the Farm Bureau Mutual Insurance Co. He purchased a new automobile and wanted to transfer the insurance. He phoned the home office of the insurance company, stated his request, and was transferred to two different girls who each stated that she did not have authority to make such a transfer and finally connected him with Pierson. Coffin stated to Pierson that he wanted to transfer his existing insurance and also to add comprehensive and collision coverage. Pierson told him that the new car was insured as requested from that moment on. Coffin had an accident in his car the next day before any change had been made in his policy. He sued the insurance company, which defended on the ground that no change had ever been made and that Pierson was merely a typing supervisor in the auto underwriters' department who had no authority to make any policy change. Was the new car covered by insurance? [Farm Bureau Mutual Insurance Company v Coffin, 136 Ind App 12, 186 NE2d 180]

40

Principal and Agent

What authority does the agent have? What are the duties and liabilities of the principal and agent to each other? These are basic questions in the agency relationship.

A. AGENT'S AUTHORITY

The fact that one person is the agent of another does not dispose of all questions. It is necessary to determine the scope of the agent's authority.

§ 40:1. Scope of Agent's Authority.

(a) Express Authority. If the principal tells the agent to perform a certain act, the agent has *express authority* to do so. Express authority can be indicated by conduct as well as by words. Accordingly, when the agent informs the principal of intended plans and the principal makes no objection to them, authorization may be indicated by such silence.

(b) Incidental Authority. An agent has implied *incidental authority* to perform any act reasonably necessary to execute the express authority given to the agent. To illustrate, if the principal authorizes the agent to purchase goods without furnishing funds to the agent to pay for them, the agent has implied incidental authority to purchase the goods on credit.

(c) Customary Authority. An agent has implied *customary authority* to do any act which, according to the custom of the community, usually accompanies the transaction for which the agent is authorized to act. For example, an agent who has express authority to receive payments from third persons has implied authority to issue receipts.

One authorized to act as a general manager has the power to make any contract necessary for the usual and ordinary conduct of business. (See p. 670, Jackson v Goodman) Likewise, an agent authorized to obtain advertising may contract for television time because the use of television as an advertising medium is customary. Authorization to contract for television time can also be regarded as incidental to a general, unrestricted authorization to advertise.[1]

An agent with express authority to receive checks in payment does not have implied authority to cash them. An employee's authority to indorse checks payable

---

[1] Columbia Broadcasting System v Stokley-Van Camp, Inc. (CA2 NY) 522 F2d 369.

to an employer does not include authority to indorse and deposit those checks into the employee's personal bank account. Authorization to a lawyer to settle a client's claim does not authorize the lawyer to indorse the client's name on a check given in settlement of the claim.

An agent does not have incidental or customary power to release or compromise debts owed to the principal or to settle disputed amounts of debts for smaller sums, even though the agent is designated as the "field representative" of the principal.

(d) Apparent Authority. A person has apparent authority as an agent when the principal by words or conduct leads a third person reasonably to believe that such person has that authority and the third person relies on that appearance.[2]

The mere possession of property does not give rise to any apparent authority of the possessor to act with respect to the property.

§ 40:2. Effect of Proper Exercise of Authority. When an agent with authority properly makes a contract with a third person that purports to bind the principal, there is by definition a binding contract between the principal and the third person. The agent is not a party to this contract. Consequently, when the owner of goods is the principal, the owner's agent is not liable for breach of warranty with respect to the goods "sold" by the agent because the owner-principal, not the agent, was the "seller" in the sales transaction.[3]

Furthermore, even when a transaction between the agent and the third person may be formalized by the execution of subsequent documents, such as a written policy of insurance after an oral agreement has been made with the agent, the later writing does not destroy the rights acquired by the principal or the third person under the agent's informal or oral contract; and parol evidence is admissible to determine the actual agreement that had been made with the agent.

§ 40:3. Duty to Ascertain Extent of Agent's Authority. A third person who deals with a person claiming to be an agent cannot rely on the statements made by the agent concerning the extent of authority. If the agent is not authorized to perform the act or is not even the agent of the principal, the transaction between the alleged agent and the third person will have no legal effect between the principal and the third person. (See p. 671, Taylor v Equitable Trust Co.)

When the third person should realize that the agent is merely a soliciting agent of an insurance company with no greater authority than to obtain an application from third persons and transmit it to the insurance company, the insurer is not bound by an agreement which such agent makes with an applicant by which the applicant had been promised unlimited medical expenses coverage, whereas the policy as delivered contained a maximum limitation on such coverage.

(a) Authority Dependent on an Event. If the authority of an agent is contingent upon the happening of some event, one may not ordinarily rely upon the statement of the agent that the event has happened.

An exception to this rule is made in cases in which the happening of the event is peculiarly within the knowledge of the agent and cannot be ascertained easily, if

---

[2] Associated Creditors' Agency v Davis, 13 Cal3d 374, 118 CalRptr 772, 530 P2d 1084.
[3] Gaito v Hoffman, 5 UCCRS 1056.

at all, by the party dealing with the agent. As an illustration, if the agent of a railroad issues a bill of lading for goods without actually receiving the goods, the railroad, as principal, is liable to one who takes the bill in good faith and for value.[4] This exception is justified because, although the authority of the agent to issue bills of lading is dependent upon receiving goods, subsequent persons taking bills of lading have no way of determining whether the agent in fact did receive the goods.

(b)   Agent's Acts Adverse to Principal. The third person who deals with an agent is required to take notice of any acts that are clearly adverse to the interest of the principal. Thus, if the agent is obviously making use of funds of the principal for the agent's personal benefit, persons dealing with the agent should recognize that the agent may be acting without authority and that they are dealing with the agent at their peril.

The only certain way that third persons can protect themselves is to inquire of the principal whether the agent is in fact the agent of the principal and has the necessary authority. If the principal states that the agent has the authority, the principal cannot later deny this authorization unless the subject matter is such that an authorization must be in writing in order to be binding.

(c)   Death of Third Person. The extent of the agent's authority becomes particularly significant when the third person dies after the transaction with the agent but before any action has been taken by the principal. If the agent had authority to contract on behalf of the principal, the agent's agreement with the third person would give rise immediately to a binding contract and the third person's subsequent death would ordinarily not affect that contract. In contrast, if the agent did not have authority to contract but only to transmit an offer from the third person, the death of the third person before the principal had accepted the offer would work a revocation of the offer and the principal could not create a contract by purporting to accept after the death of the third person.

§ 40:4. Limitations on Agent's Authority. A person who has knowledge of a limitation on the agent's authority cannot disregard that limitation. When the third person knows that the authority of the agent depends upon whether financing has been obtained, the principal is not bound by the act of the agent if the financing in fact was not obtained. (See p. 672, Citizens State Bank v Rausch) If the authority of the agent is based on a writing and the third person knows that there is such a writing, the third person is charged with knowledge of the limitations contained in it. The third person is likewise charged with such knowledge when the contract submitted indicates the existence of a limitation on the agent's authority.

If the agent informs the third person that authority is lacking to do a particular act but that the agent will endeavor to obtain authorization from the principal, the third person cannot successfully claim that the agent has apparent authority. If the third person enters into a contract on the assumption that the agent will be able to obtain authorization, the third person takes the risk that the agent will not be able to do so.

---

[4] Uniform Commercial Code § 7-301.

(a) Apparent Limitations. In some situations, it will be apparent to third persons that they are dealing with an agent whose authority is limited. When third persons know that they are dealing with an officer of a private corporation or a representative of a governmental agency, they should recognize that such person will ordinarily not have unlimited authority [5] and that a contract made with the officer might not be binding unless ratified by the principal.

(b) Secret Limitations. If the principal has clothed an agent with authority to perform certain acts but the principal gives secret instructions that limit the agent's authority, the third person is allowed to take the authority of the agent at its face value and is not bound by the secret limitations of which the third person has no knowledge.

§ 40:5. Delegation of Authority by Agent. As a general rule, an agent cannot delegate to another the authority obtained from the principal. (See p. 673, Bucholtz v Sirotkin Travel Ltd.) In other words, unless the principal expressly or impliedly consents, an agent cannot appoint *subagents* to carry out the agent's duties. The reason for this rule is that since an agent is usually selected because of some personal qualifications, it would be unfair and possibly injurious to the principal if the authority to act could be shifted by the agent to another. This is particularly true when the agent was originally appointed for the performance of a task requiring discretion or judgment. For example, an agent who is appointed to adjust claims against an insurance company cannot delegate the performance of that duty to another.

Agents, however, may authorize others to perform their work for them in the following instances:

(a) When the acts to be done involve only mechanical or ministerial duties. Thus, an agent to make application for hail insurance on wheat may delegate to another the clerical act of writing the application. And it may be shown that there is customary authority for a clerk in the office of the insurance agent to sign the agent's name so as to have the effect of a signing by the agent and be binding upon the insurance company, the agent's principal.[6]

(b) When a well-known custom recognizes such appointment. To illustrate, if one is authorized to buy or sell a grain elevator, one may do so through a broker when that is the customary method.

(c) When the appointment is justified by necessity or sudden emergency and it is impractical to communicate with the principal, and the appointment of a subagent is reasonably necessary for the protection of the interests of the principal entrusted to the agent.

(d) When it is contemplated by the parties that subagents would be employed. For example, a bank may now generally use subagents to receive payment of notes that have been left for collection since the parties contemplate that this will be done. Also, the authority to appoint subagents can be inferred where the principal knows or has reason to know that the agent employs subagents. Thus, an agent may grant

[5] Weil and Associates v Urban Renewal Agency, 206 Kan 405, 479 P2d 875.
[6] United Bonding Insurance Co. v Banco Suizo-Panameno (CA5 Fla) 422 F2d 1142.

subagents power to bind a principal fire insurance company, where the agent had a long standing practice of appointing subagents and this was known to the principal.[7]

B. DUTIES AND LIABILITIES OF PRINCIPAL AND AGENT

The creation of the principal-agent relationship gives rise not only to powers but also to duties and liabilities.

§ 40:6. Duties and Liabilities of Agent During Agency. While the agency relationship exists, the agent owes certain duties to the principal.

(a) Loyalty. An agent must be loyal or faithful to the principal. The agent must not obtain any secret profit or benefit from the agency. If the principal is seeking to buy or rent property, the agent cannot secretly obtain the property and then sell or lease it to the principal at a profit.

An agent who owns property cannot sell it to the principal without disclosing that ownership to the principal. If this is not done, the principal may avoid the contract even though the agent's conduct did not cause the principal any financial loss. Or the principal can approve the transaction and sue the agent for any secret profit obtained by the agent.

An agent cannot act as agent for both parties to a transaction unless both know of the dual capacity and agree to it. If the agent does so act without the consent of both parties, the transaction is voidable at the election of any principal who did not know of the agent's double status.

An agent must not accept secret gifts or commissions from third persons in connection with the agency. If the agent does so, the principal may sue the agent for those gifts or commissions. Such practices are condemned because the judgment of the agent may be influenced by the receipt of gifts or commissions. A principal may also recover from the agent any secret profit that the latter has made in violation of a duty of loyalty to the principal. If the agent makes a false report to the principal in order to conceal the agent's interest, the principal is entitled to recover not only the secret profits made and property acquired by the agent but may also be awarded punitive damages in order to punish and discourage such wrongdoing.

An agent is, of course, prohibited from aiding the competitors of a principal or disclosing to them information relating to the business of the principal. It is also a breach of duty for the agent to deceive a principal with false information.

(b) Obedience and Performance. An agent is under a duty to obey all lawful instructions. The agent is required to perform the services specified for the period and in the way specified. An agent who does not is liable to the principal for any harm caused. For example, if an agent is instructed to take cash payments only but accepts a check in payment; the agent is liable for the loss caused the principal when the check is dishonored by nonpayment. Likewise, when an insurance broker undertakes to obtain a policy of insurance for a principal that will provide a specified coverage but fails to obtain a policy with the proper coverage, the broker, as agent of the principal, is liable to the principal for the loss thereby caused.

---

[7] Bloom v Wolfe (ColoApp) 547 P2d 934.

If the agent violates instructions, it is immaterial that the agent acted in good faith or intended to benefit the principal. It is the fact that the agent violated the instructions and thereby caused the principal a loss which imposes a liability on the agent. In determining whether the agent has obeyed instructions, they must be interpreted in a way that a reasonable person would interpret them.

(c)   Reasonable Care. It is the duty of an agent to act with the care that a reasonable person would exercise under the circumstances. In addition, if the agent possesses a special skill, as in the case of a broker or an attorney, the agent must exercise that skill.

(d)   Accounting. An agent must account to the principal for all property or money belonging to the principal that comes into the agent's possession. The agent should, within a reasonable time, give notice of collections made and render an accurate account of all receipts and expenditures. The agency agreement may state at what intervals or on what dates such accountings are to be made.

An agent should keep the principal's property and money separate and distinct from that of the agent. If property of the agent is mingled with property of the principal so that the two cannot be identified or separated, the principal may claim all of the commingled mass. Furthermore, when funds of the principal and the agent are mixed, any loss that occurs must be borne by the agent.

(e)   Information. It is the duty of an agent to keep the principal informed of all facts relating to the agency which are relevant to protecting the principal's interests.[8] In consequence, a principal's promise to pay a bonus to an agent for information secured by the agent in the course of duty is not enforceable because the principal was entitled to that information anyway. The promise of the principal is unenforceable because it is not supported by consideration.

If the agent fails to communicate information to the principal which should have been communicated, and the principal sustains loss because of it, the principal may recover the amount of such loss from the agent.

§ 40:7. Duties and Liabilities of Agent after Termination of Agency. When the agency relationship ends, the duties of the agent continue only to the extent necessary to perform prior obligations. For example, the agent must return to the former principal any property which had been entrusted to the agent for the purpose of the agency. With the exception of such "winding up" duties, the agency relationship is terminated and the former agent can deal with the principal as freely as with a stranger. (See p. 674, Clinkenbeard v Central Southwest Oil Corp.)

§ 40:8. Enforcement of Liability of Agent. When the agent's breach of duty causes harm to the principal, the amount of the loss may be deducted from any compensation due the agent or may be recovered in an ordinary lawsuit.

When the agent handles money for the principal, the contract of employment may provide that the amount of any shortages in the agent's account may be deducted from the compensation to which the agent would otherwise be entitled.

---

[8] Restatement, Agency 2d § 381; Spritz v Brockton Savings Bank, 305 Mass 170, 25 NE2d 155.

If the agent has made a secret profit, the principal may recover that profit from the agent. In addition, the agent may forfeit the right to all compensation, without regard to whether the principal had been benefited by some of the actions of the agent and without regard to whether the principal had actually been harmed.

§ 40:9. Duties and Liabilities of Principal to Agent. The principal is under certain duties to the agent. The principal must perform the contract, compensate the agent for services, make reimbursement for proper expenditures, and under certain circumstances must indemnify the agent for loss.

(a) Employment According to Terms of Contract. When the contract is for a specified time, the principal is under the obligation to permit the agent to act as such for the term of the contract, in the absence of any just cause or contract provision which permits the principal to terminate the agency sooner. If the principal gives the agent an exclusive right to act as such, the principal cannot give anyone else the authority to act as agent nor may the principal do the act to which the exclusive agent's authority relates. If the principal or another agent does so, the exclusive agent is entitled to full compensation as though the act had been performed by the exclusive agent.

(b) Compensation. The principal must pay the agent the compensation agreed upon. If the parties have not fixed the amount of the compensation by their agreement but intended that the agent should be paid, the agent may recover the customary compensation for such services. If there is no established compensation, the agent may recover the reasonable value of the services rendered.

When one person requests another to perform services under circumstances that reasonably justify the expectation of being paid, a duty to make payment arises. For example, when one requests a broker or an attorney to act as agent, there is an implied obligation to compensate for such services.

Whether a contract is made which binds the third person may determine whether the agent is entitled to compensation. For example, a contracting agent is allowed compensation only on contracts actually made. In contrast, some soliciting agents, such as a real estate broker, will generally be entitled to compensation when the broker produces a person who is willing and able to make a contract of sale or purchase with the principal of the broker.

When the agent is employed on the contingency that there will be compensation only if a certain result is achieved, the agent is not entitled to compensation or reimbursement if the desired result is not achieved regardless of how much time or money was spent in the effort. Likewise, an agent is not entitled to compensation with respect to transactions canceled by third persons as long as the principal was not at fault.

In any case an agent may agree to work without compensation; for it is authorization to act, and not compensation for acting, that is the test of agency.

(1) Advance Payment. When agents are compensated on a basis of a percentage of the sales price of goods they sell or the contracts they make, it is customary to allow them to draw a stated amount weekly or monthly subject to adjustment at the end of some longer accounting period in the event that the commissions

actually earned should be greater than the sums paid from the drawing account. If the contract between the principal and the agent does not give the principal the right to recover overpayments, the employer does not have such a right. That is, when an agent is allowed to take advances to be charged against future commissions, the principal cannot recover the excess of the advances over the earned commissions in the absence of an express or implied agreement to that effect.

If it is not clear from the agency contract whether the principal has the right to recoup over-advances, the contract is interpreted strictly against the principal and the right to recoup is denied.

(2) Repeating Transactions. In certain industries third persons make repeated transactions with the principal. In such cases the agent who made the original contract with the third person commonly receives a certain compensation or percentage of commissions on all subsequent renewal or additional contracts. In the insurance business, for example, the insurance agent obtaining the policy-holder for the insurer receives a substantial portion of the first year's premium and then receives a smaller percentage of the premiums paid by the policyholder in the following years.

Whether an agent or an agent's estate is entitled to receive compensation on repeating transactions, either after the termination of the agent's employment or after the agent's death, depends upon the terms of the agency contract. Frequently it is provided that the right to receive compensation on repeating transactions terminates upon the termination of the agent's authority or employment by the principal.

A provision that an agent's renewal commission shall terminate if the agent accepts employment with another insurance company before the expiration of a specified period after the termination of the agent's employment is valid. There is no vested right to renewal premiums but only such right as the contract of employment confers. Such a limitation is not an illegal restraint on trade.

(3) Post-Agency Transactions. An agent is not entitled to compensation in connection with transactions, such as sales or renewals of insurance policies, occurring after the termination of the agency, even though the post-agency transactions are the result of the agent's former activities. Some contracts between a principal and an agent expressly give the agent the right to post-termination compensation, however, or may expressly deny the agent such compensation.

(c)   Reimbursement. The principal is under a duty to reimburse the agent for all disbursements made at the request of the principal and for all expenses necessarily incurred in the lawful discharge of the agency for the benefit of the principal. The agent cannot recover, however, for expenses caused by the agent's own misconduct or negligence. By way of illustration, if the agent transfers title to the wrong person, the agent cannot recover from the principal the expense incurred in correcting the error.

(d)   Indemnity. It is the duty of the principal to indemnify the agent for any losses or damages suffered on account of the agency which were not caused by the agent's fault.

When the loss sustained is not the result of obedience to the principal's instructions but of the agent's misconduct, or of an obviously illegal act, the principal is not liable for indemnification.

CASES FOR CHAPTER 40

Jackson v Goodman

69 MichApp 225, 244 NW2d 423 (1976)

A clerk in the St. Regis Hotel was killed during a robbery. Bromber, the general manager of the hotel, offered a $1,000 reward for information leading to the arrest and conviction of the killer. Jackson furnished the information and the killer was convicted. However, when Jackson claimed the reward, Goodman and the other owners of the hotel denied that Bromber had authority to offer a $1,000 reward because he had no authority to spend any amount over $50 without approval from the owners of the hotel. Jackson sued Goodman and the other owners for the $1,000 reward. A jury returned a verdict in favor of Jackson but the court entered judgment for the owners as a matter of law. Jackson appealed.

KAUFMAN, J. . . . The trial court improperly granted a judgment notwithstanding the verdict because there was sufficient evidence to present jury questions concerning . . . the presence of either inherent authority or ratification.

. . . Any individual with the authority to make a contract may offer a reward . . . The authority to contract may be inferred from the authority to manage a business. Such authority is limited to making "contracts which are incidental to such business, are usually made in it, or are reasonably necessary in conducting it." . . . One of the factors to be considered in determining the extent of authority is the custom of similar businesses at the same time and place. . . .

Other courts have presumed authority in the president of a bank to offer, on behalf of the bank, a reward for information leading to the arrest of a defaulting teller. . . . Similarly the authority to offer a reward for the arrest of persons maliciously destroying railroad tracks has been held to be within the implied authority of the railroad superintendent. . . .

The conflict resulting from an application of agency principles to the instant case is well illustrated

by the divergence between our view and that of the dissent. The basic area of disagreement involves a question of perspective. The dissent views the question of implied authority from the perspective of the business. We view this question from the perspective of the plaintiff, especially that concerning the reasonableness of his reliance on the newspaper article.

Normally, the application of rules concerning usual course of business results in an equitable outcome in line with the parties' expectations, advancement of commercial intercourse and considerations of fundamental fairness. Where the specific business exhibits a general course of behavior relative to the questioned acts, the inquiry generally will give greater focus to the specific concern than the course of conduct in similar businesses. Where, as here, the transaction is one unusual to the specific business affected, the emphasis must differ. In such a case, significant emphasis must be placed on the course of business conduct in the community at large concerning rewards and on whether the recipient party "reasonably believes that the agent is authorized to [act] . . . and has no notice that he is not so authorized." . . . A jury, as the repository of "community sense," is in a unique position to decide questions of usual course of conduct and reasonable reliance in such unusual cases.

"When there is a disputed question of agency, if there is any testimony, either direct or inferential, tending to establish it, it becomes a question of fact for the jury to determine.". . . The jury verdict should not have been disturbed.

. . . We reverse . . . and remand this cause to the trial court for entry of judgment in conformance with the jury verdict. . . .

[Judgment affirmed]

McGREGOR, J. (dissenting). . . . It was the plaintiff's theory that the reward was offered by Frank C. Bromber, a manager of the hotel, and that the offering of the reward was within Bromber's authority. . . .

The resolution of this issue largely involves the law of agency and the application of its principles to the facts of the present case. A principal is subject to liability for the acts of an agent if it can be said that: (a) the agent was authorized to do the act; (b) the agent was apparently authorized to do the act; (c) the act was within the agent's inherent authority; or (d) the act was ratified by the principal.

In the present case, Bromber cannot be said to have been authorized to offer the reward. At trial, defendant Albert Goodman testified that Bromber could not expend more than $50.00 without Goodman's express approval and that such approval was not given here. This testimony was uncontroverted by the plaintiff and, therefore, it must be assumed that Bromber did not have the actual authority to offer a reward of $1,000.00.

Nor do I find any evidence presented at trial which would justify the jury in concluding that Bromber had either the apparent or inherent authority to offer the reward. . . . Can third persons reasonably assume that a general manager of a hotel has the authority to offer a reward for information leading to the arrest and conviction of the person responsible for the murder of a hotel employee? I would hold that third persons cannot reasonably make such an assumption.

A general manager can only have the apparent or inherent authority to do those things which managers in that business at that time and place customarily do. As such, contracts entered into by general managers are only binding on the principal if they are incidental to a business such as the principal's are usually made in such a business, or are reasonably necessary in conducting such a business. I do not think that it can reasonably be said that the reward in the present case is either incidental to or reasonably necessary in conducting the hotel business. Nor do I think, in the absence of any evidence to the contrary, that it can be assumed that such rewards are usually made in the hotel business. Rather, it would be more reasonable to assume that the offering of a reward is an unusual or extraordinary event which is not customary in most businesses. Thus, since the plaintiff has failed to show that general managers of hotels, or of defendants' hotel in particular, usually offer rewards under circumstances similar to those in the present case, I conclude that there was no evidence presented which showed that Bromber had the apparent or inherent authority to offer the reward in the instant case.

Taylor v Equitable Trust Co.

269 Md 149, 304 A2d 838 (1973)

The Taylors were depositors of the Equitable Trust Company. In return for their check, Equitable gave them a treasurer's check for $20,000. Thereafter Vittetoe, a loan officer of the bank, received a long-distance telephone call from a person who identified himself as Mr. Taylor and requested that the $20,000 represented by the treasurer's check be transferred to the account of Jody Associates at Irving Trust Company in New York. Vittetoe did not know Mr. Taylor personally and replied that written instructions from Taylor would be required. Some time later, Frank Terranova appeared at the bank and described himself as the Taylors' agent, surrendered the treasurer's check, and requested that the money represented thereby be transferred to the account of Jody Associates in the Irving Trust Company. Terranova surrendered the treasurer's check which was not indorsed. Terranova also presented a letter which he had signed in his own name, addressed to Vittetoe, in which was repeated the request to transfer the $20,000.

Equitable made the transfer as requested. Taylor denied that Terranova had the authority to request such transfer and sued Equitable for damages. Judgment was entered for Equitable. Taylor appealed.

SINGLEY, J. . . . . Subtitle 3 of the UCC . . . is applicable here because the check of a bank treasurer or cashier is regarded as a draft drawn on the drawer bank, treated by UCC 3-118(a) as a note and satisfies the requirements of UCC § 3-104. UCC § 3-403(1) recognizes that the signature of an agent or other representative may be valid. Of course, the power to sign for another may be expressly given, or may be implied, or may rest on apparent authority: otherwise, the signature would be unauthorized under § 1-201(43). . . .

An unauthorized signature is wholly inoperative under § 3-404 unless the person whose signature it purports to be ratifies it or is precluded from denying it. Under § 3-401 an item containing a forged or unauthorized signature is not properly payable. . . .

There is no doubt that Equitable was negligent in not insisting on written instructions from Taylor . . . and in not verifying Terranova's authority to act for Taylor, if it proposed to act in reliance upon it. . . .

Both sides make much of the issue whether Terranova was or was not Taylor's agent. Certainly Taylor is not precluded by § 3-406 from asserting Terranova's lack of authority, because of Equitable's acknowledged failure to act in accordance with reasonable commercial standards, in making a transfer without a written direction from Taylor.

Taylor's statement that Terranova was not authorized to act for him, made in his direct testimony and again when Equitable called him as an adverse witness, went unchallenged. The existence of implied or apparent authority could only be bottomed on Terranova's letter, enclosing the check, which for all Vittetoe knew, might have been stolen. Even if we regard the letter as a representation by Terranova that he was authorized to act for Taylor, Equitable was not entitled to rely on Terranova's statement, without more. . . . In our view, Vittetoe's testimony regarding his telephone call to Miami was not enough to save the day, not only because of his equivocation and uncertainty, but because of his total disregard of even the simplest precautions to make sure that the voice at the other end was that of Taylor, a man whom he did not know.

Two comments seem particularly pertinent here: "A third person dealing with a purported agent should communicate with the principal to verify the agent's authority to sign. A written statement from the principal as to the agent's authority may also aid in avoiding any subsequent dispute as to whether such authority existed, or whether the principal had made any statement as to the authority of the apparent agent." 2 Anderson, Uniform Commercial Code, § 3-404:3 at 922. In Noah v Bowery Sav. Bank, 225 NY 284, 122 NE 235, rev'g 171 App Div 912, 155 NYS 1128 (1919), the court, in discussing the conduct of a savings bank, which permitted a withdrawal by a person other than the depositor who had possession of the passbook, said: "Lack of suspicion cannot always be the determinative factor in paying out a depositor's money. Reasonable care might demand a suspicion where from habitual indifference none in fact existed." 122 NE at 237. . . .

It is certainly true that agency could not be implied simply from Terranova's possession of the check. . . .

Judgment should have been entered in favor of Robert L. Taylor and Zena Taylor against Equita-

ble for $20,000.00 and interest should have been allowed from 26 February 1968. . . .

[Judgment reversed]

Citizens State Bank v Rausch

9 Ill App 3d 1004, 293 NE2d 678 (1973)

Rausch owned Black Acres Farm, which was subject to a first mortgage. Rausch wanted to refinance the mortgage debt and sent an agent to the Citizens State Bank with authority to make a new loan and to pledge stock as security for the new loan if a second mortgage was obtained on the farm. This condition as to obtaining a second mortgage was known to the bank. The second mortgage was not obtained but the agent and the bank made a new loan agreement, part of which obligated Rausch to deliver certain shares of stock to the bank as security. The bank sued Rausch and his wife to compel them to deliver the stock to it under the second loan agreement. Judgment was entered in their favor and the bank appealed.

STAMOS, P.J. . . . The action was initiated by plaintiff's complaint, seeking to compel delivery of stock certificates which were allegedly pledged by defendants in December, 1963 as security for the refinancing of a previous loan to Black Acres Farm, Inc. . . . A Master in Chancery . . . made the . . . recommendation . . . that plaintiff be denied relief upon its complaint, because one condition in the suretyship agreement—that defendants receive a second mortgage on Black Acres Farm as consideration—had not been fulfilled to the actual knowledge of the pledgee Bank. . . .

We . . . conclude that there was sufficient evidence supporting the Master's findings that the December pledge of stock by defendants was conditioned upon their receiving a second mortgage on Black Acres Farm, that plaintiff was actually aware of that condition at the time of the pledge agreement, and that the condition was never fulfilled. Even if we were to accept plaintiff's contention that it was unaware of the condition, a different disposition would not be warranted. The surety agreement was negotiated by a special agent on defendants' behalf. Uncontroverted evidence established that the scope of the agency was limited by the requirement that defendants receive a second mortgage on Black Acres Farm in return for their pledge of shares of stock. Accordingly, the special agent was powerless to bind the defendants to an agreement, unless it contained the consideration demanded by defendants from Black Acres Farm. A principal is bound by the acts of his special agent only insofar as such acts are in accord with the conferred authority. . . . Persons dealing with a special agent are bound, at their peril, to ascertain the nature and extent of the agent's authority. . . . We therefore hold that the Master's finding and the Chancellor's decree denying relief to plaintiff were supported by the evidence. . . .

[Judgment affirmed]

Bucholtz v Sirotkin Travel Ltd.

74 Misc 2d 180, 343 NYS2d 438 (1973)

Bucholtz made reservations through the Sirotkin Travel Agency for a three-day trip to Las Vegas. The reservations were in fact not made by the agency and Bucholtz sued the agency for damages for breach of its contract. The agency raised the defense that the mistake was the fault of another travel agency or "wholesaler" through which the agency made reservations on behalf of its client.

DONOVAN, J. . . . This small claim proceeding involves a matter of increasing importance to the traveling public, namely, the responsibility of a travel agency in connection with the sale of a tour.

Claimant engaged the defendant travel agency to make reservations for a three day trip for herself and her husband to Las Vegas. The agency advised the claimant that they would stay at the Aladdin Hotel. Changes were made in the arrival and departure time of their flight from that originally stated. At the airport tags on the plaintiff's baggage were switched so that the baggage was not directed to the Aladdin Hotel. On arrival in Las Vegas the claimant learned that no reservations had been made for herself or her husband at the Aladdin Hotel. They were required to take alternative accommodations at a motel. The motel was a half mile out of town. This created additional expense and inconvenience for the claimant and her husband in traveling to the places of interest in the town.

The law presently lacks clarity with respect to the relationship between the travel agency and its clients. Obviously the travel agency is an agent, but the question comes, whose agent? Is it the agent of a hotel or other innkeeper with whom, or for whom, the agency transacts business? Or the steamship line or airline with whom it does business? Generally the travel agency is neither an agent nor an employee of the common carriers and innkeepers with whom it may do business. . . .

The travel agent deals directly with the traveler. He must be charged with the duty of exercising reasonable care in securing passage on an appropriate carrier and lodging with an innkeeper. The money was paid over by the traveler to the defendant agency for that specific purpose.

News reports are constantly appearing with stories of travelers—many of them quite young—being stranded far from home or having vacation plans ruined because passage or lodging for which they have paid has not been provided. Who is to bear the responsibility? Is it some remote "wholesaler" who is unknown to the traveler, or the traveler himself, or the travel agency in whom the traveler has reposed his confidence?

Sometimes we must go deep into the past to find ancient principles and mold them to take care of new problems. The policy of the common law from ancient times has been to safeguard the traveler. Speaking of the rule at common law which held the innkeeper liable as an insurer of the property left in his custody by a guest, the court, in Hulett v Swift, 33 NY 571 (1865) said: "The considerations of public policy in which the rule had its origin, forbid any relaxation of its rigor. The number of travelers was few, when this custom was established for their protection. The growth of commerce and increased facilities of communication, have so multiplied the class for whose security it was designed, that its abrogation would be the removal of a safeguard against fraud, in which almost every citizen has an immediate interest. The rule is in the highest degree remedial. No public interest would be promoted, by changing the legal effect of the implied contract between the host and the guest, and relieving the former from his common law liability. Innkeepers, like carriers and other insurers, at times find their contracts burdensome; but in the profits they derive from the public, and the privileges accorded to them by the law, they find an ample and liberal compensation. The vocation would be still more profitable if coupled with new immunities; but we are not at liberty to discard the settled rules of the common law, founded on reasons which still operate in all their original force. Open robbery and violence, it is true, are less frequent as civilization advances; but the devices of fraud multiply with the increase of intelligence, and the temptations which spring from opportunity, keep pace with the growth and diffusion of wealth."

As foreseen by the court one hundred years ago, the devices of fraud have indeed multiplied.

In this case nothing was done by the travel agency to verify or confirm either the plane reservations or the hotel reservations. If this duty is the responsibility of the travel agency, then the travel agency is liable in negligence for its failure to exercise reasonable care in making the reservations.

It may be urged that the default in this respect is that of the remote "wholesaler."

Where, as here, the agent is selected because he is supposed to have some special fitness for the performance of the duties to be undertaken, the traveler is entitled to rely on the judgment and discretion of that agent as well as his honesty and financial responsibility. The agent may not evade responsibility by delegating to a subagent the carrying out of the task which has been committed to him. . . . Travel agencies may find it convenient, in the course of transacting their business, to deal with wholesalers. The news reports are so voluminous that we may take judicial notice of the vice inherent in conducting business in so loose a fashion. The wholesaler may fail to pay for accommodations or may even fail to book the accommodations and the traveler is left in a helpless situation. He either has no recourse because of financial insufficiency or he may be required to travel to a distant jurisdiction in order to maintain a suit.

Unless the principal, here the traveler, has expressly or impliedly authorized the travel agency to delegate responsibility to a second agency or "wholesaler," the responsibility must remain on the defendant travel agency. In an area so fraught with danger to the traveler, public policy demands that the travel agency be held responsible to: (a) verify or confirm the reservations and (b) use reasonable diligence in ascertaining the responsibility of any intervening "wholesaler" or tour organizer. . . .

Claimant here did not consent to any delegation of the duty owed to her by the defendant travel agency.

The defendant is liable to the claimant for the breach of its fiduciary responsibility in failing to use reasonable care to confirm the reservations. . . .

[Judgment for plaintiff]

Clinkenbeard v Central Southwest Oil Corp.

(CA5 Tex) 526 F2d 649 (1976)

The United States Department of the Interior conducted a monthly lottery of oil leases on United States land. In order to take part in the lottery, it was necessary to select the land on which to bid, file various papers, and take other steps. The Central Southwest Oil Corporation was in the business of doing this work for a monthly fee on behalf of members of the general public. Clinkenbeard retained the corporation to act for him. After about a year, he won a lease which he then sold to the corporation because Allen, the corporation president, told him the lease was not particularly valuable. The president knew that oil had been discovered on neighboring land, that there were producing oil wells in the vicinity, and knew the prices that had been paid for other neighboring leases. Allen did not tell any of this to Clinkenbeard and Clinkenbeard sold the oil lease to the corporation for a fraction of its true value. When Clinkenbeard learned the truth, he sued to rescind the sale of the lease. The court rescinded the sale on the theory that the corporation was under a fiduciary duty to Clinkenbeard at the time of the sale and had breached that duty by failing to disclose to him all information relevant to the value of the lease. The corporation appealed.

THORNBERRY, C.J. . . . Any fiduciary duty owed to Clinkenbeard had terminated at the time of the assignment in question. . . .

It is generally recognized that "an agency which is intended to continue only for the performance of a particular task terminates on the performance or completion of that task.". . . After an agency is terminated, the agent is free of any fiduciary duty to the principal arising from that relationship and may then deal with the principal on an arm's length basis. . . .

. . . The agency relationship between Central Southwest and Clinkenbeard was for the accomplishment of specific tasks: the selection of federal oil and gas properties on which to bid, the entry of bids on those properties in the Department of Interior lotteries, and notification of the results. The record is devoid of evidence indicating that Central Southwest ever undertook to do anything more than this. Thus, at the moment that Tom Allen notified Clinkenbeard that he had won a lease, the agency relationship terminated as a matter of law; *all that Central agreed to do had been done.*

This conclusion is bolstered by Clinkenbeard's unequivocal testimony at trial. He stated that he recognized that Central Southwest had done everything that he expected it to do at the time they notified him that he had won a lease. And he testified that thereafter he knew that he was dealing with Central Southwest as a potential buyer of his lease and that he was a potential seller. The objective facts of the agency relationship between Central Southwest and Clinkenbeard are those that are controlling, but this testimony clearly indicates that, even subjectively, Clinkenbeard knew that his agency relationship with Central Southwest had ended.

We recognize that this conclusion may seem harsh in light of the fact that Clinkenbeard's subjective trust of Allen may have continued beyond, or even have been augmented by, Allen's notification to him that he had won a lease. But there is a very legitimate need for definiteness in the rules that govern fiduciary relationships. Such relationships impose unusual and stringent duties while they subsist. It is only fair that those subject to such duties be reasonably able to determine their extent and duration. Moreover, we note that the Texas Supreme Court has explicitly stated that subjective trust alone is not enough to transform arms-length dealing into a fiduciary relationship. . . . Businessmen generally do trust one another, and their dealings are frequently characterized by cordiality. . . . If we should permit respondents to set aside their conveyances on such slender evidence, the security of contracts and conveyances in this state would be seriously jeopardized. . . .

Clinkenbeard argues, however, that the fiduciary duties once owed by Central Southwest to him as his agent may have continued to exist after the termination of the formal agency. As a strict matter, this is simply incorrect; the termination of the agency relationship terminates also the fiduciary duties which flow from it. . . .

. . . Because no fiduciary duty was owed by Central Southwest at the time of the assignment, reversal of the judgment in favor of Clinkenbeard is required.

[Judgment reversed]

QUESTIONS AND CASE PROBLEMS

1.   What social forces are affected by the rule that a third person must ascertain the extent of an agent's authority?
2.   Compare (a) secret limitations on authority of an agent with (b) apparent authority of an agent.
3.   An agent may secretly purchase a principal's property as long as the agent pays the reasonable market value for it. Appraise this statement.
4.   After an agency has been terminated, the agent is not entitled to further compensation. Appraise this statement.
5.   Regional Broadcasters of Michigan, Inc. owned and operated radio station WTRU. Moreschini supplied advertising material to WTRU under contract made with the station manager. When Moreschini sued Regional Broadcasters, it raised the defense that the manager had been instructed not to make any contracts on behalf of the station. Was Regional bound? [Moreschini v Regional Broadcasters, 373 Mich 496, 129 NW2d 859]
6.   Hihn and Eastland, doing business in California, were authorized to sell certain land in Texas. They in turn employed Maney, of Texas, to sell the land. He made the sale and then sued them for the commissions due him on the sale. Did Hihn and Eastland have authority to employ Maney to make the sale? [Eastland v Maney, 36 Tex Civ App 147, 81 SW 574]
7.   When two attorneys share a suite of offices, can one attorney delegate authority to the other attorney to represent a client of the first attorney without the approval of the client? [People v Betillo, 53 Misc 2d 540, 279 NYS2d 444]

8. McKinney requested E. M. Christmas, a real estate broker, to sell McKinney's property. A sale to a purchaser was effected with the contract calling for monthly installment payments by the purchaser, which payments were to be collected by the broker. When the purchaser stopped making the payments, McKinney was not notified of that fact but one of the broker's employees bought out the purchaser's contract. The broker continued making payments to McKinney as though they were being made by the purchaser. Later Christmas, the broker, resold the land to another buyer at a substantial profit. McKinney sued Christmas for this profit. Decide. [McKinney v Christmas, 143 Colo 361, 353 P2d 373]

9. An attorney received a check payable to the order of the attorney's client. The attorney indorsed the client's name and cashed the check at the bank on which it was drawn. The client then sued the bank for the amount which had been paid the attorney. The bank raised the defense that the attorney had authority to sign for the client and to receive payment on the client's behalf. Was this a valid defense? [See Aetna Casualty & Surety Co. v Traders Nat. Bank & Trust Co. (MoApp) 514 SW2d 860]

10. An insurance company directed its agent to notify the insured under a particular policy that the insured's policy was canceled. The insurance agent instructed a stenographer to notify the insured. She notified the insured. It was later claimed that this notice was not effective to cancel the policy because it had not been given by the insurer's agent. Decide. [International Service Insurance Co. v Maryland Casualty Co., (Tex Civ App) 421 SW2d 721]

11. Wiles ran a taxi business. Mullinax, an insurance broker, agreed to obtain and keep Wiles continuously covered with workmen's compensation insurance. This was done for a number of years, with Mullinax renewing the policy whenever it expired. The insurance company which had issued the policy to Wiles canceled it, and Mullinax attempted to obtain a policy from other companies. He was unable to do so but did not inform Wiles of his difficulties nor of the fact that Wiles was not covered by insurance. An employee of Wiles was killed, and a workmen's compensation claim for his death was successfully made. Wiles then learned for the first time that there was no insurance to cover this claim. Wiles sued Mullinax for the amount of the workmen's compensation claim. Decide. [Wiles v Mullinax, 267 NC 392, 148 SE2d 229]

12. Promoters were planning the formation of a new corporation. They retained an attorney to obtain a charter for the corporation. The attorney made a contract with Erickson, selling him stock of the new corporation. Did the attorney have the authority to make this contract? [Erickson v Civic Plaza National Bank, (Mo App) 422 SW2d 373]

13. Kribbs owned real estate that had been rented through his agent, Jackson, at a monthly rental of $275. When this lease terminated, Jackson and a third person, Solomon, made an agreement that if the latter obtained a new tenant for a rental of $500 a month, Jackson would pay Solomon $100 a month. Solomon obtained a new tenant who paid a monthly rental of $550. Jackson continued to send Kribbs $275 a month, less his commissions and janitor and utility costs, paid Solomon $100 a month, and kept the balance of the rental for himself. When Kribbs learned of these facts three years later, he sued Jackson, claiming from Jackson the money that he had kept for himself and which he had paid Solomon. Was Kribbs entitled to recover? [Kribbs v Jackson, 387 Pa 611, 129 A2d 490]

14. A property owner applied to an insurance agent for insurance on his property. The agent told him that he was protected immediately, and thereafter the policy was issued. The agent backdated the policy to the time of the property owner's application. Between the time when the property owner had applied for the insurance and was told that he was covered and the subsequent time when the policy was issued, the property was

damaged by a cause coming within the scope of the policy. The insurance company paid the property owner's claim on the policy and then sued the agent for indemnity on the ground that he did not have authority to backdate a policy. The agent showed that he had repeatedly made oral contracts of insurance and that the insurer then issued the policies on the basis of such oral contracts and that the policies were backdated to the date of the oral contracts. Was the agent liable to the insurer for the loss? [Lewis v Travelers Insurance Co., 51 NJ 244, 239 A2d 4]

15.   Hockett employed Snearly as an agent in connection with the sales made at the Gilette Livestock Exchange operated by Hockett. Snearly was to perform various clerical operations in connection with the agent's work, and to write checks on the account of the principal for the payment of the persons selling their cattle and for the payment of his own salary. By the terms of compensation Snearly was to receive $25 on each sale made at the Exchange up to a certain date and $30 thereafter. According to this rate of compensation, Snearly was entitled to approximately $6,000 for the period in question, but he wrote checks to himself for approximately $27,000. Hockett sued Snearly to recover the excess compensation. Snearly defended on the ground that the additional compensation was taken for extra services rendered by him. The extra work was shown to have a value of approximately $2,000. Snearly also defended on the ground that the principal had waived any right to object to an overpayment by failing to take any action sooner. Decide. [Snearly v Hockett, (Wyo) 352 P2d 230]

41 Third Persons in Agency

In agency transactions the third person has certain rights and liabilities with respect to the agent and the principal. The following discussion of those rights and liabilities is organized in terms of (1) the liability of the agent to the third person, (2) the liability of the third person to the agent, (3) the liability of the principal to the third person, (4) the liability of the principal for torts and crimes of the agent, and (5) transactions with sales personnel. The liabilities of one person, of course, are the rights of the other.

A. LIABILITY OF AGENT TO THIRD PERSON

The liability of the agent to the third person depends upon the manner in which the transaction was conducted and the nature of the agent's acts.

§ 41:1. Action of Authorized Agent of Disclosed Principal. If an agent makes a contract with a third person on behalf of a disclosed principal and has proper authority to do so and if the contract is executed properly, the agent has no personal liability on the contract. Whether the principal performs the contract or not, the agent cannot be held liable by the third party. Thus an insurance agency arranging for the insuring of a customer with a named company is not liable on the policy which the company issues to the insured. If the agent lacks authority, however, or if certain other circumstances exist, the agent may be liable.

In speaking of an agent's action as authorized or unauthorized, it must be remembered that "authorized" includes action which though originally unauthorized was subsequently ratified by the principal.[1] Once there is an effective ratification, the original action of the agent is no longer treated as unauthorized.

§ 41:2. Unauthorized Action. If a person makes a contract as agent for another but lacks authority to do so, the contract does not bind the principal. When a person purports to act as agent for a principal, an implied warranty arises that such person had authority to do so.[2] If the agent lacks authority there is a breach of this warranty and if the agent's act causes loss to the third person, that third person may generally hold the agent liable for the loss. It is no defense for the agent in such case that the agent

---

[1] Benner v Farm Bureau Mut. Ins. Co., 96 Idaho 311, 528 P2d 193.
[2] Darr Equipment Co. v Owens (TexCivApp) 408 SW2d 566.

acted in good faith or misunderstood the scope of authority. The purported agent is not liable for conduct in excess of authority when the third person knows that the agent is acting beyond the authority given by the principal.

An agent with a written authorization may avoid liability on the implied warranty of authority by showing the written authorization to the third person and permitting the third person to determine the scope of the agent's authority.

§ 41:3. No Principal with Capacity.

A person purporting to act as agent impliedly warrants that there is an existing principal and that the principal has legal capacity. If there is no principal or if the principal lacks legal capacity, the person acting as an agent is liable for any loss caused the third person.

The agent can avoid liability on the implied warranty of the existence of a principal with capacity by making known to the third person all material, pertinent facts or by obtaining the agreement of the third person that the agent shall not be liable.

§ 41:4. Disclosure of Principal.

There are three degrees to which the existence and identity of the principal may be disclosed or not disclosed. An agent's liability as a party to a contract with a third person is affected by the degree of disclosure.

(a) Disclosed Principal. When the agent makes known the identity of the principal and the fact that the agent is acting on behalf of that principal, the principal is called a *disclosed principal.* The third person dealing with an agent of a disclosed principal ordinarily intends to make a contract with the principal and not with the agent. Consequently the agent is not a party to and is not bound by the contract which is made.

(b) Partially Disclosed Principal. When the agent makes known the existence of an unknown principal but not the principal's identity, the principal is a *partially disclosed principal.* As the third party does not know the identity of the principal, the third person is making the contract with the agent and the agent is therefore a party to the contract. (See p. 693, Mawer-Gulden-Annis, Inc. v Brazilian & Columbian Coffee Co.)

(c) Undisclosed Principal. When the third person is not told or does not know that the agent is acting as an agent for anyone else, the unknown principal is called an *undisclosed principal.*[3] In such case, the third person is making the contract with the agent and the agent is a party to that contract. For example, an agent selling the goods of an undisclosed principal is the "seller" in the sales contract and is liable for breach of the implied warranty of title if the principal in fact was not the owner of the goods sold by the agent.

§ 41:5. Wrongful Receipt of Money.

If an agent obtains a payment of money from the third person by the use of illegal methods, the agent is liable to the third person.

If the third person makes an overpayment to the agent or a payment when none is due, the agent is also usually liable to the third person for the amount of

---

[3] Sago v Ashford, 145 Colo 289, 358 P2d 599.

such overpayment or payment. If the agent has acted in good faith and does not know that the payment was improperly made, however, the agent is liable to the third person only so long as the agent has possession or control of the overpayment. If the agent has remitted the overpayment to the principal before its return is demanded by the third person, the agent is not liable to the third person. In the latter case, the third person's right of action, if one exists, is only against the principal. But, payment to the principal does not relieve the agent of liability when the agent knows that the payment was not proper.

§ 41:6. Assumption of Liability. Agents may intentionally make themselves liable upon contracts with third persons. This situation frequently occurs when the agent is a well-established local brokerage house or other agency and the principal is located out of town and is not known locally.

In some situations, the agent will make a contract which will be personally binding. If the principal is not disclosed, the agent is necessarily the other contracting party and is bound by the contract. Even when the principal is disclosed, the agent may be personally bound if it was the intention of the parties that the agent was assuming a personal obligation, even though this was done in order to further the business of the principal. (See p. 694, Investment Properties of Asheville, Inc. v Allen)

§ 41:7. Execution of Contract. A simple contract that would appear to be the contract of the agent only can be shown by oral testimony, if believed, to have been intended as a contract between the principal and the third party. If the intention is established, it will be permitted to contradict the face of the written contract, and the contract as thus modified will be enforced.

To avoid any question of interpretation, James Craig, an agent for B. G. Gray, should execute an instrument by signing either *"B. G. Gray, by James Craig,"* that is, "Principal, by Agent" or *"B. G. Gray, per James Craig,"* that is, "Principal, per Agent." Such a signing is in law a signing by *Gray,* and the agent is therefore not a party to the contract. The signing of the principal's name by an authorized agent without indicating the agent's name or identity is likewise in law the signature of the principal.

If the instrument is ambiguous as to whether the agent has signed in a representative or an individual capacity, parol evidence is admissible, as between the original parties to the transaction, to establish the character in which the agent was acting. If the body of the contract states an obligation that clearly refers only to the principal, the agent is not bound by the contract even though it is signed in the agent's individual name without indicating any agency.[4]

If an agent executes a sealed instrument in those states in which a seal retains its common-law force and does so without disclosing the agency or the principal's identity, the agent is bound and cannot show that the parties did not intend this result.[5] Because of the formal character of the writing, the liability of the parties is

---

[4] Robertson v Bland (TexCivApp) 517 SW2d 676.
[5] Tooke v Thom (FlaApp) 281 So2d 34. As to the signing of commercial paper by an agent, see § 28:1(a)(2) of this book.

determined from the face of the instrument alone and it cannot be modified or contradicted by proof of intention or other matters not set forth in the writing.

§ 41:8. Failure to Obtain Commitment of Principal. In some situations, the agent is in effect an intermediary or go-between who has the duty to the third person to see to it that the principal is bound to the third person. For example, when an agent of an insurance company who has authority to write policies of insurance tells a policyholder whose fire policy has been canceled that the agent will look into the matter and that the insured should forget about it unless notified by the agent, the latter is under an obligation to make reasonable efforts to obtain the reinstatement of the policy or to notify the insured that it was not possible to do so. The agent is liable to the insured for the latter's fire loss if the agent does not obtain the reinstatement of the policy and fails to so inform the insured.

§ 41:9. Torts and Crimes. Agents are liable for harm caused third persons by the agents' fraudulent, malicious, or negligent acts. The fact that they were acting as agents at the time or that they had acted in good faith under the directions of a principal does not relieve them of liability if their conduct would impose liability upon them were they acting for themselves. The fact that they were following instructions does not shield them from liability.

If an agent commits a traditional crime, such as stealing from the third person or shooting the third person, the agent is liable for the crime without regard to the fact of acting as an agent, and without regard to whether the agent acted in self-interest or sought to advance the interest of the principal.

If an agent is guilty of fraud, the third person may avoid the transaction,[6] without regard to whether the circumstances are such that the principal would be liable for damages.

B. LIABILITY OF THIRD PERSON TO AGENT

A third party may be liable to the agent because of the manner in which the transaction was conducted or because of the acts of the third party causing harm to the agent.

§ 41:10. Action of Authorized Agent of Disclosed Principal. Ordinarily the third person is not liable to the agent for a breach of a contract that the agent has made with the third person on behalf of a disclosed principal. In certain instances, however, the third person may be liable to the agent.

§ 41:11. Undisclosed and Partially Disclosed Principal. If the agent executed the contract without informing the third person or without the third party's knowing both of the existence of the agency and the identity of the principal, the agent may sue the third party for breach of contract.

In such instances, if the contract is a simple contract, the principal may also sue the third person even though the third person thought the contract was only

---

[6] Morris Chevrolet Inc. v Pitzer (Okla) 479 P2d 958.

with the agent. In states in which the seal has lost its common-law significance, this same rule is applied to sealed contracts. In all such cases, the right of the principal to sue the third person is superior to the right of the agent to do so.

In contrast with the foregoing, if the contract is a commercial paper or a sealed contract in a state which gives the seal its common-law force, the undisclosed principal, not appearing on the instrument as a party, may not bring an action to enforce the contract.

§ 41:12. Agent Intending to Be Bound. If the third person knew that the agent was acting as an agent but nevertheless the parties intended that the agent should be personally bound by the contract, the agent may sue the third person for breach of contract.

§ 41:13. Execution of Contract. The principles that determine when an agent is liable to the third person because of the way in which a written contract was executed apply equally in determining when the third person is liable to the agent because of the way in which the contract is executed. If the agent could be sued by the third person, the third person can be sued by the agent. Thus, if the agent executes a sealed instrument in the agent's own name, only the agent can sue the third person on that instrument in a common-law state. The same rule applies if the contract is in the form of a commercial paper.

§ 41:14. Agent as Transferee. The agent may sue the third person for breach of the latter's obligation to the principal when the principal has assigned or otherwise transferred a claim or right to the agent, whether absolutely for the agent's own benefit or for the purpose of collecting the money and remitting it to the principal.

§ 41:15. Special Interest of Agent. An agent with a special interest in the subject matter of the contract may bring an action against the third person upon the latter's default. For example, a commission merchant has a right to maintain a possessory lien on goods of the principal to enforce the payment of compensation and expenses. This gives the merchant such an interest in the contract that the merchant may sue the buyer if the latter breaches the contract.

C. LIABILITY OF PRINCIPAL TO THIRD PERSON

The principal is liable to the third person for the properly authorized and executed contracts of the agent and, in certain circumstances, for the agent's unauthorized contracts.

§ 41:16. Agent's Contracts. The liability of a principal to a third person on a contract made by an agent depends upon the extent of disclosure of the principal and the form of the contract that is executed.

(a) Simple Contract Where Principal Disclosed. When a disclosed principal with contractual capacity authorizes or ratifies an agent's transaction with a third person, and when the agent properly executes a contract with the third person as an agency transaction, a binding contract exists between the principal and the third person. The principal and the third person may each sue the other in the event of a breach of the contract. The agent is not a party to the contract and is not liable for its performance and cannot sue for its breach.

The liability of a disclosed principal to a third person is not discharged by the fact that the principal gives the agent money with which to pay the third person. Consequently, the liability of a buyer for the purchase price of goods is not terminated by the fact that the buyer paid the agent the purchase price to remit to the seller.[7]

(b)   Simple Contract Where Principal Undisclosed. An undisclosed principal is liable for a simple contract made by an authorized agent. While the third person initially contracted with the agent alone, the third person upon learning of the existence of the undisclosed principal, may sue that principal. The right to sue the undisclosed principal on a simple contract is subject to two limitations. First, the third person cannot sue the principal if in good faith the principal has settled the account with the agent with respect to the contract. Some states refuse to apply this limitation, however, unless the third person has led the principal to reasonably believe that the account between the agent and the third person had been settled.

As a second limitation, the third person cannot sue the principal if the third person has elected to hold the agent and not the principal. To constitute such an election, the third person, with knowledge of the existence of the principal, must express an intention to hold the agent liable or must secure a judgment against the agent. In those jurisdictions which permit the third person to join the principal and agent as codefendants, the third party may sue both in one action, but must choose at the end of the trial the party from whom to collect, thus discharging the other.

(c)   Simple Contract Where Principal Partially Disclosed. A partially disclosed principal is liable for a simple contract made by an authorized agent. The rule as to election involving the undisclosed principal and the agent does not apply when the principal is partially disclosed. The right of the third person is not to be regarded as alternatively against either the agent or the principal but as concurrent; that is, a right against both, and therefore the third person may recover a judgment against either without discharging the other.

(d)   Contract Under Seal and Commercial Paper. If a contract is under seal in a state which preserves its common-law force, an undisclosed principal cannot sue or be sued. In a state in which the seal no longer has its common-law force, the fact that the contract made by the agent is under seal does not prohibit the third person from suing the undisclosed principal.[8]

An undisclosed principal whose name or description does not appear on commercial paper is not liable as a party thereto.[9] Thus, an undisclosed principal is not liable on commercial paper executed by an agent in the agent's own name.

§ 41:17. Payment to Agent. When the third person makes payment to an authorized agent, such payment is deemed made to the principal. (See p. 695, Liberty Mutual Ins. Co. v Enjay Chem. Co. [now Exxon]) The principal must give the third person full

---

[7] Clifton Cattle Co., Inc. v Thompson, 43 CalApp3d 11, 117 CalRptr 500.
[8] Nalbandian v Hanson Restaurant & Lounge, Inc. (Mass) 338 NE2d 335.
[9] UCC §§ 3-401, 3-403.

credit for the payment made to the agent, even though in fact the agent never remits or delivers the payment to the principal, as long as the third person made the payment in good faith and had no reason to know that the agent would be guilty of misconduct.[10]

As apparent authority has the same legal consequence as actual authority, a payment made to a person with apparent authority to receive the payment is deemed a payment to the apparent principal.

(a) Payment to Unauthorized Person. When payment by a debtor is made to a person who is not the actual or apparent agent of the creditor, such payment does not discharge the debt unless that person in fact pays the money over to the creditor.

§ 41:18. Agent's Statements. A principal is bound by a statement made by an agent while transacting business within the scope of authority. This means that the principal cannot thereafter contradict the statement of the agent and show that it is not true. Statements or declarations of an agent, in order to bind the principal, must be made at the time of performing the act to which they relate or shortly thereafter.

By the common-law rule, a third person is required to prove that the agent of the defendant had authority to make the statement which was made. Some states have reduced this burden and only require that the third person show that the agent's statements concerned a matter within the scope of the agency.[11] This means that the third person is not required to go further and prove the agent's authority to make the particular statement which was made.

§ 41:19. Agent's Knowledge. The principal is bound by knowledge or notice of any fact that is acquired by an agent while acting within the scope of actual or apparent authority.

Conversely, if the subject matter is outside the scope of the agent's authority, the agent is under no duty to inform the principal of the knowledge and the principal is not bound thereby. For example, when the agent is authorized and employed only to collect rents, the agent's knowledge of the dangerous condition of the premises is not imputed to the landlord-principal, as the reporting of such information is not part of the agent's collection duties. When a commercial paper is indorsed to the principal and the agent acting for the principal has knowledge of a matter which would be a defense to the paper, such knowledge of the agent is imputed to the principal and bars the principal from being a holder in due course. When a fact is known to the agent of the seller, the sale is deemed made by the seller with knowledge of that fact. For example, where the agent recommending and selling weed eradicator to the buyer knew that it would be used in a drainage ditch in the Mississippi River delta, a warranty of fitness for that particular purpose arose because the seller was deemed to know what the agent knew.[12] Likewise when an employee knows that there has been a pollution of water contrary to law, such knowledge is imputed to the corporate employer, even though no officer or director had in fact any knowledge thereof.[13]

---

[10] This general rule of law is restated in some states by § 2 of the Uniform Fiduciaries Act, which is expressly extended by § 1 thereof to agents, partners, and corporate officers. Similar statutory provisions are found in a number of other states.

[11] Perzinski v Chevron Chemical Co. (CA7 Wis) 503 F2d 654.

[12] Chemco Industrial Applicator Co. v duPont de Nemours and Co. (DC Mo) 366 FSupp 278.

[13] Apex Oil Co. v United States (CA8 Mo) 530 F2d 1291.

The rule that the agent's knowledge is imputed to the principal is extended in some cases to knowledge gained prior to the creation of the agency relationship. The notice and knowledge in any case must be based on reliable information. Thus, when the agent hears only rumors, the principal is not charged with notice.

(a) Exceptions. The principal is not charged with knowledge of an agent under the following circumstances: (1) when the agent is under a duty to another person to conceal such knowledge; (2) when the agent is acting adversely to the principal's interest; or (3) when the third party acts in collusion with the agent for the purpose of cheating the principal. In such cases, it is not likely that the agent would communicate knowledge to the principal. The principal is therefore not bound by the knowledge of the agent.

By definition, a defendant is not bound by a knowledge of a person who has neither actual nor apparent authority to act as agent of the defendant.

(b) Communication to Principal. As a consequence of regarding the principal as possessing the knowledge of the agent, when the law requires that a third person communicate with the principal, that duty may be satisfied by communicating with the agent. Thus, an offeree effectively communicates the acceptance of an offer to the offeror when the offeree makes such communication to the offeror's agent, and an offeror effectively communicates the revocation of an offer to the offeree by communicating the revocation to the offeree's agent.

D. LIABILITY OF PRINCIPAL FOR TORTS AND CRIMES OF AGENT

Under certain circumstances the principal may be liable to the third person for the torts or crimes of the agent or employee.

§ 41:20. Vicarious Liability for Torts and Crimes. Assume that an agent or an employee causes harm to a third person. Is the principal or employer liable for this conduct? If the conduct constitutes a crime, can the principal or employer be criminally prosecuted? The answer is that in many instances the principal or employer is liable civilly and may be prosecuted criminally. That is, the principal or employer is liable although personally free from fault and not guilty of any wrong. This concept of imposing liability for the fault of another is known as *vicarious liability.*

The situation arises both when an employer has an employee and a principal has an agent who commits the wrong. The rules of law governing the vicarious liability of the principal and the employer are the same. In the interest of simplicity, this section will be stated in terms of employees acting in the course of employment. It is to be remembered that these rules are equally applicable to agents acting within the scope of their authority. As a practical matter, some situations will only arise with agents. For example, the vicarious liability of a seller for the misrepresentations made by a salesperson will only arise when the seller appointed an agent to sell. In contrast, both the employee hired to drive a truck and the agent being sent to visit a customer could negligently run over a third person. In many situations, a person employed by another is both an employee and an agent and the tort is committed within the phase of "employee" work.

The rule of law imposing vicarious liability upon an innocent employer for the wrong of an employee is also known as the doctrine of *respondeat superior.* In modern times, this doctrine can be justified on the ground that the business should pay for the harm caused in the doing of the business, that the employer will be more careful in the selection of employees if made responsible for their actions, and that the employer may easily obtain liability insurance to protect against claims of third persons.

(a)   **Nature of Act.** The wrongful act committed by the employee may be a negligent act, an intentional act, a fraudulent act, or a violation of a governmental regulation. It may give rise only to civil liability of the employer or it may also subject the employer to prosecution for crime.

(1)   Negligent Act. Historically, the act for which liability would be imposed under the doctrine of respondeat superior was a negligent act committed within the scope of employment.

(2)   Intentional Act. Under the common law, a master was not liable for an intentional tort committed by a servant. The modern law holds that an employer is liable for the intentional tort committed by an employee for the purpose of furthering the employer's business. Thus an employer is not liable for an intentional, unprovoked assault committed by an employee upon a third person or customer of the employer because of a personal grudge or for no reason, but the employer will be held liable by the modern view when the employee's assault was committed in the belief that the employee was thereby advancing the employer's interest.[14] For example, when an employee is hired to retake property, as in the case of an employee of a finance company hired to repossess automobiles on which installments have not been paid, the employer is generally liable for the unlawful force used by the employee in retaking the property or in committing an assault upon a debtor.

(3)   Fraud. The modern decisions hold the employer liable for fraudulent acts or misrepresentations. The rule is commonly applied to a principal-agent relationship. To illustrate, when an agent makes fraudulent statements in selling stock, the principal is liable for the buyer's loss. In states which follow the common-law rule of no liability for intentional torts, the principal is not liable for the agent's fraud when the principal did not authorize or know of the fraud of the agent.

(4)   Governmental Regulation. The principal may be liable because of the agent's violation of a governmental regulation. Such regulations are most common in the areas of business and of protection of the environment. In such case, the employer may be held liable for a penalty imposed by the government. In some cases, the breach of the regulation will impose liability upon the principal in favor of a third person who is injured in consequence of the violation.

(b)   **Scope of Employment.** The mere fact that a tort or crime is committed by an employee does not necessarily impose vicarious liability upon the employer. It must

---

[14] Restatement, 2d Agency § 231; Bremen State Bank v Hartford Accident & Indemnity Co. (CA7 Ill) 427 F2d 425. Some courts follow the older rule that the employer is never liable for a willful or malicious act by an employee regardless of its purpose.

also be shown that the employee was acting within the scope of the authority if an agent, or of the course of employment, if an employee. If the agent or employee was not so acting, there is no vicarious liability. That is, when the conduct of the agent or employee is outside the scope of the agent's authority or of the course of the employee's employment, there is no vicarious liability of the principal or employer for the loss caused the third person, even though it was the fact that the agent or employee held such position which gave the agent or employee the opportunity to meet the injured person or to do the act which caused harm to that person. (See p. 697, Gandy v Cole) Consequently when an employee steals property from a customer of the employer, the employer is not liable even though it was the work of the employer which put the employee on the premises of the customer and in a position to steal the property.[15] The fact that an act was not expressly authorized by the employer, or that it was committed in violation of the employer's instructions, does not mean that the employee's act was outside the course of employment.

(1)   Departure from Employment. Situations arise in which an employee makes a departure from the course of employment. After such a departure or detour is ended and the employee is back in the course of employment, the fact that there has been such an interruption does not have any effect. Difficult questions arise when the third person is injured before the employee has fully returned to the regular course of employment. For example, suppose that a truck driver hauling the employer's goods makes a detour to see a local ballgame. After the game is over, the driver leaves the parking lot to go back to the highway. In leaving the lot, the driver hits a third person. At that moment, the driver is not doing the work of the employer. Is the employer vicariously liable? Some courts hold that the employer is liable on the theory that the departure of the employee from the course of employment was over when the personal objective of the employee was completed and the employee was returning to resume the employment. Other courts are more strict and require that the employee be either back at work or closer to the point where the departure had been made.

(2)   Dual Enterprise. In some instances, there is a *dual enterprise* or a mixing of the employee's personal activities with the work of the employer. To illustrate, the truck driver may be driving the employer's goods to the railroad station and at the same time may be taking a friend down to the station to catch a train. If the employee acts with the approval of the employer or if the doing of the employee's personal purpose does not interfere with the employment, the employee is not regarded as making a departure from the course of employment.

(3)   Borrowed Employee. In some situations, the full-time employee of one employer will be doing something for another employer and then does the wrongful act. If such *borrowed employee* was under the primary control of the temporary employer, it is the latter who is subject to vicarious liability. Hence a

---

[15] International Distributing Co., Inc. v American District Telegraph Co. (DC DistCol) 385 FSupp 871.

garage operator cannot defend against a claim for the negligent repair of an automobile on the basis that the work was done by a mechanic that was borrowed from another service station.

As the borrowed employee is not acting within the course of employment of the full-time employer, the latter is not vicariously liable for the tort or crime committed by the borrowed employee while under the control of and working for the temporary employer.

(c)   Employee of the United States. The Federal Tort Claims Act declares that the United States shall be liable vicariously whenever a federal employee driving a motor vehicle in the course of employment causes harm under such circumstances that a private employer would be liable. Contrary to the general rule, the statute exempts the employee driver from liability.

(d)   Ownership of Automobile. The ownership of the automobile driven by the employee when the third person was harmed is not controlling. The fact that it is the employer's automobile does not impose vicarious liability on the employer if in fact the employee was not acting within the course of employment at the time.

When the automobile driven by the employee is the employee's own automobile, there is some basis for inferring that the employee is not "at work" while driving the car and there is authority that the employer is not liable for the negligent driving of the employee unless it is concluded that the employer expressly or in fact authorized the employee's use of the automobile, and the mere fact that the employee was doing work for the employer at the time does not impose vicarious liability upon the employer. If the employee is involved in a collision or causes negligent harm while driving the employee's own car to or from work, the employer is ordinarily not liable to the injured person. Likewise, the employer is not liable when harm is caused to a third person while the employee is driving to or from meals or an employees' banquet.

(e)   Damages. Ordinarily the employer is liable only for compensatory damages for the torts of employees. However, when the wrongful conduct is intentionally committed or the act done in reckless disregard of the rights of others, punitive damages may be awarded to punish the wrongful conduct and to deter future similar conduct. For instance, when agents of a major finance company wrongfully repossessed an automobile, the principal was required to pay punitive damages for the wrongful acts of its agents.[16]

§ 41:21. Other Theories of Liability. If an employee is not acting within the course of employment, the employer cannot be held liable on the theory of respondeat superior. This does not mean, however, that the employer will necessarily be not liable. In some cases, the employer will be liable without regard to the nature of the act or whether the employee was acting in the course of employment.

(a)   Direct Liability of Employer. An employer is liable for the tortious and criminal consequences of acts expressly authorized. For example, if the employer instructs

---

[16] Price v Ford Motor Credit Company (MoApp) 530 SW2d 249.

an employee to highjack a competitor's truck, the employer is both civilly and criminally liable without giving any consideration to the question of whether such activity was within the course of employment of the employee. An employer is also liable upon giving defective equipment to an employee when the defect causes harm or upon giving control of proper equipment to an unfit employee and because of the latter's lack of qualifications harm is caused a third person. Thus an employer is liable when the truck given by the employer to the employee has brakes which the employer knows to be defective and the third person is injured when the employee is unable to stop the truck before hitting the third person. Likewise the employer is liable when an unfit driver is employed to drive the truck and the third person is injured because of the driver's unfitness.

(b)   Supervisory Liability. Historically, an employer was liable for the wrongful act of an employee only when the latter was acting in the course of employment. This concept is being eroded by the application of a concept of *supervisory liability* [17] that, in effect, makes the employer liable simply because it was an employee of the employer who did the wrong. Sometimes this conclusion is explained in terms that the employer was in the better position to have avoided the harm through a more careful screening of employees. This is ordinarily merely lip service to the concept that there must be fault as the basis for liability, because ordinarily it would be impossible for the employer to have screened so carefully and so prophetically as to have avoided the harm that resulted. The doctrine of supervisory liability has rather limited application, primarily because it is virtually a form of absolute liability; that is, imposing liability because harm has happened without regard to whether any fault was involved.

In the field of tort law, the concept of supervisory liability is found primarily in the case of hotels. In one case, the hotel was liable when an employee after working hours stole the keys to a guest's automobile and removed the automobile from the private parking garage to which another hotel employee had properly taken it.

(c)   Liability of Bailor. In some states a person lending an automobile to another is liable for the tort of the latter. Some states apply this to any lending but limit it to cases where the bailee is under a specified age, such as 16 years. Assume that *A* authorizes *B* to make a contract with *C* on behalf of *A* and lends *B* an automobile in order to go to *C*. In such case, even though *B* may go outside the scope of employment, *A* could still be held liable as a bailor in those states which impose the bailor's liability as above stated.

(d)   License-Sponsor Liability. In a number of states, when a minor under a specified age applies for an automobile operator's license, a parent or a person standing in the position of a parent, is required to sign the license application as a sponsor. In some states, the *license-sponsor* rule makes the sponsor jointly and severally liable with the minor for the latter's negligence in driving, although some statutes relieve the sponsor of liability if either the sponsor or the minor has filed proof of financial responsibility.

---

[17] Gilmore v Constitution Life Ins. Co. (CA10 Colo) 502 F2d 1344.

(e) Family Purpose Liability. In about half of the states, a person who owns or supplies an automobile that members of the family are permitted to use for their own purposes is vicariously liable for harm caused by the negligent operation of the vehicle by any such member of the family. The *family purpose* doctrine is repudiated in nearly half of the states as illogical and contrary to the general principles of agency law. Even when recognized, the doctrine is not applicable if the use of the vehicle is not with the permission of the owner or if the use is outside of the scope of that comtemplated.

The family purpose doctrine is not limited to cases involving minors nor to the children of a providing parent. That is, a person may be liable for providing an automobile to an adult; and the person so provided may be any family member, however related to the person providing the car. In some jurisdictions, that person may even be one who is not related to the provider, such as a household servant who is provided with or allowed to use the car for personal benefit.

Under the family purpose doctrine, it is not essential that the provider of the car be the owner of it. The essential element is that the provider is the one who has control of it and who has the power to grant or deny permission to use it, so that its use at any particular time is with the permission of the provider. Hence, the doctrine, when recognized, is applicable to impose liability upon a parent who has control of the use of the car that the child has purchased but which is used by the family only to the extent that the parent permits.

§ 41:22. Agent's Crimes. The principal is liable for the crimes of the agent committed at the principal's direction. When not authorized, however, the principal is ordinarily not liable for the crime of an agent merely because it was committed while otherwise acting within the scope of the latter's authority or employment.

Some states impose liablity on the principal when the agent has in the course of employment violated liquor sales laws, pure food laws, or laws regulating prices or prohibiting false weights. Thus, by some courts, a principal may be held criminally responsible for the sale by an agent of liquor to a minor in violation of the liquor law, even though the sale was not known to the principal and violated instructions given to the agent.

§ 41:23. Owner's Liability for Acts of an Independent Contractor. If the work is done by an independent contractor rather than by an employee, the owner is not liable for harm caused by the contractor to third persons or their property nor is the owner bound by the contracts made by the independent contractor. Likewise, the owner is ordinarily not liable for harm caused third persons by the negligence of the employees of the independent contractor.

The use of an independent contractor may also shield the owner from liability for violation of a government regulation. For example, where the pollution was caused by the exhaust from trucks of an independent contractor hired by a factory, the factory was not liable for the pollution of the environment caused by the trucks, where there was no evidence that the factory had not exercised reasonable care in selecting the contractor and it was further shown that the factory had terminated the contractor's employment as soon as the pollution complaint was made.[18]

---

[18] Aurora Metal Co. v Illinois Pollution Control Board, 30 IllApp3d 303, 333 NE2d 461.

(a) Exceptions to Owner's Immunity. There is, however, a trend toward imposing liability on the owner when the work undertaken by the independent contractor is especially hazardous in nature. That is, the law is taking the position that if the owner wishes to engage in a particular activity, the owner must be responsible for the harm it causes and cannot be insulated from such liability by the device of hiring an independent contractor to do the work.[19] In such cases, the courts regard the activity as having such a high potential of harm that the owner is not permitted to delegate to another the duty to protect the public from harm. Thus an enterprise which employs an independent contractor to act as security guard is liable for false imprisonment caused by such guard, as against the contention that the actor was an independent contractor.[20]

Regardless of the nature of the activity, the owner may be liable for the torts and contracts of the independent contractor when the owner controls the conduct of the independent contractor. For example, when the franchisor exercises a high degree of control over the franchisee, the relationship will be recognized as an agency relationship and the franchisor is bound by the action of the franchisee. Similarly, the use of an independent contractor does not insulate an owner from liability when the owner retains control of the work. Consequently, when the owner made "subcontracts" directly with the individual contractors and retained control and supervision of the construction work, the owner was deemed to be in possession; and when an employee of a contractor fell because of a defective catwalk, the owner was held liable and was not allowed to rely on the defense that the employee's employer was an independent contractor.

When the immunity based on the use of an independent contractor would make it possible for the person using the contractor to defraud others, it will be held that the employer is liable for the acts of the independent contractor and the immunity rule will be ignored. (See p. 698, Famous Music v Bay State Harness Horse Racing and Breeding Ass'n, Inc.)

(b) Undisclosed Independent Contractor. In some situations, the owner appears to be doing the act in question because the existence of the independent contractor is not disclosed or apparent. This happens most commonly when a franchisee does business under the name of the franchisor; when a concessionaire, such as a restaurant in a hotel, appears to be the hotel restaurant, although in fact it is operated by an independent concessionaire; or when the buyer of a business continues to run the business in the name of the seller. In such cases of an undisclosed independent contractor, it is generally held that the ostensible owner, that is, the franchisor, the grantor of the concession, or the seller is liable for the torts and contracts [21] of the undisclosed independent contractor.

§ 41:24. Enforcement of Claim by Third Person. A lawsuit by a third person may be brought against the agent or the principal if each is liable. In most states and in the federal

---

[19] When the contractor performs extensive or dangerous work on the premises of a customer, the contract between the contractor and the customer will commonly contain a clause by which the contractor expressly agrees to indemnify the customer for any harm occurring in the performance of the work. For example, a contractor installing heavy equipment in an industrial plant may agree to indemnify the plant for any loss sustained by the plant in the course of the installation.

[20] Dupree v Piggly Wiggly Shop Rite Foods, Inc. (TexCivApp) 542 SW2d 882.

[21] Sheraton Corp. v Kingsford Packing Co. (IndApp) 319 NE2d 852.

courts, the plaintiff may sue either or both in one action when both are liable. When both are sued, the plaintiff may obtain a judgment against both although the plaintiff will only be allowed to collect the full amount of the judgment once.

E. TRANSACTIONS WITH SALES PERSONNEL

Many transactions with sales personnel do not result in a contract with the third person with whom the salesperson deals.

§ 41:25. Soliciting Agent. The giving of an order to a salesperson ordinarily does not give rise to a contract, because ordinarily a salesperson is an agent whose authority is limited to soliciting offers from third persons and transmitting them to the principal for acceptance or rejection. Such an agent does not have authority to make a contract which will bind the principal to the third person, and the employer of the salesperson is not bound by a contract until the employer accepts the order.

(a)   Reasons for Limitation on Authority of Sales Personnel. The limitation on the authority of the salesperson is commonly based upon the fact that credit may be involved in the transaction, and the employer of the salesperson does not wish to permit its soliciting agent to make decisions as to the sufficiency of the credit standing of the buyer but wishes all of these matters to be handled by the credit management department of the home office.

Even when sales are made on a cash basis, the employer of the salesperson may want control of the order so as to avoid the danger of overselling its existing and obtainable inventory. For example, if each salesperson could bind the employer by an absolute obligation to deliver certain items and if all of the salespersons in the aggregate sold more than the seller had in inventory or could obtain at the same price at which the items in stock were purchased, the selling success of the salespersons could be an economic disaster for the employer. The employer would lose money obtaining the goods at higher prices to fill the orders in order to avoid lawsuits by buyers seeking to recover damages for nondelivery of goods.

To avoid these difficulties, it is common to limit the authority of a salesperson to that of merely a soliciting agent accepting and transmitting orders to the employer. To make this clear to buyers, order forms signed by the customer, who is given a copy, generally state that the salesperson's authority is limited in this manner and that there is no "contract" with the employer until the order is approved by the home office.

(b)   Withdrawal of Customer. From the fact that the customer giving a salesperson an order does not ordinarily have a binding contract with the employer of the salesperson until the employer approves the order, it necessarily follows that the customer is not bound by any contract until the employer aproves the order. Prior to that time, the "buyer" may withdraw from the transaction. Withdrawal under such circumstances is not a breach of contract, for, by definition, there is no contract to be broken. Likewise, if the buyer had given the salesperson any money deposit, down payment, or part payment on the purchase price, the customer on withdrawing from the transaction, is entitled to a refund of the payment which had been made.

§ 41:26. Contrast with Contracting Agent. In contrast with the consequences when the salesperson is only a soliciting agent, if the person with whom the buyer deals has authority to make contracts, there is, by definition, a binding contract between the principal and the customer from the moment that the agent agrees with the customer, that is, when the agent accepts the customer's order. Should the customer seek to withdraw from the contract thereafter, the customer must base such action on a ground which justifies the unilateral repudiation or rejection of the contract. If the customer has no such justification, the action of withdrawing is a breach of contract and the customer is liable for the seller's resulting damages. If the buyer has made any downpayment, prepayment, or deposit, the seller may deduct damages from the amount thereof before refunding any excess to the buyer. When the transaction relates to the sale of goods, the seller is entitled to retain from such advance payment either $500 or 20% of the purchase price, whichever is less, unless the seller can show that greater damages were in fact sustained.[22]

---

[22] Uniform Commercial Code § 2-718(2)(b). See § 8:6(2) of this book as to consumer protection rescission.

CASES FOR CHAPTER 41

※ Reasons only

Mawer-Gulden-Annis, Inc. v Brazilian & Colombian Coffee Co.

49 Ill App 2d 400, 199 NE2d 222 (1964)

Brazilian & Colombian Co. ordered 40 barrels of olives from Mawer-Gulden-Annis, Inc. but did not disclose that it was acting for its principal, Pantry Queen. Mawer billed and later sued Brazilian for the payment of the contract price. From a judgment in Mawer's favor, Brazilian appealed.

KLUCYNSKI, J. . . . In the instant case the trial court, upon hearing and weighing the evidence, and passing upon the credibility of the witnesses, found that Brazilian did not disclose the name of its principal at the time of contracting. We cannot hold that these findings were against the manifest weight of the evidence, especially when in its letter of June 20, 1961, . . . eight days after the confirmation and delivery, Brazilian, through Weinshenk, its president, writes, "The writer tried to contact you several times by phone and vice versa to give you the name of the buyer, but as your B/L #OZ 3990 (the bill of lading) indicates, you delivered these goods to our customers, Pantry Queen Food Products Company, and therefore you should have invoiced them for this merchandise directly.". . .

"It is a settled rule in [oral] contracts, if the agent does not disclose his agency and name his principal, he binds himself and becomes subject to all liabilities, express and implied, created by the contract and transaction, in the same manner as if he were the principal in interest. . . . And the fact that the agent is known to be a commission merchant, auctioneer, or other professional agent, makes no difference. . . ."

The duty is upon the agent, who wishes to avoid liability, to disclose the name or identity of his principal clearly and in such a manner as to bring such adequately to the actual notice of the other party, and it is not sufficient that the third person has knowledge of facts and circumstances which would, if reasonably followed by inquiry, disclose the identity of the principal. . . ."The necessity for disclosing . . . principals [is] to give the contracting party the opportunity to make inquiry as to the fact, and then to determine whether he is satisfied that such persons are the principals of the agent, and if they are, then whether such party is willing to extend credit to such principals."

The defendant's argument that the plaintiff is chargeable with knowledge of the principal from the fact that the carrier allegedly called and spoke to the shipping clerk regarding the olives and that the bill of lading made out by the shipping clerk showed Pantry Queen as the consignee, when taken together with the fact that defendant is generally known as a broker, is untenable.

Even if we assume plaintiff, from the above circumstances, had learned the identity of the principal, such information was not so timely as to relieve defendant of liability. To avoid personal liability, disclosure of the principal must be made at the time of contracting, otherwise either the agent or the subsequently disclosed principal may be held. . . . Disclosure of the principal's existence and identity subsequently has no bearing upon the relationship created at the time of the transaction. Defendant, not having informed plaintiff of the customer for whom it was purchasing, therefore, contracted as a principal, and cannot now complain if it is held liable as such. . . .

[Judgment affirmed]

Investment Properties of Asheville, Inc. v Allen

283 NC 277, 196 SE2d 262 (1973)

Investment Properties of Asheville negotiated with Allen for a long-term lease of her Acton property on which they desired to build a motel complex. Allen was represented by an agent, Norburn. Investment Properties was represented by its agent Robertson. After the lease was obtained, Investment Properties spent approximately $20,000 in preparing the land for the proposed motel. It sued Allen to recover this amount. It claimed that Norburn had agreed that Allen would reimburse Investment Properties for this amount and that he would make such payment if she did not. Allen refused to pay the amount on the ground that if Norburn had made any promise to pay for the grading, she was not bound thereby. From a judgment for Investment Properties, Allen appealed.

SHARP, J. . . . When plaintiffs rested their case against Mrs. Allen the evidence tended to show: At plaintiffs' request on 10 May 1965 Dr. Norburn had procured Mrs. Allen's signature to a contract in which she leased her Acton property to Investment Properties, Inc., for a term of 50 years at a specified monthly rental to begin not later than 10 May 1966, or earlier if plaintiffs began to receive any income from the property. The contract gave plaintiffs carte blanche in grading, reshaping, and developing the

property, but it contained no agreement that defendant would subject her land to the lien of a construction loan if plaintiffs required borrowed money to develop the premises. Dr. Norburn had previously made it quite clear to Dr. Robertson, who was acting for plaintiffs, that he was not interested in subordinating his sister's interest in the land, and plaintiffs had accepted the lease with that understanding. Shortly thereafter, however, Dr. Robertson told Dr. Norburn that Plaintiffs would not be able to finance construction of the motel complex they had planned to put on the property unless they could give the lender a first lien on the premises.*

After consulting counsel and learning the possible consequences of such a concession Dr. Norburn told Dr. Robertson that he would not try to persuade his sister to subordinate her interest in the leased premises unless plaintiffs gave her a guarantee which would save her harmless in the event the construction loan was not paid. . . .

. . . However, plaintiffs were never willing to give a guarantee satisfactory to Dr. Norburn, and he never approved any proposition which they presented to him. Neither he nor they ever submitted any of these proposals to Mrs. Allen. She never agreed to subordinate her property, and she never signed another contract of any kind with plaintiffs.

The fact that Dr. Norburn, at plaintiffs' instance, had obtained his sister's signature to the lease dated 10 May 1965 did not clothe him with apparent authority to re-negotiate the lease, and all the evidence tends to show he had no actual authority to do so. Further, the evidence tends to show that throughout their negotiations with Dr. Norburn

---

Authors' Note: If the tenant's creditor was not given a first lien and the tenant defaulted, the creditor would be able to sell the interest of the tenant in the land. This would not have much value because it is likely that the financial difficulty which led to the sale to pay the creditor would also cause the tenant to stop paying rent which would then enable the lessor to terminate the lease, so that a purchaser of the lease would in effect be getting nothing for the money invested. In contrast, if the lessor had agreed that the lessor's ownership of the land would be subordinated or made inferior to the tenant's creditor, thus giving the creditor a first lien on the land, a sale by the creditor would sell the entire interest in the property, the interests of both the lessor-owner and the tenant. This totality of interests would not be destroyed or affected by the tenant's nonpayment of rent and would have a much greater market value than that of the leasehold interest. Hence, a creditor would be willing to lend the tenant much more money if the greater value stood as security for the debt.

plaintiffs were fully aware (1) that they could not secure a construction loan for their motel project unless Mrs. Allen executed a new contract in which she agreed to give the lending institution a first lien on the leased premises; (2) that without a new contract they expended funds and graded her property at their own risk; (3) that until they could agree with Dr. Norburn upon a guarantee which he believed would protect Mrs. Allen he would not attempt to get her signature on a new lease; and (4) that even if they satisfied Dr. Norburn, he might not be able to procure her signature. Notwithstanding, plaintiffs continued to go forward with preparations to construct the motel. They cleared defendant's property of all growth and did extensive grading on it as a site for a motel. . . .

The only explanation of plaintiffs' course of conduct is the testimony of plaintiff Taylor that, "we had a guarantee for the work from a person we thought would pay." This person was certainly not Mrs. Allen. She never agreed to pay plaintiffs anything and the record contains no suggestion that she knew anyone else had done so.

Plaintiff Taylor testified that "they" charged the work done on Mrs. Allen's property to Dr. Norburn and, sometime later, he billed him for the $19,456.88—the bill for which they have sued . . . Mrs. Allen.

It is in evidence from Dr. Norburn's unrestricted testimony as a witness for the defense that, on 17 June 1965, when Dr. Robertson threatened to abandon the motel project unless plaintiffs got a new lease, Dr. Norburn told him if plaintiffs would put up one-third of the cost of the construction he felt certain his sister would execute a new contract; that, if she did not, he would pay for the grading done in the meantime. . . .

Without Dr. Norburn's testimony there is no evidence in the Allen case from which the jury could find that either she or he ever promised to pay for the grading. This testimony, however, does not help plaintiffs' case for it shows (1) that Dr. Norburn made the promise upon a condition which was not met and (2) that he made the agreement with plaintiffs in his personal capacity and not as the agent of Allen. In making his promise of 17 June 1965 to Dr. Robertson, Dr. Norburn did not profess to be acting for Mrs. Allen. He acted in his own name and pledged his credit only. Dr. Robertson understood this and was then satisfied to have it so. Plaintiffs did no grading on Mrs. Allen's property in

reliance upon any obligation on her part to pay for it. . . . When a party contracts with a known agent personally on his own credit alone, he will not be allowed afterwards to charge the principal. Having dealt with the agent as a principal he cannot set up an agent's apparent authority, on which he did not rely, so as to establish rights against a principal. . . .

We now hold, therefore, that the evidence admitted against Mrs. Allen is insufficient to establish that she or anyone purporting to act for her promised to pay for the work done on her property by Asheville Contracting Company. That being so, no question of ratification arises since "ratification is not possible unless the person making the contract, in doing so, purported to act as the agent of the person . . . claimed to be the principal.". . .

[Judgment reversed]

Liberty Mutual Ins. Co. v Enjay Chem. Co. (Now Exxon)

(DelSuper) 316 A2d 219 (1974)

E. I. duPont de Nemours & Co. licensed Enjay Chemical Company, now Exxon, and Johnson and Johnson, to use certain chemical processes, in return for which royalty payments were to be made to duPont. Liberty Mutual Insurance Company insured the fidelity of the employees of duPont. DuPont claimed that Enjay and Johnson and Johnson had not made royalty payments. The defendants asserted that they had regularly made the payments by check but that an employee of duPont, identified as C. H. D. had altered some of the checks so that he appeared as payee and then converted them. DuPont claimed that the checks which were thus converted by C. H. D. had never been paid to duPont and that the amount of those checks was still owed to it by Enjay and Johnson and Johnson. Liberty Mutual and duPont sued Enjay and Johnson and Johnson. The defendants filed a motion to dismiss the action.

PER CURIAM . . . As these checks were received C. H. D. physically altered the face thereof by typing under the payee's name (Account of C. H. D. . . . . .). C. H. D. then indorsed the checks for deposit to his personal account at the Bank of Delaware.

All royalty checks during the nine-year period were sent by defendants to E. I. duPont deNemours

Elastomer Chemicals Department, Wilmington, Delaware, 19898, Att: C. H. D., Control Division, in accordance with a written directive to that effect sent to defendants on duPont's letterhead by C. H. D.

. . . DuPont concedes that C. H. D. regularly received and indorsed checks from defendants and would indorse the checks sometimes to his personal account and sometimes to duPont's account. This series of transactions occurred over a period of nine (9) years, and not once is it shown that duPont ever challenged or countermanded C. H. D.'s authority to receive and indorse the checks which were properly paid to duPont's account. Nor did duPont ever advise defendants to deal with anyone in the Company other than C. H. D. DuPont did not repudiate C. H. D.'s authority to receive and indorse those checks where the proceeds were paid to duPont, and, therefore, it cannot be permitted to repudiate the same authority where the proceeds were diverted to C. H. D. . . .

The law in other jurisdictions supports defendants' contention that C. H. D. had authority and that payment to duPont was legally made. One factor considered is the length of time that the agent performed similar acts on behalf of the employer. . . . Here C. H. D. acted for duPont for nine years. . . .

An important factor in determining the existence of apparent authority is whether the debtor, upon sending his payments to the creditor's agent, would have any reason to suspect improper designs or acts by the agent. New Jersey, with citations of other jurisdictions, states that it is the established doctrine that when one indebted to a principal makes a payment to a duly authorized agent, having neither notice nor reason to know of any improper designs on the part of the agent, the indebtedness is discharged when the agent obtains the proceeds.

. . . It is evident from the record that nothing in the nine years of dealing between duPont's employee and the defendants was designed to put defendants on notice that he behaved improperly. It should be self-evident that the employer-creditor is responsible for the acts of his own employee. It should be equally apparent that the employer-creditor is better able to undertake his own inspection and precautions to avoid mishandling of checks by its employees, than is the debtor who sends the checks to the creditor. In our case years had gone by before duPont detected the fraud. Now duPont says that the debtor defendants should have looked

at their canceled checks, after having been returned from the presenting bank, to see if there were any fraudulent indorsements. Obviously, large companies like the defendants here would receive thousands of checks back from their banks each month. It would be extremely burdensome and expensive for defendants to look at the indorsements on the back of each returned check. It would be even more difficult for them to determine if the indorser was authorized by the creditor to indorse the particular check in question. If there was a burden, it was duPont's not the defendants. . . .

Unquestionably obligated to duPont for royalties, defendants discharged their obligation to duPont by timely delivery of a series of checks to C. H. D., duPont's duly authorized agent, which checks were paid by the payee banks. That the proceeds of those checks were fraudulently converted by duPont's own employee C. H. D. is not a circumstance which requires defendants to pay their obligations twice. . . .

To hold that payment had not been made by defendants is to create the harsh result not only of forcing defendants to pay the same obligation twice, but also of allocating the loss against a party which had not power or control over the person who caused the loss. C. H. D. was duPont's employee, not defendants and nothing defendants could have done would have insured his trustworthiness. . . .

The draftsmen of the Uniform Commercial Code have taken the position that losses caused by an unfaithful employee should be a cost of the business enterprise in the slightly different factual context of a "padded payroll" case. When the employee supplies the name of a fictitious payee. . . , the draftsmen contend that the business, rather than the bank, should bear the loss: "The principle followed is that the loss should fall upon the employer as a risk of his business enterprise rather than upon the subsequent holder or drawee. The reasons are that the employer is normally in a better position to prevent such forgeries by reasonable care in the selection or supervision of his employees, or, if he is not, is at least in a better position to cover the loss by fidelity insurance; and that the cost of such insurance is properly an expense of his business rather than of the business of the holder or drawee." Official comment 4 to § 3-405. The reasoning applies equally to third party checks made payable to duPont which C. H. D. diverted. DuPont should have exercised care in his selection and supervision. Defendants should not be held responsible for the faithlessness of duPont's employee over which it had no control, which faithlessness was permitted to continue over a period of nine (9) years. . . .

[Judgment for defendants]

Gandy v Cole

35 Mich App 695, 193 NW2d 58 (1971)

Gandy claimed that she was defrauded by Webb, that Webb was the agent of Cole, and that the latter was liable for Webb's fraud. Cole denied liability on the ground that no fraud was committed within the scope of Webb's authority. Gandy sued Cole. Judgment was entered for Cole and Gandy appealed.

DANHOF, P.J. . . . Allen L. Cole operated a business known as Allen L. Cole & Associates. This business provided various services to gas station operators and was limited solely to gas station operators. Cole's employees, referred to as field men, would call at the gas stations and examine the operation. They would do such things as check the inventory and the bookkeeping and make out tax returns. At regular intervals the gas station operator would receive a statement containing advice on how to improve his operation. The only time that the field men handled money was when they collected the fees that were owed to Cole.

Plaintiff's husband was a subscriber to Cole's services and William Webb was the field man assigned to his gas station. In 1965 plaintiff's husband was killed in an automobile accident and from that time on Webb took an active part in the management of the plaintiff's finances. At about the time of the death of plaintiff's husband. Webb gave plaintiff a business card that indicated that he was employed by Allen L. Cole & Associates, business counsellors.

Webb soon took over the management of most of the plaintiff's money, including the proceeds of the sale of the gas station and the proceeds of a life insurance policy on plaintiff's husband. Until the sale of the station the Gandy's service station bank account was continued in the names of the plaintiff and Webb. Webb wrote a check payable to Allen L. Cole & Associates on this account. The check was in payment for the services rendered by Cole.

Webb continued to control the plaintiff's finances for a considerable time. During this time Webb invested in some race horses, in partnership

with Cole, and in some gas stations. It appears that at the present time these investments are without value. Webb undertook the management of the plaintiff's funds with the understanding that he would pay her $300 per month out of these funds. For a time Webb made the $300 payments but later he decreased them to $100 per month. Plaintiff became dissatisfied and made numerous phone calls to Webb seeking an explanation. In late 1965 Webb had ceased to be employed as a field man but he still maintained an office in Cole's establishment. At no time did the plaintiff contact, or attempt to contact Cole or any of his employees regarding her finances. In 1967 the plaintiff sought legal advice and this action was commenced. About the time of the commencement of this action William Webb disappeared and as of the date of trial his whereabouts were unknown.

The plaintiff argues that Cole placed Webb in a position where he was able to defraud her, and therefore, Cole must be held liable. The law . . . is stated in 1 Restatement Agency, 2d, §§ 261, 262, pp. 570, 571, . . . "A principal who puts a servant or other agent in a position which enables the agent, while apparently acting within his authority, to commit a fraud upon third persons is subject to liability to such third persons for the fraud. A person who otherwise would be liable to another for the misrepresentations of one apparently acting for him is not relieved from liability by the fact that the servant or other agent acts entirely for his own purposes, unless the other has notice of this."

For Cole to be liable it must be found that he placed Webb in a position where he could defraud the plaintiff while apparently acting within his authority. The trial court found that Cole had not placed Webb in such a position and we agree.

The business operated by Cole was not one of the general management of an individual's business affairs. It was highly specialized, providing certain services for gas stations only. These services were limited to things such as bookkeeping, preparing tax returns, and providing advice regarding the management of the business. At no time did Allen L. Cole & Associates undertake to manage their clients' financial affairs in general. Nor, did they ever take possession of their clients' funds, and at no time did they hold themselves out as being willing to undertake such activities.

The plaintiff places heavy emphasis on the fact that Webb gave her a business card that indicated he was associated with Allen L. Cole & Associates, business counsellors. We do not believe that merely by allowing an agent to use the designation "business counsellor" Allen L. Cole placed the agent in a position which gave him the opportunity to defraud the plaintiff.

We also agree with the finding of the trial court that regardless of the position in which Cole placed Webb the plaintiff did not place any reliance on Allen L. Cole, but relied entirely on Webb in his personal capacity and not as an agent of Cole. Even in a case where an agent has been placed in a position of trust, his principal will not be liable for fraudulent acts from which he received no benefit if the agent was dealt with in a personal capacity and not as an agent. This is true even if the agent being employed by the principal is one of the things that inspires confidence in him. . . .

The trial court's conclusion that the plaintiff did not rely on Cole has ample support in the record. The plaintiff had no contact with Cole, she paid Cole no fee, and when she became suspicious she did not attempt to contact Cole. Therefore, it is reasonable to conclude that she did not rely on Cole. . . .

The plaintiff argues that the fact that a payment from Gandy's service station was made by a check signed by William Webb was sufficient notice to inform Cole that Webb was involved in the plaintiff's finances. We cannot agree. It would indeed be a heavy burden on a businessman to require that he examine every check that he receives to determine who had signed it.

The plaintiff contends that Cole ratified Webb's act by retaining benefits that were received as a result of Webb's fraud after he had learned of the fraud. Plaintiff's argument is based on the fact that in 1965 Cole received $1,040 from Webb and in 1966 Webb loaned Cole $2000. The loan was subsequently repaid and the $1,040 was received in payment for money that Webb owed Cole. The trial court found that Cole did not have knowledge that he was receiving the plaintiff's money. . . .

. . . In order to find ratification we must first find that the acts complained of were done or professedly done on the account of the principal. . . . As we have previously stated the trial court found that Webb did not deal with the plaintiff as an agent of Cole, but rather acted in his personal capacity. Since Webb was not acting or professedly acting on Cole's account, Cole cannot be held to have ratified Webb's acts. . . .

[Judgment affirmed]

O'HARA, J. (dissenting). . . . When, as in this case, a principal permits an agent to present to potential customers a business card proclaiming to all and sundry that he, the principal, is a "business counsellor" and that the card bearer is his representative, the principal had better make it his business to know what "counseling" is done, particularly when the counseling results in doing a customer of the principal out of some $15,000.

A faultless principal has no defense against dishonesty, but it does not follow that this accords a principal the right to limitless gullibility. When his employee begins dealing in race horses, lends his principal money, and gives him a check signed by the principal's customer far in excess of any amount that could possibly accrue for legitimate services rendered, I would hold as a matter of law there was an obligation upon the principal to inform himself of his agent's doings [at once].

Famous Music Corp. v Bay State Harness Horse Racing and Breeding Association, Inc.

(CA1 Mass) 554 F2d 1213 (1977)

The Bay State Harness Horse Racing and Breeding Association conducted horse races. Music was supplied for the patrons by an independent contractor hired by the Association. Some of the music played was subject to a copyright held by Famous Music Corp. and the playing of that music was a violation of the copyright. Famous Music sued the Association for copyright infringement. It raised the defense that the violation had been committed by an independent contractor. From a judgment for Famous Music Corp., the Association appealed.

MOORE, C.J. . . . To entertain its patrons when they were not absorbed in watching the races, Bay State furnished music. For this purpose, it retained Music Box, Inc. which, as an independent contractor, supplied the music and to some extent the mechanical means for its broadcast.

Bay State's president and treasurer, E. M. Loew, throughout the years was unwilling to obtain a license from the American Society of Composers, Authors and Publishers (ASCAP), of which the plaintiffs are members, and had instructed his subordinates in Bay State to instruct Music Box, Inc. not to play any ASCAP copyrighted music. Despite this admonition, on August 24, 1972 and January 6, 1973 such music was played at a time when ASCAP had monitors in the field to spot and record such transgressions.

Infringement is not disputed, but as defenses Bay State claims that (1) the infringing performances were rendered by an independent contactor for which it is not responsible, and (2) that ASCAP is barred from recovering for the infringement because it neglected to advise Bay State of its "editing service" and failed to supply Bay State with a list of its copyrighted music so that Bay State or its supplier could avoid playing it.

The courts have rejected the "independent contractor" theory, . . . and with good reason. The proprietor of a public establishment operated for a profit could otherwise reap the benefits of countless violations by orchestras, itinerant or otherwise, by merely claiming ignorance that any violation would take place. . . .

[Judgment affirmed]

QUESTIONS AND CASE PROBLEMS

1. What social forces are affected by the rule that an agent receiving an overpayment is not liable for the amount thereof when the payment was received in ignorance of the mistake and has been remitted to the principal?

2. Compare a third party beneficiary contract with a contract made by an agent on behalf of an undisclosed principal.

3. Compare the right of an agent making an undisclosed agency contract against (a) the other contracting party, and (b) the principal.

4. Compare the liability of an agent's undisclosed principal to a third person on (a) a promissory note, (b) a sealed contract, and (c) an oral contract.

5. Blanche Trembley stated that she was agent for Trembley, Inc., and in the name of that corporation she made a contract with the Puro Filter Corp. of America. There was no corporation by the name of Trembley, Inc. The Puro Filter Corp. brought an action against Trembley to recover on the contract. Was it entitled to recover? [Puro Filter Corp. v Trembley, 266 App Div 750, 41 NYS2d 472]

6. An agent received in the mail stock certificates intended for his principal. The agent forged on the certificates an indorsement from the original owner of the certificates to himself. In a lawsuit by the owner of the certificates against the principal, the owner claimed that the principal knew what the agent had done. Was he correct? [Hartford Accident & Indemnity Co. v Walston & Co., 21 NY2d 219, 287 NYS2d 58, 234 NE2d 230; adhered to 22 NY2d 672, 291 NYS2d 366, 238 NE2d 754]

7. A corporation entered into a secured transaction. On its default, the secured creditor proceeded to sell the collateral and gave notice of the sale to the president of the corporation. The corporation claimed that the notice was not sufficient because it was merely given to the president and not to the corporation. Was it correct? [A. J. Armstrong Co. v Janburt Embroidery Corp., 97 NJ Super 246, 234 A2d 737]

8. Weisz purchased a painting at an auction sale in the Parke-Burnett Galleries. It was later shown that the painting was a forgery. When Weisz sued Parke-Burnett for breach of warranty, it raised the defense that it was making the sale for the owner and therefore any warranty suit must be brought against the owner. Was it correct? [Weisz v Parke-Burnett Galleries, Inc., (NY Civil Court) 325 NYS2d 576]

9. Cooper, a plumber, was telephoned to come to a particular place of business where he met Hileman who ordered certain plumbing work performed by Cooper. When the work was finished, Hileman failed to pay the bill and claimed that he was not liable because he had been acting as an agent for Sypo, Inc. Was this defense valid? [Cooper v Hileman (SC) 222 NW2d 299]

10. Video Independent Theaters advertised in newspapers published by the Oklahoma Publishing Company. The Publishing Company would send periodic statements of the

amounts due by Video to the advertising agency Ken Guergens and Associates. The latter would then add its fee to the amount due the Publishing Company and would bill Video for the aggregate amount. On receiving payment by Video, Guergens was to deduct its fee and then transmit the balance to the Publishing Company. Guergens kept the entire amount paid by Video. The Publishing Company sued Video which claimed that it had paid the bill to Guergens. Was this a defense? [Oklahoma Publishing Company v Video Independent Theaters, Inc., (Okla) 522 P2d 1029]

11. Arley wished to insure his property in Nevada against fire. He went to Nelson, an insurance broker, and discussed the matter with Chaney, a solicitor for Nelson. It was agreed that a policy would be obtained from the Union Pacific Insurance Company and Arley was told that he was "covered." The policy was not obtained. Arley's property was destroyed by fire several months later. When he notified Nelson of his loss, the latter then obtained a policy of insurance but the insurance company canceled the policy when it learned that the property had been destroyed before the property was insured. Arley sued Chaney and Nelson. The defense was raised that they could not be liable because they had disclosed the principal and had authority to write contracts binding the principal. Was this defense valid? [Arley v Chaney, 262 Ore 69, 496 P2d 202]

12. Tongue gave Real Estate Exchange & Investors, Inc., a real estate broker, an exclusive right to sell his property at a specified price in return for a payment by Tongue of specified commissions on any sale. The Exchange offered to purchase the property from Tongue at the specified price. Tongue refused to sell it to the Exchange. The Exchange then sued Tongue for the commissions specified in the contract. Was it entitled? [Real Estate Exchange & Investors, Inc. v Tongue, 17 NC App 575, 194 SE2d 873]

13. Moritz was a guest at the Pines Hotel. While she was sitting in the lobby, Brown, a hotel employee, dropped a heavy vacuum cleaner on her knee. When she complained, he insulted her and hit her with his fist, and knocked her unconscious. She sued the hotel for damages. Was the hotel liable? [Moritz v Pines Hotel, Inc., 53 AppDiv2d 1020, 383 NYS2d 704]

14. A check was negotiated to *A*, an agent, acting on behalf of *P*, his principal. At the time *A* took the check, he knew that the goods for which the check had been originally given as payment had never been received by the drawer of the check, *D*. *P* sued *D* on the check. *D* raised the defense of failure of consideration. *P* claimed that this defense could not be raised against him because he was a holder in due course. *D* claimed that *P* was not a holder in due course because *A* knew of the defense of failure of consideration. Was *P* a holder in due course? [See American Underwriting Corp. v Rhode Island Hospital Trust Co., 111 RI 415, 303 A2d 121]

15. Phillips was employed as an automobile salesman by an automobile dealer, City Motor Company. He had a driver's license. City Motor loaned Phillips a demonstrator car. While Phillips was driving the car from a restaurant to his home, he collided with a third person. The latter sued City Motor in the District Court claiming that City Motor had been negligent in failing to obtain a copy of the driving record of Phillips from the state police before entrusting him with the automobile and claiming that City Motor benefited by having its demonstrator automobile driven on the public streets. Was City Motor liable? [Montana ex rel City Motor Co. v District Court, 166 Mont 52, 530 P2d 486]

42 Employment

The law of employment is similar to that of agency. There are material differences, however, and the relationship is commonly regulated by statutes known as labor legislation.

The civil and criminal liability of an employer for the act of an employee have been considered in the preceding chapter. This chapter deals with the contractual aspects of the employment relationship by which the parties, the employer and an individual or group of employees, agree on terms for wages, hours, working conditions, and the duration of the employment relationship.

Laws dealing with termination of employment, safe working conditions, compensation for injured employees, compensation for the unemployed, and the protection of the pension plan interests of employees are also considered in this chapter.

A. THE EMPLOYMENT RELATIONSHIP

The relationship of an employer and an employee exists when, pursuant to an express or implied agreement of the parties, one person, the *employee,* undertakes to perform services or to do work under the direction and control of another, the *employer.* In the older cases, this was described as the master-servant relationship.[1]

§ 42:1. **Nature of Relationship.** An employee without agency authority is hired only to work under the control of the employer, as contrasted with (a) an agent, who is to negotiate or make contracts with third persons on behalf of and under the control of a principal, and with (b) an independent contractor, who is to perform a contract independent of, or free from, control by the other party.

Working on the premises or under the supervision of another does not always establish that the worker is the employee of such other person.

§ 42:2. **Creation of Employment Relationship.** The relationship of employer and employee can be created only with the consent of both parties. Generally the agreement of the parties is a contract, and it is therefore subject to all of the principles applicable to contracts generally. The contract will ordinarily be express but may be implied,

---

[1] The concept of a servant is not identical to that of employee as the servant was regarded as a chattel or thing owned by the master, whereas an employee is a free person who works pursuant to a contract of employment. Frank Horton & Co., Inc. v Diggs (MoApp) 544 SW2d 313.

as when the employer accepts the rendering of services which a reasonable person would recognize as being rendered with the expectation of receiving compensation.

(a) Individual Employment Contracts. As in contracts generally, both parties must assent to the terms of the employment contract. The parties are free to make a contract on any terms they wish. Historically, wages constituted the sole reward of labor. Today, additional benefits are usually granted employees either by virtue of the contract of employment or by a federal or state statutory provision.

(b) Collective Bargaining Contracts. Collective bargaining contracts govern the rights and obligations of employers and employees in many private and public sector employment relations. Under collective bargaining, representatives of the employees bargain with a single employer or a group of employers for an agreement on wages, hours, and working conditions for the employees. The agreement worked out by the representatives of the employees, usually union officials, is generally subject to a ratification vote by the employees. Terms usually found in collective bargaining contracts are: (1) identification of the work belonging exclusively to designated classes of employees; (2) wage and benefits clauses; (3) promotion and lay-off clauses, which are generally tied in part to seniority; (4) a management's rights clause, and (5) a grievance procedure by which persons contending the contract was violated or that they were disciplined or discharged without "just cause," may have their cases determined by impartial labor arbitrators.

When there is a collective bargaining contract, the "contract of employment" in effect consists of two contracts: (1) the collective bargaining contract made by the employees' representative with the employer, and (2) the individual employment contract made by each employee with the employer. Although the individual contracts are distinct, they must conform to the basic plan or terms established by the collective bargaining contract.

(c) Special Situations. In some situations, a person who is doing something for one person is the employee of another or is not the employee of anyone.

(1) Borrowed Employee. When the regular employer loans an employee to someone else, the other person is the employer both for the purpose of determining tort liability to a third person because of a wrongful act of the employee, and for the purpose of determining workmen's compensation liability to the employee because of an injury sustained while doing the work of the temporary employer. For example, when a hotel, as a favor to one of its guests who operated a nearby restaurant, permitted the hotel handyman to do odd jobs at the guest's restaurant, the handyman, while working at the restaurant making minor repairs, was an employee of the guest for the purpose of determining workmen's compensation liability.

(2) Volunteered Services. In various shopping centers and parking lots, persons perform services for customers of the enterprise, such as loading packages in their cars. These persons are often not employees of the enterprise and receive no compensation except the tips from customers. The fact that they perform a service which might be rendered by employees of the enterprise does not make them employees. Likewise, they are not employees of the customer. This is important because it means that when the volunteer is negligent and causes

injury to another person, the third person cannot recover damages from the enterprise or the customer. Thus, when a volunteer at a parking lot was negligent in driving the customer's car from the place where it was parked to the exit of the lot and, in so doing, damaged a third person's car, the third person could not hold the customer responsible for the harm caused by the volunteer.

(3) Self-Service. The fact that customers wait on themselves in a self-service store does not make them employees of the store so as to make the store responsible to a customer injured by falling on debris dropped on the floor by another customer.[2]

§ 42:3. Duration and Termination of Employment Contract. In many instances, the employment contract will not state any time or duration. In such case, it may be terminated at any time by either party. In contrast, the employment contract may expressly state that it shall last for a specified period of time, as a contract to work as general manager for five years. In some instances, a definite duration may be implied from the circumstances.

Ordinarily a contract of employment may be terminated in the same manner as any other contract. If it is to run for a definite period of time, the employer cannot terminate the contract at an earlier date without justification for so doing. If the employment contract does not have a definite duration, it is terminable at will. In such case, the employer may terminate the employment contract at any time without regard to whether there is any cause for so doing. Laws prohibiting discrimination and retaliation, however, limit the employer's power to discharge an employee even under an "at will" contract. There is also authority that an employer may not terminate an employment contract for a purely personal reason. (See p. 709, Rabago-Alvarez v Dart Industries) Local statutes and collective bargaining contracts commonly require a period of notice of termination which the employer must give to the employee.

(a) Federal Laws. The National Labor Relations Act prohibits dismissal for union activities.[3] Title VII of the amended Civil Rights Act prohibits terminating a contract of employment for a reason amounting to discrimination because of race, sex, religion or national origin.[4] The Age Discrimination in Employment Act protects employees who are between the ages of 40 and 70 from discrimination and discharge based on age.[5]

(b) Justifiable Discharge. An employer may be justified in discharging an employee because of the employee's (1) nonperformance of duties, (2) misrepresentation or fraud in obtaining the employment, (3) disobedience to proper directions, (4) disloyalty, (5) wrongful misconduct, (6) incompetency, or (7) disability. (See p. 710, Fisher v Church of St. Mary's)

When the employer is a government or a branch of government, such as a public school system, statutes generally provide that the employer cannot terminate an employment contract without notice and hearing.

---

[2] Cameron v Bohack, 27 AppDiv2d 362, 280 NYS2d 483.
[3] 29 USC § 158(a)(3).
[4] 42 USC §§ 2000(e)-(e)(2).
[5] 29 USC §§ 621-34.

In some states, a "service letter" statute requires an employer upon request to furnish a discharged employee with a letter stating the reason for the discharge.[6]

(c)   Remedies. An employee who has been wrongfully discharged may bring against the employer an action to recover (1) wages, (2) damages for breach of contract, or (3) damages representing the value of services already performed. In certain instances, the employee may also bring (4) an action to compel the employer to specifically perform the employment contract, or (5) a proceeding under federal or state labor relations or anti-discrimination statute, seeking reinstatement with back pay and the reinstatement of full seniority rights.

§ 42:4. Duties of the Employee. The duties of an employee are determined primarily by the contract of employment with the employer. The law also implies certain obligations.

(a)   Services. Employees are under the duty to perform or hold themselves in readiness to perform such services as may be required by the contract of employment. If employees hold themselves in readiness to comply with their employer's directions, they have discharged this obligation and they will not forfeit the right to compensation because the employer has withheld directions and has thus kept them idle.

Employees impliedly agree to serve their employer honestly and faithfully. They also impliedly agree to serve the employer exclusively during the hours of employment. The employee may do other work, however, if the time and nature of such other employment are not inconsistent with the duties owed to the first employer and if the contract of employment with the first employer does not contain any provision against it.

An employee must obey reasonable regulations and requirements adopted by the employer.

Employees impliedly purport that, in performing their duties, they will exercise due care and ordinary diligence in view of the nature of the work. When skill is required, employees need exercise only ordinary skill, unless the employees have held themselves out as possessing special skills.

(b)   Trade Secrets. An employee may be given confidential trade secrets by the employer. In such case, the employee must not disclose such knowledge to others. It is immaterial that the contract of employment did not expressly prohibit such disclosure. If the employee violates this obligation, the employer may enjoin the use of the information by the person to whom it was disclosed by the employee.

Former employees who are competing with their former employer may be enjoined from utilizing information as to suppliers and customers which they obtained while employees, where such information is of vital importance to the employer's business. A court will not, however, enjoin an ex-employee from soliciting some customers of the former employer where the number solicited is a small percentage of the former employer's customers and anyone could have identified the customers as prospective buyers without having any "inside" information based on having worked for the former employer. (See p. 711, Silfen v Cream)

Employees are under no duty to refrain from divulging general information of the particular business in which they are employed. Nor are they under a duty not

---

[6] Eimer v Texaco, Inc. (CA8 Mo) 518 F2d 807.

to divulge the information of the particular business when the relation between the employer and the employee is not considered confidential. Mere knowledge and skill obtained through experience are not in themselves trade secrets, and consequently, employees may use the fruits of their experience in later employment or in working for themselves.

(c)   Inventions. In the absence of an express or implied agreement to the contrary, the inventions of an employee belong to the employee even though the latter used the time and property of the employer in their discovery, provided that the employee had not been employed for the express purpose of inventing the things or processes which were discovered. The employer has the burden of proving that the employer is entitled to the invention or process discovered by an employee in the course of employment.

If the invention is discovered during working hours and with the employer's materials and equipment, the employer has the right, called a *shop right,* to use the invention without charge in the running of the employer's business. If the employee has obtained a patent for the invention, the employee must grant the employer a nonexclusive license to use the invention without the payment of any royalty. The shop right of the employer does not give the right to make and sell machines that embody the employee's invention; it only entitles the employer to use the invention without cost in the operation of the employer's plant.

In contrast, when an employee is employed to secure certain results from experiments to be conducted in the course of employment, the inventions so discovered belong to the employer on the ground that there is a trust relationship or that there is an implied agreement by the employee to make an assignment of the inventions to the employer.[7]

In any case, an employee may expressly agree that inventions made during employment will be the property of the employer. If such a contract provision is not clear and specific, the courts are inclined to rule against the employer. An employee may also agree to assign to the employer inventions made after the termination of employment.

§ 42:5. Rights of the Employee. The rights of an employee are determined primarily by the contract of employment. As in the case of duties, the law also implies certain rights.

(a)   Compensation. The rights of an employee with respect to compensation are governed in general by the same principles that apply to the compensation of an agent. In the absence of an agreement to the contrary, when an employee is discharged, whether for cause or not, the employer must pay wages down to the expiration of the last pay period. The express terms of employment or collective bargaining contracts, or custom, frequently provide for payment of wages for fractional terminal periods, and they may even require a severance pay equal to the compensation for a full period of employment. Provisions relating to deferred compensation under a profit sharing trust for employees are liberally construed in favor of employees.[8]

---

[7] US v Dubilier Condenser Corp. 289 US 178.

[8] An employee temporarily leaving an employer to serve in the military forces of the United States is entitled to have the time served in the military forces counted as years of service for the employer in computing the pension benefits of the employee. Alabama Power Co. v Davis, 431 US 581.

(b)   Employee's Lien or Preference. Most states protect an employee's claim for compensation either by a lien or preference over other claimants of payment out of proceeds from the sale of the employer's property. These statutes vary widely in their terms. They are usually called *laborers'* or *mechanics' lien laws.* Sometimes the statutes limit their protection to workers of a particular class, such as plasterers, or brick layers. Compensation for the use of materials or machinery is ordinarily not protected by such statutes.

§ 42:6 Pension Plans. Many employers have established pension plans to benefit their employees after they retire.

(a)   The Pension Reform Act of 1974. A federal statute, also known as the Employees Retirement Income Security Act (ERISA)[9], was adopted to provide protection for the pension interests of employees.

(1)   Fiduciary Standards and Reporting. Persons administering a pension fund must handle it so as to protect the interest of the employees. The fact that an employer contributed all or part of the money does not entitle the employer to use the fund as though it were still owned by the employer. Persons administering pension plans must make detailed reports to the Secretary of Labor.

(2)   Early Vesting. The Reform Act requires the early vesting of rights of an employee.

(3)   Pension Portability. The Pension Act permits a system of voluntary participation to provide a limited pension portability so that an employee does not lose credits for years of service with one employer on going to work for another. When applicable, the employee may transfer the interest in the ex-employer's pension trust to an Individual Retirement Account (IRA) which may be retained as an individual account or may be added to the pension plan of a new employer with the latter's consent.

(4)   Actuarial Funding. The Reform Act requires that contributions be made by employers to their pension funds on a basis which is actuarially determined so that the pension fund will be sufficiently large to make the payments which will be required of it.

(5)   Termination Insurance. The Act establishes an insurance plan to protect employees when the employer goes out of business. To provide this protection, the statute creates a Pension Benefit Guaranty Corporation. In effect, this corporation guarantees that the employee will receive benefits in much the same pattern as the Federal Deposit Insurance Corporation protects bank depositors. The Guaranty Corporation is financed by small payments made by employers for every employee covered by a pension plan.

(6)   Secretary of Labor. The Act gives the Secretary of Labor extensive powers in the operation and supervision of the pension plan.

(7)   Enforcement. The Act authorizes the Secretary of Labor and employees to bring court actions to compel the observance of the statutory requirements.

---

[9] PL 93-406, 88 Stat 829, 29 USC §§ 1001-1381.

(8) ***Criminal Offenses.*** The Act makes it a crime to fire, discriminate against, or threaten any employee who exercises any right conferred by the federal statute.

§ 42:7. Attachment and Garnishment of Wages. It is generally provided that a creditor may require a third person who owes money to a debtor of the creditor to pay such amount to the creditor to satisfy the creditor's claim against the debtor. That is, if *A* has a valid claim for $100 against *B,* and *C* owes *B* $100, *A* can require *C* to pay the $100 to *A,* which thereby satisfies both *C*'s debt to *B* and *B*'s debt to *A.* The necessary legal procedure generally requires the third person to pay the money into court or to the sheriff rather than directly to the original creditor. The original creditor may also by this process usually reach tangible property belonging to the debtor which is in the custody or possession of a third person. This procedure is commonly called *attachment* and the third person is called a *garnishee.*

Under the federal Truth in Lending Act (Title I of the Federal Consumer Credit Protection Act) only a certain portion of an employee's pay can be garnisheed. Ordinarily, the amount that may be garnisheed may not exceed (a) 25 percent of the employee's weekly take-home pay or (b) the amount by which the weekly take-home pay exceeds 30 times the federal minimum wage, whichever is less.[10] The federal statute also prohibits an employer from discharging an employee because wages have been garnisheed for any one indebtedness. The federal statute does not prevent the discharge of an employee because of several garnishments based on different debts.[11]

B. UNEMPLOYMENT BENEFITS

Generally, when employees are without work through no fault of their own, they are eligible for unemployment compensation benefits.

§ 42:8. Unemployment Compensation. Unemployment compensation today is provided primarily through a federal-state system under the unemployment insurance provisions of the Social Security Act of 1935. All of the states have laws which provide similar benefits and the state agencies are loosely coordinated under the federal act. Agricultural employees, domestic employees, and state and local government employees are not covered by this federal-state system. Federal programs of unemployment compensation exist for federal civilian workers and ex-service personnel. A separate federal unemployment program applies to railroad workers.

§ 42:9. Funding. Ordinarily state unemployment compensation benefits are financed by state taxes on employer payrolls, with variations in contributions in accordance with the employer's unemployment record. A federal unemployment tax is imposed on employers, and provides funds for federal grants to the states to meet costs of administering unemployment compensation laws.

---

[10] Consumer Credit Protection Act § 303. Under the Uniform Consumer Credit Code, where adopted, this second alternative has been increased to 40 times the federal hourly minimum pay. UCCC § 5.105(2)(b). Prejudgment attachment of wages without notice and hearing is invalid. Sniadach v Family Finance Corp. 395 US 337.

[11] Cheatham v Virginia Alcoholic Beverage Control Board (CA4 Va) 501 F2d 1346.

§ 42:10. Benefits and Eligibility. The states are largely free to prescribe the amount and duration of benefits, and the conditions required for eligibility for benefits. (See p. 712, Evjen v Employment Division) In most states, the unemployed person must be available for placement in a similar job and be willing to take such employment at a comparable rate of pay. If an employee quits a job without cause, or is fired for misconduct, or becomes unemployed because of a labor dispute in which the employee actively takes part, the employee is ordinarily disqualified from receiving unemployment compensation benefits.

C. EMPLOYEE'S INJURIES

For most kinds of employment, workmen's compensation statutes govern. They provide that the injured employee is entitled to compensation for accidents occurring in the course of employment from a risk involved in that employment.

§ 42.11. Common-Law Status of Employer. In some employment situations, the common-law principles apply. Under them the employer is not an insurer of the employee's safety.[12] It is necessary, therefore, to consider the duties and defenses of an employer apart from statute.

(a) Duties. The employer is under the common-law duty to furnish an employee with a reasonably safe place in which to work, reasonably safe tools and appliances, and a sufficient number of competent fellow employees for the work involved; and to warn the employee of any unusual dangers peculiar to the employer's business. Statutes also commonly require employers to provide a safe working place or safe working conditions. Under the federal Occupational Safety and Health Act of 1970, the Secretary of the Department of Labor is authorized to set safety standards for places of employment.[13] State laws continue in force as to matters not regulated by the federal statutes.

(b) Defenses. At common law the employer is not liable to an injured employee, regardless of the employer's negligence, if the employee was guilty of contributory negligence, or if harmed by the act of a fellow employee, or if harmed by an ordinary hazard of the work, because the employee assumed such risks.

§ 42:12. Statutory Changes. The rising incidence of industrial accidents due to the increasing use of more powerful machinery and the growth of the industrial labor population, led to a demand for statutory modification of common-law rules relating to liability of employers for industrial accidents.

(a) Modification of Employer's Common-Law Defenses. One type of change by statute was to modify the defenses which an employer could assert when sued by an employee for damages. Under statutes that apply to common carriers engaged

---

[12] Workmen's compensation statutes by their terms generally do not apply to agricultural, domestic, or casual employment. In addition, in some states, the plan of workmen's compensation is optional with the employer or the employee.
[13] PL 91-596; 84 Stat 1590, 29 United States Code §§ 651 et seq. The federal statute also creates a National Institute of Occupational Health and Safety.

in interstate commerce,[14] the plaintiff must still bring an action in a court and prove the negligence of the employer or of other employees, but the burden of proving the case is made lighter by limitations on the employer's defenses.

Under the Federal Employers' Liability Act, contributory negligence is a defense only in mitigation of damages; assumption of risk is not a defense.

In many states the common-law defenses of employers whose employees are engaged in hazardous types of work have also been modified by statute.

(b) **Workmen's Compensation.** A more sweeping development was made by the adoption of workmen's compensation statutes in every state. With respect to certain industries or businesses, these statutes provide that an employee or certain relatives of a deceased employee are entitled to recover damages for the injury or death of the employee whenever the injury arose within the course of the employee's work from a risk involved in that work. In such a case, compensation is paid without regard to whether the employer or the employee was negligent, although generally no compensation is allowed for a willfully self-inflicted injury or one sustained while intoxicated.

There has been a gradual widening of the workmen's compensation statutes, so that compensation today is generally recoverable for both accident-inflicted injuries and occupational diseases. In some states compensation for occupational diseases is limited to those specified in the statute by name, such as silicosis, lead poisoning, or injury to health from radioactivity. In other states, any disease arising from an occupation is compensable.

A person must be an employee in order to be covered by workmen's compensation. A person injured while trying out for a job is covered by workmen's compensation as the "employee" of the contemplated employer.[15]

Workmen's compensation proceedings are brought before a special administrative agency or workmen's compensation board. In contrast, a common-law action for damages or an action for damages under an employer's liability statute is brought in a court of law.

Workmen's compensation statutes do not bar an employee from suing another employee for the injury caused by such other employee. Likewise, an employee may sue the employer when liability is based upon some principle not related to the employment relationship. (See p. 713, Panagos v North Detroit General Hospital)

---

[14] Federal Employer's Liability Act, 45 USC §§ 1 et seq. and the Federal Safety Appliance Act, 49 USC §§ 1 et seq.
[15] Moore v Gundelfinger, 56 MichApp 73, 223 NW2d 643.

CASES FOR CHAPTER 42

Rabago-Alvarez v Dart Industries, Inc.

55 CalApp3d 91, 127 CalRptr 222, (1976)

Yvonne Rabago-Alvarez left her job to work for Vanda, a division of Dart Industries, Inc., under the assurance that her job was permanent as long as her work was satisfactory. Some time thereafter, Yvonne's supervisor was replaced by a James Rebal. A short time later, Rebal took some customers and Yvonne to witness live adult entertainment. Yvonne refused to stay and walked out. Rebal was "angry" for her having done so and stated that she was "prudish and unbusinesslike." Thereafter, according to Yvonne, Rebal continually picked on her for matters not relating to the performance of her duties and eventually fired her "for her lack of administrative management." She sued Dart Industries for damages for breach of the employment contract. Dart Industries claimed that it was in good faith dissatisfied with the work of Yvonne. From a judgment awarding Yvonne some damages, both she and Dart Industries appealed.

ROUSE, A.J. [The court interpreted the employment contract and concluded that it could only be terminated for good cause.]

Since, . . . the defendant was not entitled to discharge plaintiff without good cause, there is no merit to defendant's contention that it was entitled to discharge plaintiff if it was in good faith dissatisfied with her performance. Even if this were the case, the trial court found, as a matter of fact, that Mr. Rebal was not in good faith dissatisfied with plaintiff's performance of her job and that he terminated her employment solely because of his personal dislike of plaintiff.

[The court then sustained the plaintiff's appeal on the ground that the lower court had improperly reduced the damages payable by the defendant by the amount that the plaintiff could have earned doing any kind of work. The court held that the duty to mitigate damages did not require the plaintiff to take any kind of work that was available and therefore the damages recovered by the plaintiff should not have been reduced by what she could have earned if she had taken any kind of job.]

Fisher v Church of St. Mary

(Wyo) 497 P2d 882 (1972)

Fisher was employed by the St. Mary's school as a teacher. Her employment was terminated because of physical disability. She sued the school for breach of contract. The case was tried without a jury. The trial court found in favor of the employer. Fisher appealed from the judgment.

MCINTYRE, C.J. . . . According to the contract in question, Mrs. Fisher agreed to teach in Saint Mary's school system for ten months commencing August 31, 1970. She was to be paid a salary of $5,800 for the year, payable in ten monthly install-

ments. She performed under the contract to November 12, 1970, at which time she suffered a cerebral hemorrhage and underwent surgery. As a result, Mrs. Fisher was hospitalized until December 13, 1970. She was again hospitalized from December 18 to December 28, 1970.

The plaintiff was paid her full salary through the month of November. For December and January she was paid the difference between her full salary and that of a substitute teacher. There is no dispute concerning any of these months. The school then hired a full-time replacement for Mrs. Fisher commencing February 1, 1971, and plaintiff's salary was terminated as of that date.

Plaintiff acknowledges she was unable to resume her teaching duties prior to April 1, 1971, but she claims she announced to defendant her intention and readiness to resume teaching as of that time. Therefore, she asserts, without qualification, her right to damages equal to her full salary for April, May and June of 1971. She suggests, apparently with some doubts about her right thereto, that she should also receive the difference between her salary and the amount paid for a substitute for the months of February and March, 1971. . . .

. . . [Was] the trial court . . . justified in finding, from the evidence before it, that plaintiff had failed to perform a sufficient portion of her contract to warrant termination on account of illness; and did the defendant in fact terminate the contract?

. . . Contracts to perform personal acts are considered as made on the implied condition that the party shall be alive and capable of performing the contract, so that death or disability, including sickness, will operate as a discharge, termination of the contract, or excuse for nonperformance.

. . . Until illness has continued long enough to be material, a contract for personal services cannot be terminated.

However, after the breach has become material or the prospective incapacity is such as to justify termination, the employer has an election to continue the contract or to terminate it. . . .

. . . If the [employment] agreement is silent on the subject, temporary disability of short duration as compared with the term of service contemplated does not of itself warrant termination of the contract. However, illness of long duration whereby the employee is rendered unable to substantially perform his duties permits the employer to treat the agreement as terminated.

. . . There is no fixed or certain formula by which it may always be determined whether the illness constitutes sufficient justification for the employer to terminate. The nature of the business and duties required by the contract, the character and possible duration of the illness, the necessities of the employer, to what extent the duties can for a time be performed by another and many other circumstances may enter into and materially influence the right to terminate.

. . . Whether justification exists for termination of a contract, under the facts and circumstances of a particular case, is usually a question of fact for the fact finder. . . .

. . . We must conclude: Whether Mrs. Fisher's employment for a ten-month period could be rightly terminated by Saint Mary's School on account of her illness and disability was a matter dependent upon such factors as length of the term, nature of the services, length of illness and nature of disability; and, while a mere temporary illness ordinarily is not sufficient reason for termination of her contract, illness and disability for such length of time as to cause serious inconvenience or injury to the school would be sufficient reason for termination of her contract.

. . . It was a question of fact for the trier to decide whether Mrs. Fisher's inability to perform was for a sufficient duration, under the circumstances of this case, to warrant termination of her contract because of illness.

It is apparent that one of the considerations in deciding what action the school would take was the length of service Mrs. Fisher had rendered and the future services she could be expected to render. Thus, the school indicated its willingness to continue plaintiff's tenure through the 1970-1971 school year if her services would be available for the following school year. On March 16, 1971, however, Mrs. Fisher advised she would not teach for Saint Mary's in the 1971-1972 school year. The school then advised plaintiff, by a letter dated March 30, 1971, that the relationship between them was terminated in all respects.

It is undisputed that Mrs. Fisher had taught two months and 12 days on her ten-month contract when she suffered her cerebral hemorrhage. She agrees she could not have returned to work before April 1, 1971. Thus, admittedly, she would have had to be absent from her duties because of illness four months and 18 days. We cannot say as a matter of law that the trial court was wrong in treating an absence of four months and 18 days a sufficient portion of the ten-month contract to materially inconvenience and injure the school and to justify termination. . . .

[Judgment affirmed]

Leo Silfen, Inc. v Cream

29 NY2d 387, 328 NYS2d 423, 278 NE2d 636 (1972)

Cream was an officer and employee of Leo Silfen, Inc. He was discharged and then went into business under the name of the Real Estate Maintenance Chemical Specialty Corporation. Through this corporation, Cream solicited former customers of his ex-employer. The latter sought to enjoin him from so doing and to recover damages. An associated corporation, Formula 33 Corporation, joined in the action as a co-plaintiff. A judgment was entered in favor of the corporations and against Cream. He appealed.

BREITEL, J. . . . Plaintiffs have failed to prove a physical appropriation or copying of confidential information, or wrongful disclosure or use of a trade secret. In particular, no trade secret protection is warranted since plaintiffs' customers are likely, if not known, users of the employers' merchandise and engaged in business at advertised locations.

Plaintiff corporations are engaged in selling building maintenance supplies to industrial and commercial users. Plaintiffs purchase their inventory from independent supply houses and then, at a substantial markup, resell to customers under their own label. Plaintiff Silfen sells soaps, polishes, waxes, finishers, and disinfectants, while plaintiff Formula 33 Corporation specializes in ice and snow melting compounds.

In 1949 defendant Cream joined Silfen, then engaged only in the paper and twine business. Cream was assigned and became solely responsible for the development of a cleaning and maintenance chemical supply division.

For each customer a separate file was kept containing: name of purchasing agent and other personnel at customer's office; temperament of purchasing agent; gratuities given; particular requirements; and past purchases. In 1961 these customer profiles were consolidated into a central filing system and measures were taken to insure that each salesman had access only to that portion of the files containing his customers.

In 1965, on the death of the principal of Silfen and the taking of control by his widow, Cream was named executive vice-president and general manager of plaintiff corporations for a term of 12 years. The written agreement between the parties provided for a base salary of $26,000 plus 25% of the aggregate net profits. The corporations reserved the right to discharge Cream if the aggregate net profits in any one year failed to exceed $35,000.

On November 17, 1967, Cream was discharged purportedly because of a decline of net profits. Cream, however, urges that he was discharged in order to make room for the new husband of the widow, the former Mrs. Silfen. Thirteen days after his discharge he set up Real Estate Maintenance Chemical Specialty Corporation and engaged in the same business as plaintiffs except limited to building owners and building managers. About three months later, in March, 1968, plaintiffs brought this action to enjoin defendants' solicitation of plaintiffs' customers. The complaint alleged that defendants had been soliciting plaintiffs' customers, that Cream had made copies of plaintiffs secret and confidential customer files, and was using such information in his solicitation. Cream admits that of a list of 1,100 customers submitted by plaintiffs defendants had solicited 47. Defendants, however, contend that the names of these customers were procured from available commercial lists compiled by commercial list houses. Defendants allege in their answer and assert in their testimony that the customers are openly engaged in business at advertised locations and their names are well known to plaintiffs' competitors.

Notably, plaintiffs did not attempt to sustain their allegation that Cream had made copies of plaintiffs' secret and confidential files, or used the recorded detail in those files with respect to each customer's "profile." The solicitation of plaintiffs' customers was at most the product of casual memory, or, as defendants would have the court believe, coincidence.* If there has been a physical taking or studied copying, the court may in a proper case enjoin solicitation, not necessarily as a violation of a trade secret, but

as an egregious breach of trust and confidence while in plaintiffs' service. . . .

Generally, where the customers are readily ascertainable outside the employer's business as prospective users or consumers of the employer's services or products, trade secret protection will not attach and courts will not enjoin the employee from soliciting his employer's customers. . . . Conversely, where the customers are not known in the trade or are discoverable only by extraordinary efforts courts have not hesitated to protect customer lists and files as trade secrets. This is especially so where the customers' patronage had been secured by years of effort and advertising effected by the expenditure of substantial time and money. . . .

The customers solicited by defendants, as apparently found by the trial court, are openly engaged in business in advertised locations and their names and addresses may readily be found by those engaged in the trade. . . .

In the absence of express agreement to that effect between the parties, or a demonstration that a customer list has the several attributes of a trade secret, courts, without more, should not enjoin an ex-employee from engaging in fair and open competition with his former employer. The limiting effects upon the former employee with respect to his ability to earn a living are marked and obvious. . . .

In concluding, it may be stated expressly what was earlier implied, namely, that if defendants had been shown to have appropriated by copying, studied memory, or by some other manner which does not now come to mind, the detailed information in the customer files there would be a case quite different from this. The record shows no such appropriation with respect to a single customer, let alone many customers to an extent barring reliance on casual memory. Instead, it shows that defendants solicited 47 of the 1,100 customers submitted on a list prepared by plaintiffs from its confidential files. The point is that in the circumstances described names of customers alone involved no trade secret and there was no wrongful conduct by defendants. If trade secrets there were, they consisted of the data in the carefully secured and segregated files.

[Judgment reversed]

Evjen v Employment Agency

22 OrApp 372, 539 P2d 662 (1975)

Evjen was a full-time employee for Boise Cascade. At the same time, he was a full-time student

---

* In passing it should be noted that defendants do not argue that otherwise protectible information might be exempted if it is shown that the employee's appropriation was the result of experience or memory and not physical taking or copying. There are authorities which suggest that an employee may use in competition with his former employer the names, even lists, of customers retained in his memory. . . .

at the Chemeta Community College. He was laid off as part of a general economy move by the employer. He applied for unemployment compensation. The referee found that Evjen never missed work in order to go to classes, that Evjen could not afford to go to school without working, and that in case of any conflict between work and school, work came first. The referee held Evjen was entitled to unemployment compensation. The Appeals Board reversed this decision and Evjen appealed.

SCHWAB, C.J. . . . In order for an unemployed individual to obtain unemployment insurance benefits he must prove, among other things, that "he is able to work, available for work, and is actively seeking and unable to obtain suitable work." ORS 657.155. When such an individual files a claim for benefits ORS 657.265 provides that an authorized representative of the Administrator of the Employment Division shall compute and promptly notify claimant of his entitlement to benefits, if any. If the claimant or one of his affected employers does not agree with the determination he may ask for a hearing, ORS 657.265(4), before a referee, ORS 657.270.

If the Administrator or any interested party is not satisfied with the referee's decision, he may have the matter reviewed by the Employment Appeals Board. ORS 657.275. . . .

In *Callaghan v Morgan* . . . in affirming an order denying benefits to an unemployed community college student we stated:

"All cases cited to us indicate that he who seeks to obtain unemployment compensation benefits while regularly attending school has a heavy burden to overcome. . . ." What has transpired since then is set forth in *Minniti v Employment Division* . . . .

". . . On appeal, while reiterating that an individual's status as a student creates a substantial burden to be overcome in establishing eligibility under ORS 657.155, we clarified our earlier opinion by explicitly ruling that unequivocal testimony indicating a willingness on the part of a claimant to forego educational opportunities *together with* additional facts demonstrating that his education is 'secondary' to employment might serve to meet that burden. . . . The Board's order was then reversed and remanded for a further determination of whether claimant was entitled to benefits.

"We did not . . . decide that an unequivocal statement of an intent to compromise one's educational interests in order to

obtain employment would—in and of itself—be sufficient to overcome the burden imposed upon a student seeking unemployment benefits. As we noted in our previous opinion, citing *Couchman v Industrial Commission*, . . .

"A determination of the availability for employment is one for which an all-inclusive rule cannot be stated, but rather must be made within the context of the factual situation presented by each case. . . ."

Although we have not so categorized school attendance in any of our opinions, both the referee and the Employment Appeals Board speak of enrollment in school as creating a "presumption" of non-availability for work. There is authority for the proposition that evidence of this type creates an inference rather than a presumption . . . However, we need not consider that distinction here.

"Ordinarily whether an inference or presumption has been overcome is a question for the jury, but if the evidence is of such character that but one reasonable deduction can be made therefrom the court may so declare as a matter of law. . . ." *Judson v Bee Hive Auto Service Co.* . . .

This is such a case. The only evidence presented at the hearing was claimant's testimony. Nothing in his testimony was in any way inconsistent with his statement that work came first. The referee found him credible. The Employment Appeals Board, in a review of the record only, has no basis for arriving at a different result on the issue of credibility. On the record here we find as a matter of law that the referee's decision was correct.

[Judgment reversed]

Panagos v North Detroit General Hospital

35 Mich App 554, 192 NW2d 542 (1971)

Ruth Panagos was employed by the North Detroit General Hospital. While eating lunch in the hospital cafeteria, she cut her mouth on a foreign particle contained in a piece of pie which she had purchased in the cafeteria. She sued the hospital for damages. The defendant moved to dismiss the claim on the theory that any claim of the plaintiff could only be asserted as a workmen's compensation claim. The trial court refused to dismiss the action. Judgment was entered for the plaintiff. The defendant appealed.

BURNS, P.J. . . . Did the trial court err in denying the motion to dismiss which was based on the ground that the Workmen's Compensation Department has exclusive original jurisdiction to determine whether an injury arose out of and in the course of employment with defendant?

MCLA § 412.1 (Stat Ann 1968 Rev § 17.151) provides in part: "Section 1. An employee, who receives a personal injury arising out of and in the course of his employment by an employer who is at the time of such injury subject to the provisions of this act, shall be paid compensation in the manner and to the extent hereinafter provided."

Defendant contends that the Workmen's Compensation Department has exclusive jurisdiction to determine whether an injury arose "out of and in the course of" plaintiff's employment. Thus, contends defendant, it is the Department which determines whether any given injury is within the purview of the Workmen's Compensation Act.

In Herman v Theis (1968), 10 Mich App 684, 160 NW2d 365, plaintiff was injured when he fell asleep while driving home. He brought a tort action against his employer contending that the employer was negligent in overworking the plaintiff. The court stated:

"Plaintiff states in his brief to this Court that the injuries may have arisen 'out of' his employment by defendant, but denies that they were 'in the course of' his employment and reminds us that defendant also denied this in his answer. This Court will not engage in this evaluation of the facts of any of the merits of the claim, as such issues were not decided by a lower court or board, and we find that plaintiff's 'opinion' is mere conjecture, unsupported by any decision which we could re-examine. Jurisdiction for the determination of those issues concerning exclusiveness and conditions of liability initially must lie with the compensation department and plaintiff may not waive such jurisdiction by filing an action at law and merely stating that C.L.S. 1961, § 412.1 (Stat. Ann. 1960 Rev. § 17.151) does not apply to his situation. Rather, the workmen's compensation department is the forum which properly considers questions of employment relationship, injury, and compensation (C.L. 1948, § 413.16 [Stat. Ann. 1960 Rev. § 17.190]), and it must determine whether its

jurisdiction is proper, based on findings of 'exclusiveness' and 'conditions of liability,' the decision concerning the jurisdiction then being appealable to the appeal board and the courts, if plaintiff disagrees, as he does here. The question as to 'out of and in the course of' is one of fact, and not of law, and it is the function of the department to consider the facts and circumstances in determining 'exclusive' jurisdiction. . . .

'Based upon the bare allegations of plaintiff's declaration we cannot and should not venture an answer as to whether or not such arose out of and in the course of employment. This is more properly a matter for determination of the workmen's compensation department, if such forum is yet available to plaintiff.' " Herman v Theis, supra, at 689, 690, 160 NW 2d at 368.

Defendant contends that the above language by this Court stands for the proposition that the question of whether a given injury arose "out of and in the course of employment" must first be decided by the Workmen's Compensation Board before any resort to the courts may be had. However, the Court stated at p 691, 160 NW2d at p 369:

"To accept plaintiff's argument would be to deny the employer the right to have his liability *as an employer* determined by the forum established by statute to determine it whenever the plaintiff believed that the department might not agree that such a relationship existed. Thus, we have found that a plaintiff's remedy against an employer based on an injury allegedly arising out of an employment relationship properly belongs within the Workmen's Compensation Department for initial determination as to jurisdiction and liability."

In Herman, plaintiff's cause of action was based upon the employment relationship. Plaintiff contended that defendant overworked the plaintiff thus causing him to fall asleep while driving his car and to injure himself.

In the case at bar plaintiff's cause of action is not based upon the fact that she was employed by the defendant hospital. The case is based entirely upon the fact that there was deleterious material in a piece of pie which she had purchased in her employer's cafeteria.

The court in Herman quoted the following from a concurring opinion in Totten v Detroit Aluminum & Brass Corporation (1955), 344 Mich 414, 419, 73 NW2d 882:

> " 'It is also conceivable that there are circumstances under which an employee may recover damages based on the negligence of his employer, or his workmen, entirely unrelated to the relationship of employee which the claimant bears to the defendant employer.' " Herman v Theis, supra, p 691, 160 NW2d p 369.

Plaintiff's present case is based upon the vendor-vendee relationship. The whole theory of the cause of action has nothing to do with the fact that plaintiff also happened to be employed by the defendant. We see no need for plaintiff to first seek relief from the Workmen's Compensation Department when it is clear that the employee-employer relationship is unrelated to the cause of action. Nor do we find any statutory mandate which would require a plaintiff to first appear before the Workmen's Compensation Department just because the defendant is also the plaintiff's employer. . . .

[Judgment affirmed]

QUESTIONS AND CASE PROBLEMS

1. What social forces are affected by the shop right rule applicable to inventions of an employee?

2. Compare (a) an employee and (b) an independent contractor.

3. Compare the creation of an agency relationship and an employment relationship.

4. Compare the protection of trade secrets and the concept of common-law copyright.

5. Faunce was employed by the Boost Co., which manufactured a soft drink. After some years he left its employ and began manufacturing a different soft drink. The company claimed that he was using trade secrets learned while he was in its employ and sought to enjoin him. It was proved that the soft drink made by the defendant was not the same as that made by the plaintiff; that the difference between one soft drink and another was primarily due to the one percent of the volume that represented flavoring; and that the drink made by the defendant could be made by anyone in the soft drink business on the basis of general knowledge of the trade. Was Boost entitled to an injunction? [Boost Co. v Faunce, 17 NJ Super 458, 86 A2d 283]

6. Buffo was employed by the Baltimore & Ohio Railroad Co. With a number of other workers he was removing old brakes from railroad cars and replacing them with new brakes. In the course of the work, rivet heads and scrap from the brakes accumulated on the tracks under the cars, but these were removed only occasionally when the men had time. Buffo, while holding an air hammer in both arms, was crawling under a car when his foot slipped on scrap on the ground, which caused him to strike and injure his knee. He sued the railroad for damages under the Federal Employers' Liability Act. Decide. [Buffo v Baltimore & Ohio Railroad Co., 364 Pa 437, 72 A2d 593]

7. Bandag, Inc. was in the business of recapping used automobile tires. Mornings was employed as its chief chemist. In the course of his work, he discovered a new process for bonding treads to tires that were being recapped. He was not employed to discover such a process, and no agreement had ever been made with Bandag as to the ownership of any discoveries made by Mornings. Bandag sued Mornings, claiming that, as employer, it was entitled to the ownership of the process which had been developed in the course of Mornings' employment. Was Bandag entitled to the invention? [Bandag, Inc. v Mornings, 259 Iowa 998, 146 NW2d 916]

8. The Central Lumber Co. furnished material to Schroeder for the construction of certain buildings. It also loaned her $465 to enable her to pay the men working in the construction.

A mechanics' lien law gave a lien to persons furnishing materials, machinery, or fixtures for the construction of buildings. Was the company entitled to a lien for the $465? [Central Lumber Co. v Schroeder, 164 La 759, 114 So 644]

9.   Thouron did part-time housework in Acree's home in return for an hourly pay and free transportation to and from her home in Acree's automobile driven by Acree's full-time chauffeur. While she was being driven to Acree's house to work, there was a collision because of the chauffeur's negligence. Thouron sued Acree for damages caused by the negligence of the latter's chauffeur. The workmen's compensation law was not applicable since it excluded domestic employees. The liability of the employer was thus governed by common law. Decide. [Thouron v Acree, 54 Del 117, 174 A2d 702]

10.   Baugh was employed by the Lummus Cotton Gin Co. The contract of employment stated that his employment was "conditional on . . . conduct and service being satisfactory to us, we to be the sole judge. . . ." After some time the company discharged Baugh solely because it could not afford to employ him longer. Baugh sued the company. Was it liable for breach of contract? [Lummus Cotton Gin Co. v Baugh, 29 Ga App 498, 116 SE 51]

11.   Moore was an electronics engineer employed by the United States. While traveling under a work assignment from one air base to another, he ran into and injured Romitti, who then sued the United States. The United States raised the defense that Moore was not acting within the course of his employment while driving to the new job assignment. Was this defense valid? [United States v Romitti (CA9 Cal) 363 F2d 662]

12.   An employer provided an annual outing for his employees, which was held on a working day. Any employee not attending the outing was required to report to work as usual. An employee was killed on the outing. Was his death covered by workmen's compensation? [Lybrand, Ross Bros. & Montgomery v Industrial Commission, 36 Ill 2d 410, 223 NE2d 150]

13.   Complitano was an employee of Steel & Alloy Tank Co. The city in which the plant was located sponsored a softball league. Complitano and other employees of Steel & Alloy formed a team which represented the employer in the league. All games were played after hours and off the premises and were managed and controlled in all respects by the employees. Steel & Alloy made a financial contribution to the support of the team but had no other interest in it. Complitano was injured while playing in one of the games and filed a claim for workmen's compensation on the theory that the activity was of mutual benefit to the employer and the claimant. Decide. [Complitano v Steel & Alloy Tank Co., 63 NJ Super 444, 164 A2d 792]

Part Nine • Partnerships and Special Ventures

43 Creation and Termination of Partnerships

The single or sole proprietorship is the most common form of business organization, but many businesses have two or more owners. The partnership is a very common form of multiple ownership.

A. NATURE AND CREATION

Modern partnership law shows traces of Roman law, the law merchant, and the common law of England. A Uniform Partnership Act (UPA) has been widely adopted.[1]

§ 43:1. Definition. A *partnership* or copartnership is a legal relationship created by the voluntary "association of two or more persons to carry on as co-owners a business for profit."[2] The persons so associated are called *partners*. While each partner is the agent of the partnership, a partner is not regarded as an "employee" of the partnership.

§ 43:2. Characteristics of a Partnership. A partnership can be described in terms of its characteristics:

(a) A partnership is a voluntary contractual relation; it is not imposed by law. Because of the intimate and confidential nature of the partnership relation, courts do not attempt to thrust a partner upon anyone.

(b) The relation of partnership usually involves contributions by the members of capital, labor, or skill, or a combination of these.

(c) The parties are associated as co-owners and principals to transact the business of the firm.

---

[1] This Act has been adopted in all states except Georgia and Louisiana; and it is in force in the District of Columbia, Guam, and the Virgin Islands.

[2] Uniform Partnership Act, § 6(1); Carle v Carle Tool & Engineering Co. 33 NJSuper 469, 110 A2d 568.

(d) A partnership is organized for the pecuniary profit of its members. If profit is not its object, the group will commonly be an unincorporated association.

The trend of the law is to treat a partnership as a separate legal person, although historically and technically it is merely a group of individuals with each partner being the owner of a fractional interest in the common enterprise. The Uniform Partnership Act does not make the partnership a separate entity and therefore suit cannot be brought by the firm in its firm name,[3] in the absence of a special statute or procedural rule so providing. Some courts also regard a partnership as distinct from the individual partners so that a partnership cannot claim the benefit of a personal immunity possessed by an individual partner. (See p. 727, Mathews v Wosek)

As a partnership is based upon the agreement of the parties, the characteristics and attributes of the partnership relationship are initially a matter of the application of general principles of contract law, upon which the principles of partnership law are superimposed.

§ 43:3. Purposes of a Partnership. A partnership, whether it relates to the conduct of a business or a profession, may be formed for any lawful purpose. A partnership cannot be formed to carry out immoral or illegal acts, or acts that are contrary to public policy. When there is an illegal purpose, the partners cannot sue on the contracts that involve the illegality. Moreover, in such cases, the partners cannot seek the aid of courts to settle their affairs among themselves. In addition, if the conduct of the partnership constitutes a crime, all persons involved in the commission of the crime are subject to punishment.

§ 43:4. Classification of Partnerships. Ordinary partnerships are classified as general and special partnerships, and as trading and nontrading partnerships. The ordinary partnership is distinguished from the statutory limited partnership.[4]

(a) **General and Special Partnerships.** A *general partnership* is created for the general conduct of a particular kind of business, such as hardware business or a manufacturing business. A *special partnership* is formed for a single transaction, such as the purchase and resale of a certain building.

(b) **Trading and Nontrading Partnerships.** A *trading partnership* is organized for the purpose of buying and selling, such as a firm engaged in the retail grocery business. A *nontrading partnership* is one organized for a purpose other than engaging in commerce, such as the practice of law or medicine.

§ 43:5. Firm Name. In the absence of a statutory requirement, a partnership need not have a firm name, although it is customary to have one. The partners may, as a general rule, adopt any firm name they desire. They may use a fictitious name or even the name of a stranger. There are, however, certain limitations upon the adoption of a firm name:

(a) The name cannot be the same as or be deceptively similar to the name of another firm for the purpose of attracting its patrons.

---

[3] Allgeier v Martin and Associates (MoApp) 508 SW2d 524.
[4] See Chapter 45.

(b) Some states prohibit the use of the words "and company" unless they indicate an additional partner.

(c) Most states require the registration of a fictitious partnership name.

§ 43:6. Classification of Partners.

(a) *General partners* are those who publicly and actively engage in the transaction of firm business.

(b) *Nominal partners* hold themselves out as partners or permit others to hold them out as such. They are not in fact partners, but in some instances they may be held liable as partners.

(c) *Silent partners* are those who, although they may be known to the public as partners, take no active part in the business.

(d) *Secret partners* are those who take an active part in the management of the firm but who are not known to the public as partners.

(e) *Dormant partners* are ones who take no active part in transacting the business and who remain unknown to the public.

§ 43:7. Who May Be Partners. In the absence of statutory provisions to the contrary, persons who are competent to contract may form a partnership. A minor may become a partner, but may avoid the contract of partnership and withdraw.

In general, the capacity of an insane person to be a partner is similar to that of a minor, except that an adjudication of insanity usually makes subsequent agreements void rather than merely voidable. An enemy alien may not be a partner, but other aliens may enter into the relationship. A corporation, unless expressly authorized by statute or its certificate of incorporation, may not act as a partner. The modern statutory trend, however, is to permit corporations to become partners.

§ 43:8. Creation of Partnership. A partnership is a voluntary association and exists because the parties agree to be in partnership. If there is no agreement, there is no partnership. If the parties agree that the legal relationship between them shall be such that they in fact operate a business for profit as co-owners, a partnership is created even though the parties may not have labeled their new relationship a "partnership." The law is concerned with the substance of what is done rather than the name. Conversely, a partnership does not arise if the parties do not agree to the elements of a partnership, even though they call it a partnership. Thus, the fact that an agreement described the signers as constituting a "partnership" did not make them a partnership when in fact they were not operating a business as co-owners for profit.[5]

The manner in which an enterprise is described in a tax return or an application for a license is significant in determining whether it is a partnership as against a person making the return or the application. The mere fact that the enterprise is described as a partnership is not controlling or binding, however, as to a person named as a partner in the return or in the application if that person did not know of its preparation, did not sign it, and did not know what it said. When the parties are in fact employer and employee, there is no partnership even though the employer files a partnership form of income tax return. (See p. 728, Chaiken v Employment Security Commission)

---

[5] Havens v Woodfill, 148 Ind App 366, 266 NE2d 221.

§ 43:9. Partnership Agreement. As a general rule, partnership agreements need not be in writing. A partnership agreement must be in writing, however, if it is within the provision of the statute of frauds that a contract which cannot be performed within one year must be in writing. In some situations the agreement may come under the provision of the statute that requires a transfer of interest in land to be in writing. Generally, however, the agreement need not be written solely because the partnership is formed to engage in the business of buying and selling real estate.

Even when unnecessary, it is always desirable to have the partnership agreement in writing to avoid subsequent controversies as to mutual rights and duties. The formal document that is prepared to evidence the contract of the parties is termed a *partnership agreement, articles of partnership,* or *articles of copartnership.*

§ 43:10. Determining Existence of Partnership. Whether a partnership exists is basically a matter of proving the intention of the parties.

As in the case of agency, the burden of proving the existence of a partnership is upon the person who claims that one exists.[6]

When the parties have not clearly indicated the nature of their relationship, the law has developed the following guides to aid in determining whether the parties have created a partnership:

(a)   Control. The presence or absence of control of a business enterprise is significant in determining whether there is a partnership and whether a particular person is a partner.

(b)   Sharing Profits and Losses. The fact that the parties share profits and losses is strong evidence of a partnership.

(c)   Sharing Profits. An agreement that does not provide for sharing losses but does provide for sharing profits is evidence that the parties are partners, as it is assumed that they will also share losses. Sharing profits is prima facie evidence of a partnership; but a partnership is not to be inferred when profits are received in payment of (1) a debt, (2) wages, (3) rent, (4) an annuity to a deceased partner's surviving spouse or representative, (5) interest, or (6) payment for the goodwill of the business. The fact that one doctor receives one half of the net income does not establish that that doctor is a partner of another doctor where the doctor was guaranteed a minimum annual amount and the federal income tax and social security contributions were deducted from the payments to the doctor, thus indicating that the relationship was employer and employee.[7] If there is no evidence of the reason for receiving the profits, a partnership of the parties involved exists. (See p. 729, Cutler v Bowen)

(d)   Gross Returns. The sharing of gross returns is itself very slight, if any, evidence of partnership. To illustrate, in a case in which one party owned a show that was exhibited upon land owned by another under an agreement to divide the gross proceeds, no partnership was proven because there was no co-ownership or community of interest in the business. Similarly, it was not established that there was a partnership when it was shown that a farmer rented an airplane to a pilot to do aerial chemical

---

[6] Falkner v Falkner, 24 MichApp 633, 180 NW2d 491.
[7] UPA § 7(4).

spraying under an agreement by which the pilot would pay the farmer, as compensation for the use of the plane, a share of the fees which the pilot received.

(e) Co-Ownership. Neither the co-ownership of property nor the sharing of profits or rents from property which two or more persons own creates a partnership. Thus the fact that a person acquires a 49 percent interest in a trailer park does not establish that such person is a partner.[8] This in itself does not establish that the co-owners are together conducting the trailer park business for profit. Conversely, the mere fact that there is a sharing of the income from property by joint owners does not establish that they are partners.

(f) Contribution of Property. The fact that all persons have not contributed to the enterprise does not establish that the enterprise is not a partnership. A partnership may be formed even though some of its members furnish only skill or labor.

(g) Fixed Payment. When a person who performs continuing services for another receives a fixed payment for such services, not dependent upon the existence of profit and not affected by losses, that person is not a partner.

§ 43:11. Partners as to Third Persons. In some instances, persons who are in fact not partners may be held accountable to third persons as though they were partners. This liability arises when they conduct themselves in such a manner that others are reasonably led to believe that they are partners and to act in reliance on that belief to their injury.[9] A person who is held liable as a partner under such circumstances is termed a nominal partner, a partner by estoppel, or an ostensible partner.

Partnership liability may arise by estoppel when a person who in fact is not a partner is described as a partner in a document filed with the government, provided the person so described has in some way participated in the filing of the document and the person claiming the benefit of the estoppel had knowledge of that document and relied on the statement. For example, suppose that the partnership of *A* and *B*, in registering its fictitious name, names *A*, *B*, and *C* as partners and the registration certificate is signed by all of them. If a creditor who sees this registration statement extends credit to the firm in reliance in part on the fact that *C* is a partner, *C* has a partner's liability insofar as that creditor is concerned.

Conversely, no estoppel arises when the creditor does not know of the existence of the registration certificate and consequently does not rely thereon in extending credit to the partnership. Likewise, such liability does not arise when *C* does not know of the certificate.

(a) Effect of Estoppel. The existence of a partnership by estoppel means only that the fact of nonpartnership cannot be raised as a defense against a third person in whose favor the estoppel operates. That is, when creditor *C* sues *A* and claims that *A* is liable for the debt of the partnership because *A* is a partner, *A* cannot show that *A* in fact is not a partner or that there is no partnership. In contrast, this estoppel does not make the apparent partner a member of a partnership when in fact there is no partnership. Consequently, the fact that the third person is protected

---

[8] Sandberg v Jacobson, 253 CalApp3d 663, 61 CalRptr 436.
[9] UPA § 16(1).

does not entitle the apparent partner to a share of the profits earned by the other persons who appear to be such person's partner; because the fact remains that the apparent partner and the other persons are not partners.

§ 43:12. Partnership Property. In general, partnership property consists of all the property contributed by the partners or acquired for the firm or with its funds.[10] There is usually no limitation upon the kind and amount of property that a partnership may acquire. The firm may own real as well as personal property, unless it is prohibited from doing so by statute or by the partnership agreement.

The parties may agree that real estate owned by one of the partners should become partnership property. When this intent exists, the particular property constitutes partnership property even though it is still in the name of the original owner.

(a)   Title to Personal Property in Firm Name. A partnership may hold and transfer the title to personal property in the firm name, whether the name is fictitious or consists of the names of living people. Thus, a partnership may hold a security interest in personal property in the firm name, such as "Keystone Cleaners."

(b)   Title to Real Property in Firm Name. A majority of states now permit a partnership to hold or transfer the title to real property in the firm name alone, without regard to whether or not the name is fictitious.[11]

(c)   Transferees of Firm's Real Property. In order for a transfer of a firm's real property to be technically correct, (1) it must have been made by a partner or agent with the authority to make the transfer and (2) it must have been made in the name of the holder of the title. When both conditions have been satisfied, the transferee has legal title as against the partnership.

If the transfer was authorized but was not made in the name of the title holder, the transferee acquires equitable title to the property and the right to have a proper instrument of conveyance executed. When the transfer of the partnership property was not authorized, the firm may recover the property from the transferee if the transferee knew that it was firm property or did not purchase it for value. When the title to the firm property is recorded but not in the name of the firm, a person who purchases from the record holder in good faith, for value, and without notice or knowledge of the partnership title, may keep the property.

A conveyance by a partner of partnership property, even though without authority, cannot be recovered by the partnership where it has been reconveyed by the grantee to a buyer for value and without notice or knowledge that the partner who had made the original conveyance had exceeded that partner's authority.

(d)   Title to Partnership Property in Name of Individual Partner. Frequently property that in fact is partnership property appears of record as owned by one of the partners. This may arise when the property in question was owned by that individual before the partnership was formed and though contributed to the partnership when it was organized, the former owner never went through the formality of transferring title to the partnership. The situation may also arise when a member of an existing

---

[10] UPA § 8; All Florida Sand v Lawler Construction Co. 209 Ga 720, 75 SE2d 559.
[11] UPA § 8(3), (4).

partnership uses partnership funds to acquire property and either through a clerical mistake or in order to deceive the other partners, the title to the property is taken in the name of the acting partner. In such cases, the partner holding the title will be treated as a trustee holding the property for the benefit and use of the partnership, just as though the property were held in the name of the partnership.

§ 43:13. Tenancy in Partnership. Partners hold title to firm property by *tenancy in partnership*.[12] The characteristics of such a tenancy are:

(a) Each partner has an equal right to use firm property for partnership purposes in the absence of a contrary agreement.

(b) A partner possesses no interest in any specific item of partnership property that can be voluntarily sold, assigned, or mortgaged by a partner.

(c) A creditor of a partner cannot proceed against any specific items of partnership property.[13] The creditor can only proceed against the partner's interest in the partnership. This is done by applying to a court for a *charging order*. By this procedure, the share of any profits that would be paid to the debtor-partner is paid to a receiver on behalf of the creditor or the court may direct the sale of the interest of the debtor-partner in the partnership.

(d) On the death of a partner, the partnership property vests in the surviving partners for partnership purposes and is not subject to the rights of the surviving spouse of the deceased partner.

§ 43:14. Assignment of Partner's Interest. Although a partner cannot transfer specific items of partnership property, in the absence of authority to so act on behalf of the partnership, a partner's interest in the partnership may be voluntarily assigned by the partner.[14] The assignee does not become a partner without the consent of the other partners. Without this consent, the assignee is only entitled to receive the assignor's share of the profits during the continuance of the partnership and the assignor's interest upon the dissolution of the firm. The assignee has no right to participate in the management of the partnership; nor does the assignee have a right to inspect the books of the partnership. Assignment of a partner's interest does not in itself cause dissolution of the firm.

B. DISSOLUTION AND TERMINATION

Partnerships may be dissolved by the acts of the partners, by order of a court, or by operation of law. Dissolution changes the legal status of both the partnership and the individual partners.

§ 43:15. Effect of Dissolution. Dissolution ends the right of the partnership to exist as a going concern. It is followed by a winding-up period, upon the conclusion of which the partnership's legal existence is terminated.

---

[12] UPA § 25(1); Williams v Dovell, 202 Md 646, 96 A2d 484.
[13] UPA § 25(2)(c).
[14] UPA § 27.

Dissolution reduces the authority of the partners. From the moment of dissolution, the partners lose authority to act for the firm, "except so far as may be necessary to wind up partnership affairs or to complete transactions begun but not then finished."[15] The vested rights of the partners are not extinguished by dissolving the firm, and the existing liabilities remain. Thus, when the partnership is dissolved by the death of a partner, the estate of the deceased partner is liable to the same extent as the deceased partner.

§ 43:16. Dissolution by Act of Parties.

(a) **Agreement.** A partnership may be dissolved in accordance with the terms of the original agreement of the parties, as by the expiration of the period for which the relation was to continue or by the performance of the object for which it was organized.[16] The relation may also be dissolved by subsequent agreement, as when the partners agree to dissolve the firm before the lapse of the time specified in the articles of partnership or before the attainment of the object for which the firm was created.

(b) **Withdrawal.** A partner has the power to withdraw from the partnership at any time; but if the withdrawal violates the partnership agreement, the withdrawing partner becomes liable to the copartners for damages for breach of contract. When the relation is for no definite purpose or time, a partner may withdraw without liability at any time, unless a sudden withdrawal would do irreparable damage to the firm. (See p. 730, Langdon v Hurdle)

(c) **Expulsion.** A partnership is dissolved by the expulsion of any partner from the business in accordance with such a power conferred by the agreement between the partners.

(d) **Alienation of Interest.** Neither a voluntary sale of a partner's interest nor an involuntary sale for the benefit of creditors works a dissolution of the partnership.

§ 43:17. Dissolution by Operation of Law.

(a) **Death.** An ordinary partnership is dissolved immediately upon the death of any partner, even when the agreement provides for the continuance of the business. Thus, when the executor of a deceased partner carries on the business with the remaining partner, there is legally a new firm.

(b) **Bankruptcy.** Bankruptcy of the firm or of one of the partners causes the dissolution of the firm; insolvency alone does not.

(c) **Illegality.** A partnership is dissolved "by an event which makes it unlawful for the business of the partnership to be carried on or for the members to carry it on in partnership." To illustrate, when it is made unlawful by statute for judges to engage in the practice of law, a law firm is dissolved when one of its members becomes a judge.

---

[15] UPA § 33.
[16] UPA § 31(1)(a).

(d)   War. A partnership is ordinarily dissolved when there is war between the governments to which the different partners owe allegiance.

§ 43:18. Dissolution by Decree of Court. When a partnership is to continue for a specified time, there are several situations in which one partner is permitted to obtain its dissolution through a decree of court. A court will not order the dissolution for trifling causes or temporary grievances that do not involve a permanent harm or injury to the partnership.

The filing of a complaint seeking a judicial dissolution does not in itself cause a dissolution of the partnership as it is the decree of court which has that effect.[17]

A partner may obtain a decree of dissolution for any of the following reasons:

(a)   Insanity. A partner has been judicially declared insane or of unsound mind.

(b)   Incapacity. One of the parties has become incapable of performing the terms of the partnership agreement.

(c)   Misconduct. One of the partners has been guilty of conduct that substantially tends to affect prejudicially the continuance of the business. The habitual drunkenness of a partner is a sufficient cause for judicial dissolution.

(d)   Impracticability. One of the partners persistently or wilfully acts in such a way that it is not reasonably practicable to carry on the partnership business. Dissolution will be granted where dissensions are so serious and persistent as to make continuance impracticable, or where all confidence and cooperation between the parties have been destroyed.

(e)   Lack of Success. The partnership cannot continue in business except at a loss.

(f)   Equitable Circumstances. A decree of dissolution will be granted under any other circumstances that equitably call for a dissolution. Such a situation exists when one partner has been induced by fraud to enter into the partnership.

§ 43:19. Notice of Dissolution. The rule that dissolution terminates the authority of the partners to act for the firm requires some modification. Under some circumstances, one partner may continue to possess the power to make a binding contract.

(a)   Notice to Partners. When the firm is dissolved by the act of a partner, notice must be given to the other partners unless that partner's act clearly showed an intent to withdraw from or to dissolve the firm. If the withdrawing partner acted without notice to the other partners, such partner is bound as between them upon contracts created for the firm. "Where the dissolution is caused by the act, death, or bankruptcy of a partner, each partner is liable to his copartners for his share of any liability created by any partner acting for the partnership as if the partnership had not been dissolved unless (1) the dissolution being by act of any partner, the partner acting for the partnership had knowledge of the dissolution, or (2) the dissolution being by the death or bankruptcy of a partner, the partner acting for the partnership had knowledge or notice of the death or bankruptcy." [18]

---

[17] Cooper v Isaacs (CA DistCol) 448 F2d 1202.
[18] UPA § 34.

(b)   Notice to Third Persons. When dissolution is caused by the act of a partner or of the partners, notice must be given to third parties. A notice should expressly state that the partnership has been dissolved. Circumstances from which a termination may be inferred are generally not sufficient notice. Thus, the fact that the partnership checks added "Inc." after the partnership name is not sufficient notice that the partnership does not exist and that the business has been incorporated.

Actual notice of dissolution must be given to persons who have dealt with the firm. To persons who have had no dealings with the firm, a publication of the fact is sufficient. Such notice may be by newspaper publication, by posting a placard in a public place, or by any similar method. Failure to give proper notice continues the power of each partner to bind the others in respect to third persons on contracts within the scope of the business.

When dissolution has been caused by operation of law, notice to third persons is not required. As between the partners, however, the UPA requires knowledge or notice of dissolution by death and bankruptcy. And it has been held that when the third party dealing with the partnership is not informed of the death of a partner, the surviving partners and the firm are bound by a notice sent by the third person to the deceased partner.

§ 43:20. Winding up Partnership Affairs. In the absence of an express agreement permitting continuation of the business by the surviving partners, they must wind up the business and account for the share of any partner who has withdrawn, been expelled, or has died. If the remaining partners continue the business and use that partner's distributive share in so doing, that partner is entitled to that share, together with interest or the profit earned thereon.

Although the partners have no authority after dissolution to create new obligations, they retain authority to do acts necessary to wind up the business. (See p. 731, King v Stoddard) When dissolution is obtained by court decree, the court may appoint a receiver to conduct the winding up of the partnership business. This may be done in the usual manner or the receiver may sell the business as a going concern to those partners who wish to continue its operation.[19]

With a few exceptions, all partners have the right to participate in the winding up of the business.[20]

When the firm is dissolved by the death of one partner; the partnership property vests in the surviving partners for the purpose of administration. They must collect and preserve the assets, pay the debts, and with reasonable promptness make an accounting to the representative of the deceased partner's estate. In connection with these duties, the law requires the highest degree of integrity. A partner cannot purchase any of the partnership property without the consent of the other partners.

§ 43:21. Distribution of Assets. Creditors of the firm have first claim on the assets of the partnership. Difficulty arises when there is a contest between the creditors of the firm and the creditors of the individual partners. The general rule is that firm creditors have first claim on assets of the firm, and the individual creditors share in the remaining assets, if there are any.

---

[19] Wolf v Murrane (Iowa) 199 NW2d 90.
[20] UPA § 37.

Conversely, creditors of the individual partners have priority in the distribution of the individual assets; the claims of the firm creditors may be satisfied out of the individual partner's assets only after claims of individual creditors are settled.

After the firm liabilities to nonpartners have been paid, the assets of the partnership are distributed as follows: (1) each partner is entitled to a refund of advances made to or for the firm; (2) contributions to the capital of the firm are then returned; (3) the remaining assets, if any, are divided equally as profits among the partners unless there is some other agreement. If the partnership has sustained a loss, the partners share it equally in the absence of a contrary agreement.

Distribution of partnership assets must be made on the basis of actual value when it is clear that the book values are merely nominal or arbitrary amounts.[21]

A provision in a partnership agreement that on the death of a partner the interest of that partner shall pass to that partner's surviving spouse is valid and takes effect as against the contention that it is not valid because it does not satisfy the requirements applicable to wills.

§ 43:22. Continuation of Partnership Business. As a practical matter, the business of the partnership is commonly continued after dissolution and winding up. In all cases, however, there is a technical dissolution, winding up, and a termination of the life of the original partnership. If the business continues, either with the surviving partners, or with them and additional partners, it is a new partnership. Again, as a practical matter, the liquidation of the old partnership may in effect be merely a matter of bookkeeping entries with all parties in interest recontributing or relending to the new business any payment to which they would be entitled from the liquidation of the original partnership.

If any dispute arises, however, it must be determined on the basis that the original partnership had ceased to exist and that the parties in interest had reached a new partnership agreement. Thus, the executor of a deceased partner has no rights in running or winding up the business in the absence of the consent of the other partners either contained in the original partnership agreement or obtained upon the death of the partner in question. The right of such executor is limited to demanding an accounting from the surviving partners upon the completion of the winding up of the partnership affairs. Consequently, a representative of the individual estate of a deceased partner does not have any right to complete a contract between a third person and the partnership.

---

[21] Mahan v Mahan, 107 Ariz 517, 489 P2d 1197.

CASES FOR CHAPTER 43

Mathews v Wosek

44 Mich App 706, 205 NW2d 813 (1973)

Wosek Delivery Service was a partnership composed of Richard and his wife, Kathleen. Richard was driving a partnership automobile. Mathews was a passenger in the automobile when it was struck by a train. Mathews and Wosek were acting within the scope of their employment by Love Brothers, Inc. By virtue of the appropriate workmen's compensation act, Richard Wosek as a fellow servant of Mathews could not be sued by Mathews. Mathews sued the Wosek partnership which raised the defense that as Mathews could not have sued Wosek individually, Mathews could not sue the Wosek partnership. From a judgment against him, Mathews appealed.

LEVIN, J. . . . Section 13 of the Uniform Partnership Act, reads: ". . . (Partnership bound by partner's wrongful act). Where, by any wrongful act or omission of any partner acting in the ordinary course of the business of the partnership, or with the authority of his copartners, loss or injury is caused to any person not being a partner in the partnership, or any penalty is incurred, the partnership is liable therefor *to the same extent as the partner so* acting or omitting to act.". . .

In Caplan v Caplan, 268 NY 445, 198 NE 23, 101 A.L.R. 1223 (1935), a wife, injured in an automobile collision caused by her husband's negligence, commenced an action against a partnership of which her husband was a member. The collision had occurred while her husband was driving on partnership business. The New York Court of Appeals ruled that the interspousal immunity of the husband also immunized the partnership from liability.

The reasoning of the New York Court focused on the nature of a partnership. The Court declared that a partnership is not a "separate entity." It stressed that the mutual liability of the partners resulted from agreement. The Court reasoned that when a tortfeasor partner is free of personal liability, and thus liability could not be truly mutual in fact, it would be anomalous to hold the other partners liable. . . .

In Eule v Eule Motor Sales, 34 NJ 537, 170 A2d 241 (1961), the New Jersey Supreme Court . . . ruled, on facts similar to those in the New York case of Caplan v Caplan, *supra,* that a partnership was subject to liability. . . .

Starting from the premise that the immunity of an agent would not save a *corporation* from liability (a premise with which the New York Court also began), the New Jersey Court was unable to find any distinction "of practical significance" between these two classes of enterprise organization.

The New Jersey Court viewed the partnership as an entity in itself, not merely the aggregate of the various partners. The plaintiff in the New Jersey case sought to hold the partnership as an entity, not the individual partners: "The action is against the partnership as such, and a judgment for plaintiff accordingly would bind the partnership assets and not the partners individually.". . .

The New Jersey Court declared . . . that the tort-feasor partner's obligation "to contribute if partnership assets should be insufficient to meet partnership liabilities" is not a bar to the imposition of liability against the partnership because . . . "[p]artners contemplate liability for negligent operation of their vehicles, and either expect to share it or to provide against it by insurance. Surely partners do not contemplate a different approach with respect to injuries to the spouse of one of them merely because the agency of the hurt happens to be the husband rather than some other partnership representative. In terms of what men expect, the wife's claim is no different from any other."

In saying that a partnership is liable "to the same extent as the partner," the draftsmen of the Uniform Partnership Act may have either intended to limit liability or, . . . have intended affirmatively to state the common-law obligation to make compensation. Either interpretation would be consistent with the language employed.

The question presented is not free of doubt. We must choose one of two arguably sound positions. We choose the result reached by the New Jersey Supreme Court. An immunity from liability should be given a strict construction. . . . Persons frequently act concurrently in more than one role. Where litigants have a dual relationship, one of which is consistent with the imposition of liability, we see no compelling reason to prefer the relationship which bars recovery.

The tendency of the law of partnership has been to emphasize to a greater extent than at earlier stages of the law's development the entity aspects of a partnership. . . .

[Judgment reversed and action remanded]

Chaiken v Employment Security Commission

(Del Super) 274 A2d 707 (1971)

Chaiken and two others ran a barber shop. The Delaware Employment Security Commission claimed that the other two persons were employees of Chaiken and that Chaiken had failed to pay the unemployment compensation tax assessed against employers. He defended on the ground that he had not "employed" the other two and that all three were partners. From a decision that they were employees, Chaiken appealed.

STOREY, J. . . . Chaiken contends that he and his "partners":

(1) properly registered the partnership name and names of partners in the Prothonotary's office, . . .

(2) properly filed federal partnership information returns and paid federal taxes quarterly on an estimated basis, and

(3) duly executed partnership agreements.

Of the three factors, the last is most important. Agreements of "partnership" were executed between Chaiken and Mr. Strazella, a barber in the shop, and between Chaiken and Mr. Spitzer, similarly situated. The agreements were nearly identical. The first paragraph declared the creation of a partnership and the location of business. The second provided that Chaiken would provide barber chair, supplies, and licenses, while the other partner would provide tools of the trade. The paragraph also declared that upon dissolution of the partnership, ownership of items would revert to the party providing them. The third paragraph declared that the income of the partnership would be divided 30% for Chaiken, 70% for Strazella; 20% for Chaiken and 80% for Spitzer. The fourth paragraph declared that all partnership policy would be decided by Chaiken, whose decision was final. The fifth paragraph forbade assignment of the agreement without permission of Chaiken. The sixth paragraph required Chaiken to hold and distribute all receipts. The final paragraph stated hours of work for Strazella and Spitzer and holidays.

The mere existence of an agreement labelled "partnership" agreement and the characterization of signatories as "partners" does not conclusively prove the existence of a partnership. Rather, the intention of the parties, as explained by the wording of the agreement, is paramount. . . .

A partnership is defined as an association of two or more persons to carry on as co-owners a business for profit. . . . As co-owners of a business, partners have an equal right in the decision making process. 6 Del.C. § 1518 (5). But this right may be abrogated by agreement of the parties without destroying the partnership concept, provided other partnership elements are present. . . .

Thus, while paragraph four reserves for Chaiken all right to determine partnership policy, it is not standing alone, fatal to the partnership concept. Co-owners should also contribute valuable consideration for the creation of the business. Under paragraph two, however, Chaiken provides the barber chair (and implicitly the barber shop itself), mirror, licenses and linen, while the other partners merely provide their tools and labor—nothing more than any barber-employee would furnish. Standing alone, however, mere contribution of work and skill can be valuable consideration for a partnership agreement. . . .

Most importantly, co-owners carry on "a business for profit." The phrase has been interpreted to mean that partners share in the profits and the losses of the business. The intent to divide the profits is an indispensable requisite of partnership. . . . Paragraph three of the agreement declares that each partner shall share in the income of the business. There is no sharing of the profits, and as the agreement is drafted, there are no profits. . . .

It is the conclusion of this Court that Chaiken did not carry the burden of proving the existence of partnerships with Spitzer and Strazella. . . . Since . . . no partnership at law exists, the facts support the Commission's finding . . .

[Judgment affirmed]

Cutler v Bowen

(Utah) 543 P2d 1349 (1975)

Bowen owned and operated the Havana Club in a rented building. He made an agreement with Cutler, the bartender, that she would operate the club, purchase supplies, pays bills, keep the books, and hire and fire employees. Cutler and Bowen were each to receive $100 a week and to divide the net profits. The Club was operated under this arrangement until the building was taken by the Redevelopment Agency. The Agency paid the Club $10,000 damages for disruption of business. The Club was terminated because a suitable new location could not be found. Cutler then sued Bowen for one-half of the sum paid by the Redevelopment Agency on the theory that they had been a partnership. From a judgment in favor of Cutler, Bowen appealed.

CROCKETT, J. . . . The defendant contended that he was the sole owner of the entire business; and that the plaintiff's status was merely that of an employee. . . . Plaintiff took the position that, conceding the defendant was the owner of the physical assets of the business as above stated, insofar as the going concern and goodwill value, [she was] a partner in the business. . . .

When parties join in an enterprise, it is usually in contemplation of success and making profits, and is often without much concern about who will bear losses. However, when they so engage in a venture for their mutual benefit or profit, that is generally held to be a partnership, in which the law imposes upon them both liability for debts or losses that may occur. . . .

On the question whether profits shared should be regarded simply as wages, it is important to consider the degree to which a party participates in the management of the enterprise and whether the relationship is such that the party shares generally in the potential profits or advantages and thus should be held responsible for losses or liability incurred therein. . . .

It is not shown here that any occasion arose where the plaintiff's responsibility for debts or other liabilities of the business was tested. However, throughout the four years in which she operated and managed the Club, . . . it was her responsibility to see that all bills were paid, including the rental on the lease, employees' salaries, the costs of all purchases, licenses and other expenses of the business. During that time she saw the defendant Bowen only infrequently for the purpose of rendering an accounting and dividing the profits. It is further pertinent that the parties reported their income tax as a partnership.

Under the arrangement as shown and as found by the trial court, a good case can be made out that it was largely through the capability, experience, and efforts of the plaintiff that, in addition to the physical plant, there existed a separate asset in the value of the "going concern and goodwill" of the business, which was being lost by its displacement. On the basis of what has been said above, we see nothing to persuade us to disagree with the view taken by the trial court [that Cutler and Bowen were partners.]

The failure of the parties to find another suitable location, and the cessation of operation of the Havana Club, was properly regarded as a termination of the partnership. The rule governing the rights of the parties in such circumstances is that after all debts and liabilities of the partnership have been satisfied, each partner should be repaid his contributions thereto, and any remainder allocated as their interests appear.

From the circumstances shown in evidence as discussed herein, there appears to be a reasonable basis for the trial court's view that, except for the physical assets, which belonged to the defendant and to which the plaintiff makes no claim, the further asset of the business: that is, the value of what is called going concern and goodwill belonged to the two of them as partners in the enterprise; and that

when the business could not be relocated, the $10,000 should properly be regarded as compensation for the loss . . . of the business; and that the partners having lost their respective equal shares in the going business operation, they should also share equally in the compensation for its loss. . . .

[Judgment affirmed]

Langdon v Hurdle

17 NC App 530, 195 SE2d 72 (1973)

Langdon, Hurdle, and Hoffman formed a medical partnership. Five years and one day later the partnership ceased to do business. In a lawsuit brought by Langdon against Hurdle and Hoffman, Hurdle counterclaimed for damages from Hoffman for withdrawing from the partnership. Judgment was entered for Hoffman on the counterclaim and Hurdle appealed.

GRAHAM, J. . . . The position taken by appellant [Hurdle] in his brief is that his codefendant [Hoffman] has wrongfully dissolved the partnership and that appellant is entitled to recover for damages resulting therefrom. His counterclaim, however, seems grounded more upon the theory that during the existence of the partnership, appellee failed to perform in the manner contemplated by the agreement. Among the many grievances set forth by Hurdle are that Hoffman permitted his wife to engage in discussions of partnership business with Hurdle; took excessive time off from his professional duties; refused to visit Hurdle's patients on weekends and afternoons when Hurdle would be off duty; was unfriendly, hostile, uncooperative, and failed to observe professional courtesy and ethics with Hurdle.

In view of the unsatisfactory relationship between the partners, as reflected by the complaints as set forth above, it would seem reasonable to expect appellant to rejoice at the termination of the partnership. However, he alleges that Hoffman wrongfully left the partnership office on 1 August 1971 and set up a separate office, abandoning the partnership. Hurdle says Hoffman had no right to do this and that in doing so he breached the partnership agreement and must respond in damages. We disagree.

The partnership agreement did not provide that the partnership was to continue for any specified period. Paragraph 10 of the agreement expressly provides that a withdrawing partner is to receive payment for his share of the partnership assets. The only penalty set forth for withdrawal is a provision that should Hoffman leave the partnership during the first five years of the partnership, he would be prohibited from practicing urology in Fayetteville or within a thirty-five mile radius thereof for five years from the date of his departure. This provision is not applicable since the alleged withdrawal by Hoffman did not occur within five years after the partnership originated.

The partnership contemplated by the agreement entered by the partners was a partnership at will. A partnership is a partnership at will unless some agreement to the contrary can be proved. . . . [This court has previously held] "The significance of the partnership being one at will, i.e., without any definite term or undertaking to be accomplished, is that the termination by the election of a partner is not a breach of contract. Having the legal right to terminate, it would seem that there is no liability for its exercise whatever the motive, and whatever may be the injurious consequences to co-partners, who have neglected to protect themselves by an agreement to continue for a definite term. . . . According to the majority view, the only difference, so far as concerns the rights of dissolution by one partner, between a partnership for an indefinite period and one for a specified term is that in the case of a partnership for a definite term a dissolution before the expiration of the stipulated time is a breach of agreement which subjects such partner to a claim for damages for breach of contract if the dissolution is not justified, whereas the dissolution of a partnership at will affords the other partner no grounds for complaint; in either case the action of one partner actually dissolves the partnership. . . . In view of the rule . . . that a partner may exercise his right to dissolve a partnership at will for any reason which he deems sufficient, or even arbitrarily, he is not liable for damages which have resulted to his co-partners by reason of such action. The Uniform Partnership Act . . . provides that dissolution of the partnership is brought about 'without violation of the agreement between the partners . . . by the express will of any partner when no definite term or particular undertaking is specified.' ". . .

As a matter of law, Hoffman committed no legal wrong in withdrawing from the partnership.

[Judgment affirmed]

King v Stoddard

28 Cal App 3d 708, 104 Cal Rptr 903 (1972)

The Stoddard family, father, mother, and son, were a partnership which published a newspaper, the Walnut Kernel. The parents died and the son kept running the paper. King performed accounting services for the paper. When he was not paid, he sued the son and the executors of the estates of the deceased partners, the parents, claiming that his bill was a partnership liability for which each was liable. The executors defended on the ground that the son as surviving partner did not have authority to employ an accountant but was only authorized to wind up the partnership business. To this defense it was answered that the newspaper was continued in order to preserve its asset value as a going concern, so that it could be sold, and that the running of the paper was therefore part of the winding up process, which, if true, would give the surviving partner the authority to employ the accountant. From a judgment in favor of the accountant, the executors appealed.

BROWN A.J. . . . The estate's liability was predicated upon the court's finding that the services were rendered during the process of winding up the partnership operation of the Walnut Kernel newspaper. We have concluded that the trial court erred and that the continuation of the business was not a winding up of the affairs of the partnership.

The partnership was dissolved by operation of law upon the deaths of Alda and Lyman E. Stoddard, Sr. . . . "In general a dissolution operates only with respect to future transactions; as to everything past the partnership continues until all pre-existing matters are terminated.". . .

. . . [UPA § 35] provides that "[a]fter dissolution a partner can bind the partnership . . . (a) By any act appropriate for winding up partnership affairs. . . ."

It is this latter provision upon which the court based its decision that the estates of the deceased partners were liable for the accounting services performed after dissolution. The court found that "LYMAN STODDARD, JR.'S continuation of the WALNUT KERNEL business was an appropriate act for winding up the partnership, since the assets of the business would have substantial value only if it was a going business. . . .

We disagree with this finding. It is probably true that there might have been advantages to the partnership to sell the business as a going business, but the indefinite continuation of the partnership business is contrary to the requirement for winding up of the affairs upon dissolution. In Harvey v Harvey, 90 Cal App 2d 549, 554, 203 P2d 112, 115-

116, the court disapproved a finding that the business and assets of a partnership were of such character as to render its liquidation impracticable and inadvisable until a purchaser could be found. The court stated: "In effect it [the finding] authorizes the indefinite continuation of the partnership after the death of a partner, a procedure not in accordance with section 571 of the Probate Code. Respondents counter with the argument that the business is such that it cannot be wound up profitably, and the estate given its share. But this argument overlooks the distinction between winding up a business and winding up the partnership interest in that business.". . .

Even if we assume that a situation might exist where continuation of the business for a period would be appropriate to winding up the partnership interest, such a situation did not exist here. The record reflects the fact that the surviving partner was not taking action to wind up the partnership as was his duty

. . . nor did the estates consent in any way to a delay. Rather, their insistence on winding up took the form of an effort to sell the business and a suit to require an accounting. There is nothing in the record upon which to base the argument made by respondents that appellants consented to their continued employment. The fact that they did not object is of no relevance. They had no right to direct and did not participate in the operation of the business. Therefore, the determination that the acts of the accountants were rendered during a winding up process is not based upon substantial evidence. . . .

We conclude that the services of respondents were rendered after the dissolution resulting from the deaths of the partners, Lyman, Sr., and Alda Stoddard, and do not constitute services during the "winding up" processes of the partnership. . . .

[Judgment reversed]

QUESTIONS AND CASE PROBLEMS

1. What social forces are affected by the rule that distribution of partnership assets must be made on the basis of actual value when it is clear that the book values are merely nominal or arbitrary amounts?

2. If an income tax return incorrectly states that *C* is a partner of *A* and *B,* compare the effect of the return's being signed by (a) *C* and by (b) *A.*

3. In proving that *A* and *B* are partners, compare the effect of proof that they (a) share gross returns, (b) are co-owners of property used in or by a business, or (c) share profits.

4. Compare the requirement of notice to third persons when (a) an agency is terminated, and (b) a partnership is dissolved.

5. Gordon Elliot was a member of a partnership. He withdrew from the partnership. Subsequently he was divorced from his wife, and the divorce decree awarded to his wife his interest in the partnership assets. Did this make her a partner? [Elliot v Elliot, 88 Idaho 81, 396 P2d 719]

6. Bates and Huffman formed a partnership to run a shoe business. In a lawsuit between the partners, Huffman claimed that the partnership agreement was void because Bates was a minor. Was he correct? [Huffman v Bates, (Mo App) 348 SW2d 363]

7. The National Acceptance Co., a partnership, entered into a contract obligating it to make certain payments to the General Machinery & Supply Co. Later, General Machinery claimed that it was not bound by the contract because some of the partners of National were minors and could avoid their contract. Was this a valid defense for General Machinery? [General Machinery & Supply Co. v National Acceptance Co., (Colo App) 472 P2d 735]

8. Williams owned and operated a bakery business. His two sons were employed in the business and from time to time received a share of the profits as a bonus. The father and one of the sons died. The administrator of the son's estate, the First National Bank, then sued the estate of the father for an accounting, claiming that the father and the

two sons were a partnership and that the deceased son's estate was therefore entitled to a one-third share. Decide. [First National Bank v Williams, 142 Ore 648, 20 P2d 222]

9. Saunders and Cooper orally agreed to purchase, renovate, and operate several rooming houses, a restaurant, and a grocery store. It was later claimed that no partnership had been formed because there was no written agreement. Was there a partnership? [Cooper v Saunders-Hunt (DistColApp) 365 A2d 626]

10. The Consolidated Loan Co. was owned and operated by three partners. After the death of two of the partners, the surviving partner, Salabes, made an agreement with the estates of the other two to continue the partnership. Thereafter Salabes brought an action for a decree that she "is now the sole remaining partner in, or the sole proprietress of, Consolidated Loan Company" subject to the interests of the estates of the deceased partners. Was she the sole owner of the enterprise? [Miller v Salabes, 225 Md 53, 169 A2d 671]

11. A suit was brought by the heirs of members of a partnership to determine the right to the proceeds of sale of certain real estate. The real estate had been purchased by the partnership with partnership money and in the partnership name. The real estate was not used in the partnership business but was held only for investment purposes. It was claimed by the heirs that this real estate was not subject to the provisions of the Uniform Partnership Act governing tenancy by partnership because it was not used in the business. Were they correct? [Brown v Brown, 45 Tenn App 78, 320 SW2d 721]

12. Peoples was an employee of Trans Texas Properties, a business which was owned by Filip. Peoples made an advertising contract with Cox Enterprises on behalf of Trans Texas and gave Cox a credit application which stated that Elliott was one of the owners of Trans Texas. When the bill for the advertising for Trans Texas was not paid, Cox sued Filip and Elliott. When Elliott showed that he was in fact not an owner or partner of Trans Texas, Cox claimed that Elliott was a partner by estoppel because he had not denied the statement made by Peoples in the credit application and had not exercised reasonable care to guard against the making of such misstatements. Was Elliott a partner by estoppel? [Cox Enterprises, Inc. v Filip (TexCivApp) 538 SW2d 836]

13. Simpson and Balaban, as partners, owned and operated the Desert Cab Company. Simpson died. The administrator of his estate obtained a court order authorizing the sale of Simpson's interest in the partnership and in the physical assets of the partnership. Was this order proper? [Balaban v Bank of Nevada, 86 Nev 862, 477 P2d 860]

14. A lease was executed by which *L* rented a property to *I*. Thereafter *C* claimed that *L* and *I* were in fact partners and that the agreement between *L* and *I* was drawn in the form of a lease so as to shield *L* from the liability to which he would be subject as a partner. Was such evidence admissible? [Goodpasture Grain & Milling Co. v Buck, 77 NMex 609, 426 P2d 586]

44 Powers and Duties of Partners

The powers and duties of the partners are determined by a combination of the law of agency and the law of contracts.

A. AUTHORITY OF PARTNERS

The scope of a partner's authority is determined by the partnership agreement and by the nature of the partnership relation.

§ 44:1. Authority of Majority of Partners. When there are more than two partners in a firm, the decision of the majority prevails in matters involving the manner in which the ordinary functions of the business will be conducted. To illustrate, a majority of the partners of a firm decide to increase the firm's advertising and enter into a contract for that purpose. The transaction is valid and binds the firm and all of the partners.

The act of the majority is not binding if it contravenes the partnership agreement. For such matters, unanimous action is required.[1] Thus, the majority of the members cannot change the nature of the business against the protests of the minority.

When there are two or any other even number of partners, there is the possibility of an even division on a matter that requires majority approval. In such a case no action can be taken, and the partnership is deadlocked. When the partners are evenly divided on any question, one partner has no authority to act. (See p. 745, Summers v Dooley) If the division is over a basic issue and the partners persist in the deadlock so that it is impossible to continue the business, any one of the partners may petition the court to order the dissolution of the firm.

§ 44:2. Express Authority of Individual Partners. An individual partner may have express authority to do certain acts, either because the partnership agreement so declares or because a sufficient number of partners have agreed thereto.

A partner's authority to act for the firm is similar to that of an agent to act for a principal. Thus, in addition to the express authority, a partner has the authority to do those acts which are customary for a member of a partnership conducting the particular business of the partnership. As in the case of an agent, the acts of a partner in excess of authority do not ordinarily bind the partnership.

---

[1] Uniform Partnership Act, § 18(h).

§ 44:3. Customary Authority of Individual Partners. A partner, by virtue of being a co-manager of the business, customarily has certain powers necessary and proper to carry out that business. In the absence of express limitation, the law will therefore imply that a partner has such powers. The scope of such powers varies with the nature of the partnership and also with the business customs and usages of the area in which the partnership operates.

The following are the more common of the customary or implied powers of individual partners:

(a) Contracts. A partner may make any contract necessary to the transaction of the firm business. A partner cannot make a contract of guaranty, however, merely to induce a third person to purchase from the partnership.

When a plaintiff sues on a promissory note or other contract executed by a partner who does not possess express authority to enter into such transaction, the plaintiff has the burden of proving that the making of the contract or the giving of commercial paper was "usual" for a business of the character of the partnership.

(b) Sales. A partner may sell the firm's goods in the regular course of business and make the usual warranties incidental to such sales. This authority, however, is limited to the goods held for sale by the partnership.

(c) Purchases. A partner may purchase any kind of property within the scope of the business, and for this purpose may pledge the credit of the firm. This authority is not affected by the fact that the partner subsequently misuses or keeps the property instead of turning it over to the firm.

(d) Loans. A partner in a trading firm may borrow money for partnership purposes. In doing so, the partner may execute commercial paper in the firm name or give security, such as a mortgage or a pledge of the personal property of the firm. If the third person acts in good faith, the transaction is binding even though the partner misappropriates the money. A partner in a non-trading partnership does not ordinarily possess the power to borrow.

(e) Insurance. A partner may insure the firm property, cancel a policy of insurance, or make proof of loss and accept a settlement for the loss.

(f) Employment. A partner may hire such employees and agents as are necessary to carry out the purpose of the enterprise.

(g) Claims against Firm. A partner has the authority to compromise, adjust, and pay bona fide claims against the partnership. A partner may pay debts out of the firm funds or may pay them by transfering firm property. Although a partner has no authority to pay personal debts from firm assets, a partner's creditors are protected if they receive such payments in good faith and without knowledge that the partner has paid them from firm assets.

(h) Claims of Firm. A partner may adjust, receive payment of, and release debts and other claims of the firm. In so doing, a partner may take money or commercial paper but, as a general rule, cannot accept goods in payment. One who makes a proper payment is protected even though the partner to whom the payment is made embezzles the money or fails to account to the firm for the payment.

(i)   Admissions. A partner may bind the firm by admissions or statements that are adverse to the interests of the partnership if they are made in regard to firm affairs and in pursuance of firm business. For example, when a buyer takes a purchase back to the partnership's store, the admission by the partner then in the store that the product was defective binds the firm.

(j)   Notice. A partner may receive notice of matters affecting the partnership affairs, and such notice, in the absence of fraud, is binding on the other partners.[2]

§ 44:4. Limitations on Authority.

The partners may agree to limit the normal powers of each partner. When a partner, contrary to such an agreement, negotiates a contract for the firm with a third person, the firm is bound if the third person was unaware of the agreement. In such a case, the partner violating the agreement is liable to the other partners for any loss caused by the breach of the limitation. If the third person knew of the limitation, however, the firm would not be bound.[3]

A third person cannot assume that the partner has all the authority which the partner purports to have. If there is anything that would put a reasonable person on notice that the partner's powers are limited, the third person is bound by that limitation.

The third person must be on the alert for the following situations in particular, as they warn that the partner with whom the third person deals either has restricted authority or no authority at all:

(a)   Nature of Business. A third person must take notice of limitations arising out of the nature of the business. A partnership may be organized for a particular kind of business, trade, or profession, and third persons are presumed to know the limitations commonly imposed on partners in such an enterprise. Thus, an act of a partner that would ordinarily bind a commercial firm, such as the issuance of a note, would not bind a partnership engaged in a profession. A partner in a trading partnership has much greater powers than one in a nontrading firm.

(b)   Scope of Business. A third person must recognize and act in accordance with limitations that arise from the scope of the business. A partner cannot bind the firm to a third person in a transaction not within the scope of the firm's business unless the partner had express authority to do so. Thus, when a partner in a dental firm speculates in land or when a partner in a firm dealing in automobiles buys television sets for resale, the third person, in the absence of estoppel or express authority, cannot hold the other partners liable on such a contract. The scope of the business is a question of fact to be determined by the jury from the circumstances of each case. In general, it means the activities commonly recognized as a part of a given business at a given place and time. The usual scope, however, may be enlarged by agreement or by conduct.

(c)   Termination of Partnership. A third person must watch for the termination of the partnership relation, either when the partnership is terminated under conditions requiring no notice or when notice of the termination has been properly given.

[2] UPA § 12.
[3] UPA § 9(4).

(d) **Adverse Interest.** A third person must take notice of an act of a partner that is obviously against the interest of the firm. To illustrate, if a partner issues a promissory note in the firm name and delivers it to a creditor in payment of a personal obligation, the creditor risks nonpayment because such an act may be a fraud upon the firm.

§ 44:5. Prohibited Transactions. There are certain transactions into which a partner cannot enter on behalf of the partnership unless the partner is expressly authorized to do so. A third person entering into such a transaction does so at the risk that the partner has not been so authorized.

The following are prohibited transactions:

(a) **Cessation of Business.** A partner cannot bind the firm by a contract that would make it impossible for the firm to conduct its usual business.

A partner does not have implied authority to sell the business, goodwill, and assets of a partnership business. (See p. 745, Feingold v Davis)

(b) **Suretyship.** A partner has no implied authority to bind the firm by contracts of surety, guaranty, or indemnity for purposes other than the firm business.

(c) **Arbitration.** A partner cannot submit controversies of the firm to arbitration "unless authorized by the other partners or unless they have abandoned the business." [4]

(d) **Confession of Judgment.** A partner cannot confess judgment against the firm upon one of its obligations, because all partners should have an opportunity to defend in court, except when the other partners consent or when they have abandoned the business. [5]

(e) **Assignment for Creditors.** A partner cannot ordinarily make a general assignment of firm property for the benefit of creditors, unless authorized by the other partners or unless they have abandoned the business. [6]

(f) **Personal Obligations.** A partner cannot discharge personal obligations or claims of the firm by interchanging them in any way.

(g) **Sealed Instruments.** Instruments under seal are binding upon the firm when they are made in the usual course of business. In a minority of the states, however, a partner cannot bind copartners by an instrument under seal.

B. DUTIES, RIGHTS, REMEDIES, AND LIABILITIES OF PARTNERS

The duties, rights, remedies, and liabilities between the partners are influenced, to a large extent, by the high standards of fair dealing necessary for the successful operation of the partnership form of business.

§ 44:6. Duties of Partners. In many respects, the duties of a partner are the same as those of an agent.

---

[4] UPA § 9(3)(e).
[5] UPA § 9(3)(d).
[6] UPA § 9(3)(a).

(a)   **Loyalty and Good Faith.** Each partner must act in the highest good faith toward the others and one must not take any advantage over the others by the slightest misrepresentation or concealment.[7] Each partner owes a duty of loyalty to the firm which requires a partner's devotion to the firm's business and bars the making of any secret profit at the expense of the firm, the use of the firm's property for personal benefit, or the exploitation for personal gain of a business opportunity of the partnership. A partner's duties to the firm must be observed above the furtherance of the partner's own personal interest. To illustrate, when one partner renewed a lease of the building occupied by the firm but the lease was renewed in the name of that partner alone, that partner was compelled to hold the lease for the firm on the ground that the failure to renew the lease in the name of the firm was a breach of the duties of good faith and loyalty owed to the firm.

A partner, in the absence of an agreement to the contrary, is required to give undivided time and energy to the furtherance of the business of the partnership. In any case, a partner cannot promote a competing business. If the partner does so, the partner is liable for damages sustained by the partnership. To illustrate, two persons form a partnership for the purpose of making and selling hats, and one of them, unknown to the other, engages in an individual enterprise of selling hats. The partnership, not having agreed to this competition, may compel the competing partner to account for the profits obtained from the competing business.

The obligation of a partner to refrain from competing with the partnership continues after the termination of the partnership if the partnership agreement contains a valid anticompetitive covenant. (See p. 746, Grund v Wood) In the absence of any such restriction, or if the restriction agreed upon is held invalid, a partner is free to compete with the remaining partners, even though they continue the partnership business.

(b)   **Obedience.** Each partner is under the obligation to perform all duties and to obey all restrictions imposed by the partnership agreement or by the vote of the requisite number of partners. Consequently, each partner must observe any limitation imposed by a majority of the partners with respect to the ordinary details of the partnership business. If a majority of the partners operating a retail store decide that no sales shall be made on credit, a partner who is placed in charge of the store must obey this limitation. If a third person does not know of the limitation, the managing partner will have the power to make a binding sale on credit to such person. If the third person does not pay the bill and the firm thereby suffers loss, the partner who violated the "no-credit" limitation is liable to the firm for the loss caused by such disobedience.

(c)   **Reasonable Care.** A partner must use reasonable care in transacting the business of the firm and is liable for any loss resulting from a failure to do so. A partner is not liable, however, for honest mistakes or errors of judgment.

(d)   **Information.** A partner has the duty to inform the partnership of matters relating to the partnership and must "render on demand true and full information of all

---

[7] Skone v Quanco Farms, 261 CalApp2d 237, 68 CalRptr 26.

things affecting the partnership to any partner or the legal representative of any deceased partner or partner under legal disability." [8]

The obligation to inform embraces matters relating to the purchase by one partner of the interest of another and to matters relating to the liquidation of the partnership (see p. 747, Bovy v Graham, Cohen & Wampold).

(e) Accounting. A partner transacting any business for the firm must make and keep, or turn over to the proper person, correct records thereof.

If the partners have delegated to one of the partners the task of keeping the books and accounts for all the business of the firm, the record keeper must keep proper records. If they are disputed, the record keeper has the burden of proving their accuracy, which means that if it is not shown that the records are correct, the record keeper will be held liable.

When an action is brought to compel a partner to account, the court may require the making of an audit by a disinterested third person.

When a partnership is organized for an illegal purpose or for conducting a lawful business in an unlawful manner, a wrongdoing partner cannot obtain an accounting by the partnership. For example, where the members of an engineering partnership did not have the license required for engineering work, one of the partners, an unlicensed engineer, could not require the other partners to account.[9]

§ 44:7. Rights of Partners as Owners. Each partner, in the absence of a contrary agreement, has the following rights, which stem from the fact that the partner is a co-owner of the partnership business.

(a) Management. Each partner has a right to take an equal part in transacting the business of the firm. To illustrate, three persons enter into a partnership. The first contributes $10,000 in cash; the second, property valued at $7,500; and the third, services in actually running the business. Each partner has an equal right to participate in the conduct of the partnership business. It is immaterial that one partner contributed more than another or that one contributed only services.

As an incident of the right to manage the partnership, each partner has the right to possession of the partnership property for the purposes of the partnership.

(b) Inspection of Books. All partners are equally entitled to inspect the books of the firm. "The partnership books shall be kept, subject to any agreement between the partners, at the principal place of business of the partnership, and every partner shall at all times have access to and may inspect and copy any of them." [10]

(c) Share of Profits. Each partner is entitled to a share of the profits. The partners may provide, if they so wish, that profits shall be shared in unequal proportions. In the absence of such a provision in the partnership agreement, each partner is entitled to an equal share of the profits without regard to the amount of capital contributed or services performed for the partnership.

---

[8] UPA, § 20.
[9] Griffin v Cafarelli, 38 AppDiv2d 847, 330 NYS2d 110.
[10] UPA § 19.

The right to profits is regarded as personal property regardless of the nature of the partnership business. Upon the death of a partner, the right to a share of the profits and an accounting passes to the dead partner's executor or administrator.

(d)   Compensation. In the absence of a contrary agreement, a partner is not entitled to compensation for services performed for the partnership. This is so even though the services are unusual or more extensive than the services rendered by the other partners. Consequently when one partner becomes seriously ill and the other partners transact all of the firm's business, they are not entitled to compensation for these services, because the sickness of a partner is considered a risk assumed in the relation. No agreement can be implied that the active partner is to be compensated, even though the services rendered by the active partner are such that ordinarily they would be rendered in the expectation of receiving compensation. As an exception, "a surviving partner is entitled to reasonable compensation for services performed in winding up the partnership affairs." [11]

To illustrate the effect of an agreement of the partners, they may agree that one of the partners shall devote full time as manager of the business and that a salary shall be paid for such services in addition to the managing partner's share of the profits.

(e)   Repayment of Loans. A partner is entitled to the return of any money advanced to or for the firm. These amounts, however, must be separate and distinct from original or additional contributions to the capital of the firm.

(f)   Payment of Interest. In the absence of an agreement to the contrary, contributions to capital do not draw interest. The theory is that the profits constitute sufficient compensation. The partners, of course, may agree to pay interest on the capital contributions and, in any case, interest will run on such contributions from the date when repayment of capital is due.[12]

Advances by a partner in the form of loans are treated as if they were made by a stranger and bear interest from the date the advance is made.[13]

(g)   Contribution and Indemnity. A partner who pays more than a proportionate share of the debts of the firm has a right to contribution from the other partners. Under this principle, if an employee of a partnership negligently injures a third person while acting within the scope of employment and the injured party collects damages from one partner, the latter may enforce contribution from the other partners in order to divide the loss equally between them.

The partnership must indemnify every partner for payments made and personal liabilities reasonably incurred in the ordinary and proper conduct of its business or for the preservation of its business or property.[14] A partner has no right, however, to indemnity or reimbursement if the partner has (1) acted in bad faith, (2) negligently caused the necessity for payment, or (3) previously agreed to bear the expense alone.

(h)   Distribution of Capital. Every partner is entitled to receive a share of the firm property upon dissolution after the payment of all creditors and the repayment of

---

[11] UPA § 18(f).
[12] UPA § 18(d).
[13] UPA § 18(c).
[14] UPA § 18(b).

loans made to the firm by partners. Unless otherwise stated in the partnership agreement, all partners are entitled to the return of their capital contributions.

After such distribution is made, each partner is the sole owner of the fractional part distributed to that partner, rather than a co-owner of all the property as during the existence of the partnership

§ 44:8. Remedies of Partners. The remedies available to the members of a firm are, in some instances, limited because of the peculiar relation of the partners and because of the nature of their claims. In the following discussion the distinction between actions at law and actions in equity is preserved, although in most states and in the federal courts today there is only a civil action.

(a) Actions at Law. An action on a partnership claim can only be brought by the partnership. Local procedure determines whether such suit is to be brought in the firm name or in the names of all the partners. A partner cannot maintain an action at law against the firm upon a claim against the partnership. A partnership cannot bring an action at law against one of its members on claims that the firm holds against that partner. In the absence of statute, a partnership cannot maintain an action against another firm when they have partners in common.

One partner cannot maintain an action at law against another on claims involving partnership transactions. There are two exceptions to this general rule: (1) when the claim has been distinguished from the firm dealings by agreement, and (2) when the firm accounts have been balanced and show the amount to be due.

Partners may sue each other at law in those cases in which there is no necessity of investigating the partnership accounts. Situations of this kind exist when a partner dissolves the relation in violation of the partnership agreement, when a partner fails to furnish capital or services as agreed, or when a partner wrongfully causes injury to a partner that in no way involves the partnership.

(b) Actions in Equity. The proper tribunal to settle all controversies growing out of partnership transactions is a court of equity. For example, an action by a partner to recover a share of profits should be brought in equity. The powers and the procedure of this court are such as to enable it to settle fully problems that arise in winding up the affairs of the firm.

In many instances, an accounting is sought in connection with the dissolution of the firm. A partner is entitled to an accounting (1) if wrongly excluded from the partnership business or the possession of its property by the other partners; (2) if the right exists under the terms of any agreement; (3) if the partner is a trustee; or (4) if other circumstances render an accounting just and reasonable.[15]

§ 44:9. Liability of Partners and Partnership as to Particular Acts. The liability of a partnership and of the partners for the acts of individual partners and of employees is governed by the same principles as apply to the liability of an employer or a principal for the acts of an employee or agent.

(a) Contracts. All members of the firm are liable on contracts made by a partner for the partnership and in its name if they were made within the scope of the partner's

---

[15] UPA § 22.

real or apparent authority. This is true even though the partners may be unknown to the third persons. Thus, a dormant partner, when discovered, can be held liable with the others.

When a partner, acting on behalf of the partnership, makes an authorized, simple contract but does so in the partner's own name, the firm and the other partners are liable as undisclosed principals.

When a partner with necessary authority executes commercial paper in the name of the firm, the firm and every partner is bound thereby, even though the individual partners did not sign the paper. If a partner signs commercial paper in the partner's own name, the partnership and the other partners cannot sue or be sued thereon as undisclosed principals. While partnership law determines the authority of a partner to enter into transactions on behalf of the firm, the Uniform Commercial Code governs how commercial paper is to be executed by a partner.

When a borrowing partner gives the lender a promissory note for the partner's personal obligation, the partnership and the other partners cannot be liable thereon, even though the borrowing partner used the money for the benefit of the partnership.[16]

The fact that a partner has either express or implied authority to bind the partnership does not in itself establish that a contract made by the partner is a partnership contract, as distinguished from the individual contract of the partner. As in the case of agency situations generally, a contract between the third person and the principal, here the partnership, does not arise when that is not the intention of the parties. Consequently, where a third person and a partner make a contract intending to bind the partner individually, rather than the partnership, no contract liability of the partnership is created. Care must be taken to distinguish this situation from that in which the partnership is not disclosed and in which the third person has the intention of dealing with the partner only, as in such cases the partnership and the other partners may be bound or have rights under the rules governing undisclosed principals who act through authorized agents.

(b)   Torts. All partners are liable for torts, such as fraud, trespass, negligence, and assaults, committed by one partner while transacting firm business.[17] Accordingly, a partnership formed to manage real estate is liable for a battery inflicted by one partner upon a tenant in collecting the rent.[18] The members of a firm are also liable for breach of trust by a partner in respect to goods or money of a third person held by the firm.

When a partner is guilty of fraud in dealing with a third person, the partnership is liable for the consequences even though the commission of fraud was not within the scope of the partner's authority.

When one partner is guilty of misconduct with respect to a third person, the partnership and the other partners may be vicariously liable for such misconduct. The circumstances may be such that the other partners are themselves liable for their own failing to take steps to protect the third person's interest. The partnership is not liable for a tort that has no relation to the partnership business. This is so

---

[16] Edwards Feed Mill v Johnson (TexCivApp) 302 SW2d 151.
[17] UPA § 13.
[18] Soden v Starkman (FlaApp) 218 So2d 763.

even though the partnership has been informed of the partner's conduct but did not take any action thereon.

(c) Crimes. The partners of a firm and the partnership itself are liable for certain crimes committed by a partner in the course of the business, such as selling goods without obtaining a necessary vendor's license or selling in violation of a statute prohibiting sale. A partnership, as distinct from the individual partners, may be fined for committing the crime of violating the federal law establishing regulations for the safe transportation in interstate commerce of explosives and other dangerous articles.[19] If carrying on the firm business does not necessarily involve the commission of the act constituting a crime, the firm and the partners not participating in the commission of the crime or authorizing its commission generally are not criminally liable. This exception is not recognized in some cases, such as the making of prohibited sales to minors or sales of adulterated products.

§ 44:10. Nature of Partner's Liability. By virtue of the Uniform Partnership Act, partners are jointly liable on all firm contracts. They are jointly and severally liable for all torts committed by an employee or one of the partners in the scope of the partnership business. When partners are liable for the wrongful injury caused a third person, the latter may sue all or any number of the members of the firm.

§ 44:11. Extent of Partner's Liability. Each member of the firm is individually and unlimitedly liable for the debts of the partnership regardless of the member's investment or interest in the firm. Moreover, the individual property of a partner may be sold in satisfaction of a judgment, even before the firm property has been exhausted.

(a) Liability for Breach of Duty. When a partner violates a duty owed to the partnership, the partner's liability is determined by the general principles of law applicable to such conduct.

When one partner commits a fraud upon another partner, the injured partner may recover both compensatory and exemplary damages from the wrongdoing partner.

(b) Liability of New Partners. A person admitted as a partner into an existing partnership is limitedly liable for all the obligations of the partnership arising before such admission. This is a limited liability in that the pre-admission claim may be satisfied only out of partnership property and does not extend to the individual property of the newly-admitted partner.[20] The incoming partner does not become personally liable for pre-admission claims unless the incoming partner expressly promises to pay such claims.

(c) Effect of Dissolution on Partner's Liability. A partner remains liable after dissolution of the partnership unless expressly released by the creditors or unless all claims against the partnership have been satisfied. The dissolution of the partnership does not of itself discharge the existing liability of any partner. The individual property

---

[19] United States v A & P Trucking Co., 358 US 121.
[20] UPA § 17; see also UPA § 41(1), (7).

of a deceased partner is liable for the obligations of the partnership which were incurred while the deceased partner was alive, but the individual creditors of the deceased partner have priority over the partnership creditors with respect to such property.[21]

§ 44:12. Enforcement of Partner's Liability. The manner in which the civil liability of a partner may be enforced depends upon the form of the lawsuit brought by the creditor. The firm may have been sued in the name of all the individual partners doing business as the partnership, as "Plaintiff v *A, B,* and *C,* doing business as the Ajax Warehouse." In such a case, those partners named are bound by the judgment against the firm if they have been properly served in the suit. Partners either not named [22] or not served are generally not bound by the judgment.

When there is a dispute on the point, the question of whether one partner was acting in the scope of the partnership business at a particular time is a question to be submitted to the jury.

When a judgment is obtained against a partner, it may be enforced against the non-partnership assets of that partner in the same way as a judgment would be enforced against any judgment debtor. The creditor may enforce judgment against the partner's interest in the partnership only by obtaining a charging order against that interest. (See p. 748, Myrick v Second National Bank)

If the judgment binds an individual partner, the creditor may enforce the judgment against the partner before, at the same time, or after the creditor seeks to enforce the judgment against the firm or other partners who are also bound by the judgment. If a partner is not bound by a judgment, the creditor must bring another lawsuit against the partner in which the creditor establishes that the defendant is a partner in the particular partnership and that a judgment was entered against the partnership for a partnership liability. When this is established, a judgment is entered in favor of the creditor against the particular partner. The creditor may then have execution on this judgment against the property of the partner.

§ 44:13. Suit in Firm Name. At common law, a partnership could not sue or be sued in the firm name, on the theory that there was no legal person by that name. If the partnership were composed of *A, B,* and *C,* it was necessary for them to sue or be sued as *A, B,* and *C.* If the firm name was "The *X* Bakery," some states required that they appear in the action as "*A, B,* and *C,* trading as the *X* Bakery." By statute or court rule, this principle of the common law has been abolished in many states, and a partnership may sue or be sued either in the names of the partners or in the firm name.

The identity of the parties in an action is determined by the nature of the obligation on which the action is brought. If the action is brought on commercial paper held by one partner, the action must be brought in that partner's name, although this could be changed by indorsing the paper to the firm.

---

[21] UPA § 36.
[22] Fazzi v Peters, 68 Cal2d 590, 68 CalRptr 170, 440 P2d 242.

CASES FOR CHAPTER 44

Summers v Dooley

94 Idaho 87, 481 P2d 318 (1971)

Summers and Dooley formed a partnership to collect trash. Summers became unable to work and he hired a third man to do his work and paid him out of his personal funds. Summers suggested to Dooley that the third man be paid from the partnership funds but Dooley refused to do so. Finally Summers sued Dooley for reimbursement for the money he had spent to pay the third man. From a judgment for Dooley, Summers appealed.

DONALDSON, J. . . . Summers continued to operate the business using the third man and in October of 1967 instituted suit in the district court for $6,000 against his partner, the gravamen of the complaint being that Summers has been required to pay out more than $11,000 in expenses, incurred in the hiring of the additional man, without any reimbursement from either the partnership funds or his partner. After trial before the court, sitting without a jury, Summers was granted only partial relief and he has appealed. He urges in essence that the trial court erred by failing to conclude that he should be reimbursed for expenses and costs connected in the employment of extra help in the partnership business.

The principal thrust of appellant's contention is that in spite of the fact that one of the two partners refused to consent to the hiring of additional help, nonetheless, the non-consenting partner retained profits earned by the labors of the third man and therefore the non-consenting partner should be estopped from denying the need and value of the employee, and has by his behavior ratified the act of the other partner who hired the additional man.

The issue presented for decision by this appeal is whether an equal partner in a two man partnership has the authority to hire a new employee in disregard of the objection of the other partner and then attempt to charge the dissenting partner with the costs incurred as a result of his unilateral decision.

The State of Idaho has enacted specific statutes with respect to the legal concept known as "partnership." Therefore any solution of partnership problems should logically begin with an application of the relevant code provision.

In the instant case the record indicates that although Summers requested his partner Dooley to agree to the hiring of a third man, such requests were not honored. In fact Dooley made it clear that he was "voting no" with regard to the hiring of an additional employee.

An application of the relevant statutory provisions and pertinent case law to the factual situation presented by the instant case indicates that the trial court was correct in its disposal of the issue since a majority of the partners did not consent to the hiring of the third man. I.C. § 53-318(8) provides: "Any difference arising as to ordinary matters connected with the partnership business may be decided by a *majority of the partners*. . . ." It is the opinion of this Court that the preceding statute is of a mandatory rather than permissive nature. . . .

A careful reading of the statutory provision indicates that subsection 5 bestows *equal rights in the management and conduct of the partnership business* upon all of the partners. The concept of equality between partners with respect to management of business affairs is a central theme and recurs throughout the Uniform Partnership law. . . . Business differences must be decided by a majority of the partners.

". . . If the partners are equally divided, those who forbid a change must have their way.". . .

In the case at bar one of the partners continually voiced objection to the hiring of the third man. He did not sit idly by and acquiesce in the actions of his partner. Under these circumstances it is manifestly unjust to permit recovery of an expense which was incurred individually and not for the benefit of the partnership but rather for the benefit of one partner.

[Judgment affirmed]

Feingold v Davis

444 Pa 399, 282 A2d 291 (1971)

William and Charlotte Davis, husband and wife, conducted the Davis Nursing Home as a partnership. William made a contract to sell the home and all its assets and goodwill to Feingold. Charlotte refused to recognize the contract. Feingold sued William and Charlotte to obtain a decree of specific performance of the sales contract. Judgment was entered against the plaintiff and he appealed.

POMEROY, J. . . . Under Section 10(4) of the Uniform Partnership Act, . . . a conveyance by one partner of real estate (and by the same token an agreement to make a conveyance) titled in the names of all the partners, passes the equitable interest of the partnership, subject, however, to an important proviso, viz., that the act is within the authority of paragraph (1) of Section 9 of the Partnership Act. Section 9(1) makes a partner an agent of the partnership *"for the purpose of its business,"* and makes the act of a partner "for apparently carrying on in the usual way the business of the partnership" binding on a partnership unless in fact the partner has no such authority, and the person with whom he is dealing knows he has not. The transaction here involved was manifestly not the carrying on in the usual way of the business of the partnership, but the converse; it was the sale of the business, including goodwill and apparently all other assets, except cash. Under paragraph (2) of the same Section 9, such a transaction is not binding on the partnership unless authorized by all partners. Similarly, paragraph (3) provides that all partners must authorize, *inter alia,* the disposition of the goodwill of the business or the doing of "any other act which would make it impossible to carry on the ordinary business of the partnership."

. . . At least insofar as the contemplated conveyance relates to real estate, the non-signing partner's authorization to the one purporting to act for the partnership must be in writing in order to be binding. Nothing in Section 9 of the Partnership Act dealing with the extent of a partner's agency relationship with the firm provides or suggests that the requisite authority of the partners for whom one partner is acting can be less than written authority where real estate is involved. There is no reason to suppose that the unequivocal and long-standing requirement of the Statute of Frauds that an agent to sell real estate must be authorized to do so in writing in order to charge his principal is not applicable to a partnership agent, and we hold that the authority must be so evidenced. . . . In the case at bar no partnership articles or any other writing evidencing the authority of William Davis was produced. His copartner and

the firm were therefore not bound by the binder agreement. . . .

[Judgment affirmed]

Grund v Wood

(Colo App) 490 P2d 955 (1971)

Grund, Wood, and others were partners in a medical partnership. Paragraph 10.5 of the partnership agreement stated that a partner withdrawing from the partnership would not practice medicine within a five-mile radius of the partnership clinic for a period of two years after his withdrawal. It was further stated that if a withdrawing partner violated this convenant, he would forfeit $1,300 for every month that he had been a partner, not to exceed $15,600. The agreement further recited, "Such amount shall be deemed to be liquidated damages." Grund withdrew from the medical partnership. He sued to obtain his share of the partnership assets. Wood claimed that Grund had violated the anticompetitive covenant and held back $15,600. The lower court awarded the plaintiff his share of assets less $15,600. Grund appealed.

PIERCE, J. . . . Plaintiff [assigns as] error . . . the trial court's finding that paragraph 10.5 of the partnership agreement was a valid and enforceable liquidated damage provision rather than an unenforceable penalty or forfeiture. We cannot agree with plaintiff's contention.

Where a contract has been made not to engage in a particular profession within a stated area, it has been the policy of courts to construe such an agreement as being for liquidated damages rather than a penalty when the evidence shows that the stipulated amount of damages is reasonable and is not unjust, oppressive, or disproportionate to the damage that would result from the breach of such a covenant. . . . In Farthing v San Mateo Clinic, 143 Cal App 2d 385, 299 P2d 977, a noncompetition agreement providing for liquidated damages was upheld where a retiring partner's rights to his unpaid partnership interest would be forfeited upon his resumption of practice within a proscribed area. The liquidated damages provision there was similarly based upon a scale determined by the length of time a withdrawing partner had been a member of the partnership. Therein, the court stated:

"There is no way of calculating the future loss that will be suffered through the loss of this group of patients. . . . It is obvious that the measure selected is reasonably related to the anticipated loss. The interest in accounts receivable of a partner who was nearing parity would be much greater than that of one at the bottom of the scale, and a better established partner usually would take a much greater share of business from the clinic than would a partner who was not as well established."

. . . The trial court found . . . that it was the intention of the parties to provide for liquidated damages in the agreement and the method for assessing those damages was reasonable. [We] hold its determination that paragraph 10.5 was a valid and enforceable liquidated damages provision was proper. . . .

[Judgment affirmed]

Bovy v Graham, Cohen & Wampold

17 WashApp 567, 564 P2d 1175 (1977)

Bovy was a partner in the law partnership of Graham, Cohen and Wampold. The partnership was dissolved. It was then realized that the partnership agreement did not make adequate provision for the distribution of fees upon dissolution. The parties entered into a supplementary agreement or addendum to the original partnership agreement with specified how fees should be divided upon dissolution. Bovy sued the partnership to compel compliance with the addendum. The partnership raised the defense that Bovy had not fully disclosed the number of cases in which he claimed a contingent fee and that the addendum would not have been agreed to if the actual facts had been known. The lower court granted specific performance of the addendum and the partnership appealed.

REED, J. . . . The addendum agreement was repudiated by defendants, who had continued as partners. As justification for their repudiation, defendants cite Bovy's failure to disclose the number and value of his contingent fee files at the time the addendum was negotiated. Defendants further argue that they would never have agreed to the addendum had they known the true extent of Bovy's work in progress. In support of their contention defendants

refer to portions of the record containing both Bovy's admission that he did not disclose the extent of his files, and his acknowledgment that he had only one file subject to the agreement. On appeal we are presented with the issue of whether, after dissolution of the partnership, Bovy was subject to a fiduciary duty of disclosure, whereby he was required to divulge the number and value of his contingent fee files during the negotiation of the addendum agreement. We hold that a duty of full disclosure does exist during the winding up of partnership affairs, that Bovy breached this fiduciary duty of disclosure, and that such nondisclosure makes it improper to specifically enforce the addendum agreement in favor of plaintiff Bovy.

. . . The relationship among partners is fiduciary in character and imposes upon the partners the obligation of candor and utmost good faith in their dealings with each other. . . . That the fiduciary standard is a high one is aptly expressed in the following quotation from Justice Cardozo's opinion in *Meinhard v Salmon,* 249 N.Y. 458, 164 N.E. 545, 546, 62 A.L.R. 1(1928).

"Copartners, owe to one another . . . the duty of the finest loyalty. Many forms of conduct permissible in a workaday world for those acting at arm's length, are forbidden to those bound by fiduciary ties. A trustee is held to something stricter than the morals of the market place. Not honesty alone, but the punctilio of an honor the most sensitive, is then the standard of behavior. As to this there has developed a tradition that is unbending and inveterate. Uncompromising rigidity has been the attitude of courts of equity when petitioned to undermine the rule of undivided loyalty by the "disintregrating erosion" of particular exceptions. . . . Only thus has the level of conduct for fiduciaries been kept at a level higher than that trodden by the crowd."

The good faith obligation of a fiduciary relationship not only demands that a partner should not make any false statement to his copartner, but also that he abstain from any and all concealment concerning matters pertaining to the partnership business . . . The partnership relationship is a fiduciary character which carries with it the requirement of utmost good faith and loyalty and the obligation of each member of the partnership to make full disclosure of all known information that is significant and material to the affairs or property of the partnership.

We now turn to the question of what effect dissolution of the partnership has upon the fiduciary relationship of copartners. . . . While there may be a relaxation of a partner's duties to his copartner in matters that look beyond the business of the newly-dissolved partnership, the good faith and full disclosure exacted of partners continues during the winding up of the partnership affairs. . . . During negotiations pursuant to a dissolution, each partner must deal fairly with his copartners and must not conceal from them important matters within his own knowledge concerning the business of the partnership. . . . Even though personal relations between partners have deteriorated to the extent that neither partner has any confidence in the other (as is presumably the case in many partnership dissolutions), that fact does not relieve the partners of their fiduciary obligations to each other. . . . We conclude that plaintiff Bovy was obligated to fully disclose any information pertaining to the winding up of partnership affairs. Bovy's breach of the confidential relationship and duty of disclosure existing among partners bars him from seeking performance of the addendum agreement . . .

[Judgment reversed]

Myrick v Second National Bank

(FlaApp) 335 So2d 343 (1976)

The Port Richey Shopping Village was owned and operated by a partnership. Myrick and his wife were two of the partners. They owed money to the Second National Bank. The Second National Bank obtained a judgment against the Myricks and directed the sheriff to sell the Myricks' interest in the shopping village. Myrick and his wife filed a motion to prevent the sale. The court refused to do so. The Myricks appealed.

SCHEB, J. . . . The plaintiff instructed the sheriff to levy on the defendants' interest in the partnership known as Port Richey Shopping Village, a joint venture. On April 19, 1976, the trial court denied the Myricks' motion to set aside the levy and cancel the notice of sale, holding: ". . . that a partnership interest is property as defined in Florida Statute 56.061, that is subject to levy and sale under execution and that *Lott v Padgett,* [153 Fla. 308,] 14 So.2d 669 has not been superseded by the Uni-

form Partnership Act, and . . . is controlling . . ." This appeal ensued.

We think the trial judge's reliance upon *Lott v Padgett* was error. *Lott,* decided by our Supreme Court in 1943, correctly stated the common law that a debtor's interest in a partnership was susceptible to being seized by legal process; however, this doctrine was superseded by adoption of the Uniform Partnership Act (U.P.A.) in 1973. Fla.Stat. § 620.56, et seq. The U.P.A. changed the common law nature of a partnership interest. Under Fla.Stat. § 620.685, a [partner's] interest in the partnership is personal property; i.e., his share of the profits and all surplus. And § 620.575(3) provides that the new Act shall be interpreted and construed as to make uniform the law of those states which have enacted it; . . .

Section 620.695(1) of the act provides: On application to a court having jurisdiction by any judgment creditor of a partner, the court may charge the interest of the debtor partner with payment of the unsatisfied amount of the judgment with interest, and may then or later appoint a receiver of his share of the profits and of any other money due or to become due to him from the partnership, and make all other orders to take the actions that the debtor partner might have made or that the circumstances of the case may require.

Plaintiff argues that § 620.695 merely furnishes a creditor with an additional remedy and . . . does not limit the rights of creditors with respect to a partner's interest in the partnership.

The point is one of first impression in Florida since Florida's adoption of the U.P.A. Section 620.695 is adopted from Section 28 of the Act and it has been held that its purpose is to protect non-debtor partners. . . . The distinction for which plaintiff argues appears inconsistent with the language of Section 28 as to the proper method for a judgment creditor to reach the interest of a partner in the partnership. . . . We do not think this provision justifies an immediate levy and sale. Rather, the charging order is the essential first step, and all further proceedings must occur under the supervision of the court, which may take all appropriate actions, including the appointment of a receiver if necessary, to protect the interests of the various parties. The reason for prohibiting a levy on partnership assets for debts of individual partners is to prevent disruption of the partnership business and the consequent injustice to other partners , . . . These same considerations weigh against immediate levy and sale of a partner's share in the partnership when less disruptive measures may afford the same and perhaps even a greater level of protection to a judgment creditor.

California and New York have rejected the contention made by plaintiff here, that a levy on a partner's interest in the partnership is permissible under the Act. . . . Other cases decided under the U.P.A. state that a charging order is the proper procedure to reach the partnership interest.

[Judgment reversed and action remanded]

QUESTIONS AND CASE PROBLEMS

1. What social forces are affected by the rule governing the authority of a majority of the partners?

2. A partnership owns and operates an automobile dealership. With respect to authority to sell one of the automobiles held by the dealership for sale, compare the authority of (a) an agent of the partnership, and (b) a partner in the partnership.

3. Compare the effect of a secret limitation on the authority of (a) an agent, and (b) a partner.

4. Compare the right of a partner to engage in a business which competes with the firm (a) while still a partner, and (b) after leaving the partnership.

5. Elrod and Hansford were partners under the name of Walter Elrod & Co. Hansford purchased on credit from the firm of Dawson Blakemore & Co. certain merchandise for the firm. Before the sale, Elrod had notified Dawson Blakemore & Co. that he would not be bound to pay for any purchase for the firm made on credit by Hansford. Thereafter Dawson Blakemore & Co. brought an action against the members of Walter Elrod & Co. to recover the price of the goods. Elrod contended that he was not bound by the contract made by Hansford. Decide. [Dawson Blakemore & Co. v Elrod, 105 Ky 624, 49 SW 465]

6. O'Bryan, Sullivan, and Davis were partners engaged in operating freight steamers on the Yukon River. Sullivan purchased in the firm name and received from Merrill certain lumber for the construction of firm warehouses at terminal points for the storage of freight. In an action on the contract of sale brought by Merrill against the members of the firm, it was contended that some of the partners had no power to bind the firm on this kind of contract. Do you agree with this contention? [Merrill v O'Bryan, 48 Wash 415, 93 P 917]

7. Delay and Foster entered into a partnership. Thereafter Foster wrongfully dissolved the partnership. Delay brought an action at law against Foster to recover damages arising out of the wrongful dissolution and breach of the partnership agreement. The defendant contended that the plaintiff was not entitled to bring an action at law but should have brought an action in equity. Do you agree? [Delay v Foster, 34 Idaho 691, 203 P 461]

8. Phillips and Harris were partners in the business of selling used cars. While driving a partnership automobile on partnership business, Harris negligently collided with Cook. Cook sued Phillips and Harris. Are Phillips and the partnership liable for the harm caused by Harris? [Phillips v Cook, 239 Md 215, 210 A2d 143]

9. Kittilsby and Vevelstad were partners doing work on a mining claim known as the Sea Level Claim. Kittilsby did the assessment work for one year and then went to Seattle, upon the promise of Vevelstad to do the work for the following year. Vevelstad did not do the work, and the claim became open to location. Vevelstad procured Singleton, who was to act for him, to locate and prove a claim covering the same district. After Singleton had conveyed the claim to him for a nominal consideration, Vevelstad sold

the claim to the Juneau Sea Level Copper Mines. Thereafter Kittilsby brought an action against Vevelstad to recover half of the proceeds of the sale. Was he entitled to judgment? [Kittilsby v Vevelstad, 103 Wash 126, 173 P 744]

10. Wilke, President of the Commercial Bank of Webster City, Iowa, and Wright entered into a farming and stock-raising partnership. The business was conducted under the name of Wilke and Wright Farm Co. The agreement stipulated that Wilke was "to have control and management of said business." Thereafter, Wright sold some partnership cattle to Gross and Gidley, cattle buyers, who resold the cattle to Simon. In an action brought against Simon to recover the cattle, Wilke alleged that Wright had no authority to sell them. Decide. [Wilke v Simon, 46 SD 422, 193 NW 666]

11. The St. John Transportation Co., a corporation, made a contract with the firm of Bilyeu & Herstel, contractors, by which the latter was to construct a ferryboat. Herstel, a member of the firm of contractors, executed a contract in the firm name with Benbow for certain materials and labor in connection with the construction of the ferryboat. In an action brought by Benbow to enforce a lien against the ferryboat, called The James Johns, it was contended that all members of the firm were bound by the contract made by Herstel. Do you agree? [Benbow v The James Johns, 56 Ore 554, 108 P 634]

12. Bosquez and Gonzalez were partners in the business of selling radio broadcasting time. Bosquez borrowed money from Burns and gave Burns a promissory note which obligated the partnership as maker. Burns later sued the two partners and the firm on the note. Gonzalez raised the defense that Bosquez had no authority to execute the note. Was he correct? [Burns v Gonzalez (TexCivApp) 439 SW2d 128]

13. Milton Smith, Maude Smith, and Warren Ten Brook were partners doing business as "Greenwood Sales & Service." Pretending to act on behalf of the partnership, Ten Brook borrowed $6,000 from Holloway, giving her a note that was signed: "Greenwood Sales & Service, by Warren Ten Brook, Partner." In fact, Ten Brook borrowed the $6,000 so that he could make his capital contribution to the partnership. The check so obtained from Holloway was payable to the order of the partnership and was in fact deposited by Ten Brook in the partnership account. When the note was not paid, Holloway sued all of the partners. The other partners claimed that neither the partnership nor they were bound by Ten Brook's unauthorized act committed for his personal gain. Was this defense valid? [Holloway v Smith, 197 Va 334, 88 SE2d 909]

14. Henslee and Boyd formed a partnership to operate a sawmill business. As part of the agreement, Henslee agreed to sell timber to the partnership at the prevailing market prices. Boyd later sued Henslee to set aside the agreement on the ground of fraud and breach of partnership duties. One of the objections made by Boyd was that Henslee had refused to sell timber to the partnership as required by the agreement. Henslee replied that he had refused to sell because the partnership could not pay in cash. Boyd then answered that Henslee should not have insisted on a cash sale since that would use up the partnership's ready cash. Was Henslee guilty of a breach of his partnership duty? [Henslee v Boyd, 235 Ark 369, 360 SW2d 505]

15. Petrikis, Ellis, and others, who were partners, signed an agreement stating: "We, the undersigned, hereby agree to sell our interests in the partnership business. If and when the sale takes place and after all bills are accounted for, the remainder of the money is to be divided according to the share each partner now attains in the said business." Petrikis then began negotiations to sell the business to Hanges and finally made a contract selling the business to him for $17,500. Ellis, one of the partners, refused to accept the terms of the contract. Hanges then notified the partners that he called the deal off, whereupon the partners brought suit against him for breach of contract. Was Hanges liable for breach of contract? [Petrikis v Hanges, 111 Cal App 2d 734, 245 P2d 39]

45 Special Ventures

New forms of business organizations are evolving to meet modern business and investment needs. This has both a positive and a negative aspect. As to the positive, it is necessary to employ that form of structure or organization which will permit the doing of the desired work or the attainment of the desired goal in the most efficient manner. As to the negative, how can the enterprise and the participants be protected from the hazards that may arise?

Initially, the entrepreneur and society tend to follow existing patterns. This is due in part to the fact that the old familiar patterns and devices have been working reasonably well.

In this chapter, a number of forms of special ventures are considered. In addition to these, the enterprise may be based upon an agency, a partnership, or a corporation.

A. PURPOSE OF SPECIAL VENTURES

Today's special venture may be either permanent or temporary. Down to the middle of this century, persons organizing a business generally hoped to stay in that business the rest of their lives or for many years. Today it is common to form temporary ventures.

In many instances, the special venture is merely a new use of an old form of organization in order to obtain a particular advantage, generally a tax advantage. Thus we find both general and limited partnerships being employed as tax-saving devices. Similarly, leases may form an essential link in structuring a business, as in the case of a lease to a franchisee or a sale and leaseback when it is so structured that the net effect of it is to provide the lessee with working capital.

B. FRANCHISES

The use of franchises has expanded rapidly in recent years as a method of controlling and financing operations by the franchisor and as a method of investment and participation by the franchisee.

§ 45:1. Definitions. A *franchise* has been defined by the Federal Trade Commission for the purpose of one of its investigations as "an arrangement in which the owner of a trademark, tradename, or copyright licenses others, under specified conditions or limitations, to use the trademark, tradename, or copyright in purveying goods or services." The *franchisor* is the party granting the franchise, and the *franchisee* is the person to whom the franchise is given.

§ 45:2. The Franchisor and the Franchisee. Theoretically the relationship between the franchisor and the franchisee is an arm's-length relationship between two independent contractors, their respective rights being determined by the contract existing between them.

(a) Prices. Depending upon the nature of the business, the franchisor may be content to charge the franchisee according to the franchisor's established price scale or contract and is not concerned with the prices or charges of the franchisee in dealing with its customers. Franchisor-manufacturers of brand name or trademark products are very often desirous of having the retail prices of their products maintained. As a general rule, any agreement between a franchisor and a franchisee to control or fix prices is a violation of the antitrust laws and is illegal per se.

(b) Purchase of Materials and Supplies. A provision requiring the franchisee to purchase materials and supplies exclusively from the franchisor when competitive goods are freely available is illegal as a tying arrangement in violation of the antitrust laws.

(c) Geographic Limitations. A restriction on the territory in which the franchisee may resell products and the customers to whom the products may be sold may be a violation of the antitrust law.[1] Such so-called "location practices" are not illegal where they do not prevent franchisees from selling to customers outside of the territory nor bar them from advertising beyond such territory.

(d) Standards. The franchise device is frequently used as a means of maintaining standards. Ordinarily there should be no question as to the validity of provisions seeking to maintain standards as a franchisor has a legitimate interest in maintaining standards in order to protect name and reputation.

(e) Duration and Termination. The franchise may last for as long as the parties agree. Commonly it runs for a short period of time, such as a year, so that the franchise holder is well aware that in order to stay in business the terms of the franchise contract must be followed.

Franchise contracts generally specify the causes for which the franchisor may terminate the franchise, such as the franchisee's death, bankruptcy, failure to make payments, or failure to meet sales quotas. Franchise contracts frequently contain an arbitration provision under which a neutral party is to make a final and binding determination on whether or not a breach of the contract had occurred sufficient to justify cancellation of the franchise. The arbitration provision may provide that the franchisor can appoint a trustee to run the business of the franchisee while the arbitration proceedings are pending.

Holders of automobile dealership franchises are protected from bad faith termination of their dealerships by the federal Automobile Dealers' Day in Court Act.[2] When an automobile manufacturer makes arbitrary and unreasonable demands and

---

[1] Continental T.V., Inc. v GTE Sylvania, Inc. 433 US 36.
[2] 15 USC § 1222. Several states have similar statutes.

thereafter terminates the dealer's franchise for failure to comply with the demands, the manufacturer is liable for the damages caused thereby. (See p. 760, Shor-Line Rambler, Inc. v American Motors) However, a manufacturer is justified in terminating an automobile dealership for failing to maintain the required sales quota where the manufacturer has given the dealer repeated warnings, the quota is reasonable, and the quota has been reduced to reflect local economic conditions.[3]

In many states, gasoline dealerships are protected from arbitrary termination either by general statutes protecting all franchisees or by special statutes protecting only gasoline dealerships. Typically a gasoline franchisee (1) rents the gas station from the oil company, and (2) enters into a dealership contract with the company to operate that station. When the lease provides that it may be terminated on notice, the company, by terminating the lease, is able to indirectly terminate the dealership contract because the dealer cannot perform the obligations under that contract without the rented station. Generally, a lease allowing the franchisor to terminate upon notice is given literal effect, which means that the lessor may give the terminating notice without regard to whether there is any cause for terminating the lease. However, if there is a statute stating that the dealership contract cannot be terminated without cause, there is authority that the franchisor may not exercise the power in the lease to terminate the lease unless there is good cause for terminating the dealership contract.[4]

When the relationship between the franchisor and the franchisee is created primarily for the sale of products manufactured by the franchisor, the rights of the parties are governed by the law of sales of Article 2 of the Uniform Commercial Code.

(f) Statutory Regulation. There continue to be statutory reform movements, both at the federal and state levels, to provide general protection for the franchise holder. In one sense this is merely another effort on the part of society to equalize the bargaining positions of the parties who in theory are bargaining equals but who in actual practice are not. Viewed in this light, the modern movement for consumer protection and the movement for the protection of franchise holders are closely related.

Protective regulation of franchisees generally relates to problems of fraud in the sale of the franchise and protecting the franchisee from unreasonable demands and termination by the franchisor. The sale of the franchise may be fraudulent, with the franchisor misrepresenting the "get rich quick" aspects and the scope of the enterprise. Members of the employee class are particularly vulnerable to the sales appeal of the franchisor, for the franchise is sold as a way to obtain financial independence and to "be your own boss." Too often the franchise operation exists only on paper so that the individual franchise is worth very little. The franchisee in such case is in the same position as the defrauded buyer of corporate stock. Because of this similarity, a number of courts hold that the laws governing the fraudulent sale of securities are applicable to the fraudulent sale of franchises. Other courts refuse to apply the security sale laws to the sale of franchises. (See p. 761, Brown v Computer System, Inc.) Some states have adopted *franchise investment laws* under which a franchisee deceived by a misleading statement in a prospectus may sue for damages.

---

[3] Clifford Jacobs Motors, Inc. v Chrysler Corp. (DC Ohio) 357 FSupp 564.
[4] Shell Oil Co. v Marinello, 63 NJ 402, 307 A2d 598.

§ 45:3. The Franchisor and Third Persons. Generally the franchisor is not liable in any way to a third person dealing with or affected by the franchise holder. This freedom from liability, while at the same time maintaining control over the general pattern of operations, is one of the reasons franchisors grant franchises. If the negligence of the franchisee causes harm to a third person, the franchisor is not liable because the franchisee is regarded as an independent contractor. (See p. 761, B. P. Oil Corporation v Mabe)

When the franchisee makes a contract with a third person, the franchisor is not liable on the contract as the franchisee is not the agent of the franchisor and does not have any authority to bind the franchisor by contract.

(a)   Actual Control. An exception is made to the foregoing rules when the franchisor exercises such actual control over the operations of the franchisee that the latter is not to be regarded as an independent contractor but rather as an employee or agent of the franchisor.[5] This conclusion is likely to be reached when the franchisee makes contracts in the name of the franchisor, the franchisor controls the hiring and firing of employees of the franchisee, and the franchisor alone can adjust customer complaints. Likewise, when a franchisee is highly controlled by the franchisor, the franchisor will be liable to a customer of the franchisee where a consumer protection statute seeks to protect consumers from exploitation by being charged for unused lessons, services, or goods.

(b)   Product Liability. When the franchise involves the resale of goods manufactured or obtained by the franchisor and supplied to the franchisee, there is a growing likelihood that, if the product causes harm to the franchisee's customer, the franchisor will be liable to the customer on theories of warranty [6] or strict tort liability. Similarly, when a franchisor establishes the standards under which franchisees make products, the franchisor is liable to an injured person as though the franchisor were a manufacturer or seller, even though the manufacturing franchisee is an independent contractor.

§ 45:4. The Franchisee and Third Persons. When the franchise holder has any contract relationship or contact with a third person, the contract or tort liability of the franchisee is the same as though there were no franchise. For example, if the franchise is to operate a restaurant, the franchise holder is liable to a customer for breach of an implied warranty of the fitness of the food for human consumption to the same extent as though the franchise holder were running an independent restaurant. If the franchise holder negligently causes harm to a third person, as by running over that person with a truck used in the enterprise, the conclusion is the same and the tort liability of the franchise holder is determined by the principles which would be applicable if no franchise existed. The franchise holder is liable on a contract made in the franchise holder's own name. The fact that there is a franchise does not add to or subtract from the liability which the franchisee would have in the same situation had there been no franchise.

---

[5] Murphy v Holiday Inns, Inc. (Va) 219 SE2d 874.
[6] UCC §§ 2-313, 2-314.

C. SPECIAL VENTURE ORGANIZATIONS

When joint or common participation is sought, a special venture organization might be formed instead of a decentralized structure, such as that in a franchise system, or instead of a standard organization, such as a corporation.

§ 45:5. Limited Partnership. A common form of modified partnership is the limited partnership. This form of partnership is solely a creature of statute: the Uniform Limited Partnership Act (ULPA).[7]

In a *limited partnership* certain members contribute capital without liability for firm debts beyond the loss of their investment. These members are known as *limited partners*. The partners who manage the business and are personally liable for the firm debts are *general partners*. A limited partnership can be formed by "one or more general partners and one or more limited partners." [8]

Unlike a general partnership, this special form can be created only by executing a certificate setting forth the essential details of the partnership and the relative rights of the partners. The certificate, when executed, must be recorded in the office of the official in charge of public records, such as the Recorder of Deeds, of the county in which the principal place of business of the partnership is located. When there is no proper filing of the limited partnership certificate, the participants have the status and liability of general partners in a general partnership.

The limited partner contributes cash or property but not services. With certain exceptions, the limited partner's name cannot appear in the firm name. The limited partner's rights are limited to receiving a share of the profits and the return of capital upon dissolution; the limited partner cannot exercise any control over the business. If improper use is made of the limited partner's name, giving the public the impression of being an active partner, or if the limited partner exercises any control over the business, the limited partner loses the protection of limited liability and becomes liable without limit as a general partner.

Limited partners cannot withdraw their capital contribution when it is needed to pay creditors.

Participation in the affairs of the business by the limited partners can only give rise to a liability to creditors of the partnership. The general partner cannot claim that such participation makes the limited partners bound to share in the losses of the enterprise.

The dissolution and winding up of limited partnerships is governed by the same principles applicable to general partnerships. In many respects, the ULPA follows the general pattern of the UPA, and a general partner in a limited partnership has the same rights and liabilities as a partner in a general partnership.[9]

§ 45:6. Joint Venture. A *joint venture,* or joint adventure, is a relationship in which two or more persons combine their labor or property for a single undertaking and share

---

[7] This Act has been adopted in all states except Louisiana, and is in force in the District of Columbia and the Virgin Islands.

[8] Uniform Limited Partnership Act, § 1.

[9] North Peachtree I-285 Properties, Ltd. v Hicks, 136 GaApp 426, 221 SE2d 607.

profits and losses equally, or as otherwise specified. Where several contractors pool all their assets in order to construct one tunnel, the relationship is a joint venture.

A joint venture is similar in many respects to a partnership, but it differs primarily in that the joint venture typically relates to the prosecution of a single enterprise or transaction, although its accomplishment may require several years, while a partnership is generally a continuing business or activity.[10] This is not an exact definition because a partnership may be expressly created for a single transaction. Because this distinction is so insubstantial, many courts hold that a joint venture is subject to the same principles of law as partnerships.[11] Thus, the duties owed by the joint venturers to each other are the same as in the case of partnerships, with the result that when the joint venturers agree to acquire and develop a certain tract of land but some of the venturers secretly purchase the land in their own names, the other joint venturers are entitled to damages for this breach of the duty of loyalty.

An agreement for farming operations that provides for sharing expenses and profits, or an agreement to purchase real estate for development and resale, will often be regarded as a joint venture.

It is essential that there be a community of interest or purpose and that each coadventurer have an equal right to control the operations or activities of the undertaking. The actual control of the operations may be entrusted to one of the joint adventurers. Thus, the fact that one joint adventurer is placed in control of the farming and livestock operations of the undertaking and appears to be the owner of the land does not destroy the joint adventure relationship.

As in the case of partnerships, a minor may be a member of a joint venture.

It is generally essential that the joint venture be for a business or commercial purpose.

The fact that there is a common business objective or goal does not establish that the persons seeking that objective or goal are engaged in a joint venture. The relationship may be merely a contract employing an independent contractor or an employee, or a sales contract. In determining whether a relationship is one of employment or a joint venture, it is often important to determine whether one person carries workers' compensation insurance with respect to the other, whether Social Security taxes are paid with respect to the other, and whether federal withholding tax deductions are made from the share of profits received by any of the persons involved. Persons who are joint venturers will ordinarily have unlimited joint and several liability with respect to obligations of the enterprise, without regard to whether they have signed any agreement or commercial paper executed on behalf of the venture.

(a) Duration of Joint Venture. When a joint venture agreement states the time for which the venture is to last, such specification will be given effect. In the absence of a fixed duration provision, a joint venture is ordinarily terminable at the will of any participant,[12] except that when the joint venture clearly relates to a particular transaction, such as the construction of a specified bridge, the joint venture ordinarily lasts until the particular transaction or project is completed or becomes impossible to complete.

---

[10] Ramacciotti v Simpkins (IllApp2d) 266 NE2d 700.
[11] Pedersen v Manitowoc Co. 25 NY2d 412, 306 NYS2d 903, 255 NE2d 146.
[12] Maimon v Telman, 40 Ill2d 535, 240 NE2d 652.

The term "joint venture" is descriptive of a relationship rather than of a structure or organization. Thus two joint venturers may organize a corporation for the purpose of carrying out their joint venture of constructing an apartment building. The relationship between the two is a joint venture even though the organization or structure employed is a corporation.

Sight is frequently lost of this distinction between relationship and structure for the reason that many joint ventures have no formal structure and therefore the relationship is the aspect which attracts attention.

(b) Third Person Liability. The conclusion that persons are joint venturers often becomes important when a suit is brought by or against a third person for personal injuries or property damage. If there is a joint venture, the fault or negligence of one venturer will be imputed to the other venturer so that the other venturer will lose the lawsuit because of the misconduct of the co-venturer.

§ 45:7. Mining Partnership. A *mining partnership* is an association formed for the purpose of conducting mining operations. In some states it is declared by statute that a mining partnership exists when two or more persons engage in working a mine claim. Apart from statute, the formation of such a partnership is a matter of intention, as in the case of an ordinary partnership, evidenced by words or conduct of the parties. The intent to create a mining partnership must be shown.

In many respects the mining partnership is governed by the same principles as an ordinary partnership. The authority of a mining partner to bind the mining partnership, however, is more limited than in the case of a general partnership. Ordinarily that authority is limited to matters that are necessary and proper or usual for the working of the mine. Moreover, the interest of a partner in a mining partnership is transferable, and the transferee becomes a partner in the partnership in the transferor's place without regard to the wishes of the other partners. Similarly, there is no dissolution when the interest of a partner passes to another person by operation of law, or when a partner becomes bankrupt or dies. Profits and losses, unless otherwise stipulated, are shared proportionately according to the contributions made or shares held by each partner.

§ 45:8. Syndicate. A *syndicate* is generally defined as an association of persons formed to conduct a particular business transaction, generally of a financial nature. Thus, a syndicate may be formed by which its members agree to contribute sufficient money to purchase the control of a railroad. One of the common types of this form of business is the *underwriting syndicate,* which is an organization of investment banks formed for the purpose of marketing large issues of stocks and bonds.

A syndicate may be incorporated, in which case it has the attributes of an ordinary corporation. If it is not incorporated, it is treated in many respects the same as a general partnership, although it is held that, as in the case of the mining partnership, the personal factor or relationship between the partners is not important. When this is so held, it also follows that the interest of each member is freely transferable and that the member's transferee succeeds to the member's rights.

§ 45:9. Unincorporated Association. An *unincorporated association* is a combination of two or more persons for the furtherance of a common nonprofit purpose. No particular form of organization is required, and any conduct or agreement indicating an attempt to associate or work together for a common purpose is sufficient. Social clubs, fraternal associations, and political parties are common examples of unincorporated associations.

The authority of an unincorporated association over its members is governed by ordinary principles of contract law, and an association cannot expel a member for a ground which is not expressly authorized by the contract between the association and the member.[13]

Generally the members of an unincorporated association are not liable for the debts or liabilities of the association by the mere fact that they are members. It is generally required to show that they authorized or ratified the act in question. (See p. 763, Libby v Perry) If either authorization or ratification by a particular member can be shown, that member is unlimitedly liable as in the case of a general partner.

Except when otherwise provided by statute, an unincorporated association does not have any legal existence, such as has a corporation, apart from the members who compose it. Thus, an unincorporated association cannot sue or be sued in its own name.

§ 45:10. Cooperative.

A *cooperative* consists of a group of two or more independent persons or enterprises which cooperate with respect to a common objective or function. Thus, farmers may pool their farm products and sell them as a group. Consumers may likewise pool their orders and purchase goods in bulk.

(a)   Incorporated Cooperative. Statutes commonly provide for the special incorporation of cooperative enterprises. Such statutes often provide that any excess of payments over cost of operation shall be refunded to each participant member in direct proportion to the volume of business which the member has done with the cooperative. This contrasts with the payment of a dividend by an ordinary business corporation in which the payment of dividends is proportional to the number of shares held by the shareholder and is unrelated to the extent of the shareholder's business activities with the enterprise. The fact that a cooperative is incorporated does not convert it into a corporation for all purposes, and it retains its fundamental characteristic of an association designed to render services to its members. (See p. 764, Lambert v Fisherman's Dock Cooperative, Inc.)

(b)   Antitrust Law Exemption. As the agreement by the members of sellers' cooperatives that all products shall be sold at a common price is an agreement to fix prices, the sellers' cooperative is basically an agreement in restraint of trade and a violation of antitrust laws. The Capper-Volstead Act of 1922 expressly exempts normal selling activities of farmers' and diarymen's cooperatives from the operation of the federal Sherman Antitrust Act as long as the cooperatives do not conspire with outsiders to fix prices.

§ 45:11. Business Trusts.

A *business trust, common-law trust,* or *Massachusetts trust* arises when the owners of property transfer the ownership to one or more persons, called *trustees,*

---

[13] Cunningham v Independent Soap & Chemical Workers, 207 Kan 812, 486 P2d 1316 (holding labor union without authority to expel members for crossing picket line and working during strike).

to be managed for business purposes by the trustees for the benefit of the original owners, called *beneficiaries.* In addition to the transfer of the legal title to the trustee or trustees, *trust certificates* or *trust shares* are issued to the beneficiaries as evidence of their interest, and profits are divided proportionally among the holders of the certificates.

Like shares in a corporation, shares in a business trust may be transferred. Unlike a corporation, the holders of the shares do not have control of the trustees running the business, as do shareholders of the board of directors of a corporation. Some courts hold that the business trust is merely a trust and the fact that it is designed for business operations, rather than to pay money for the support of certain persons or institutions, does not prevent the ordinary trust relationship law from applying. Other courts hold that for the purpose of taxation or the regulation of the business, the business trust is to be classified as a corporation with its rights and duties determined accordingly.

One of the objectives of the business trust is to achieve a limited liability for the beneficiaries. In most jurisdictions, the beneficiaries are not liable for the debts of the business trust if they have relinquished all control over management to the trustees. The same conclusion is reached if a clause in the agreement establishing the trust states that the beneficiary shall not be liable, at least with respect to persons dealing with the trust with knowledge or notice of such a limitation. In order to meet the requirement of providing knowledge of such a limitation to such third persons, it is common for the stationery of the business trust to state that such a limitation exists.

§ 45:12. Joint-Stock Company. *Joint-stock companies* are of common-law origin, although in a number of states they are now regulated by statute. This form of association has features resembling both a partnership and a corporation, or a business trust. Like a corporation, the shares of its members are transferable. The management of the company is generally delegated to designated persons because as a general rule membership is much larger than that of an ordinary partnership. The business is usually conducted under an impersonal name.

§ 45:13. Expansion of Participant Liability. The fact that the relationship between persons is not a partnership, a joint venture, or a similar organization does not necessarily establish that a member of the enterprise is not liable to third persons. There is a judicial trend in favor of imposing liability on persons participating in an enterprise or economic activity when it may be reasonably foreseen that harm may be caused third persons. This concept is distinct from the supervisory and vicarious liability of an employer for the acts of an employee, or the product liability of a manufacturer or seller, but the same underlying force of protecting the third person or the consumer may be seen at work.

For example, under this new view it has been held that a savings and loan association financing a home construction project owed a duty to purchasers of the homes to see that the houses were not defectively constructed; and when cutting corners on construction costs made the homes defective but private buyers could not determine this fact for themselves, the savings and loan association was liable on a negligence basis to the purchasers even though there was no privity of contract between them, and the failure in duty of the governmental building inspectors did not relieve the association of such liability.[14]

As an aspect of participant liability, the character of one participant may affect the status of another. For example, where a state government and a private enterprise are joint venturers or partners in a profit-making venture, the discriminatory conduct of the private enterprise may be deemed "state action" within the meaning of the constitutional guarantee of equal protection.[15]

---

[14] Connor v Great Western Savings and Loan Ass'n, 69 Cal2d 850, 73 CalRptr 369, 447 P2d 609 (a dissenting opinion was filed on the ground that the financer had no control over the construction work and that any duty owed by the financer was to its shareholders and not to the purchasers of the homes). California Civil Code § 3434 was amended after the Connor decision so as to limit the Connor doctrine by prohibiting liability of a lender to third persons for the negligent construction work of a borrower as long as the lender does not engage in any nonlending activity and is not a party to any misrepresentations. Bradley v Craig, 274 CalApp2d 466, 79 CalRptr 401, refused to apply the Connor concept in an individual construction loan transaction when the lender was deemed to do nothing more than lend money.

[15] Burton v Wilmington Parking Authority, 365 US 715. See also Lucas v Wisconsin Electric Power Company (CA7 Wis) 466 F2d 638 cert den 409 US 1114.

CASES FOR CHAPTER 45

Shor-Line Rambler v American Motors Sales Corp.

(CA7 Ill) 543 F2d 601 (1976)

Schoenbacher owned an American Motors franchise known as Shor-Line Rambler, Inc. American Motors notified him that within ninety days he must make specified extensive personnel changes and an expansion of facilities. When he failed to do so, American Motors terminated his franchise. Shor-Line then sued for damages under the Automobile Dealers' Day in Court Act on the theory that in terminating the franchise, American Motors had not acted in good faith. From a judgment for Shor-Line Rambler, American Motors appealed.

CAMPBELL, S.D.J. . . . The verdict was abundantly supported by evidence which established that Shor-Line had suffered faithfully through the hard years with American Motors and that as recently as 1971, American Motors had reported that Shor-Line's facilities were adequate. Then, abruptly in 1972 Shor-Line was given 90 days to totally change its character. Not only were extensive personnel changes required, but new facilities were requested, all of which demanded unreasonable and unrealistic expenses for the dealer.

Despite Shor-Line's efforts to comply with some of the demands, American Motors terminated the franchise. The evidence supports the jury's finding against American Motors.

The issue of American Motors' bad faith involves its intentions as manifested by its actions. This is a factual determination for the jury. . . . Therefore, even though some evidence was introduced to support the contention that American Motors may have been justified in terminating Shor-Line, the jury heard the evidence and returned its verdict. We find no basis for disturbing this verdict on appeal. . . . The damages awarded to Shor-Line were not contrary to the manifest weight of the evidence. Shor-Line's expert witness testified as to his estimate of the damages over a ten-year period. Even though this information was introduced by Shor-Line, American Motors never objected to the use of the ten-year period. Further, a statement made by the President of American Motors, William Luneberg, was introduced into evidence:

". . . by the end of this decade, we'll get one-half a million car sales, and I don't care what the hell the market is then." American Motors' General Sales Manager agreed with Luneberg's projection. Based on this evidence, the jury was justified in determining the damages over a ten-year period. It was properly a question for the jury to determine, Auto-west, Inc. v Peugeot, Inc. 434 F.2d 556 (2d Cir. 1970), and likewise will not be disturbed on appeal.

Apart from the ten-year time frame, future profits are a reasonable damages award. In an action under the Automobile Dealer's Day in Court Act, the Tenth Circuit has held that "[t]o be meaningful, such damages must include the amount of money that the dealer could have obtained in the future from the profits from his franchise.". . . It was not unreasonable for the jury to infer that Shor-Line would have received profits during this ten-year period but for the termination . . .

[Judgment affirmed]

Brown v Computer Credit System, Inc.

128 Ga App 429, 197 SE2d 165 (1973)

Computer Credit System operated a computerized credit card system. Brown paid $10,000 as a fee for a franchise to sell membership in the system to local stores. Brown sued to recover the $10,000, basing his claim on the local statute which provided that the purchaser of unregistered securities could sue the seller to recover the purchase price. From a judgment for Computer, Brown appealed.

EBERHARDT, P.J. . . . Brown appeals, raising the sole question of whether the agreement is a "security" subject to the provisions of the Securities Act. . . .

In Georgia Market Centers, Inc. v Fortson, 225 Ga 854, 171 SE2d 620, the Supreme Court held that a similar agreement was not a security within the ambit of the [Georgia] Securities Act. . . . The test adopted there . . . is that an "investment contract" . . . is a security if the scheme involves an investment of money in a common enterprise with profits to come solely from the efforts of others, provided that the person investing capital supplies no more than token participation. There, however, as here, the investor is entitled to no return under the agreement except through his own efforts. In the instant case the agreement provides that the only way for Brown to realize profits is to sell the company's services within his territory, and that he has no right to participate in the company's profits or losses except to the extent of profits derived from business produced by his sales activities. He may, of course, procure the assistance of others in selling the service to merchants. Hence, under the test laid

down in the *Market Centers* case . . . we hold that the "Master Franchise Agreement" involved here is not a "security" within the meaning of the Securities Act.

It is urged that the test [above] set forth . . . is not adequate to meet the ever increasing flood of "franchise" systems which are being sold across the country, and that the test of an "investment contract" should be expanded to include the consideration of whether the franchisee's money is being used as risk capital by the franchisor. However, we are bound by the ruling in *Market Centers* that where the contract promises no return to the franchisee except in connection with his own efforts, the contract is not a "security" within the meaning of the Securities Act. . . .

[Judgment affirmed]

B. P. Oil Corporation v Mabe

(MdApp) 370 A2d 554 (1977)

The B. P. Oil company leased an automobile service station to Faison. Mabe drove his automobile into this service station for water. The attendant poured water into the radiator. The water apparently contained some gasoline. There was an explosion and Mabe was injured. He sued the B. P. Oil Corporation for his injury on the theory that Faison was the corporation's agent and the corporation was therefore liable for the negligence which led to the explosion. From a judgment for Mabe, the oil corporation appealed.

SMITH, J. . . . We conclude that Mabe failed to establish either actual agency or agency by estoppel. . . .

The service station in question was painted yellow and green, said to be the BP colors. There was a large BP sign on a pole hanging over the station; BP insignia appeared on the gasoline pumps; there was a tow truck present with a BP sign on it, and the attendant in question wore a uniform with yellow and green BP emblems on his jacket and cap.

The service station building was leased by the owner to Faison. He leased it to BP who in turn leased it back to Faison. Gasoline tanks, pumps and signs were owned by BP. Under the agreement between Faison and BP, Faison was required to "furnish, install and display continuously on the exterior of the station at a point visible and accessible to the public, a legible sign showing that [he was] occupying said station under a lease and [was] the sole owner of the business." Mabe was asked by his attorney whether there was "any sign up that said anything about being operated by anybody other than BP," to which he replied in the negative. The record is otherwise silent as to such a sign.

Under the agreement between BP and Faison he was to buy a minimum of 180,000 gallons of gasoline per year, which works out to 15,000 gallons per month. He testified, however, that he "was only buying 400 gallons of gasoline per week," a reason given for the fact that he did not participate in any promotion of BP, saying that he could not "afford to on that."

. . . The profit to be derived by Faison from the operation of the service station in question came . . . from the difference between the buying price and selling price of the gasoline and other items sold by him after deduction of other expenses of operation.

Faison was paid no salary or commission by BP. Any employees were hired, fired, and paid by him. He was required to make no reports to BP relative to his sales and service operation. He paid his own sales and other taxes. BP had no control over the hours of station operation, the hours of operation being fixed by Faison. Faison paid cash on delivery for that which he bought. If he did not have the money to pay, he did not obtain the product. He provided his own uniforms and said that BP never told him that he had to wear a uniform of any kind.

We first address ourselves to whether actual agency was established. . . .

The presence or absence of control is an essential element in determining whether a master-servant relationship exists. . . .

Cases from other jurisdictions . . . have recognized control as a necessary element and have found insufficient evidence of control to warrant a conclusion of the existence of a master-servant relationship and thus of actual agency in factual situations analogous to the case at bar. . . .

[Citing cases the court said:]

"It is indeed a matter of common knowledge and practice that distinctive colors and trademark signs are displayed at gasoline stations by independent dealers of petroleum product suppliers. These signs and emblems represent no more than notice to the motorist that a

given company's products are being marketed at the station. . . .

"Whether relation of master and servant does in fact exist between lessor of gasoline station and its lessee so as to render the doctrine of respondeat superior applicable, depends on whether lessor has the right to control, or exercises the right to control, lessee in the details of the work to be performed in the operation and management of the station."

The evidence adduced on behalf of Mabe simply does not show that BP controlled Faison's operations. Accordingly, actual agency was not established.

The law applicable to such an agency [by estoppel] is that stated in Restatement (Second) of Agency § 267 (1958):

"One who represents that another is his servant or other agent and thereby causes a third person justifiably *to rely* upon the care or skill of such apparent agent is subject to liability to the third person for harm caused by the lack of care or skill of the one appearing to be a servant or other agent as if he were such." (Emphasis added.)

. . . Reliance is necessary to establish agency by estoppel. . . .

"Estoppel is always a matter personal to the individual asserting it and he must therefore show that he was misled by the appearances relied upon. It is not enough that he might have been, or that some one else was, so misled. It must also appear that he had reasonable cause to believe that the authority existed; mere belief without cause, or belief in the face of facts that should have put him on his guard is not enough.". . .

A number of courts around the country have stated the law in the above fashion and have failed, in circumstances analogous to the case at bar, to find liability upon a defendant such as BP in the instant case.

Reynolds v Skelly Oil Co., 227 Iowa 163, 287 N.W. 823 (1939), where the court said:

"The argument of appellee that the Skelly Oil Company was estopped because of the signs displayed and that, because of such signs, there was a presumption that the station was owned by the Skelly Oil Company has no support in reason or authority. As well argue that, because the word 'Chevrolet' or 'Buick' is displayed in front of a place of business, General Motors would be estopped to claim that it was not the owner of the business. It is a matter of common knowledge that these trademark signs are displayed throughout the country by independent dealers.". . .

. . . We need not discuss any factors of agency by estoppel other than that of reliance because Mabe has fallen far short of having established any such reliance when he entered Faison's service station.

Mabe . . . said he was attracted to Faison's station by "nothing except for the [fact that it was a] BP station, [and it] had BP signs, BP gas, BP pumps." This, added to the statement of Mabe that his reason for choosing the station in question was that he "always buy[s] BP gasoline, always deal[s] with BP," is but little different from a statement that one always buys a particular make of shoes, wears clothes with a certain label, drives an automobile produced by a certain manufacturer, eats a certain brand of breakfast cereal, or smokes a certain kind of cigarette. In short, the record lacks any evidence of reliance upon the part of Mabe. There has been comment in some of the cases and in the brief of Mabe relative to advertising which may have enticed prospective customers into places of business. The record in this instance is completely silent as to any advertising on the part of BP.

. . . There is no evidence of any kind of reliance on the part of Mabe and no evidence of actual agency. . . .

[Judgment reversed and action remanded]

Libby v Perry

(Me) 311 A2d 527 (1973)

National Guard units based at the Augusta State Armory held an annual New Year's Eve dance. The dance was run and funds were handled by an Armory Committee which was composed of officers from the various guard units at the Armory. Perry was a member of the Armory Committee. Libby was a paying guest at the dance and on leaving fell on ice in the parking lot. He sued Perry and the other members of the Armory Committee. The evidence showed that every member of the committee had taken some part in planning or running the dance

with the exception of Turner who took no part and was absent from all meetings of the committee. Judgment was entered in favor of Libby against all defendants and they appealed.

DUFRESNE, C.J. . . . The Armory Committee, [is] a voluntary unincorporated association and a nonentity at common law. . . .

Mr. Perry testified it was his opinion that on becoming an officer he automatically became a member of the Armory Committee. In the absence of any evidence that the official duties of an officer in the National Guard required participation in an association organized to conduct social activities, albeit for the benefit of the Guard, acceptance of membership in such association must be viewed as voluntary on the part of the accepting member, subjecting him to whatever liability the law applicable to voluntary unincorporated associations may impose.

A voluntary unincorporated association, formed to accomplish a common purpose, is duty bound to use the same care to avoid injury to others as natural persons are individually, but mere membership in the associate body does not make all the members liable for any and all unlawful or negligent acts of their associates. . . .

In the case of a voluntary association such as the Armory Committee, dedicated by the mandate of its bylaws to promote social services for the immediate benefit of its members and the ultimate interest of the National Guard units located at the Augusta Armory, while at the same time enhancing good public relations between the Guard and the area residents through their sponsored social events, individual members of the association do not, merely by virtue of their membership in such association, subject themselves to liability for injuries sustained as a result of the negligent conduct of their associates or their agents in the running of the social event sponsored by the association. Liability attaches only to those members of the association who are shown to have actively participated in the affair resulting in plaintiff's injuries. . . .

In the instant case, the evidence was sufficient to support the factual inference that the Armory Committee had assumed control of the premises . . . The defect which caused the plaintiff's fall and consequential injuries was shown to have existed for a sufficient period of time to have permitted protective action such as salting and sanding and that the members of the Armory Committee or their agents, in charge of the affair, in the exercise of reasonable care should have known of, or discovered, the dangerous condition caused by the frozen ruts in the immediate approaches to the steps leading to the armory building where the dance was being held. The minutes of the meeting of the Committee in April 1966, indicating a unanimous vote of the attending members setting the charge of $2.00 per person for the New Year's Eve ball, establishes not only their presence at the meeting, but also, by justifiable inference, an active participation in the planned event by the defendants Pillsbury, Nichols, Bryant, Laflin, Perry, Fenderson, Quinn, Colford and Weymouth. The defendants Madore and Tondreau were shown to have approved the affair by the evidentiary records showing that they respectively held the office of treasurer during the period of planning and staging of the dance. The jury could have inferred active participation of the other defendants Musk, Lasso, Jacques, Hayes, Gagnon, Morang, Liscomb, Richards, and Drapeau, by reason of their attendance record immediately prior to the holding of the event. Defendant Storr's direct involvement was evidenced by the fact that he applied for the use of the Armory. The record, on the other hand, is silent respecting defendant Turner's participation in, or attendance at, the meeting of the Committee in April, 1966 and indicates that he was absent from the October, November and December, 1966 meetings which preceded the dance. Under such circumstances, it was error as a matter of law for the jury to find the defendant Turner responsible to the plaintiff with the other defendants on the mere evidence that he was a member of the Armory Committee. All the other defendants actively participated, aided, and abetted in the affair and are responsible to the plaintiff for the wrongful acts of omission of their associates or their agents in carrying out the social event duly authorized by the association. . . .

In the instant case, all the actively participating defendant members of the Armory Committee owed the plaintiff. . . the positive duty of exercising through their associates or agents in charge of the dance reasonable care to provide him with walkways or areaways reasonably safe from unreasonable risk of harm in the light of the totality of the existing circumstances. . . .

[Judgment reversed as to Turner but sustained as to other defendants]

Lambert v Fisherman's Dock Cooperative, Inc.

115 NJ Super 424, 280 A2d 193 (1971)

Lambert was a member of the Fisherman's Dock Cooperative, Inc. The cooperative changed its bylaws to provide that when a shareholder's membership in the cooperative was terminated, the shareholder was to receive what had been paid for the shares rather than the book value of the shares. Lambert's membership was terminated and he claimed that he was entitled to the book value of the shares in spite of the contrary bylaw. Lambert sued Fisherman's Dock and a judgment was entered in his favor. Fisherman's Dock appealed.

LABRECQUE, J.A.D. . . . Briefly stated, plaintiff's theory of recovery was that when he purchased his two shares of the association's stock he was purchasing a "growth" stock; since the net worth of the association increased substantially in value thereafter, his interest had increased in proportion; thus he should be paid an amount equal to the net worth of the association, regardless of its liquidity. He argued that by changing the bylaws the association destroyed the "growth potential" of his shares, and thus breached its contract with him as a shareholder.

The court below appears to have accepted plaintiff's theory as to the nature of his relationship with the association. It held that the provision in the bylaws fixing the amount to be paid an expelled member for his stock constituted a contract between plaintiff and defendant and vested in plaintiff certain rights which could not be altered without his assent, even though all of the other shareholders, acting in concert, agreed. He ruled that it made no difference whether the corporation was one formed under Title 34 of the Revised Statutes or one formed under Title 14; that the association's stock bore all of the essential characteristics of stock issued by corporations formed primarily for profit. We find ourselves in disagreement.

A cooperative association is a unique institution, differing in many of its essentials from a corporation organized for profit. The relationship between such an association and one of its members is in many respects the antithesis of that which exists between a corporation organized under the General Corporation Act and its stockholders. The latter exists for the purpose of making a profit for its stockholders and its activities are geared to the accomplishment of that end. The amount of dividends paid each stockholder, as well as the number of votes he may cast, depend upon the number of shares held by him. . . .

A cooperative association, on the other hand, has been defined as a democratic association of persons organized to furnish themselves an economic service under a plan that eliminates entrepreneur profit and that provides for substantial equality of ownership and control. . . . In general, each shareholder has equal ownership and exercises an equal share in the control of the association, regardless of the number of shares of stock he holds. . . . By its very nature a cooperative is not designed to make a profit, and the return on capital, if authorized, is limited. . . . Usually, such profits as may be realized from the association's activities are proportionately divided among the shareholders on the basis of the amount of their patronage during the period the profit was earned. . . .

A significant characteristic of a cooperative is the right of the association to restrict ownership of its shares to those availing themselves of its services, to restrict the number of shares held by a member and to prohibit or limit transfers of stock. . . .

A cooperative may also specify how members may withdraw or otherwise be separated from membership, and the amount to be paid them upon such withdrawal or separation. . . .

Plaintiff contends that upon the cancellation of his stock he was entitled to receive its fair book value as prescribed by the appropriate section of the bylaws in effect at the time the stock was issued to him. Defendant contends that the section of the bylaws which was in effect at the time plaintiff's membership was terminated governs; hence he is entitled to receive no more than the cost of acquisition of his stock. Plaintiff counters that the amended bylaws could not affect his rights under the original bylaws in the absence of his assent to the new bylaws.

We hold that the amended bylaws controlled the redemption of defendant's shares in 1965, and that he thereby became entitled to receive only the price he had paid for his shares. Defendant had no vested right to his proportionate share of the "full book value" of the assets of the cooperative, regardless of how that term might be defined. To permit a member who voluntarily withdraws or who is no longer eligible to membership, to take with him a share of the association's assets based upon his stock holdings, would not only pose the possibility of financial ruin to such an association but would run contrary to the very principles which govern its existence. . . .

[Judgment reversed]

QUESTION AND CASE PROBLEMS

1. What social forces are affected by the federal Automobile Dealers Day in Court Act?

2. Compare a special partnership and a joint venture.

3. Compare a franchise and a contract.

4. Compare a limited and a general partnership with respect to (a) formality of creation, (b) duration, and (c) liability of partners.

5. Food Caterers, Inc. of East Hartford Connecticut, obtained a franchise from Chicken Delight, Inc. to use that name at its store and agreed to the product standards and controls specified by the franchisor. The franchise contract required the franchisee to maintain a free delivery service in order to deliver hot, freshly prepared food to customers. The franchisee used a delivery truck which bore no sign or name. Its employee Carfiro drove the truck in making a delivery of food. He negligently struck and killed McLaughlin. The victim's estate sued Chicken Delight on the theory that Carfiro was its agent because he was doing the work which Chicken Delight required to be done and which benefited Chicken Delight. Was Carfiro the agent of Chicken Delight? [McLaughlin's Estate v Chicken Delight, Inc., 164 Conn 317, 321 A2d 456]

6. Simpson and Saunders each had a used car dealer's license. They made an agreement to run their businesses independently but to share a lot, the building thereon, the furnishings, and the use of a telephone. Bates sued both Simpson and Saunders claiming that they were joint venturers and therefore both were liable for the fraudulent conduct of Simpson. Was Saunders liable? [Bates v Simpson, 121 Utah 165, 239 P2d 749]

7. A limited partnership owned and operated a marina under the name of West River Marina, Ltd. Radack was the general partner. McCully and others were limited partners. The partnership did not pay its debts and a foreclosure action was brought against it. McCully and other limited partners petitioned the court for permission to intervene in the foreclosure action on the theory that the action was a sham which was planned by Radack and others as a way of wiping out the interests of the limited partners and thus acquiring the property for themselves. Radack and the others objected to the intervention on the ground that limited partners have no voice in the management of a limited partnership and therefore could not take part in litigation. Should the intervention be allowed? [McCully v Radack, 27 Md App 350, 340 A2d 374]

8. Nissan was the distributor of Datsuns in the United States. Randy's Datsun and two other dealers held dealer franchises for the Salt Lake City area and were in competition with each other. The other two dealers complained to Nissan that Randy's was cutting prices. Nissan warned Randy to maintain higher prices and attempted to persuade Randy to move outside the city. Randy refused because the last dealer to go there had gone bankrupt. A shortage of Datsuns arose and Nissan allocated the limited supply by a formula which had the effect of reducing the supply to Randy's and increasing the supply to the other two dealers. Thereafter Nissan notified Randy's that he would not renew the franchise agreement with Randy's. Randy's sued Nissan for damages for bad faith termination of the franchise in violation of the federal Automobile Dealers' Franchise Act. Was Nissan liable? [Randy's v Nissan Motor Corp. (CA10 Utah) 533 F2d 510]

9. Woods Mill was a limited partnership formed for the construction of an apartment complex. Financial difficulties arose and some of the limited partners discussed the economic problems with their general partner. One of the limited partners visited the construction site and complained as to the manner in which the work was being done. Thereafter the building contractor defaulted. The limited partners were sued for the breach of the contract on the theory that they had so participated in the business that they were liable as general partners. Were they liable? [Trans-Am Builders Inc. v Woods Mill Ltd., 133 GaApp 411, 210 SE2d 866]

10. Brenner was in the scrap iron business. Almost daily Plitt loaned Brenner money with which to purchase scrap iron. The agreement of the parties was that when the scrap was sold, Plitt would be repaid and would receive an additional sum as compensation for making the loan. The loans were to be repaid in any case, without regard to whether Brenner made a profit. A dispute arose as to the relationship between the two men. Plitt claimed that it was a joint venture. Decide. [Brenner v Plitt, 182 Md 348, 34 A2d 853]

11. Merrilees, Hopkins, Mayer, and Adams formed a limited partnership but did not record their partnership agreement until 49 days after the partnership business began operations. Stowe, a creditor, claimed that a general partnership had been created because of the delay in filing the agreement. Decide. [Stowe v Merrilees, 6 Cal App 2d 217, 44 P2d 368]

Part Ten • Corporations

46 Nature, Creation, and Termination of Corporations

The corporation is one of the most important forms of business organization. To the large-scale enterprise it offers an easier way to finance itself by means of dividing its ownership into many small units that can be sold to a wide economic range of customers. In addition to assisting financing operations, the corporate device offers a limited liability to the persons interested in the enterprise and a perpetual succession not affected by the death of any particular owner or by the transfer of the shares of any particular owner. Because of its limited liability, the corporation is also popular with many smaller businesses.

A. NATURE AND CLASSES

A *corporation* is an entity, an artificial legal being, created by government grant and endowed with certain powers. That is, the corporation exists in the eyes of the law as a person, separate and distinct from the people who own the corporation.

This concept means that property of the corporation is not owned by the persons who own shares in the corporation, but by the corporation. Debts of the corporation are debts of this artificial person and not of the people running the corporation or owning shares of stock in it. The corporation can sue and be sued in its own name with respect to corporate rights and liabilities, but the shareholders cannot sue or be sued as to those rights and liabilities. Furthermore, a parent corporation and its subsidiary corporation are regarded as separate entities. (See p. 780, Branmar Theater Co. v Branmar, Inc.)

A corporation is formed by obtaining approval of a *certificate of incorporation, articles of incorporation,* or a *charter* from the state or national government.[1] The

---

[1] In speaking of corporate matters, one is likely to become confused by the use of the terms "charter," "articles of incorporation," and "certificate of incorporation." Under the modern statute the word "charter" is generally replaced with "certificate of incorporation." That is, an application is filed for a certificate of incorporation rather than requesting or petitioning the government to grant or issue a charter. The application for a certificate of incorporation is accompanied by the blueprint of the proposed corporation or its articles of incorporation. The approval of the application in effect makes "official" the right of the corporation to exist and to follow the pattern or blueprint of the articles of incorporation.

persons who developed the idea of forming a corporation and who induce others to join in the enterprise are called *promoters.* The persons who make the application for the charter are called *incorporators.*

§ 46:1. Classifications of Corporations.

(a) Public, Private, and Quasi-Public Corporations. A *public corporation* is one established for governmental purposes and for the administration of public affairs. A city is a public or municipal corporation acting under authority granted to it by the state.

A *private corporation* is one established by private interests, whether for charitable and benevolent purposes or for purposes of finance, industry, and commerce. Private corporations are often called "public" in business circles when the stock is sold to the public.

A *quasi-public corporation,* which is also known as a public service corporation or a public utility, is a private corporation furnishing services upon which the public is particularly dependent. Examples of this class of corporation are those operating railroads, canals, and bridges or those supplying gas, electricity, and water. Such corporations are usually given special franchises and powers, such as the power of eminent domain.

(b) Public Authorities. In the twentieth century, the public is increasingly demanding that government perform services. Some of these are performed directly by government. Others are performed by separate corporations or *authorities* that are created by government. For example, a city parking facility may be organized as a separate *municipal parking authority.* A public low-cost housing project may be operated as an independent *housing authority.*

(c) Domestic and Foreign Corporations. If a corporation has been created under the law of a particular state or nation, it is called a *domestic corporation* with respect to that state or nation. Any other corporation going into that state or nation is called a *foreign corporation.* Thus a corporation holding a Texas charter is a domestic corporation in Texas but a foreign corporation in all other states and nations. This distinction becomes important in considering the extent of control that may be exercised by a government over corporations operating within its territorial boundaries. Whether a corporation is domestic is determined without regard to the residence of its shareholders or incorporators, or the state in which it conducts business. A corporation created under the law of one nation is classified as an *alien corporation* in other nations.

(d) Special Service Corporations. Corporations formed for transportation, banking, insurance, savings and loan operations, and similar specialized functions, are subject to separate codes or statutes with regard to their organization. In addition, federal and state laws and administrative agencies regulate in detail the manner in which their business is conducted.

(e) Close Corporations. A corporation whose shares are held by a single shareholder or a closely-knit group of shareholders is known as a *close corporation.* The shares are not traded publicly. Many such corporations are small firms which in the past would have operated as proprietorships or partnerships but are incorporated either to obtain the advantages of limited liability or a tax benefit, or both.

It would be foolish to require a close corporation to follow the same procedure as a large corporation; and statutes have in many states liberalized the corporation law when close corporations are involved, as by permitting their incorporation by a smaller number of persons, allowing them to have a one-person board of directors, and eliminating the requirement of formal meetings.[2]

(f) Professional Corporations. In every state, a corporation may be organized for the purpose of conducting a profession. The fact that professional persons may form a corporation does not permit a converse conclusion that any corporation may render professional services. To some extent a corporation may supply professional services to its members.[3]

(g) Nonprofit Corporations. A *nonprofit corporation* (or an eleemosynary corporation) is one that is organized for charitable or benevolent purposes, such as certain hospitals, homes, and universities.[4] Special procedure for incorporation is sometimes prescribed, with provision being made for a detailed examination and hearing as to the purpose, function, and methods of raising money for the enterprise.

§ 46:2. Power to Create a Corporation. Since by definition a corporation is created by government grant, the right to be a corporation must be obtained from the proper government.

(a) Federal Power. The federal government may create corporations whenever appropriate to carry out the powers granted to it.

(b) State Power. Generally a state by virtue of its police power may create any kind of corporation for any purpose. Most states have a *general corporation code* that lists certain requirements, and anyone who satisfies the requirements and files the necessary papers with the government may automatically become a corporation. The American Bar Association has proposed a Model Business Corporation Act (ABA MBCA).[5] There is no uniform corporation act.

§ 46:3. Regulation of Corporations. In addition to determining whether a corporate power exists, it is necessary to consider whether there is any government regulation imposed

---

[2] This distinction between big and little corporations is part of the same current of legal development that in the Uniform Commercial Code has given rise to the distinction between the merchant seller or buyer, on the one hand, and the casual seller or buyer, on the other.

[3] A labor union has a constitutional right to employ a lawyer on a salary basis to provide free legal services for union members. United Mine Workers v Illinois State Bar Association, 389 US 217. A union may also recommend to its members individual attorneys for the purpose of suing under the federal Employers' Liability Act and may obtain the commitment of such attorneys that they will not charge more than 25 percent of any recovery. United Transportation Union v State Bar of Michigan, 401 US 576.

[4] Gilbert v McLeod Infirmary, 219 SC 174, 64 SE2d 524. The Committee on Corporate Laws of the American Bar Association has prepared a Model Non-Profit Corporation Act as a companion to the Model Business Association Act. The Non-Profit Corporation Act has formed the basis for nonprofit corporation statutes in Alabama, Iowa, Nebraska, North Carolina, North Dakota, Ohio, Oregon, Texas, Virginia, Washington, Wisconsin, and the District of Columbia.

[5] This Act or its later revisions has been adopted, or has influenced legislation in a substantial number of states.

upon the exercise of that power. Both the federal and state governments, by virtue of their power to create corporations, can exercise control over them.

Domestic corporations are regulated by the provisions of the code or general statutes under which they are organized and also by the tax laws and general laws of the state of their origin. A foreign corporation is also subject to regulation and taxation in every state in which it does business, except as later noted. Generally a foreign corporation must register to do business within the state.

In regulating a corporation, state and national governments must observe certain limitations because corporations come within the protection of certain constitutional guarantees.

(a)   The Corporation as a Person. The Constitution of the United States prohibits the national government and the state governments from depriving any "person" of life, liberty, or property without due process of law. Many state constitutions contain a similar limitation upon their respective state governments. A corporation is regarded as a "person" within the meaning of such provisions.

The federal Constitution prohibits a state from denying to any "person" within its jurisdiction the equal protection of the laws. No such express limitation is placed upon the federal government, although the due process clause binding the federal government is liberally interpreted so that it prohibits substantial inequality of treatment.

While a corporation is regarded as a "person" with respect to rights and liabilities, a corporation is not regarded as a person within a statute which uses the term to refer to natural persons. Thus, a corporation cannot claim that its lawsuit should be given priority at trial because a state statute grants such a priority to a "person" 65 years old or over.

(b)   The Corporation as a Citizen. For certain purposes, such as determining the right to bring a lawsuit in a federal court, a corporation is today deemed a "citizen" of any state in which it has been incorporated and of the state where it has its principal place of business, without regard to the actual citizenship of the individual persons owning the stock of the corporation. Thus, the corporation incorporated in New York is a New York corporation even though its shareholders are citizens of many other states. Likewise, a Delaware corporation having its principal place of business in New York is deemed a citizen of New York as well as Delaware.[6] An environmental protection law authorizing any "citizen" to bring suit to prevent pollution permits a corporation to bring such a suit.

The federal Constitution prohibits states from abridging "the privileges or immunities of citizens of the United States." A corporation, however, is not regarded as a "citizen" within the clause. Thus, with one exception, a foreign corporation has no constitutional right to do business in another state if that other state wishes to exclude it. For example, Pennsylvania can deny a New York corporation the right to come into Pennsylvania to do business. As a practical matter, most states do not exclude foreign corporations but seize upon this power as justifying special regulation or taxation. On this basis it is commonly provided that a foreign corporation must

---

[6] 28 United States Code § 1332(c).

register or even take out a domestic charter, file copies of its charter, pay certain taxes, or appoint a resident agent before it can do business within the state.

As an exception to the power of a state, a state cannot require a license or registration of a foreign interstate commerce corporation or impose a tax on the right to engage in such a business.

The citizenship of a corporation is ordinarily not affected by the fact that it acquires the stock or assets of another corporation.

§ 46:4. Ignoring the Corporate Entity.

Ordinarily each corporation will be regarded and treated as a separate legal person and the law will not look behind a corporation to see who owns or controls it.

The fact that a parent or holding company and a subsidiary company have officers and directors or shareholders in common is not sufficient ground for ignoring the separate corporate entity of each corporation. Thus an employee of a subsidiary corporation cannot sue the parent corporation for injuries sustained at work.[7]

The fact that two corporations have identical shareholders does not justify a court in regarding the two corporations as being one. Likewise the fact that there is a close working relationship between two corporations does not in itself constitute any basis for ignoring their separate corporate entities when they in fact are separately run enterprises.

In some instances, the corporate entity is ignored, however, and rights and liabilities are determined as though there were no corporation and as though the shareholders were the persons doing the act performed by the corporation, meaning that they do not obtain the various advantages of being a corporation. It is frequently held that the inadequate capitalization of a corporation is a strong factor in reaching the conclusion that the corporate entity is to be disregarded.[8]

(a) Prevention of Fraud or Illegality. When the corporation is formed to perpetrate a fraud or to conceal illegality, a court will ordinarily ignore the corporate entity, or as it is figuratively called, "pierce the corporate veil." [9] For example, if enemy aliens are not eligible to purchase or own particular kinds of property, they cannot organize an American corporation and purchase the property in the name of the corporation. In such a case, a court will look behind the corporation to see that the alien enemies are really the persons involved and will not allow them to defeat the law by the device of forming a corporation. Similarly a buyer under a requirements contract remains liable even though the buyer incorporates the business in the effort to avoid the contract obligation.

When a person engages in business and uses the corporation as a mask by which to hide from a person being defrauded, the law will ignore the separate corporate entity and will hold the wrongdoer liable for the acts of the corporation on the theory that it is the *alter ego* of the wrongdoer.

---

[7] Fanfan v Berwin Corp. (DC Pa) 362 FSupp 793.

[8] Automotriz Del Golfo v Resnick, 47 Cal2d 792, 306 P2d 1.

[9] It is likely that the enforcement of the obligation of good faith imposed by Uniform Commercial Code § 1-203 will result in ignoring a corporate entity in some cases. Thompson v United States (CA8 Tex) 408 F2d 1075.

(b)   Prevention of Injustice. Disregarding the corporate entity is not limited to cases of actual fraud or illegality. The corporate entity may also be disregarded to prevent injustice or inequitable consequences. (See p. 781, Cohen v Williams)

(c)   Functional Reality. When a corporation is in effect merely a department of a large enterprise, as when a large manufacturer incorporates its marketing department, it is likely that the separate corporate character of the incorporated department will be ignored.

In some instances a court will hold that there is such an identity between a local subsidiary corporation doing business within the state and the foreign parent corporation that the latter may be regarded as doing business within the state. For example, where the question was whether the parent corporation was doing business within the state, it was concluded that since the marketing corporation was admittedly doing business within the state and since it was merely a department or branch of the parent holding corporation, the holding corporation was to be deemed doing business within the state; as opposed to the contention that the corporation doing business within the state was a different legal person distinct from the parent holding corporation.

The concept of the unity of a parent corporation and its incorporated subsidiary has been carried even to the extent of holding the subsidiary responsible for the tort of the parent corporation.

(1)   Independent Subsidiary Corporation. The close functional relation between a parent corporation and a subsidiary does not require that a court ignore the separate corporate entity of the subsidiary. If the subsidiary is in fact operating independently of the parent, its separate identity will not be ignored. Thus, a parent corporation will be regarded as distinct from its subsidiary when the parent and the subsidiary are each operated by its own management which makes decisions independently of the other.

(2)   Actual Control of Subsidiary Corporation. When a parent corporation exercises actual control over a wholly owned subsidiary, the parent corporation will be held liable for the wrongs that the parent corporation commits under the guise of subsidiary corporation action.

(d)   Obtaining Advantages of Corporate Existence. The court will not go behind the corporate identity merely because the corporation has been formed to obtain tax savings or to obtain limited liability for its shareholders. Likewise, the corporate entity will not be ignored merely because the corporation does not have sufficient assets to pay the claims against it.

The fact that recognizing the corporate entity has the effect of preventing creditors of the corporation from reaching assets which would otherwise be held by the shareholders, in whose hands they would be subject to the claims of the creditors, is not in itself a ground for refusing to recognize the corporate entity. It is immaterial that one individual is the only shareholder in the corporation.

B. CREATION OF THE CORPORATION

All states have general laws governing the creation of corporations by persons who comply with the provisions of the statutes.

§ 46:5. Promoters. Corporations frequently come into existence as the result of the activities of one or more persons known as *promoters,* although there is no legal requirement for the services of a promoter in the formation of a corporation.

The promoter brings together persons interested in the enterprise, aids in obtaining subscriptions to stock, and sets in motion the machinery which leads to the formation of the corporation itself.

A corporation is not liable on a contract made by its promoter for its benefit unless it takes some affirmative action to adopt such contract. Such action may be express words of adoption, or the adoption of the contract may be inferred from the corporation's accepting the benefits thereof. (See p. 783, Fortune Furniture v Mid-South Plastic) A corporation may also become bound by such contracts by assignment or by novation.

The promoter is personally liable for all contracts made in behalf of the corporation before its existence unless exempted by the terms of the agreement or by the circumstances surrounding it. When a promoter makes a contract on behalf of a corporation to be formed thereafter, the promoter is liable thereon if the corporation is not formed, in the absence of an agreement that the promoter should not be so liable.

A promoter is liable for all torts committed in connection with the promoter's activities. The corporation is not ordinarily liable for the torts of the promoter, but it may become liable by its conduct after incorporation. Thus, when a corporation, with actual or implied notice of the fraud of the promoter, assumes the promoter's contract, it is liable for the promoter's fraud which induced the other party to enter into the contract.

A promoter stands in a fiduciary relation to the corporation and to stock subscribers, and cannot make secret profits at their expense. Accordingly, if a promoter makes a secret profit on a sale of land to the corporation, the promoter must account to the corporation for this profit; that is, the promoter must surrender the profit to it. The promoter may be held guilty of embezzlement if the promoter converts property that should have gone to the corporation.

The corporation is not liable in most states for the expenses and services of the promoter unless it subsequently promises to pay for them or unless its charter or a statute imposes such liability upon it.

§ 46:6. Incorporation. One or more natural persons, or a domestic or a foreign corporation, may act as incorporators of a corporation by signing and filing articles of incorporation with the designated government official. These articles are filed in duplicate.[10] The designated official, upon being satisfied that the articles conform to the statutory requirements indorses "approved" or "filed" and the date on each copy. The official then retains one copy and returns the other copy to the corporation.[11]

Statutes may require the incorporators to give some form of public notice, as by advertising in a newspaper, of the intention to form the corporation.

§ 46:7. Application for Incorporation. The application for incorporation sets forth certain information about the new corporation.

---

[10] American Bar Association Model Business Corporation Act, § 53.
[11] ABA MBCA § 55.

Part 10 / Corporations

(a)   Name of Proposed Corporation. Subject to certain limitations, the incorporators may select any name.

(b)   Object of Proposed Corporation. A corporation may be formed for any lawful purpose.

When the applicants for a charter satisfy the statutory requirements, they are entitled to a charter and cannot be refused a charter for a ground not stated in the statute.[12]

Some states also require a statement of the means to be used to attain the object of the corporation. This is particularly common in the case of nonprofit or charitable corporations.

(c)   Capital Stock. The amount of capital stock to be authorized and the number and value of the shares into which it is divided must be specified.

The ABA Model Business Corporation Act requires that the articles of incorporation contain a description of the classes of shares, the number of shares in each class, and the relative rights of each class.[13] Other statutes have similar requirements.

(d)   Place of Business. The location of the principal office or place of business of the proposed corporation must be stated.

(e)   Duration. The period during which the proposed corporation is to exist must be set forth. In a number of states limitations are imposed upon the number of years a corporation may exist, the maximum ranging from 20 to 100 years. Commonly, provision is made for a renewal or extension of corporate life. Many states permit the incorporators to select perpetual life for the corporation.

(f)   Directors and Officers. In many states the number of directors or the names and addresses of directors for the first year must be stated. Sometimes additional information regarding the directors is required. In some instances the names and addresses of the officers for the first year must also be stated.

The purpose of requiring the naming of the first board of directors is to provide the corporation with a body to govern or manage the corporation during the interval from the moment that the corporate life begins until the organization meeting of the shareholders is held. In some states that do not require the naming of the first board of directors in this manner, the incorporators have the power of management during this period.

(g)   Incorporators. The names and addresses of the incorporators must be given, along with the number of shares subscribed by each. Sometimes the method of payment for those shares must also be stated.

(h)   Registered Office and Agent. The trend of current statutes is to require a corporation to give a specific office address and the name of an agent, which are described as the "registered" office and the "registered" agent.[14] The object of such provisions

---

[12] Gay Activists Alliance v Lomenzo, 31 NY2d 965, 341 NYS2d 108, 293 NE2d 255 (Secretary of State may not refuse charter because the purposes are violative of "public policy" and the corporate name is "not appropriate").

[13] ABA MBCA § 54.

[14] ABA MBCA § 12.

is to provide information to the world as to where someone can be found, to whom to give notice, or where to effect legal service upon the corporation.

§ 46:8. The Charter. After the application for a certificate of incorporation or a charter is filed, the fee paid, and other conditions precedent fulfilled, an administrative official, such as the secretary of state, examines the papers. If the requirements of the law have been met, a certificate of incorporation, license, or charter is issued and recorded or filed, as specified by the terms of the local statute.

Under the Model Business Corporation Act, corporate existence begins upon the issuance of the certificate by the state official.[15] In some states corporate existence does not begin until an organization meeting is held under the charter to put the corporation in operation, and in others, not until a report on the organization meeting is made. The statute may declare that the charter shall be void if the certificate of organization is not properly filed within the prescribed time. In a few states there is an additional requirement of a local recording of the certificate of incorporation.

The charter not only creates the corporation but also confers contractual rights and imposes contractual duties as between the state, the corporation, and the shareholders. In theory it is required that the corporation accept the charter which is given to it; but unless expressly required by statute, it is not necessary for the corporation to inform any state officer that the charter is accepted. The acceptance can be inferred from conduct, such as holding an organization meeting.

Since the charter is regarded as a contract, the corporation is protected from subsequent change or modification by the clause of the federal Constitution that prohibits states from impairing the obligation of contracts. This does not mean that in no case can the rights given by a charter be modified. Under many statutes it is expressly provided that the charter granted by the state is subject to the power reserved by the state to change the charter should it desire to do so. Independently of such a reservation, the rule has developed that permits the state, under the exercise of its police power, to modify existing contracts, including corporate charters, to further the public health, safety, morals, or general welfare.

§ 46:9. Proper and Defective Incorporation. If the legal procedure for incorporation has been followed, the corporation has a perfect legal right to exist. It is then called a *corporation de jure,* meaning that it is a corporation by virtue of law.

Assume that there is some defect in the corporation which is formed. If the defect is not a material one, the law usually will overlook the defect and hold that the corporation is a corporation de jure.

The ABA MBCA abolishes objections to irregularities and defects in incorporating. It provides that the "certificate of incorporation shall be conclusive evidence that all conditions required to be performed by the incorporators have been complied with and that the corporation has been incorporated under this Act."[16] Many state

---

[15] ABA MBCA § 56.

[16] ABA MBCA § 56. The Model Act expressly excepts "a proceeding to cancel or revoke the certificate of incorporation or for involuntary dissolution of the corporation." The provision would likewise not be operative when the original corporate existence was for a specified number of years which had expired, the corporation then becoming a de facto corporation if it continued to do business without obtaining an extension of its corporate life.

statutes follow this pattern. Such an approach is based upon the practical consideration that when countless people are purchasing shares of stock and entering into business transactions with thousands of corporations, it becomes an absurdity to expect that anyone is going to make the detailed search that would be required to determine whether a given corporation is a de jure corporation.[17]

(a)   De Facto Corporation. The defect in the incorporation may be so substantial that the law cannot ignore it and will not accept the corporation as a de jure corporation. Yet there may be sufficient compliance so that the law will recognize that there is a corporation. When this occurs, the association is called a *de facto corporation.* It exists in fact but not by right, and the state may bring proceedings to have the corporate charter revoked because of the defect. If, however, the state does not take proceedings against the defective corporation, the de facto corporation has all the rights and privileges of a regular lawful or de jure corporation, and third persons contracting with it cannot avoid their contracts on the ground that the corporation was merely a de facto corporation. The de facto corporation is, in a sense, like a voidable contract. It can be set aside by the state; but unless the state acts, the corporation is lawful with respect to the entire world.

Although there is conflict among the authorities, most courts hold that a de facto corporation must meet four tests: (1) there must be a valid law under which the corporation could have been properly incorporated; (2) the attempt to organize the corporation must have been made in good faith; (3) there must have been a genuine attempt to organize in compliance with the requirements of the statute; and (4) there must be a use of the corporate powers.

(b)   Partnership v Corporation by Estoppel. The defect in incorporation may be so great that the law will not accept the corporation even as a de facto corporation, let alone as a de jure corporation. In such a case, in the absence of a statute making the incorporation conclusive, there is no corporation. If the incorporators proceed to run the business in spite of such irregularity, they may be held liable as partners.[18]

The partnership liability rule is sometimes not applied when the third person dealt with the business as though it were a corporation. In such instances, it is stated that the third person is estopped from denying that the "corporation" with which the business was transacted has legal existence. In effect, there is *corporation by estoppel* with respect to that creditor.

C. DISSOLUTION OR TERMINATION

A corporation may be dissolved or terminated by agreement, insolvency, reorganization proceedings, or forfeiture of charter. Some statutes provide for the dissolution of corporations by court decree.

---

[17] This trend and the reasons therefore may be compared to those involved in the concept of the negotiability of commercial paper. Note the similar protection from defenses given to the person purchasing shares for value and without notice. Uniform Commercial Code § 8-202.

[18] In a minority of states the court will not hold the individuals liable as partners, but will hold liable the person who committed the act on behalf of the business on the theory that such person was an agent who acted without authority and is therefore liable for breach of the implied warranties of the existence of a principal possessing capacity and of proper authorization. Doggrell v Great Southern Box Co. (CA6 Tenn) 206 F2d 671.

§ 46:10. Dissolution by Agreement.

(a) **Expiration of Time.** If the incorporators have selected a corporate life of a stated number of years, the corporate existence automatically terminates upon the expiration of that period.

(b) **Surrender of Charter.** The shareholders may terminate the corporate existence by surrendering the charter to the government. The surrender is not effective until the state accepts the charter. The state's acceptance of a surrender of the charter ends the corporate existence and generally extinguishes the liability of the corporation for debts.

§ 46:11. Insolvency, Bankruptcy, and Reorganization.

(a) **Insolvency.** The insolvency of a corporation does not in itself terminate the corporate existence. Statutes in some states, however, provide that when the corporation is insolvent, creditors may commence proceedings to dissolve the corporation. Sometimes the statute merely dissolves the corporation as to creditors. This situation is sometimes called a *de facto dissolution* or *quasi dissolution.*

(b) **Bankruptcy.** When a corporation is adjudicated bankrupt, a sale of all its assets will be ordered. This leaves the corporation without any assets with which to do business unless there should be a surplus above the amount required to pay off the debts of the corporation. The bankruptcy proceeding does not, however, terminate the legal existence of the corporation.

(c) **Reorganization.** When a reorganization of a corporation occurs under the federal bankruptcy laws, the corporate existence is not terminated. If the reorganization is successful, the result is the same as though the corporation merely exchanged obligations and securities. Under state law, however, reorganization proceedings generally result in formation of a new corporation.

§ 46:12. Forfeiture of Charter.
The government that granted the charter may forfeit or revoke the charter for good cause. Sometimes the legislature provides in a general statute that the charter of any corporation shall be automatically forfeited when certain acts are committed or omitted.

Common grounds for forfeiture are fraudulent incorporation; *willful nonuser,* that is, failure to exercise powers; or *misuser,* that is, abuse of corporate powers and franchises. When it is claimed that a corporation has abused its privileges, such acts must be willful, serious, and injurious to the public. The action against the corporation to forfeit its charter must be brought by and in the name of the government, meaning ordinarily an action by the attorney general of the state. Forfeiture of a charter is an extreme penalty. Because of its severity, it is rarely used.

In a number of states when a corporation does not pay its taxes, its power to do business is suspended. Some states impose personal liability upon the officers and directors for such taxes.

§ 46:13. Judicial Dissolution.
In some states, provision is made for the judicial dissolution of a corporation when its management is deadlocked and the deadlock cannot be broken

by the shareholders. In some states, a "custodian" may be appointed for a corporation when the shareholders are unable to break a deadlock in the board of directors and irreparable harm is threatened or sustained by the corporation because of the deadlock.

D. CONSOLIDATIONS, MERGERS, AND CONGLOMERATES

Two or more corporations may be combined to form a new structure or enterprise. This may be a consolidation, a merger, or the formation of a conglomerate.

§ 46:14. Definitions.

(a) **Consolidation.** In a *consolidation* of two or more corporations, the separate corporate existences cease, and a new corporation with the property and the assets of the old corporations comes into being.

When a consolidation is effected, the new corporation ordinarily succeeds to the rights, powers, and immunities of its component parts. Limitations, however, may be prescribed by certificate of incorporation, constitution, or statute. As a general rule, the consolidation corporation is subject to all the liabilities of the constituent corporations.

(b) **Merger.** *Merger* differs from consolidation in that, when two corporations merge, one absorbs the other. One corporation preserves its original charter and identity and continues to exist, and the other disappears and its corporate existence terminates. Most states provide a short form or simplified pattern of merger upon the vote of either 90 or 95% of the stockholders.

Usually if a stockholder dissents from a proposed consolidation or merger, or if a stockholder fails to convert existing shares into stock of the new or continuing corporation, the dissenting stockholder or the corporation may make application to the courts to appraise the value of the stock held. The new or continuing corporation is then required to pay the value of the stock to the stockholder, and the stockholder is required to transfer the stock to the new or continuing corporation. In effect, the court orders the new or continuing corporation to buy the stock from the dissenting stockholder.

(c) **Conglomerate.** *Conglomerate* is the term describing the relationship of a parent corporation to subsidiary corporations engaged in diversified fields of activity unrelated to the field of activity of the parent corporation. For example, a wiring manufacturing corporation that owns all the stock of a newspaper corporation and of a drug manufacturing corporation would be described as a conglomerate. In contrast, if the wire manufacturing company owned a mill to produce the metal used in making the wire and owned a mine which produced the ore that was used by the mill, the relationship would probably be described as an *integrated industry* rather than as a conglomerate. This is merely a matter of usage, rather than of legal definition. Likewise, when the parent company is not engaged in production or the rendering of services, it is customary to call it a holding company.

Without regard to whether the enterprise is a holding company, or whether the group of businesses constitute a conglomerate or an integrated industry, each part is a distinct corporation to which the ordinary corporation law applies. In some instances additional principles apply because of the nature of the relationship existing between the several corporations involved. In some instances the entity of one of the corporations in the conglomerate group may be ignored.

§ 46:15. Legality. Consolidations, mergers, and asset acquisitions between enterprises are often prohibited by federal antitrust legislation on the ground that the effect is to lessen competition in interstate commerce. A business corporation may not merge with a charitable corporation because this would divert the assets of the respective corporations to purposes not intended by their shareholders.[19]

Conglomerates are lawful; but there is a movement to amend or interpret the antimerger provision, Section 7 of the Clayton Act, so as to subject conglomerates to the same limitations as apply to consolidations and mergers.

§ 46:16. Liability of Enterprise.

(a) Liability of Successor Enterprise. Generally the enterprise engaging in or continuing the business after a merger or consolidation will be subject to the contract obligations and debts of the original corporations.

The corporation which absorbs another corporation by merger is generally liable for the contracts of the corporation which was absorbed, and it is no defense that the third party does not have any contract with the absorbing corporation. (See p.784, Gaswint v Case)

The liability of a successor corporation on a contract of the earlier corporation may arise from conduct showing a novation or agreement that the successor be substituted for the earlier corporation. To illustrate, where there was a supply contract between corporations *A* and *B*, and *C* became the successor to corporation *B*, and thereafter *A* and *C* did business just as though *C* were *B*, it will be concluded that there was an agreement that *C* should have all the rights and liabilities of *B* under the original *A-B* contract.

(1) Liability of Purchaser of Assets. The mere fact that one corporation acquires the business or purchases the assets of another corporation does not make the purchasing corporation liable for the debts of the selling corporation where there is no consolidation or merger of the two corporations, nor an assumption of debts by the purchasing corporation, nor any design to defraud the creditors of the selling corporation. (See p.784, Comstock v Great Lakes Distributing Co.)

(b) Liability of Component Enterprise. An existing business may be acquired by another corporation under a variety of circumstances. How does the acquisition affect the rights and liabilities of the business that is acquired? For example, when corporation *A* buys out corporation *B*, what becomes of the rights and liabilities of corporation *B?*

When there is a formal consolidation or merger, statutes commonly provide expressly for the transfer of rights and liabilities to the surviving corporation or the new corporation. The contract of sale or agreement between corporation *A* and corporation *B* will ordinarily expressly assign *B's* rights to *A* and contain an assumption

[19] Stevens Bros. Foundation, Inc. v Commissioner of Internal Revenue (CA8 TaxCt) 324 F2d 633, cert den 376 US 969, reh den 377 US 920.

by *A* of the liabilities of *B*. In accord with general principles of contract law, *A* can sue as assignee of the assigned rights and third persons can sue on the transferred liabilities on the theory that they are third party beneficiaries of such assumption.

Liability on the part of the acquiring corporation does not, however, follow in all cases.

CASES FOR CHAPTER 46

Branmar Theatre Co. v Branmar, Inc.

(Del Ch) 264 A2d 526 (1970)

The Branmar Theatre Co., a family corporation, leased a theatre from Branmar, Inc. The lease prohibited it from transferring the theatre. The holders of the stock of Branmar Theatre Co. sold their stock to the Schwartzes. The lessor (Branmar, Inc.) claimed that this was a violation of the antiassignment provision and threatened to cancel the lease. Branmar Theatre Co. thereafter brought an action for a declaratory judgment to enjoin the cancellation of the lease.

SHORT, V.C. . . . Plaintiff was incorporated under the laws of Delaware on June 7, 1967. The owners of its outstanding capital stock were the Robert Rappaport family of Cleveland, Ohio. On June 9, 1967, plaintiff and defendant entered into a lease agreement for a motion picture theatre in the Branmar Shopping Center, New Castle County, Delaware. The lease, 16 pages in length, recites that the lessor is to erect a theatre building in the shopping center. It provides for the payment of rent by the lessee to the lessor of $27,500 per year plus a percentage of gross admissions receipts, plus 5 percent of any amounts paid to the lessee by refreshment concessionaires. The percentage of admissions figure is regulated by the type of attractions in the theatre, the minimum being 5 percent and the maximum 10. The lease provides for a 20-year term with an option in the lessee to renew for an additional 10 years. The lessee is to provide the lessor with a loan of $60,000, payable in installments, to be used for construction. The lessee is to provide, at its cost, whatever fixtures and equipment are necessary to operate the theatre. Paragraph 12 of the lease, the focal point of this lawsuit, provides:

"Lessee [tenant] shall not sublet, assign, transfer or in any manner dispose of the said premises or any part thereof, for all or any part of the term hereby granted, without the prior written consent of the Lessor [landlord], such consent shall not be unreasonably withheld."

Joseph Luria, the principal for Branmar Shopping Center testified at trial that he negotiated the lease agreement with Isador Rappaport; that he made inquiries about Rappaport's ability to manage a theatre and satisfied himself that Rappaport had the competence and the important industry connections to successfully operate the theatre. It appears that Rappaport and his son operate a successful theatre in Cleveland, Ohio, and have owned and operated theatres elsewhere.

Following execution of the lease, the Rappaports were approached by Muriel Schwartz and Reba Schwartz, operators of 10 theatres in the Delaware and neighboring Maryland area, with an offer to manage the theatre for the Rappaports who had no other business interests in the Wilmington area. This offer was not accepted, but the Schwartzes subsequently agreed with the Rapports to purchase the lease from plaintiff and have it assigned to them. An assignment was executed by plaintiff to the Schwartzes. Defendant rejected the assignment under the power reserved in Paragraph 12 of the lease. On May 29, 1969, the Schwartzes purchased the outstanding shares of plaintiff from the Rappaports. Upon receipt of notice of the sale, defendant advised plaintiff that it considered the sale of the shares to the Schwartzes to be a breach of Paragraph 12 of the lease and the lease to be null and void.

The theatre building is now substantially completed and ready for occupancy. The Schwartzes are ready and willing to perform under the lease agreement. Defendant intends to substitute a new tenant, Sameric Theatres, for the corporate plaintiff, contending that Sameric is a better qualified operator than the Schwartzes.

Defendant argues that the sale of stock was in legal effect an assignment of the lease by the Rappaports to the Schwartzes, was in breach of Paragraph 12 of the lease, and that it was therefore justified in terminating plaintiff's leasehold interest. That in the absence of fraud, and none is charged here, transfer of stock of a corporate lessee is ordinarily not a violation of a clause prohibiting assignment is clear from the authorities. . . . Defendant contends, however, that this is not the ordinary case. Here, it says, due to the nature of the motion picture business, the performance required was by the Rappaports personally. But while defendant's negotiations were with a member of the Rappaport family when the lease was executed, it chose to let the theatre to a corporation whose stock might foreseeably be transferred by the then stockholders. In the preparation of the lease, a document of 16 pages, defendant was careful to spell out in detail the rights and duties of the parties. It did not, however, see fit to provide for forfeiture in the event the stocholders sold their shares. Had this been the intent, it would have been a simple matter to have so provided. . . . "When plaintiff chose to deal with a corporation as its tenant, it must also have known that shares of stock therein might be owned by different stockholders and were subject to assignment to others in the ordinary course of business. The inhibitions against assignment run as to the lease itself and not to the stock in the lessee corporation. . . . Had the parties to the lease intended that the sale and transfer by one or more stockholders in the lessee corporation . . . of their shares of stock therein was to be deemed to be an assignment or attempted assignment of the lease itself, such fact should have been expressed in the lease in clear and unequivocal language.". . .

Defendant suggests that since "the Rappaports" could not assign the lease without its consent, they should not be permitted to accomplish the same result by transfer of their stock. But the rule that precludes a person from doing indirectly what he cannot do directly has no application to the present case. The attempted assignment was not by the Rappaports but by plaintiff corporation, the sale of stock by its stockholders. Since defendant has failed to show circumstances to justify ignoring the corporation's separate existence, reliance upon the cited rule is misplaced.

I find that the sale of stock by the Rappaports to the Schwartzes was not an assignment within the terms of Paragraph 12 of the lease and that the [lease] remains in full force and effect. . . .

[Judgment for plaintiff]

Cohen v Williams

294 Ala 417, 318 So2d 279 (1975)

Daisy Burrell sued the Mobile Roofing and Construction Company, Inc. She obtained a judgment against the corporation. The corporation then went out of business. Daisy Burrell died and Daisy Lee Williams, her personal representative, sued Philip F. Cohen, who was the only stockholder, director, and officer of the corporation. Judgment was entered against Cohen on the theory that he and the corporation were identical. Cohen appealed.

EMBRY, J. . . . The complaint invoked equitable principles to enforce that judgment against Cohen personally on the theory that Cohen so controlled the corporation, and conducted its business, as to make it merely his instrumentality and to permit the fiction of separate corporate entity to continue would allow the corporation to evade its just responsibilities.

. . . Mobile Roofing was incorporated twenty-five to twenty-eight years prior to trial. It subcontracted home construction work, taking mortgages which were immediately assigned to a bank. Its subcontractors were paid with the funds derived from the assignments.

Sometime prior to 1967 Daisy Burrell contracted with Mobile Roofing for it to construct a house for her. During the term of that contract Cohen became the sole stockholder, director and officer of that corporation although at various times prior thereto there had been as many as two other stockholders, directors and officers. In June 1971 Daisy Burrell recovered judgment against Mobile Roofing in the amount of $11,000 on a cause or causes of action arising from that contract or the conduct of Mobile Roofing during its existence. Cohen "dissolved" the corporation because of the judgment by going out of business (there was no evidence that the "dissolution" was effected by compliance with legal formalities).

For ten or twelve years prior to trial there had been no meetings of stockholders or directors; no minutes of any meetings existed. Cohen had freely withdrawn money from profits of Mobile Roofing; he had borrowed money on an insurance policy and paid debts of the "dissolved" corporation with these personal funds but had not paid on the Burrell judgment. After hearing this evidence the trial court entered judgment against Cohen personally in the sum of $11,000.

. . . Was this an appropriate case, in furtherance of the ends of justice, to treat Mobile Roofing and Construction Company, Inc., a corporation, and Philip F. Cohen—the individual owning all its stock and assets—as identical?

We find the evidence sufficient to support the decree to this effect, therefore affirm.

One of the most lucid expressions of the general rule pertaining to the disregard of corporate entity is found at 18 Am Jur 2d, Corporations, § 14, p.559.

"The doctrine that a corporation is a legal entity existing separate and apart from the persons composing it is a legal theory introduced for purposes of convenience and to subserve the ends of justice. The concept cannot, therefore, be extended to a point beyond its reason and policy, and when invoked in support of an end subversive of this policy, will be disregarded by the courts. Thus, in an appropriate case and in furtherance of the ends of justice, a corporation and the individual or individuals owning all its stock and assets will be treated as identical."

It is basic that a corporation is a distinct and separate entity from the individuals who compose it as stockholders or who manage it as directors or officers. . . . This is not a rule cast in concrete but rather this court has always looked to substance over form. In a proper case, when the corporate form is being used to evade personal responsibility this court has not been hesitant to disregard the corporate form and impose liability on the person controlling the corporation and subverting it to his personal use by the conduct of its business in a manner to make it merely his instrumentality. . . .

In addition to the facts summarized in this opinion there was abundant evidence from which the trial court could properly deduce that Mobile Roofing was a fictional shield employed by Cohen to avoid personal responsibility. Let us hasten to add that limitation of personal liability is one of the *valid* attributes of the corporate entity. The limitation of liability to the corporate assets must give way to imposition of personal liability where the actions

of those in control of the corporation denigrate the purpose of limited liability, that purpose being to encourage investment of risk capital. . . .

A homing signal guiding one to agreement with the trial court's conclusion that Mobile Roofing was a device utilized by Cohen to evade personal liability was evidence that the impending Burrell judgment against the corporation caused him to "dissolve" the corporation and assume personal responsibility for corporate liabilities, save and except the Burrell judgment.

This court pointed out . . . that actual fraud is not necessarily a predicate for discarding the theory of separate corporate existence. It may also be discarded to prevent injustice or inequitable consequences. . . .

Cohen argues that he did not consistently disregard the corporate entity and that imposition of personal liability should not be made as to a contract entered into with the corporation during the years it validly existed as a corporation. This argument misconceives the issue. This is an action to make Cohen liable for a judgment against the corporation. It is not an action on the contract made with the corporation; judgment against it liquidated the damages recovered in this action. The complaint alleges and the answer admits that plaintiff first sought to collect the judgment from the corporation. Because of Cohen's "dissolution" of the corporation, there were no assets from which the judgment could be collected. Cohen personally assumed liability for all corporate debts except the judgment. By the "dissolution" he sought to evade the judgment. These are precisely the type of acts which a court in the exercise of its inherent equitable powers may view to differentiate the form from the substance.

Cohen also contends that in order to "pierce the corporate veil" (an overworked cliche) it must be shown that the corporation was formed for the purpose of perpetrating fraud upon its customers or creditors. The "dissolution" to avoid consequences of the judgment is only another evidentiary factor tending to the deduction that Mobile Roofing was the *alter ego* of Cohen. A corporation "dissolved" to evade creditors can enjoy no more standing as an entity separate and apart from its sole stockholders and *alter ego*, who "dissolved" it for that purpose, than a corporation formed to accomplish such evasion. . . . To permit either would eradicate the equitable principles which underlie the reasons for disregarding the separate corporate entity in the particular case under the particular circumstances, as we have already discussed. . . .

[Judgment affirmed]

Fortune Furniture Mfg. Co. v Mid-South Plastic Fabric Co.

(Miss) 310 So2d 725 (1975)

Walker made a contract in the name of Mid-South Plastic Fabric Company with the Fortune Furniture Manufacturing Company. Mid-South was not then in existence, but it was incorporated several weeks later. Mid-South sold goods to Fortune. When Mid-South sued Fortune for the purchase price, Fortune counterclaimed, alleging a breach of the contract which Walker had made. Mid-South claimed that it was not bound by the pre-incorporation contract. The jury concluded that Mid-South was bound, but the trial court rejected this verdict. Fortune appealed.

GILLESPIE, C.J. . . . Fortune was engaged in manufacturing furniture in Okolona, Mississippi. On or before July 8, 1968, Phil Stillpass, who lived in New York, and W. E. Walker, who lived in Okolona, called at the office of Fortune and talked to Sidney Whitlock, President of Fortune, about plastics. Stillpass was in the business of selling plastics and Fortune needed plastics in the manufacture of furniture. A tentative oral agreement was reached whereby a company by the name of Mid-South would sell plastics to Fortune. Whitlock told Walker and Stillpass to send him a letter containing the terms of the contract. On July 8, 1968, the following letter was mailed to Whitlock and received in due course:

Mr. Sidney Whitlock, President
Fortune Furniture Manufacturers, Inc.
Okolona, Mississippi 38860

Dear Sid:

This is to confirm the agreement entered into this date between myself and Phil Stillpass on behalf of Mid-South Plastic Co., Inc. and you on behalf of Fortune Furniture Manufacturing Co. Inc.

We agree to maintain expanded and 21 oz. Plastic in the warehouse of Mid-South Furniture Suppliers, Inc. in sufficient amounts to supply all of the plastic for your plant's use, and if for any reason we do not have the necessary plastic you will be at liberty to purchase the plastic from any other source and we will pay the difference in price paid the other source and our current price.

We also agree to pay Fortune a 2% rebate on the gross sale price of our plastic as an advertisement aid to your Company which rebate to be paid at your request.

We assure you that all fabrics you need will be in our warehouse at all times and we appreciate your agreeing to buy all of your plastics from us.

Very truly yours,

W. E. Walker, President

Mid-South was organized with a corporate charter dated July 22, 1968. Stillpass was elected chairman and secretary-treasurer and W. E. Walker was elected president. . . .

Is Mid-South bound by the letter?

The principal argument of Mid-South is that the letter dated July 8, 1968, written by Walker, purportedly on behalf of Mid-South and as president thereof, is not binding because Mid-South did not come into existence until July 22, 1968, the date of the charter. It is contended by Mid-South that the letter could not have been the act or the creation of Mid-South which was not then a corporate entity and that there was no ratification or adoption of the contract by affirmative action of the company after its incorporation.

The general rule is that a contract made by promoters with a view towards incorporation will be binding upon the corporation if it accepts benefits of the contract with the full knowledge of the terms of the contract. . . .

There are several theories upon which corporations have been held liable, including the theory of adoption and the theory of ratification. In Pearl Realty Co. v Wells, 164 Miss 300, 145 So 102 (1933), the Court spoke in terms of "ratification" and upheld a contract for services rendered in obtaining a cancellation of a lease to a lot upon which Pearl Realty Company subsequently erected a building. Pearl Realty Company was incorporated after the negotiations between the promoter of the corporation and Wells. In concluding that the corporation had ratified the contract made by the promoters, the Court said: "It is permissible for promoters to make contracts which, if ratified by corporations after they are organized, will bind the corporations." . . .

An analysis of Pearl Realty Company indicates that the term "ratification" in that opinion does not refer to any formal act of the corporation, but rather that the corporation adopted the contract and received the benefits of it with full knowledge on the part of all parties concerned in the corporation's organization of the manner and conditions under which it had been obtained. The Court held that under such circumstances the contract was binding on the corporation.

The general rule is that adoption may be implied from the acts or acquiescence of a corporation without express acceptance or ratification, and the adopting corporation will be liable if its responsible officers have or are chargeable with knowledge of the facts upon which it acts. . . .

Stillpass and Walker, the only executive officers of Mid-South, initiated and concluded the agreement that was reduced to writing in the letter to Fortune. Stillpass admitted that Mid-South would not have been organized without Fortune's account. The jury was fully justified in finding that these two officers had full knowledge of the terms of the contract and took advantage of it to sell more than $1,000,000 in goods to Fortune as a result of the contract. We are of the opinion that the jury was justified under the evidence in finding that Mid-South was bound by the terms of the letter of July 8, 1968.

[Judgment reversed]

Gaswint v Case

(Ore) 509 P2d 19 (1973)

Gaswint was employed by an Oregon corporation, Amigo Motor Homes, Inc. The stock of the corporation was acquired by Black Diamond Enterprises, Inc. Some time thereafter Gaswint was discharged. He sued Case, a corporate officer, and the two corporations for damages for breach of contract. Black Diamond asserted that it was not liable to the plaintiff because it had never made any contract with him. A judgment was entered in favor of Gaswint, from which judgment an appeal was taken.

TONGUE, J. . . . Defendants contend that Black Diamond, a Tennessee corporation, was entitled to a judgment of nonsuit because there was no evidence that it was a party to the agreement dated August 14, 1969, and that there was no evidence that it agreed to employ plaintiff for a period of one year or that it had agreed to assume the liabilities of Amigo.

There was evidence, however, that there had been a merger between Black Diamond and Amigo and that Black Diamond had acquired all of the capital stock of Amigo.

Under 8A Tenn Code Ann, § 48-905(e) and also under ORS 57.480(5), Black Diamond, as the "surviving" corporation in the merger, was responsible and liable for the obligations of Amigo, including its obligations under the agreement of August 14, 1969. . . . Therefore, plaintiff was not required to prove an express agreement by Black Diamond to hire plaintiff or to assume the liabilities of Amigo. . . .

[Judgment affirmed]

Comstock v Great Lakes Distributing Company

209 Kan 306, 496 P2d 1308 (1972)

Comstock was injured when an automobile jack collapsed. The jack had been manufactured by the Vulcan Manufacturing Company. In 1963, subsequent to the manufacturing of this particular jack, the controlling interest in Vulcan passed from its then existing shareholders and was acquired by a new investor, Verplank. Vulcan was not able to pay its debts and stopped doing business in 1965. Its assets were then sold at a sheriff's public auction sale. The equipment of Vulcan which had been purchased at the sheriff's sale was resold two times thereafter and a substantial part was ultimately purchased by Great Lakes. Great Lakes rented space from the owner of the building in which the Vulcan business had been conducted and began repairing and manufacturing automobile jacks.

Comstock sued Vulcan, Great Lakes, and others to recover damages for his injury. From a judgment for the defendants, Comstock appealed.

KAUL, J. . . . The basis of plaintiff's action against Great Lakes is that it is merely a continuation of Vulcan, or in the alternative there was a de facto merger of Vulcan and Great Lakes. In order to support his claim, plaintiff attempts to compare the corporate composition of Vulcan prior to 1963 with the corporate makeup of Great Lakes, which did not exist until 1965. Plaintiff ignores the complete change in Vulcan's corporate composition during the period 1963-1965 due to the intervening acquisition by Verplank. At the time of the alleged continuation or merger, the parties who were stockholders, officers and directors of Vulcan prior to 1963 no longer had such status. The continuation or merger into Great Lakes, claimed by plaintiff, must be considered with reference to Vulcan as it was composed under the

Verplank operation when the jack in question was manufactured and when Vulcan ceased doing business, not as it was in 1963 when acquired by Verplank. In other words, June 8, 1965, when Vulcan ceased doing business, serves as the point of reference for the consideration of the issue of continuance or merger.

. . . Both parties accept the general rule of nonliability of a transferee corporation for the prior debts of the transferor and the exceptions thereto: . . . "Generally where one corporation sells or otherwise transfers all of its assets to another corporation, the latter is not liable for the debts and liabilities of the transferor, except: (1) where the purchaser expressly or impliedly agrees to assume such debts; (2) where the transaction amounts to a consolidation or merger of the corporation; (3) where the purchasing corporation is merely a continuation of the selling corporation; and (4) where the transaction is entered into fraudulently in order to escape liability for such debts.". . .

Plaintiff admits the rule of nonliability, which we have quoted, is the law of this jurisdiction, but attempts to impose liability on Great Lakes on the theory of consolidation or merger under exception (2), or in the alternative on the theory that Great Lakes was merely a continuation of Vulcan under exception (3). The record does not support either theory.

We shall first direct our attention to the claim of consolidation or merger. . . . "Strictly speaking, a consolidation signifies such a union as necessarily results in the creation of a new corporation and the termination of the constituent ones, whereas a merger signifies the absorption of one corporation by another, which retains its name and corporate identity with the added capital, franchises and powers of a merged corporation.". . .

In the instant case there is no evidence of direct dealing between Vulcan and Great Lakes. Vulcan never sold, transferred or delivered anything to Great Lakes. Some of the equipment and machinery formerly owned by Vulcan is now owned by Great Lakes. The testimony of Judge Plunkett, which is undisputed, was that the machinery and equipment were sold at a sheriff's auction to a Dale Thule and L. L. Hurst, Jr., after competitive bidding by several bidders. Thule was described as the owner of an automotive equipment business and Hurst as owner of the Edwards Manufacturing Company. Thereafter, the First Heartland Investment Company, to

protect its investment, bid in the machinery and equipment within the statutory time. Later part of the machinery and equipment was sold to Great Lakes and the remainder to Lakes Center Switch Company of Winona, Minnesota. . . .

There is no evidence that any assets, tangible or intangible, passed directly from Vulcan to Great Lakes. Nor is there any evidence that any of the original purchasers of Vulcan's property at foreclosure sales acted as "strawmen" to accomplish a transfer of ownership from Vulcan to Great Lakes.

The portion of the machinery and equipment formerly owned by Vulcan, which eventually came into the hands of Great Lakes, passed through first and second purchasers following a foreclosure sale before acquisition by Great Lakes. . . . "When a corporation purchases the franchises and property of another corporation at a sale under a decree foreclosing a mortgage thereon, or other judicial sale, or where natural persons purchase at such sale and afterwards transfer to a corporation, the new corporation is not liable for the debts of the old company, provided they are not prior liens on the property, and provided their payment has not been assumed, nor their payment imposed by the foreclosure decree or by statute. So where an individual purchases the assets of a corporation at a foreclosure sale and then resells to a new company composed largely of the members of the company whose assets were sold, and there is no fraud, the new company is not liable for the debts of the old. . . ." . . .

By the undisputed evidence, Great Lakes acquired the machinery and equipment as a bona fide purchaser; it does not own any interest in the building formerly owned by Vulcan, but only occupies a part of it as a tenant. Other assets of Vulcan were purchased or acquired by other parties. The acquisition of some Vulcan property by Great Lakes, under the circumstances described, does not tend to show a consolidation, merger or mere continuation as those terms have been defined.

Is there any evidence tending to show that Great Lakes was merely a continuation or reincarnation of Vulcan? None of the incorporators of Great Lakes were stockholders or officers of Vulcan at the time Great Lakes was chartered in February of 1965. Vulcan was a going business under the control of, and operated by, Verplank at that time and continued as a corporate entity. There was testimony that the directors or stockholders of Vulcan held a meeting as late as October 1965. Great Lakes did not come into being as a result of a reincorporation of Vulcan or by amendment of the Vulcan corporate charter. . . .

. . . There is no evidence in the instant case of any direct dealings between the two corpora- tions—no transfer of capital stock, assets, contracts or franchises and no evidence of any agreement or understanding between the two corporations. . . .

[Judgment affirmed]

QUESTIONS AND CASE PROBLEMS

1. What social forces are affected by the recognition of a corporation as a distinct legal entity?

2. Compare the terms "charter," "articles of incorporation," and "certificate of incorporation."

3. Compare a close corporation and a professional corporation.

4. Compare consolidations, mergers, and conglomerates.

5. Robinson was a salesman of the Realty Investment Consultants, Inc. (R.I.C., Inc.). Kramer was president, treasurer, and director of the corporation and owned all of its stock. Robinson contacted Ferrarell in answer to the latter's letter of inquiry in response to a newspaper ad of R.I.C. Robinson executed a contract with Ferrarell on behalf of R.I.C. and signed the contract as agent for that corporation. Subsequently, Ferrarell sued Robinson and Kramer for breach of the contract by R.I.C. Were they liable? [Ferrarell v Robinson, 11 Ariz App 473, 465 P2d 610]

6. Greenberg organized the PSG Company in order to obtain certain tax advantages. He owned all of the stock of the corporation and was its principal officer. El Salto sued PSG Co. and Greenberg, claiming that the corporation was liable for damages for discriminatory price practices and that Greenberg was also liable for such damages on the theory that PSG was the alter ego of Greenberg. Is Greenberg liable to El Salto on the facts above stated? [El Salto v PSG Co., (CA9 Ore) 444 F2d 477]

7. An action was brought by Alabama Tank Lines and other carriers against the Martin Truck Line, claiming that the truck line was operating without the necessary certificate of the state Public Service Commission. It was shown that Martin Truck Line had obtained a certificate at a time when all of its stock was owned by Thornbury, Cook, and Edwards. The stock was thereafter sold to Houghland and Page. No approval of the transfer of stock to them was obtained from the Public Service Commission. Was Martin Truck Line entitled to continue to do business under the certificate that had been originally issued? [Martin Truck Line v Alabama Tank Lines, 261 Ala 163, 73 So2d 756]

8. Middlesex Apartments, Inc., owned a tract of land. Mar Building, Inc., a corporation, was formed to act as building contractor to construct an apartment complex on the land owned by Middlesex. Weiner and Blashinsky were officers of Mar. Mar contracted with Middlesex to construct the apartments for $680,000. This figure had no relationship to the actual cost of construction which was probably $900,000. Mar did not have sufficient assets to pay the subcontractors doing work in the construction. The subcontracts made by Mar stipulated that the subcontractors would not assert any liens against the apartment building. Mar became insolvent and the subcontractors were not paid. Most of them settled their claims for 25 cents on the dollar. Three who did not, brought suit and sought to pierce the corporate veil of Mar in order to hold Middlesex, Weiner, and Blashinsky directly liable. Were the defendants liable? [Yacker v Weiner, 109 NJ Super, 351, 263 A2d 188]

9. Mulley was a promoter of a corporation not yet formed, Collier County Developers, Inc. He made a contract as promoter with Vodopich for services in selling certain real estate. Vodopich later sued Mulley for breach of the contract. Mulley claimed that he was not liable because Vodopich knew that the corporation had not yet been formed. Was he correct? [Vodopich v Collier County Developers, Inc. (FlaApp) 319 So2d 43]

10. *A* made a contract with *B* on behalf of *X* Corporation. *B* knew that *X* Corporation was not yet formed. Thereafter *X* Corporation was properly organized, but *B* refused to perform its contract on the ground that *X* had not been in existence when the contract was made. Was this a valid defense? [330 Michigan Avenue, Inc. v. Cambridge Hotel, Inc., (Fla App) 183 So2d 725]

11. North Gate Corporation leased property to National Food Stores. The lease contained a provision that neither the corporation nor its "beneficiaries" would engage in a competing business within a specified radius. Some shareholders of North Gate Corporation engaged in such a business within the prohibited area. National Food Stores claimed that the restriction on "beneficiaries" applied to "shareholders" of North Gate. Were the shareholders bound by the anticompetitive covenant? [North Gate Corporation v National Food Stores, Inc., 30 Wis 2d 317, 140 NW2d 744]

12. Corporation *A* owed money to *B*. The debt was guaranteed by *C*. Corporation *A* merged with Corporation *D*, with *D* being the surviving corporation. *D* failed to pay the debt to *B*, who then sued *C* on the guarantee. *C* denied liability on the ground that he had guaranteed the debt of Corporation *A* and that as Corporation *A* was no longer in existence, he, *C*, was not bound by any guarantee. Was this defense valid? [Essex International, Inc. v Clamage, (CA7 Ill) 440 F2d 547]

13. The Maid of the Mist Steamboat Co. was organized for operating sight-seeing steamships on the Niagara River. It had a fifty-year charter which expired in 1942. No one realized that fact until 1947. In that year an application was made under the New York law to renew the charter of the corporation. During the intervening period from 1942 to 1947 the corporation had continued to do business as usual. What kind of corporation was it during that period? [Garzo v Maid of the Mist Steamboat Co., 303 NY 516, 104 NE2d 882]

14. Adams and two other persons were promoters for a new corporation, the Aldrehn Theaters Co. The promoters retained Kridelbaugh to perform legal services in connection with the incorporation of the new business and promised to pay him $1,500. The corporation was incorporated through Kridelbaugh's services, and the promoters became its only directors. Kridelbaugh attended a meeting of the board of directors at which he was told that he should obtain a permit for the corporation to sell stock because the directors wished to pay him for his prior services. The promoters failed to pay Kridelbaugh, and he sued the corporation. Was the corporation liable? [Kridelbaugh v Aldrehn Theaters Co., 195 Iowa 147, 191 NW 803]

15. A labor union made a collective bargaining agreement with Interscience Publishers, Inc. The contract made no provision that it was binding on successors of the contracting parties. Later, for general business reasons and not as an antilabor measure, Interscience merged with and disappeared into another publishing corporation, John Wiley & Sons, Inc. The former's employees, with a few exceptions, worked for Wiley. Thereafter the labor union claimed that Wiley was required to submit to arbitration, in accordance with the terms of the contract with Interscience, certain questions relating to employees who had worked for Interscience but were working for Wiley after the merger. Wiley claimed that it was not bound by the arbitration agreement with Interscience. Decide. [John Wiley & Sons v Livingston, 376 US 543]

16. A corporation was formed for the purpose of doing the laundry work for a cooperating group of hospitals. The local tax assessors claimed that the laundry corporation was required to pay the same taxes as any other laundry corporation. The hospitals claimed that the laundry corporation had the same "charitable" status as the hospitals, which, if true, would exempt it from the taxes in question. Was it exempt? [Children's Hospital Medical Center v Board of Assessors, 353 Mass 35, 227 NE2d 908]

17. Akel and his wife organized and incorporated the Akel Corporation. Prior to the actual incorporation, they obtained from Dooley a lease of property in which the Akel Corporation was named as the tenant. Dooley had no information as to whether the corporation was in existence. The corporation was in fact incorporated prior to the commencement of the lease. Later Dooley sued Akel and his wife for the rent. They claimed that they were not liable as individuals because the corporation was the tenant. Decide. [Akel v Dooley, (Fla App) 185 So2d 491]

18. The Drackett Co. manufactured a bathroom fixture cleaner named "Vanish." All of the products of this company were sold by its wholly owned subsidiary, "The Drackett Products Co." The subsidiary had no other business, and all of the income of the parent company was obtained from the subsidiary company's sales. Shirley purchased a can of Vanish. When she used it, chemical fumes caused extreme damage to her lungs. She sued Drackett Products Co., claiming that it was negligent. It defended on the ground that it did not make the product, that it was not negligent because it had no reason to foresee that any harm would result, and that it could not be liable for any fault of the manufacturing corporation. Was this a valid defense? [Shirley v The Drackett Products Co., 26 Mich App 644, 182 NW2d 726]

47 Corporate Powers

By common law and by virtue of the statute under which it is incorporated, a corporation has certain powers. Some of the powers possessed by a corporation are the same as those powers held by a natural person, such as the right to own property. Others are distinct powers not possessed by natural persons, such as the power to exist perpetually in those states where this is allowed.

§ 47:1. Nature and Limitations of Corporate Powers. All corporations do not have the same powers. For example, those that operate banks, insurance companies, savings and loan associations, and railroads generally have special powers.

Except for limitations in the federal Constitution or the state's own constitution, a state may grant to a corporation any powers that it chooses. In addition, a corporation has certain powers that are incidental to corporate existence. These powers are implied because they are reasonably necessary to carry out and make effective the expressly granted powers. Moreover, in exercising their powers, corporations have a choice of employing any lawful means. The ABA MBCA broadly authorizes a corporation "to have and exercise all powers necessary or convenient to effect its purpose." [1] Many state statutes make a similar "catchall" grant of powers.

§ 47:2. Particular Powers.

(a)   Perpetual Succession. One of the distinctive features of a corporation is its perpetual succession or continuous life—the power to continue as a unit forever or for a stated period of time regardless of changes in stock ownership. If no period is fixed for its duration, the corporation will exist indefinitely unless it is legally dissolved. When the period is limited, the corporation may in many states extend the period by meeting additional requirements of the statute. In view of such power of extension, a corporation may make a long-term contract running beyond the termination date of its certificate of incorporation.

(b)   Corporate Name. A corporation must have a name to identify it. As a general rule it may select any name for this purpose. It may not, however, select for its exclusive use a name that all may lawfully use, such as a descriptive name, or one that another firm has the exclusive right to use.

---

[1] The American Bar Association Model Business Corporation Act (ABA MBCA) § 4(2).

Most statutes require that the corporate name contain some word indicating the corporate character [2] and that it shall not be the same as or deceptively similar to the name of another corporation. Some statutes likewise prohibit the use of a name which is likely to mislead the public. The ABA MBCA states that the corporate name "shall not contain any word or phrase which indicates or implies that it is organized for any purpose other than one or more of the purposes contained in its articles of incorporation." [3] Under such a provision it would be improper to include in the corporate name the word "electronic" or "computerized" when such a word had no relation to the actual work of the corporation and the purpose of including such word in the corporate name was to take advantage of the current popularity of those words and thus attract investors to purchase the corporate stock or customers to deal with the corporation. In some states a name similar to one in use may be rejected even though the similarity is not so extreme as to be deceptive but is merely confusing.[4]

(c)   Corporate Seal. A corporation may have a distinctive seal. However, a corporation need not use a seal in the transaction of business unless it is required by statute to use a seal or unless a natural person in transacting that business would be required to use a seal.

(d)   Bylaws. The shareholders of a corporation have inherent power to make bylaws to supplement the charter of the corporation, but the right to do so is commonly expressed by statute.

Bylaws are adopted by the action of the shareholders, but some statutes provide for the adoption of bylaws by the directors unless otherwise provided. Action by the state or an amendment of the corporation charter is not required to make the bylaws effective. The difference between bylaws and provisions of a charter is a practical consideration. The charter represents provisions that should endure throughout the life of the corporation. The *bylaws* represent more detailed provisions for governing the corporation, which might become undesirable in the course of events, and therefore should not be given the same permanence as the charter. This distinction is not always observed, and there is frequently a tendency to put much detail into the charter. No actual harm is done by so doing, except that it makes the charter unnecessarily long and also makes a change more difficult since state approval is required to amend the charter, while bylaws can be changed by corporate action.

The bylaws are subordinate to the general law of the state, including the statute under which the corporation is formed, as well as to the charter of the corporation. Bylaws that conflict with such superior authority or which are in themselves unreasonable are invalid. Bylaws that are valid are binding upon all shareholders regardless of whether they know of the existence of those bylaws or were among the majority

---

[2] ABA MBCA § 8(a) declares that the corporate name must contain the word "corporation," "company," "incorporated," "limited," or an abbreviation of one of such words.

With respect to a professional corporation, there may be some additional requirement that the name indicate the nature of the services rendered in addition to the fact that it is a corporation. For example, it may be necessary to have the name of "Jones Accounting Associates, Inc." rather than merely "Jones Associates, Inc."

[3] ABA MBCA § 8(b).

[4] New York Business Corporation Law § 301(a)(2).

which consented to their adoption. Bylaws are not binding upon third persons, however, unless they have notice or knowledge of them.

(e)   Stock. A corporation may issue stock and certificates representing such stock.[5]

(f)   Borrowing Money. Corporations have the implied power to borrow money in carrying out their authorized business purposes. For example, a fire insurance company may borrow money to pay losses due on its policies. Statutes commonly prohibit corporations from raising the defense of usury.

(g)   Execution of Commercial Paper. The power to issue or indorse commercial paper, or to accept drafts, is implied when the corporation has the power to borrow money and when such means are appropriate and ordinarily used to further the authorized objectives of the corporation.

    Such transactions, however, are unauthorized when they are not related to, or if they are detrimental to, the furtherance of the corporate business. For example, it is beyond the power of a corporation to be an accommodation party on a note given by someone buying its stock.

(h)   Bonds. A corporation having the power to borrow money has the implied power to issue various types of bonds.

    The bonds issued by a corporation are subject to Article 8 of the Uniform Commercial Code. If the bonds satisfy the requirements of UCC § 3-104, they are governed by Article 3 of the Code on commercial paper as far as negotiation is concerned.

    Ordinarily conditions inserted in the corporate bonds for the protection of the bondholders have the effect of making the bonds nonnegotiable and therefore not within the scope of Article 3 of the Uniform Commercial Code, and only Article 8 applies to them.

(i)   Transferring Property. The corporate property may be leased, assigned for the benefit of creditors, or sold. (See p. 795, Wilmington Memorial Co., Inc. v Silverbrook Cemetery Co.) In many states, however, a solvent corporation may not transfer all of its property except with the consent of all or a substantial majority of its shareholders. In any case, the sale must be for a fair price.

    A corporation, having power to incur debts, may mortgage or pledge its property as security for those debts. This rule does not apply to franchises of public service companies, such as street transit systems and gas and electric companies.

(j)   Acquisition of Property. Although the power to acquire and hold property is usually given in the charter, a corporation always has the implied power to acquire and hold such property as is reasonably necessary for carrying out its express powers. In some states the power of a corporation to hold property is restricted as to the method of acquiring it, or is limited as to the quantity or the value of the property or the period of time for which it may be held. Restrictions on holding real estate are also imposed upon corporations by the constitutions of some states.

---

[5] Statutes in many states authorize a corporation to issue stock rights and warrants. See, for example, 8 Delaware Code § 157.

(1)   Investments. Modern corporation codes generally provide that a corporation may acquire the stock of other corporations.

(2)   Holding Companies. A corporation owning stock of another corporation may own such a percentage of the stock of the other company that it controls the latter's operations. In such a case, the first company is commonly called a *holding company.* Sometimes a holding company is organized solely for the purpose of controlling other companies called *operating* or *subsidiary companies.*

The device of a holding company may be socially desirable or undesirable depending upon the circumstances under which it operates. If it is merely a device to coordinate different phases of an economic activity, the holding company is a proper device. If its object is to eliminate competition between the operating companies whose stock is held, it may be illegal under state or federal antitrust laws. It is no objection, however, that the subsidiary company engages in a business in which the holding company could not lawfully engage. (See p. 796, Connecticut General Life Ins. Co. v Superintendent of Insurance)

The fact that a corporation owns its subsidiary does not give it an unlimited right to control the subsidiary. Some degree of restriction is placed on the parent corporation in requiring "fairness" in its dealings with the subsidiary.[6]

(k)   Acquisition of Own Stock. Generally a corporation may purchase its own stock, if it is solvent at the time and the purchase does not impair capital. Sometimes a more precise standard is specified.[7] The Model Act permits a corporation to acquire its own shares ". . . only to the extent of unreserved and unrestricted earned surplus available therefore. . . ."[8] In a few states corporations are denied implied power to purchase their own stock, but they are permitted to receive it as a gift, in payment of a debt, or as security for a debt.

Stock which is reacquired by the corporation that issued it is commonly called *treasury stock.* Ordinarily the treasury stock is regarded as still being issued or outstanding stock.[9] As such, the shares are not subject to the rule that original shares cannot be issued for less than par. They can be sold by the corporation at any price. Under the Model Act, "treasury shares may be disposed of by the corporation for such consideration expressed in dollars as may be fixed from time to time by the board of directors."

Although treasury stock retains the character of outstanding stock, it has an inactive status while it is held by the corporation. Thus, the treasury shares cannot be voted nor can dividends be declared on them.

The reacquisition by a corporation of its shares and the holding of them as treasury shares is to be distinguished from what occurs upon the redemption of shares. When shares are redeemed, they are automatically canceled.

---

[6] Sinclair Oil Corp. v Levien (Del) 280 A2d 717.

[7] A corporation may not purchase its own shares "if . . . the present fair value of the remaining assets . . . would be less than one fourth . . . times the amount of its liabilities to creditors." Arkansas Business Corporation Act § 5; Ark Stat Ann § 64-105.

[8] ABA MBCA § 6.

[9] When a corporation reacquires its own shares, it has the choice of "retiring" them and thus restoring them to the status of authorized but unissued shares or to treat them as still issued and available for transfer. It is the latter which are described as treasury shares.

Stock which is surrendered is not considered to be outstanding, whether it is retained as treasury shares or is formally canceled. (See p. 798, Jack Cole-Dixie Highway Co. v Red Ball Motor Freight, Inc.)

(l) Business in Another State. A corporation has the inherent power and generally is expressly authorized to engage in business in other states. This grant of power by the incorporating state does not exempt the corporation, however, from satisfying the restrictions imposed by the foreign state in which it seeks to do business.

(m) Participation in Enterprise. Corporations may generally participate in an enterprise to the same extent as individuals. They may enter into joint ventures. The modern statutory trend is to permit a corporation to be a member of a partnership. A corporation may be a limited partner. The Model Act authorizes a corporation "to be a promoter, partner, member, associate, or manager of any partnership, joint venture, trust or other enterprise." [10]

When the power to be a participant in an enterprise is not expressly granted to a corporation, there is a conflict as to whether it has implied authority to be a participant. When the relationship is of a permanent character or is of such a nature as to subject the corporation to the control of the outside enterprise, it is likely that the courts will refuse to imply a power to be a participant. For example, in the absence of express statutory authorization to be a partner, a corporation cannot be a member of a general partnership. Many modern corporation codes expressly grant this power.

In addition to the question of corporate power to participate in an enterprise, such participation is subject to and may be illegal under the federal antitrust legislation. [11]

(n) Employee Benefit and Aid. The ABA MBCA empowers a corporation "to pay pensions and establish pensions plans, pension trusts, profit sharing plans, stock bonus plans, stock option plans, and other incentive plans for any or all of its directors, officers, and employees." [12]

Corporations have such power under most state codes either by express provision or by judicial decision. Such power is possessed by a professional corporation, and the existence of such power is a major reason for the forming of a professional corporation. The various employee benefit plans enable either the professional corporation or its members or both to obtain an advantage in the computation of federal income tax liability that would not otherwise be open to them as individuals or as partners.

(o) Charitable Contributions. The Model Act authorizes a corporation without any limitation "to make donations for the public welfare or for charitable, scientific, or educational purposes." In some states some limitation is imposed upon the amount that can be donated for charitable purposes. The federal income tax law tends to set a limitation on charitable contributions, since corporations ordinarily will not make contributions in an amount greater than may be claimed as a deduction for the purpose of federal income tax computation.

---

[10] ABA MBCA § 4(p).
[11] United States v Penn-Olin Chemical Co. 378 US 158.
[12] ABA MBCA § 4(o).

(p) Civic Improvement. The Model Act also authorizes a corporation "to transact any lawful business which the board of directors shall find will be in aid of governmental policy." Under such broad authorization a corporation may aid in a military war, in a war on poverty, and take part in measures to prevent civil strife.

§ 47:3. Ultra Vires Acts. When a corporation acts in excess of or beyond the scope of the powers granted by its charter and the statute under which it was organized, then the corporation's act is described as *ultra vires.* Such an act is improper because it is a violation of the obligation of the corporation to the state. It is also improper with respect to shareholders and creditors of the corporation because corporate funds have been diverted to unauthorized uses.

As an illustration of the latter point, assume that a corporation is created and authorized to manufacture television sets. Various persons purchase stock in the corporation, lend it money, or sell to it on credit because of their estimate of the worth of the television business in general and of the corporation as a television manufacturing company in particular. Assume that the corporation has funds that it uses for the ultra vires purpose of lending to persons to buy homes. Many of the shareholders and creditors would probably never have become associated with the corporation if it had been organized for that purpose. The fact that the ultra vires use of the money may be better economically or socially than the authorized use does not alter the fact that the shareholders' and the creditors' money is not used the way they intended.

(a) Ultra Vires Acts and Illegality Distinguished. Although it is not lawful for a corporation to perform ultra vires acts, the objection to the commission of such acts is distinct from the objection of illegality. (See p. 798, Ladd Estate Co. v Wheatley) In the case of illegality, the act would be wrong regardless of the nature of the person or the association committing it. The fact that an act is ultra vires merely means that this particular corporation does not have permission from the government to do the act. Thus, it would ordinarily be beyond the powers of a business corporation, and therefore ultra vires, to engage in a charitable enterprise, such as the building of a church or college. But the activity would hardly be termed illegal.

(b) Effect of Ultra Vires Contracts. There is some conflict in the law as to the effect of an ultra vires contract. Under the modern statutory trend, ultra vires cannot be raised to attack the validity of any act, contract, or transfer of property,[13] except as noted under § 47:3(c). This trend is recognized by the Model Act which declares that "no act of a corporation and no conveyance or transfer of real or personal property to or by a corporation shall be invalid by reason of the fact that the corporation was without capacity or power to do such act or to make or receive such a conveyance or transfer." [14]

In the absence of statute, most courts recognize ultra vires as a defense but refuse to apply it in a particular case if it would be inequitable and work a hardship.

The courts also refuse to recognize it as a defense against the holder of a commercial paper on which the corporation, without authority, became an accommodation party. Likewise, a transfer of real or personal property cannot be set aside on the

---

[13] ABA MBCA § 7; Inter-Continental Corp. v Moody (TexCivApp) 411 SW2d 578.
[14] ABA MBCA § 7.

ground that it is ultra vires. Here the object of the law is to preserve the security of titles even though the result is to permit the wrongful acts of the corporation to stand.

In most states if the ultra vires contract has been completely performed, neither party can rescind the contract on the ground that it was originally ultra vires. Conversely, if neither party to the ultra vires contract has performed, the court will neither enforce the contract nor hold either party liable for a breach of the contract. A person who has benefited by the ultra vires act cannot refuse to pay for the value which was received on the ground that the transaction was ultra vires. (See p. 798, Total Automation v Illinois National Bank & Trust Co.)

(c) Remedies for Ultra Vires Acts. In all states (1) a shareholder may obtain an injunction to stop the board of directors or other persons involved from entering into an ultra vires transaction; (2) the corporation, or a shareholder acting on behalf of the corporation, may sue the persons who made or approved the contract in order to recover damages for the loss caused the corporation by the ultra vires act; and (3) an action may be brought by the attorney general of the state to revoke the charter on the ground of its serious or repeated violation.

When an action is brought to enjoin or set aside corporate action on the ground that it is ultra vires, there is no requirement that the plaintiffs show that the corporation or they are in any way harmed, as each shareholder has a right to see that the corporation does not do an act which is not authorized. Similarly, when the attorney general brings an action to forfeit the corporate charter because of ultra vires acts, there is no requirement of proof of damage to the corporation; as a practical matter, a court is more likely to forfeit the charter if harm to the community can be shown.

In contrast, when shareholders bring a derivative action to recover damages on behalf of the corporation for the harm caused by the ultra vires acts, the plaintiffs must necessarily show the extent to which the corporation has been harmed. However, the shareholders are not required to prove what individual harm they have sustained.

CASES FOR CHAPTER 47

Wilmington Memorial Co., Inc. v Silverbrook Cemetery Co.

(Del Ch) 287 A2d 405 (1972)

The Silverbrook Cemetery Company sold bronze grave markers. The Wilmington Memorial Company also sold bronze gravemarkers and claimed that the cemetery company did not have authority to make such sales. The charter of the cemetery company gave it power to sell "personal estate of every kind" and a general power to make all contracts and do all acts necessary for the conducting of the cemetery. Wilmington Memorial brought an action for a declaratory judgment against the cemetery. The cemetery moved for summary judgment in its favor.

SHORT, V.C. . . . The cemetery itself comprises sixty acres of land upon which an office building, a crematorium and two garages have been constructed. The burial grounds are divided into two distinct sections: a traditional stone monument area and a memorial park area in which all graves are marked by flat bronze memorials set in the ground flush to the surface.

Defendant's sale of bronze markers is the subject of this action. Up to this time it has never sold any stone monuments. Defendant has been selling bronze markers since 1950 and during the years 1966, 1967 and 1968 averaged between fifty and sixty individual sales per year. These sales accounted for ninety-five per cent of the total bronze markers installed in the cemetery. No sales have been made by defendant to customers who have not purchased burial lots in the cemetery. Marker sales are usually conducted in the main office in which sample memorials are on display, or by letter to the customer sometime after a burial. The standard 24 inch by 12 inch marker is sold for $135 including the cost of installation. Though there is no requirement that lot owners purchase markers exclusively from defendant, it requires that all bronze markers purchased from third parties must be installed by defendant at a charge of $50 for the standard size marker. The cost of installation is charged to the third party dealer. In contrast, outside monument dealers are permitted to install stone monuments in the traditional cemetery section. Defendant readily admits that installation does not require skilled labor. It also admits that a substantial part of the installation charge represents profit.

Plaintiff company, incorporated in 1960 under the General Corporation Law, has been in the monument business since 1937. Its place of doing business is located in the proximate vicinity of defendant's cemetery. A major portion of its business is in the sale of granite monuments. However, it has been selling bronze markers in competition with defendant since 1950.

Plaintiff contends that defendant's sale of markers is in violation of its charter. The charter does not expressly provide for the sale of markers. However, it does expressly carry the broad general powers "to purchase . . . personal estate of every kind and the same to . . . sell . . . ," and "to enter into any and all contracts . . . proper to be in the conduct of its business [as a cemetery company]." These provisions clearly indicate the legislative intent to grant to Silverbrook the power to engage in activities related to the business of operating a cemetery. Burial of and memorializing the dead are certainly related activities. As the court said in Clagett v Vestry of Rock Creek Parish, DC, 241 F Supp 950: "grave and marker . . . are so intimately related to the extent that the suggestion of one suggests the other." See also, People ex rel. Guettler v Mount Olive Cemetery Ass'n, 26 Ill 2d 156, 186 NE2d 39 (markers and monuments); State v Lakewood Cemetery Ass'n, 93 Minn 191, 101 NW 161 (greenhouse);

Wing v Forest Lawn Cemetery Ass'n, 15 Cal 2d 472, 101 P2d 1099 (mortuary). I am satisfied that Silverbrook's charter, by necessary implication, confers the power to sell grave markers.

Plaintiff charges that defendant's tax exempt status permits it to compete unfairly with its taxable competitors. Under Silverbrook's charter the "cemetery grounds, with the buildings" are exempt from taxation. At the present time bronze markers are on display in a corner of Silverbrook's office building and a garage on the grounds is being used, among other things, for storing and assembling markers. Since Silverbrook pays no taxes on the cemetery grounds or any of its buildings, plaintiff argues that it is afforded an unfair economic advantage. Assuming, without deciding, that plaintiff has standing to raise this issue, I am satisfied that it must be resolved in defendant's favor. The selling of markers having been found to be an activity authorized by Silverbrook's charter the exemption of its property from taxes does not qualify its right to exercise all the privileges granted thereby. Daily Monument Co. v Crown Hill Cemetery Ass'n, 114 Ohio App 143, 176 NE2d 268. Moreover, the only advantage occasioned to defendant of which plaintiff can complain would be the exemption from taxes on that portion of cemetery property which is used to display and store markers. On the evidence adduced this advantage, if any, is de minimis.

Plaintiff contends that defendant's well-developed relationship with the purchasers of grave lots enables it to unfairly approach the same customers for the sale of markers. Defendant admits that it "is in the inevitable enviable position of having the first opportunity to approach the purchasers." However, it is not unusual in our economic system that such a relationship produces an advantage over competitors. I see nothing unfair or inequitable in such an advantage. And this is particularly so where, as here, there is no showing that defendant's sale of markers is tied directly or indirectly by contract to the sale of grave lots. . . .

. . . Defendants' motion for summary judgment is granted.

Connecticut General Life Insurance Co. v Superintendent of Insurance

10 NY2d 42, 217 NYS2d 39, 176 NE2d 63 (1961)

Connecticut General Life Insurance Co. is a Connecticut insurance company which obtained a license to write life insurance policies in New York.

It thereafter proposed to acquire 80 percent or more of the common stock of the National Fire Insurance Co. of Hartford, a fire and casualty insurance company licensed to write policies in New York. The New York State Superintendent of Insurance brought an action for a declaratory judgment to have the Connecticut company prohibited from writing life policies in New York if it acquired such stock because, through its subsidiary, it would then be writing fire and casualty insurance in New York. From a decision in favor of the Superintendent, the insurance company appealed.

FOSTER, J. . . . Undoubtedly [the New York statutes] forbid a foreign life insurance company licensed in this State from engaging in the business of writing fire or casualty insurance. . . . The real issue involved in this case is whether or not, by purchasing controlling interest in a fire or casualty company, the parent life insurance company actually is engaging in that business. . . . As appellant [insurance company] appropriately points out, the Legislature, in the Insurance Law, has used express language to prohibit certain activity through or by subsidiaries when that was its intention. [The Court then listed the specific sections of the statute expressly applying to holding companies and subsidiaries.]

The Insurance Law is replete with additional express references to subsidiaries and affiliates. . . . From these . . . and from the absence of express references to subsidiaries in [the sections here applicable], we may infer properly that the Legislature did not intend that the limitations [here applicable] be extended by implication to cover parent-subsidiary situations. This is a well-established canon of statutory construction. . . .

Such a construction, of course, is consistent with the general rule . . . that in no legal sense can the business of a corporation be said to be that of its stockholders . . . or the business of a subsidiary corporation be said to be that of a parent. . . . It is consistent also with the settled rule that a subsidiary corporation may engage in a business forbidden to its parent, unless the subsidiary entity is used as a cloak to cover for fraud or illegality. . . . On this issue we agree with the dissent below that the Superintendent may not presuppose, "without justification, that the plaintiff will utilize a fire or casualty subsidiary as a mere agent or tool to evade the provisions of said sections," and that "We are bound to assume that the mandate of the statute will be respected and that a subsidiary or plaintiff doing a

fire or casualty business will carry on in the usual way, namely, as an independent corporate entity." Appellant, in seeking to purchase a controlling interest in a fire insurance company, admittedly desires to improve its competitive position, and to enable its agents to offer to the public both life insurance and casualty and fire insurance. This does not, as the Superintendent argues, mean that appellant desires to engage in the fire or casualty insurance business. If the time comes that appellant, through the guise of a subsidiary, actually engages in that business, that will be time enough to refuse to renew appellant's license.

No public policy would be offended by consummation of the proposed acquisition. Appellant's admitted assets, capital, and surplus apparently are sufficient to insure against insolvency and to protect policyholders in this State. . . .

[Judgment reversed]

DESMOND, C.J., (dissenting). . . . The majority opinion says: "No public policy would be offended by consummation of the proposed acquisition." We think this State's policy of protecting the trustheld funds of life insurers from any and all diversions is plain, compelling, and essential and that it positively forbids what petitioner is trying to do. . . .

A life insurance company holds it policyholders' funds in trust for the protection of their beneficiaries against want. Those trust funds, conservatively and prudently invested to serve the high trust purpose on the happening of the inevitable event insured against, should not be subjected even in the most remote way to the hazards of other kinds of insurance. Nor should the life insurer's trusteed funds be, by investment in other insurance stocks, indirectly subjected to the other company's less restrictive investment policies. If any further explanation of the public policy is sought, it can be found in the Armstrong Committee Reports of 1906 (see Vol. 10, p. 385 et seq.) which described the life insurance companies of that day as transacting through stock ownership "the business of banks and trust companies," reminded us of the life companies' duty of conservatism in investment, rejected the idea that life companies should be allowed to make more money by speculation, and warned that a life insurer which gets control of companies in other business will end up by managing those other companies and thus engaging in their separate businesses. . . .

[DYE and BURKE, JJ., concur in the dissent]

Jack Cole—Dixie Highway Co. v Red Ball Motor Freight, Inc.

(Miss) 254 So2d 734 (1971)

As part of a business purchase and reorganization, it was agreed that all preferred stock of Dixie Highway should be surrendered and thereafter the Jack Cole—Dixie Highway Co. would have only common stock. An amendment to a corporate charter was prepared which declared that there should only be common stock. This amendment was agreed to on January 22, 1965. The amendment declared that it would be effective when filed for record, which occurred in one county on January 23 and in another county on January 27, 1965. A lawsuit was brought in which the question arose as to the date on which the preferred stock was canceled, as this determined whether the preferred stock should be classified as outstanding securities. The trial court held that the preferred stock had been surrendered on January 22, 1965. An appeal was taken from that determination.

BRADY, J. . . . The effective date of the amendment is of no consequence to the disposition of this case since the amendment itself was not required for the cancellation of the corporation's preferred stock. There is a wide distinction between the authorized capital stock of a corporation and its actual capital stock. While an amendment to the articles of incorporation would be required to increase or decrease the amount of the "authorized" capital stock of the company, no amendment was required to reduce the amount of actual stock outstanding, this being a matter solely for agreement between the stockholders and the corporation. Whenever a stockholder surrenders his stock to the corporation, the stock is no longer outstanding, regardless of whether the corporation cancels the stock or simply retains the stock as treasury stock; and further, in either event, such stock no longer constitutes a present liability of the corporation. . . .

The intent of Dixie . . . is especially apparent from Dixie's federal income tax return for the year 1965, which reported the surrender and cancellation of all the preferred stock of the corporation on January 22, 1965. . . . There are many other instances where various reports, financial statements, and applications reflected this same intent.

The trial court held that the aforesaid acts constituted a valid surrender and cancellation of the

5,500 shares of preferred stock on January 22, 1965, and that the preferred stock could no longer be considered as constituting outstanding securities, debts or obligations of Dixie. . . .

[Judgment affirmed]

Ladd Estate Company v Wheatley

246 Ore 627, 426 P2d 878 (1967)

The Ladd Estate Company brought suit on a promissory note made by Wheatley and guaranteed by Westover Tower, Inc. Westover claimed that its guaranty of the note was not binding because Wheatley was a director of the corporation when the guaranty was made and the guaranty was therefore ultra vires and illegal as it violated a statute prohibiting loans to directors. The lower court entered judgment for Ladd and Westover appealed.

LUSK, J. . . . The claim that the giving of the guaranty was an illegal act is based upon ORS 57.226, which reads: "No loans shall be made by a corporation to its officers or directors, and no loans shall be made by a corporation secured by its shares." The court found that Wheatley was a director at the time the guaranty was given. . . . An act of a corporation in contravention of a statute specifically prohibiting it is illegal and unenforceable. . . . We think, however, that the transaction, though admittedly ultra vires, is not denounced by ORS 57.226. That statute prohibits the making of "loans" by a corporation to its officers or directors. Concededly, the guaranty in question was not a loan. Counsel for Westover characterize it in their brief as "an executory agreement to make a loan to an officer and director." It was not even that, for it was only a conditional agreement. "The guarantee of a loan is not a loan. To guarantee a loan is to undertake to pay a debt or perform a duty, in case of the failure of another person primarily liable for such payment or performance. Ball Electric Light Co. v Child, 68 Conn 522, 525, 37 A 391. The making of a loan creates an absolute obligation: the guaranteeing a loan a conditional obligation. . . ."

[Judgment affirmed]

Total Automation v Illinois National Bank & Trust Co.

40 IllApp3d 266, 351 NE2d 879 (1976)

Total Automation, a corporation, had a checking account in the Illinois National Bank. Total owed

money to the bank's travel department. The bank deducted the amount of the travel bill from the checking account balance. Creditors of Total Automation brought an action on its behalf against the bank, claiming that the bank had no right to set off the travel agency debt because it was ultra vires for a national bank to operate a travel department. From a judgment for the bank, the plaintiff appealed.

RECHENMACHER, J. . . . The plaintiff in this appeal has raised the single issue of ultra vires, contending that the bank had no right to set-off because the operation of a travel agency by a national bank is an ultra vires act. Hence, it argues, the debt owed by the plaintiff to the bank's travel agency department was not a valid debt and therefore the right of set-off is not available to the bank. . . .

In support of its ultra vires argument the plaintiff cites the case of *Arnold Tours Inc. v Camp,* 472 F.2d 427 (1972), where the United States Court of Appeals (First Circuit) held that a national bank does not have the power under its charter, pursuant to the National Bank Act, to conduct a full-fledged travel agency. . . . The operation of a travel agency by a national bank is the act which plaintiff claims is ultra vires and therefore a defense. Plaintiff is not aggrieved as a private person by having to pay for services it used, nor can it be heard to say it is aggrieved as a member of the public by a departure

from sound public policy relating to banking, since the plaintiff voluntarily entered into the ultra vires transaction and reaped its benefits.

Generally speaking, the defense of ultra vires is not favored by the courts where it is raised by a private party seeking to avoid payment for a benefit received and where there is no matter of public policy involved. . . .

A national bank is a creature of Congress and strictly amenable to federal laws insofar as its duties and powers are concerned. Its authority to engage in a particular transaction with a private citizen cannot be questioned by a party to that transaction for the purpose of avoiding the transaction. . . . In 10 Am Jur 2d *Banks* § 276 (1963) it is said:

"It is also to be taken into consideration that where the provisions of the National Bank Act prohibit certain acts by banks or their officers, without imposing any penalty or forfeiture applicable to particular transactions which have been executed, their validity can be questioned only by the United States, and not by private parties."

We see no merit in the ultra vires contention raised by the plaintiff. . . .

[Judgment affirmed]

QUESTIONS AND CASE PROBLEMS

1. What social forces are affected by the rule of law permitting corporations to issue certificates representing shares of stock?

2. Compare (a) an ultra vires act and (b) an illegal act.

3. Compare the power of a corporation to (a) give a promissory note to represent a loan to the corporation, and (b) be an accommodation indorser on a note given in payment for the issue of its own corporate stock.

4. Compare (a) a promissory note and (b) a corporate bond.

5. The Central Mutual Auto Insurance Co. was a Michigan corporation. A foreign corporation, the Central Mutual Insurance Co., was granted a license to do business in Michigan. Central Mutual Auto Insurance Co. brought an action to prevent the foreign corporation from doing business within Michigan under that name. Decide. [Central Mutual Auto Insurance Co. v Central Mutual Insurance Co., 275 Mich 554, 267 NW 733]

6. In an action by the Federal Savings State Bank as the holder of a note against Grimes, the maker of the note, the authority of the corporate payee, the Industrial Mutual Life Insurance Co., to accept the note from the maker was questioned. It was argued that the corporate payee possessed the power because there was no statute expressly prohibiting

the exercise of that power. Was this argument valid? [Federal Savings State Bank v Grimes, 156 Kan 55, 131 P2d 894]

7. The Bank of Campbellsville was practically owned by the men who were its directors and officers. They personally owed a debt to Marshall, one of their depositors, for money they had borrowed from him to use to run the bank. Marshall overdrew his account in the bank. The directors and officers then agreed with him that the bank would pay the overdraft for Marshall and that their debt to him would be reduced by the amount of such payment. This was done. The bank later became insolvent, and Webster was appointed to liquidate the bank. He claimed that the overdraft agreement was ultra vires and that Marshall should be required to pay back to the bank the full amount of the overdraft. Marshall brought an action for a declaratory judgment for the purpose of determining his rights. Was he required to pay the full amount of the overdraft? [Marshall v Webster, 287 Ky 692, 155 SW2d 13]

8. A husband, *H*, borrowed money from bank *B*. *B* promised to insure the loan so that if *H* died before the debt was repaid, the proceeds of the insurance policy would pay off the debt. *B* failed to obtain the insurance, and *H* died owing a balance on the debt. *H*'s widow sued the bank to cancel the balance remaining on the theory that if *B* had obtained the insurance as it had promised to do, there would not be any balance. *B* defended on the ground that it could not have obtained the insurance because it would have been ultra vires for it to have done so. Was this defense valid? [Robichaud v Athol Credit Union, 352 Mass 351, 225 NE2d 347]

9. The Hartford Small Business Capital Corporation made ultra vires loans to various persons and corporations. The federal Small Business Administration, was appointed the receiver of the corporation. It sued Segal who was a director of the corporation, claiming that he was liable for the loss which such loans had caused the corporation. He raised the defense that he was not liable because there had not been any intent to defraud anyone. Was this a valid defense? [Small Business Administration v Segal (DC Conn) 383 FSupp 198]

10. An employee of the Archer Pancoast Co., a corporation, was killed as the result of falling through a hatchway in a building occupied by the company as a factory. Hoffman, superintendent of the factory, called Noll, an undertaker, and arranged for the funeral. Hoffman agreed to pay Noll $100 for his services. After performing the work, Noll brought an action against the Archer Pancoast Co. to recover the agreed sum. The defendant raised the defense of ultra vires. Decide. [Noll v Archer Pancoast Co., 60 App Div 414, 69 NYS 1007]

11. The Philadelphia Electric Co. was incorporated "for the purpose of supplying heating, lighting, and power by electricity to the public." The company supplied electricity but in addition began to sell electrical appliances. An action was brought by the attorney general against the corporation to forfeit its charter for engaging in ultra vires acts. Decide. [Commonwealth of Pennsylvania ex rel. Baldrige, Attorney General v Philadelphia Electric Co., 300 Pa 577, 151 A 344]

12. A bylaw of the Coleman Realty Co. provided that the corporation could not sell its stock to a person not a shareholder without first offering to sell it at its book value to the corporation or to the remaining shareholders in proportion to their interests. This bylaw was later repealed at a shareholders' meeting by the vote of Mrs. Ludgate who owned a majority of the stock. Bechtold, a minority shareholder, brought an action to declare that the repeal of the bylaw was invalid and had no effect. Was the repeal of the bylaw effective? [Bechtold v Coleman Realty Co., 367 Pa 208, 79 A2d 661]

48 Corporate Stock and Shareholders

The ownership of a corporation is divided among the shareholders. The rights and liabilities that are possessed by those who acquire stock are different from the rights and liabilities of those who are owners of proprietorships or partnerships.

A. CORPORATE STOCK

The ownership of a fractional part of a corporation is evidenced by the share or stock of the shareholder or stockholder. "Share" and "stock" have the same meaning.

§ 48:1. Nature of Stock. Membership in a corporation is usually based upon ownership of one or more shares of stock of the corporation. Each share represents a fractional interest in the total property possessed by the corporation. Each share confers the right to receive the dividends, when declared, and the right to participate in a distribution of capital upon the dissolution of the corporation. The shareholder does not own or have an interest in any specific property of the corporation; the corporation is the owner of all of its property.

(a) Capital and Capital Stock. *Capital* refers to the net assets of the corporation. *Capital stock* refers to the declared money value of the outstanding stock of the corporation.

(b) Valuation of Stock. Corporate stock commonly has a specified *par value*. This means that the person subscribing to the stock and acquiring it from the corporation must pay that amount. When stock is issued by the corporation for a price greater than the par value, some statutes provide that only the par value amount is to be treated as stated capital, the excess being allocated to surplus.[1]

Shares may be issued with no par value. In such a case no amount is stated in the certificate, and the amount that the subscriber pays the corporation is determined by the board of directors.

The value found by dividing the value of the corporate assets by the number of shares outstanding is the *book value* of the shares. The *market value* of a share of stock is the price at which it can be voluntarily bought or sold.

---

[1] California Corporations Code, § 1901.

§ 48:2. Certificate of Stock. The corporation ordinarily issues a *certificate of stock* or share certificate as evidence of the shareholder's ownership of stock. Although the issuance of such certificates is not essential either to the existence of a corporation or to the ownership of its stock, it is an almost universal practice since it is a convenient method of proving ownership and since it makes transfer of ownership easier.

Any form of certificate that identifies the interest owned by a person in the corporation is sufficient.

§ 48:3. Kinds of Stock. The stock of a corporation may be divided into two or more classes.

(a) Preferences. *Common stock* is ordinary stock that has no preferences. Each share usually entitles the holder to one vote and to a share of the profits in the form of dividends, when declared, and to participate in the distribution of capital upon dissolution of the corporation. *Preferred stock* has a priority over common stock. The priority may be with respect to dividends. Preferred stock may also have a priority over common stock in the distribution of capital upon dissolution of the corporation. Preferred stock is ordinarily nonvoting.

(1) Cumulative Preferred Stock. Ordinarily the right to receive dividends is dependent upon the declaration of dividends by the board of directors for that particular period of time. If there is no fund from which the dividends may be declared or if the directors do not declare them from an available fund, the shareholder has no right to dividends. The fact that a shareholder has not received dividends for the current year does not in itself give the right to accumulate or carry over into the next year a claim for those dividends.

It is sufficient that the articles of incorporation manifest an intent that the preferred stock be cumulative, as where it was stated that no dividends could be paid upon the common stock until unpaid dividends for all preceding years have been paid to the preferred shareholders. It was immaterial that the articles did not expressly state that the right to dividends was "cumulative" or that the dividends were not guaranteed.

In the absence of a statement that the right to dividends is noncumulative, it is frequently held that preferred stock has the right to cumulate dividends, particularly with respect to each year in which there was a surplus available for dividend declaration.

If the right to dividends on preferred stock does not accumulate, it is possible for the directors to defeat the rights of preferred shareholders in favor of the common shareholders. To illustrate, assume that in a corporation in which there are equal amounts of outstanding common and preferred stock, a surplus is available in each of five years for the declaration of a 6 percent dividend on the preferred stock of $100 par value but that nothing is available for the common stock. If the board of directors declared no dividends until the fifth year and if the preferred shareholders were not permitted to accumulate their preferences for the prior years, they would receive only 6 percent or $6 a share in the fifth year and the holders of common stock could receive the balance, whereas the common shareholders would have received nothing had dividends of $6 been declared annually on the preferred stock.

(2) ***Participating Preferred Stock.*** Sometimes the preferred stock is given the right of participation. After the common shares receive dividends or a capital distribution equal to that first received by the preferred stock, both kinds share equally in the balance.

(b) **Duration of Shares.** Ordinarily shares continue to exist for the life of the corporation. Under modern statutes, however, any kind of shares, whether common or preferred, may be made terminable at an earlier date.

(1) ***Redeemable Shares.*** *Redeemable shares* are surrendered to the corporation, which pays the shareholder the par value of the shares or such amount as is stated in the redemption agreement. Redeemed shares ordinarily cease to exist after redemption, as distinguished from being owned by the corporation as treasury stock.

(2) ***Convertible Shares.*** *Convertible shares* entitle the shareholder to exchange owned shares for a different type of share or for bonds of the corporation. Convertible unsecured bonds that may be converted into stock are more common than shares which may be converted into bonds.

(c) **Fractional Shares.** Modern statutes expressly authorize a corporation to issue fractional shares or to issue script or certificates representing such fractional shares that can be sold or combined for the acquisition of whole shares. In some states the holder of a fractional share is entitled to vote, to receive dividends, and to participate in the distribution of corporate assets upon liquidation.

B. ACQUISITION OF SHARES

Shares of stock may be acquired by (1) subscription, either before or after the corporation is organized, or (2) transfer of existing shares from a shareholder or from the corporation.

§ 48:4. Statute of Frauds. A contract for the sale of corporate shares must be evidenced by a writing or it cannot be enforced.[2] The writing must show that there has been a contract for the sale of a stated quantity of described securities at a defined or stated price. The writing must be signed in the manner required of a writing for the sale of goods.

No writing is required for instructions between a customer and a broker because, although such instructions contemplate the subsequent making of a sale, the giving of the instructions does not constitute a contract of sale. (See p. 816, Reinhart v Rauscher Pierce Securities Corp.)

§ 48:5. Subscription. A *stock subscription* is a contract or an agreement to buy a specific number and kind of shares when they are issued. As in the case of any other contract, the agreement to subscribe to shares of a corporation is subject to avoidance for fraud.

---

[2] UCC § 8-319(a).

(a)   Subscription before Incorporation. In many states a preincorporation subscription of shares is regarded as an offer to the corporation. By this view it is necessary for the corporation to accept the subscription offer either expressly or by conduct. A few states hold that such subscriptions automatically become binding contracts when the organization has been completed.

In some states the preincorporation subscription is irrevocable for a stated period.[3] The ABA MBCA provides that "a subscription for shares of a corporation to be organized shall be irrevocable for a period of six months, unless otherwise provided by the terms of the subscription agreement or unless all of the subscribers consent to the revocation of such subscription."[4] As in the case of any contract, there may be a rescission upon proper grounds.

Generally a subscriber is not entitled to receive a share certificate until the price of the shares has been paid.

(b)   Subscription after Incorporation. Subscriptions may be made after incorporation. In that event the transaction is like any other contract with the corporation. The offer of the subscription may come from the subscriber or from the corporation, but in either case there must be an acceptance. Upon acceptance the subscriber immediately becomes a shareholder with all the rights, privileges, and liabilities of a shareholder even though the subscriber has not paid any of the purchase price. The transaction, however, may only be a contract for the future issue of shares rather than a present subscription.

§ 48:6. Transfer of Shares. In the absence of a valid restriction, a shareholder may transfer shares to anyone.

(a)   Restrictions on Transfer. Restrictions on the transfer of stock are valid provided they are not unreasonable. In order to prevent its stock from going into the hands of strangers, it is lawful to require that the corporation or other stockholders be given the first right to purchase stock before a shareholder may sell it to an outsider.[5] (See p. 816, Irwin v West End Development Company) A provision giving a corporation the right to purchase a shareholder's shares upon death is valid.

The provision of the ABA Model Business Corporation Act has been followed in many states to authorize "any provision . . . for the regulation of the internal affairs of the corporation, including any provision restricting the transfer of shares."[6]

A restriction upon the right to transfer is not valid as against the purchaser of the certificate unless the restriction is conspicuously noted on the certificate or unless the transferee has actual knowledge of the restriction.

In any case, a restriction on the transfer of stock is strictly interpreted. For example, a restriction on the sale of stock is not applicable to a "gift" of stock made in accordance with the Gifts to Minors Act.

(b)   Interest Transferred. The transfer of shares may be absolute, that is, it may divest all ownership and make the transferee the full owner, or it may be merely for security, as when stock is pledged to secure the repayment of a loan. Since it is

---

[3] New York Business Corporation Law § 503(a).
[4] ABA MBCA § 17.
[5] Groves v Prickett (CA9 Cal) 420 F2d 1119.
[6] ABA MBCA § 54(h).

an essential element of a pledge transaction that the pledgee be able to sell the pledged property upon default, the pledge of stock requires the delivery to the pledgee of the stock certificate together with a separate assignment of or an indorsement on the stock certificate in favor of the pledgee or bearer. When this is done, the pledgee will be able to transfer title to the shares in case of default.

§ 48:7. Mechanics of Transfer. The ownership of shares is transferred by the delivery of the certificate of stock indorsed by its owner in blank, or to a specified person; or by the delivery of the certificate by such person accompanied by a separate assignment or power of attorney executed by the owner.[7] A transfer made in this manner is effective as between the parties even though the corporate charter or bylaws specify that shares cannot be transferred until a transfer is made on the books of the corporation or the records of a corporate transfer agent.

A delivery from the owner of the shares directly to the transferee is not required. It can be made to an intermediary. When there is no delivery of the share certificate to anyone, however, there is no transfer of ownership of the shares. (See p. 818, Pedersen v Brantner)

A physical transfer of the certificate without a necessary indorsement is effective as between the parties because indorsement is only necessary to make a transferee a "bona fide" purchaser as against third parties.

The owner of a security can prove continued ownership of a security by showing that what appears to be a proper indorsement on the security is actually unauthorized. Upon so doing, the owner recovers the security from the transferee of the security. The owner may not do so, however, if (1) the owner has ratified the unauthorized indorsement or (2) the security was obtained by a purchaser for value without notice of any adverse claim who in good faith surrendered the indorsed security to the issuer or its transfer agent and received a new, re-issued, or re-registered security.

In the latter case, the remedy of the true owner is restricted to the issuer and its transfer agent. The owner may hold them liable for money damages for improper registration. As an alternative, the owner may require the issuance of a replacement security unless this would result in the overissue of outstanding stock, in which case the issuer must purchase a like security for the owner or pay the owner the value of the original security.[8]

In general, the transfer agent stands in the same position as the corporation with respect to its stock and must make a formal transfer whenever the corporation would itself be required to recognize a transfer. When a corporation or its transfer agent wrongfully refuses to register a transfer of shares of stock, the new owner of the shares may bring suit for damages sustained and in some states may sue for the value of the shares on the theory of conversion.

§ 48:8. Effect of Transfer.

(a) Validity of Transfer. As a transfer of shares is a transfer of ownership, the transfer must in general satisfy the requirements governing any other transfer of

---

[7] UCC § 8-309. The second alternative of a delivery of an unindorsed certificate is designed to keep the certificate "clean," as when the transfer is for a temporary or special purpose as in the case of a pledge of the certificate as security for a loan.

[8] UCC § 8-104, 8-311, 8-404.

property or agreement to transfer property. As between the parties, a transfer may be set aside for any ground that would warrant similar relief under property law. If the transfer of stock has been obtained by duress, the transferor may obtain a rescission of the transfer.

(b) Negotiability. Under the common law, the transferee of shares of stock had no greater right than the transferor because the certificate and the shares represented by the certificate were nonnegotiable. By statute, the common-law rule has been changed by imparting negotiability to the certificate. Just as various defenses cannot be asserted against the holder in due course of a commercial paper, it is provided that similar defenses cannot be raised against the person acquiring the certificate in good faith and for value. As against such a person, the defenses cannot be raised that the transferor did not own the shares, or did not have authority to deliver the certificate, or that the transfer was made in violation of a restriction upon transfer not known to such person and not noted conspicuously on the certificate.

The fact that corporate stock has the quality of negotiability does not make it commercial paper within Article 3 of the Uniform Commercial Code. Shares of stock are classified under the UCC as investment securities; and Article 8, as supplemented by the continuing non-Code law which has not been displaced,[9] is the source of the law governing the rights of the parties to the transaction involving such securities. Nevertheless, courts may look to Article 3 for guidance when a question regarding an investment security cannot be resolved on the basis of the language in Article 8 alone.

(c) Secured Transaction. Corporate stock is frequently delivered to a creditor as security for a debt owed by the shareholder. Thus, a debtor borrowing money from a bank may deliver shares of stock to the bank as collateral security for the repayment of the loan, or a broker's customer purchasing stock on margin may leave the stock in the possession of the broker as security for the payment of any balance due. The delivery of the security to the creditor gives rise to a perfected security interest without any filing by the creditor. In itself the pledge does not make the pledgee of the corporate stock the owner of the stock nor of any of the assets of the corporation.

(d) Effect of Transfer on Corporation. Until there is a transfer on its books, the corporation is entitled to treat as the owner the person whose name is on the books.[10] The corporation may properly refuse to recognize the transferee when the corporation is given notice or has knowledge that the transfer is void or in breach of trust. In such a case the corporation properly refuses to effect a transfer until the rights of the parties have been determined.

The corporation may also refuse to register the transfer of shares when the outstanding certificate is not surrendered to it, in the absence of satisfactory proof that it has been lost, destroyed, or stolen.

§ 48:9. Lost, Destroyed, and Stolen Securities. The owner of a lost, destroyed, or stolen security is entitled to a replacement security if the owner files a sufficient indemnity

---

[9] UCC § 1-103.
[10] UCC § 8-207.

bond and requests the new security within a reasonable time before the issuer has notice that the original certificate has been aquired by a bona fide purchaser. If after the issue of the new security, a bona fide purchaser appears with the original security, the corporation must register a transfer of the security to that person and accept such person as the owner of the shares.[11] (See p. 818, Weller v American Telephone and Telegraph Co.)

§ 48:10. Protection of the Public.

(a) **State Regulation.** In order to protect the public from the sale of securities of nonexistent or worthless corporations, many states have adopted regulations called *blue-sky laws.* The statutes vary in detail. Some impose a criminal penalty for engaging in fraudulent practices, while others require the licensing of dealers in securities and approval by a government agency before a given security can be sold to the public.[12]

The state blue-sky laws are subject to the very important limitation that they can apply only to intrastate transactions and cannot apply to sales made in interstate commerce. Likewise they commonly exempt sales to merchant buyers of securities, that is, persons in the business of purchasing securities or who frequently do so, such as mutual funds, and apply only to sales to members of the general public.

(b) **Federal Regulation.** The Securities Act of 1933 and the Securities Exchange Act of 1934 provide the basic framework for the federal regulation of the sale of securities in interstate commerce. The 1933 Act deals with the original distribution of securities by the issuing corporations, while the 1934 Act is concerned with the secondary distribution of securities in the national securities exchanges and in the . over-the-counter markets.

§ 48:11. Securities Act of 1933.
The 1933 Act prohibits the offer or sale of securities to the public in interstate commerce before a *registration statement* has been filed with the Securities and Exchange Commission (SEC). The seller must also provide a *prospectus* to the purchasers of the securities setting forth the key information contained in the registration statement. The object is to provide the interested investor with detailed information about the security and the enterprise. The SEC does not approve or disapprove the securities as being good or bad investments but only reviews the form and content of the registration statement and the prospectus to assure full disclosure.

(a) **Applicability.** The statute applies to the issuing of stocks and bonds and any other form of investment contract by an issuer, underwriter, or dealer.

(b) **Registration Statement Exemption.** The issuing of some securities is exempt from the requirement of a registration statement. Registration is not required for issues of $500,000 or less, nor for issues by a government or a nonprofit corporation. The statute does not apply to transactions between private investors, nor to private offerings to a limited number of persons who would otherwise have access to the kinds of information set forth in the registration statement.[13]

---

[11] UCC § 8-405(1), (2), (3).
[12] Harvey v Davis, 69 Cal3d 362, 71 CalRptr 129, 444 P2d 705.
[13] Securities Act Amendment of 1964, PL 88-467, 78 Stat 565, 15 USC § 781(g)(1)(B).

(c) Liability for Fraud. The federal Act imposes civil liability and criminal penalties for fraudulent statements made in connection with the issuance of securities whether or not exempt from the registration statement requirements. Civil and criminal liability is also imposed for false statements made in the registration statement, and for the omission of material matter therefrom. The same liability applies to fraudulent statements in and omissions from a stock prospectus.

Any investor who sustains loss because of the false statements or omissions of the registration statement may sue to recover damages.

(d) Criminal Penalties. The Act declares it unlawful for any issuer, underwriter, or dealer in securities to send either the securities or a prospectus for them in interstate commerce or the mails without having first registered the issue with the Securities and Exchange Commission.

A criminal penalty is imposed for failure to register or for making false statements to the Commission. The Commission may enjoin any practice that violates the act, and persons injured may bring suit for civil damages against the violator.

§ 48:12. Securities Exchange Act of 1934. The 1934 Act was designed to prevent fraudulent and manipulative practices in the secondary distribution of securities, that is, their sale on national security exchanges and in the over-the-counter market.

(a) Registration Requirements. Exchanges, brokers, and dealers who deal in the securities traded in interstate commerce or on any national security exchange must register if they have assets of $1 million or more and 500 or more shareholders.

A registrant is required to file periodic reports in order to keep the registration information up to date.

(b) Disclosure of Ownership and Short-Swing Profit. Corporate directors and officers owning registered securities of their corporation and any shareholder owning more than ten percent of any class of the issuer's securities must file with the SEC a statement as to such ownership and must report any sale made within the preceding month.

If such a person sells at a profit any of such securities in less than six months after their purchase, the profit is called a *short-swing profit.* The corporation may sue the director, officer, or stockholder for the short-swing profit and may recover that profit even though there was no fraudulent intent in making the profit.[14]

(c) Insider Information. Anyone in possession of material inside information about a corporation, such as a discovery which it has made or action with respect to dividends, must either disclose it to the investing public or abstain from trading in the corporation's stock until such information has been disclosed. Investors who lack that information and have sold their stock at a loss, may recover damages from any insider who has made unfair use of the undisclosed information.[15]

(d) Anti-Fraud Provisions. The Act makes it unlawful for any person to manipulate prices and create the appearance of active trading in securities or to make a false

---

[14] Securities Act of 1934, § 16(a), (b).
[15] Securities Act of 1934, § 10(b), Rule 10(b)(5).

or misleading statement of any material fact in a report or a financial document. This applies to all securities, whether registered or not as long as use is made of the mails, interstate commerce, or a national stock exchange.

A civil action for damages may be brought by any injured party who purchased or sold securities because of false, misleading, or undisclosed information.[16]

Criminal penalties may also be imposed for willful violations of the Act, or the SEC regulations or rules.

C. RIGHTS OF SHAREHOLDERS

The control of the shareholders over the corporation is indirect. Periodically, ordinarily once a year, the shareholders elect directors and through this means can control the corporation. At other times, however, the shareholders have no right or power to control the corporate activity so long as it is conducted within lawful channels.

§ 48:13. Ownership Rights.

(a) Certificate of Stock. A shareholder has the right to have a properly executed certificate as evidence of ownership of shares.

(b) Transfer of Shares. Subject to certain valid restrictions, a shareholder has the right to transfer the shares, and may sell the shares at any price or transfer them as a gift.

§ 48:14. Right to Vote. The right to vote means the right to vote at shareholders' meetings for the election of directors and on such other special matters as must be passed upon by the shareholders. As an illustration of the latter, a proposal to change the capital structure of the corporation or a proposal to sell all or substantially all the assets of the corporation must be approved by the shareholders.

A shareholder may vote in any manner. The shareholder owes no duty to the corporation, or to other shareholders, to act in a way which will be for their interest. The fact that a shareholder is also a director of the corporation does not restrict this freedom of voting nor does it disqualify the shareholder from voting on any issue on which other shareholders are entitled to vote.

(a) Who May Vote. Ordinarily only those common shareholders in whose name the stock appears on the books of the corporation are entitled to vote. Generally the directors may fix a date for determining the shareholders who may vote.[17]

When a shareholder has pledged shares as security, the shareholder may generally continue to vote the shares, and the pledgee is not entitled to vote the shares unless a transfer of the shares is made to the pledgee by the corporation.[18]

(b) Number of Votes. Each shareholder is ordinarily entitled to one vote for each voting share. In some states, however, the number of votes allowed to each shareholder is limited by statute.

---

[16] Blue Chip Stamps v Manor Drug Store, 421 US 723.
[17] ABA MBCA § 30.
[18] ABA MBCA § 33.

In most states *cumulative voting* in the election of directors may be provided for or automatically exists when the contrary is not stated in the charter or articles of incorporation.[19] In nearly half of the states cumulative voting is mandatory, being imposed by either constitution or statute. On the other hand, a few states prohibit cumulative voting.

Under a cumulative voting plan, each shareholder has as many votes as the number of shares owned multiplied by the number of directors to be elected. The votes can be distributed among directors in any manner.

There is a conflict of authority as to the validity of a provision for the election of the directors by classes, as when directors serve for three years and one-third of the directors are elected each year. In some jurisdictions such a provision is held invalid as impairing the right of cumulative voting. In other jurisdictions, such a system is valid, and cumulative voting is exercised as to the directors within each class to be elected at each election.

(c)   Voting by Proxy. A shareholder has the right to authorize another to vote the shares owned by the shareholder. This is known as *voting by proxy.* In the absence of restrictions to the contrary, any person, even one not a shareholder, may act as a proxy. Ordinarily authority to act as a proxy may be conferred by an informal written instrument.[20] The corporation law of a particular state may expressly require that a proxy be signed. There is also some statutory recognition of the visual transmission of a proxy as in the case of a "photogram" appearing to have been transmitted by a shareholder.[21]

(d)   Voting Agreements and Trusts. Shareholders, as a general rule, are allowed to enter into an agreement by which they concentrate their voting strength for the purpose of controlling the management.

A *voting trust* exists when by agreement a group of shareholders, or all of the shareholders, transfer their shares in trust to one or more persons as trustees who are authorized to vote the stock during the life of the trust agreement. In general, such agreements have been upheld if their object is lawful. In some juridictions such trusts cannot run beyond a specified number of years. There are some signs of a relaxation as to this matter. Several states have abandoned any time limitation, several have extended the time limitation, and many states provide for an extension or renewal of the agreement.

§ 48:15. Preemptive Offer of Shares. If the capital stock of a corporation is increased, shareholders ordinarily have the preemptive right to subscribe to such percentage of the new shares as their old shares bore to the former total of capital stock. This right is given in order to enable shareholders to maintain their relative interests in the corporation.

The existence of a preemptive right may make impossible the concluding of a transaction in which the corporation is to transfer a block of stock as consideration.

---

[19] ABA MBCA § 33.

[20] See, for example, the regulations of the Securities and Exchange Commission, Rule X-14A-4. By statute it has been declared in at least one jurisdiction that "a telegram . . . is a sufficient writing." In a few states an oral proxy is valid.

[21] North Carolina Gen Stat § 55-68(a).

Moreover, practical difficulties arise as to how stock should be allocated among shareholders of different classes. For these reasons, the trend of corporation statutes has been toward the abolition of the preemptive right and court decisions have made many exceptions to the requirement.[22]

§ 48:16. Inspection of Books. A shareholder has the right to inspect the books of the shareholder's corporation. The request for inspection must be made in good faith, for proper motives, and at a reasonable time and place.[23] The Model Act authorizes inspection of corporate records "for any proper purpose." [24]

The purpose of inspection must be reasonably related to the shareholder's interest as a shareholder. A shareholder is entitled to inspect the records to determine the financial condition of the corporation, the quality of its management, and any matters relating to rights or interests in the corporate business, such as the value of stock; to obtain information needed for a lawsuit against the corporation or its directors or officers; or in order to organize the other shareholders into an "opposition" party to remove the board of directors at the next election; or to buy the shares of other shareholders. (See p. 819, Skoglund v Ormand Industries, Inc.)

Inspection has frequently been refused when it was sought merely from idle curiosity or for "speculative purposes." Inspection has sometimes been denied on the ground that it was merely sought to obtain a mailing list of persons who would be solicited to buy products of another enterprise. Inspection has also been refused where the object of the shareholder was to advance political or social beliefs without regard to the welfare of the corporation.

Many cases deny the right of inspection when it would be harmful to the corporation or is sought only for the purpose of annoying, harrassing, or causing vexation, or for the purpose of aiding competitors of the corporation. In contrast, the right of inspection is so broadly recognized in some states that the fact that the shareholder may make an improper use of the information obtained does not bar inspection.

The ABA MBCA seeks to prevent the abuse of the power to inspect corporate books by limiting the right of inspection to persons who have owned the stock for not less than 6 months or who own not less than 5 percent of all the outstanding shares of the corporation. As a further safeguard, the Model Act requires that the request for inspection be made by "written demand stating the purpose thereof." [25]

Inspection need not be made personally. A shareholder may employ an accountant or an attorney to examine the records. The Model Act declares that the shareholder "shall have the right to examine, in person, or by agent or attorney, at any reasonable time or times, for any proper purpose its relevant books and records of account, minutes, and record of shareholders and to make extracts therefrom."

---

[22] ABA MBCA § 26. The Model Act in effect takes a neutral position by proposing one section that declares that shareholders have no preemptive right, except as expressly stated in the articles of incorporation; and an alternative provision declaring that they have such right, except to the extent expressly denied by the articles or by the alternative section. In recognition of the necessity that the corporation have a free hand in using a block of stock as payment, even the latter alternative section declares that the preemptive right does not exist as to "any shares sold otherwise than for cash."

[23] Sanders v Pacific Gamble Robinson Co. 250 Minn 265, 84 NW2d 919.

[24] ABA MBCA § 52.

[25] ABA MBCA § 52.

(a)   Form of Books. There are generally no legal requirements as to the form of corporate books and records. The Model Act recognizes that corporate books and records may be stored in modern data storage systems. "Any books, records, and minutes may be in written form or in any other form capable of being converted into written form within a reasonable time."

(b)   Financial Statements. In recognition of the widespread practice of corporations preparing formal financial statements, the Model Act requires a corporation to send such a statement to a shareholder upon request. It provides that "upon the written request of any shareholder . . . , the corporation shall mail to such shareholder . . . its most recent financial statements showing in reasonable detail its assets and liabilities, and the results of its operations." [26] A number of states have similar provisions.

§ 48:17.   Dividends. A shareholder has the right to receive a proportion of dividends as they are declared, subject to the relative rights of other shareholders to preferences, accumulation of dividends, and participation. However, there is no absolute right to receive dividends.

(a)   Funds Available for Declaration of Dividends. Statutes commonly provide that no dividends may be declared unless there is a "surplus" for their payment. This surplus is generally calculated as the amount of the corporate assets in excess of all outstanding liabilities and outstanding shares of the corporation.

As an exception to these rules, a wasting assets corporation may pay dividends out of current net profits without regard to the preservation of the corporate assets. *Wasting assets corporations* include those enterprises that are designed to exhaust or use up the assets of the corporation (as by extracting oil, coal, iron, and other ores), as compared with a manufacturing plant where the object is to preserve the plant as well as to continue to manufacture. A wasting assets corporation may also be formed for the purpose of buying and liquidating a bankrupt's stock of merchandise.

In some states statutes provide that dividends may be declared from current net profits, without regard to the existence of a deficit from former years, or from surplus.

If dividends are about to be declared from an unlawful source, an injunction can be obtained to stop their declaration or payment. If the payment has already been made, the directors responsible for the action may be sued individually and be made to indemnify the corporation for the loss they have caused it by the improper payment if they acted negligently or in bad faith in declaring the dividends.

(b)   Discretion of Directors. Assuming that a fund is available for the declaration of dividends, it is then a matter primarily within the discretion of the board of directors whether a dividend shall be declared. The fact that there is a surplus which could be used for dividends does not determine that they must be declared. This rule is not affected by the nature of the shares. Thus, the fact that the shareholders hold cumulative preferred shares does not give them any right to demand a declaration of dividends or to interfere with an honest exercise of discretion by the directors.

---

[26] ABA MBCA § 52.

In general, a court will refuse to substitute its judgment for the judgment of the directors of the corporation and will interfere with their decision as to dividend declaration only when it is shown that their conduct is harmful to the welfare of the corporation or its shareholders. The courts, however, will compel the declaration of a dividend when it is apparent that the directors have amassed a surplus beyond any practical business need.

Once dividends are duly declared, a debtor-creditor relation exists between the corporation and the shareholders as to those dividends. The shareholder may accordingly sue the corporation to recover the amount of lawfully declared dividends if it fails to pay them.

(c)   Form of Dividends. Customarily, a dividend is paid in money; but it may be paid in property, such as a product manufactured by the corporation, in shares of other corporations held by the corporation, or in shares of the corporation itself.

(d)   Effect of Transfer of Shares. In determining who is entitled to dividends, it is immaterial when the surplus from which the distribution is made was earned. As between the transferor and the transferee, if the dividend is in cash or property other than the shares of the corporation declaring the dividend, the person who was the owner on the date the dividend was declared is entitled to the dividend. Thus, if a cash dividend is declared before a transfer is made, the transferor is entitled to it. If the transfer was made before the declaration date, the transferee is entitled to it. In applying this rule, it is immaterial when distribution of the dividend is made.

The rule that the date of declaration determines the right to a cash dividend is subject to modification by the corporation. The board of directors in declaring the dividend may state that it will be payable to those who will be the holders of record on a later specified date.

If the dividend consists of shares in the corporation declaring the dividend, ownership is determined by the date of distribution. Whichever party is the owner of the shares when the stock dividend is distributed is entitled to the stock dividend. The reason for this variation from the cash dividend rule lies in the fact that the declaration of a stock dividend has the effect of diluting the existing corporate assets among a larger number of shares.[27] The value of the holding represented by each share is accordingly diminished. Unless the person who owns the stock on the date when distribution is made receives a proportionate share of the stock dividend, the net effect will be to lessen that person's holding.

The transferor and transferee may enter into any agreement they choose with respect to dividends.

These rules determine the right to dividends as between transferor and transferee. Regardless of what those rights may be, the corporation is generally entitled to continue to recognize the transferor as a shareholder until it has been notified that a transfer has been made and the corporate records are accordingly changed. If the corporation, believing that the transferor is still the owner of the shares, sends a dividend to which the transferee is entitled, the transferee cannot sue the corporation. In that

---

[27] Geier v Mercantile-Safe Deposit & Trust Co., 273 MdApp 102, 328 A2d 311.

case, the remedy of the transferee is to sue the transferor for the dividend that the latter has received.

§ 48:18. Capital Distribution. Upon the dissolution of the corporation, the shareholders are entitled to receive any balance of the corporate assets that remains after the payment of all creditors. Certain classes of stock may have a preference or priority in this distribution.

§ 48:19. Shareholders' Actions. When the corporation has the right to sue its directors or officers or third persons for damages caused by them to the corporation or for breach of contract, one or more shareholders may bring such action if the corporation refuses to do so. This is a *derivative* (secondary) *action* in that the shareholder enforces only the cause of action of the corporation, and any money recovery is paid into the corporate treasury.

An action cannot be brought by minority shareholders, however, if the action of the corporate directors or officers has been ratified by a majority of the shareholders acting in good faith and if the matter is of such a nature that had such majority originally authorized the acts of the directors or officers, there would not have been any wrong.

Shareholders may also intervene or join in an action brought against the corporation when the corporation refuses to defend the action against it or is not doing so in good faith. Otherwise the shareholders may take no part in an action by or against the corporation.

Shareholders in a deadlocked corporation may bring an action to obtain a dissolution of the corporation.

D. LIABILITIES OF SHAREHOLDERS

The shareholder is ordinarily protected from liability for the acts of the corporation. Some exceptions are made by statute.

§ 48:20. Limited Liability. The liability of a shareholder is generally limited. This means that the shareholder is not personally responsible for the debts and liabilities of the corporation. The capital contributed by the shareholders may be exhausted by the claims of creditors, but there is no personal liability for any unpaid balance.

§ 48:21. Exceptions to Limited Liability. Liability may be imposed upon a shareholder as though there were no corporation when either the court ignores the corporate entity because of the particular circumstances of the case, or when the corporation is so defectively organized that it is deemed not to exist.

(a) Wage Claims. Statutes sometimes provide that the shareholders shall be unlimitedly liable for the wage claims of corporate employees. This principle has been abandoned in some states in recent years or has been confined to the major shareholders of corporations of which the stock is not sold publicly.

(b) Unpaid Subscriptions. Most states prohibit the issuance of par value shares for less than par or except for "money, labor done, or property actually received." Whenever shares issued by a corporation are not fully paid for, the original subscriber receiving the shares or any transferee who does not give value, or who knows that the shares were not fully paid, may be liable for the unpaid balance if the corporation is insolvent and the money is required to pay the creditors.[28]

If the corporation has issued the shares as fully paid, or has given them as a bonus, or has agreed to release the subscriber for the unpaid balance, the corporation cannot recover that balance. The fact that the corporation is thus barred does not prevent the creditors of the corporation from bringing an action to compel payment of the balance. The same rules are applied when stock is issued as fully paid in return for property or services which were overvalued so that the stock is not actually paid for in full. There is a conflict of authority, however, as to whether the shareholder is liable from the mere fact that the property or services given for the shares were in fact overvalued by the directors or whether in addition it must be shown that the directors had acted in bad faith in making the erroneous valuation. The trend of modern statutes is to prohibit disputing the valuation placed by the corporation on services or property in the absence of proof of fraud.

If a statute makes void the shares issued for less than par, they may be canceled upon suit of the corporation.

(c) Unauthorized Dividends. If dividends are improperly paid out of capital, the shareholders generally are liable to creditors to the extent of such depletion of capital. In some states the liability of the shareholder depends on whether the corporation was insolvent at the time, whether debts were existing at the time, and whether the shareholders had notice of the source of the dividend.

§ 48:22. The Professional Corporation. The liability of a shareholder in a professional corporation is limited to the same degree as that of a shareholder in an ordinary business corporation. Several fact situations may arise.

(a) Act of Shareholder in Creating Liability. If a shareholder in a professional corporation, such as a corporation of physicians, negligently drives the company car in going to attend a patient, or is personally obligated on a contract made for the corporation, or is guilty of malpractice, the shareholder is liable without limit for the liability that has been created. This is the same rule of law that applies in the case of the ordinary business corporation. Professional corporation statutes generally repeat the rule with respect to malpractice liability by stating that the liability of a shareholder for malpractice is not affected by the fact of incorporation.

(b) Malpractice Liability of an Associate. The liability of a shareholder in a professional corporation for the malpractice of an associate is not clear. If Doctors *A, B,* and *C* are a partnership, each is unlimitedly liable for any malpractice liability incurred by the others. Assume that Doctors *A, B,* and *C* are a professional corporation, will *A* be liable for the malpractice of *C?* If the orthodox rule applicable to business corporations applies here, the answer is "no liability." The statutory reference to malpractice liability is generally not very clear, and it is possible that a conservative court will interpret the statutory preservation of malpractice liability as preserving liability when such liability would exist if there were a partnership.

---

[28] Under ABA MBCA § 25, the transferee is protected if the shares were acquired in good faith without knowledge or notice that they were not fully paid.

(c)   Ordinary Torts. If an ordinary tort, meaning one not related to malpractice, is committed, each shareholder is protected from liability for the acts of others. For example, assume that in order to aid a patient, a medical corporation sends its secretary after hours with medicine to a patient's home. In the course of the trip the secretary negligently runs over a pedestrian. In such a case both the secretary and the corporation would be liable for the harm caused the pedestrian. Would a shareholder be liable? It should be concluded that a shareholder would not be liable. Here the ordinary rule of limited liability of a shareholder should apply. Since the situation described does not involve "malpractice," there is no possibility of concluding that there is a liability of a shareholder under a malpractice exception to the general rule of limited liability. Consequently, in the absence of an express contrary statement in the professional corporation statute, a shareholder in the professional corporation is shielded from liability in the case of ordinary torts of others.

Under the proposed ABA Model Professional Corporation Act, three alternative provisions as to liability of shareholders are proposed: limited liability as in a business corporation, vicarious personal liability as in a partnership, and personal liability limited in amount conditioned upon financial responsibility in the form of insurance or a surety bond.[29]

---

[29] American Bar Association Model Professional Corporation Act, § 11(d).

CASES FOR CHAPTER 48

Reinhart v Rauscher Pierce Securities Corp.

83 NMex 194, 490 P2d 240 (1971)

Reinhart owned shares of unlisted stock. Rauscher Pierce Securities Corp. was a stockbroker. Rauscher agreed to sell Reinhart's stock when its value fell more than ten percent of the original cost to Reinhart. The stock fell more than ten percent but Rauscher failed to sell it. Reinhart sued Rauscher for damages. The defense was raised that there was no liability because the contract was oral and a writing was required to make the contract binding. From a judgment for Rauscher, Reinhart appealed.

SUTIN, J. . . . On the statute of frauds defense, defendants contend the oral contract was not to be performed within one year from the date of the agreement. . . . Reinhart never said he wanted defendants to hold his stock for a year or more. He could terminate the agency within a year. It was capable of performance within a year. Therefore, the rule does not apply. . . .

The statute of frauds does not apply to the relationship between a broker and customer which creates a relation of trust and confidence. . . .

It has been suggested that . . . [UCC §]8-319, . . . entitled Statute of Frauds, is applicable here. It is not because a "sale of securities" did not take place in this case. The facts here established an agency relationship, not a sale. Lindsey v Stein Bros. and Boyce, Inc., 222 Tenn. 149, 433 S.W. 2d 669 (1968). 21 A.L.R.3d 964, 977, § 4(d); 3 Anderson, Uniform Commercial Code, Second Edition, § 8-319:5, p. 789.

[Judgment reversed action remanded]

Irwin v West End Development Co.

(CA10 Colo) 481 F2d 34 (1973)

The Taylors owned stock in the West End Development Company, a corporation. They sold their stock to Vroom, an officer of the corporation, in violation of a transfer restriction contained in the articles of incorporation. This restriction required that any stockholder selling shares must first offer to every existing stockholder a proportion of the shares being sold, the proportion being the same as the percentage of the stock which the other shareholder already owned. The other five stockholders in the corporation brought a lawsuit to compel

Vroom to hold the stock as constructive trustee * for the benefit of all stockholders in order to give effect to the transfer restriction. Vroom raised the defense that the restriction was not binding. From a decision in favor of the plaintiffs, the corporation and Vroom appealed.

BARRETT, C.J. . . . Vroom contends that the Court erred in impressing a constructive trust on his stock purchased from the Taylors because Article IV, Paragraph 6 of the Articles of Incorporation is not enforceable. It states:

> No shareholder shall sell or transfer any outstanding shares of the capital stock issued by the corporation to such shareholder, excepting to the other shareholders, in the proportion which the number of shares owned by each bears to the total shares outstanding, without the prior consent of the owners or at least two-thirds (⅔) of the shares entitled to vote at the shareholders' meeting . . .

Vroom alleges that the provision is unintelligible, unworkable, and too uncertain in its terms to be enforced or to give the appellees their pro-rata rights to the purchase of stock sold to Vroom by the Taylors. . . . Vroom argues that it is also an unreasonable restraint on the alienation of the corporation stock.

. . . The law prohibits an absolute restriction against transferability, but if a restriction does not amount to an effective prohibition against transferability, then the test is reasonableness. Thus, a "first refusal" provision is valid. . . . The trial court recognized that the provision contained ambiguities but it construed them against the drafter and gave the provision a reasonable meaning . . . to . . . provide a workable and equitable result. The trial court stated that instead of stating "in proportion which the number of shares owned by each bears to the total shares outstanding," the draftsman meant to state, "in the proportion which the number of shares owned by each bears to the total shares not offered for sale." Vroom was, or should have been, well aware of the provisions contained in the Articles of Incorporation. He should have offered the Taylors' stock to [other shareholders] on a pro-rata basis before purchasing

it entirely for himself . . . A constructive trust was imposed by the trial court because Vroom would be unjustly enriched by being permitted to keep the 30.76 shares. The trust arose because of unconscionable conduct by Vroom in obtaining the shares from the Taylors for his sole benefit. . . .

Vroom contends that the provisions of Section 15 of the Uniform Stock Transfer Act barred the trial court's impression of a constructive trust upon the Taylor stock. It states:

> There shall be no lien in favor of a corporation upon the shares represented by a certificate issued by such corporation and there shall be no restriction upon the transfer of shares so represented by virtue of any bylaw of such corporation, or otherwise, unless the right of the corporation to such a lien or the restriction is stated upon the certificate. 1963 C.R.S. 31-11-14.

Vroom alleges that the effect of the statute is to render ineffective the restrictive provisions of Article IV, Paragraph 6 of the Articles of Incorporation because the restrictions were not set forth upon the stock certificates sold by Taylors to Vroom.

Section 15 of the Uniform Stock Transfer Act was superseded by [UCC §] 8-204 which states:

> Unless noted conspicuously on the security, a restriction on transfer imposed by the issuer even though otherwise lawful is ineffective except against a person with actual knowledge of it.

. . . The failure to note the restriction on the certificates is no bar to its enforcement against Vroom who had actual notice of it. The trial court went further and stated that in any event, Vroom is estopped from setting up the absence of the restriction from the face of the stock certificate as a defense, inasmuch as he owed a fiduciary duty to the other stockholders. Vroom breached his contractual and fiduciary duties to the appellees when he purchased the Taylor stock without honoring the agreement he had previously made to permit the other stockholders to share in the purchase. The only equitable solution is the one the trial court arrived at, i.e., the imposition of a constructive trust on the 30.76 shares of stock purchased by Vroom from the Taylors. In this regard, we note that Vroom will share on a pro-rata basis, notwithstanding his breach.

[Judgment imposing trust on purchased shares affirmed]

---

* Authors' note: A *constructive trust* is a trust which the law implies, although none exists, when property has been wrongfully acquired, in order to compel the wrongdoer to hold such property for the benefit of the persons who should have received it. See § 53:10 of this book.

Pedersen v Brantner

(MoApp) 502 SW2d 25 (1973)

Linhart owned shares of stock in the First National Bank. She borrowed money from the bank and pledged the stock as security. She thereafter decided to transfer 70 head of cattle and the shares of stock to her son. She could not deliver the shares certificate to him because it was held by the bank. She therefore executed a bill of sale reciting the transfer of the cattle and the stock to the son. She gave him the bill of sale and he had the bill recorded. After her death, the son brought an action to determine the ownership of the stock. From a judgment against him, he appealed.

SHANGLER, P.J. . . . Appellant stakes his right to ownership of the stock on the theory that delivery to him of the bill of sale was symbolic delivery of title to the stock. The Uniform Stock Transfer Act, [provides:]

> Title to a certificate and to shares represented thereby can be transferred *only* (1) By *delivery* of the certificate *indorsed* either in blank or to a specified person appearing by the certificate to be the owner of the shares represented thereby; or (2) By *delivery* of the certificate *and* a separate document containing a written assignment of the certificate. . . . (emphasis supplied) An attempted transfer of title to a certificate or to the shares represented thereby without delivery of the certificate shall have the effect of a promise to transfer; and the obligation, if any, imposed by such a promise shall be determined by the law governing the formation and performance of contracts.

Thus, the statute clearly provides that title to shares of stock follows the certificate and an attempted sale of stock without actual delivery of the certificate has the effect of a promise to transfer, which gives rise to an obligation on the transferor determinable by the law of contracts. . . .

The conveyance by bill of sale does not conform to the requirements of the Uniform Stock Transfer Act , . . . [The Uniform Stock Transfer Act was] repealed effective July 1, 1965. The transaction we consider occurred before the effective date of Article 8 of the Uniform Commercial Code, which now covers the subject. Therefore, this action is to be determined upon the basis of the repealed law.

. . . The transferability of shares in national banks is not governed by different rules from those which are ordinarily applied to the transfers of shares in other corporate bodies.

[Judgment affirmed]

Weller v American Telephone and Telegraph Co.

(DelCh) 290 A2d 842 (1972)

Weller owned stock of the American Telephone and Telegraph Company and of the General Electric Company. Her signature was forged on the stock certificates and the shares were then sold in the open market. The purchasers obtained the registration of the transfer of the shares to them. Weller then sued the two corporations and demanded that they replace the securities which she originally owned. The defendants raised the defense that Weller had failed to notify them within a reasonable time of the wrongful taking of the securities.

MARVEL, V.C. . . . In 1968, Gertrude L. Weller, a 94-year-old widow, was invited to live in the home of Mr. and Mrs. Kenneth Jumper. This change of residence came about because the plaintiff had known Mrs. Jumper for many years and was also acquainted with Mr. Jumper, who had performed various helpful services for her in the past. Because of her lonely circumstances and advanced age, she was more than delighted to accept the Jumpers' proposal. . . .

Thereafter, because of her age and poor health, plaintiff gradually surrendered more and more responsibility concerning the details of her business affairs to Mr. Jumper. . . .

In February, 1970, after having moved to her nephew's to live, following disclosure to some extent of Mr. Jumper's actual nature, Mrs. Weller ascertained that for over a period of almost two years she had been systematically defrauded by Mr. Jumper . . .

The trial evidence is to the effect that Mr. Jumper . . . forged plaintiff's name to plaintiff's stock certificates . . .

§ 8-404(2) of the Uniform Commercial Code provides that where an issuer has registered a transfer of a security in the name of a person not entitled to it, such issuer on demand must deliver a like security to the true owner, provided, . . . the owner has acted pursuant to subsection (1) of the section which follows. § 8-404(2)(b). Subsection (1) of the following section provides that the owner of such a security must notify the issuer of the wrongful taking complained of within a reasonable time after he has notice of a lost or wrongfully taken certificate, Section 8-405(1).

Defendants argue that in the case at bar plaintiff failed to notify the issuers within a "reasonable time," as such phrase is defined in the statute. It contends that plaintiff should have known some twenty-two months before she notified the issuing corporations that Mr. Jumper had converted her stock certificates. Defendants go on to point out that had plaintiff made a casual examination of her bank book or bank statement, it would have been brought to her attention that dividend checks accruing on the shares here in issue were not being deposited to her credit.

In order to determine whether or not Mrs. Weller notified the issuer within a "reasonable time" after she had "noticed" that her shares had been transferred as a result of forgery, it is necessary to determine the meaning of these two phrases as employed in the statute.

The definition section of Article 8 provides . . . : "In addition Article 1 contains general definitions and principles of construction and interpretation applicable throughout this Article." Section 8-102(6). Article 1, provides that a person has "notice" of a fact when he has actual knowledge of it, has received notification, or ". . . from all the facts and circumstances known to him at the time in question, he has reason to know that it exists." Section 1-201 (25). Article 1 also provides: "What is a reasonable time for taking any action depends on the nature, purpose and circumstances of such action." Section 1-204(2).

In the case at bar we are concerned with the affairs of a 94-year-old woman, who while a guest in another's home, was persuaded to allow one of her hosts, whom she trusted, to handle her affairs. I am accordingly satisfied that Mrs. Weller, a lonely and trusting person of advanced years and of infirm mind and body, had every reasonable right to trust a family which took her in and which she had known intimately before she moved into its home. Furthermore, in light of her reliance on the perpetrator of the acts which deprived her of title to her securities and her own age and decrepitude, she having among other things broken a hip while at the Jumpers, I do not think Mrs. Weller can be charged with unreasonable action in not checking her accounts from time to time. I therefore conclude in view of all of the surrounding circumstances that Mrs. Weller did not have the required statutory notice of Mr. Jumper's dishonesty until February 19 or 20, 1970, and that she thereafter notified the issuers of her stolen securities within a reasonable time.

Accordingly, plaintiff is entitled to the entry of an order providing for the issuance to her of 500 shares of American Telephone and Telegraph Company common stock together with accrued and unpaid dividends, as well as 200 shares of General Electric Company common stock together with accrued and unpaid dividends , . . .

Skoglund v Ormand Industries, Inc.

(DelCh) 372 A2d 204 (1976)

Ormand Industries engaged in outdoor advertising in California. Skoglund and Ackerly together owned about 90,000 shares of Ormand. In addition, Skoglund and Ackerly ran outdoor advertising companies in Seattle. They believed that Ormand was being mismanaged and served a written request on the corporation to inspect the corporate books since 1973. The request also asked for a list of Ormand's stockholders. The corporation refused to permit this inspection on the ground that it was too broad and that the fact that the applicants ran similar businesses showed that their request was not made for a proper purpose. Skoglund and Ackerly brought an action to compel Ormand to allow the inspection.

BROWN, V.C. . . . The right of a stockholder to inspect the stock list and books and records of his corporation is measured by the propriety of his purpose. The test for a "proper purpose" is that it be "reasonably related to such person's interest as a stockholder." . . . If a proper purpose is established, it is no defense of itself that the stockholder may also have another, or secondary purpose which may be improper. . . . However, even though the purpose may be proper in the sense that it is reasonably related to the person's interest as a stockholder, it must also not be adverse to the interests of the corporation. To this extent a stockholder's right of inspection is a qualified right depending upon the facts of the particular case. . . . In this case the defendant corporation charges that the plaintiffs' motivation in seeking inspection is improper for several reasons. . . .

To begin with, it is no secret that the plaintiffs, along with several other interested persons, seek to gain control of the defendant corporation (hereafter "Ormand") and to oust its present management. Plaintiffs' group has filed a . . . statement to this effect with the Securities and Exchange Commission.

Plaintiff Skoglund is an eminently successful businessman who first became a stockholder of Ormand in July 1972. Plaintiff Ackerley is a business associate of Skoglund who first acquired his Ormand shares in May 1975. In the past Skoglund has bought and sold several communications corporations engaged in the outdoor advertising business. Ackerley also has knowledge and experience in the communications business and presently heads Ackerley Communications Inc., a closely held Seattle outdoor advertising company in which Skoglund is a major shareholder. Having followed the progress of Ormand somewhat closely since becoming shareholders, plaintiffs rely on three distinct factors as justification for their inspection demand.

First, based upon their personal knowledge and expertise in the outdoor advertising business, coupled with an examination of the financial information contained in Ormand's annual reports, plaintiffs contend that Ormand's outdoor advertising subsidiary, which forms a significant part of Ormand's operation, is being mismanaged at best and, in all likelihood, is being looted. According to Ackerley, Ormand's net income of $35,000 on $6.25 million of outdoor advertising sales, as reflected in the 1975 annual report, is unbelievable and indicates that something is terribly wrong. Ackerley also finds the lease cost of advertising space of 17 per cent to 18 per cent, again as computed from the annual report figures, to be far out of line with industry standards. Plaintiffs say that unless they are permitted an examination of the corporate books and financial records, there is no way they can ascertain where the money is going and for what.

Second, plaintiffs rely on various public disclosures by Ormand which, to them, indicate questionable, if not improper, transactions. . . .

The third and significant factor which plaintiffs say has prompted them to act stems from a meeting by Ackerley with one Robert M. Brunson, former president of Ormand's communications subsidiary. Brunson had resigned his position ostensibly because of improper manipulations of corporate finances by Jarrell Ormand which he could not ignore. Brunson produced a list of alleged improprieties including the use of Ormand funds for numerous of Jarrell Ormand's personal expenses, including some $50,000 to $75,000 for work on his private residence. An Ormand employee charged to the company's payroll is said to have actually worked at Jarrell Ormand's home. Corporate credit with advertising customers was allegedly used for the personal benefit of Jarrell Ormand, his family members and certain of his personal friends. And at least seven members of Jarrell Ormand's family are said to be on the corporate payroll, with plaintiffs having doubt as to the value of services rendered by some of them. While plaintiffs acknowledge that the $100,000 or so involved in the matters revealed by Brunson may be a mere drop in the bucket concerning the overall mismanagement they fear, they nonetheless feel that as shareholders they have a right to examine the corporate records to ascertain the accuracy of the charges and to contact other shareholders concerning their findings.

To begin with, Ormand contends that under Delaware law a shareholder may not review generally all books and records of his corporation, but rather is limited to those pertaining to the specific matters on which he has based his right to inspect. . . . Reliance is also placed on the fact that plaintiffs are in a competitive position with Ormand because of their outdoor advertising interests in the Seattle area. Finally, Ormand contends that on the evidence presented plaintiffs have admitted that they have no immediate or future need for the list of shareholders.

I deal first with its argument that plaintiffs are not entitled to review all the minute books and all the corporate financial records of Ormand . . . covering the period of January 1, 1973 to the present . . . .

Ormand relies on three Delaware precedents , . . .

[Those] authorities, however, as I read them, do not establish such an inflexible principle of our corporate law, even though they do indicate, as well they should, that shareholder inspection, if otherwise proper, should be reasonably confined to information concerning the event or circumstances which caused the shareholder to become interested in the first place. . . .

It cannot be overlooked that the reason for the demand here is to investigate the likelihood of general corporate mismanagement and improper transactions, a purpose which warrants inspection of books and records under our decisional law. . . .

From the evidence presented in this case, I am of the opinion that if the plaintiffs are otherwise entitled to inspection and examination of the corporate books and records for the purpose of ascertaining the possible existence of corporate mismanagement and waste, then their right should not be limited to those transactions and conditions which have been heretofore brought to their attention and which have aroused their suspicions. Rather it should extend to the corporate minutes and financial records in general during the period into which they seek to inquire, especially where the time span is reasonably related to the specific events cited as the basis for the demand . . .

I turn next to Ormand's contention that inspection should be denied due to the ownership interests of plaintiffs in other outdoor advertising businesses. On this point Ormand relies on the assertion that Ackerley and Skoglund, because of their ownership interests in other outdoor advertising concerns, are in a competitive posture to the outdoor advertising interest of Ormand.

Ormand argues that inspection of the corporate books and records, . . . should be denied so as to provide "the assurance that the information disclosed to shareholders is not for the purpose of injuring the corporate business or building up a rival concern." . . .

Here plaintiffs have offered evidence to justify their concern as stockholders in the management of Ormand's business, and I am not persuaded that they are using this as a guise to obtain otherwise confidential information concerning Ormand's operation of its outdoor advertising interests. While some information best unseen by competitors may well come to their attention by inspection, the unfortunate fact of the matter is that it is within Ormand's advertising operation that plaintiffs suspect the majority of the mismanagement to be taking place. Moreover, plaintiffs are not directly competing in the same local market area as Ormand since their main outdoor advertising interests are being conducted in Seattle, and it is their very experience in outdoor advertising which they feel qualifies them to question the propriety of Ormand's similar activity.

. . . I conclude that the ownership interests of plaintiffs in other outdoor advertising companies is not sufficient under the facts presented to defeat their right of inspection.

. . . I am satisfied that plaintiffs have established a proper purpose to support their demand to examine the books and records of the corporation for the time period stated, and that the propriety of or motivation behind any accompanying purpose is not sufficient to show either overriding bad faith on their part or imminent threat to the business interests of Ormand. . . .

[Judgment for plaintiff]

QUESTIONS AND CASE PROBLEMS

1. What social forces are affected by the rule requiring that a transfer restriction be known to the transferee or conspicuously noted on the share certificate?

2. Compare (a) common stock, (b) redeemable shares, and (c) convertible shares.

3. Compare the effect of an oral contract (a) by *A* to sell 100 shares of *X* corporation stock to *B,* and (b) by stockbroker *C* to sell *A*'s stock in the *X* corporation when the market price reaches $10.00 a share.

4. Compare the effect of the physical delivery of (a) a stock certificate signed in blank by the registered shareholder, (b) an assignment of the stock signed by the registered shareholder, and (c) an assignment of the stock signed by the registered shareholder accompanied by the unindorsed share certificate.

5. Smallwood made a contract to purchase stock of the Re-Mark Chemical Co. from Moretti. Moretti did not deliver the stock certificate to Smallwood but gave him a written assignment of 5,000 shares and directed the company to issue 5,000 shares to Smallwood. There was a delay in issuing the certificate because of certain stock registration problems. Meanwhile four dividends were declared on the stock. They were received by Moretti, who paid them to Smallwood, who accepted them without question. Shortly thereafter

the Re-Mark Co. went into bankruptcy reorganization, and Smallwood then sought to set aside the purchase from Moretti. He claimed that the purchase was not effective because no stock certificate had been issued to him and therefore he had not been given the legal title to the stock. Was he entitled to set the sale aside? [Smallwood v Moretti, (Fla App) 128 So2d 628]

6. A dealer sold goods to a corporation. When the corporation failed to pay him, he sued *X* who owned a block of shares of the corporation and had been active in organizing the corporation. Was *X* liable? [Blond Lighting Fixture Supply Co. v Funk, (Tex Civ App) 392 SW2d 586]

7. Siebrecht organized a corporation called the Siebrecht Realty Co. and then transferred his building to the corporation in exchange for its stock. The corporation rented different parts of the building to different tenants. Elenkrieg, an employee of one of the tenants, fell and was injured because of the defective condition of a stairway. She sued Siebrecht individually on the ground that the corporation had been formed by him for the purpose of securing limited liability. Decide. [Elenkrieg v Siebrecht, 238 NY 254, 144 NE 519]

8. Buechner was a minority shareholder in Fishback, Inc. Rouse was the majority stockholder in the corporation. Buechner claimed that Rouse had mismanaged the corporation and thereby caused losses which reduced the value of Buechner's stock in the corporation. Beuchner sued Rouse for the loss of the value of his stock. Was Buechner entitled to recover? [Buechner v Rouse (ColoApp) 538 P2d 117]

9. Dixon requested to inspect the books of G. S. & M. Company. The objection was raised that he did not own 5% or more of the corporate stock. If this is true, is Dixon barred from inspecting the books? [See G. S. & M. Co. v Dixon, 220 Ga 329, 138 SE2d 662]

10. *A* owned corporate stock. He told *B* that he was going to give the stock to *B* and handed the stock certificate to *B*. *B* requested that *A* indorse the certificate. *A* refused to do so. Who was the owner of the stock? [See Smith v Augustine, 82 Misc 2d 326, 368 NYS2d 675]

11. Chandler owned stock in a corporation. The stock was taxed by the town of New Gloucester as property owned by Chandler. Sweetsir, the proper official, sued Chandler for the taxes due. Chandler defended on the ground that the stock should be taxed as evidence of a debt, the same as a bond, and that the tax as assessed was therefore unlawful. Was his contention valid? [Sweetsir v Chandler, 98 Maine 145, 56 A 584]

12. Lehman was a shareholder of the National Benefit Insurance Co., which had been incorporated under the laws of Iowa. He brought an action to compel the corporation to permit him to inspect and copy records and documents of the corporation. It was admitted that he had the right to inspect the papers. Did he have a right to make copies of them? [Lehman v National Benefit Insurance Co., 243 Iowa 1348, 53 NW2d 872]

13. *K* owned shares of stock in the *J* corporation. He left the shares of stock lying on top of a desk in his office. Many people continually passed through the office and one day *K* realized that someone had taken the shares of stock from the top of his desk. *K* applied to the *J* corporation for the issuance of a duplicate stock certificate. The corporation refused to issue a duplicate on the ground that it was *K*'s own fault that the original certificate had been stolen. *K* claimed that he was entitled to a new certificate even though he had been at fault. Was he correct? [See Ibanez v Farmers Underwriters Asso., 14 Cal 3d 390, 121 CalRptr 256, 534 P2d 1336.]

14. Corporation *A* wished to employ *B*. Negotiations were conducted by telephone. In order to induce *B* to accept employment, the proper representative of corporation *A* promised *B* that in addition to a money salary, *B* would receive a specified number of shares of stock of corporation *A* for each year of employment. *B* went to work for corporation

A and received his money salary but three years went by with no stock being delivered to him. *B* then sued *A* corporation to compel it to issue the stock. It raised the defense that the agreement to give *B* stock could not be enforced because it was not evidenced by a writing as required by UCC § 8-319. Was this a valid defense? [See Bingham v Wells, Rich, Greene, Inc., 34 AppDiv2d 924, 311 NYS2d 508; Butcher v United States Invest. Corp., 236 Pa Super 8, 344 A2d 583.]

15. Elizabeth Szabo, who owned stock of the American Telephone & Telegraph Co., was notified by the company that there had been a three-for-one split of the company's stock effective as of April 24, 1959, and that on May 29, 1959, the company would prepare and mail to her an additional stock certificate representing twice the number of shares already held by her. Upon receiving the notice from the company, Szabo indorsed on her certificate a transfer to herself and her son as joint tenants with the right of survivorship. She delivered the indorsed certificate to the stock transfer agent of the corporation but directed him to hold up the transfer of the stock until the new certificate for the split shares was available. The stock transfer agent was also notified to have the new certificate made out to Szabo and her son as joint tenants with the right of survivorship. Three days before the new certificate for the stock split was issued, Szabo died. Her son claimed the original shares of stock from her estate and the new shares issued on the stock split. Was he entitled to all these shares? [Szabo's Estate, 10 NY2d 123, 217 NYS2d 593, 176 NE2d 395]

16. The stock of *X* Corporation was subject to certain transfer restrictions. When *X* Corporation was dissolved, *A*, a shareholder, then sold his stock to *B* but did not comply with the stock transfer restrictions. It was claimed that *B* had not acquired any of the rights of *A* by such transfer. Was this correct? [Mischer v Burke, (Tex Civ App) 456 SW2d 550]

49 Management of Corporations

A corporation is managed, directly or indirectly, by its shareholders, board of directors, and officers.

Since the shareholders elect the directors, they indirectly determine the management policies of the business.[1] Without express authorization by the corporation, however, a shareholder cannot bind it by contract.

§ 49:1. Meetings of Shareholders. To have legal effect, action by the shareholders must be taken at a regular or special meeting. The time and place of regular or stated meetings are usually prescribed by the articles of incorporation or bylaws. Notice to shareholders of such meetings is ordinarily not required, but it is usually given as a matter of good business practice. Some statutes require that notice be given of all meetings, and generally notice must be given specifying the subject matter when the meeting is of an unusual character. Unless otherwise prescribed, special meetings are called by the directors. It is sometimes provided that a special meeting may be called by a certain percentage of shareholders.[2] Notice of the day, hour, and the place of a special meeting must be given to all shareholders. The notice must also include a statement of the nature of the business to be transacted. No other business may be transacted at such a meeting.

(a) Quorum. A valid meeting requires the presence of a quorum of the voting shareholders. In order to constitute a quorum, usually a specified number of shareholders or a number authorized to vote a stated proportion of the voting stock must attend.[3] If a quorum is present, a majority of those present may act with respect to any matter, unless there is an express requirement of a greater affirmative vote.

When a meeting opens with a quorum, the quorum generally is not thereafter broken if shareholders leave the meeting and those remaining are not sufficient to constitute a quorum. This principle is designed to prevent obstructionist tactics by dissenting shareholders.

---

[1] When the voting stock of a large corporation is widely held by small shareholders scattered over an extensive geographic area, this indirect control is not very effective and management tends to determine the policies of the corporation.

[2] New York Business Corporation Law § 603.

[3] The American Bar Association Model Business Corporation Act provides that unless stated in the articles of incorporation, a majority of the voting shares constitutes a quorum and that, in specifying the quorum in the articles, it cannot be set at less than one third of the shares entitled to vote at the particular meeting. ABA MBCA § 32.

(b)   No Meeting Action. A number of statutes provide for corporate action by shareholders without holding a meeting. The ABA MBCA provides that "Any action required by this Act to be taken at a meeting of the shareholders of a corporation, or any action which may be taken at a meeting of the shareholders, may be taken without a meeting if they consent in writing, setting forth the action so taken [and] signed by all of the shareholders entitled to vote with respect to the subject matter thereof." [4] Such provisions give flexibility of operation, which is needed by the small or close corporation.

§ 49:2. Directors. The management of a corporation is usually under the guidance of a board of directors elected by the shareholders. Most states now permit the number of directors to be fixed by the bylaws. Many specify that the board of directors shall consist of not less than three directors. A few authorize one or more directors. [5] Professional corporation legislation often authorizes or is interpreted as authorizing a one- or two-person board of directors.

Statutory provisions for the classification of directors are common. The Model Act provides that when the board consists of nine or more members, the directors may be divided "into two or three classes, each class to be as nearly equal in number as possible." [6]

(a)   Qualifications. Eligibility for membership on a board of directors is determined by statute, certificate of incorporation, or bylaw. In the absence of a contrary provision, any person is eligible for membership, including a nonresident, a minor, or even a person who is not a shareholder.

Bylaws may require that a director own stock in the corporation, although ordinarily this requirement is not imposed. A director who is also a shareholder has a dual capacity and has rights both as a director and as a shareholder.

(b)   Powers of Directors. The board of directors has authority to manage the corporation. The court will not interfere with the board's discretion in the absence of illegal conduct or fraud harming the rights of creditors, shareholders, or the corporation.

The board of directors may enter into any contract or transaction necessary to carry out the business for which the corporation was formed. The board may appoint officers and other agents to act for the company, or it may delegate authority to one or more of its members to do so. For example, it may appoint several of its own members as an executive committee to act for the board between board meetings.

(c)   Conflict of Interests. A director is disqualified from taking part in corporate action with respect to a matter in which the director has a conflicting interest. Since it cannot be known how the other directors would have acted if they had known of the conflict of interest, the corporation generally may avoid any transaction because of the director's disqualification.

A number of states provide by statute that the conflict of interest of a director does not impair the transaction or contract entered into or authorized by the board

---

[4] ABA MBCA § 145.
[5] Delaware Ann § 141(b). See also ABA MBCA § 36.
[6] ABA MBCA § 37.

of directors if the disqualified director disclosed the interest and the contract or transaction is fair and reasonable with respect to the corporation.

§ 49:3. Meetings of Directors. Theoretically, action by directors can only be taken at a proper meeting of the board. (See p. 831, Stone v American Lacquer Solvents Co.) Bylaws sometimes require the meeting to be held at a particular place. Most states expressly provide that the directors may meet either in or outside of the state of incorporation. Directors who participate without objection in a meeting irregularly held as to place or time other than as specified in the bylaws cannot object later. Generally a director is not allowed to vote by proxy.

Most states permit action to be taken by the board of directors without the holding of an actual meeting. It is commonly provided when such action is taken that it be set forth in writing and signed by all the directors. Moreover, when the directors and shareholders are the same persons, there is no objection to running a corporation in an informal manner. It is not necessary that the board of directors then act by means of a formal meeting.

§ 49:4. Liability of Directors. In dealing with the corporation, the directors act in a fiduciary capacity, as it is to their care that the stockholders have entrusted the control of the corporate property and the management of the business.

Directors must perform their duties in good faith, in a manner the director reasonably believes to be in the best interests of the corporation, and with such care as an ordinarily prudent person in a like position would use under similar circumstances. A director is liable for the illegal payment of dividends, the illegal purchase by the corporation of its own shares, and illegal distributions of the assets of the corporation upon liquidation.[7]

In performing their duties, directors may in good faith rely on information prepared by others such as officers or employees of the corporation, lawyers, accountants, or a committee of the board upon which the director does not serve.

Directors who have acted in good faith and have exercised reasonable care will not be liable for losses resulting from their management of the corporation.

Directors of a corporation are not personally liable for wrongs committed by the corporation merely by virtue of the fact that they are directors. It must be shown that they have authorized or ratified the improper conduct or have in some way participated therein.

(a) Director's Liability for Conflict of Interests. When a director violates the rule prohibiting conflicting interests, the corporation may recover any secret profit made by the director. The ordinary rule of agency law as to loyalty determines liability. When the corporation has sustained loss because it has taken the action advocated by the disqualifed director, it will generally be able to hold the director liable for the loss by applying the agency principles of loyalty and the duty to inform of matters relevant to the transaction, namely the director's personal interests.

---

[7] ABA MBCA § 48. The earlier version of the Model Act also imposed liability upon directors for loans made to officers and directors and for the amount of capital not paid into the corporation if it commenced doing business before it obtained $1,000. These two provisions were deleted from the present version of the Model Act, although they are found in a number of state statutes which have followed the earlier Model Act.

(b) **Action against Director.** Actions against directors should be brought by the corporation. If the corporation fails to act, as is the case when the directors alleged to be liable control the corporation, one or more shareholders may bring the action in a representative capacity for the corporation.

(c) **Removal of Directors.** Ordinarily directors are removed by the vote of the shareholders. In some states the board of directors may remove a director and elect a successor on the ground that the director removed (1) did not accept office; (2) failed to satisfy the qualifications for office; (3) was continuously absent from the state without a leave of absence granted by the board, generally for a period of six months or more; (4) was adjudicated a bankrupt; (5) was convicted of a felony; (6) was unable to perform the duties of director because of any illness or disability, generally for a period of six months or more; or (7) has been judicially declared of unsound mind.[8]

The Model Act provides for removal of directors "with or without cause" by a majority vote of the shareholders.[9]

§ 49:5. Officers of the Corporation.

Corporations will generally have a president, at least one vice-president, a secretary, and a treasurer. Corporation codes generally expressly permit the same person to be both secretary and treasurer. In larger corporations there will often be a recording secretary and a corresponding secretary.

Sometimes the officers are elected by the shareholders but usually they are appointed by the board of directors. The Model Act follows the general pattern of providing for the selection of officers by the board of directors.[10] Ordinarily no particular formality need be observed in making such appointments. There are seldom particular qualifications required of officers. Unless prohibited, a director may hold an executive office. The Model Act and state statutes commonly provide that one person may hold two or more corporate offices. In some instances, a limitation is imposed, as by the Model Act, which prohibits the same person from being both president and secretary of the corporation.

§ 49:6. Powers of Officers.

The officers of a corporation are its agents. Consequently, their powers are controlled by the law of agency. As in the case of any other agency, the third person has the burden of proving that a particular officer has the authority which such officer purports to have. Moreover, if the third person knows that a particular act requires the adoption of a resolution by the board of directors, no reliance on the apparent authority of the president or other corporate officer to perform the act is justified. This means that even though the third person does in fact rely on the appearance of authority, the corporation is not bound by the act of its president or officer.

The fact that the officer or employee acting on behalf of the corporation is a major shareholder does not give the officer or employee any greater agency powers. Moreover, in all cases, the person dealing with the officer or employee is charged with knowledge of any limitation on authority contained in the recorded corporate charter. (See p. 833, Newberry v Barth, Incorporated)

---

[8] See California Corporations Code § 807, recognizing grounds (1), (2), (5), and (7).
[9] ABA MBCA § 39.
[10] ABA MBCA § 50.

(a)   President. It is sometimes held that in the absence of some limitation upon authority, the president of a corporation has by virtue of that office the authority to act as agent on behalf of the corporation within the scope of the business in which the corporation is empowered to engage. It has also been held, however, that the president has such broad powers only when the president is the general manager of the corporation, and then such powers stem from the office of general manager and not from that of president. In any event, the president does not have authority by virtue of that office to make a contract which because of its unusual character would require action by the board of directors. The president, therefore, cannot make a contract to fix long-term or unusual contracts of employment, to bind the corporation as a guarantor, to release a claim of the corporation, or to promise that the corporation will later repurchase shares when issued to a subscriber.

It is ordinarily held that the president of a business corporation is not authorized to execute commercial paper in the name of the corporation although the president may do so when authorized by the board of directors to borrow money for the corporation.

(b)   Other Officers and Employees. The authority of corporate employees and other officers, such as secretary or treasurer, is generally limited to the duties of their offices. The authority may, however, be extended by the conduct of the corporation, in accordance with the general principles governing apparent authority based on the conduct of the principal. An unauthorized act may, of course, be ratified. The authority of the general manager of the corporation is determined by principles of ordinary agency law.

§ 49:7. Liability of Officers. The relation of the officers to the corporation, like that of the directors, is fiduciary in nature. For this reason, the officers are liable for secret profits made in connection with or at the expense of the business of the corporation.

If an officer diverts a corporate opportunity, the corporation may recover from the officer the profit of which the corporation has been thus deprived. (See p. 834, Abbott Redmont Thinlite Corp. v Redmont) This is an application of the prohibition against secret profits applicable to ordinary agents. Thus the president of a contracting corporation must account to the corporation for a secret profit which the president or a member of the president's family made on the letting of a subcontract.

The advent of the age of computers has not changed the basic principles of law determining the liability of corporate officers but gives rise to new situations to which the old principles will be applied. When computers are used, management may be liable for failure to exercise proper care in their use. Management may also be liable for failing to utilize computers.

Under some state statutes regulating the sale of corporate securities, an officer taking part in a sale which violates the statute is liable without regard to knowledge or lack of knowledge that the sale violated the statute. When the corporation has violated a statute designed to protect health or environment, corporate officers may be held liable for having failed to prevent the violation.

Officers are liable for willful or negligent acts that cause a loss to the corporation. On the other hand, they are not liable for mere errors in judgment committed while exercising their discretion, provided they have acted with reasonable prudence and care.

§ 49:8. Agents and Employees of Corporation.
The authority, rights, and liabilities of an agent of a corporation are governed by the same rules applicable when the principal is a natural person.

The authority of corporate employees is governed by general agency principles. The construction supervisor of a construction corporation does not have implied authority to modify the terms of the contract between the corporation and a supplier of building materials.

§ 49:9. Indemnification of Officers, Directors, Employees, and Agents.
While performing what they believe to be their duty, officers, directors, employees, and agents of corporations may commit acts for which they are later sued or criminally prosecuted. The Model Act broadly authorizes the corporation to indemnify such persons if they acted in good faith and in a manner reasonably believed to be in or not opposed to the interests of the corporation and had no reason to believe that their conduct was unlawful.[11]

In some states statutory provision is made requiring the corporation to indemnify directors and officers for reasonable expenses incurred by them in defending unwarranted suits brought against them by shareholders. Such statutes have been adopted to induce responsible persons to accept positions of corporate responsibility.

§ 49:10. Corporate Minutes.
Minutes are ordinarily kept of meetings of the shareholders and of the directors of a corporation. The keeping of accurate minutes is important not only for the purpose of preserving continuity in management policies but also because of the consequence that the action taken may have with respect to the liability of individual persons, with respect to tax liability of individual persons, or with respect to tax liability of the corporation. The minutes are not conclusive, however, and they may be supplemented or contradicted by parol evidence.

§ 49:11. Liability of Management to Third Persons.
Ordinarily the management of a corporation, meaning its directors, officers, and executive employees, is not liable to third persons for the effect upon such third persons of their management or advice. The liability of a director or officer for misconduct ordinarily is a liability which may be enforced only by the corporation or by shareholders bringing a derivative action on behalf of the corporation. Ordinarily, directors or officers are not liable to a third person for loss caused by the negligent performance of their duties as directors or officers, even though because of such negligence the corporation is in turn liable to the third person to whom the corporation owed the duty to use care or was under a contract obligation to render a particular service.

Officers and managers of a corporation are not liable for the economic consequence of their advice upon third persons, even though they caused the corporation to refuse to deal with or to break its contract with such third persons, as long as the officers and managers acted in good faith to advance the interests of the corporation. Thus, a person who has a contract with the corporation which is not renewed because of the adverse vote of the directors cannot sue the directors for damages even though they were "wrong" in their decision as such a matter was merely an error in judgment for which there is no tort liability. Similarly when a banker makes a contract to

---

[11] ABA MBCA § 5(a).

lend money to a corporation, the promoter-president of the corporation is not liable to the banker for malicious interference with contract when the promoter-president causes the corporation to break its contract to borrow the money from the banker and instead obtains from a different lender a larger loan at a lower rate of interest, as the circumstances fail to show that there was any malice on the part of the promoter-president.[12]

As exceptions to the above rule, directors and officers in control of management may be liable directly to an injured person when the directors or officers commit a tort or direct the commission of a tort upon the third person, as when they take an active part in causing the corporation to conspire to enter into a monopoly or trust agreement to the detriment of the third person. Similarly when corporate officers or directors cause a bad check to be issued with knowledge that there are not sufficient funds on deposit to pay the check, they are personally liable to the payee. (See p. 836, Klockner v Keser)

If a director or an officer makes an individual capacity contract, the director or officer is personally liable thereon to the other person and is not protected from liability by the fact that the motive was to act on behalf of the corporation. When a corporate officer, director, or employee is liable to a third person, it is no defense that the corporation may also be liable to the third person.

§ 49:12. Criminal Liability. Officers and directors, as in the case of agents generally, are personally responsible for any crimes committed by them even when they act in behalf of the corporation. At the local level they may be criminally responsible for violation of ordinances relating to sanitation, safety, and hours of closing. At the state level they may be criminally liable for conducting a business without obtaining necessary licenses or after the corporate certificate of incorporation was forfeited for failing to file reports or pay taxes. At the national level they may be prosecuted for violation of the federal antitrust laws.[13]

The president of a national food chain corporation has been held criminally liable under the Federal Food, Drug, and Cosmetic Act on the ground that food in the corporation's warehouse had been exposed to rodent contamination.[14]

A number of states impose criminal liability upon the person, corporate officer, or agent who conducts local business on behalf of a foreign corporation that has not qualified to engage in such business.[15]

§ 49:13. Corporate Debts and Taxes. As the corporation is a separate legal person, debts and taxes owed by the corporation are ordinarily the obligations of the corporation only. Consequently, neither directors nor officers are individually liable for the corporate debts or taxes, even though it may have been their acts which gave rise to the debts or their neglect which resulted in the failure to pay the taxes.

In some states civil liability for corporate debts is imposed upon the officers and directors of the corporation when it improperly engages in business. Some states

---

[12] H. F. Philipsborn & Co. v Suson, 59 Ill2d 465, 322 NE2d 45.
[13] United States v Wise, 370 US 405.
[14] United States v Park, 421 US 658.
[15] California Corporation Code § 6803.

make the directors and officers personally liable for taxes that the corporation has neglected to pay.[16]

§ 49:14. Protection of Shareholders. Various devices and limitations have developed to protect shareholders both from misconduct by management and from the action of the majority of the shareholders. Shareholders may protect themselves by voting at the next annual election for new directors, and also officers, if the latter are elected; or they may take special remedial action at a special meeting of shareholders called for that purpose. In any case, the objecting shareholders may bring a legal action when the management misconduct complained of constitutes a legal wrong. When the complaining shareholders represent so small a minority that they could not win an election, the lawsuit is the only practical remedy.

§ 49:15. Irregular Procedure. There is a strong judicial tendency to ignore the effects of a procedural error or irregularity when the circumstances are such that it can be concluded that all or substantially all of the shareholders have agreed to or waived any objection to the procedure which was followed. (See p. 837, Coastal Pharmaceutical Co. v Goldman) Thus, irregularities with respect to the place and notice of a meeting of the board of directors will be ignored in the case of a closely held corporation when all of the directors attended and participated in the meeting or acquiesced in action taken at such meeting. A third person sued by the corporation cannot challenge the right of the corporation to sue on the ground that corporate procedure requirements have not been observed.

Likewise, when the corporation has received the benefit of a transaction, it will be estopped from claiming that there was some irregularity in the corporate procedure followed. As in the case of agency generally, a corporation may ratify acts of its officers or directors that were unauthorized.

---

[16] West Virginia v Calco Awning and Window Corp. 153 WVa 524, 170 SE2d 362 (corporate officers liable for consumer sales tax).

CASES FOR CHAPTER 49

Stone v American Lacquer Solvents Company

463 Pa 417, 345 A2d 174 (1975)

Harold Stone was the chairman of the board of directors of the American Lacquer Solvents Company. The board of directors adopted a resolution declaring that after his death his widow would be entitled to a pension. The resolution specifically stated that it could not be revoked without Stone's consent. Stone later wrote to the board stating that he wished the resolution revoked. At a subsequent special meeting of the board of directors, the pension resolution was revoked. After Stone died, his widow sued the corporation for the pension. It defended on the ground that the pension resolution had been revoked. The widow claimed that the revocation was not effective on the theory that the special meeting was irregular. Judgment was entered for the corporation and the widow appealed.

EAGEN, J. . . . On March 2, 1968, Stone and his wife suffered a marital dispute while residing in Coral Gables, Florida. Following this Stone contacted his son-in-law Robert Shaw, President and General Manager of American, who was visiting in Florida at the time, and told him he wanted the Resolution providing a pension for his wife canceled. Shaw contacted the company's counsel and, acting in accordance with his advice as to the procedure to be followed, prepared a letter from Stone to the board of directors of American saying, "It is my wish that the Resolution dated December 7, 1967 concerning a pension for my wife Rachel be rescinded." Stone signed and personally delivered the letter to Shaw on March 3rd.

On March 11, 1968, Shaw convened a special meeting of the board of directors of American. Five of the seven members of the board attended the meeting and when Stone's letter was brought to their attention, they voted unanimously to rescind the Resolution of December 7, 1967. Stone was not notified the meeting was to be held and did not attend.

Stone died on November 1, 1968, and when American refused to pay his widow, Rachel Stone, the pension provided for in the Resolution of December 7, 1967, she instituted this action seeking specific performance. The trial court ruled the Resolution, providing for the payment of the pension, had been validly rescinded by the board at the meeting of March 11, 1968, and hence, the plaintiff had no cause of action. The correctness of this ruling is challenged by this appeal.

As a general rule the directors of a corporation may bind a corporation only when they act at a legal meeting of the board. . . . If they purport to act at a meeting which is not a legal meeting, their action is not that of the corporation, and the corporation, absent ratification or acquiescence, is not bound. . . .

As to special meetings of the board of directors of a corporation, the general rule in Pennsylvania is that such a meeting held without notice to some or any of the directors and in their absence is illegal, and action taken at such a meeting, although by a majority of the directors, is invalid absent ratification or estoppel. . . . However, this notice requirement may be waived by a director either prior or subsequent to the special meeting, provided such waiver is in writing. . . . Additionally, any action which may properly be taken at a meeting of a board of directors of a corporation may be effected and is binding without a meeting, if a consent in writing setting forth the action so taken is signed by each and every member of the board and filed with the secretary of the corporation. . . .

A reading of the trial court's opinion filed in support of its decree upholding the legality of the board's action of March 11, 1968, rescinding the board's prior Resolution providing for the payment

of the pension to the plaintiff was based on three grounds, any one of which, if correct, would warrant its ruling.

First, the court concluded that Stone's letter of March 3, 1968, constituted a consent to the board's subsequent action rescinding the pension Resolution. The difficulty with this position is that the applicable statute requires that such a consent be executed after the meeting and that it specifically set forth the action taken, and that it be filed with the secretary of the corporation. Stone's letter does not meet these requirements.

Secondly, the court concluded Stone's letter of March 3, 1968, constituted a waiver of receipt of notice of the meeting of March 11, 1968. The difficulty with this position is that the letter does not refer to the meeting or indicate in any way that notice thereof is waived. The letter amounts to no more than an expression of desire or consent to rescind the pension Resolution.

In connection with its conclusion that Stone's letter constituted a waiver of notice of the meeting, the court reasoned that no purpose would be served by Stone's presence at the meeting since the other directors were merely acceding to Stone's wishes and request. This analysis overlooks the rationale for the salutory rule that all directors receive notice of special meetings. That rationale is that "each member of a corporate body has the right of consultation with the others, and has the right to be heard upon all questions considered, and it is presumed that if the absent members had been present they might have dissented, and their arguments might have convinced the majority of the unwisdom of their proposed action and thus have produced a different result." *Holcombe v Trenton White City Co.,* 80 N.J. Eq. 122, 82 A. 618 (1912), aff'd, without opinion, 82 N.J. Eq. 364, 91 A. 1069 (1913). We agree with this rationale and, in view of the presumption embodied therein, we cannot concur in the trial court's premise that Stone and the other directors were of one mind as regards the pension rescission. In relation to this, we specifically note that another member of the board of directors failed to attend the meeting of March 11, 1968, and there is nothing in the record to show if he received notice of the meeting, or ever consented to the action taken at the meeting.

Finally, the court concluded that the rescinding resolution of the board was voidable only and that Stone's silence and failure to object thereto prior to his death amounted to a ratification. The difficulty with this position is that there is nothing in the record to show that Stone was ever made aware that the meeting of March 11, 1968, had been held or knew the rescinding resolution had been adopted by the board. Under the circumstances, it cannot be said a ratification was effected.

[Judgment reversed]

Newberry v Barth, Incorporated

(Iowa) 252 NW2d 711 (1977)

Barth, Incorporated, owned an apartment complex. The charter of the corporation was locally recorded and stated that the property of the corporation could not be sold without the consent of the preferred stockholders. The only preferred shareholder of Barth was the federal housing commissioner (FHA). Florence Barth was a major shareholder and manager of the apartments. Following the death of her husband, the other major shareholder, Florence made a contract to sell the apartment complex to Newberry. She believed that she had the authority to do so. The contract was never performed and Newberry brought suit for specific performance against her and the corporation. The trial court ordered the specific performance of the contract and the defendants appealed.

REYNOLDSON, J. . . . Barth, Incorporated [is an Iowa corporation]. The apartment complex was its principal asset. It was purchased from Florence Barth and her husband Paul Barth who died July 29, 1968.

Florence Barth had listed this real estate for sale with the Mack Gable Agency on August 13, 1968 for a sale price of $220,000 terms "cash or possible 45000 down." The listing agreement disclosed the owner as "Barth, Inc." Mrs. Barth testified she thought she had authority to list the property on behalf of the corporation.

At all times pertinent here the articles of incorporation were a matter of record in Black Hawk county recorder's office and in the office of the Secretary of State. . . .

These articles provided the corporation could not take the following actions without prior consent of the preferred shareholders: . . . assign, transfer, dispose of or encumber any real or personal property. . . . Mrs. Barth, who managed the apartment operation, was permitted to draw as wages $133.28 per month. . . .

The articles authorized five preferred shares and 490 common shares. The common shares were owned by Paul Barth, president, 233 shares; Florence Barth, secretary-treasurer, 232 shares; and Addison P. Clark, vice-president, 25 shares. Following Paul Barth's death the office of president was left vacant. His will bequeathed his property to his wife, but the trial record is unclear whether his estate was still being probated and whether his stock had ever been transferred to Florence Barth.

The November 7, 1968 real estate contract, drafted by Mack Gable, called for a purchase price of $210,000 . . . The seller was designated as Florence Barth. . . .

The purchaser, plaintiff Newberry, thought Florence Barth owned the property, but admitted . . . she had never said so.

In defense against the action, defendants assert Florence Barth had no authority to bind the corporation and therefore the latter cannot be compelled to perform the contract. . . .

Trial court found both defendants were bound by the sales transaction and ordered both to specifically perform the contract. . . .

Trial court's findings declared, "The court concludes that . . . Florence Barth['s] . . . contracting to sell the Barth apartments is binding upon the Barth Corporation."

There is little record support for this finding, . . .

The plaintiff is charged with constructive notice of the recorded articles of incorporation. *Dempster Mfg. Co. v Downs,* 126 Iowa 80, 83, 101 N.W. 735, 736 (1904) ("The corporation is created by the adoption of the articles. These form the very basis of its existence. Every one who deals with it or its stock is charged with knowledge of their contents.") These articles placed many restrictions on Mrs. Barth's ability to manage the corporation. Almost every major decision required prior approval of the preferred stockholders.

Contrary to trial court's finding, there is no evidence Florence Barth "could readily deliver the corporate property." There was no corporate action approving the sale or even authorizing her to list the corporate assets for sale. Fully as important, there was no prior consent of the preferred stockholder.

Neither is the corporation bound by the attempted sale of virtually all of its assets by Mrs. Barth.

A recorded deed gave Newberry constructive notice that Barth, Incorporated owned the apartment complex. . . . Florence Barth was thus an agent for a disclosed principal. . . .

. . . Mrs. Barth had no actual authority to sell this property. . . . Moreover, the articles specifically prohibited conveyance of real estate without prior consent of the preferred stockholders.

Implied authority of a corporate officer or agent includes all such incidental authority as is necessary, usual and proper to effectuate the main authority expressly conferred. . . . But although a general or managing officer will be presumed, in absence of proof to the contrary, to have authority to contract in the usual course of corporate business, . . . this implied authority ordinarily does not extend to contracts for the sale of the fixed assets of the corporation . . .

We next consider whether Mrs. Barth had apparent authority to sell this real estate, examining the conduct of the principal to third persons. . . .

In this case the only action taken by the corporation was to install Mrs. Barth as apartment manager. By so doing, it clothed her with authority to perform the usual and necessary actions of an apartment manager. However, the corporation did nothing to indicate to third persons, and specifically the plaintiff, that Mrs. Barth had authority to sell the real estate. Plaintiff was unaware of the existence of the corporate defendant.

It is clear Florence Barth had no apparent authority to bind Barth, Incorporated to this contract. . . .

Nor do we find, in this case, there was any "inherent agency" to bind the corporation to the real estate contract. Inherent agency power is derived from the nature of the position held by the agent and extends to acts generally within the powers of persons holding such position. . . . It is generally held no officer or agent of a corporation, by virtue of his office alone, has any authority to sell or make a contract for the sale of the corporation's real estate. . . .

[Judgment reversed and action remanded]

Abbott Redmont Thinlite Corp. v Redmont

(CA2 NY) 475 F2d 85 (1973)

Redmont was the president of Abbott Redmont Thinlite Corporation. He left that corporation and ran the Circle Redmont Corporation in competition with his former employer. In so doing, it was claimed that he diverted five contracts from his former employer to his company. The former employer sued Redmont and Circle Redmont Corporation to recover the profit of which the former employer was deprived. Judgment was entered for the employer as to part of its claim and it appealed.

OAKES, C.J. . . . The issue here presented is whether the appellees, Rudolph R. Redmont and circle Redmont Corporation, deprived the appellant, Abbott Redmont Thinlite Corporation, of a business opportunity in which it had a "tangible expectancy," and thereby violated Redmont's obligations as a former officer-employee of appellant. . . .

Appellee Redmont, who had previously worked in the glass block business, joined appellant Abbott in 1960 as president of Abbott Redmont Thinlite Corporation. Abbott Redmont's business consisted of furnishing and installing glass block skylights, including toplights (glass blocks set in aluminum grids, generally used in schools) and rooflights (glass blocks set in anti-corrosive concrete grids, generally used in sewage plants). The method used to sell these lights was to discover through trade journals and other sources what construction projects were in the course of design. Once aware of this, Abbott would contact the architect who was in the process of working up the designs for those projects, and attempt to convince him to write into the design the use of skylights and other specifications which Abbott's products line would fulfill. Part of appellee Redmont's job was to contact such architects and to convince them of the advisability of employing Abbott's products in their final design. As of the time in question, up to and including the date when Redmont quit his employ with Abbott and began his own company, Circle Redmont Corporation (Circle), Abbott was the sole distributor in the metropolitan New York area for the particular products with which this action is concerned. Therefore, once the proper requirements were, or named product was, written into the architect's specifications, to all intents and purposes Abbott was assured of the required subcontract. Once Abbott's products had been incorporated into the plans and specifications by the architect, the projects were then in the regular course put out for bid to general contractors. When the general contractor was chosen Abbott would enter into a formal subcontract with the general contractor to furnish and install the Abbott product.

There are five projects here involved.* Appellee Redmont, while in the employ of Abbott, had proceeded to contact the architects for each of these five projects and to write Abbott product specifications into each of the projects. In each case Redmont had also prepared a bid for submission to the general contractor who had been successful in obtaining the general construction contract (or the owner himself if the owner chose to build without a general contractor). Redmont concededly retained knowledge of the amounts of the bids which he had prepared while in Abbott's employ after his employment ceased.

In early 1966 Owens-Illinois, the producer of the glass block used in all of Abbott's products, announced that it was discontinuing the production of glass block. Soon afterward, in February, 1966, Products Research Corporation (PRC), which made the aluminum grids for the toplights and inserted the Owens-Illinois glass block in the grids and from which Abbott purchased the complete toplight sections, informed Abbott that as a result of Owens-Illinois' action, it was leaving the glass block business.

. . . Redmont . . . left Abbott on April 1, 1966. . . .

Redmont, meanwhile, had established his own company, Circle, and had found another source of supply for rooflights and toplights. On the dates given below, Redmont, acting by and for Circle, entered into contracts for toplight and rooflight work on projects for which he had persuaded the architects to write in Abbott product specifications while working for Abbott:

Job	Date of Redmont's Contract
Plainfield Public Library..............	4/18/66
Oakland High School	6/ 2/66
Junior High School 144	7/20/66
Riverdale Girls School	8/ 5/66
Manhattan Pumping Station.........	8/ 5/66

As stated, the central questions for determination here are whether Abbott Redmont Thinlite Corporation had a "tangible expectancy," . . . in the five contracts listed above and whether Redmont violated his fiduciary duty by diverting that expectancy to his own profit. Although Redmont had left the employ of Abbott at the time he contracted with the general contractors for these projects, he was taking advantage of a corporate opportunity which he had helped obtain for Abbott and which would have almost certainly been Abbott's but for Redmont's departure. Redmont, we believe, had an obligation which carried over after he left Abbott not to exploit projects which would have clearly brought profits to Abbott but for his competition. . . . Once Abbott's specifications were written into the architect's plans it was almost a certainty that Abbott would get the final subcontract to install its lights. While occasionally the architect's specifications would be changed, the record shows that this happened very rarely. Thus, it was not merely an "expectancy," but almost a certainty that Redmont's work on these five deals would secure the final contract for Abbott. . . . Redmont did take business which, but for his entry into direct competition with Abbott, would have been Abbott's if Redmont had not departed. . . .

The degree of likelihood of realization from the opportunity is, however, the key to whether an expectancy is tangible. . . .

The high degree of likelihood that, but for Redmont's competition, Abbott would have been awarded these contracts is combined here with the fact that Redmont benefited by information as a result of his employment at Abbott—knowledge of the details of the specifications, knowledge of the contractor's requirements, knowledge of Abbott's probable costs—which made Abbott peculiarly vulnerable to his competition on the specific deals here in question. While this is not the kind of information that, like customers' lists, is "confidential" in the sense of the term that might in and of itself create liability on use, . . . it was information obtained in the course of his employment. A former employee may, of course, go into competition with his ex-employer and can use general information concerning the method of business and names of customers of his ex-employer in his new venture. . . . But he cannot, as here, utilize specific information he obtained during his employment to deprive his ex-employer of customers with whom he knows a deal is in the process of completion. The use of specific information on deals in progress obtained while in Abbott's employ, and the *degree of likelihood* that but for Redmont's competition Abbott would have been awarded

---

* Job	Type
Plainfield Library...............	Toplight
Oakland High School	Toplight
Junior High School 144	Toplight
Riverdale Girls School	Toplight
Manhattan Pumping Station......	Rooflight

the contract, dictate our holding that Redmont violated his fiduciary obligations to Abbott by submitting competing bids.

But Abbott had a "tangible expectancy" in the four toplight contracts only until June 7, 1966, when PRC canceled Abbott's toplight orders, leaving Abbott without a source of supply. Abbott had ample warning from PRC that these orders would be canceled if Abbott did not submit shop drawings to PRC by June 6, 1966. Abbott's failure to submit the requested drawings constitutes intentional abandonment . . . of its contract rights in the toplight projects on which contracts were signed after that, *i.e.,* the Junior High School 144 project and the Riverdale Girls School project. It is not clear from the record how long Abbott retained its supply of glass blocks for rooflights for the Manhattan Pumping Station, the one rooflight project after Owens-Illinois went out of the glass block business. Absent any such supply, Abbott cannot complain of any loss by misappropriation of its "opportunity" since it would have abandoned the opportunity in any event. On this the record is not clear.

We reverse as to the Plainfield Public Library and Oakland High School projects, affirm as to the Junior High School 144 and Riverdale Girls School projects, and remand for further findings in respect to the Manhattan Pumping Station project and for the award of damages in accordance with this opinion.

Klockner v Keser

(Colo App) 488 P2d 1135 (1971)

Klockner and Combellick were directors and officers of K.M.S., a corporation engaged in the business of auctioning automobiles. The corporation sold some automobiles for Keser and gave him a check in payment of the proceeds. At the time the check was issued, Klockner and Combellick knew that the account of the corporation was overdrawn. When the check was dishonored by the bank, Keser sued them. They defended on the ground that the delivering of the bad check was the act of the corporation and that they were not liable for the wrong caused by the corporation. A judgment was entered in favor of Keser against Klockner and Combellick and they appealed.

DUFFORD, J. . . . The corporation commenced business in November 1965 with a cash reserve of $44,000. Its gross auction sales exceeded

$400,000 per month. Sellers of automobiles received a check from the corporation on the day their automobiles were auctioned and sold. Buyers frequently paid the corporation with drafts on out-of-town banks. The delay in collecting the draft proceeds (referred to in the testimony as "draft-lag") created recurring cash shortages in the corporation's bank account. Shortly after the corporation commenced business, to provide operating capital for the corporation and to meet the problem of draft-lags, Klockner, Combellick, and Sapp executed personal notes to the bank and the bank credited the amount of the notes to the corporation's account to cover checks to sellers. When the draft proceeds were collected, the bank deposited them in the corporation account and the corporation then issued checks in payment of the directors' personal notes. This manner of financing continued throughout the corporation's existence.

From November 1965 until May 1966, the corporation's books showed a loss every month with the possible exception of May. By the end of May, the corporation's cash reserves had dwindled to $14,000. From June 1966 until the end of September 1966, when the corporation ceased doing business, no financial statements were prepared.

In July, 1966, Combellick, refused to execute any more short term notes. Also, at about this time, efforts were made to sell or lease the corporation or its assets as a going business. On September 13, 1966, an agreement, approved by the defendants, was entered into between the corporation and the bank, whereby the bank was authorized to apply the corporation's draft proceeds as they were received against the obligations owed by the directors to the bank on their personal notes. Towards the end of August 1966 and through the first 15 days of September 1966, the short-term financing was reduced considerably, and most of the draft proceeds were used to repay the individual notes of the directors. These payments on the directors' short-term notes and other payments constituted a withdrawal of nearly $24,000 from the corporation's bank account within approximately 20 days prior to September 15, 1966, and totally depleted the corporation's cash reserves. On September 15, 1966, plaintiffs received checks from the corporation . . . in the amount of $20,913.50. On the date the checks were issued, the corporation's account was over-drawn $9,592.66, and on the approximate date the checks were presented for payment, the account was overdrawn in the amount of $41,231.54.

. . . The record supports . . . finding . . . fraudulent misrepresentations on the part of the defendants.

A person who writes a check impliedly represents that there are sufficient funds in the account upon which it is drawn. . . . In the instant case, . . . the defendants, as directors and officers of the corporation, authorized the corporation to continue doing business until the end of September 1966. Continuing business necessitated, of course, the issuance of checks to sellers of automobiles, such as the plaintiffs. The approval or sanction by the directors or officers of a corporation to acts of fraudulent misrepresentation is a sufficient basis for holding them personally liable for damages arising from such fraudulent acts. . . .

Considering the facts of this case, we hold that the record supports the trial court's finding that the defendants "knew or should have known" of the overdrawn status of the corporation's bank account at the time in question. We also hold, pursuant to what we consider to be the better reasoned authorities, that although officers and directors of a corporation may not be held liable for the torts of a corporation solely by reason of their office, they may be held liable personally for the results of tortious, fraudulent misrepresentations where they approved of and sanctioned the making of such representations and knew or should have known of the falsity of the representations and the consequential damages which were likely to result therefrom. . . .

[Judgment affirmed]

Coastal Pharmaceutical Co. v Goldman

213 Va 831, 195 SE2d 848 (1973)

Goldman brought an action to rescind a contract with Coastal Pharmaceutical Company on the ground that the contract had never been authorized nor ratified by Coastal.

Goldman owned the stock of Ghent Arms Corp. which operated a nursing home. Because of Ghent's poor financial condition, Goldman contracted to transfer his stock to Coastal Pharmaceutical Co., which would make the Ghent Corp. a wholly-owned subsidiary of Coastal. Thereafter Goldman learned that Coastal was on the verge of bankruptcy and sought to rescind the contract on the ground that the contract had never been expressly authorized nor ratified by Coastal. Judgment was entered for Goldman and Coastal appealed.

POFF, J. . . . The crucial question involved is whether the chancellor was correct in his ruling that because Coastal never authorized execution of the agreement by formal corporate action or ratified it by timely corporate action or by implication, the agreement "never became a valid mutually binding and enforceable contract." . . .

We consider first Goldman's argument that neither the board of directors nor the stockholders [of Coastal] formally authorized Gay [who acted as agent of Coastal] to execute the contract and that the contract was therefore null and void.

This court has held that a corporation cannot escape liability for commercial commitments made by its officers in the name of the corporation by asserting a lack of *de jure* authorization by its board of directors. . . .

Necessarily, the converse is also true; a corporation cannot be required to assume liabilities of such a contract and be denied its benefits. If implied or *de facto* authorization is sufficient to bind the corporation and its stockholders to obligations, it is sufficient to validate their rights.

Corporations are creatures of statutory law. The same law which creates them provides procedures for the conduct of their affairs. Ordinarily, corporate conduct must conform to those procedures. But the total complex of corporate law acknowledges that all corporations are not alike and recognizes that strict statutory conformity, seldom practiced faithfully by the largest and most sophisticated corporations, is impractical if not impossible for others. For the law to close its eyes to the differences and attempt to compress all corporations into a neat little mold would be to forsake realism for legalism and often to sacrifice justice for standardization. As we said in Brewer v First Nat'l Bank, 202 Va 807, 812-813, 120 SE2d 273, 278 (1961): "While it is salutary, and in some instances mandatory, that these rules be followed, it is generally recognized that where there is a family, or close corporation, such as the one involved in this case, in which the stockholders, officers and directors ignore the requirements of the statutes and corporate by-laws, and conduct its business in an informal manner, the actions so taken may, nonetheless, be binding upon the corporation. . . . In this case, the agreement of January 17, 1955, was not authorized at a formal meeting of the board of directors of the corporation, nor was the writing executed in the proper manner. However, it is clear from the actions of the parties, from the circumstances surrounding and subsequent to the execution of the agreement, and from the agreement itself, that it was intended, by all concerned, to be the *act of the corporation.*" . . .

. . . Under the facts of this case, Gay was vested by Coastal with *de facto* authority to execute the contract as an "act of the corporation" within the spirit of the rule in *Brewer.*

The dispositive facts of this case, as distinguished from facts not relevant to the specific basis of the Chancellor's decree, are not in dispute. For a period of more than a year preceding execution of the contract, Coastal and Ghent arms were negotiating some form of combination. Goldman was the sole owner of one corporation and part owner of the other. The physical combination between the two corporations began originally in December 1969 when, under a $3,500.00 loan from Coastal to Ghent Arms, Gay, Coastal's managing director, went on Ghent Arms' payroll to serve both corporations. The combination took further form after Gay became Coastal's president a month later and, with other Coastal employees, assumed managerial authority over the nursing home. During 1970, with the home's financial condition improving, Coastal's stockholders, moribund for seven years, held three meetings, all of which Goldman attended. Although the minutes of these meetings were inartistically drafted and did not record conventional resolutions or categorical votes on informal motions, they clearly reflect a corporate purpose to authorize Coastal's officers to pursue the steps preliminary to corporate acquisition of the nursing home.

On January 17, 1971, Coastal's stockholders met again. That meeting and its date are both significant. At that point in time, an attorney was preparing a written contract to incorporate the oral agreement reached by Gay and Goldman a few days before; five days later, the written contract would be signed and pre-dated to January 17, 1971.

At that meeting, Coastal's stockholders treated Ghent Arms as their own. After hearing Gay's report of Ghent Arms' financial status, they proceeded to elect a board of directors for Ghent Arms Corporation for the year 1971, and they closed the meeting with a standing ovation commending Gay's management of the affairs of the corporation. In light of the preparatory action taken at earlier meetings, this exercise of dominion over the nursing home and the endorsement of Gay's conduct can be interpreted only as a corporate affirmation of the oral agreement Gay had made with Goldman and an implied authority for Gay to validate that agreement by signing the written contract.

Goldman contends that since this authority did not spring from the action of the board of directors, execution of the contract cannot be an "act of the corporation." True, directors normally conduct the business of the corporation. True, the several meetings in which the contract was authorized were called "stockholders' meetings." But, except for the minutes of the March 31, 1970 meeting (which did not record those present), the minutes show that all members of the board of directors attended all meetings. Nothing in these minutes indicates an objection by any director or any of the sixty-six stockholders. So far as the record discloses, until Goldman decided on March 9, 1971 to rescind the contract, approval was unanimous, enthusiastic, and uninterrupted from beginning to end. . . .

[Judgment reversed and action remanded]

QUESTIONS AND CASE PROBLEMS

1. What social forces are affected by the rule that a person dealing with a corporate officer is charged with knowledge of any limitation on the officer's authority contained in the recorded corporate charter?

2. With respect to authority to bind the enterprise, compare (a) a partner and (b) a shareholder.

3. Directors must always own stock of the corporation in order to insure that they will be attentive to their duties. Appraise this statement.

4. Compare the indemnification of (a) agents and (b) corporate officers.

5. The president of the Atlantic & North Carolina Railroad Co. published in one newspaper a notice of a special meeting of stockholders to be held in Newbern, North Carolina.

After the stockholders assembled, they adjourned to meet in Morehead City on the same day. After reassembling, the stockholders voted to authorize a lease of the corporate property to the Howland Improvement Co. Twenty days later the regular annual meeting of the corporation was held. A resolution was then introduced by Foy, at the instance of Hill, instructing the proper officers to bring a suit to set the lease aside. The stockholders' meeting voted to take no action on this resolution and voted that it be tabled. On behalf of himself and other stockholders, Hill then brought a suit against the railroad company to have the lease annulled. He contended that the lease was not properly authorized because the notice of the meeting had not been given as required by the bylaws and because the meeting had not been held at the place of call. Was the special meeting properly held? [Hill v Atlantic & North Carolina Railroad Co., 143 NC 539, 55 SE 854]

6. Sacks claimed that when he was a salesman for Helene Curtis Industries, its president, Stein, made an oral contract with him to the effect that Sacks was to act as the sales manager of the corporation at a compensation of a straight salary and a percentage of the increased volume of the corporation's sales. The corporation later refused to pay compensation on this basis and asserted that it had never been informed of any such agreement. The corporation denied that the contract had in fact been made and asserted that the president had no authority to make such an agreement. Was the agreement binding on the corporation? [Sacks v Helene Curtis Industries, 340 Ill App 76, 91 NE2d 127]

7. The directors of the American Founders Life Insurance Co. made a contract with the Colorado Management Corp. for certain services. American Founders later sued for the return of the money paid to Colorado on the ground that the contract could be set aside because it had been approved by American Founders at a board of directors' meeting at which only six of the eight directors were present and three of these directors were also directors of Colorado and two of them were also officers of Colorado. The bylaws of American Founders required a majority, which was five, to constitute a quorum for a directors' meeting. Was American Founders entitled to recover? [Colorado Management Corp. v American Founders Life Insurance Co., 145 Colo 413, 359 P2d 665]

8. Miller was president and Holcomb was treasurer of Chewning Motors, a Michigan corporation. After 1958 they had nothing to do with the business, no corporate meetings were held, no new officers were selected, and the corporation did not file the annual reports required by statute. Eberts Cadillac Co. was owed money by Chewning Motors. It sued Miller and Holcomb on the basis that a Michigan statute imposed liability on corporate officers in such cases. The statute provided with respect to the annual reports that "any officer . . . of such corporation so in default who has neglected or refused to join in making such report . . . shall be liable for all debts of such corporation contracted during the period of such neglect or refusal." They raised the defense that they had not taken any part in the corporate business during the years in which the reports should have been filed. Is this a valid defense? [Eberts Cadillac Co. v Miller, 10 MichApp 370, 159 NW2d 217]

9. Ponder was the president of the Long Beach Motel Hotel Corporation. He requested a quotation from General Electric on air conditioners for the hotel. He was sent a quotation, on the basis of which he sent in a purchase order on behalf of the corporation. General Electric rejected this order made in the name of the corporation and in effect stated that it would only sell to Ponder personally. A new purchase order was sent to Ponder which showed him individually as the buyer. He signed his name but then added "Pres." When General Electric sued him for the purchase price, he claimed that he had signed on behalf of the corporation and that General Electric knew that it was dealing with the corporation. Was he bound by the contract? [General Electric Co. v Ponder, (La App) 234 So2d 786]

10. Heyl and others were directors of Western Inn Corporation. The corporation desired to construct a motel but financial difficulties developed. Outside financing did not prove possible, and finally Heyl and several other directors loaned the money to the corporation. At the time of each loan, all details were made known to, and approved by, the board of directors and the shareholders. As part of the loan agreement with Heyl and the others, a mortgage on the corporation's hotel property was given to them. Thereafter the corporation defaulted on the loan agreement, and Heyl and the other directors who had loaned the corporation the money foreclosed on the mortgage and purchased the hotel property at the foreclosure sale. The Western Inn Corporation sued Heyl and the directors on the theory that they had committed a breach of their fiduciary duty as directors by purchasing the corporation property for themselves at the foreclosure sale and that they therefore held the property as constructive trustees for the corporation. Was the corporation correct? [Western Inn Corp. v Heyl, (Tex Civ App) 452 SW2d 752]

11. Cholfin and his wife were two of the three directors of the Allied Freightways Corporation. Cholfin ran the business, and his wife and the other director took no active part in its management. Cholfin unlawfully used $16,587.25 of the corporate funds to pay his own debts and $3,086.39 of the corporate funds to pay those of his wife. Allied Freightways brought suit to recover from the Cholfins the money improperly spent from the corporation. Allied Freightways claimed that each of the defendants was liable for the full amount of all improper expenditures. Was this correct? [Allied Freightways v Cholfin, 325 Mass 630, 91 NE2d 765]

12. AT&T has contracts with five subsidiary corporations by which AT&T furnishes certain services for each subsidiary and each subsidiary is under contract to pay AT&T compensation of 2½ percent of gross revenues of the subsidiary. Kutik owned shares in AT&T. He brought a lawsuit against Taylor and other directors of AT&T and the five subsidiaries. Kutik claimed that in the preceding six years AT&T had only collected 1% instead of 2½% from each of the subsidiaries. Were the directors liable? [Kutik v Taylor, 364 NYS2d 387]

13. Anthony Yee was the president of the Waipahu Auto Exchange, a corporation. As part of his corporate duties, he arranged financing for the company. The Federal Services Finance Corporation drew twelve checks payable to the order of the Waipahu Auto Exchange. These were then indorsed by its president: "Waipahu Auto Exchange, Limited, by Anthony Yee, President," and were cashed at two different banks. The Bishop National Bank of Hawaii, on which the checks were drawn, charged its depositor, Federal Services, with the amount of these checks. Federal Services then sued Bishop National Bank to restore to its account the amount of these twelve checks on the theory that Bishop National Bank had improperly made payment on the checks because Anthony Yee had no authority to cash them. Did Yee have authority to indorse and cash the checks? [Federal Services Finance Corp. v Bishop National Bank of Hawaii, (CA9 Haw) 190 F2d 442]

Part Eleven • Real Property

50 Nature and Ownership of Real Property

The law of real property is technical and to a large extent uses a vocabulary drawn from the days of feudalism. Much of the earlier law of real property is no longer of practical importance in the modern business world. The following discussion is therefore a simplified presentation of the subject.

A. NATURE OF REAL PROPERTY

Real property has special characteristics of permanence and uniqueness that have strongly influenced the rules that society has developed to resolve disputes concerning real property.

§ 50:1. Definitions. *Real property* includes (a) land, (b) buildings and fixtures, and (c) rights in the land of another.

(a)   Land. *Land* means more than the surface of the earth. It embraces the soil and all things of a permanent nature affixed to the ground, such as herbs, grass, or trees, and other growing, natural products. The term also includes the waters upon the ground and things that are embedded beneath the surface. For example, coal, oil, and marble embedded beneath the surface form part of the land.

Technically, land is considered as extending downward to the earth's center and upward indefinitely. The Uniform Aeronautics Act states that the owner of land owns the space above, subject to the right of aircraft in flight which does not interfere with the use of the land and is not dangerous to persons or property lawfully on the land.[1]

---

[1] The Uniform Aeronautics Act (UAA) has been adopted in Arizona, Delaware, Georgia, Hawaii, Idaho, Indiana, Maryland, Minnesota, Missouri, Montana, Nevada, New Jersey, North Carolina, North Dakota, Pennsylvania, South Carolina, South Dakota, Tennessee, Utah, Vermont, and Wisconsin, but was withdrawn by the Commissioners on Uniform State Laws in 1943.

(b)   Buildings and Fixtures. A *building* includes any structure placed on or beneath the surface of land, without regard to its purpose or use. A *fixture* is personal property that has been attached to the earth or placed in a building in such a way or under such circumstances that it is deemed part of the real property.

(c)   Rights in Land of Another. These rights include *easements,* such as the right to cross another's land, and *profits,* such as the right to take coal from another's land.

§ 50:2. Easements. An *easement* is not only a right in the land of another, but it is a right that belongs to the land which is benefited. The benefited land is called the *dominant tenement,* and the land which is subject to the easement is called the *servient tenement.*

An easement is an interest in land and therefore an oral promise to create an easement is not binding because of the statute of frauds.

(a)   Creation of Easement. An easement may be created in several ways.

(1) An easement may be created by deed.

(2) An easement may be created by implication when one conveys part of the land that has been used as a dominant estate in relation to the part retained. To illustrate, if water or drain pipes run from the part conveyed through the part retained, there is an implied right to have such use continued. In order that an easement will be implied in such a case, the use must be apparent, continuous, and reasonably necessary.

(3) An easement may also be created by implication when it is necessary to the use of the land conveyed. This ordinarily arises when one subdivides land and sells a portion to which no entry can be made, except over the land retained or over the land of a stranger. The grantee's right to use the land retained by the grantor for the purpose of going to and from the land conveyed is known as a *way of necessity.*

(4) An easement may be created by estoppel, as when the grantor states that the plot conveyed is bounded by a street. If in such case, the grantor owns the adjoining land, the public cannot be denied the right to use the area which the owner has described as a street.

(5) An easement may be created by prescription by adverse use for a statutory period. No easement is acquired if the use of the land is with the permission of the owner. This adverse use by which an easement is acquired is similar to the adverse possession by which title is acquired as is discussed in § 50:28.

(b)   Termination of Easement. Once an easement has been granted, it cannot be destroyed by the act of the grantor. A "revocation" attempted without the easement owner's consent has no effect.

An easement may be lost by nonuse when there are surrounding circumstances which show an intent to abandon the easement. For example, where a service transit system had an easement to maintain trolley tracks, it could be found that there was an abandonment of the easement when the tracks were removed and all surface transportation was discontinued. Likewise, where the owner of the easement planted a flowerbed on the land across the end of the path of the easement, the intent to abandon the easement was evident.

§ 50:3. Licenses. A *license* is a personal, revocable privilege to do an act or series of acts upon the land of another. Unlike an easement, a license is not an interest in land. The person allowed to come into the house to use the phone has a license. The advertising company that has permission to paint a sign on the side of a building also has a license.

A license may be terminated at the will of the licensor and continues only as long as the licensor is the owner of the land. (See p. 856, Bunn v Offutt)

§ 50:4. Liens. Real property may be subject to liens that arise by the voluntary act of the owner of the land, such as the lien of a mortgage which is created when the owner voluntarily borrows money and the land is made security for the repayment of the debt. Liens may also arise involuntarily as in the case of tax liens, judgment liens, and mechanics' liens. In the case of taxes and judgments, the liens provide a means for enforcing the obligations of the owner of the land to pay the taxes or the judgment.

Mechanics' liens give persons furnishing labor and materials in the improvement of real estate the right to proceed against the real estate for the collection of the amounts due them. If the owner had dealt directly with such persons, the mechanics' lien is a remedy in addition to the right to enforce the contract of the owner. If the claimant did not have a contract directly with the owner, as in the case of a person furnishing labor or materials to the contractor who dealt with the owner, the claimant has no contract claim against the owner. Mechanics' liens are created by statutes which regulate in detail the kinds of claims for which liens may be imposed and the procedure to be followed.

§ 50:5. Duration and Extent of Ownership. The interest held by a person in real property may be defined in terms of the period of time for which such person will remain the owner, as (1) a fee simple estate or (2) a life estate. These estates are termed *freehold estates.* In addition, either of these estates may be subject to a condition or may expire or terminate upon the happening of a specified contingency. Although a person may own property for a specified number of years this interest is not regarded as a freehold estate, but is a *leasehold estate* and is subject to special rules of law.

(a) Fee Simple Estate. An *estate in fee,* a *fee simple* or a *fee simple absolute,* lasts forever. The owner of such fee has the absolute and entire interest in the land. The important characteristics of this estate are as follows: (1) it is alienable during life; (2) it is alienable by will; (3) it descends to heirs generally if not devised (transferred by will); (4) it is subject to rights of the owner's surviving spouse; and (5) it is liable for debts of the owner before or after death.

Statutes commonly declare that a deed conveying property will be held to convey a fee simple estate if nothing is stated that limits the grantee to a lesser estate.

(b) Life Estate. A *life estate* (or life tenancy), as its name indicates, lasts only during the life of a person, ordinarily its owner. Upon the owner's death, no interest remains to pass to heirs or by will.

B. FIXTURES

By the concept of fixtures, personal property changes to real property and third persons and creditors may acquire rights therein.

§ 50:6. Definition. A *fixture* is personal property that is attached to the earth or placed in a building in such a way or under such circumstances that it is deemed part of the real property.

A person buys a refrigerator, an air conditioner, or a furnace, or some other item that is used in a building, and then has the item installed. The question whether the item is a fixture and therefore part of the building can arise in a variety of situations. (1) The real estate tax assessor assesses the building and adds in the value of the item on the theory that it is part of the building. (2) The buyer of the item owns the building and then sells the building, and the buyer of the building claims that the item stays with the building. (3) The buyer places a mortgage on the building, and the mortgagee claims that the item is bound by the mortgage. (4) The buyer is a tenant in the building in which the item is installed and the landlord claims that the item must stay in the building when the tenant leaves. (5) The buyer does not pay in full for the item, and the seller of the item has a security interest that the seller asserts against the buyer of the item or against the landlord of the building in which the buyer installs the item. The seller of the item may be asserting a claim against the mortgagee of the building or against the buyer of the building.

The determination of the rights of these parties depends upon the common law of fixtures, as occasionally modified by statute.[2]

§ 50:7. Tests of a Fixture. In the absence of an agreement between the parties, the courts apply three tests to determine whether the personal property has become a fixture:

(a) Annexation. Generally the personal property becomes a fixture if it is so attached to the realty that it cannot be removed without materially damaging the realty or destroying the personal property itself. If the property is so affixed as to lose its specific identity, such as bricks in a wall, it becomes part of the realty. Where railroad tracks are so placed as to be immovable, they are to be deemed fixtures.

(b) Adaptation. Personal property especially adapted or suited to the building may constitute a fixture. By the *institutional* or *industrial plant doctrine,* machinery reasonably necessary for the operation of an industrial plant usually becomes part of the realty when installed, without regard to whether it is physically attached or not. This principle does not apply to office equipment and trucks used in the operation of the enterprise.

(c) Intent. The true test is the intention of the person affixing the property at the time it was affixed.

In the absence of direct proof of such intent, it is necessary to resort to the nature of the property, the method of its attachment, and all the surrounding circumstances to determine what the intent was. (See p. 844, Premonstratensian Fathers v Badger Mutual Fire Ins. Co.)

[2] The Uniform Commercial Code regulates the priority of security interests in fixtures, UCC § 9-313, but does not determine when an item is a fixture.

The size, method of attaching, and cost of removal are significant in determining whether it was intended that attached property should become a fixture. For example, a pre-fabricated, glass-lined silo was held to be a fixture where it was 70 feet high, 20 feet around, weighed 35,000 pounds, was firmly attached to a special concrete base set in the ground for that purpose, and would cost $7,000 to move. These factors when coupled with the fact that a silo was clearly adapted to the use of the farm land established that a farmer-purchaser had attached the silo to the land with the intention that it should be a permanent addition.[3]

The fact that machinery installed in a plant would be very difficult and expensive to move and so delicate that the moving would cause damage and unbalancing is significant in reaching the conclusion that the owner of the plant had installed the equipment as a permanent addition and thus had the intent which would make the equipment become fixtures. When the floors in a large apartment house are of concrete which is covered with a thin sheet of plywood to which is stapled wall to wall carpeting, the carpeting constitutes a fixture which cannot be removed from the building as removal would probably destroy the carpeting, it having been cut to size, and the carpeting being necessary to make the building livable as an apartment.

§ 50:8. Movable Machinery and Equipment. Machinery and equipment that is movable is ordinarily held not to constitute fixtures, even though, in order to move it, it is necessary to unbolt it from the floor or to disconnect electrical wires or water pipes.

It is ordinarily held that refrigerators and freezers, and gas and electric ranges are not fixtures and do not lose their character as personal property when they are readily removable upon disconnecting pipes or unplugging wires. A portable window air conditioner which rests on a rack which is fixed to the window sill by two screws and is connected directly to the building only by an electric cord plug is not a fixture.

The mere fact that an item may be "unplugged," however, does not establish that it is not a fixture. For example, a computer and its related hardware constituted "fixtures" when there was such a mass of wires and cables under the floor that the installation gave the impression of permanence.

§ 50:9. Trade Fixtures. Equipment which is attached to a rented building by a tenant for use in trade or business is ordinarily removable by the tenant upon permanently leaving the premises.[4] Such equipment is commonly called a *trade fixture*.

C. LIABILITY TO THIRD PERSONS FOR CONDITION OF REAL PROPERTY

In the case of real estate, liability is ordinarily based upon occupancy. That is, the person in possession may be liable for harm to the third person caused by a condition of the premises, even though the occupier is not the owner but is merely a tenant renting the premises.

§ 50:10. Status-of-Plaintiff Common-Law Rule. Under the common law, liability to a person injured on real estate was controlled by the status of the injured person, that is,

---

[3] Wisconsin Department of Revenue v A. O. Smith Harvestore Products, Inc., 72 Wis2d 60, 240 NW2d 357.

[4] Lemmons v United States (Ct Cl) 496 F2d 864.

whether the person injured was a trespasser, a licensee, or an invitee. A different duty was owed by the occupier of land to each of these three categories.

(a)   **Trespassers.** As to *trespassers,* the occupier ordinarily owes only the duty of refraining from causing intentional harm once the presence of the trespasser is known; but the occupier is not under any duty to warn of dangers or to make the premises safe to protect the trespasser from harm. The most significant exception to this rule arises in the case of small children who, although trespassers, are generally afforded greater protection through the *attractive nuisance doctrine.* For example, the owner of a private residential swimming pool was liable for the drowning of a 5-year old child when the owner did not maintain adequate fencing around the pool, since the placing of such fencing would not have imposed a great burden.

(b)   **Licensees.** As to *licensees,* who are on the premises with the permission of the occupier, the latter owes the duty of warning of nonobvious dangers that are known to the occupier. For example, a host must warn a guest of a known danger. Consequently where a sliding glass door was "invisible" when the patio lights were on and the house lights were off, the host must warn guests of the presence of the glass and is liable when the guest is injured in shattering the glass when reaching for a phone which was in fact on the other side of the glass.[5]

In contrast, the occupier owes no duty to the licensee to take any steps to learn of the presence of unknown dangers.

(c)   **Invitees.** As to *invitees,* whose presence is sought to further the economic interest of the occupier, such as customers, there is a duty to take reasonable steps to discover any danger and a duty to warn the invitee or to correct the danger. For example, a store must make a reasonable inspection of the premises to determine that there is nothing on the floor that would be dangerous, such as a slippery substance that might cause a patron to fall, and must either correct the condition or appropriately rope off the danger area or give suitable warning. If the occupier of the premises fails to conform to the degree of care described and harm results to an invitee on the premises, the occupier is liable for such harm.

In most states the courts have expanded the concept of invitees beyond the category of those persons whose presence will economically benefit the occupier so that it includes members of the public who are invited when it is apparent that such persons cannot be reasonably expected to make an inspection of the premises before making use of them and that they would not be making repairs to correct any dangerous condition. Some courts have also made inroads into the prior law by treating a recurring licensee, such as a letter carrier, as an invitee.

§ 50:11. Negligence Rule. Several courts have begun a strong new trend in ignoring these common-law distinctions and holding the occupier liable according to ordinary negligence standards; that is, when the occupier as a reasonable person should foresee from the circumstances that harm would be caused a third person, the occupier has the duty to take reasonable steps to prevent such harm, without regard to whether the

---

[5] Natal v Phoenix Assurance Co. (La) 305 So2d 438.

potential victim would be traditionally classified as a trespasser, a licensee, or an invitee.[6] (See p. 859, Basso v Miller)

Under this rule, the occupier of a store and parking lot who knows that people customarily cut across the lot to patronize a neighboring coffee shop is liable to such a pedestrian who is injured by falling down the edge of the parking lot where a retaining wall has fallen away, when such occupier knew or should have known that pedestrians would cross the lot during the night and a reasonably prudent person would foresee that in the dark the condition of the lot made harm to such persons probable.[7]

§ 50:12. Intermediate Rule. Some courts have taken an intermediate position and have merely abolished the distinction between licensees and invitees so that the occupier owes the same duty of care to all lawful visitors, and whether one is a licensee or an invitee is merely a circumstance to be considered by the jury in applying the ordinary rule of negligence. On this basis it has been held that a police officer may recover from the occupier of premises upon falling and being injured on accumulated ice on the premises, although entering for the purpose of serving a parking violation summons.

In some states, the distinction between licensees and invitees has been retained in name but destroyed in fact by requiring an occupier to warn the licensee of unknown dangers of which the occupier in the exercise of reasonable care should have known, or by classifying a licensee as an invitee.[8]

D. CO-OWNERSHIP OF REAL PROPERTY

All interests in particular real property may be held in severalty, that is by one person alone. As explained in Chapter 20, ownership in severalty also exists when title is held in the form of "A or B."

§ 50:13. Multiple Ownership. Several persons may have concurrent interests in the same real property. The forms of multiple ownership for real property are the same as those for personal property.[9]

When co-owners sell property, they hold the proceeds of sale by the same type of tenancy as they held the original property.

§ 50:14. Condominiums. A *condominium* is a combination of co-ownership and individual ownership. For example, persons owning an office building or an apartment house by condominium are co-owners of the land and of the halls, lobby, elevators, stairways and exits; yards, gardens, and surrounding land; incinerator, laundry rooms, and other areas used in common; but each apartment or office in the building is individually owned by its occupant.

---

[6] Rowland v Christian, 69 Cal2d 108, 70 CalRptr 97, 443 P2d 561.

[7] Ward v Enevold, 31 ColoApp 333, 504 P2d 1108.

[8] Caroff v Liberty Lumber Co., 146 NJ Super 353, 369 A2d 983 (holding that a public officer, such as a police officer or health inspector, who enters premises in the performance of official duties, has the same status as a business invitee when injured because of a condition of the premises).

[9] See Chapter 20.

(a) **Control and Expense.** In some states, the owners of the various units in the condominium have equal voice in the management and share an equal part of its expenses. In others, control and liability for expenses are shared by a unit owner in the same ratio that the value of the unit bears to the value of the entire condominium project. In all states, the unit owners have an equal right to use the common areas.

The owner of each condominium unit makes such repairs as are required by the owner's deed or contract of ownership, and the owner is prohibited from making any major change which would impair or damage the safety or value of an adjoining unit. Any changes or improvements made to outside walls must ordinarily be consistent with the existing pattern of the building.

(b) **Collection of Expenses from Unit Owner.** When a unit owner fails to pay the owner's share of taxes, operating expenses, and repairs, it is commonly provided that a lien may be entered against that owner's unit for the amount which is due. If payment is not then made, some condominium statutes authorize the association to sell the delinquent owner's rights in the unit.

(c) **Tort Liability.** Most condominium projects fail to make provision as to the liability of unit owners for a tort occurring in the common areas. A few states expressly provide that when a third person is injured in the common areas a suit may only be brought against the condominium association and any judgment recovered is a charge against the association to be paid off as a common expense. When the condominium association is incorporated, the same result should be obtained by applying ordinary principles of corporation law under which liability for torts occurring on the premises of the corporation are not the liability of the individual shareholders.

(d) **Cooperatives Distinguished.** Ownership in a condominium is to be distinguished from ownership in a cooperative. A cooperative will typically be a corporation renting apartments to persons who are also owners of stock of the corporation. The apartment complex is owned only by the corporation and the only "ownership" interests of the stockholders is as tenants of their respective apartments or offices.

§ 50:15. Advantages of Condominium Ownership.

(a) **Freedom from Enterprise Liability.** The owner of a unit is not liable personally for an enterprise liability nor may the unit of the owner be taken to pay for such a liability. For example, even though the total enterprise be sold for taxes or to pay a tort judgment in favor of a third person injured on the common premises, the ownership of the individual units remains unchanged.

(b) **Transferability of Unit.** The condominium unit is property which the unit owner can transfer as freely as any other kind of property. Because of this transferability of the unit, it is easier for the unit owner to raise money by mortgaging the unit than would be the case if the enterprise were run as an apartment house or cooperative and the unit owner would have merely a fractional interest or a leasehold interest to put up as security.

(c) **Tax Deductions.** A deduction for mortgage interest and property taxes paid may be claimed by the unit owners on their individual income tax returns. Over a period of time, the unit owner can thus effect a tax savings which in effect will lower the cost of the condominium unit.

E. TRANSFER OF REAL PROPERTY BY DEED

Although many of the technical limitations of the feudal and earlier common-law days have disappeared, much of the law relating to the modern deed originated in those days. For this reason, the drawing of a deed to transfer the title to land should be entrusted only to one who knows exactly what must be done.

§ 50:16. Definitions. A *deed* is an instrument or writing by which an owner or *grantor* transfers or conveys an interest in land to a new owner called a *grantee* or transferee.

Unlike a contract, no consideration is required to make a deed effective.[10] Although consideration is not required to make a valid deed or transfer of title by deed, the absence of consideration may be evidence to show that the transfer is made by the owner in fraud of creditors who may then be able to set aside the transfer.

Real property, as in the case of personal property, may either be sold or given as a gift. However, a deed is necessary to transfer title to land, even though it is a gift.

§ 50:17. Classification of Deeds. Deeds may be classified in terms of the interest conveyed as (1) a *quitclaim deed,* which transfers merely whatever interest, if any, the grantor may have in the property, without specifying that interest in any way, and (2) a *warranty deed,* which purports to transfer a specified interest and which warrants or guarantees that such interest is transferred.

A deed may also be classified as a common-law deed or a statutory deed. The *common-law deed* is a long form that sets forth the details of the transaction. The *statutory deed* in substance merely recites that a named person is making a certain conveyance to a named grantee. It is generally held that the existence of a statute authorizing a short form of deed does not preclude the use of the common-law form.

§ 50:18. Execution of Deeds. Ordinarily a deed must be signed, by signature or mark, or sealed by the grantor. In order to have the deed recorded, statutes generally require that two or more witnesses sign the deed and that the grantor then acknowledge the deed before a notary public or other officer. In the interest of legibility, it is frequently required that the signatures of the parties be followed by their printed or typewritten names.

In many states the statute that authorizes a short or simplified form of deed also declares that no seal is required to make effective a writing which purports to convey an interest in land.

A deed must be executed and delivered by a person having capacity. It may be set aside by the grantor on the ground of the fraud of the grantee provided that innocent third persons have not acquired rights in the land.

---

[10] Robinson v Thompson, 192 Neb 428, 222 NW2d 123.

The deed remains binding as between the grantor and the grantee even though it has not been acknowledged or recorded.

§ 50:19. Delivery of Deeds. A deed has no effect and title does not pass until the deed has been delivered. Delivery is a matter of intent as shown by words and conduct; no particular form of ceremony is required. The essential intent in delivering a deed is not merely that the grantor intends to hand over physical control and possession of the paper on which the deed is written, but that the grantor intends thereby to transfer the ownership of the property described in the deed. That is, the grantor must deliver the deed with the intent that it should take effect as a deed and convey an interest in the property.

A deed is ordinarily made effective by handing it to the grantee with the intention that the grantee should thenceforth be the owner of the property described in the deed. A delivery may also be made by placing the deed, addressed to the grantee, in the mail or by giving it to a third person with directions to hand it to the grantee. Where the grantor mailed the deed to the grantee, there was a valid delivery by the act of mailing and the grantee's interest was not affected by the fact that the grantor committed suicide later that day and the deed was not received by the grantee until after the grantor's death.

When a deed is delivered to a third person for the purpose of delivery to the grantee upon the happening of some event or contingency, the transaction is called a *delivery in escrow.* No title passes until the fulfillment of the condition or the happening of the event or contingency.

An effective delivery of a deed may be made symbolically as by delivering to the grantee the key to a locked box and informing the grantee that the deed to the property is in the box.

§ 50:20. Acceptance of Deeds. Generally there must be an acceptance by the grantee. In all cases an acceptance is presumed. However, the grantee may disclaim the transfer if the grantee acts within a reasonable time after learning that the transfer has been made.

§ 50:21. Recording of Deeds. If the owner of lands desires to do so, the deed may be recorded in the office of a public official sometimes called a recorder or commissioner of deeds. The recording is not required to make the deed effective to pass title, but it is done so that the public will know that the grantee is the present owner and thereby prevent the former owner from making any other transaction relating to the property. The recording statutes provide that a person purchasing land from the last holder of record will take title free of any unrecorded claim to the land of which the purchaser does not have notice or knowledge.

The fact that a deed is recorded charges everyone with knowledge of its existence even though they in fact do not know of it because they have neglected to examine the record. The recording of a deed, however, is only such notice if the deed was properly executed. Likewise, the grantee of land cannot claim any protection by virtue of the recording of a deed when (1) a claim is made by one whose title is superior to that of the owner of record; (2) the grantee already had notice or knowledge of the adverse claim when title was acquired; (3) a person acting under a hostile claim was then in possession of the land; (4) the grantee received the land as a gift; or (5) the transfer to the grantee was fraudulent.

§ 50:22. Additional Protection of Buyers. Apart from the protection given to buyers and third persons by the recorded title to property, a buyer may generally also be protected by procuring title insurance or an *abstract of title,* which is a summarized report of the title to the property as shown by the records, together with a report of all judgments, mortgages, and similar claims against the property that have been recorded.

§ 50:23. Cancellation of Deeds. A deed, although delivered, acknowledged, and recorded, may be set aside or cancelled by the grantor upon proof of such circumstances as would warrant the setting aside of a contract. For example, when a conveyance is made in consideration of a promise to support the grantor, the failure of the grantee to perform will ordinarily justify cancellation of the deed.

§ 50:24. Grantor's Warranties.

(a)   **Warranties of Title.** In the common-law deed the grantor may expressly warrant or make certain covenants as to the title conveyed. The statutes authorizing a short form of deed provide that unless otherwise stated in the deed, the grantor shall be presumed to have made certain warranties of title.

The more important of the covenants or warranties of title which the grantor may make are: (1) *covenant of seizin,* or guarantee that the grantor owns the exact estate conveyed; (2) *covenant of right to convey,* or guarantee that the grantor, if not the owner, as in the case of an agent, has the right or authority to make the conveyance; (3) *covenant against encumbrances,* or guarantee that the land is not subject to any right or interest of a third person, such as a lien or easement; (4) *covenant for quiet enjoyment,* or covenant by the grantor that the grantee's possession of the land shall not be disturbed either by the grantor, in the case of a limited covenant, or by the grantor or any person claiming title under the grantor, in the case of a general covenant; and (5) *covenant for further assurances,* or promise that the grantor will execute any additional documents that may be required to perfect the title of the grantee.

(b)   **Fitness for Use.** In the absence of an express warranty in the deed, no warranty as to fitness arises under the common law in the sale or conveyance of real estate. Thus, by the common law there is no implied warranty that a house is reasonably fit for habitation, even though it is a new house sold by the builder.[11]

When a home is purchased directly from the builder, many courts imply a warranty that it was constructed in good workmanlike manner but do not go so far as to impose a warranty that the house is fit to use or free from defects. Similarly, a buyer may have some protection against defects due to poor design of the building

---

[11] Mitchem v Johnson, 7 Ohio2d 66, 218 NE2d 594. No warranty arises under the Sales Article of the UCC since its provisions apply only to sales of "goods." Vernali v Centrella, 28 ConnSupp 476, 266 A2d 200. In any case, the buyer of a house must give notice of any defects within a reasonable time after the buyer learns or should have learned of the defects. Pollard v Saxe & Yolles Development Co., 12 Cal3d 374, 115 CalRptr 648, 525 P2d 88 (extending the concept of UCC § 2-607(3), although recognizing that it was applicable only to the sale of goods).

when purchasing a home from the contractor who prepared the building plans and specifications. In such a case, the contractor may be held liable if, because of a defect in the plans and specifications, the building when constructed is not fit for the purpose for which it was constructed. And a builder is liable for fraud when intentionally concealing defects in the construction which a buyer could not discover by inspection.

In accord with a modern trend, approximately half of the states hold that when a builder or real estate developer sells a new house to a home buyer, an implied warranty that the house and foundation are fit for occupancy or use arises without regard to whether the house was purchased before, during, or after completion of construction. (See p. 861, Humber v Morton) This warranty will not be implied against the first buyer when the house is resold, but there is authority that the second buyer may sue the original contractor for breach of the implied warranty, as against the contention that lack of privity of contract barred suit.[12]

(c)   Damages for Breach of Grantor's Warranties. When the grantor has broken a warranty, whether express or implied, the grantor is liable for the loss caused the grantee thereby.

§ 50:25. Grantee's Covenants. In a deed the grantee may agree to do or to refrain from doing certain acts. Such an agreement becomes a binding contract between the grantor and the grantee. The grantor may sue the grantee for its breach. When the covenant of the grantee relates directly to the property conveyed, such as an agreement to maintain fences on the property or that the property shall be used only for residential purposes, it is said not only that the covenant is binding between the grantor and the grantee but also that it *runs with the land.* This means that anyone acquiring the grantee's land from the grantee is also bound by the covenant of the grantee, even though this subsequent owner had not made any such agreement with anyone.

The right to enforce the covenant also runs with the land owned by the grantor to whom the promise was made. Thus, if *A* owns adjoining tracts of land and conveys one of them to *B* and *B* covenants to maintain the surface drainage on the land so that it will not flood *A*'s land, the benefit of this covenant will run with the land retained by *A*. If *A* sells the remaining tract of land to *C, B* is bound to perform the covenant so as to benefit the neighboring tract even though it is now owned by *C.*

A covenant which provides that the grantee shall refrain from certain conduct is termed a *restrictive* (or negative) *covenant.* It runs with the land in the same manner as a covenant that calls for the performance of an act, that is, an *affirmative covenant.*

§ 50:26. Scope of Grantee's Restrictive Covenants. A restrictive covenant may impose both a limitation on the kind of structure that can be erected on the land and the use which may be made.

A covenant restricting the owner to one single-family private dwelling bars the owner from building a duplex apartment.

(a)   General Building Scheme. When a tract of land is developed and individual lots or homes are sold to separate purchasers, it is common to use the same restrictive

---

[12] Barnes v MacBrown and Co., Inc., 264 Ind 227, 342 NE2d 619.

covenants in all deeds in order to impose uniform restrictions and patterns on the property. Any person acquiring a lot within the tract is bound by the restrictions if they are in the deed or a prior recorded deed, or the grantee has notice or knowledge of such restrictions. Any person owning one of the lots in the tract may bring suit against another lot owner to enforce the restrictive covenant. The effect is to create a zoning code based upon the agreement of the parties in their deeds, as distinguished from one based upon government regulation.

(b)   Restraints on Alienation. The covenants of the grantee may restrict the sale or transfer of the property. It is lawful to provide that the grantor shall have the option to purchase the property, or that if the grantee offers to sell it to anyone, the grantor will be given an opportunity to match the price that a third person is willing to pay. Restrictions on the grantee's right to sell the property are not enforceable when the restriction discriminates against potential buyers because of race, color, creed, or national origin.

F. OTHER METHODS OF TRANSFERRING REAL PROPERTY

Title to real property can also be acquired by eminent domain and by adverse possession.

§ 50:27. Eminent Domain. By *eminent domain* property is taken from its private owner and the title is acquired by the taking government or public authority. Two important questions arise: namely, whether there is a taking of property, and whether the property is taken for a public use. In respect to the first, it is not necessary that the owner be physically deprived of the property. It is sufficient that the normal use of the property has been impaired or lost. As to the second, it is not necessary that the public at large actually use the property. It is sufficient that it is appropriated for the public benefit.

§ 50.28. Adverse Possession. Title to land may be acquired by holding it adversely to the true owner for a certain period of time. In such a case, the possessor gains title by *adverse possession*. If such possession is maintained, the possessor automatically becomes the owner of the property, even though the possessor admittedly had no lawful claim to the land.

In order to acquire title in this manner, possession must be (1) actual, (2) visible and notorious, (3) exclusive, (4) hostile, and (5) continuous for a required period of time.

Commonly the period of time is 21 years but statutes may provide 10 to 20 years. Occupation of land in the mistaken belief that one is the owner is a "hostile" possession. (See p. 862, Somon v Murphy Fabrication & Erection Co.)

G. MORTGAGES

An agreement that creates an interest in real property as security for an obligation and which is to cease upon the performance of the obligation is a *mortgage*. The person whose interest in the property is given as security is the *mortgagor*. The person who receives the security is the *mortgagee*.

§ 50:29. Characteristics of Mortgage. There are three outstanding characteristics of a mortgage: (1) the termination of the mortgagee's interest upon the performance of the obligation secured by the mortgage; (2) the right of the mortgagee to enforce the mortgage by foreclosure upon the mortgagor's failure to perform; and (3) the mortgagor's right to redeem or regain the property. In any case, however, the intention of the parties determines whether there is a mortgage.

§ 50:30. Property Subject to Mortgage. In general, any form of property that may be sold or conveyed may be mortgaged. It is immaterial whether the right is a present right or a future interest, or merely a right in the land of another. It is not necessary that the mortgagor have complete or absolute ownership in the property. The mortgagor may mortgage any interest, legal or equitable, divided or undivided.

§ 50:31. Form of Mortgage. As a mortgage upon real property transfers an interest in the property, it must be in writing by virtue of the statute of frauds.

As a general rule, no particular form of language is required, provided the language used expresses the intent of the parties to create a mortgage. In many states, the substance of a mortgage is practically identical to that of a deed with the exception that a mortgage contains a defeasance clause, a description of the obligation secured, and sometimes a covenant to pay or perform the obligation. The *defeasance clause* states that the mortgage shall cease to have any effect when the obligation is performed, as when the debt of the mortgagor is paid. In many states, statutes provide a form of mortgage that may be used.

Special forms of mortgages have been developed in the case of mortgages securing the payment of corporate bonds and mortgages given to finance real estate developments.

The federal Real Estate Settlement Procedure Act (RESPA) [13] requires that a buyer who is obtaining a mortgage be furnished with an itemized statement setting forth the details of the loan and also be given an instructive manual prepared by HUD (Housing and Urban Development).

§ 50:32. Recording or Filing of Mortgage. An unrecorded mortgage is valid and binding between the parties to it. The heirs or donees of a mortgagor cannot defend against the mortgage on the ground that it has not been recorded. Recording statutes in most states, however, provide that purchasers or creditors who give value and act in good faith in ignorance of an unrecorded mortgage may enforce their respective rights against the property without regard to the existence of the unrecorded mortgage. Accordingly, the purchaser of the land in good faith for value from the mortgagor holds the land free of the unrecorded mortgage, and the mortgagee's only remedy is against the mortgagor on the debt due the mortgagee. The mortgagee can proceed against the transferee only if the mortgagee can prove that the transferee of the land did not purchase it in good faith, for value, and in ignorance of the unrecorded mortgage.

§ 50:33. Repairs and Improvements. In the absence of an agreement to the contrary, a mortgagor is under no duty to make improvements or to restore or repair parts of the premises that are destroyed or damaged through no fault of the mortgagor.

---

[13] PL 93-533, PL 94-205, 12 USC § 2601 et seq.

A mortgagee, when in possession, must make reasonable and necessary repairs in order to preserve the property and is entitled to reimbursement for such repairs. Ordinarily, however, the mortgagee may not charge to the mortgagor expenditures for valuable or enduring improvements.

§ 50:34. Taxes, Assessments, and Insurance. The duty to pay taxes and assessments rests upon the mortgagor. In the absence of an agreement, neither party is under a duty to insure the mortgaged property. Both parties, however, may insure their respective interests. It is common practice for the mortgagor to obtain a single policy of insurance on the property payable to the mortgagee and the mortgagor as their interests may appear.

If the mortgagor fails to perform the duty of paying taxes, assessments, or insurance premiums, the mortgagee is entitled to make such payments and to receive reimbursement.

§ 50:35. Impairment of Security. The mortgagor is liable to the mortgagee for any damage to the property, caused by the mortgagor's fault, that impairs the security of the mortgage by materially reducing the value of the property. Both the mortgagor and the mortgagee have a right of action against a third person who wrongfully injures the property.

§ 50:36. Transfer of Interest.

(a)   Transfer by Mortgagor. The mortgagor may ordinarily transfer the land without the consent of the mortgagee. Such a transfer passes only the interest of the mortgagor and does not divest or impair the mortgage if properly recorded.

The transfer of the property by the mortgagor does not affect the liability of the mortgagor to the mortgagee. Unless the latter has agreed to substitute the mortgagor's grantee for the mortgagor, the latter remains liable for the mortgage debt as though no transfer had been made.

(b)   Liability of Mortgagor's Transferee. The purchaser of mortgaged property does not become personally liable for the mortgaged debt unless the purchaser expressly assumes that debt. Such an assumption of the debt does not release the mortgagor from liability to the mortgagee unless the mortgagee agrees to such substitution of parties.

(c)   Transfer by Mortgagee. In most states, a mortgage may be transferred or assigned by the mortgagee. A few states hold that a mortgage is nonassignable and that the title of the mortgagee can only be transferred by a formal conveyance or deed.

§ 50:37. Rights of Mortgagee After Default. Upon the mortgagor's default, the mortgagee in some states is entitled to obtain possession of the property and collect the rents or to have a receiver appointed for that purpose. In all states, the mortgagee may enforce the mortgage by *foreclosure* or sue to enforce the mortgaged debt.

Generally it is provided that upon any default under the terms of the mortgage agreement, the mortgagee has the right to declare that the entire mortgaged debt is due even though the default related only to an installment or to the doing of some act, such as maintaining insurance on the property or producing receipts for taxes.

A sale on the foreclosure of the mortgage destroys the mortgage, and the property passes to the buyer at the sale free of the mortgage. But the extinction of the mortgage by foreclosure does not destroy the debt that was secured by the mortgage. The mortgagor remains liable for any unpaid balance or deficiency, although by statute, the mortgagor is generally given credit for the fair value of the property if it was purchased by the mortgagee.

§ 50:38. Rights of Mortgagor After Default.

(a)   Stay of Foreclosure. In certain cases, authorized by statute, a *stay* (or delay) *of foreclosure* may be obtained by the mortgagor to prevent undue hardship.

(b)   Redemption. The *right of redemption* means the right of the mortgagor to free the property of the mortgage lien after default. By statute in many states, the right may be exercised during a certain time following foreclosure and sale of the mortgaged land.

CASES FOR CHAPTER 50

Bunn v Offutt

216 Va 681, 222 SE2d 522 (1976)

Bunn and his wife claimed that they had an easement to enter and use the swimming pool on neighboring land. They based their claim on a contract that had been made between the former owners of the land and the owners of the neighboring land. The Bunns brought an action against the owners of the neighboring land to establish their right to use the pool. From a judgment for the defendants, the Bunns appealed.

HARRISON, J. . . . On July 9, 1962, Temco, Inc. conveyed to Harvey W. Wynn and Rosabelle G. Wynn property known as 900 South Wakefield Street in Arlington. Prior thereto, on January 26, 1962, the Wynns had signed a contract of purchase prepared by the seller's agent. In this contract is found the following provision: "Use of apartment swimming pool to be available to purchaser and his family." The Wynns testified that the agent, Willis L. Lawrence, told them that the use of the pool went with the ownership of the home being purchased, and that subsequent purchasers would have the right to use the pool. The pool is located in an adjoining apartment complex which was being developed by appellees at the time. The Wynns said the sales agent emphasized that use of this pool would be a desirable feature in the event they subsequently

decided to sell the property. No reference was made to the pool in the deed from Temco to the Wynns.

On May 31, 1969, the Bunns contracted in writing to buy the property from the Wynns through the latter's agent, Sonnett Realty Co., Inc. While no reference to the pool was made in the contract, the Wynns and a representative of Sonnett told the Bunns that the use of the pool went with the purchase of the property. However, the deed, dated July 18, 1969, conveying the property from the Wynns to the Bunns contains no reference to the pool. After the purchase was effected, and when the Bunns requested passes from appellees showing their entitlement to the use of the pool, their request was refused.

The rights of the parties depend upon the nature of the transaction in 1962 between appellees, as sellers, and Mr. and Mrs. Wynn, as purchasers.

The testimony of Offutt, owner of appellee corporations, is unequivocal that at no time did he ever intend to extend the privilege of using the swimming pool beyond the original purchasers of certain houses (including 900 South Wakefield Street) which were located adjacent to his apartment development. He said that at one time he thought he would experience difficulty in selling the houses without an added inducement, and therefore included in his sales contract a clause to the effect that the use of the apartment swimming pool would be available to the purchaser and his family. Offutt further testified he never intended the right to run with the land and inure to successors in interest and in fact had never extended pool privileges to any one beyond the first purchasers.

The dispositive issue in this case is whether the language in the contract, "Use of apartment swimming pool to be available to purchaser and his family," amounted to a grant of a mere license to the Wynns and their family; or whether the Wynns acquired thereby a private easement across the land of appellees to the swimming pool and to the use of the pool, which easement was thereafter transferred to the Bunns.

A license has been described as "a right, given by some competent authority to do an act which without such authority would be illegal, a tort, or a trespass." . . . A license is personal between the licensor and the licensee and cannot be assigned. . . . And a grant which creates any interest or estate in land is not a license. Such a grant creates an easement. . . .

An easement has been described as "a privilege without profit, which the owner of one tenement has a right to enjoy in respect of that tenement in or over the tenement of another person; by reason whereof the latter is obliged to suffer, or refrain from doing something on his own tenement to the advantage of the former". . . .

> "Easements correspond to the servitudes of the civil law, and consist (1) of privileges on the part of one person to use the land of another (the servient tract) in a particular manner and for a particular purpose, or (2) of rights to demand that the owner of the servient tract refrain from certain uses of his own land, the privileges or rights in either case not being inconsistent with a general property in the owner of the servient tract. The easement further involves the right of freedom in its exercise from interference by the owner of the servient tract or other persons. Examples of easements are rights of way, of drainage, or light and air, etc." [Footnotes omitted] 1 Minor on Real Property (2d Ed., Ribble), § 87.

Easements may be created by express grant or reservation, by implication, by estoppel or by prescription. The only rights acquired by the Wynns in the property of appellees were acquired by deed from Temco. The provisions of the contract were merged in this deed. However, the deed is silent as to the pool, and the contract made the use of the pool available only to "purchaser and his family." The trial court found this language consistent with appellees' theory that a mere license only was granted to the purchasers and their families, and not an interest in land or an estate of inheritance; that the absence of any provision regarding the swimming pool in the deed to the Wynns was sufficient to preclude any easement by grant or reservation; and that the evidence and exhibits failed to show that an easement was created by estoppel, necessity or prescription. The trial court further found that no easement had been created by implication for there was neither a showing of a preexisting use of the easement prior to the conveyance by Temco to the Wynns, nor any showing that the use of the swimming pool was essential to the beneficial enjoyment of the land conveyed.

The Wynns and their family were given a mere license to use the swimming pool. It was not an interest running with the land that could subsequently be transferred by them.

[Judgment affirmed]

Premonstratensian Fathers v Badger Mutual Fire Ins. Co.

46 Wis 2d 362, 175 NW2d 337 (1970)

In 1958 a supermarket was constructed and owned by Jacobs Realty Corporation. The market contained five large walk-in coolers or refrigerators. Title to the market was thereafter transferred to the Premonstratensian Fathers and was insured against fire by Badger Mutual Insurance Company. The building was severely damaged by fire and the insurer paid approximately $80,000 for the building damage. The Fathers claimed an additional $20,000 for the destruction of the coolers. The insurer refused to pay this amount and asserted that the coolers were not owned by the Fathers. From a judgment for the Fathers, the insurer appealed.

HANSE, N.J. . . . If the coolers are determined to be common-law fixtures, and were such at the time of the construction of the building and the installation of the coolers, then they would have passed to the Fathers under the warranty deed of March 7, 1960, and they would be insured under the terms of the policy. The issue then is whether these coolers constitute fixtures.

The rule which has developed . . . as to what constitutes a fixture is not really a comprehensive definition, but rather a statement of the factors which are to be applied to the facts and circumstances of

858

a particular case to determine whether or not the property in question does constitute a fixture. . . .

ANNEXATION

. . . An object will not acquire the status of a fixture unless it is in some manner or means . . . attached or affixed, either actually or constructively, to the realty." . . . The trial court ably pointed out the physical facts which led to its conclusion that there is indeed annexation in this case. The more important of these are as follows: (1) The exterior walls of the cooler, in four instances, constituted the interior wall of another room. (2) In the two meat coolers, a meat hanging and tracking system was built into the coolers. These tracks were used to move large cuts of meats from the cooler area into the meat preparation areas, and were suspended from the steel girders of the building structure by means of large steel bolts. These bolts penetrated through the roof of the cooler supporting wooden beams, which, in turn, supported the tracking system. The tracking in the coolers was a part of a system of tracking throughout the rear portion of the supermarket. (3) The coolers were attached to hardwood plank which was, in turn, attached to the concrete floor of the supermarket. The attachment of the plank to the floor was accomplished through the use of a ramsetting gun. The planks were laid on the floor, and the bolts were driven through them into the concrete floor, where they then exploded, firmly fixing the coolers into place. There was a material placed on the planks which served both as an adhesive and as an insulation. (4) The floor of the coolers was specially sloped during the construction of the building so that the slope would carry drainage into a specially constructed drain in the concrete. In addition, four of the coolers were coated with a protective coating to seal the floors. In the freezer, a special concrete buildup was constructed in the nature of a trough, the purpose of which was to carry away moisture as frozen chickens melted. (5) A refrigeration unit was built into each cooler. The unit was suspended from the ceiling of the cooler, and tubing was run through the wall of the cooler to compressors located elsewhere in the store. (6) Electric lights and power receptacles were built into each cooler and were connected by electrical wiring through the walls and the ceiling of the cooler to the store's electrical power supply. (7) The walls of the cooler were interlocked, and set into the splines,

the hardwood planks ramset into the concrete floor, in tongue and groove fashion.

These factors adequately support the conclusion that the coolers were indeed physically annexed to the premises. The insurers argue that the coolers were removable without material injury to the premises, which detracts from the annexation. There was a dispute in the evidence introduced at the trial, with the insurers' expert testifying that this type of cooler was easily severable from the building, while one of the members of the Jacobs family testified that when he removed some of the bolts from the floor following the fire, large sections of concrete would crack on the floor. This was a conflict for resolution by the trial court. In any event, the element of removability without material damage to the building no longer enjoys the position of prominence in the law of fixtures which it once held. It is now only one of the factors which is to be considered by the trial court. . . .

ADAPTATION

Adaptation refers to the relationship between the chattel and the use which is made of the realty to which the chattel is annexed. The use of the realty was that of a retail grocery, commonly known as a supermarket. This was the intent of the parties at the time of the construction of the building, and the intent of the parties throughout the entire history of the business. The fact of operation has borne out this intent. In a business which carries fresh foods, frozen foods, produce, meats and butter, coolers used for storage and handling of these perishables are patently related to the use of the building. In fact, it would be hard to picture any equipment more closely related to the operation of a supermarket, where large quantities of perishables must, of necessity, be purchased for storage and processing.

The insurers raise a number of points to dispute this finding. They state: The coolers were not custom made; the coolers are useful not to the building, but to the use to which the building is put; the coolers could have been used anywhere; other coolers could have been used. There is no requirement that the coolers be custom made, but only that they be adapted to the use to which the building is put. The test here is not the adaptability to the building, but the adaptability to the use to which the building is put. The fact that other coolers could have been used, or that these coolers could have been used elsewhere, does not alter the fact that there was a close connection between these coolers and the retail grocery business conducted on the property. . . .

INTENT

This court has repeatedly held that intent is the primary determinant of whether a certain piece of property has become a fixture. The relevant intent is that of the party making the annexation. At the time of the construction of the supermarket and the installation of the coolers, both the Jacobs Realty Corporation and the Jacobs Brothers Stores, Inc., were in existence as separate legal entities. The title to the land in question was registered in the name of the Jacobs Realty Corporation, but the exact status of Jacobs Brothers Stores, Inc., is unclear at that date. There is no definitive evidence which demonstrates whether it was the Jacobs Realty Corporation or the Jacobs Brothers Stores, Inc., which purchased the coolers and caused them to be installed on the premises. The invoice from the manufacturer was sent to the "Jacobs Bros. Super Market," a nonexistent legal entity. The evidence introduced at the trial as to who paid for the coolers consisted of the testimony of Henry Jacobs. He did not remember which of the corporations issued the check in payment of the coolers; many of their records were burned; John, Norbert and Henry Jacobs paid for them through one of the corporations; and he was inclined to think it was Jacobs Realty Corporation that purchased them. Thus, there is no evidence from which it can be positively asserted that either Jacobs Realty Corporation or Jacobs Brothers Stores, Inc., purchased the coolers.

In its decision, the trial court found, as a reasonable and legitimate inference from all the facts and circumstances surrounding the placement of the coolers onto the realty, that there was an intention that the coolers become a permanent accession to the realty; that when Jacobs Realty Corporation conveyed the land together with all buildings and improvements thereon to Jacobs Brothers Stores, Inc., the intention still prevailed that the coolers were a permanent accession to the realty; and that the same intention still prevailed when Jacobs Brothers Stores, Inc., conveyed the building and improvements to the plaintiff, and when the plaintiff leased the premises (the land, with all buildings and improvements thereon) back to the corporation as lessee. . . .

The coolers were fixtures when installed; passed to Jacobs Brothers Stores, Inc., through the warranty deed; subsequently passed to the Fathers through that warranty deed; and are in fact fixtures within the meaning of the coverage clause of the insurance policy in this case. . . .

[Judgment affirmed]

Basso v Miller

40 NY2d 233, 386 NYS2d 564 (1976)

Ice Caves Mountain, Inc., operated a scenic park as a tourist attraction. One of the patron's fell into a crevice. Among the people coming to the patron's rescue were Miller and Basso. These two were riding on a motorcycle driven by Miller. When they arrived at the Ice Caves, they were told by Ms. Ballentine not to go to the scene of the accident as there was enough help. They nevertheless proceeded and took part in the rescue operation without any objection from those in charge. In returning from the rescue scene, the motorcycle hit some holes in the motor trail, went out of control and threw both riders onto rocks. Basso sued Miller and Ice Caves. A judgment was entered in favor of Basso against the defendants and they appealed. Ice Caves appealed on the ground that the trial court had improperly instructed the jury that if it found that Basso was a licensee, Ice Cave then owed him a duty not to let him get harmed because of a dangerous condition of the roadway and was required to advise him of the condition which caused harm. Ice Caves claimed that this put too heavy a duty on it.

COOKE, J. . . . Ice Caves contends, and correctly so, that the New York standard has been that as a licensee a plaintiff must take the premises as he finds them, and that the owner thereof is liable only if he is found to have committed affirmative acts of negligence or if a trap existed or there was concealed danger not likely to be discovered. . . . There is only a duty to warn of known dangerous defects which the defendant "should know or suspect that the licensee will not discover himself after a reasonable inspection of the premises.". . .

In New York, for long, it has been the status of the plaintiff which has been determinative of the duty and, often, the ascribing of status has been a difficult task. In the instant case, for example, much of the testimony in the nearly 1,000-page record was elicited in order to enable the jury to classify the plaintiff as a trespasser, licensee or invitee. As a further complication, not only did the jury have to weigh and evaluate the differing testimony as to status at any particular time, but also had to determine whether the status of the plaintiff shifted as the afternoon turned to evening. As the trial court explained, under one view of the facts, it was possible for the jury to have labeled plaintiff a trespasser when he entered without permission and against the wishes of Ms. Ballentine, a licensee when seen but not ejected by Mr. Grau, the "boss," in the parking lot, and an invitee when assisting in the rescue. This being so, it remains a curiosity of the law that the duty owed to plaintiff on exit may have been many times greater than that owed him on his entrance, though he and the premises all the while remained the same.

Rather than to demand continued attempts to fit a plaintiff into one of the three rigid categories, the court pauses instead to reflect, to reconsider the necessity for such classification and to state today that the distinctions need no longer be made. Taking a broad view, we note that nearly 20 years have passed since the distinctions between licensees and invitees have been abolished by statute in England (Occupiers' Liability Act [1957], 5 & 6 Eliz. 2, ch. 31) and since the United States Supreme Court in *Kermarec v Compagnie Generale,* 358 U.S. 625, 630-631, 79 S.Ct. 406, 3 L.Ed.2d 550, leveled direct criticism at this aspect of tort law. In its determination that such categories have no place in admiralty law, the *Kermarec* court made these cogent comments . . . :

> "The distinctions which the common law draws between licensee and invitee were inherited from a culture deeply rooted to the land, a culture which traced many of its standards to a heritage of feudalism. In an effort to do justice in an industrialized urban society, with its complex economic and individual relationships, modern common-law courts have found it necessary to formulate increasingly subtle verbal refinements, to create subclassifications among traditional common-law catgories, and to delineate fine gradations in the standards of care which the landowner owes to each. Yet even within a single jurisdiction, the classifications and subclassifications bred by the common law have produced confusion and conflict. As new distinctions have been spawned, older ones have become obscured. Through this semantic morass the common law has moved, unevenly and with hesitation, towards imposing on owners and occupiers a

single duty of reasonable care in all the circumstances."

New York courts are not unmindful of the adoption of the single standard of care in several of our sister States. Beginning with the 1968 California Supreme Court decision in *Rowland v Christian,* 69 Cal. 2d 108, 70 Cal.Rptr.97,443 P.2d 561, we have observed the growing number of well-reasoned decisions abandoning the common-law distinctions and adopting the simple rule of reasonable care under the circumstances. . . . We have . . . today abandoned the classifications entirely and announced our adherence to the single standard of reasonable care under the circumstances whereby foreseeability shall be a measure of liability. . . . This standard of reasonable care should be no different than that applied in the usual negligence action. Contributory and, now, comparative negligence, as well as assumption of the risk, all fit into their respective places, to be invoked when appropriate.

Indeed as the duty was so clearly stated in *Smith v Arbaugh's Rest.* "A landowner must act as a reasonable man in maintaining his property in a reasonably safe condition in view of all the circumstances, including the likelihood of injury to others, the seriousness of the injury, and the burden of avoiding the risk." Application of the single rule in the instant case exemplifies its good sense, for the duty of keeping the roads of Ice Caves Mountain in repair should not vary with the status of the person who uses them but, rather, with the foreseeability of their use and the possibility of injury resulting therefrom. While the likelihood of a plaintiff's presence had been an implicit consideration in the determination of status and the duty commensurate therewith, it now becomes a primary independent factor in determining foreseeability and the duty of the owner or occupier will vary with the likelihood of plaintiff's presence at the particular time and place of the injury. While status is no longer determinative, considerations of who plaintiff is and what his purpose is upon the land are factors which, if known, may be included in arriving at what would be reasonable care under the circumstances.

Of course, before it becomes appropriate for the jury to consider all such questions, the court, as it would in the usual negligence action, must make the threshold determination as to whether the plaintiff, by introducing adequate evidence on each element, has made out a case sufficient in law to support a favorable jury verdict. Only in those cases where there arises a real question as to the landowner's negligence should the jury be permitted to proceed. In all others, where proof of any essential element falls short, the case should go no further. While the rigid status classifications are to be dispensed with, the function of the court and the standard of proof remain the same.

The failure of the court to properly instruct the jury [requires a new trial].

[Judgment reversed and action remanded]

Humber v Morton

(Tex) 426 SW2d (1968)

Humber purchased a new house from Morton who was in the business of building and selling new houses. The first time that she lit a fire in the fireplace, the house caught on fire because of a defect in the fireplace and the house was partially damaged. She sued Morton who defended in part on the theory that the rule of caveat emptor, or "Let the buyer beware," barred the suit. From a judgment in favor of Morton, Humber appealed.

NORVELL, J. . . . We are of the opinion that the courts erred in holding as a matter of law that Morton was not liable to Mrs. Humber because the doctrine of caveat emptor applied to the sale of a new house by a "builder-vendor" and consequently no implied warranty that the house was fit for human habitation arose from the sale. Accordingly, we reverse the judgments of the courts below and remand the cause to the district court for a . . . trial upon the merits. . . .

It is undisputed that Morton built the house and then sold it as a new house. Did he thereby impliedly warrant that such house was constructed in a good workmanlike manner and was suitable for human habitation? We hold that he did. Under such circumstances, the law raises an implied warranty. . . .

Does the doctrine of caveat emptor apply to the sale of a new house by a builder-vendor?

Originally, the two great systems of jurisprudence applied different doctrines to sales of both real and personal property. The rule of the common law—caveat emptor—was fundamentally based upon the premise that the buyer and seller dealt at arm's length, and that the purchaser had means and opportunity to gain information concerning the subject matter of the sale which were equal to those of the seller. . . .

In 1884, the Supreme Court of the United States applied the doctrine of implied warranty, the antithesis of caveat emptor, to a real property situation involving false work and pilings driven into the bed of the Maumee River. . . .

While in numerous common-law jurisdictions, the caveat emptor doctrine as applied to the vendor-builder, new-house situation has overstayed its time, it was said by way of dicta in a Texas Court of Civil Appeals case in 1944 that: "By offering the (new) house for sale as a new and complete structure, appellant impliedly warranted that it was properly constructed and of good material and specifically that it had a good foundation. . . ."

This decision has been described as "a preview of things to come.". . . See also, Williston on Contracts (3rd Ed Jaeger) § 926A, wherein it is said: "It would be much better if this enlightened approach (implied warranty, Jones v Gatewood, 381 P2d 158 [Okla]) were generally adopted with respect to the sale of new houses for it would tend to discourage much of the sloppy work and jerry-building that has become perceptible over the years.". . .

The Glisan case (Glisan v Smolenske), 153 Colo 274, 387 P2d 260 (1963), was factually similar to the hypothetical example heretofore set out in this opinion. Smolenske had agreed to purchase a house from Glisan while it was under construction. The court propounded and answered the implied warranty question, thusly:

"Was there an implied warranty that the house, when completed, would be fit for habitation? There is a growing body of law on this question, which, if followed, requires an answer in the affirmative. . . ."

While it is not necessary for us to pass upon a situation in which the vendor-purchaser relationship is absent, the case of Schipper v Levitt & Sons, 44 NJ 70, 207 A2d 314 (1965), is important as much of the reasoning set forth in the opinion is applicable here. The Supreme Court of New Jersey . . . placed emphasis upon the close analogy between a defect in a new house and a manufactured chattel. The opinion states:

"The law should be based on current concepts of what is right and just and the judiciary should be alert to the never-ending need for keeping its common-law principles abreast of the times. Ancient distinctions which make no sense in today's society and tend to discredit the law should be readily rejected. . . ."

If at one time in Texas the rule of caveat emptor had application to the sale of a new house by a vendor-builder, that time is now past. The decisions and legal writings herein referred to afford numerous examples and situations illustrating the harshness and injustice of the rule when applied to the sale of new houses by a builder-vendor. . . . Obviously, the ordinary purchaser is not in a position to ascertain when there is a defect in a chimney flue, or vent of a heating apparatus, or whether the plumbing work covered by a concrete slab foundation is faulty. . . .

The caveat emptor rule as applied to new houses is an anachronism patently out of harmony with modern home buying practices. It does a disservice not only to the ordinary prudent purchaser but to the industry itself by lending encouragement to the unscrupulous, fly-by-night operator and purveyor of shoddy work.

The judgments of the courts below are reversed and the cause remanded for trial in accordance with this opinion.

Somon v Murphy Fabrication & Erection Co.

(WVa) 232 SE2d 524 (1977)

Somon owned the land next to the land owned by Murphy Fabrication & Erection Co. Somon occupied a portion of Murphy's land because Somon wrongly thought that his property was wider than it actually was. He was thus in possession of an area of approximately 80 feet by 500 feet in the belief that he was the rightful owner. When Murphy sought to oust Somon from this area, Somon claimed that he had acquired title by adverse possession. Murphy answered that there had not been any adverse possession because Somon had acted under a claim of right. From a judgment for Somon, Murphy appealed.

MILLER, J. . . . One who seeks to assert title to a tract of land under the doctrine of adverse possession must prove each of the following elements for the requisite statutory period: * (1) That he has held the tract adversely or hostilely; (2) That the possession has been actual: (3) That it has been open and notorious (sometimes stated in the cases as visible and notorious); (4) That possession has been exclusive; (5) That possession has been continuous; . . .

---

* Such person is technically referred to as the "disseisor."

For the element of "hostile" or "adverse" possession, the person claiming adverse possession must show that his possession of the property was against the right of the true owner and is inconsistent with the title of the true owner. The word "hostile" is synonymous with the word "adverse" and need not and does not import that the disseisor must show ill will or malevolence to the true owner. . . .

For "actual" possession, there must be an exercising of dominion over the property and the quality of the acts of dominion are governed by the location, condition and reasonable uses which can be made of the property. . . .

For possession to be open and notorious, it is generally meant that the acts asserting dominion over the property must be of such a quality to put a person of ordinary prudence on notice of the fact that the disseisor is claiming the land as his own. . . . Proof of actual knowledge on the part of the true owner is ordinarily not required. . . .

The element of "exclusive" possession relates to the fact that the disseisor must show that others do not have possession, although this does not mean that sporadic use by others defeats this element since it only need be the type of possession which would characterize an owner's use. . . . Exclusivity has also been applied to the concept of dominion over the entire tract, but this may not in all circumstances be essential. . . .

For the possession to be "continuous" is merely to state that it must last for the statutory period, which, as we have seen, is the fundamental basis for the doctrine of adverse possession. . . .

Turning from these abstract principles to the case at hand, we note the following salient facts: Somon obtained his deed in 1953 and prior to the actual conveyance had walked the boundary of the tract, including the old fence line, with his grantor. In this regard he stated that the old fence, standing in what is now the disputed area, was in existence and did constitute a portion of the fence line that enclosed the entire property. Prior to receiving his grant, he had leased the property from his grantor and had utilized it primarily for grazing cattle with occasional cutting of timber and hunting, and these uses continued after he obtained title to the property. He also made some repairs to the old fence in the disputed area, and this was corroborated by a neighbor.

The record is clear that from 1953 until 1973, when Murphy through its attorney advised that the fence line was on its property, Somon was not disturbed in his uses of the disputed area by Murphy or anyone claiming through Murphy.

Murphy's attack to Somon's claim of adverse possession rests upon a broad front with the initial contention that none of the elements were proven.

We do not believe that this position can be sustained under the facts. It appears that for the statutory period the old fence line formed part of the entire fence line that the testimony indicated surrounded Somon's farm. There was an enclosure coupled with the grazing of cattle and cutting of timber, which has been held to be sufficient to establish necessary elements of adverse possession. . . .

The one challenge that appears of merit is Murphy's assertion that since Somon thought the boundary line was the old fence line, he did not intend to possess the disputed area adversely or hostilely. The argument is advanced that Somon, being mistaken in believing that his deed description carried to the fence line north of Painters Run, when in fact it did not, never intended to lay adverse claim to the disputed area. In effect he could not claim adversely as he had a bona fide belief that he owned the area.

It is, perhaps, sufficient to comment briefly on the two major and opposite views that have evolved in this area. One advances a subjective test; the other an objective one. Those courts that follow the subjective test reason that the element of hostile and adverse connotes a mental intent and therefore if one entertains a belief that he holds the disputed area by virtue of his title document, he does not possess it with the requisite adverse or hostile intent. The other view looks on the physical acts and concludes that if physical dominion has been exercised over the disputed area, this is sufficient to satisfy the adverse or hostile element. . . .

Proof is more certain if limited to objective evidence. The physical evidence of possession should alert the true owner that an adverse claim is made. . . . It is also compatible with the claim of title that must be shown in order to satisfy this element of the doctrine of adverse possession in this type of case. This is true since the actual boundaries of the disputed area have been shown not to lie within the title instrument, thus giving rise to the "mistake" in the first instance. The only way the disseisor can hold is by showing actual dominion over the disputed area, which is the basis for a claim of title. . . .

[Judgment affirmed]

QUESTIONS AND CASE PROBLEMS

1. What social forces are affected by recognizing the right of aircraft to fly over land at such a height that the flight does not interfere with the use of the land and is not dangerous to persons or property on the land?

2. Compare (a) an easement, (b) a profit, and (c) a fixture.

3. When a trespasser falls down an unguarded hole on the land on which that person is a trespasser, the occupier of the land is liable for such harm. Appraise this statement.

4. Compare the status of an apartment "owner" in (a) a condominium and (b) a cooperative.

5. Price sued Whisnant, as guardian for McRary, who had cut and removed trees from certain land. Price claimed title on the basis that he owned the land by adverse possession. He proved that for a period of more than 20 years he had from time to time entered on the land and cut and removed logs. Was Price the owner of the land? [Price v Whisnant, 236 NC 381, 72 SE2d 851]

6. Bradham and others, trustees of the Mount Olivet Church, brought an action to cancel a mortgage on the church property that had been executed by Davis and others as trustees of the church and given to Robinson as mortgagee. It was found by the court that the church was not indebted to the mortgagee for any amount. Should the mortgage be canceled? [Bradham v Robinson, 236 NC 589, 73 SE2d 555]

7. Miller executed a deed to real estate, naming Mary Zieg as grantee. He placed the deed in an envelope on which was written, "To be filed at my death," and put the

envelope and deed in a safe deposit box in the National Bank. The box had been rented in the names of Miller and Mary Zieg. After his death Mary removed the deed from the safe deposit box. Moseley, as executor under Miller's will, brought an action against Mary to declare the deed void. Decide. [Moseley v. Zieg, 180 Neb 810, 146 NW2d 72]

8. Digirolamo owned a tract of land near the Philadelphia Gun Club. During shooting contests held by the club, buckshot from the contestant's guns sometimes fell on his land. He sued the club to compel it to stop. The club claimed that as it had held these contests for over 21 years, it had acquired an easement to do so. Decide. [Digirolamo v Philadelphia Gun Club, 371 Pa 40, 89 A2d 357]

9. Henry Lile owned a house. When the land on which it was situated was condemned for a highway, he removed the house to the land of his daughter, Sarah Crick. In the course of construction work, blasting damaged the house and Sarah Crick sued the contractors, Terry & Wright. They claimed that Henry should be joined in the action as a plaintiff and that Sarah could not sue by herself because it was Henry's house. Were the defendants correct? [Terry & Wright v Crick, (Ky) 418 SW2d 217]

10. Sears, Roebuck and Co. supplied the Seven Palms Motor Inn with window drapes and rods and matching bedspreads. When payment was not made, it claimed that these were fixtures for which a mechanics's lien could be asserted. Were they fixtures? [Sears, Roebuck and Co. v Seven Palms Motor Inn, Inc., (Mo) 530 SW2d 695]

11. The land for the Mira Loma Subdivision had been conveyed by the Enfield Realty Co. to Hallie Houston by a deed which stated, "No mercantile business of any kind shall ever be carried on, on the premises hereby conveyed; . . . it being understood that all improvements to be created on said premises shall be built and used for residence purposes only, excepting such improvements as may be proper for use in connection with a residence." By subsequent conveyances MacDonald and Merritt acquired three lots in the subdivision, and title to 27 other lots was conveyed to other owners. MacDonald and Merritt brought an action against the other lot owners to obtain a decree declaring that they could subdivide their three lots and erect duplex homes. Were they entitled to such a decree? [MacDonald v Painter, (Tex) 441 SW2d 179]

12. By a sealed writing, called a "lease," *A* declared that his neighbor *B* had the right to drive over a driveway in the rear of *A*'s house. *B* later claimed that he had an easement. *A* denied this and contended that *B* had a "lease." Was *A* correct? [Rice v Reich, 51 Wis 2d 205, 186 NW2d 269]

13. Davis Store Fixtures sold certain equipment on credit to Head, who installed it in a building which was later used by the Cadillac Club. When payment was not made, Davis sought to repossess the equipment. If the equipment constituted fixtures, this could not be done. The equipment consisted of a bar for serving drinks, a bench, and a drainboard. The first two were attached to the floor or wall with screws, and the drainboard was connected to water and drainage pipes. Did the equipment constitute fixtures? [Davis Store Fixtures v Cadillac Club, 60 Ill App 2d 106, 207 NE2d 711]

14. Smikahl sold to Hansen a tract of land on which there were two houses and four trailer lots equipped with concrete patios and necessary connections for utility lines. The tract purchased by Hansen was completely surrounded by the land owned by Smikahl and third persons. In order to get onto the highway, it was necessary to cross the Smikahl tract. Several years later, Smikahl put a barbed wire fence around his land. Hansen sued to prevent obstruction to travel between his land and the highway over the Smikahl land. Smikahl defended on the ground that no such right of travel had been given to Hansen. Was he correct? [Hansen v Smikahl. 173 Neb 309, 113 NW2d 210]

51 Leases

A lease exists whenever one person holds possession of the real property of another under an agreement.

A. CREATION AND TERMINATION

The person who owns the real property and permits the occupation of the premises is known as the *lessor* or *landlord*. The *lessee* or *tenant* is the one who occupies the property. A *lease* establishes the relationship of landlord and tenant.

Basically a lease parallels a bailment in which there is an agreement to make the bailment and a subsequent transfer of possession to carry out that agreement. In the case of a lease, there is the lease contract and the interest thereafter acquired by the tenant when possession is delivered under the lease contract. The common law looked at the transfer of possession and regarded the lease as merely the creation of an interest in land. The modern law looks at the contract and regards the lease as the same as the renting of an automobile. With this new approach, typical contract law concepts of unconscionability, mitigation of damages, and the implication of warranties are brought into the law of leases.

§ 51:1. Creation of the Lease Relationship. The relationship of landlord and tenant is created by an express or implied contract. An oral lease is valid at common law, but statutes in most states require written leases for certain tenancies. Many statutes provide that a lease for a term exceeding three years must be in writing. Statutes in other states require written leases when the term exceeds one year.

(a) Antidiscrimination. Statutes in many states prohibit an owner who rents property for profit from discriminating against prospective tenants on the basis of race, color, religion, or national origin. Enforcement of such statutes is generally entrusted to an administrative agency.

(b) Covenants and Conditions. Some obligations of the parties in the lease are described as covenants. Thus, a promise by the tenant to make repairs is called a *covenant to repair*. Sometimes it is provided that the lease shall be forfeited or terminated upon a breach of a promise, and that provision is then called a *condition* rather than a covenant.

(c) Other Agreements. The lease may be the only agreement between the parties. In contrast, there may also be a separate guaranty or a letter of credit to protect the landlord from breach by the tenant. The tenant, in addition to holding under the lease may also hold a franchise from the lessor.

(d) Unconscionability. At common law, the parties to a lease had a relatively uncontrolled freedom to include such terms as they choose. As the lease is increasingly treated as a contract, some states require that leases conform to the concept of conscionability and follow the pattern of UCC § 2-302.[1] A provision in a residential lease stating that curtailment of services by the landlord would not constitute an eviction unless caused willfully or by gross negligence and that such interruption would not entitle the tenant to any compensation is unconscionable and does not bar the tenant from suing for breach of the warranty of habitability. Similarly, a provision in a lease declaring that the landlord would not be responsible for interruptions in the various services provided tenants will not protect the landlord when the air-conditioning system was out of operation for six weeks in midsummer.

§ 51:2. Essential Elements. The following elements are necessary in the establishment of the relation of landlord and tenant:

(a) The occupying of the land must be with the express or implied consent of the landlord.

(b) The tenant must occupy the premises in subordination to the rights of the landlord.

(c) A reversionary interest in the land must remain in the landlord. That is, the landlord must be entitled to retake the possession of the land upon the expiration of the lease.

(d) The tenant must have an estate of present possession in the land. This means a right to be in possession of the land now.

§ 51:3. Classification of Tenancies

(a) Tenancy for Years. A *tenancy for years* is one under which the tenant has an estate of definite duration. The term "for years" is used to describe such a tenancy even though the duration of the tenancy is for only one year or for less than a year.

(b) Tenancy from Year to Year. A *tenancy from year to year* is one under which a tenant, holding an estate in land for an indefinite duration, pays an annual, monthly, or weekly rent. A distinguishing feature of this tenancy is the fact that it does not terminate at the end of a year, month, or week except upon proper notice.

In almost all states a tenancy from year to year is implied if the tenant holds over after a tenancy for years with the consent of the landlord, as shown by an express statement or by conduct such as continuing to accept rent.[2] The lease will frequently state that a holding over shall give rise to a tenancy from year to year unless written notice to the contrary be given.

---

[1] Flam v Herrmann, 395 NYS2d 136.

[2] In some jurisdictions, when rent is accepted from a tenant holding over after the expiration of the term of the lease and there is no agreement to the contrary, there results only a periodic tenancy from month to month rather than a tenancy from year to year. Bay West Realty Co. v Christy (NY CivCt) 61 Misc2d 891, 310 NYS2d 348.

(c)   Tenancy at Will. When land is held for an indefinite period, which may be terminated at any time by the landlord or the tenant, a *tenancy at will* exists. A person who enters into possession of land for an indefinite period with the owner's permission but without any agreement as to rent is a tenant at will.

Statutes in some states and decisions in others require advance notice of termination of this type of tenancy.

(d)   Tenancy by Sufferance. When a tenant holds over without permission of the landlord, the latter may treat the tenant as a trespasser or as a tenant. Until the landlord elects to do one or the other, a *tenancy by sufferance* exists.

§ 51:4. Termination of Lease. A lease is generally not terminated by the death, insanity, or bankruptcy of either party, except in the case of a tenancy at will. Provisions in a lease giving the landlord the right to terminate the lease under certain conditions are generally strictly construed.

Leases may be terminated in the following ways:

(a)   Termination by Notice. A lease may give the landlord the power to terminate it by giving notice to the tenant. In states which follow the common law, it is immaterial why the landlord terminates the lease by notice. In some states, statutes prohibit a landlord from terminating a lease in order to retaliate against a tenant for having exercised lawful rights possessed by the tenant. Under such a statute a lessor may not terminate a lease to retaliate for the good faith action of a tenant in seeking to enforce rights under the lease or in reporting violations of health, safety, or building codes.[3] A tenant in a public housing project has even greater protection than a tenant in a privately owned apartment against termination, as the lease may not be terminated as long as the tenant continues to pay rent and does no act which by itself would justify a termination of the lease.[4]

(b)   Expiration of Term in a Tenancy for Years. When a tenancy for years exists, the relation of landlord and tenant ceases upon the expiration of the term, without any requirement that one party give the other any notice of termination. Express notice to end the term may be required of either or both parties by provisions of the lease, except when a statute prohibits the landlord from imposing such a requirement.

(c)   Notice in a Tenancy from Year to Year. In the absence of an agreement of the parties, notice is now usually governed by statute. Thirty or sixty days' notice is generally required to end a tenancy from year to year. As to tenancies for periods of less than a year, the provisions of the statutes commonly require notice of only one week.

(d)   Release. The relation of landlord and tenant is terminated if the landlord makes a release or conveyance of the landlord's interest in the land to the tenant. A tenant may at any time purchase the rented property if the landlord and the tenant agree. In addition, the lease may give the tenant the option of purchasing at a stated time or at a stated price.

---

[3] Parkin v Fitzgerald, 307 Minn 423, 240 NW2d 828.
[4] Escalera v New York City Housing Authority (CA2 NY) 425 F2d 853 cert den 400 US 853.

(e)   **Merger.** If the tenant acquires the landlord's interest in any manner, as by inheritance or purchase, the leasehold interest is said to disappear by merger into the title to the land now held by the former tenant.

(f)   **Surrender.** A surrender or giving up of the tenant's estate to the landlord terminates the tenancy if the surrender is accepted by the landlord. A surrender may be made expressly or impliedly. An express surrender must, under the statute of frauds, be in writing and be signed by the person making the surrender or by an authorized agent.

A surrender by operation of law occurs when the acts of the parties clearly show that both consider that the premises have been surrendered as when the premises have been abandoned by the tenant and the return has been accepted by the landlord. An acceptance may be inferred from the conduct of the landlord, but such conduct must clearly indicate an intention to accept. A tenant's offer to surrender a lease is accepted by the landlord's executing a new lease with a tenant's sublessee.[5]

(g)   **Forfeiture.** The landlord may terminate the lease by forfeiting the relation because of the tenant's misconduct or breach of a condition, if a term of the lease or a statute so provides. In the absence of such a provision, the landlord may only claim damages for the breach. Terminating the relationship by forfeiture is not favored by the courts.

(h)   **Destruction of Property.** If a lot and building on it are leased, either an express provision in the lease or a statute generally releases the tenant from liability when the building is destroyed, or reduces the amount of rent in proportion to the loss sustained. Such statutes do not impose upon the landlord any duty to repair or restore the property to its former condition.

When the lease covers rooms or an apartment in a building, a destruction of the leased premises terminates the lease.

(i)   **Fraud.** As a lease is based on a contract, a lease may be avoided when the circumstances are such that a contract could be avoided for fraud.

§ 51:5. Notice of Termination. When notice of termination is required, no particular words are necessary to constitute a sufficient notice, provided the words used clearly indicate the intention of the party. The notice, whether given by the landlord or the tenant, must be definite. Statutes sometimes require that the notice be in writing. In the absence of such a provision, however, oral notice is generally held to be sufficient.

§ 51:6. Renewal of Lease. When a lease terminates for any reason, it is ordinarily a matter for the landlord and the tenant to enter into a new agreement if they wish to extend or renew the lease. The power to renew the lease may be stated negatively by declaring that the lease runs indefinitely, as from year to year, subject to being terminated by either party by giving written notice a specified number of days or months before the termination date. If it is not clear whether a renewal provision gives the tenant only the right to renew for one term of the lease or whether it gives the right to

---

[5] Weisberg v Loughridge, 253 CalApp2d 278, 61 CalRptr 563.

renew indefinitely for an unlimited number of times, the law will interpret the lease strictly as permitting only one additional term.

A retaliatory refusal to renew a lease is prohibited. Consequently, where it had been the practice of the landlord to allow expired leases to continue on a month to month basis, the landlord could not refuse to do this and evict the tenant for the purpose of retaliating for the latter's activity in a tenant's association, even though a statute declared that the lessor was entitled to possession immediately upon the expiration of a fixed period lease.[6]

A tenant in a housing project which is heavily financed and controlled by the federal government has in effect a perpetual right of renewal, as such tenant cannot be evicted merely because the lease has expired.

B. RIGHTS AND DUTIES OF PARTIES

The rights and duties of the landlord and tenant are based upon principles of real estate law and contract law. With the rising tide of consumer protectionism, the tendency is increasing to treat the relationship as merely a contract and to govern the rights and duties of the parties by general principles of contract law.

§ 51:7. Possession. Possession involves both the right to acquire possession at the beginning of the lease and the right to retain possession until the lease is ended. The modern lease commonly provides that if the lessor is late in making the premises available to the tenant, the commencement of the lease shall be postponed until the lessor notifies the tenant that occupancy is ready and the lease then runs for its original term from that later date.

(a) Tenant's Right to Acquire Possession. By making a lease, the lessor impliedly covenants to give possession of the premises to the tenant at the agreed time. If the landlord rents a building which is being constructed, there is an implied covenant that it will be ready for occupancy at the commencement of the term of the lease.

(b) Tenant's Right to Retain Possession. After the tenant has entered into possession, the tenant has the exclusive possession and control of the premises as long as the lease continues and so long as there is no default under the lease, unless the lease otherwise provides. Thus, the tenant can refuse to allow the lessor to enter the property for the purpose of showing it to prospective customers, although today most leases expressly give this right to the landlord.

If the landlord interferes with this possession by evicting the tenant, the landlord commits a wrong for which the tenant is afforded legal redress. An *eviction* occurs when the tenant is deprived of the possession, use, and enjoyment of the premises by the interference of the lessor or the lessor's agent. If the landlord wrongfully deprives the tenant of the use of one room when the tenant is entitled to use an entire apartment or building, there is a *partial eviction.*

(c) Covenant for Quiet Enjoyment. Most written leases today contain an express promise by the landlord to respect the possession of the tenant, called a *covenant*

---

[6] Golphin v Park Monroe Associates (DistColApp) 353 A2d 314.

for quiet enjoyment. Such a provision protects the tenant from interference with possession by the landlord or the landlord's agent, but it does not impose liability upon the landlord for the unlawful acts of third persons. Thus, such a covenant does not require the landlord to protect a tenant from damage by a rioting mob. Moreover, to constitute a breach of the warranty of quiet enjoyment, there must be an eviction of the tenant from some or all of the rented premises and this must be caused by the act of the landlord. Consequently, no breach of this warranty is shown when the industrial tenant remains in possession and is merely dissatisfied with the excessive noise caused by the printing plant in the floor above, the tenant having rented its floor at a lower rent because of the printing plant and with full knowledge that it was located overhead.[7]

(d)   Constructive Eviction. An eviction may be actual or constructive. It is a *constructive eviction* when some act or omission of the landlord substantially deprives the tenant of the use and enjoyment of the premises. (See p. 878, Cherberg v Peoples National Bank)

It is essential in a constructive eviction that the landlord intended to deprive the tenant of the use and enjoyment of the premises. This intent may, however, be inferred from conduct. A tenant cannot claim a constructive eviction by a particular condition unless the tenant in fact has left the premises because of that condition. If the tenant continues to occupy the premises for more than a reasonable time after the acts claimed to constitute a constructive eviction, a waiver arises and the tenant cannot thereafter abandon the premises and claim to have been evicted.[8]

(e)   Retaliatory Eviction. A landlord may not evict a tenant in order to retaliate against the tenant because the tenant has exercised statutory or constitutional rights.

§ 51:8.   Use of Premises. The lease generally specifies the use to which the tenant may put the property and authorizes the landlord to adopt regulations with respect to the use of the premises that are binding upon the tenant as long as they are reasonable, lawful, and not in conflict with the terms of the lease. In the absence of express or implied restrictions, a tenant is entitled to use the premises for any lawful purpose for which they are adapted or for which they are ordinarily employed,[9] or in a manner contemplated by the parties in executing the lease. A provision specifying the use to be made of the property is strictly construed against the tenant.

(a)   Change of Use. The modern lease will in substance make a change of use a condition subsequent so that if the tenant uses the property for any purpose other than the one specified, the landlord has the option of declaring the lease terminated.

(b)   Continued Use of Property. With the increased danger of damage to the premises by vandalism or fire when the building is vacant and because of the common insurance provision making a fire insurance policy void when a vacancy continues for a specified

---

[7] Finkelstein v Levinson, (NY Civil Court) 343 NYS2d 849.

[8] Maki v Nikula, 220 Or 180, 355 P2d 770. Some states prohibit a landlord of residential property from "willfully" turning off the utilities of a tenant for the purpose of evicting the tenant. Wolfe v Fox, (CalApp) 137 CalRptr 258 (imposing a civil penalty of $100 a day for every day that utilities are shut off).

[9] Delta Wild Life & Forestry, Inc. v Bear Kelso Plantation, Inc. (Miss) 281 So2d 683.

time, the modern lease will ordinarily require the tenant to give the landlord notice of nonuse or vacancy of the premises. Likewise, in many situations, it is important to the landlord that the tenant operate a particular business. For example, when the landlord operated a truck stop station and rented an adjacent diner to a tenant, the operation of the diner during reasonable hours was an essential part of the transaction. Hence, there may be a duty on the tenant to make use of the premises as a counterpart of the right to possession.

(c)   Rules. The modern lease generally contains a blanket agreement by the tenant to abide by the provisions of rules and regulations adopted by the landlord. These rules are generally binding on the tenant whether they exist at the time the lease was made or were thereafter adopted.

(d)   Restriction of Animals. A restriction in a lease prohibiting the keeping of pets is valid.

§ 51:9. Rent. The tenant is under a duty to pay rent as compensation for the landlord. The amount of rent agreed to by the parties may be subject to governmental limitations establishing maximum amounts that can be charged.

The time of payment of rent is ordinarily fixed by the lease. When the lease does not control, rent generally is not due until the end of the term. Statutes or custom, however, may require rent to be paid in advance when the agreement of the parties does not regulate the point. Rent that is payable in crops is generally payable at the end of the term.

If the lease is assigned, the assignee is liable to the landlord for the rent. The assignment, however, does not in itself discharge the tenant from the duty to pay the rent. The landlord thus may bring an action for the rent against either the original tenant or the assignee, or both, but is entitled to only one satisfaction. A sublessee ordinarily is not liable to the original lessor for rent, unless that liability has been expressly assumed or is imposed by statute.

§ 51:10. Repairs and Condition of Premises. In the absence of an agreement to the contrary, the tenant has the duty to make those repairs that are necessary to prevent waste and decay of the premises, and is liable for *permissive waste* on failing to do so. When the landlord leases only a portion of the premises, or leases the premises to different tenants, the landlord is under a duty to make repairs to connecting parts, such as halls, basements, elevators, and stairways, which are under the landlord's control. When the landlord makes repairs, reasonable care must be exercised to make them in a proper manner; but the landlord is not automatically liable as an insurer if the tenant is injured after the landlord has made the repairs.

(a)   Inspection of Premises. Most states deny the landlord the right to enter the leased premises to inspect them for waste and need for repairs except when the right is expressly reserved in the lease. It is customary for leases of apartments and commercial property to reserve to the landlord the right to enter to inspect the premises and to make repairs.

(b)   Housing Laws. Various laws protect tenants, as by requiring landlords to observe specified safety, health, and fire prevention standards. Some statutes require that a landlord who leases a building for dwelling purposes must keep it in a condition fit for habitation. Leases commonly require the tenant to obey local ordinances and laws relating to the care and use of the premises. If compliance with a law requires the making of repairs, such a provision imposes upon the tenant the duty to make the repairs necessary to comply with the law.

(c) **Warranty of Habitability.** At common law a landlord was not bound by a warranty that the premises were fit for use unless the lease contained an express warranty to that effect. A strong modern trend in the law rejects this view and implies in residential leases of furnished and unfurnished property a warranty that the premises are habitable. (See p. 878, King v Moorehead) If the landlord breaches this warranty, the tenant is entitled to damages. These damages may be set off against the rent which is due, or if no rent is due, the tenant may bring an independent lawsuit to recover damages from the landlord.[10]

(d) **Abatement and Escrow Payment of Rent.** In order to protect tenants from unsound living conditions, statutes sometimes provide that a tenant is not required to pay rent as long as the premises are not fit to live in. As a compromise, some statutes require the tenant to continue to pay the rent but require that it be paid into an escrow or agency account from which it is paid to the landlord only on proof that the necessary repairs have been made to the premises.

§ 51:11. **Improvements.** In the absence of special agreement, neither the tenant nor the landlord is under the duty to make improvements, as contrasted with repairs. Either party may, however, make a covenant for improvements, in which case a failure to perform will result in liability in an action for damages for breach of contract brought by the other party. In the absence of an agreement to the contrary, improvements that are attached to the land become part of the realty and belong to the landlord.

§ 51:12. **Taxes and Assessments.** In the absence of an agreement to the contrary, the landlord and not the tenant is usually under a duty to pay taxes or assessments. If the tax or assessment, however, is chargeable to improvements made by the tenant that do not become a part of the property, the tenant is liable.

When the premises are assigned by the tenant, the assignee is bound by any covenants of the tenant to pay taxes and assessments. Such covenants are said to "run with the land." The fact that the assignee is bound by the covenants does not, however, discharge the tenant from liability.

A sublessee is not bound by the covenants of the tenant, but may expressly assume them. In the latter case, likewise, the tenant is not discharged unless the landlord consents thereto.

§ 51:13. **Tenant's Deposit.** A landlord may require a tenant to make a deposit to protect the landlord from any default on the part of the tenant.

(a) **Custody.** In some states, protection is given the tenant who is required to make a payment to the landlord as a "deposit" to insure compliance with the lease. It is

---

[10] Jarrell v Hartman, 48 IllApp3d 985, 363 NE2d 626.

sometimes provided that the landlord hold such payment as a trust fund and inform the tenant of any bank in which the money is deposited, and be subject to a penalty if the money is used before the tenant has breached the lease.

(b)   Refund. Once paid by the tenant, it frequently happens that the landlord will keep the entire deposit, even though it is in excess of any claim against the tenant, and tenants will not bring suit because the amount involved is too small to justify an action. Tenant protection statutes sometimes remedy this situation by requiring the landlord to refund any part of the deposit in excess of the amount actually needed to compensate for the breach by the tenant. Under such a statute, it is immaterial that the tenant had agreed that the deposit was nonrefundable.

§ 51:14. Remedies of Landlord.

(a)   Landlord's Lien. In the absence of an agreement or statute so providing, the landlord does not have a lien upon the personal property or crops of the tenant for money due for rent. The parties may create by express or implied contract a lien in favor of the landlord for rent, and also for advances, taxes, or damages for failure to make repairs.

In the absence of a statutory provision, the lien of the landlord is superior to the claims of others, except prior lienors and bona fide purchasers without notice.

(b)   Suit for Rent. Whether or not the landlord has a lien for unpaid rent, the landlord may sue the tenant on the latter's obligation to pay rent as specified in the lease or, if payment of rent is not specified, the landlord may enforce a quasi-contractual obligation to pay the reasonable value of the use and occupation of the property. In some jurisdictions, the landlord is permitted to bring a combined action to recover the possession of the land and the overdue rent at the same time.

(c)   Distress. The common law devised a speedy remedy to aid the landlord in collecting rent. It permitted seizure of personal property found on the premises and allowed the landlord to hold such property until the arrears of rent were paid. This right was known as *distress.* It was not an action against the tenant for rent but merely a right to retain the property as security until the rent was paid. Statutes have generally either abolished or greatly modified the right of distress.[11]

(d)   Recovery of Possession. The lease commonly provides that upon the breach of any of its provisions by the tenant, such as the failure to pay rent, the lease shall terminate or the landlord may exercise the option to declare the lease terminated. When the lease is terminated for any reason, the landlord then has the right to evict the tenant and retake possession of the property.

At common law, the landlord, when entitled to possession, could regain it without resorting to legal proceedings. This *right of reentry* is available in many states even when the employment of force is necessary. Other states deny the right to use force.

---

[11] A landlord's distraint statute which permits distraint without notice and hearing is unconstitutional even though distraint is an old common-law remedy. Van Ness Industries, Inc. v Claremont Painting & Decorating Co., 129 NJSuper 507, 324 A2d 102. A Uniform Residential Landlord and Tenant Act has been adopted in Alaska, Arizona, Florida, Hawaii, Kansas, Kentucky, Montana, Nebraska, New Mexico, Oregon, Tennessee, and Virginia.

Modern cases hold that a landlord cannot lock out a tenant for overdue rent and must employ legal process to regain possession even though the lease expressly gives the landlord the right to self-help.

A state statute permitting a landlord to lock out a tenant and to hold the tenant's property for nonpayment of rent is unconstitutional as a denial of due process when the landlord may so act without any prior notice to the tenant nor judicial hearing, and the statute is not cured by the fact that the tenant can obtain the property by filing a bond for double the amount of the landlord's claim.

The landlord may resort to legal process to evict the tenant in order to enforce the right to possession of the premises. The action of ejectment is ordinarily used. In addition to the common-law remedies, statutes in many states provide a summary remedy to recover possession that is much more efficient than the slow common-law remedies. Unless expressly stated, a statutory remedy does not replace those of the common law, but is merely cumulative. In many states today, the landlord brings an action of trespass or a civil action to recover possession.

(e) **Landlord's Duty to Mitigate Damages.** If the tenant leaves the premises before the expiration of the lease, is the landlord under any duty to rerent the premises in order to reduce the rent or damages for which the departing tenant will be liable? By the common law and majority rule, a tenant owns an estate in land and if the tenant abandons it there is no duty on the landlord to seek to find a new tenant for the premises. A modern minority view, now held in one fourth of the states, places greater emphasis on the contractual aspects of a lease, so that when the tenant abandons the property and thereby defaults or breaks the contract, the landlord is under the duty to seek to mitigate the damages caused by the tenant's breach and must make reasonable effort to rerent the property.[12] (See p. 880, Lefrak v Lambert) Likewise it has been held that when the tenant produces a substitute tenant, the landlord must rerent to the substitute tenant if there is no valid reason for rejecting the substitute.

C. LIABILITY FOR INJURY ON PREMISES

When the tenant, a member of the tenant's family, or a third person is injured by a condition of the premises, the question arises as to who is liable for the damages sustained by the injured person.

§ 51:15. Landlord's Liability to Tenant. In the absence of a covenant to keep the premises in repair, the landlord is ordinarily not liable to the tenant for the latter's personal injuries caused by the defective condition of the premises that are placed under the control of the tenant by the lease. Likewise, the landlord is not liable for the harm caused by an obvious condition that was known to the tenant at the time the lease was made. For example, a landlord is not liable for the fatal burning of a tenant whose clothing was set on fire by an open-faced radiant gas heater.

The landlord is liable to the tenant for injuries caused by latent or nonapparent defects of which the landlord had knowledge. A new trend is beginning to appear

---

[12] Dushoff v Phoenix Company, 22 ArizApp 445, 528 P2d 637 (commercial lease).

which makes foreseeability of harm the test of the landlord's liability rather than the mechanical test of whether the landlord had control of the part of the premises involved. (See p. 881, Sargent v Ross)

In a number of states, by decision or statute, a landlord is liable to a tenant or a child or guest of the tenant where there is a defect which makes the premises dangerously defective, even though the landlord did not have any knowledge of the defect. Other states refuse to apply this strict tort liability concept.

(a) Crimes of Third Persons. Ordinarily the landlord is not liable to the tenant for crimes committed on the premises by third persons, as when a third person enters the premises and commits larceny or murder.[13] The landlord is not required to establish any security system to protect the tenant from crimes of third persons. Housing regulations apply only to the physical characteristics and use of the premises. They do not impose any duty on the landlord to maintain a security system to protect tenants from unlawful acts of third persons. In contrast, when a landlord does not maintain the security system that existed when the lease was entered into, the landlord may be liable for the harm sustained by the tenant by the illegal acts of third persons whose misconduct was foreseeable.

Thus, the landlord of a large apartment complex had the duty of taking reasonable steps to protect against the entry of third persons onto the premises and the commission of crimes by them, when such crimes were being repeatedly committed and the landlord had eliminated a lobby guard and a garage attendant who had performed security duties when the tenant first moved into the apartment building. Likewise where the tenant has repeatedly reported that the deadlock on the apartment door was broken, the landlord is liable for the tenant's loss when a thief enters through the door because such conduct was foreseeable. Similarly, a landlord is liable to a tenant for a criminal assault committed upon the tenant by a third person who gained entrance to the apartment house complex by the use of the pass key, where this pattern of crime had been frequent but the landlord had not taken any protective measures to prevent repetition.[14]

(b) Limitation of Liability. A provision in a lease excusing or exonerating the landlord from liability is generally valid, regardless of the cause of the tenant's loss. A number of courts, however, have restricted the landlord's power to limit liability in the case of residential as distinguished from commercial, leasing; so that a provision in a residential lease that the landlord shall not be liable for damage caused by water, snow, or ice is void. A modern trend holds that clauses limiting liability of the landlord are void with respect to harm caused by the negligence of the landlord when the tenant is a residential tenant generally or is a tenant of a government low-cost housing project. (See p. 882, Crowell v Housing Authority)

Third persons on the premises, even though with the consent of the tenant, are generally not bound by such a clause and may therefore sue the landlord when they sustain injuries. Thus, it has been held that members of the tenant's family, employees, and guest, are not bound where they do not sign the lease, although there is authority to the contrary.

---

[13] Smith v Chicago Housing Authority, 36 IllApp3d 967, 344 NE2d 536.
[14] Smith v General Apartment Co., 13 GaApp 927, 213 SE2d 74.

(c) Indemnification of Landlord. The modern lease commonly contains a provision declaring that the tenant will indemnify the landlord for any liability of the landlord to a third person which arises in connection with the rented premises.

§ 51:16. Landlord's Liability to Third Persons. The landlord is ordinarily not liable to third persons injured because of the condition of the premises when the landlord is not in possession of them. If the landlord retains control over a portion of the premises, such as hallways or stairways, however, liability exists for injuries to third persons caused by failure to exercise proper care in connection with that part of the premises. The modern trend of cases imposes liability on the landlord when a third person is harmed by a condition that the landlord had contracted with the tenant to correct or had contracted to keep the premises in repair.[15]

§ 51:17. Tenant's Liability to Third Persons. A tenant in complete possession has control of the property and is therefore liable when the tenant's failure to use due care under the circumstances causes harm to (1) licensees, such as a person allowed to use a telephone, and (2) invitees, such as customers entering a store. With respect to both classes, the liability is the same as an owner in possession of property. It is likewise immaterial whether the property is used for residential or business purposes, provided the tenant has control of the area where the injury occurs.

    The liability of the tenant to third persons is not affected by the fact that the landlord may have contracted in the lease to make repairs which, if made, would have avoided the injury. The tenant can be protected, however, in the same manner that the landlord can, by procuring public liability insurance for indemnity against loss from claims of third persons.

D. TRANSFER OF RIGHTS

    Both the landlord and the tenant have property and contract rights with respect to the lease. When either makes a transfer of them, questions arise as to the rights and liabilities of the transferee.

§ 51:18. Transfer of Landlord's Reversionary Interest. The reversionary interest of the landlord may be transferred voluntarily by the landlord, or involuntarily by a judicial or execution sale. The tenant then becomes the tenant of the new owner of the reversionary interest, and the new owner is bound by the terms of the lease.

    When the landlord assigns the reversion, the assignee is, in the absence of an agreement to the contrary, entitled to subsequent accruals of rent. The rent may, however, be reserved in an assignment or a reversion. The landlord also has the right to assign the lease independent of the reversion, or to assign the rent independent of the lease.

    Upon the transfer of the lessor's reversionary interest, the transferee, the new landlord, becomes bound by the obligations stated in the lease, such as a covenant to repair. The new landlord is not liable, however, for damages for any breach of a

---

[15] Putnam v Stout, 38 NY2d 607, 381 NYS2d 848.

covenant committed by the former landlord unless the new landlord has expressly assumed liability for such prior breaches.

§ 51:19. Tenant's Assignment of Lease and Sublease. An *assignment of a lease* is a transfer by the tenant of the tenant's entire interest in the premises to a third person. A tenancy for years may be assigned by the tenant unless the latter is restricted from so doing by the terms of the lease or by a statute. A *sublease* is a transfer of any part of the premises by the tenant to a third person, the *sublessee,* for a period less than the term of the lease.

Whether the transaction between the tenant and the third person is a sublease or an assignment is determined by the effect of the transaction. If the entire interest of the tenant is transferred to the third person, the transaction is an assignment of the lease, without regard to whether the parties have described the transaction as a sublease or as an assignment. In contrast, if there is some interest left over after the interest of the third person expires, the relationship is a sublease.

(a)   Limitations on Rights. The lease may contain provisions denying the right to assign or sublet or imposing specified restrictions on the privilege of assigning or subletting. Such restrictions enable the landlord to obtain protection from new tenants who would damage the property or be financially irresponsible.

Restrictions in the lease are construed liberally in favor of the tenant. An ineffectual attempt to assign or sublet does not violate a provision prohibiting such acts. This is equally true when the tenant merely permits someone else to use the land.

As a provision restricting the right of the tenant to assign the lease or requiring the landlord's written consent thereto is for the benefit of the landlord, it may be waived by the landlord.

(b)   Effect of Assignment or Sublease. An express covenant or promise by the sublessee is necessary to impose liability on the sublessee for the obligations of the lease. In contrast, when the lease is assigned, the assignee becomes bound by the terms of the lease upon taking possession of the property.

Neither the act of subletting nor the landlord's agreement to it releases the original tenant from liability under the terms of the original lease.

When a lease is assigned, the original tenant remains liable for the rent which becomes due thereafter. If the assignee renews or extends the lease by virtue of an option contained therein, the original tenant is likewise liable for the rent for such extended period in the absence of a contrary agreement or novation by which the landlord agrees that the assignee shall be deemed substituted as tenant and the original tenant shall be released from further liability.

It is customary and desirable for the tenant to require the sublessee to covenant or promise to perform all obligations under the original lease and to indemnify the tenant for any loss caused by the default of the sublessee. An express covenant or promise by the sublessee is necessary to impose such liability. The fact that the sublease is made "subject" to the terms of the original lease merely recognizes the superiority of the original lease but does not impose any duty upon the sublessee to perform the tenant's obligations under the original lease. If the sublessee promises to assume the obligations of the original lease, the landlord, as a third party beneficiary, may sue the sublessee for breach of the provisions of the original lease.

CASES FOR CHAPTER 51

Cherberg v Peoples National Bank

88 Wash2d 595, 564 P2d 1137 (1977)

The Joshua Green Corporation owned and operated the Lewis Building. The Cherbergs rented part of the building and opened a restaurant. Thereafter the Peoples National Bank demolished the adjoining building which left the south wall of the Lewis Building in a dangerous condition. The city building department condemned the building as unsafe. The Cherbergs requested the Green Corporation to repair the south wall. It refused to do so. The Cherbergs claimed that this was a violation of the lease and sued the bank and the Green Corporation. The trial court directed a verdict in favor of the bank and entered a judgment for the Cherbergs against the Joshua Green Corporation. The intermediate appellate court reversed and remanded the action. The Cherbergs filed a petition to review this reversal.

UTTER, A.J. . . . The lease between the parties required the lessee to make necessary repairs to maintain the demised premises, excepting the outside walls and other structural components of the building, and reserved to the lessor the use of the roof and outside walls of the building. The lease does not contain an express covenant concerning the responsibility to maintain the structural components of the building.

An implied duty on the part of the lessor exists to make those repairs mandated by competent government authority where, as here, the appropriate authority determines that, in the interest of the public welfare, a defective condition of a building must be remedied. . . . The evidence presented established that the refusal of the respondent to take action to fulfill this duty, within a reasonable time after notification from the City, breached an implied covenant of quiet enjoyment and resulted in an actionable constructive eviction. . . .

The area requiring repair was not a part of the demised premises but was an area of the building over which the landlord had expressly retained control.

A landlord has a duty to maintain, control and preserve retained portions of the premises subject to a leasehold in a manner rendering the demised premises adequate for the tenant's use and safe for occupancy by both the tenant and his invitees. . . . Failure to fulfill this duty results in liability on the part of the lessor for injury caused thereby, . . . and failure to fulfill this duty, by omission to repair, can in a proper case constitute an actionable constructive eviction. . . .

The willful refusal to adequately maintain retained portions of a building so as to allow the tenant to enjoy the benefical use of the demised portion of the building is a breach of an implied duty owed by the landlord to the tenant under Washington law. On these facts this breach of duty was sufficient to constitute an actionable constructive eviction, and provides a basis for the conclusion that the landlord was liable for any damages stemming from that breach, . . . independent of any directive to repair issued by the City of Seattle. . . .

[Judgment reversed]

King v Moorehead

(MoApp) 495 SW2d 65 (1973)

King leased a single-family dwelling to Moorehead. He brought an action against her to recover the premises because of nonpayment of rent and in order to collect the unpaid rent. Moorehead raised the defense that the house was not habitable and that it violated the housing code. Judgment was entered for King and Moorehead appealed.

SHANGLER, J. . . . At early common law, a lease was considered a conveyance of an estate in land and was equivalent to a sale of the premises for the term of the [lease]. . . . As a purchaser of an estate in land, the tenant was subject to the strict property rule of *caveat emptor*—let the buyer beware. The lessee's eyes were his bargain. He had the duty to inspect the property for defects and took the land as he found it. . . . There was no implied warranty by the lessor that the leased premises were habitable or fit. The common law traditionally assumed that the landlord and tenant were of equal bargaining power. So, if the tenant wished to protect himself as to the fitness of the premises, he could exact an express covenant from the landlord for that purpose. . . .

The law of leasehold originated in an era of agrarian economy which assumed that the land was the most important feature of the conveyance. . . .

Although the early agrarian lease was viewed as a conveyance, the authorities agree that the modern lease is both a conveyance and a contract. With the change from an agricultural to an urban society, the function of the lease has also changed. The land itself, once the central reason for the lease, is of no value to an urban dweller. The minds of the parties to a modern lease contemplate more than the mere delivery of possession and the fixing of rent. The urban lessee seeks and expects "a well known package of goods and service—a package which includes not merely walls and ceilings, but also adequate heat, light and ventilation, serviceable plumbing facilities, secure windows and doors, proper sanitation and proper maintenance.". . .

In recent years those courts which have considered the question have uniformly rejected the applicability of *caveat emptor* to residential leases and have implied a warranty of habitability and fitness for use of the premises on principles of contract law. . . .

Considerations which justify reappraisal of common law principles of landlord and tenant in favor of an implied warranty of habitability in residential leases include (1) the contemporary housing shortage and resultant inequality in bargaining power between the landlord and tenant; . . . (2) housing codes which impose repair, maintenance and other standards of habitability upon landlords; . . . (3) the common experience that the landlord has superior knowledge of the condition of the premises, including any latent defects, and that the housing requirements and violations are usually known or made known to the landlord; . . . (4) a residential lessee is a purchaser of "a well known package of services" who must rely on the skill and honesty of the supplier to assure the quality of such services, and thus a residential tenant is entitled to the benefit of consumer protection law. . . .

The social realities, legislative policies, and judicial disposition to re-examine an outworn common-law doctrine which have prompted these courts to imply a warranty of habitability in residential leases obtain also in Missouri. [The court referred to the various building codes.]

It is consistent with these legislative policies that in every residential lease there be an implied warranty by the landlord that the dwelling is habitable and fit for living at the inception of the term and that it will remain so during the entire term. The warranty of the landlord is that he will provide facilities and services vital to the life, health, and safety of the tenant and to the use of the premises for residential purposes. It is an obligation which the landlord fulfills by substantial compliance with the relevant provisions of an applicable housing code. . . .

We are drawn to this conclusion also by the compelling analogy of another development in the law. In Missouri the rule of *caveat emptor* has steadily given way to a warranty of fitness for use implied by law, without any agreement, in sales transactions. The history of this demise is given in Smith v Old Warson Development Company, 479 S.W.2d 795 (Mo. banc 1972). In *Smith,* the court determined that an implied warranty of fitness is read into a contract for the sale of a new home by a vendor-builder. . . .

We now [hold] that a warranty of habitability is implied by operation of law in every residential lease.

We adopt the view that a lease is not only a conveyance but also gives rise to a contractual relationship between the landlord and tenant from which the law implies a warranty of habitability and fitness by the landlord. Under contract principles a tenant's obligation to pay rent is dependent upon the landlord's performance of his obligation to provide a habitable dwelling during the tenancy. . . .

The implied warranty of habitability remedy developed, in measure, as response to a chronic and prolonged housing shortage, particularly for those of low income. . . . Common law constructive eviction, (based upon a fiction which the implied warranty remedy discards) could be claimed only by a tenant who abandoned the premises within a reasonable time. Abandonment was required to maintain the fiction of an eviction and thus the breach of the dependent convenant of quiet enjoyment. The effect of the abandonment requirement was to prevent a tenant from remaining in possession without paying rent. . . . Constructive eviction has proved an insufficient remedy for those most likely to have resort to it, low income tenants. The dilemma it raises for them is that they must continue to pay rent and endure the conditions of untenantability or abandon the premises and hope to find another dwelling which, in these times of severe housing shortage, is likely to be as uninhabitable as the last.

This dilemma is avoided by recognizing that the modern lease is a bilateral contract so that the tenant's obligation for rent is dependent upon the landlord's performance of his responsibilities, among them, his implied warranty of habitability. Breach of this duty justifies retention of possession by the tenant and withholding of rent until habitability has been restored. A tenant who retains possession, however, shall be required to deposit the rent as it becomes due . . . pending the litigation. . . . This procedure assures the landlord that those rents adjudicated for distribution to him will be available to correct the defects in habitability, and will also encourage the landlord to minimize the tenant's damages by making tenantable repairs at the earliest time. Also, for good cause and in a manner consistent with the ultimate right between the parties, a trial court will have discretion to make partial distribution to the landlord before final adjudication when to deny it would result in irreparable loss to him. We conclude also that this procedure is that most compatible with policy of our Legislature, of the Housing Code of Kansas City and of the implied warranty of habilitability remedy itself that there be preserved and maintained an adequate supply of habitable dwellings.

[Judgment reversed and action remanded]

Lefrak v Lambert

(Civil Court NY) 390 NYS2d 959 (1976)

Lambert and his wife rented an apartment from Lefrak. They left the apartment when a child was born because they could not afford to pay the rent. The apartment was not rerented and the landlord sued them for 17 months rent. The Lamberts claimed that the landlord should have attempted to mitigate their liability by finding a new tenant for the apartment.

POSNER, J. . . . The plaintiff is well known and respected in this city as one of the largest (if not *the* largest) individual owner of residential apartment houses. The apartment in question is one of five thousand in the privately owned development known as "Lefrak City." The defendants are a young couple . . . The common law for centuries is that a landlord is under no obligation to mitigate damages stemming from the tenant's breach of the lease agreement. . . .

This court finds, that as a matter of law, seventeen months is an unreasonable period of time for a middle-class apartment in a middle-class neighborhood to remain vacant, absent proof by the landlord that a good faith effort was made to re-rent. . . .

There is no longer good reason—if there ever was—why leases should be governed by rules different from those applying to contracts in general. . . . The greatest strength of the common law is its ability to adapt to changing conditions. It is a living, growing, changing thing and nowhere is that growth and that change more evident than in the law of landlord-tenant. Courts across the nation are rejecting the conveyance theory of landlord-tenant law in favor of simple contract law. . . .

If ever there was good reason to treat leases as a conveyance, that reason no longer exists. With the possible exception of cooperative and condominium apartments where our income tax laws require some vestige of ownership, residential landlords and tenants do not consider the renting of an apartment as a conveyance. It is the owner who keeps title, takes depreciation, deducts real estate taxes and interest and maintains all of the indicia of ownership. A tenant does no more than contract for a package of goods and services to be supplied. . . .

The modern concept of a lease . . . is that a lease is a contract and that the contract principle of interdependency of covenants should be applied. Further, recognition has been given, that the landlord and tenant are not in equal bargaining positions. Both the courts and the legislature have applied these principles in matters dealing with (1) the right to sublet, (2) the warranty of habitability, and (3) in striking out unconscionable clauses. The only major area not yet dealt with by the appellate courts and legislature of this state is this question of "Mitigation of Damages." A number of other states have responded judicially. . . . There is direct authority, as well as dicta, which takes the view, respecting the duty of the landlord in this regard, that it is the duty of a landlord on wrongful abandonment of the premises by his tenant, to make reasonable efforts to reduce the damages from the breach by reletting the premises to a new tenant. . . .

If the lease is now viewed as a contract, then all the rules of law regarding contracts should apply, including the requirement that the injured party make a reasonable effort to mitigate damages. . . .

There is something basically unjust, basically unreasonable and, therefore basically not legal about a landlord in an urban society with a housing shortage having no obligation to try to re-rent an apartment and mitigate damages. There is something unfair about permitting tenants to be in a different category than other persons entering into a contract. . . .

Since the plaintiff has failed to establish that he acted in good faith to mitigate damages, the court finds that he was entitled only to a reasonable period of time in which to re-rent. In this case that was three (3) months. Therefore, adding the three months to the two months unpaid at the time tenants vacated and subtracting the $502 security plus $45 payment made in September, 1975, plaintiff is entitled to a judgment in the sum of $743 for unpaid rent and $148 for legal expenses (20% × $743) for a total of $891 with statutory costs.

Sargent v Ross

113 NH 388, 308 A2d 528 (1973)

Sargent rented a second floor apartment in an apartment house owned by Ross. Anna, the four-year-old daughter of Sargent fell from an outdoor stairway and was killed. Suit was brought for her death against Ross. She defended on the ground that she did not have control over the stairway and therefore was not liable for its condition. The jury returned a verdict in favor of the plaintiff. Ross moved to set aside the verdict.

KENISON, C.J. . . . The determination of the question of which party had control of the defective part of the premises causing the injury has generally been considered dispositive of the landlord's liability. . . . But the control test is insufficient since it substitutes a facile and conclusive test for a reasoned consideration of whether due care was exercised under all the circumstances. . . .

There was evidence from which the jury could find that the landlord negligently designed or constructed a stairway which was dangerously steep or that she negligently failed to remedy or adequately warn the deceased of the danger.

. . . The inflexibility of . . . the control [test] is pointedly demonstrated by this case. A child is killed by a dangerous condition of the premises. Both husband and wife tenants testify that they could do nothing to remedy the defect because they did not own the house nor have authority to alter the defect. But the landlord claims that she should not be liable because the stairs were not under her control. Both of these contentions are premised on the theory that the other party should be responsible. So the orthodox analysis would leave us with neither landlord nor tenant responsible for dangerous conditions on the premises. This would be both illogical and intolerable, particularly since neither party then would

have any legal reason to remedy or take precautionary measures with respect to dangerous conditions. In fact, the traditional "control" rule actually discourages a landlord from remedying a dangerous condition since his repairs may be evidence of his control. . . . Nor can there be serious doubt that ordinarily the landlord is best able to remedy dangerous conditions, particularly where a substantial alteration is required.

In recent years, immunities from tort liability affording "special protection in some types of relationships have been steadily giving way" in this and other jurisdictions. . . . [Citing several cases the court said:]

> "Considerations of human safety within an urban community dictate that the landowner's relative immunity, which is primarily supported by values of the agrarian past, be modified in favor of negligence principles of landowner liability.". . .
> "In modern times the immunities have rightly though gradually, been giving way to the overriding social view that where there is foreseeability of substantial harm landowners, as well as other members of society, should generally be subjected to a reasonable duty of care to avoid it.". . .

We think that now is the time for the landlord's limited tort immunity to be relegated to the history books where it more properly belongs.

. . . We today discard the rule of "caveat lessee" and the doctrine of landlord nonliability in tort to which it gave birth. We thus bring up to date the other half of landlord-tenant law. Henceforth, landlords as other persons must exercise reasonable care not to subject others to an unreasonable risk of harm. . . . A landlord must act as a reasonable person under all of the circumstances including the likelihood of injury to others, the probable seriousness of such injuries, and the burden of reducing or avoiding the risk. . . .

The abiding respect of this court for precedent and stability in the law is balanced by an appreciation of the need for responsible growth and change in rules that have failed to keep pace with modern developments in social and juridical thought. When we abolished the tort immunity of a parent from suit by his child, another artificial and inequitable exception to the general rules of tort liability, we made the following observation which is equally pertinent to this case: "If after thorough examination a prior judicial decision seems manifestly out of accord with modern conditions of life, it should not be followed as a controlling precedent. . . . Finding no supportable rationale upon which this judicially created exception to the ordinary rules of liability can be predicated, justice demands and reason dictates that a change be made from the previous holding in such a situation.". . .

Our decision will shift the primary focus of inquiry for judge and jury from the traditional question of "who had control?" to a determination of whether the landlord, and the injured party, exercised due care under all the circumstances. Perhaps even more significantly, the ordinary negligence standard should help insure that a landlord will take whatever precautions are reasonably necessary under the circumstances to reduce the likelihood of injuries from defects in his property. It is appropriate that the landlord who will retain ownership of the premises and any permanent improvements should bear the cost of repairs necessary to make the premises safe. . . .

The charge [to the jury] clearly set forth the elements of ordinary negligence which were presented by the court as a prerequisite to a finding of liability. . . . Thus, the jury could find that the defendant was negligent in the design or construction of the steep stairway or in failing to take adequate precautionary measures to reduce the risk of injury. We have carefully reviewed the record and conclude that there is sufficient evidence, on the basis of the principles set forth above, to support the verdict of the jury which had the benefit of a view. . . . Both plaintiff and the wife tenant testified that the stairs were too steep, and the husband tenant testified that his wife complained to him of this fact. While the defendant landlord did not testify, the jury could find that she knew that this steep stairway was frequently used by the young children for whom her daughter-in-law was the regular, daily babysitter. In any event, the use of these steps by young children should have been anticipated by the defendant. . . .

The verdict of the jury is sustained. . . .

Crowell v Housing Authority

(Tex) 495 SW2d 887 (1973)

Crowell rented an apartment from the Housing Authority of the City of Dallas. The gas heater in the apartment was defective and carbon monoxide from the heater killed Crowell. His son, Lewis, sued **the Housing Authority under the Texas Survival Statute to recover medical expenses and damages for the pain and suffering of his father. The Housing Authority raised the defense that the lease expressly declared that the Authority would not be liable for any damages. The lower court held that this provision barred the action. Crowell appealed.**

WALKER, J. [The lease between the respondent, the Housing Authority, and Crowell declared:]

". . . nor shall the Landlord nor any of its representatives or employees be liable for any damage to person or property of the Tenant, his family, or his visitors, which might result from the condition of these or other premises of the Landlord, from theft or from any cause whatsoever."

A somewhat similar provision was upheld in Manius v Housing Authority of City of Pittsburgh, 350 Pa 512, 39 A2d 614. The courts of two other jurisdictions concluded that it is contrary to public policy to allow a housing authority to exempt itself by contract from liability to its own tenants for negligence in the performance of its duty to provide safe and sanitary housing for persons of low income. Thomas v Housing Authority of City of Bremerton, 71 Wash 2d 69, 426 P2d 836; Housing Authority of Birmingham Dist v Morris, 244 Ala 557, 14 So2d 527. We approve and adopt the latter view.

Agreements exempting a party from future liability for negligence are generally recognized as valid and effective except where, because of the relationship of the parties, the exculpatory provision is contrary to public policy or the public interest. If the contract is between private persons who bargain from positions of substantially equal strength, the agreement is ordinarily enforced by the courts. The exculpatory agreement will be declared void, however, where one party is at such disadvantage in bargaining power that he is practically compelled to submit to the stipulation. It is generally held, for example, that a contract exempting an employer from all liability for negligent injury of his employees in the course of their employment is void as against public policy. The same rule applies to agreements exempting public utilities from liability for negligence in the performance of their duty of public service. . . .

The rules applicable to public utilities have been applied by some courts to innkeepers and public warehousemen. . . . There is a definite tendency to extend the same rules to other professional bailees such as garagemen and owners of parking lots and parcel checkrooms. These bailees are under no public duty, but they deal with the public and the indispensable need for their services deprives the customer of any real bargaining power. . . .

The same considerations lead us to the conclusion that the exculpatory agreement in the present case is contrary to public policy. Respondent [Housing Authority] is a public body organized for the declared public purpose, among others, of providing safe and sanitary dwelling accommodations to persons of low income. It may lease accommodations only to families or persons who lack sufficient income

to enable them, without financial assistance, to live in decent, safe and sanitary dwellings without overcrowding. . . . As pointed out by the court in *Thomas,* the situation of respondent and its tenants presents a classic example of unequal bargaining power. The terms of the contract are dictated by respondent, and a prospective tenant has no choice but to accept them if he and his family are to enjoy decent housing accommodations not otherwise available to them. We hold that the exculpatory provision quoted above is contrary to public policy and void in so far as it purports to affect respondent's liability in the present case. . . .

[Judgment reversed and action remanded]

QUESTIONS AND CASE PROBLEMS

1. What social forces are affected by the rule governing the duty of a landlord to relet premises wrongfully abandoned by a tenant?

2. Compare (a) an actual eviction of the tenant, (b) a constructive eviction of the tenant, and (c) a breach of the warranty of habitability.

3. Compare (a) a sale of a house, (b) a lease of a house, and (c) a contract for services.

4. The landlord of an apartment complex is under the duty to provide a safe place in which to live and therefore must maintain a security guard system to protect from the commission of such crimes as are reasonably foreseeable. Appraise this statement.

5. Stockham owned certain real estate. For a consideration he gave to the Borough Bill Posting Co. the exclusive privilege of erecting and using a signboard to be located on the land for bill posting purposes. He reserved the right, in case the property was sold or required for building purposes, to cancel all privileges upon returning to the company, a pro rata amount of the consideration. In an action brought by Stockham against the company, it was contended that a landlord-tenant relationship had been created. Do you agree? [Stockham v Borough Bill Posting Co., 144 App Div 642, 129 NYS 745]

6. *A* leased property to *B*. The lease declared that *A* should pay the taxes assessed against the property because of any "improvements" while *B* would pay the portion of taxes assessed against the property because of trade fixtures installed by him. Certain changes were made to the building by *B*. A dispute arose as to whether these were "improvements" or "trade fixtures." Who pays the additional real estate taxes assessed because of such changes if it cannot be determined whether they are improvements or trade fixtures? [Allied Stores Corp. v North West Bank, 2 Wash App 2d 778, 469 P2d 993]

7. Clay, who owned a tract of land, permitted Hartney to occupy a cabin on the land. There was no agreement as to the length of time that it could be occupied, and either could terminate the relationship when he chose. There was no provision for rent. Hartney died. The next day Clay closed up the cabin and put Hartney's possessions outside the door. Paddock, who was appointed the executor under Hartney's will, claimed the right to occupy the cabin. Was he entitled to do so? [Paddock v Clay, 138 Mont 541, 357 P2d 1]

8. The Old Dover Tavern, Inc. rented a building from Amershadian to conduct a "business under the style and trade name of 'Old Dover Tavern, Inc.' engaging in the serving

and selling [of] cigars, tobacco and all kinds of drinks and beverages of any name, nature and description." Thereafter, the tenant claimed that it was entitled to sell cold foods, such as sandwiches, on the theory that such sale was "incidental to the sale of beverages." The Corporation brought an action to establish that it was so entitled. Was it? [Old Dover Tavern, Inc. v Amershadian (MassApp) 318 NE2d 191]

9. Martin leased a building for a 5-year period to a new tenant after making repairs to the building to fit it for the tenant and after having paid approximately $1,000 as commissions to a real estate agent to obtain the tenant. Under the lease the tenant was required to pay the last five months' rent in advance, or approximately $3,000. During the term of the lease the tenant defaulted in the payment of rent and Martin, acting within the terms of the lease, terminated it. Lochner, the receiver who was thereafter appointed for the tenant, sued for the return of the advance rent on the ground that there could be no "rent" due for an unexpired portion of a lease which had been terminated by the landlord and the landlord would be unjustly enriched if he were allowed to retain the advance payment. Decide. [Lochner v Martin, 218 Md 519, 147 A2d 749]

10. Joy White rented an apartment in an apartment house operated by Ridgleawood, Inc. After some discussion, she gave her apartment over to Allan and took a more expensive apartment in the same apartment house. Ridgleawood accepted rent from both White and Allan for the respective apartments. When Allan damaged his apartment, Ridgleawood sued White on the ground she was liable for the conduct of her assignee. Decide. [Ridgleawood, Inc. v White, (Tex Civ App) 380 SW2d 766]

11. Catanese leased premises for use as a drug store from Saputa. Catanese moved his store to another location but continued to pay the rent to Saputa. Saputa entered the premises without the permission of Catanese and made extensive alterations to the premises to suit two physicians who had agreed to rent the premises from Saputa. Catanese informed Saputa that he regarded the making of the unauthorized repairs as ground for canceling the lease. Saputa then sued Catanese for the difference between the rent Catanese agreed to pay and the rent the doctors agreed to pay for the remainder of the term of the Catanese lease. Was Catanese liable for such rent? [Saputa v Catanese, (La App) 182 So2d 826]

12. Thompson rented property to Fletcher. Thompson sold the property to Bryan in February. Thereafter Thompson refused to accept Fletcher's offer of rent payments for March and April, but Fletcher did not know that the property had been sold. In April, Bryan declared the lease forfeited for nonpayment of rent. Decide. [Fletcher v Bryan, 76 NMex 221, 413 P2d 885]

13. Phillips Petroleum, Inc. leased a service station to Prather. McWilliam was a customer at the service station and was injured when a rusted window fell from the wall and hit her. She sued Phillips Petroleum. Was Phillips liable? [McWilliam v Phillips Petroleum, Inc., 269 Ore 526, 525 P2d 1011]

14. Championship Sports rented the Municipal Convention Hall of the City of Miami Beach for one day for the purpose of holding a world championship boxing match "and for no other purpose whatsoever without the written consent of the lessor indorsed on this lease . . ." As required by law, the City Boxing Commission ordered that a knee injury of the champion be examined. The medical report advised that the champion should undergo surgery and should not participate in the scheduled fight. The Commission recommended that the champion not fight. The fight was postponed and the money paid by ticket holders was refunded by the City. Was Championship Sports required to pay the rent for the hall to Miami Beach? [City of Miami Beach v Championship Sports, Inc., (FlaApp) 200 So2d 583]

Part Twelve • Estates

52 Decedents' Estates

The law of decedents' estates is governed by the statutes and the court decisions in the several states. A step toward national uniformity was taken in 1969 when the American Bar Association and the National Conference of Commissioners on Uniform State Laws approved a Uniform Probate Code (UPC) and submitted it to the states for adoption.[1]

A. WILLS

After all of the debts of a decedent are paid, distribution is made of any balance of the estate to those entitled to receive it. If the decedent made a valid will, it determines which persons are entitled to receive the property. If the decedent did not make a valid will, the distribution is determined by the intestate law.

§ 52:1. Definitions. *Testate distribution* describes the distribution that is made when the decedent leaves a valid will. A *will* is ordinarily a writing that provides for a distribution of property upon the death of the writer but which confers no rights prior to that time. A man who makes a will is called a *testator;* a woman, a *testatrix.*

The person to whom property is left by a will is a *beneficiary.* A gift of personal property by will is a *legacy* or *bequest,* in which case the beneficiary may also be called a *legatee.* A gift of real property by will is a *devise,* in which case the beneficiary may be called a *devisee.*

The will may identify the beneficiary by name or by description or by specifying the work or activity in which the beneficiary is engaged.

---

[1] The Uniform Probate Code has been adopted in Alaska, Arizona, Colorado, Florida, Hawaii, Idaho, Minnesota, Montana, Nebraska, New Mexico, North Dakota, and Utah. In 1975 a number of minor amendments were made to the Code.

§ 52:2. Parties to Will.

(a)   **Testator.** Generally the right to make a will is limited to persons 18 and older. In a few states a girl of 12 years or over, or a boy of 14 years or over, may make a will disposing of personal property. The testator must always have *testamentary capacity*. (See p. 897, Mangan v Mangan) In order to have testamentary capacity, a person must have sufficient mental capacity to understand that the writing which is being executed is a will, that is, that it disposes of the person's property after death, and must also have a reasonable appreciation of the identity of relatives and friends and of the nature and extent of the property which may exist at death.

The excessive and continued use of alcohol, producing mental deterioration, may be sufficient to justify the conclusion that the decedent lacked testamentary capacity.

(b)   **Beneficiary.** Generally there is no restriction with respect to the capacity of the beneficiary. In the case of a charitable corporation, a statute may set a maximum upon the amount of property that it may own.

When part of a decedent's estate passes to a minor, it is ordinarily necessary to appoint a guardian to administer such interest for the minor. Two common exceptions are: (1) If there is a will which directs that any share payable to a minor be held by a particular person as trustee for the minor, the minor's interest will be so held and a guardian is not required; (2) Statutes often provide that if the estate or interest of the minor is not large, it may be paid directly to the minor or to the parent or person by whom the minor is maintained.

§ 52:3. Testamentary Intent.

There cannot be a will unless the testator manifests an intention to make a provision that will be effective only upon death. This is called a *testamentary intent*.[2] Ordinarily this is an intention that certain persons shall become the owners of certain property upon the death of the testator. But a writing also manifests a testamentary intent when the testator only designates an executor and does not make any disposition of property.[3]

§ 52:4. Form.

(a)   **Writing.** There cannot be a valid will unless it conforms to the statute of wills, and there is a considerable variety of detail among the states. Generally a will must be in writing.

A will may be written on two or more sheets of paper as long as they are securely fastened together or as long as the sense of the writing of the various pages links them together.[4] A will may also incorporate by reference another writing or memorandum that is in existence at the time the will is written and which is clearly identified in the will.

(b)   **Signature.** A written will must be signed by the testator. In the absence of a provision of the statute stating that the will must be signed "in writing," a rubber

---

[2] Van Voast's Estate, 127 Mont 450, 266 P2d 377.
[3] Sapery's Estate, 28 NJ 599, 147 A2d 777.
[4] Cole v Webb, 220 Ky 817, 295 SW 1035.

stamp signature has been held sufficient. It is common, however, to require a written signature.

Generally a will must be signed at the bottom or end. The purpose of this requirement is to prevent unscrupulous persons from taking a will that has been validly signed and writing or typing additional provisions in the space below the signature.

(c)   Attestation and Publication. *Attestation* is the act of witnessing the execution of a will. Generally it includes signing the will as a witness, after a clause which recites that the witness has observed the execution of the will or that the decedent acknowledges the writing as the decedent's will. This clause is commonly called an *attestation clause*. Statutes often require that attestation be made by the witnesses in the presence of the testator and in the presence of each other.

Publication is the act of the testator of informing the attesting witnesses that the document which is signed before them or is shown to them is the decedent's will. (See p. 898, Arnold v Parry) The law varies between states as to the necessity of publication.

In some states witnesses are not required. In others, either two or three are required. When witnesses are required, it is generally specified that they be credible or competent and that they have no interest in the will. Thus, a witness who will personally gain financially by the will is disqualified. Generally a person is not disqualified on the ground of interest because of being named as executor, or because of being an officer or member of a group named as a beneficiary of the will.

(d)   Date. There is generally no requirement that a will be dated. In a few states a date is required in the case of a will written completely in the handwriting of the decedent.[5] It is advisable, however, to date a will, for when there are several wills, the most recent prevails with respect to conflicting provisions.

§ 52:5. Modification of Will.
A will may be modified by executing a codicil. A *codicil* is a separate writing that amends a will. The will, except as changed by the codicil, remains the same. The result is as though the testator rewrote the will, substituting the provisions of the codicil for those provisions of the will that are inconsistent with the codicil. A codicil must be executed with all the formality of a will and is treated in all other respects the same as a will.

A will cannot be modified merely by crossing out a clause and writing in what the testator wishes. Such an interlineation is not operative unless it is executed with the same formality required of a will, or in some states unless the will is republished in its interlineated form.

§ 52:6. Revocation of Will.

(a)   Revocation by Act of Testator. A will is revoked when the testator destroys, burns, or tears the will, or crosses out the provisions of the will with the intention to revoke it. The revocation may be in whole or in part.

---

[5] Succession of Sarrazin, 223 La 286, 65 So2d 602.

In many states a will may be revoked by a later writing executed with the same formality as a will which merely declares that the will is revoked.[6] Such a writing is effective even though it does not make any disposition of the property of the testator. In any case, a revocation that does not comply with the formal requirements of wills is not effective.[7]

A testator must have the same degree of mental capacity to revoke a will as is required to make a will.[8] Moreover, the revoking act must be the testator's free, volitional act. A later will or writing revoking a former will is therefore ineffective if it is a forgery or if it was obtained through fraud, duress, undue influence, or mistake.

(b)   Revocation by Operation of Law. In certain instances statutes provide that a change of circumstances has the effect of a revocation. Thus it may be provided that when a person marries after executing a will, the will is revoked or is presumed revoked,[9] unless it was made in contemplation of marriage or unless it provided for the future spouse. In some states the revocation is not total but only to the extent of allowing the spouse to take such share of the estate as that to which the spouse would have been entitled had there been no will.

It is also commonly provided that the birth or adoption of a child after the execution of a will works a revocation or partial revocation of the will as to that child. In the case of a partial revocation, the child is entitled to receive the same share as though the testator had died intestate.

The divorce of the testator does not in itself work a revocation; but the majority of courts hold that if a property settlement is carried out on the basis of the divorce, a prior will of the testator is revoked, at least to the extent of the legacy given to the divorced spouse.[10]

§ 52:7. Probate of Will. *Probate* is the act by which the proper court or official accepts a will and declares that the instrument satisfies the statutory requirements as the will of the testator. Until a will is probated, it has no legal effect.

When witnesses have signed a will, generally they must appear and state that they saw the testator sign the will. If those witnesses cannot be found, have died, or are outside the jurisdiction, the will may be probated nevertheless. When no witnesses are required, it is customary to require two or more persons to identify the signature of the testator at time of probate.

After the probate witnesses have made their statements under oath, the officer or court will ordinarily admit the will to probate in the absence of any particular circumstances indicating that the writing should not be probated. A certificate or decree which officially declares that the will is the will of the testator and has been admitted to probate is then issued.

Any qualified person wishing to object to the probate of the will on the ground that it is not a proper will may appear before the official or court prior to the entry

---

[6] Harchuck v Campana, 139 Conn 549, 95 A2d 566.

[7] Bancker's Estate, (FlaApp) 232 So2d 431.

[8] Hiler v Cude, 248 Ark 1065, 455 SW2d 891.

[9] Kent's Estate, 4 Ill 2d 81, 122 NE2d 229.

[10] Mosely v Mosely, 217 Ark 536, 231 SW2d 99.

of the decree of probate or may petition after probate to have the probate of the will set aside.

§ 52:8. Will Contest. The probate of a will may be refused or set aside on the ground that the will is not the free expression of the intention of the testator. It may be attacked on the ground of (1) lack of mental capacity to execute a will, (2) undue influence, duress, fraud, or mistake existing at the time of the execution of the will that induced or led to its execution,[11] or (3) forgery. With the exception of mental capacity, these concepts mean the same as they do in contract law.

If it is found that any one of these elements exists, the probate of the will is refused or set aside. The decedent's estate is then distributed as if there had been no will unless an earlier will can be probated.

Testators sometimes include in their wills a provision that any beneficiary contesting the will shall forfeit all interest under the will. Most courts hold such an *in terrorem clause* valid, although some make an exception when the contest is brought by the beneficiary in good faith and for probable cause. There is a difference of interpretation as to what action by a beneficiary constitutes a "contest" of the will. Generally a proceeding brought merely for an interpretation of provisions of the will is not a contest.[12]

§ 52:9. Special Types of Wills. A *holographic will* is one that is written by the testator entirely by hand. In many states no distinction is made between a holographic and other wills. In other states the general body of the law of wills applies, but certain variations are established. Thus it may be required that a holographic be dated.[13]

A *nuncupative will* is an oral will made and declared by the testator in the presence of witnesses to be a will. Generally it can be made only with respect to personal property during the last illness of the testator.

It is commonly provided that a nuncupative will cannot be probated unless the witnesses reduce it to writing and sign the writing within a certain period of time after the declaring of the will.

Soldiers and sailors generally may make an oral or a written will of their personal estate without complying with the formalities required of other wills. It is sufficient that testamentary intent be shown.

A will made by a soldier or sailor is not revoked by the termination of the testator's period of service. It remains in force on returning to civilian life, and it can only be revoked in the same manner as any other will.

§ 52:10. Election to Take Against the Will. In order to protect the husband or wife of a testator, the surviving spouse may generally ignore the provisions of a will and elect to take against the will. In such a case the surviving spouse receives the share of the estate which that spouse would have received had the testator died without leaving a will, or a fractional share specified by statute.

The right to take against the will is generally barred by certain specified kinds of misconduct of the surviving spouse. Thus, if the spouse is guilty of such desertion

---

[11] Thompson's Will, 248 NC 588, 104 SE2d 280.
[12] Griffin v Sturges, 131 Conn 471, 40 A2d 758.
[13] Moody's Estate, 118 CalApp2d 300, 257 P2d 709.

or nonsupport as would have justified the decedent in obtaining a divorce, it is usually provided that the surviving spouse cannot elect to take against the will.

§ 52:11. Disinheritance. With two exceptions,[14] any person may be disinherited or excluded from sharing in the estate of a decedent. A person who would inherit if there were no will is excluded from receiving any part of a decedent's estate if the decedent has left a will giving everything to other persons.[15]

§ 52:12. Construction of Will. The will of a decedent is to be interpreted according to the ordinary or plain meaning evidenced by its words. The court will strive to give effect to every provision of the will in order to avoid concluding that any part of the decedent's estate was not disposed of by the will.

(a)   Surrounding Circumstances. In interpreting a will, the court is not limited to considering only the exact words written on the will but may interpret those words in the light of the circumstances surrounding its execution, the identity of the beneficiaries, and the nature of the property of the decedent. (See p. 900, Bostwick v Hurstel)

(b)   Anti-Lapse Statutes. If the beneficiary named in the testator's will has died before the testator, and the testator did not make any alternate provision applicable in such case, the gift ordinarily does not lapse because *anti-lapse* statutes commonly provide that the gift to the deceased beneficiary shall not lapse but that the children or heirs of that beneficiary may take the legacy in the place of the deceased beneficiary. (See p. 901, Murray v Willett) An anti-lapse statute does not apply if the testator specifies a disposition which should be made of the gift if the original legatee has died.

B. INTESTACY

If the decedent does not effectively dispose of all property by will or does not have a will, the decedent's property is distributed to certain relatives. Since such persons acquire or succeed to the rights of the decedent and since the circumstance under which they do so is the absence of an effective will, it is said that they acquire title by *intestate succession.*

The right of intestate succession or inheritance is not a basic right of the citizen or an inalienable right but exists only because the state legislature so provides. It is within the power of the state legislature to modify or destroy the right to inherit property.[16]

§ 52:13. Plan of Intestate Distribution. Although wide variations exist among the statutory provisions of the states, a common pattern of intestate distribution can be observed:

(a)   Spouses. The surviving spouse of the decedent, whether husband or wife, shares in the estate. Generally the amount received is a fraction which varies with the

---

[14] The exceptions to this rule are based (a) upon the election of a spouse to take against the will and (b) in certain cases upon the partial revocation of a will by a subsequent marriage, birth, or adoption.

[15] Fagel v Fagel, 140 IndApp 663, 225 NE2d 776; affirmed 250 Ind 27, 234 NE2d 628.

[16] Maxwell v Bugbee, 250 US 525; Orr v Gilman, 183 US 278.

number of children and other heirs. If no blood relations survive, the spouse is generally entitled to take the entire estate. Otherwise the surviving spouse ordinarily receives a one-half or one-third share of the estate.

(b) **Lineals.** *Lineals* or *lineal descendants* are blood descendants of the decedent. That portion of the estate which is not distributed to the surviving spouse is generally distributed to lineals.

(c) **Parents.** If the estate has not been fully distributed by this time, the remainder is commonly distributed to the decedent's parents.

(d) **Collateral Heirs.** These are persons who are not descendants of the decedent but who are related through a common ancestor. Generally brothers and sisters and their descendants share any part of the estate that has not already been distributed.

Statutes vary as to how far distribution will be made to the descendants of brothers and sisters. Under some statutes a degree of relationship is specified, such as first cousins, and no person more remotely related to the decedent is permitted to share in the estate. If the entire estate is not distributed within the permitted degree of relationship, the property that has not been distributed is given to the state government. This right of the state to take the property is the *right of escheat.* Under some statutes the right of escheat arises only when there is no relative of the decedent, however remotely related.

(e) **Distribution Per Capita and Per Stirpes.** The fact that different generations of distributees may be entitled to receive the estate creates a problem of determining the proportions in which distribution is to be made. When all the distributees stand in the same degree of relationship to the decedent, *distribution* is made *per capita,* each receiving the same share. Thus, if the decedent is survived by three children, *A, B,* and *C,* each of them is entitled to receive one third of the estate.

If the distributees stand in different degrees of relationship, distribution is made in as many equal parts as there are family lines or stirpes represented in the nearest generation. Parents take to the exclusion of their children or subsequent descendants; and when members of the nearest generation have died, their descendants take by way of representation. This is called *distribution per stirpes* or *stirpital distribution.*

(f) **Murder of Decedent.** Statutes generally provide that a person who murders the decedent cannot inherit from the victim by intestacy. In the absence of such a statute, some courts hold that the inheritance cannot be denied, while others refuse to allow inheritance under such circumstances.[17]

Statutes prohibiting an heir from inheriting when the ancestor is murdered are strictly construed so that the heir is not excluded when negligence causes the death of the ancestor, even though the heir has been convicted of involuntary manslaughter for such death.

(g) **Death of Distributee after Decedent.** The persons entitled to distribution of a decedent's estate are determined as of the date of death. If a distributee dies thereafter, the rights of the distributee are not lost but pass from the original decedent's estate to the deceased distributee's estate.

---

[17] Reagan v Brown, 59 NM 423, 285 P2d 789.

(h) Simultaneous Death. The Uniform Simultaneous Death Act [18] provides that where survivorship cannot be established, "the property of each person shall be disposed of as if he had survived the other." [19]

C. ADMINISTRATION OF DECEDENTS' ESTATES

A decedent's estate consists of the assets that a person owns at death. It must be determined who is entitled to receive that property. If the decedent owed debts, those debts must be paid first. After that, any balance is to be distributed according to the terms of any will, or by the intestate law if the decedent did not leave a will.

§ 52:14. Definitions. The decedent has the privilege of naming in the will the person who will administer the estate. A man named in a will to administer the estate of the decedent is an *executor;* a woman, an *executrix.* If the decedent failed to name an executor or did not leave a will, the law permits another person, usually a close relative, to obtain the appointment of someone to wind up the estate. This person is an *administrator* or *administratrix.*

In certain special instances a temporary administrator may be appointed. Thus, if there is a will contest, an *administrator pendente lite* may be appointed; that is, an administrator who serves during the litigation for the purpose of preserving the estate.

Administrators and executors are often referred to generally as *personal representatives* of the decedents since they represent the decedents or stand in their place.

§ 52:15. When Administration Is Not Necessary. No administration is required when the decedent did not own any property at the time of death or when all the property owned was jointly owned with another person who acquired the decedent's interest by right of survivorship. Thus, if all of the property of a husband and wife is held as tenants by the entireties, no administration is required upon the death of either of them because the other automatically acquires the entire estate free of any debts or liabilities of the decedent.

In some states special statutes provide for a simplified administration when the decedent leaves only a small estate, commonly under $1,000 to $5,000. In many states, if all of the parties in interest (creditors and relatives of the decedent) can agree on what shares or amounts each one is to receive, it is possible for a *settlement agreement* to be made by which the estate is divided without any formal or court proceedings.

§ 52:16. Appointment of Personal Representative. Both executors and administrators must be appointed to act as such by a court or officer designated by law. The appointment is made by granting to the personal representative *letters testamentary,* in the case

---

[18] This Act has been adopted for the District of Columbia and the Panama Canal Zone and in every state except Louisiana and Ohio.
[19] Special provision is made in the case of beneficiaries, joint tenants, tenants by entireties, community property, and insurance policies.

of an executor, or *letters of administration,* in the case of an administrator. For the appointment of a personal representative, an application or petition is filed with the court or officer setting forth the details of the decedent's death, stating that the decedent, if a resident of the state, lived within the county or, if a nonresident, that property of the decedent is within the county, and reciting the facts which justify the appointment of the personal representative.

(a)   Person Entitled to Act as Personal Representative. If the decedent has named an executor, that person has the right to act as personal representative or to decline to do so.[20] If no executor has been named, an administrator is appointed.

The right to act as administrator is regulated by statutes, which generally give the right to administer to the surviving spouse; but if there is no surviving spouse or if the spouse declines, the right is given to the next of kin.

If there is no next of kin or if they decline, the right is given to the creditors of the decedent. This priority is based on the belief that the existence of a relationship or monetary interest will insure a better administration of the estate than otherwise. In the absence of proper persons being willing to apply, it is sometimes provided that the court or officer can appoint as administrator "any fit person."

In specifying the classes of persons who are eligible for appointment as administrators, a state may not declare a blanket preference for men; and whether a man should be appointed instead of a woman must be decided on the merits of each case as it arises.[21] In some states, a public official called a *public administrator* will be appointed.

(b)   Oath and Bond. A personal representative who is appointed, is required to take an oath and to file a bond that the estate will be properly administered according to law. In some states an executor is not required to furnish a bond if a resident of the state and in sound financial condition or if the testator has expressly directed that no bond be required.

§ 52:17. Proof of Claims against the Estate. The statutes vary widely with respect to the presentation of claims against a decedent's estate. In very general terms the statutes provide for some form of public notice of the grant of letters, as by advertisement. Creditors are then required to give notice of their claims within a period specified either by statute or a court order, as within six months. In most states the failure to present the claim within the specified time bars the claim.[22] (See p. 902, Glass v Benkert) In other states the creditor may assert a late claim with respect to any assets of the estate remaining in the hands of the representative at the time that the creditor asserts the claim.

If the claim is secured by a mortgage, there is no need to give notice in order to preserve the mortgage lien. The mortgagee may proceed to enforce the mortgage against the land even though the personal representative was not given notice of the claim. Notice is required, however, if the mortgagee wishes to be paid from the general assets of the estate in the hands of the personal representative, as distinguished from the mortgaged land.

---

[20] Adams v Readnour, 134 Ky 230, 120 SW 279.
[21] Reed v Reed, 404 US 71.
[22] State ex rel Paramount Publix Corp. v District Court, 90 Mont 281, 1 P2d 335.

In many states any claim against the estate must be made in writing, sworn to as true, and delivered to the personal representative.

(a)   Nature of Claims.

(1)   Funeral Expenses. In most jurisdictions a personal representative either cannot or will not be appointed before the burial of the decedent. Accordingly, it is the surviving spouse or the next of kin who has the responsibility of arranging for the burial of the decedent. Most states allow a claim for funeral expenses against the estate even though the funeral arrangements had been contracted for by a member of the family and the personal representative had not ordered or authorized such action.[23]

The funeral expenses must be reasonable and in harmony with the estate and social standing of the decedent. If the court deems the funeral bill excessive, it may allow the undertaker only part of the bill as a charge against the estate. The party who contracted with the undertaker will then remain liable for the balance.

In the case of a minor decedent, the father, if solvent, must pay the funeral expenses.

(2)   Administration Expenses. The estate is charged with the expenses of its administration. These include the cost of the personal representative's bond, if any; the fee charged by the court or clerk for the grant of the letters to the personal representative; the cost of advertising and giving notice when required; the cost of filing the account; the cost of any particular services, such as bringing suit against third persons; and the compensation of the personal representative and the estate's attorney.

(3)   Family Allowance. Most states make some provision for the immediate necessities of a decedent's family during the period of administration. The widow, or the children, and in some instances the husband of a decedent, are generally entitled to receive a certain portion of the estate for this purpose. In some states the granting of this allowance lies within the discretion of the court; while in others it is a matter of right. It most commonly takes the form of a specified sum of money, although in some states it is the right to take certain specified articles of property or to live in the house of the decedent for a specified time. It is immaterial whether the decedent left a will or, if there is a will, whether the claimant receives anything under the decedent's will.

The right of a spouse to receive this allowance is generally barred by conduct on the claimant's part that would have entitled the decedent to obtain a divorce. Thus a wife who is guilty of deserting her husband is not entitled, upon his death, to receive the family allowance from his estate.

The family allowance is ordinarily not subject to the claim of creditors. This means that the person entitled to the allowance may receive it even though there will not be enough to pay creditors after the allowance has been deducted.

(4)   Debts and Liabilities of the Decedent. Generally any debt or liability of the decedent existing at the time of death may be asserted against the estate.

---

[23] Home Undertaking Co. v Joliff, 172 Wash 78, 19 P2d 654.

(b) Priority of Claims. When the estate of a decedent is insolvent, that is, when it is not sufficiently large to pay all debts and taxes, the law generally provides that certain claims shall be paid first. Although there is great variation of detail, the most common pattern of priority provides for the payment of claims against the estate in the following order: (1) funeral expenses; (2) administration expenses; (3) family allowance; (4) claims due the United States; [24] (5) expenses of the last illness; (6) debts due state, county, and city governments; (7) claims for wages; (8) lien claims; (9) all other debts.

Assuming a state in which the priorities are as stated, the effect is that the decedent's estate is first used to pay the claims listed in (1). If any balance remains, claims (2) are paid. If any balance remains, claims (3) are paid, and so on. If there are several claimants within a particular class, but not enough money to pay each in full, they share proportionately the balance remaining and creditors in lower priorities receive nothing.

§ 52:18. Powers and Duties of Personal Representative.
The powers and duties of the personal representative relate to the collection of the assets of the estate; the care and preservation of the assets; the management of the estate; the prosecution and defense of lawsuits to which the estate is a party; the payment of debts of the decedent, administration expenses, federal estate taxes and state taxes; accounting to the extent required by law; and distributing the estate to those entitled to it. Apart from special powers that a decedent may confer upon an executor, the powers of an executor and administrator are the same.

(a) Performance. A personal representative is under the duty to administer the estate according to law. An executor must also comply with directions contained in the will.

(b) Due Care and Loyalty. A personal representative has the duty of exercising due care and loyalty.[25]

(c) Possession and Preservation of Estate. The personal representative has the task of collecting the assets of the estate and subsequently of distributing them to the persons entitled to them. An executor or administrator has the duty to defend the estate against adverse claims.

It is customary for the personal representative to deposit cash of the estate in a bank. In some states this is specifically required by statute. The deposit in any case must be made in the representative's name as representative, that is, as *John Jones, Administrator of the Estate of Henry Brown, Deceased,* or in the name of the estate, as *Estate of Henry Brown, Deceased.* In either case checks on the account would be signed by John Jones as administrator of the named estate.

(d) Payment of Debts. The personal representative has the duty to pay the debts of the decedent, taxes, and the expenses of administering the estate.

(e) Inventory and Appraisal. The personal representative must make a list or inventory of the assets of the decedent's estate. With this inventory must be an appraisal

---

[24] 31 USC § 191.
[25] In re Stewart, 145 Ore 460, 28 P2d 642.

of the value of the various items so that the value of each bequest or distributive share and the total value of the estate can be determined.

Generally the inventory and the appraisal are restricted to personal property, although some statutes require the listing of real estate as well. A number of states allow the omission of certain types of personal property, such as clothing, Bibles, and school books.

(f)   Monument or Tombstone. The personal representative has the duty to erect a tombstone or monument on the grave of the decedent.

(g)   Investments. Since the function of the personal representative is to distribute the estate, the representative ordinarily has no authority to make investments. Sometimes the duty to do so will be implied when, because of litigation or the nature of the assets, there will be a long delay in the distribution of the estate.

(h)   Administration of Real Estate. Whether the administrator has any duty or power with respect to real estate of the decedent depends upon the law of the particular state. At common law only the personal property of a decedent was administered by a personal representative. Real estate of the decedent vested upon death in heirs or devisees.

In most states this rule has been modified to the extent that where it is necessary to pay debts of the decedent, the personal representative may take control of the real estate and rent or sell it for that purpose. In some states the distinction between real and personal property is abolished, and the personal representative has the same administrative control over real estate of the decedent as over personal property.[26]

In the absence of a statutory provision, generally the personal assets of the decedent must be consumed in the payment of debts before the real estate can be touched for that purpose.

Whether the personal representative is under a duty to insure the real estate depends upon whether, under the circumstances, a reasonable person would obtain insurance.

(i)   Continuation of Business. In the absence of statute or an express direction in the will, an executor does not have the right to continue the business of the decedent.

(j)   Determination of Proper Distributees. It is the duty of the personal representative to ascertain by the exercise of reasonable diligence the proper persons to whom distribution is to be made.[27] For example, if an estate is to be divided among the brothers of the decedent, the personal representative should ascertain as far as can reasonably be done the identity and whereabouts of all of the brothers. Or if a spouse is disqualified from sharing in the estate, the personal representative must make that fact known to the court.

After the rights of the parties who are entitled to the estate have been determined, the personal representative is under the duty to make distribution in accordance with those rights.

(k)   Accounting. A personal representative is under the same duty to account as an agent.

---

[26] Peterson v Peterson, 173 Kan 636, 251 P2d 221.
[27] In re Maher, 195 Wash 126, 79 P2d 984.

(l) Liability of Personal Representative. If misconduct of the executor or the administrator or failure to act causes loss to the estate, such representative may be required to indemnify the estate for the amount of the loss which has been caused. The decree or order imposing liability is commonly called a *surcharge*.

§ 52:19. Termination of Authority of Personal Representative.
The termination of the authority of a personal representative ordinarily has no retroactive effect. The validity of transactions completed before the termination of authority is not affected.

(a) Discharge of the Representative. After the administration of the estate is completed, the personal representative applies to the court to be discharged. Once a discharge is entered, authority to act is terminated.

(b) Revocation of Grant of Letters. The letters may have been erroneously granted. The letters will, in such a case, be revoked.

Letters will also be revoked when they have been granted in the wrong county, or when the person appointed was not qualified. Thus, letters of administration granted to the decedent's apparent widow will be revoked when it is shown that she had not been the decedent's wife.

Letters of administration will be revoked when it is later found that the decedent left a will and the will is admitted to probate. Conversely, letters testamentary will be revoked when the will is set aside as being invalid.

(c) Resignation. In most states the personal representative can resign if permission of the court is obtained. This request will ordinarily be granted if a good cause for resignation is shown and the estate will not be prejudiced thereby.[28]

(d) Removal. In most states, statutes have been adopted which specify the grounds for the removal of a personal representative. In general, these include any delinquency, misconduct, or personal incapacity of a nature sufficiently serious as to interfere with the administration of the estate. Thus a personal representative may be removed for failure to file required papers, or for fraud, misappropriation of funds of the estate, or a loss of personal competence or fitness to act as administrator. A personal representative may also be removed for representing an interest adverse to the estate.[29]

---

[28] State ex rel Russell v Mueller, 332 Mo 758, 60 SW2d 48.
[29] Watkin's Estate, 114 Vt 109, 41 A2d 180.

CASES FOR CHAPTER 52

Mangan v Mangan

(MoApp) 554 SW2d 418 (1977)

Ralph Mangan wrote a will in 1968 and two later wills in 1972. The later wills reduced the share given to his brother, Edward. Ralph died six months after writing the third will. The third will was admitted to probate. Edward appealed from the decree of probate and claimed that the third will was not valid on the theory that Ralph lacked testamentary capacity when he wrote the will.

HOGAN, J. . . . On November 16, 1971, the testator sustained a gunshot wound either as a result of an accident while cleaning his gun, or perhaps as the result of an attempt to take his own life. Testator was hospitalized for the treatment of that wound and he remained hospitalized until December 22, 1971, at which time he was moved to a nursing home. On February 26, 1972, the testator left the nursing home and took up residence with his brother, Edward, the petitioner here. He remained with Edward until April 5, 1972, when he was again hospitalized with a bleeding ulcer, arteriosclerotic cardiovascular disease, and other secondary ailments. On May 9, 1972, the testator was again moved to the nursing home where he remained until he expired August 22, 1972. On June 6, 1972, testator was adjudicated an incompetent.

While the testator was in the nursing home from December 1971 to February 1972 he executed two wills. The first of these wills was executed January 19, 1972, and the second on February 23, 1972. The provisions of these wills differ considerably from those of the February, 1968 will in that Edward L. Mangan's share of the estate is greatly reduced, and that part left to Joseph J. Mangan, Jr., is substantially increased.

The contestant (petitioner) sought to invalidate both wills executed in 1972, on the grounds that the testator lacked testamentary capacity and was unduly influenced by Joseph Mangan, Jr., and his wife, Helen, on both occasions. To support his contention that the testator lacked testamentary capacity in 1972, petitioner had some evidence that as early as the summer of 1971, Ralph A. Mangan was confused and disoriented; and while he was hospitalized in 1971 and thereafter, was thoroughly disoriented because of his advanced age, arteriosclerosis, and the trauma of the gunshot wound. . . .

The proponents * had the evidence of many witnesses that during his first stay in the hospital and later at the nursing home testator appeared competent. Further, the proponents' witnesses more or less uniformly stated that the testator was a self-reliant person who attended to all his business affairs even after the 1972 wills had been executed. . . . There was testimony that Helen Mangan contacted an attorney about the January 19, 1972, will upon the testator's instruction, and that the attorney went over that will in detail with the testator. The attorney who prepared the final will—the will admitted by the Probate Court of Greene County—was called, and having detailed his past acquaintance with the Mangan family and having gone over in some detail his observation of the testator prior to the actual

* Authors' note: A proponent is the person who proposes or offers a writing for probate as the will of a decedent.

execution of the February 23, 1972, will, gave it as his opinion that the testator was of sound and disposing mind, that testator "was capable, competent and that he did know . . . what he wanted and what the objects of his bounty were." The testator, according to this attorney, "mentioned dollars amounts . . . street addresses and that sort of thing"; the testator also "went over various names," mentioning a number of "nephews, cousins and so on." In substance, this attorney testified that at and near the time the February 23, 1972, will was drafted and executed, the testator . . . knew the nature and extent of his property and the persons who were the natural objects of his bounty, and appreciated his natural obligations to those persons. Such . . . are the requirements for testamentary capacity. . . .

The fact that the testator made an unequal or even unjust distribution of his property does not of itself [invalidate a will]. A man has the right to will his property to whomsoever he chooses, and the beneficiary in his will is not bound to account for the choice. . . .

There was evidence from two physicians that at times the testator was confused and disoriented as a result of cerebral arteriosclerosis and the medication given him to palliate his anxieties. However, these physicians testified, in substance, that patients suffering from cerebral arteriosclerosis enjoy periods of lucidity, that the testator was given a drug to improve his cerebral circulation, and both physicians were . . . unable to state with reasonable certainty that the testator lacked testamentary capacity on February 23, 1972. The attorney who prepared the final will testified that upon the basis of his observation, the testator had testamentary capacity when he executed that will. . . . The contestant makes a great deal of the fact that the testator mistook the first names of some of his collateral kindred. Contestant argues that this lack of memory, if such it was, clearly demonstrates testamentary incompetence. We do not agree; the testator had a great many kinsmen, and he could have had testamentary capacity without knowing whether all of them were alive, and without remembering the names of all his nephews. . . .

[Decree affirmed]

Arnold v Parry

(IndApp) 363 NE2d 1055 (1977)

The Indiana statute requires that a will be signed by the testator and by two witnesses and specifies that "the testator shall signify to the attesting

witnesses that the instrument is his will." Lamb
wanted to sign a will. Either he or his attorney informed two witnesses that it was Lamb's will which
he was signing and they then signed it as witnesses.
After the death of Lamb, the will was admitted to
probate. An appeal was taken from the decree of
probate by Arnold, a relative who would inherit if
there were no will. He claimed that the will was
not entitled to probate on the ground that the statute
had not been satisfied because the evidence did not
establish that Lamb had informed the witnesses that
the writing was his will. The validity of the will
was defended by Parry, the executor, and by a legatee named in the will.

BUCHANAN, P.J. . . . Arnold says the will
was improperly executed, because the only surviving
attesting witness, Mrs. Hilda Johnson, could not positively state that the testator published his will by
signifying to her that she was witnessing his signature
on his will as required by [Indiana Code] 29-1-5-3
Signatures

Sec. 3. (a) The execution of a will, other than
a nuncupative will, must be by the signature
of the testator and of at least two (2) witnesses
as follows:

(1) *The testator shall signify to the attesting
witnesses that the instrument is his will
and either*

(i) Himself sign, or

(ii) Acknowledge his signature already made,
or

(iii) At his direction and in his presence have
someone else sign his name for him. . . .

Defendants . . . on the other hand, point out
that it can be inferred from Mrs. Johnson's testimony
that either Mr. Lamb or his attorney in the presence
of Mr. Lamb stated to her that the document was
Mr. Lamb's will and that this is sufficient publication. . . .

It is our opinion that there is sufficient evidence of publication of the will to comply with the
statute.

Publication is the act of making it known in
the presence of witnesses that the instrument to be
executed is the last will and testament of the testator.
. . . The purpose of publication is not to inform
the witnesses that the document is a will, but rather
to make sure that the witnesses are aware the testator
knows he is about to execute a will. The likelihood

of fraud is lessened if the witnesses know the testator
understands the testamentary character of the instrument he is about to execute. . . .

The pertinent part of the statute is Sec. 3(a)(1)
which provides unambiguously that "The testator
shall signify to the attesting witnesses that the instrument is his will and either . . ." So a will is published
if the testator signifies to the attesting witnesses it
is his will.

How may this be done? Must the "sign" come
only from the testator as an utterance from him,
as Arnold maintains? . . .

The publication requirements seem to be
closely analogous to the requirement in some jurisdictions that a testator request the witnesses to sign.

The request for the witnesses to sign may come
from the testator's attorney or the scrivener of the
will, and is justified as coming from the testator on
any agency theory. . . .

The instrument is published as the testator's
will if done so in his presence, and he need not further
assent to it by word or deed. The fact that he does
not deny it is his will is sufficient *. . . .

We conclude that Mr. Lamb's will was sufficiently published because he signified it to be his
will by the act of signing it after it had been referred
to as his will thereby fulfilling the purpose of the
statute by making the witnesses aware that Mr. Lamb
knew he was signing his will. . . .

[Decree of probate affirmed]

---

* It is evident that an able-bodied testator, in full
possession of his faculties, who stands by in the immediate
presence of a lawyer-scrivener and a prospective witness
to the execution of a will, and hears the scrivener tell the
witness that the document before them is the testator's
last will and testament and that the latter desires him to
witness the execution of the instrument, is adopting the
declaration of the will as his own act and communicating
his publication of it to the witness fully and unequivocally
by signing it then and there, and remaining in the presence
of the witness while the latter signs it in his turn. In such
case, there being nothing else to indicate the contrary,
"enough" has been "said or done in the presence of and
with the knowledge of the testator to cause the witnesses
to understand distinctly that the testator desires them to
know that the paper produced is his will which they are
to attest as such." *In re DuBois' Estate,* 9 NJ Super 280,
285, 76 A2d 33, 36. (AppDiv 1950). To require, over and
above the foregoing, a nod of the head or a murmur or
other objective manifestation by the testator of concurrence
as an absolute prerequisite to a legally operative declaration
in such circumstances would, in our judgment come close
to substituting a fetish for a rule of reason.

Bostwick v Hurstel

364 Mass 282, 304 NE2d 186 (1973)

In the first clause of her will, Cecile Bostwick bequeathed 25 shares of stock in the American Telephone and Telegraph Company (A.T.&T.) to James Bostwick. By the next clause of her will she bequeathed "all remaining shares of stock in . . . [A.T.&T.] which I may own at the time of my decease" to two nephews and nieces. Subsequent to writing the will, all of the A.T.&T. stock was sold. Thereafter additional stock of that company was purchased and additional new shares were received by virtue of stock splits. When Cecile died, 150 shares were the equivalent of 25 shares when the will was written. James claimed 150 shares under her will. The nephews and nieces asserted that at most James was only entitled to 25 shares. From a decree allowing James only 25 shares, he appealed.

QUIRICO, J. . . . "The important question presented to us is whether the bequest of twenty-five shares of stock to [James Bostwick] was a specific bequest which would entitle him to the resulting 150 shares as of the date of the death of the testatrix, . . . or whether it was a general bequest of shares which would entitle him to only twenty-five shares after the two splits. . . ."

The manner in which we framed the issue and the two cases cited are indicative of the way this court has traditionally approached the question whether legatees should benefit from stock splits: we have first determined whether the testamentary gift (hereinafter called "legacy" or "bequest") in the will was general or specific, and then applied the result thought to follow automatically from the chosen label. If the bequest was found to be general, indicating that the testator did not have in mind particular property of his own at the time he executed his will, the legatee has only received the exact number of shares specified in the will; if, on the other hand, it was found that the testator intended to separate out and bequeath particular shares then in his possession, the bequest was termed specific and the legatee received the specified shares as well as the accretions created by the stock split. . . .

The approach used . . . of first labeling the gift as general or specific and then applying the seemingly automatic consequences is the one we have used in all our prior and subsequent cases concerned with shares created by stock splits. . . .

The two principal difficulties with the general versus specific classification approach are that it fails to consider the testator's intent with specific reference to the additional shares created by a stock split and that it also fails to recognize the basic nature of a stock split. As was stated by the Supreme Court of Rhode Island in a case involving the same issue we consider here, "It is readily apparent from an understanding of the basic elementary principles of corporate security law that a change in the number of shares of stock attributable to a split in the stock of the corporation occuring, as it does here, between the execution of the will and the death of the testator should be considered one of form and not substance. . . . A stock split in no way alters the substance of the testator's total interest or rights in the corporation. . . . [It] is merely a dividing up of the outstanding shares of a corporation into a greater number of units without disturbing the stockholder's original proportional participating interest in the corporation." Egavian v Egavian, 102 RI 740, 746, 232 A2d 789, 793 (1967). Thus, for example, in a situation where a testator executes a will leaving 100 shares of a certain stock to a named legatee and the stock splits two for one between the time the will was executed and the testator's death, if the court denies the legatee's right to receive the additional 100 shares, his legacy will be thereby reduced to only half of the corporate interest which the testator originally intended to bequeath. Furthermore, this result will ordinarily be due to a corporate decision over which the testator had little or no control. It is highly doubtful that this is the ultimate result the testator intended, although the unquestioned rule of construction in this jurisdiction is to give effect to the testator's intent where possible. . . .

In cases involving stock splits, the majority of courts today hold that the legatee of a bequest of shares of stock is entitled to additional shares created by stock splits occurring in the interval between the execution of a testator's will and his death. . . . The theories by which they have arrived at such a result vary, but it is clear that many jurisdictions have concluded that the general or specific classification approach is overly rigid and formalistic, and have rejected it for a rule which is more in line with the testator's intent. . . .

The rule is based on the sound premise that . . . the additional shares created by a stock split merely indicate a change in form, with the stockholder's proportionate interest or ownership in the corporation, his rights to dividends and rights upon dissolution remaining the same. Furthermore, we believe the rule comports more often with a testator's intent regarding such additional shares than is true of our gift classification approach. As observed by several courts, in most cases the probable intent of the testator is to give a legatee the proportion of ownership in a corporation represented by the shares bequeathed on the date of the will's execution, since any other interpretation would mean the testator intended to subject his bequest to change or even negation by subsequent corporate actions over which he probably had little or no control. . . . Finally, it seems that the rule would obviate the necessity for continuously litigating the question whether a particular bequest of stock is general or specific when stock splits are involved, since the rule does not call initially for a determination of fact.

On the strength of the foregoing reasons, we today adopt the rule established in Egavian v Egavian, 102 RI 740, 747-748, 232 A2d 789 (1967), . . . and hold that, in the absence of anything manifesting a contrary intent, a legatee of a bequest of stock is entitled to the additional shares received by a testator as a result of a stock split occurring in the interval between the execution of his will and his death. . . .

Applying the rule adopted to the facts of the case before us we hold that Bostwick is entitled to the 125 shares in addition to the twenty-five bequeathed.

The testatrix wanted Bostwick to enjoy the full value of the twenty-five A.T.&T. shares she had bequeathed and was giving him her interest in the corporation which these shares represented at the time she executed her will. The two subsequent stock splits created a sixfold increase in the number of A.T.&T. shares, so that when the testatrix died the fractional interest in the corporation represented by the bequeathed twenty-five shares was only a sixth of what it had been when her will was executed. Therefore, at the time of the testatrix's death, the interest she bequeathed to Bostwick consisted of 150 shares, and not twenty-five.

[Judgment reversed and action remanded]

Murray v Willett

36 MdApp 551, 373 A2d 1303 (1977)

Murray wrote a will by which he left all his property to his sisters Mary and Isabel. He further provided "in the event of the prior decease of Isabel, her share is to go to Mary. In the event of the prior decease [of] Mary, her share is to go to Isabel." Mary died in 1971 and was survived by a son. Isabel died in 1973 and was survived by a son. Murray died thereafter. The sons of the two sisters claimed that they were entitled to the estate of Murray. Other relatives of Murray claimed that the gifts to the named sisters had lapsed and that Murray's estate therefore passed to them. The court held that the sons of the two sisters were entitled to the estate. The other relatives appealed.

GILBERT, C.J. . . . The difficulty . . . in the instant case is occasioned by the phrase "of the prior decease." Those words give rise to two distinct inferences. The phrase could be argued to mean, first, that each sister must survive the other in order to take under the will, or, second, that each sister must survive the testator before she may take under the will.

Had the testator been cognizant of and heeded the message in the "Minutes and Advices of the Yearly Meeting of Friends Held in London" (1802), that "[f]riends are earnestly recommended to employ persons skillful in law, and of good repute, to make their wills; as great inconvenience and loss, and sometimes the ruin of families, have happened through the unskillfulness of some who have taken upon them[selves] to make wills . . ." , it is likely that this litigation would never have arisen. . . .

We believe this case to be controlled by [Maryland Estate & Trusts Code Annotated] § 4-403, which provides . . .

"(a) *Death of legatee prior to testator.* Unless a contrary intent is expressly indicated in the will, a legacy may not lapse or fail because of the death of a legatee after the execution of the will but prior to the death of the testator if the legatee is:

(1) Actually and specifically named as legatee;

(2) Described or in any manner referred to, designated, or identified as legatee in the will; or

(3) A member of a class in whose favor a legacy is made.

(b) *Effect of death of legatee.* A legacy described in subsection (a) shall have the same effect and operation in law to direct the distribution of the property directly from the estate of the person who owned the property to those persons who would have taken the property if the legatee had died, testate or intestate, owning the property."

As we view the will in the case now before us, there is no "expressed" or "indicated" intent therein to demonstrate that the testator was desirous of having his estate, or any portion thereof, pass by way of intestacy. The clause can only reasonably be interpreted, therefore, to mean that Murray devised his estate to his two sisters, Mary and Isabel, in equal shares with the proviso that if either sister was not alive at his death, then the surviving sister would inherit the whole of the estate. Because both sisters predeceased Murray, it is safe to infer, in the light of the anti-lapse statute, § 4-403, that Murray intended for the children of Mary and Isabel to take by way of representation the share that the child's mother would have taken had she survived Murray. . . .

[Judgment affirmed]

Glass v Benkert

18 CalApp3d 126, 95 CalRptr 735 (1971)

An airplane piloted by Benkert crashed. The crash killed the pilot and his passenger, Milton Glass. The pilot's wife was appointed administratrix of his estate. She gave notice of her appointment by means of newspaper publication, informing the public that anyone with a claim against Benkert or his estate should file that claim with her within six months after the date the notice was first published. The filing of claims within such period was required by statute. More than six months after the publication date, a claim was filed with her on behalf of the children of Milton Glass by which the children sought to recover damages for the death of their father. Benkert's administratrix asserted that the claim of the children of Glass was barred because it had not been filed with her within the statutory six-month period. The children of Glass contended that the six-months' limitation was not binding on them because they were minors. The court held that the children were barred and they appealed.

REPPY, A.J. . . . Section 707 [of the Probate Code] provides in relevant part: "All claims for dam-

ages for . . . death of a person . . . must be filed or presented within the time limited in the notice or as extended by the provisions of Sections 702 and 709 of this code; and *any claim* not so filed or presented is *barred forever*. . . ." (Italics supplied). There is no express exception for minors. In Artukovich v Astendorf, 21 Cal2d 329, 131 P2d 831, the Supreme Court, construing Political Code section 4075, acknowledged the Legislature's intent to balance the questions of public policy involved in each instance and held that where statutes make no exception for minors, none may be implied. . . . The court stated: "[N]o exception in favor of minors or persons laboring under other disabilities may be written into said section under the guise of judicial interpretation. . . . 'The solicitude of the law in protecting a minor in his contractual and other relationships is limited and not general in application.' . . . [P]ractically every special consideration which has been extended to . . . [minors] is . . . covered by statute. Thus there are statutory provisions extending special consideration to minors with respect to the time within which certain proceedings must be commenced [citations], but the special consideration extended is expressly limited to the proceedings therein mentioned. We find no similar provisions extending special consideration to minors in statutes prescribing the time within which claims must be filed or the time within which proceedings must be commenced upon rejected claims either in probate proceedings [citation] or in liquidation proceedings.". . .

There are strong policy reasons for the legislative decision not to toll the pertinent limitations period during minority which are exemplified in the instant case. The defendant's decedent died leaving heirs who must be provided for and an estate which must be distributed. Tying up the estate for up to 21 years waiting for a minor claimant to reach majority would place a considerable hardship on the heirs. Also, the heirs could be forced to defend several separate actions, one as each minor claimant reached majority.

[Judgment affirmed]

QUESTIONS AND CASE PROBLEMS

1. What social forces are affected by allowing a person to give property after death by means of leaving a will?
2. Compare an ordinary gift and a gift by will with respect to (a) intent, (b) formality, and (c) delivery.

3. Compare alteration of commercial paper, discharge of a contract by agreement, and revocation of a will with respect to (a) intent, (b) formality, and (c) parties.

4. Compare a will and a contract with respect to (a) signing, (b) publication, and (c) subscribing witnesses.

5. Probate of the will of Vivian Lingenfelter was opposed. It was shown that the testatrix was sick, highly nervous, and extremely jealous and that she committed suicide a week after executing the will. In support of the will, it was shown that she understood the will when she discussed it with an attorney; that her husband was seriously ill when she wrote the will; that he died the following day; and that she grieved his death. A proceeding was brought to determine whether the will was entitled to be probated. Decide. [Lingenfelter's Estate, 38 Cal2d 571, 241 P2d 990]

6. By his will, James Kidd left the balance of his estate to anyone engaging in obtaining scientific proof that there exists a soul which leaves the human body upon death. The bequest was claimed by the Neurological Sciences Foundation of the Barrow Neurological Institute. The Foundation was engaged in research with respect to the normal and abnormal functioning of the human nervous system. Was it entitled to the bequest? [Kidd's Estate, 106 Ariz 554, 479 P2d 697]

7. Ewing died intestate. One of his brothers arranged for his funeral with the Lilly Funeral Home. The Home presented its bill to the estate, but the estate refused to pay it. Was the estate liable for the bill in view of the fact that the funeral had not been ordered by the estate? [Ewing's Estate, 234 Iowa 950, 14 NW2d 633]

8. Field executed a will. Upon her death the will was found in her safe deposit box, but the part of the will containing the fifth bequest was torn from the will. This torn fragment was also found in the box. There was no evidence that anyone other than Field had ever opened the box. A proceeding was brought to determine whether the will was entitled to be probated. Decide. [Flora v Hughes, 312 Ky 478, 228 SW2d 27]

9. Roberts bequeathed the balance of her estate to her son Watkins. She bequeathed $1.00 to her grandson Richard. Watkins died before Roberts. Richard and two other children of Watkins claimed the balance of the estate by virtue of the anti-lapse statute. In opposition to Richard, it was claimed that since Roberts had disinherited him by leaving him $1.00 he could not take a larger share and that the anti-lapse statute was inapplicable. Decide. [Roberts' Estate, 9 Cal App 2d 747, 88 Cal Rptr 396]

10. Anna Miller wrote a will 11 pages long and enclosed it in an envelope, which she sealed. She then wrote on the envelope, "My last will & testament," and signed her name below this statement. This was the only place where she signed her name on any of the papers. Could this writing be admitted to probate as her will? [Miller's Executor v Shannon, (Ky) 299 SW2d 103]

11. Morris wrote a letter to the secretary of the First National Bank reading: "Always has been a letter to you, sealed & stamped to be forwarded if needed by accident to me—with frequent changes, latest not complete because of a change in charity set up— one half for crippled children & one half for S P C A You will act for me . . . one thing is for sure & now a place to dispose of things—Short's bill first—Inventory is in my box and here I have some precious bits & pieces. Thank you always." The letter was signed by Morris. Can this letter be probated after her death? [Morris' Estate, 268 Cal 2d 638, 74 Cal Rptr 32]

12. *A* bequeathed the balance of her estate to *B* and *C* "if they both be living at the time of my demise and if one shall have predeceased me then all of my estate to the one remaining." Both *B* and *C* died before *A*. *B* was survived by a daughter, *D*. *C* was not survived by any children or grandchildren. *A* was survived by *E,* a nephew, the child of a deceased brother. *E* and *D* each claimed the estate of *A*. The claim of *D* was based on the anti-lapse statute. The claim of *E* was based on the fact that he was the

closest living relative of *A*. Who was entitled to *A*'s estate? [See Kerr's Estate, (CADistCol) 433 F2d 479]

13.   Plate was about to sign his will. He began writing his name. He made one stroke of the pen on the paper and then laid the pen down stating, "I can't sign it now." The will was offered for probate. Decide. [Plate's Estate, 148 Pa 55, 23 A 1038]

14.   E. J. White wrote by hand and signed the following: "To Whom it May concern. If anything should happen to me, I want all My Property & otherthing & Bonds divided between Marvin, Arlene & my sisters. Eight Thousand to Earls children, the House 311 North 25 Ave. to Marvin. sell the property. I will finish this later." No change or addition was ever made to this writing. She died seven years later. This writing was offered for probate as her will. Objection was made to the probate on the ground that the last sentence showed that the writing had not been made with testamentary intent. Was this objection valid? [Maines v Davis (Miss) 227 So2d 844]

53 Trusts

A transfer of property to one person with the understanding that it will be held or used for the benefit of another person is a *trust.*

§ 53:1. Definitions. The owner of the property who creates the trust is the *settlor,* the word being taken from the old legal language of "settling the property in trust." The settlor is sometimes called the donor or trustor. The person to whom the property is transferred in trust is the *trustee.* The person for whose benefit the trustee holds the property is the *beneficiary* (or *cestui que trust*).

Property held in trust is sometimes called the *trust corpus, trust fund, trust estate,* or *trust res.* A distinction is made between the *principal,* or the property in trust, and the *income* which is earned by the principal and distributed by the trustee.

Although an express trust is ordinarily created by a transfer of property, the settlor may retain the property as trustee for the beneficiary. The fact that there is a duty to make a payment does not create a trust.[1]

If the trust is created to take effect within the lifetime of the settlor, it is a *living trust* or an *inter vivos trust.* If the trust is provided for in the settlor's will and is to become effective only when the will takes effect after death, the trust is called a *testamentary trust.*

§ 53:2. Creation of Trusts.

(a) Consideration. Since a trust is a transfer of property, consideration is not required, although the absence of consideration may show that the trust is a transfer in fraud of creditors.

(b) Legality. A trust may generally be created for any lawful purpose. A trust is invalid when it is for an unlawful purpose or is in fraud of creditors. A trust may also be void in whole or in part for violating the *rule against perpetuities.* This rule prohibits a person from creating by any transfer, whether in trust or not, a "floating" interest in property that will not become definite (or vested) until a date further away than 21 years after the death of persons alive at the time that the owner of the property attempts to create the interest. For example, the owner of property who has no children cannot create a trust for grandchildren. The law is opposed to tying up property for such long periods of time because no one would know who was the owner of the property until all possible grandchildren were born.

---

[1] Milwaukee v Firemen's Relief Association, 34 Wis2d 350, 149 NW2d 589.

When a trust violates the rule against perpetuities, courts will sustain it as far as is lawfully possible,[2] illustrative of the social force of seeking to enforce intent, subject to the superior social force of protecting the general welfare.

(c)   Capacity of Beneficiary. The capacity of the beneficiary of the trust to hold property or to contract is immaterial. Many trusts are created because the beneficiary lacks legal or actual capacity to manage the property.

(d)   Formality. In creating a trust, it is common practice to execute a writing, called a *trust agreement* or *deed of trust.* No particular form of language is necessary to create a trust so long as the property, the trust purpose, and the beneficiaries are designated. If an inter vivos trust relates to an interest in land, the statute of frauds requires that the trust be evidenced by writing setting forth the details of the trust. When the trust depends upon a transfer of title to land, there must be a valid transfer of the title to the trustee.

A trust in personal property may be declared orally without any writing.[3] If a trust is created by the will of the settlor, there must be a writing which meets the requirements of a will. The same is true when the trust is not intended to come into existence until the death of the settlor.

In the absence of a specific requirement of the statute of frauds as to land or the statute of wills, any conduct or writing which shows an intent to create a trust will be given effect. (See p. 910, Barnette v McNulty)

(e)   Intention. An intention to impose a duty on the trustee with respect to specific property must be expressed. It is not necessary, however, that the word "trust" or "trustee" be used. The settlor will ordinarily name a trustee, but failure to do so is not fatal to the trust because a trustee will be appointed by the court.

(f)   Active Duty. A trust does not exist unless an active duty is placed upon the trustee to manage the property in some manner or to exercise discretion or judgment. A bare direction to hold the property in trust without any direction as to its use or distribution is not sufficient for an active duty. Thus, when a decedent transferred $5,000 to a trustee to be held in trust for *A,* no trust was created. In such a case, the intended beneficiary is entitled to receive the property outright as though the decedent had not attempted to create a trust.

(g)   Identity of Beneficiary. Every trust must have a beneficiary. In a private trust the beneficiaries must be identified by name, description, or designation of the class to which the beneficiaries belong. In a charitable trust it is sufficient that the beneficiaries be members of the public at large or a general class of the public.

Trusts for religious masses, for the maintenance of grave monuments, or for the care of particular animals are technically invalid because there is no human, identified beneficiary; but such trusts are nevertheless enforced because of the social interests that are involved.

In the absence of a statute otherwise providing, leaving property in trust for the perpetual care of a private grave is generally void as a violation of the rule against perpetuities.

---

[2] In re Hop's Estate, (Hawaii) 469 P2d 183.
[3] Monell v College of Physicians and Surgeons, 198 CalApp2d 38, 17 CalRptr 744.

(h)   Acceptance of Trust. As the performance of a trust imposes duties upon the trustee, a trustee may renounce or reject the trust, but acceptance will be presumed in the absence of a disclaimer. A renunciation, however, does not affect the validity of the trust because a court will appoint a substitute trustee if the settlor does not do so.

It is necessary that the beneficiary accept the trust, but the beneficiary's consent will be presumed in the absence of disclaimer.

§ 53:3. Nature of Beneficiary's Interest. The effect of a transfer in trust is to divide the property so that the legal title is given to the trustee and the *equitable title* or beneficial interest is given to the beneficiary. The beneficiary may ordinarily transfer or assign such interest in the trust, and the beneficiary's creditors may reach that interest in satisfaction of their claims. An exception arises when the settlor has restricted the trust in such a way that the beneficiary cannot assign nor creditors reach the interest, creating what is commonly called a *spendthrift trust*.[4]

§ 53:4. Powers of Trustee. A trustee can exercise only those powers that are given by law or the trust instrument or those which the court will construe as being impliedly given.[5] Modern trusts commonly give the trustee discretion to make decisions on matters that could not be foreseen by the settlor. For example, the trustee may be authorized to expend principal as well as income when in the trustee's opinion it is necessary for the education or medical care of a beneficiary. The trustee must exercise discretion in a reasonable manner. (See p. 911, Mesler v Holly)

§ 53:5. Duties of Trustee.

(a)   Performance. A trustee is under the duty to carry out the trust according to its terms and is personally liable for any loss sustained from an unjustified failure to perform such duties. A trustee cannot delegate the performance of personal duties.[6]

(b)   Due Care. The trustee is under a duty to use reasonable skill, prudence, and diligence in the performance of trust duties. More simply stated, the trustee must use the care which would be exercised by a reasonable person under the circumstances.[7]

(c)   Loyalty. A trustee is not permitted to profit personally from the position as trustee, other than to receive the compensation allowed by contract or by law.

(d)   Possession and Preservation of Trust Property. The trustee is under a duty to take possession of trust property and to preserve it from loss or damage. If the property includes accounts receivable or outstanding debts, the trustee is under the duty to collect them.

(e)   Defense of Trust. The trustee must defend the trust when its validity is disputed in court.

---

[4] Wilson v United States, (CA3 Pa) 372 F2d 232.
[5] Rosencrans v Fry, 12 NJ 88, 95 A2d 905.
[6] Hill v Irons, 92 Ohio App 141, 109 NE2d 699.
[7] Mereto's Estate, 373 Pa 308, 96 A2d 115.

(f) Production of Income. Either by express or implied direction, the trustee is required to invest the money or property in enterprises or transactions that will yield an income to the estate.[8]

A trustee is generally permitted to invest in bonds of the United States, or of instrumentalities of the United States; bonds of states, cities, and counties, subject to certain restrictions; first mortgages on real estate when the mortgage does not represent more than a specified percentage of the value of the land; and mortgage bonds of certain types of corporations. Most states now permit a trustee to invest in corporate stocks. Court approval is generally required for investments in real estate.

The device of the *common trust fund* has been legalized in a number of states. Under this plan the trustee, often a bank which is a trustee for a number of small trusts, pools the assets of all the trusts into a common trust fund. Each trust is given certificates in the fund proportionate to the size of its contribution. The fund is then invested in such investments as mortgages on large buildings and factories, in which the individual trust funds could not have been invested directly because of their small size.

(g) Accounting and Information. A trustee must keep accurate records so that it can be determined whether the trust has been properly administered. Upon request by a beneficiary, the trustee must furnish information with respect to the trust. Periodically, or at certain times, as determined by the law in each state, a trustee must file an account in court at which time the court passes upon the stewardship of the trust.

§ 53:6. Remedies for Breach of Trust. A breach of trust may occur in a variety of ways, which in turn affects the remedies available. These remedies include:

(a) Money judgment against trustee for loss caused,

(b) Injunction or order to compel the trustee to do or refrain from doing an act.

(c) Criminal prosecution of the trustee for misconduct.

(d) Tracing and recovery of trust property which has been converted by the trustee,[9] unless the property had been acquired by a bona fide purchaser who gave value and purchased without notice of the breach of trust.

(e) Judgment against surety on the trustee's bond for loss caused the trust by the trustee's default.

(f) Removal of the trustee for misconduct.

(g) Suit against third persons who participated in a breach of trust.

§ 53:7. Termination of Trust. A trust may be terminated (1) in accordance with its terms; (2) because of the impossibility of attaining the object of the trust; (3) by revocation by the settlor, when allowed by the terms of the trust; [10] (See p. 912, Rosenauer v Title Insurance and Trust Co.) (4) by merger of all interests in the same person;

---

[8] Lynch v John M. Redfield Foundation, 9 CalApp3d 293, 88 CalRptr 86.
[9] General Association of D.S.D.A., Inc. v General Association of D.S.D.A., (TexCivApp) 410 SW2d 256.
[10] D.A.R. v Washburn College, 160 Kan 583, 164 P2d 129.

and (5) upon the request of all the beneficiaries when there is no express purpose that requires continuation of the trust.[11]

§ 53:8. **Tentative Trusts.** The law has developed a peculiar trust theory to govern a bank deposit made by *A* in an account marked *"A, in trust for B."*[12] In the absence of any evidence showing an intention to create a formal trust by this method of deposit, a true trust is not created. Such a deposit is regarded as creating a *tentative trust* which the depositor and the depositor's creditors are permitted to treat as though there were no trust; but if the depositor dies, any money that remains in the account after creditors are paid belongs to the person named as the beneficiary.[13] (See p. 913, Wright's Estate) Some states refuse to recognize tentative trusts, while others have expressly authorized them by statute.

§ 53:9. **Charitable Trusts.**

(a) **Purpose.** *Charitable trusts* may be created for any purpose that advances the public welfare. These include trusts to: (1) maintain or propagate religion, religious education, and missionary work; (2) further health and relieve human suffering by establishing institutions or by direct aid of food, clothing, shelter, and medical care to the needy; (3) found or maintain educational institutions, museums, libraries, or aid students or teachers; (4) care for and maintain public cemeteries; (5) erect monuments to public men or national heroes; (6) construct and maintain public buildings or improvements, such as an irrigation system or a playground; (7) further patriotism; and (8) prevent cruelty to animals.

(b) **Cy Pres Doctrine.** In the absence of a contrary provision in the trust agreement, the law will not permit a charitable trust to end even though the original purpose has been accomplished or can no longer be achieved, or because the beneficiary no longer exists. In such a case the courts apply the *cy pres doctrine,* an abbreviation of the Norman French words "cy pres comme possible" or "as near as possible." By this doctrine the court directs that the trust fund be held for another purpose that will be as near as possible to that intended by the settlor.

If, however, it is clear that the settlor intended the trust to be performed exactly as specified or not at all, the trust fails when it is not possible to follow directions.

(c) **Limitations.** In most aspects a charitable trust is the same as a private trust. In some states additional limitations are imposed. Thus a maximum amount may be set on the property that a charitable corporation may own. In some states a decedent is limited as to the amount of property which can be left to charity when the decedent is survived by near relatives. When an absolute gift is made to a charity, the charity generally must hold it in trust for the purposes of the charity.

§ 53:10. **Implied Trusts.** In certain instances trusts are implied in order to carry out the presumed intention of the parties [14] or to protect the former owner of property from the fraud

---

[11] First National Bank v Taylor, 5 ArizApp 327, 426 P2d 663.
[12] Del Bello v Westchester County Bar Ass'n, 19 NY2d 466, 280 NYS2d 651, 227 NE2d 579.
[13] Bearinger's Estate, 336 Pa 253, 9 A2d 342.
[14] Kellow v Bumgardner, 196 Va 247, 835 SE2d 391.

of the present owner. When the court implies a trust to carry out the presumed intent of the parties, the trust is called a *resulting trust;* when it implies a trust to correct or prevent a wrong, it is called a *constructive trust.*[15]

(a)   Purchase Money Resulting Trust. The most common resulting trust arises when a person pays for the purchase of property but title to the property is taken in the name of another person. It is then presumed that the titleholder was intended to hold as trustee for the benefit of the person paying the money. To give effect to this presumption, a resulting trust is generally imposed upon the property and the titleholder. This means that the titleholder cannot use the property but must dispose of it as directed by the person paying the money. This presumption is not conclusive and may be overcome by evidence showing that it was the intention of the person paying the money to lend the money to the person taking title or to make a gift of the property. If the person paying the money is the husband or parent of the person taking title, there is a presumption that the payment was made as a gift, in which case a resulting trust does not arise unless the presumption of a gift is overcome by contrary evidence.[16]

(b)   Constructive Trust of Improperly Acquired Property. When a person has acquired title to property by unlawful or unfair means or in breach of a duty as an agent or trustee, the law will make such person hold it as constructive trustee for the person who has been unjustly deprived of the property.[17] (See p. 915, Simonds v Simonds) Thus if an agent privately purchases property that was to be purchased for the principal, the latter may hold the agent as constructive trustee of that property.

(c)   Statutory Trust. In some instances, statutes declare that a person receiving property or money holds it as trustee for a particular purpose. In a number of states, when an owner makes a payment to a construction contractor, the latter holds the money as trustee for the benefit of unpaid labor and suppliers of materials.[18]

---

[15] Pray v Babbitt, 247 CalApp2d 109, 55 CalRptr 279.
[16] Hanley v Hanley, 14 Ill2d 566, 152 NE2d 879.
[17] Cordoba v Wiswall, 7 ArizApp 144, 436 P2d 922.
[18] B. F. Farnell Co. v Monahan, 58 Mich 552, 141 NW2d 58.

CASES FOR CHAPTER 53

Barnette v McNulty

21 ArizApp 583, 516 P2d 583 (1974)

Wilson Barnette owned 201 shares of Van Pack of Arizona, a corporation. He signed a form called "declaration of trust" in which he declared himself to hold these shares as trustee for Margaret, his wife. Wilson did not indorse the share certificate nor notify the corporation to change the listing of his name as the shareholder. After his death, Margaret claimed the shares by virtue of the trust provisions. Wilson's executor claimed the shares on the ground that no trust had ever been created, and that in any case, the trust had been revoked. From a decision in favor of the executor, the widow appealed.

HOWARD, J. . . . The essential elements of a trust are: (a) A competent settlor and trustee; (b) clear and unequivocal intent to create a trust; (c) an ascertainable trust res; and (d) sufficiently identifiable beneficiaries.

Appellee [executor] contends that no trust was created in this instance because the settlor, Mr. Barnette, failed to have the stock transferred on the corporation books to himself as trustee and did not execute the assignment on the reverse side of the stock certificates. We do not agree with this contention. The owner of shares of stock in a corporation may make himself trustee of the shares for another by oral or written declaration of the trust without a delivery of any document to the beneficiary or any change in the corporation's records. . . . Where the settlor is also the trustee, Scott on Trusts, 3rd Ed. § 32.5 states:

> "We have been considering the situation that arises when the owner of property conveys it to another person as Trustee. Where he declares himself Trustee of the property, however, it is obvious that the delivery of the subject matter . . . is neither necessary nor appropriate. Since his intention is to retain title to the property, although he is to hold it for the benefit of another, it is clear that it would be inconsistent with his intention for him to surrender the property."

Further, Restatement (Second) of Trusts, § 17 at 59 states: "A trust may be created by: (a) a declaration by the owner of property that he holds it as Trustee for another person; . . . ." The comment on clause (a) states that "if the owner of property declares himself trustee of the property, a trust may be created without a transfer of title to the property." It is therefore clear that Mr. Barnette created a valid trust.

[The court sustained the widow's claim that a valid trust had been created but held that the trust had been revoked and affirmed the judgment of the lower court in favor of the executor.]

Mesler v Holly

(FlaApp) 318 So2d 530 (1975)

Frederick Way transferred property to himself and Elaine Holly as trustees for the benefit of Frederick for life. On his death, Gussler replaced him as co-trustee and the trust continued for the benefit of Elaine. The trust declaration gave her and Gussler "absolute discretion [to] distribute so much of the trust estate as the co-trustees deem necessary to maintain the standard of living to which Elaine J. Holly has become accustomed. . . . It is the intent of the settlor to grant a life estate to Elaine J. Holly with right of invasion of principal in order to maintain the standard of living to which Elaine J. Holly has become accustomed." The trust declaration provided that on the death of Elaine the fund held in trust should pass to another trust created by the settlor for the benefit of his great grandchildren. A suit was brought by these children against Holly and Gussler claiming that they were spending too much of the trust fund and that they were never stating what was done with the money. The trustees defended on the ground that they had been given "absolute discretion." The lower court sustained this defense and dismissed the action. The plaintiffs appealed.

McNulty, C.J. . . . Even though a grant of "absolute discretion" to a fiduciary is very broad, it does not relieve a trustee from the exercise of good faith or from being judicious in his administration of the trust, which administration is always subject to review by the court in appropriate instances. Likewise, a trustee is always subject to accountability to remaindermen where discretion is improperly, arbitrarily, or capriciously exercised.

Moreover, . . . where, as here, a trustee is also the sole lifetime beneficiary, such factor is a viable judicial consideration in determining whether the trustee is properly exercising discretionary powers. Concededly, determination of Elaine J. Holly's standard of living is, in the first instance, a function and responsibility of the trustees. While perhaps a court should not fix the criteria for exercise of the discretionary power of the trustees to invade the principal, it certainly may review the exercise of such power. We think, too, that when a trustee is peculiarly influential in making such determination for her own benefit, her discretion in the premises becomes particularly vulnerable to a challenge by remaindermen. And, we apprehend the legitimacy of the plaintiffs' concern where, as here, (1) there is no requirement for the trustees to post a bond for faithful performance of their duties, (2) either trustee may withdraw funds from any bank account in the name of the trust, and (3), as the trial court determined, there is no specific requirement in the trust instrument to furnish any inventory, accounting or other information to the remaindermen beneficiaries until their eligibility for receiving distribution.

Clearly, a trustee who is also a beneficiary and who is given a power, or discretion, to invade the trust principal has a fiduciary obligation to the remaindermen to keep her demands within reasonable limits. Even an unlimited power of invasion is subject to implied limitations to protect the remaindermen.

We hold, therefore, that allegations that a trustee is the sole lifetime beneficiary, that she has not furnished any accounts or reports of her administration to the remaindermen, and that she is not confining her invasions of principal to reasonable limits, as may be set out in the complaint, give rise to an inference of abuse of discretion by the trustee and are sufficient to require the trustee to respond. Trustees are accountable to the courts and their performance may be controlled by the courts. If the evidence discloses any abuse of discretion on the part of a trustee or co-trustees in distributing principal to a lifetime beneficiary, particularly if such beneficiary is a trustee, then the trial court can order appropriate adjustments to correct any abuses in the past and take steps (e.g., to require bonding of trustees, periodic accountings to remaindermen and appropriate supervisory measures) to prevent abuses in the future. . . .

[Judgment reversed and action remanded]

Rosenauer v Title Insurance and Trust Co.

30 CalApp3d 300, 106 CalRptr 321 (1973)

Elizabeth Rosenauer transferred property in trust to the Title Insurance and Trust Company (TI) under a written declaration of trust which specified that she could amend or change the trust "at any time during her lifetime . . . by an instrument in writing executed by [her] and delivered to the trustee." The trust declaration made no statement as to a total revocation of the trust but § 2280 of the California Civil Code declares "unless expressly made irrevocable by the instrument creating the trust, every voluntary trust shall be revocable by the testator by writing filed with the trustee." By her will, Elizabeth expressly revoked the trust. After her death the will was admitted to probate. Robert Rosenauer, the executor under the will, brought an action to determine if the trust had been revoked. The court held that the will did not revoke the trust. The executor appealed.

COMPTON, A.J. . . . According to plaintiff, [the Civil Code] embodies the California preference for free alienability of property and revocability of trusts. Thus he contends that the statute should control regardless of the recitals in the trust instrument concerning the method of revocation. Plaintiff's position is that since the statute contains no requirement that the revocation be filed with the trustee during the life of the trustor and since the statute does not exclude "will" from the definition of a "writing," his filing of the will with the TI after the death of deceased complies with the statute.

The Restatement of Trusts, section 330(1), comment (j) provides as follows:

> "If the settlor reserves a power to revoke the trust only in a particular manner or under particular circumstances, he can revoke the trust only in that manner or under those circumstances. If the settlor reserves a power to revoke the trust by transaction inter vivos, as for example, by a notice to the trustee, he cannot revoke the trust by his will."

Case law throughout the country is found to be in support of the Restatement view.

In Leahy v Old Colony Trust Co., 326 Mass 49, 93 NE2d 238, the Supreme Judicial Court of Massachusetts held that a trust was not revoked by a will under facts similar to our own case. In so holding the court stated at page 240:

> "Plainly Jennie M. Luhrs could not alter or revoke the trust except in accordance with some power to do so reserved in the trust instrument. . . . The power of amendment or revocation, reserved in the trust instrument, was a power to do so only 'during the lifetime of said Jennie M. Luhrs.' A will does not take effect during the lifetime of the testator, but operates only from and after his death."

In National Shawmut Bank of Boston v Joy, 315 Mass 457, 470-471, 53 NE2d 113, 122, it was said:

> . . . "A testamentary disposition becomes operative only upon and by reason of the death of the owner who makes it. It operates only upon what he leaves at his death. If the interest in question passes from the owner presently, while he remains alive, the transfer is inter vivos and not testamentary. Accordingly, it is settled that a power to revoke 'during the lifetime' of the settlor, which means by a revocation taking effect before the death of the settlor cannot be exercised by a will that in

the nature of things cannot take effect before the death of the testator.''. . .

While Civil Code section 2280 was undoubtedly intended to liberalize the power of revocation in California we do not believe it was intended to operate as a nullification of a trustor's plainly expressed preference for a mode of revocation.

The thrust of the statute is to remove any doubt concerning the revocability of a voluntary trust which is silent on the subject and it cannot be construed as creating an exclusive method for the exercise of the power when as here the trust is not silent but instead quite specific.

[Judgment affirmed]

Wright's Estate

17 IllApp3d 894, 308 NE2d 319 (1974)

Charles Wright opened a savings account in the Farmers State Bank. The account was marked "Charles Wright, Pay on Death to Mary Lowe." It was not intended that Mary should have any right to withdraw money from the account while Charles was alive. Charles thereafter died. By his will, he left his entire estate to his sons. Nothing was said in the will about the bank account. Both Mary and the sons claimed the balance on deposit in the account. The lower court entered judgment in favor of the sons and Mary appealed.

ALLOY, J. . . . It is principally maintained by appellant that decedent, in opening and maintaining the account in question, established a so-called "Totten" or tentative trust, which device was recognized as valid in Illinois by our Supreme Court in the case of In re Petralia, 32 Ill2d 134, 204 NE2d 1 (1965) by the following language (at 138, 20 NE2d at 3).

"We accept the position adopted by the American Law Institute in Section 58 of the Restatement (second) of Trusts: 'Where a person makes a deposit in a savings account in a bank or other savings organization in his own name as trustee for another person intending to reserve a power to withdraw the whole or any part of the deposit at any time during his lifetime and to use as his own whatever he may withdraw, or otherwise revoke the trust, the intended trust is enforceable by the beneficiary

upon the death of the depositor as to any part remaining on deposit on his death if he has not revoked the trust.' "

In support of the proposition that a recognized "Totten" or tentative trust was here created, appellant refers us to, *inter alia,* the following circumstances: at the time the account in question was opened, the decedent apparently withdrew $2,000 from his regular savings account (held in his name alone) and immediately used such money to fund the new account. Further, decedent continued to make significant deposits to the account in question throughout the rest of his life, while making only one withdrawal of $500, which withdrawal was "made up" with a deposit in the amount of $500 only 9 days later. Decedent and appellant were affectionate friends; their plans for marriage being thwarted, however, by the condition of decedent's health.

Appellant points out that the primary object of all rules of construction in interpretation is to arrive at and give effect to the mutual intentions of the parties as expressed in the whole agreement and the circumstances surrounding the transaction.

"In the interpretation of any particular trust agreement, the Court is required to examine the entire agreement and it may also consider the relation of the parties, their connection with the subject matter of the agreement, the circumstances under which it was made, and the purpose for which it was made.''. . .

Appellee, on the other hand, argues that "payable on death" accounts in banks are alien to the common law, and until rendered effective by affirmative legislative action, they must be held violative of public policy unless in compliance with the Statute of Wills (Ill.Rev.Stat. 1971, ch. 3, § 43). It is further maintained by appellee that the evidence adduced below failed to establish that decedent created a "present interest" in appellant in the purported trust *res* during the lifetime of decedent, a recognized requisite of a valid *inter vivos* trust. . . . In support of these conclusions, appellee relies heavily upon the case of In re Estate of Gubala, 81 IllApp2d 378, 225 NE2d 646 (1st Dist., 1967), where a "payable on death" account held in a savings and loan association was upheld, but only because of the existence of specific enabling legislation providing therefor (Ill. Rev.Stat., ch. 32, § 770(c)), which legislation is not applicable to accounts held in banks.

While the court in *Gubala* categorized "payable on death" accounts as pure testamentary dispositions, we do not think that is perforce true in all cases where the words "payable on death" or their equivalent appear in the title of an account. We believe, rather, that each case must be decided upon its own facts, and although it is true that the words "Pay upon Death" appear in the name of the account *sub judice,* it is also true that largely all of the indicia surrounding the creation of a "Totten" trust are equally in being. Thus, it was shown below that decedent and appellant had been close and affectionate friends; that, indeed, marriage had been contemplated, but rejected due to decedent's ill health. Decedent clearly established the account in question with an intent to benefit appellant, as he apparently transferred funds from an account held in his name alone in order to originally fund the new account, which named appellant a beneficiary thereof, and while it is true that he manifested an intent that appellant's possession and enjoyment of the account would not occur until his death, that is a feature of many *inter vivos* trusts given judicial sanction. . . .

"The Declaration of trust immediately creates an equitable interest in the beneficiaries although the enjoyment of the interest is postponed until the death of the settlor, and although the interest may be divested by the exercise of the power of revocation. The fact that the beneficiary's actual enjoyment of the trust is contingent on [the settlor's] death without having revoked the trust by withdrawing the balance in the account does not negate the existence of a present interest in the [beneficiary] during [the settlor's] lifetime, even though that interest may have been highly destructible."

Under the circumstances, we do not believe it may properly be said, as maintained by appellee, that appellant had no "present interest" in the account during the lifetime of decedent. On the contrary, she was a beneficiary named in the account and in our judgment thus held a present, although wholly defeasible, interest therein contemporaneous with decedent's superior rights. The latter's death, however, terminated his rights, and rendered appellant's indefeasible.

That we find, in accordance with the foregoing, that a tentative trust has been here established would seem to end our inquiry. However, a further argument advanced by appellant in our view serves as a basis for an alternate holding which we deem to be valid whether or not decedent established a trust in creating the account in question. We accordingly deem it wise to consider appellant's alternate theory, which maintains that the decedent in this case entered into a perfectly valid contract with the bank naming her as a third-party beneficiary thereto. As such, she is entitled to whatever funds were contained in the account at decedent's death, pursuant to the explicit terms of the contract. In support of this proposition, we are referred, *inter alia* to 4 Corbin on Contracts, Sec. 783, at pages 89-90 (1951), where it is said as follows:

"Rarely has the third party been regarded as the beneficiary of a contract between A [the depositor] and the bank. This is due either to insufficient analysis or to the uncertainty and conflict that until recently existed in third party beneficiary law. In all cases, so long as there is no fraud on A's creditors, C [the named beneficiary] should get the money that A has not drawn out . . . as . . . beneficiary of the banking debtor's promise to the creditor [depositor].". . .

We find appellant's third-party beneficiary contract theory quite compelling and entirely consistent with sound principles of jurisprudence. (See: Dudley v Uptown National Bank of Moline, 25 IllApp2d 514, 527-529, 167 NE2d 257 (2d Dist., 1960), where the third-party beneficiary theory advanced herein was made, but was found by the court to be inapplicable under the facts before it.) It is absolutely clear that decedent named appellant as the death beneficiary of the account in question, and it is equally clear that he entered into a binding contractual arrangement with the bank in connection therewith. There being no rights of creditors or a surviving spouse here in question, we see no legally cogent reason for thwarting the decedent's clear dispositive intent concerning the sums held in the account at decedent's death.

In accordance with the foregoing, we find that decedent either established a valid "Totten" trust with respect to the account in question, or entered into a valid third-party beneficiary contract naming appellant as the beneficiary thereof. In either case, appellant is entitled to all sums in the account at the time of decedent's death.

[Judgment reversed and action remanded]

Simonds v Simonds

58 AppDiv2d 305, 396 NYS2d 547 (1977)

Mary was the wife of Frederick Simonds. She was the beneficiary of insurance policies on his life. Later they were divorced and as part of the settlement agreement, Frederick agreed to maintain insurance on his life and that not less than $7,000 of the insurance proceeds should be payable to Mary. Frederick allowed the policies of insurance to lapse but later acquired other policies in which Reva, his second wife, and Gayle, their daughter, were named as beneficiaries. On his death, Reva and Gayle claimed the insurance proceeds. Mary brought a suit claiming that they should be declared to hold $7,000 of such insurance proceeds as constructive trustees for Mary. From a decision in Mary's favor, Reva and Gayle appealed.

SIMONS, J. . . . We are asked to determine whether plaintiff had a vested interest in this subsequently acquired policy and, if so, whether the court may impose a constructive trust in her favor upon the proceeds. Defendant contends that we may not, because the policy was not one of the original policies in which plaintiff acquired a vested right but new insurance . . . and because she has not been guilty of any wrong-doing. It is her contention that plaintiff is limited to a legal action against the estate for breach of contract. . . .

Normally, one who purchases a life insurance policy and pays the premiums may change the beneficiary at will if he retains that right under the terms of the policy . . . However, the separation agreement between plaintiff and decedent contained mutual promises and agreements to forbear which constituted legal consideration and created a vested right in plaintiff to the extent of $7,000 in the insurance policies on decendent's life, notwithstanding any right which he possessed to change the beneficiary under the terms of the policies. After the execution of the separation agreement, the designation of plaintiff as beneficiary became irrevocable and could not be changed without her consent . . .

If the insurer has paid over the proceeds to the substituted beneficiary, a plaintiff may proceed directly against the substituted beneficiary and obtain relief by way of a constructive trust. . . .

In this case, however, the original policies subject to the agreement no longer existed at the time

of decedent's death. They had lapsed and had been replaced. . . . Because the original policies were no longer in existence, defendant contends that relief by use of a constructive trust is improper because there is no *res* against which a trust may be imposed. This argument misapprehends the nature of constructive trusts.

A constructive trust is not a trust at all in the substantive sense of the word. It is a remedial device created by the court to compel a person who holds legal title to property subject to an equitable duty to convey to another, to do so because he would be unjustly enriched if he were permitted to retain the property. The defendant is not compelled to convey the property because he is a trustee; he is a trustee because the court determines that he has an equitable duty to convey it (Restatement, Restitution, § 160, Comments [a], [c]). . . .

> "A constructive trust is the formula through which the conscience of equity finds expression. When property has been acquired in such circumstances that the holder of the legal title may not in good conscience retain the beneficial interest, equity converts him into a trustee.". . .

Since a constructive trust is only a remedial device fashioned by equity to right a wrong, formal requirements of substantive trust law need not be found before a court may grant relief. . . .

Decedent might have defeated plaintiff's remedy here by allowing these insurance policies to lapse without replacing them. She would then have possessed no alternative except a contract action against the estate. . . . However, decedent replaced the lapsed policies, not in the principal amount of the original policies, $21,000, but with new insurance having a face value in excess of $55,000, and the equitable rights of plaintiff attached to those replacement policies as decedent had agreed they would and as the divorce decree ordered that they should. . . . For purposes of restitution, the necessity of a *res,* if a *res* is required, is easily satisfied by tracing these life insurance proceeds, specifically promised to plaintiff, into the hands of defendant.

Defendant concedes the existence of the policies, the execution of the separation agreement and the validity of the decree enforcing it. By the terms of the contract and decree, plaintiff acquired equitable rights in the prior policies and their replacements and the only issue remaining is whether a constructive trust may be imposed upon $7,000 plus interest from the proceeds of those policies now in defendant's hands.

It is frequently said that the remedy of constructive trust is used to correct some act of fraud or breach of duty or confidence. Our courts have enumerated the elements which must exist before a constructive trust may be imposed: (1) a confidential relationship, (2) a promise, (3) a transfer in reliance thereon, and (4) unjust enrichment. The mere breach of the agreement is not sufficient to impose a constructive trust. Decedent must have abused a confidential or fiduciary relationship. . . . At the time the parties executed this separation agreement a confidential relationship existed between them during which plaintiff was induced to give up her legal marital rights in exchange for decedent's mutual promises which expressly included his promise to provide insurance. . . . When the decedent subsequently breached his promise and failed to maintain the insurance, his estate was unjustly enriched because the premium expenses which he incurred were limited to satisfying his financial responsibilities to his child and second wife. In doing so, he ignored his contract obligation to plaintiff, an obligation he assumed because his responsibility for regular support payments had been reduced in consideration of the deferred payment of life insurance proceeds to plaintiff upon his death. Property which should have been paid to her or to her benefit was diverted by him to other uses.

Decedent's wrong is clear enough and if defendant participated in it, a trust might readily be imposed against her. . . . Plaintiff does not allege any wrong on defendant's part, however, and defendant contends that since she is innocent of any wrongdoing, a constructive trust may not be imposed upon her.

The right to this relief does not depend upon the commission of a tort or a crime by the possessor of the property, and the enrichment may be unjust although not unlawful or wrongful. Thus, it is said that a constructive trust may be imposed upon property transferred by mistake or even in a case in which it has been received by an innocent donee, if the donee is unjustly enriched. . . .

Unless the recipient of the property is a bona fide purchaser, she may not retain property which decedent has transferred to her in violation of plaintiff's equitable rights. . . .

Obviously, this defendant was a donee and not a bona fide purchaser. Without giving consideration, she received $7,000 in life insurance proceeds which decedent had promised for good and valuable consideration to pay to plaintiff. It is against equity and good conscience that defendant be permitted to retain the money. . . . The circumstances in this case permit the inference that the decedent and defendant have been unjustly enriched by decedent's failure to keep his contract . . . and the imposition of a constructive trust on the insurance proceeds in defendant's possession is appropriate to secure a just result to this plaintiff. . . .

[Judgment affirmed]

QUESTIONS AND CASE PROBLEMS

1. What social forces are affected by the rule of law authorizing the enforcement or application of constructive trusts?

2. Compare an executor, a trustee, and an agent with respect to (a) formality of appointment, (b) fiduciary duty, and (c) duration of authority.

3. Compare a tentative trust and a true trust with respect to (a) intent, (b) revocability, and (c) rights of creditors.

4. Compare an absolute gift to (a) a charity and (b) a private person with respect to the rights of the donee in each case.

5. Berry owned a business which he transferred by deed to his sons in trust to operate and to pay the income in a specified manner. Some years later, after the death of Berry and of several of the sons, a suit was brought by some of the beneficiaries to require the trustee to invest $104,000 that had been held in the trust and remained uninvested

for 14 years and to compel the trustee to insure the trust property that had not been covered by insurance. Decide. [Berry v McCourt, 1 Ohio App2d 172, 204 NE2d 235]

6. William and Walter Asher were trustees under the will of J. M. Asher, deceased. As trustees, they loaned money to themselves at a low rate of interest, without security, and paid commissions to themselves from principal. Morrison, a beneficiary of the trust, brought an action to have them removed as trustees. Decide. [Morrison v Asher, (MoApp) 361 SW2d 844]

7. By his will, Owsley left money to Bell as trustee to hold as a scholarship fund to pay tuition for worthy students attending "Carthage College, Carthage, Illinois." After her death, Carthage College moved to Wisconsin. Another college in Carthage, Illinois claimed that the trust fund should be held for its benefit under the cy pres doctrine. Was it correct? [Bell v Carthage College, 103 IllApp2d 289, 243 NE2d 23]

8. By his will, Biles, directed that the balance of his estate be given to such charitable organization or organizations as his executors should select. Objection was made that this gave the executors authority to apply the cy pres doctrine. Was this correct? [Biles v Martin (Ala) 259 So2d 258]

9. Burton wrote a will of 3 sentences. In the first she named her brother as the "executor and trustee" of her estate. In the next sentence she left her property to her brother. In the last sentence she stated "My Brother knows my wishes and will carry them out, to the best of his ability." After her death, the brother claimed her entire estate for himself. The heirs claimed that there was no trust and that the estate should therefore pass to them. Was the brother correct? [Burton v Irwin, 212 Va 104, 181 SE2d 624]

Appendix • How to Find the Law

In order to determine what the law on a particular question or issue is, it may be necessary to examine (1) compilations of constitutions, treaties, statutes, executive orders, proclamations, and administrative regulations; (2) reports of state and federal court decisions; (3) digests of opinions; (4) treatises on the law; and (5) loose-leaf services.

Compilations

In the consideration of a legal problem in business it is necessary to determine whether the matter is affected or controlled by the Constitution, national or state; by a national treaty; by an Act of Congress or a state legislature, or by a city ordinance; by a decree or proclamation of the President of the United States, a governor, or a mayor; or by a regulation of a federal, state, or local administrative agency.

Each body or person that makes laws, regulations, or ordinances usually will compile and publish at the end of each year or session all of the matter that it has adopted. In addition to the periodical or annual volumes, it is common to compile all the treaties, statutes, regulations, or ordinances in separate volumes. To illustrate, the federal Anti-Injunction Act may be cited as the Act of March 23, 1932, 47 Stat 70, 29 USC Sections 101 et seq. This means that this law was enacted on March 23, 1932, and that this law can be found at page 70 in Volume 47 of the reports that contain all of the statutes adopted by the Congress.

The second part of the citation, 29 USC Sections 101 et seq., means that in the collection of all of the federal statutes, which is known as the United States Code, the full text of the statute can be found in the sections of the 29th title beginning with Section 101.

Court Decisions

For complicated or important legal cases or when an appeal is to be taken, a court will generally write an *opinion,* which explains why the court made the decision. Appellate courts as a rule write opinions. The great majority of these decisions, particularly in the case of the appellate courts, are collected and printed. In order to avoid confusion, the opinions of each court will ordinarily be printed in a separate set of reports, either by official reporters or private publishers.

In the reference "Pennoyer v Neff, 95 US 714, 24 LEd 565," the first part states the names of the parties. It does not necessarily tell who was the plaintiff and who was the defendant. When an action is begun in a lower court, the first name is that of the plaintiff and the second name that of the defendant. When the case is appealed, generally the name of the person taking the appeal appears on the records of the higher court as the first one and that of the adverse party as the second. Sometimes, therefore, the original order of the names of the parties is reversed.

The balance of the reference consists of two citations. The first citation, 95 US 714, means that the opinion which the court filed in the case of Pennoyer and Neff may be found on page 714 of the 95th volume of a series of books in which are printed officially the opinions of the United States Supreme Court. Sometimes the same opinion is printed in two different sets of volumes. In the example, 24 LEd 565 means that in the 24th volume of another set of books, called *Lawyers' Edition,* of the United States Supreme Court Reports, the same opinion begins on page 565.

In opinions by a state court there are also generally two citations, as in the case of "Morrow v Corbin, 122 Tex 553, 62 SW2d 641." This means that the opinion in the lawsuit between Morrow and Corbin may be found in the 122d volume of the reports of the highest court of Texas, beginning on page 553; and also in Volume 62 of the *Southwestern Reporter,* Second Series, at page 641.

The West Publishing Company publishes a set of sectional reporters covering the entire United States. They are called sectional because each reporter, instead of being limited to a particular court or a particular state, covers the decisions of the courts of a particular section of the country. Thus the decisions of the courts of Arkansas, Kentucky, Missouri, Tennessee, and Texas are printed by the West Publishing company as a group in a sectional reporter called the *Southwestern Reporter.*[1] Because of the large number of decisions involved, generally only the opinions of the state appellate courts are printed. A number of states [2] have discontinued publication of the opinions of their courts, and those opinions are now found only in the West reporters.

The reason for the "Second Series" in the Southwestern citation is that when there were 300 volumes in the original series, instead of calling the next volume 301, the publisher called it Volume 1, Second Series. Thus 62 SW2d Series really means the 362d volume of the *Southwestern Reporter.* Six to eight volumes appear in a year for each geographic section.

In addition to these state reporters, the West Publishing Company publishes a *Federal Supplement,* which primarily reports the opinions of the Federal District Courts; the *Federal Reporter,* which primarily reports the decisions of the United States Courts of Appeals; and the *Supreme Court Reporter,* which reports the decisions of the United States Supreme Court. The Supreme Court decisions are also reported in a separate set called the *Lawyers' Edition,* published by the Lawyers Co-operative Publishing Company.

The reports published by the West Publishing Company and Lawyers Co-operative Publishing Company are unofficial reports, while those bearing the name or abbreviation of the United States or of a state, such as "95 US 714" or "122 Tex 553" are official reports. This means that in the case of the latter, the particular court, such as the United States Supreme Court, has officially authorized that its decisions be printed and that by federal statute such official printing is made. In the case of the unofficial reporters, the publisher prints the decisions of a court on its own initiative. Such opinions are part

---

[1] The sectional reporters are: Atlantic—A. (Connecticut, Delaware, District of Columbia, Maine, Maryland, New Hampshire, New Jersey, Pennsylvania, Rhode Island, Vermont); Northeastern—N.E. (Illinois, Indiana, Massachusetts, New York, Ohio); Northwestern—N.W. (Iowa, Michigan, Minnesota, Nebraska, North Dakota, South Dakota, Wisconsin); Pacific—P. (Alaska, Arizona, California, Colorado, Hawaii, Idaho, Kansas, Montana, Nevada, New Mexico, Oklahoma, Oregon, Utah, Washington, Wyoming); Southeastern—S.E. (Georgia, North Carolina, South Carolina, Virginia, West Virginia); Southwestern—S.W. (Arkansas, Kentucky, Missouri, Tennessee, Texas); and Southern—So. (Alabama, Florida, Louisiana, Mississippi). There is also a special New York State reporter known as the New York Supplement and a special California State reporter known as the California Reporter.
[2] See, for example, Alaska, Florida, Iowa, Kentucky, Louisiana, Maine, Mississippi, Missouri, North Dakota, Oklahoma, Texas, and Wyoming.

of the public domain and not subject to any copyright or similar restriction.

Digests of Opinions

The reports of court decisions are useful only if one has the citation, that is, the name and volume number of the book and the page number of the opinion one is seeking. For this reason, digests of the decisions have been prepared. These digests organize the entire field of law under major headings, which are then arranged in alphabetic order. Under each heading, such as "Contracts," the subject is divided into the different questions that can arise with respect to that field. A master outline is thus created on the subject. This outline includes short paragraphs describing what each case holds and giving its citation.

Treatises and Restatements

Very helpful in finding a case or a statute are the treatises on the law. These may be special books, each written by an author on a particular subject, such as *Williston on Contracts, Bogert on Trusts, Fletcher on Corporations,* or they may be general encyclopedias, as in the case of *American Jurisprudence, American Jurisprudence, Second,* and *Corpus Juris Secundum.*

Another type of treatise is found in the restatements of the law prepared by the American Law Institute. Each restatement consists of one or more volumes devoted to a particular phase of the law, such as the *Restatement of the Law of Contracts, Restatement of the Law of Agency,* and *Restatement of the Law of Property.* In each restatement the American Law Institute, acting through special committees of judges, lawyers, and professors of law, has set forth what the law is; and in many areas where there is no law or the present rule is regarded as unsatisfactory, the restatement specifies what the Institute deems to be the desirable rule.

Loose-Leaf Services

A number of private publishers, notably Commerce Clearing House and Prentice-Hall, publish loose-leaf books devoted to particular branches of the law. Periodically the publisher sends to the purchaser a number of pages that set forth any decision, regulation, or statute made or adopted since the prior set of pages was prepared. Such services are unofficial.

Glossary

A

abandon: give up or leave employment; relinquish possession of personal property with intent to disclaim title.

abate: put a stop to a nuisance; reduce or cancel a legacy because the estate of the decedent is insufficient to make payment in full.

ab initio: from the beginning.

abrogate: recall or repeal; make void or inoperative.

absolute liability: liability for an act that causes harm even though the actor was not at fault.

absolute privilege: protection from liability for slander or libel given under certain circumstances to statements regardless of the fact that they are false or maliciously made.

abstract of title: history of the transfers of title to a given piece of land, briefly stating the parties to and the effect of all deeds, wills, and judicial proceedings relating to the land.

acceleration clause: provision in a contract or any legal instrument that upon a certain event the time for the performance of specified obligations shall be advanced; for example, a provision making the balance due upon debtor's default.

acceptance: unqualified assent to the act or proposal of another; as the acceptance of a draft (bill of exchange), of an offer to make a contract, of goods delivered by the seller, or of a gift or a deed.

accession: acquisition of title to personal property by virtue of the fact that it has been attached to property already owned or was the offspring of an owned animal.

accessory after the fact: one who after the commission of a felony knowingly assists the felon.

accessory before the fact: one who is absent at the commission of the crime but who aided and abetted its commission.

accident: an event that occurs even though a reasonable person would not have foreseen its occurrence, because of which the law holds no one responsible for the harm caused.

accommodation party: a person who signs a commercial paper to lend credit to another party to the paper.

accord and satisfaction: an agreement to substitute a different performance for that called for in the contract and the performance of that substitute agreement.

accretion: the acquisition of title to additional land when the owner's land is built up by gradual deposits made by the natural action of water.

acknowledgment: an admission or confirmation, generally of an instrument and usually made before a person authorized to administer oaths, as a notary public; the purpose being to declare that the instrument was executed by the person making the instrument, or that it was a voluntary act or that that person desires that it be recorded.

action: a proceeding to enforce any right.

action in personam: an action brought to impose liability upon a person, such as a money judgment.

action in rem: an action brought to declare the status of a thing, such as an action to declare the title to property to be forfeited because of its illegal use.

action of assumpsit: a common-law action brought to recover damages for breach of a contract.

action of ejectment: a common-law action brought to recover the possession of land.

action of mandamus: a common-law action brought to compel the performance of a ministerial or clerical act by an officer.

action of quo warranto: a common-law action brought to challenge the authority of an officer to act or to hold office.

action of replevin: a common-law action brought to recover the possession of personal property.

action of trespass: a common-law action brought to recover damages for a tort.

act of bankruptcy: any of the acts specified by the national bankruptcy law which, when committed by the debtor within the four months preceding the filing of the petition in bankruptcy, is proper ground for declaring the debtor a bankrupt.

act of God: a natural phenomenon that is not reasonably foreseeable.

administrative agency: a governmental commission or board given authority to regulate particular matters.

administrator—administratrix: the person (man—woman) appointed to wind up and settle the estate of a person who has died without a will.

adverse possession: the hostile possession of real estate, which when actual, visible, notorious, exclusive, and continued for the required time, will vest the title to the land in the person in such adverse possession.

advisory opinion: an opinion that may be rendered in a few states when there is no actual controversy before the court and the matter is submitted by private persons, or in some instances by the governor of the state, to obtain the court's opinion.

affidavit: a statement of facts set forth in written form and supported by the oath or affirmation of the person making the statement setting forth that such facts are true on the basis of actual knowledge or on information and belief. The affidavit is executed before a notary public or other person authorized to administer oaths.

affinity: the relationship that exists by virtue of marriage.

affirmative covenant: an express undertaking or promise in a contract or deed to do an act.

agency: the relationship that exists between a person identified as a principal and another by virtue of which the latter may make contracts with third persons on behalf of the principal. (Parties—principal, agent, third person)

agency coupled with an interest in the authority: an agency in which the agent has given a consideration or has paid for the right to exercise the authority granted to him.

agency coupled with an interest in the subject matter: an agency in which for a consideration the agent is given an interest in the property to which the agency relates.

agency shop: a union contract provision requiring that non-union employees pay to the union the equivalent of union dues in order to retain their employment.

agent: one who is authorized by the principal or by operation of law to make contracts with third persons on behalf of the principal.

allonge: a paper securely fastened to a commercial paper in order to provide additional space for indorsements.

alluvion: the additions made to land by accretion.

alteration: any material change of the terms of a writing fraudulently made by a party thereto.

ambulatory: not effective and therefore may be changed, as in the case of a will that is not final until its maker has died.

amicable action: an action that all parties agree should be brought and which is begun by the filing of

such an agreement, rather than by serving the adverse parties with process. Although the parties agree to litigate, the dispute is real, and the decision is not an advisory opinion.

amicus curiae: literally, a friend of the court; one who is appointed by the court to take part in litigation and to assist the court by furnishing an opinion in the matter.

annexation: attachment of personal property to realty in such a way as to make it become real property and part of the realty.

annuity: a contract by which the insured pays a lump sum to the insurer and later receives fixed annual payments.

anomalous indorser: a person who signs a commercial paper but is not otherwise a party to the instrument.

anticipatory breach: the repudiation by a promisor of the contract prior to the time that performance is required when such repudiation is accepted by the promisee as a breach of the contract.

anti-injunction acts: statutes prohibiting the use of injunctions in labor disputes except under exceptional circumstances; notably the federal Norris-La Guardia Act of 1932.

Anti-Petrillo Act: a federal statute that makes it a crime to compel a radio broadcasting station to hire musicians not needed, to pay for services not performed, or to refrain from broadcasting music of school children or from foreign countries.

antitrust acts: statutes prohibiting combinations and contracts in restraint of trade, notably the federal Sherman Antitrust Act of 1890, now generally inapplicable to labor union activity.

appeal: taking the case to a reviewing court to determine whether the judgment of the lower court or administrative agency was correct. (Parties—appellant, appellee)

appellate jurisdiction: the power of a court to hear and decide a given class of cases on appeal from another court or administrative agency.

arbitration: the settlement of disputed questions, whether of law or fact, by one or more arbitrators by

whose decision the parties agree to be bound. Increasingly used as a procedure for labor dispute settlement.

assignment: transfer of a right. Generally used in connection with personal property rights, as rights under a contract, commercial paper, an insurance policy, a mortgage, or a lease. (Parties—assignor, assignee)

assumption of risk: the common-law rule that an employee could not sue the employer for injuries caused by the ordinary risks of employment on the theory that the employee had assumed such risks by undertaking the work. The rule has been abolished in those areas governed by workmen's compensation laws and most employers' liability statutes.

attachment: the seizure of property of, or a debt owed to, the debtor by the service of process upon a third person who is in possession of the property or who owes a debt to the debtor.

attractive nuisance doctrine: a rule imposing liability on a landowner for injuries sustained by small children playing on the land when the landowner permits a condition to exist or maintains equipment that a reasonable person should realize would attract small children who could not realize the danger. The rule does not apply if an unreasonable burden would be imposed on the landowner in taking steps to protect the children.

authenticate: make or establish as genuine, official, or final, as by signing, countersigning, sealing, or any other act indicating approval.

B

bad check laws: laws making it a criminal offense to issue a bad check with intent to defraud.

baggage: such articles of necessity or personal convenience as are usually carried for personal use by passengers of common carriers.

bail: variously used in connection with the release of a person or property from the custody of the law, referring (a) to the act of releasing or bailing, (b) to the persons who assume liability in the event that the released person does not appear or it is held that the property should not be released, and (c) to the bond or sum of money that is furnished the court or other official as indemnity for nonperformance of the obligation.

bailee's lien: a specific, possessory lien of the bailee on the goods for work done to them. Commonly extended by statute to any bailee's claim for compensation and eliminating the necessity of retention of possession.

bailment: the relation that exists when personal property is delivered into the possession of another under an agreement, express or implied, that the identical property will be returned or will be delivered in accordance with the agreement. (Parties—bailor, bailee)

bankruptcy: a procedure by which one unable to pay debts may be declared a bankrupt, after which all assets in excess of any exemption claim are surrendered to the court for administration and distribution to creditors, and the debtor is given a discharge that releases from the unpaid balance due on most debts.

bearer: the person in physical possession of commercial paper payable to bearer, a document of title directing delivery to bearer, or an investment security in bearer form.

beneficiary: the person to whom the proceeds of a life insurance policy are payable, a person for whose benefit property is held in trust, or a person given property by a will.

bequest: a gift of personal property by will.

bill of exchange (draft): an unconditional order in writing by one person upon another, signed by the person giving it, and ordering the person to whom it is directed to pay on demand or at a definite time a sum certain in money to order or to bearer.

bill of lading: a document issued by a carrier reciting the receipt of goods and the terms of the contract of transportation. Regulated by the federal Bills of Lading Act or the Uniform Commercial Code.

bill of sale: a writing signed by the seller reciting that the personal property therein described has been sold to the buyer.

binder: a memorandum delivered to the insured stating the essential terms of a policy to be executed in the future, when it is agreed that the contract of insurance is to be effective before the written policy is executed.

blank indorsement: an indorsement that does not name the person to whom the paper, document of title, or investment security is negotiated.

blue-sky laws: state statutes designed to protect the public from the sale of worthless stocks and bonds.

boardinghouse keeper: one regularly engaged in the business of offering living accommodations to permanent lodgers or boarders.

bona fide: in good faith; without any fraud or deceit.

bond: an obligation or promise in writing and sealed, generally of corporations, personal representatives, trustees; fidelity bonds.

boycott: a combination of two or more persons to cause harm to another by refraining from patronizing or dealing with such other person in any way or inducing others to so refrain; commonly an incident of labor disputes.

bulk sales acts: statutes to protect creditors of a bulk seller. Notice must be given creditors, and the bulk sale buyer is liable to the seller's creditors if the statute is not satisfied. Expanded to "bulk transfers" under the UCC.

business trust: a form of business organization in which the owners of the property to be devoted to the business transfer the title of the property to trustees with full power to operate the business.

C

cancellation: a crossing out of a part of an instrument or a destruction of all legal effect of the instrument, whether by act of party, upon breach by the other party, or pursuant to agreement or decree of court.

capital: net assets of a corporation.

capital stock: the declared money value of the outstanding stock of the corporation.

cash surrender value: the sum paid the insured on the surrender of a policy to the insurer.

cause of action: the right to damages or other judicial relief when a legally protected right of the plaintiff is violated by an unlawful act of the defendant.

caveat emptor: let the buyer beware. This maxim has been nearly abolished by warranty and strict tort liability concepts.

certificate of protest: a written statement by a notary public setting forth the fact that the holder had presented the commercial paper to the primary party and that the latter had failed to make payment.

cestui que trust: the beneficiary or person for whose benefit the property is held in trust.

charter: the grant of authority from a government to exist as a corporation. Generally replaced today by a certificate of incorporation approving the articles of incorporation.

chattel mortgage: a security device by which the owner of personal property transfers the title to a creditor as security for the debt owed by the owner to the creditor. Replaced under the Uniform Commercial Code by a secured transaction. (Parties—chattel mortgagor, chattel mortgagee)

chattels personal: tangible personal property.

chattels real: leases of land and buildings.

check: an order by a depositor on a bank to pay a sum of money to a payee; a bill of exchange drawn on a bank and payable on demand.

chose in action: intangible personal property in the nature of claims against another, such as a claim for accounts receivable or wages.

chose in possession: tangible personal property.

circumstantial evidence: relates to circumstances surrounding the facts in dispute from which the trier of fact may deduce what had happened.

civil action: in many states a simplified form of action combining all or many of the former common-law actions.

civil court: a court with jurisdiction to hear and determine controversies relating to private rights and duties.

closed shop: a place of employment in which only union members may be employed. Now generally prohibited.

codicil: a writing by one who has made a will which is executed with all the formality of a will and is treated as an addition to or modification of the will.

coinsurance: a clause requiring the insured to maintain insurance on property up to a stated amount and providing that to the extent that this is not done the insured is to be deemed a coinsurer with the insurer, so that the latter is liable only for its proportionate share of the amount of insurance required to be carried.

collateral note: a note accompanied by collateral security.

collective bargaining: the process by which the terms of employment are agreed upon through negotiations between the employer or employers within a given industry or industrial area and the union or the bargaining representative of the employees.

collective bargaining unit: the employment area within which employees are by statute authorized to select a bargaining representative, who is then to represent all the employees in bargaining collectively with the employer.

collusion: an agreement between two or more persons to defraud the government or the courts, as by obtaining a divorce by collusion when no grounds for a divorce exist, or to defraud third persons of their rights.

color of title: circumstances that make a person appear to be the owner when in fact not the owner, as the existence of a deed appearing to convey the property to a given person gives color of title although the deed is worthless because it is in fact a forgery.

commission merchant: a bailee to whom goods are consigned for sale.

common carrier: a carrier that holds out its facilities to serve the general public for compensation without discrimination.

common law: the body of unwritten principles originally based on the usages and customs of the community which were recognized and enforced by the courts.

common stock: stock that has no right or priority over any other stock of the corporation as to dividends or distribution of assets, upon dissolution.

common trust fund: a plan by which the assets of small trust estates are pooled into a common fund, each trust being given certificates representing its proportionate ownership of the fund, and the pooled fund is then invested in investments of large size.

community property: the cotenancy held by husband and wife in property acquired during their marriage under the law of some of the states, principally in the southwestern United States.

complaint: the initial pleading filed by the plaintiff in many actions which in many states may be served as original process to acquire jurisdiction over the defendant.

composition of creditors: an agreement among creditors that each shall accept a part payment as full payment in consideration of the other creditors doing the same.

concealment: the failure to volunteer information not requested.

conditional estate: an estate that will come into being upon the satisfaction of a condition precedent or that will be terminated upon the satisfaction of a condition subsequent.

conditional sale: a credit transaction by which the buyer purchases on credit and promises to pay the purchase price in installments, while the seller retains the title to the goods, together with the right of repossession upon default, until the condition of payment in full has been satisfied. The conditional sale

is replaced under the Uniform Commercial Code by a secured transaction.

confidential relationship: a relationship in which, because of the legal status of the parties or their respective physical or mental conditions or knowledge, one party places full confidence and trust in the other.

conflict of laws: the body of law that determines the law of which state is to apply when two or more states are involved in the facts of a given case.

confusion of goods: the mixing of goods of different owners that under certain circumstances results in one of the owners becoming the owner of all the goods.

consanguinity: relationship by blood.

consideration: the promise or performance that the promisor demands as the price of the promise.

consignment: a bailment made for the purpose of sale by the bailee. (Parties—consignor, consignee)

consolidation of corporations: a combining of two or more corporations in which the corporate existence of each one ceases and a new corporation is created.

constructive: an adjective employed to indicate that the noun which is modified by it does not exist but the law disposes of the matter as though it did; as a constructive bailment or a constructive trust.

contingent beneficiary: the person to whom the proceeds of a life insurance policy are payable in the event that the primary beneficiary dies before the insured.

contract: a binding agreement based upon the genuine assent of the parties, made for a lawful object, between competent parties, in the form required by law, and generally supported by consideration.

contract carrier: a carrier who transports on the basis of individual contracts that it makes with each shipper.

contract to sell: a contract to make a transfer of title in the future as contrasted with a present transfer.

contribution: the right of a co-obligor who has paid more than a proportionate share to demand that the other obligor pay the amount of the excess payment made.

contributory negligence: negligence of the plaintiff that contributes to injury and at common law bars from recovery from the defendant although the defendant may have been more negligent than the plaintiff.

conveyance: a transfer of an interest in land, ordinarily by the execution and delivery of a deed.

cooling-off period: a procedure designed to avoid strikes by requiring a specified period of delay before the strike may begin during which negotiations for a settlement must continue.

cooperative: a group of two or more persons or enterprises that act through a common agent with respect to a common objective, as buying or selling.

copyright: a grant to an author or artist of an exclusive right to publish and sell the copyrighted work for the life of the author or artist and fifty years thereafter.

corporation: an artificial legal person or being created by government grant, which for many purposes is treated as a natural person.

cost plus: a method of determining the purchase price or contract price by providing for the payment of an amount equal to the costs of the seller or contractor to which is added a stated percentage as the profit.

costs: the expenses of suing or being sued, recoverable in some actions by the successful party, and in others, subject to allocation by the court. Ordinarily they do not include attorney's fees or compensation for loss of time.

counterclaim: a claim that the defendant in an action may make against the plaintiff.

covenants of title: covenants of the grantor in a deed that guarantee such matters as the right to make the conveyance, ownership of the property, freedom of the property from encumbrances, or that the grantee will not be disturbed in the quiet enjoyment of the land.

crime: a violation of the law that is punished as an offense against the state or government.

cross complaint: a claim that the defendant may make against the plaintiff.

cross-examination: the examination made of a witness by the attorney for the adverse party.

cumulative voting: a system of voting for directors in which each shareholder has as many votes as the number of voting shares owned multiplied by the number of directors to be elected, which votes can be distributed for the various candidates as desired.

cy pres doctrine: the rule under which a charitable trust will be carried out as nearly as possible in the way the settlor desired, when for any reason it cannot be carried out exactly in the way or for the purposes expressed.

D

damages: a sum of money recovered to redress or make amends for the legal wrong or injury done.

damnum absque injuria: loss or damage without the violation of a legal right, or the mere fact that a person sustains a loss does not mean that legal rights have been violated.

declaratory judgment: a procedure for obtaining the decision of a court on a question before any action has been taken or loss sustained. It differs from an advisory opinion in that there must be an actual, imminent controversy.

dedication: acquisition by the public or a government of title to land when it is given over by its owner to use by the public and such gift is accepted.

deed: an instrument by which the grantor (owner of land) conveys or transfers the title to a grantee.

de facto: existing in fact as distinguished from as of right, as in the case of an officer or a corporation purporting to act as such without being elected to the office or having been properly incorporated.

deficiency judgment: a personal judgment for the amount still remaining due the mortgagee after foreclosure, which is entered against any person liable on the mortgage debt. Statutes generally require the mortgagee to credit the fair value of the property against the balance due when the mortgagee has purchased the property. Also, a similar judgment entered by a creditor against a debtor in a secured transaction under Article 9 of the UCC.

del credere agent: an agent who sells goods for the principal and who guarantees to the principal that the buyer will pay for the goods.

delegation: the transfer to another of the right and power to do an act.

de minimis non curat lex: a maxim that the law is not concerned with trifles. Not always applied, as in the case of the encroachment of a building over the property line, in which case the law will protect the landowner regardless of the extent of the encroachment.

demonstrative evidence: evidence that consists of visible, physical objects, as a sample taken from the wheat in controversy or a photograph of the subject matter involved.

demonstrative legacy: a legacy to be paid or distributed from a specified fund or property.

demurrage: a charge made by the carrier for the unreasonable detention of cars by the consignor or consignee.

demurrer: a pleading that may be filed to attack the sufficiency of the adverse party's pleading as not stating a cause of action or a defense.

dependent relative revocation: the doctrine recognized in some states that if a testator revokes or cancels a will in order to replace it with a later will, the earlier will is to be deemed revived if for any reason the later will does not take effect or no later will is executed.

deposition: the testimony of a witness taken out of court before a person authorized to administer oaths.

devise: a gift of real estate made by will.

directed verdict: a direction by the trial judge to the jury to return a verdict in favor of a specified party to the action.

directors: the persons vested with control of the corporation, subject to the elective power of the shareholders.

discharge in bankruptcy: an order of the bankruptcy court discharging the bankrupt debtor from the unpaid balance of most claims.

discharge of contract: termination of a contract by performance, agreement, impossibility, acceptance of breach, or operation of law.

discovery: procedures for ascertaining facts prior to the time of trial in order to eliminate the element of surprise in litigation.

dishonor by nonacceptance: the refusal of the drawee to accept a draft (bill of exchange).

dishonor by nonpayment: the refusal to pay a commercial paper when properly presented for payment.

dismiss: a procedure to terminate an action by moving to dismiss on the ground that the plaintiff has not pleaded a cause of action entitling the plaintiff to relief.

disparagement of goods: the making of malicious, false statements as to the quality of the goods of another.

distress for rent: the common-law right of the lessor to enter the premises when the rent has not been paid and to seize all personal property found on the premises. Statutes have modified or abolished this right in many states.

distributive share: the proportionate part of the estate of the decedent that will be distributed to an heir or legatee, and also as devisee in those jurisdictions in which real estate is administered as part of the decedent's estate.

domestic bill of exchange: a draft drawn in one state and payable in the same or another state.

domestic corporation: a corporation that has been incorporated by the state as opposed to incorporation by another state.

domicile: the home of a person or the state of incorporation, to be distinguished from a place where a person lives but does not regard as home, or a state in which a corporation does business but in which it was not incorporated.

double indemnity: a provision for payment of double the amount specified by the insurance contract if death is caused by an accident and occurs under specified circumstances.

double jeopardy: the principle that a person who has once been placed in jeopardy by being brought to trial at which the proceedings progressed at least as far as having the jury sworn cannot thereafter be tried a second time for the same offense.

draft: see bill of exchange.

draft-varying acceptance: one in which the acceptor's agreement to pay is not exactly in conformity with the order of the instrument.

due care: the degree of care that a reasonable person would exercise to prevent the realization of harm, which under all the circumstances was reasonably forseeable in the event that such care were not taken.

due process of law: the guarantee by the 5th and 14th amendments of the federal Constitution and of many state constitutions that no person shall be deprived of life, liberty, or property without due process of law. As presently interpreted, this prohibits any law, either state or federal, that sets up an unfair procedure or the substance of which is arbitrary or capricious.

duress: conduct that deprives the victim of free will and which generally gives the victim the right to set aside any transaction entered into under such circumstances.

E

easement: a permanent right that one has in the land of another, as the right to cross another's land or easement of way.

eleemosynary corporation: a corporation organized for a charitable or benevolent purpose.

embezzlement: a statutory offense consisting of the unlawful conversion of property entrusted to the wrongdoer.

eminent domain: the power of a government and certain kinds of corporations to take private property against the objection of the owner, provided the taking is for a public purpose and just compensation is made therefor.

encumbrance: a right held by a third person in or a lien or charge against property, as a mortgage or judgment lien on land.

equity: the body of principles that originally developed because of the inadequacy of the rules then applied by the common-law courts of England.

erosion: the loss of land through a gradual washing away by tides or currents, with the owner losing title to the lost land.

escheat: the transfer to the state of the title to a decedent's property when the owner of property dies intestate not survived by anyone capable of taking the property as heir.

escrow: a conditional delivery of property or of a deed to a custodian or escrow holder, who in turn makes final delivery to the grantee or transferee when a specified condition has been satisfied.

estate: the extent and nature of one's interest in land; the assets constituting a decedent's property at the time of death, or the assets of a bankrupt.

estate in fee simple: the largest estate possible in which the owner has the absolute and entire property in the land.

estoppel: the principle by which a person is barred from pursuing a certain course of action or of disputing the truth of certain matters.

evidence: that which is presented to the trier of fact as the basis on which the trier is to determine what happened.

exception: an objection, as an exception to the admission of evidence on the ground that it was hearsay; a clause excluding particular property from the operation of a deed.

ex contractu: a claim or matter that is founded upon or arises out of a contract.

ex delicto: a claim or matter that is founded upon or arises out of a tort.

execution: the carrying out of a judgment of a court, generally directing that property owned by the defendant be sold and the proceeds first used to pay the execution or judgment creditor.

exemplary damages: damages in excess of the amount needed to compensate for the plaintiff's injury, which are awarded in order to punish the defendant for malicious or wanton conduct; also punitive.

exoneration: an agreement or provision in an agreement that one party shall not be held liable for loss; the right of the surety to demand that those primarily liable pay the claim for which the surety is secondarily liable.

expert witness: one who has acquired special knowledge in a particular field through practical experience, or study, or both, whose opinion is admissible as an aid to the trier of fact.

ex post facto law: a law making criminal an act that was lawful when done or that increases the penalty when done. Such laws are generally prohibited by constitutional provisions.

extraordinary bailment: a bailment in which the bailee is subject to unusual duties and liabilities, as a hotelkeeper or common carrier.

F

factor: a bailee to whom goods are consigned for sale.

factors' acts: statutes protecting persons who buy in good faith for value from a factor although the goods had not been delivered to the factor with the consent or authorization of their owner.

fair employment practice acts: statutes designed to eliminate discrimination in employment in terms of race, religion, national origin, or sex.

fair labor standards acts: statutes, particularly the federal statute, designed to prevent excessive hours of employment and low pay, the employment of young children, and other unsound practices.

featherbedding: the exaction of money for services not performed, which is made an unfair labor practice generally and a criminal offense in connection with radio broadcasting.

Federal Securities Act: a statute designed to protect the public from fraudulent securities.

Federal Securities Exchange Act: a statute prohibiting improper practices at and regulating security exchanges.

Federal Trade Commission Act: a statute prohibiting unfair methods of competition in interstate commerce.

fellow-servant rule: a common-law defense of the employer that barred an employee from suing an employer for injuries caused by a fellow employee.

felony: a criminal offense that is punishable by confinement in prison or by death, or that is expressly stated by statute to be a felony.

financial responsibility laws: statutes that require a driver involved in an automobile accident to prove financial responsibility in order to retain a license, which responsibility may be shown by procuring public liability insurance in a specified minimum amount.

financing factor: one who lends money to manufacturers on the security of goods to be manufactured thereafter.

firm offer: an offer stated to be held open for a specified time, which must be so held in some states even in the absence of an option contract, or under the Code, with respect to merchants.

fixture: personal property that has become so attached to or adapted to real estate that it has lost its character as personal property and is part of the real estate.

Food, Drug, and Cosmetic Act: a federal statute prohibiting the interstate shipment of misbranded or adulterated foods, drugs, cosmetics, and therapeutic devices.

forbearance: refraining from doing an act.

foreclosure: procedure for enforcing a mortgage resulting in the public sale of the mortgaged property and less commonly in merely barring the right of the mortgagor to redeem the property from the mortgage.

foreign (international) bill of exchange: a bill of exchange made in one nation and payable in another.

foreign corporation: a corporation incorporated under the laws of another state.

forgery: the fraudulent making or altering of an instrument that apparently creates or alters a legal liability of another.

franchise: (a) a privilege or authorization, generally exclusive, to engage in a particular activity within a particular geographic area, as a government franchise to operate a taxi company within a specified city, or a private franchise as the grant by a manufacturer of a right to sell products within a particular territory or for a particular number of years; (b) the right to vote.

fraud: the making of a false statement of a past or existing fact with knowledge of its falsity or with reckless indifference as to its truth with the intent to cause another to rely thereon, and such person does rely thereon and is harmed thereby.

freight forwarder: one who contracts to have goods transported and, in turn, contracts with carriers for such transportation.

fructus industriales: crops that are annually planted and raised.

fructus naturales: fruits from trees, bushes, and grasses growing from perennial roots.

fungible goods: goods of a homogenous nature of which any unit is the equivalent of any other unit or is treated as such by mercantile usage.

future advance mortgage: a mortgage given to secure additional loans to be made in the future as well as an original loan.

G

garnishment: the name given in some states to attachment proceedings.

general creditor: a creditor who has a claim against the debtor but does not have any lien on any of the debtor's property, whether as security for debt or by way of a judgment or execution upon a judgment.

general damages: damages that in the ordinary course of events follow naturally and probably from the injury caused by the defendant.

general legacy: a legacy to be paid out of the assets generally of the decedent without specifying any particular fund or source from which the payment is to be made.

general partnership: a partnership in which the partners conduct as co-owners a business for profit, and each partner has a right to take part in the management of the business and has unlimited liability.

gift causa mortis: a gift made by the donor in the belief that death was immediate and impending, which gift is revoked or is revocable under certain circumstances.

grace period: a period generally of 30 or 31 days after the due date of a premium of life insurance in which the premium may be paid.

grand jury: a jury not exceeding 23 in number that considers evidence of the commission of crime and prepares indictments to bring offenders to trial before a petty jury.

grant: convey real property; an instrument by which such property has been conveyed, particularly in the case of a government.

gratuitous bailment: a bailment in which the bailee does not receive any compensation or advantage.

grievance settlement: the adjustment of disputes relating to the administration or application of existing contracts as compared with disputes over new terms of employment.

guarantor: one who undertakes the obligation of guaranty.

guaranty: an undertaking to pay the debt of another if the creditor first sues the debtor and is unable to recover the debt from the debtor or principal. (In some instances the liability is primary, in which case it is the same as suretyship.)

H

hearsay evidence: statements made out of court which are offered in court as proof of the information contained in the statements, which, subject to many exceptions, are not admissible in evidence.

hedging: the making of simultaneous contracts to purchase and to sell a particular commodity at a future date with the intention that the loss on one transaction will be offset by the gain on the other.

heirs: those persons specified by statute to receive the estate of a decedent not disposed of by will.

holder: the person in possession of a commercial paper payable to that person as payee or indorsee, or the person in possession of a commercial paper payable to bearer.

holder in due course: a holder of a commercial paper who is favored and is given an immunity from certain defenses.

holder through a holder in due course: a person who is not a holder in due course but is a holder of the paper after it was held by some prior party who was a holder in due course, and who is given the same rights as a holder in due course.

holographic will: a will written by hand.

hotelkeeper: one regularly engaged in the business of offering living accommodations to all transient persons.

hung jury: a petty jury that has been unable to agree upon a verdict.

I

ignorantia legis non excusat: ignorance of the law is not an excuse.

implied contract: a contract expressed by conduct or implied or deduced from the facts. Also used to refer to a quasi-contract.

imputed: vicariously attributed to or charged to another, as the knowledge of an agent obtained while acting in the scope of authority is imputed to the principal.

incidental authority: authority of an agent that is reasonably necessary to execute express authority.

incontestable clause: a provision that after the lapse of a specified time the insurer cannot dispute the policy on the ground of misrepresentation or fraud of the insured or similar wrongful conduct.

in custodia legis: in the custody of the law.

indemnity: the right of a person secondarily liable to require that a person primarily liable pay for loss sustained when the secondary party discharges the obligation which the primary party should have discharged; the right of an agent to be paid the amount of any loss or damage sustained without fault because of obedience to the principal's instructions; an undertaking by one person for a consideration to pay another person a sum of money to indemnify that person when a specified loss is incurred.

independent contractor: a contractor who undertakes to perform a specified task according to the terms of a contract but over whom the other contracting party has no control except as provided for by the contract.

indictment: a formal accusation of crime made by a grand jury which accusation is then tried by a petty or trial jury.

inheritance: the interest which passes from the decedent to the decedent's heirs.

injunction: an order of a court of equity to refrain from doing (negative injunction) or to do (affirmative or mandatory injunction) a specified act. Its use in labor disputes has been greatly restricted by statute.

in pari delicto: equally guilty; used in reference to a transaction as to which relief will not be granted to either party because both are equally guilty of wrongdoing.

insolvency: an excess of debts and liabilities over assets or inability to pay debts as they mature.

insurable interest: an interest in the nonoccurrence of the risk insured against, generally because such occurrence would cause financial loss, although sometimes merely because of the close relationship between the insured and the beneficiary.

insurance: a plan of security against risks by charging the loss against a fund created by the payments made by policyholders.

intangible personal property: an interest in an enterprise, such as an interest in a partnership or stock of a corporation, and claims against other persons, whether based on contract or tort.

interlineation: a writing between the lines or adding to the provisions of a document, the effect thereof depending upon the nature of the document.

interlocutory: an intermediate step or proceeding that does not make a final disposition of the action and from which ordinarily no appeal may be taken.

international bill of exchange: a bill or draft made in one nation and payable in another.

interpleader: a form of action or proceeding by which a person against whom conflicting claims are made may bring the claimants into court to litigate their claims between themselves, as in the case of a bailee when two persons each claim to be the owner of the bailed property, or an insurer when two persons each claim to be the beneficiary.

inter se: among or between themselves, as the rights of partners inter se or as between themselves.

inter vivos: any transaction which takes place between living persons and creates rights prior to the death of any of them.

intestate: the condition of dying without a will as to any property.

intestate succession: the distribution made as directed by statute of property owned by a decedent not effectively disposed of by will.

ipso facto: by the very act or fact in itself without any further action by any one.

irrebuttable presumption: a presumption which cannot be rebutted by proving that the facts are to the contrary; not a true presumption but merely a rule of law described in terms of a presumption.

irreparable injury to property: an injury that would be of such a nature or inflicted upon such an interest that it would not be reasonably possible to compensate the injured party by the payment of money damages because the property in question could not be purchased in the open market with the money damages which the defendant could be required to pay.

J

joint and several contract: a contract in which two or more persons are jointly and severally obligated or are jointly and severally entitled to recover.

joint contract: a contract in which two or more persons are jointly liable or jointly entitled to performance under the contract.

joint stock company: an association in which the shares of the members are transferable and control is delegated to a group or board.

joint tenancy: the estate held by two or more jointly with the right of survivorship as between them, unless modified by statute.

joint venture: a relationship in which two or more persons combine their labor or property for a single undertaking and share profits and losses equally unless otherwise agreed.

judgment: the final sentence, order, or decision entered into at the conclusion of the action.

judgment note: a promissory note containing a clause authorizing the holder of the note to enter judgment against the maker of the note if it is not paid when due. Also called cognovit note.

judgment n.o.v.: a judgment which may be entered after verdict upon the motion of the losing party on the ground that the verdict is so wrong that a judgment should be entered the opposite of the verdict, or non obstante veredicto (notwithstanding the verdict).

judgment on the pleadings: a judgment which may be entered after all the pleadings are filed when it is clear from the pleadings that a particular party is entitled to win the action without proceeding any further.

judicial sale: a sale made under order of court by an officer appointed to make the sale or by an officer having such authority as incident to the office. The sale may have the effect of divesting liens on the property.

jurisdiction: the power of a court to hear and determine a given class of cases; the power to act over a particular defendant.

jurisdictional dispute: a dispute between rival labor unions which may take the form of each claiming that particular work should be assigned to it.

justifiable abandonment by employee: the right of an employee to abandon employment because of nonpayment of wages, wrongful assault, the demand for the performance of services not contemplated, or injurious working conditions.

justifiable discharge of employee: the right of an employer to discharge an employee for nonperformance of duties, fraud, disobedience, disloyalty, or incompetence.

L

laches: the rule that the enforcement of equitable rights will be denied when the party has delayed so long that rights of third persons have intervened or the death or disappearance of witnesses would prejudice any party through the loss of evidence.

land: earth, including all things imbedded in or attached thereto, whether naturally or by the act of man.

last clear chance: the rule that a defendant who had the last clear chance to have avoided injuring the plaintiff is liable even though the plaintiff had also been contributorily negligent. In some states also called the humanitarian doctrine.

law of the case: matters decided in the course of litigation which are binding on the parties in the subsequent phases of litigation.

leading questions: questions which suggest the desired answer to the witness, or assume the existence of a fact which is in dispute.

lease: an agreement between the owner of property and a tenant by which the former agrees to give possession of the property to the latter in consideration of the payment of rent. (Parties—landlord or lessor, tenant or lessee)

leasehold: the estate or interest of a tenant in rented land.

legacy: a gift of personal property made by will.

legal tender: such form of money as the law recognizes as lawful and declares that a tender thereof in the proper amount is a proper tender which the creditor cannot refuse.

letters of administration: the written authorization given to an administrator as evidence of appointment and authority.

letters testamentary: the written authorization given to an executor as evidence of appointment and authority.

levy: a seizure of property by an officer of the court in execution of a judgment of the court, although in many states it is sufficient if the officer is physically in the presence of the property and announces the fact that it is "seized," but then allows the property to remain where it was found.

lex loci: the law of the place where the material facts occurred as governing the rights and liabilities of the parties.

lex loci contractus: the law of the place where the contract was made as governing the rights and liabilities of the parties to a contract with respect to certain matters.

lex loci fori: the law of the state in which the action is brought as determining the rules of procedure applicable to the action.

lex loci sitae rei: the law of the place where land is located as determining the validity of acts done relating thereto.

libel: written or visual defamation without legal justification.

license: a personal privilege to do some act or series of acts upon the land of another, as the placing of a sign thereon, not amounting to an easement or a right of possession.

lien: a claim or right against property existing by virtue of the entry of a judgment against its owner or by the entry of a judgment and a levy thereunder on the property, or because of the relationship of the claimant to the particular property, such as an unpaid seller.

life estate: an estate for the duration of a life.

limited jurisdiction: a court with power to hear and determine cases within certain restricted categories.

limited liability: loss of contributed capital or investment as maximum liability.

limited partnership: a partnership in which at least one partner has a liability limited to the loss of the capital contribution made to the partnership, and such a partner neither takes part in the management of the partnership nor appears to the public to be a partner.

lineal consanguinity: the relationship that exists when one person is a direct descendant from the other.

liquidated damages: a provision stipulating the amount of damages to be paid in event of default or breach of contract.

liquidation: the process of converting property into money whether of particular items of property or all the assets of a business or an estate.

lis pendens: the doctrine that certain types of pending actions are notice to everyone so that if any right is acquired from a party to such action, the transferee takes that right subject to the outcome of the pending action.

lobbying contract (illegal): a contract by which one party agrees to attempt to influence the action of a legislature or Congress, or any members thereof, by improper means.

lottery: any plan by which a consideration is given for a chance to win a prize.

lucri causa: with the motive of obtaining gain or pecuniary advantage.

M

majority: of age, as contrasted with being a minor; more than half of any group, as a majority of stockholders.

malice in fact: an intention to injure or cause harm.

malice in law: a presumed intention to injure or cause harm when there is no privilege or right to do the act in question, which presumption cannot be contradicted or rebutted.

maliciously inducing breach of contract: the wrong of inducing the breach of any kind of contract with knowledge of its existence and without justification.

malum in se: an offense that is criminal because contrary to the fundamental sense of a civilized community, as murder.

malum prohibitum: an offense that is criminal not because inherently wrong but is prohibited for the convenience of society, as overtime parking.

marshalling assets: the distribution of a debtor's assets in such a way as to give the greatest benefit to all creditors.

martial law: government exercised by a military commander over property and persons not in the armed forces, as contrasted with military law which governs the military personnel.

mechanics' lien: protection afforded by statute to various types of laborers and persons supplying materials, by giving them a lien on the building and land that has been improved or added to by them.

mens rea: the mental state that must accompany an act to make the act a crime. Sometimes described as the "guilty mind," although appreciation of guilt is not required.

merger by judgment: the discharge of a contract through being merged into a judgment which is entered in a suit on the contract.

merger of corporations: a combining of corporations by which one absorbs the other and continues to exist, preserving its original charter and identity while the other corporation ceases to exist.

misdemeanor: a criminal offense which is neither treason nor a felony.

misrepresentation: a false statement of fact although made innocently without any intent to deceive.

mobilia sequuntur personam: the maxim that personal property follows the owner and in the eyes of the law is located at the owner's domicile.

moratorium: a temporary suspension by statute of the enforcement of debts or the foreclosure of mortgages.

mortgage: an interest in land given by the owner to a creditor as security for the payment to the creditor of a debt, the nature of the interest depending upon the law of the state where the land is located. (Parties—mortgagor, mortgagee)

multiple insurers: insurers who agree to divide a risk so that each is only liable for a specified portion.

N

National Labor Management Relations Act: the federal statute, also known as the Taft-Hartley Act, designed to protect the organizational rights of labor and to prevent unfair labor practices by management or labor.

natural and probable consequences: those ordinary consequences of an act which a reasonable person would foresee.

negative covenant: an undertaking in a deed to refrain from doing an act.

negligence: the failure to exercise due care under the circumstances in consequence of which harm is proximately caused to one to whom the defendant owed a duty to exercise due care.

negligence per se: an action which is regarded as so improper that it is declared by law to be negligent in itself without regard to whether due care was otherwise exercised.

negotiable instruments: drafts, promissory notes, checks, and certificates of deposit in such form that greater rights may be acquired thereunder than by taking an assignment of a contract right; called negotiable commercial paper by the Code.

negotiation: the transfer of a commercial paper by indorsement and delivery by the person to whom then payable in the case of order paper, and by physical transfer in the case of bearer paper.

nominal damages: a nominal sum awarded the plaintiff in order to establish that legal rights have been violated although the plaintiff in fact has not sustained any actual loss or damages.

Norris-LaGuardia Anti-Injunction Act: a federal statute prohibiting the use of the injunction in labor disputes, except in particular cases.

notice of dishonor: notice given to parties secondarily liable that the primary party to the instrument has refused to accept the instrument or to make payment when it was properly presented for that purpose.

novation: the discharge of a contract between two parties by their agreeing with a third person that such third person shall be substituted for one of the original parties to the contract, who shall thereupon be released.

nudum pactum: a mere promise for which there is no consideration given and which therefore is ordinarily not enforceable.

nuisance: any conduct that harms or prejudices another in the use of his land or which harms or prejudices the public.

nuisance per se: an activity which is in itself a nuisance regardless of the time and place involved.

nuncupative will: an oral will made and declared by the testator in the presence of witnesses to be a will; generally made during the testator's last illness.

O

obiter dictum: that which is said in the opinion of a court in passing or by the way, but which is not necessary to the determination of the case and is therefore not regarded as authoritative as though it were actually involved in the decision.

obliteration: any erasing, writing upon, or crossing out that makes all or part of a will impossible to read, and which has the effect of revoking such part when done by the maker of the will with the intent of effecting a revocation.

occupation: taking and holding possession of property; a method of acquiring title to personal property after it has been abandoned.

open-end mortgage: a mortgage given to secure additional loans to be made in the future as well as the original loan.

operation of law: the attaching of certain consequences to certain facts because of legal principles that operate automatically, as contrasted with consequences which arise because of the voluntary action of a party designed to create those consequences.

opinion evidence: evidence not of what the witness observed but the conclusion drawn from what the witness has observed, or, in the case of expert witnesses, what has been observed in tests or experiments or what has been heard in court.

option contract: a contract to hold an offer to make a contract open for a fixed period of time.

P

paper title: the title of a person evidenced only by deeds or matter appearing of record under the recording statutes.

parol evidence rule: the rule that prohibits the introduction in evidence of oral or written statements made prior to or contemporaneously with the execution of a complete written contract, deed, or instrument, in the absence of clear proof of fraud, accident, or mistake causing the omission of the statement in question.

passive trust: a trust that is created without imposing any duty to be performed by the trustee and is therefore treated as an absolute transfer of the title to the trust beneficiary.

past consideration: something that has been performed in the past and which therefore cannot be consideration for a promise made in the present.

patent: the grant to an inventor of an exclusive right to make and sell an invention for a nonrenewable period of 17 years; a deed to land given by a government to a private person.

pawn: a pledge of tangible personal property rather than of documents representing property rights.

pecuniary legacy: a general legacy of a specified amount of money without indicating the source from which payment is to be made.

per autre vie: limitation of an estate. An estate held by *A* during the lifetime of *B* is an estate of *A* per autre vie.

per curiam opinion: an opinion written "by the court" rather than by a named judge when all the judges of the court are so agreed on the matter that it is not deemed to merit any discussion and may be simply disposed of.

perpetual succession: a phrase describing the continuing life of the corporation unaffected by the death of any stockholder or the transfer by stockholders of their stock.

perpetuities, rule against: a rule of law that prohibits the creation of an interest in property which will not become definite or vested until a date further away than 21 years after the death of persons alive at the time the owner of the property attempts to create the interest.

per se: in, through, or by itself.

person: a term that includes both natural persons, or living people, and artificial persons, as corporations which are created by act of government.

personal defenses: limited defenses that cannot be asserted by the defendant against a holder in due course. This term is not expressly used in Uniform Commercial Code.

per stirpes: according to the root or by way of representation. Distribution among heirs related to the decedent in different degrees, the property being divided into lines of descent from the decedent and the share of each line then divided within the line by way of representation.

petty jury: the trial jury of twelve. Also petit jury.

picketing: the placing of persons outside of places of employment or distribution so that by words or banners they may inform the public of the existence of a labor dispute.

pleadings: the papers filed by the parties in an action in order to set forth the facts and frame the issues to be tried, although under some systems, the pleadings merely give notice or a general indication of the nature of the issues.

pledge: a bailment given as security for the payment of a debt or the performance of an obligation owed to the pledgee. (Parties—pledgor, pledgee)

police power: the power to govern; the power to adopt laws for the protection of the public health, welfare, safety, and morals.

policy: the paper evidencing the contract of insurance.

polling the jury: the process of inquiring of each juror individually in open court as to whether the verdict announced in court was agreed to.

possession: exclusive dominion and control of property.

possessory lien: a right to retain possession of property of another as security for some debt or obligation owed the lienor which right continues only as long as possession is retained.

possibility of reverter: the nature of the interest held by the grantor after conveying land outright but subject to a condition or provision that may cause the grantee's interest to become forfeited and the interest to revert to the grantor or heirs.

postdate: to insert or place a later date on an instrument than the actual date on which it was executed.

power of appointment: a power given to another, commonly a beneficiary of a trust, to designate or appoint who shall be beneficiary or receive the fund after his death.

power of attorney: a written authorization to an agent by the principal.

precatory words: words indicating merely a desire or a wish that another use property for a particular purpose but which in law will not be enforced in the absence of an express declaration that the property shall be used for the specified purpose.

pre-emptive offer of shares: the right, subject to many exceptions, that each shareholder has that whenever the capital stock of the corporation is increased to be allowed to subscribe to such a percentage of the new shares as the shareholder's old shares bore to the former total capital stock.

preferred creditor: a creditor who by some statute is given the right to be paid first or before other creditors.

preferred stock: stock that has a priority or preference as to payment of dividends or upon liquidation, or both.

preponderance of evidence: the degree or quantum of evidence in favor of the existence of a certain fact when from a review of all the evidence it appears more probable that the fact exists than that it does not. The actual number of witnesses involved is not material nor is the fact that the margin of probability is very slight.

prescription: the acquisition of a right to use the land of another, as an easement, through the making of hostile, visible, and notorious use of the land, continuing for the period specified by the local law.

presumption: a rule of proof which permits the existence of a fact to be assumed from the proof that another fact exists when there is a logical relationship between the two or when the means of disproving the assumed fact are more readily within the control or knowledge of the adverse party against whom the presumption operates.

presumption of death: the rebuttable presumption which arises that a person has died when that person has been continuously absent and unheard of for a period of 7 years.

presumption of innocence: the presumption of fact that a person accused of crime is innocent until shown guilty of the offense charged.

presumption of payment: a rebuttable presumption that one performing continuing services which would normally be paid periodically, as weekly or monthly, has in fact been paid when a number of years have passed without any objection or demand for payment having been made.

presumptive heir: a person who would be the heir if the ancestor should die at that moment.

pretrial conference: a conference held prior to the trial at which the court and the attorneys seek to simplify the issues in controversy and eliminate matters not in dispute.

price: the consideration for sale of goods.

prima facie: such evidence as by itself would establish the claim or defense of the party if the evidence were believed.

primary beneficiary: the person designated as the first one to receive the proceeds of a life insurance policy, as distinguished from a contingent beneficiary who will receive the proceeds only if the primary beneficiary dies before the insured.

primary liability: the liability of a person whose act or omission gave rise to the cause of action and who in all fairness should therefore be the one to pay the victim even though others may also be liable for misconduct.

principal: one who employs an agent; the person who, with respect to a surety, is primarily liable to the third person or creditor.

principal in the first degree: one who actually engages in the commission or perpetration of a crime.

principal in the second degree: one who is actually or constructively present at the commission of the crime and who aids and abets in its commission.

private carrier: a carrier owned by the shipper, such as a company's own fleet of trucks.

privileged communication: information which the witness may refuse to testify to because of the relationship with the person furnishing the information, as husband-wife, attorney-client.

privilege from arrest: the immunity from arrest of parties, witnesses, and attorneys while present within the jurisdiction for the purpose of taking part in other litigation.

privity: a succession or chain of relationship to the same thing or right, as privity of contract, privity of estate, privity of possession.

probate: the procedure for formally establishing or proving that a given writing is the last will and testament of the person purporting to have signed it.

product liability: liability imposed upon the manufacturer or seller of goods for harm caused by a defect in the goods, embracing liability for (1) negligence, (2) fraud, (3) breach of warranty, and (4) strict tort.

profit à prendre: the right to take a part of the soil or produce of another's land, such as timber or water.

promissory estoppel: the doctrine that a promise will be enforced although it is not supported by consideration when the promisor should have reasonably expected that the promise would induce action or forbearance of a definite and substantial character on the part of the promisee, and injustice can only be avoided by enforcement of the promise.

promissory note: an unconditional promise in writing made by one person to another, signed by the maker engaging to pay on demand, or at a definite time, a sum certain in money to order or to bearer. (Parties—maker, payee)

promissory representation: a representation made by the applicant to the insurer as to what is to occur in the future.

promissory warranty: a representation made by the applicant to the insurer as to what is to occur in the future which the applicant warrants will occur.

promoters: the persons who plan the formation of the corporation and sell or promote the idea to others.

proof: the probative effect of the evidence; the conclusion drawn from the evidence as to the existence of particular facts.

property: the rights and interests one has in anything subject to ownership.

pro rata: proportionately, or divided according to a rate or standard.

protest: the formal certificate by a notary public or other authorized person that proper presentment of a commercial paper was made to the primary party and that such party defaulted, the certificate commonly also including a recital that notice was given to secondary parties.

proximate cause: the act which is the natural and reasonably foreseeable cause of the harm or event which occurs and injures the plaintiff.

proximate damages: damages which in the ordinary course of events are the natural and reasonably foreseeable result of the defendant's violation of the plaintiff's rights.

proxy: a written authorization by a shareholder to another person to vote the stock owned by the shareholder; the person who is the holder of such a written authorization.

public charge: a person who because of a personal disability or lack of means of support is dependent upon public charity or relief for sustenance.

public domain: public or government owned lands.

public easement: a right of way for use by members of the public at large.

public policy: certain objectives relating to health, morals, and integrity of government that the law seeks to advance by declaring invalid any contract which conflicts with those objectives even though there is no statute expressly declaring such contract illegal.

punitive damages: damages in excess of those required to compensate the plaintiff for the wrong done, which are imposed in order to punish the defendant because of the particularly wanton or willful character of wrongdoing; also exemplary.

purchase-money mortgage: a mortgage given by the purchaser of land to the seller to secure the seller for the payment of the unpaid balance of the purchase price, which the seller purports to lend the purchaser.

purchaser in good faith: a person who purchases without any notice or knowledge of any defect of title, misconduct, or defense.

Q

qualified acceptance: An acceptance of a draft that varies the order of the draft in some way.

qualified indorsement: an indorsement that includes words such as "without recourse" evidencing the intent that the indorser shall not be held liable for the failure of the primary party to pay the instrument.

quantum meruit: an action brought for the value of the services rendered the defendant when there was no express contract as to the payment to be made.

quantum valebant: an action brought for the value of goods sold the defendant when there was no express contract as to the purchase price.

quasi: as if, as though it were, having the characteristics of; a modifier employed to indicate that the subject is to be treated as though it were in fact the noun which follows the word "quasi:" as in quasi contract, quasi corporation, quasi public corporation.

quid pro quo: literally "what for what." An early form of the concept of consideration by which an action for debt could not be brought unless the defendant had obtained something in return for the obligation sued upon.

quitclaim deed: a deed by which the grantor purports only to give up whatever right or title the grantor may have in the property without specifying or warranting transfer of any particular interest.

quorum: the minimum number of persons, shares represented, or directors who must be present at a meeting in order that business may be lawfully transacted.

R

ratification by minor: the approval of a contract given by a minor after attaining majority.

ratification of agency: the approval of the unauthorized act of an agent or of a person who is not an agent for any purpose after the act has been done, which has the same effect as though the act had been authorized before it was done.

ratio decidendi: the reason or basis for deciding the case in a particular way.

ratio legis: the reason for a principle or rule of law.

real defenses: certain defenses (universal) that are available against any holder of a commercial paper, although this term is not expressly used by the Uniform Commercial Code.

real evidence: tangible objects that are presented in the courtroom for the observation of the trier of fact as proof of the facts in dispute or in support of the theory of a party.

real property: land and all rights in land.

reasonable care: the degree of care that a reasonable person would take under all the circumstances then known.

rebate: a refund made by the seller or the carrier of part of the purchase price or freight bill. Generally illegal as an unfair method of competition.

rebuttable presumption: a presumption which may be overcome or rebutted by proof that the actual facts were different than those presumed.

receiver: an impartial person appointed by a court to take possession of and manage property for the protection of all concerned.

recognizance: an obligation entered into before a court to do some act, such as to appear at a later date for a hearing. Also called a contract of record.

redemption: the buying back of one's property, which has been sold because of a default, upon paying the amount which had been originally due together with interest and costs.

referee: an impartial person selected by the parties or appointed by a court to determine facts or decide matters in dispute.

referee in bankruptcy: a referee appointed by a bankruptcy court to hear and determine various matters relating to bankruptcy proceedings.

reformation: a remedy by which a written instrument is corrected when it fails to express the actual intent of both parties because of fraud, accident, or mistake.

registration of titles: a system generally known as the Torrens system of permanent registration of title to all land within the state.

reimbursement: the right of one paying money on behalf of another, which such other person should have paid, to recover the amount of the payment from such other person.

release of liens: an agreement or instrument by which the holder of a lien on property such as a mortgage lien, releases the property from the lien although the debt itself is not discharged.

remedy: the action or procedure that is followed in order to enforce a right or to obtain damages for injury to a right.

remote damages: damages which were in fact caused by the defendant's act but the possibility that such damages should occur seemed so improbable and unlikely to a reasonable person that the law does not impose liability for such damages.

renunciation of duty: the repudiation of one's contractual duty in advance of the time for performance, which repudiation may be accepted as an anticipatory breach by the other contracting party.

renunciation of right: the surrender of a right or privilege, as the right to act as administrator or the right to receive a legacy under the will of a decedent.

reorganization of corporation: procedure devised to restore insolvent corporations to financial stability through readjustment of debt and capital structure either under the supervision of a court of equity or of bankruptcy.

repossession: any taking again of possession although generally used in connection with the act of a secured seller in taking back the property upon the default of the credit buyer.

representations: any statements, whether oral or written, made to give the insurer the information which it needs in writing the insurance, and which if false and relating to a material fact will entitle the insurer to avoid the contract.

representative capacity: action taken by one on behalf of another, as the act of a personal representative on behalf of a decedent's estate, or action taken both on one's behalf and on behalf of others, as a shareholder bringing a representative action.

rescission upon agreement: the setting aside of a contract by the action of the parties as though the contract had never been made.

rescission upon breach: the action of one party to a contract to set the contract aside when the other party is guilty of a breach of the contract.

residuary estate: the balance of the decedent's estate available for distribution after all administrative expenses, exemptions, debts, taxes, and legacies have been paid.

res inter alios acta: the rule that transactions and declarations between strangers having no connection with the pending action are not admissible in evidence.

res ipsa loquitur: the permissible inference that the defendant was negligent in that the thing speaks for itself when the circumstances are such that ordinarily the plaintiff could not have been injured had the defendant not been at fault.

res judicata: the principle that once a final judgment is entered in an action between the parties, it is binding upon them and the matter cannot be litigated again by bringing a second action.

respondeat superior: the doctrine that the principal or employer is vicariously liable for the unauthorized torts committed by an agent or employee while acting within the scope of the agency or the course of the employment, respectively.

restraints on alienation: limitations on the ability of the owner to convey freely as he chooses. Such limitations are generally regarded as invalid.

restrictive covenants: covenants in a deed by which the grantee agrees to refrain from doing specified acts.

restrictive indorsement: an indorsement that prohibits the further transfer, constitutes the indorsee the agent of the indorser, vests the title in the indorsee in trust for or to the use of some other person, is conditional, or is for collection or deposit.

resulting trust: a trust that is created by implication of law to carry out the presumed intent of the parties.

retaliatory statute: a statute that provides that when a corporation of another state enters the state it shall be subject to the same taxes and restrictions as would be imposed upon a corporation from the retaliating state if it had entered the other state. Also reciprocity statutes.

reversible error: an error or defect in court proceedings of so serious a nature that on appeal the appellate court will set aside the proceedings of the lower court.

reversionary interest: the interest that a lessor has in property which is subject to an outstanding lease.

revival of judgment: the taking of appropriate action to preserve a judgment, in most instances to continue the lien of the judgment that would otherwise expire after a specified number of years.

revival of will: the restoration by the writer of a will which had previously been revoked.

rider: a slip of paper executed by the insurer and intended to be attached to the insurance policy for the purpose of changing it in some respect.

riparian rights: the right of a person through whose land runs a natural watercourse to use the water free from unreasonable pollution or diversion by upper riparian owners and blocking by lower riparian owners.

risk: the peril or contingency against which the insured is protected by the contract of insurance.

Robinson-Patman Act: a federal statute designed to eliminate price discrimination in interstate commerce.

run with the land: the concept that certain covenants in a deed to land are deemed to "run" or pass with the land so that whoever owns the land is bound by or entitled to the benefit of the covenants.

S

sale or return: a sale in which the title to the property passes to the buyer at the time of the transaction but the buyer is given the option of returning the property and restoring the title to the seller.

scienter: knowledge, referring to those wrongs or crimes which require a knowledge of wrong in order to constitute the offense.

scope of employment: the area within which the employee is authorized to act with the consequence that a tort committed while so acting imposes liability upon the employer.

seal: at common law an impression on wax or other tenacious material attached to the instrument. Under modern law, any mark not ordinarily part of the signature is a seal when so intended, including the letters "L.S." and the word "seal," or a pictorial representation of a seal, without regard to whether they had been printed or typed on the instrument before its signing.

sealed verdict: a verdict that is rendered when the jury returns to the courtroom during an adjournment of the court, the verdict then being written down and sealed and later affirmed before the court when the court is in session.

secondary evidence: copies of original writings or testimony as to the contents of such writings which are admissible when the original cannot be produced and the inability to do so is reasonably explained.

secured transaction: a credit sale of goods or a secured loan that provides special protection for the creditor.

settlor: one who settles property in trust or creates a trust estate.

severable contract: a contract the terms of which are such that one part may be separated or severed from the other, so that a default as to one part is not necessarily a default as to the entire contract.

several contracts: separate or independent contracts made by different persons undertaking to perform the same obligation.

severalty: sole ownership of property by one person.

severed realty: real property that has been cut off and made moveable, as by cutting down a tree, and which thereby loses its character as real property and becomes personal property.

shareholder's action: an action brought by one or more shareholders on behalf of themselves and on behalf of all shareholders generally and of the corporation to enforce a cause of action of the corporation against third persons.

sheriff's deed: the deed executed and delivered by the sheriff to the purchaser at a sale conducted by the sheriff.

Sherman Antitrust Act: a federal statute prohibiting combinations and contracts in restraint of interstate trade, now generally inapplicable to labor union activity.

shop right: the right of an employer to use in business without charge an invention discovered by an employee during working hours and with the employer's material and equipment.

sight draft: a draft or bill of exchange payable on sight or when presented for payment.

sitdown strike: a strike in which the employees remain in the plant and refuse to allow the employer to operate it.

slander: defamation of character by spoken words or gestures.

slander of title: the malicious making of false statements as to a seller's title.

slowdown: a slowing down of production by employees without actual stopping work.

social security acts: statutes providing for assistance for the aged, blind, unemployed, and similar classes of persons in need.

special agent: an agent authorized to transact a specific transaction or to do a specific act.

special damages: damages that do not necessarily result from the injury to the plaintiff but at the same time are not so remote that the defendant should not be held liable therefor provided that the claim for special damages is properly made in the action.

special indorsement: an indorsement that specifies the person to whom the instrument is indorsed.

special jurisdiction: a court with power to hear and determine cases within certain restricted categories.

specific (identified) goods: goods which are so identified to the contract that no other goods may be delivered in performance of the contract.

specific lien: the right of a creditor to hold particular property or assert a lien on particular property of the debtor because of the creditor's having done work on or having some other association with the property; as distinguished from having a lien generally against the assets of the debtor merely because the debtor is indebted to the lienholder.

specific performance: an action brought to compel the adverse party to perform a contract on the theory that merely suing for damages for its breach will not be an adequate remedy.

spendthrift trust: a trust, which to varying degrees, provides that creditors of the beneficiary shall not be able to reach the principal or income held by the trustee and that the beneficiary shall not be able to assign any interest in the trust.

spoliation: an alteration or change made to a written instrument by a person who has no relationship to or interest in the writing. It has no effect as long as the terms of the instrument can still be ascertained.

stare decisis: the principle that the decision of a court should serve as a guide or precedent and control the decision of a similar case in the future.

status quo ante: the original positions of the parties to a contract prior to the making of the contract or the doing of some other act.

Statute of Frauds: a statute, which in order to prevent fraud through the use of perjured testimony, requires that certain types of transactions be evidenced in writing in order to be binding or enforceable.

Statute of Limitations: a statute that restricts the period of time within which an action may be brought.

stop delivery: the right of an unpaid seller under certain conditions to prevent a carrier or a bailee from delivering goods to the buyer.

stop payment: an order by a depositor to the bank to refuse to make payment of a check when presented for payment.

strict tort liability: a product liability theory which imposes liability on the manufacturer, seller, or distributor of goods for harm caused by defective goods.

sublease: a transfer of the premises by the lessee to a third person, the sublessee or subtenant, for a period of less than the term of the original lease.

subpoena: a court order directing a person to appear as a witness. In some states also it is the original process that is to be served on the defendant in order to give the court jurisdiction over the defendant.

subrogation: the right of a party secondarily liable to stand in the place of the creditor after making payment to the creditor and to enforce the creditor's right against the party primarily liable in order to obtain indemnity from such primary party.

subsidiary corporation: a corporation that is controlled by another corporation through the ownership by the latter of a controlling amount of the voting stock of the former.

subsidiary term: a provision of a contract that is not fundamental or does not go to the root of the contract.

substantial performance: the equitable doctrine that a contractor substantially performing a contract in good faith is entitled to recover the contract price less damages for noncompletion or defective work.

substantive law: the law that defines rights and liabilities.

substitution: discharge of contracts by substituting another in its place.

subtenant: one who rents the leased premises from the original tenant for a period of time less than the balance of the lease to the original tenant.

sui generis: in a class by itself, or its own kind.

sui juris: legally competent, possessing capacity.

summary judgment: a judgment entered by the court when no substantial dispute of fact is present, the court acting on the basis of affidavits or depositions which show that the claim or defense of a party is a sham.

summons: a writ by which an action was commenced under the common law.

supersedeas: a stay of proceedings pending the taking of an appeal or an order entered for the purpose of effecting such a stay.

suretyship: an undertaking to pay the debt or be liable for the default of another.

surrender: the yielding up of the tenant's leasehold estate to the lessor in consequence of which the lease terminates.

survival acts: statutes which provide that causes of action shall not terminate on death but shall survive and may be enforced by or against a decedent's estate.

survivorship: the right by which a surviving joint tenant or tenant by the entireties acquires the interest of the predeceasing tenant automatically upon the death of such tenant.

symbolic delivery: the delivery of goods by delivery of the means of control, as a key or relevant document of title, as a negotiable bill of lading.

syndicate: an association of individuals formed to conduct a particular business transaction, generally of a financial nature.

T

tacking: adding together successive periods of adverse possession of persons in privity with each other in order to constitute a sufficient period of continuous adverse possession to vest title thereby.

Taft-Hartley Act: popular name for the National Labor Management Relations Act of 1947.

tenancy at sufferance: the holding over by a tenant after a lease has expired of the rented land without the permission of the landlord and prior to the time that the landlord has elected to treat such possessor as a trespasser or a tenant.

tenancy at will: the holding of land for an indefinite period that may be terminated at any time by the landlord or by the landlord and tenant acting together.

tenancy for years: a tenancy for a fixed period of time, even though the time is less than a year.

tenancy from year to year: a tenancy which continues indefinitely from year to year until terminated.

tenancy in common: the relation that exists when two or more persons own undivided interests in property.

tenancy in partnership: the ownership relation that exists between partners under the Uniform Partnership Act.

tender of payment: an unconditional offer to pay the exact amount of money due at the time and place specified by the contract.

tender of performance: an unconditional offer to perform at the time and in the manner specified by the contract.

tentative trust: a trust which arises when money is deposited in a bank account in the name of the depositor "in trust for" a named person.

terminable fee: an estate that terminates upon the happening of a contingency without any entry by the grantor or heirs, as a conveyance for "so long as" the land is used for a specified purpose.

testamentary: designed to take effect at death, as by disposing of property or appointing a personal representative.

testate: the condition of leaving a will upon death.

testate succession: the distribution of an estate in accordance with the will of the decedent.

testator—testatrix: a man—woman who makes a will.

testimonium clause: a concluding paragraph in a deed, contract, or other instrument, reciting that the instrument has been executed on a specified date by the parties.

testimony: the answers of witnesses under oath to questions given at the time of the trial in the presence of the trier of fact.

theory of the case: the rule that when a case is tried on the basis of one theory, the appellant in taking an appeal cannot argue a different theory to the appellate court.

third party beneficiary: a third person whom the parties to a contract intend to benefit by the making of the contract and to confer upon such person the right to sue for breach of the contract.

tie-in sale: the requirement imposed by the seller that the buyer of particular goods or equipment also purchase certain other goods from the seller in order to obtain the original property desired.

time draft: a bill of exchange payable at a stated time after sight or at a definite time.

title insurance: a form of insurance by which the insurer insures the buyer of real property against the risk of loss should the title acquired from the seller be defective in any way.

toll the statute: stop the running of the period of the Statute of Limitations by the doing of some act by the debtor.

Torrens System: see registration of titles.

tort: a private injury or wrong arising from a breach of a duty created by law.

trade acceptance: a draft or bill of exchange drawn by the seller of goods on the purchaser at the time of sale and accepted by the purchaser.

trade fixtures: articles of personal property which have been attached to the freehold by a tenant and which are used for or are necessary to the carrying on of the tenant's trade.

trademark: a name, device, or symbol used by a manufacturer or seller to distinguish goods from those of other persons.

trade name: a name under which a business is carried on and, if fictitious, it must be registered.

trade secrets: secrets of any character peculiar and important to the business of the employer that have been communicated to the employee in the course of confidential employment.

treason: an attempt to overthrow or betray the government to which one owes allegiance.

treasury stock: stock of the corporation which the corporation has reacquired.

trier of fact: in most cases a jury, although it may be the judge alone in certain classes of cases, as in equity, or in any case when jury trial is waived, or an administrative agency or commission is involved.

trust: a transfer of property by one person to another with the understanding or declaration that such property be held for the benefit of another, or the holding of property by the owner in trust for another, upon a declaration of trust, without a transfer to another person. (Parties—settlor, trustee, beneficiary.)

trust corpus: the fund or property that is transferred to the trustee or held by the settlor as the body or subject matter of the trust.

trust deed: a form of deed which transfers the trust property to the trustee for the purposes therein stated, particularly used when the trustee is to hold the title to the mortgagor's land in trust for the benefit of the mortgage bondholders.

trustee de son tort: a person who is not a trustee but who has wrongly intermeddled with property of another and who is required to account for the property as though an actual trustee.

trustee in bankruptcy: an impartial person elected to administer the bankrupt's estate.

trust receipt: a credit security device under which the wholesale buyer executes a receipt stating that the buyer holds the purchased goods in trust for the person financing the purchase. The trust receipt is replaced by the secured transaction under the UCC.

U

uberrima fides: utmost good faith, a duty to exercise the utmost good faith which arises in certain relationships, as that between an insurer and the applicant for insurance.

ultra vires: an act or contract which the corporation does not have authority to do or make.

underwriter: an insurer.

undisclosed principal: a principal on whose behalf an agent acts without disclosing to the third person the fact of agency or the identity of the principal.

undue influence: the influence that is asserted upon another person by one who dominates that person.

unfair competition: the wrong of employing competitive methods that have been declared unfair by statute or an administrative agency.

unfair labor practice acts: statutes that prohibit certain labor practices and declare them to be unfair labor practices.

unincorporated association: a combination of two or more persons for the furtherance of a common nonprofit purpose.

union contract: a contract between a labor union and an employer or group of employers prescribing the general terms of employment of workers by the latter.

union shop: under present unfair labor practice statutes, a place of employment where nonunion workers may be employed for a trial period of not more than 30 days after which the nonunion workers must join the union or be discharged.

universal agent: an agent authorized by the principal to do all acts that can lawfully be delegated to a representative.

usury: the lending of money at greater than the maximum rate of interest allowed by law.

V

vacating of judgment: the setting aside of a judgment.

valid: legal.

verdict: the decision of the trial or petty jury.

void: of no legal effect and not binding on anyone.

voidable: a transaction that may be set aside by one party thereto because of fraud or similar reason but which is binding on the other party until the injured party elects to avoid.

voidable preference: a preference given by the bankrupt to a creditor, but which may be set aside by the trustee in bankruptcy.

voir dire examination: the preliminary examination of a juror or a witness to ascertain fitness to act as such.

volenti non fit injuria: the maxim that the defendant's act cannot constitute a tort if the plaintiff has consented thereto.

voluntary nonsuit: a means of the plaintiff's stopping a trial at any time by moving for a voluntary nonsuit.

voting trust: the transfer by two or more persons of their shares of stock of a corporation to a trustee who is to vote the shares and act for such shareholders.

W

waiver: the release or relinquishment of a known right or objection.

warehouse receipt: a receipt issued by the warehouser for stored goods. Regulated by the Uniform Commercial Code, which clothes the receipt with some degree of negotiability.

warranties of indorser of commercial paper: the implied covenants made by an indorser of a commercial paper distinct from any undertaking to pay upon the default of the primary party.

warranties of insured: statements or promises made by the applicant for insurance which if false will entitle the insurer to avoid the contract of insurance in many jurisdictions.

warranties of seller of goods: warranties consisting of express warranties that relate to matters forming part of the basis of the bargain; warranties as to title and right to sell; and the implied warranties which the law adds to a sale depending upon the nature of the transaction.

warranty deed: a deed by which the grantor conveys a specific estate or interest to the grantee and makes one or more of the covenants of title.

warranty of authority: an implied warranty of an agent of the authority exercised by the agent.

warranty of principal: an implied warranty of an agent that the agent is acting for an existing principal who has capacity to contract.

watered stock: stock issued by a corporation as fully paid when in fact it is not.

will: an instrument executed with the formality required by law, by which a person makes a disposition of property to take effect upon death or appoints a personal representative.

willful: intentional as distinguished from accidental or involuntary. In penal statutes, with evil intent or legal malice, or without reasonable ground for believing one's act to be lawful.

Wool Products Labeling Act: a federal statute prohibiting the misbranding of woolen fabrics.

workmen's compensation: a system providing for payments to workers because they have been injured from a risk arising out of the course of their employment while they were employed at their employment or have contracted an occupational disease in that manner, payment being made without consideration of the negligence or lack of negligence of any party.

Y

year and a day: the common-law requirement that death result within a year and a day in order to impose criminal liability for homicide.

Z

zoning restrictions: restrictions imposed by government on the use of property for the advancement of the general welfare.

Uniform Commercial Code

TITLE

AN ACT

To be known as the Uniform Commercial Code, Relating to Certain Commercial Transactions in or regarding Personal Property and Contracts and other Documents concerning them, including Sales, Commercial Paper, Bank Deposits and Collections, Letters of Credit, Bulk Transfers, Warehouse Receipts, Bills of Lading, other Documents of Title, Investment Securities, and Secured Transactions, including certain Sales of Accounts, Chattel Paper, and Contract Rights; Providing for Public Notice to Third Parties in Certain Circumstances; Regulating Procedure, Evidence and Damages in Certain Court Actions Involving such Transactions, Contracts or Documents; to Make Uniform the Law with Respect Thereto; and Repealing Inconsistent Legislation.

ARTICLE 1

GENERAL PROVISIONS

PART 1

SHORT TITLE, CONSTRUCTION, APPLICATION AND SUBJECT MATTER OF THE ACT

§ 1—101. Short Title

This Act shall be known and may be cited as Uniform Commercial Code.

§ 1—102. Purposes; Rules of Construction; Variation by Agreement

(1) This Act shall be liberally construed and applied to promote its underlying purposes and policies.

(2) Underlying purposes and policies of this Act are

    (a) to simplify, clarify and modernize the law governing commercial transactions;

    (b) to permit the continued expansion of commercial practices through custom, usage and agreement of the parties;

    (c) to make uniform the law among the various jurisdictions.

(3) The effect of provisions of this Act may be varied by agreement, except as otherwise provided in this Act and except that the obligations of good faith, diligence, reasonableness and care prescribed by this Act may not be disclaimed by agreement, but the parties may by agreement determine the standards by which the performance of such obligations is to be measured if such standards are not manifestly unreasonable.

(4) The presence in certain provisions of this Act of the words "unless otherwise agreed" or words of similar import does not imply that the effect of other provisions may not be varied by agreement under subsection (3).

1

(5) In this Act unless the context otherwise requires

(a) words in the singular number include the plural, and in the plural include the singular;

(b) words of the masculine gender include the feminine and the neuter, and when the sense so indicates, words of the neuter gender may refer to any gender.

§ 1—103. Supplementary General Principles of Law Applicable

Unless displaced by the particular provisions of this Act, the principles of law and equity, including the law merchant and the law relative to capacity to contract, principal and agent, estoppel, fraud, misrepresentation, duress, coercion, mistake, bankruptcy, or other validating or invalidating cause shall supplement its provisions.

§ 1—104. Construction Against Implicit Repeal

This Act being a general act intended as a unified coverage of its subject matter, no part of it shall be deemed to be impliedly repealed by subsequent legislation if such construction can reasonably be avoided.

§ 1—105. Territorial Application of the Act; Parties' Power to Choose Applicable Law

(1) Except as provided hereafter in this section, when a transaction bears a reasonable relation to this state and also to another state or nation, the parties may agree that the law either of this state or of such other state or nation shall govern their rights and duties. Failing such agreement, this Act applies to transactions bearing an appropriate relation to this state.

(2) Where one of the following provisions of this Act specifies the applicable law, that provision governs and a contrary agreement is effective only to the extent permitted by the law (including the conflict of laws rules) so specified:

Rights of creditors against sold goods. Section 2—402.

Applicability of the Article on Bank Deposits and Collections. Section 4—102.

Bulk transfers subject to the Article on Bulk Transfers. Section 6—102.

Applicability of the Article on Investment Securities. Section 8—106.

Perfection provisions of the Article on Secured Transactions. Section 9—103.

§ 1—106. Remedies to Be Liberally Administered

(1) The remedies provided by this Act shall be liberally administered to the end that the aggrieved party may be put in as good a position as

if the other party had fully performed, but neither consequential or special nor penal damages may be had except as specifically provided in this Act or by other rule of law.

(2) Any right or obligation declared by this Act is enforceable by action unless the provision declaring it specifies a different and limited effect.

§ 1—107. Waiver or Renunciation of Claim or Right After Breach

Any claim or right arising out of an alleged breach can be discharged in whole or in part without consideration by a written waiver or renunciation signed and delivered by the aggrieved party.

§ 1—108. Severability

If any provision or clause of this Act or application thereof to any person or circumstances is held invalid, such invalidity shall not affect other provisions or applications of the Act which can be given effect without the invalid provision or application, and to this end the provisions of this Act are declared to be severable.

§ 1—109. Section Captions

Section captions are parts of this Act.

PART 2

GENERAL DEFINITIONS AND PRINCIPLES OF INTERPRETATION

§ 1—201. General Definitions

Subject to additional definitions contained in the subsequent Articles of this Act which are applicable to specific Articles or Parts thereof, and unless the context otherwise requires, in this Act:

(1) "Action" in the sense of a judicial proceeding includes recoupment, counterclaim, set-off, suit in equity and any other proceedings in which rights are determined.

(2) "Aggrieved party" means a party entitled to resort to a remedy.

(3) "Agreement" means the bargain of the parties in fact as found in their language or by implication from other circumstances including course of dealing or usage of trade or course of performance as provided in this Act (Sections 1—205 and 2—208). Whether an agreement has legal consequences is determined by the provisions of this Act, if applicable; otherwise by the law of contracts (Section 1—103). (Compare "Contract.")

(4) "Bank" means any person engaged in the business of banking.

(5) "Bearer" means the person in possession of an instrument, document of title, or security payable to bearer or indorsed in blank.

(6) "Bill of lading" means a document evidencing the receipt of goods for shipment issued by a person engaged in the business of transporting or forwarding goods, and includes an airbill. "Airbill" means a document serving for air transportation as a bill of lading does for marine or rail transportation, and includes an air consignment note or air waybill.

(7) "Branch" includes a separately incorporated foreign branch of a bank.

(8) "Burden of establishing" a fact means the burden of persuading the triers of fact that the existence of the fact is more probable than its non-existence.

(9) "Buyer in ordinary course of business" means a person who in good faith and without knowledge that the sale to him is in violation of the ownership rights or security interest of a third party in the goods buys in ordinary course from a person in the business of selling goods of that kind but does not include a pawnbroker. All persons who sell minerals or the like (including oil and gas) at wellhead or minehead shall be deemed to be persons in the business of selling goods of that kind. "Buying" may be for cash or by exchange of other property or on secured or unsecured credit and includes receiving goods or documents of title under a preexisting contract for sale but does not include a transfer in bulk or as security for or in total or partial satisfaction of a money debt.

(10) "Conspicuous": A term or clause is conspicuous when it is so written that a reasonable person against whom it is to operate ought to have noticed it. A printed heading in capitals (as: NON-NEGOTIABLE BILL OF LADING) is conspicuous. Language in the body of a form is "conspicuous" if it is in larger or other contrasting type or color. But in a telegram any stated term is "conspicuous." Whether a term or clause is "conspicuous" or not is for decision by the court.

(11) "Contract" means the total legal obligation which results from the parties' agreement as affected by this Act and any other applicable rules of law. (Compare "Agreement.")

(12) "Creditor" includes a general creditor, a secured creditor, a lien creditor and any representative of creditors, including an assignee for the benefit of creditors, a trustee in bankruptcy, a receiver in equity and an executor or administrator of an insolvent debtor's or assignor's estate.

(13) "Defendant" includes a person in the position of defendant in a cross-action or counterclaim.

(14) "Delivery" with respect to instruments, documents of title, chattel paper or securities means voluntary transfer of possession.

(15) "Document of title" includes bill of lading, dock warrant, dock receipt, warehouse receipt or order for the delivery of goods, and also any other document which in the regular course of business or financing is treated as adequately evidencing that the person in possession of it is entitled to receive, hold and dispose of the document and the goods it covers. To be a document of title a document must purport to be issued by or addressed to a bailee and purport to cover goods in the bailee's possession which are either identified or are fungible portions of an identified mass.

(16) "Fault" means wrongful act, omission or breach.

(17) "Fungible" with respect to goods or securities means goods or securities of which any unit is, by nature or usage of trade, the equivalent of any other like unit. Goods which are not fungible shall be deemed fungible for the purposes of this Act to the extent that under a particular agreement or document unlike units are treated as equivalents.

(18) "Genuine" means free of forgery or counterfeiting.

(19) "Good faith" means honesty in fact in the conduct or transaction concerned.

(20) "Holder" means a person who is in possession of a document of title or an instrument or an investment security drawn, issued or indorsed to him or to his order or to bearer or in blank.

(21) To "honor" is to pay or to accept and pay, or where a credit so engages, to purchase or discount a draft complying with the terms of the credit.

(22) "Insolvency proceedings" includes any assignment for the benefit of creditors or other proceedings intended to liquidate or rehabilitate the estate of the person involved.

(23) A person is "insolvent" who either has ceased to pay his debts in the ordinary course of business or cannot pay his debts as they become due or is insolvent within the meaning of the federal bankruptcy law.

(24) "Money" means a medium of exchange authorized or adopted by a domestic or foreign government as a part of its currency.

(25) A person has "notice" of a fact when
    (a) he has actual knowledge of it; or
    (b) he has received a notice or notification of it; or
    (c) from all the facts and circumstances known to him at the time in question he has reason to know that it exists.
A person "knows" or has "knowledge" of a fact when he has actual knowledge of it. "Discover" or "learn" or a word or phrase of similar import refers to knowledge rather than to reason to know. The time and circumstances under which a notice or notification may cease to be effective are not determined by this Act.

(26) A person "notifies" or "gives" a notice or notification to another by taking such steps as may be reasonably required to inform the other in ordinary course whether or not such other actually comes to know of it. A person "receives" a notice or notification when

    (a) it comes to his attention; or

    (b) it is duly delivered at the place of business through which the contract was made or at any other place held out by him as the place for receipt of such communications.

(27) Notice, knowledge or a notice or notification received by an organization is effective for a particular transaction from the time when it is brought to the attention of the individual conducting that transaction, and in any event from the time when it would have been brought to his attention if the organization had exercised due diligence. An organization exercises due diligence if it maintains reasonable routines for communicating significant information to the person conducting the transaction and there is reasonable compliance with the routines. Due diligence does not require an individual acting for the organization to communicate information unless such communication is part of his regular duties or unless he has reason to know of the transaction and that the transaction would be materially affected by the information.

(28) "Organization" includes a corporation, government or governmental subdivision or agency, business trust, estate, trust, partnership or association, two or more persons having a joint or common interest, or any other legal or commercial entity.

(29) "Party," as distinct from "third party," means a person who has engaged in a transaction or made an agreement within this Act.

(30) "Person" includes an individual or an organization (See Section 1—102).

(31) "Presumption" or "presumed" means that the trier of fact must find the existence of the fact presumed unless and until evidence is introduced which would support a finding of its nonexistence.

(32) "Purchase" includes taking by sale, discount, negotiation, mortgage, pledge, lien, issue or re-issue, gift or any other voluntary transaction creating an interest in property.

(33) "Purchaser" means a person who takes by purchase.

(34) "Remedy" means any remedial right to which an aggrieved party is entitled with or without resort to a tribunal.

(35) "Representative" includes an agent, an officer of a corporation or association, and a trustee, executor or administrator of an estate, or any other person empowered to act for another.

(36) "Rights" includes remedies.

(37) "Security interest" means an interest in personal property or fixtures which secures payment or performance of an obligation. The retention or reservation of title by a seller of goods notwithstanding shipment or delivery to the buyer (Section 2—401) is limited in effect to a reservation of a "security interest." The term also includes any interest of a buyer of accounts or chattel paper which is subject to Article 9. The special property interest of a buyer of goods on identification of such goods to a contract for sale under Section 2—401 is not a "security interest," but a buyer may also acquire a "security interest" by complying with Article 9. Unless a lease or consignment is intended as security, reservation of title thereunder is not a "security interest" but a consignment is in any event subject to the provisions on consignment sales (Section 2—326). Whether a lease is intended as security is to be determined by the facts of each case; however, (a) the inclusion of an option to purchase does not of itself make the lease one intended for security, and (b) an agreement that upon compliance with the terms of the lease the lessee shall become or has the option to become the owner of the property for no additional consideration or for a nominal consideration does make the lease one intended for security.

(38) "Send" in connection with any writing or notice means to deposit in the mail or deliver for transmission by any other usual means of communication with postage or cost of transmission provided for and properly addressed and in the case of an instrument to an address specified thereon or otherwise agreed, or if there be none to any address reasonable under the circumstances. The receipt of any writing or notice within the time at which it would have arrived if properly sent has the effect of a proper sending.

(39) "Signed" includes any symbol executed or adopted by a party with present intention to authenticate a writing.

(40) "Surety" includes guarantor.

(41) "Telegram" includes a message transmitted by radio, teletype, cable, any mechanical method of transmission, or the like.

(42) "Term" means that portion of an agreement which relates to a particular matter.

(43) "Unauthorized" signature or indorsement means one made without actual, implied or apparent authority and includes a forgery.

(44) "Value." Except as otherwise provided with respect to negotiable instruments and bank collections (Sections 3—303, 4—208 and 4—209) a person gives "value" for rights if he acquires them

    (a) in return for a binding commitment to extend credit or for the extension of immediately available credit whether or not drawn upon and whether or not a charge-back is provided for in the event of difficulties in collection; or

(b) as security for or in total or partial satisfaction of a preexisting claim; or

(c) by accepting delivery pursuant to a preexisting contract for purchase; or

(d) generally, in return for any consideration sufficient to support a simple contract.

(45) "Warehouse receipt" means a receipt issued by a person engaged in the business of storing goods for hire.

(46) "Written" or "writing" includes printing, typewriting or any other intentional reduction to tangible form.

§ 1—202. Prima Facie Evidence by Third Party Documents

A document in due form purporting to be a bill of lading, policy or certificate of insurance, official weigher's or inspector's certificate, consular invoice, or any other document authorized or required by the contract to be issued by a third party shall be prima facie evidence of its own authenticity and genuineness and of the facts stated in the document by the third party.

§ 1—203. Obligation of Good Faith

Every contract or duty within this Act imposes an obligation of good faith in its performance or enforcement.

§ 1—204. Time; Reasonable Time; "Seasonably"

(1) Whenever this Act requires any action to be taken within a reasonable time, any time which is not manifestly unreasonable may be fixed by agreement.

(2) What is a reasonable time for taking any action depends on the nature, purpose and circumstances of such action.

(3) An action is taken "seasonably" when it is taken at or within the time agreed or, if no time is agreed, at or within a reasonable time.

§ 1—205. Course of Dealing and Usage of Trade

(1) A course of dealing is a sequence of previous conduct between the parties to a particular transaction which is fairly to be regarded as establishing a common basis of understanding for interpreting their expressions and other conduct.

(2) A usage of trade is any practice or method of dealing having such regularity of observance in a place, vocation or trade as to justify an expectation that it will be observed with respect to the transaction in question. The existence and scope of such a usage are to be proved as facts. If it is established that such a usage is embodied in a written trade code or similar writing the interpretation of the writing is for the court.

(3) A course of dealing between parties and any usage of trade in the vocation or trade in which they are engaged or of which they are or should be aware give particular meaning to and supplement or qualify terms of an agreement.

(4) The express terms of an agreement and an applicable course of dealing or usage of trade shall be construed wherever reasonable as consistent with each other; but when such construction is unreasonable, express terms control both course of dealing and usage of trade and course of dealing controls usage of trade.

(5) An applicable usage of trade in the place where any part of performance is to occur shall be used in interpreting the agreement as to that part of the performance.

(6) Evidence of a relevant usage of trade offered by one party is not admissible unless and until he has given the other party such notice as the court finds sufficient to prevent unfair surprise to the latter.

§ 1—206. Statute of Frauds for Kinds of Personal Property Not Otherwise Covered

(1) Except in the cases described in subsection (2) of this section, a contract for the sale of personal property is not enforceable by way of action or defense beyond five thousand dollars in amount or value of remedy unless there is some writing which indicates that a contract for sale has been made between the parties at a defined or stated price, reasonably identifies the subject matter, and is signed by the party against whom enforcement is sought or by his authorized agent.

(2) Subsection (1) of this section does not apply to contracts for the sale of goods (Section 2—201) nor of securities (Section 8—319) nor to security agreements (Section 9—203).

§ 1—207. Performance or Acceptance Under Reservation of Rights

A party who with explicit reservation of rights performs or promises performance or assents to performance in a manner demanded or offered by the other party does not thereby prejudice the rights reserved. Such words as "without prejudice," "under protest" or the like are sufficient.

§ 1—208. Option to Accelerate at Will

A term providing that one party or his successor in interest may accelerate payment or performance or require collateral or additional collateral "at will" or "when he deems himself insecure" or in words of similar import shall be construed to mean that he shall have power to do so only if he in good faith believes that the prospect of payment or performance is impaired. The burden of establishing lack of good faith is on the party against whom the power has been exercised.

§ 1—209. Subordinated Obligations
An obligation may be issued as subordinated to payment of another obligation of the person obligated, or a creditor may subordinate his right to payment of an obligation by agreement with either the person obligated or another creditor of the person obligated. Such a subordination does not create a security interest as against either the common debtor or a subordinated creditor. This section shall be construed as declaring the law as it existed prior to the enactment of this section and not as modifying it.

ARTICLE 2
SALES

PART 1

SHORT TITLE, GENERAL CONSTRUCTION AND SUBJECT MATTER

§ 2—101. Short Title
This Article shall be known and may be cited as Uniform Commercial Code—Sales.

§ 2—102. Scope; Certain Security and Other Transactions Excluded From This Article
Unless the context otherwise requires, this Article applies to transactions in goods; it does not apply to any transaction which although in the form of an unconditional contract to sell or present sale is intended to operate only as a security transaction nor does this Article impair or repeal any statute regulating sales to consumers, farmers or other specified classes of buyers.

§ 2—103. Definitions and Index of Definitions
(1) In this Article, unless the context otherwise requires,
  (a) "Buyer" means a person who buys or contracts to buy goods.
  (b) "Good faith" in the case of a merchant means honesty in fact and the observance of reasonable commercial standards of fair dealing in the trade.
  (c) "Receipt" of goods means taking physical possession of them.
  (d) "Seller" means a person who sells or contracts to sell goods.
(2) Other definitions applying to this Article or to specified Parts thereof, and the sections in which they appear are:
"Acceptance." Section 2—606.
"Banker's credit." Section 2—325.
"Between merchants." Section 2—104.
"Cancellation." Section 2—106(4).
"Confirmed credit." Section 2—325.
"Conforming to contract." Section 2—106.
"Contract for sale." Section 2—106.
"Cover." Section 2—712.
"Entrusting." Section 2—403.
"Financing agency." Section 2—104.
"Future goods." Section 2—105.
"Goods." Section 2—105.
"Identification." Section 2—501.
"Installment contract." Section 2—612.
"Letter of Credit." Section 2—325.
"Lot." Section 2—105.
"Merchant." Section 2—104.
"Overseas." Section 2—323.
"Person in position of seller." Section 2—707.
"Present sale." Section 2—106.
"Sale." Section 2—106.
"Sale on approval." Section 2—326.
"Sale or return." Section 2—326.
"Termination." Section 2—106.
(3) The following definitions in other Articles apply to this Article:
"Check." Section 3—104.
"Consignee." Section 7—102.
"Consignor." Section 7—102.
"Consumer goods." Section 9—109.
"Dishonor." Section 3—507.
"Draft." Section 3—104.
(4) In addition Article 1 contains general definitions and principles of construction and interpretation applicable throughout this Article.

§ 2—104. Definitions: "Merchant"; "Between Merchants"; "Financing Agency"
(1) "Merchant" means a person who deals in goods of the kind or otherwise by his occupation

holds himself out as having knowledge or skill peculiar to the practices or goods involved in the transaction or to whom such knowledge or skill may be attributed by his employment of an agent or broker or other intermediary who by his occupation holds himself out as having such knowledge or skill.

(2) "Financing agency" means a bank, finance company or other person who in the ordinary course of business makes advances against goods or documents of title or who by arrangement with either the seller or the buyer intervenes in ordinary course to make or collect payment due or claimed under the contract for sale, as by purchasing or paying the seller's draft or making advances against it or by merely taking it for collection whether or not documents of title accompany the draft. "Financing agency" includes also a bank or other person who similarly intervenes between persons who are in the position of seller and buyer in respect to the goods (Section 2—707).

(3) "Between merchants" means in any transaction with respect to which both parties are chargeable with the knowledge or skill of merchants.

§ 2—105. Definitions: Transferability; "Goods"; "Future" Goods; "Lot"; "Commercial Unit"

(1) "Goods" means all things (including specially manufactured goods) which are movable at the time of identification to the contract for sale other than the money in which the price is to be paid, investment securities (Article 8) and things in action. "Goods" also includes the unborn young of animals and growing crops and other identified things attached to realty as described in the section on goods to be severed from realty (Section 2—107).

(2) Goods must be both existing and identified before any interest in them can pass. Goods which are not both existing and identified are "future" goods. A purported present sale of future goods or of any interest therein operates as a contract to sell.

(3) There may be a sale of a part interest in existing identified goods.

(4) An undivided share in an identified bulk of fungible goods is sufficiently identified to be sold although the quantity of the bulk is not determined. Any agreed proportion of such a bulk or any quantity thereof agreed upon by number, weight or other measure may to the extent of the seller's interest in the bulk be sold to the buyer who then becomes an owner in common.

(5) "Lot" means a parcel or a single article which is the subject matter of a separate sale or delivery, whether or not it is sufficient to perform the contract.

(6) "Commercial unit" means such a unit of goods as by commercial usage is a single whole for purposes of sale and division of which materially impairs its character or value on the market or in use. A commercial unit may be a single article (as a machine) or a set of articles (as a suite of furniture or an assortment of sizes) or a quantity (as a bale, gross, or carload) or any other unit treated in use or in the relevant market as a single whole.

§ 2—106. Definitions: "Contract"; "Agreement"; "Contract for Sale"; "Sale"; "Present Sale"; "Conforming" to Contract; "Termination"; "Cancellation"

(1) In this Article unless the context otherwise requires, "contract" and "agreement" are limited to those relating to the present or future sale of goods. "Contract for sale" includes both a present sale of goods and a contract to sell goods at a future time. A "sale" consists in the passing of title from the seller to the buyer for a price (Section 2—401). A "present sale" means a sale which is accomplished by the making of the contract.

(2) Goods or conduct, including any part of a performance, are "conforming" or conform to the contract when they are in accordance with the obligations under the contract.

(3) "Termination" occurs when either party pursuant to a power created by agreement or law puts an end to the contract otherwise than for its breach. On "termination" all obligations which are still executory on both sides are discharged but any right based on prior breach or performance survives.

(4) "Cancellation" occurs when either party puts an end to the contract for breach by the other and its effect is the same as that of "termination" except that the cancelling party also retains any remedy for breach of the whole contract or any unperformed balance.

§ 2—107. Goods to Be Severed From Realty: Recording

(1) A contract for the sale of minerals or the like (including oil and gas) or a structure or its materials to be removed from realty is a contract for the sale of goods within this Article if they are to be severed by the seller, but until severance a purported present sale thereof which is not effective as a transfer of an interest in land is effective only as a contract to sell.

(2) A contract for the sale apart from the land of growing crops or other things attached to realty and capable of severance without material harm thereto but not described in subsection (1) or of timber to be cut is a contract for the sale of goods within this Article whether the subject matter is to be severed by the buyer or by the seller even though it forms part of the realty at the time of contracting,

and the parties can by identification effect a present sale before severance.

(3) The provisions of this section are subject to any third party rights provided by the law relating to realty records, and the contract for sale may be executed and recorded as a document transferring an interest in land and shall then constitute notice to third parties of the buyer's rights under the contract for sale.

PART 2

FORM, FORMATION AND READJUSTMENT OF CONTRACT

§ 2—201. Formal Requirements; Statute of Frauds

(1) Except as otherwise provided in this section, a contract for the sale of goods for the price of $500 or more is not enforceable by way of action or defense unless there is some writing sufficient to indicate that a contract for sale has been made between the parties and signed by the party against whom enforcement is sought or by his authorized agent or broker. A writing is not insufficient because it omits or incorrectly states a term agreed upon but the contract is not enforceable under this paragraph beyond the quantity of goods shown in such writing.

(2) Between merchants, if within a reasonable time a writing in confirmation of the contract and sufficient against the sender is received and the party receiving it has reason to know its contents, it satisfies the requirements of subsection (1) against such party unless written notice of objection to its contents is given within 10 days after it is received.

(3) A contract which does not satisfy the requirements of subsection (1) but which is valid in other respects is enforceable

  (a) if the goods are to be specially manufactured for the buyer and are not suitable for sale to others in the ordinary course of the seller's business and the seller, before notice of repudiation is received and under circumstances which reasonably indicate that the goods are for the buyer, has made either a substantial beginning of their manufacture or commitments for their procurement; or

  (b) if the party against whom enforcement is sought admits in his pleading, testimony or otherwise in court that a contract for sale was made, but the contract is not enforceable under this provision beyond the quantity of goods admitted; or

  (c) with respect to goods for which payment has been made and accepted or which have been received and accepted (Sec. 2—606).

§ 2—202. Final Written Expression: Parol or Extrinsic Evidence

Terms with respect to which the confirmatory memoranda of the parties agree or which are otherwise set forth in a writing intended by the parties as a final expression of their agreement with respect to such terms as are included therein may not be contradicted by evidence of any prior agreement or of a contemporaneous oral agreement but may be explained or supplemented

  (a) by course of dealing or usage of trade (Section 1—205) or by course of performance (Section 2—208); and

  (b) by evidence of consistent additional terms unless the court finds the writing to have been intended also as a complete and exclusive statement of the terms of the agreement.

§ 2—203. Seals Inoperative

The affixing of a seal to a writing evidencing a contract for sale or an offer to buy or sell goods does not constitute the writing a sealed instrument and the law with respect to sealed instruments does not apply to such a contract or offer.

§ 2—204. Formation in General

(1) A contract for sale of goods may be made in any manner sufficient to show agreement, including conduct by both parties which recognizes the existence of such a contract.

(2) An agreement sufficient to constitute a contract for sale may be found even though the moment of its making is undetermined.

(3) Even though one or more terms are left open a contract for sale does not fail for indefiniteness if the parties have intended to make a contract and there is a reasonably certain basis for giving an appropriate remedy.

§ 2—205. Firm Offers

An offer by a merchant to buy or sell goods in a signed writing which by its terms gives assurance that it will be held open is not revocable, for lack of consideration, during the time stated or if no time is stated for a reasonable time, but in no event may such period of irrevocability exceed three months; but any such term of assurance on a form supplied by the offeree must be separately signed by the offeror.

§ 2—206. Offer and Acceptance in Formation of Contract

(1) Unless otherwise unambiguously indicated by the language or circumstances

  (a) an offer to make a contract shall be construed as inviting acceptance in any manner and by any medium reasonable in the circumstances;

  (b) an order or other offer to buy goods for prompt or current shipment shall be construed as inviting acceptance either by a prompt promise to ship or by the prompt or current shipment of conforming or non-conforming goods, but such a shipment of non-conforming goods does not constitute an acceptance if the seller seasonably notifies the buyer that the shipment is offered only as an accommodation to the buyer.

(2) Where the beginning of a requested performance is a reasonable mode of acceptance, an offeror who is not notified of acceptance within a reasonable time may treat the offer as having lapsed before acceptance.

§ 2—207. Additional Terms in Acceptance or Confirmation

(1) A definite and seasonable expression of acceptance or a written confirmation which is sent within a reasonable time operates as an acceptance even though it states terms additional to or different from those offered or agreed upon, unless acceptance is expressly made conditional on assent to the additional or different terms.

(2) The additional terms are to be construed as proposals for addition to the contract. Between merchants such terms become part of the contract unless:

  (a) the offer expressly limits acceptance to the terms of the offer;

  (b) they materially alter it; or

  (c) notification of objection to them has already been given or is given within a reasonable time after notice of them is received.

(3) Conduct by both parties which recognizes the existence of a contract is sufficient to establish a contract for sale although the writings of the parties do not otherwise establish a contract. In such case the terms of the particular contract consist of those terms on which the writings of the parties agree, together with any supplementary terms incorporated under any other provisions of this Act.

§ 2—208. Course of Performance or Practical Construction

(1) Where the contract for sale involves repeated occasions for performance by either party with knowledge of the nature of the performance and opportunity for objection to it by the other, any course of performance accepted or acquiesced in without objection shall be relevant to determine the meaning of the agreement.

(2) The express terms of the agreement and any such course of performance, as well as any course of dealing and usage of trade, shall be construed whenever reasonable as consistent with each other; but when such construction is unreasonable, express terms shall control course of performance and course of performance shall control both course of dealing and usage of trade (Section 1—205).

(3) Subject to the provisions of the next section on modification and waiver, such course of performance shall be relevant to show a waiver or modification of any term inconsistent with such course of performance.

§ 2—209. Modification, Rescission and Waiver

(1) An agreement modifying a contract within this Article needs no consideration to be binding.

(2) A signed agreement which excludes modification or rescission except by a signed writing cannot be otherwise modified or rescinded, but except as between merchants such a requirement on a form supplied by the merchant must be separately signed by the other party.

(3) The requirements of the statute of frauds section of this Article (Section 2—201) must be satisfied if the contract as modified is within its provisions.

(4) Although an attempt at modification or rescission does not satisfy the requirements of subsection (2) or (3) it can operate as a waiver.

(5) A party who has made a waiver affecting an executory portion of the contract may retract the waiver by reasonable notification received by the other party that strict performance will be required of any term waived, unless the retraction would be unjust in view of a material change of position in reliance on the waiver.

§ 2—210. Delegation of Performance; Assignment of Rights

(1) A party may perform his duty through a delegate unless otherwise agreed or unless the other party has a substantial interest in having his original promisor perform or control the acts required by the contract. No delegation of performance relieves the party delegating of any duty to perform or any liability for breach.

(2) Unless otherwise agreed, all rights of either seller or buyer can be assigned except where the assignment would materially change the duty of the other party, or increase materially the burden or risk imposed on him by his contract, or impair materially his chance of obtaining return performance. A right to damages for breach of the whole contract or a right arising out of the assignor's due performance of his entire obligation can be assigned despite agreement otherwise.

(3) Unless the circumstances indicate the contrary, a prohibition of assignment of "the contract" is to be construed as barring only the delegation to the assignee of the assignor's performance.

(4) An assignment of "the contract" or of "all my rights under the contract" or an assignment in similar general terms is an assignment of rights and, unless the language or the circumstances (as in an assignment for security) indicate the contrary, it is a delegation of performance of the duties of the assignor, and its acceptance by the assignee constitutes a promise by him to perform those duties. This promise is enforceable by either the assignor or the other party to the original contract.

(5) The other party may treat any assignment which delegates performance as creating reasonable grounds for insecurity and may without prejudice to his rights against the assignor demand assurances from the assignee (Section 2—609).

PART 3

GENERAL OBLIGATION AND CONSTRUCTION OF CONTRACT

§ 2—301. General Obligations of Parties

The obligation of the seller is to transfer and deliver and that of the buyer is to accept and pay in accordance with the contract.

§ 2—302. Unconscionable Contract or Clause

(1) If the court as a matter of law finds the contract or any clause of the contract to have been unconscionable at the time it was made, the court may refuse to enforce the contract, or it may enforce the remainder of the contract without the unconscionable clause, or it may so limit the application of any unconscionable clause as to avoid any unconscionable result.

(2) When it is claimed or appears to the court that the contract or any clause thereof may be unconscionable, the parties shall be afforded a reasonable opportunity to present evidence as to its commercial setting, purpose and effect to aid the court in making the determination.

§ 2—303. Allocation or Division of Risks

Where this Article allocates a risk or a burden as between the parties "unless otherwise agreed," the agreement may not only shift the allocation but may also divide the risk or burden.

§ 2—304. Price Payable in Money, Goods, Realty, or Otherwise

(1) The price can be made payable in money or otherwise. If it is payable in whole or in part in goods each party is a seller of the goods which he is to transfer.

(2) Even though all or part of the price is payable in an interest in realty the transfer of the goods and the seller's obligations with reference to them are subject to this Article, but not the transfer of the interest in realty or the transferor's obligations in connection therewith.

§ 2—305. Open Price Term

(1) The parties, if they so intend, can conclude a contract for sale even though the price is not settled. In such a case, the price is a reasonable price at the time for delivery if

  (a) nothing is said as to price; or
  (b) the price is left to be agreed by the parties and they fail to agree; or
  (c) the price is to be fixed in terms of some agreed market or other standard as set or recorded by a third person or agency and it is not so set or recorded.

(2) A price to be fixed by the seller or by the buyer means a price for him to fix in good faith.

(3) When a price left to be fixed otherwise than by agreement of the parties fails to be fixed through fault of one party, the other may at his option treat the contract as cancelled or himself fix a reasonable price.

(4) Where, however, the parties intend not to be bound unless the price be fixed or agreed and it is not fixed or agreed, there is no contract. In such a case, the buyer must return any goods already received or if unable so to do must pay their reasonable value at the time of delivery and the seller must return any portion of the price paid on account.

§ 2—306. Output, Requirements and Exclusive Dealings

(1) A term which measures the quantity by the output of the seller or the requirements of the buyer means such actual output or requirements as may occur in good faith, except that no quantity unreasonably disproportionate to any stated estimate or in the absence of a stated estimate to any normal or otherwise comparable prior output or requirements may be tendered or demanded.

(2) A lawful agreement by either the seller or the buyer for exclusive dealing in the kind of goods concerned imposes, unless otherwise agreed, an obligation by the seller to use best efforts to supply the goods and by the buyer to use best efforts to promote their sale.

§ 2—307. Delivery in Single Lot or Several Lots

Unless otherwise agreed all goods called for by a contract for sale must be tendered in a single delivery and payment is due only on such tender; but where the circumstances give either party the right to make or demand delivery in lots, the price if it can be apportioned may be demanded for each lot.

§ 2—308. Absence of Specified Place for Delivery

Unless otherwise agreed

    (a) the place for delivery of goods is the seller's place of business or, if he has none, his residence; but

    (b) in a contract for sale of identified goods which to the knowledge of the parties at the time of contracting are in some other place, that place is the place for their delivery; and

    (c) documents of title may be delivered through customary banking channels.

§ 2—309. Absence of Specific Time Provisions; Notice of Termination

(1) The time for shipment or delivery or any other action under a contract if not provided in this Article or agreed upon shall be a reasonable time.

(2) Where the contract provides for successive performances but is indefinite in duration, it is valid for a reasonable time; but unless otherwise agreed may be terminated at any time by either party.

(3) Termination of a contract by one party, except on the happening of an agreed event, requires that reasonable notification be received by the other party and an agreement dispensing with notification is invalid if its operation would be unconscionable.

§ 2—310. Open Time for Payment or Running of Credit; Authority to Ship Under Reservation

Unless otherwise agreed

    (a) payment is due at the time and place at which the buyer is to receive the goods even though the place of shipment is the place of delivery; and

    (b) if the seller is authorized to send the goods, he may ship them under reservation, and may tender the documents of title, but the buyer may inspect the goods after their arrival before pay-ment is due unless such inspection is inconsistent with the terms of the contract (Section 2—513); and

    (c) if delivery is authorized and made by way of documents of title otherwise than by subsection (b), then payment is due at the time and place at which the buyer is to receive the documents regardless of where the goods are to be received; and

    (d) where the seller is required or authorized to ship the goods on credit, the credit period runs from the time of shipment but postdating the invoice or delaying its dispatch will correspondingly delay the starting of the credit period.

§ 2—311. Options and Cooperation Respecting Performance

(1) An agreement for sale which is otherwise sufficiently definite (subsection (3) of Section 2—204) to be a contract is not made invalid by the fact that it leaves particulars of performance to be specified by one of the parties. Any such specification must be made in good faith and within limits set by commercial reasonableness.

(2) Unless otherwise agreed, specifications relating to assortment of the goods are at the buyer's option and, except as otherwise provided in subsections (1) (c) and (3) of Section 2—319, specifications or arrangements relating to shipment are at the seller's option.

(3) Where such specification would materially affect the other party's performance but is not seasonably made or where one party's cooperation is necessary to the agreed performance of the other but is not seasonably forthcoming, the other party in addition to all other remedies

    (a) is excused for any resulting delay in his own performance; and

    (b) may also either proceed to perform in any reasonable manner or after the time for a material part of his own performance treat the failure to specify or to cooperate as a breach by failure to deliver or accept the goods.

§ 2—312. Warranty of Title and Against Infringement; Buyer's Obligation Against Infringement

(1) Subject to subsection (2), there is in a contract for sale a warranty by the seller that

    (a) the title conveyed shall be good, and its transfer rightful; and

(b) the goods shall be delivered free from any security interest or other lien or encumbrance of which the buyer at the time of contracting has no knowledge.

(2) A warranty under subsection (1) will be excluded or modified only by specific language or by circumstances which give the buyer reason to know that the person selling does not claim title in himself or that he is purporting to sell only such right or title as he or a third person may have.

(3) Unless otherwise agreed a seller who is a merchant regularly dealing in goods of the kind warrants that the goods shall be delivered free of the rightful claim of any third person by way of infringement or the like but a buyer who furnishes specifications to the seller must hold the seller harmless against any such claim which arises out of compliance with the specifications.

§ 2—313. Express Warranties by Affirmation, Promise, Description, Sample

(1) Express warranties by the seller are created as follows:

(a) Any affirmation of fact or promise made by the seller to the buyer which relates to the goods and becomes part of the basis of the bargain creates an express warranty that the goods shall conform to the affirmation or promise.

(b) Any description of the goods which is made part of the basis of the bargain creates an express warranty that the goods shall conform to the description.

(c) Any sample or model which is made part of the basis of the bargain creates an express warranty that the whole of the goods shall conform to the sample or model.

(2) It is not necessary to the creation of an express warranty that the seller use formal words such as "warrant" or "guarantee" or that he have a specific intention to make a warranty, but an affirmation merely of the value of the goods or a statement purporting to be merely the seller's opinion or commendation of the goods does not create a warranty.

§ 2—314. Implied Warranty: Merchantability; Usage of Trade

(1) Unless excluded or modified (Section 2—316), a warranty that the goods shall be merchantable is implied in a contract for their sale if the seller is a merchant with respect to goods of that kind. Under this section, the serving for value of food or drink to be consumed either on the premises or elsewhere is a sale.

(2) Goods to be merchantable must be at least such as

(a) pass without objection in the trade under the contract description; and

(b) in the case of fungible goods, are of fair average quality within the description; and

(c) are fit for the ordinary purposes for which such goods are used; and

(d) run, within the variations permitted by the agreement, of even kind, quality and quantity within each unit and among all units involved; and

(e) are adequately contained, packaged, and labeled as the agreement may require; and

(f) conform to the promises or affirmations of fact made on the container or label if any.

(3) Unless excluded or modified (Section 2—316), other implied warranties may arise from course of dealing or usage of trade.

§ 2—315. Implied Warranty: Fitness for Particular Purpose

Where the seller at the time of contracting has reason to know any particular purpose for which the goods are required and that the buyer is relying on the seller's skill or judgment to select or furnish suitable goods, there is unless excluded or modified under the next section an implied warranty that the goods shall be fit for such purpose.

§ 2—316. Exclusion or Modification of Warranties

(1) Words or conduct relevant to the creation of an express warranty and words or conduct tending to negate or limit warranty shall be construed wherever reasonable as consistent with each other; but, subject to the provisions of this Article on parol or extrinsic evidence (Section 2—202), negation or limitation is inoperative to the extent that such construction is unreasonable.

(2) Subject to subsection (3), to exclude or modify the implied warranty of merchantability or any part of it, the language must mention merchantability and in case of a writing must be conspicuous, and to exclude or modify any implied warranty of fitness the exclusion must be by a writing and conspicuous. Language to exclude all implied warranties of fitness is sufficient if it states, for example, that "There are no warranties which extend beyond the description on the face hereof."

(3) Notwithstanding subsection (2)

(a) unless the circumstances indicate otherwise, all implied warranties are excluded by expressions like "as is," "with all faults" or other language which in common understanding calls the buyer's attention to the exclusion of warranties and makes plain that there is no implied warranty; and

(b) when the buyer before entering into the contract has examined goods or the sample or model as fully as he desired or has refused to examine the goods, there is no implied warranty with regard to defects which an examination ought in the circumstances to have revealed to him; and

(c) an implied warranty can also be excluded or modified by course of dealing or course of performance or usage of trade.

(4) Remedies for breach of warranty can be limited in accordance with the provisions of this Article on liquidation or limitation of damages and on contractual modification of remedy (Sections 2—718 and 2—719).

§ 2—317. Cumulation and Conflict of Warranties Express or Implied

Warranties whether express or implied shall be construed as consistent with each other and as cumulative, but if such construction is unreasonable the intention of the parties shall determine which warranty is dominant. In ascertaining that intention the following rules apply:

(a) Exact or technical specifications displace an inconsistent sample or model or general language of description.

(b) A sample from an existing bulk displaces inconsistent general language of description.

(c) Express warranties displace inconsistent implied warranties other than an implied warranty of fitness for a particular purpose.

§ 2—318. Third Party Beneficiaries of Warranties Express or Implied

Note: *If this Act is introduced in the Congress of the United States this section should be omitted. (States to select one alternative.)*

Alternative A

A seller's warranty whether express or implied extends to any natural person who is in the family or household of his buyer or who is a guest in his home if it is reasonable to expect that such person may use, consume or be affected by the goods and who is injured in person by breach of the warranty.

A seller may not exclude or limit the operation of this section.

Alternative B

A seller's warranty whether express or implied extends to any natural person who may reasonably be expected to use, consume or be affected by the goods and who is injured in person by breach of the warranty. A seller may not exclude or limit the operation of this section.

Alternative C

A seller's warranty whether express or implied extends to any person who may reasonably be expected to use, consume or be affected by the goods and who is injured by breach of the warranty. A seller may not exclude or limit the operation of this section with respect to injury to the person of an individual to whom the warranty extends.

§ 2—319. F.O.B. and F.A.S. Terms

(1) Unless otherwise agreed, the term F.O.B. (which means "free on board") at a named place, even though used only in connection with the stated price, is a delivery term under which

(a) when the term is F.O.B. the place of shipment, the seller must at that place ship the goods in the manner provided in this Article (Section 2—504) and bear the expense and risk of putting them into the possession of the carrier; or

(b) when the term is F.O.B. the place of destination, the seller must at his own expense and risk transport the goods to that place and there tender delivery of them in the manner provided in this Article (Section 2—503);

(c) when under either (a) or (b) the term is also F.O.B. vessel, car or other vehicle, the seller must in addition at his own expense and risk load the goods on board. If the term is F.O.B. vessel, the buyer must name the vessel and, in an appropriate case, the seller must comply with the provisions of this Article on the form of bill of lading (Section 2—323).

(2) Unless otherwise agreed, the term F.A.S. vessel (which means "free alongside") at a named port, even though used only in connection with the stated price, is a delivery term under which the seller must

(a) at his own expense and risk deliver the goods alongside the vessel in the manner usual in that port or on a dock designated and provided by the buyer; and

(b) obtain and tender a receipt for the goods in exchange for which the carrier is under a duty to issue a bill of lading.

(3) Unless otherwise agreed in any case falling within subsection (1) (a) or (c) or subsection (2) the buyer must seasonably give any needed instructions for making delivery, including, when the term is F.A.S. or F.O.B., the loading berth of the vessel and, in an appropriate case, its name and sailing date. The seller may treat the failure of needed instructions as a failure of cooperation under this Article (Section 2—311). He may also at his option move the goods in any reasonable manner preparatory to delivery or shipment.

(4) Under the term F.O.B. vessel or F.A.S., unless otherwise agreed, the buyer must make payment against tender of the required documents and the seller may not tender nor the buyer demand delivery of the goods in substitution for the documents.

§ 2—320. C.I.F. and C. & F. Terms

(1) The term C.I.F. means that the price includes in a lump sum the cost of the goods and the insurance and freight to the named destination. The term C. & F. or C.F. means that the price so includes cost and freight to the named destination.

(2) Unless otherwise agreed and even though used only in connection with the stated price and destination, the term C.I.F. destination or its equivalent requires the seller at his own expense and risk to

(a) put the goods into the possession of a carrier at the port for shipment and obtain a negotiable bill or bills of lading covering the entire transportation to the named destination; and

(b) load the goods and obtain a receipt from the carrier (which may be contained in the bill of lading) showing that the freight has been paid or provided for; and

(c) obtain a policy or certificate of insurance, including any war risk insurance, of a kind and on terms then current at the port of shipment in the usual amount, in the currency of the contract, shown to cover the same goods covered by the bill of lading and providing for payment of loss to the order of the buyer or for the account of whom it may concern; but the seller may add to the price the amount of the premium for any such war risk insurance; and

(d) prepare an invoice of the goods and procure any other documents required to effect shipment or to comply with the contract; and

(e) forward and tender with commercial promptness all the documents in due form and with any indorsement necessary to perfect the buyer's rights.

(3) Unless otherwise agreed, the term C. & F. or its equivalent has the same effect and imposes upon the seller the same obligations and risks as a C.I.F. term except the obligation as to insurance.

(4) Under the term C.I.F. or C. & F., unless otherwise agreed the buyer must make payment against tender of the required documents and the seller may not tender nor the buyer demand delivery of the goods in substitution for the documents.

§ 2—321. C.I.F. or C. & F.: "Net Landed Weights"; "Payment on Arrival"; Warranty of Condition on Arrival

Under a contract containing a term C.I.F. or C. & F.

(1) Where the price is based on or is to be adjusted according to "net landed weights," "delivered weights," "out turn" quantity or quality or the like, unless otherwise agreed the seller must reasonably estimate the price. The payment due on tender of the documents called for by the contract is the amount so estimated, but after final adjustment of the price a settlement must be made with commercial promptness.

(2) An agreement described in subsection (1) or any warranty of quality or condition of the goods on arrival places upon the seller the risk of ordinary deterioration, shrinkage and the like in transportation but has no effect on the place or time of identification to the contract for sale or delivery or on the passing of the risk of loss.

(3) Unless otherwise agreed, where the contract provides for payment on or after arrival of the goods the seller must before payment allow such preliminary inspection as is feasible; but if the goods are lost, delivery of the documents and payment are due when the goods should have arrived.

§ 2—322. Delivery "Ex-Ship"

(1) Unless otherwise agreed, a term for delivery of goods "ex-ship" (which means from the carrying vessel) or in equivalent language is not restricted to a particular ship and requires delivery from a ship which has reached a place at the named port of destination where goods of the kind are usually discharged.

(2) Under such a term, unless otherwise agreed

(a) the seller must discharge all liens arising out of the carriage and furnish the buyer with a direction which puts the carrier under a duty to deliver the goods; and

(b) the risk of loss does not pass to the buyer until the goods leave the ship's tackle or are otherwise properly unloaded.

§ 2—323. Form of Bill of Lading Required in Overseas Shipment; "Overseas"

(1) Where the contract contemplates overseas shipment and contains a term C.I.F. or C. & F. or F.O.B. vessel, the seller unless otherwise agreed must obtain a negotiable bill of lading stating that the goods have been loaded on board or, in the case of a term C.I.F. or C. & F., received for shipment.

(2) Where in a case within subsection (1) a bill of lading has been issued in a set of parts, unless otherwise agreed, if the documents are not to be sent from abroad the buyer may demand tender of the full set; otherwise only one part of the bill of lading need be tendered. Even if the agreement expressly requires a full set

(a) due tender of a single part is acceptable within the provisions of this Article on cure of improper delivery (subsection (1) of Section 2—508); and

(b) even though the full set is demanded, if the documents are sent from abroad the person tendering an incomplete set may nevertheless require payment upon furnishing an indemnity which the buyer in good faith deems adequate.

(3) A shipment by water or by air or a contract contemplating such shipment is "overseas" insofar as by usage of trade or agreement it is subject to the commercial, financing or shipping practices characteristic of international deep water commerce.

§ 2—324. "No Arrival, No Sale" Term

Under a term "no arrival, no sale" or terms of like meaning, unless otherwise agreed,

(a) the seller must properly ship conforming goods and if they arrive by any means he must tender them on arrival, but he assumes no obligation that the goods will arrive unless he has caused the non-arrival; and

(b) where without fault of the seller the goods are in part lost or have so deteriorated as no longer to conform to the contract or arrive after the contract time, the buyer may proceed as if there had been casualty to identified goods (Section 2—613).

§ 2—325. "Letter of Credit" Term; "Confirmed Credit"

(1) Failure of the buyer seasonably to furnish an agreed letter of credit is a breach of the contract for sale.

(2) The delivery to seller of a proper letter of credit suspends the buyer's obligation to pay. If the letter of credit is dishonored, the seller may on seasonable notification to the buyer require payment directly from him.

(3) Unless otherwise agreed, the term "letter of credit" or "banker's credit" in a contract for sale means an irrevocable credit issued by a financing agency of good repute and, where the shipment is overseas, of good international repute. The term "confirmed credit" means that the credit must also carry the direct obligation of such an agency which does business in the seller's financial market.

§ 2—326. Sale on Approval and Sale or Return; Consignment Sales and Rights of Creditors

(1) Unless otherwise agreed, if delivered goods may be returned by the buyer even though they conform to the contract, the transaction is

(a) a "sale on approval" if the goods are delivered primarily for use, and

(b) a "sale or return" if the goods are delivered primarily for resale.

(2) Except as provided in subsection (3), goods held on approval are not subject to the claims of the buyer's creditors until acceptance; goods held on sale or return are subject to such claims while in the buyer's possession.

(3) Where goods are delivered to a person for sale and such person maintains a place of business at which he deals in goods of the kind involved, under a name other than the name of the person making delivery, then with respect to claims of creditors of the person conducting the business the goods are deemed to be on sale or return. The provisions of this subsection are applicable even though an agreement purports to reserve title to the person making delivery until payment or resale or uses such words as "on consignment" or "on memorandum." However, this subsection is not applicable if the person making delivery

(a) complies with an applicable law providing for a consignor's interest or the like to be evidenced by a sign, or

(b) establishes that the person conducting the business is generally known by his creditors to be substantially engaged in selling the goods of others, or

(c) complies with the filing provisions of the Article on secured Transactions (Article 9).

(4) Any "or return" term of a contract for sale is to be treated as a separate contract for sale within the statute of frauds section of this Article (Section 2—201) and as contradicting the sale aspect of the contract within the provisions of this Article on parol or extrinsic evidence (Section 2—202).

§ 2—327. Special Incidents of Sale on Approval and Sale or Return

(1) Under a sale on approval, unless otherwise agreed

    (a) although the goods are identified to the contract, the risk of loss and the title do not pass to the buyer until acceptance; and

    (b) use of the goods consistent with the purpose of trial is not acceptance but failure seasonably to notify the seller of election to return the goods is acceptance, and if the goods conform to the contract acceptance of any part is acceptance of the whole; and

    (c) after due notification of election to return, the return is at the seller's risk and expense but a merchant buyer must follow any reasonable instructions.

(2) Under a sale or return, unless otherwise agreed

    (a) the option to return extends to the whole or any commercial unit of the goods while in substantially their original condition, but must be exercised seasonably; and

    (b) the return is at the buyer's risk and expense.

§ 2—328. Sale by Auction

(1) In a sale by auction, if goods are put up in lots each lot is the subject of a separate sale.

(2) A sale by auction is complete when the auctioneer so announces by the fall of the hammer or in other customary manner. Where a bid is made while the hammer is falling in acceptance of a prior bid, the auctioneer may in his discretion reopen the bidding or declare the goods sold under the bid on which the hammer was falling.

(3) Such a sale is with reserve unless the goods are in explicit terms put up without reserve. In an auction with reserve, the auctioneer may withdraw the goods at any time until he announces completion of the sale. In an auction without reserve, after the auctioneer calls for bids on an article or lot, that article or lot cannot be withdrawn unless no bid is made within a reasonable time. In either case a bidder may retract his bid until the auctioneer's announcement of completion of the sale, but a bidder's retraction does not revive any previous bid.

(4) If the auctioneer knowingly receives a bid on the seller's behalf or the seller makes or procures such a bid, and notice has not been given that liberty for such bidding is reserved, the buyer may at his option avoid the sale or take the goods at the price of the last good faith bid prior to the completion of the sale. This subsection shall not apply to any bid at a forced sale.

PART 4

TITLE, CREDITORS AND GOOD FAITH PURCHASERS

§ 2—401. Passing of Title; Reservation for Security; Limited Application of This Section

Each provision of this Article with regard to the rights, obligations and remedies of the seller, the buyer, purchasers or other third parties applies irrespective of title to the goods except where the provision refers to such title. Insofar as situations are not covered by the other provisions of this Article and matters concerning title become material the following rules apply:

(1) Title to goods cannot pass under a contract for sale prior to their identification to the contract (Section 2—501), and unless otherwise explicitly agreed the buyer acquires by their identification a special property as limited by this Act. Any retention or reservation by the seller of the title (property) in goods shipped or delivered to the buyer is limited in effect to a reservation of a security interest. Subject to these provisions and to the provisions of the Article on Secured Transactions (Article 9), title to goods passes from the seller to the buyer in any manner and on any conditions explicitly agreed on by the parties.

(2) Unless otherwise explicitly agreed, title passes to the buyer at the time and place at which the seller completes his performance with reference to the physical delivery of the goods, despite any reservation of security interest and even though a document of title is to be delivered at a different time or place; and in particular and despite any reservation of a security interest by the bill of lading

    (a) if the contract requires or authorizes the seller to send the goods to the buyer but does not require him to deliver them at destination, title passes to the buyer at the time and place of shipment; but

(b) if the contract requires delivery at destination, title passes on tender there.

(3) Unless otherwise explicitly agreed, where delivery is to be made without moving the goods,

    (a) if the seller is to deliver a document of title, title passes at the time when and the place where he delivers such documents; or

    (b) if the goods are at the time of contracting already identified and no documents are to be delivered, title passes at the time and place of contracting.

(4) A rejection or other refusal by the buyer to receive or retain the goods, whether or not justified, or a justified revocation of acceptance revests title to the goods in the seller. Such revesting occurs by operation of law and is not a "sale."

§ 2—402. Rights of Seller's Creditors Against Sold Goods

(1) Except as provided in subsections (2) and (3), rights of unsecured creditors of the seller with respect to goods which have been identified to a contract for sale are subject to the buyer's rights to recover the goods under this Article (Sections 2—502 and 2—716).

(2) A creditor of the seller may treat a sale or an identification of goods to a contract for sale as void if as against him a retention of possession by the seller is fraudulent under any rule of law of the state where the goods are situated, except that retention of possession in good faith and current course of trade by a merchant-seller for a commercially reasonable time after a sale or identification is not fraudulent.

(3) Nothing in this Article shall be deemed to impair the rights of creditors of the seller

    (a) under the provisions of the Article on Secured Transactions (Article 9); or

    (b) where identification to the contract or delivery is made not in current course of trade but in satisfaction of or as security for a preexisting claim for money, security or the like and is made under circumstances which under any rule of law of the state where the goods are situated would apart from this Article constitute the transaction a fraudulent transfer or voidable preference.

§ 2—403. Power to Transfer; Good Faith Purchase of Goods; "Entrusting"

(1) A purchaser of goods acquires all title which his transferor had or had power to transfer except that a purchaser of a limited interest acquires rights only to the extent of the interest purchased.

A person with voidable title has power to transfer a good title to a good faith purchaser for value. When goods have been delivered under a transaction of purchase, the purchaser has such power even though

    (a) the transferor was deceived as to the identity of the purchaser, or

    (b) the delivery was in exchange for a check which is later dishonored, or

    (c) it was agreed that the transaction was to be a "cash sale" or

    (d) the delivery was procured through fraud punishable as larcenous under the criminal law.

(2) Any entrusting of possession of goods to a merchant who deals in goods of that kind gives him power to transfer all rights of the entruster to a buyer in ordinary course of business.

(3) "Entrusting" includes any delivery and any acquiescence in retention of possession regardless of any condition expressed between the parties to the delivery or acquiescence and regardless of whether the procurement of the entrusting or the possessor's disposition of the goods have been such as to be larcenous under the criminal law.

(4) The rights of other purchasers of goods and of lien creditors are governed by the Articles on Secured Transactions (Article 9), Bulk Transfers (Article 6) and Documents of Title (Article 7).

PART 5

PERFORMANCE

§ 2—501. Insurable Interest in Goods; Manner of Identification of Goods

(1) The buyer obtains a special property and an insurable interest in goods by identification of existing goods as goods to which the contract refers even though the goods so identified are non-conforming and he has an option to return or reject them. Such identification can be made at any time and in any manner explicitly agreed to by the parties. In the absence of explicit agreement, identification occurs

    (a) when the contract is made, if it is for the sale of goods already existing and identified;

    (b) if the contract is for the sale of future goods other than those described in paragraph (c), when goods are shipped, marked or otherwise designated by the seller as goods to which the contract refers;

    (c) when the crops are planted or otherwise become growing crops or the young are conceived, if the contract is for the sale of unborn young to be born within twelve months after contracting or for the sale of crops to be harvested within twelve months or the next normal harvest season after contracting whichever is longer.

(2) The seller retains an insurable interest in goods so long as title to or any security interest in the goods remains in him; and where the identification is by the seller alone, he may until default or insolvency or notification to the buyer that the identification is final substitute other goods for those identified.

(3) Nothing in this section impairs any insurable interest recognized under any other statute or rule of law.

§ 2—502.   Buyer's Right to Goods on Seller's Insolvency

(1) Subject to subsection (2), and even though the goods have not been shipped, a buyer who has paid a part or all of the price of goods in which he has a special property under the provisions of the immediately preceding section may, on making and keeping good a tender of any unpaid portion of their price, recover them from the seller if the seller becomes insolvent within ten days after receipt of the first installment on their price.

(2) If the identification creating his special property has been made by the buyer, he acquires the right to recover the goods only if they conform to the contract for sale.

§ 2—503.   Manner of Seller's Tender of Delivery

(1) Tender of delivery requires that the seller put and hold conforming goods at the buyer's disposition and give the buyer any notification reasonably necessary to enable him to take delivery. The manner, time and place for tender are determined by the agreement and this Article, and in particular

    (a) tender must be at a reasonable hour, and, if it is of goods, they must be kept available for the period reasonably necessary to enable the buyer to take possession; but

    (b) unless otherwise agreed, the buyer must furnish facilities reasonably suited to the receipt of the goods.

(2) Where the case is within the next section respecting shipment, tender requires that the seller comply with its provisions.

(3) Where the seller is required to deliver at a particular destination, tender requires that he comply with subsection (1) and also, in any appropriate case, tender documents as described in subsections (4) and (5) of this section.

(4) Where goods are in the possession of a bailee and are to be delivered without being moved

    (a) tender requires that the seller either tender a negotiable document of title covering such goods or procure acknowledgement by the bailee of the buyer's right to possession of the goods; but

    (b) tender to the buyer of a nonnegotiable document of title or of a written direction to the bailee to deliver is sufficient tender unless the buyer seasonably objects, and receipt by the bailee of notification of the buyer's rights fixes those rights as against the bailee and all third persons; but risk of loss of the goods and of any failure by the bailee to honor the nonnegotiable document of title or to obey the direction remains on the seller until the buyer has had a reasonable time to present the document or direction, and a refusal by the bailee to honor the document or to obey the direction defeats the tender.

(5) Where the contract requires the seller to deliver documents

    (a) he must tender all such documents in correct form, except as provided in this Article with respect to bills of lading in a set (subsection (2) of Section 2—323); and

    (b) tender through customary banking channels is sufficient and dishonor of a draft accompanying the documents constitutes nonacceptance or rejection.

§ 2—504.   Shipment by Seller

Where the seller is required or authorized to send the goods to the buyer and the contract does not require him to deliver them at a particular destination, then, unless otherwise agreed, he must

    (a) put the goods in the possession of such a carrier and make such a contract for their transportation as may be reasonable having regard to the nature of the goods and other circumstances of the case; and

    (b) obtain and promptly deliver or tender in due form any document necessary to enable the buyer to obtain possession of the goods or otherwise required by the agreement or by usage of trade; and

    (c) promptly notify the buyer of the shipment.

Failure to notify the buyer under paragraph (c) or to make a proper contract under paragraph (a) is a ground for rejection only if material delay or loss ensues.

§ 2—505. Seller's Shipment Under Reservation

(1) Where the seller has identified goods to the contract by or before shipment

    (a) his procurement of a negotiable bill of lading to his own order or otherwise reserves in him a security interest in the goods. His procurement of the bill to the order of a financing agency or of the buyer indicates in addition only the seller's expectation of transferring that interest to the person named.

    (b) a nonnegotiable bill of lading to himself or his nominee reserves possession of the goods as security but except in a case of conditional delivery (subsection (2) of Section 2—507) a nonnegotiable bill of lading naming the buyer as consignee reserves no security interest even though the seller retains possession of the bill of lading.

(2) When shipment by the seller with reservation of a security interest is in violation of the contract for sale it constitutes an improper contract for transportation within the preceding section but impairs neither the rights given to the buyer by shipment and identification of the goods to the contract nor the seller's powers as a holder of a negotiable document.

§ 2—506. Rights of Financing Agency

(1) A financing agency by paying or purchasing for value a draft which relates to a shipment of goods acquires to the extent of the payment or purchase, and in addition to its own rights under the draft and any document of title securing it, any rights of the shipper in the goods, including the right to stop delivery and the shipper's right to have the draft honored by the buyer.

(2) The right to reimbursement of a financing agency which has in good faith honored or purchased the draft under commitment to or authority from the buyer is not impaired by subsequent discovery of defects with reference to any relevant document which was apparently regular on its face.

§ 2—507. Effect of Seller's Tender; Delivery on Condition

(1) Tender of delivery is a condition to the buyer's duty to accept the goods and, unless otherwise agreed, to his duty to pay for them. Tender entitles the seller to acceptance of the goods and to payment according to the contract.

(2) Where payment is due and demanded on the delivery to the buyer of goods or documents of title, his right as against the seller to retain or dispose of them is conditional upon his making the payment due.

§ 2—508. Cure by Seller of Improper Tender or Delivery; Replacement

(1) Where any tender or delivery by the seller is rejected because non-conforming and the time for performance has not yet expired, the seller may seasonably notify the buyer of his intention to cure and may then within the contract time make a conforming delivery.

(2) Where the buyer rejects a non-conforming tender which the seller had reasonable grounds to believe would be acceptable with or without money allowance, the seller may if he seasonably notifies the buyer have a further reasonable time to substitute a conforming tender.

§ 2—509. Risk of Loss in the Absence of Breach

(1) Where the contract requires or authorizes the seller to ship the goods by carrier

    (a) if it does not require him to deliver them at a particular destination, the risk of loss passes to the buyer when the goods are duly delivered to the carrier even though the shipment is under reservation (Section 2—505); but

    (b) if it does require him to deliver them at a particular destination and the goods are there duly tendered while in the possession of the carrier, the risk of loss passes to the buyer when the goods are there duly so tendered as to enable the buyer to take delivery.

(2) Where the goods are held by a bailee to be delivered without being moved, the risk of loss passes to the buyer

    (a) on his receipt of a negotiable document of title covering the goods; or

    (b) on acknowledgment by the bailee of the buyer's right to possession of the goods; or

    (c) after his receipt of a nonnegotiable document of title or other written direction to deliver, as provided in subsection (4) (b) of Section 2—503.

(3) In any case not within subsection (1) or (2), the risk of loss passes to the buyer on his receipt of the goods if the seller is a merchant; otherwise the risk passes to the buyer on tender of delivery.

(4) The provisions of this section are subject to contrary agreement of the parties and to the provisions of this Article on sale on approval (Section 2—327) and on effect of breach on risk of loss (Section 2—510).

§ 2—510.   Effect of Breach on Risk of Loss

(1) Where a tender or delivery of goods so fails to conform to the contract as to give a right of rejection, the risk of their loss remains on the seller until cure or acceptance.

(2) Where the buyer rightfully revokes acceptance, he may to the extent of any deficiency in his effective insurance coverage treat the risk of loss as having rested on the seller from the beginning.

(3) Where the buyer, as to conforming goods already identified to the contract for sale, repudiates or is otherwise in breach before risk of their loss has passed to him, the seller may to the extent of any deficiency in his effective insurance coverage treat the risk of loss as resting on the buyer for a commercially reasonable time.

§ 2—511.   Tender of Payment by Buyer; Payment by Check

(1) Unless otherwise agreed, tender of payment is a condition to the seller's duty to tender and complete any delivery.

(2) Tender of payment is sufficient when made by any means or in any manner current in the ordinary course of business unless the seller demands payment in legal tender and gives any extension of time reasonably necessary to procure it.

(3) Subject to the provisions of this Act on the effect of an instrument on an obligation (Section 3—802), payment by check is conditional and is defeated as between the parties by dishonor of the check on due presentment.

§ 2—512.   Payment by Buyer Before Inspection

(1) Where the contract requires payment before inspection, non-conformity of the goods does not excuse the buyer from so making payment unless
   (a) the non-conformity appears without inspection; or
   (b) despite tender of the required documents, the circumstances would justify injunction against honor under the provisions of this Act (Section 5—114).

(2) Payment pursuant to subsection (1) does not constitute an acceptance of goods or impair the buyer's right to inspect or any of his remedies.

§ 2—513.   Buyer's Right to Inspection of Goods

(1) Unless otherwise agreed and subject to subsection (3), where goods are tendered or delivered or identified to the contract for sale, the buyer has a right before payment or acceptance to inspect them at any reasonable place and time and in any reasonable manner. When the seller is required or authorized to send the goods to the buyer, the inspection may be after their arrival.

(2) Expenses of inspection must be borne by the buyer but may be recovered from the seller if the goods do not conform and are rejected.

(3) Unless otherwise agreed and subject to the provisions of this Article on C.I.F. contracts (subsection (3) of Section 2—321), the buyer is not entitled to inspect the goods before payment of the price when the contract provides
   (a) for delivery "C.O.D." or on other like terms; or
   (b) for payment against documents of title, except where such payment is due only after the goods are to become available for inspection.

(4) A place or method of inspection fixed by the parties is presumed to be exclusive but, unless otherwise expressly agreed, it does not postpone identification or shift the place for delivery or for passing the risk of loss. If compliance becomes impossible, inspection shall be as provided in this section unless the place or method fixed was clearly intended as an indispensable condition, failure of which avoids the contract.

§ 2—514.   When Documents Deliverable on Acceptance; When on Payment

Unless otherwise agreed, documents against which a draft is drawn are to be delivered to the drawee on acceptance of the draft if it is payable more than three days after presentment; otherwise, only on payment.

§ 2—515.   Preserving Evidence of Goods in Dispute

In furtherance of the adjustment of any claim or dispute
   (a) either party on reasonable notification to the other, and for the purpose of ascertaining the facts and preserving evidence, has the right to inspect, test and sample the goods including such of them as may be in the possession or control of the other; and
   (b) the parties may agree to a third party inspection or survey to determine the conformity or condition of the goods and may agree that the findings shall be binding upon them in any subsequent litigation or adjustment.

PART 6

BREACH, REPUDIATION AND EXCUSE

§ 2–601. Buyer's Rights on Improper Delivery

Subject to the provisions of this Article on breach in installment contracts (Section 2—612) and unless otherwise agreed under the sections on contractual limitations of remedy (Sections 2—718 and 2—719), if the goods or the tender of delivery fail in any respect to conform to the contract, the buyer may

> (a) reject the whole; or
>
> (b) accept the whole; or
>
> (c) accept any commercial unit or units and reject the rest.

§ 2—602. Manner and Effect of Rightful Rejection

(1) Rejection of goods must be within a reasonable time after their delivery or tender. It is ineffective unless the buyer seasonably notifies the seller.

(2) Subject to the provisions of the two following sections on rejected goods (Sections 2—603 and 2—604),

> (a) after rejection any exercise of ownership by the buyer with respect to any commercial unit is wrongful as against the seller; and
>
> (b) if the buyer has before rejection taken physical possession of goods in which he does not have a security interest under the provisions of this Article (subsection (3) of Section 2—711), he is under a duty after rejection to hold them with reasonable care at the seller's disposition for a time sufficient to permit the seller to remove them; but
>
> (c) the buyer has no further obligations with regard to goods rightfully rejected.

(3) The seller's rights with respect to goods wrongfully rejected are governed by the provisions of this Article on Seller's remedies in general (Section 2—703).

§ 2—603. Merchant Buyer's Duties as to Rightfully Rejected Goods

(1) Subject to any security interest in the buyer (subsection (3) of Section 2—711), when the seller has no agent or place of business at the market of rejection, a merchant buyer is under a duty after rejection of goods in his possession or control to follow any reasonable instructions received from the seller with respect to the goods and in the absence of such instructions to make reasonable efforts to sell them for the seller's account if they are perishable or threaten to decline in value speedily. Instructions are not reasonable if on demand indemnity for expenses is not forthcoming.

(2) When the buyer sells goods under subsection (1), he is entitled to reimbursement from the seller or out of the proceeds for reasonable expenses of caring for and selling them, and if the expenses include no selling commission then to such commission as is usual in the trade or, if there is none, to a reasonable sum not exceeding ten per cent on the gross proceeds.

(3) In complying with this section, the buyer is held only to good faith and good faith conduct hereunder is neither acceptance nor conversion nor the basis of an action for damages.

§ 2—604. Buyer's Options as to Salvage of Rightfully Rejected Goods

Subject to the provisions of the immediately preceding section on perishables, if the seller gives no instructions within a reasonable time after notification of rejection the buyer may store the rejected goods for the seller's account or reship them to him or resell them for the seller's account with reimbursement as provided in the preceding section. Such action is not acceptance or conversion.

§ 2—605. Waiver of Buyer's Objections by Failure to Particularize

(1) The buyer's failure to state in connection with rejection a particular defect which is ascertainable by reasonable inspection precludes him from relying on the unstated defect to justify rejection or to establish breach

> (a) where the seller could have cured it if stated seasonably; or
>
> (b) between merchants when the seller has after rejection made a request in writing for a full and final written statement of all defects on which the buyer proposes to rely.

(2) Payment against documents made without reservation of rights precludes recovery of the payment for defects apparent on the face of the documents.

§ 2—606. What Constitutes Acceptance of Goods

(1) Acceptance of goods occurs when the buyer

> (a) after a reasonable opportunity to inspect the goods signifies to the seller that the goods are conforming or that he will take or retain them in spite of their non-conformity; or
>
> (b) fails to make an effective rejection (subsection (1) of Section 2—602), but such acceptance does not occur until

the buyer has had a reasonable opportunity to inspect them; or

(c) does any act inconsistent with the seller's ownership; but if such act is wrongful as against the seller it is an acceptance only if ratified by him.

(2) Acceptance of a part of any commercial unit is acceptance of that entire unit.

§ 2—607. Effect of Acceptance; Notice of Breach; Burden of Establishing Breach After Acceptance; Notice of Claim or Litigation to Person Answerable Over

(1) The buyer must pay at the contract rate for any goods accepted.

(2) Acceptance of goods by the buyer precludes rejection of the goods accepted and if made with knowledge of a non-conformity cannot be revoked because of it unless the acceptance was on the reasonable assumption that the non-conformity would be seasonably cured but acceptance does not of itself impair any other remedy provided by this Article for non-conformity.

(3) Where a tender has been accepted

(a) the buyer must within a reasonable time after he discovers or should have discovered any breach notify the seller of breach or be barred from any remedy; and

(b) if the claim is one for infringement or the like (subsection (3) of Section 2—312) and the buyer is sued as a result of such a breach, he must so notify the seller within a reasonable time after he receives notice of the litigation or be barred from any remedy over for liability established by the litigation.

(4) The burden is on the buyer to establish any breach with respect to the goods accepted.

(5) Where the buyer is sued for breach of a warranty or other obligation for which his seller is answerable over

(a) he may give his seller written notice of the litigation. If the notice states that the seller may come in and defend and that if the seller does not do so he will be bound in any action against him by his buyer by any determination of fact common to the two litigations, then unless the seller after seasonable receipt of the notice does come in and defend he is so bound.

(b) if the claim is one for infringement or the like (subsection (3) of Section 2—312), the original seller may demand in writing that his buyer turn over to

him control of the litigation including settlement or else be barred from any remedy over and if he also agrees to bear all expense and to satisfy any adverse judgment, then unless the buyer after seasonable receipt of the demand does turn over control the buyer is so barred.

(6) The provisions of subsections (3), (4) and (5) apply to any obligation of a buyer to hold the seller harmless against infringement or the like (subsection (3) of Section 2—312).

§ 2—608. Revocation of Acceptance in Whole or in Part

(1) The buyer may revoke his acceptance of a lot or commercial unit whose non-conformity substantially impairs its value to him if he has accepted it

(a) on the reasonable assumption that its non-conformity would be cured and it has not been seasonably cured; or

(b) without discovery of such non-conformity if his acceptance was reasonably induced either by the difficulty of discovery before acceptance or by the seller's assurances.

(2) Revocation of acceptance must occur within a reasonable time after the buyer discovers or should have discovered the ground for it and before any substantial change in condition of the goods which is not caused by their own defects. It is not effective until the buyer notifies the seller of it.

(3) A buyer who so revokes has the same rights and duties with regard to the goods involved as if he had rejected them.

§ 2—609. Right to Adequate Assurance of Performance

(1) A contract for sale imposes an obligation on each party that the other's expectation of receiving due performance will not be impaired. When reasonable grounds for insecurity arise with respect to the performance of either party, the other may in writing demand adequate assurance of due performance and until he receives such assurance may, if commercially reasonable, suspend any performance for which he has not already received the agreed return.

(2) Between merchants, the reasonableness of grounds for insecurity and the adequacy of any assurance offered shall be determined according to commercial standards.

(3) Acceptance of any improper delivery or payment does not prejudice the aggrieved party's right to demand adequate assurance of future performance.

(4) After receipt of a justified demand, failure to provide within a reasonable time, not exceeding thirty days, such assurance of due performance as is adequate under the circumstances of the particular case is a repudiation of the contract.

§ 2—610. Anticipatory Repudiation

When either party repudiates the contract with respect to a performance not yet due, the loss of which will substantially impair the value of the contract to the other, the aggrieved party may

    (a) for a commercially reasonable time await performance by the repudiating party; or

    (b) resort to any remedy for breach (Section 2—703 or Section 2—711), even though he has notified the repudiating party that he would await the latter's performance and has urged retraction; and

    (c) in either case suspend his own performance or proceed in accordance with the provisions of this Article on the seller's right to identify goods to the contract notwithstanding breach or to salvage unfinished goods (Section 2—704).

§ 2—611. Retraction of Anticipatory Repudiation

(1) Until the repudiating party's next performance is due, he can retract his repudiation unless the aggrieved party has since the repudiation cancelled or materially changed his position or otherwise indicated that he considers the repudiation final.

(2) Retraction may be by any method which clearly indicates to the aggrieved party that the repudiating party intends to perform, but must include any assurance justifiably demanded under the provisions of this Article (Section 2—609).

(3) Retraction reinstates the repudiating party's rights under the contract with due excuse and allowance to the aggrieved party for any delay occasioned by the repudiation.

§ 2—612. "Installment Contract"; Breach

(1) An "installment contract" is one which requires or authorizes the delivery of goods in separate lots to be separately accepted, even though the contract contains a clause "each delivery is a separate contract" or its equivalent.

(2) The buyer may reject any installment which is non-conforming if the non-conformity substantially impairs the value of that installment and cannot be cured or if the non-conformity is a defect in the required documents; but if the non-conformity does not fall within subsection (3) and the seller gives adequate assurance of its cure, the buyer must accept that installment.

(3) Whenever non-conformity or default with respect to one or more installments substantially impairs the value of the whole contract, there is a breach of the whole. But the aggrieved party reinstates the contract if he accepts a non-conforming installment without seasonably notifying of cancellation or if he brings an action with respect only to past installments or demands performance as to future installments.

§ 2—613. Casualty to Identified Goods

Where the contract requires for its performance goods identified when the contract is made, and the goods suffer casualty without fault of either party before the risk of loss passes to the buyer, or in a proper case under a "no arrival, no sale" term (Section 2—324) then

    (a) if the loss is total the contract is avoided; and

    (b) if the loss is partial or the goods have so deteriorated as no longer to conform to the contract the buyer may nevertheless demand inspection and at his option either treat the contract as avoided or accept the goods with due allowance from the contract price for the deterioration or the deficiency in quantity but without further right against the seller.

§ 2—614. Substituted Performance

(1) Where without fault of either party the agreed berthing, loading, or unloading facilities fail or an agreed type of carrier becomes unavailable or the agreed manner of delivery otherwise becomes commercially impracticable but a commercially reasonable substitute is available, such substitute performance must be tendered and accepted.

(2) If the agreed means or manner of payment fails because of domestic or foreign governmental regulation, the seller may withhold or stop delivery unless the buyer provides a means or manner of payment which is commercially a substantial equivalent. If delivery has already been taken, payment by the means or in the manner provided by the regulation discharges the buyer's obligation unless the regulation is discriminatory, oppressive or predatory.

§ 2—615. Excuse by Failure of Presupposed Conditions

Except so far as a seller may have assumed a greater obligation and subject to the preceding section on substituted performance:

    (a) Delay in delivery or nondelivery in whole or in part by a seller who complies with paragraphs (b) and (c) is not a breach of his duty under a contract for sale if performance as agreed has been made impracticable by the occurrence of a contingency the non-occurrence of which was a basic assumption on which the contract was made or by compliance in good faith with any applicable foreign or domestic governmental regulation or order whether or not it later proves to be invalid.

(b) Where the causes mentioned in paragraph (a) affect only a part of the seller's capacity to perform, he must allocate production and deliveries among his customers but may at his option include regular customers not then under contract as well as his own requirements for further manufacture. He may so allocate in any manner which is fair and reasonable.

(c) The seller must notify the buyer seasonably that there will be delay or non-delivery and, when allocation is required under paragraph (b), of the estimated quota thus made available for the buyer.

§ 2—616. Procedure on Notice Claiming Excuse

(1) Where the buyer receives notification of a material or indefinite delay or an allocation justified under the preceding section, he may by written notification to the seller as to any delivery concerned; and where the prospective deficiency substantially impairs the value of the whole contract under the provisions of this Article relating to breach of installment contracts (Section 2—612), then also as to the whole,

(a) terminate and thereby discharge any unexecuted portion of the contract; or

(b) modify the contract by agreeing to take his available quota in substitution.

(2) If, after receipt of such notification from the seller, the buyer fails so to modify the contract within a reasonable time not exceeding thirty days, the contract lapses with respect to any deliveries affected.

(3) The provisions of this section may not be negated by agreement except insofar as the seller has assumed a greater obligation under the preceding section.

PART 7

REMEDIES

§ 2—701. Remedies for Breach of Collateral Contracts Not Impaired

Remedies for breach of any obligation or promise collateral or ancillary to a contract for sale are not impaired by the provisions of this Article.

§ 2—702. Seller's Remedies on Discovery of Buyer's Insolvency

(1) Where the seller discovers the buyer to be insolvent, he may refuse delivery except for cash including payment for all goods theretofore delivered under the contract, and stop delivery under this Article (Section 2—705).

(2) Where the seller discovers that the buyer has received goods on credit while insolvent, he may reclaim the goods upon demand made within ten days after the receipt, but if misrepresentation of solvency has been made to the particular seller in writing within three months before delivery the ten day limitation does not apply. Except as provided in this subsection, the seller may not base a right to reclaim goods on the buyer's fraudulent or innocent misrepresentation of solvency or of intent to pay.

(3) The seller's right to reclaim under subsection (2) is subject to the rights of a buyer in ordinary course or other good faith purchaser under this Article (Section 2—403). Successful reclamation of goods excludes all other remedies with respect to them.

§ 2—703. Seller's Remedies in General

Where the buyer wrongfully rejects or revokes acceptance of goods or fails to make a payment due on or before delivery or repudiates with respect to a part or the whole, then with respect to any goods directly affected and, if the breach is of the whole contract (Section 2—612), then also with respect to the whole undelivered balance, the aggrieved seller may

(a) withhold delivery of such goods;

(b) stop delivery by any bailee as hereafter provided (Section 2—705);

(c) proceed under the next section respecting goods still unidentified to the contract;

(d) resell and recover damages as hereafter provided (Section 2—706);

(e) recover damages for non-acceptance (Section 2—708) or in a proper case the price (Section 2—709);

(f) cancel.

§ 2—704. Seller's Right to Identify Goods to the Contract Notwithstanding Breach or to Salvage Unfinished Goods

(1) An aggrieved seller under the preceding section may

    (a) identify to the contract conforming goods not already identified if at the time he learned of the breach they are in his possession or control;

    (b) treat as the subject of resale goods which have demonstrably been intended for the particular contract even though those goods are unfinished.

(2) Where the goods are unfinished an aggrieved seller may, in the exercise of reasonable commercial judgment for the purposes of avoiding loss and of effective realization, either complete the manufacture and wholly identify the goods to the contract or cease manufacture and resell for scrap or salvage value or proceed in any other reasonable manner.

§ 2—705. Seller's Stoppage of Delivery in Transit or Otherwise

(1) The seller may stop delivery of goods in the possession of a carrier or other bailee when he discovers the buyer to be insolvent (Section 2—702) and may stop delivery of carload, truckload, planeload or larger shipments of express or freight when the buyer repudiates or fails to make a payment due before delivery or if for any other reason the seller has a right to withhold or reclaim the goods.

(2) As against such buyer, the seller may stop delivery until

    (a) receipt of the goods by the buyer; or

    (b) acknowledgment to the buyer by any bailee of the goods except a carrier that the bailee holds the goods for the buyer; or

    (c) such acknowledgment to the buyer by a carrier by reshipment or as warehouseman; or

    (d) negotiation to the buyer of any negotiable document of title covering the goods.

(3) (a) To stop delivery the seller must so notify as to enable the bailee by reasonable diligence to prevent delivery of the goods.

    (b) After such notification the bailee must hold and deliver the goods according to the directions of the seller, but the seller is liable to the bailee for any ensuing charges or damages.

    (c) If a negotiable document of title has been issued for the goods, the bailee is not obliged to obey a notification to stop until surrender of the document.

    (d) A carrier who has issued a nonnegotiable bill of lading is not obliged to obey a notification to stop received from a person other than the consignor.

§ 2—706. Seller's Resale Including Contract for Resale

(1) Under the conditions stated in Section 2—703 on seller's remedies, the seller may resell the goods concerned or the undelivered balance thereof. Where the resale is made in good faith and in a commercially reasonable manner, the seller may recover the difference between the resale price and the contract price together with any incidental damages allowed under the provisions of this Article (Section 2—710), but less expenses saved in consequence of the buyer's breach.

(2) Except as otherwise provided in subsection (3) or unless otherwise agreed, resale may be at public or private sale including sale by way of one or more contracts to sell or of identification to an existing contract of the seller. Sale may be as a unit or in parcels and at any time and place and on any terms but every aspect of the sale including the method, manner, time, place and terms must be commercially reasonable. The resale must be reasonably identified as referring to the broken contract, but it is not necessary that the goods be in existence or that any or all of them have been identified to the contract before the breach.

(3) Where the resale is at private sale, the seller must give the buyer reasonable notification of his intention to resell.

(4) Where the resale is at public sale

    (a) only identified goods can be sold except where there is a recognized market for a public sale of futures in goods of the kind; and

    (b) it must be made at a usual place or market for public sale if one is reasonably available and except in the case of goods which are perishable or threaten to decline in value speedily the seller must give the buyer reasonable notice of the time and place of the resale; and

    (c) if the goods are not to be within the view of those attending the sale, the notification of sale must state the place where the goods are located and provide for their reasonable inspection by prospective bidders; and

    (d) the seller may buy.

(5) A purchaser who buys in good faith at a resale takes the goods free of any rights of the original buyer even though the seller fails to comply with one or more of the requirements of this section.

(6) The seller is not accountable to the buyer for any profit made on any resale. A person in the position of a seller (Section 2—707) or a buyer who has rightfully rejected or justifiably revoked acceptance must account for any excess over the amount of his security interest, as hereinafter defined (subsection (3) of Section 2—711).

§ 2—707. "Person in the Position of a Seller"

(1) A "person in the position of a seller" includes, as against a principal, an agent who has paid or become responsible for the price of goods on behalf of his principal or anyone who otherwise holds a security interest or other right in goods similar to that of a seller.

(2) A person in the position of a seller may as provided in this Article withhold or stop delivery (Section 2—705) and resell (Section 2—706) and recover incidental damages (Section 2—710).

§ 2—708. Seller's Damages for Nonacceptance or Repudiation

(1) Subject to subsection (2) and to the provisions of this Article with respect to proof of market price (Section 2—723), the measure of damages for nonacceptance or repudiation by the buyer is the difference between the market price at the time and place for tender and the unpaid contract price together with any incidental damages provided in this Article (Section 2—710), but less expenses saved in consequence of the buyer's breach.

(2) If the measure of damages provided in subsection (1) is inadequate to put the seller in as good a position as performance would have done, then the measure of damages is the profit (including reasonable overhead) which the seller would have made from full performance by the buyer, together with any incidental damages provided in this Article (Section 2—710), due allowance for costs reasonably incurred and due credit for payments or proceeds of resale.

§ 2—709. Action for the Price

(1) When the buyer fails to pay the price as it becomes due, the seller may recover, together with any incidental damages under the next section, the price

    (a) of goods accepted or of conforming goods lost or damaged within a commercially reasonable time after risk of their loss has passed to the buyer; and

    (b) of goods identified to the contract if the seller is unable after reasonable effort to resell them at a reasonable price or the circumstances reasonably indicate that such effort will be unavailing.

(2) Where the seller sues for the price, he must hold for the buyer any goods which have been identified to the contract and are still in his control except that if resale becomes possible he may resell them at any time prior to the collection of the judgment. The net proceeds of any such resale must be credited to the buyer and payment of the judgment entitles him to any goods not resold.

(3) After the buyer has wrongfully rejected or revoked acceptance of the goods or has failed to make a payment due or has repudiated (Section 2—610), a seller who is held not entitled to the price under this section shall nevertheless be awarded damages for nonacceptance under the preceding section.

§ 2—710. Seller's Incidental Damages

Incidental damages to an aggrieved seller include any commercially reasonable charges, expenses or commissions incurred in stopping delivery, in the transportation, care and custody of goods after the buyer's breach, in connection with return or resale of the goods or otherwise resulting from the breach.

§ 2—711. Buyer's Remedies in General; Buyer's Security Interest in Rejected Goods

(1) Where the seller fails to make delivery or repudiates or the buyer rightfully rejects or justifiably revokes acceptance, then with respect to any goods involved, and with respect to the whole if the breach goes to the whole contract (Section 2—612), the buyer may cancel and whether or not he has done so may in addition to recovering so much of the price as has been paid

    (a) "cover" and have damages under the next section as to all the goods affected whether or not they have been identified to the contract; or

    (b) recover damages for nondelivery as provided in this Article (Section 2—713).

(2) Where the seller fails to deliver or repudiates, the buyer may also

    (a) if the goods have been identified recover them as provided in this Article (Section 2—502); or

    (b) in a proper case obtain specific performance or replevy the goods as provided in this Article (Section 2—716).

(3) On rightful rejection or justifiable revocation of acceptance, a buyer has a security interest

in goods in his possession or control for any payments made on their price and any expenses reasonably incurred in their inspection, receipt, transportation, care and custody and may hold such goods and resell them in like manner as an aggrieved seller (Section 2—706).

§ 2—712. "Cover"; Buyer's Procurement of Substitute Goods

(1) After a breach within the preceding section, the buyer may "cover" by making in good faith and without unreasonable delay any reasonable purchase of or contract to purchase goods in substitution for those due from the seller.

(2) The buyer may recover from the seller as damages the difference between the cost of cover and the contract price together with any incidental or consequential damages as hereinafter defined (Section 2—715), but less expenses saved in consequence of the seller's breach.

(3) Failure of the buyer to effect cover within this section does not bar him from any other remedy.

§ 2—713. Buyer's Damages for Nondelivery or Repudiation

(1) Subject to the provisions of this Article with respect to proof of market price (Section 2—723), the measure of damages for nondelivery or repudiation by the seller is the difference between the market price at the time when the buyer learned of the breach and the contract price together with any incidental and consequential damages provided in this Article (Section 2—715), but less expenses saved in consequence of the seller's breach.

(2) Market price is to be determined as of the place for tender or, in cases of rejection after arrival or revocation of acceptance, as of the place of arrival.

§ 2—714. Buyer's Damages for Breach in Regard to Accepted Goods

(1) Where the buyer has accepted goods and given notification (subsection (3) of Section 2—607), he may recover as damages for any non-conformity of tender the loss resulting in the ordinary course of events from the seller's breach as determined in any manner which is reasonable.

(2) The measure of damages for breach of warranty is the difference at the time and place of acceptance between the value of the goods accepted and the value they would have had if they had been as warranted, unless special circumstances show proximate damages of a different amount.

(3) In a proper case any incidental and consequential damages under the next section may also be recovered.

§ 2—715. Buyer's Incidental and Consequential Damages

(1) Incidental damages resulting from the seller's breach include expenses reasonably incurred in inspection, receipt, transportation and care and custody of goods rightfully rejected, any commercially reasonable charges, expenses or commissions in connection with effecting cover and any other reasonable expense incident to the delay or other breach.

(2) Consequential damages resulting from the seller's breach include

    (a) any loss resulting from general or particular requirements and needs of which the seller at the time of contracting had reason to know and which could not reasonably be prevented by cover or otherwise; and

    (b) injury to person or property proximately resulting from any breach of warranty.

§ 2—716. Buyer's Right to Specific Performance or Replevin

(1) Specific performance may be decreed where the goods are unique or in other proper circumstances.

(2) The decree for specific performance may include such terms and conditions as to payment of the price, damages, or other relief as the court may deem just.

(3) The buyer has a right of replevin for goods identified to the contract if after reasonable effort he is unable to effect cover for such goods or the circumstances reasonably indicate that such effort will be unavailing or if the goods have been shipped under reservation and satisfaction of the security interest in them has been made or tendered.

§ 2—717. Deduction of Damages From the Price

The buyer on notifying the seller of his intention to do so may deduct all or any part of the damages resulting from any breach of the contract from any part of the price still due under the same contract.

§ 2—718. Liquidation or Limitation of Damages; Deposits

(1) Damages for breach by either party may be liquidated in the agreement but only at an amount which is reasonable in the light of the anticipated or actual harm caused by the breach, the difficulties of proof of loss, and the inconvenience or nonfeasibility of otherwise obtaining an adequate remedy. A term fixing unreasonably large liquidated damages is void as a penalty.

(2) Where the seller justifiably withholds delivery of goods because of the buyer's breach, the buyer is entitled to restitution of any amount by which the sum of his payments exceeds

    (a) the amount to which the seller is entitled by virtue of terms liquidating the seller's damages in accordance with subsection (1), or

    (b) in the absence of such terms, twenty percent of the value of the total performance for which the buyer is obligated under the contract or $500, whichever is smaller.

(3) The buyer's right to restitution under subsection (2) is subject to offset to the extent that the seller establishes

    (a) a right to recover damages under the provisions of this Article other than subsection (1), and

    (b) the amount or value of any benefits received by the buyer directly or indirectly by reason of the contract.

(4) Where a seller has received payment in goods, their reasonable value or the proceeds of their resale shall be treated as payments for the purposes of subsection (2); but if the seller has notice of the buyer's breach before reselling goods received in part performance, his resale is subject to the conditions laid down in this Article on resale by an aggrieved seller (Section 2—706).

§ 2—719. Contractual Modification or Limitation of Remedy

(1) Subject to the provisions of subsections (2) and (3) of this section and of the preceding section on liquidation and limitation of damages,

    (a) the agreement may provide for remedies in addition to or in substitution for those provided in this Article and may limit or alter the measure of damages recoverable under this Article, as by limiting the buyer's remedies to return of the goods and repayment of the price or to repair and replacement of non-conforming goods or parts; and

    (b) resort to a remedy as provided is optional unless the remedy is expressly agreed to be exclusive, in which case it is the sole remedy.

(2) Where circumstances cause an exclusive or limited remedy to fail of its essential purpose, remedy may be had as provided in this Act.

(3) Consequential damages may be limited or excluded unless the limitation or exclusion is unconscionable. Limitation of consequential damages for injury to the person in the case of consumer goods is prima facie unconscionable but limitation of damages where the loss is commercial is not.

§ 2—720. Effect of "Cancellation" or "Rescission" on Claims for Antecedent Breach

Unless the contrary intention clearly appears, expressions of "cancellation" or "rescission" of the contract or the like shall not be construed as a renunciation or discharge of any claim in damages for an antecedent breach.

§ 2—721. Remedies for Fraud

Remedies for material misrepresentation or fraud include all remedies available under this Article for non-fraudulent breach. Neither rescission or a claim for rescission of the contract for sale nor rejection or return of the goods shall bar or be deemed inconsistent with a claim for damages or other remedy.

§ 2—722. Who Can Sue Third Parties for Injury to Goods

Where a third party so deals with goods which have been identified to a contract for sale as to cause actionable injury to a party to that contract

    (a) a right of action against the third party is in either party to the contract for sale who has title to or a security interest or a special property or an insurable interest in the goods; and if the goods have been destroyed or converted, a right of action is also in the party who either bore the risk of loss under the contract for sale or has since the injury assumed that risk as against the other;

    (b) if at the time of the injury the party plaintiff did not bear the risk of loss as against the other party to the contract for sale and there is no arrangement between them for disposition of the recovery, his suit or settlement is, subject to his own interest, as a fiduciary for the other party to the contract;

    (c) either party may with the consent of the other sue for the benefit of whom it may concern.

§ 2—723. Proof of Market Price: Time and Place

(1) If an action based on anticipatory repudiation comes to trial before the time for performance with respect to some or all of the goods, any damages based on market price (Section 2—708 or Section 2—713) shall be determined according to the price of such goods prevailing at the time when the aggrieved party learned of the repudiation.

(2) If evidence of a price prevailing at the times or places described in this Article is not readily available, the price prevailing within any reasonable time before or after the time described or at any other place which in commercial judgment or under usage of trade would serve as a reasonable substitute for the one described may be used, making any proper allowance for the cost of transporting the goods to or from such other place.

(3) Evidence of a relevant price prevailing at a time or place other than the one described in this Article offered by one party is not admissible unless and until he has given the other party such notice as the court finds sufficient to prevent unfair surprise.

§ 2—724. Admissibility of Market Quotations

Whenever the prevailing price or value of any goods regularly bought and sold in any established commodity market is in issue, reports in official publications or trade journals or in newspapers or periodicals of general circulation published as the reports of such market shall be admissible in evidence. The circumstances of the preparation of such a report may be shown to affect its weight but not its admissibility.

§ 2—725. Statute of Limitations in Contracts for Sale

(1) An action for breach of any contract for sale must be commenced within four years after the cause of action has accrued. By the original agreement, the parties may reduce the period of limitation to not less than one year but may not extend it.

(2) A cause of action accrues when the breach occurs, regardless of the aggrieved party's lack of knowledge of the breach. A breach of warranty occurs when tender of delivery is made, except that where a warranty explicitly extends to future performance of the goods and discovery of the breach must await the time of such performance the cause of action accrues when the breach is or should have been discovered.

(3) Where an action commenced within the time limited by subsection (1) is so terminated as to leave available a remedy by another action for the same breach, such other action may be commenced after the expiration of the time limited and within six months after the termination of the first action unless the termination resulted from voluntary discontinuance or from dismissal for failure or neglect to prosecute.

(4) This section does not alter the law on tolling of the statute of limitations nor does it apply to causes of action which have accrued before this Act becomes effective.

ARTICLE 3

COMMERCIAL PAPER

PART 1

SHORT TITLE, FORM AND INTERPRETATION

§ 3—101. Short Title

This Article shall be known and may be cited as Uniform Commercial Code—Commercial Paper.

§ 3—102. Definitions and Index of Definitions

(1) In this Article unless the context otherwise requires

   (a) "Issue" means the first delivery of an instrument to a holder or a remitter.

   (b) An "order" is a direction to pay and must be more than an authorization or request. It must identify the person to pay with reasonable certainty. It may be addressed to one or more such persons jointly or in the alternative but not in succession.

   (c) A "promise" is an undertaking to pay and must be more than an acknowledgment of an obligation.

   (d) "Secondary party" means a drawer or indorser.

   (e) "Instrument" means a negotiable instrument.

(2) Other definitions applying to this Article and the sections in which they appear are:

   "Acceptance." Section 3—410.
   "Accommodation party." Section 3—415.
   "Alteration." Section 3—407.
   "Certificate of deposit." Section 3—104.
   "Certification." Section 3—411.
   "Check." Section 3—104.
   "Definite time." Section 3—109.
   "Dishonor." Section 3—507.
   "Draft." Section 3—104.
   "Holder in due course." Section 3—302.
   "Negotiation." Section 3—202.

"Note." Section 3—104.

"Notice of dishonor." Section 3—508.

"On demand." Section 3—108.

"Presentment." Section 3—504.

"Protest." Section 3—509.

"Restrictive Indorsement." Section 3—205.

"Signature." Section 3—401.

(3) The following definitions in other Articles apply to this Article:

"Account." Section 4—104.

"Banking Day." Section 4—104.

"Clearing house." Section 4—104.

"Collecting bank." Section 4—105.

"Customer." Section 4—104.

"Depositary Bank." Section 4—105.

"Documentary Draft." Section 4—104.

"Intermediary Bank." Section 4—105.

"Item." Section 4—104.

"Midnight deadline." Section 4—104.

"Payor bank." Section 4—105.

(4) In addition Article 1 contains general definitions and principles of construction and interpretation applicable throughout this Article.

§ 3—103. Limitations on Scope of Article

(1) This Article does not apply to money, documents of title or investment securities.

(2) The provisions of this Article are subject to the provisions of the Article on Bank Deposits and Collections (Article 4) and Secured Transactions (Article 9).

§ 3—104. Form of Negotiable Instruments; "Draft"; "Check"; "Certificate of Deposit"; "Note"

(1) Any writing to be a negotiable instrument within this Article must

(a) be signed by the maker or drawer; and

(b) contain an unconditional promise or order to pay a sum certain in money and no other promise, order, obligation or power given by the maker or drawer except as authorized by this Article; and

(c) be payable on demand or at a definite time; and

(d) be payable to order or to bearer.

(2) A writing which complies with the requirements of this section is

(a) a "draft" ("bill of exchange") if it is an order;

(b) a "check" if it is a draft drawn on a bank and payable on demand;

(c) a "certificate of deposit" if it is an acknowledgment by a bank of receipt of money with an engagement to repay it;

(d) a "note" if it is a promise other than a certificate of deposit.

(3) As used in other Articles of this Act, and as the context may require, the terms "draft," "check," "certificate of deposit" and "note" may refer to instruments which are not negotiable within this Article as well as to instruments which are so negotiable.

§ 3—105. When Promise or Order Unconditional

(1) A promise or order otherwise unconditional is not made conditional by the fact that the instrument

(a) is subject to implied or constructive conditions; or

(b) states its consideration, whether performed or promised, or the transaction which gave rise to the instrument, or that the promise or order is made or the instrument matures in accordance with or "as per" such transaction; or

(c) refers to or states that it arises out of a separate agreement or refers to a separate agreement for rights as to prepayment or acceleration; or

(d) states that it is drawn under a letter of credit; or

(e) states that it is secured, whether by mortgage, reservation of title or otherwise; or

(f) indicates a particular account to be debited or any other fund or source from which reimbursement is expected; or

(g) is limited to payment out of a particular fund or the proceeds of a particular source, if the instrument is issued by a government or governmental agency or unit; or

(h) is limited to payment out of the entire assets of a partnership, unincorporated association, trust or estate by or on behalf of which the instrument is issued.

(2) A promise or order is not unconditional if the instrument

(a) states that it is subject to or governed by any other agreement; or

(b) states that it is to be paid only out of a particular fund or source except as provided in this section.

§ 3—106. Sum Certain

(1) The sum payable is a sum certain even though it is to be paid

    (a) with stated interest or by stated installments; or

    (b) with stated different rates of interest before and after default or a specified date; or

    (c) with a stated discount or addition if paid before or after the date fixed for payment; or

    (d) with exchange or less exchange, whether at a fixed rate or at the current rate; or

    (e) with costs of collection or an attorney's fee or both upon default.

(2) Nothing in this section shall validate any term which is otherwise illegal.

§ 3—107. Money

(1) An instrument is payable in money if the medium of exchange in which it is payable is money at the time the instrument is made. An instrument payable in "currency" or "current funds" is payable in money.

(2) A promise or order to pay a sum stated in a foreign currency is for a sum certain in money and, unless a different medium of payment is specified in the instrument, may be satisfied by payment of that number of dollars which the stated foreign currency will purchase at the buying sight rate for that currency on the day on which the instrument is payable or, if payable on demand, on the day of demand. If such an instrument specifies a foreign currency as the medium of payment the instrument is payable in that currency.

§ 3—108. Payable on Demand

Instruments payable on demand include those payable at sight or on presentation and those in which no time for payment is stated.

§ 3—109. Definite Time

(1) An instrument is payable at a definite time if by its terms it is payable

    (a) on or before a stated date or at a fixed period after a stated date; or

    (b) at a fixed period after sight; or

    (c) at a definite time subject to any acceleration; or

    (d) at a definite time subject to extension at the option of the holder, or to extension to a further definite time at the option of the maker or acceptor or automatically upon or after a specified act or event.

(2) An instrument which by its terms is otherwise payable only upon an act or event uncertain as to time of occurrence is not payable at a definite time even though the act or event has occurred.

§ 3—110. Payable to Order

(1) An instrument is payable to order when by its terms it is payable to the order or assigns of any person therein specified with reasonable certainty, or to him or his order, or when it is conspicuously designated on its face as "exchange" or the like and names a payee. It may be payable to the order of

    (a) the maker or drawer; or

    (b) the drawee; or

    (c) a payee who is not maker, drawer or drawee; or

    (d) two or more payees together or in the alternative; or

    (e) an estate, trust or fund, in which case it is payable to the order of the representative of such estate, trust or fund or his successors; or

    (f) an office, or an officer by his title as such in which case it is payable to the principal but the incumbent of the office or his successors may act as if he or they were the holder; or

    (g) a partnership or unincorporated association, in which case it is payable to the partnership or association and may be indorsed or transferred by any person thereto authorized.

(2) An instrument not payable to order is not made so payable by such words as "payable upon return of this instrument properly indorsed."

(3) An instrument made payable both to order and to bearer is payable to order unless the bearer words are handwritten or typewritten.

§ 3—111. Payable to Bearer

An instrument is payable to bearer when by its terms it is payable to

    (a) bearer or the order of bearer; or

    (b) a specified person or bearer; or

    (c) "cash" or the order of "cash," or any other indication which does not purport to designate a specific payee.

§ 3—112. Terms and Omissions Not Affecting Negotiability

(1) The negotiability of an instrument is not affected by

    (a) the omission of a statement of any consideration or of the place where the instrument is drawn or payable; or

    (b) a statement that collateral has been given to secure obligations either on the instrument or otherwise of an obligor on the instrument or that in case of default on those obligations the holder may realize on or dispose of the collateral; or

(c) a promise or power to maintain or protect collateral or to give additional collateral; or

(d) a term authorizing a confession of judgment on the instrument if it is not paid when due; or

(e) a term purporting to waive the benefit of any law intended for the advantage or protection of any obligor; or

(f) a term in a draft providing that the payee by indorsing or cashing it acknowledges full satisfaction of an obligation of the drawer; or

(g) a statement in a draft drawn in a set of parts (Section 3—801) to the effect that the order is effective only if no other part has been honored.

(2) Nothing in this section shall validate any term which is otherwise illegal.

§ 3—113. Seal

An instrument otherwise negotiable is within this Article even though it is under a seal.

§ 3—114. Date, Antedating, Postdating

(1) The negotiability of an instrument is not affected by the fact that it is undated, antedated or postdated.

(2) Where an instrument is antedated or postdated, the time when it is payable is determined by the stated date if the instrument is payable on demand or at a fixed period after date.

(3) Where the instrument or any signature thereon is dated, the date is presumed to be correct.

§ 3—115. Incomplete Instruments

(1) When a paper, whose contents at the time of signing show that it is intended to become an instrument, is signed while still incomplete in any necessary respect, it cannot be enforced until completed; but when it is completed in accordance with authority given, it is effective as completed.

(2) If the completion is unauthorized, the rules as to material alteration apply (Section 3—407), even though the paper was not delivered by the maker or drawer; but the burden of establishing that any completion is unauthorized is on the party so asserting.

§ 3—116. Instruments Payable to Two or More Persons

An instrument payable to the order of two or more persons,

(a) if in the alternative, is payable to any one of them and may be negotiated, discharged or enforced by any of them who has possession of it;

(b) if not in the alternative, is payable to all of them and may be negotiated, discharged or enforced only by all of them.

§ 3—117. Instruments Payable With Words of Description

An instrument made payable to a named person with the addition of words describing him

(a) as agent or officer of a specified person is payable to his principal but the agent or officer may act as if he were the holder;

(b) as any other fiduciary for a specified person or purpose is payable to the payee and may be negotiated, discharged or enforced by him;

(c) in any other manner is payable to the payee unconditionally and the additional words are without effect on subsequent parties.

§ 3—118. Ambiguous Terms and Rules of Construction

The following rules apply to every instrument:

(a) Where there is doubt whether the instrument is a draft or a note, the holder may treat it as either. A draft drawn on the drawer is effective as a note.

(b) Handwritten terms control typewritten and printed terms, and typewritten control printed.

(c) Words control figures except that if the words are ambiguous figures control.

(d) Unless otherwise specified, a provision for interest means interest at the judgment rate at the place of payment from the date of the instrument, or if it is undated from the date of issue.

(e) Unless the instrument otherwise specifies, two or more persons who sign as maker, acceptor or drawer or indorser and as a part of the same transaction are jointly and severally liable even though the instrument contains such words as "I promise to pay."

(f) Unless otherwise specified, consent to extension authorizes a single extension for not longer than the original period. A consent to extension, expressed in the instrument, is binding on secondary parties and accommodation makers. A holder may not exercise his option to extend an instrument over the objection of a maker or acceptor or other party who in accordance with Section 3—604 tenders full payment when the instrument is due.

§ 3—119. Other Writings Affecting Instrument

(1) As between the obligor and his immediate obligee or any transferee, the terms of an instrument may be modified or affected by any other written agreement executed as a part of the same transaction, except that a holder in due course is not affected by any limitation of his rights arising out of the separate written agreement if he had no notice of the limitation when he took the instrument.

(2) A separate agreement does not affect the negotiability of an instrument.

§ 3—120. Instruments "Payable Through" Bank

An instrument which states that it is "payable through" a bank or the like designates that bank as a collecting bank to make presentment but does not of itself authorize the bank to pay the instrument.

§ 3—121. Instruments Payable at Bank

Note: *If this Act is introduced in the Congress of the United States this section should be omitted. (States to select either alternative)*

Alternative A—

A note or acceptance which states that it is payable at a bank is the equivalent of a draft drawn on the bank payable when it falls due out of any funds of the maker or acceptor in current account or otherwise available for such payment.

Alternative B—

A note or acceptance which states that it is payable at a bank is not of itself an order or authorization to the bank to pay it.

§ 3—122. Accrual of Cause of Action

(1) A cause of action against a maker or an acceptor accrues,
(a) in the case of a time instrument, on the day after maturity;
(b) in the case of a demand instrument, upon its date or, if no date is stated, on the date of issue.

(2) A cause of action against the obligor of a demand or time certificate of deposit accrues upon demand, but demand on a time certificate may not be made until on or after the date of maturity.

(3) A cause of action against a drawer of a draft or an indorser of any instrument accrues upon demand following dishonor of the instrument. Notice of dishonor is a demand.

(4) Unless an instrument provides otherwise, interest runs at the rate provided by law for a judgment
(a) in the case of a maker, acceptor or other primary obligor of a demand instrument, from the date of demand;
(b) in all other cases from the date of accrual of the cause of action.

PART 2

TRANSFER AND NEGOTIATION

§ 3—201. Transfer: Right to Indorsement

(1) Transfer of an instrument vests in the transferee such rights as the transferor has therein, except that a transferee who has himself been a party to any fraud or illegality affecting the instrument or who as a prior holder had notice of a defense or claim against it cannot improve his position by taking from a later holder in due course.

(2) A transfer of a security interest in an instrument vests the foregoing rights in the transferee to the extent of the interest transferred.

(3) Unless otherwise agreed, any transfer for value of an instrument not then payable to bearer gives the transferee the specifically enforceable right to have the unqualified indorsement of the transferor. Negotiation takes effect only when the indorsement is made and until that time there is no presumption that the transferee is the owner.

§ 3—202. Negotiation

(1) Negotiation is the transfer of an instrument in such form that the transferee becomes a holder. If the instrument is payable to order, it is negotiated by delivery with any necessary indorsement; if payable to bearer, it is negotiated by delivery.

(2) An indorsement must be written by or on behalf of the holder and on the instrument or on a paper so firmly affixed thereto as to become a part thereof.

(3) An indorsement is effective for negotiation only when it conveys the entire instrument or any unpaid residue. If it purports to be of less, it operates only as a partial assignment.

(4) Words of assignment, condition, waiver, guaranty, limitation or disclaimer of liability and the

like accompanying an indorsement do not affect its character as an indorsement.

§ 3—203. Wrong or Misspelled Name

Where an instrument is made payable to a person under a misspelled name or one other than his own, he may indorse in that name or his own or both; but signature in both names may be required by a person paying or giving value for the instrument.

§ 3—204. Special Indorsement; Blank Indorsement

(1) A special indorsement specifies the person to whom or to whose order it makes the instrument payable. Any instrument specially indorsed becomes payable to the order of the special indorsee and may be further negotiated only by his indorsement.

(2) An indorsement in blank specifies no particular indorsee and may consist of a mere signature. An instrument payable to order and indorsed in blank becomes payable to bearer and may be negotiated by delivery alone until specially indorsed.

(3) The holder may convert a blank indorsement into a special indorsement by writing over the signature of the indorser in blank any contract consistent with the character of the indorsement.

§ 3—205. Restrictive Indorsements

An indorsement is restrictive which either
  (a) is conditional; or
  (b) purports to prohibit further transfer of the instrument; or
  (c) includes the words "for collection," "for deposit," "pay any bank," or like terms signifying a purpose of deposit or collection; or
  (d) otherwise states that it is for the benefit or use of the indorser or of another person.

§ 3—206. Effect of Restrictive Indorsement

(1) No restrictive indorsement prevents further transfer or negotiation of the instrument.

(2) An intermediary bank, or a payor bank which is not the depositary bank, is neither given notice nor otherwise affected by a restrictive indorsement of any person except the bank's immediate transferor or the person presenting for payment.

(3) Except for an intermediary bank, any transferee under an indorsement which is conditional or includes the words "for collection," "for deposit," "pay any bank," or like terms (subparagraphs (a) and (c) of Section 3—205) must pay or apply any value given by him for or on the security of the instrument consistently with the indorsement and to the extent that he does so he becomes a holder

for value. In addition, such transferee is a holder in due course if he otherwise complies with the requirements of Section 3—302 on what constitutes a holder in due course.

(4) The first taker under an indorsement for the benefit of the indorser or another person (subparagraph (d) of Section 3—205) must pay or apply any value given by him for or on the security of the instrument consistently with the indorsement and, to the extent that he does so, he becomes a holder for value. In addition, such taker is a holder in due course if he otherwise complies with the requirements of Section 3—302 on what constitutes a holder in due course. A later holder for value is neither given notice nor otherwise affected by such restrictive indorsement unless he has knowledge that a fiduciary or other person has negotiated the instrument in any transaction for his own benefit or otherwise in breach of duty (subsection (2) of Section 3—304).

§ 3—207. Negotiation Effective Although It May Be Rescinded

(1) Negotiation is effective to transfer the instrument although the negotiation is
  (a) made by an infant, a corporation exceeding its powers, or any other person without capacity; or
  (b) obtained by fraud, duress or mistake of any kind; or
  (c) part of an illegal transaction; or
  (d) made in breach of duty.

(2) Except as against a subsequent holder in due course, such negotiation is in an appropriate case subject to rescission, the declaration of a constructive trust or any other remedy permitted by law.

§ 3—208. Reacquisition

Where an instrument is returned to or reacquired by a prior party, he may cancel any indorsement which is not necessary to his title and reissue or further negotiate the instrument; but any intervening party is discharged as against the reacquiring party and subsequent holders not in due course and, if his indorsement has been cancelled, is discharged as against subsequent holders in due course as well.

PART 3

RIGHTS OF A HOLDER

§ 3—301. Rights of a Holder

The holder of an instrument whether or not he is the owner may transfer or negotiate it and, except as otherwise provided in Section 3—603 on payment or satisfaction, discharge it or enforce payment in his own name.

§ 3—302. Holder in Due Course

(1) A holder in due course is a holder who takes the instrument

    (a) for value; and

    (b) in good faith; and

    (c) without notice that it is overdue or has been dishonored or of any defense against or claim to it on the part of any person.

(2) A payee may be a holder in due course.

(3) A holder does not become a holder in due course of an instrument:

    (a) by purchase of it at judicial sale or by taking it under legal process; or

    (b) by acquiring it in taking over an estate; or

    (c) by purchasing it as part of a bulk transaction not in regular course of business of the transferor.

(4) A purchaser of a limited interest can be a holder in due course only to the extent of the interest purchased.

§ 3—303. Taking for Value

A holder takes the instrument for value

    (a) to the extent that the agreed consideration has been performed or that he acquires a security interest in or a lien on the instrument otherwise than by legal process; or

    (b) when he takes the instrument in payment of or as security for an antecedent claim against any person whether or not the claim is due; or

    (c) when he gives a negotiable instrument for it or makes an irrevocable commitment to a third person.

§ 3—304. Notice to Purchaser

(1) The purchaser has notice of a claim or defense if

    (a) the instrument is so incomplete, bears such visible evidence of forgery or alteration, or is otherwise so irregular as to call into question its validity, terms or ownership or to create an ambiguity as to the party to pay; or

    (b) the purchaser has notice that the obligation of any party is voidable in whole or in part, or that all parties have been discharged.

(2) The purchaser has notice of a claim against the instrument when he has knowledge that a fiduciary has negotiated the instrument in payment of or

as security for his own debt or in any transaction for his own benefit or otherwise in breach of duty.

(3) The purchaser has notice that an instrument is overdue if he has reason to know

    (a) that any part of the principal amount is overdue or that there is an uncured default in payment of another instrument of the same series; or

    (b) that acceleration of the instrument has been made; or

    (c) that he is taking a demand instrument after demand has been made or more than a reasonable length of time after its issue. A reasonable time for a check drawn and payable within the states and territories of the United States and the District of Columbia is presumed to be thirty days.

(4) Knowledge of the following facts does not of itself give the purchaser notice of a defense or claim

    (a) that the instrument is antedated or postdated;

    (b) that it was issued or negotiated in return for an executory promise or accompanied by a separate agreement, unless the purchaser has notice that a defense or claim has arisen from the terms thereof;

    (c) that any party has signed for accommodation;

    (d) that an incomplete instrument has been completed, unless the purchaser has notice of any improper completion;

    (e) that any person negotiating the instrument is or was a fiduciary;

    (f) that there has been default in payment of interest on the instrument or in payment of any other instrument, except one of the same series.

(5) The filing or recording of a document does not of itself constitute notice within the provisions of this Article to a person who would otherwise be a holder in due course.

(6) To be effective, notice must be received at such time and in such manner as to give a reasonable opportunity to act on it.

§ 3—305. Rights of a Holder in Due Course

To the extent that a holder is a holder in due course, he takes the instrument free from

(1) all claims to it on the part of any person; and

(2) all defenses of any party to the instrument with whom the holder has not dealt except

(a) infancy, to the extent that it is a defense to a simple contract; and

(b) such other incapacity, or duress, or illegality of the transaction, as renders the obligation of the party a nullity; and

(c) such misrepresentation as has induced the party to sign the instrument with neither knowledge nor reasonable opportunity to obtain knowledge of its character or its essential terms; and

(d) discharge in insolvency proceedings; and

(e) any other discharge of which the holder has notice when he takes the instrument.

§ 3—306. Rights of One Not Holder in Due Course

Unless he has the rights of a holder in due course, any person takes the instrument subject to

(a) all valid claims to it on the part of any person; and

(b) all defenses of any party which would be available in an action on a simple contract; and

(c) the defenses of want or failure of consideration, nonperformance of any condition precedent, nondelivery, or delivery for a special purpose (Section 3—408); and

(d) the defense that he, or a person through whom he holds the instrument, acquired it by theft, or that payment or satisfaction to such holder would be inconsistent with the terms of a restrictive indorsement. The claim of any third person to the instrument is not otherwise available as a defense to any party liable thereon unless the third person himself defends the action for such party.

§ 3—307. Burden of Establishing Signatures, Defenses and Due Course

(1) Unless specifically denied in the pleadings, each signature on an instrument is admitted. When the effectiveness of a signature is put in issue

(a) the burden of establishing it is on the party claiming under the signature; but

(b) the signature is presumed to be genuine or authorized except where the action is to enforce the obligation of a purported signer who has died or become incompetent before proof is required.

(2) When signatures are admitted or established, production of the instrument entitles a holder to recover on it unless the defendant establishes a defense.

(3) After it is shown that a defense exists, a person claiming the rights of a holder in due course has the burden of establishing that he or some person under whom he claims is in all respects a holder in due course.

PART 4

LIABILITY OF PARTIES

§ 3—401. Signature

(1) No person is liable on an instrument unless his signature appears thereon.

(2) A signature is made by use of any name, including any trade or assumed name, upon an instrument, or by any word or mark used in lieu of a written signature.

§ 3—402. Signature in Ambiguous Capacity

Unless the instrument clearly indicates that a signature is made in some other capacity, it is an indorsement.

§ 3—403. Signature by Authorized Representative

(1) A signature may be made by an agent or other representative, and his authority to make it may be established as in other cases of representation. No particular form of appointment is necessary to establish such authority.

(2) An authorized representative who signs his own name to an instrument

(a) is personally obligated if the instrument neither names the person represented nor shows that the representative signed in a representative capacity;

(b) except as otherwise established between the immediate parties, is personally obligated if the instrument names the person represented but does not show that the representative signed in a representative capacity, or if the instrument does not name the person represented but does show that the representative signed in a representative capacity.

(3) Except as otherwise established, the name of an organization preceded or followed by the name and office of an authorized individual is a signature made in a representative capacity.

§ 3—404. Unauthorized Signatures

(1) Any unauthorized signature is wholly inoperative as that of the person whose name is signed unless he ratifies it or is precluded from denying

it; but it operates as the signature of the unauthorized signer in favor of any person who in good faith pays the instrument or takes it for value.

(2) Any unauthorized signature may be ratified for all purposes of this Article. Such ratification does not of itself affect any rights of the person ratifying against the actual signer.

§ 3—405. Impostors; Signature in Name of Payee

(1) An indorsement by any person in the name of a named payee is effective if

(a) an impostor by use of the mails or otherwise has induced the maker or drawer to issue the instrument to him or his confederate in the name of the payee; or

(b) a person signing as or on behalf of a maker or drawer intends the payee to have no interest in the instrument; or

(c) an agent or employee of the maker or drawer has supplied him with the name of the payee intending the latter to have no such interest.

(2) Nothing in this section shall affect the criminal or civil liability of the person so indorsing.

§ 3—406. Negligence Contributing to Alteration or Unauthorized Signature

Any person who by his negligence substantially contributes to a material alteration of the instrument or to the making of an unauthorized signature is precluded from asserting the alteration or lack of authority against a holder in due course or against a drawee or other payor who pays the instrument in good faith and in accordance with the reasonable commercial standards of the drawee's or payor's business.

§ 3—407. Alteration

(1) Any alteration of an instrument is material which changes the contract of any party thereto in any respect, including any such change in

(a) the number or relations of the parties; or

(b) an incomplete instrument, by completing it otherwise than as authorized; or

(c) the writing as signed, by adding to it or by removing any part of it.

(2) As against any person other than a subsequent holder in due course.

(a) alteration by the holder which is both fraudulent and material discharges any party whose contract is thereby changed unless that party assents or is precluded from asserting the defense;

(b) no other alteration discharges any party and the instrument may be enforced according to its original tenor, or as to incomplete instruments, according to the authority given.

(3) A subsequent holder in due course may in all cases enforce the instrument according to its original tenor, and when an incomplete instrument has been completed, he may enforce it as completed.

§ 3—408. Consideration

Want or failure of consideration is a defense as against any person not having the rights of a holder in due course (Section 3—305), except that no consideration is necessary for an instrument or obligation thereon given in payment of or as security for an antecedent obligation of any kind. Nothing in this section shall be taken to displace any statute outside this Act under which a promise is enforceable notwithstanding lack or failure of consideration. Partial failure of consideration is a defense pro tanto whether or not the failure is in an ascertained or liquidated amount.

§ 3—409. Draft Not an Assignment

(1) A check or other draft does not of itself operate as an assignment of any funds in the hands of the drawee available for its payment, and the drawee is not liable on the instrument until he accepts it.

(2) Nothing in this section shall affect any liability in contract, tort or otherwise arising from any letter of credit or other obligation or representation which is not an acceptance.

§ 3—410. Definition and Operation of Acceptance

(1) Acceptance is the drawee's signed engagement to honor the draft as presented. It must be written on the draft, and may consist of his signature alone. It becomes operative when completed by delivery or notification.

(2) A draft may be accepted although it has not been signed by the drawer or is otherwise incomplete or is overdue or has been dishonored.

(3) Where the draft is payable at a fixed period after sight and the acceptor fails to date his acceptance, the holder may complete it by supplying a date in good faith.

§ 3—411. Certification of a Check

(1) Certification of a check is acceptance. Where a holder procures certification, the drawer and all prior indorsers are discharged.

(2) Unless otherwise agreed, a bank has no obligation to certify a check.

(3) A bank may certify a check before returning it for lack of proper indorsement. If it does so, the drawer is discharged.

§ 3—412. Acceptance Varying Draft

(1) Where the drawee's proffered acceptance in any manner varies the draft as presented, the holder may refuse the acceptance and treat the draft as dishonored in which case the drawee is entitled to have his acceptance cancelled.

(2) The terms of the draft are not varied by an acceptance to pay at any particular bank or place in the United States, unless the acceptance states that the draft is to be paid only at such bank or place.

(3) Where the holder assents to an acceptance varying the terms of the draft, each drawer and indorser who does not affirmatively assent is discharged.

§ 3—413. Contract of Maker, Drawer and Acceptor

(1) The maker or acceptor engages that he will pay the instrument according to its tenor at the time of his engagement or as completed pursuant to Section 3—115 on incomplete instruments.

(2) The drawer engages that upon dishonor of the draft and any necessary notice of dishonor or protest he will pay the amount of the draft to the holder or to any indorser who takes it up. The drawer may disclaim this liability by drawing without recourse.

(3) By making, drawing or accepting, the party admits as against all subsequent parties including the drawee the existence of the payee and his then capacity to indorse.

§ 3—414. Contract of Indorser; Order of Liability

(1) Unless the indorsement otherwise specifies (as by such words as "without recourse"), every indorser engages that upon dishonor and any necessary notice of dishonor and protest he will pay the instrument according to its tenor at the time of his indorsement to the holder or to any subsequent indorser who takes it up, even though the indorser who takes it up was not obligated to do so.

(2) Unless they otherwise agree, indorsers are liable to one another in the order in which they indorse, which is presumed to be the order in which their signatures appear on the instrument.

§ 3—415. Contract of Accommodation Party

(1) An accommodation party is one who signs the instrument in any capacity for the purpose of lending his name to another party to it.

(2) When the instrument has been taken for value before it is due, the accommodation party is liable in the capacity in which he has signed even though the taker knows of the accommodation.

(3) As against a holder in due course and without notice of the accommodation, oral proof of the accommodation is not admissible to give the accommodation party the benefit of discharges dependent on his character as such. In other cases, the accommodation character may be shown by oral proof.

(4) An indorsement which shows that it is not in the chain of title is notice of its accommodation character.

(5) An accommodation party is not liable to the party accommodated, and if he pays the instrument has a right of recourse on the instrument against such party.

§ 3—416. Contract of Guarantor

(1) "Payment guaranteed" or equivalent words added to a signature mean that the signer engages that if the instrument is not paid when due he will pay it according to its tenor without resort by the holder to any other party.

(2) "Collection guaranteed" or equivalent words added to a signature mean that the signer engages that if the instrument is not paid when due he will pay it according to its tenor, but only after the holder has reduced his claim against the maker or acceptor to judgment and execution has been returned unsatisfied, or after the maker or acceptor has become insolvent or it is otherwise apparent that it is useless to proceed against him.

(3) Words of guaranty which do not otherwise specify guarantee payment.

(4) No words of guaranty added to the signature of a sole maker or acceptor affect his liability on the instrument. Such words added to the signature of one of two or more makers or acceptors create a presumption that the signature is for the accommodation of the others.

(5) When words of guaranty are used, presentment, notice of dishonor and protest are not necessary to charge the user.

(6) Any guaranty written on the instrument is enforceable notwithstanding any statute of frauds.

§ 3—417. Warranties on Presentment and Transfer

(1) Any person who obtains payment or acceptance and any prior transferor warrants to a person who in good faith pays or accepts that

    (a) he has a good title to the instrument or is authorized to obtain payment or acceptance on behalf of one who has a good title; and

    (b) he has no knowledge that the signature of the maker or drawer is unauthorized, except that this warranty is not given by a holder in due course acting in good faith

    (i) to a maker with respect to the maker's own signature; or

    (ii) to a drawer with respect to the drawer's own signature, whether or not the drawer is also the drawee; or

    (iii) to an acceptor of a draft if the holder in due course took the draft after the acceptance or obtained the acceptance without knowledge that the drawer's signature was unauthorized; and

(c) the instrument has not been materially altered, except that this warranty is not given by a holder in due course acting in good faith

    (i) to the maker of a note; or

    (ii) to the drawer of a draft whether or not the drawer is also the drawee; or

    (iii) to the acceptor of a draft with respect to an alteration made prior to the acceptance if the holder in due course took the draft after the acceptance, even though the acceptance provided "payable as originally drawn" or equivalent terms; or

    (iv) to the acceptor of a draft with respect to an alteration made after the acceptance.

(2) Any person who transfers an instrument and receives consideration warrants to his transferee and if the transfer is by indorsement to any subsequent holder who takes the instrument in good faith that

(a) he has a good title to the instrument or is authorized to obtain payment or acceptance on behalf of one who has a good title and the transfer is otherwise rightful; and

(b) all signatures are genuine or authorized; and

(c) the instrument has not been materially altered; and

(d) no defense of any party is good against him; and

(e) he has no knowledge of any insolvency proceeding instituted with respect to the maker or acceptor or the drawer of an unaccepted instrument.

(3) By transferring "without recourse," the transferor limits the obligation stated in subsection (2) (d) to a warranty that he has no knowledge of such a defense.

(4) A selling agent or broker who does not disclose the fact that he is acting only as such gives the warranties provided in this section, but if he makes such disclosure warrants only his good faith and authority.

§ 3—418. Finality of Payment or Acceptance

Except for recovery of bank payments as provided in the Article on Bank Deposits and Collections (Article 4) and except for liability for breach of warranty on presentment under the preceding section, payment or acceptance of any instrument is final in favor of a holder in due course, or a person who has in good faith changed his position in reliance on the payment.

§ 3—419. Conversion of Instrument; Innocent Representative

(1) An instrument is converted when

    (a) a drawee to whom it is delivered for acceptance refuses to return it on demand; or

    (b) any person to whom it is delivered for payment refuses on demand either to pay or to return it; or

    (c) it is paid on a forged indorsement.

(2) In an action against a drawee under subsection (1), the measure of the drawee's liability is the face amount of the instrument. In any other action under subsection (1), the measure of liability is presumed to be the face amount of the instrument.

(3) Subject to the provisions of this Act concerning restrictive indorsements, a representative, including a depositary or collecting bank, who has in good faith and in accordance with the reasonable commercial standards applicable to the business of such representative dealt with an instrument or its proceeds on behalf of one who was not the true owner, is not liable in conversion or otherwise to the true owner beyond the amount of any proceeds remaining in his hands.

(4) An intermediary bank or payor bank which is not a depositary bank is not liable in conversion solely by reason of the fact that proceeds of an item indorsed restrictively (Sections 3—205 and 3—206) are not paid or applied consistently with the restrictive indorsement of an indorser other than its immediate transferor.

PART 5

PRESENTMENT, NOTICE OF DISHONOR AND PROTEST

§ 3—501. When Presentment, Notice of Dishonor, and Protest Necessary or Permissible

(1) Unless excused (Section 3—511), presentment is necessary to charge secondary parties as

follows:

(a) presentment for acceptance is necessary to charge the drawer and indorsers of a draft where the draft so provides, or is payable elsewhere than at the residence or place of business of the drawee, or its date of payment depends upon such presentment. The holder may at his option present for acceptance any other draft payable at a stated date;

(b) presentment for payment is necessary to charge any indorser;

(c) in the case of any drawer, the acceptor of a draft payable at a bank or the maker of a note payable at a bank, presentment for payment is necessary, but failure to make presentment discharges such drawer, acceptor or maker only as stated in Section 3—502(1) (b).

(2) Unless excused (Section 3—511)

(a) notice of any dishonor is necessary to charge any indorser;

(b) in the case of any drawer, the acceptor of a draft payable at a bank or the maker of a note payable at a bank, notice of any dishonor is necessary, but failure to give such notice discharges such drawer, acceptor or maker only as stated in Section 3—502(1) (b).

(3) Unless excused (Section 3—511), protest of any dishonor is necessary to charge the drawer and indorsers of any draft which on its face appears to be drawn or payable outside of the states, territories, dependencies and possessions of the United States, the District of Columbia and the Commonwealth of Puerto Rico. The holder may at his option make protest of any dishonor of any other instrument and in the case of a foreign draft may on insolvency of the acceptor before maturity make protest for better security.

(4) Notwithstanding any provision of this section, neither presentment nor notice of dishonor nor protest is necessary to charge an indorser who has indorsed an instrument after maturity.

§ 3—502. Unexcused Delay; Discharge

(1) Where without excuse any necessary presentment or notice of dishonor is delayed beyond the time when it is due

(a) any indorser is discharged; and

(b) any drawer or the acceptor of a draft payable at a bank or the maker of a note payable at a bank who because the drawee or payor bank becomes insolvent during the delay is deprived of funds maintained with the drawee or payor bank to cover the instrument may discharge his liability by written assignment to the holder of his rights against the drawee or payor bank in respect of such funds, but such drawer, acceptor or maker is not otherwise discharged.

(2) Where without excuse a necessary protest is delayed beyond the time when it is due, any drawer or indorser is discharged.

§ 3—503. Time of Presentment

(1) Unless a different time is expressed in the instrument, the time for any presentment is determined as follows:

(a) where an instrument is payable at or a fixed period after a stated date, any presentment for acceptance must be made on or before the date it is payable;

(b) where an instrument is payable after sight, it must either be presented for acceptance or negotiated within a reasonable time after date or issue whichever is later;

(c) where an instrument shows the date on which it is payable, presentment for payment is due on that date;

(d) where an instrument is accelerated, presentment for payment is due within a reasonable time after the acceleration;

(e) with respect to the liability of any secondary party, presentment for acceptance or payment of any other instrument is due within a reasonable time after such party becomes liable thereon.

(2) A reasonable time for presentment is determined by the nature of the instrument, any usage of banking or trade and the facts of the particular case. In the case of an uncertified check which is drawn and payable within the United States and which is not a draft drawn by a bank, the following are presumed to be reasonable periods within which to present for payment or to initiate bank collection:

(a) with respect to the liability of the drawer, thirty days after date or issue whichever is later; and

(b) with respect to the liability of an indorser, seven days after his indorsement.

(3) Where any presentment is due on a day which is not a full business day for either the person making presentment or the party to pay or accept, presentment is due on the next following day which is a full business day for both parties.

(4) Presentment to be sufficient must be made at a reasonable hour, and, if at a bank, during its banking day.

§ 3—504. How Presentment Made

(1) Presentment is a demand for acceptance or payment made upon the maker, acceptor, drawee or other payor by or on behalf of the holder.

(2) Presentment may be made
    (a) by mail, in which event the time of presentment is determined by the time of receipt of the mail; or
    (b) through a clearing house; or
    (c) at the place of acceptance or payment specified in the instrument or, if there be none, at the place of business or residence of the party to accept or pay. If neither the party to accept or pay nor anyone authorized to act for him is present or accessible at such place, presentment is excused.

(3) It may be made
    (a) to any one of two or more makers, acceptors, drawees or other payors; or
    (b) to any person who has authority to make or refuse the acceptance or payment.

(4) A draft accepted or a note made payable at a bank in the United States must be presented at such bank.

(5) In the cases described in Section 4—210 presentment may be made in the manner and with the result stated in that section.

§ 3—505. Rights of Party to Whom Presentment Is Made

(1) The party to whom presentment is made may without dishonor require
    (a) exhibition of the instrument; and
    (b) reasonable identification of the person making presentment and evidence of his authority to make it if made for another; and
    (c) that the instrument be produced for acceptance or payment at a place specified in it, or if there be none at any place reasonable in the circumstances; and
    (d) a signed receipt on the instrument for any partial or full payment and its surrender upon full payment.

(2) Failure to comply with any such requirement invalidates the presentment, but the person presenting has a reasonable time in which to comply and the time for acceptance or payment runs from the time of compliance.

§ 3—506. Time Allowed for Acceptance or Payment

(1) Acceptance may be deferred without dishonor until the close of the next business day following presentment. The holder may also in a good faith effort to obtain acceptance, and without either dishonor of the instrument or discharge of secondary parties, allow postponement of acceptance for an additional business day.

(2) Except as a longer time is allowed in the case of documentary drafts drawn under a letter of credit, and unless an earlier time is agreed to by the party to pay, payment of an instrument may be deferred without dishonor pending reasonable examination to determine whether it is properly payable, but payment must be made in any event before the close of business on the day of presentment.

§ 3—507. Dishonor; Holder's Right of Recourse; Term Allowing Re-Presentment

(1) An instrument is dishonored when
    (a) a necessary or optional presentment is duly made and due acceptance or payment is refused or cannot be obtained within the prescribed time or in case of bank collections the instrument is seasonably returned by the midnight deadline (Section 4—301); or
    (b) presentment is excused and the instrument is not duly accepted or paid.

(2) Subject to any necessary notice of dishonor and protest, the holder has upon dishonor an immediate right of recourse against the drawers and indorsers.

(3) Return of an instrument for lack of proper indorsement is not dishonor.

(4) A term in a draft or an indorsement thereof allowing a stated time for re-presentment in the event of any dishonor of the draft by nonacceptance if a time draft or by nonpayment if a sight draft gives the holder as against any secondary party bound by the term an option to waive the dishonor without affecting the liability of the secondary party and he may present again up to the end of the stated time.

§ 3—508. Notice of Dishonor

(1) Notice of dishonor may be given to any person who may be liable on the instrument by or on behalf of the holder or any party who has himself

received notice, or any other party who can be compelled to pay the instrument. In addition, an agent or bank in whose hands the instrument is dishonored may give notice to his principal or customer or to another agent or bank from which the instrument was received.

(2) Any necessary notice must be given by a bank before its midnight deadline and by any other person before midnight of the third business day after dishonor or receipt of notice of dishonor.

(3) Notice may be given in any reasonable manner. It may be oral or written and in any terms which identify the instrument and state that it has been dishonored. A misdescription which does not mislead the party notified does not vitiate the notice. Sending the instrument bearing a stamp, ticket or writing stating that acceptance or payment has been refused or sending a notice of debit with respect to the instrument is sufficient.

(4) Written notice is given when sent although it is not received.

(5) Notice to one partner is notice to each although the firm has been dissolved.

(6) When any party is in insolvency proceedings instituted after the issue of the instrument, notice may be given either to the party or to the representative of his estate.

(7) When any party is dead or incompetent, notice may be sent to his last known address or given to his personal representative.

(8) Notice operates for the benefit of all parties who have rights on the instrument against the party notified.

§ 3—509. Protest; Noting for Protest

(1) A protest is a certificate of dishonor made under the hand and seal of a United States consul or vice consul or a notary public or other person authorized to certify dishonor by the law of the place where dishonor occurs. It may be made upon information satisfactory to such person.

(2) The protest must identify the instrument and certify either that due presentment has been made or the reason why it is excused and that the instrument has been dishonored by nonacceptance or nonpayment.

(3) The protest may also certify that notice of dishonor has been given to all parties or to specified parties.

(4) Subject to subsection (5), any necessary protest is due by the time that notice of dishonor is due.

(5) If, before protest is due, an instrument has been noted for protest by the officer to make protest, the protest may be made at any time thereafter as of the date of the noting.

§ 3—510. Evidence of Dishonor and Notice of Dishonor

The following are admissible as evidence and create a presumption of dishonor and of any notice of dishonor therein shown:

(a) a document regular in form as provided in the preceding section which purports to be a protest;

(b) the purported stamp or writing of the drawee, payor bank or presenting bank on the instrument or accompanying it stating that acceptance or payment has been refused for reasons consistent with dishonor;

(c) any book or record of the drawee, payor bank, or any collecting bank kept in the usual course of business which shows dishonor, even though there is no evidence of who made the entry.

§ 3—511. Waived or Excused Presentment, Protest or Notice of Dishonor or Delay Therein

(1) Delay in presentment, protest or notice of dishonor is excused when the party is without notice that it is due or when the delay is caused by circumstances beyond his control and he exercises reasonable diligence after the cause of the delay ceases to operate.

(2) Presentment or notice or protest as the case may be is entirely excused when

(a) the party to be charged has waived it expressly or by implication either before or after it is due; or

(b) such party has himself dishonored the instrument or has countermanded payment or otherwise has no reason to expect or right to require that the instrument be accepted or paid; or

(c) by reasonable diligence the presentment or protest cannot be made or the notice given.

(3) Presentment is also entirely excused when

(a) the maker, acceptor or drawee of any instrument except a documentary draft is dead or in insolvency proceedings instituted after the issue of the instrument; or

(b) acceptance or payment is refused but not for want of proper presentment.

(4) Where a draft has been dishonored by nonacceptance, a later presentment for payment and any notice of dishonor and protest for nonpayment are excused unless in the meantime the instrument has been accepted.

(5) A waiver of protest is also a waiver of presentment and of notice of dishonor even though protest is not required.

(6) Where a waiver of presentment or notice or protest is embodied in the instrument itself, it is binding upon all parties; but where it is written above the signature of an indorser, it binds him only.

PART 6

DISCHARGE

§ 3—601. Discharge of Parties

(1) The extent of the discharge of any party from liability on an instrument is governed by the sections on

> (a) payment or satisfaction (Section 3—603); or
>
> (b) tender of payment (Section 3—604); or
>
> (c) cancellation or renunciation (Section 3-605); or
>
> (d) impairment of right of recourse or of collateral (Section 3—606); or
>
> (e) reacquisition of the instrument by a prior party (Section 3—208); or
>
> (f) fraudulent and material alteration (Section 3—407); or
>
> (g) certification of a check (Section 3—411); or
>
> (h) acceptance varying a draft (Section 3—412); or
>
> (i) unexcused delay in presentment or notice of dishonor or protest (Section 3—502).

(2) Any party is also discharged from his liability on an instrument to another party by any other act or agreement with such party which would discharge his simple contract for the payment of money.

(3) The liability of all parties is discharged when any party who has himself no right of action or recourse on the instrument

> (a) reacquires the instrument in his own right; or
>
> (b) is discharged under any provision of this Article, except as otherwise provided with respect to discharge for impairment of recourse or of collateral (Section 3—606).

§ 3—602. Effect of Discharge Against Holder in Due Course

No discharge of any party provided by this Article is effective against a subsequent holder in due course unless he has notice thereof when he takes the instrument.

§ 3—603. Payment or Satisfaction

(1) The liability of any party is discharged to the extent of his payment or satisfaction to the holder even though it is made with knowledge of a claim of another person to the instrument unless prior to such payment or satisfaction the person making the claim either supplies indemnity deemed adequate by the party seeking the discharge or enjoins payment or satisfaction by order of a court of competent jurisdiction in an action in which the adverse claimant and the holder are parties. This subsection does not, however, result in the discharge of the liability

> (a) of a party who in bad faith pays or satisfies a holder who acquired the instrument by theft or who (unless having the rights of a holder in due course) holds through one who so acquired it; or
>
> (b) of a party (other than an intermediary bank or a payor bank which is not a depositary bank) who pays or satisfies the holder of an instrument which has been restrictively indorsed in a manner not consistent with the terms of such restrictive indorsement.

(2) Payment or satisfaction may be made with the consent of the holder by any person including a stranger to the instrument. Surrender of the instrument to such a person gives him the rights of a transferee (Section 3—201).

§ 3—604. Tender of Payment

(1) Any party making tender of full payment to a holder when or after it is due is discharged to the extent of all subsequent liability for interest, costs and attorney's fees.

(2) The holder's refusal of such tender wholly discharges any party who has a right of recourse against the party making the tender.

(3) Where the maker or acceptor of an instrument payable otherwise than on demand is able and ready to pay at every place of payment specified in the instrument when it is due, it is equivalent to tender.

§ 3—605. Cancellation and Renunciation

(1) The holder of an instrument may even without consideration discharge any party

> (a) in any manner apparent on the face of the instrument or the indorsement, as by intentionally cancelling the instrument or the party's signature by destruction or mutilation, or by striking out the party's signature; or
>
> (b) by renouncing his rights by a writing signed and delivered or by surrender

of the instrument to the party to be discharged.

(2) Neither cancellation nor renunciation without surrender of the instrument affects the title thereto.

§ 3—606. Impairment of Recourse or of Collateral

(1) The holder discharges any party to the instrument to the extent that, without such party's consent, the holder

    (a) without express reservation of rights releases or agrees not to sue any person against whom the party has to the knowledge of the holder a right of recourse or agrees to suspend the right to enforce against such person the instrument or collateral or otherwise discharges such person, except that failure or delay in effecting any required presentment, protest or notice of dishonor with respect to any such person does not discharge any party as to whom presentment, protest or notice of dishonor is effective or unnecessary; or

    (b) unjustifiably impairs any collateral for the instrument given by or on behalf of the party or any person against whom he has a right of recourse.

(2) By express reservation of rights against a party with a right of recourse, the holder preserves

    (a) all his rights against such party as of the time when the instrument was originally due; and

    (b) the right of the party to pay the instrument as of that time; and

    (c) all rights of such party to recourse against others.

PART 7

ADVICE OF INTERNATIONAL SIGHT DRAFT

§ 3—701. Letter of Advice of International Sight Draft

(1) A "letter of advice" is a drawer's communication to the drawee that a described draft has been drawn.

(2) Unless otherwise agreed, when a bank receives from another bank a letter of advice of an international sight draft the drawee bank may immediately debit the drawer's account and stop the running of interest pro tanto. Such a debit and any resulting credit to any account covering outstanding drafts leaves in the drawer full power to stop payment or otherwise dispose of the amount and creates no trust or interest in favor of the holder.

(3) Unless otherwise agreed and except where a draft is drawn under a credit issued by the drawee, the drawee of an international sight draft owes the drawer no duty to pay an unadvised draft but if it does so and the draft is genuine, may appropriately debit the drawer's account.

PART 8

MISCELLANEOUS

§ 3-801. Drafts in a Set

(1) Where a draft is drawn in a set of parts, each of which is numbered and expressed to be an order only if no other part has been honored, the whole of the parts constitutes one draft but a taker of any part may become a holder in due course of the draft.

(2) Any person who negotiates, indorses or accepts a single part of a draft drawn in a set thereby becomes liable to any holder in due course of that part as if it were the whole set, but as between different holders in due course to whom different parts have been negotiated, the holder whose title first accrues has all rights to the draft and its proceeds.

(3) As against the drawee, the first presented part of a draft drawn in a set is the part entitled to payment, or if a time draft to acceptance and payment. Acceptance of any subsequently presented part renders the drawee liable thereon under subsection (2). With respect both to a holder and to the drawer, payment of a subsequently presented part of a draft payable at sight has the same effect as payment of a check notwithstanding an effective stop order (Section 4—407).

(4) Except as otherwise provided in this section, where any part of a draft in a set is discharged by payment or otherwise the whole draft is discharged.

§ 3—802. Effect of Instrument on Obligation for Which It Is Given

(1) Unless otherwise agreed, where an instrument is taken for an underlying obligation

    (a) the obligation is pro tanto discharged if a bank is drawer, maker or acceptor of the instrument and there is no recourse on the instrument against the underlying obligor; and

    (b) in any other case the obligation is suspended pro tanto until the instrument is due or, if it is payable on demand, until its presentment. If the instrument is dishonored, action may be maintained on either the instrument or the obligation; discharge of the underlying obligor on the instrument also discharges him on the obligation.

(2) The taking in good faith of a check which is not postdated does not of itself so extend the time on the original obligation as to discharge a surety.

§ 3—803. Notice to Third Party

Where a defendant is sued for breach of an obligation for which a third person is answerable over under this Article, he may give the third person written notice of the litigation, and the person notified may then give similar notice to any other person who is answerable over to him under this Article. If the notice states that the person notified may come in and defend and that if the person notified does not do so, he will in any action against him by the person giving the notice be bound by any determination of fact common to the two litigations, then unless after seasonable receipt of the notice, the person notified does come in and defend he is so bound.

§ 3—804. Lost, Destroyed or Stolen Instruments

The owner of an instrument which is lost, whether by destruction, theft or otherwise, may maintain an action in his own name and recover from any party liable thereon upon due proof of his ownership, the facts which prevent his production of the instrument and its terms. The court may require security indemnifying the defendant against loss by reason of further claims on the instrument.

§ 3—805. Instruments Not Payable to Order or to Bearer

This Article applies to any instrument whose terms do not preclude transfer which is otherwise negotiable within this Article but which is not payable to order or to bearer, except that there can be no holder in due course of such an instrument.

ARTICLE 4

BANK DEPOSITS AND COLLECTIONS

PART 1

GENERAL PROVISIONS AND DEFINITIONS

§ 4—101. Short Title

This Article shall be known and may be cited as Uniform Commercial Code—Bank Deposits and Collections.

§ 4—102. Applicability

(1) To the extent that items within this Article are also within the scope of Articles 3 and 8, they are subject to the provisions of those Articles. In the event of conflict the provisions of this Article govern those of Article 3 but the provisions of Article 8 govern those of this Article.

(2) The liability of a bank for action or nonaction with respect to any item handled by it for purposes of presentment, payment or collection is governed by the law of the place where the bank is located. In the case of action or nonaction by or at a branch or separate office of a bank, its liability is governed by the law of the place where the branch or separate office is located.

§ 4—103. Variation by Agreement; Measure of Damages; Certain Action Constituting Ordinary Care

(1) The effect of the provisions of this Article may be varied by agreement except that no agreement can disclaim a bank's responsibility for its own lack of good faith or failure to exercise ordinary care or can limit the measure of damages for such lack or failure; but the parties may by agreement determine the standards by which such responsibility is to be measured if such standards are not manifestly unreasonable.

(2) Federal Reserve regulations and operating letters, clearing house rules, and the like, have the effect of agreements under subsection (1), whether or not specifically assented to by all parties interested in items handled.

(3) Action or nonaction approved by this Article or pursuant to Federal Reserve regulations or operating letters constitutes the exercise of ordinary care and, in the absence of special instructions, action or nonaction consistent with clearing house rules and the like or with a general banking usage not disapproved by this Article, prima facie constitutes the exercise of ordinary care.

(4) The specification or approval of certain procedures by this Article does not constitute disapproval of other procedures which may be reasonable under the circumstances.

(5) The measure of damages for failure to exercise ordinary care in handling an item is the amount of the item reduced by an amount which could not have been realized by the use of ordinary care, and where there is bad faith it includes other damages, if any, suffered by the party as a proximate consequence.

§ 4—104. Definitions and Index of Definitions

(1) In this Article unless the context otherwise requires

   (a) "Account" means any account with a bank and includes a checking, time, interest or savings account;

   (b) "Afternoon" means the period of a day between noon and midnight;

   (c) "Banking day" means that part of any day on which a bank is open to the public for carrying on substantially all of its banking functions;

   (d) "Clearing house" means any association of banks or other payors regularly clearing items;

   (e) "Customer" means any person having an account with a bank or for whom a bank has agreed to collect items and includes a bank carrying an account with another bank;

   (f) "Documentary draft" means any negotiable or nonnegotiable draft with accompanying documents, securities or other papers to be delivered against honor of the draft;

   (g) "Item" means any instrument for the payment of money even though it is not negotiable but does not include money;

   (h) "Midnight deadline" with respect to a bank is midnight on its next banking day following the banking day on which it receives the relevant item or notice or from which the time for taking action commences to run, whichever is later;

   (i) "Property payable" includes the availability of funds for payment at the time of decision to pay or dishonor;

   (j) "Settle" means to pay in cash, by clearing house settlement, in a charge or credit or by remittance, or otherwise as instructed. A settlement may be either provisional or final;

   (k) "Suspends payments" with respect to a bank means that it has been closed by order of the supervisory authorities, that a public officer has been appointed to take it over or that it ceases or refuses to make payments in the ordinary course of business.

(2) Other definitions applying to this Article and the sections in which they appear are:

"Collecting bank"	Section 4—105.
"Depositary bank"	Section 4—105.
"Intermediary bank"	Section 4—105.
"Payor bank"	Section 4—105.
"Presenting bank"	Section 4—105.
"Remitting bank"	Section 4—105.

(3) The following definitions in other Articles apply to this Article:

"Acceptance"	Section 3—410.
"Certificate of Deposit"	Section 3—104.
"Certification"	Section 3—411.
"Check"	Section 3—104.
"Draft"	Section 3—104.
"Holder in due course"	Section 3—302.
"Notice of dishonor"	Section 3—508.
"Presentment"	Section 3—504.
"Protest"	Section 3—509.
"Secondary party"	Section 3—102.

(4) In addition Article 1 contains general definitions and principles of construction and interpretation applicable throughout this Article.

§ 4—105. "Depositary Bank"; "Intermediary Bank"; "Collecting Bank"; "Payor Bank"; "Presenting Bank"; "Remitting Bank"

In this Article unless the context otherwise requires:

   (a) "Depositary bank" means the first bank to which an item is transferred for collection even though it is also the payor bank;

   (b) "Payor bank" means a bank by which an item is payable as drawn or accepted;

   (c) "Intermediary bank" means any bank to which an item is transferred in course of collection except the depositary or payor bank;

   (d) "Collecting bank" means any bank handling the item for collection except the payor bank;

   (e) "Presenting bank" means any bank presenting an item except a payor bank;

   (f) "Remitting bank" means any payor or intermediary bank remitting for an item.

§ 4—106. Separate Office of a Bank

A branch or separate office of a bank [maintaining its own deposit ledgers] is a separate bank for the purpose of computing the time within which and determining the place at or to which action may be taken or notices or orders shall be given under this Article and under Article 3.

Note: *The brackets are to make it optional with the several states whether to require a branch to maintain its own deposit ledgers in order to be considered to be a separate bank for certain purposes under Article 4. In some states, "maintaining its own deposit ledgers" is a satisfactory test. In others, branch banking practices are such that this test would not be suitable.*

§ 4—107. Time of Receipt of Items

(1) For the purpose of allowing time to process items, prove balances and make the necessary entries on its books to determine its position for the day, a bank may fix an afternoon hour of 2 p.m. or later as a cutoff hour for the handling of money and items and the making of entries on its books.

(2) Any item or deposit of money received on any day after a cutoff hour so fixed or after the close of the banking day may be treated as being received at the opening of the next banking day.

§ 4—108. Delays

(1) Unless otherwise instructed, a collecting bank in a good faith effort to secure payment may, in the case of specific items and with or without the approval of any person involved, waive, modify or extend time limits imposed or permitted by this Act for a period not in excess of an additional banking day without discharge of secondary parties and without liability to its transferor or any prior party.

(2) Delay by a collecting bank or payor bank beyond time limits prescribed or permitted by this Act or by instructions is excused if caused by interruption of communication facilities, suspension of payments by another bank, war, emergency conditions or other circumstances beyond the control of the bank provided it exercises such diligence as the circumstances require.

§ 4—109. Process of Posting

The "process of posting" means the usual procedure followed by a payor bank in determining to pay an item and in recording the payment including one or more of the following or other steps as determined by the bank:

(a) verification of any signature;
(b) ascertaining that sufficient funds are available;
(c) affixing a "paid" or other stamp;
(d) entering a charge or entry to a customer's account;
(e) correcting or reversing an entry or erroneous action with respect to the item.

PART 2

COLLECTION OF ITEMS: DEPOSITARY AND COLLECTING BANKS

§ 4—201. Presumption and Duration of Agency Status of Collecting Banks and Provisional Status of Credits; Applicability of Article; Item Indorsed "Pay Any Bank"

(1) Unless a contrary intent clearly appears and prior to the time that a settlement given by a collecting bank for an item is or becomes final (subsection (3) of Section 4—211 and Sections 4—212 and 4—213), the bank is an agent or subagent of the owner of the item and any settlement given for the item is provisional. This provision applies regardless of the form of indorsement or lack of indorsement and even though credit given for the item is subject to immediate withdrawal as of right or is in fact withdrawn; but the continuance of ownership of an item by its owner and any rights of the owner to proceeds of the item are subject to rights of a collecting bank such as those resulting from outstanding advances on the item and valid rights of setoff. When an item is handled by banks for purposes of presentment, payment and collection, the relevant provisions of this Article apply even though action of parties clearly establishes that a particular bank has purchased the item and is the owner of it.

(2) After an item has been indorsed with the words "pay any bank" or the like, only a bank may acquire the rights of a holder

(a) until the item has been returned to the customer initiating collection; or
(b) until the item has been specially indorsed by a bank to a person who is not a bank.

§ 4—202. Responsibility for Collection; When Action Seasonable

(1) A collecting bank must use ordinary care in

(a) presenting an item or sending it for presentment; and
(b) sending notice of dishonor or nonpayment or returning an item other than a documentary draft to the bank's transferor [or directly to the depositary bank under subsection (2) of Section 4—212] *(see note to Section 4—212)* after learning that the item has not been paid or accepted, as the case may be; and
(c) settling for an item when the bank receives final settlement; and

(d) making or providing for any necessary protest; and

(e) notifying its transferor of any loss or delay in transit within a reasonable time after discovery thereof.

(2) A collecting bank taking proper action before its midnight deadline following receipt of an item, notice or payment acts seasonably; taking proper action within a reasonably longer time may be seasonable but the bank has the burden of so establishing.

(3) Subject to subsection (1) (a), a bank is not liable for the insolvency, neglect, misconduct, mistake or default of another bank or person or for loss or destruction of an item in transit or in the possession of others.

§ 4—203. Effect of Instructions

Subject to the provisions of Article 3 concerning conversion of instruments (Section 3—419) and the provisions of both Article 3 and this Article concerning restrictive indorsements, only a collecting bank's transferor can give instructions which affect the bank or constitute notice to it; and a collecting bank is not liable to prior parties for any action taken pursuant to such instructions or in accordance with any agreement with its transferor.

§ 4—204. Methods of Sending and Presenting; Sending Direct to Payor Bank

(1) A collecting bank must send items by reasonably prompt method taking into consideration any relevant instructions, the nature of the item, the number of such items on hand, and the cost of collection involved and the method generally used by it or others to present such items.

(2) A collecting bank may send

(a) any item direct to the payor bank;

(b) any item to any nonbank payor if authorized by its transferor; and

(c) any item other than documentary drafts to any nonbank payor, if authorized by Federal Reserve regulation or operating letter, clearing house rule or the like.

(3) Presentment may be made by a presenting bank at a place where the payor bank has requested that presentment be made.

§ 4—205. Supplying Missing Indorsement; No Notice from Prior Indorsement

(1) A depositary bank which has taken an item for collection may supply any indorsement of the customer which is necessary to title unless the item contains the words "payee's indorsement required" or the like. In the absence of such a require-

ment, a statement placed on the item by the depositary bank to the effect that the item was deposited by a customer or credited to his account is effective as the customer's indorsement.

(2) An intermediary bank, or payor bank which is not a depositary bank, is neither given notice nor otherwise affected by a restrictive indorsement of any person except the bank's immediate transferor.

§ 4—206. Transfer Between Banks

Any agreed method which identifies the transferor bank is sufficient for the item's further transfer to another bank.

§ 4—207. Warranties of Customer and Collecting Bank on Transfer or Presentment of Items; Time for Claims

(1) Each customer or collecting bank who obtains payment or acceptance of an item and each prior customer and collecting bank warrants to the payor bank or other payor who in good faith pays or accepts the item that

(a) he has a good title to the item or is authorized to obtain payment or acceptance on behalf of one who has a good title; and

(b) he has no knowledge that the signature of the maker or drawer is unauthorized, except that this warranty is not given by any customer or collecting bank that is a holder in due course and acts in good faith

(i) to a maker, with respect to the maker's own signature; or

(ii) to a drawer, with respect to the drawer's own signature, whether or not the drawer is also the drawee; or

(iii) to an acceptor of an item, if the holder in due course took the item after the acceptance or obtained the acceptance without knowledge that the drawer's signature was unauthorized; and

(c) the item has not been materially altered, except that this warranty is not given by any customer or collecting bank that is a holder in due course and acts in good faith

(i) to the maker of a note; or

(ii) to the drawer of a draft whether or not the drawer is also the drawee; or

(iii) to the acceptor of an item with respect to an alteration made prior to the acceptance if the holder in due course took the item after the acceptance, even though the acceptance provided "payable as originally drawn" or equivalent terms; or

(iv) to the acceptor of an item with respect to an alteration made after the acceptance.

(2) Each customer and collecting bank who transfers an item and receives a settlement or other consideration for it warrants to his transferee and to any subsequent collecting bank who takes the item in good faith that

(a) he has a good title to the item or is authorized to obtain payment or acceptance on behalf of one who has a good title and the transfer is otherwise rightful; and

(b) all signatures are genuine or authorized; and

(c) the item has not been materially altered; and

(d) no defense of any party is good against him; and

(e) he has no knowledge of any insolvency proceeding instituted with respect to the maker or acceptor or the drawer of an unaccepted item.

In addition, each customer and collecting bank so transferring an item and receiving a settlement or other consideration engages that upon dishonor and any necessary notice of dishonor and protest he will take up the item.

(3) The warranties and the engagement to honor set forth in the two preceding subsections arise notwithstanding the absence of indorsement or words of guaranty or warranty in the transfer or presentment and a collecting bank remains liable for their breach despite remittance to its transferor. Damages for breach of such warranties or engagement to honor shall not exceed the consideration received by the customer or collecting bank responsible plus finance charges and expenses related to the item, if any.

(4) Unless a claim for breach of warranty under this section is made within a reasonable time after the person claiming learns of the breach, the person liable is discharged to the extent of any loss caused by the delay in making claim.

§ 4—208. Security Interest of Collecting Bank in Items, Accompanying Documents and Proceeds

(1) A bank has a security interest in an item and any accompanying documents or the proceeds of either

(a) in case of an item deposited in an account, to the extent to which credit

given for the item has been withdrawn or applied;

(b) in case of an item for which it has given credit available for withdrawal as of right, to the extent of the credit given whether or not the credit is drawn upon and whether or not there is a right of charge-back; or

(c) if it makes an advance on or against the item.

(2) When credit which has been given for several items received at one time or pursuant to a single agreement is withdrawn or applied in part, the security interest remains upon all the items, any accompanying documents or the proceeds of either. For the purpose of this section, credits first given are first withdrawn.

(3) Receipt by a collecting bank of a final settlement for an item is a realization on its security interest in the item, accompanying documents and proceeds. To the extent and so long as the bank does not receive final settlement for the item or give up possession of the item or accompanying documents for purposes other than collection, the security interest continues and is subject to the provisions of Article 9 except that

(a) no security agreement is necessary to make the security interest enforceable (subsection (1) (b) of Section 9—203); and

(b) no filing is required to perfect the security interest; and

(c) the security interest has priority over conflicting perfected security interests in the item, accompanying documents or proceeds.

§ 4—209. When Bank Gives Value for Purposes of Holder in Due Course

For purposes of determining its status as a holder in due course, the bank has given value to the extent that it has a security interest in an item provided that the bank otherwise complies with the requirements of Section 3—302 on what constitutes a holder in due course.

§ 4—210. Presentment by Notice of Item Not Payable by, Through or at a Bank; Liability of Secondary Parties

(1) Unless otherwise instructed, a collecting bank may present an item not payable by, through or at a bank by sending to the party to accept or pay a written notice that the bank holds the item for acceptance or payment. The notice must be sent in time to be received on or before the day when presentment is due, and the bank must meet any

requirement of the party to accept or pay under Section 3—505 by the close of the bank's next banking day after it knows of the requirement.

(2) Where presentment is made by notice and neither honor nor request for compliance with a requirement under Section 3—505 is received by the close of business on the day after maturity or in the case of demand items by the close of business on the third banking day after notice was sent, the presenting bank may treat the item as dishonored and charge any secondary party by sending him notice of the facts.

§ 4—211. Media of Remittance; Provisional and Final Settlement in Remittance Cases

(1) A collecting bank may take in settlement of an item

    (a) a check of the remitting bank or of another bank on any bank except the remitting bank; or

    (b) a cashier's check or similar primary obligation of a remitting bank which is a member of or clears through a member of the same clearing house or group as the collecting bank; or

    (c) appropriate authority to charge an account of the remitting bank or of another bank with the collecting bank; or

    (d) if the item is drawn upon or payable by a person other than a bank, a cashier's check, certified check or other bank check or obligation.

(2) If before its midnight deadline the collecting bank properly dishonors a remittance check or authorization to charge on itself or presents or forwards for collection a remittance instrument of or on another bank which is of a kind approved by subsection (1) or has not been authorized by it, the collecting bank is not liable to prior parties in the event of the dishonor of such check, instrument or authorization.

(3) A settlement for an item by means of a remittance instrument or authorization to charge is or becomes a final settlement as to both the person making and the person receiving the settlement

    (a) if the remittance instrument or authorization to charge is of a kind approved by subsection (1) or has not been authorized by the person receiving the settlement and in either case the person receiving the settlement acts seasonably before its midnight deadline in presenting, forwarding for collection or paying the instrument or authorization,—at the time the remittance instrument or authorization is finally paid by the payor by which it is payable;

    (b) if the person receiving the settlement has authorized remittance by a nonbank check or obligation or by a cashier's check or similar primary obligation of or a check upon the payor or other remitting bank which is not of a kind approved by subsection (1) (b),—at the time of the receipt of such remittance check or obligation; or

    (c) if in a case not covered by sub-paragraphs (a) or (b) the person receiving the settlement fails to seasonably present, forward for collection, pay or return remittance instrument or authorization to it to charge before its midnight deadline,—at such midnight deadline.

§ 4—212. Right of Charge-Back or Refund

(1) If a collecting bank has made provisional settlement with its customer for an item and itself fails by reason of dishonor, suspension of payments by a bank or otherwise to receive a settlement for the item which is or becomes final, the bank may revoke the settlement given by it, charge back the amount of any credit given for the item to its customer's account or obtain refund from its customer whether or not it is able to return the items, if by its midnight deadline or within a longer reasonable time after it learns the facts it returns the item or sends notification of the facts. These rights to revoke, charge-back and obtain refund terminate if and when a settlement for the item received by the bank is or becomes final (subsection (3) of Section 4—211 and subsections (2) and (3) of Section 4—213).

[(2) Within the time and manner prescribed by this section and Section 4—301, an intermediary or payor bank, as the case may be, may return an unpaid item directly to the depositary bank and may send for collection a draft on the depositary bank and obtain reimbursement. In such case, if the depositary bank has received provisional settlement for the item, it must reimburse the bank drawing the draft and any provisional credits for the item between banks shall become and remain final.]

Note: *Direct returns is recognized as an innovation that is not yet established bank practice, and therefore, Paragraph 2 has been bracketed. Some lawyers have doubts whether it should be included in legislation or left to development by agreement.*

(3) A depositary bank which is also the payor may charge-back the amount of an item to its customer's account or obtain refund in accordance with the section governing return of an item received by

a payor bank for credit on its books. (Section 4—301)

(4) The right to charge-back is not affected by

(a) prior use of the credit given for the item; or

(b) failure by any bank to exercise ordinary care with respect to the item but any bank so failing remains liable.

(5) A failure to charge-back or claim refund does not affect other rights of the bank against the customer or any other party.

(6) If credit is given in dollars, as the equivalent of the value of an item payable in a foreign currency, the dollar amount of any charge-back or refund shall be calculated on the basis of the buying sight rate for the foreign currency prevailing on the day when the person entitled to the charge-back or refund learns that it will not receive payment in ordinary course.

§ 4—213. Final Payment of Item for Payor Bank; When Provisional Debits and Credits Become Final; When Certain Credits Become Available for Withdrawal

(1) An item is finally paid by a payor bank when the bank has done any of the following, whichever happens first:

(a) paid the item in cash; or

(b) settled for the item without reserving a right to revoke the settlement and without having such right under statute, clearing house rule or agreement; or

(c) completed the process of posting the item to the indicated account of the drawer, maker or other person to be charged therewith; or

(d) made a provisional settlement for the item and failed to revoke the settlement in the time and manner permitted by statute, clearing house rule or agreement.

Upon a final payment under subparagraphs (b), (c) or (d), the payor bank shall be accountable for the amount of the item.

(2) If provisional settlement for an item between the presenting and payor banks is made through a clearing house or by debits or credits in an account between them, then to the extent that provisional debits or credits for the item are entered in accounts between the presenting and payor banks or between the presenting and successive prior collecting banks seriatim, they become final upon final payment of the item by the payor bank.

(3) If a collecting bank receives a settlement for an item which is or becomes final (subsection (3) of Section 4—211, subsection (2) of Section 4—213), the bank is accountable to its customer for the amount of the item and any provisional credit given for the item in an account with its customer becomes final.

(4) Subject to any right of the bank to apply the credit to an obligation of the customer, credit given by a bank for an item in an account with its customer becomes available for withdrawal as of right

(a) in any case where the bank has received a provisional settlement for the item,—when such settlement becomes final and the bank has had a reasonable time to learn that the settlement is final;

(b) in any case where the bank is both a depositary bank and a payor bank and the item is finally paid,—at the opening of the bank's second banking day following receipt of the item.

(5) A deposit of money in a bank is final when made but, subject to any right of the bank to apply the deposit to an obligation of the customer, the deposit becomes available for withdrawal as of right at the opening of the bank's next banking day following receipt of the deposit.

§ 4—214. Insolvency and Preference

(1) Any item in or coming into the possession of a payor or collecting bank which suspends payment and which item is not finally paid shall be returned by the receiver, trustee or agent in charge of the closed bank to the presenting bank or the closed bank's customer.

(2) If a payor bank finally pays an item and suspends payments without making a settlement for the item with its customer or the presenting bank which settlement is or becomes final, the owner of the item has a preferred claim against the payor bank.

(3) If a payor bank gives or a collecting bank gives or receives a provisional settlement for an item and thereafter suspends payments, the suspension does not prevent or interfere with the settlement becoming final if such finality occurs automatically upon the lapse of certain time or the happening of certain events (subsection (3) of Section 4—211, subsections (1) (d), (2) and (3) of Section 4—213).

(4) If a collecting bank receives from subsequent parties settlement for an item which settlement is or becomes final and suspends payments without making a settlement for the item with its customer which is or becomes final, the owner of the item has a preferred claim against such collecting bank.

PART 3

COLLECTION OF ITEMS: PAYOR BANKS

§ 4—301. Deferred Posting; Recovery of Payment by Return of Items; Time of Dishonor

(1) Where an authorized settlement for a demand item (other than a documentary draft) received by a payor bank otherwise than for immediate payment over the counter has been made before midnight of the banking day of receipt, the payor bank may revoke the settlement and recover any payment if before it has made final payment (subsection (1) of Section 4—213) and before its midnight deadline it

    (a) returns the item; or

    (b) sends written notice of dishonor or nonpayment if the item is held for protest or is otherwise unavailable for return.

(2) If a demand item is received by a payor bank for credit on its books, it may return such item or send notice of dishonor and may revoke any credit given or recover the amount thereof withdrawn by its customer, if it acts within the time limit and in the manner specified in the preceding subsection.

(3) Unless previous notice of dishonor has been sent, an item is dishonored at the time when for purposes of dishonor it is returned or notice sent in accordance with this section.

(4) An item is returned:

    (a) as to an item received through a clearing house, when it is delivered to the presenting or last collecting bank or to the clearing house or is sent or delivered in accordance with its rules; or

    (b) in all other cases, when it is sent or delivered to the bank's customer or transferor or pursuant to his instructions.

§ 4—302. Payor Bank's Responsibility for Late Return of Item

In the absence of a valid defense such as breach of a presentment warranty (subsection (1) of Section 4—207), settlement effected or the like, if an item is presented on and received by a payor bank the bank is accountable for the amount of

    (a) a demand item other than a documentary draft whether properly payable or not if the bank, in any case where it is not also the depositary bank, retains the item beyond midnight of the banking day of receipt without settling for it or, regardless of whether it is also the depositary bank, does not pay or return the item or send notice of dishonor until after its midnight deadline; or

    (b) any other properly payable item unless within the time allowed for acceptance or payment of that item the bank either accepts or pays the item or returns it and accompanying documents.

§ 4—303. When Items Subject to Notice, Stop-Order, Legal Process or Setoff; Order in Which Items May Be Charged or Certified

(1) Any knowledge, notice or stop-order received by, legal process served upon or setoff exercised by a payor bank, whether or not effective under other rules of law to terminate, suspend or modify the bank's right or duty to pay an item or to charge its customer's account for the item, comes too late to so terminate, suspend or modify such right or duty if the knowledge, notice, stop-order or legal process is received or served and a reasonable time for the bank to act thereon expires or the setoff is exercised after the bank has done any of the following:

    (a) accepted or certified the item;

    (b) paid the item in cash;

    (c) settled for the item without reserving a right to revoke the settlement and without having such right under statute, clearing house rule or agreement;

    (d) completed the process of posting the item to the indicated account of the drawer, maker or other person to be charged therewith or otherwise has evidenced by examination of such indicated account and by action its decision to pay the item; or

    (e) become accountable for the amount of the item under subsection (1) (d) of Section 4—213 and Section 4—302 dealing with the payor bank's responsibility for late return of items.

(2) Subject to the provisions of subsection (1), items may be accepted, paid, certified or charged to the indicated account of its customer in any order convenient to the bank.

PART 4

RELATIONSHIP BETWEEN PAYOR BANK AND ITS CUSTOMER

§ 4—401. When Bank May Charge Customer's Account

(1) As against its customer, a bank may charge against his account any item which is otherwise properly payable from that account even though the charge creates an overdraft.

(2) A bank which in good faith makes payment to a holder may charge the indicated account of its customer according to
> (a) the original tenor of his altered item; or
> (b) the tenor of his completed item, even though the bank knows the item has been completed unless the bank has notice that the completion was improper.

§ 4—402. **Bank's Liability to Customer for Wrongful Dishonor**

A payor bank is liable to its customer for damages proximately caused by the wrongful dishonor of an item. When the dishonor occurs through mistake, liability is limited to actual damages proved. If so proximately caused and proved, damages may include damages for an arrest or prosecution of the customer or other consequential damages. Whether any consequential damages are proximately caused by the wrongful dishonor is a question of fact to be determined in each case.

§ 4—403. **Customer's Right to Stop Payment; Burden of Proof of Loss**

(1) A customer may by order to his bank stop payment of any item payable for his account but the order must be received at such time and in such manner as to afford the bank a reasonable opportunity to act on it prior to any action by the bank with respect to the item described in Section 4—303.

(2) An oral order is binding upon the bank only for fourteen calendar days unless confirmed in writing within that period. A written order is effective for only six months unless renewed in writing.

(3) The burden of establishing the fact and amount of loss resulting from the payment of an item contrary to a binding stop payment order is on the customer.

§ 4—404. **Bank Not Obligated to Pay Check More Than Six Months Old**

A bank is under no obligation to a customer having a checking account to pay a check, other than a certified check, which is presented more than six months after its date, but it may charge its customer's account for a payment made thereafter in good faith.

§ 4—405. **Death or Incompetence of Customer**

(1) A payor or collecting bank's authority to accept, pay or collect an item or to account for proceeds of its collection if otherwise effective is not rendered ineffective by incompetence of a customer of either bank existing at the time the item is issued or its collection is undertaken if the bank does not know of an adjudication of incompetence. Neither death nor incompetence of a customer revokes such authority to accept, pay, collect or account until the bank knows of the fact of death or of an adjudication of incompetence and has reasonable opportunity to act on it.

(2) Even with knowledge a bank may for 10 days after the date of death pay or certify checks drawn on or prior to that date unless ordered to stop payment by a person claiming an interest in the account.

§ 4—406. **Customer's Duty to Discover and Report Unauthorized Signature or Alteration**

(1) When a bank sends to its customer a statement of account accompanied by items paid in good faith in support of the debit entries or holds the statement and items pursuant to a request or instructions of its customer or otherwise in a reasonable manner makes the statement and items available to the customer, the customer must exercise reasonable care and promptness to examine the statement and items to discover his unauthorized signature or any alteration on an item and must notify the bank promptly after discovery thereof.

(2) If the bank establishes that the customer failed with respect to an item to comply with the duties imposed on the customer by subsection (1), the customer is precluded from asserting against the bank
> (a) his unauthorized signature or any alteration on the item if the bank also establishes that it suffered a loss by reason of such failure; and
> (b) an unauthorized signature or alteration by the same wrongdoer on any other item paid in good faith by the bank after the first item and statement was available to the customer for a reasonable period not exceeding fourteen calendar days and before the bank receives notification from the customer of any such unauthorized signature or alteration.

(3) The preclusion under subsection (2) does not apply if the customer establishes lack of ordinary care on the part of the bank in paying the item(s).

(4) Without regard to care or lack of care of either the customer or the bank, a customer who does not within one year from the time the statement and items are made available to the customer (subsection (1)) discover and report his unauthorized signature or any alteration on the face or back of the item or does not within 3 years from that time discover and report any unauthorized indorsement is

precluded from asserting against the bank such un-authorized signature or indorsement or such alteration.

(5) If under this section a payor bank has a valid defense against a claim of a customer upon or resulting from payment of an item and waives or fails upon request to assert the defense, the bank may not assert against any collecting bank or other prior party presenting or transferring the item a claim based upon the unauthorized signature or alteration giving rise to the customer's claim.

§ 4—407. Payor Bank's Right to Subrogation on Improper Payment

If a payor bank has paid an item over the stop payment order of the drawer or maker or other-wise under circumstances giving a basis for objection by the drawer or maker, to prevent unjust enrich-ment and only to the extent necessary to prevent loss to the bank by reason of its payment of the item, the payor bank shall be subrogated to the rights

(a) of any holder in due course on the item against the drawer or maker; and

(b) of the payee or any other holder of the item against the drawer or maker either on the item or under the transac-tion out of which the item arose; and

(c) of the drawer or maker against the payee or any other holder of the item with respect to the transaction out of which the item arose.

PART 5

COLLECTION OF DOCUMENTARY DRAFTS

§ 4—501. Handling of Documentary Drafts; Duty to Send for Presentment and to Notify Cus-tomer of Dishonor

A bank which takes a documentary draft for collection must present or send the draft and accom-panying documents for presentment and, upon learn-ing that the draft has not been paid or accepted in due course, must seasonably notify its customer of such fact even though it may have discounted or bought the draft or extended credit available for withdrawal as of right.

§ 4—502. Presentment of "On Arrival" Drafts

When a draft or the relevant instructions re-quire presentment "on arrival," "when goods arrive"

or the like, the collecting bank need not present until in its judgment a reasonable time for arrival of the goods has expired. Refusal to pay or accept because the goods have not arrived is not dishonor; the bank must notify its transferor of such refusal but need not present the draft again until it is instructed to do so or learns of the arrival of the goods.

§ 4—503. Responsibility of Presenting Bank for Documents and Goods; Report of Reasons for Dishonor; Referee in Case of Need

Unless otherwise instructed and except as pro-vided in Article 5, a bank presenting a documentary draft

(a) must deliver the documents to the drawee on acceptance of the draft if it is payable more than three days after presentment; otherwise, only on pay-ment; and

(b) upon dishonor, either in the case of presentment for acceptance or present-ment for payment, may seek and fol-low instructions from any referee in case of need designated in the draft or if the presenting bank does not choose to utilize his services it must use diligence and good faith to ascer-tain the reason for dishonor, must no-tify its transferor of the dishonor and of the results of its effort to ascertain the reasons therefor and must request instructions.

But the presenting bank is under no obligation with respect to goods represented by the documents except to follow any reasonable instructions seasonably re-ceived; it has a right to reimbursement for any ex-pense incurred in following instructions and to pre-payment of or indemnity for such expenses.

§ 4—504. Privilege of Presenting Bank to Deal With Goods; Security Interest for Expenses

(1) A presenting bank which, following the dishonor of a documentary draft, has seasonably re-quested instructions but does not receive them within a reasonable time may store, sell, or otherwise deal with the goods in any reasonable manner.

(2) For its reasonable expenses incurred by action under subsection (1), the presenting bank has a lien upon the goods or their proceeds, which may be foreclosed in the same manner as an unpaid seller's lien.

ARTICLE 5
LETTERS OF CREDIT

§ 5—101. Short Title
This Article shall be known and may be cited as Uniform Commercial Code—Letters of Credit.

§ 5—102. Scope
(1) This Article applies
  (a) to a credit issued by a bank, if the credit requires a documentary draft or a documentary demand for payment; and
  (b) to a credit issued by a person other than a bank, if the credit requires that the draft or demand for payment be accompanied by a document of title; and
  (c) to a credit issued by a bank or other person, if the credit is not within subparagraphs (a) or (b) but conspicuously states that it is a letter of credit or is conspicuously so entitled.

(2) Unless the engagement meets the requirements of subsection (1), this Article does not apply to engagements to make advances or to honor drafts or demands for payment, to authorities to pay or purchase, to guarantees or to general agreements.

(3) This Article deals with some but not all of the rules and concepts of letters of credit as such rules or concepts have developed prior to this act or may hereafter develop. The fact that this Article states a rule does not by itself require, imply or negate application of the same or a converse rule to a situation not provided for or to a person not specified by this Article.

§ 5—103. Definitions
(1) In this Article unless the context otherwise requires
  (a) "Credit" or "letter of credit" means an engagement by a bank or other person, made at the request of a customer and of a kind within the scope of this Article (Section 5—102), that the issuer will honor drafts or other demands for payment upon compliance with the conditions specified in the credit. A credit may be either revocable or irrevocable. The engagement may be either an agreement to honor or a statement that the bank or other person is authorized to honor.
  (b) A "documentary draft" or a "documentary demand for payment" is one honor of which is conditioned upon the presentation of a document or documents. "Document" means any paper including document of title, security, invoice, certificate, notice of default and the like.
  (c) An "issuer" is a bank or other person issuing a credit.
  (d) A "beneficiary" of a credit is a person who is entitled under its terms to draw or demand payment.
  (e) An "advising bank" is a bank which gives notification of the issuance of a credit by another bank.
  (f) A "confirming bank" is a bank which engages either that it will itself honor a credit already issued by another bank or that such a credit will be honored by the issuer or a third bank.
  (g) A "customer" is a buyer or other person who causes an issuer to issue a credit. The term also includes a bank which procures issuance or confirmation on behalf of that bank's customer.

(2) Other definitions applying to this Article and the sections in which they appear are:
  "Notation of Credit."   Section 5—108.
  "Presenter."   Section 5—112(3).

(3) Definitions in other Articles applying to this Article and the sections in which they appear are:

"Accept" or "Acceptance."	Section 3—410.
"Contract for sale."	Section 2—106.
"Draft."	Section 3—104.
"Holder in due course."	Section 3—302.
"Midnight deadline."	Section 4—104.
"Security."	Section 8—102.

(4) In addition, Article 1 contains general definitions and principles of construction and interpretation applicable throughout this Article.

§ 5—104. Formal Requirements; Signing
(1) Except as otherwise required in subsection (1) (c) of Section 5—102 on scope, no particular form of phrasing is required for a credit. A credit must be in writing and signed by the issuer, and a confirmation must be in writing and signed by the confirming bank. A modification of the terms of a credit or confirmation must be signed by the issuer or confirming bank.

(2) A telegram may be a sufficient signed writing if it identifies its sender by an authorized authentication. The authentication may be in code and the authorized naming of the issuer in an advice of credit is a sufficient signing.

§ 5—105. Consideration

No consideration is necessary to establish a credit or to enlarge or otherwise modify its terms.

§ 5—106. Time and Effect of Establishment of Credit

(1) Unless otherwise agreed, a credit is established

(a) as regards the customer, as soon as a letter of credit is sent to him or the letter of credit or an authorized written advice of its issuance is sent to the beneficiary; and

(b) as regards the beneficiary, when he receives a letter of credit or an authorized written advice of its issuance.

(2) Unless otherwise agreed, once an irrevocable credit is established as regards the customer, it can be modified or revoked only with the consent of the custromer; and once it is established as regards the beneficiary, it can be modified or revoked only with his consent.

(3) Unless otherwise agreed after a revocable credit is established, it may be modified or revoked by the issuer without notice to or consent from the customer or beneficiary.

(4) Notwithstanding any modification or revocation of a revocable credit, any person authorized to honor or negotiate under the terms of the original credit is entitled to reimbursement for or honor of any draft or demand for payment duly honored or negotiated before receipt of notice of the modification or revocation and the issuer in turn is entitled to reimbursement from its customer.

§ 5—107. Advice of Credit; Confirmation; Error in Statement of Terms

(1) Unless otherwise specified, an advising bank by advising a credit issued by another bank does not assume any obligation to honor drafts drawn or demands for payment made under the credit, but it does assume obligation for the accuracy of its own statement.

(2) A confirming bank by confirming a credit becomes directly obligated on the credit to the extent of its confirmation as though it were its issuer and acquires the rights of an issuer.

(3) Even though an advising bank incorrectly advises the terms of a credit it has been authorized to advise, the credit is established as against the issuer to the extent of its original terms.

(4) Unless otherwise specified, the customer bears as against the issuer all risks of transmission and reasonable translation or interpretation of any message relating to a credit.

§ 5—108. "Notation Credit"; Exhaustion of Credit

(1) A credit which specifies that any person purchasing or paying drafts drawn or demands for payment made under it must note the amount of the draft or demand on the letter or advice of credit is a "notation credit."

(2) Under a notation credit

(a) a person paying the beneficiary or purchasing a draft or demand for payment from him acquires a right to honor only if the appropriate notation is made; and by transferring or forwarding for honor the documents under the credit, such a person warrants to the issuer that the notation has been made; and

(b) unless the credit or a signed statement that an appropriate notation has been made accompanies the draft or demand for payment, the issuer may delay honor until evidence of notation has been procured which is satisfactory to it; but its obligation and that of its customer continue for a reasonable time not exceeding thirty days to obtain such evidence.

(3) If the credit is not a notation credit

(a) the issuer may honor complying drafts or demands for payment presented to it in the order in which they are presented and is discharged pro tanto by honor of any such draft or demand;

(b) as between competing good faith purchasers of complying drafts or demands, the person first purchasing has priority over a subsequent purchaser even though the later purchased draft or demand has been first honored.

§ 5—109. Issuer's Obligation to Its Customer

(1) An issuer's obligation to its customer includes good faith and observance of any general banking usage but, unless otherwise agreed, does not include liability or responsibility

(a) for performance of the underlying contract for sale or other transaction between the customer and the beneficiary; or

(b) for any act or omission of any person other than itself or its own branch or for loss or destruction of a draft, demand or document in transit or in the possession of others; or

(c) based on knowledge or lack of knowledge of any usage of any particular trade.

(2) An issuer must examine documents with care so as to ascertain that on their face they appear to comply with the terms of the credit but, unless otherwise agreed, assumes no liability or responsibility for the genuineness, falsification or effect of any document which appears on such examination to be regular on its face.

(3) A nonbank issuer is not bound by any banking usage of which it has no knowledge.

§ 5—110. Availability of Credit in Portions; Presenter's Reservation of Lien or Claim

(1) Unless otherwise specified, a credit may be used in portions in the discretion of the beneficiary.

(2) Unless otherwise specified, a person by presenting a documentary draft or demand for payment under a credit relinquishes upon its honor all claims to the documents and a person by transferring such draft or demand or causing such presentment authorizes such relinquishment. An explicit reservation of claim makes the draft or demand non-complying.

§ 5—111. Warranties on Transfer and Presentment

(1) Unless otherwise agreed, the beneficiary, by transferring or presenting a documentary draft or demand for payment, warrants to all interested parties that the necessary conditions of the credit have been complied with. This is in addition to any warranties arising under Articles 3, 4, 7 and 8.

(2) Unless otherwise agreed, a negotiating, advising, confirming, collecting or issuing bank presenting or transferring a draft or demand for payment under a credit warrants only the matters warranted by a collecting bank under Article 4 and any such bank transferring a document warrants only the matters warranted by an intermediary under Articles 7 and 8.

§ 5—112. Time Allowed for Honor or Rejection; Withholding Honor or Rejection by Consent; "Presenter"

(1) A bank to which a documentary draft or demand for payment is presented under a credit may without dishonor of the draft, demand or credit

(a) defer honor until the close of the third banking day following receipt of the documents; and

(b) further defer honor if the presenter has expressly or impliedly consented thereto.

Failure to honor within the time here specified constitutes dishonor of the draft or demand and of the credit [except as otherwise provided in subsection (4) of Section 5—114 on conditional payment].

> **Note:** *The bracketed language in the last sentence of subsection (1) should be included only if the optional provisions of Section 5—114(4) and (5) are included.*

(2) Upon dishonor the bank may unless otherwise instructed fulfill its duty to return the draft or demand and the documents by holding them at the disposal of the presenter and sending him an advice to that effect.

(3) "Presenter" means any person presenting a draft or demand for payment for honor under a credit even though that person is a confirming bank or other correspondent which is acting under an issuer's authorization.

§ 5—113. Indemnities

(1) A bank seeking to obtain (whether for itself or another) honor, negotiation or reimbursement under a credit may give an indemnity to induce such honor, negotiation or reimbursement.

(2) An indemnity agreement inducing honor, negotiation or reimbursement

(a) unless otherwise explicitly agreed applies to defects in the documents but not in the goods; and

(b) unless a longer time is explicitly agreed expires at the end of ten business days following receipt of the documents by the ultimate customer unless notice of objection is sent before such expiration date. The ultimate customer may send notice of objection to the person from whom he received the documents and any bank receiving such notice is under a duty to send notice to its transferor before its midnight deadline.

§ 5—114. Issuer's Duty and Privilege to Honor; Right to Reimbursement

(1) An issuer must honor a draft or demand for payment which complies with the terms of the relevant credit regardless of whether the goods or documents conform to the underlying contract for sale or other contract between the customer and the beneficiary. The issuer is not excused from honor

of such a draft or demand by reason of an additional general term that all documents must be satisfactory to the issuer, but an issuer may require that specified documents must be satisfactory to it.

(2) Unless otherwise agreed, when documents appear on their face to comply with the terms of a credit but a required document does not in fact conform to the warranties made on negotiation or transfer of a document of title (Section 7—507) or of a security (Section 8—306) or is forged or fraudulent or there is fraud in the transaction

   (a) the issuer must honor the draft or demand for payment, if honor is demanded by a negotiating bank or other holder of the draft or demand which has taken the draft or demand under the credit and under circumstances which would make it a holder in due course (Section 3—302) and in an appropriate case would make it a person to whom a document of title has been duly negotiated (Section 7—502) or a bona fide purchaser of a security (Section 8—302); and

   (b) in all other cases, as against its customer, an issuer acting in good faith may honor the draft or demand for payment despite notification from the customer of fraud, forgery or other defect not apparent on the face of the documents but a court of appropriate jurisdiction may enjoin such honor.

(3) Unless otherwise agreed, an issuer which has duly honored a draft or demand for payment is entitled to immediate reimbursement of any payment made under the credit and to be put in effectively available funds not later than the day before maturity of any acceptance made under the credit.

[(4) When a credit provides for payment by the issuer on receipt of notice that the required documents are in the possession of a correspondent or other agent of the issuer

   (a) any payment made on receipt of such notice is conditional; and

   (b) the issuer may reject documents which do not comply with the credit, if it does so within three banking days following its receipt of the documents; and

   (c) in the event of such rejection, the issuer is entitled by charge-back or otherwise to return of the payment made.]

[(5) In the case covered by subsection (4), failure to reject documents within the time specified in sub-paragraph (b) constitutes acceptance of the documents and makes the payment final in favor of the beneficiary.]

Note: *Subsections (4) and (5) are bracketed as optional. If they are included the bracketed language in the last sentence of Section 5— 112(1) should also be included.*

§ 5—115. Remedy for Improper Dishonor or Anticipatory Repudiation

(1) When an issuer wrongfully dishonors a draft or demand for payment presented under a credit, the person entitled to honor has, with respect to any documents, the rights of a person in the position of a seller (Section 2—707) and may recover from the issuer the face amount of the draft or demand, together with incidental damages under Section 2—710 on seller's incidental damages and interest but less any amount realized by resale or other use or disposition of the subject matter of the transaction. In the event no resale or other utilization is made the documents, goods or other subject matter involved in the transaction must be turned over to the issuer on payment of judgment.

(2) When an issuer wrongfully cancels or otherwise repudiates a credit before presentment of a draft or demand for payment drawn under it, the beneficiary has the rights of a seller after anticipatory repudiation by the buyer under Section 2—610 if he learns of the repudiation in time reasonably to avoid procurement of the required documents. Otherwise the beneficiary has an immediate right of action for wrongful dishonor.

§ 5—116. Transfer and Assignment

(1) The right to draw under a credit can be transferred or assigned only when the credit is expressly designated as transferable or assignable.

(2) Even though the credit specifically states that it is nontransferable or nonassignable, the beneficiary may, before performance of the conditions of the credit, assign his right to proceeds. Such an assignment is an assignment of an account under Article 9 on Secured Transactions and is governed by that Article except that

   (a) the assignment is ineffective until the letter of credit or advice of credit is delivered to the assignee which delivery constitutes perfection of the security interest under Article 9; and

   (b) the issuer may honor drafts or demands for payment drawn under the credit until it receives a notification of the assignment signed by the beneficiary which reasonably identifies the credit involved in the assignment and contains a request to pay the assignee; and

(c) after what reasonably appears to be such a notification has been received the issuer may without dishonor refuse to accept or pay even to a person otherwise entitled to honor until the letter of credit or advice of credit is exhibited to the issuer.

(3) Except where the beneficiary has effectively assigned his right to draw or his right to proceeds, nothing in this section limits his right to transfer or negotiate drafts or demands drawn under the credit.

§ 5—117. Insolvency of Bank Holding Funds for Documentary Credit

(1) Where an issuer or an advising or confirming bank or a bank which has for a customer procured issuance of a credit by another bank becomes insolvent before final payment under the credit and the credit is one to which this Article is made applicable by paragraphs (a) or (b) of Section 5—102(1) on scope, the receipt or allocation of funds or collateral to secure or meet obligations under the credit shall have the following results:

(a) to the extent of any funds or collateral turned over after or before the insolvency as indemnity against or specifically for the purpose of payment of drafts or demands for payment drawn under the designated credit, the drafts or demands are entitled to payment in preference over depositors or other general creditors of the issuer or bank; and

(b) on expiration of the credit or surrender of the beneficiary's rights under it unused any person who has given such funds or collateral is similarly entitled to return thereof; and

(c) a charge to a general or current account with a bank if specifically consented to for the purpose of indemnity against or payment of drafts or demands for payment drawn under the designated credit falls under the same rules as if the funds had been drawn out in cash and then turned over with specific instructions.

(2) After honor or reimbursement under this section, the customer or other person for whose account the insolvent bank has acted is entitled to receive the documents involved.

ARTICLE 6

BULK TRANSFERS

§ 6—101. Short Title

This Article shall be known and may be cited as Uniform Commercial Code—Bulk Transfers.

§ 6—102. "Bulk Transfers"; Transfers of Equipment; Enterprises Subject to This Article; Bulk Transfers Subject to This Article

(1) A "bulk transfer" is any transfer in bulk and not in the ordinary course of the transferor's business of a major part of the materials, supplies, merchandise or other inventory (Section 9—109) of an enterprise subject to this Article.

(2) A transfer of a substantial part of the equipment (Section 9—109) of such an enterprise is a bulk transfer if it is made in connection with a bulk transfer of inventory, but not otherwise.

(3) The enterprises subject to this Article are all those whose principal business is the sale of merchandise from stock, including those who manufacture what they sell.

(4) Except as limited by the following section,

all bulk transfers of goods located within this state are subject to this Article.

§ 6—103. Transfers Excepted From This Article

The following transfers are not subject to this Article:

(1) Those made to give security for the performance of an obligation;

(2) General assignments for the benefit of all the creditors of the transferor, and subsequent transfers by the assignee thereunder;

(3) Transfers in settlement or realization of a lien or other security interests;

(4) Sales by executors, administrators, receivers, trustees in bankruptcy, or any public officer under judicial process;

(5) Sales made in the course of judicial or administrative proceedings for the dissolution or reorganization of a corporation and of which notice is sent to the creditors of the corporation pursuant to order of the court or administrative agency;

(6) Transfers to a person maintaining a known place of business in this State who becomes bound to pay the debts of the transferor in full and gives public notice of that fact, and who is solvent after becoming so bound;

(7) A transfer to a new business enterprise organized to take over and continue the business, if public notice of the transaction is given and the new enterprise assumes the debts of the transferor and he receives nothing from the transaction except an interest in the new enterprise junior to the claims of creditors;

(8) Transfers of property which is exempt from execution.

Public notice under subsection (6) or subsection (7) may be given by publishing once a week for two consecutive weeks in a newspaper of general circulation where the transferor had its principal place of business in this state an advertisement including the names and addresses of the transferor and transferee and the effective date of the transfer.

§ 6—104. Schedule of Property, List of Creditors

(1) Except as provided with respect to auction sales (Section 6—108), a bulk transfer subject to this Article is ineffective against any creditor of the transferor unless:

(a) The transferee requires the transferor to furnish a list of his existing creditors prepared as stated in this section; and

(b) The parties prepare a schedule of the property transferred sufficient to identify it; and

(c) The transferee preserves the list and schedule for six months next following the transfer and permits inspection of either or both and copying therefrom at all reasonable hours by any creditor of the transferor, or files the list and schedule in (a public office to be here identified).

(2) The list of creditors must be signed and sworn to or affirmed by the transferor or his agent. It must contain the names and business addresses of all creditors of the transferor, with the amounts when known, and also the names of all persons who are known to the transferor to assert claims against him even though such claims are disputed. If the transferor is the obligor of an outstanding issue of bonds, debentures or the like as to which there is an indenture trustee, the list of creditors need include only the name and address of the indenture trustee and the aggregate outstanding principal amount of the issue.

(3) Responsibility for the completeness and accuracy of the list of creditors rests on the transferor, and the transfer is not rendered ineffective by errors or omissions therein unless the transferee is shown to have had knowledge.

§ 6—105. Notice to Creditors

In addition to the requirements of the preceding section, any bulk transfer subject to this Article, except one made by auction sale (Section 6—108), is ineffective against any creditor of the transferor unless at least ten days before he takes possession of the goods or pays for them, whichever happens first, the transferee gives notice of the transfer in the manner and to the persons hereafter provided (Section 6—107).

[§ 6—106. Application of the Proceeds

In addition to the requirements of the two preceding sections:

(1) Upon every bulk transfer subject to this Article for which new consideration becomes payable except those made by sale at auction, it is the duty of the transferee to assure that such consideration is applied so far as necessary to pay those debts of the transferor which are either shown on the list furnished by the transferor (Section 6—104) or filed in writing in the place stated in the notice (Section 6—107) within thirty days after the mailing of such notice. This duty of the transferee runs to all the holders of such debts, and may be enforced by any of them for the benefit of all.

(2) If any of said debts are in dispute, the necessary sum may be withheld from distribution until the dispute is settled or adjudicated.

(3) If the consideration payable is not enough to pay all of the said debts in full, distribution shall be made pro rata.]

Note: *This section is bracketed to indicate division of opinion as to whether or not it is a wise provision, and to suggest that this is a point on which State enactments may differ without serious damage to the principle of uniformity.*

In any State where this section is omitted, the following parts of sections, also bracketed in the text, should also be omitted, namely:

Section 6—107(2) (e).
6—108(3) (c).
6—109(2).

In any State where this section is enacted, these other provisions should be also.

Optional Subsection (4)

[(4) The transferee may within ten days after he takes possession of the goods pay the consideration into the (specify court) in the county where the transferor had its principal place of business in this state and thereafter may discharge his duty under this section by giving notice by registered or certified mail to all the persons to whom the duty runs that the consideration has been paid into that court and that they should file their claims there. On motion of any interested party, the court may order the distribution of the consideration to the persons entitled to it.]

Note: *Optional subsection (4) is recommended for those states which do not have a general statute providing for payment of money into court.*

§ 6—107.   The Notice

(1) The notice to creditors (Section 6—105) shall state:

    (a) that a bulk transfer is about to be made; and

    (b) the names and business addresses of the transferor and transferee, and all other business names and addresses used by the transferor within three years last past so far as known to the transferee; and

    (c) whether or not all the debts of the transferor are to be paid in full as they fall due as a result of the transaction, and if so, the address to which creditors should send their bills.

(2) If the debts of the transferor are not to be paid in full as they fall due or if the transferee is in doubt on that point, then the notice shall state further:

    (a) the location and general description of the property to be transferred and the estimated total of the transferor's debts;

    (b) the address where the schedule of property and list of creditors (Section 6—104) may be inspected;

    (c) whether the transfer is to pay existing debts and if so, the amount of such debts and to whom owing;

    (d) whether the transfer is for new consideration and if so, the amount of such consideration and the time and place of payment; [and]

    [(e) if for new consideration, the time and place where creditors of the transferor are to file their claims.]

(3) The notice in any case shall be delivered personally or sent by registered or certified mail to all the persons shown on the list of creditors furnished by the transferor (Section 6—104) and to all other persons who are known to the transferee to hold or assert claims against the transferor.

Note: *The words in brackets are optional. See Note under § 6—106.*

§ 6—108.   Auction Sales; "Auctioneer"

(1) A bulk transfer is subject to this Article even though it is by sale at auction, but only in the manner and with the results stated in this section.

(2) The transferor shall furnish a list of his creditors and assist in the preparation of a schedule of the property to be sold, both prepared as before stated (Section 6—104).

(3) The person or persons other than the transferor who direct, control or are responsible for the auction are collectively called the "auctioneer." The auctioneer shall:

    (a) receive and retain the list of creditors and prepare and retain the schedule of property for the period stated in this Article (Section 6—104);

    (b) give notice of the auction personally or by registered or certified mail at least ten days before it occurs to all persons shown on the list of creditors and to all other persons who are known to him to hold or assert claims against the transferor; [and]

    [(c) assure that the net proceeds of the auction are applied as provided in this Article (Section 6—106).]

(4) Failure of the auctioneer to perform any of these duties does not affect the validity of the sale or the title of the purchasers; but if the auctioneer knows that the auction constitutes a bulk transfer, such failure renders the auctioneer liable to the creditors of the transferor as a class for the sums owing to them from the transferor up to but not exceeding the net proceeds of the auction. If the auctioneer consists of several persons their liability is joint and several.

Note: *The words in brackets are optional. See Note under § 6—106.*

§ 6—109.   What Creditors Protected; [Credit for Payment to Particular Creditors]

(1) The creditors of the transferor mentioned in this Article are those holding claims based on transactions or events occurring before the bulk transfer, but creditors who become such after notice to creditors is given (Sections 6—105 and 6—107) are not entitled to notice.

[(2) Against the aggregate obligation imposed by the provisions of this Article concerning the application of the proceeds (Section 6—106 and subsection (3) (c) of 6—108), the transferee or auctioneer is entitled to credit for sums paid to particular creditors of the transferor, not exceeding the sums believed in good faith at the time of the payment to be properly payable to such creditors.]

Note: *The words in brackets are optional. See Note under § 6—106.*

§ 6—110. Subsequent Transfers

When the title of a transferee to property is subject to a defect by reason of his noncompliance with the requirements of this Article, then:

(1) a purchaser of any of such property from such transferee who pays no value or who takes with notice of such noncompliance takes subject to such defect, but

(2) a purchaser for value in good faith and without such notice takes free of such defect.

§ 6—111. Limitation of Actions and Levies

No action under this Article shall be brought nor levy made more than six months after the date on which the transferee took possession of the goods unless the transfer has been concealed. If the transfer has been concealed, actions may be brought or levies made within six months after its discovery.

Note to Article 6: Section 6—106 is bracketed to indicate division of opinion as to whether or not it is a wise provision, and to suggest that this is a point on which State enactments may differ without serious damage to the principle of uniformity.

In any State where Section 6—106 is not enacted, the following parts of sections, also bracketed in the text, should also be omitted, namely:

> *Sec. 6—107(2) (e).*
> *6—108(3) (c).*
> *6—109(2).*

In any State where Section 6—106 is enacted, these other provisions should be also.

ARTICLE 7

WAREHOUSE RECEIPTS, BILLS OF LADING AND OTHER DOCUMENTS OF TITLE

PART 1

GENERAL

§ 7—101. Short Title

This Article shall be known and may be cited as Uniform Commercial Code—Documents of Title.

§ 7—102. Definitions and Index of Definitions

(1) In this Article, unless the context otherwise requires:

(a) "Bailee" means the person who by a warehouse receipt, bill of lading or other document of title acknowledges possession of goods and contracts to deliver them.

(b) "Consignee" means the person named in a bill to whom or to whose order the bill promises delivery.

(c) "Consignor" means the person named in a bill as the person from whom the goods have been received for shipment.

(d) "Delivery order" means a written order to deliver goods directed to a warehouseman, carrier or other person who in the ordinary course of business issues warehouse receipts or bills of lading.

(e) "Document" means document of title as defined in the general definitions in Article 1 (Section 1—201).

(f) "Goods" means all things which are treated as movable for the purposes of a contract of storage or transportation.

(g) "Issuer" means a bailee who issues a document except that in relation to an unaccepted delivery order it means the person who orders the possessor of goods to deliver. Issuer includes any person for whom an agent or employee purports to act in issuing a document if the agent or employee has real or apparent authority to issue documents, notwithstanding that the issuer received no goods or that the goods were misdescribed or that in any other respect the agent or employee violated his instructions.

(h) "Warehouseman" is a person engaged in the business of storing goods for hire.

(2) Other definitions applying to this Article or to specified Parts thereof, and the sections in which they appear are:

> "Duly negotiate."   Section 7—501.
> "Person entitled under the document."
>   Section 7—403(4).

(3) Definitions in other Articles applying to this Article and the sections in which they appear are:

> "Contract for sale."   Section 2—106.
> "Overseas."   Section 2—323.
> "Receipt" of goods.   Section 2—103.

(4) In addition, Article 1 contains general definitions and principles of construction and interpretation applicable throughout this Article.

§ 7—103. Relation of Article to Treaty, Statute, Tariff, Classification or Regulation

To the extent that any treaty or statute of the United States, regulatory statute of this State or tariff, classification or regulation filed or issued pursuant thereto is applicable, the provisions of this Article are subject thereto.

§ 7—104. Negotiable and Nonnegotiable Warehouse Receipt, Bill of Lading or Other Document of Title

(1) A warehouse receipt, bill of lading or other document of title is negotiable

    (a) if by its terms the goods are to be delivered to bearer or to the order of a named person; or

    (b) where recognized in overseas trade, if it runs to a named person or assigns.

(2) Any other document is nonnegotiable. A bill of lading in which it is stated that the goods are consigned to a named person is not made negotiable by a provision that the goods are to be delivered only against a written order signed by the same or another named person.

§ 7—105. Construction Against Negative Implication

The omission from either Part 2 or Part 3 of this Article of a provision corresponding to a provision made in the other Part does not imply that a corresponding rule of law is not applicable.

PART 2

WAREHOUSE RECEIPTS: SPECIAL PROVISIONS

§ 7—201. Who May Issue a Warehouse Receipt; Storage Under Government Bond

(1) A warehouse receipt may be issued by any warehouseman.

(2) Where goods including distilled spirits and agricultural commodities are stored under a statute requiring a bond against withdrawal or a license for the issuance of receipts in the nature of warehouse receipts, a receipt issued for the goods has like effect as a warehouse receipt even though issued by a person who is the owner of the goods and is not a warehouseman.

§ 7—202. Form of Warehouse Receipt; Essential Terms; Optional Terms

(1) A warehouse receipt need not be in any particular form.

(2) Unless a warehouse receipt embodies within its written or printed terms each of the following, the warehouseman is liable for damages caused by the omission to a person injured thereby:

    (a) the location of the warehouse where the goods are stored;

    (b) the date of issue of the receipt;

    (c) the consecutive number of the receipt;

    (d) a statement whether the goods received will be delivered to the bearer, to a specified person, or to a specified person or his order;

    (e) the rate of storage and handling charges, except that where goods are stored under a field warehousing arrangement a statement of that fact is sufficient on a nonnegotiable receipt;

    (f) a description of the goods or of the packages containing them;

    (g) the signature of the warehouseman, which may be made by his authorized agent;

    (h) if the receipt is issued for goods of which the warehouseman is owner, either solely or jointly or in common with others, the fact of such ownership; and

    (i) a statement of the amount of advances made and of liabilities incurred for which the warehouseman claims a lien or security interest (Section 7—209). If the precise amount of such advances made or of such liabilities incurred is, at the time of the issue of the receipt, unknown to the warehouseman or to his agent who issues it, a statement of the fact that advances have been made or liabilities incurred and the purpose thereof is sufficient.

(3) A warehouseman may insert in his receipt any other terms which are not contrary to the provisions of this Act and do not impair his obligation of delivery (Section 7—403) or his duty of care (Section 7—204). Any contrary provisions shall be ineffective.

§ 7—203. Liability for Non-Receipt or Misdescription

A party to or purchaser for value in good faith of a document of title other than a bill of lading relying in either case upon the description therein of the goods may recover from the issuer damages caused by the non-receipt or misdescription of the goods, except to the extent that the document conspicuously indicates that the issuer does not know whether any part or all of the goods in fact were received or conform to the description, as where the description is in terms of marks or labels or kind, quantity or condition, or the receipt or description is qualified by "contents, condition and quality unknown," "said to contain" or the like, if such indication be true, or the party or purchaser otherwise has notice.

§ 7—204. Duty of Care; Contractual Limitation of Warehouseman's Liability

(1) A warehouseman is liable for damages for loss of or injury to the goods caused by his failure to exercise such care in regard to them as a reasonably careful man would exercise under like circumstances but, unless otherwise agreed, he is not liable for damages which could not have been avoided by the exercise of such care.

(2) Damages may be limited by a term in the warehouse receipt or storage agreement limiting the amount of liability in case of loss or damage, and setting forth a specific liability per article or item, or value per unit of weight, beyond which the warehouseman shall not be liable; provided, however, that such liability may on written request of the bailor at the time of signing such storage agreement or within a reasonable time after receipt of the warehouse receipt be increased on part or all of the goods thereunder, in which event increased rates may be charged based on such increased valuation, but that no such increase shall be permitted contrary to a lawful limitation of liability contained in the warehouseman's tariff, if any. No such limitation is effective with respect to the warehouseman's liability for conversion to his own use.

(3) Reasonable provisions as to the time and manner of presenting claims and instituting actions based on the bailment may be included in the warehouse receipt or tariff.

(4) This section does not impair or repeal . . .

Note: *Insert in subsection (4) a reference to any statute which imposes a higher responsibility upon the warehouseman or invalidates contractual limitations which would be permissible under this Article.*

§ 7—205. Title Under Warehouse Receipt Defeated in Certain Cases

A buyer in the ordinary course of business of fungible goods sold and delivered by a warehouseman who is also in the business of buying and selling such goods takes free of any claim under a warehouse receipt even though it has been duly negotiated.

§ 7—206. Termination of Storage at Warehouseman's Option

(1) A warehouseman may, on notifying the person on whose account the goods are held and any other person known to claim an interest in the goods, require payment of any charges and removal of the goods from the warehouse at the termination of the period of storage fixed by the document, or, if no period is fixed, within a stated period not less than thirty days after the notification. If the goods are not removed before the date specified in the notification, the warehouseman may sell them in accordance with the provisions of the section on enforcement of a warehouseman's lien (Section 7—210).

(2) If a warehouseman in good faith believes that the goods are about to deteriorate or decline in value to less than the amount of his lien within the time prescribed in subsection (1) for notification, advertisement and sale, the warehouseman may specify in the notification any reasonable shorter time for removal of the goods and in case the goods are not removed, may sell them at public sale held not less than one week after a single advertisement or posting.

(3) If as a result of a quality or condition of the goods of which the warehouseman had no notice at the time of deposit, the goods are a hazard to other property or to the warehouse or to persons, the warehouseman may sell the goods at public or private sale without advertisement on reasonable notification to all persons known to claim an interest in the goods. If the warehouseman after a reasonable effort is unable to sell the goods, he may dispose of them in any lawful manner and shall incur no liability by reason of such disposition.

(4) The warehouseman must deliver the goods to any person entitled to them under this Article upon due demand made at any time prior to sale or other disposition under this section.

(5) The warehouseman may satisfy his lien from the proceeds of any sale or disposition under this section but must hold the balance for delivery on the demand of any person to whom he would have been bound to deliver the goods.

§ 7—207. Goods Must Be Kept Separate; Fungible Goods

(1) Unless the warehouse receipt otherwise provides, a warehouseman must keep separate the goods covered by each receipt so as to permit at all times identification and delivery of those goods, except that different lots of fungible goods may be commingled.

(2) Fungible goods so commingled are owned in common by the persons entitled thereto, and the warehouseman is severally liable to each owner for

that owner's share. Where because of overissue a mass of fungible goods is insufficient to meet all the receipts which the warehouseman has issued against it, the persons entitled include all holders to whom overissued receipts have been duly negotiated.

§ 7—208. Altered Warehouse Receipts

Where a blank in a negotiable warehouse receipt has been filled in without authority, a purchaser for value and without notice of the want of authority may treat the insertion as authorized. Any other unauthorized alteration leaves any receipt enforceable against the issuer according to its original tenor.

§ 7—209. Lien of Warehouseman

(1) A warehouseman has a lien against the bailor on the goods covered by a warehouse receipt or on the proceeds thereof in his possession for charges for storage or transportation (including demurrage and terminal charges), insurance, labor, or charges present or future in relation to the goods, and for expenses necessary for preservation of the goods or reasonably incurred in their sale pursuant to law. If the person on whose account the goods are held is liable for like charges or expenses in relation to other goods whenever deposited and it is stated in the receipt that a lien is claimed for charges and expenses in relation to other goods, the warehouseman also has a lien against him for such charges and expenses whether or not the other goods have been delivered by the warehouseman. But against a person to whom a negotiable warehouse receipt is duly negotiated, a warehouseman's lien is limited to charges in an amount or at a rate specified on the receipt or if no charges are so specified then to a reasonable charge for storage of the goods covered by the receipt subsequent to the date of the receipt.

(2) The warehouseman may also reserve a security interest against the bailor for a maximum amount specified on the receipt for charges other than those specified in subsection (1), such as for money advanced and interest. Such a security interest is governed by the Article on Secured Transactions (Article 9).

(3) (a) A warehouseman's lien for charges and expenses under subsection (1) or a security interest under subsection (2) is also effective against any person who so entrusted the bailor with possession of the goods that a pledge of them by him to a good faith purchaser for value would have been valid but is not effective against a person as to whom the document confers no right in the goods covered by it under Section 7—503.

(b) A warehouseman's lien on household goods for charges and expenses in rela-

tion to the goods under subsection (1) is also effective against all persons if the depositor was the legal possessor of the goods at the time of deposit. "Household goods" means furniture, furnishings and personal effects used by the depositor in a dwelling.

(4) A warehouseman loses his lien on any goods which he voluntarily delivers or which he unjustifiably refuses to deliver.

§ 7—210. Enforcement of Warehouseman's Lien

(1) Except as provided in subsection (2), a warehouseman's lien may be enforced by public or private sale of the goods in block or in parcels, at any time or place and on any terms which are commercially reasonable, after notifying all persons known to claim an interest in the goods. Such notification must include a statement of the amount due, the nature of the proposed sale and the time and place of any public sale. The fact that a better price could have been obtained by a sale at a different time or in a different method from that selected by the warehouseman is not of itself sufficient to establish that the sale was not made in a commercially reasonable manner. If the warehouseman either sells the goods in the usual manner in any recognized market therefor, or if he sells at the price current in such market at the time of his sale, or if he has otherwise sold in conformity with commercially reasonable practices among dealers in the type of goods sold, he has sold in a commercially reasonable manner. A sale of more goods than apparently necessary to be offered to insure satisfaction of the obligation is not commercially reasonable except in cases covered by the preceding sentence.

(2) A warehouseman's lien on goods other than goods stored by a merchant in the course of his business may be enforced only as follows:

(a) All persons known to claim an interest in the goods must be notified.

(b) The notification must be delivered in person or sent by registered or certified letter to the last known address of any person to be notified.

(c) The notification must include an itemized statement of the claim, a description of the goods subject to the lien, a demand for payment within a specified time not less than ten days after receipt of the notification, and a conspicuous statement that unless the claim is paid within that time the goods will be advertised for sale and sold by auction at a specified time and place.

(d) The sale must conform to the terms of the notification.

(e) The sale must be held at the nearest suitable place to that where the goods are held or stored.

(f) After the expiration of the time given in the notification, an advertisement of the sale must be published once a week for two weeks consecutively in a newspaper of general circulation where the sale is to be held. The advertisement must include a description of the goods, the name of the person on whose account they are being held, and the time and place of the sale. The sale must take place at least fifteen days after the first publication. If there is no newspaper of general circulation where the sale is to be held, the advertisement must be posted at least ten days before the sale in not less than six conspicuous places in the neighborhood of the proposed sale.

(3) Before any sale pursuant to this section, any person claiming a right in the goods may pay the amount necessary to satisfy the lien and the reasonable expenses incurred under this section. In that event, the goods must not be sold but must be retained by the warehouseman subject to the terms of the receipt and this Article.

(4) The warehouseman may buy at any public sale pursuant to this section.

(5) A purchaser in good faith of goods sold to enforce a warehouseman's lien takes the goods free of any rights of persons against whom the lien was valid, despite noncompliance by the warehouseman with the requirements of this section.

(6) The warehouseman may satisfy his lien from the proceeds of any sale pursuant to this section but must hold the balance, if any, for delivery on demand to any person to whom he would have been bound to deliver the goods.

(7) The rights provided by this section shall be in addition to all other rights allowed by law to a creditor against his debtor.

(8) Where a lien is on goods stored by a merchant in the course of his business, the lien may be enforced in accordance with either subsection (1) or (2).

(9) The warehouseman is liable for damages caused by failure to comply with the requirements for sale under this section and, in case of willful violation, is liable for conversion.

PART 3

BILLS OF LADING: SPECIAL PROVISIONS

§ 7—301. Liability for Non-Receipt or Misdescription; "Said to Contain"; "Shipper's Load and Count"; Improper Handling

(1) A consignee of a nonnegotiable bill who has given value in good faith or a holder to whom a negotiable bill has been duly negotiated relying in either case upon the description therein of the goods, or upon the date therein shown, may recover from the issuer damages caused by the misdating of the bill or the nonreceipt or misdescription of the goods, except to the extent that the document indicates that the issuer does not know whether any part or all of the goods in fact were received or conform to the description, as where the description is in terms of marks or labels or kind, quantity, or condition or the receipt or description is qualified by "contents or condition of contents of packages unknown," "said to contain," "shipper's weight, load and count" or the like, if such indication be true.

(2) When goods are loaded by an issuer who is a common carrier, the issuer must count the packages of goods if package freight and ascertain the kind and quantity if bulk freight. In such cases, "shipper's weight, load and count" or other words indicating that the description was made by the shipper are ineffective except as to freight concealed by packages.

(3) When bulk freight is loaded by a shipper who makes available to the issuer adequate facilities for weighing such freight, an issuer who is a common carrier must ascertain the kind and quantity within a reasonable time after receiving the written request of the shipper to do so. In such cases, "shipper's weight" or other words of like purport are ineffective.

(4) The issuer may by inserting in the bill the words "shipper's weight, load and count" or other words of like purport indicate that the goods were loaded by the shipper; and if such statement be true, the issuer shall not be liable for damages caused by the improper loading. But their omission does not imply liability for such damages.

(5) The shipper shall be deemed to have guaranteed to the issuer the accuracy at the time of shipment of the description, marks, labels, number, kind, quantity, condition and weight, as furnished by him; and the shipper shall indemnify the issuer against damage caused by inaccuracies in such particulars. The right of the issuer to such indemnity shall in no way limit his responsibility and liability under the contract of carriage to any person other than the shipper.

§ 7—302. Through Bills of Lading and Similar Documents

(1) The issuer of a through bill of lading or other document embodying an undertaking to be performed in part by persons acting as its agents or by connecting carriers is liable to anyone entitled to recover on the document for any breach by such other persons or by a connecting carrier of its obligation under the document but, to the extent that the bill covers an undertaking to be performed overseas or in territory not contiguous to the continental United States or an undertaking including matters other than transportation, this liability may be varied by agreement of the parties.

(2) Where goods covered by a through bill of lading or other document embodying an undertaking to be performed in part by persons other than the issuer are received by any such person, he is subject with respect to his own performance while the goods are in his possession to the obligation of the issuer. His obligation is discharged by delivery of the goods to another such person pursuant to the document, and does not include liability for breach by any other such persons or by the issuer.

(3) The issuer of such through bill of lading or other document shall be entitled to recover from the connecting carrier or such other person in possession of the goods when the breach of the obligation under the document occurred, the amount it may be required to pay to anyone entitled to recover on the document therefor, as may be evidenced by any receipt, judgment, or transcript thereof, and the amount of any expense reasonably incurred by it in defending any action brought by anyone entitled to recover on the document therefor.

§ 7—303. Diversion; Reconsignment; Change of Instructions

(1) Unless the bill of lading otherwise provides, the carrier may deliver the goods to a person or destination other than that stated in the bill or may otherwise dispose of the goods on instructions from

    (a) the holder of a negotiable bill; or

    (b) the consignor on a nonnegotiable bill notwithstanding contrary instructions from the consignee; or

    (c) the consignee on a nonnegotiable bill in the absence of contrary instructions from the consignor, if the goods have arrived at the billed destination or if the consignee is in possession of the bill; or

    (d) the consignee on a nonnegotiable bill if he is entitled as against the consignor to dispose of them.

(2) Unless such instructions are noted on a negotiable bill of lading, a person to whom the bill is duly negotiated can hold the bailee according to the original terms.

§ 7—304. Bills of Lading in a Set

(1) Except where customary in overseas transportation, a bill of lading must not be issued in a set of parts. The issuer is liable for damages caused by violation of this subsection.

(2) Where a bill of lading is lawfully drawn in a set of parts, each of which is numbered and expressed to be valid only if the goods have not been delivered against any other part, the whole of the parts constitute one bill.

(3) Where a bill of lading is lawfully issued in a set of parts and different parts are negotiated to different persons, the title of the holder to whom the first due negotiation is made prevails as to both the document and the goods, even though any later holder may have received the goods from the carrier in good faith and discharged the carrier's obligation by surrender of his part.

(4) Any person who negotiates or transfers a single part of a bill of lading drawn in a set is liable to holders of that part as if it were the whole set.

(5) The bailee is obliged to deliver in accordance with Part 4 of this Article against the first presented part of a bill of lading lawfully drawn in a set. Such delivery discharges the bailee's obligation on the whole bill.

§ 7—305. Destination Bills

(1) Instead of issuing a bill of lading to the consignor at the place of shipment, a carrier may at the request of the consignor procure the bill to be issued at destination or at any other place designated in the request.

(2) Upon request of anyone entitled as against the carrier to control the goods while in transit and on surrender of any outstanding bill of lading or other receipt covering such goods, the issuer may procure a substitute bill to be issued at any place designated in the request.

§ 7—306. Altered Bills of Lading

An unauthorized alteration or filling in of a blank in a bill of lading leaves the bill enforceable according to its original tenor.

§ 7—307. Lien of Carrier

(1) A carrier has a lien on the goods covered by a bill of lading for charges subsequent to the date of its receipt of the goods for storage or transportation (including demurrage and terminal charges) and

for expenses necessary for preservation of the goods incident to their transportation or reasonably incurred in their sale pursuant to law. But against a purchaser for value of a negotiable bill of lading, a carrier's lien is limited to charges stated in the bill or the applicable tariffs, or if no charges are stated then to a reasonable charge.

(2) A lien for charges and expenses under subsection (1) on goods which the carrier was required by law to receive for transportation is effective against the consignor or any person entitled to the goods unless the carrier had notice that the consignor lacked authority to subject the goods to such charges and expenses. Any other lien under subsection (1) is effective against the consignor and any person who permitted the bailor to have control or possession of the goods unless the carrier had notice that the bailor lacked such authority.

(3) A carrier loses his lien on any goods which he voluntarily delivers or which he unjustifiably refuses to deliver.

§ 7—308. Enforcement of Carrier's Lien

(1) A carrier's lien may be enforced by public or private sale of the goods, in block or in parcels, at any time or place and on any terms which are commercially reasonable, after notifying all persons known to claim an interest in the goods. Such notification must include a statement of the amount due, the nature of the proposed sale and the time and place of any public sale. The fact that a better price could have been obtained by a sale at a different time or in a different method from that selected by the carrier is not of itself sufficient to establish that the sale was not made in a commercially reasonable manner. If the carrier either sells the goods in the usual manner in any recognized market therefor or if he sells at the price current in such market at the time of his sale or if he has otherwise sold in conformity with commercially reasonable practices among dealers in the type of goods sold, he has sold in a commercially reasonable manner. A sale of more goods than apparently necessary to be offered to ensure satisfaction of the obligation is not commercially reasonable except in cases covered by the preceding sentence.

(2) Before any sale pursuant to this section, any person claiming a right in the goods may pay the amount necessary to satisfy the lien and the reasonable expenses incurred under this section. In that event the goods must not be sold, but must be retained by the carrier subject to the terms of the bill and this Article.

(3) The carrier may buy at any public sale pursuant to this section.

(4) A purchaser in good faith of goods sold to enforce a carrier's lien takes the goods free of

any rights of persons against whom the lien was valid, despite noncompliance by the carrier with the requirements of this section.

(5) The carrier may satisfy his lien from the proceeds of any sale pursuant to this section but must hold the balance, if any, for delivery on demand to any person to whom he would have been bound to deliver the goods.

(6) The rights provided by this section shall be in addition to all other rights allowed by law to a creditor against his debtor.

(7) A carrier's lien may be enforced in accordance with either subsection (1) or the procedure set forth in subsection (2) of Section 7—210.

(8) The carrier is liable for damages caused by failure to comply with the requirements for sale under this section and in case of willful violation is liable for conversion.

§ 7—309. Duty of Care; Contractual Limitation of Carrier's Liability

(1) A carrier who issues a bill of lading, whether negotiable or nonnegotiable, must exercise the degree of care in relation to the goods which a reasonably careful man would exercise under like circumstances. This subsection does not repeal or change any law or rule of law which imposes liability upon a common carrier for damages not caused by its negligence.

(2) Damages may be limited by a provision that the carrier's liability shall not exceed a value stated in the document if the carrier's rates are dependent upon value and the consignor by the carrier's tariff is afforded an opportunity to declare a higher value or a value as lawfully provided in the tariff, or, where no tariff is filed, he is otherwise advised of such opportunity; but no such limitation is effective with respect to the carrier's liability for conversion to its own use.

(3) Reasonable provisions as to the time and manner of presenting claims and instituting actions based on the shipment may be included in a bill of lading or tariff.

PART 4

WAREHOUSE RECEIPTS AND BILLS OF LADING: GENERAL OBLIGATIONS

§ 7—401. Irregularities in Issue of Receipt or Bill or Conduct of Issuer

The obligations imposed by this Article on an issuer apply to a document of title regardless of the fact that

    (a) the document may not comply with the requirements of this Article or of any other law or regulation regarding its issue, form or content; or

(b) the issuer may have violated laws regulating the conduct of his business; or

(c) the goods covered by the document were owned by the bailee at the time the document was issued; or

(d) the person issuing the document does not come within the definition of warehouseman, if it purports to be a warehouse receipt.

§ 7—402. Duplicate Receipt or Bill; Overissue

Neither a duplicate nor any other document of title purporting to cover goods already represented by an outstanding document of the same issuer confers any right in the goods, except as provided in the case of bills in a set, overissue of documents for fungible goods and substitutes for lost, stolen or destroyed documents. But the issuer is liable for damages caused by his overissue or failure to identify a duplicate document as such by conspicuous notation on its face.

§ 7—403. Obligation of Warehouseman or Carrier to Deliver; Excuse

(1) The bailee must deliver the goods to a person entitled under the document who complies with subsections (2) and (3), unless and to the extent that the bailee establishes any of the following:

(a) delivery of the goods to a person whose receipt was rightful as against the claimant;

(b) damage to or delay, loss or destruction of the goods for which the bailee is not liable [, but the burden of establishing negligence in such cases is on the person entitled under the document];

Note: *The brackets in (1) (b) indicate that State enactments may differ on this point without serious damage to the principle of uniformity.*

(c) previous sale or other disposition of the goods in lawful enforcement of a lien or on warehouseman's lawful termination of storage;

(d) the exercise by a seller of his right to stop delivery pursuant to the provisions of the Article on Sales (Section 2—705);

(e) a diversion, reconsignment or other disposition pursuant to the provisions of this Article (Section 7—303) or tariff regulating such right;

(f) release, satisfaction or any other fact affording a personal defense against the claimant;

(g) any other lawful excuse.

(2) A person claiming goods covered by a document of title must satisfy the bailee's lien where the bailee so requests or where the bailee is prohibited by law from delivering the goods until the charges are paid.

(3) Unless the person claiming is one against whom the document confers no right under Sec. 7—503(1), he must surrender for cancellation or notation of partial deliveries any outstanding negotiable document covering the goods, and the bailee must cancel the document or conspicuously note the partial delivery thereon or be liable to any person to whom the document is duly negotiated.

(4) "Person entitled under the document" means holder in the case of a negotiable document, or the person to whom delivery is to be made by the terms of or pursuant to written instructions under a nonnegotiable document.

§ 7—404. No Liability for Good Faith Delivery Pursuant to Receipt or Bill

A bailee who in good faith, including observance of reasonable commercial standards, has received goods and delivered or otherwise disposed of them according to the terms of the document of title or pursuant to this Article is not liable therefor. This rule applies even though the person from whom he received the goods had no authority to procure the document or to dispose of the goods and even though the person to whom he delivered the goods had no authority to receive them.

PART 5

WAREHOUSE RECEIPTS AND BILLS OF LADING: NEGOTIATION AND TRANSFER

§ 7—501. Form of Negotiation and Requirements of "Due Negotiation"

(1) A negotiable document of title running to the order of a named person is negotiated by his indorsement and delivery. After his indorsement in blank or to bearer, any person can negotiate it by delivery alone.

(2) (a) A negotiable document of title is also negotiated by delivery alone when by its original terms it runs to bearer.

(b) When a document running to the order of a named person is delivered to him, the effect is the same as if the document had been negotiated.

(3) Negotiation of a negotiable document of title after it has been indorsed to a specified person requires indorsement by the special indorsee as well as delivery.

(4) A negotiable document of title is "duly negotiated" when it is negotiated in the manner

stated in this section to a holder who purchases it in good faith without notice of any defense against or claim to it on the part of any person and for value, unless it is established that the negotiation is not in the regular course of business or financing or involves receiving the document in settlement or payment of a money obligation.

(5) Indorsement of a nonnegotiable document neither makes it negotiable nor adds to the transferee's rights.

(6) The naming in a negotiable bill of a person to be notified of the arrival of the goods does not limit the negotiability of the bill nor constitute notice to a purchaser thereof of any interest of such person in the goods.

§ 7—502. Rights Acquired by Due Negotiation

(1) Subject to the following section and to the provisions of Section 7—205 on fungible goods, a holder to whom a negotiable document of title has been duly negotiated acquires thereby:

(a) title to the document;

(b) title to the goods;

(c) all rights accruing under the law of agency or estoppel, including rights to goods delivered to the bailee after the document was issued; and

(d) the direct obligation of the issuer to hold or deliver the goods according to the terms of the document free of any defense or claim by him except those arising under the terms of the document or under this Article. In the case of a delivery order, the bailee's obligation accrues only upon acceptance and the obligation acquired by the holder is that the issuer and any indorser will procure the acceptance of the bailee.

(2) Subject to the following section, title and rights so acquired are not defeated by any stoppage of the goods represented by the document or by surrender of such goods by the bailee, and are not impaired even though the negotiation or any prior negotiation constituted a breach of duty or even though any person has been deprived of possession of the document by misrepresentation, fraud, accident, mistake, duress, loss, theft or conversion, or even though a previous sale or other transfer of the goods or document has been made to a third person.

§ 7—503. Document of Title to Goods Defeated in Certain Cases

(1) A document of title confers no right in goods against a person who before issuance of the document had a legal interest or a perfected security interest in them and who neither

(a) delivered or entrusted them or any document of title covering them to the bailor or his nominee with actual or apparent authority to ship, store or sell or with power to obtain delivery under this Article (Section 7—403) or with power of disposition under this Act (Sections 2—403 and 9—307) or other statute or rule of law; nor

(b) acquiesced in the procurement by the bailor or his nominee of any document of title.

(2) Title to goods based upon an unaccepted delivery order is subject to the rights of anyone to whom a negotiable warehouse receipt or bill of lading covering the goods has been duly negotiated. Such a title may be defeated under the next section to the same extent as the rights of the issuer or a transferee from the issuer.

(3) Title to goods based upon a bill of lading issued to a freight forwarder is subject to the rights of anyone to whom a bill issued by the freight forwarder is duly negotiated; but delivery by the carrier in accordance with Part 4 of this Article pursuant to its own bill of lading discharges the carrier's obligation to deliver.

§ 7—504. Rights Acquired in the Absence of Due Negotiation; Effect of Diversion; Seller's Stoppage of Delivery

(1) A transferee of a document, whether negotiable or nonnegotiable, to whom the document has been delivered but not duly negotiated, acquires the title and rights which his transferor had or had actual authority to convey.

(2) In the case of a nonnegotiable document, until but not after the bailee receives notification of the transfer, the rights of the transferee may be defeated

(a) by those creditors of the transferor who could treat the sale as void under Section 2—402; or

(b) by a buyer from the transferor in ordinary course of business if the bailee has delivered the goods to the buyer or received notification of his rights; or

(c) as against the bailee by good faith dealings of the bailee with the transferor.

(3) A diversion or other change of shipping instructions by the consignor in a nonnegotiable bill of lading which causes the bailee not to deliver to

the consignee defeats the consignee's title to the goods if they have been delivered to a buyer in ordinary course of business and in any event defeats the consignee's rights against the bailee.

(4) Delivery pursuant to a nonnegotiable document may be stopped by a seller under Section 2—705, and subject to the requirement of due notification there provided. A bailee honoring the seller's instructions is entitled to be indemnified by the seller against any resulting loss or expense.

§ 7—505. Indorser Not a Guarantor for Other Parties

The indorsement of a document of title issued by a bailee does not make the indorser liable for any default by the bailee or by previous indorsers.

§ 7—506. Delivery Without Indorsement: Right to Compel Indorsement

The transferee of a negotiable document of title has a specifically enforceable right to have his transferor supply any necessary indorsement, but the transfer becomes a negotiation only as of the time the indorsement is supplied.

§ 7—507. Warranties on Negotiation or Transfer of Receipt or Bill

Where a person negotiates or transfers a document of title for value otherwise than as a mere intermediary under the next following section, then unless otherwise agreed he warrants to his immediate purchaser only, in addition to any warranty made in selling the goods,

    (a) that the document is genuine; and
    (b) that he has no knowledge of any fact which would impair its validity or worth; and
    (c) that his negotiation or transfer is rightful and fully effective with respect to the title to the document and the goods it represents.

§ 7—508. Warranties of Collecting Bank as to Documents

A collecting bank or other intermediary known to be entrusted with documents on behalf of another or with collection of a draft or other claim against delivery of documents warrants by such delivery of the documents only its own good faith and authority. This rule applies even though the intermediary has purchased or made advances against the claim or draft to be collected.

§ 7—509. Receipt or Bill: When Adequate Compliance With Commercial Contract

The question whether a document is adequate to fulfill the obligations of a contract for sale or the conditions of a credit is governed by the Articles on Sales (Article 2) and on Letters of Credit (Article 5).

PART 6

WAREHOUSE RECEIPTS AND BILLS OF LADING: MISCELLANEOUS PROVISIONS

§ 7—601. Lost and Missing Documents

(1) If a document has been lost, stolen or destroyed, a court may order delivery of the goods or issuance of a substitute document and the bailee may without liability to any person comply with such order. If the document was negotiable, the claimant must post security approved by the court to indemnify any person who may suffer loss as a result of non-surrender of the document. If the document was not negotiable, such security may be required at the discretion of the court. The court may also in its discretion order payment of the bailee's reasonable costs and counsel fees.

(2) A bailee who without court order delivers goods to a person claiming under a missing negotiable document is liable to any person injured thereby, and if the delivery is not in good faith becomes liable for conversion. Delivery in good faith is not conversion if made in accordance with a filed classification or tariff or, where no classification or tariff is filed, if the claimant posts security with the bailee in an amount at least double the value of the goods at the time of posting to indemnify any person injured by the delivery who files a notice of claim within one year after the delivery.

§ 7—602. Attachment of Goods Covered by a Negotiable Document

Except where the document was originally issued upon delivery of the goods by a person who had no power to dispose of them, no lien attaches by virtue of any judicial process to goods in the possession of a bailee for which a negotiable document of title is outstanding unless the document be first surrendered to the bailee or its negotiation enjoined, and the bailee shall not be compelled to deliver the goods pursuant to process until the document is surrendered to him or impounded by the court. One who purchases the document for value without notice of the process or injunction takes free of the lien imposed by judicial process.

§ 7—603. Conflicting Claims; Interpleader

If more than one person claims title or possession of the goods, the bailee is excused from delivery until he has had a reasonable time to ascertain the validity of the adverse claims or to bring an action to compel all claimants to interplead and may compel such interpleader, either in defending an action for nondelivery of the goods, or by original action, whichever is appropriate.

ARTICLE 8

INVESTMENT SECURITIES

PART 1

SHORT TITLE AND GENERAL MATTERS

§ 8—101. Short Title

This Article shall be known and may be cited as Uniform Commercial Code—Investment Securities.

§ 8—102. Definitions and Index of Definitions

(1) In this Article, unless the context otherwise requires

   (a) A "security" is an instrument which

      (i) is issued in bearer or registered form; and

      (ii) is of a type commonly dealt in upon securities exchanges or markets or commonly recognized in any area in which it is issued or dealt in as a medium for investment; and

      (iii) is either one of a class or series or by its terms is divisible into a class or series of instruments; and

      (iv) evidences a share, participation or other interest in property or in an enterprise or evidences an obligation of the issuer.

   (b) A writing which is a security is governed by this Article and not by Uniform Commercial Code—Commercial Paper even though it also meets the requirements of that Article. This Article does not apply to money.

   (c) A security is in "registered form" when it specifies a person entitled to the security or to the rights it evidences and when its transfer may be registered upon books maintained for that purpose by or on behalf of an issuer or the security so states.

   (d) A security is in "bearer form" when it runs to bearer according to its terms and not by reason of any indorsement.

(2) A "subsequent purchaser" is a person who takes other than by original issue.

(3) A "clearing corporation" is a corporation all of the capital stock of which is held by or for a national securities exchange or association registered under a statute of the United States such as the Securities Exchange Act of 1934.

(4) A "custodian bank" is any bank or trust company which is supervised and examined by state or federal authority having supervision over banks and which is acting as custodian for a clearing corporation.

(5) Other definitions applying to this Article or to specified Parts thereof and the sections in which they appear are:

"Adverse claim."	Section 8—301.
"Bona fide purchaser."	Section 8—302.
"Broker."	Section 8—303.
"Guarantee of the signature."	Section 8—402.
"Intermediary Bank."	Section 4—105.
"Issuer."	Section 8—201.
"Overissue."	Section 8—104.

(6) In addition Article 1 contains general definitions and principles of construction and interpretation applicable throughout this Article.

§ 8—103. Issuer's Lien

A lien upon a security in favor of an issuer thereof is valid against a purchaser only if the right of the issuer to such lien is noted conspicuously on the security.

§ 8—104. Effect of Overissue; "Overissue"

(1) The provisions of this Article which validate a security or compel its issue or reissue do not apply to the extent that validation, issue or reissue would result in overissue; but

   (a) if an identical security which does not constitute an overissue is reasonably available for purchase, the person entitled to issue or validation may compel the issuer to purchase and deliver such a security to him against surrender of the security, if any, which he holds; or

(b) if a security is not so available for purchase, the person entitled to issue or validation may recover from the issuer the price he or the last purchaser for value paid for it, with interest from the date of his demand.

(2) "Overissue" means the issue of securities in excess of the amount which the issuer has corporate power to issue.

§ 8—105. Securities Negotiable; Presumptions

(1) Securities governed by this Article are negotiable instruments.

(2) In any action on security

(a) unless specifically denied in the pleadings, each signature on the security or in a necessary indorsement is admitted;

(b) when the effectiveness of a signature is put in issue, the burden of establishing it is on the party claiming under the signature but the signature is presumed to be genuine or authorized;

(c) when signatures are admitted or established, production of the instrument entitles a holder to recover on it unless the defendant establishes a defense or a defect going to the validity of the security; and

(d) after it is shown that a defense or defect exists, the plaintiff has the burden of establishing that he or some person under whom he claims is a person against whom the defense or defect is ineffective (Section 8—202).

§ 8—106. Applicability

The validity of a security and the rights and duties of the issuer with respect to registration of transfer are governed by the law (including the conflict of laws rules) of the jurisdiction of organization of the issuer.

§ 8—107. Securities Deliverable; Action for Price

(1) Unless otherwise agreed and subject to any applicable law or regulation respecting short sales, a person obligated to deliver securites may deliver any security of the specified issue in bearer form or registered in the name of the transferee or indorsed to him or in blank.

(2) When the buyer fails to pay the price as it comes due under a contract of sale, the seller may recover the price

(a) of securities accepted by the buyer; and

(b) of other securities if efforts at their resale would be unduly burdensome or if there is no readily available market for their resale.

PART 2

ISSUE—ISSUER

§ 8—201. "Issuer"

(1) With respect to obligations on or defenses to a security, "issuer" includes a person who

(a) places or authorizes the placing of his name on a security (otherwise than as authenticating trustee, registrar, transfer agent or the like) to evidence that it represents a share, participation or other interest in his property or in an enterprise or to evidence his duty to perform an obligation evidenced by the security; or

(b) directly or indirectly creates fractional interests in his rights or property which fractional interests are evidenced by securities; or

(c) becomes responsible for or in place of any other person described as an issuer in this section.

(2) With respect to obligations on or defenses to a security, a guarantor is an issuer to the extent of his guaranty whether or not his obligation is noted on the security.

(3) With respect to registration of transfer (Part 4 of this Article), "issuer" means a person on whose behalf transfer books are maintained.

§ 8—202. Issuer's Responsibility and Defenses; Notice of Defect or Defense

(1) Even against a purchaser for value and without notice, the terms of a security include those stated on the security and those made part of the security by reference to another instrument, indenture or document or to a constitution, statute, ordinance, rule, regulation, order or the like to the extent that the terms so referred to do not conflict with the stated terms. Such a reference does not of itself charge a purchaser for value with notice of a defect going to the validity even though the security expressly states that a person accepting it admits such notice.

(2) (a) A security other than one issued by a government or governmental agency

or unit even though issued with a defect going to its validity is valid in the hands of a purchaser for value and without notice of the particular defect unless the defect involves a violation of constitutional provisions in which case the security is valid in the hands of a subsequent purchaser for value and without notice of the defect.

(b) The rule of subparagraph (a) applies to an issuer which is a government or governmental agency or unit only if either there has been substantial compliance with the legal requiremants governing the issue or the issuer has received a substantial consideration for the issue as a whole or for the particular security and a stated purpose of the issue is one for which the issuer has power to borrow money or issue the security.

(3) Except as otherwise provided in the case of certain unauthorized signatures on issue (Section 8—205), lack of genuineness of a security is a complete defense even against a purchaser for value and without notice.

(4) All other defenses of the issuer including nondelivery and conditional delivery of the security are ineffective against a purchaser for value who has taken without notice of the particular defense.

(5) Nothing in this section shall be construed to effect the right of a party to a "when, as and if issued" or a "when distributed" contract to cancel the contract in the event of a material change in the character of the security which is the subject of the contract or in the plan or arrangement pursuant to which such security is to be issued or distributed.

§ 8—203. Staleness as Notice of Defects or Defenses

(1) After an act or event which creates a right to immediate performance of the principal obligation evidenced by the security or which sets a date on or after which the security is to be presented or surrendered for redemption or exchange, a purchaser is charged with notice of any defect in its issue or defense of the issuer

(a) if the act or event is one requiring the payment of money or the delivery of securities or both on presentation or surrender of the security and such funds or securities are available on the date set for payment or exchange and he takes the security more than one year after that date; and

(b) if the act or event is not covered by paragraph (a) and he takes the security more than two years after the date set for surrender or presentation or the date on which such performance became due.

(2) A call which has been revoked is not within subsection (1).

§ 8—204. Effect of Issuer's Restrictions on Transfer

Unless noted conspicuously on the security, a restriction on transfer imposed by the issuer even though otherwise lawful is ineffective except against a person with actual knowledge of it.

§ 8—205. Effect of Unauthorized Signature on Issue

An unauthorized signature placed on a security prior to or in the course of issue is ineffective except that the signature is effective in favor of a purchaser for value and without notice of the lack of authority if the signing has been done by

(a) an authenticating trustee, registrar, transfer agent or other person entrusted by the issuer with the signing of the security or of similar securities or their immediate preparation for signing; or

(b) an employee of the issuer or of any of the foregoing entrusted with responsible handling of the security.

§ 8—206. Completion or Alteration of Instrument

(1) Where a security contains the signatures necessary to its issue or transfer but is incomplete in any other respect

(a) any person may complete it by filling in the blanks as authorized; and

(b) even though the blanks are incorrectly filled in, the security as completed is enforceable by a purchaser who took it for value and without notice of such incorrectness.

(2) A complete security which has been improperly altered, even though fraudulently, remains enforceable but only according to its original terms.

§ 8—207. Rights of Issuer With Respect to Registered Owners

(1) Prior to due presentment for registration of transfer of a security in registered form, the issuer or indenture trustee may treat the registered owner as the person exclusively entitled to vote, to receive notifications and otherwise to exercise all the rights and powers of an owner.

(2) Nothing in this Article shall be construed to affect the liability of the registered owner of a security for calls, assessments or the like.

§ 8—208. Effect of Signature of Authenticating Trustee, Registrar or Transfer Agent

(1) A person placing his signature upon a security as authenticating trustee, registrar, transfer agent or the like warrants to a purchaser for value without notice of the particular defect that

(a) the security is genuine; and

(b) his own participation in the issue of the security is within his capacity and within the scope of the authorization received by him from the issuer; and

(c) he has reasonable grounds to believe that the security is in the form and within the amount the issuer is authorized to issue.

(2) Unless otherwise agreed, a person by so placing his signature does not assume responsibility for the validity of the security in other respects.

PART 3

PURCHASE

§ 8—301. Rights Acquired by Purchaser; "Adverse Claim"; Title Acquired by Bona Fide Purchaser

(1) Upon delivery of a security, the purchaser acquires the rights in the security which his transferor had or had actual authority to convey except that a purchaser who has himself been a party to any fraud or illegality affecting the security or who as a prior holder had notice of an adverse claim cannot improve his position by taking from a later bona fide purchaser. "Adverse claim" includes a claim that a transfer was or would be wrongful or that a particular adverse person is the owner of or has an interest in the security.

(2) A bona fide purchaser, in addition to acquiring the rights of a purchaser, also acquires the security free of any adverse claim.

(3) A purchaser of a limited interest acquires rights only to the extent of the interest purchased.

§ 8—302. "Bona Fide Purchaser"

A "bona fide purchaser" is a purchaser for value in good faith and without notice of any adverse claim who takes delivery of a security in bearer form or of one in registered form issued to him or indorsed to him or in blank.

§ 8—303. "Broker"

"Broker" means a person engaged for all or part of his time in the business of buying and selling securities, who in the transaction concerned acts for, or buys a security from or sells a security to a customer. Nothing in this Article determines the capacity in which a person acts for purposes of any other statute or rule to which such person is subject.

§ 8—304. Notice to Purchaser of Adverse Claims

(1) A purchaser (including a broker for the seller or buyer but excluding an intermediary bank) of a security is charged with notice of adverse claims if

(a) the security whether in bearer or registered form has been indorsed "for collection" or "for surrender" or for some other purpose not involving transfer; or

(b) the security is in bearer form and has on it an unambiguous statement that it is the property of a person other than the transferor. The mere writing of a name on a security is not such a statement.

(2) The fact that the purchaser (including a broker for the seller or buyer) has notice that the security is held for a third person or is registered in the name of or indorsed by a fiduciary does not create a duty of inquiry into the rightfulness of the transfer or constitute notice of adverse claims. If, however, the purchaser (excluding an intermediary bank) has knowledge that the proceeds are being used or that the transaction is for the individual benefit of the fiduciary or otherwise in breach of duty, the purchaser is charged with notice of adverse claims.

§ 8—305. Staleness as Notice of Adverse Claims

An act or event which creates a right to immediate performance of the principal obligation evidenced by the security or which sets a date on or after which the security is to be presented or surrendered for redemption or exchange does not of itself constitute any notice of adverse claims except in the case of a purchase

(a) after one year from any date set for such presentment or surrender for redemption or exchange; or

(b) after six months from any date set for payment of money against presentation or surrender of the security if funds are available for payment on that date.

§ 8—306. Warranties on Presentment and Transfer

(1) A person who presents a security for registration of transfer or for payment or exchange

warrants to the issuer that he is entitled to the registration, payment or exchange. But a purchaser for value without notice of adverse claims who receives a new, reissued or re-registered security on registration of transfer warrants only that he has no knowledge of any unauthorized signature (Section 8—311) in a necessary indorsement.

(2) A person by transferring a security to a purchaser for value warrants only that

    (a) his transfer is effective and rightful; and

    (b) the security is genuine and has not been materially altered; and

    (c) he knows no fact which might impair the validity of the security.

(3) Where a security is delivered by an intermediary known to be entrusted with delivery of the security on behalf of another or with collection of a draft or other claim against such delivery, the intermediary by such delivery warrants only his own good faith and authority even though he has purchased or made advances against the claim to be collected against the delivery.

(4) A pledgee or other holder for security who redelivers the security received, or after payment and on order of the debtor delivers that security to a third person makes only the warranties of an intermediary under subsection (3).

(5) A broker gives to his customer and to the issuer and a purchaser the warranties provided in this section and has the rights and privileges of a purchaser under this section. The warranties of and in favor of the broker acting as an agent are in addition to applicable warranties given by and in favor of his customer.

§ 8—307. Effect of Delivery Without Indorsement; Right to Compel Indorsement

Where a security in registered form has been delivered to a purchaser without a necessary indorsement, he may become a bona fide purchaser only as of the time the indorsement is supplied, but against the transferor the transfer is complete upon delivery and the purchaser has a specifically enforceable right to have any necessary indorsement supplied.

§ 8—308. Indorsement, How Made; Special Indorsement; Indorser Not a Guarantor; Partial Assignment

(1) An indorsement of a security in registered form is made when an appropriate person signs on it or on a separate document an assignment or transfer of the security or a power to assign or transfer it or when the signature of such person is written without more upon the back of the security.

(2) An indorsement may be in blank or special. An indorsement in blank includes an indorsement to bearer. A special indorsement specifies the person to whom the security is to be transferred, or who has power to transfer it. A holder may convert a blank indorsement into a special indorsement.

(3) "An appropriate person" in subsection (1) means

    (a) the person specified by the security or by special indorsement to be entitled to the security; or

    (b) where the person so specified is described as a fiduciary but is no longer serving in the described capacity,—either that person or his successor; or

    (c) where the security or indorsement so specifies more than one person as fiduciaries and one or more are no longer serving in the described capacity,—the remaining fiduciary or fiduciaries, whether or not a successor has been appointed or qualified; or

    (d) where the person so specified is an individual and is without capacity to act by virtue of death, incompetence, infancy or otherwise,—his executor, administrator, guardian or like fiduciary; or

    (e) where the security or indorsement so specifies more than one person as tenants by the entirety or with right of survivorship and by reason of death all cannot sign,—the survivor or survivors; or

    (f) a person having power to sign under applicable law or controlling instrument; or

    (g) to the extent that any of the foregoing persons may act through an agent,—his authorized agent.

(4) Unless otherwise agreed, the indorser by his indorsement assumes no obligation that the security will be honored by the issuer.

(5) An indorsement purporting to be only of part of a security representing units intended by the issuer to be separately transferable is effective to the extent of the indorsement.

(6) Whether the person signing is appropriate is determined as of the date of signing and an indorsement by such a person does not become unauthorized for the purposes of this Article by virtue of any subsequent change of circumstances.

(7) Failure of a fiduciary to comply with a controlling instrument or with the law of the state having jurisdiction of the fiduciary relationship, including any law requiring the fiduciary to obtain

court approval of the transfer, does not render his indorsement unauthorized for the purposes of this Article.

§ 8—309. Effect of Indorsement Without Delivery

An indorsement of a security whether special or in blank does not constitute a transfer until delivery of the security on which it appears or, if the indorsement is on a separate document, until delivery of both the document and the security.

§ 8—310. Indorsement of Security in Bearer Form

An indorsement of a security in bearer form may give notice of adverse claims (Section 8—304) but does not otherwise affect any right to registration the holder may possess.

§ 8—311. Effect of Unauthorized Indorsement

Unless the owner has ratified an unauthorized indorsement or is otherwise precluded from asserting its ineffectiveness

    (a) he may assert its ineffectiveness against the issuer or any purchaser other than a purchaser for value and without notice of adverse claims who has in good faith received a new, reissued or re-registered security on registration of transfer; and

    (b) an issuer who registers the transfer of a security upon the unauthorized indorsement is subject to liability for improper registration (Section 8—404).

§ 8—312. Effect of Guaranteeing Signature or Indorsement

(1) Any person guaranteeing a signature of an indorser of a security warrants that at the time of signing

    (a) the signature was genuine; and

    (b) the signer was an appropriate person to indorse (Section 8—308); and

    (c) the signer had legal capacity to sign.

But the guarantor does not otherwise warrant the rightfulness of the particular transfer.

(2) Any person may guarantee an indorsement of a security and by so doing warrants not only the signature (subsection 1) but also the rightfulness of the particular transfer in all respects. But no issuer may require a guarantee of indorsement as a condition to registration of transfer.

(3) The foregoing warranties are made to any person taking or dealing with the security in reliance on the guarantee, and the guarantor is liable to such person for any loss resulting from breach of the warranties.

§ 8—313. When Delivery to the Purchaser Occurs; Purchaser's Broker as Holder

(1) Delivery to a purchaser occurs when

    (a) he or a person designated by him acquires possession of a security; or

    (b) his broker acquires possession of a security specially indorsed to or issued in the name of the purchaser; or

    (c) his broker sends him confirmation of the purchase and also by book entry, or otherwise, identifies a specific security in the broker's possession as belonging to the purchaser; or

    (d) with respect to an identified security to be delivered while still in the possession of a third person, when that person acknowledges that he holds for the purchaser; or

    (e) appropriate entries on the books of a clearing corporation are made under Section 8—320.

(2) The purchaser is the owner of a security held for him by his broker, but is not the holder except as specified in subparagraphs (b), (c) and (e) of subsection (1). Where a security is part of a fungible bulk, the purchaser is the owner of a proportionate property interest in the fungible bulk.

(3) Notice of an adverse claim received by the broker or by the purchaser after the broker takes delivery as a holder for value is not effective either as to the broker or as to the purchaser. However, as between the broker and the purchaser, the purchaser may demand delivery of an equivalent security as to which no notice of an adverse claim has been received.

§ 8—314. Duty to Deliver, When Completed

(1) Unless otherwise agreed, where a sale of a security is made on an exchange or otherwise through brokers

    (a) the selling customer fulfills his duty to deliver when he places such a security in the possession of the selling broker or of a person designated by the broker or if requested causes an acknowledgment to be made to the selling broker that it is held for him; and

    (b) the selling broker including a correspondent broker acting for a selling customer fulfills his duty to deliver by placing the security or a like security in the possession of the buying broker or a person designated by him or by effecting clearance of the sale in accordance with the rules of the exchange on which the transaction took place.

(2) Except as otherwise provided in this section and unless otherwise agreed, a transferor's duty to deliver a security under a contract of purchase is not fulfilled until he places the security in form to be negotiated by the purchaser in the possession of the purchaser or of a person designated by him or at the purchaser's request causes an acknowledgment to be made to the purchaser that it is held for him. Unless made on an exchange, a sale to a broker purchasing for his own account is within this subsection and not within subsection (1).

§ 8—315. Action Against Purchaser Based Upon Wrongful Transfer

(1) Any person against whom the transfer of a security is wrongful for any reason, including his incapacity, may against anyone except a bona fide purchaser reclaim possession of the security or obtain possession of any new security evidencing all or part of the same rights or have damages.

(2) If the transfer is wrongful because of an unauthorized indorsement, the owner may also reclaim or obtain possession of the security or new security even from a bona fide purchaser if the ineffectiveness of the purported indorsement can be asserted against him under the provisions of this Article on unauthorized indorsements (Section 8—311).

(3) The right to obtain or reclaim possession of a security may be specifically enforced and its transfer enjoined and the security impounded pending the litigation.

§ 8—316. Purchaser's Right to Requisites for Registration of Transfer on Books

Unless otherwise agreed, the transferor must on due demand supply his purchaser with any proof of his authority to transfer or with any other requisite which may be necessary to obtain registration of the transfer of the security but if the transfer is not for value a transferor need not do so unless the purchaser furnishes the necessary expenses. Failure to comply with a demand made within a reasonable time gives the purchaser the right to reject or rescind the transfer.

§ 8—317. Attachment or Levy Upon Security

(1) No attachment or levy upon a security or any share or other interest evidenced thereby which is outstanding shall be valid until the security is actually seized by the officer making the attachment or levy, but a security which has been surrendered to the issuer may be attached or levied upon at the source.

(2) A creditor whose debtor is the owner of a security shall be entitled to such aid from courts of appropriate jurisdiction, by injunction or otherwise, in reaching such security or in satisfying the claim by means thereof as is allowed at law or in equity in regard to property which cannot readily be attached or levied upon by ordinary legal process.

§ 8—318. No Conversion by Good Faith Delivery

An agent or bailee who in good faith (including observance of reasonable commercial standards if he is in the business of buying, selling or otherwise dealing with securities) has received securities and sold, pledged or delivered them according to the instructions of his principal is not liable for conversion or for participation in breach of fiduciary duty although the principal had no right to dispose of them.

§ 8—319. Statute of Frauds

A contract for the sale of securities is not enforceable by way of action or defense unless

(a) there is some writing signed by the party against whom enforcement is sought or by his authorized agent or broker sufficient to indicate that a contract has been made for sale of a stated quantity of described securities at a defined or stated price; or

(b) delivery of the security has been accepted or payment has been made but the contract is enforceable under this provision only to the extent of such delivery or payment; or

(c) within a reasonable time a writing in confirmation of the sale or purchase and sufficient against the sender under paragraph (a) has been received by the party against whom enforcement is sought and he has failed to send written objection to its contents within ten days after its receipt; or

(d) the party against whom enforcement is sought admits in his pleading, testimony or otherwise in court that a contract was made for sale of a stated quantity of described securities at a defined or stated price.

§ 8—320. Transfer or Pledge within a Central Depository System

(1) If a security

(a) is in the custody of a clearing corporation or a custodian bank or a nominee of either subject to the instructions of the clearing corporation; and

(b) is in bearer form or indorsed in blank by an appropriate person or registered in the name of the clearing corporation or custodian bank or a nominee of either; and

(c) is shown on the account of a transferor or pledgor on the books of the clearing corporation;

then, in addition to other methods, a transfer or pledge of the security or any interest therein may be effected by the making of appropriate entries on the books of the clearing corporation reducing the account of the transferor or pledgor and increasing the account of the transferee or pledgee by the amount of the obligation or the number of shares or rights transferred or pledged.

(2) Under this section, entries may be with respect to like securities or interests therein as a part of a fungible bulk and may refer merely to a quantity of a particular security without reference to the name of the registered owner, certificate or bond number or the like and, in appropriate cases, may be on a net basis taking into account other transfers or pledges of the same security.

(3) A transfer or pledge under this section has the effect of a delivery of a security in bearer form or duly indorsed in blank (Section 8—301) representing the amount of the obligation or the number of shares or rights transferred or pledged. If a pledge or the creation of a security interest is intended, the making of entries has the effect of a taking of delivery by the pledgee or a secured party (Sections 9—304 and 9—305). A transferee or pledgee under this section is a holder.

(4) A transfer or pledge under this section does not constitute a registration of transfer under Part 4 of this Article.

(5) That entries made on the books of the clearing corporation as provided in subsection (1) are not appropriate does not affect the validity or effect of the entries nor the liabilities or obligations of the clearing corporation to any person adversely affected thereby.

PART 4

REGISTRATION

§ 8—401. Duty of Issuer to Register Transfer

(1) Where a security in registered form is presented to the issuer with a request to register transfer, the issuer is under a duty to register the transfer as requested if

(a) the security is indorsed by the appropriate person or persons (Section 8—308); and

(b) reasonable assurance is given that those indorsements are genuine and effective (Section 8—402); and

(c) the issuer has no duty to inquire into adverse claims or has discharged any such duty (Section 8—403); and

(d) any applicable law relating to the collection of taxes has been complied with; and

(e) the transfer is in fact rightful or is to a bona fide purchaser.

(2) Where an issuer is under a duty to register a transfer of a security, the issuer is also liable to the person presenting it for registration or his principal for loss resulting from any unreasonable delay in registration or from failure or refusal to register the transfer.

§ 8—402. Assurance that Indorsements Are Effective

(1) The issuer may require the following assurance that each necessary indorsement (Section 8—308) is genuine and effective

(a) in all cases, a guarantee of the signature (subsection (1) of Section 8—312) of the person indorsing; and

(b) where the indorsement is by an agent, appropriate assurance of authority to sign;

(c) where the indorsement is by a fiduciary, appropriate evidence of appointment or incumbency;

(d) where there is more than one fiduciary, reasonable assurance that all who are required to sign have done so;

(e) where the indorsement is by a person not covered by any of the foregoing, assurance appropriate to the case corresponding as nearly as may be to the foregoing.

(2) A "guarantee of the signature" in subsection (1) means a guarantee signed by or on behalf of a person reasonably believed by the issuer to be responsible. The issuer may adopt standards with respect to responsibility provided such standards are not manifestly unreasonable.

(3) "Appropriate evidence of appointment or incumbency" in subsection (1) means

(a) in the case of a fiduciary appointed or qualified by a court, a certificate issued by or under the direction or supervision of that court or an officer thereof and dated within sixty days before the date of presentation for transfer; or

(b) in any other case, a copy of a document showing the appointment or a certificate issued by or on behalf of a person reasonably believed by the issuer to be responsible or, in the absence of such a document or certificate, other evidence reasonably deemed by the issuer to be appropriate. The issuer may adopt standards with respect to such evidence provided such standards are not manifestly unreasonable. The issuer is not charged with notice of the contents of any document obtained pursuant to this paragraph (b) except to the extent that the contents relate directly to the appointment or incumbency.

(4) The issuer may elect to require reasonable assurance beyond that specified in this section but if it does so and, for a purpose other than that specified in subsection 3(b), both requires and obtains a copy of a will, trust, indenture, articles of copartnership, bylaws or other controlling instrument it is charged with notice of all matters contained therein affecting the transfer.

§ 8—403. Limited Duty of Inquiry

(1) An issuer to whom a security is presented for registration is under a duty to inquire into adverse claims if

(a) a written notification of an adverse claim is received at a time and in a manner which affords the issuer a reasonable opportunity to act on it prior to the issuance of a new, reissued or re-registered security and the notification identifies the claimant, the registered owner and the issue of which the security is a part and provides an address for communications directed to the claimant; or

(b) the issuer is charged with notice of an adverse claim from a controlling instrument which it has elected to require under subsection (4) of Section 8—402.

(2) The issuer may discharge any duty of inquiry by any reasonable means, including notifying an adverse claimant by registered or certified mail at the address furnished by him or, if there be no such address, at his residence or regular place of business that the security has been presented for registration of transfer by a named person, and that

the transfer will be registered unless within thirty days from the date of mailing the notification, either

(a) an appropriate restraining order, injunction or other process issues from a court of competent jurisdiction; or

(b) an indemnity bond sufficient in the issuer's judgment to protect the issuer and any transfer agent, registrar or other agent of the issuer involved, from any loss which it or they may suffer by complying with the adverse claim is filed with the issuer.

(3) Unless an issuer is charged with notice of an adverse claim from a controlling instrument which it has elected to require under subsection (4) of Section 8—402 or receives notification of an adverse claim under subsection (1) of this section, where a security presented for registration is indorsed by the appropriate person or persons the issuer is under no duty to inquire into adverse claims. In particular

(a) an issuer registering a security in the name of a person who is described as a fiduciary is not bound to inquire into the existence, extent, or correct description of the fiduciary relationship and thereafter the issuer may assume without inquiry that the newly registered owner continues to be the fiduciary until the issuer receives written notice that the fiduciary is no longer acting as such with respect to the particular security;

(b) an issuer registering transfer on an indorsement by a fiduciary is not bound to inquire whether the transfer is made in compliance with a controlling instrument or with the law of the state having jurisdiction of the fiduciary relationship, including any law requiring the fiduciary to obtain court approval of the transfer; and

(c) the issuer is not charged with notice of the contents of any court record or file or other recorded or unrecorded document even though the document is in its possession and even though the transfer is made on the indorsement of a fiduciary to the fiduciary himself or to his nominee.

§ 8—404. Liability and Non-Liability for Registration

(1) Except as otherwise provided in any law relating to the collection of taxes, the issuer is not liable to the owner or any other person suffering

loss as a result of the registration of a transfer of a security if

    (a) there were on or with the security the necessary indorsements (Section 8—308); and

    (b) the issuer had no duty to inquire into adverse claims or has discharged any such duty (Section 8—403).

(2) Where an issuer has registered a transfer of a security to a person not entitled to it, the issuer on demand must deliver a like security to the true owner unless

    (a) the registration was pursuant to subsection (1); or

    (b) the owner is precluded from asserting any claim for registering the transfer under subsection (1) of the following section; or

    (c) such delivery would result in overissue, in which case the issuer's liability if governed by Section 8—104.

§ 8—405. Lost, Destroyed and Stolen Securities

(1) Where a security has been lost, apparently destroyed or wrongfully taken and the owner fails to notify the issuer of that fact within a reasonable time after he has notice of it and the issuer registers a transfer of the security before receiving such a notification, the owner is precluded from asserting against the issuer any claim for registering the transfer under the preceding section or any claim to a new security under this section.

(2) Where the owner of a security claims that the security has been lost, destroyed or wrongfully taken, the issuer must issue a new security in place of the original security if the owner

    (a) so requests before the issuer has notice that the security has been acquired by a bona fide purchaser; and

    (b) files with the issuer a sufficient indemnity bond; and

    (c) satisfies any other reasonable requirements imposed by the issuer.

(3) If, after the issue of the new security, a bona fide purchaser of the original security presents it for registration of transfer, the issuer must register the transfer unless registration would result in overissue, in which event the issuer's liability is governed by Section 8—104. In addition to any rights on the indemnity bond, the issuer may recover the new security from the person to whom it was issued or any person taking under him except a bona fide purchaser.

§ 8—406. Duty of Authenticating Trustee, Transfer Agent or Registrar

(1) Where a person acts as authenticating trustee, transfer agent, registrar, or other agent for an issuer in the registration of transfers of its securities or in the issue of new securities or in the cancellation of surrendered securities

    (a) he is under a duty to the issuer to exercise good faith and due diligence in performing his functions; and

    (b) he has with regard to the particular functions he performs the same obligation to the holder or owner of the security and has the same rights and privileges as the issuer has in regard to those functions.

(2) Notice to an authenticating trustee, transfer agent, registrar or other such agent is notice to the issuer with respect to the functions performed by the agent.

ARTICLE 9

SECURED TRANSACTIONS; SALES OF ACCOUNTS AND CHATTEL PAPER

PART 1

SHORT TITLE, APPLICABILITY AND DEFINITIONS

§ 9—101. Short Title

This Article shall be known and may be cited as Uniform Commercial Code—Secured Transactions.

§ 9—102. Policy and Subject Matter of Article

(1) Except as otherwise provided in Section 9—104 on excluded transactions, this Article applies

    (a) to any transaction (regardless of its form) which is intended to create a security interest in personal property or fixtures including goods, documents, instruments, general intangibles, chattel paper or accounts; and also

    (b) to any sale of accounts or chattel paper.

(2) This Article applies to security interests created by contract including pledge, assignment, chattel mortgage, chattel trust, trust deed, factor's lien, equipment trust, conditional sale, trust receipt, other lien or title retention contract and lease or consignment intended as security. This Article does not apply to statutory liens except as provided in Section 9—310.

(3) The application of this Article to a security interest in a secured obligation is not affected by the fact that the obligation is itself secured by a transaction or interest to which this Article does not apply.

Note: *The adoption of this Article should be accompanied by the repeal of existing statutes dealing with conditional sales, trust receipts, factor's liens where the factor is given a non-possessory lien, chattel mortgages, crop mortgages, mortgages on railroad equipment, assignment of accounts and generally statutes regulating security interests in personal property.*

Where the state has a retail installment selling act or small loan act, that legislation should be carefully examined to determine what changes in those acts are needed to conform them to this Article. This Article primarily sets out rules defining rights of a secured party against persons dealing with the debtor; it does not prescribe regulations and controls which may be necessary to curb abuses arising in the small loan business or in the financing of consumer purchases on credit. Accordingly there is no intention to repeal existing regulatory acts in those fields by enactment or re-enactment of Article 9. See Section 9—203(4) and the Note thereto.

§ 9—103. Perfection of Security Interests in Multiple State Transactions

(1) Documents, instruments and ordinary goods.

    (a) This subsection applies to documents and instruments and to goods other than those covered by a certificate of title described in subsection (2), mobile goods described in subsection (3), and minerals described in subsection (5).

    (b) Except as otherwise provided in this subsection, perfection and the effect of perfection or non-perfection of a security interest in collateral are governed by the law of the jurisdiction where the collateral is when the last event occurs on which is based the assertion that the security interest is perfected or unperfected.

    (c) If the parties to a transaction creating a purchase money security interest in goods in one jurisdiction understand at the time that the security interest attaches that the goods will be kept in another jurisdiction, then the law of the other jurisdiction governs the perfection and the effect of perfection or non-perfection of the security interest from the time it attaches until thirty days after the debtor receives possession of the goods and thereafter if the goods are taken to the other jurisdiction before the end of the thirty-day period.

    (d) When collateral is brought into and kept in this state while subject to a security interest perfected under the law of the jurisdiction from which the collateral was removed, the security interest remains perfected, but if action is required by Part 3 of this Article to perfect the security interest,

        (i) if the action is not taken before the expiration of the period of perfection in the other jurisdiction or the end of four months after the collateral is brought into this state, whichever period first expires, the security interest becomes unperfected at the end of that period and is thereafter deemed to have been unperfected as against a person who became a purchaser after removal;

        (ii) if the action is taken before the expiration of the period specified in subparagraph (i), the security interest continues perfected thereafter;

        (iii) for the purpose of priority over a buyer of consumer goods (subsection (2) of Section 9—307), the period of the effectiveness of a filing in the jurisdiction from which the collateral is removed is governed by the rules with respect to perfection in subparagraphs (i) and (ii).

(2) Certificate of title.

    (a) This subsection applies to goods covered by a certificate of title issued under a statute of this state or of another jurisdiction under the law of which indication of a security interest on the certificate is required as a condition of perfection.

(b) Except as otherwise provided in this subsection, perfection and the effect of perfection or non-perfection of the security interest are governed by the law (including the conflict of laws rules) of the jurisdiction issuing the certificate until four months after the goods are removed from that jurisdiction and thereafter until the goods are registered in another jurisdiction, but in any event not beyond surrender of the certificate. After the expiration of that period, the goods are not covered by the certificate of title within the meaning of this section.

(c) Except with respect to the rights of a buyer described in the next paragraph, a security interest, perfected in another jurisdiction otherwise than by notation on a certificate of title, in goods brought into this state and thereafter covered by a certificate of title issued by this state is subject to the rules stated in paragraph (d) of subsection (1).

(d) If goods are brought into this state while a security interest therein is perfected in any manner under the law of the jurisdiction from which the goods are removed and a certificate of title is issued by this state and the certificate does not show that the goods are subject to the security interest or that they may be subject to security interests not shown on the certificate, the security interest is subordinate to the rights of a buyer of the goods who is not in the business of selling goods of that kind to the extent that he gives value and receives delivery of the goods after issuance of the certificate and without knowledge of the security interest.

(3) Accounts, general intangibles and mobile goods.

(a) This subsection applies to accounts (other than an account described in subsection (5) on minerals) and general intangibles and to goods which are mobile and which are of a type normally used in more than one jurisdiction, such as motor vehicles, trailers, rolling stock, airplanes, shipping containers, road building and construction machinery and commercial harvesting machinery and the like, if the goods are equipment or are inventory leased or held for lease by the debtor to others, and are not covered by a certificate of title described in subsection (2).

(b) The law (including the conflict of laws rules) of the jurisdiction in which the debtor is located governs the perfection and the effect of perfection or non-perfection of the security interest.

(c) If, however, the debtor is located in a jurisdiction which is not a part of the United States, and which does not provide for perfection of the security interest by filing or recording in that jurisdiction, the law of the jurisdiction in the United States in which the debtor has its major executive office in the United States governs the perfection and the effect of perfection or non-perfection of the security interest through filing. In the alternative, if the debtor is located in a jurisdiction which is not a part of the United States or Canada and the collateral is accounts or general intangibles for money due or to become due, the security interest may be perfected by notification to the account debtor. As used in this paragraph, "United States" includes its territories and possessions and the Commonwealth of Puerto Rico.

(d) A debtor shall be deemed located at his place of business if he has one, at his chief executive office if he has more than one place of business, otherwise at his residence. If, however, the debtor is a foreign air carrier under the Federal Aviation Act of 1958, as amended, it shall be deemed located at the designated office of the agent upon whom service of process may be made on behalf of the foreign air carrier.

(e) A security interest perfected under the law of the jurisdiction of the location of the debtor is perfected until the expiration of four months after a change of the debtor's location to another jurisdiction, or until perfection would have ceased by the law of the first jurisdiction, whichever period first expires.

Unless perfected in the new jurisdiction before the end of that period, it becomes unperfected thereafter and is deemed to have been unperfected as against a person who became a purchaser after the change.

(4) Chattel paper.

The rules stated for goods in subsection (1) apply to a possessory security interest in chattel paper. The rules stated for accounts in subsection (3) apply to a non-possessory security interest in chattel paper, but the security interest may not be perfected by notification to the account debtor.

(5) Minerals.

Perfection and the effect of perfection or non-perfection of a security interest which is created by a debtor who has an interest in minerals or the like (including oil and gas) before extraction and which attaches thereto as extracted, or which attaches to an account resulting from the sale thereof at the wellhead or minehead are governed by the law (including the conflict of laws rules) of the jurisdiction wherein the wellhead or minehead is located.

§ 9—104. Transactions Excluded from Article

This Article does not apply

(a) to a security interest subject to any statute of the United States, to the extent that such statute governs the rights of parties to and third parties affected by transactions in particular types of property; or

(b) to a landlord's lien; or

(c) to a lien given by statute or other rule of law for services or materials except as provided in Section 9—310 on priority of such liens; or

(d) to a transfer of a claim for wages, salary or other compensation of an employee; or

(e) to a transfer by a government or governmental subdivision or agency; or

(f) to a sale of accounts or chattel paper as part of a sale of the business out of which they arose, or an assignment of accounts or chattel paper which is for the purpose of collection only, or a transfer of a right to payment under a contract to an assignee who is also to do the performance under the contract or a transfer of a single account to an assignee in whole or partial satisfaction of a preexisting indebtedness; or

(g) to a transfer of an interest in or claim in or under any policy of insurance,

except as provided with respect to proceeds (Section 9—306) and priorities in proceeds (Section 9—312); or

(h) to a right represented by a judgment (other than a judgment taken on a right to payment which was collateral); or

(i) to any right of setoff; or

(j) except to the extent that provision is made for fixtures in Section 9—313, to the creation or transfer of an interest in or lien on real estate, including a lease or rents thereunder; or

(k) to a transfer in whole or in part of any claim arising out of tort; or

(l) to a transfer of an interest in any deposit account (subsection (1) of Section 9—105), except as provided with respect to proceeds (Section 9—306) and priorities in proceeds (Section 9—312).

§ 9—105. Definitions and Index of Definitions

(1) In this Article unless the context otherwise requires:

(a) "Account debtor" means the person who is obligated on an account, chattel paper or general intangible;

(b) "Chattel paper" means a writing or writings which evidence both a monetary obligation and a security interest in or a lease of specific goods, but a charter or other contract involving the use or hire of a vessel is not chattel paper. When a transaction is evidenced both by such a security agreement or a lease and by an instrument or a series of instruments, the group of writings taken together constitutes chattel paper;

(c) "Collateral" means the property subject to a security interest, and includes accounts and chattel paper which have been sold;

(d) "Debtor" means the person who owes payment or other performance of the obligation secured, whether or not he owns or has rights in the collateral, and includes the seller of accounts or chattel paper. Where the debtor and the owner of the collateral are not the same person, the term "debtor" means the owner of the collateral in any provision of the Article dealing with the collateral, the obligor in any provision dealing with the obligation, and may include both where the context so requires;

(e) "Deposit account" means a demand, time, savings, passbook or like account maintained with a bank, savings and loan association, credit union or like organization, other than an account evidenced by a certificate of deposit;

(f) "Document" means document of title as defined in the general definitions of Article 1 (Section 1—201), and a receipt of the kind described in subsection (2) of Section 7—201;

(g) "Encumbrance" includes real estate mortgages and other liens on real estate and all other rights in real estate that are not ownership interests;

(h) "Goods" includes all things which are movable at the time the security interest attaches or which are fixtures (Section 9—313), but does not include money, documents, instruments, accounts, chattel paper, general intangibles, or minerals or the like (including oil and gas) before extraction. "Goods" also includes standing timber which is to be cut and removed under a conveyance or contract for sale, the unborn young of animals, and growing crops;

(i) "Instrument" means a negotiable instrument (defined in Section 3—104), or a security (defined in Section 8—102) or any other writing which evidences a right to the payment of money and is not itself a security agreement or lease and is of a type which is in ordinary course of business transferred by delivery with any necessary indorsement or assignment;

(j) "Mortgage" means a consensual interest created by a real estate mortgage, a trust deed on real estate, or the like;

(k) An advance is made "pursuant to commitment" if the secured party has bound himself to make it, whether or not a subsequent event of default or other event not within his control has relieved or may relieve him from his obligation;

(l) "Security agreement" means an agreement which creates or provides for a security interest;

(m) "Secured party" means a lender, seller or other person in whose favor there is a security interest, including a person to whom accounts or chattel paper have been sold. When the holders of obligations issued under an indenture of trust, equipment trust agreement or the like are represented by a trustee or other person, the representative is the secured party;

(n) "Transmitting utility" means any person primarily engaged in the railroad, street railway or trolley bus business, the electric or electronics communications transmission business, the transmission of goods by pipeline, or the transmission or the production and transmission of electricity, steam, gas or water, or the provision of sewer service.

(2) Other definitions applying to this Article and the sections in which they appear are:

"Account."	Section 9—106.
"Attach."	Section 9—203.
"Construction mortgage."	Section 9—313(1).
"Consumer goods."	Section 9—109(1).
"Equipment."	Section 9—109(2).
"Farm products."	Section 9—109(3).
"Fixture."	Section 9—313(1).
"Fixture filing."	Section 9—313(1).
"General intangibles."	Section 9—106.
"Inventory."	Section 9—109(4).
"Lien creditor."	Section 9—301(3).
"Proceeds."	Section 9—306(1).
"Purchase money security interest."	Section 9—107.
"United States."	Section 9—103.

(3) The following definitions in other Articles apply to this Article:

"Check."	Section 3—104.
"Contract for sale."	Section 2—106.
"Holder in due course."	Section 3—302.
"Note."	Section 3—104.
"Sale."	Section 2—106.

(4) In addition Article 1 contains general definitions and principles of construction and interpretation applicable throughout this Article.

§ 9—106. Definitions: "Account"; "General Intangibles"

"Account" means any right to payment for goods sold or leased or for services rendered which is not evidenced by an instrument or chattel paper, whether or not it has been earned by performance. "General intangibles" means any personal property (including things in action) other than goods, accounts, chattel paper, documents, instruments, and money. All rights to payment earned or unearned under a charter or other contract involving the use or hire of a vessel and all rights incident to the charter or contract are accounts.

§ 9—107. Definitions: "Purchase Money Security Interest"

A security interest is a "purchase money security interest" to the extent that it is

(a) taken or retained by the seller of the collateral to secure all or part of its price; or

(b) taken by a person who, by making advances or incurring an obligation, gives value to enable the debtor to acquire rights in or the use of collateral, if such value is in fact so used.

§ 9—108. When After-Acquired Collateral Not Security for Antecedent Debt

Where a secured party makes an advance, incurs an obligation, releases a perfected security interest, or otherwise gives new value which is to be secured in whole or in part by after-acquired property, his security interest in the after-acquired collateral shall be deemed to be taken for new value and not as security for an antecedent debt if the debtor acquires his rights in such collateral either in the ordinary course of his business or under a contract of purchase made pursuant to the security agreement within a reasonable time after new value is given.

§ 9—109. Classification of Goods; "Consumer Goods"; "Farm Products"; "Inventory"

Goods are

(1) "consumer goods" if they are used or bought for use primarily for personal, family or household purposes;

(2) "equipment" if they are used or bought for use primarily in business (including farming or a profession) or by a debtor who is a non-profit organization or a governmental subdivision or agency or if the goods are not included in the definitions of inventory, farm products or consumer goods;

(3) "farm products" if they are crops or livestock or supplies used or produced in farming operations or if they are products of crops or livestock in their unmanufactured states (such as ginned cotton, wool-clip, maple syrup, milk and eggs), and if they are in the possession of a debtor engaged in raising, fattening, grazing or other farming operations. If goods are farm products, they are neither equipment nor inventory;

(4) "inventory" if they are held by a person who holds them for sale or lease or to be furnished under contracts of service or if he has so furnished them, or if they are raw materials, work in process or materials used or consumed in a business. Inven-

tory of a person is not to be classified as his equipment.

§ 9—110. Sufficiency of Description

For the purposes of this Article, any description of personal property or real estate is sufficient whether or not it is specific if it reasonably identifies what is described.

§ 9—111. Applicability of Bulk Transfer Laws

The creation of a security interest is not a bulk transfer under Article 6 (see Section 6—103).

§ 9—112. Where Collateral Is Not Owned by Debtor

Unless otherwise agreed, when a secured party knows that collateral is owned by a person who is not the debtor, the owner of the collateral is entitled to receive from the secured party any surplus under Section 9—502(2) or under Section 9—504(1), and is not liable for the debt or for any deficiency after resale, and he has the same right as the debtor

(a) to receive statements under Section 9—208;

(b) to receive notice of and to object to a secured party's proposal to retain the collateral in satisfaction of the indebtedness under Section 9—505;

(c) to redeem the collateral under Section 9—506;

(d) to obtain injunctive or other relief under Section 9—507(1); and

(e) to recover losses caused to him under Section 9—208(2).

§ 9—113. Security Interests Arising Under Article on Sales

A security interest arising solely under the Article on Sales (Article 2) is subject to the provisions of this Article except that to the extent that and so long as the debtor does not have or does not lawfully obtain possession of the goods

(a) no security agreement is necessary to make the security interest enforceable; and

(b) no filing is required to perfect the security interest; and

(c) the rights of the secured party on default by the debtor are governed by the Article on Sales (Article 2).

§ 9—114. Consignment

(1) A person who delivers goods under a consignment which is not a security interest and who would be required to file under this Article by paragraph (3) (c) of Section 2—326 has priority over a

secured party who is or becomes a creditor of the consignee and who would have a perfected security interest in the goods if they were the property of the consignee, and also has priority with respect to identifiable cash proceeds received on or before delivery of the goods to a buyer, if

      (a) the consignor complies with the filing provision of the Article on Sales with respect to consignments (paragraph (3) (c) of Section 2—326) before the consignee receives possession of the goods; and

      (b) the consignor gives notification in writing to the holder of the security interest, if the holder has filed a financing statement covering the same types of goods before the date of the filing made by the consignor; and

      (c) the holder of the security interest receives the notification within five years before the consignee receives possession of the goods; and

      (d) the notification states that the consignor expects to deliver goods on consignment to the consignee, describing the goods by item or type.

(2) In the case of a consignment which is not a security interest and in which the requirements of the preceding subsection have not been met, a person who delivers goods to another is subordinate to a person who would have a perfected security interest in the goods if they were the property of the debtor.

PART 2

VALIDITY OF SECURITY AGREEMENT AND RIGHTS OF PARTIES THERETO

§ 9—201. General Validity of Security Agreement

Except as otherwise provided by this Act, a security agreement is effective according to its terms between the parties, against purchasers of the collateral and against creditors. Nothing in this Article validates any charge or practice illegal under any statute or regulation thereunder governing usury, small loans, retail installment sales, or the like, or extends the application of any such statute or regulation to any transaction not otherwise subject thereto.

§ 9—202. Title to Collateral Immaterial

Each provision of this Article with regard to rights, obligations and remedies applies whether title to collateral is in the secured party or in the debtor.

§ 9—203. Attachment and Enforceability of Security Interest; Proceeds; Formal Requisites

(1) Subject to the provisions of Section 4—208 on the security interest of a collecting bank and Section 9—113 on a security interest arising under the Article on Sales, a security interest is not enforceable against the debtor or third parties with respect to the collateral and does not attach unless

      (a) the collateral is in the possession of the secured party pursuant to agreement, or the debtor has signed a security agreement which contains a description of the collateral and in addition, when the security interest covers crops growing or to be grown or timber to be cut, a description of the land concerned; and

      (b) value has been given; and

      (c) the debtor has rights in the collateral.

(2) A security interest attaches when it becomes enforceable against the debtor with respect to the collateral. Attachment occurs as soon as all of the events specified in subsection (1) have taken place unless explicit agreement postpones the time of attaching.

(3) Unless otherwise agreed, a security agreement gives the secured party the rights to proceeds provided by Section 9—306.

(4) A transaction, although subject to this Article, is also subject to . . . . *, and in the case of conflict between the provisions of this Article and any such statute, the provisions of such statute control. Failure to comply with any applicable statute has only the effect which is specified therein.

Note: *At* * *in subsection (4) insert reference to any local statute regulating small loans, retail installment sales and the like.*

The foregoing subsection (4) is designed to make it clear that certain transactions, although subject to this Article, must also comply with other applicable legislation.

This Article is designed to regulate all the "security" aspects of transactions within its scope. There is, however, much regulatory legislation, particularly in the consumer field, which supplements this Article and should not be repealed by its enactment. Examples are small loan acts, retail installment selling acts and the like. Such acts may provide for licensing and rate regulation and may prescribe particular forms of contract. Such provisions should remain in force despite the enactment of this Article. On the other hand if a retail installment selling act contains provisions on filing, rights on default, etc., such provisions should be repealed as inconsistent with this Article except that inconsistent provisions as to deficiencies, penalties, etc., in the Uniform Consumer Credit Code and other recent related legislation should remain because those statutes were drafted after the substantial enactment of the Article and with the intention of modifying certain provisions of this Article as to consumer credit.

§ 9—204. After-Acquired Property; Future Advances

(1) Except as provided in subsection (2), a security agreement may provide that any or all obligations covered by the security agreement are to be secured by after-acquired collateral.

(2) No security interest attaches under an after-acquired property clause to consumer goods other than accessions (Section 9—314) when given as additional security unless the debtor acquires rights in them within ten days after the secured party gives value.

(3) Obligations covered by a security agreement may include future advances or other value whether or not the advances or value are given pursuant to commitment (subsection (1) of Section 9—105).

§ 9—205. Use or Disposition of Collateral Without Accounting Permissible

A security interest is not invalid or fraudulent against creditors by reason of liberty in the debtor to use, commingle or dispose of all or part of the collateral (including returned or repossessed goods) or to collect or compromise accounts or chattel paper, or to accept the return of goods or make repossessions, or to use, commingle or dispose of proceeds, or by reason of the failure of the secured party to require the debtor to account for proceeds or replace collateral. This section does not relax the requirements of possession where perfection of a security interest depends upon possession of the collateral by the secured party or by a bailee.

§ 9—206. Agreement Not to Assert Defenses Against Assignee; Modification of Sales Warranties Where Security Agreement Exists

(1) Subject to any statute or decision which establishes a different rule for buyers or lessees of consumer goods, an agreement by a buyer or lessee that he will not assert against an assignee any claim or defense which he may have against the seller or lessor is enforceable by an assignee who takes his assignment for value, in good faith and without notice of a claim or defense, except as to defenses of a type which may be asserted against a holder in due course of a negotiable instrument under the Article on Commercial Paper (Article 3). A buyer who as part of one transaction signs both a negotiable instrument and a security agreement makes such an agreement.

(2) When a seller retains a purchase money security interest in goods, the Article on Sales (Article 2) governs the sale and any disclaimer, limitation or modification of the seller's warranties.

§ 9—207. Rights and Duties When Collateral is in Secured Party's Possession

(1) A secured party must use reasonable care in the custody and preservation of collateral in his possession. In the case of an instrument or chattel paper, reasonable care includes taking necessary steps to preserve rights against prior parties unless otherwise agreed.

(2) Unless otherwise agreed, when collateral is in the secured party's possession

(a) reasonable expenses (including the cost of any insurance and payment of taxes or other charges) incurred in the custody, preservation, use or operation of the collateral are chargeable to the debtor and are secured by the collateral;

(b) the risk of accidental loss or damage is on the debtor to the extent of any deficiency in any effective insurance coverage;

(c) the secured party may hold as additional security any increase or profits (except money) received from the collateral, but money so received, unless remitted to the debtor, shall be applied in reduction of the secured obligation;

(d) the secured party must keep the collateral identifiable but fungible collateral may be commingled;

(e) the secured party may repledge the collateral upon terms which do not impair the debtor's right to redeem it.

(3) A secured party is liable for any loss caused by his failure to meet any obligation imposed by the preceding subsections but does not lose his security interest.

(4) A secured party may use or operate the collateral for the purpose of preserving the collateral or its value or pursuant to the order of a court of appropriate jurisdiction or, except in the case of consumer goods, in the manner and to the extent provided in the security agreement.

§ 9—208. Request for Statement of Account or List of Collateral

(1) A debtor may sign a statement indicating what he believes to be the aggregate amount of unpaid indebtedness as of a specified date and may send it to the secured party with a request that the statement be approved or corrected and returned to the debtor. When the security agreement or any other record kept by the secured party identifies the collateral, a debtor may similarly request the secured party to approve or correct a list of the collateral.

(2) The secured party must comply with such a request within two weeks after receipt by sending a written correction or approval. If the secured party claims a security interest in all of a particular type of collateral owned by the debtor, he may indicate that fact in his reply and need not approve or correct an itemized list of such collateral. If the secured party without reasonable excuse fails to comply, he is liable for any loss caused to the debtor thereby; and if the debtor has properly included in his request a good faith statement of the obligation or a list of the collateral or both, the secured party may claim a security interest only as shown in the statement against persons misled by his failure to comply. If he no longer has an interest in the obligation or collateral at the time the request is received, he must disclose the name and address of any successor in interest known to him; and he is liable for any loss caused to the debtor as a result of failure to disclose. A successor in interest is not subject to this section until a request is received by him.

(3) A debtor is entitled to such a statement once every six months without charge. The secured party may require payment of a charge not exceeding $10 for each additional statement furnished.

PART 3

RIGHTS OF THIRD PARTIES; PERFECTED AND UNPERFECTED SECURITY INTERESTS; RULES OF PRIORITY

§ 9—301. Persons Who Take Priority Over Unperfected Security Interests; Rights of "Lien Creditor"

(1) Except as otherwise provided in subsection (2), an unperfected security interest is subordinate to the rights of

(a) persons entitled to priority under Section 9—312;

(b) a person who becomes a lien creditor before the security interest is perfected;

(c) in the case of goods, instruments, documents, and chattel paper, a person who is not a secured party and who is a transferee in bulk or other buyer not in ordinary course of business or is a buyer of farm products in ordinary course of business, to the extent that he gives value and receives delivery of the collateral without knowledge of the security interest and before it is perfected;

(d) in the case of accounts and general intangibles, a person who is not a secured party and who is a transferee, to the extent that he gives value without knowledge of the security interest and before it is perfected.

(2) If the secured party files with respect to a purchase money security interest before or within ten days after the debtor receives possession of the collateral, he takes priority over the rights of a transferee in bulk or of a lien creditor which arise between the time the security interest attaches and the time of filing.

(3) A "lien creditor" means a creditor who has acquired a lien on the property involved by attachment, levy or the like and includes an assignee for benefit of creditors from the time of assignment, and a trustee in bankruptcy from the date of the filing of the petition or a receiver in equity from the time of appointment.

(4) A person who becomes a lien creditor while a security interest is perfected takes subject to the security interest only to the extent that it secures advances made before he becomes a lien creditor or within 45 days thereafter or made without knowledge of the lien or pursuant to a commitment entered into without knowledge of the lien.

§ 9—302. When Filing Is Required to Perfect Security Interest; Security Interests to Which Filing Provisions of This Article Do Not Apply

(1) A financing statement must be filed to perfect all security interests except the following:

(a) a security interest in collateral in possession of the secured party under Section 9—305;

(b) a security interest temporarily perfected in instruments or documents without delivery under Section 9—304 or in proceeds for a 10 day period under Section 9—306;

(c) a security interest created by an assignment of a beneficial interest in a trust or a decedent's estate;

(d) a purchase money security interest in consumer goods; but filing is required for a motor vehicle required to be registered; and fixture filing is required for priority over conflicting interests in fixtures to the extent provided in Section 9—313;

(e) an assignment of accounts which does not alone or in conjunction with other assignments to the same assignee transfer a significant part of the outstanding accounts of the assignor;

(f) a security interest of a collecting bank (Section 4—208) or arising under the Article on Sales (see Section 9—313) or covered in subsection (3) of this section;

(g) an assignment for the benefit of all the creditors of the transferor, and subsequent transfers by the assignee thereunder.

(2) If a secured party assigns a perfected security interest, no filing under this Article is required in order to continue the perfected status of the security interest against creditors of and transferees from the original debtor.

(3) The filing of a financing statement otherwise required by this Article is not necessary or effective to perfect a security interest in property subject to

(a) a statute or treaty of the United States which provides for a national or international registration or a national or international certificate of title or which specifies a place of filing different from that specified in this Article for filing of the security interest; or

(b) the following statutes of this state; [list any certificate of title statute covering automobiles, trailers, mobile homes, boats, farm tractors, or the like, and any central filing statute *.]; but during any period in which collateral is inventory held for sale by a person who is in the business of selling goods of that kind, the filing provisions of this Article (Part 4) apply to a security interest in that collateral created by him as debtor; or

(c) a certificate of title statute of another jurisdiction under the law of which indication of a security interest on the certificate is required as a condition of perfection (subsection (2) of Section 9—103).

(4) Compliance with a statute or treaty described in subsection (3) is equivalent to the filing of a financing statement under this Article, and a security interest in property subject to the statute or treaty can be perfected only by compliance therewith except as provided in Section 9—103 on multiple state transactions. Duration and renewal of perfection of a security interest perfected by compliance with the statute or treaty are governed by the provisions of the statute or treaty; in other respects the security interest is subject to this Article.

* Note: *It is recommended that the provisions of certificate of title acts for perfection of security interests by notation on the certificates should be amended to exclude coverge of inventory held for sale.*

§ 9—303. When Security Interest Is Perfected; Continuity of Perfection

(1) A security interest is perfected when it has attached and when all of the applicable steps required for perfection have been taken. Such steps are specified in Sections 9—302, 9—304, 9—305 and 9—306. If such steps are taken before the security interest attaches, it is perfected at the time when it attaches.

(2) If a security interest is originally perfected in any way permitted under this Article and is subsequently perfected in some other way under this Article, without an intermediate period when it was unperfected, the security interest shall be deemed to be perfected continuously for the purposes of this Article.

§ 9—304. Perfection of Security Interest in Instruments, Documents, and Goods Covered by Documents; Perfection by Permissive Filing; Temporary Perfection Without Filing or Transfer of Possession

(1) A security interest in chattel paper or negotiable documents may be perfected by filing. A security interest in money or instruments (other than instruments which constitute part of chattel paper) can be perfected only by the secured party's taking possession, except as provided in subsections (4) and (5) of this section and subsections (2) and (3) of Section 9—306 on proceeds.

(2) During the period that goods are in the possession of the issuer of a negotiable document therefor, a security interest in the goods is perfected by perfecting a security interest in the document, and any security interest in the goods otherwise perfected during such period is subject thereto.

(3) A security interest in goods in the possession of a bailee other than one who has issued a negotiable document therefor is perfected by issuance

of a document in the name of the secured party or by the bailee's receipt of notification of the secured party's interest or by filing as to the goods.

(4) A security interest in instruments or negotiable documents is perfected without filing or the taking of possession for a period of 21 days from the time it attaches to the extent that it arises for new value given under a written security agreement.

(5) A security interest remains perfected for a period of 21 days without filing where a secured party having a perfected security interest in an instrument, a negotiable document or goods in possession of a bailee other than one who has issued a negotiable document therefor

    (a) makes available to the debtor the goods or documents representing the goods for the purpose of ultimate sale or exchange or for the purpose of loading, unloading, storing, shipping, transshipping, manufacturing, processing or otherwise dealing with them in a manner preliminary to their sale or exchange, but priority between conflicting security interests in the goods is subject to subsection (3) of Section 9—312; or

    (b) delivers the instrument to the debtor for the purpose of ultimate sale or exchange or of presentation, collection, renewal or registration of transfer.

(6) After the 21 day period in subsections (4) and (5), perfection depends upon compliance with applicable provisions of this Article.

§ 9—305. When Possession by Secured Party Perfects Security Interest Without Filing

A security interest in letters of credit and advices of credit (subsection (2) (a) of Section 5—116), goods, instruments, money, negotiable documents or chattel paper may be perfected by the secured party's taking possession of the collateral. If such collateral other than goods covered by a negotiable document is held by a bailee, the secured party is deemed to have possession from the time the bailee receives notification of the secured party's interest. A security interest is perfected by possession from the time possession is taken without relation back and continues only so long as possession is retained, unless otherwise specified in this Article. The security interest may be otherwise perfected as provided in this Article before or after the period of possession by the secured party.

§ 9—306. "Proceeds"; Secured Party's Rights on Disposition of Collateral

(1) "Proceeds" includes whatever is received upon the sale, exchange, collection or other disposition of collateral or proceeds. Insurance payable by reason of loss or damage to the collateral is proceeds, except to the extent that it is payable to a person other than a party to the security agreement. Money, checks, deposit accounts, and the like are "cash proceeds." All other proceeds are "noncash proceeds."

(2) Except where this Article otherwise provides, a security interest continues in collateral notwithstanding sale, exchange or other disposition thereof unless the disposition was authorized by the secured party in the security agreement or otherwise, and also continues in any identifiable proceeds including collections received by the debtor.

(3) The security interest in proceeds is a continuously perfected security interest if the interest in the original collateral was perfected, but it ceases to be a perfected security interest and becomes unperfected ten days after receipt of the proceeds by the debtor unless

    (a) a filed financing statement covers the original collateral and the proceeds are collateral in which a security interest may be perfected by filing in the office or offices where the financing statement has been filed and, if the proceeds are acquired with cash proceeds, the description of collateral in the financing statement indicates the types of property constituting the proceeds; or

    (b) a filed financing statement covers the original collateral and the proceeds are identifiable cash proceeds; or

    (c) the security interest in the proceeds is perfected before the expiration of the ten day period.

Except as provided in this section, a security interest in proceeds can be perfected only by the methods or under the circumstances permitted in this Article for original collateral of the same type.

(4) In the event of insolvency proceedings instituted by or against a debtor, a secured party with a perfected security interest in proceeds has a perfected security interest only in the following proceeds:

    (a) in identifiable noncash proceeds and in separate deposit accounts containing only proceeds;

(b) in identifiable cash proceeds in the form of money which is neither commingled with other money nor deposited in a deposit account prior to the insolvency proceedings;

(c) in identifiable cash proceeds in the form of checks and the like which are not deposited in a deposit account prior to the insolvency proceedings; and

(d) in all cash and deposit accounts of the debtor in which proceeds have been commingled with other funds, but the perfected security interest under this paragraph (d) is

(i) subject to any right to setoff; and

(ii) limited to an amount not greater than the amount of any cash proceeds received by the debtor within ten days before the institution of the insolvency proceedings, less the sum of (I) the payments to the secured party on account of cash proceeds received by the debtor during such period and (II) the cash proceeds received by the debtor during such period to which the secured party is entitled under paragraphs (a) through (c) of this subsection (4).

(5) If a sale of goods results in an account or chattel paper which is transferred by the seller to a secured party and if the goods are returned to or are repossessed by the seller or the secured party, the following rules determine priorities:

(a) If the goods were collateral at the time of sale, for an indebtedness of the seller which is still unpaid, the original security interest attaches again to the goods and continues as a perfected security interest if it was perfected at the time when the goods were sold. If the security interest was originally perfected by a filing which is still effective, nothing further is required to continue the perfected status; in any other case, the secured party must take possession of the returned or repossessed goods or must file.

(b) An unpaid transferee of the chattel paper has a security interest in the goods against the transferor. Such security interest is prior to a security interest asserted under paragraph (a) to the extent that the transferee of the chattel

paper was entitled to priority under Section 9—308.

(c) An unpaid transferee of the account has a security interest in the goods against the transferor. Such security interest is subordinate to a security interest asserted under paragraph (a).

(d) A security interest of an unpaid transferee asserted under paragraph (b) or (c) must be perfected for protection against creditors of the transferor and purchasers of the returned or repossessed goods.

§ 9—307. Protection of Buyers of Goods

(1) A buyer in ordinary course of business (subsection (9) of Section 1—201), other than a person buying farm products from a person engaged in farming operations, takes free of a security interest created by his seller even though the security interest is perfected and even though the buyer knows of its existence.

(2) In the case of consumer goods, a buyer takes free of a security interest even though perfected if he buys without knowledge of the security interest, for value and for his own personal, family or household purposes unless prior to the purchase the secured party has filed a financing statement covering such goods.

(3) A buyer other than a buyer in ordinary course of business (subsection (1) of this section) takes free of a security interest to the extent that it secures future advances made after the secured party acquires knowledge of the purchase, or more than 45 days after the purchase, whichever first occurs, unless made pursuant to a commitment entered into without knowledge of the purchase and before the expiration of the 45 day period.

§ 9—308. Purchase of Chattel Paper and Instruments

A purchaser of chattel paper or an instrument who gives new value and takes possession of it in the ordinary course of his business has priority over a security interest in the chattel paper or instrument

(a) which is perfected under Section 9—304 (permissive filing and temporary perfection) or under Section 9—306 (perfection as to proceeds) if he acts without knowledge that the specific paper or instrument is subject to a security interest; or

(b) which is claimed merely as proceeds of inventory subject to a security interest (Section 9—306) even though he knows that the specific paper or instrument is subject to the security interest.

§ 9—309. Protection of Purchasers of Instruments and Documents

Nothing in this Article limits the rights of a holder in due course of a negotiable instrument (Section 3—302) or a holder to whom a negotiable document of title has been duly negotiated (Section 7—501) or a bona fide purchaser of a security (Section 8—301), and such holders or purchasers take priority over an earlier security interest even though perfected. Filing under this Article does not constitute notice of the security interest to such holders or purchasers.

§ 9—310. Priority of Certain Liens Arising by Operation of Law

When a person in the ordinary course of his business furnishes services or materials with respect to goods subject to a security interest, a lien upon goods in the possession of such person given by statute or rule of law for such materials or services takes priority over a perfected security interest unless the lien is statutory and the statute expressly provides otherwise.

§ 9—311. Alienability of Debtor's Rights: Judicial Process

The debtor's rights in collateral may be voluntarily or involuntarily transferred (by way of sale, creation of a security interest, attachment, levy, garnishment or other judicial process) notwithstanding a provision in the security agreement prohibiting any transfer or making the transfer constitute a default.

§ 9—312. Priorities Among Conflicting Security Interests in the Same Collateral

(1) The rules of priority stated in other sections of this Part and in the following sections shall govern when applicable: Section 4—208 with respect to the security interests of collecting banks in items being collected, accompanying documents and proceeds; Section 9—103 on security interests related to other jurisdictions; Section 9—114 on consignments.

(2) A perfected security interest in crops for new value given to enable the debtor to produce the crops during the production season, and given not more than three months before the crops become growing crops by planting or otherwise, takes priority over an earlier perfected security interest to the extent that such earlier interest secures obligations due more than six months before the crops become growing crops by planting or otherwise, even though

the person giving new value had knowledge of the earlier security interest.

(3) A perfected purchase money security interest in inventory has priority over a conflicting security interest in the same inventory and also has priority in identifiable cash proceeds received on or before the delivery of the inventory to a buyer if

(a) the purchase money security interest is perfected at the time the debtor receives possession of the inventory; and

(b) the purchase money secured party gives notification in writing to the holder of the conflicting security interest if the holder had filed a financing statement covering the same types of inventory (i) before the date of the filing made by the purchase money secured party, or (ii) before the beginning of the 21 day period where the purchase money security interest is temporarily perfected without filing or possession (subsection (5) of Section 9—304); and

(c) the holder of the conflicting security interest receives the notification within five years before the debtor receives possession of the inventory; and

(d) the notification states that the person giving the notice has or expects to acquire a purchase money security interest in inventory of the debtor, describing such inventory by item or type.

(4) A purchase money security interest in collateral other than inventory has priority over a conflicting security interest in the same collateral or its proceeds if the purchase money security interest is perfected at the time the debtor receives possession of the collateral or within ten days thereafter.

(5) In all cases not governed by other rules stated in this section (including cases of purchase money security interests which do not qualify for the special priorities set forth in subsections (3) and (4) of this section), priority between conflicting security interests in the same collateral shall be determined according to the following rules:

(a) Conflicting security interests rank according to priority in time of filing or perfection. Priority dates from the time a filing is first made covering the collateral or the time the security interest is first perfected, whichever is earlier, provided that there is no period thereafter when there is neither filing nor perfection.

(b) So long as conflicting security interests are unperfected, the first to attach has priority.

(6) For the purposes of subsection (5), a date of filing or perfection as to collateral is also a date of filing or perfection as to proceeds.

(7) If future advances are made while a security interest is perfected by filing or the taking of possession, the security interest has the same priority for the purposes of subsection (5) with respect to the future advances as it does with respect to the first advance. If a commitment is made before or while the security interest is so perfected, the security interest has the same priority with respect to advances made pursuant thereto. In other cases, a perfected security interest has priority from the date the advance is made.

§ 9—313. Priority of Security Interests in Fixtures

(1) In this section and in the provisions of Part 4 of this Article referring to fixture filing, unless the context otherwise requires

(a) goods are "fixtures" when they become so related to particular real estate that an interest in them arises under real estate law

(b) a "fixture filing" is the filing in the office where a mortgage on the real estate would be filed or recorded of a financing statement covering goods which are or are to become fixtures and conforming to the requirements of subsection (5) of Section 9—402

(c) a mortgage is a "construction mortgage" to the extent that it secures an obligation incurred for the construction of an improvement on land including the acquisition cost of the land, if the recorded writing so indicates.

(2) A security interest under this Article may be created in goods which are fixtures or may continue in goods which become fixtures, but no security interest exists under this Article in ordinary building materials incorporated into an improvement on land.

(3) This Article does not prevent creation of an encumbrance upon fixtures pursuant to real estate law.

(4) A perfected security interest in fixtures has priority over the conflicting interest of an encumbrancer or owner of the real estate where

(a) the security interest is a purchase money security interest, the interest of the encumbrancer or owner arises before the goods become fixtures, the

security interest is perfected by a fixture filing before the goods become fixtures or within ten days thereafter, and the debtor has an interest of record in the real estate or is in possession of the real estate; or

(b) the security interest is perfected by a fixture filing before the interest of the encumbrancer or owner is of record, the security interest has priority over any conflicting interest of a predecessor in title of the encumbrancer or owner, and the debtor has an interest of record in the real estate or is in possession of the real estate; or

(c) the fixtures are readily removable factory or office machines or readily removable replacements of domestic appliances which are consumer goods, and before the goods become fixtures the security interest is perfected by any method permitted by this Article; or

(d) the conflicting interest is a lien on the real estate obtained by legal or equitable proceedings after the security interest was perfected by any method permitted by this Article.

(5) A security interest in fixtures, whether or not perfected, has priority over the conflicting interest of an encumbrancer or owner of the real estate where

(a) the encumbrancer or owner has consented in writing to the security interest or has disclaimed an interest in the goods as fixtures; or

(b) the debtor has a right to remove the goods as against the encumbrancer or owner. If the debtor's right terminates, the priority of the security interest continues for a reasonable time.

(6) Notwithstanding paragraph (a) of subsection (4) but otherwise subject to subsections (4) and (5), a security interest in fixtures is subordinate to a construction mortgage recorded before the goods become fixtures if the goods become fixtures before the completion of the construction. To the extent that it is given to refinance a construction mortgage, a mortgage has this priority to the same extent as the construction mortgage.

(7) In cases not within the preceding subsections, a security interest in fixtures is subordinate to the conflicting interest of an encumbrancer or owner of the related real estate who is not the debtor.

(8) When the secured party has priority over all owners and encumbrancers of the real estate,

he may, on default, subject to the provisions of Part 5, remove his collateral from the real estate but he must reimburse any encumbrancer or owner of the real estate who is not the debtor, and who has not otherwise agreed, for the cost of repair of any physical injury, but not for any diminution in value of the real estate caused by the absence of the goods removed or by any necessity of replacing them. A person entitled to reimbursement may refuse permission to remove until the secured party gives adequate security for the performance of this obligation.

§ 9—314. Accessions

(1) A security interest in goods which attaches before they are installed in or affixed to other goods takes priority as to the goods installed or affixed (called in this section "accessions") over the claims of all persons to the whole except as stated in subsection (3) and subject to Section 9—315(1).

(2) A security interest which attaches to goods after they become part of a whole is valid against all persons subsequently acquiring interests in the whole except as stated in subsection (3) but is invalid against any person with an interest in the whole at the time the security interest attaches to the goods who has not in writing consented to the security interest or disclaimed an interest in the goods as part of the whole.

(3) The security interests described in subsections (1) and (2) do not take priority over
    (a) a subsequent purchaser for value of any interest in the whole; or
    (b) a creditor with a lien on the whole subsequently obtained by judicial proceedings; or
    (c) a creditor with a prior perfected security interest in the whole to the extent that he makes subsequent advances
if the subsequent purchase is made, the lien by judicial proceedings obtained or the subsequent advance under the prior perfected security interest is made or contracted for without knowledge of the security interest and before it is perfected. A purchaser of the whole at a foreclosure sale other than the holder of a perfected security interest purchasing at his own foreclosure sale is a subsequent purchaser within this section.

(4) When under subsections (1) or (2) and (3), a secured party has an interest in accessions which has priority over the claims of all persons who have interests in the whole, he may, on default, subject to the provisions of Part 5, remove his collateral from the whole but he must reimburse any encumbrancer or owner of the whole who is not the debtor and who has not otherwise agreed for the cost of

repair of any physical injury but not for any diminution in value of the whole caused by the absence of the goods removed or by any necessity for replacing them. A person entitled to reimbursement may refuse permission to remove until the secured party gives adequate security for the performance of this obligation.

§ 9—315. Priority When Goods Are Commingled or Processed

(1) If a security interest in goods was perfected and subsequently the goods or a part thereof have become part of a product or mass, the security interest continues in the product or mass if
    (a) the goods are so manufactured, processed, assembled or commingled that their identity is lost in the product or mass; or
    (b) a financing statement covering the original goods also covers the product into which the goods have been manufactured, processed or assembled.
In a case to which paragraph (b) applies, no separate security interest in that part of the original goods which has been manufactured, processed or assembled into the product may be claimed under Section 9—314.

(2) When under subsection (1) more than one security interest attaches to the product or mass, they rank equally according to the ratio that the cost of the goods to which each interest originally attached bears to the cost of the total product or mass.

§ 9—316. Priority Subject to Subordination

Nothing in this Article prevents subordination by agreement by any person entitled to priority.

§ 9—317. Secured Party Not Obligated on Contract of Debtor

The mere existence of a security interest or authority given to the debtor to dispose of or use collateral does not impose contract or tort liability upon the secured party for the debtor's acts or omissions.

§ 9—318. Defenses Against Assignee; Modification of Contract After Notification of Assignment; Term Prohibiting Assignment Ineffective; Identification and Proof of Assignment

(1) Unless an account debtor has made an enforceable agreement not to assert defenses or claims arising out of a sale as provided in Section 9—206, the rights of an assignee are subject to
    (a) all the terms of the contract between the account debtor and assignor and

any defense or claim arising therefrom; and

(b) any other defense or claim of the account debtor against the assignor which accrues before the account debtor receives notification of the assignment.

(2) So far as the right to payment or a part thereof under an assigned contract has not been fully earned by performance, and notwithstanding notification of the assignment, any modification of or substitution for the contract made in good faith and in accordance with reasonable commercial standards is effective against an assignee unless the account debtor has otherwise agreed, but the assignee acquires corresponding rights under the modified or substituted contract. The assignment may provide that such modification or substitution is a breach by the assignor.

(3) The account debtor is authorized to pay the assignor until the account debtor receives notification that the amount due or to become due has been assigned and that payment is to be made to the assignee. A notification which does not reasonably identify the rights assigned is ineffective. If requested by the account debtor, the assignee must seasonably furnish reasonable proof that the assignment has been made; and unless he does so, the account debtor may pay the assignor.

(4) A term in any contract between an account debtor and an assignor is ineffective if it prohibits assignment of an account or prohibits creation of a security interest in a general intangible for money due or to become due or requires the account debtor's consent to such assignment or security interest.

PART 4

FILING

§ 9—401. Place of Filing; Erroneous Filing; Removal of Collateral

First Alternative Subsection (1)

(1) The proper place to file in order to perfect a security interest is as follows:

(a) when the collateral is timber to be cut or is minerals or the like (including oil and gas) or accounts subject to subsection (5) of Section 9—103, or when the financing statement is filed as a fixture filing (Section 9—313) and the collateral is goods which are or are to become fixtures, then in the office where a mortgage on the real estate would be filed or recorded;

(b) in all other cases, in the office of the [Secretary of State].

Second Alternative Subsection (1)

(1) The proper place to file in order to perfect a security interest is as follows:

(a) when the collateral is equipment used in farming operations, or farm products, or accounts or general intangibles arising from or relating to the sale of farm products by a farmer, or consumer goods, then in the office of the . . . . in the county of the debtor's residence or if the debtor is not a resident of this state then in the office of the . . . . in the county where the goods are kept, and in addition when the collateral is crops growing or to be grown in the office of the . . . . in the county where the land is located;

(b) when the collateral is timber to be cut or is minerals or the like (including oil and gas) or accounts subject to subsection (5) of Section 9—103, or when the financing statement is filed as a fixture filing (Section 9—313) and the collateral is goods which are or are to become fixtures, then in the office where a mortgage on the real estate would be filed or recorded;

(c) in all other cases, in the office of the [Secretary of State].

Third Alternative Subsection (1)

(1) The proper place to file in order to perfect a security interest is as follows:

(a) when the collateral is equipment used in farming operations, or farm products, or accounts or general intangibles arising from or relating to the sale of farm products by a farmer, or consumer goods, then in the office of the . . . . in the county of the debtor's residence or if the debtor is not a resident of this state then in the office of the . . . . in the county where the goods are kept, and in addition when the collateral is crops growing or to be grown in the office of the . . . . in the county where the land is located;

(b) when the collateral is timber to be cut or is minerals or the like (including oil and gas) or accounts subject to subsection (5) of Section 9—103, or when the financing statement is filed as a fixture filing (Section 9—313) and the collateral is goods which are or are to become fixtures, then in the office where a mortgage on the real estate would be filed or recorded;

(c) in all other cases, in the office of the [Secretary of State] and in addition, if the debtor has a place of business in only one county of this state, also in the office of . . . . of such county, or, if the debtor has no place of business in this state, but resides in the state, also in the office of . . . . of the county in which he resides.

Note: *One of the three alternatives should be selected as subsection (1).*

(2) A filing which is made in good faith in an improper place or not in all of the places required by this section is nevertheless effective with regard to any collateral as to which the filing complied with the requirements of this Article and is also effective with regard to collateral covered by the financing statement against any person who has knowledge of the contents of such financing statement.

(3) A filing which is made in the proper place in this state continues effective even though the debtor's residence or place of business or the location of the collateral or its use, whichever controlled the original filing, is thereafter changed.

Alternative Subsection (3)

[(3) A filing which is made in the proper county continues effective for four months after a change to another county of the debtor's residence or place of business or the location of the collateral, whichever controlled the original filing. It becomes ineffective thereafter unless a copy of the financing statement signed by the secured party is filed in the new county within said period. The security interest may also be perfected in the new county after the expiration of the four-month period; in such case, perfection dates from the time of perfection in the new county. A change in the use of the collateral does not impair the effectiveness of the original filing.]

(4) The rules stated in Section 9—103 determine whether filing is necessary in this state.

(5) Notwithstanding the preceding subsections, and subject to subsection (3) of Section 9—302, the proper place to file in order to perfect a security interest in collateral, including fixtures, of a transmitting utility is the office of the [Secretary of State]. This filing constitutes a fixture filing (Section 9—313) as to the collateral described therein which is or is to become fixtures.

(6) For the purposes of this section, the residence of an organization is its place of business if it has one or its chief executive office if it has more than one place of business.

Note: *Subsection (6) should be used only if the state chooses the Second or Third Alternative Subsection (1).*

§ 9—402. Formal Requisites of Financing Statement; Amendments; Mortgage as Financing Statement

(1) A financing statement is sufficient if it gives the names of the debtor and the secured party, is signed by the debtor, gives an address of the secured party from which information concerning the security interest may be obtained, gives a mailing address of the debtor and contains a statement indicating the types, or describing the items, of collateral. A financing statment may be filed before a security agreement is made or a security interest otherwise attaches. When the financing statement covers crops growing or to be grown, the statement must also contain a description of the real estate concerned. When the financing statement covers timber to be cut or covers minerals or the like (including oil and gas) or accounts subject to subsection (5) of Section 9—103, or when the financing statement is filed as a fixture filing (Section 9—313) and the collateral is goods which are or are to become fixtures, the statement must also comply with subsection (5). A copy of the security agreement is sufficient as a financing statement if it contains the above information and is signed by the debtor. A carbon, photographic or other reproduction of a security agreement or a financing statement is sufficient as a financing statement if the security agreement so provides or if the original has been filed in this state.

(2) A financing statement which otherwise complies with subsection (1) is sufficient when it is signed by the secured party instead of the debtor if it is filed to perfect a security interest in

(a) collateral already subject to a security interest in another jurisdiction when it is brought into this state, or wh the debtor's location is changed t state. Such a financing statem state that the collateral w into this state or that the tion was changed to such circumstance

(b) proceeds under security inter eral was p statemen collateral; o.

(c) collateral as to which the filing has lapsed; or

(d) collateral acquired after a change of name, identity or corporate structure of the debtor (subsection (7)).

(3) A form substantially as follows is sufficient to comply with subsection (1):

Name of debtor (or assignor) . . . . . .
Address . . . .
Name of secured party (or assignee) . .
Address . . . .

1. This financing statement covers the following types (or items) of property:
    (Describe) . . . .

2. (If collateral is crops) The above described crops are growing or are to be grown on:
    (Describe Real Estate) . . . .

3. (If applicable) The above goods are to become fixtures on *
    (Describe Real Estate) . . . .
    and this financing statement is to be filed [for record] in the real estate records. (If the debtor does not have an interest of record) The name of a record owner is . . . .

4. (If products of collateral are claimed) Products of the collateral are also covered.

(use whichever is applicable) { . . . .
Signature of Debtor (or Assignor)
. . . .
Signature of Secured Party (or Assignee)

(4) A financing statement may be amended by filing a writing signed by both the debtor and the secured party. An amendment does not extend the period of effectiveness of a financing statement. If any amendment adds collateral, it is effective as to the added collateral only from the filing date of the amendment. In this Article, unless the context otherwise requires, the term "financing statement" means the original financing statement and any amendments.

(5) A financing statement covering timber to be cut or covering minerals or the like (including oil and gas) or accounts subject to subsection (5) of Section 9—103, or a financing statement filed as

a fixture filing (Section 9—313) where the debtor is not a transmitting utility, must show that it covers this type of collateral, must recite that it is to be filed [for record] in the real estate records, and the financing statement must contain a description of the real estate [sufficient if it were contained in a mortgage of the real estate to give constructive notice of the mortgage under the law of this state]. If the debtor does not have an interest of record in the real estate, the financing statement must show the name of a record owner.

(6) A mortgage is effective as a financing statement filed as a fixture filing from the date of its recording if

(a) the goods are described in the mortgage by item or type; and

(b) the goods are or are to become fixtures related to the real estate described in the mortgage; and

(c) the mortgage complies with the requirements for a financing statement in this section other than a recital that it is to be filed in the real estate records; and

(d) the mortgage is duly recorded.

No fee with reference to the financing statement is required other than the regular recording and satisfaction fees with respect to the mortgage.

(7) A financing statement sufficiently shows the name of the debtor if it gives the individual, partnership or corporate name of the debtor, whether or not it adds other trade names or names of partners. Where the debtor so changes his name or, in the case of an organization, its name, identity or corporate structure that a filed financing statement becomes seriously misleading, the filing is not effective to perfect a security interest in collateral acquired by the debtor more than four months after the change, unless a new appropriate financing statement is filed before the expiration of that time. A filed financing statement remains effective with respect to collateral transferred by the debtor even though the secured party knows of or consents to the transfer.

(8) A financing statement substantially complying with the requirements of this section is effective even though it contains minor errors which are not seriously misleading.

Note: *Language in brackets is optional.*
Note: *Where the state has any special recording system for real estate other than the usual grantor-grantee index (as, for instance, a tract system or a title registration or Torrens system) local adaptations of subsection (5) and Section 9—403(7) may be necessary. See Mass. Gen. Laws Chapter 106, Section 9—409.*

---

* Where appropriate substitute either "The above [ ] is standing on . . . ." or "The above miner[als or t]he like (including oil and gas) or accounts will be [financed] at the wellhead or minehead of the well or mine [locate]n . . . ."

§ 9—403. What Constitutes Filing; Duration of Filing; Effect of Lapsed Filing; Duties of Filing Officer

(1) Presentation for filing of a financing statement and tender of the filing fee or acceptance of the statement by the filing officer constitutes filing under this Article.

(2) Except as provided in subsection (6), a filed financing statement is effective for a period of five years from the date of filing. The effectiveness of a filed financing statement lapses on the expiration of the five-year period unless a continuation statement is filed prior to the lapse. If a security interest perfected by filing exists at the time insolvency proceedings are commenced by or against the debtor, the security interest remains perfected until termination of the insolvency proceedings and thereafter for a period of sixty days or until expiration of the five-year period, whichever occurs later. Upon lapse, the security interest becomes unperfected, unless it is perfected without filing. If the security interest becomes unperfected upon lapse, it is deemed to have been unperfected as against a person who became a purchaser or lien creditor before lapse.

(3) A continuation statement may be filed by the secured party within six months prior to the expiration of the five year period specified in subsection (2). Any such continuation statement must be signed by the secured party, identify the original statement by file number and state that the original statement is still effective. A continuation statement signed by a person other than the secured party of record must be accompanied by a separate written statement of assignment signed by the secured party of record and complying with subsection (2) of Section 9—405, including payment of the required fee. Upon timely filing of the continuation statement, the effectiveness of the original statement is continued for five years after the last date to which the filing was effective whereupon it lapses in the same manner as provided in subsection (2) unless another continuation statement is filed prior to such lapse. Succeeding continuation statements may be filed in the same manner to continue the effectiveness of the original statement. Unless a statute on disposition of public records provides otherwise, the filing officer may remove a lapsed statement from the files and destroy it immediately if he has retained a microfilm or other photographic record, or in other cases after one year after the lapse. The filing officer shall so arrange matters by physical annexation of financing statements to continuation statements or other related filings, or by other means, that if he physically destroys the financing statements of a period more than five years past, those which have been continued by a continuation statement or which are still effective under subsection (6) shall be retained.

(4) Except as provided in subsection (7), a filing officer shall mark each statement with a file number and with the date and hour of filing and shall hold the statement or a microfilm or other photographic copy thereof for public inspection. In addition, the filing officer shall index the statement according to the name of the debtor and shall note in the index the file number and the address of the debtor given in the statement.

(5) The uniform fee for filing and indexing and for stamping a copy furnished by the secured party to show the date and place of filing for an original financing statement or for a continuation statement shall be $. . . . . . . if the statement is in the standard form prescribed by the [Secretary of State] and otherwise shall be $. . . . . . . , plus in each case, if the financing statement is subject to subsection (5) of Section 9—402, $. . . . . . . The uniform fee for each name more than one required to be indexed shall be $. . . . . . . The secured party may at his option show a trade name for any person and an extra uniform indexing fee of $. . . . . . . shall be paid with respect thereto.

(6) If the debtor is a transmitting utility (subsection (5) of Section 9—401) and a filed financing statement so states, it is effective until a termination statement is filed. A real estate mortgage which is effective as a fixture filing under subsection (6) of Section 9—402 remains effective as a fixture filing until the mortgage is released or satisfied of record or its effectiveness otherwise terminates as to the real estate.

(7) When a financing statement covers timber to be cut or covers minerals or the like (including oil and gas) or accounts subject to subsection (5) of Section 9—103, or is filed as a fixture filing, [it shall be filed for record and] the filing officer shall index it under the names of the debtor and any owner of record shown on the financing statement in the same fashion as if they were the mortgagors in a mortgage of the real estate described, and, to the extent that the law of this state provides for indexing of mortgages under the name of the mortgagee, under the name of the secured party as if he were the mortgagee thereunder, or where indexing is by description in the same fashion as if the financing statement were a mortgage of the real estate described.

Note: *In states in which writings will not appear in the real estate records and indices unless actually recorded, the bracketed language in subsection (7) should be used.*

§ 9—404. Termination Statement

If a financing statement covering consumer goods is filed on or after . . . . , then within one month or within ten days following written demand by the debtor after there is no outstanding secured obligation and no commitment to make advances, incur obligations or otherwise give value, the secured party must file with each filing officer with whom the financing statement was filed, a termination statement to the effect that he no longer claims a security interest under the financing statement, which shall be identified by file number. In other cases whenever there is no outstanding secured obligation and no commitment to make advances, incur obligations or otherwise give value, the secured party must on written demand by the debtor send the debtor, for each filing officer with whom the financing statement was filed, a termination statement to the effect that he no longer claims a security interest under the financing statement, which shall be identified by file number. A termination statement signed by a person other than the secured party of record must be accompanied by a separate written statement of assignment signed by the secured party of record complying with subsection (2) of Section 9—405, including payment of the required fee. If the affected secured party fails to file such a termination statement as required by this subsection, or to send such a termination statement within ten days after proper demand therefor, he shall be liable to the debtor for one hundred dollars, and in addition for any loss caused to the debtor by such failure.

(2) On presentation to the filing officer of such a termination statement, he must note it in the index. If he has received the termination statement in duplicate, he shall return one copy of the termination statement to the secured party stamped to show the time of receipt thereof. If the filing officer has a microfilm or other photographic record of the financing statement, and of any related continuation statement, statement of assignment and statement of release, he may remove the originals from the files at any time after receipt of the termination statement, or if he has no such record, he may remove them from the files at any time after one year after receipt of the termination statement.

(3) If the termination statement is in the standard form prescribed by the [Secretary of State], the uniform fee for filing and indexing the termination statement shall be $. . . . . , and otherwise shall be $. . . . . , plus in each case an additional fee of $. . . . . . . for each name more than one against which the termination statement is required to be indexed.

Note: *The date to be inserted should be the effective date of the revised Article 9.*

§ 9—405. Assignment of Security Interest; Duties of Filing Officer; Fees

(1) A financing statement may disclose an assignment of a security interest in the collateral described in the financing statement by indication in the financing statement of the name and address of the assignee or by an assignment itself or a copy thereof on the face or back of the statement. On presentation to the filing officer of such a financing statement the filing officer shall mark the same as provided in Section 9—403(4). The uniform fee for filing, indexing and furnishing filing data for a financing statement so indicating an assignment shall be $. . . . . . . if the statement is in the standard form prescribed by the [Secretary of State] and otherwise shall be $. . . . . , plus in each case an additional fee of $. . . . . . . for each name more than one against which the financing statement is required to be indexed.

(2) A secured party may assign of record all or part of his rights under a financing statement by the filing in the place where the original financing statement was filed of a separate written statement of assignment signed by the secured party of record and setting forth the name of the secured party of record and the debtor, the file number and the date of filing of the financing statement and the name and address of the assignee and containing a description of the collateral assigned. A copy of the assignment is sufficient as a separate statement if it complies with the preceding sentence. On presentation to the filing officer of such a separate statement, the filing officer shall mark such separate statement with the date and hour of the filing. He shall note the assignment on the index of the financing statement, or in the case of a fixture filing, or a filing covering timber to be cut, or covering minerals or the like (including oil and gas) or accounts subject to subsection (5) of Section 9—103, he shall index the assignment under the name of the assignor as grantor and, to the extent that the law of this state provides for indexing the assignment of a mortgage under the name of the assignee, he shall index the assignment of the financing statement under the name of the assignee. The uniform fee for filing, indexing and furnishing filing data about such a separate statement of assignment shall be $. . . . . . . if the statement is in the standard form prescribed by the [Secretary of State] and otherwise shall be $. . . . . , plus in each case an additional fee of $. . . . . . . for each name more than one against which the statement of assignment is required to be indexed. Notwithstanding the provisions of this subsection, an assignment of record of a security interest in a fixture

contained in a mortgage effective as a fixture filing (subsection (6) of Section 9—402) may be made only by an assignment of the mortgage in the manner provided by the law of this state other than this Act.

(3) After the disclosure or filing of an assignment under this section, the assignee is the secured party of record.

§ 9—406. Release of Collateral; Duties of Filing Officer; Fees

A secured party of record may by his signed statement release all or a part of any collateral described in a filed financing statement. The statement of release is sufficient if it contains a description of the collateral being released, the name and address of the debtor, the name and address of the secured party, and the file number of the financing statement. A statement of release signed by a person other than the secured party of record must be accompanied by a separate written statement of assignment signed by the secured party of record and complying with subsection (2) of Section 9—405, including payment of the required fee. Upon presentation of such a statement of release to the filing officer, he shall mark the statement with the hour and date of filing and shall note the same upon the margin of the index of the filing of the financing statement. The uniform fee for filing and noting such a statement of release shall be $. . . . . . . if the statement is in the standard form prescribed by the [Secretary of State] and otherwise shall be $. . . . . . . , plus in each case an additional fee of $. . . . . . . for each name more than one against which the statement of release is required to be indexed.

[§ 9—407. Information From Filing Officer]

[(1) If the person filing any financing statement, termination statement, statement of assignment, or statement of release, furnishes the filing officer a copy thereof, the filing officer shall upon request note upon the copy the file number and date and hour of the filing of the original and deliver or send the copy to such person.]

[(2) Upon request of any person, the filing officer shall issue his certificate showing whether there is on file on the date and hour stated therein, any presently effective financing statement naming a particular debtor and any statement of assignment thereof and if there is, giving the date and hour of filing of each such statement and the names and addresses of each secured party therein. The uniform fee for such a certificate shall be $. . . . . . . if the request for the certificate is in the standard form prescribed by the [Secretary of State] and otherwise shall be $. . . . . . . Upon request the filing officer

shall furnish a copy of any filed financing statement or statement of assignment for a uniform fee of $. . . . . . . per page.]

Note: *This section is proposed as an optional provision to require filing officers to furnish certificates. Local law and practices should be consulted with regard to the advisability of adoption.*

§ 9—408. Financing Statements Covering Consigned or Leased Goods

A consignor or lessor of goods may file a financing statement using the terms "consignor," "consignee," "lessor," "lessee" or the like instead of the terms specified in Section 9—402. The provisions of this Part shall apply as appropriate to such a financing statement but its filing shall not of itself be a factor in determining whether or not the consignment or lease is intended as security (Section 1—201(37)). However, if it is determined for other reasons that the consignment or lease is so intended, a security interest of the consignor or lessor which attaches to the consigned or leased goods is perfected by such filing.

PART 5

DEFAULT

§ 9—501. Default; Procedure When Security Agreement Covers Both Real and Personal Property

(1) When a debtor is in default under a security agreement, a secured party has the rights and remedies provided in this Part and, except as limited by subsection (3), those provided in the security agreement. He may reduce his claim to judgment, foreclose or otherwise enforce the security interest by any available judicial procedure. If the collateral is documents, the secured party may proceed either as to the documents or as to the goods covered thereby. A secured party in possession has the rights, remedies and duties provided in Section 9—207. The rights and remedies referred to in this subsection are cumulative.

(2) After default, the debtor has the rights and remedies provided in this Part, those provided in the security agreement and those provided in Section 9—207.

(3) To the extent that they give rights to the debtor and impose duties on the secured party, the rules stated in the subsections referred to below may not be waived or varied except as provided with respect to compulsory disposition of collateral (subsection (3) of Section 9—504 and Section 9—505) and

with respect to redemption of collateral (Section 9—506) but the parties may by agreement determine the standards by which the fulfillment of these rights and duties is to be measured if such standards are not manifestly unreasonable:

(a) subsection (2) of Section 9—502 and subsection (2) of Section 9—504 insofar as they require accounting for surplus proceeds of collateral;

(b) subsection (3) of Section 9—504 and subsection (1) of Section 9—505 which deal with disposition of collateral;

(c) subsection (2) of Section 9—505 which deals with acceptance of collateral as discharge of obligation;

(d) Section 9—506 which deals with redemption of collateral; and

(e) subsection (1) of Section 9—507 which deals with the secured party's liability for failure to comply with this Part.

(4) If the security agreement covers both real and personal property, the secured party may proceed under this Part as to the personal property or he may proceed as to both the real and the personal property in accordance with his rights and remedies in respect of the real property, in which case the provisions of this Part do not apply.

(5) When a secured party has reduced his claim to judgment, the lien of any levy which may be made upon his collateral by virtue of any execution based upon the judgment shall relate back to the date of the perfection of the security interest in such collateral. A judicial sale, pursuant to such execution, is a foreclosure of the security interest by judicial procedure within the meaning of this section, and the secured party may purchase at the sale and thereafter hold the collateral free of any other requirements of this Article.

§ 9—502. Collection Rights of Secured Party

(1) When so agreed, and in any event on default, the secured party is entitled to notify an account debtor or the obligor on an instrument to make payment to him whether or not the assignor was theretofore making collections on the collateral, and also to take control of any proceeds to which he is entitled under Section 9—306.

(2) A secured party who by agreement is entitled to charge back uncollected collateral or otherwise to full or limited recourse against the debtor and who undertakes to collect from the account debtors or obligors must proceed in a commercially reasonable manner and may deduct his reasonable expenses of realization from the collections. If the

security agreement secures an indebtedness, the secured party must account to the debtor for any surplus, and unless otherwise agreed, the debtor is liable for any deficiency. But, if the underlying transaction was a sale of accounts or chattel paper, the debtor is entitled to any surplus or is liable for any deficiency only if the security agreement so provides.

§ 9—503. Secured Party's Right to Take Possession After Default

Unless otherwise agreed, a secured party has on default the right to take possession of the collateral. In taking possession, a secured party may proceed without judicial process if this can be done without breach of the peace or may proceed by action. If the security agreement so provides, the secured party may require the debtor to assemble the collateral and make it available to the secured party at a place to be designated by the secured party which is reasonably convenient to both parties. Without removal, a secured party may render equipment unusable and may dispose of collateral on the debtor's premises under Section 9—504.

§ 9—504. Secured Party's Right to Dispose of Collateral After Default; Effect of Disposition

(1) A secured party after default may sell, lease or otherwise dispose of any or all of the collateral in its then condition or following any commercially reasonable preparation or processing. Any sale of goods is subject to the Article on Sales (Article 2). The proceeds of disposition shall be applied in the order following to

(a) the reasonable expenses of retaking, holding, preparing for sale or lease, selling, leasing and the like and, to the extent provided for in the agreement and not prohibited by law, the reasonable attorneys' fees and legal expenses incurred by the secured party;

(b) the satisfaction of indebtedness secured by the security interest under which the disposition is made;

(c) the satisfaction of indebtedness secured by any subordinate security interest in the collateral if written notification of demand therefor is received before distribution of the proceeds is completed. If requested by the secured party, the holder of a subordinate security interest must seasonably furnish reasonable proof of his interest, and unless he does so, the secured party need not comply with his demand.

(2) If the security interest secures an indebtedness, the secured party must account to the debtor for any surplus, and, unless otherwise agreed, the debtor is liable for any deficiency. But if the underlying transaction was a sale of accounts or chattel paper, the debtor is entitled to any surplus or is liable for any deficiency only if the security agreement so provides.

(3) Disposition of the collateral may be by public or private proceedings and may be made by way of one or more contracts. Sale or other disposition may be as a unit or in parcels and at any time and place and on any terms but every aspect of the disposition including the method, manner, time, place and terms must be commercially reasonable. Unless collateral is perishable or threatens to decline speedily in value or is of a type customarily sold on a recognized market, reasonable notification of the time and place of any public sale or reasonable notification of the time after which any private sale or other intended disposition is to be made shall be sent by the secured party to the debtor, if he has not signed after default a statement renouncing or modifying his right to notification of sale. In the case of consumer goods, no other notification need be sent. In other cases, notification shall be sent to any other secured party from whom the secured party has received (before sending his notification to the debtor or before the debtor's renunciation of his rights) written notice of a claim of an interest in the collateral. The secured party may buy at any public sale; and if the collateral is of a type customarily sold in a recognized market or is of a type which is the subject of widely distributed standard price quotations, he may buy at private sale.

(4) When collateral is disposed of by a secured party after default, the disposition transfers to a purchaser for value all of the debtor's rights therein, discharges the security interest under which it is made and any security interest or lien subordinate thereto. The purchaser takes free of all such rights and interests even though the secured party fails to comply with the requirements of this Part or of any judicial proceedings

    (a) in the case of a public sale, if the purchaser has no knowledge of any defects in the sale and if he does not buy in collusion with the secured party, other bidders or the person conducting the sale; or

    (b) in any other case, if the purchaser acts in good faith.

(5) A person who is liable to a secured party under a guaranty, indorsement, repurchase agreement or the like and who receives a transfer of collat-

eral from the secured party or is subrogated to his rights has thereafter the rights and duties of the secured party. Such a transfer of collateral is not a sale or disposition of the collateral under this Article.

§ 9—505. Compulsory Disposition of Collateral; Acceptance of the Collateral as Discharge of Obligation

(1) If the debtor has paid sixty percent of the cash price in the case of a purchase money security interest in consumer goods or sixty percent of the loan in the case of another security interest in consumer goods and has not signed after default a statement renouncing or modifying his rights under this Part, a secured party who has taken possession of collateral must dispose of it under Section 9—504; and if he fails to do so within ninety days after he takes possession, the debtor at his option may recover in conversion or under Section 9—507(1) on secured party's liability.

(2) In any other case involving consumer goods or any other collateral, a secured party in possession may, after default, propose to retain the collateral in satisfaction of the obligation. Written notice of such proposal shall be sent to the debtor if he has not signed after default a statement renouncing or modifying his rights under this subsection. In the case of consumer goods, no other notice need be given. In other cases, notice shall be sent to any other secured party from whom the secured party has received (before sending his notice to the debtor or before the debtor's renunciation of his rights) written notice of a claim of an interest in the collateral. If the secured party receives objection in writing from a person entitled to receive notification within twenty-one days after the notice was sent, the secured party must dispose of the collateral under Section 9—504. In the absence of such written objection, the secured party may retain the collateral in satisfaction of the debtor's obligation.

§ 9—506. Debtor's Right to Redeem Collateral

At any time before the secured party has disposed of collateral or entered into a contract for its disposition under Section 9—504 or before the obligation has been discharged under Section 9—505(2), the debtor or any other secured party may, unless otherwise agreed in writing after default, redeem the collateral by tendering fulfillment of all obligations secured by the collateral as well as the expenses reasonably incurred by the secured party in retaking, holding and preparing the collateral for disposition, in arranging for the sale, and to the extent provided in the agreement and not prohibited by law, his reasonable attorneys' fees and legal expenses.

§ 9—507. Secured Party's Liability for Failure to Comply With This Part

(1) If it is established that the secured party is not proceeding in accordance with the provisions of this Part, disposition may be ordered or restrained on appropriate terms and conditions. If the disposition has occurred, the debtor or any person entitled to notification or whose security interest has been made known to the secured party prior to the disposition has a right to recover from the secured party any loss caused by a failure to comply with the provisions of this Part. If the collateral is consumer goods, the debtor has a right to recover in any event an amount not less than the credit service charge plus ten percent of the principal amount of the debt or the time price differential plus 10 percent of the cash price.

(2) The fact that a better price could have been obtained by a sale at a different time or in a different method from that selected by the secured party is not of itself sufficient to establish that the sale was not made in a commercially reasonable manner. If the secured party either sells the collateral in the usual manner in any recognized market therefor, or if he sells at the price current in such market at the time of his sale, or if he has otherwise sold in conformity with reasonable commercial practices among dealers in the type of property sold, he has sold in a commercially reasonable manner. The principles stated in the two preceding sentences with respect to sales also apply as may be appropriate to other types of disposition. A disposition which has been approved in any judicial proceeding or by any bona fide creditors' committee or representative of creditors shall conclusively be deemed to be commercially reasonable, but this sentence does not indicate that any such approval must be obtained in any case nor does it indicate that any disposition not so approved is not commercially reasonable.

ARTICLE 10

EFFECTIVE DATE AND REPEALER

See Article 11 for Transition Provisions for those jurisdictions adopting the 1972 amendments.

§ 10—101. Effective Date

This Act shall become effective at midnight on December 31st following its enactment. It applies to transactions entered into and events occurring after that date.

§ 10—102. Specific Repealer; Provision for Transition

(1) The following acts and all other acts and parts of acts inconsistent herewith are hereby repealed:

(Here should follow the acts to be specifically repealed including the following:

    Uniform Negotiable Instruments Act
    Uniform Warehouse Receipts Act
    Uniform Sales Act
    Uniform Bills of Lading Act
    Uniform Stock Transfer Act
    Uniform Conditional Sales Act
    Uniform Trust Receipts Act
    Also any acts regulating:
        Bank collections
        Bulk sales
        Chattel mortgages
        Conditional sales

        Factor's lien acts
        Farm storage of grain and similar acts
        Assignment of accounts receivable)

(2) Transactions validly entered into before the effective date specified in Section 10—101 and the rights, duties and interests flowing from them remain valid thereafter and may be terminated, completed, consummated or enforced as required or permitted by any statute or other law amended or repealed by this Act as though such repeal or amendment had not occurred.

Note: *Subsection (1) should be separately prepared for each state. The foregoing is a list of statutes to be checked.*

§ 10—103. General Repealer

Except as provided in the following section, all acts and parts of acts inconsistent with this Act are hereby repealed.

§ 10—104. Laws Not Repealed

[(1)] The Article on Documents of Title (Article 7) does not repeal or modify any laws prescribing the form or contents of documents of title or the services or facilities to be afforded by bailees, or otherwise regulating bailees' businesses in respects not specifically dealt with herein; but the fact that such laws are violated does not affect the status of a document of title which otherwise complies with the definition of a document of title (Section 1—201).

[(2) This act does not repeal . . . .
. . . . *,
cited as the Uniform Act for the Simplification of Fiduciary Security Transfers, and if in any respect there is any inconsistency between that Act and the Article of this Act on investment securities (Article 8) the provisions of the former Act shall control.]

Note: *At * in subsection (2) insert the statutory reference to the Uniform Act for the Simplification of Fiduciary Security Transfers if such Act has previously been enacted. If it has not been enacted, omit subsection (2).*

ARTICLE 11

EFFECTIVE DATE AND TRANSITION PROVISIONS

This material has been numbered Article 11 to distinguish it from Article 10, the transition provision of the 1962 Code, which may still remain in effect in some states to cover transition problems from pre-Code law to the original Uniform Commercial Code. Adaptation may be necessary in particular states. The terms "[old Code]" and "[new Code]" and "[old U.C.C.]" and "[new U.C.C.]" are used herein, and should be suitably changed in each state.

This draft was prepared by the Reporters and has not been passed upon by the Review Committee, the Permanent Editorial Board, the American Law Institute, or the National Conference of Commissioners on Uniform State Laws. It is submitted as a working draft which may be adapted as appropriate in each state.

§ 11—101. Effective Date

This Act shall become effective at 12:01 A.M. on_____, 19__.

§ 11—102. Preservation of Old Transition Provision

The provisions of [here insert reference to the original transition provision in the particular state] shall continue to apply to [the new U.C.C.] and for this purpose the [old U.C.C. and new U.C.C.] shall be considered one continuous statute.

§ 11—103. Transition to [New Code]—General Rule

Transactions validly entered into after [effective date of old U.C.C.] and before [effective date of new U.C.C.], and which were subject to the provisions of [old U.C.C.] and which would be subject to this Act as amended if they had been entered into after the effective date of [new U.C.C.] and the rights, duties and interests flowing from such transactions remain valid after the latter date and may be terminated, completed, consummated or enforced as required or permitted by the [new U.C.C.]. Security interests arising out of such transactions which are perfected when [new U.C.C.] becomes effective shall remain perfected until they lapse as provided in [new U.C.C.], and may be continued as permitted by [new U.C.C.], except as stated in Section 11—105.

§ 11—104. Transition Provision on Change of Requirement of Filing

A security interest for the perfection of which filing or the taking of possession was required under [old U.C.C.] and which attached prior to the effective date of [new U.C.C.] but was not perfected shall be deemed perfected on the effective date of [new U.C.C.] if [new U.C.C.] permits perfection without filing or authorizes filing in the office or offices where a prior ineffective filing was made.

§ 11—105. Transition Provision on Change of Place of Filing

(1) A financing statement or continuation statement filed prior to [effective date of new U.C.C.] which shall not have lapsed prior to [the effective date of new U.C.C.] shall remain effective for the period provided in the [old Code], but not less than five years after the filing.

(2) With respect to any collateral acquired by the debtor subsequent to the effective date of [new U.C.C.], any effective financing statement or continuation statement described in this section shall apply only if the filing or filings are in the office or offices that would be appropriate to perfect the security interests in the new collateral under [new U.C.C.].

(3) The effectiveness of any financing statement or continuation statement filed prior to [effective date of new U.C.C.] may be continued by a continuation statement as permitted by [new U.C.C.], except that if [new U.C.C.] requires a filing in an office where there was no previous financing statement, a new financing statement conforming to Section 11—106 shall be filed in that office.

(4) If the record of a mortgage of real estate would have been effective as a fixture filing of goods described therein if [new U.C.C.] had been in effect on the date of recording the mortgage, the mortgage shall be deemed effective as a fixture filing as to such goods under subsection (6) of Section 9—402 of the [new U.C.C.] on the effective date of [new U.C.C.].

§ 11—106. Required Refilings

(1) If a security interest is perfected or has priority when this Act takes effect as to all persons or as to certain persons without any filing or recording, and if the filing of a financing statement would be required for the perfection or priority of the security interest against those persons under [new U.C.C.], the perfection and priority rights of the security interest continue until 3 years after the effective date of [new U.C.C.]. The perfection will then lapse unless a financing statement is filed as provided in subsection (4) or unless the security interest is perfected otherwise than by filing.

(2) If a security interest is perfected when [new U.C.C.] takes effect under a law other than [U.C.C.] which requires no further filing, refiling or recording to continue its perfection, perfection continues until and will lapse 3 years after [new U.C.C.] takes effect, unless a financing statement is filed as provided in subsection (4) or unless the security interest is perfected otherwise than by filing, or unless under subsection (3) of Section 9—302 the other law continues to govern filing.

(3) If a security interest is perfected by a filing, refiling or recording under a law repealed by this Act which required further filing, refiling or recording to continue its perfection, perfection continues and will lapse on the date provided by the law so repealed for such further filing, refiling or recording

unless a financing statement is filed as provided in subsection (4) or unless the security interest is perfected otherwise than by filing.

(4) A financing statement may be filed within six months before the perfection of a security interest would otherwise lapse. Any such financing statement may be signed by either the debtor or the secured party. It must identify the security agreement, statement or notice (however denominated in any statute or other law repealed or modified by this Act), state the office where and the date when the last filing, refiling or recording, if any, was made with respect thereto, and the filing number, if any, or book and page, if any, of recording and further state that the security agreement, statement or notice, however denominated, in another filing office under the [U.C.C.] or under any statute or other law repealed or modified by this Act is still effective. Section 9—401 and Section 9—103 determine the proper place to file such a financing statement. Except as specified in this subsection, the provisions of Section 9—403(3) for continuation statements apply to such a financing statement.

§ 11—107. Transition Provisions as to Priorities

Except as otherwise provided in [Article 11], [old U.C.C.] shall apply to any questions of priority if the positions of the parties were fixed prior to the effective date of [new U.C.C.]. In other cases questions of priority shall be determined by [new U.C.C.].

§ 11—108. Presumption that Rule of Law Continues Unchanged

Unless a change in law has clearly been made, the provisions of [new U.C.C.] shall be deemed declaratory of the meaning of the [old U.C.C.].

Index of Cases

Subject Index

A*

absolute guarantee, *584*

absolute liability, 48; consumer protection, 49; for industrial activity, 49; wild animals, 49

absolute ownership, *306*

absolute privilege, to slander, 54

abstract of title, *851*

acceleration, power of, 469

acceptance, *499;* apparent qualifications, 151; of bilateral contract, 154; communication of, 154; containing additional requests, 152; containing provision for clerical matters, 152; delay in acting on application as, 153; draft-varying, 501; effect of buyer's, on breach, 403; exercise of option as, 154; form of, 501; general, *501;* of guaranty contract, 154; implied terms in, 151; kinds of, 501; by mail or telegraph, 154; manner of, 152; nature of, 151; of offer, 150; revocation of, 442; silence as, 153; by telephone, 155; of trust, 907; of unilateral contract, 154; of unordered goods and tickets, 153; unqualified, 151; what constitutes, of goods, 403; who may accept, 152

acceptor, *460, 499*

accession, *310*

accessory, after the fact, *35;* before the fact, *35;* to a crime, *35*

accident, and parol evidence rule, 231

accommodation party, 462; liability of 463

accord, *272*

accord and satisfaction, 272

accounting, of agent, 667

acquiescence, by principal, 651

act of God, 275, 329, *348*

adequacy of consideration, 195; exceptions to rule, 196

---

* Where the entry is italicized in the text, the page reference is in italic type.

adhesion, contract of, 243

administration of estate, not necessary when, 892

administrative agencies, 5

administrative agency, 83; constitutional limitations on investigation by, 86; decentralization of functions, 86; and environmental protection, 98; finality of determination by, 89; inspection of premises, 86; open meetings of, 89; pattern of procedure, 87; power to compel production of papers, 86; public participation, 89; punishment and enforcement powers of, 88; regulation of business by, 213

administrative hearing, 87

administrative law, *83*

administrative regulations, *3;* notice of, 90

administrator, *84, 892;* executive powers of, 85; judicial powers of, 85; legislative powers of, 84; powers of, 84; public, *893*

administrator pendente lite, *892*

administratrix, *892*

adverse claim, to commercial paper, 520; defendant's assertion of, 520; effect of, 520; ignorance of, to commercial paper, 514; knowledge of, to commercial paper, 531; what constitutes, 520

adverse interest, of partner, 737

adverse possession, *853*

advertising, deceptive, 108; labels and packaging, 109; retractive, *109*

affirmative covenant, *852*

after-acquired property, 578

Age Discrimination in Employment Act, 703

Agencies, administrative, 5; private, 5

agency, *647;* administrative, 83; authorization by appointment, 650; authorization by conduct, 651; coupled with an interest, 650; creating, 650; duties and liabilities of agent after termination, 667; duties and liabilities of agent

1

E

G

N

O

guished from gift, 360; distinguished from option to purchase, *360;* effect of on title, 387; by entrustee, 388; fraud and other defenses, 365; home solicitation, 111; illegal, 365; implied conditions, 364; insurable interest, 378; nature and legality, 359; law of contracts applicable, 361; modification of contract, 364; parol evidence rule, 364; referral, 111; and statute of frauds, 367; subject matter of, 359; terms of transaction, 379; UCC applicable, 361; usage of trade and course of dealing, 364

sale of goods, *359*

sale or return, *385*

sales contract, action for breach of warranty, 444; action for conversion or recovery of goods, 446; buyer's action for damages for nondelivery, 444; buyer's resale of goods, 446; cancellation by buyer, 445; cancellation by seller, 441; completion or salvage of, 439; assignment of, 406; duties of the parties, 401; formality of, 367; nature of writing required, 367; non-code claims, 439; non-UCC local requirements, 369; oral, 368; reclamation of goods on seller's insolvency, 443; rejection of improper delivery, 442; remedies for breach, 438; remedies of buyer, 442; remedies for fraud of seller, 446; remedies of seller, 439; repossession of goods by seller, 442; resale by seller, 441; seller's action for damages, 441; seller's action for purchase price, 442; statute of limitations, 438

sales personnel, limitations on authority of, 692; transactions with, 692

sample, *419*

satisfaction, of commercial paper, 531

seal, 364; as substitute for consideration, 197

seal of approval, 109

secret partner, *719*

secured credit sale, *559;* of equipment, 581; of inventory, 577

secured credit sales of equipment, filing, 581; use of collateral, 581

secured credit sale of inventory, rights and remedies after default, 580

secured loan transactions, 581

secured transaction, proceeds of collateral, 578

security interest, assignment of, 580; in after-acquired property, 578; use of property and extent of, 577

secured seller, buyer's remedies for violation of UCC by, 567

secured transaction, 387, *559;* rights of parties after default, 565; waiver of defenses, 564

securities, federal regulation, 807; insider information, 808; short-swing profit, *808;* state regulation, 807

Securities Act of 1933, 807

Securities Exchange Act of 1934, 807

security agreement, 560

security interest, priority of repair and storage liens, 563; interstate, 562; filing not required, 562; perfected, *562;* perfection of, *561;* reservation of, 386; in future transactions, 561; attaches when, *560;* creation of, 560; in goods being manufactured, 583

self-service stores, 383, 703

seller, action for damages, 441; action for purchase price, 442; cancellation by, 441; domination of market by, 181; duty to deliver, 401; goods retained by, 389; implied warranties of, 418; protection of, 390; protection of creditors of, 390; remedies for fraud of, 446; repossession of goods by, 442; resale by, 441

selling on consignment, *345*

service of process, 10

servicemark, *308*

servient tenement, *842*

settlement agreement, *892*

settlement options, life insurance, *621*

settlor, *905*

setoffs, in assignment, 258

several contracts, *244*

severalty, *316*

shareholder, exceptions to limited liability of, 814; liability of, 814; limited liability of, 814; meetings of, 824; ownership rights, 809; protection of, 831; remedies of, 814; rights of, 809; right to inspect books, 811; right to receive dividends, 812; right to share in capital distribution, 814; right to vote, 809

shareholders' meetings, no action, 825; quorum, 824

sheriff, *7*

Sherman Act, 69; punishment and civil remedy provided, 69